Cases in
Strategic Management

Cases in Strategic Management

Fifth Edition

Charles W. L. Hill
University of Washington

Gareth R. Jones
Texas A&M University

HOUGHTON MIFFLIN COMPANY

Boston   New York

For Alexandra, Elizabeth, Charlotte, and Michelle

    C.W.L.H.

For Jennifer, Nicholas, and Julia

    G.R.J.

Sponsoring Editor: *George Hoffman*
Senior Associate Editor: *Susan M. Kahn*
Senior Project Editor: *Maria Morelli*
Editorial Assistants: *Cecilia Molinari, Tanius Stamper*
Production/Design Coordinator: *Jennifer Meyer Dare*
Manufacturing Coordinator: *Sally Culler*
Marketing Manager: *Melissa Russell*

Cover image and design: Harold Burch, Harold Burch Design, New York City

Netscape Communicator browser window copyright © 1999 Netscape Communication Corporation. Used with permission.

Printed in the U.S.A.

Library of Congress Catalog Card number: 00-104964

ISBN: 0-618-07147-4

123456789-KPT-04 03 02 01 00

Contents

Section C   Corporate Level: Domestic and Global Cases   C391

Preface

In its fourth edition, *Strategic Management: An Integrated Approach* became the most widely used strategic management textbook on the market. This overwhelming support and acceptance has led us to build on this foundation for this new edition of *Cases in Strategic Management*. We have continued to strive for currency to ensure that cutting edge issues are addressed, and we believe that we have written and collected a set of strategic management cases that are the best ever.

The 41 cases that we have selected for this edition will appeal, we are certain, to students and professors alike, both because these cases are intrinsically interesting and because of the number of strategic management issues they illuminate. These cases will provide students with a broad overview of the field of strategic management and will give them the opportunity to do some in-depth analysis of strategic issues.

The cases fall into three clearly defined categories: cases dealing with small business, which highlight problems and issues in running entrepreneurially based companies; business-level cases, which focus on the way that companies create value and competitive advantage in different industry conditions; and corporate-level cases, which examine how value is created or lost through such strategies as diversification and merger. The organizations discussed in the cases range from large, well-known ones, for which students can do research in order to update the information, to small, entrepreneurial businesses that illustrate the uncertainty and challenge of the strategic management process. In addition, the selections include many international cases, and most of the other cases contain some element of global strategy. There is enough variety in these cases and depth and breadth of coverage to satisfy the needs of most professors. Refer to the table of contents for a complete listing of the cases with brief descriptions. A grid that outlines the topical coverage of each case can be found in the *Instructor's Resource Manual: Cases.*

To help students learn how to effectively analyze and write a case study, we continue to include a special section on this subject. This section includes a checklist and explanation of areas to consider when analyzing, writing, and presenting a case study, suggested research tools, and an explanation of the role and methods of financial analysis.

We feel that our entire selection is unrivaled in breadth and depth. We have been fortunate to have a large number of cases to draw on from case authors, many of whom use our books. We are grateful to the other case authors who have contributed to this edition.

Jacqueline M. Abbey
Georgetown University

Frank C. Barnes
University of North Carolina, Charlotte

M. Edgar Barrett
Thunderbird—The American Graduate School of International Management

Christopher A. Bartlett
Harvard Business School

Julian Birkinshaw
Richard Ivey School of Business, The University of Western Ontario

Brad Brown
University of Virginia

Lew G. Brown
University of North Carolina at Greensboro

James W. Camerius
Northern Michigan University

Kristen M. Cashman
University of North Carolina at Greensboro

Lisa Chadderdon
Harvard Business School

James W. Clinton
University of Northern Colorado

Isaac Cohen
San Jose State University

Harold Dyck
California State University—San Bernardino

Michael I. Eizenberg
Bentley College

Vidya Gargeya
University of North Carolina at Greensboro

Madelyn Gengelbach
University of Missouri at Kansas City

Sue Greenfeld
California State University—San Bernardino

Irene Hagenbuch
Bentley College

Alan N. Hoffman
Bentley College

Harold F. Hogan, Jr.
Harvard Business School

Margaret Johnston
University of Washington

Javad Kargar
North Carolina Central University

Mike Keeffe
Southwest Texas State University

Robert Kennedy
Harvard Business School

Charles A. Kivett
University of North Carolina at Greensboro

Suresh Kotha
University of Washington

Jeffrey A. Krug
University of Illinois at Urbana—Champaign

Sharon Ungar Lane
Bentley College

Kevin B. Lowe
University of North Carolina at Greensboro

Michael Lubatkin
University of Connecticut

John H. Lundin
University of North Carolina at Greensboro

Stewart C. Malone
University of Virginia

Bill Middlebrook
Southwest Texas State University

Cynthia Montgomery
Harvard Business School

Richard Moxon
University of Washington

Karen L. Newman
Georgetown University

Stanley D. Nollen
Georgetown University

George M. Puia
Indiana State University

Krishnan Ramaya
University of Southern Indiana

John K. Ross III
Southwest Texas State University

Frank T. Rothaermel
Michigan State University

Don K. Sowers
University of North Carolina at Greensboro

Marilyn L. Taylor
University of Missouri at Kansas City

Robin Teigland
Richard Ivey School of Business, The University of Western Ontario (Canada)

Jorge Touché
Thunderbird—The American Graduate School of International Management

Suzanne Uhlen
Lund University (Sweden)

Roderick E. White
Richard Ivey School of Business, The University of Western Ontario (Canada)

Tony R. Wingler
University of North Carolina at Greensboro

TEACHING AND LEARNING AIDS

Taken together, the teaching and learning features of *Cases in Strategic Management* provide a package that is unsurpassed in its coverage.

For the Instructor

A comprehensive **Instructor's Resource Manual** created especially to accompany the casebook offers complete teaching notes for each case in this collection. These teaching notes cover all aspects of a company's strategy and structure. We also provide a series of questions that can be given to students to help them focus on the significant issues in each case. We have found these to be useful in leading students to think strategically, especially at the beginning of the strategy course, when they lack the tools to pull out the significant issues.

Videos pertaining to several of the cases and concepts in the book are available to instructors. They help highlight many issues of interest and can be used to spark class discussion.

An **Web site** contains features to aid instructors including downloadable files from the *Instructor's Resource Manual* and the Video Guide. Additional materials on the student Web site may also be of use to instructors.

For the Student

A student **Web site** provides help for students as they make their way through the course. The Web site features links to the companies highlighted in the cases and links to other sites of general interest while studying strategic management. It also includes the section on analyzing a case study and writing a case study analysis.

ACKNOWLEDGMENTS

This book is the product of far more than two authors. We are grateful to George Hoffman, our executive editor, and Melissa Russell, our marketing manager, for their help in promoting and developing the book and for providing us with timely feedback and information from professors and reviewers that have allowed us to shape the book to meet the needs of its intended market. We are also grateful to Susan Kahn, senior development editor, for ably coordinating the planning of our book and for managing the creation of the ancillary materials, and to Maria Morelli for her adept handling of production. We are also grateful to the case authors for allowing us to use their materials. We also want to thank the departments of management at the University of Washington and Texas A&M University for providing the setting and atmosphere in which the book could be written, and the students of these universities who reacted to and provided input for many of our ideas. In addition, the following reviewers of this and earlier editions gave us valuable suggestions regarding the case selection.

Ken Armstrong
Anderson University

Kunal Banerji
West Virginia University

Glenn Bassett
University of Bridgeport

Thomas H. Berliner
The University of Texas at Dallas

Richard G. Brandenburg
University of Vermont

Steven Braund
University of Hull

Philip Bromiley
University of Minnesota

Geoffrey Brooks
Western Oregon State College

Lowell Busenitz
University of Houston

Gene R. Conaster
Golden State University

Steven W. Congden
University of Hartford

Catherine M. Daily
Ohio State University

Robert DeFillippi
Suffolk University Sawyer School of Management

Helen Deresky
SUNY—Plattsburgh

Gerald E. Evans
The University of Montana

John Fahy
Trinity College, Dublin

Patricia Feltes
Southwest Missouri State University

Mark Fiegener
Oregon State University

Isaac Fox
Washington State University

Craig Galbraith
University of North Carolina at Wilmington

Scott R. Gallagher
Rutgers University

Eliezer Geisler
Northeastern Illinois University

Gretchen Gemeinhardt
University of Houston

Lynn Godkin
Lamar University

Robert L. Goldberg
Northeastern University

Graham L. Hubbard
University of Minnesota

Tammy G. Hunt
University of North Carolina at Wilmington

James Gaius Ibe
Morris College

W. Grahm Irwin
Miami University

Jonathan L. Johnson
University of Arkansas Walton College of Business Administration

Marios Katsioloudes
University of South Carolina Coastal Carolina College

Robert Keating
University of North Carolina at Wilmington

Geoffrey King
California State University—Fullerton

Rico Lam
University of Oregon

Robert J. Litschert
Virginia Polytechnic Institute and State University

Franz T. Lohrke
Louisiana State University

Lance A. Masters
California State University—San Bernardino

Robert N. McGrath
Embry-Riddle Aeronautical University

Charles Mercer
Drury College

Van Miller
University of Dayton

Joanna Mulholland
West Chester University of Pennsylvania

Francine Newth
Providence College

Paul R. Reed
Sam Houston State University

Rhonda K. Reger
Arizona State University

Malika Richards
Indiana University

Ronald Sanchez
University of Illinois

Joseph A. Schenk
University of Dayton

Brian Shaffer
University of Kentucky

Pradip K. Shukla
Chapman University

Dennis L. Smart
University of Nebraska at Omaha

Barbara Spencer
Clemson University

Lawrence Steenberg
University of Evansville

Kim A. Stewart
University of Denver

Ted Takamura
Warner Pacific College

Bobby Vaught
Southwest Missouri State

Robert P. Vichas
Florida Atlantic University

Daniel L. White
Drexel University

Edgar L. Williams, Jr.
Norfolk State University

Finally, thanks are due to our families for their patience and support during the revision process. We especially thank our wives, Alexandra Hill and Jennifer George, for their ever increasing support and affection.

Charles W. L. Hill
Gareth R. Jones

PART FIVE

Cases in Strategic Management

INTRODUCTION

Analyzing a Case Study and Writing a Case Study Analysis

WHAT IS CASE STUDY ANALYSIS?

Case study analysis is an integral part of a course in strategic management. The purpose of a case study is to provide students with experience of the strategic management problems faced by actual organizations. A case study presents an account of what happened to a business or industry over a number of years. It chronicles the events that managers had to deal with, such as changes in the competitive environment, and charts the managers' response, which usually involved changing the business- or corporate-level strategy. The cases in Part V of this book cover a wide range of issues and problems that managers have had to confront. Some cases are about finding the right business-level strategy to compete in changing conditions. Some are about companies that grew by acquisition, with little concern for the rationale behind their growth, and how growth by acquisition affected their future profitability. Each case is different because each organization is different. The underlying thread in all the cases, however, is the use of strategic management techniques to solve business problems.

Cases prove valuable in a strategic management course for several reasons. First, cases provide you, the student, with experience of organizational problems that you probably have not had the opportunity to experience firsthand. In a relatively short period of time, you will have the chance to appreciate and analyze the problems faced by many different companies and to understand how managers tried to deal with them.

Second, cases illustrate the theory and content of strategic management—that is, all the information presented to you in the previous chapters of this book. This information has been collected, discovered, and distilled from the observations, research, and experience of managers and academicians. The meaning and implications of this information are made clearer when they are applied to case studies. The theory and concepts help reveal what is going on in the companies studied and allow you to evaluate the solutions that specific companies adopted to deal with their problems. Consequently, when you analyze cases, you will be like a detective who, with a set of conceptual tools, probes what happened and what or who was responsible and then marshals the evidence that provides the solution. Top managers enjoy the thrill of testing their problem-solving abilities in the real world. It is important to remember, after all, that no one knows what the right answer is. All that managers can do is to make the best guess. In fact, managers say repeatedly that they are happy if they are right only half the time in solving strategic problems. Strategic management is an uncertain game, and using cases to see how theory can be put into practice is one way of improving your skills of diagnostic investigation.

Third, case studies provide you with the opportunity to participate in class and to gain experience in presenting your ideas to others. Instructors may sometimes call on students as a group to identify what is going on in a case, and through classroom discussion the issues in and solutions to the case problem will reveal themselves. In such a situation, you will have to organize your views and conclusions so that you can present them to the class. Your classmates may have analyzed the issues differently from you, and they will want you to argue your points before they will accept your conclusions; so be prepared for debate. This mode of discussion is an example of the dialectical approach to decision making that you may recall from Chapter 1. This is how decisions are made in the actual business world.

Instructors also may assign an individual, but more commonly a group, to analyze the case before the whole class. The individual or group probably will be responsible for a thirty- to forty-minute presentation of the case to the class. That presentation must cover the issues involved, the problems facing the company, and a series of recommendations for resolving the problems. The discussion then will be thrown open to the class, and you will have to defend your ideas. Through such discussions and presentations, you will experience how to convey your ideas effectively to others. Remember that a great deal of managers' time is spent in these kinds of situations, presenting their ideas and engaging in discussion with other managers, who have their own views about what is going on. Thus, you will experience in the classroom the actual process of strategic management, and this will serve you well in your future career.

If you work in groups to analyze case studies, you also will learn about the group process involved in working as a team. When people work in groups, it is often difficult to schedule time and allocate responsibility for the case analysis. There are always group members who shirk their responsibilities and group members who are so sure of their own ideas that they try to dominate the group's analysis. Most of the strategic management takes place in groups, however, and it is best if you learn about these problems now.

ANALYZING A CASE STUDY

As just mentioned, the purpose of the case study is to let you apply the concepts of strategic management when you analyze the issues facing a specific company. To analyze a case study, therefore, you must examine closely the issues with which the company is confronted. Most often you will need to read the case several times— once to grasp the overall picture of what is happening to the company and then several times more to discover and grasp the specific problems.

Generally, detailed analysis of a case study should include eight areas:

1. The history, development, and growth of the company over time

2. The identification of the company's internal strengths and weaknesses

3. The nature of the external environment surrounding the company

4. A SWOT analysis

5. The kind of corporate-level strategy pursued by the company

6. The nature of the company's business-level strategy

7. The company's structure and control systems and how they match its strategy

8. Recommendations

To analyze a case, you need to apply the concepts taught in this course to each of these areas. Where to look for a review of the concepts you need to use is obvious from the chapter titles. For example, to analyze the company's environment, you would use Chapter 3, on environmental analysis.

To help you further, we next offer a summary of some of the steps you can take to analyze the case material for each of the eight points we have just noted.

1. *Analyze the company's history, development, and growth.* A convenient way to investigate how a company's past strategy and structure affect it in the present is to chart the critical incidents in its history—that is, the events that were the most unusual or the most essential for its development into the company it is today. Some of the events have to do with its founding, its initial products, how it made new-product market decisions, and how it developed and chose functional competencies to pursue. Its entry into new businesses and shifts in its main lines of business are also important milestones to consider.

2. *Identify the company's internal strengths and weaknesses.* Once the historical profile is completed, you can begin the SWOT analysis. Use all the incidents you have charted to develop an account of the company's strengths and weaknesses as they have emerged historically. Examine each of the value creation functions of the company, and identify the functions in which the company is currently strong and currently weak. Some companies might be weak in marketing; some might be strong in research and development. Make lists of these strengths and weaknesses. The table on page C14 gives examples of what might go in these lists.

3. *Analyze the external environment.* The next step is to identify environmental opportunities and threats. Here you should apply all the concepts from Chapter 3, on industry and macroenvironments, to analyze the environment the company is confronting. Of particular importance at the industry level is Porter's five forces model and the stage of the life cycle model. Which factors in the macroenvironment will appear salient depends on the specific company being analyzed. However, use each concept in turn (for instance, demographic factors) to see whether it is relevant for the company in question.

Having done this analysis, you will have generated both an analysis of the company's environment and a list of opportunities and threats. The table on page C14 also lists some common environmental opportunities and threats that you might look for, but the list you generate will be specific to your company.

4. *Evaluate the SWOT analysis.* Having identified the company's external opportunities and threats as well as its internal strengths and weaknesses, you need to consider what your findings mean. That is, you need to balance strengths and weaknesses against opportunities and threats. Is the company in an overall strong competitive position? Can it continue to pursue its current business- or corporate-level strategy profitably? What can the company do to turn weaknesses into strengths and threats into opportunities? Can it develop new functional, business, or corporate strategies to accomplish this change? *Never merely generate the SWOT*

analysis and then put it aside. Because it provides a succinct summary of the company's condition, a good SWOT analysis is the key to all the analyses that follow.

5. *Analyze corporate-level strategy.* To analyze a company's corporate-level strategy, you first need to define the company's mission and goals. Sometimes the mission and goals are stated explicitly in the case; at other times you will have to infer them from available information. The information you need to collect to find out the company's corporate strategy includes such factors as its line(s) of business and the nature of its subsidiaries and acquisitions. It is important to analyze the relationship among the company's businesses. Do they trade or exchange resources? Are there gains to be achieved from synergy? Alternatively, is the company just running a portfolio of investments? This analysis should enable you to define the corporate strategy that the company is pursuing (for example, related or unrelated diversification, or a combination of both) and to conclude whether the company operates in just one core business. Then, using your SWOT analysis, debate the merits of this strategy. Is it appropriate, given the environment the company is in? Could a change in corporate strategy provide the company with new opportunities or transform a weakness into a strength? For example, should the company diversify from its core business into new businesses?

Other issues should be considered as well. How and why has the company's strategy changed over time? What is the claimed rationale for any changes? Often it is a good idea to analyze the company's businesses or products to assess its situation and identify which divisions contribute the most to or detract from its competitive advantage. It is also useful to explore how the company has built its portfolio over time. Did it acquire new businesses, or did it internally venture its own? All these factors provide clues about the company and indicate ways of improving its future performance.

6. *Analyze business-level strategy.* Once you know the company's corporate-level strategy and have done the SWOT analysis, the next step is to identify the company's business-level strategy. If the company is a single-business company, its business-level strategy is identical to its corporate-level strategy. If the company is in many businesses, each business will have its own business-level strategy. You will need to identify the company's generic competitive strategy—differentiation, low cost, or focus—and its investment strategy, given the company's relative competitive position and the stage of the life cycle. The company also may market different products using different business-level strategies. For example, it may offer a low-cost product range and a line of differentiated products. Be sure to give a full account of a company's business-level strategy to show how it competes.

Identifying the functional strategies that a company pursues to build competitive advantage through superior efficiency, quality, innovation, and customer responsiveness and to achieve its business-level strategy is very important. The SWOT analysis will have provided you with information on the company's functional competencies. You should further investigate its production, marketing, or research and development strategy to gain a picture of where the company is going. For example, pursuing a low-cost or a differentiation strategy successfully requires a very different set of competencies. Has the company developed the right ones? If it has, how can it exploit them further? Can it pursue both a low-cost and a differentiation strategy simultaneously?

The SWOT analysis is especially important at this point if the industry analysis, particularly Porter's model, has revealed the threats to the company from the environment. Can the company deal with these threats? How should it change its business-level strategy to counter them? To evaluate the potential of a company's business-level strategy, you must first perform a thorough SWOT analysis that captures the essence of its problems.

Once you complete this analysis, you will have a full picture of the way the company is operating and be in a position to evaluate the potential of its strategy. Thus, you will be able to make recommendations concerning the pattern of its future actions. However, first you need to consider strategy implementation, or the way the company tries to achieve its strategy.

7. *Analyze structure and control systems.* The aim of this analysis is to identify what structure and control systems the company is using to implement its strategy and to evaluate whether that structure is the appropriate one for the company. As we discuss in Chapter 13, different corporate and business strategies require different structures. Chapter 13 provides you with the conceptual tools to determine *the degree of fit between the company's strategy and structure.* For example, does the company have the right level of vertical differentiation (for instance, does it have the appropriate number of levels in the hierarchy or decentralized control?) or horizontal differentiation (does it use a functional structure when it should be using a product structure?)? Similarly, is the company using the right integration or control systems to manage its operations? Are managers being appropriately rewarded? Are the right rewards in place for encouraging cooperation among divisions? These are all issues that should be considered.

In some cases there will be little information on these issues, whereas in others there will be a lot. Obviously, in writing each case you should gear the analysis toward its most salient issues. For example, organizational conflict, power, and politics will be important issues for some companies. Try to analyze why problems in these areas are occurring. Do they occur because of bad strategy formulation or because of bad strategy implementation?

Organizational change is an issue in most of the cases because the companies are attempting to alter their strategies or structures to solve strategic problems. Thus, as a part of the analysis, you might suggest an action plan that the company in question could use to achieve its goals. For example, you might list in a logical sequence the steps the company would need to follow to alter its business-level strategy from differentiation to focus.

8. *Make recommendations.* The last part of the case analysis process involves making recommendations based on your analysis. Obviously, the quality of your recommendations is a direct result of the thoroughness with which you prepared the case analysis. The work you put into the case analysis will be obvious to the professor from the nature of your recommendations. Recommendations are directed at solving whatever strategic problem the company is facing and at increasing its future profitability. Your recommendations should be in line with your analysis; that is, they should follow logically from the previous discussion. For example, your recommendations generally will center on the specific ways of changing functional, business, and corporate strategy and organizational structure and control to improve business performance. The set of recommendations will be specific to each case, and so it is difficult to discuss these recommendations here. Such recommendations

might include an increase in spending on specific research and development projects, the divesting of certain businesses, a change from a strategy of unrelated to related diversification, an increase in the level of integration among divisions by using task forces and teams, or a move to a different kind of structure to implement a new business-level strategy. Again, make sure your recommendations are mutually consistent and are written in the form of an action plan. The plan might contain a timetable that sequences the actions for changing the company's strategy and a description of how changes at the corporate level will necessitate changes at the business level and subsequently at the functional level.

After following all these stages, you will have performed a thorough analysis of the case and will be in a position to join in class discussion or present your ideas to the class, depending on the format used by your professor. Remember that you must tailor your analysis to suit the specific issue discussed in your case. In some cases, you might completely omit one of the steps in the analysis because it is not relevant to the situation you are considering. You must be sensitive to the needs of the case and not apply the framework we have discussed in this section blindly. The framework is meant only as a guide and not as an outline that you must use to do a successful analysis.

WRITING A CASE STUDY ANALYSIS

Often, as part of your course requirements, you will need to present your instructor with a written case analysis. This may be an individual or a group report. Whatever the situation, there are certain guidelines to follow in writing a case analysis that will improve the evaluation your work will receive from your instructor. Before we discuss these guidelines and before you use them, make sure that they do not conflict with any directions your instructor has given you.

The structure of your written report is critical. Generally, if you follow the steps for analysis discussed in the previous section, *you already will have a good structure for your written discussion.* all reports begin with an *introduction* to the case. In it you outline briefly what the company does, how it developed historically, what problems it is experiencing, and how you are going to approach the issues in the case write-up. Do this sequentially by writing, for example, "First, we discuss the environment of Company X. . . . Third, we discuss Company X's business-level strategy. . . . Last, we provide recommendations for turning around Company X's business."

In the second part of the case write-up, the strategic-analysis section, do the SWOT analysis, analyze and discuss the nature and problems of the company's business-level and corporate strategy, and then analyze its structure and control systems. Make sure you use plenty of headings and subheadings to structure your analysis. For example, have separate sections on any important conceptual tool you use. Thus, you might have a section on Porter's five forces model as part of your analysis of the environment. You might offer a separate section on portfolio techniques when analyzing a company's corporate strategy. Tailor the sections and subsections to the specific issues of importance in the case.

In the third part of the case write-up, present your solutions and recommendations. Be comprehensive, and make sure they are in line with the previous analysis so that the recommendations fit together and move logically from one to the next.

The recommendations section is very revealing because, as mentioned earlier, your instructor will have a good idea of how much work you put into the case from the quality of your recommendations.

Following this framework will provide a good structure for most written reports, though obviously it must be shaped to fit the individual case being considered. Some cases are about excellent companies experiencing no problems. In such instances, it is hard to write recommendations. Instead, you can focus on analyzing why the company is doing so well, using that analysis to structure the discussion. Following are some minor suggestions that can help make a good analysis even better.

1. Do not repeat in summary form large pieces of factual information from the case. The instructor has read the case and knows what is going on. Rather, use the information in the case to illustrate your statements, to defend your arguments, or to make salient points. Beyond the brief introduction to the company, you must avoid being *descriptive;* instead, you must be *analytical.*

2. Make sure the sections and subsections of your discussion flow logically and smoothly from one to the next. That is, try to build on what has gone before so that the analysis of the case study moves toward a climax. This is particularly important for group analysis, because there is a tendency for people in a group to split up the work and say, "I'll do the beginning, you take the middle, and I'll do the end." The result is a choppy, stilted analysis because the parts do not flow from one to the next, and it is obvious to the instructor that no real group work has been done.

3. Avoid grammatical and spelling errors. They make the paper sloppy.

4. Some cases dealing with well-known companies end in 1993 or 1994 because no later information was available when the case was written. If possible, do a library search for more information on what has happened to the company in subsequent years. Following are sources of information for performing this search:

The Internet with its World Wide Web is the place to start your research. Very often you can download copies of a company's annual report from its Web site, and many companies also keep lists of press releases and articles that have been written about them. Thoroughly search the company's Web site for information such as the company's history and performance, and download all relevant information at the beginning of your project. Yahoo is a particularly good search engine to use to discover the address of your company's Web site, although others work as well.

Compact disk sources such as Lotus One Source and InfoTrac provide an amazing amount of good information, including summaries of recent articles written on specific companies that you can then access in the library.

F&S Predicasts provide a listing on a yearly basis of all the articles written about a particular company. Simply reading the titles gives an indication of what has been happening in the company.

Annual reports on a Form 10-K often provide an organization chart.

Companies themselves provide information if you write and ask for it.

Fortune, BusinessWeek, and *Forbes* have many articles on companies featured in the cases in this book.

Standard & Poor's industry reports provide detailed information about the competitive conditions facing the company's industry. Be sure to look at this journal.

5. Sometimes instructors hand out questions for each case to help you in your analysis. Use these as a guide for writing the case analysis. They often illuminate the important issues that have to be covered in the discussion.

If you follow the guidelines in this section, you should be able to write a thorough and effective evaluation.

GUIDELINES FOR THE STRATEGIC MANAGEMENT PROJECT

The case study guidelines just discussed also can be followed to help you conduct research for the Strategic Management Project Modules that are at the end of every chapter in this book. In order to answer the questions contained in each module, for example, it is necessary to locate and access articles on your chosen company in the same way that you will update the information on companies highlighted in the case studies. Obviously, however, you need to collect more information on your chosen company because it is *your case.*

The guidelines also can be used to help you to write your Strategic Management Project. The experience you develop from analyzing one or more of the companies in the case studies and writing the resulting report should help you improve the analytical skills needed for the Strategic Management Project. Essentially, in your Strategic Management Project, you are writing about and analyzing a company at the same time to show how that company creates value through its strategy and structure.

THE ROLE OF FINANCIAL ANALYSIS IN CASE STUDY ANALYSIS

Another important aspect of analyzing a case study and writing a case study analysis is the role and use of financial information. A careful analysis of the company's financial condition immensely improves a case write-up. After all, financial data represent the concrete results of the company's strategy and structure. Although analyzing financial statements can be quite complex, a general idea of a company's financial position can be determined through the use of ratio analysis. Financial performance ratios can be calculated from the balance sheet and income statement. These ratios can be classified into five different subgroups: profit ratios, liquidity ratios, activity ratios, leverage ratios, and shareholder-return ratios. These ratios should be compared with the industry average or the company's prior years of performance. It should be noted, however, that deviation from the average is not necessarily bad; it simply warrants further investigation. For example, young companies will have purchased assets at a different price and will likely have a different capital structure than older companies. In addition to ratio analysis, a company's cash flow position is of critical importance and should be assessed. Cash flow shows how much actual cash a company possesses.

■ Profit Ratios

Profit ratios measure the efficiency with which the company uses its resources. The more efficient the company, the greater is its profitability. It is useful to compare a company's profitability against that of its major competitors in its industry. Such a comparison tells whether the company is operating more or less efficiently than its rivals. In addition, the change in a company's profit ratios over time tells whether its performance is improving or declining.

A number of different profit ratios can be used, and each of them measures a different aspect of a company's performance. The most commonly used profit ratios are as follows:

1. *Gross profit margin.* The gross profit margin simply gives the percentage of sales available to cover general and administrative expenses and other operating costs. It is defined as follows:

$$\text{Gross Profit Margin} = \frac{\text{Sales Revenue} - \text{Cost of Goods Sold}}{\text{Sales Revenue}}$$

2. *Net profit margin.* Net profit margin is the percentage of profit earned on sales. This ratio is important because businesses need to make a profit to survive in the long run. It is defined as follows:

$$\text{Net Profit Margin} = \frac{\text{Net Income}}{\text{Sales Revenue}}$$

3. *Return on total assets.* This ratio measures the profit earned on the employment of assets. It is defined as follows:

$$\text{Return on Total Assets} = \frac{\text{Net Income Available to Common Stockholders}}{\text{Total Assets}}$$

Net income is the profit after preferred dividends (those set by contract) have been paid. Total assets include both current and noncurrent assets.

4. *Return on stockholders' equity.* This ratio measures the percentage of profit earned on common stockholders' investment in the company. In theory, a company attempting to maximize the wealth of its stockholders should be trying to maximize this ratio. It is defined as follows:

$$\text{Return on Stockholders' Equity} = \frac{\text{Net Income Available to Common Stockholders}}{\text{Stockholders' Equity}}$$

■ Liquidity Ratios

A company's liquidity is a measure of its ability to meet short-term obligations. An asset is deemed liquid if it can be readily converted into cash. Liquid assets are current assets such as cash, marketable securities, accounts receivable, and so on. Two commonly used liquidity ratios are as follows:

1. *Current ratio.* The current ratio measures the extent to which the claims of short-term creditors are covered by assets that can be quickly converted into cash. Most companies should have a ratio of at least 1, because failure to meet these commitments can lead to bankruptcy. The ratio is defined as follows:

$$\text{Current Ratio} = \frac{\text{Current Assets}}{\text{Current Liabilities}}$$

2. *Quick ratio.* The quick ratio measures a company's ability to pay off the claims of short-term creditors without relying on the sale of its inventories. This is a valuable measure since in practice the sale of inventories is often difficult. It is defined as follows:

$$\text{Quick Ratio} = \frac{\text{Current Assets} - \text{Inventory}}{\text{Current Liabilities}}$$

■ Activity Ratios

Activity ratios indicate how effectively a company is managing its assets. The following two ratios are particularly useful.

1. *Inventory turnover.* This measures the number of times inventory is turned over. It is useful in determining whether a firm is carrying excess stock in inventory. It is defined as follows:

$$\text{Inventory Turnover} = \frac{\text{Cost of Goods Sold}}{\text{Inventory}}$$

Cost of goods sold is a better measure of turnover than sales, since it is the cost of the inventory items. Inventory is taken at the balance sheet date. Some companies choose to compute an average inventory, beginning inventory, plus ending inventory, but for simplicity use the inventory at the balance sheet date.

2. *Days sales outstanding (DSO), or average collection period.* This ratio is the average time a company has to wait to receive its cash after making a sale. It measures how effective the company's credit, billing, and collection procedures are. It is defined as follows:

$$\text{DSO} = \frac{\text{Accounts Receivable}}{\text{Total Sales}/360}$$

Accounts receivable is divided by average daily sales. The use of 360 is the standard number of days for most financial analysis.

■ Leverage Ratios

A company is said to be highly leveraged if it uses more debt than equity, including stock and retained earnings. The balance between debt and equity is called the *capital structure.* The optimal capital structure is determined by the individual company. Debt has a lower cost because creditors take less risk; they know they will get their interest and principal. However, debt can be risky to the firm because if enough profit is not made to cover the interest and principal payments, bankruptcy can occur.

Three commonly used leverage ratios are as follows:

1. *Debt-to-assets ratio.* The debt-to-asset ratio is the most direct measure of the extent to which borrowed funds have been used to finance a company's investments. It is defined as follows:

$$\text{Debt-to-Assets Ratio} = \frac{\text{Total Debt}}{\text{Total Assets}}$$

Total debt is the sum of a company's current liabilities and its long-term debt, and total assets are the sum of fixed assets and current assets.

2. *Debt-to-equity ratio.* The debt-to-equity ratio indicates the balance between debt and equity in a company's capital structure. This is perhaps the most widely used measure of a company's leverage. It is defined as follows:

$$\text{Debt-to-Equity Ratio} = \frac{\text{Total Debt}}{\text{Total Equity}}$$

3. *Times-covered ratio.* The times-covered ratio measures the extent to which a company's gross profit covers its annual interest payments. If the times-covered ratio declines to less than 1, then the company is unable to meet its interest costs and is technically insolvent. The ratio is defined as follows:

$$\text{Times-Covered Ratio} = \frac{\text{Profit Before Interest and Tax}}{\text{Total Interest Charges}}$$

■ Shareholder-Return Ratios

Shareholder-return ratios measure the return earned by shareholders from holding stock in the company. Given the goal of maximizing stockholders' wealth, providing shareholders with an adequate rate of return is a primary objective of most companies. As with profit ratios, it can be helpful to compare a company's shareholders returns against those of similar companies. This provides a yardstick for determining how well the company is satisfying the demands of this particularly important group of organizational constituents. Four commonly used ratios are as follows:

1. *Total shareholder returns.* Total shareholder returns measure the returns earned by time $t + 1$ on an investment in a company's stock made at time t. (Time t is the time at which the initial investment is made.) Total shareholder returns include both dividend payments and appreciation in the value of the stock (adjusted for stock splits) and are defined as follows:

$$\text{Total Shareholder Returns} = \frac{\text{Stock Price } (t + 1)\text{-Stock Price } (t) + \text{Sum of Annual Dividends per Share}}{\text{Stock Price } (t)}$$

Thus, if a shareholder invests $2 at time t, and at time $t +1$ the share is worth $3, while the sum of annual dividends for the period t to $t + 1$ has amounted to $0.2, total shareholder returns are equal to $(3 - 2 + 0.2)/2 = 0.6$, which is a 60 percent return on an initial investment of $2 made at time t.

2. *Price-earnings ratio.* The price-earnings ratio measures the amount investors are willing to pay per dollar of profit. It is defined as follows:

$$\text{Price-Earnings Ratio} = \frac{\text{Market Price per Share}}{\text{Earnings per Share}}$$

3. *Market to book value.* Another useful ratio is market to book value. This measures a company's expected future growth prospects. It is defined as follows:

$$\text{Market to Book Value} = \frac{\text{Market Price per Share}}{\text{Earnings per Share}}$$

4. *Dividend yield.* The dividend yield measures the return to shareholders received in the form of dividends. It is defined as follows:

$$\text{Dividend Yield} = \frac{\text{Dividend per Share}}{\text{Market Price per Share}}$$

Market price per share can be calculated for the first of the year, in which case the dividend yield refers to the return on an investment made at the beginning of the year. Alternatively, the average share price over the year may be used. A company must decide how much of its profits to pay to stockholders and how much to reinvest in the company. Companies with strong growth prospects should have a lower dividend payout ratio than mature companies. The rationale is that shareholders can invest the money elsewhere if the company is not growing. The optimal ratio depends on the individual firm, but the key decider is whether the company can produce better returns than the investor can earn elsewhere.

■ Cash Flow

Cash flow position is simply cash received minus cash distributed. The net cash flow can be taken from a company's statement of cash flows. Cash flow is important for what it tells us about a company's financing needs. A strong positive cash flow enables a company to fund future investments without having to borrow money from bankers or investors. This is desirable because the company avoids the need to pay out interest or dividends. A weak or negative cash flow means that a company has to turn to external sources to fund future investments. Generally, companies in strong-growth industries often find themselves in a poor cash flow position (because their investment needs are substantial), whereas successful companies based in mature industries generally find themselves in a strong cash flow position.

A company's internally generated cash flow is calculated by adding back its depreciation provision to profits after interest, taxes, and dividend payments. If this figure is insufficient to cover proposed new-investment expenditures, the company has little choice but to borrow funds to make up the shortfall or to curtail investments. If this figure exceeds proposed new investments, the company can use the excess to build up its liquidity (that is, through investments in financial assets) or to repay existing loans ahead of schedule.

CONCLUSION

When evaluating a case, it is important to be *systematic*. Analyze the case in a logical fashion, beginning with the identification of operating and financial strengths and weaknesses and environmental opportunities and threats. Move on to assess the value of a company's current strategies only when you are fully conversant with the SWOT analysis of the company. Ask yourself whether the company's current strategies make sense, given its SWOT analysis. If they do not, what changes need to be made? What are your recommendations? Above all, link any strategic recommendations you may make to the SWOT analysis. State explicitly how the strategies you identify take advantage of the company's strengths to exploit environmental opportunities, how they rectify the company's weaknesses, and how they counter environmental threats. Also, do not forget to outline what needs to be done to implement your recommendations.

TABLE 1

A SWOT Checklist

Potential internal strengths
Many product lines?
Broad market coverage?
Manufacturing competence?
Good marketing skills?
Good materials management systems?
R&D skills and leadership?
Information system competencies?
Human resource competencies?
Brand name reputation?
Portfolio management skills?
Cost of differentiation advantage?
New-venture management expertise?
Appropriate management style?
Appropriate organizational structure?
Appropriate control systems?
Ability to manage strategic change?
Well-developed corporate strategy?
Good financial management?
Others?

Potential environmental opportunities
Expand core business(es)?
Exploit new market segments?
Widen product range?
Extend cost or differentiation advantage?
Diversify into new growth businesses?
Expand into foreign markets?
Apply R&D skills in new areas?
Enter new related businesses?
Vertically integrate forward?
Vertically integrate backward?
Enlarge corporate portfolio?
Overcome barriers to entry?
Reduce rivalry among competitors?
Make profitable new acquisitions?
Apply brand name capital in new areas?
Seek fast market growth?
Others?

Potential internal weaknesses
Obsolete, narrow product lines?
Rising manufacturing costs?
Decline in R&D innovations?
Poor marketing plan?
Poor material management systems?
Loss of customer good will?
Inadequate human resources?
Inadequate information systems?
Loss of brand name capital?
Growth without direction?
Bad portfolio management?
Loss of corporate direction?
Infighting among divisions?
Loss of corporate control?
Inappropriate organizational
   structure and control systems?
High conflict and politics?
Poor financial management?
Others?

Potential environmental threats
Attacks on core business(es)?
Increases in domestic competition?
Increase in foreign competition?
Change in consumer tastes?
Fall in barriers to entry?
Rise in new or substitute products?
Increase in industry rivalry?
New forms of industry competition?
Potential for takeover?
Existence of corporate raiders?
Increase in regional competition?
Changes in demographic factors?
Changes in economic factors?
Downturn in economy?
Rising labor costs?
Slower market growth?
Others?

Small Business, Entrepreneurship, and Ethics Cases

CASE 1

Artistic Impressions, Inc.: Developing An Entrepreneurial Growth Strategy

This case was prepared by James W. Camerius of Northern Michigan University and James W. Clinton of the University of Northern Colorado.

INTRODUCTION

"I think that there's plenty of opportunity out there and I don't think that we're scratching the surface in the African-American market," suggested Bart Breighner, president and chief executive officer of Artistic Impressions, Inc. "But the reality is that African-Americans make up only 10 percent of this country's population of close to 300 million. I want the whole shot, so we're going to do things to grow the Caucasian market."

Bart Breighner was excited and optimistic about the future of the company he had created. Artistic Impressions was a rapidly growing direct seller of affordable art works for the home and office. The firm had a plan to achieve sales of $25 million in 1998. Twice ranked in the top 500 fastest-growing private companies in the United States, according to *INC.* magazine, the company had its sales increase more than 962 percent in the past five years.

Artistic Impressions, with corporate offices and distribution center in Lombard, Illinois, a western suburb of Chicago, sold paintings and other art works through more than 2,700 salespeople in over forty states, primarily to African-Americans.

This case is intended to be used as a basis for class discussion rather than as an illustration of either effective or ineffective handling of the situation. This case was prepared by James W. Camerius, Northern Michigan University, and James W. Clinton, University of Northern Colorado. Used by permission.

The selling was done by means of home art shows—a form of the direct marketing party plan. The corporate strategy was based on a perceived market need and a compensation system designed to reward salespeople with substantial commissions. Breighner was certain he had positioned the firm for future growth. Breighner called a meeting of his staff to discuss repositioning the firm for the future. He asked the staff to respond to the following issues: "What do we need to do to get us where we want to go, to reach the kind of customer we want to reach, and to recruit and maintain the kind of sales force that will grow the business?"

BART BREIGHNER

Bart Breighner had graduated from the University of Maryland. In 1962, he was making $4,500 a year as a teacher of high school math. Six years later, he earned $100,000 a year as a manager for World Book Encyclopedia. He had a thirty-year track record in the direct selling field, primarily with World Book Encyclopedia. In his twenty-one years with World Book, he had built field sales organizations. For the last seven of those years, he held the position of executive vice president and director of North American sales. Reflecting on that period, he said:

> They sent me through the Harvard University Advanced Management Program. As part of my job responsibility, I traveled around the world.... that was an exciting career. But the company

was sold twice, and I wasn't politically adept at dealing with the paternalistic environment. I wasn't comfortable and I did move on. I decided to become an entrepreneur.

Breighner next entered the loan consulting business on a freelance basis, by starting a small but profitable financial planning company. He left after a short period of time to become a consultant to Bee Line Fashions, an $80 million company experiencing financial difficulties. Tiring again of the corporate environment, he left after six months because "We could not agree on how we were going to salvage [the company]. . . . it was going way down. At that point, I said, Hey, who was I kidding? I'm too rambunctious to report to someone else."

After additional experience in training and recruiting programs, Breighner decided to return to direct selling. "I missed direct sales and the psychic rewards the business offers," he recalled. "I looked into possibilities and capital requirements." He surveyed the field to identify an unsatisfied market need. He felt that he wanted to "control his own destiny" at that midcareer point in his life. A number of fields in direct sales are relatively crowded— such as nutrition and cosmetic and facial products—but there are very few successful home enhancement companies. Consequently, he founded Artistic Impressions, Inc., in 1985.

In 1995, in his book, *Face to Face Selling*, Breighner detailed the steps individuals needed to take in order to get started and succeed in sales— steps such as setting goals, preparing mentally, and developing a sales presentation. The book also explored what Breighner called "the art of creative confrontation" to effectively deal with others. He used many of his own experiences throughout the book, citing creative sales techniques for new and experienced salespeople.

Breighner believed that his initial motivation to enter direct selling came from a popular platform speaker whom he had met early in his career. When asked why he was still working in the field at the age of seventy, the speaker said, "I need the money."

When Breighner started Artistic Impressions, he intended it to become the dominant company in the industry. "Success is intentional," he said. Breighner was a finalist several times for the Entrepreneur of the Year award sponsored by Ernst & Young, an accounting and consulting firm. He also created a comprehensive videotape series for training his sales force, with an emphasis on building confidence in even the most inexperienced new consultant. He also served on the board of directors of the Direct Selling Association, an industry organization located in Washington, D.C.

THE DIRECT SALES ENVIRONMENT

The direct selling industry consisted of a few well-established companies and many smaller firms that sold a broad range of products, such as toys, animal food, plant-care products, clothing, computer software, and financial services. Avon (cosmetics), Amway Corporation (home cleaning products), Shaklee Corporation (vitamins and health foods), World Book, Encyclopaedia Britannica, Tupperware (plastic dishes and food containers), Kirby (vacuum cleaners), and Mary Kay (cosmetics) dominated this market. By the 1980s, analysts believed that the industry was in a mature stage of development, including a high concentration of firms selling nutritional products (vitamins) and facial products (cosmetics).

Spectacular sales growth, characteristic of the 1960s and 1970s, had given way in most firms to a pattern of stagnant revenues and profits. The industry found it difficult to attract new salespeople, who were typically responsible for generating much of a company's sales growth. Industry problems were blamed on the increasing number of men and women who worked full time, which made it difficult to find enough recruits for part-time sales and to reach sales targets. An improved economy, too, was faulted, for it encouraged some potential customers to avoid purchasing items from part-time salespeople and shop instead at established retail stores for more expensive products. In addition, the marketplace had become more sophisticated, forcing manufacturers to develop new, more upscale, products and modify existing ones, which were outdated.

As Breighner saw it, Artistic Impressions offered a career in direct sales that would appeal to individuals who wanted to be independent, successful businesspeople,—and particularly to those in other careers who feared being displaced through corporate downsizing. Breighner also believed that successful professionals who were frustrated in their present positions and wanted a midcareer change would find satisfaction in selling his company's products. "Our people, who are independent contractors, see our company as a vehicle for obtaining financial independence," he suggested.

On reviewing the direct selling field in 1984, Breighner concluded that there were very few successful "home enhancement companies." A major competitor in the field was a firm called Home Interiors, with annual sales of about $500 million. Several smaller companies were less of a threat. Breighner indicated that while he respected their product lines and their business methods, he felt that the market would support and probably needed an art product for the home that was more upscale than what was available. He perceived an opening for a different kind of company.

THE ORGANIZATION

Artistic Impressions was a privately held, multilevel direct sales organization. A multilevel organization is one in which a hierarchical network of distributors is created to sell and distribute a product line. What distinguishes this approach is the fact that each distributor in the network is not only seeking to make retail sales of goods and services to the final consumer, but is also looking for distributors to join his or her distribution network. By recruiting and training new distributors, the recruiter becomes a master distributor who earns sales commissions and bonuses on the retail sales of all distributors within the network. Artistic Impressions' primary business was selling framed art by means of the party plan. The party plan method of at-home retailing requires a salesperson to make sales presentations in the home of a host or hostess who has invited potential customers to a "party." Usually, the party plan includes various games and other entertainment activities, in which participants receive small inexpensive gifts. Closing the sale occurs when the salesperson takes orders from the people attending the party.

According to the company's mission statement, "Artistic Impressions exists to provide quality art at affordable prices to enhance the American home." But, Breighner noted, the primary goal of the firm, or any company, was to survive, and the second goal was to be consistently profitable—"profit is not something that is left over."

Although Breighner was Caucasian, African-Americans made up 90 percent of his company's sales force, as well as 90 percent of its customers. As Breighner explained,

It wasn't intentional. It just went that way, because of the direction of the organization. We got some powerful management and sales people with exceptional educational and professional backgrounds who just happened to be African-American. I would like to have a blended company, that is, a company that reflects the population as a whole. Some people call this diversity.

Given the customer base, the primary focus of the company's product line was art that would appeal to African-Americans. "We have a very large African-American community," Deborah Thompson-Widmer, the company's director of promotions and communications, who is Caucasian, pointed out, adding that "It's very hard to find African-American art out there. We hit a gold mine . . . [in this area], and [our products] really met a need."

A former associate dean of admissions at Ripon College in Wisconsin, Thompson-Widmer oversaw three departments at Artistic Impressions. Field service processed new applications for sales representatives, monitored the productivity of sales representatives, and generated reports for team managers. Promotions sought to motivate the sales force by developing incentives such as contests, customer specials, and hostess specials. The third department, marketing, developed promotional materials and videos. Thompson-Widmer stressed the importance for the company of

a whole trend in the economy where people are staying home more, they're doing more things at home, they're entertaining in the home, and they want to decorate the home. That has helped us. So many people don't go to galleries because they don't think they can afford gallery art. So many people want to decorate but they don't get to the store, they don't know what to get.

Artistic Impressions discovered that religious art appealed greatly to the African-American community. In two paintings, *The Last Supper*, by the artist R. Williams, and *Praying Hands*, the flesh tones were darker than in other portrayals. The company's version appeared as a replica of an original painting, but done in darker flesh tones. The design was also available as a figurine. Other art works depicted African-Americans in various true-to-life situations. The product line also included landscapes, florals, still lifes, and abstracts that had a broader appeal and did not emphasize ethnic background as strongly.

Another emerging market niche that the company was just beginning to explore was Hispanic art. Thompson-Widmer noted that

> We have a very strong group of sellers in Puerto Rico. They're asking for more and more Hispanic art. We've started to branch into that because the marketplace is telling us that we have a segment of people saying this is what we need, and that's where we are going. We're in a really big growth spurt now. Sales for the year are up 30 percent. We're booming in the number of recruits coming in and the number of states we're in. It's a very exciting process. We really want to stay in the United States. We did Puerto Rico because it's easy to ship. If there was a direction we would go first, it probably would be Canada.

THE PROCESS

Identifying a Market Need

In the 1980s, marketing studies conducted by World Book Encyclopedia revealed that the field of home beautification was going to grow in the future. "I made a mental note at that time that the field was hot and was going to continue to be hot," Bart Breighner recalled. "I made lists of what business I could be in. Later that factor plus my more than twenty years of experience of recruiting, training, and developing direct sales people combined to show me a way to capitalize on my assets."

During his trips to Europe, Breighner came to enjoy art in general and accumulated a collection of moderately priced art works. While searching for a new residence in the western suburbs of Chicago, he observed that the art decorating people's homes was not very attractive. Often, ordinary posters served as the centerpiece of home decoration. He felt that he could provide products to the American public that would enhance their quality of life. Hence, he defined the nature of the business as "home enhancement." The core of his strategy was to (1) find a need, (2) develop a product to fill it, and (3) develop a compensation system that would allow the firm to fulfill its objectives and at

the same time provide above average income for its sales force. Entry-level participants were to be known as consultants. The marketing program at Artistic Impressions was based on "consultants who take pride in making homes and offices more attractive by offering beautiful, affordable pieces of artwork in the comfort of a home or office."

Although first-year sales reached $500,000, the company lost $120,000. The following year's sales tripled to $1.5 million, doubled the next year to $3 million, were $5 million in the fourth year, and $6.5 million the fifth. The company currently recorded ninety-one months of consecutive increases over the previous month. Breighner anticipated doubling sales over the next three years.

THE PRODUCT LINE

The product line featured more than 375 hand-painted originals, serigraphs, lithographs and prints, with over 150 specialized framing options. The company also sold limited edition figurines and collector plates. These items were illustrated in a 100-page company catalog. The art came from thousands of artists from around the world. In addition, the company also sold a broad spectrum of art created by artists with whom it had contracted on an independent basis—for instance, H. Hargrove, a popular creator of Americana. As mentioned earlier, it also sold ethnic and religious art, which it felt could interest a diverse audience but appealed primarily to African-Americans and other ethnic groups.

Renee DeRosa was in charge of product development. She attended art shows around the country, and artists contacted her about their work. A product committee reviewed the art to evaluate its market potential. The committee also worked with regional managers to identify regional tastes. Customer tastes and preferences filtered up from the field to the product committee, which made the marketing decision. Committee members followed trends in decorating, color schemes, and styles, knowing that what was popular in California might not be in New York.

To introduce new products, Artistic Impressions' management periodically published new catalog supplements. The 1998 supplement showed several examples of a new process, developed by the company, called stochastic reproduction. It is a technique for producing tones and colors with sharper and clearer imaging. It allowed colors and images to "jump off the canvas" and provide a "lifelike appearance."

As Breighner recalls:

We were in business only two years when a Korean-American, who was in the forefront of replicating painting on canvas from original oil paintings, came to work for Artistic. We started producing paintings on canvas, what we call lithographic canvas. That was the key. It revolutionized our business. Some people call them prints on canvas, because they're reproductions from an original oil painting. We also developed a studio and hired some foreign artists—Koreans, Chinese, and Russian. We have the technology to reproduce the same abstract painting over and over.

PROMOTION

As stated earlier, the marketing system of Artistic Impressions comprised approximately 2,700 salespeople, who operated in more than forty states. In 1997, representatives of the company conducted more than 40,000 art shows. They arranged with hosts to invite friends, relatives, and acquaintances into living rooms to view sixty or more paintings, many of which were originals. Guests were pre-screened before each home so that the show could be customized for them. Consultants could request any type of artwork. If the person hosting the show wanted contemporary works in burgundies and greens, he or she would be sent twenty to thirty paintings with these color schemes.

When a show was scheduled, the consultant arrived at the host's home and displayed the artwork on an easel with up to forty framed samples. After the show, the guests, often including both husbands and wives, had an opportunity to buy the paintings. Typically, five to ten people attended a show and the presentation lasted about an hour. Future hosts were often selected from guests at the show. Hosts were eligible to purchase paintings from the company's product line at substantial discounts.

A consultant could earn up to $50 an hour for a show. The person hosting it would get 10 percent of the show's sales, which averaged $1,000—or $100 off a piece of artwork. If two of his or her guests ask to do a show in the future, he or she would get another $100 off another piece of artwork for each hostess. The typical art consultant who worked one night a week earned more than $10,000 a year. Special incentives to motivate associates included discounts on art, prizes, and trips to London, Switzerland, Hawaii, and Acapulco, Mexico. Commissions for consultants started at 22 percent and increased, depending on sales volume. "The consultants get about $8,000 in inventory they can use and trade every week through resupply to get new paintings for the shows," Thompson-Widmer said. "Our consultants do nothing more than set up shows, sell, get the commission, recruit more people, and we take care of the other aspects of the business."

The corporate sales training program, called "The System Works," was provided free to consultants by corporate management. Sales consultants were encouraged to qualify for management opportunities by recruiting others to become consultants. In this multilevel organization, consultants were eligible to initially become sales directors after recruiting three people as consultants. As sales directors, they earned commissions and bonuses on sales made by their new recruits. "The sales director gets an override, a percentage payback for training the consultants under them. The override increases with each level. We always pay four levels down," Thompson-Widmer explained. "Everything is based on current production, team building and team sales volume."

The first level of management was the sales director, and the next level, the regional manager. The regional manager supervised two sales directors. A regional manager with a team of two sales directors and twenty-four consultants scheduling, on average, two weekly shows each, could earn more than $50,000 annually. Some of the senior managers supervised several hundred independent contractors. The next level, zone manager, included two regions with twelve people each plus six people under them plus the individual. The top level was the executive manager, who supervised four zones in the hierarchy: consultants, sales directors, regional managers, and zone managers. Commission and bonuses increased as one moved up the hierarchy. In 1998, the sales force was primarily African-American. It was headed by Cedric Hill, also an African-American, who was president of the sales division. Before joining the Artistic Impressions management team, Hill was an aerospace engineer working at NASA. Hill and his team generated $8 million worth of sales within five years of joining the company.

To motivate sales associates, the company held an annual convention at a hotel in the Chicago area. The three-day event was designed as a business and networking environment. It featured a series of meetings of active consultants, team competition, new product introduction, entertainment, motivational sessions, and sales performance recognition. The artists who created the artwork sold by the company attended the convention, displaying their latest work and meeting with the company's representatives. Each year, Artistic Impressions recognized top achievers at all levels in personal sales, number of shows given, recruiting of new consultants, and so forth. Those attending the convention paid their own expenses. "We hold two regional meetings every year for our managers and keep training them," said Thompson-Widmer. "We also send our trainers from our corporate office to help train in the field as well. We pretty much run our business interacting with about seventy to seventy-five regional and zone managers. Although we send out mailings to all our representatives, our focus is to hit the regional managers."

The company did no national or regional advertising. Publicity was limited to feature stories on the company and its activities in magazines such as *Black Enterprise.*

DISTRIBUTION

Sales associates were not required to purchase inventory or deliver merchandise. The company shipped all products by United Parcel Service (UPS) from a distribution center adjacent to corporate headquarters in Lombard, Illinois, to the show host, who delivered them to customers. Approximately 7,000 framed paintings per week were shipped to show hosts.

PRICE

Listed prices of art works included the choice of frame from a basic line of thirty frames. The price range for the majority of artwork sold was $69 to $149. The company was concerned that the price of its product be kept within an affordable range for its customers. If customers chose the artwork of an upscale designer or a specialized, higher-quality, museum frame, they paid additional charges. Designer frames ranged in price from $10 to $30 more, depending on the size of the frame. The museum line of frames was available in only two sizes and sold for either $60 or $80. Frame liners were also available and cost from $10 to $30, depending on the size of artwork selected. Limited editions of figurines and plates sold exclusively by Artistic Impressions started at $29.95. Some special figurines emulated original paintings also sold by the company. R. Williams's *The Last Supper* was one such work, priced at $159.

CORPORATE RESPONSIBILITY

Artistic Impressions created a partnership with the National Foundation for Teaching Entrepreneurship (NFTE). Breighner served as its chairman, maintaining that it was important to "donate your talents as well as money to organizations of this type." He had raised more than $500,000 in the last five years for NFTE. NFTE provided entrepreneurial and motivational training for inner city youth, along with a practical plan for exiting poverty. Breighner intended to sponsor about twelve summer camps, to be offered free to inner city youth from up to a dozen U.S. cities. The Direct Selling Association honored Artistic Impressions with the "Vision for Tomorrow" award in recognition of its "contribution to support and launch the careers of disadvantaged youth."

THE CHALLENGE

Breighner was certain that he had positioned Artistic Impressions for continued success by appealing to a wider market. Others on his executive team were not so sure. They felt that the company was already struggling in 1998 just to get 7,000 mostly African-American paintings out to current customers. Some thought that any attempt to enter new markets would distract from the highly successful niche strategy that the company had developed since its inception. But Breighner held his ground:

The business we're in is selling art, framed art, and we do it primarily with a party plan, the home show method. But we're going to redo the mission because frankly, we're an opportunity-driven company.

References

Artistic Impressions, Inc. "Share the Exciting World of Art." Company sales brochure, 1998.

Artistic Impressions, Inc. Catalog Supplement, 1998.

Breighner, Bart. *Face to Face Selling*. Indianapolis: Park Avenue Publications, 1995.

Camerius, J. W., and J. W. Clinton. Interview with Bart Breighner, founder and president of Artistic Impressions, Inc. Lombard, Ill., May 12, 1998.

——. Interview with Deborah Thompson-Widmer, director of promotions and communications, Artistic Impressions, Inc. Lombard, Illinois, May 12, 1998.

Kuratko, D. F., and R. M. Hodgetts, *Entrepreneurship: A Contemporary Approach*. Fort Worth: Dryden Press, 1998.

Pride, W. M., and O. C. Ferrell. *Marketing: Concepts and Strategies*. Boston: Houghton Mifflin Company, 1993.

CASE 2

Brithinee Electric Revisited: "… *Raising the Standards*"

This case was prepared by Harold Dyck and Sue Greenfeld of California State University, San Bernadino.

INTRODUCTION

As teenagers, identical twins Wallace Jr. and Don Brithinee helped when their father, Wallace Sr., started Brithinee Electric in 1963. Back then, the entire business consisted of repairing electric motors. Providing service to customers with critical motor repair needs became an enduring philosophy of Brithinee Electric. On occasion, this meant "working around the clock." Hard work eventually earned the twin brothers Ph.D.'s in mathematics from the University of California, Riverside, by the time they were twenty-three years old, and led to the success of the firm in the succeeding decades. This success is demonstrated by various industry and manufacturers' awards presented to Brithinee Electric, proudly displayed in the lobby. Upstairs in the entrance to the conference room are pictures of Wally and Don Brithinee with distinguished political figures, including former head of the Joint Chiefs of Staff, General Colin Powell, and former British Prime Minister Margaret Thatcher.

Brithinee Electric repairs industrial motors, distributes motor-control devices, and designs and builds control panels, primarily for municipalities

and other businesses. In 1988, when this Colton, California, firm marked its twenty-five years in business, it had twenty-three employees, and $4.6 million in revenue. In subsequent years, a case study about it appeared in three strategic management textbooks.[1] The most pressing issues facing the company then included employee development, job rotation, overdependence on the "Brithinee boys," and a possible expansion. As the company was located in the Inland Empire (about 50 miles directly east of Los Angeles), an expansion would have meant serving the San Diego area with a new facility there. At that time, the company had an implied mission based on quality and service but no formal mission statement.

By 1999, Brithinee Electric had made many improvements and experienced a number of market developments. The company had witnessed a recession, lost a $1 million per year customer, observed dramatic changes in its industry, and improved employee training. It was less concerned about job rotation, had solved most of the overdependence issues, and had decided not to expand to San Diego. The firm also formalized a mission statement that included "enabling the customer" as an aim. The Brithinee philosophy means empowering their multiethnic employees to "provide literature, materials, specifications, and some learning opportunities for our customers." In addition, the company recently added the words "Brithinee Electric … Raising the Standards" to its "Customer Bill of Rights" (see Figures 1 and 2).

This case is intended to be used as the basis for class discussion rather than as an illustration of either effective or ineffective handling of the situation. This case was prepared by Harold Dyck, Ph.D., and Susan Greenfeld, D.B.A., California State University, San Bernardino. It was presented at North Armerican Case Research Association meeting, Sonoma, California, October 1999. Used by permission.

FIGURE 1

Brithinee's Mission Statement

Brithinee Electric

Our mission

to delight our customers by delivering products and services of superior quality, thereby raising their expectations.

Having grown their company to fifty employees and $6.7 million in revenues, Wally and Don Brithinee, sole owners of Brithinee Electric, now face different issues, many not foreseen in 1988. For example, the competition for selling electric motors is far more serious today than eleven years ago, and the market has changed toward more sophisticated control devices. Brithinee Electric faces these questions: How does an independent motor rewinding shop position itself for the twenty-first century? How can it distinguish itself from the competition? Can it position itself as a high-quality service provider when the customers don't understand the need for the standards? Figure 3 presents

FIGURE 2

Brithinee's Customer Bill of Rights

CUSTOMER BILL OF RIGHTS

At Brithinee Electric, we believe both the customer and the supplier of electrical hardware and service will benefit if the purchase decision is an informed one. Assert your rights as customer by getting to know your vendor's business practices. Get maximum value by comparing the vendor's commitment as well as the price.

As a customer of Brithinee Electric, you have the right to expect:

RELIABILITY
*   Stable workforce
*   Work references
*   Sound financial condition
*   Environmental responsibility

QUALITY
*   Qualified personnel
*   Documentation
*   Pride in workmanship
*   Best available technology

COMMUNICATION
*   Before and after tests reports
*   Prompt and accurate quotations
*   Product and service alternatives
*   Accurate itemized invoices

COMMITMENT
*   Service
*   Investment in technology and our facility
*   Investment in inventory
*   Problem solving

BRITHINEE
ELECTRIC
... Raising the Standards

FIGURE 3

Brithinee Electric's
Organization Chart

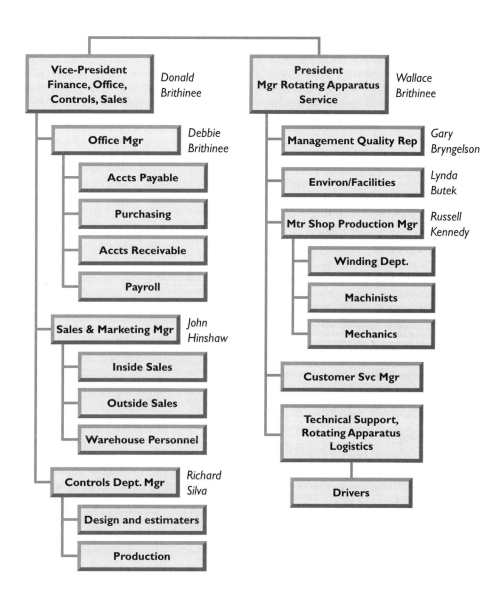

the current organizational chart, showing Wally
and Don Brithinee and key Brithinee personnel.

COMPANY HISTORY

Wallace Brithinee Sr. started Brithinee Electric in
1963 after two previous ventures did not work out.
However, these earlier ventures were the spring-
board for the formation of this third endeavor in repairing industrial motors. Even as young boys,
Wally and Don Brithinee were learning the rewinding business and worked alongside their father in
starting and developing the fledgling company.

In 1970, when Lincoln Electric, a large manufacturer of electric motors, came out with an appealing
low-price motor, the Brithinees made a strategic decision to become distributors in addition to repairing motors. This allowed the company to offer a
choice to the customer: replace or repair. By 1972,
Brithinee Electric had seven employees and enough
business to feel optimistic about the future—so it
built a 10,000 square-foot facility, which was expanded to 16,750 square feet seven years later. By
1980, the company had twenty-three employees,
and in 1982, Wallace Sr. stepped down, with Wally
and Don Brithinee taking over the business.

In 1987, Brithinee had about $4.5 million in rev-
enue, 75 percent of it from sales distribution (primarily for Toshiba and Baldor) and 25 percent from
repair of motors. Building customized control

panels, a new venture with one full-time employee, was not material enough to be listed as a separate category in the company's financial statements.

Various governmental agencies and utilities in the United States and Canada place the energy use of electric motors in industry at about 70 percent of total electrical energy consumption—roughly equivalent to the energy consumption of all passenger automobiles. Just as poor repair practices can increase gasoline consumption in an automobile, poor repair practices performed in the repair of an electric motor can decrease its energy efficiency. Thus, when Iraq invaded Kuwait in August 1990, threatening Western oil supplies, legislators in the United States and Canada revised energy legislation from the 1970s. Regulators, noting that the motor horsepower repaired far exceeds the horsepower sold new, studied the repair process for electric motors, as well as the purchasing practices of industrial firms. Although draconian measures such as licensing schemes or even the banning of motor repair in favor of replacement with new, energy-efficient models were being considered, the sentiment for less government intervention led to voluntary-compliance programs that seek to transform the market.

Besides trying to reduce U.S. dependence on foreign oil, the U.S. government signed several climate-change treaties (for instance, Rio de Janeiro and Kyoto) and agreed to reduce greenhouse gas emissions. Since fossil-fuel power plants are large contributors to such emissions, it will be necessary to decrease their loads to reach the targeted reductions, and electric motor-driven systems are a large component of the load. Hence, heightened environmental concerns can be seen as a further contributor to the pressure to improve electric motor repair practices.

While the industrial user of an electric motor–driven system may not be greatly motivated by the distant feel of U.S. treaties or global warming, such a user is highly motivated by both the potential for greater reliability of the machinery stemming from improved repair practices and by the prospect of lower power bills. Consequently, Wally Brithinee, as the chairman of the Engineering Committee of the Electrical Apparatus Service Association (EASA), took the lead in developing a set of standards and guidelines for repair of electric motors that met most of the regulators' objections. These became the "building blocks" for the motor repair industry, ush-

ering in a "market transformation." These standards also became a marketing tool for Brithinee Electric.

In 1991, the company experienced its first significant decline in revenues. It "hit a brick wall," says Don Brithinee. The United States suffered a recession, which Brithinee weathered with some pain. The company also lost its $1 million per year customer, "through no fault of their own." This customer was lost because it could not accommodate the change in the size of the variable frequency drive that Brithinee was supplying. The total revenue declined further in 1992 before turning upward and resuming a growth mode. In 1996, revenue finally exceeded that of 1990. Brithinee takes pride in the fact that no one was laid off during the downturn, though some employees were asked to use their accumulated vacation time.

In 1992, Brithinee made three changes to accommodate the rebuilding of large quantities of locomotive motors from the Electro-Motive Division (EMD) of General Motors and to expand inventory space. First, it acquired a second 13,000 square-foot building (called the "680 Building" because of its address) about 100 yards south of the old site. This building cost $495,000, for which the company spent $141,000 for remodeling. Second, it moved $500,000 of inventory out of the main building into the new building, enlarged the winding machine shop areas, and dedicated special floor space to EMD. Third, it established more stringent quality procedures than had previously existed.

Acquiring the new building pushed Brithinee Electric in a new strategic direction: designing and building control panels. Previously, Brithinee "dabbled" in making control panels, but now that became a significant part of the business. The company prefers not to be dependent on one industry. Its main work is in water pumping and treatment, rock crushing, cement facilities, and the food industry, including wineries and breweries. The decline in aerospace and defense orders in the early 1990s taught many southern California businesses not to have all their eggs in one basket.

The expansion of control panels was a "Y in the road," says Don. "It is a different beast . . . it's a cleaner operation . . . it's not a repair operation at all. It is an assembly of new electronic components." As part of this new focus, in 1992, Brithinee hired Richard Silva, who was instrumental in attaining Underwriter Laboratories (UL) certification for the company. Consequently, Square D and Telemecanique, both subsidiaries of Groupe Schneider, a French multinational corporation, became major new customers.

In addition, Lynda Butek, the environmental/facilities coordinator, who works directly for Wally Brithinee, was responsible for the 1992 installation of a closed-loop aqueous parts washer for loads weighing up to 20,000 pounds. Previously, the company had to dispose of large quantities of water from a washdown area. Figures 4 and 5 show the current facilities.

In 1997, the original "620 building" underwent a major renovation, costing $315,000. As he describes the changes Wally states the reasons for the remodeling:

> . . . to control the environment in the manufacturing area, and to make it reflect the quality of the products produced there. In that regard, we had specific goals and tasks. One was to reduce noise and increase the desirability of the eastern one-third of the building as a work area. That area has certain processes with air handlers and pumps that generate audible noise. These include

the paint booth exhaust; the sand-blast cabinet and dust collector; and the parts washer, with its array of pumps. We evaluated all the lighting in the building and greatly increased it. . . .

At the same time, controls were centralized so that it would be easy to reduce lighting and electrical consumption when personnel were not in the work area. During the remodel, we added insulation with value of R–30 and covered the ceiling with a white plastic sheath. That moderated temperatures, further reduced noise, and increased the effectiveness of the light. The effects were dramatic.

Shop offices were enlarged, allowing better supervisory control at the plant floor. A laser printer was added, with fax-modem, and the shop offices became much more efficient. There was far less cause for drivers, delivery persons, and shop personnel to come into the business office. The offices of this building were redone to eliminate the large, open office area. As we had grown, the open area seemed to create many

FIGURE 4

Layout of the 620 Building

FIGURE 5

Layout of the
680 Building

distractions to the tasks at hand and to offer
sound interference for telephone conversations.

The conference room that existed was reshaped and enlarged, and today is fitted with a
table for executive meetings. The decor has
been completely redone from its early 1970s
look, to a more modern look.

As other shops in Southern California have
closed, larger motors are coming in for repairs at
Brithinee. Wanting to handle larger stators and ro-
tors, the company is adding a vacuum pressure im-
pregnation (VPI) tank as an integral part of their
repair facility. Putting in the new VPI tank required
digging a 10- to 12-foot pit and getting various environmental protection permits.

Brithinee primarily uses personal selling to establish relationships, and it benefits from word-of-
mouth advertising. In late 1997, the company hired
Cyd Sandefur as an assistant to Don Brithinee to
work on advertising and other special projects.

Today, total revenues are at $6.99 million, with
43 percent from repair work, 26 percent from motor
sales, and the remaining 31 percent from custom-

made control panel sales. Whereas eleven years
earlier the accounting records were separated into
statements for repairs and statements for sales, today
there is a single consolidated statement. This system
gives the company the flexibility to move people
from one area to another but loses the detailed information concerning specific labor charges.

INDUSTRY DYNAMICS

At the end of the 1980s, sales of new motors grew
at a 20 percent rate. As the industry edged into the
1990s, the market matured, prices came down and
reliability went up. Features became more user-
friendly. The product became more standardized,
and was more widely sold in consumer markets. By
the late 1990s, competition heated up to the point
that twelve out of thirteen of Toshiba's top distributors in variable-frequency drives (inverters) decreased their year-to-year purchases. "What
changed was better competition from some premium brand names," states Don. Brithinee Electric
could not keep pace as a straight-forward distribu-

tor, and its market share of new motor sales dropped, contrary to its expectations.

The variable-frequency drives greatly changed the industry by increasing motor system efficiency, reducing energy consumption, and shifting market demand. These drives introduce high-voltage pulses, thousands each second, into the motor windings, resulting in "partial discharge" and corona. This produces highly corrosive ozone and charged particles that erode the organic insulation from the windings. These problems could cost customer goodwill while increasing costs to rework a motor. When a motor winding fails, the entire job must be redone. Previously, insulation life could be ten to twelve years without a failure, but with the new electronic frequency drives, wire failures could occur within a few hundred hours of operation.

Before the failure mechanism was known (and it is still under investigation), the Engineering Committee of the EASA met with researchers from various laboratories and from manufacturers of the basic building-block materials within a motor winding. The purpose was to make sure that the needs of the repair industry were known and to inform that there was an increase in winding failures not easily explained by inspection and analysis used in the past. If and when more resistant materials became available, the motor repair industry should not be the last to find out.

The development of the microprocessor-controlled variable-frequency drive paralleled that of the computer during the 1990s. This created opportunities for improved process control as well as energy efficiency of the driven system. Roughly during the same time, the Energy Policy Act of 1992 (EPACT) caused motor manufacturers to redesign industrial electric motors to be more energy-efficient. The design changes generally included increasing the active materials in the stator and rotor. In the stator (the part that is usually rewound), those active materials are the laminated steel sheets ("core iron") and the copper wire. In the case of the wire, the designer increases the cross-section of the conductor, while the length of the wire is reduced, thus reducing winding resistance. But these design changes usually result in increased difficulty for coil insertion (trying to stuff more copper into a very crowded frame and core). Thus, the repair industry needed thinner, tougher, slicker insulation in order to maintain the energy

efficiency of the motor, yet have resistance to the harsh electrical environment from the variable-frequency drive that may be applied.

Meetings with Du Pont's Nomex and Kevlar researchers and marketers in Richmond, Virginia, as well as with key industry suppliers of wire (Essex Group, Phelps Dodge) and resins (P. D. George Company), reiterated all these issues. Additionally, EASA's Engineering Committee met several times with the technical subsection of the NEMA Motors and Generators Committee, so that every effort was made to strengthen the information ties between manufacturers and the repair industry. The result was guidelines for motor rewinding that provide both an energy-efficient rewind and a winding that can give long life in the variable-frequency applications, using materials that are readily available.

While chairing the EASA committee, Wally Brithinee recognized that there were marketing issues for Brithinee Electric in winding an "inverter-duty" motor. It enhanced the relationship with several motor manufacturers, and helped to distinguish the windings coming out of his company's facility as perhaps superior to the new motors' windings.

In 1999, Brithinee Electric had less repair competition than it did in the eleven previous years. The large manufacturers with repair shops had withdrawn from Southern California. Don says, "The playing field is a lot more level when we are competing with another independent company than with the captive business of a major manufacturer. That has brought some positive changes for us because we don't have the pressure of competing with some of the majors."

The closings included ASEA Brown Boveri, a Swiss company, which was a 30,000 square foot shop, 30 miles to the west of Brithinee Electric. Electro-Motive Division of General Motors folded its motor repair facility in Los Angeles, while Reliance Electric shut its shop in Anaheim. Westinghouse had been gone for a number of years, and General Electric did little repair of high-voltage motors and no longer did rewind. The last big captive shop was owned by McGraw-Edison, which was sold to MagneTek. This company in turn sold the operation to Eastern Electric, which uses a much smaller staff. Since the majors have vanished, opportunities for independents in the industry have improved. Don wonders: Why did the "big boys" leave the market? Do they know something we don't know? How can Brithinee capitalize on these industry changes?

EXTERNAL AND GOVERNMENTAL INTERFACES

As part of their commitment to educating and raising the expectations of their customers, Wally Brithinee and Lynda Butek have taken on leadership roles within EASA. Wally, we saw earlier, became chair of the Engineering Committee. Lynda became chair of the Environmental Affairs Committee, renamed the Governmental Affairs Committee, and also serves on the Insurance and Safety Committee. She says that involvement in the EASA "really helped the business from a technical standpoint." This committee work has kept Brithinee abreast of the newest materials and technology and given it the opportunity to initiate and maintain contacts with wire, insulation materials, and equipment manufacturers.

In addition, the company works closely with several regulatory agencies, including the South Coast Air Quality Management District (SCAQMD) and the Air Resources Board (ARB) of California, to help streamline regulations. There are several agencies in California with overlapping jurisdictions, but they do not appear to communicate with each other. Every year, Lynda fills out three sets of forms with basically the same information for three different state agencies. For example, she recalls a report which took her half a day to prepare. Brithinee owed $6.95 for particulate matter emissions (for example, sulfur oxide, methane, hydrogen oxide, 1.1.1 trichloroethane and carbon monoxide). Lynda questions the reasonableness of all these agencies and considers how to best streamline the processes to minimize repetition and how to gather the information with the least disruptions of work. She believes, "that California is still the toughest state to get permits in." Wally adds that whatever happens in California is closely watched by the industry in other states. As Wally reflects on his involvement with EASA and various agencies, he ponders how to best influence government regulatory policies. Is there anything he can do to minimize agency overlap and duplication of effort for

the industry? How can EASA lobby state and federal agencies to become more business-friendly while also protecting society?

OPERATIONS

Motor Repair—"Your Emergencies Are Our Concern"

Brithinee repairs motors up to 1000 HP, 4000 volts, and currently up to 5 tons. According to Wally Brithinee, "95 percent of all motors 200 horsepower and above can be expected to be repaired once in their lifetime." Motor repair begins with the receiving of incoming electrical motors. Using contract drivers and its own fleet of trucks, Brithinee picks up and delivers customers' motors, or customers will bring the motors to the shop. The motors then undergo initial inspection and testing before being dismantled. The core is tested and the old windings are burned off in a temperature-controlled oven. Then a second core test is performed. The motors are rewound with new quadruple-build or inverter-duty magnet wire. Connections are made and an inspection performed before additional assembly and final testing. Approximately 70 percent of the motor is used in the remanufacture; most of the rest is recycled. The finished motor repair can maintain energy efficiency within $\frac{1}{2}$ percent of what the motor was designed for. Finally the motor is prepared for shipping and delivery to the customer. Brithinee does not repair motors on site due to liability, the difficulty associated with burning off the old windings, the use of chemicals, rewinding, assembly, and bonding of the new wire inside the industrial motor (see Figure 6).

The Motor Repair Workflow

Russ Kennedy, production manager since 1988, oversees the workflow from start to finish. He makes the work assignments and ensures that finished goods are delivered in a timely fashion. He documents the initial conditions of incoming motors using one of three digital cameras, and the images are stored electronically on a Macintosh. This has improved the process "tremendously" over the previously used Polaroids. Benefits include lower

FIGURE 6

Flow Chart for
Motor Repair

Workers walk into Russ's office and pick up their assignments—with the photos on them. The motors are placed in bins both alphabetically and numerically. Supposedly, every job has a home, but with three shifts and uneven pallet sizes, workers on limited occasions will put a motor "wherever," and finding that motor "can become an Easter egg hunt," says Russ. Brithinee still has jobs in the shop from 1995. For example, a company that owns a $30,000 motor may not have sufficient funds in its budget to get it repaired immediately, so it just leaves the motor with Brithinee. Although Brithinee has cleared out a significant number of these older jobs, its management still wonders, "at what point do you provide service to your customers by storing the motors *gratis* vs. charging for that storage?"

A typical repair can range from $600 to $7,000. The job comes in, an estimate is made by fax or phone, and the customer is allowed to respond to the quote before the repair proceeds. Motors are scheduled for repair based on customer need as determined at a daily production meeting, at which the day and night shift production and customer service team discusses work-in-progress. At that time, the team determines the priority for open jobs and discusses what work will be performed during the night shifts. In the early 1990s, EASA created laminated charts with acceptable tolerance values to allow the workers to compare the fit of each part. These charts are placed at each workstation. Various agencies now recommend that customers patronize repair facilities using the guidelines developed by EASA.

Russ color codes the work orders: green for go, red for stop, and orange for a "hot" rush job. Orange jobs go to the head of the queue. Russ cites the case where the City of Riverside didn't have water for ten city blocks, and Brithinee Electric worked through the night to complete the rush job. The customer pays a premium for the overtime when that happens. Jobs may be assigned by worker's ability. A priority job can preempt another job, "by the minute," says Russ. The repair of a "hot" rush job from a very big customer may begin before a quote has been accepted, causing consternation in the accounts receivable department. This department has the responsibility to satisfy the customer's purchasing and accounting needs. Brithinee wonders: how to provide a procedure that meets the needs of the accounting department without holding up

costs, more flexibility, more views of each motor, and file-handling capability. Having a picture associated electronically with the work order has decreased the number of misunderstandings with workers and customers. For example, one customer, after delivery of the repaired motor, inquired about a missing part. A picture cleared up the problem.

emergency work? Besides, one of Wally's goals is to reduce Brithinee's overtime costs. Three-fourths of the costs of repair is labor while one-fourth goes for parts and material.

Layout and Work Stoppages

With from 75 to 110 work orders open at any one time and eighteen workers on the day shift, five on the swing shift, and three on graveyard shift, there is never any time a worker is idle. Occasionally, a machine may be idle when workers are pulled off a machine to work on a rush job. There used to be bottlenecks in the shop floor area and it was thought that more space would remedy the problem. A consultant hired to redesign the plant layout interviewed everyone and made suggestions about restructuring the work area to get a better workflow. She told them, Russ recalls, that "you don't need more room, you just need to change the way you do things." Previously, process work crossed paths too frequently from department to department. The company corrected the problem by relocating aisles and increasing their size, adding electrical outlets and lighting, and improving each workstation. The more hazardous repair operations were separated out to a specific area.

Other problems included work stoppages, which would occur when work crews ran out of propane gas. No one was monitoring the gas level. Regular deliveries by a propane gas vendor freed workers to concentrate on the task at hand. Russ wonders: what is the appropriate level of outsourcing? Besides the delivery of gas propane, are there any other areas which Brithinee should consider?

Customer Reports

Beginning in 1993, Brithinee Electric began providing to the customer a previously internal computer report on why a motor fails. Brithinee decided to share this information with its customers to add value to the service it provides, and to raise the level of their expectations.

This report explains what was found, how the motor tested when it came in, and how it tests when it goes out. Included are specifics about vibration, resistance of the winding, and types of bearings installed, which provide a baseline for the motor's performance. Wally says, "We don't expect [the customer] to even ask for what they really

need. . . . With our training and outreach programs through the Department of Energy, [we ask ourselves] 'how do you get the user of electrical motor systems to develop or purchase a good system—for both efficiency and reliability?'"

Lynda Butek says, "Brithinee Electric has always had a reputation for quality . . . and that reputation has tripled in the last nine to ten years. Wally has instituted a very rigorous testing and reporting system for our customers that they didn't even know they wanted." She indicates that at first customers appeared to ignore the report, but "now you try not to send it and you get a phone call. 'Where is my report? I need my report!'" Not only do customers expect to receive the report from Brithinee; now they also expect to obtain such a report from Brithinee's competitors.

Customized Control Panels

Customized control panels involve building industrial integrated systems, dealing with programmable logic controllers, motor controls, and variable frequency drives. Brithinee sees itself as neither a mass producer nor a low-price leader. From one employee in 1987, this department now has grown to eight employees. Sometimes the workload for control panels expands, and up to nine people are "borrowed" from the repair side to complete a project. Brithinee is a niche player, specializing in drives and soft-start applications, which reduce stresses associated with each motor start and increase the longevity of the motor. A control panel can cost $1,000 to $10,000 in labor time to design. Brithinee sometimes charges separately for designing the control panel and related software, and for manufacture.

When Brithinee hired Richard Silva, the controls department manager, in 1992, one of his first assignments was to establish the necessary procedures in order to manufacture control panels listed with Underwriters Laboratories, under UL Standard 508 and, later, UL845. While Underwriters Laboratories does not share liability, the UL label does convey that the listed product meets accepted safety standards in its construction, thereby reducing the risk of liability. "It legitimizes you. . . . It has been real good for our business. It has opened doors, and been a plus for us," says Richard Silva.

Richard indicates that Brithinee will "overdesign" a product, meaning that it builds to guarantee product performance. If the panel fails, it hurts the company in two ways: (1) the costs to send someone to fix the problem and (2) the company's reputation is damaged. "First time, every time we want it to work," says Richard. For example, Brithinee uses a larger-size wire and will dip it in tin to lessen problems associated with heat. Brithinee also investigates where the panel will be installed and serviced and it takes into account environmental conditions, such as heat, moisture, and wind. One panel shipped to the United Arab Emirates was designed with parts that would be available locally if the need should arise.

For the UL845, Richard works with several large companies, including Square D. Square D finds Brithinee's control panel operations very flexible. Brithinee can build control panels in a hurry, faster than Square D's own plant can do. As Richard describes the sales sequence, "Brithinee is a subcontractor to Square D who sells the product to a distributor who sells it to an electrical contractor who will sell it to the general contractor who actually sells to the municipality or utility company." Square D also supplies Brithinee with some control panel parts. Thus, Square D is both a supplier and a customer and represents major dollars with few billings.

Candace Winn, manager of Square D's Oceanside, California plant, describes her company's relationship with Brithinee as "unique." She says, "We talk to them all the time on the phone three to six times a day. . . . They have a real knack for educating the customer." She feels confident that when she gets a job from Brithinee it is done correctly, and she almost considers the firm to be a sister company. David Whitney, senior sales engineer at Square D, who calls on industrial-type end-users in Orange County and part of Los Angeles County, characterizes the Square D–Brithinee relationship as more like a partnership than as a customer-supplier one. He remarks, "There is a lot of trust and shared information. . . . Brithinee has a lot of product expertise. They will see what our customers want and design it for them."

AutoCAD drawing adds to Brithinee's flexibility and allows the company to get its product to the market faster by compressing the design phase. For a job with design specifications, the length of the project could be years, and they might not even win the bid. Once a project is approved, it typically takes four to six weeks to build a control panel. The longest lead time is acquiring the metal structure that houses the electrical components. Building the control panel might take only a week or two.

In scheduling a control panel job, Richard plans for unexpected delays, but the control panel department takes special pride in having so far met all the deadlines for shipping their products. Richard affirms that "we have never, ever, ever missed a ship date. Never. We will never miss a ship date. . . . I have been here Saturday and Sunday to make a ship date. . . . It is important to us. You are only as good as your reputation."

Richard explains that the UL508 directory looks "like a telephone directory," but there are only twenty companies in the United States with the UL845 certification. Other companies with the UL845 are very large corporations, such as Siemens, Allen-Bradley, and Square D. More than the UL508 certification, the UL845 has elevated the visibility of Brithinee Electric and helped it obtain more business.

Several Brithinee individuals mention that repair costs are well known and manageable, but a good system for determining the labor costs and profit on control panels has eluded them. Richard explains that "labor has been a real problem. Until recently, we did not have a good way to keep track of accounting hours." Sometimes Brithinee would not know for six months whether it made money on a job. For bidding on a job, Brithinee bases its estimates on historical data, but each job can be unique and variable. Richard ponders what it would take to get the feedback he needs to make better bids, win more contracts, and increase the profitability of the firm.

ISO AND EASA Q CERTIFICATIONS

The International Organization for Standardization (ISO) created worldwide guidelines to promote operational efficiency, improve productivity, and reduce costs. The ISO 9000 concept took off in the early 1990s and has helped to define world-class quality systems. Most large manufacturers (for instance, Toshiba, General Motors, and Square D) are ISO 9000.

There are three models of ISO 9000: 9001, 9002, and 9003. (However, a new revision is expected to have only one model.) The most rigorous of the ISO standards is the ISO 9001, which means that the company has certification in design, engineering, and manufacturing, whereas ISO 9002 means qualification in just manufacturing. The ISO standards guarantee a formalized system to create a product in a consistent manner. They do not guarantee quality in terms of customer satisfaction as measured against expectations.

The Electrical Apparatus Service Association (EASA) has initiated a related standard, the EASA Q. Lynda Butek asserts that this standard " is *more* than the ISO 9002 ... [it is 9002] plus specific procedures only having to do with motor rewind. It also includes a customer satisfaction audit of certain selected customers, which the ISO 9002 does not have." The EASA Q was put together by the Technical Services Committee of EASA, chaired by Wally Brithinee.

Russ Kennedy says that movement toward EASA Q and ISO 9002 "makes my job easier with the documentation. Procedures are being implemented that everyone's following. It helps change the mindset of a 20-year mechanic to conform to today's standards and regulations. . . . It's a great adventure we're in right now. It makes work very interesting, and these guys [the Brithinee brothers] are behind it."

On the other hand, is ISO really necessary given the company's UL certification? Candace Winn, at Square D, says that it is the *UL* certifications that distinguish Brithinee from other control panel makers. Of the three certifications (that is, UL845, ISO 9002, and EASA Q), the UL845 is "drastically important," she says.

The pressure for achieving ISO 9002 is internally driven. "It is not a big market issue here in Southern California," says Wally. Other industries (i.e., paper and petroleum) are moving toward ISO 9000 certification, but there is no market pressure for Brithinee. "Most of our customers are not terribly concerned about [our being ISO 9002 certified]," says Don. "For our size business, it doesn't seem to be an expectation."

In some industries, ISO helps a company compete on the global scene, but none of Brithinee's repair work is international due to the high cost of transporting heavy industrial motors. A few international sales of control panels systems occur, though, since the value per pound is significantly higher.

Brithinee designed process flow charts for its jobs with GM's Electro-Motive Division, where procedures were more standardized than in their other rewinding business. These procedures include calibration of all measuring instruments. A byproduct of the GM work has been the addition of similar systems for Brithinee's other motor repair work.

While ISO 9000 certification is not a major issue for Brithinee (which already has a relationship with GM), GM uses it as a screen to prequalify when selecting new vendors.

According to Don, Brithinee Electric would like to avoid errors in office and administration (such as invoicing), in the repair shop, and in the control systems areas. It would like to develop systems in how to provide feedback, detection and prevention of errors. "Every point seems to be a spot in which we can make savings." For example, Brithinee sold a vehicle and verbally canceled the cellular telephone service associated with that vehicle. The provider stated it did not need anything in writing to cancel the telephone number. Debbie Brithinee, the firm's office manager and Don's wife, wrote a memo to staff members to watch out that no further charges came through on that telephone number. Something got lost in the procedure, and sixteen months later they realized that they had been charged $70 a month for a telephone number that had zero calls on it. The telephone company refused to refund the money. Don wonders whether it is worth the time and energy to change cellular telephone vendors, or could better procedures have prevented this error from occurring in the first place?

Another costly error occurred with a large customized control panel order when the individual quoting the price made a mistake in handling the spreadsheet. Accidentally, 18 percent of the materials were not added into the cost, virtually wiping out any profit—all because the line was not included in a summation. This was the largest job Brithinee has ever had. If a company has significant customized business, how does it create standardized systems and procedures? Can standardized procedures catch mistakes in Brithinee's processes? ISO certification of procedures may be one way to prevent procedural errors.

ISO 9000 certification is a popular movement in other industries, and Don and Wally Brithinee wonder if ISO certification could make their company more competitive in the electrical apparatus industry. Could it add value? David Whitney at Square D remarks that Brithinee would be smart to attain ISO 9000 as many big customers, such as Boeing, sometimes ask about quality programs, and "it certainly helps to be able to say 'we are working with customers with ISO.'"

Don wonders if achieving ISO 9002 would "awaken that interest" in the firm's customers?

Brithinee is getting virtually no external pressure from its customers to become ISO certified. The principal benefit would be the internal side—the savings associated with going through the process of developing these systems. "Our goal will eventually be to achieve ISO 9002, but we are still a ways off.... We are working on a number of fronts towards that end," says Wally. He also ponders the question: Is the year 2000 a realistic goal for achieving this certification?

THE VALUE CHAIN, RELATIONSHIP MARKETING, AND ADVERTISING

The value chain is defined as the sum of activities from start to finish that add value. These activities include procurement, design, assembly, remanufacture, distribution, marketing, and service. Relationship marketing involves creating and maintaining long-term relationships with external and internal customers. These concepts are part of Brithinee's long-term strategy.

Brithinee Electric is more engaged in value-added activities and in creating longer-term relationships with both suppliers and customers than it had been in 1987. Ten years ago, Brithinee did not have much value-added assembly. The contract with EMD Locomotive provided one value-added dimension in the repair shop. Most sales in 1987 were off-the-shelf packages for Toshiba and Baldor. Brithinee Electric was not good at retaining that type of sales. It lacked retail outlets and could not compete with aggressive discount houses entering this market in the early 1990s. However, control panels added new opportunities for its business, capitalizing on its interest in customized high-tech products and services in the electrical apparatus industry.

Relationship marketing is also evident with Square D, where Brithinee actually helps David Whitney (at Square D) sell to his customers. Brithinee becomes an extension of Square D's value-added chain, and vice versa. "My customer may be a water district and I may ask where do they get their motors repaired and suggest to the customer that they contact Brithinee," comments Dave.

Two outside salespeople generate business by calling on customers and identifying new prospects, whether in the repair area, sales, or control panels. Its competitors sometimes refer a customer to Brithinee, and it reciprocates on occasion

when it cannot fulfill a customer's request. Bill Gaborko at C&M Electric, a small local competitor, receives telephone referrals from Brithinee to handle single-phase motors. C&M does not do large motors, and it refers those customers to Brithinee.

The Brithinee philosophy is to grow and maintain the business primarily with existing customers, but also go after new customers. "Getting a new customer is the most expensive part of a business," says John Hinshaw, the sales and marketing manager. The company looks for new "business starts" in the Inland Empire.

John confirms that the computer-generated repair reports given to customers on the problems found and the job done has helped raise customers' expectations and that those customers now require the same information from Brithinee's competitors. He also stresses, like Richard Silva, the value of the UL label and sees it as the most important certification in generating sales locally, especially for the control panel side of the business. For example, the city of Los Angeles does not care about ISO 9000. "For electrical safety, UL is it," John comments.

Brithinee is exploring new ways to generate sales because it would like to run its three shifts at full strength and to increase revenues and profit margins. Using a Dun & Bradstreet "Marketplace" CD-ROM set, it has identified hundreds of prospects that are like its client base. The company has also discovered that sometimes its repair customers don't know about the control side of the business, and vice versa.

In order to reach out to a new customer base, Don Brithinee and Cyd Sandefur have been attending a marketing class at a local community college. She helps Don create presentation material for seminars and find other ways as well to familiarize the public with the company and its work. The presentations have been given to groups of customers or through the EASA trade organization, both on-site and out in the field. These seminars cover such topics as how to hook up and safely use industrial motors, how to make the equipment run better, and how to do maintenance planning. Wally believes that, "customers are better customers when they know what we do."

Don and Cyd have also toyed with the idea of creating a supply chain to Arizona and northern California because there are carrier services that guarantee overnight delivery. Cyd says that they are still in the infancy stage of their marketing efforts and are considering what further steps Brithinee could take to market itself.

ACCOUNTING AND INFORMATION TECHNOLOGY

Before she was hired by Brithinee Electric, Debbie Brithinee, Don's wife, had worked for seventeen years in accounting, purchasing, and trust operations in a county government, overseeing a $70 million budget. Periodically, she helped on special projects for the Brithinee firm before becoming Brithinee's office manager in 1990. She is now responsible for Brithinee's general ledger and other types of accounting. Table 1 presents an eleven-year overview of Brithinee's financial status, including its balance sheet and income statement.

In 1998, at the request of employees, Brithinee introduced a 401(k) profit-sharing plan. It was implemented after companywide meetings and a vote. Until then, the company had placed annual bonuses into a guaranteed fund that could not be tapped by the employees. With the 401(k) plan, Brithinee is committing funds monthly, which is difficult since the company does not know how profitable it will be at year's end. Debbie says that

"our financial statements look very different month-to-month than they did in prior years. . . . it was a big step for us to go into the 401(k)." Employees are fully vested in the 401(k) the first day they begin work. The two advantages of the 401(k), as Wally sees it are that the employees are both aware of the plan throughout the year and control the funds. The question he wrestles with, however, is how to ensure that employees "understand a tie-in between . . . [their] performance and the company's performance," for if the employees "are to succeed, the company needs to succeed."

Another accounting issue is the difficulty of measuring labor associated with control panel projects. "We don't do cost accounting," Debbie says. "In the repair shop, we have done considerable analysis on what goes into a repair. . . . But in the control panel area, it's very, very difficult to get a handle on that. That's what we're working on now." She would like to know what systems would capture information to solve this problem. Could the company develop better methods to account for the dramatic differences that occur between initial estimates and the actual building of the control panel? These differences include labor uncertainty and changes in the prices of parts. Customer design changes can also complicate the process. Debbie wonders whether the firm can overcome its

TABLE 1

Brithinee Electric's Financial Statements, 1988–1998

	Balance Sheet			
	1988	*1989*	*1990*	*1991*
Assets				
Current assets	1,278,365	1,644,500	1,551,245	1,229,799
Fixed assets less accumulated depreciation	121,739	82,625	139,922	193,562
Other assets	14,716	14,716	14,716	7,876
Total	1,414,820	1,741,841	1,705,884	1,431,238
Liabilities and Shareholders' Equity				
Current liabilities	356,096	563,656	332,276	328,377
Longterm liabilities				
Shareholders' equity	1,058,724	1,178,184	1,373,607	1,102,860
Total	1,414,820	1,741,841	1,705,884	1,431,238
Income Statement				
Gross income	4,836,401	5,372,555	5,643,979	4,530,838
Cost of goods sold	3,349,853	3,766,378	3,751,243	3,013,072

reluctance to adjust the original estimate once changes occur. Tracking purchase orders is problematic, according to Cyd Sandefur, who is doing the tracking manually. She says that "things change in the middle of the project. Something will be quoted that doesn't work." This means renegotiation for parts and prices.

In terms of information technology, Don states, "We enjoy our computers . . . we probably have thirty computers scattered around . . . versus only one or two ten years ago. . . . This is a big plus." These computers include both Macintosh and Windows NT-based machines operating on the same network. The software they use allows both types of machines to work side by side entering orders, sending mail, accessing data files and exchanging data across the network. The company has created its local area network (LAN) and is on the Internet but does not have its own Web site. Don reflects, "I don't find that most of the customers we deal with would find their way to us through [a Web site] . . . not yet." The company is seeking lower-cost ways of reaching its customers.

Regarding the company's use of computers, Wally calls them "a shop tool." He created the spreadsheets that track progress of motors through the repair processes. "It is not universally acknowledged that you would put computers in the shop area," he says. Don further elaborates that "we don't have an integrated system for our order entry and accounting." Brithinee has purchased some custom software to reduce paperwork and streamline processes, but it has yet to be implemented. The goal is to reduce the amount of hours devoted to accounting, and Don wonders how best to achieve it.

PERSONNEL ISSUES

Brithinee Electric's reputation for dealing with emergencies tends to attract more emergencies. "Always being in a panic mode" was wearing its personnel down. To respond to this problem and to create a less stressful organizational climate, Brithinee undertook two actions: it contracted with a psychological consultant who could assist the company in its hiring practices, and it added a second and third shift.

In 1996, the industrial psychologist began pretesting applicants, a process intended to comply with employment discrimination laws. "We have been trying to put together a company of more like-minded people," states Don. "We have managed to remove some personnel who were a problem for us. . . . This has made the organizational environment more pleasant and conveyed a better image

Balance Sheet						
1992	1993	1994	1995	1996	1997	1998 (Proj)
1,105,523	1,997,596	1,125,322	1,195,479	1,269,494	1,501,129	1,446,709
271,273	223,745	293,329	240,558	363,180	406,165	441,091
2,087	6,896	6,896	6,896	1,093	2,004	1,951
1,378,883	1,228,238	1,425,546	1,442,933	1,633,767	1,909,299	1,889,752
540,978	376,593	3,787,799	292,863	305,465	550,758	351,239
		28,079	19,036	26,708	36,106	27,662
837,905	851,644	1,018,668	1,131,034	1,301,593	1,322,434	1,510,850
1,378,883	1,228,237	1,425,546	1,442,933	1,633,767	1,909,299	1,889,752
4,405,211	4,968,783	5,127,066	5,995,404	5,696,261	6,490,431	7,027,731
3,045,850	3,260,598	3,344,487	2,854,561	3,525,998	4,370,105	4,483,012

to our customers and even our vendors." Brithinee profiled both potential employees and, with their permission, the existing employees. This has given the company insights as to why certain personalities work well together and others do not. As Russ Kennedy explains, "We want people to fit . . . the Brithinee profile."

Another aspect of the current employee tests resulted in people being moved around. "This seems to be working out a lot better," comments Lynda Butek. In addition, Brithinee has instituted drug testing for preemployment screening and created a "no-tolerance drug usage policy." Employees using illegal drugs were removed. Among them was an individual who had crashed a truck, and was creating morale problems. His dismissal boosted morale in the shop. While some may view such firings as harsh, one employee describes the management style at Brithinee as "very forgiving." For example, the company allows people the flexibility to make mistakes, and most employees seem to appreciate this.

In hiring additional personnel for a second and third shift, it was important to choose those with the "right characteristics." Brithinee used to have attrition due to employee burnout. Now, the work is shared by a broader group of workers with similar goals. In addition, the company has three or four "all purpose, no purpose" utility people at the entry level. "We have grown on all fronts . . . [and now] we take emergencies more in stride," says Russ.

Brithinee Electric suffers from some growth-related problems common to small, family-owned businesses. Long-time employees remember working side by side with Don and Wally and have difficulty following the chain of command. The psychologist has aided the company by redefining job descriptions and creating more fully and carefully documented employee manuals. He has also helped Wally and Don communicate better with each other. Wally mentions that he is sold on the value of using a psychologist to help managers better understand their staff and adopt a team approach.

As for pay increases—always a significant personnel issue—they are determined by Don and Wally, who factor in profitability, labor market conditions, and the value of the individual to the company. Employees cannot expect to get a yearly pay raise.

GROWTH AND THE FUTURE

As Brithinee looks into the future, Don and Wally consider how best to grow revenues by 10 to 15 percent in an industry predicted to shrink by 2 percent per year. Should they remain focused and expand their existing electrical motors, sales, and control panels departments, or should they diversify into other areas? The questioning involves not just growth, but also what areas the company should grow in. Predictions as to where the business will grow are hard to make. For example, since 1988 the rewinding portion of the business grew by 180 percent. Wally comments, "I would have never expected that. . . . We've never been good at predictions here." Brithinee Electric forecasts its earnings only one year at a time, but its consultant suggests that it set longer-term goals.

In reflecting on future business opportunities, Wally notes that the water industry nationwide is expected to spend $40 billion in upgrades of water and wastewater treatment facilities in the near future, a significant part of which will finance conversion to variable-frequency drives. "Upgrading fits our controls arena," he says. "This is our greatest potential area for growth." Brithinee already runs three shifts, but the second and third shift are skeleton crews. Should the firm expand to fully staffed crews, and if so, how soon? Expanding the repair side for handling larger-size motors, however, would require extensive capital investment. As Wally puts it, "everything would have to be upsized to another level greater than what we have." He sees the intensive struggle for capital and wonders where the capital might come from.

Another possibility for growth is to expand the facility by acquiring more land. The company has already acquired the vacant lot of about 5 acres between its two current buildings. According to Lynda Butek, it is a "strange piece of property" because it also wraps around the back of both buildings, a cul-de-sac, and extends to the next street. What would be the best use for it: expanding the warehouse, making it into a parking lot or a control panel area, or erecting another building in order to handle more repair work?

As the Brithinee brothers contemplate what will best prepare them for the twenty-first century, they ask whether quality is enough to ensure expansion for the company? Will attaining ISO 9000 and EASA Q enhance the business as much as they hope it will? Will educating its customers continue to create a niche for Brithinee? What other activities can Brithinee implement to "raise the standards" and "define the level of expectations" of its customers? Finally, as the brothers celebrate their fiftieth birthday, the issues of retirement and succession loom in the future.

If and when Don and Wally Brithinee should decide to limit their involvement in the business or leave it altogether, the typical exit strategies would include (1) closing the business; (2) being bought out by partners or employees; (3) selling to outsiders and relinquishing all ties to the business; (4) positioning the firm for a merger or acquisition but remaining as active board members and/or as employees; (5) passing the business to the next generation; (6) hiring a CEO/president to run the firm; (7) leasing the facilities and equipment; or (8) going public. A merger or acquisition by a large U.S. corporation would seem unlikely given that major U.S. players have essentially left the industry. However, there are some lesser known American, as well as British, firms that might be interested in this company. As for the next generation, Don and Deborah Brithinee have one child, Nicole, aged ten, while Wally remains single. The brothers carry substantial life and disability insurance policies on each other.

References

Electrical Apparatus Service Association, Inc. (EASA), "Understanding A-C Motor Efficiency," pamphlet, 1994.

——, "How to Get the Most from Your Electric Motors," pamphlet, 1997.

——, "EASA AR 100 1998 Recommended Practice," pamphlet, 1998.

Greenfeld, S. "Brithinee Electric." Case study in Smith, Arnold and Bizzell, *Business Strategy and Policy.* Boston: Houghton-Mifflin, 1991, pp. 180–200. Also in Stahl and Grisby, *Strategic Management for Decision Making,* Boston: PWS-Kent Publishing Co., 1992, pp. 368–387; and in Dess & Miller, *Strategic Management.* New York: McGraw-Hill, 1993), pp. 393–410.

Nailen, Richard L. "Building A Service Company's Numbers with Higher Mathematics." *Electrical Apparatus,* December 1997.

"You Got It Off the Ground and Flying, Now How Do You Safely Land It?" *Los Angeles Times,* December 16, 1998, p. C8.

CASE 3

Wizards of the Coast

This case was prepared by Frank T. Rothaermel of Michigan State University and Suresh Kotha and Richard Moxon of the University of Washington.

The excitement was high among the top managers of Wizards of the Coast, the world's leading adventure gaming company, as they sat down to review progress over the first half of 1997. The company had just completed the acquisition of a major competitor, and with the opening of its first gaming entertainment center, it was pioneering a whole new retail concept. After three years of tremendous growth fueled by one hit product, followed by an unexpected downturn in revenues in 1996, Wizards looked to be on the rebound. But everyone knew that the company still had to prove that it had a sustainable growth strategy for the future.

CREATING THE MAGIC

In 1997, Wizards of the Coast was a privately held company best known for the world's leading adventure trading-card game, *Magic: The Gathering®*. Since its release in 1993, more than 5 million consumers worldwide had embraced the game, which was available in nine languages and played in over fifty-two countries. (See Appendix A for a description of *Magic®*.)

The Genesis

Wizards of the Coast was founded by Peter Adkison and a group of other young professionals in 1990

to develop role-playing games. Adkison had been intrigued by strategy and role-playing games ever since early childhood. He recalls playing games as a youngster all night long under the comforters of his bed using a flashlight, so that his mother would think he was asleep when she took a peek into the room during the early night hours. In high school, he developed a passion for the *Dungeons & Dragons® (D&D)* adventure role-playing game. (See Appendix B for a description of *D&D*.) It seemed natural to him to turn this hobby into a business. After graduating from college, Adkison worked for Boeing as a computer systems analyst but was eager to start his own venture. He recalls, "I was a small cog in a huge machine that itself was a small cog in a huge machine." Adkison and six of his friends kept their jobs but began developing role-playing games in their spare time.

In 1991, Adkison met Richard Garfield in a chat room on the Internet. At the time, Garfield was a doctoral student in combinational mathematics at the University of Pennsylvania and was known as an avid game player who had been designing his own games since he was a teenager. When the two got together at a game convention, the concept for *Magic®* was born. Adkison had the idea that there was a need for a fantasy role-playing game that was portable and could be played anywhere in no more than an hour. He thought that maybe it should be a card game. Garfield had also been interested in fantasy games since playing a game called *Cosmic Encounter* in the 1980s. One of the pieces in *Cosmic Encounter* had special powers. By invoking these powers, a player could change the rules of the game. This intrigued Garfield, and he wondered what would happen if all the pieces were magic, each one altering the game in some unique way. He believed that this idea could lead to a fantasy board game, but Adkison persuaded him to focus on cards instead and to think about a format in which players could trade cards.

Garfield came back a few weeks later with a prototype of *Magic: The Gathering®*. The idea was to combine a fantasy game concept, where players controlled the acts of mystical characters, with a trading-card format, where players could buy and sell collectible cards similar to those of their sports heroes. As Garfield remembers, "The concept of a trading-card game was one of the only 'Eureka!' experiences I've had." Adkison emphasizes the point that the first prototype of *Magic®* resembled very closely the later commercialized version of *Magic®:* "We still have the original, hand-drawn cards, and gosh, if you know how to play *Magic®*, you can play just fine with that very first game."

Operating out of the basement of Adkison's home as an eight-person company, Wizards of the Coast released *Magic: The Gathering®* in August 1993. The game became an overnight success. The first printing of 10 million cards, which was expected to last a year, sold out in just six weeks. According to one owner of a game store, "My initial order was for 24 units, my second order was for 572, and my third was to send everything you've got in the warehouse." With its sales success also came critical acclaim and the winning of several game and toy industry awards.

After *Magic's* instant splash, Garfield quit his new teaching position at Whitman College and began to pursue his true passion as a game inventor with Wizards of the Coast. Adkison made Garfield an equity partner in Wizards of the Coast and fully dedicated his then fledgling firm to creating fantasy card games. Adkison too quit his job at Boeing to become the president and CEO of Wizards of the Coast. (See Figure 1 for a timeline of Wizards of the Coast.)

Products and Customers

Magic® cards were sold in starter decks of sixty randomly selected cards for about $8.95, and booster packs of eight or fifteen cards for about $2.95 retail price. Even though these were the recommended retail prices, it was not uncommon for retailers to unbundle decks and to mark up the prices of highly demanded cards. The cards featured original artwork that appealed to fantasy-game players and collectors. As a consequence, *Magic®* cards were both collected and traded, with a card's price determined by its strategic role and its collector value. Each deck was unique, so no two players had identical sets of cards. Players traded cards in order to create a deck with desired characteristics.

According to the chief game developer for Wizards of the Coast, twenty-seven-year old George Skaff Elias, the typical *Magic®* player is a person with a good education, disposable income, and an affinity for computers. While the game is most popular with males in their teens or twenties, the game also caught on with younger teens and with older men and women as well. College dormitories are a particular breeding ground for new "gamers." Compared with the typical player of a board game such as Monopoly, the player of *Magic®* sees the game more like a hobby, something on which to spend a significant amount of time and money.

Manufacturing and Distribution

Wizards contracted out the design, manufacturing, and packaging of its cards and other products. Most of its *Magic®* cards were designed by independent artists, who earned royalties from their sales by Wizards. The tremendous royalty payments due to the unexpected success of *Magic®* were initially a problem for Wizards, but it was solved in a friendly round of renegotiations with the artists. In the beginning, the company relied only on one supplier, Carta Mundi in Belgium, since no other firm could deliver the quality needed along with the ability to do the sophisticated card sorting that was required. During the first two years of booming popularity, manufacturing capacity was the single biggest constraint on the growth of Wizards. Carta Mundi was in 1997 still the largest supplier, but other suppliers were contracted as the game grew and as they were able to meet Wizards' standards.

Wizards built a widespread network to market its cards. Most adventure games were sold through small game, comic, or hobby shops, which were often mom-and-pop stores, supplied through relatively small distributors. These shops were critical for reaching the serious gamers and accounted for about 75 percent of the company's sales. Wizards allocated new card series to these stores, and there was often a feeding frenzy as consumers rushed to get an edge with new cards. As the popularity of *Magic®* rose, Wizards was able to enter national

FIGURE 3.1

Timeline of Wizards of the Coast

1990   Wizards of the Coast is formed as a sole proprietorship by Peter Adkison (May).

Wizards of the Coast is incorporated (December).

1991   Adkison meets Richard Garfield on the Internet.

First play-test version of *Magic: The Gathering*® is distributed.

Wizards acquires the Talislanta role-playing game line from Bard Games.

1992   Wizards releases its first new product, *The Primal Order*®.

Six other role-playing products are released.

Palladium sues Wizards for trademark infringement in its product *The Primal Order*®.

Garfield Games is formed to launch *Magic: The Gathering*®.

1993   Wizards lays off all its employees.

Everyone stays on to launch *Magic,* being paid in stock.

The Palladium lawsuit is settled.

Magic: The Gathering® is launched to record sales.

The *Duelist Convocation (DCI)* is started to provide tournament play for *Magic*®.

All employees are hired back.

The company moves from "the basement" to real offices.

The *Duelist* magazine is launched.

Garfield Games and Wizards of the Coast merge.

1994   Five expansions for *Magic* are released.

Jyhad®, the second trading-card game, based on the Vampire RPG, is released.

First world championships for *Magic* are held in Seattle.

First European office is opened in Glasgow.

1995   *Netrunner*®, WotC's third trading-card game, is released.

The *Everyway*® role-playing game is released.

Wizards buys Andon, a convention management company.

The *Magic: The Gathering*® computer game is released by Microprose.

More than thirty employees are laid off in company's largest downsizing.

All game divisions are divested except for trading-card games.

1996   The *Magic: The Gathering*® $1,000,000 Pro Tour is launched in New York.

The Wizards of the Coast tournament center opens at corporate headquarters.

The BattleTech trading-card game is released.

Wizards gains the contract to run Origins, the second largest game convention in the United States.

1997   The Wizards of the Coast Game Center opens in Seattle.

Wizards acquires TSR Inc.

Wizards acquires Five Rings Publishing Group.

First Wizards retail store opens in Seattle.

toy chains such as Toys 'R' Us, bookstores such as Barnes & Noble, and discounters such as Target. These stores did not have the same atmosphere and appeal as the small retailers but were more effective for reaching the mass market.

The Wizards Culture

While developing the systems needed to manage a much larger enterprise, Adkison was trying to preserve the creative culture that was present when the company was formed. Leading by example, for many years he refused to have his own office or even a cubicle. On his business cards and memos, his position and title was stated as "CEO and janitor." He saw the company as similar to a small software firm, with a casual, creative atmosphere that tolerated individualism and creativity, expressed, for example, in eccentric clothing, body piercing, and frequent nerf wars among employees. But over the years, the atmosphere had become more reserved, and Adkinson now even has a corner office.

Wizards' executives and employees tended to be very committed to the gaming concept. Garfield, the inventor of *Magic®*, sees adventure games as the "intellectual counterpart of sports—they keep you mentally fit." He believes that with playing *Magic®* comes "a lot of stealth education," whether it is art appreciation because of the beautiful cards or enhanced literacy because of the occasional quote from Shakespeare. Garfield also believes that *Magic®* is a strategic game that could be played successfully only when the player has a good understanding of strategy, probability, and chance.

Adkison, however, recognized that devoted gamers did not always make successful executives.

> There's nobody in the company who's ever managed a company this size, including me. We're trying to balance the desire for top-notch people to take us to the next level with the desire to stay true to people who founded the company. And that is very, very tough. We faced a lot of organizational problems when hiring people on top of an existing layer. None of the people who reported to me in 1993 report to me now. Many of them are still here, but experienced managers have come into the organization between them and myself. Our board of directors has evolved also, going from a board

composed mainly of founders and management to a board with several outside directors, who have a lot of gray hair.

As Adkison pointed out, the firm hired experienced managers from established toy companies, used consultants on strategy and operational issues, and brought outsiders into its board of directors. In the meantime, Adkison himself completed an MBA degree in 1997 at the University of Washington Business School. He knew that he would need to continue strengthening the organization if it was to create a sustainable strategy for growth. Some of the newly hired professionals, who came with strong credentials, did not fit in well at Wizards and were asked to leave after a short time. Adkison made the transition from an entrepreneur to a traditional CEO as he deepened his theoretical understanding of business as well as his management skills and combined both with his intuitive feel for the gaming business.

THE ADVENTURE GAMING INDUSTRY

Wizards' executives defined the company as part of the adventure gaming industry, which is itself part of the much larger toy industry. They followed publications of the *Toy Manufacturers of America*, as well as the more specialized *Comics Retailer*, a monthly publication that had in-depth reports on gaming developments. Total U.S. toy industry sales in 1996 were estimated at more than $17 billion, of which the biggest single category was video games. Outside of video games, the games/puzzles category accounted for approximately $1.4 billion of sales. Role-playing, trading-card and war games, the segments in which Wizards competed most directly, accounted for about $350 million to $500 million in 1996 according to *Comics Retailer*, while the Game Manufacturers Association estimated gaming sales at $750 million.

The adventure gaming industry began in the 1960s with the development of a number of war games. The industry was revolutionized and began rapid growth in the early 1970s with the introduction of *Dungeons & Dragons®*, the first popular role-playing game. The game attracted players with its complexity and with the opportunity for players to exercise their creativity. The industry was revolutionized once again in the early 1990s with the introduction of *Magic*®. By 1997, *Dungeons & Dragons*® and *Magic*® were still the top-selling role-playing and trading-card games. The rest of the industry consisted of another major competitor, Games Workshop, a UK-based company with revenues of more than $100 million, and many smaller competitors. Industry observers estimated that the most serious potential future competition would come from companies invading adventure games from other industries.

Although there was no clear distinction between adventure and family games, what made adventure games unique was the fact that people pursued these games as a serious hobby, sometimes dedicating many hours a week to playing a certain game. In Adkison's words, "The Magic player is a hobby gamer, meaning it is a person that would rather game than do anything else. If this person could, he or she would play all the time. The constraint people are facing is the time they have to play." This commitment of hobby players led some critics to characterize players of *Dungeons & Dragons*® and *Magic*® as members of a cult.

Industry executives, however, feel that this is an unfair image and see most gamers as devoted to the intellectual and creative challenges offered by the games. According to a survey conducted by the *Game Manufacturers Association,* adventure game enthusiasts are young, literate and are doing well in scholastic endeavors. The survey results indicate that a majority of them are indeed very young—about 31 percent are between ten and fourteen years of age, about 37 percent are between fifteen and eighteen years old, and 32 percent are nineteen years or older. The survey also revealed that about 82 percent of the respondents indicated that they maintain a grade-point average of 3.0 or better in high school or college, and about 65 percent said that they read thirty-six or more books a year. About 80 percent described themselves as book readers.

Another issue facing the gaming industry is the rise of the Internet and of computer-based games. Most people in the industry regarded typical video games as representing completely different customer experiences: either lonely quests through fantasy worlds or "shoot-em-up" arcade-like games. But the Internet offered the possibility of role-playing and trading-cards in a virtual world.

GROWING THE MAGIC

The success of *Magic*® put Wizards on an explosive growth trajectory. Sales of about $200,000 in 1993 rocketed to $57 million in 1994 and $127 million in 1995. Adkison muses: "Our margins are fantastic, just like Microsoft's on software, because we basically sell intellectual property. We have basically zero marginal cost." Wizards and Adkison had become instant entrepreneurial superstars. The company grew to about 500 employees and in 1996 moved to a brand-new, 178,000-square-foot office complex down the street from Boeing's job center in Renton, Washington. It had also opened several international sales offices.

Growth, however, brought problems. Staffing became close to chaotic. For instance, Adkison found that someone who had been on the payroll for several months had never really been hired by anybody. According to Adkison, "I've made so many mistakes, it's not even funny, and that is not counting the mistakes I made last week." Many of the gamers who started with the company were not ready to move into managerial roles. On the other hand, some managers who were brought in from outside could not work well with the gamers.

As it was already the dominant adventure trading-card game, there was not much growth potential for *Magic*® in taking an increasing share of this market. Wizards focused instead on extending the *Magic*® brand name into other products and in reaching the mass market to increase the overall size of the adventure trading-card industry. At the same time, Wizards had begun promoting *Magic*® tournaments in an effort to give the game added legitimacy and defend it from competing games.

Extending the Brand

Adkison was now attempting to leverage the *Magic*® brand name through licensing into books, computer games, and other products. With the popularity of *Magic*®, Wizards was able to pick and choose its opportunities. For example, *Magic*® appeared as a book series, published by Harper-Collins, with more than half a million copies sold. It was also out in two CD-ROM computer games. Wizards' executives felt that bookstores were a logical market for Wizards' products, since *Magic*® players tended to be heavy readers, and *Magic*® itself was often played in bookstores.

Magic® merchandise had been extended through licensing into prepaid phone cards, clothing, card albums and protectors, a *Magic*® strategy guide and encyclopedia, and calendars. Wizards had also reached an agreement with an Internet development and design company to develop interactive CD-ROM products to serve as guides to the fantasy worlds created by Wizards. Wizards had also received movie and television offers, but no agreements had been reached so far. Licensing revenues were estimated to be about $1 million annually.

Going for the Mass Market

The dream of Wizards and other adventure game developers was the mass-market role-playing game. Selling a normal board game was a one-shot revenue of less than $10 to a game company, but customers could spend up to $500 per year on a role-playing game. A mass-market hit could easily create a billion-dollar company.

In the summer of 1997, Wizards introduced a more mainstream version of *Magic*® named *Portal*®. The game was targeted at a broader audience, such as younger teens and families, and was launched with a media campaign of close to $5 million. The aim was to move toward a consumer other than the core gamer, who had made *Magic*® a magical success. *Portal*® would be distributed through mass-market retailers such as Toys 'R' Us and Target. Wizards also introduced the so-called Arc System games. The Arc System game is a generic trading-card game system, which allows the development of card decks based on a variety of popular characters from television, such as Xena, the Warrior Princess. Those decks can also be intermingled.

But Wizards saw risks in the mass market as well. *Magic*® gamers were attracted to the atmosphere of game stores and to the experience of the game, not just the game itself. Mass-market retailers, on the other hand, saw games as "boxes." And given their tremendous buying power, Wizards would not enjoy the same margins that it did on its *Magic*® sales.

Developing Tournaments

To sustain and increase *Magic*® sales, Wizards was attempting to professionalize the activity of playing *Magic*®, transforming it into a legitimate sport. Noted Adkison, "It's been proven that sports are very sustainable. They hold people's attention for a long time." One part of the strategy was to create players with celebrity standing who could then push the game's popularity in the mass market.

Tournaments had been organized informally in the first years of *Magic*®, many of them held in and sponsored by the game stores selling *Magic*®. And hundreds of tournaments were held each year. In 1996, the company organized a six-city professional tournament series that offered $1 million in prizes and scholarships. Wizards also created a computer-based global ranking for all professional players, accessible at the Wizards home page (www.wizards.com). In the United States, more than 50,000 tournament players competed in thirty leagues.

The *Magic*® World Championships generated such interest that they were carried on television by ESPN for the first time in 1997. Players from more than forty countries competed for individual and team titles and for $250,000 in prize money. Wizards was able to attract a corporate partner, MCI Telecommunications, to sponsor the world championships. According to one news analysis, the partnership gave legitimacy to Wizards and provided a mass audience, while MCI was able to tap an attractive audience by being associated with a "cool" event. According to the company that brokered the deal, *Magic*® players were especially attractive because of their passion for the game and their desire to collect everything associated with it. "You've never seen loyalty like this. It's unrivaled across any other product or service category," one analyst stated. MCI agreed to sponsor Wizard's *Magic*® tournaments in exchange for exclusive worldwide rights to produce and distribute *Magic*® prepaid telephone cards featuring the artwork of *Magic*® cards.

Wizards also published a variety of magazines connected with its games. *The Duelist* featured information on upcoming *Magic*® tournaments and articles and tips from celebrity players. The *Dragon* magazine, which came to Wizards with the acquisition of the *Dungeons & Dragons*® game, had been published since the 1970s.

Opening Game Centers

In May 1997, Wizards of the Coast opened its first retail and gaming store, a 34,000-square-foot Wizards of the Coast Game Center located in Seattle, close to the campus of the University of Washington. Figure 2 shows pictures of the game center. Designed as the first entertainment center solely aimed at adventure gamers, it offered an extensive array of arcade video games, sold games and associated merchandise, offered food and beverages, and provided a place to meet and compete with other trading-card gamers. It was also intended to be a site for tournaments. According to Adkison,

> The game center is sort of like Nike Town or Planet Hollywood. Playing is a serious hobby for the Magic player. Therefore, we decided to create the ultimate gaming and retail environment. This is a club, a hangout, a place for the devoted game players to go and know they can play any time. I was inspired by Starbucks' concept of the 'third place.' I wanted to create a third place for the gamer, a place between home and school or work. Starbucks inspired us but we want to make it even better.

Wizards hoped that game centers would create an even stronger game playing community. The company also hoped that game centers could expand the interest in games and encourage people to consider games as an entertainment choice, like going to the movies or out to dinner. Just as the Cineplex concept broadened to the moviegoing public, Wizards hoped that "gameplexes" could do the same thing for games. The first Wizards of the Coast Game Center carried many competitive games, but Wizards games were featured prominently.

Lisa Stevens, one of the original founders and vice president of Location-Based Entertainment, comments: "Our strategic intent was driven by the quest 'to make games as big as movies.' We were all inspired by that quest. And then we ask ourselves, what made the movies big? Basically, the invention of the Cineplex, where you could go as a group and see different movies. That is why we offer different games in our retail stores, even games from some of our competitors." Another objective behind game centers was to improve the retail distribution of the Wizards product line. The company was disappointed with the support given by traditional retail-

FIGURE 2

Wizards of the Coast Game Center in Seattle's University District ers to the games and felt that it knew better than retailers how to retail and support its games.

Wizards knew that the success of game centers was not a sure thing. Other companies, such as Gameworks, had introduced family entertainment centers with very limited success. Wizards was encouraged, however, by the success of the U.K.-based Games Workshop, with its gaming centers featuring the popular game *Warhammer*®. Adkison pointed out: "We have the brand but we need to improve distribution. Target and other stores help sustain the sales but those stores don't create new players, that's what we do in our retail stores."

Product Development

Wizards had developed and marketed what was viewed as many great games, but none was able to replicate *Magic's*® success. Although Adkison remained optimistic, he realized that repeating that tremendous success would be difficult. "We have several things we're working on in R&D that could turn out to be like *Magic*®. But in the gaming business, you can't bank on that success. We have to learn to make money with smaller releases."

The adventure game industry had developed largely as a result of two runaway hits, first *Dungeons & Dragons*®, and then *Magic*®. Adkison expected that another hit would one day revolutionize the industry once again. But it seemed unlikely that the same company would be responsible for the next revolution. Wizards needed to position itself to succeed even if it was not the one to develop this next hit.

Besides aggressively promoting *Magic*®, Wizards of the Coast had applied for a patent on *Magic*®, covering not the design of the cards but the method of play. It was set on collecting royalty payments from imitators, which had blossomed in recent years. Entry barriers to the game industry were relatively low, and Wizards estimated that there were more than 100 games trying to compete with *Magic*®.

Adkison recognized that Wizards of the Coast was still a one-product company, whose future was tightly linked to the success of *Magic*®: "*Magic*® provides over 90 percent of our cash flow. It is obviously our primary focus. The big strategic issue with *Magic*® is to develop its potential to become a 'classic game' that yields steady profits year after year. I wouldn't mind being a $500 million to $1 billion company. We want to make games as big as the movies."

Acquisitions

Wizards had recently completed two major acquisitions: Five Rings Publishing, the developer of the *Legends of the Five Rings*® trading-card game; and TSR, the creator of the pioneering *Dungeons & Dragons*® adventure game. The latter acquisition brought the number one (Wizards) and number three (TSR) of the adventure gaming industry under one roof in 1997. The number two of the industry is the publicly traded company Games Workshop from the United Kingdom. Adkison comments on Wizards' acquisition strategy:

> Looking at hobby gaming industry means that you need to look at a horizontally narrowed focused segment. And there are only three games in the hobby category out there: 1) *Magic*®, 2) *Dungeons & Dragons*®, and 3) *Warhammer*® [owned by Games Workshop]. And the sweet thing is that we own two of those three. One thing I have learned in my competitive analysis course in MBA-school is that it may be better to be a big player in a small market than to be a small player in a big market. And we want to be a big player.

However, integrating these acquisitions had been a major challenge for Wizards. It had to sort out TSR's very serious financial difficulties, and it moved the TSR operations and many of its staff from Wisconsin to its Seattle area headquarters.

Wizards had also confirmed reports that it had held discussions with Westend Games, which had the license for a Star Wars role-playing game, and another for a DC Comics role-playing game. There were other small game companies that might also make attractive acquisition candidates.

Global Expansion

Wizards estimated that *Magic*® was played in more than fifty countries by more than 5 million players. The company now had international offices in Antwerp, London, and Paris, and it planned to open other offices in Europe and Asia soon. Adkison noted that international sales had been very important in sustaining the company during the downturn in U.S. sales in 1996. The international market still had a lot of expansion potential.

BEYOND *MAGIC*®: CHALLENGES FACING PETER ADKISON

In December 1995, Wizards had a round of downsizing as Adkison was attempting to focus the company on *Magic*®. Wizards divested itself of the product lines that were not primarily trading-card games. The company's growth came to a sudden halt in 1996, when sales fell off to $117 million. According to Adkison, while the cause was partly the inevitable leveling-off in the growth of *Magic's*® customer base, the downturn was also due to the fragmentation of the retail game stores. The success of *Magic*® had drawn many entrepreneurs into the game store business, but there was not enough room for all of them. The resulting shakeout caused some distributors to go under, and this hit Wizards too.

In addition, many imitators offered role-playing adventure games on-line, and Wizards' executives worried that such games might replace the face-to-face experience of Wizards' *Magic*® and *Dungeons & Dragons*®. Adkison recognized that the company would have to respond to the Internet challenge: "Currently, we are looking at e-commerce, and how to sell on-line. Should we ignore it or crush it?"

While sales in 1997 were expected to be close to the same level as in 1996, Adkison was aiming at future growth. "We certainly can operate at a slow growth mode and make nice profits," he said. "But we are focused on growing the company more rapidly in the future." Part of the pressure for growth was coming from its original investors. Many of them were friends of the original entrepreneurs, came from modest backgrounds, and had become rich from their investment in Wizards. But this wealth was all on paper, and many wanted to cash out some of their investments. But to take the company public at an attractive price, Wizards would need to have a good growth story for new investors. Hence it was critical to develop a sustainable growth strategy. This was the central issue facing Wizards' executives as they sat down in mid 1997 to discuss Wizards' future.

APPENDIX A: MAGIC: THE GATHERING®

The game *Magic: The Gathering*® combines elements of chess, bridge, and the 1970s role-playing game *Dungeons & Dragons.*® *Magic*® is a trading-card game in which the two players are rival wizards dueling for control of a magical "universe" called *Dominia*. Each player starts out with twenty life points, or lives. The goal is to reduce the opponent's life points from twenty to zero before the opponent has reduced your life points to zero.

Before starting the game, each player builds a deck of at least forty cards from his or her collection of cards and then plays that deck against the opponent's deck. Each player begins by shuffling his or her deck and drawing seven cards. The players take turns; each player's turn is made up of a series of actions, such as playing cards and attacking the opponent. There are several types of elaborately illustrated cards a player can chose from. For example, lands are the most basic, providing the magical energy a player needs to play all other cards. Creatures can fight for the player either by attacking the opponent or by fighting off the opponent's creatures. Other cards represent spells that a player can cast to hurt the opponent or help his or her creatures. The basic strategy of *Magic* lies in choosing when to play what card and when to use what creatures to attack the opponent or protect yourself. More complex strategies involve combining cards to make them more powerful and choosing which cards to use in the player's deck to make it most effective. Games usually last between fifteen minutes and half an hour; however, some games can last up to several hours.

One of the key features of *Magic*® is that each game played is unique since each player starts out with a deck of 40 cards individually selected from among the more than 4,000 different cards sold. It is not uncommon for a player to own several hundred or even thousands of cards. Each player tries to assemble his or her favorite 40 cards out of the pool he or she owns according to the player's intended strategy. This ingenious twist encourages players to buy or trade for new cards to enhance their powers and strategic game options.

In addition, the game is in permanent evolution since new cards are constantly released and older cards are retired by Wizards of the Coast. These retired cards gain instant status as collectibles to be bought, sold, and traded in hobby stores, on college campuses, and on the Internet. New cards are issued in different sets and limited editions; many cards are even printed in limited numbers. These perpetual expansions have kept the game novel and contributed to its phenomenal growth as players engage in frantic buying and trading of cards in a fantasy arms race to create a competitive advantage in their individualist starter deck. Since most of the strategy in *Magic*® is assembling the unassailable deck, serious players have spent hundreds, if not thousands, of dollars to create their dream deck. This has led to the criticism that affluent players are more likely to win than their poorer counterparts.

With each expansion, *Dominia,* the fantasy multiverse where the wizards battle, also expands. "Think of *Dominia* as a beach," says Wizards spokeswoman Sue-Lane Wood. "Each expansion is a grain of sand on that beach, each its own universe." Currently, *Magic*® has undergone just a dozen or so extensions. However, the possible number of expansions is limited only by the imagination and the players' willingness to remain bewitched. Here are samples of *Magic*® cards.

Samples of
Magic® Cards

APPENDIX B: DUNGEONS & DRAGONS®

The *Dungeons & Dragons*® role-playing game, commonly known as *D&D,* evolved from historical war gaming, in which armchair generals lined up armies of painted miniature figurines on tabletops, decorated to look like battlefields, and staged skirmishes that were either historical or theoretical. Troop movements were negotiated with the help of rulers, and combat was resolved through the roll of dice and consultation of tables. Role-playing began with an idea to put aside the role of an entire army and take up the role of an individual character, who would infiltrate a castle through the sewers below to open the drawbridge and let in the invading army. This scenario proved so popular that the designer ran it repeatedly, for numerous friends and fellow wargamers, eventually substituting fantasy monsters for castle guards as obstacles to be overcome. Eventually, one of the players, Gary Gygax, volunteered to create standard rules for the new game, and he added rules for playing spell-casting wizards to offer an alternative to role-playing a warrior. These new rules were first published in Gygax's wargaming periodical *Chainmail,* but in 1974 he developed a full set of rules and called them *Dungeons & Dragons*®.

Over the next twenty-five years, *D&D* would be distributed in twenty-two countries and translated into more than a dozen languages. The *Advanced Dungeons & Dragons*® game expanded on the original in 1978, and the second-edition *AD&D*® game hit the market in 1989. Over a dozen *campaign settings*—distinct worlds in which to play *D&D*— were published over the years, and novels, computer games, board games, cartoons, comic books, and other media built upon the brand. Throughout its life, the *D&D* game frequently has been misunderstood, condemned, associated with nerds, and given up for dead, yet it retains near-universal brand recognition even among people who have never played it, and sales of the game are rising.

How D&D Is Played

Although computer games are simulating the traditional game with increasing efficiency, *D&D* is played with paper, pencil, dice, and rulebooks. A character is created by rolling dice to determine his or her basic physical and mental attributes, then the player chooses the character's profession (for example, fighter or wizard), equips the character for the road, joins with a group of friends who also have created characters, and goes on an adventure. One of the players takes on the special role of *Dungeon Master.* This person presents the situation at hand to the rest of the players, who react in character to cooperatively tell a story and enjoy the adventure together. For example, the Dungeon Master may say something like this, "You cross the drawbridge and enter the Castle of Nightmares, ready to seek and recover the famed *Staff of the Magi,* but a group of creatures steps from the shadows within to block your way. What will you do?" Each of the players in turn declares what his or her character intends to do—call out a greeting or threat, draw a weapon and prepare for battle, cast a spell, or anything else the player imagines the char-

acter might do under the circumstances—and then dice are rolled to determine the order in which actions take place and whether or not they are successful. (The Dungeon Master plays the role of every person and creature met by the adventuring party). Rounds of action continue until the encounter is resolved. The player-characters then move on and continue to explore the castle until they achieve their goal (in this case, finding the Staff) or until their characters are either captured or killed by the inhabitants of the castle. Collectively, they tell the story of the adventure, and collectively they work to succeed (or fail). Assuming the party is successful, they gain *experience points,* grow more powerful, and move on to even more challenging scenarios. Ongoing campaigns may last for years, with groups playing every week for hours at a time.

CASE 4

American Council for International Studies (ACIS): Striving to Stay Small

This case was prepared by Michael I. Eizenberg, Sharon Ungar Lane, and Alan N. Hoffman of Bentley College.

In the spring of 1977 four young middle-level managers at American Leadership Study Groups (ALSG) concluded that they were unhappy with the way their company was being run. As they saw it, senior management was out of touch with the day-to-day activities of the company and with long-range planning. After thoroughly discussing their concerns, Michael Eizenberg, aged twenty-nine, John Hannyngton, aged twenty-five, Peter Jones, aged twenty-seven, and David Stitt, aged twenty-six, decided that they would leave ALSG and go out on their own. They were convinced that they had the right combination of skills, experience, expertise, and commitment to build their own organization.

They soon enlisted the support of Linda Van Huss, ALSG's leading field sales person. Clandestinely, they created a business plan, sought legal advice, and among them invested $100,000 in cash. In addition, their close working relationships with Djohn Andersen and Miriam Zumpolle secured them $200,000 in backing from the Scandinavian Student Travel Service.

This case is intended to be used as the basis for class discussion rather than as an illustration of either effective or ineffective handling of the situation. This case was prepared by Michael I. Eizenberg, Sharon Unger Lane, and Alan N. Hoffman, Bentley College. Used by permission.

ACIS: THE EARLY YEARS

The American Council for International Studies, or ACIS, was conceived as an educational travel organization that enabled teachers to lead their students on educational trips abroad. Its goal was to create a highly efficient hands-on infrastructure, which would foster close partnerships with teachers so that they would return each year with a new group of student travelers. Senior managers' involvement in the day-to-day running of the organization to forge these partnerships was crucial and differentiated ACIS from its competitors.

In August 1978, ACIS was launched with a mailing to high schools throughout the United States. Its first brochure was a simple 32-page black-and-white catalog, whose prices were only a few percentage points lower than those in the glossy 100-page brochures of their much more established competition. The founders were counting on their personal relations with teachers, as well as their expertise, to bring in an initial base of customers. Sales during the first few months were much lower than they expected. Clients felt some personal loyalty, but were finally influenced by a sense of stability they had in working with a well-established organization.

"We didn't really understand the risk we were taking until we were actually out on our own,"

TABLE I

Overview of Educational Travel Organizations in 1979

Name	Year Founded	Estimated Number of Clients	Estimated Revenue	Location
American Institute for Foreign Study (AIFS)	1965	15,000	$25 million	Greenwich, Conn.
CHA	1966	17,000	$27 million	Philadelphia, Pa.
American Leadership Study Group (ALSG)	1966	12,000	$20 million	Worcester, Mass.
American Council for International Studies (ACIS)	1978	2,300	$3 million	Boston, Mass.

Eizenberg, the ACIS president, recalls. "Within the organization we were extremely confident of ourselves and our abilities. It wasn't until we were actually in our own sparsely furnished offices that we understood how much we had depended on the infrastructure we had previously worked within. All of a sudden, we understood the risk we were taking. There was a moment of pause, but we became stronger and more focused. We pulled harder together, and there was added intensity and purpose to our work. We realized that if we were going to make it, it would be because we had the strength and determination to make it happen."

Business did not pour into ACIS. Van Huss drove to high schools all over the South, virtually collaring the teachers who, she knew, led groups. New leads were followed up immediately with unprecedented levels of personal service. Despite its best efforts, when the sales season ended in January, ACIS had signed up only 2,300 participants—roughly 16 percent of what the established organizations were carrying, and about 30 percent below their own worst-case projections.

AIRLINE DEREGULATION

Throughout the 1960s and 1970s, all tour operators, including organizations offering educational trips, relied upon the inexpensive flights to Europe offered by charter companies. Only when charter flights were full did organizations turn to the scheduled airlines for a few seats at significantly higher rates. The managers at ACIS were stunned to discover that they did not have enough passengers to make even the smallest charter flight operation possible. They had never considered having to rely totally on the scheduled carriers. Now they assumed they were going to have to grab a few seats here and there from a variety of carriers, at rates well above their budgets.

However, by the end of the 1970s, travelers' disenchantment with charter flights and the Airline Deregulation Act of 1978 began to have an impact. The skies were opening up to new competition on routes between the United States and the United Kingdom. Laker Airways was already beginning to provide scheduled service between New York and London; and British Airways and the U.S. flag carriers were faced with significant low-priced competition in their most lucrative transatlantic market.

The ACIS managers had nurtured contacts at British Airways, but British Airways had in the past been reluctant to seek the lower-priced traffic of customers such as ACIS. In early December, a call came from British Airways indicating its willingness to reconsider its position. An exploratory breakfast the next day with district manager Jim Kivlehan turned into an all-day session. By lunchtime, they had established that ACIS passengers could fly from all thirteen British Airways gateways in the United States so that it would not be necessary for passengers to fly to New York to board a charter flight. By late afternoon, British Airways had decided it would be willing to provide service to points beyond London with convenient connections on British European Airways. By the end of the day, the majority of ACIS passengers were placed at rates below original budgets on British Airways' scheduled 747s. The remaining passengers were placed on other foreign flag carriers in groups of forty or fifty at higher rates. The end result was much better than originally anticipated.

Its early foothold in selling scheduled service at new competitive rates from gateways throughout the United States suddenly gave ACIS a significant competitive advantage. Its small size in 1979 allowed the company to shift its passengers easily from charters to scheduled flights, and direct scheduled airline service from multiple U.S. gateways quickly became a defining characteristic of ACIS. Larger, more established companies lacked the impetus to change, and their existing infrastructures made such a major change difficult to implement. They had thrived with charters and controlled significant market share; they would only gradually make the shift that ACIS had made in one morning.

IT'S GREAT TO BE SMALL

ACIS's organizational structure was simple. Eizenberg was president. He handled flights, general management, and corporate functions. Stitt and Jones were responsible for telephone sales in Boston, Van Huss was in charge of field sales throughout the Southeast, and Hannyngton directed overseas operations. All four were Vice Presidents. There were three other full-time employees.

When prospective trip leaders spoke to Jones, Stitt, or Van Huss, they had direct access to Hannyngton's strong organizational abilities overseas and Eizenberg's grasp of the emerging opportunities in the deregulated airline industry. All decisions were made within the small management group. When they disagreed, they considered various solutions until they found one that worked from all points of view. Everyone was on hand, accessible, and deeply committed to the common goal of doing their best for each customer.

The integration of sales, flight, and overseas arrangements was spontaneous. The whole organization, its customers, and suppliers benefited greatly from the fact that commitments were made

quickly and decisively. Active communication led to constant and thorough review.

Close partnerships were forged with teachers who led groups. Especially careful attention was paid to selecting staff in Europe, who would be ACIS's frontline representatives overseas and in day-to-day charge of all educational and operational components. ACIS executives were also always highly visible abroad, pitching in to ensure high levels of customer satisfaction. As the dollar strengthened during the early and mid 1980s, ACIS significantly improved hotel quality without passing on major price increases, adding substantially to its own bottom line. Teachers frequently commented that ACIS's programs kept improving every year.

The years from 1980 to 1985 were outstanding for ACIS. Enrollments grew 25 to 30 percent each year. Tangible excitement pulsed through the organization. Everything kept getting better. Airline seats were plentiful and the dollar had more and more purchasing power abroad. When Eurodollar interest rates soared to 20 percent, ACIS's bottom line rose substantially as well. Profitability was high enough each year to support building a larger organization with higher ongoing and infrastructure expenses. Most importantly, the word was spreading to high school teachers everywhere that ACIS offered a genuinely interesting educational experience, great quality, and exceptional personal service.

In 1981, ACIS began investing in a Data General computer system, and Mike Tenney was hired as system architect. He created an integrated database for sales, marketing, operations, and administration. Embedded "notepads" allowed sales and operations staff to make modifications to ACIS's expanding range of preplanned itineraries and keep track of special customer requests and sales commitments, permitting the selling process to remain responsive to special customers and changing market conditions. By 1983, there was E-mail throughout the Boston office and a modem link with Atlanta. By 1984, many ACIS managers had Macintoshes on their desks and used emulation software to access travel information in the Data General computer system.

1985: GROWTH AND PROSPERITY

In 1985, ACIS had acquired a historic brownstone building for its headquarters in Boston and opened sales offices in Atlanta, Chicago, and Los Angeles. In addition, it had acquired a small office building for its European headquarters in London, opened an operations office in Paris, and invested in start-up companies to handle arrangements in Madrid and Rome. Its customer base was loyal and solid and enthusiastically referred new customers to ACIS. The organization had excellent working relationships with all major airlines. The overseas network provided high-quality services, and the educational experience was beneficial to all involved. However, ACIS's core infrastructure in 1985 remained surprisingly small. Seventeen people worked in Boston, four in Atlanta, one in Chicago and Los Angeles, and two in London and Paris. Revenues were now in the same range as those of its largest competitors, and it provided superior service with many fewer staff members.

"Both 1984 and 1985 were incredible years," Eizenberg recalls. "The marketplace had a definite rhythm. The dollar was stronger than it had ever been. Suddenly it was 10 francs to the dollar, not 5. Everyone wanted to go to Europe, the airlines had plenty of seats to sell, and we had great trips to offer at very good prices. It was as if we were dancing to the beat of our customers and our suppliers. Each of us at ACIS had developed a lot of our own patterns, but we danced together. It felt like we all had parts in an amazing piece of choreography." ACIS's sales season for spring and summer 1986 ended just before the Christmas holidays of 1985 and had set another record. Everyone in the organization felt great heading home for the holiday break.

TERRORISM STRIKES THE ROME AIRPORT

On December 27, 1985, as terminals were jammed with hundreds of holiday travelers waiting at the check-in counters, Leonardo da Vinci Airport in Rome was attacked by terrorists. At 9:03 A.M. a man threw a grenade toward an espresso bar. Other terrorists showered the 820-foot-long terminal with bullets. Within five minutes the attack was over, leaving fifteen people dead and seventy-four wounded. Minutes later, the terror was repeated at Schwechat Airport in Vienna as terrorists opened fire with AK-47 automatic rifles and rolled three hand grenades across the floor like bowling balls toward their victims. The result: thirty-seven dead and forty-seven wounded. The entire civilized world was outraged and feared what terrorists might do next.

Airport authorities had been on guard because of a November 26, 1985, U.S. Federal Aviation Administration (FAA) alert for terrorist threats. Interpol, the international Paris-based anticrime organization, had issued a similar warning. But heightened security at the airports in both Rome and Vienna had not prevented the attacks because precautions had been taken mainly in the boarding areas and around the planes themselves, whereas the terrorists attacked places away from the boarding gates, where people were allowed to move freely. The aim clearly was to massacre innocent, defenseless civilians.

The impact on international travel was immediate. No one wanted to go to Europe. It seemed as though everyone who had signed up for an ACIS trip no longer had any intention of going. The switchboard was overwhelmed with phone calls insisting that trips be canceled and all monies refunded. ACIS received 7,000 cancellations and demands for refunds in just two days. Its remaining 8,000 passengers were likely to cancel as well.

For the first few days, everyone at ACIS was stunned trying to deal with the panic. "At first, we simply did our best to buy time and try to calm everybody down. We assured them that we were a responsible organization, and could be counted on in this difficult situation," Eizenberg explains. "No matter what we said, it was clear that the situation was far beyond anything we could control. A sense of panic prevailed that we increasingly felt helpless to do anything about. Cancellations kept streaming in, along with demands for full refunds."

Perhaps 30 percent of prospective participants were willing to take a wait-and-see attitude. The predominant view from the marketplace called for ACIS to cancel all trips and make full refunds. However, doing so would have had severe financial consequences. After all the work and money already expended, the whole of 1986 stood to be a total loss.

The ACIS participant contract contained clear language about cancellation penalties, entitling ACIS to keep $250 from the deposit of anyone who canceled. Enforcing these penalties would give ACIS the same level of income from those who chose to cancel as it would earn from those who chose to participate.

Although the U.S. State Department informed ACIS that there were no travel advisories indicating that travel to Europe was unsafe or that there was a significant threat of future terrorist attacks, ACIS

TABLE 2

Overview of Educational Travel Organizations in 1985

Name	Year Founded	Estimated Number of Clients	Estimated Revenue	Location
American Institute for Foreign Study (AIFS)	1965	14,000	$25 million	Greenwich, Conn.
CHA	1966	16,000	$27 million	Philadelphia, Pa.
American Leadership Study Group (ALSG)	1966	13,000	$21 million	Worcester, Mass.
American Council for International Studies (ACIS)	1978	15,300	$24 million	Boston, Mass.

could not sell this view in the marketplace. However, enforcing cancellation penalties would have alienated the goodwill ACIS had worked so hard to build up. After all its success and good luck, ACIS faced a no-win situation: either risk losing the market or face losing a significant percentage of its capital.

"After a week, even the most loyal ACIS teachers were growing impatient for answers. They needed an immediate solution that would work with students, parents, and school administrators," Eizenberg recalls. "On January 7, we announced we were amending the cancellation policies stated in our catalogue and were offering full refunds of all monies except for a $35 registration/processing fee and a $150 credit which could be used on a future trip abroad with ACIS."

Everyone at ACIS felt that the offer was an extremely fair and generous solution under the circumstances. Most parents, teachers, and school administrators also acknowledged the good faith the offer represented. Still, processing the 8,000 cancellations was discouraging to everyone at ACIS. ACIS's fine reputation had been thoroughly tested, but not tarnished.

ACIS had built up financial reserves during its good years, and they would have been dangerously drained had 1986 been a total loss. But the year turned out quite well. Retaining the $35 registration/processing fee guaranteed the organization $500,000 in 1986 income. Interest income on deposits and future credits contributed another $350,000. Six thousand passengers ended up traveling, yielding $250,000 in operating income. Airlines eager to generate sales came through with $250,000 in promotional support. By the spring the dollar had dropped 12 percent in value, and the organization sold off $3 million in excess foreign exchange contracts. This brought in an additional $350,000. By year's end, ACIS both showed a respectable profit while preserving its greatest asset, the goodwill of its customers.

While ACIS withstood the unprecedented events of 1986 quite well, the feeling that it could not withstand two or three similar years in rapid succession persisted. When the sales season for 1987 began in September 1986, the market had not gotten over the shock either. The substantially weaker U.S. dollar and lower U.S. interest rates were not helping. By October, it was clear that the market would recover only to about 75 percent of its previous level and that profitability would be reduced to about half of what it was in 1985.

THE ACQUISITION OF ACIS

In late October of 1986, Eizenberg spoke with Bertil Hult, owner of EF, the world's largest educational travel organization. EF had begun as a small language school for Swedish students who wanted to study English in the United Kingdom. By 1986, EF was operating various language and exchange programs for more than 50,000 participants worldwide. Hult wanted to expand his position in the U.S. market and asked if ACIS would be interested in becoming part of his large and diversified organization. He suggested that they meet at his offices in Santa Barbara.

"I really didn't expect much when I flew out. There were four of us with significant ownership positions in ACIS, and I knew that it would take $5,000,000 for a deal to be worthwhile for all of us. I couldn't imagine anyone paying that much for ACIS in the current market environment. At the meetings, I was extremely impressed with Bertil and the other EF senior managers I met," Eizenberg recalls. "Late the following afternoon we got around to discussing the number. Bertil's jaw dropped when I mentioned the $5 million figure. He'd thought we were in bad financial shape after 1986, but we weren't. I remember his saying that with EF's management, worldwide resources, and marketing expertise, he could quickly build a company much larger and more competitive than ACIS for a lot less than $5 million. The meeting ended cordially, but I realized that EF was never going to pay the money it would take to make us all happy, and there was no way we were going to sell for less."

A week later, at the annual meeting of the Council for Standards in International Education (CSIET) in Washington, D.C., Eizenberg sat with one of the EF executives he had met in Santa Barbara. Hank Kahn, a divisional president of American Institute for Foreign Study (AIFS), observed Eizenberg's rapport with his EF colleagues and asked what was going on between him and EF. Eizenberg told Kahn that EF was interested in acquiring ACIS and added that the number being discussed was $5 million.

AIFS, Inc. had become a publicly traded company (NASDAQ) in February 1986. At that time, it was the parent company of the American Institute for Foreign Study, Inc. The institute operated a diversified group of programs all in the field of international education. These included College Semester Summer Study Abroad, High School Academic and Travel programs, and several inbound programs (including Camp America, Homestay in America, Academic Year in America, and Au Pair in America). It also owned Richmond College, a fully accredited American university in London. In November 1986, AIFS; Inc. acquired ELS English Language Schools as its second subsidiary. In the spring of 1987, Roger Walther, president and cofounder of AIFS; Inc., announced his intention to acquire ACIS, one of his largest competitors in the outbound high school market, in order to propel the firm to dominance in the international student travel industry.

In June 1987, AIFS, Inc. acquired ACIS for $4.75 million combined cash and stock, plus earn-out incentives worth an additional $1.5 million over five years. ACIS thus became AIFS, Inc.'s third subsidiary. The management for all AIFS, outbound high school programs became the responsibility of the ACIS management team, and ACIS became the single brand name for all ACIS and AIFS outbound high school programs (see Figure 1).

Eizenberg remained as president and CEO of ACIS and also joined the board of AIFS, Inc., and the board of trustees of Richmond College. Jones, Hannyngton, and Van Huss retained their positions as senior managers at ACIS, keeping intact the entrepreneurial team that had created the company.

The late 1980s were a time of expansive growth for AIFS, Inc. With the acquisition of the two new subsidiaries sales volume grew from $33,049,000 in 1986 to $95,604,000 in 1988. The high school subsidiary accounted for approximately 40 percent of gross sales in 1988, and AIFS, Inc. returned to a leadership position in this important market area.

The original owners of ACIS stayed on as the management team of the organization. The ACIS subsidiary underwent regular review by the AIFS, Inc. board, but it continued to function with a great deal of autonomy. ACIS achieved all of the performance goals established in the original acquisition agreement and received the maximum amount payable under the terms of the earn-out. The 1990s brought new challenges and new opportunities for AIFS, Inc. and for the management team of the ACIS subsidiary.

1990: WAR IN IRAQ/KUWAIT

In August, 1990, Iraqi military forces invaded and occupied the small neighboring Kuwait, and in January 1991 Desert Storm was launched against Iraq. Iraq capitulated on February 28. ACIS enrollments in 1991 suffered much as they had in 1986. Enrollments had been low during the fall. When the war erupted in January, ACIS experienced a 50 percent cancellation rate. By the time the war ended, it was too late to renew interest in ACIS's 1991 programs. As in 1986, ACIS kept a small processing fee and refunded the balance of all monies paid except for

FIGURE I

Organizational Chart of AIFS, Inc. and Subsidiaries, 1997

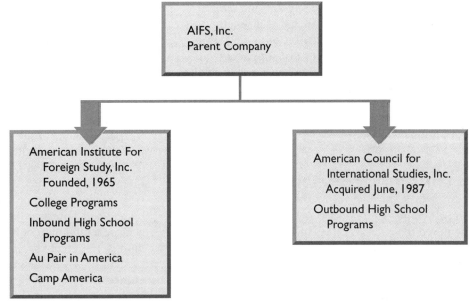

Note: the management for all AIFS outbound high school programs became the responsibility of the ACIS management team in 1988. ACIS became the single brand name for all ACIS and AIFS outbound high school programs in 1989.

$150, which could be used as a credit on a future trip with ACIS. However, ACIS recognized that the low participant numbers offered a chance to regroup and began looking at its 1992 planning with a new sense of urgency.

NEW LOOK, NEW IDEAS, NEW BUSINESS

In January 1992, Charlotte Dietz, the vice president of marketing, initiated a series of focus group meetings and several marketing initiatives that were destined to change the face of ACIS entirely. A "partnership committee" of twenty-five teachers came to Boston to discuss their views of international travel in general and ACIS in particular. The loyalty the teachers felt to ACIS was stronger than anyone within the organization had imagined. They reinforced the view that the quality of ACIS programs abroad and its level of personal service prior to departure was markedly superior to that of its competitors. The teachers genuinely wanted to help spread the word about the superiority of ACIS programs. The problem was that CHA, EF, ACIS and ALSG all had beautiful four-color brochures emphasizing the high quality each organization offered.

All that differentiated them was price; and in this regard, ACIS was at a disadvantage.

ACIS's marketing plan for 1992 was a strategic breakthrough. It focused on three key areas: (1) mobilizing ACIS's loyal customer base, (2) enhancing and differentiating ACIS's written materials, and (3) making ACIS's commitment to quality tangible and accessible to new teachers.

In early July, a personal letter of thanks was sent to the entire ACIS mailing list. The letter also solicited referrals, offering a $100 stipend per new teacher enrolled. The mailing yielded new leads, which in turn yielded a lot of new business.

The 1992 ACIS catalog was published in late August 1991. Its look was revolutionary. The presentation was of the highest quality; it looked more like a coffee-table book than a travel brochure. On the cover was a reproduction of Maximilien Luce's impressionist masterpiece "Le Quai St-Michel et Notre Dame." Beautiful four-color photographs adorned the inside pages. Interesting vignettes created exciting itineraries. Teacher testimonials expressed satisfaction and loyalty. ACIS's brochure finally conveyed its unique vision of educational travel.

Participant numbers skyrocketed in 1992. Flight costs were kept substantially below budget. More than 100 new couriers were selected and trained. All departments and overseas offices maintained very high levels of performance. Continuing airline and hotel overcapacity meant that suppliers were genuinely grateful for any and all business and willingly helped solve any problems that arose. ACIS finished the year with record profitability. The original founders of ACIS received the balance of their earn-out.

A LONG-TIME COMPETITOR EXITS

In September 1991, Milestone Educational Institute acquired the assets of ALSG. In June, 1993, Milestone went out of business leaving more than 5,000 students and teachers without trips at the last minute. The ACIS management team immediately set about helping the stranded travelers, supported by $100,000 of corporate funds for the cause to provide free or substantially reduced rates to the stranded groups. Continental Airlines provided free tickets for all passengers ALSG had booked with Continental. Several communities held local fund-raising events. EF also offered a reduced rate plan. Passports, a new entrant started by Gil Markle, the original founder of ALSG, provided support as well. Within ten days, the majority of stranded travelers were setting off on trips. ACIS benefited tremendously from the goodwill its actions created during the crisis, adding substantially to its bottom line for many years to come.

A GOOD IDEA

In 1993, ACIS managers read *Service Breakthroughs,* a book by James Heskett, Earl Sasser, and Christopher Hart, all Harvard Business School professors. ACIS was already committed to providing high quality. *Service Breakthroughs* made high quality crucial and insisted that a key step to achieving it was establishing parameters so that quality could be objectively measured. Questionnaires were individually prepared for each teacher to evaluate every service, measure overall satisfaction, and compare ACIS to other travel organizations.

The overall level of teacher satisfaction was exceptionally high: 96.5 percent indicated that they planned to travel with ACIS again, and 98

percent indicated they would recommend ACIS to a colleague. More than 75 percent of experienced teachers indicated that ACIS was "outstandingly better" than its lower-priced competitors, and an additional 20 percent indicated that ACIS was "better."

The reports also collated statistical data about satisfaction ratings for each hotel and every meal, the performance of the courier, and overall predeparture service, as well as the educational content of the trip. Overall ratings were high, although there were some disparities. Statistical standards were established according to type of service. To be retained, hotels and restaurants were required to achieve a minimum of 80 percent good/excellent ratings, 15 percent average, and not more than 5 percent poor. Couriers were required to achieve ratings of at least 80 percent excellent, 15 percent good, and 5 percent average. Educational content required an overall 95 percent rating of excellent.

The "Teacher Evaluation Report" was distributed to all ACIS staff and immediately became the standard by which the organization measured itself. Key numbers from this report were published in ACIS's 1994 teacher brochure to emphasize teacher satisfaction.

EVERYTHING IS GREAT, BUT . . .

ACIS's 1994 results were outstanding. It gained a significant portion of the market share that ALSG had previously controlled, and the dollar increased in value. Altogether, it made for an extremely impressive bottom line.

Each of the functional departments maintained high levels of performance even with all the growth. However, the significant increase in volume began to strain internal systems. In its 1994 brochure, ACIS offered ninety-two different programs, many of which could be modified with extra days or additional features. Sales staff also regularly made minor adjustments at the request of teachers. The notepad feature of the now ten-year-old database allowed the noting of these modifications and adjustments but did not integrate them into the actual database structure. At lower volume levels, it was feasible for all the departments to work with the notepads, but not as volume increased.

TABLE 3

Overview of Educational Travel Organizations in 1994

Name	Year Founded	Estimated Number of Participants	Estimated Revenue	Location
EF	1986	70,000	$120 million	Cambridge, Mass.
CHA	1966	35,000	$ 70 million	Philadelphia, Pa.
ACIS	1978	35,000	$ 80 million	Boston, Mass.
Passports	1993	2,300	$ 3 million	Spencer, Mass.

Until seventy-five days prior to departure, ACIS "free sold" from a wide-open inventory of more than ninety itineraries. Some teachers had groups as small as five or six participants; others as large as forty or fifty. For efficient operation in Europe, they all had to be divided into bus groups of thirty-five to forty-five. Eighty percent of the time this happened as part of the natural flow of demand. However, significant numbers of teachers were asked to switch dates or change their programs to fit a coherent operational structure. The large variety of programs offered by ACIS meant that this consolidation process became more complex as the number of participants and the number of itineraries offered grew.

Airline and hotel capacity was beginning to show signs of tightening, and it was extremely challenging to find the space needed during the peak demand periods. The premise of unlimited capacity was questioned.

Twice in 1994 the organization ground to a virtual halt while the issues surrounding consolidating groups and finding the required air and hotel capacity were resolved. ACIS was uncharacteristically performing like a large, unwieldy company. Often ACIS senior managers had to step in to solve problems that went beyond what staff members could address.

The hands-on work of ACIS senior staff during these periods helped maintain overall morale within the organization and a high satisfaction level among teachers. Teachers were frequently given extra benefits when their trip plans needed to be changed. Customer satisfaction results were extremely high in 1994, with nearly 99 percent of teachers saying that they would recommend ACIS to a colleague. Enrollment figures and profitability came in at record levels. By the time of the 1995 sales meeting in August 1994, the intense months of the previous year were a distant memory.

YIELD MANAGEMENT AND GLOBAL ALLIANCES

Before the Airline Deregulation Act of 1978, the U.S. government carefully regulated the number of scheduled flights allowed on all international and domestic routes, and all airlines were required to charge the same governmentally regulated rates. As soon as the Deregulation Act took effect, upstarts such as People's Express, Laker, New York Air, Southwest, and Midway moved into previously protected routes, and airline capacity more than doubled. The established carriers also scrambled to expand route systems. The extra capacity created a bonanza for travel industry wholesalers such as ACIS. Airlines needed help filling all the seats that were coming into the market. High-volume wholesalers were able to leverage huge discounts from carriers desperate for business. Wholesalers in every market segment prospered while the airlines themselves lost billions year after year.

In response, the established carriers began to develop yield management systems. The early systems lacked the sophistication and the computer capability to manage seat inventory for maximum yield. Carriers either sold too many cheap seats and didn't hold back sufficient seat inventory for higher-paying customers, or they held back too many high-priced seats and flew empty airplanes.

In 1988, Bell Laboratories patented a mathematical formula that could perform rapid calculations on fare problems with literally thousands of variables. During the next five years further advances in software enabled the yield and inventory control departments at major airlines to perform complicated passenger demand and rate-per-seat calculations on a flight by flight basis. Computer-driven yield-control calculations decided the number of cheap seats available on every flight.

In 1991, the U.S. government granted antitrust immunity to a global alliance between Northwest Airlines and KLM Royal Dutch Airlines. This global alliance permitted Northwest and KLM to code-share using the same aircraft on previously competitive routes, and to enter into joint marketing agreements that covered their entire route systems. Delta Airlines entered into a similar global alliance with Swiss Air and Sabena, and United Airlines entered an alliance with Lufthansa and SAS. An alliance between British Airways and American Airlines is awaiting government approval. These alliances reduced the amount of capacity partners made available on competitive routes to passenger demand.

By 1994, the unprecedented airline losses, which occurred in the first fourteen years after deregulation, had turned into record profits.

1995: UPGRADING ACIS INFORMATION SYSTEMS

In 1995, senior management recognized that the problem of communication between the strong functional departments needed to be addressed. A core inventory of trips was established, and the group reservations department was put in charge of overall coordination of the sales, flights, and overseas departments. But the two initiatives yielded only small improvements in overall coordination. The large variety of trips that ACIS offered made selling into the core inventory extremely difficult, especially in the competitive market in which ACIS was operating. Airlines were releasing less of their flight inventory to wholesale group sales. By the time the

ACIS group reservations department had the opportunity to provide overall coordination, a lot of the least expensive airline space was already gone.

Mike Tenney, a senior vice president at the company, was at work on writing the code for a new Oracle database system. In the meantime, each department was forced to find complex, inefficient, and undocumented "work-arounds" to cope with the limitations of the now twelve-year-old computer system. Annually, ACIS experienced two extremely difficult and stressful time periods, when the overall organizational flow stopped while the expectations and demands of groups were made to fit within available airline and hotel space. In 1995, the two periods lasted six weeks instead of four. For the first time, significant airlines cost overruns were incurred for about 3 percent of ACIS passengers. The dollar also weakened at a time when ACIS was "long" dollars. These two factors reduced ACIS profitability by about 20 percent from the record levels achieved the year before. Although 1995 was a good year, management was concerned that it would no longer always be easy to find the cheap airline seats that ACIS's budgeting depended on.

Stephen Cummings, also a senior vice president, installed a wide area network using frame relay technology. This gave all 100 ACIS employees in the United States and Europe instant access to the Business Basic database, as well as several secondary databases developed in Lotus Notes. The Microsoft Office Suite was installed on all ACIS servers worldwide. Lotus Notes Mail was used companywide and ACIS began gathering teacher E-mail addresses to facilitate electronic communication with teachers. A Web site was established with basic information about ACIS and its most popular programs.

But it was increasingly clear that the overall organizational design of the company did not work effectively within the constraints of limited airline and hotel capacity, and there was as much of a battle for cheap seats as there was for passengers. The organization was being stretched to its limits for longer periods of time than ever before.

NEW CHALLENGES FOR 1996

ACIS faced new challenges at every turn. EF already had a mailing out that guaranteed extremely low prices for 1996. In addition, experienced employees from Milestone created a new competitor, National Educational Travel Council (NETC), which had secured substantial backing from a group of U.K. investors and offered high-quality, small-company service at low prices.

ACIS senior managers also realized that the overall dynamics of the business were changing because cheap seats were becoming a scarce commodity and were often sold out, especially during busy periods. And it had become increasingly difficult to find well-located high-quality hotels within ACIS's budgets. ACIS's commitment to maintaining consistently high quality also drove trip fees up, because services receiving lower customer satisfaction had to be replaced with more expensive ones, increasing the price differential between ACIS and its lower-priced competitors. Customers willing to pay the larger price differential were harder to find. At the same time, the dollar was dropping in value in Europe, and ACIS was long dollars for the entire 1996 season.

Senior management was very concerned about losing market share, especially to NETC. Something had to be done to keep prices down. The best way to hold the line was to get more business in sooner to increase efficiency and ensure the best access to the maximum number of cheap seats and lowest-priced good-quality land arrangements.

ACIS: BEGINNING TO LOSE THAT "SMALL FEELING"

ACIS announced its most aggressive pricing strategy ever, contingent on participants meeting early enrollment deadlines. They did, and by October 15 enrollments were at record levels. The deluge of registrations stretched ACIS processing capabilities to their limits. The new enrollment deadlines added another degree of complexity to the already strained computer system. In processing early registration, there was definite advantage when the group reservations department could position groups so that they meshed well with the expectations of teachers and the availability of flights and overseas arrangements. Frequently, however, there was no readily apparent solution, and it became extremely complex to negotiate an outcome that was acceptable to the different functional departments, because each had limitations and requirements that it felt compelled to meet. In effect, this meant that 25 percent of all groups booked could not readily

flow through the system. This was further complicated by the notepad structure of the old database system, which dealt with minor modifications to itineraries by noting them as text in an "exceptions" field, and did not integrate them into the overall database structure.

The 1996 strategy worked only insofar as it preserved and expanded ACIS's market share. It kept NETC from gaining market share solely at the expense of ACIS. However, ACIS began to feel like a big company. The organization ground to a halt for extended periods to resolve discrepancies between teacher expectation and operational requirements. But as high quality remained a driving concern, ACIS again received extremely high teacher satisfaction ratings.

Despite the surge in enrollment numbers, profitability for 1996 dropped to its lowest level in several years: lower prices yielded decreased margins and high enrollment led to long dollars while the value of the dollar plummeted. In addition, the strategy of having participants book early so that ACIS would have better access to lower-priced airline seats was only partly successful. The cost savings were more than offset by cost overages on the last 5 percent of passengers booked, reducing profitability.

THE NEED TO GET SMALL AGAIN

January 1996 was a crucial month at ACIS. Eizenberg had returned after spending three months in the Advanced Management Program at Harvard Business School. Passenger numbers were at a record high, but airlines were increasingly imposing capacity limitations. Hotel space was tight. The twelve-year-old reservation and group management system was being stretched to its limits. Consolidating groups into a workable structure was more complex than ever before. Everyone in the organization displayed incredible dedication, but there was also more than enough stress and frustration.

ACIS had five major functional departments: administration, flights, group reservations, overseas, and sales. Meetings were held to consider the challenges the organization faced. They began with a strategic overview of the growth and development of ACIS, and proceeded to a discussion of how a combination of once extremely favorable external conditions had become much more challenging. Six common themes emerged:

- Profitability needed to improve.

- The database system caused a lot of problems.

- There were difficulties in communicating between departments and offices.

- The staff in one department did not know what the staff in another department did.

- Competition made it hard to find new clients and low-cost airline seats.

- Sometimes ACIS felt like a big, clumsy company.

"The problems we faced would have been unthinkable in the early days of ACIS," Eizenberg recalls. "Then profitability had increased year after year. In those days it was great when the computer had worked right, but we were close enough to what we were doing that it didn't matter as much when it didn't. Sure, we had written memos to document what we were doing, but the most important communication happened spontaneously when we simply spoke to each other every day. When there were seven, eight, nine, ten of us, we worked so closely together that we always knew what the other was doing. Selling was much easier when we had a smaller number of programs. We knew the exact details of each program so well that it was simple to convince potential clients about our superior product. Years before, we could move the whole organization in an instant to take advantage of inexpensive airline seats when they became available. Back then we proved that a highly motivated team working together with the right combination of capabilities and experience could accomplish just about anything. Peter Jones, my partner from the earliest days of the organization, was skeptical at first but he climbed on board when I told him it was time to reinvent the old ACIS. The only difference was this time we'd be coaches."

1997: ANOTHER DIFFICULT YEAR FOR EDUCATIONAL TRAVEL

Sales started slowly for 1997. The crash of TWA Flight 800 in July 1996 had cast a shadow over educational travel. In addition, the dollar was weak when ACIS entered into foreign exchange contracts to establish pricing rates for its 1997 programs. This forced the company to significantly increase prices to bring its margins back to workable levels. There were also difficulties in implementing the new Oracle database system. Together, all these factors contributed to a significant decline in 1997 sales compared with sales in the previous two years.

APPENDIX: AIFS, INC., 1997

Board of Directors
Cyril J.H. Taylor
Chairman of the Board

Robert N. Brennan
Vice Chairman
President and COO, American Institute for Foreign Study, Inc.

Michael I. Eizenberg
President and CEO, American Council for International Studies, Inc.

Walter McCann
President, Richmond College

Peter Tcherepnine
Executive Vice President
Loeb Partners Corporation

Headquarters
AIFS, Inc.
102 Greenwich Avenue
Greenwich, Connecticut 06830

Subsidiaries
American Institute for Foreign Study
102 Greenwich Avenue
Greenwich, Connecticut 06820

37 Queens Gate
London, SW7 5HR

American Council for International Studies
19 Bay State Road
Boston, Massachusetts 02181

Subsidiary Officers

American Institute for Foreign Study

Cyril J.H. Taylor
Chairman and CEO

Robert N. Brennan
President and COO

Peter Lasalandra
Senior Vice President

William Gertz
Senior Vice President

John Linakis
Senior Vice President

Robert Cristadoro
Vice President

Barbara Cartledge
Vice President

Dennis Regan
Vice President

Paul Moonves
Senior Vice President and Treasurer

American Council for International Studies

Michael I. Eizenberg
President and CEO

Peter Jones
Managing Director

Tom Jones
Executive Vice President

Rebecca Tabaczynski
Executive Vice President

Linda Van Huss
Executive Vice President

Charlotte Dietz
Senior Vice President

Stephen Cummings
Senior Vice President

Michael Tenney
Senior Vice President

CASE 5

Replacements, LTD.

This case was prepared by Lew G. Brown, Tony R. Wingler, Vidya Gargeya, John H. Lundin, Kevin B. Lowe, Don K. Sowers, Kristen M. Cashman, and Charles A. Kivett, of the Joseph M. Bryan School of Business and Economics, University of North Carolina at Greensboro.

A HOBBY BECOMES A BUSINESS

On September 5, 1997, just a little before 1:30 P.M., a group of faculty members and an undergraduate research fellow from the University of North Carolina at Greensboro assembled outside the front entrance to Replacements, Ltd. The company's headquarters was located just off Interstate highways 85 and 40 on Greensboro's eastern edge. As the group waited for everyone to arrive, a steady stream of customers entered and left the company's large, first-floor showroom.

Once everyone was present, the group entered the building, and Doug Anderson, the company's executive vice president, escorted the visitors to the second-floor conference room. Waiting there were Ron Swanson, the chief information officer; Scott Fleming, the vice president of operations; and Kelly Smith, the chief financial officer. (See Figure 1 for the company's organization chart.)

A few minutes later, Bob Page, the company's president, entered the conference room. Like all the officers, he was casually dressed, wearing a dark blue knit shirt that bore the Replacements, Ltd.,

logo. Following closely behind Page were his two miniature black and tan dachshunds, Trudy and Toby. Page always had the two dogs with him at work, and they had free run of the executive office area. It was not unusual for them to enter and leave meetings, perhaps carrying chew-toys with them.

After the introductions, Page began:

I'm not comfortable making speeches, but I do like to talk about the company's history. So I thought I would just do that as a way of helping you begin gathering information for your case.

I was born on a small tobacco farm in Rockingham County, near the city of Reidsville. I have two brothers and a sister. We grew up working on the farm. When the time came, I went to North Carolina State University. After two years, I decided to transfer to UNC Chapel Hill, where I majored in accounting. After graduation, the Army drafted me. I got out in 1970, went to work for an accounting firm, and later earned my CPA.

After about four years, for some reason, I took a job as an auditor with the State of North Carolina. From the first day, I hated the job. I just didn't like politics and all the rules and regulations. I was very unhappy.

About this time, I guess to get away from my unhappiness at work, I started going to flea markets, buying and selling things on consignment. It was not unusual for me to leave work on a

This case is intended to be used as the basis for class discussion rather than as an illustration of either effective or ineffective handling of the situation. This case was prepared by Lew G. Brown, Tony R. Wingler, Vidya Gargeya, John H. Lundin, Kevin B. Lowe, Don K. Sowers, Kristen M. Cashman, and Charles A. Kivett, University of North Carolina at Greensboro. Used by permission.

FIGURE I

Replacements, Ltd., Organizational Chart

Source: Replacements, Ltd.

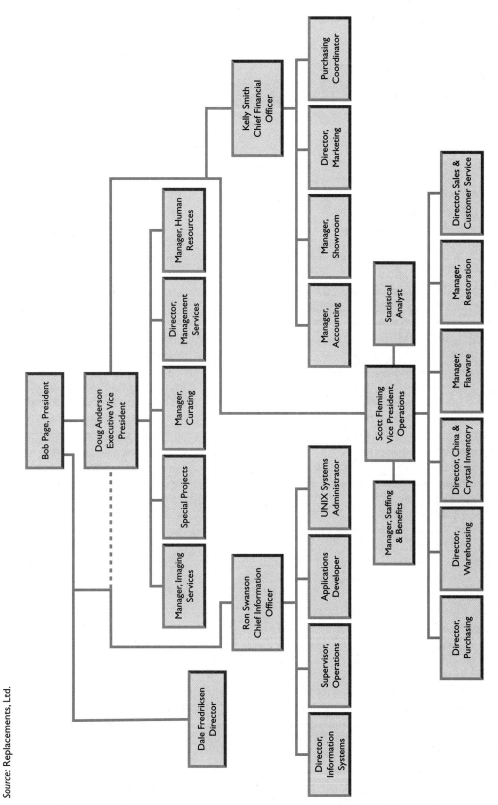

Friday afternoon and drive all night in order to be at a flea market, say, in Nashville, Tennessee, the next morning.

People learned about my hobby and began to ask me to keep an eye out for various things, especially china patterns. Perhaps they had broken a piece of their china and found that the manufacturer no longer made that pattern. Or, perhaps they had never had a full set and now wanted to complete it. When I got a request, I'd make a note on a 3-by-5 index card and put it in an old recipe box. When I was at a flea market and found a china pattern that someone needed, I'd buy it. When I got home, I'd drop them a line or give them a call.

I was still working for the state at this time. Word of my hobby spread, and I found myself getting more and more requests. I'd come home at night and find lots of mail and phone messages. I set up a card table in my bedroom to keep up with the paperwork. I packed orders for mailing on my kitchen floor.

By 1981, I was working late almost every night. I'd sold about $53,000 worth of china, etc., the previous year. I finally got up the nerve to quit my job with the state in March and to try to make a go of my hobby. My friends thought I was crazy to leave a good job with the state in order to sell used "dishes." But I wanted to do something enjoyable and fun. I thought I'd be better off in the long run.

The first thing I needed was more space, because I'd filled up my apartment. I rented about 500–600 square feet in a building in Greensboro. I needed some way to haul all the stuff I bought around, so I bought a used van for $3,000. Funny. I had to put up my old Toyota as collateral to buy the van. I hired a part-time college student to pack orders for me, and I did the rest. I still went on buying trips every weekend.

By September that year, 1981, I had incorporated the business as Replacements and bought a 2,000-square-foot building that the owner financed for me. I had several part-time employees by then, and it didn't take long to run out of space. So I started looking for another location. Zoning regulations were a real problem.

I found a place with 4,000 square feet. We filled it up in a year. This was sometime in 1982.

I got two more adjoining lots, and we built a 15,000-square-foot building.

Sometime around 1986, we moved again. This time to a place with 40,000 square feet, and the company was up to fifty employees. That same year, I was nearly killed in a car wreck while on one of my trips and had to spend nearly five months in a wheelchair.

By 1989, I realized we needed more space. This time I was going to look around to find a piece of land that was big enough so that we wouldn't have to move again. Moving is such a nightmare. A friend happened to see this 87-acre parcel where we are now. I bought it, and we built 105,000 square feet. It took two teams four months to move the inventory. It was 20 miles one way from the old place. Operating during that period was also a nightmare, because you were never sure where anything was. Often a piece you needed was still at the old place, and we'd have to make a special trip just to get it.

In 1994, we expanded, adding 120,000 square feet this time. As you'll see when you tour the building, we're about full again.

Today, we have about 500 employees here and about 1,500 dealers out scouring flea markets, auctions, etc., looking for stuff they can buy and then sell to Replacements so we can then sell it to our customers. We publish a quarterly index that lists 95,000 patterns and what we will pay a dealer, or an individual, for any of the pieces in those patterns. We have 4 million pieces in our inventory. We also buy from manufacturers when they discontinue a pattern, and we handle current lines. We also buy silverware and flatware, collectibles, and crystal. We now get about 26,000 calls in an average week. Our sales this year will be about $60 million. [See Figure 2] Not bad for selling used "dishes." And we're the largest company like this in the world. Our nearest competitor has less than $3 million in sales and ten employees. We really don't have any competition.

And, I'm happy. I'm the sole owner of this business, yet I still live in the same 1,300-square-foot house I have lived in since I bought it for $55,000 fourteen years ago. I drive a seven-year-old Ford Explorer. I really enjoy helping folks find and replace that piece that broke. China,

FIGURE 2

Replacements, Ltd.:
Total Sales
vs. Employees

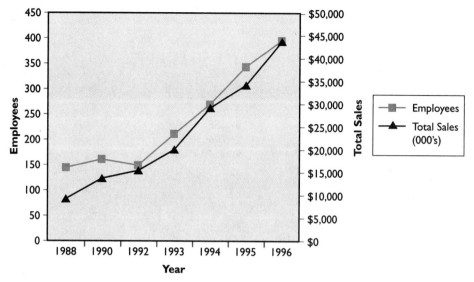

Source: Replacements, Ltd.

crystal, and all that is so personal. We have people come in here and bring their entire set of china and crystal. They may be going into a retirement home and don't have room for it and don't have family to give it to. They ask us to find one buyer so the set won't be broken up. And we do. I take customer calls every day. This business is all about helping people out and making them happy.

I know you folks are from the business school. We're glad you're here. We're always looking for new ideas. But, you need to understand, we don't have a business plan. We don't have a strategy. We don't have a marketing plan. We don't have budgets. We don't have much of that stuff you teach, but we've been pretty successful.

THE TABLETOP MARKET

Page had obviously identified a large, untapped market, but no one knew just how large the market for used china, crystal, and flatware was. There were no market studies or market research reports on it.

However, information was available on the retail "tabletop" market. *HFN* magazine presented an analysis of the industry in its September 1997 issue. Tables 1 and 2 give summary statistics from that report and information on the major manufacturers in the tabletop market. The tabletop market included dinnerware, glassware and crystal, and flatware. The dinnerware market included *housewares* (so-called "everyday" or casual dinnerware), sold by mass merchandisers, *upstairs casual* (casual or everyday dinnerware with somewhat higher prices than mass-market prices), and *upstairs formal* (including formal china). The term *upstairs* implies a higher-priced, more formal item. Crystal included stemware—crystal pieces with a base and a stem supporting the portion that would hold the beverage, such as a wine glass. Flatware included sterling silver, silverplate (utensils that were plated with silver), and stainless steel pieces.

The *HFN* article noted several industry trends:

- Lifestyle stores and home superstores such as Linens and Things and Bed, Bath, and Beyond were responsible for much of the industry's growth.

- There was a move to open-stock selling, that is, allowing customers to buy individual items rather than requiring that they buy full place settings or

TABLE 1

The Tabletop Industry, 1996

A. Total Market:		
Category	Retail Dollar Volume	Percent of Total
Dinnerware	$1.659 billion	40.3%
Glassware and crystal	$1.706 billion	41.4%
Flatware	$ .753 billion	18.3%
Total market	$4.117 billion	100% +3.3% from 1995

B. Dinnerware Analysis:		
Category	Retail Dollar Volume	Percent of Total
Housewares, mass market	$934.2 million	56.3%
Upstairs formal	$431.2 million	26% −2% from 1995
Upstairs casual	$293.6 million	17.7%
Total dinnerware	$1.659 billion	100% +2% from 1995

C. Crystal Analysis:		
Category	Retail Dollar Volume	Percent of Total
Crystal giftware	$455.7 million	68.1%
Crystal stemware	$175.3 million	26.2% +1.92% from 1995
Crystal barware	$ 38.1 million	5.7%
Total crystal	$669.2 million	100% +5% from 1995

D. Flatware Analysis:		
Category	Retail Dollar Volume	Percent of Total
Stainless steel	$535.9 million	72%
Sterling silver	$152.0 million	20% No Change from 1995
Silverplate	$ 65.0 million	8%
Total flatware	$752.9 million	100% +5% from 1995

sets of items. Some brides, for example, were requesting just dinner plates. Some consumers were mixing formal and casual tableware.

■ A shift from formal to casual was taking place, as evidenced by the switch to more casual dress in business settings. Color had become more important in casual china.

■ Baby boomers were saving for retirement and, at the same time, to deal with stressful lifestyles, were eating out more often and spending more on leisure.

■ In upstairs tabletop, upstairs casual dinnerware and crystal stemware were doing well, but analysts did not regard formal china as a growth

TABLE 2

Major Manufacturers of Upstairs Tableware

- **Lenox, Inc.** Estimated 1996 sales: $370 million. Parent: Brown-Forman, Corp. Subsidiaries: Dansk International Designs, Ltd.; Gorham, Inc.; Kirk Stieff Company.

- **Mikasa, Inc.** Estimated 1996 sales: $372.3 million. Public company with headquarters in London.

- **Noritake Company, Inc.** Estimated 1996 sales: $51 million. Parent: Noritake Company, Ltd. Headquarters in London.

- **Royal China and Porcelain Companies, Inc.** Estimated 1993 sales: $30 million. Parent: Royal Worcester Spode, Ltd. Headquarters in London.

- **Royal Doulton USA, Inc.** Estimated 1992 sales: $8.4 million. Parent Pearson, Inc. Headquarters in London.

- **Waterford Wedgwood PLC., Inc.** Estimated 1996 sales: $636.7 million. (Wedgwood Group (china) = $378 million, Waterford Crystal = $259 million).

- **Oneida Silversmiths Division.** Estimated 1996 sales: $270 million. Parent: Oneida, Ltd. (Oneida Ltd. 1997 sales = $376.9 million; 54% of sales from consumer tableware).

- **Reed and Barton Corporation.** Estimated 1995 sales: $43 million. Private company with headquarters in London.

- **Syratech Corporation.** Estimated 1996 sales: $270.9 million. Silver, silverplated, and sterling brands marketed under Wallace, International Silver, and Westmoreland brand names. Wallace Silversmiths, Inc., 1996 sales estimated at $75 million. Corporate revenues include sale of casual furniture.

- **Durand International.** Estimated 1994 sales: $24 million. Manufactures lead crystal. Private subsidiary with headquarters in London.

Source: HFN Magazine, September 1997, pp. 5-29

opportunity. Noritake, the second largest formal china manufacturer, had targeted the self-purchase customer and the "encore" bride. Although manufacturers of formal tableware were responding to the casual trend, they were not neglecting the formal.

MARKETING AT REPLACEMENTS

"As Bob Page often says, 'We'll try anything—once,'" Kelly Smith observed as he discussed Replacements' marketing strategy. The company's chief financial officer, Smith also headed its marketing efforts. He had joined Replacements in 1995, af-

ter graduating from Wake Forest University with a degree in accounting, getting his CPA, and working for Arthur Anderson, Kayser Roth (a textile firm), and NationsBank.

For example, in June 1994, the company decided to try advertising in *Parade* magazine, the magazine that's inserted in Sunday newspapers all across the country. The people at *Parade* had been trying to get us to advertise. So we advertised only in the West Coast edition, thinking there'd be consumers, especially in California, who'd be interested in our service; and advertising in one region would give us a chance to see how *Parade* worked. It so happened that the first ad followed a major California earthquake by only a couple of months. Apparently there were a lot of people who'd lost some or all of their china and crystal in the quake. The Monday morning following the Sunday ad, our telephones rang off the hook. We had over 3,000 phone calls that day, which at that time was really a huge volume of calls for one day. It was by far our record day. And for a long time that record stood.

Just to give you an idea of how we have grown, yesterday we had—let me look at my daily call record a second—yes, we had 4,800 calls yesterday. That's a pretty normal day now.

I know you're interested in what I think the big issues are from a marketing perspective. Well, the first issue is how we can continue to find the right media to generate new leads, new customers. Historically, we've been space-ad driven. We've not done a lot of prospecting, direct mailing, buying lists, like a lot of direct marketing companies do. What little we've done, we've found to be unsuccessful if we didn't have the names of patterns associated with customer names; that is, we know what particular patterns each customer on the list owns. We've talked to bridal stores to try to get the list of clients who bought a certain pattern when we learn that a manufacturer has discontinued that particular pattern, but we really haven't had much luck with that. The big challenge is finding the right media to help us sustain our growth rate. We know it's out there; it's just a question of finding it.

A second problem we face is having a more defined customer contact strategy. Once we get a name on file, we tend to send them quotes several times a year. We have seasonal sales and sales on select patterns. We've some general controls on this; but in theory, we could send out lots of quotes for just a little bit of inventory. We don't do any analysis of our customers' buying histories, and we rarely purge our database. We need to come up with a strategy to generate sales without spewing quotes out of our building. But, we know how important quoting is. In July 1995, we stopped quoting for a month while we converted to a new computer system; and sales plummeted. We all became sensitized to how important the quoting process is to maintaining sales growth. But I

was doing some estimating just last week. If you're on file with one pattern, you'll probably get four to six mailings a year from us. If you, however, had eight patterns, you might get forty-eight mailings a year—and they'd all come in the same old, nice-looking envelope. So we've got to figure out what we call "smart quoting."

TARGET MARKET

Smith then described the market that Replacements goes after.

Our target market is anyone who has china, crystal, sterling, or flatware patterns where they need to replace a broken or missing piece or just want to complete their set but the pattern is no longer produced. We also offer collectible items, like Hummel figurines, for people who like to collect those kinds of things.

We had a study several years ago. We determined that our typical customer was between 45 and 75 years old and was generally an affluent female. I wish I could find that study, but I can't seem to put my hands on it.

FINDING THE PRODUCT

Obtaining the product requires intermediaries, Smith explained.

I guess the first question a lot of people have is how do we get all the things we have to sell. Well, I said this is an unusual business. Unlike other retailers, we can't call up the manufacturer and say, send us 100 suits in assorted sizes.

The primary source of our product is the 1,500 or so active independent, individual suppliers who buy china, etc., anywhere they can find it. It might be at a flea market, an estate auction, or an antique store. The supplier can look up a particular pattern and piece in that pattern in our index to see what we'll pay for it. [See Figure 3.] Then the supplier can buy the piece for something less than what we will pay. The supplier makes money on the spread, just as we do when we sell the piece for more than we paid the supplier.

That supplier then boxes up any pieces he/she may have and sends them to us. Each morning we'll get from 300 to 500 boxes deliv-

FIGURE 3

Sample Line from a Page in Replacements' Supplier Index[1]

China

Pattern: Noritake	N	Pla	CS	DP	LP	SP	BB	CR	SU
Lilac Time	2483	13.5	1	11	9	1	.50	3	4

Lilac Time (con)		OV	RV	PLI	PL2	PL3	FR	CER	SO
		2	21	24	1	41	6	7	10

Lilac Time (con)		CSS	GR	BD	S/P	TP	CP	CV	DE
		17	27	23	15	45	45	49	9

Lilac Time (con)		CH	REL	MUG	BOU
		33	10	10	12

Code Key

Code	Description	Code	Description
PLA	Place setting, consisting of:	**CER**	Cereal bowl (rim or coupe)
CS	Cup and saucer	**SO**	Soup bowl (rim or coupe, 7"-9")
DP	Dinner plate (10" to 10-3/4")	**CSS**	Cream soup and saucer
SP	Salad plate (round, 8" to 8-3/4")	**GR**	Gravy boat with stand (1 or 2 pieces)
BB	Bread and butter (6" to 7-3/4")	**BD**	Butter dish with lid
LP	Luncheon plate (round, 9" to 9-1/2")	**S/P**	Salt and pepper set
CR	Creamer	**TP**	Tea pot with lid (short and stout)
SU	Sugar bowl with lid	**CP**	Coffee pot with lid (tall and thin)
OV	Oval vegetable bowl (9"-11")	**CV**	Covered vegetable (oval or round)
RV	Round vegetable bowl (8"-11")	**DE**	DemiTasse cup and saucer
PLI	Platter One (10" to 13-7/8")	**CH**	Chop plate (round platter, 12"-14")
PL2	Platter Two (14" to 15-7/8")	**REL**	Relish (7"-10")
PL3	Platter Three (16"-18")	**MUG**	Mug
FR	Fruit/Dessert bowl (4" to 5'3/4")	**BOU**	Bouillon soup & saucer

[1]Figures listed under the codes for type of piece are in dollars. For example, 13.5 listed for a place setting of Noritake Lilac Time means that Replacements will pay $13.50 for a four-piece place setting consisting of a cup and saucer, dinner plate, salad plate, and bread and butter plate.

ered to us in Greensboro—about 250,000 pieces a month. It's like Christmas every day. We never know what's coming until we open the boxes.

Once we open the box, we inspect the contents and compare them to the paperwork the supplier has completed and included with the shipment. That paperwork includes the supplier's statement as to what he/she expects us to pay. We grade the merchandise, enter it in the computer, and send it to inventory. The paperwork then goes to accounting so that we can pay the supplier. We pay the suppliers within fourteen days, and sometimes sooner. Some of the suppli-

ers just do this as a hobby. For others, it's their job. Last year we paid sixty-one different suppliers more than $20,000 each, with a few earning in the six-figure range. We want being a supplier to be a reliable and stable source of income.

One problem is that, as in any business, about 20 percent of the suppliers produce about 80 percent of the product. We have a lot of inactive suppliers. We had about 3,000 suppliers two years ago. All it cost was $15 a year to be a supplier and get our index, which we publish four times a year. But it cost us $25 a year just to publish the indexes for that supplier. The index contains general information for our suppliers and lists what we will pay for every piece of every china, crystal and glass-ware, flatware, and collectible item. The index is about two inches thick.

So in January 1996, we started the STAR sup-plier program. We raised the annual membership fee to $100. For this, the member got the indexes free, access to a special 800 number, twenty-four-hour turnaround on quotes, electronic payment to the supplier's bank account, and a 1 percent rebate on all sales to us once the supplier passed $5,000 in a year. The 1 percent rebate applied to all $5,000 plus the amount above that level. That program helped a little, but we still had too many people who didn't sell anything to us.

So we've just revised the program again. Now, you have to sell us at least $2,000 in the prior year in order to be a STAR supplier. If you sold less than $500, it will cost you $400 to be a member. We're probably down to about 1,500 suppliers now. They account for about 85 per-cent of our supply.

About 8 to 10 percent of our supply comes from manufacturers. When a manufacturer de-cides to discontinue a pattern, we will buy its inventory of that pattern. The manufacturers de-cided about five years ago that it was cheaper to let us handle the small orders for remnants. They'll also often sell active patterns to us as they would to any other dealer, with us getting a standard discount from their recommended re-tail price. We have active accounts with most manufacturers now. In fact, we are Noritake's biggest customer.

The final 5 to 7 percent of our supply comes from individuals. [Table 3 summarizes sales by product type.] People may just walk into our showroom and sell to us. Sometimes they have inherited the items and don't want them or would rather have the money. Other times, the person is going through a divorce and wants to sell the items.

We estimate that we have about 95,000 pat-terns and over 4 million pieces in inventory. We also offer collectibles like rare figurines, col-lectible plates, past Christmas ornaments, etc. For all our products, we offer a thirty-day, money-back, satisfaction guarantee.

We also have a couple of other 'products.' We offer a free pattern-identification service. We have several curators who work with customers to identify patterns. Often a person doesn't know the manufacturer's or the pattern's name. They can send us a picture, tracing, or an actual piece; and our staff will conduct the research to identify the pattern and manufacturer. We also offer a flatware restoration and cleaning service and have considered offering a china repair ser-vice. We repair china now for resale, but we have never offered that service to our customers.

PRICE

Smith next described the company's approach to pricing.

Bob understands supply and demand so well. From the very beginning he was developing his buying-pricing model so we can buy the inven-tory we need, not buy the inventory we don't need, and move the inventory that we have.

Bob uses a pricing matrix that has customer groups down one axis, that is, the number of customers we have for a pattern. For example, do we have one to ten customers or eleven to twenty, and so forth. The other axis is the num-ber of pieces we have in stock. At the intersec-tion of each row and column is the percentage of the retail price that we're willing to pay for an item. So if we have a lot of customers for a pattern and not much inventory, we'll pay 50 percent of retail, which is the most we'll pay for anything. At the other end of the scale, if we have lots of inventory and not many customers, we'll only pay 5 percent of retail. Bob set up these parameters years ago. We continue to find ways to add layers of screening to make pricing more advantageous for us. We have minimum/maximum/absolute pricing we set for particular patterns that can override the matrix based on all sorts of factors. There may be a particular pattern that we really want, and we'll pay a certain price for items in that pat-tern regardless of what the matrix might say.

Pricing is a continuous process. Literally every day, Bob's setting up special pricing scales for certain patterns or groups of patterns. By changing the retail prices, we automatically change the buying prices by action of the ma-trix. So, if we need more dinner plates in a pat-tern, we can raise the retail price to reflect

TABLE 3

Replacements, Ltd.: Sales by Product Type

Product Type	1995	1996	1997
China	$23,280,361	$29,180,113	$34,107,173
Crystal	2,911,824	3,594,419	4,134,168
Flatware	4,986,811	6,778,454	9,097,704
Collectibles	365,474	676,207	884,495
Showroom	1,128,235	1,665,924	1,573,174
Totals	$32,672,705	$41,895,117	$49,796,714

Source: Replacements, Ltd.

demand. This increases the buying price. At some price point, our buyers will seek out that pattern; or if they or others are holding that pattern, at some price they'll be willing to sell. We started getting away from the standardized pricing scales to more customized pricing about one and a half to two years ago. This is Bob's biggest time consumer and his most important job. Although there'll always need to be judgment in this, we need to systematize our pricing in order to reduce the amount of fine tuning or tweaking we do now.

THE SHOWROOM

The Replacements showroom, Smith noted, is more than a place for selling.

In addition to selling directly to our customers by mail, we also operate a showroom here so customers can stop by and make purchases. Bob started a showroom several years ago. It was probably only about 200 square feet— pretty much of an afterthought. But more and more people kept stopping by, so the showroom had to grow. Now it takes 12,000 square feet, and we have about 100,000 people per month visiting it. We also offer guided tours every half-hour from 8:30 A.M. to 8:00 P.M., seven days a week, year-round. Part of our showroom is our museum, which has over 2,000 unique pieces of china, crystal, and silver on display.

PROMOTION

Smith introduced Mark Klein and described his background and his duties as the company's director of marketing.

He's responsible for all our communications work. He directs a graphic artist, a media placement coordinator, a manufacturer's liaison, and a senior merchandising analyst who takes care of developing and placing all our ads. He also supervises our mailing operation, which involves a manager and seven employees. Before joining us last September, Mark worked ten years with Hecht's Department Stores as a buyer of housewares, china, and furniture, and then served as a field sales representative for a furniture company for six years. He has a degree in marketing and management from Virginia Tech.

Smith then asked Klein to discuss Replacements' advertising program. Klein responded:

Okay, Kelly. Our advertising's obviously very important in generating leads. We track our advertising very carefully so we can determine which are the best magazines to use for advertising.

I guess it'd be good to start by summarizing our print advertising program. I've prepared for you this table, which summarizes our print advertising program for September 1996 through August 1997. [See Figure 4.] During this period, we advertised in eighty-four magazines.

FIGURE 4

Advertising Analysis For Publications Advertised in 9/96–8/97

Publication*	Code	ROI	Ad Cost	Total Sales	New Clients
Better Homes & Gardens Ad-Monthly Pub-Monthly 1½" Listing 1/3 pg in 3/96	GB	$7.76	$62,295	$966,862	8,801
Colonial Homes Ad-Bimonthly Pub-Monthly 1/12 Pg BW	CH	$13.75	$8,444	$232,280	1,942
Country Living Ad-Monthly Pub-Bimonthly 1/3 Pg Masthead out May 96, 16M Classified Word Ad	CL	$35.40	$7,166	$507,273	4,208
Good Housekeeping Ad-Monthly Pub-Monthly 1" Listing remnant 7/96, 25M	GH	$7.91	$27,437	$433,917	3,735
Gourmet Ad-Monthly Pub-Monthly STF Calico blue starting in Dec 96 1/12 Page, BW	GT	$6.60	$23,099	$305,065	2,002
House Beautiful Ad-Monthly Pub-Monthly 1/12 Page 4-C	HB	$8.18	$41,889	$685,364	4,526
Martha Stewart Living Ad-Monthly Pub-Monthly Vil Holly in Dec 96 issue 1/12 Page 4/C, 10x/yr.	MS	$6.27	$30,490	$382,570	5,403
New Yorker Ad-Weekly Pub-Weekly 1½" weekly 1/6 thru 7/7/97	YO	$3.30	$54,137	$357,708	1,857
Smithsonian Ad-Monthly Pub-Monthly 2" Listing/makegood 3/97	SM	$5.71	$23,709	$270,819	1,605
Southern Living Ad-Monthly Pub-Monthly 39 words, Prepaid Oct-Dec 97 Prepay 3 mos. 10% discount	SL	$106.87	$9,567	$2,044.962	12,122
Sunset Ad-Monthly Pub-Monthly 4-C Test ad Oct, Nov, Dec 96, JB BW 1/12 pg 1/12 Page, 2/97 Coach Scenes	TU	$10.77	$18,117	$390,238	2,668
Victoria Ad-Monthly Pub-Monthly 1/3 4C in 3/96, 12M	VI	$6.94	$24,345	$337,898	5,286
Yankee Ad-Monthly Pub-Monthly	YA	$5.27	$27,417	$289,030	2,320
Subtotal—All but Parade		$8.39	$552,346	$9,265,633	75,286
Parade Ad-Monthly Pub-Monthly	—	$2.58	$1,049,263	$6,246,195	89,572
TOTAL—All publications		$4.84	$1,601,609	$15,511,828	164,858

*Specific publications listed are the top fourteen in terms of total sales. Subtotal and total figures include *all* publications.
Source: Replacements, Ltd.

This table summarizes the top fourteen magazines in terms of the sales dollars the advertising generated. It shows basic information on the magazine and our ad, the code our telemarketers use when they record that magazine as the source of a new customer, the return on investment from the ad, the cost of the ad, and the number of new sales and clients it generated in the period. We calculate the ROI measure by taking 50 percent of the total sales amount (which assumes an average 50 percent gross margin on sales) and dividing that by the cost of the ad. This figure then gives us the gross margin dollars generated for each dollar of ad cost. If this number drops below 1.0, then we drop that magazine unless there's some other factor working.

We also track sales for magazines in which we didn't advertise during the past twelve months. You see, once a person becomes a client and we include the client in our database, we designate the source of that client. Our operators ask the clients on their first call how they heard about Replacements. If a client says he/she saw our ad in the *New York Times Magazine*, then we put that code in the client's file. From then on, we credit all purchases that client may make to that magazine. Sometimes we may have discontinued our ads in that magazine, but we still track our sales for those customers by that magazine.

Many of these magazines also have sections where they list the advertisers in that edition and allow readers to circle a number on a card to request information from that advertiser. This information comes to us from the magazines, and we have to enter the information manually and then mail the person a Replacements' brochure. We track these inquiries and sales from the inquiries also.

At this juncture, Smith suggested that Klein also tell how the company keeps track of its other client sources. Klein agreed:

Good point. I also prepared a list of our top 16 client sources from other than publications. I took these from an overall list of about 150 such sources. For example, if a customer calls in and says he/she was referred to us by an antique store, we would code that customer as "AS." The exhibit shows that in the past twelve

months we had over $462,000 in sales to such customers. This table also shows the sales we credit to our lists, that is, lists of customers we've purchased over the years. You'll see on the exhibit a listing for the "C.C.M. List" or the "W. D. C. List." You'll notice also the listing for "Department Store Referral." Many people will go to a department store if they break a piece of china or need additional pieces. If the store doesn't carry that pattern or if it's discontinued, often the store personnel will refer the customer to us. The Discovery Channel has a show called "Start to Finish" that runs about a five-minute segment on Replacements. It's run the segment about twelve to fifteen times over the past two years. Every time it runs, we get a burst of telephone calls. In fact, you can "see" the calls move across the country as the show airs in different time zones.

The largest total sales dollar item is the "friend or relative" entry. You can see the importance of word of mouth; but, frankly, we wonder if this entry isn't just a catch-all when our operators are busy. For example, when someone calls and indicates that she saw our ad in *American Country Collectibles* magazine, the operator may not know the code for that magazine. If not, he/she must go to another screen and scroll through a list to find the code. This takes time, and our operators are very busy. We think that in such a case it is easy just to enter the code for friend or relative (FR) and save the time and trouble of looking.

Smith confirmed that "having our operators get accurate information is one of our biggest concerns," as this information is crucial for tracking. Klein continued, focusing again on advertising.

I think Kelly mentioned earlier that we are space-ad driven. We've tried a little television and radio advertising, but they just don't seem to work very well for us. We've too much information we need to communicate, and we can't seem to do it effectively in thirty seconds or a minute. Plus, we find that people need to see sample items in the ad.

For example, here's a sample ad from *Parade*. [See Figure 5.] You'll notice the line of plates across the bottom. One might assume that we just pick some sample plates for the ad, but we select each individual plate/pattern very

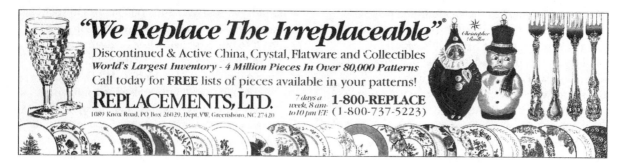

FIGURE 5

Sample *Parade* Ad

Source: Replacements, Ltd.

carefully based on our inventory and the number of customers who might want that pattern. We'll have people call in who'll say that they recognize their pattern as being the fifth plate from the left in the ad. So our operators must have copies of the ads with pattern names noted so they can help the customers.

Our staff does all of the creative work in developing our ads. Until 1995, we used outside companies to do this. We think we can do it just as well; and by placing the ads ourselves, we save the 15 percent fee we'd have paid an advertising agency to do that.

Despite our focus on print ads, we're trying to get a TV ad with Visa, the credit card folks. You may remember that Visa has these ads in which it features unique or unusual businesses and notes that the establishments don't take American Express. We think we fit Visa's criteria, and Bob has a personal goal of getting Replacements in one of those ads. We even filmed a sample ad to show Visa. We haven't had any luck yet. Visa is also developing some radio ads with the same theme, but we're not sure Replacements will work as well on radio.

We're always looking for new home-and-shelter-type publications in which to advertise. Bob encourages us to try anything. One of the greatest things about working here is that we don't have an ad budget—so if we come up with an idea we like, we just try it. Although we don't have a budget, we spend about 3 to 4

percent of revenue on advertising. We just seem to hit that range. We could certainly spend more, but we find there is a "wear-out" factor with our advertising. For example, we only advertise once a month in *Parade*. Our ad is on the page with the 'Intelligence Report' feature, the second most-read page in the magazine. But our space is always the same size and our ads look alike even though we change them. If we advertised every week, we'd just speed up the wear-out factor.

Personal Selling

As telemarketing is very important to Replacements, Klein offered some specifics about the process, also describing how calls are followed up.

I've mentioned our telemarketing staff several times, so perhaps I should discuss this process in more detail. We've about seventy full-time staff in this area who operate from 8 A.M. to 10 P.M. daily, year-round. When we're not open, we record messages by voice mail and return the calls the next day. About 90 percent of our sales are by telephone, with the remaining 10 percent occurring in our showroom. Our operators will handle about 26,000 calls a week. We have five T-1 lines into the building, each T-1 being twenty-four lines. Even though you have to add twenty-four lines at a time, we'll add a T-1 before we really need it because we want customers to be able to get in. It is rare that all of our lines are busy, but it has happened. People can also E-mail us at ReplaceLtd@aol.com.

The first time a customer calls our 1–800-Re-place number, he/she's typically seen one of our ads and is interested in getting a free list of pat-terns we carry and other basic information. Our operators try to establish rapport. Our goal in that first call is to get the customer's name and ad-dress and the names of any patterns he/she owns and a particular piece request. This is critical to us knowing how to price and how to adjust our pricing matrix. As I've noted, we also record how the customer came to call us, through an ad, a re-ferral, or however. So our goal is to get that cus-tomer on file with as much specific information as possible. Finally, our operators are supposed to conclude the call by asking if the customer has any other china, crystal, silver, flatware, glassware, everyday stoneware, etc., needs that we can help them with. This is a way to educate the customer about our other offerings. So many customers think we only carry china.

We have over 2.5 million customers on file. However, one problem is that many records are so old that we are not sure if the information, such as which pieces they want, is still valid. If a customer calls in who is already on our system, the operator just punches in the customer's phone number to call up his/her information.

So we have a standard format that our opera-tors follow. The typical operator will take 70 to 110 calls per day. We try to hire people with telephone experience. They need the ability to sit at a desk all day and take calls. We put them through a month's training. New employees can take monitored calls in about two weeks. They have to learn the computer screens and how to work them. They'll sit and listen as an experi-enced person takes calls.

Because we can get bursts of calls from time to time, we've developed a system so that other staff members working in other functional areas are trained to handle phone calls and take or-ders. Even our managers, including Bob, do this. When someone calls, our automatic system an-swers before the first ring and delivers a prere-corded message. At the end of the message, the call goes to an operator, depending on which number the customer selects from the menu. The computer monitors incoming traffic, and

whenever there are more than two calls in the queue, the queue beginning whenever the sys-tem answers a call, we have bells that ring in certain offices. For example, bells will ring in the accounting office, the mailroom, and other support departments. The bells also ring in sev-eral of the managers' offices like Kelly's and Bob's. A light in the telephone operators' room goes on so that an operator who's getting ready to go on a break, for example, knows to wait.

That's our standard system. We also have what we call a "Code 2." Anyone who is in-volved in the system can call a Code 2. They do this by announcing over the intercom that we have a Code 2. We don't have any specific rules about when to do this. For example, we've a display on our phones that tells us how many calls are in queue and what the maximum wait time is. If I notice that there are more than three calls in the queue and wait time is twenty sec-onds, I'll call a Code 2. We do this over the intercom rather than with bells so that back-up staff will hear it even if they aren't at their desks.

As a result of this system, we can handle the peak-call periods. Our average wait time is *eight seconds*. If we do have calls that are blocked due to our lines being busy or customers aban-don a call, we have a system that captures their phone numbers; and we'll call them the next day to see if we can help them.

We've five supervisors who monitor calls for quality-control purposes, and we produce daily reports that keep up with every detail. We know how many calls each person takes, the av-erage talk time, and lots of other information. I noted that managers serve as Code 2 backups. Bob Page, for example, took sixty-nine calls yes-terday. That's high, but he enjoys taking the calls. It allows him, and all of us, to keep in touch with customers.

We also have a similar phone system with twenty operators in our purchasing depart-ment. These folks deal with our suppliers. We have twelve people in our customer service area, handling questions, returns, or problem or-ders. We're considering consolidating all three groups and using the phone system to route calls to each operator based on that operator's skills and responsibilities.

Now once a person has called, talked to an operator, and been added to the system as a new client, we'll have their patterns on file. The next day, we send that person a quote that lists his/her patterns and the prices for the pieces that we have in stock. We send these letters first class because we found that bulk mail was too slow. We also can send just a brochure.

If the person calling wants a dinner plate in a certain pattern and we don't have that pattern in stock, we ask the customer if he/she would like to be in our "call collect first" program. This means the customer says he/she'll accept a collect call if the piece he/she is looking for comes in. We'll call them before we send out letters to other customers who're looking for that same pattern or piece. This used to be an actual collect call; but we found we were spending so much time trying to complete the collect call, so we just started paying for it ourselves. But by the customer saying he/she'll accept a collect call, we know we have a more serious customer.

When we get more pieces in on a pattern than we need to satisfy our "call collect" customers, we send out a mailing to others in the database who are looking for that pattern. These and all the other quotes we mail, with the exception of that first quote, go third class bulk, with about a ten-day delivery time. We have some decision rules that determine when and if we do a wider mailing.

Independent of these mailings are our sales runs. These account for the bulk of our mailings. We group patterns into various groups to balance the size of our mailings. Based on our sales history and inventory, the computer will calculate a discount and generate sales quotes. We go through that sales cycle about five times a year with each cycle being about three weeks and each mailing ranging from 240,000 to 375,000 letters. If we still have inventory after a sales run, we may discount the item even more the next time. One to two times a year, we go through the process of quoting everybody at full price. [See Figure 6.]

So you can see how, as I mentioned earlier, someone could get lots of mailings from us over the period of a year. This can get expensive, and we don't want to overwhelm people with quotes. So we have to work constantly on and think about our customer-contact strategy. Are there more efficient and effective ways to contact customers once we find them and get them on our system?

OPERATIONS MANAGEMENT AND INFORMATION SYSTEMS

Taking Inventory

Scott Fleming, Replacements' vice president for operations, had just left the inventory area and entered the company's first-floor showroom on his way back to his second-floor office. He noticed Ron Swanson, chief information officer, who had just finished talking to one of the sales associates who helped showroom customers. In the background, another group of visitors was departing on a Replacements' tour—as groups did every thirty minutes.

Fleming had worked for Replacements for seven years during the 1980s. He left the company for four years before returning in 1994. Swanson had joined Replacements in early 1996 as chief information officer. He brought twenty-seven years of experience, including twenty years with county government in Iowa; five years with Sara Lee; and two years with CMI, a textile manufacturer.

Fleming called out to Swanson:

I was just on the way up to see if I could catch you. I've just been back in the inventory area. As you know, we had a tremendous number of shipments come in yesterday, and the pieces are beginning to work their way back to inventory. The staff is really pushed. Bob has always believed that the more inventory we have, the more we can sell. But no matter how fast we grow, it seems that the inventory grows faster. I'm concerned that we need to tackle this problem strategically. I think keeping track of inventory is taxing our information system.

On an average day, Replacements' supplier network shipped 300 to 500 boxes via surface carriers (such as UPS), resulting in the company receiving more than 50,000 pieces in an average week. In turn, the company shipped about 35,000 pieces a week to meet customer orders. (See Figure 7.)

At the beginning of any given day, the company had no listing of the items that would be delivered

FIGURE 6

1997 Sales Cycle 4—Sales Run
Work Process Schedule

Group	Group's Previous Sale Ends	Sale Dates	Begin Process	Greenbar to Bob	Greenbar from Bob	Start Printing	Finish Printing	Finish Mailing	Number of Customers
11&13	6/18/97	7/16-8/7	6/24	6/25	6/27	6/30	7/6	7/7	271,568
15&2	6/25/97	7/23-8/14	6/26	6/27	6/30	7/7	7/12	7/13	239,821
1&3	7/2/97	7/30-8/20	6/27	6/30	7/1	7/13	7/19	7/21	261,169
4&5	7/9/97	8/6-8/27	7/1	7/2	7/3	7/20	7/26	7/28	313,466
6&7	7/16/97	8/13-9/3	7/21	7/22	7/24	7/27	8/2	8/4	314,709
8&9	7/23/97	8/20-9/10	7/28	7/29	8/1	8/3	8/9	8/11	317,805
10&11	7/30/97	8/27-9/17	8/4	8/5	8/7	8/10	8/16	8/18	360,137
16	8/6/97	9/3-9/24	8/11	8/12	8/14	8/17	8/23	8/25	371,760
17&14	8/13/97	9/10-10-1	8/18	8/19	8/21	8/24	8/31	9/1	375,468

Group 11 Hutchenreuter Crustal—Kaysons
Lenox Crystal
Group 13 Ken Kraft China—Mauser Mfg. Co. Silver (omit Mikasa & Metlox China)
International Silver (Lufberry—Zephyr)
Group 15 Moncrief—Oscar de la Renta Silver
Group 2 Royal Dalton
Red Wing China—Royal Saxony
Gorham Silver (252H—Imperial Chrysanthemum)
Group 1 Old Abbey—Rewcrest (omit Royal Doulton)
Oneida (Modjeska)—Oneida (Young Love)
Rosenthal
Group 3 Royal Sealy—Sheffield (omit RW)
Group 4 Shafford—Warwick China (omit Syracuse) (omit Towle)
Group 5 Gorham Silver (Imperial—Zodiac)
Waterford—Zylstra (omit Wedgwood China)
Allan Adler Silver—Booths

Group 6 Wedgwood
Borsumy Fine Chila—Crown Empire (omit Castleton)
Group 7 Castleton
Towle
Ceralene Raynaud—Englishtown Crafts
Group 8 Enesco China—Freeman (omit Fostoria)
Group 9 Fostoria
Frigast Silver—Hibbard, Spencer, Bart (omit Haviland)
Group 10 International Silver (1810—Lovelace)
Haviland
Johnson Brothers
Group 12 Lenox China
Group 16 Noritake, Wallace Silver
Group 17 Metlox, Royal Worcester, Syracuse
Oneida/Heirloom Silver (Abington)—Oneida/Heirloom Monte Carlo
Group 14 Mikasa
Spode China

Source: Replacements, Ltd.

to its docks that day. A shipment's contents were known only after warehouse employees opened the box. Once employees opened the boxes, they used computer terminals to enter data on the pieces received. They then sent the pieces to the appropriate area (china, crystal, or flatware), where other employees carefully inspected each piece and determined the amount that Replacements would pay to the supplier for each one. The employees then issued payment orders and sent them to the accounting department. They also assigned each piece to a specific location in one of more than 59,000 bins arranged in 16-feet-high shelves and then transferred the piece to inventory. Defective items were sent to appropriate areas for restoration and then placed in inventory.

The company stocked about 73,000 china patterns from 1,300 manufacturers; 12,500 crystal patterns from 265 manufacturers; and 9,600 flatware patterns from 439 manufacturers. The total

FIGURE 7

Layout of
Replacements, Ltd.

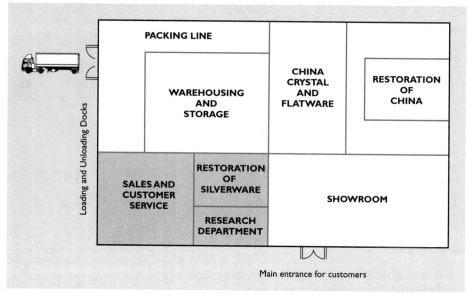

Note: Administration offices are located on the second and third floor above sales and customer service, restoration of silverware, and research department section of the building (as shown by the shaded area).

inventory amounted to more than 4 million individual pieces.

Fleming spoke about some of the problems:

> One of my concerns is that we have so many new people. They're good employees, but they don't yet know the patterns. Although they can quickly learn to find the more commonly ordered patterns, it's hard for them to find the rarer, less frequently ordered patterns. Further, I'm concerned that it is easy for a new employee who is working hard to put a piece in the wrong place. As a result, it could be lost forever! There's no telling how much lost inventory we have floating around on those shelves.
>
> And on top of that, we estimate that about 7 percent of the items we receive are broken in shipment; and we break another 2 percent while we are handling them. So we've got a quality problem on top of an information problem.

Swanson asked how his department could help. Fleming responded:

> I wish I had some new ideas, Ron. Frankly, I am at my wit's end trying to solve this inventory/quality management problem without an accurate information system. And, to add to the confusion, we're unable to handle all the calls we receive from both our suppliers and customers.

Replacements received about 5,000 calls from customers and suppliers in a typical fourteen-hour day. About fifty-six salespeople and sixty-one purchasing employees handled most of the calls. In addition, there were more than eighty others who helped handle telephone calls when needed—including Page, as mentioned earlier. Jack Whitley Jr., the director of sales and customer service, felt that the company needed to add from four to fourteen full-time employees to handle the telephone calls. Fleming explained:

> Our phone records tell us that customers abandon about 1 percent of all calls. I wish I could do something about that. That translates to more than a half million dollars in revenue! Also, many times we find that a particular item sought by a customer is not available in our inventory. However, in all likelihood a supplier could find that item within a few months. But we have no system in place by which we can correlate the receipt of that item to the earlier customer request. I really have no idea how much money we may be losing on that account.

History of Replacements' Information Systems

The earliest system used to remember customers' names and patterns was simply Page's handwritten 3-by-5 file cards. After about three years, the manual system was unable to keep up with the growth in customers and inventory.

In 1985, Replacements purchased a Data General (DG) minicomputer. The installation automated both the china and flatware inventory and the customer list.

Two years later, the company hired an internal programming staff to develop both batch and data-entry functions to support the company's operations. This group subsequently developed the first on-line systems, which were referred to as "green screen-COBOL-interactive" systems.

In 1993, the company installed the first local area networks (LANs), and PCs began to replace the terminals. Even though the PCs possessed computing capability, they employed a "terminal emulation" interface, which used only a small portion of their total capability. Eventually, the DG system grew to 300 terminals, with 220 of them being PCs.

Later in 1993, the DG system's scalability (the ability to increase the system to meet demand) became an issue. Replacements' management decided to look into two alternative solutions:

1. Expanding the existing, proprietary DG platform by changing to the UNIX operating system using Oracle database software
2. Moving to a more "open" system of Hewlett-Packard hardware with the UNIX operating system and Sybase database software

Both options required a database conversion from the old INFOS database management system. Replacements hired an independent consulting firm to supply the project manager for the projected conversion. The task of translating the database structures from the hierarchical INFOS database to the relational Oracle database proved more difficult than the consulting firm had projected. The initial implementation date was delayed over nine months. During this period, many of the development staff left Replacements. After eighteen months of working to convert the database, the management team decided to implement the new system immediately. Managers had considered different cut-over approaches; but the main problem was that only one computer was available, and it could only run one operating system and database at a time. The team decided that an immediate cut-over from the old to the new system would happen over a long holiday weekend: "Tomorrow we go live!" That holiday weekend was the July 4 weekend, 1995.

Problems riddled the changeover from the start. The new system lost recently entered orders. Critical inventory updates failed. Important data was lost somewhere in the system. The new system came apart, and system users rapidly lost confidence in its precision and reliability. In some instances, when a customer called to place an order, the order taker would run back into the warehouse to verify the existence of the inventory before confirming the order. Because of the problems with lost orders, some orders were handwritten and hand-filled to ensure inventory availability and delivery. One executive remarked, "This came as close as anything to completely destroying the business."

Eventually, the new system became more reliable, and the employees became more confident in its ability to reflect inventory and to execute necessary transactions accurately. During this period, Replacements' programmers found lots of errors in the programming modules. This revelation made the managers realize that they needed to be more proactive in their system's design and development.

It took the internal programmers almost a year to repair the system installed on July 4, 1995. By then, they had also implemented a limited fail-safe system that provided redundancy by making possible the operation of major functions if the primary system failed. The backup system did not have the capability to run the entire operation, but it would prevent a total shutdown. In order to keep the vital operations functioning, the group decided that the system would suspend noncritical operations in the event of a primary computer failure.

Toward the end of 1995, managers decided that they needed to take a more strategic view in the information systems area. A six-month search ensued to select a chief information officer (CIO), and Swanson was hired as Replacements' first CIO in May 1996. At this time, most of the information system's staff was also new on the job. The information services provided consisted of basic maintenance only—that is, keeping what was running operational.

After five months on the job, Swanson submitted his initial vision of what was needed. The report, entitled "A Proposal for Strategic Direction," recommended a change in hardware platform, a change to a new financial system, a change to database servers, and a change in application development tools. As a result, Replacements developed a new financial system on the IBM AS400, moved to a Microsoft NT Server on a 10/100 megabit local area network to provide access to data and images pertaining to china and flatware, and implemented Powerbuilder, a comprehensive application development tool. A new call center was implemented to enhance the capacity for handling incoming calls. Replacements also began leasing rather than purchasing hardware.

Information Systems Challenges

Replacements faced many questions and challenges in the information systems area. How could the functional areas integrate their operations, and how could the systems ensure that the data collected were current and accurate? What upgrade path should the company take to enhance the performance of the major processors (DGs and IBM)? Could operations and marketing help to design a more effective system to support their needs? Did Replacements have the information architecture to guide its processing and application decisions into the twenty-first century? In which IS competencies should Replacements invest? Should IS merely support the other functional areas at Replacements, or were there some areas where IS should take the lead?

CORPORATE STRATEGY

Finding Respect

Bob Page looked out his window toward Interstates 85/40. It was snowing heavily—very unusual for the first week of December in North Carolina. It was Friday, and everyone was exhausted but energized by the last two weeks' hectic activities. Sales on Monday had reached a record high of $417,000, smashing the previous one-day record of $286,000 set just a year ago, on December 5, 1996. Tuesday's sales had topped $375,000.

A reporter from the *Wall Street Journal* had visited Replacements earlier in the week and made several follow-up telephone calls about an article that the paper would publish in late December. An issue of *Southern Living* that included an article on Replacements had just hit the newsstands. The president of Wedgwood USA and a representative from the office in England had come to see Page. Five years ago, Page had gone to England to see someone at Wedgwood only to be stood up. Now, it was Wedgwood that approached Replacements.

Trudy, one of his two dachshunds, interrupted his thoughts, begging for a dog treat. Her puppies would arrive in three weeks. Several employees had already adopted them and, like their parents, the puppies would come to work every day.

Page had never envisioned it being like this. He had thought that he would be lucky to have six employees. Now there were 500 people in the Replacements family, 50 hired in the last two months. He had known there was demand, but he had never dreamed how much of a demand there was. He shared his view of the company and its strengths.

> It's not something that business school professors would want to hear, but we really don't talk about the bottom line. That would almost never come up in a conversation here. Our philosophy is that we do the things that we believe in and the bottom line will take care of itself. We take care of our customers.
>
> I think that just by doing the things that we're doing today, sales are going to continue to grow. The articles in *Southern Living* and in the *Wall Street Journal*—that's exposure. More and more people find out about us, yet half of our business still comes from word of mouth.
>
> There are dozens and dozens of companies that've started up since I started Replacements, but they're still on a level like when I operated out of my attic. We recently bought out a competitor in Washington State, and its entire inventory and office furniture fit in two tractor-trailers. We ship out two tractor-trailer loads of merchandise daily.
>
> We've established an impeccable reputation with our suppliers. They know that they can trust us to send them their money. I've heard some horror stories that when they've sent someone else something it would take them six months to get their money. In other cases, I've heard that the company said that it was going to pay one price and after they have shipped it the

company said, "Well we're not going to pay that." I think that our real focus on computers and our index have made us different. We have one competitor who was sending out letters to our suppliers asking them to get our index but not let us know what they were doing. On certain items they would pay $2.00 or $5.00 per piece more—but then told the suppliers not to ship anything without telling them.

We recently purchased the mailing list of one of our former competitors. It also wanted to sell its inventory, but it had such depth in the pieces that it had. It had a fifty-year supply of cups and saucers in one pattern! What we look at is buying a lot of different pieces, but not in huge amounts. They just kept accumulating pieces, but it was their buying system that didn't work for them. They might pay $15 for a cup and saucer and then they would automatically pay $15 for the dinner plate because the system was so rigid. We may be paying $1 for the cup and saucer and $25 for the dinner plate based on demand or how much inventory we already have.

Our customers can't find the product anywhere else. Some of our patterns are more than 100 years old. We couple that with the level of customer service that we provide. What would it take for a substantial competitor to emerge? Money, experience, a customer list, inventory, and a period of time. At this time, I'm not really concerned about competitors, because if someone had all the money in the world, they wouldn't have the inventory. We have the largest stockpile in the world of discontinued products. It would take a competitor a period of time to accumulate the inventory.

When we put out our indexes, the first ones to buy them are our competitors. Of course, a lot of our competitors sell a good portion of their inventory to us. They don't have the client base that we do. It has taken us all these years to accumulate $2\frac{1}{2}$ million customers. You couldn't do that overnight. If you had all the customers, what would you sell them? Now we have made lots of mistakes over the years. For example, we were buying a pattern called Sylvia from a German manufacturer. It turned out that Sylvia was a shape, not a pattern, and now we have 25 patterns with a Sylvia shape. This is something that was listed in our book, and if someone brought

a piece in we would buy it—but it wasn't what we thought we were buying. These are the kinds of things that other people are going to have to learn, too. We have knowledge here that nobody else would have. And we keep documenting things. We have over 2,200 old Noritake patterns, forty years old or older. When we publish our book, it's just going to be a killer book. This is doing a service to the world.

We are constantly adding patterns. We computer-image hundreds of patterns a week. We'd love for our customers and suppliers to have access to this knowledge. We have suppliers who fax things in here or bring a piece in or try to describe it over the phone. If they had access to some of this knowledge, it would make it easier. Here is an example of a pattern to which we have assigned a number. For our purposes, it is an identifiable pattern. This would save on our own research time. We may also want to have customers place their own orders.

We entered the silver business because we kept getting more and more requests from people asking why we didn't handle silver, too. And, of course, we already had our mailing list. It's fairly cost effective to add silver. With our supplier base, we just had to let them know we were in the silver business. It was a natural expansion of our business . . . all tableware.

Refurbishment is a business that we want to do at some point when we get caught up ourselves. We have a large new kiln that we're operating; and in the last couple of weeks, we have gotten fire polishing for beveling stemware. We lost some pieces before we perfected that. There's a lot of experimentation involved. With the china patterns, we keep records of the temperature to fire various patterns, which patterns we can fire, and which we can't. We get better at what we do as time goes on. We have the ability to launch the business now, but we are processing so many things that we already bought but can't sell until we refurbish. If someone came in right now, we could do it—but we don't have the manpower. It's very time consuming, and it's a real art.

I went to England four or five years ago to meet with people from Wedgwood, and the man who I had an appointment with was out of town. Now, they want us to be their worldwide distributor for closeouts. The president of Wedgwood USA and another man from England were here. They approached us about this arrangement—we did not approach them. They have their own matching center for recently discontinued patterns (patterns discontinued within the last five years). They shared information with us on the total sales of various patterns in all markets. They gave us a breakdown of sales by those patterns in the United States, the United Kingdom, Japan, and Australia. They want to sell us all the company's discontinued inventory, and they would refer to us all the customers who are looking for discontinued merchandise. We would supply that from the United States.

Over the years, we've bought thousands of pieces of stemware from Lenox crystal in recent patterns that have been out of production for three or four years. We had such demand that they'd produce those just for us. They also would have produced some of their china patterns for us if they still had some of the decals to decorate the pieces. Once they've discontinued patterns, they'll sell them out to us because they want to dispose of them. They also have outlet stores, but we sell more Lenox pieces than all their outlet stores combined.

Back four or five years ago, we had a dip in employee morale. I'd say that now our employee morale is way up there. Everyone's working really hard. And we have people who're really thrilled to be here. It's really great. It's demanding, very demanding; but it's positive adrenaline for the most part. I really enjoy it.

I still try very hard to know everyone by name. I'd know 95 percent of them. We've got so many new ones. I get a picture of everybody, and they fill out a questionnaire giving a little bit of information about themselves, what attracted them to Replacements, and what's the most interesting thing about them. I took these home last night. In my spare time, I look at their pictures and read their comments. When we had twenty-five employees, I knew everybody and their brothers and sisters. I miss some of that, but I am still very close to a lot of people here. I like to think that this is my extended family.

It's our real intent to take care of our people. We've higher expectations of our employees than most places. Right now, they're over-

worked because it's our busy season. I think that people either love it here, or they hate it. Typically, people who just want a job won't be here long. We have others who just couldn't think of working anywhere else. They just love being here. And it's a very diverse group. For example, there's a guy who we hired down in imaging who's a vegetarian and is really new-wave looking. But he wrote the nicest little thing. He started working here through a temporary agency. And he wrote that this is the neatest job that he'd ever worked at or heard about, and he had been looking for over a year. He's very enthusiastic about being here. We want people who are really glad to be here. We feel like attitude is the most important thing.

There's a learning curve. The new employees train for two or three weeks out in the warehouse before they ever have anyone on the phone, and then they are not proficient at what they do. It takes six months to a year to really get familiar with the products, and still they wouldn't have the depth of knowledge needed to put that customer on file and send them a list. There are so many times that I get a customer on the phone and think that if somebody else in phone sales had gotten that customer that they'd not be able to talk them through and get the information to put that customer on file and send them a list. I'm able to talk them through because of my product knowledge. Right now our employee is just looking at a computer screen; it will be very educational when we get pictures on the screen and he or she can see what the product looks like.

The thing I love to do is to go to flea markets and antique shops and buy things. What would I do if I didn't own Replacements? I love what I do. I really enjoy it. I'm overworked right now. I enjoy going out in the warehouse and working. I go out there every day. And, of course, I do a lot of the identification. There were 750 pieces of mail today. Some days there are 1,100 or 1,200, so it was fairly light today. I go through and I can identify up to $\frac{1}{2}$ of the pieces that come in. I love to take sales calls. I get ideas from everything I do, whether it's the mail or sales calls. If I'm out of town for a few days, I can hardly wait to get back. I'm always ready to get back."

CASE 6

The Scaffold Plank Incident

This case was prepared by Stewart C. Malone and Brad Brown of the University of Virginia.

What had started as a typically slow February day in the lumber business had turned into a moral dilemma. With 12 inches of snow covering the ground, construction (and lumber shipments) had ground to a halt and on the 26th of the month, the company was still $5,000 below break-even point. In the three years since he had been in the business, Bob Hopkins knew that a losing February was nothing unusual, but the country seemed to be headed for a recession, and as usual, housing starts were leading the way into the abyss.

Bob had gone to work for a commercial bank immediately after college but soon found the bureaucracy to be overwhelming and his career progress appeared to be written in stone. At the same time he was considering changing jobs, one of his customers, John White, offered him a job at White Lumber Company. The job was as a "trader," a position that involved both buying and selling lumber. The compensation was incentive-based and there was no cap on how much a trader could earn. White Lumber, although small in size, was one of the bank's best accounts. John White was not only a director of the bank but one of the community's leading citizens.

It was a little after 8:00 A.M. when Bob received a call from Stan Parrish, the lumber buyer at Quality Lumber. Quality was one of White Lumber's best retail dealer accounts, and Bob and Stan had established a good relationship.

"Bob, I need a price and availability on 600 pieces of 3 × 12 Doug fir-rough-sawn—2 & better

grade—16-feet long," said Stan, after exchanging the usual pleasantries.

"No problem, Stan. We could have those ready for pickup tomorrow and the price would be $470 per thousand board feet."

"The price sounds good, Bob. I'll probably be getting back to you this afternoon with a firm order," Stan replied.

Bob poured a third cup of coffee and mentally congratulated himself. Not bad, he thought—a two-truck order and a price that guaranteed full margin. It was only a half-hour later that Mike Fayerweather, his partner, asked Bob if he had gotten any inquiries on a truck of 16-foot scaffold plank. As Bob said he hadn't, alarm bells began to go off in his brain. While Stan had not said anything about scaffold plank, the similarities between the inquiries seemed to be more than coincidence.

While almost all lumber undergoes some sort of grading, the grading rules on scaffold plank were unusually restrictive. Scaffold planks are the wooden planks that are suspended between metal supports, often many stories above the ground. When you see painters and window-washers six stories in the air, they generally are standing on scaffold plank. The lumber had to be free of most of the natural defects found in ordinary construction lumber and had to have unusually high strength in flexing. Most people would not be able to tell certified scaffold plank from ordinary lumber, but it was covered by its own rules in the grading book, and if you were working ten stories above the ground, you definitely wanted to have certified scaffold plank underneath you. White Lumber did not carry scaffold plank, but its rough 3 × 12s certainly would fool all but the expertly trained eye.

This case is intended to be used as a basis for class discussion rather than as an illustration of either effective or ineffective handling of the situation. This case was prepared by Stewart C. Malone and Brad Brown, University of Virginia. Used by permission.

At lunch, Bob discussed his concerns about the inquiry with Mike.

"Look, Bob, I just don't see where we have a problem. Stank didn't specify scaffold plank, and you didn't quote him on scaffold plank," observed Mike. "We aren't even certain that the order is for the same material."

"I know all that, Mike," said Bob, "but we both know that four inquiries with the same tally is just too big a coincidence, and three of those inquiries were for Paragraph 171 scaffold plank. It seems reasonable to assume that Stan's quotation is for the same stuff."

"Well, it's obvious that our construction lumber is a good deal cheaper than the certified plank. If Stan is quoting based on our 2 & better grade and the rest of his competition is quoting on scaffold plank, then he will certainly win the job," Mike said.

"Maybe I should call Stan back and get more information on the specifications of the job. It may turn out that this isn't a scaffold plank job, and all of these problems will just disappear."

The waitress slipped the check between the two lumbermen. "Well, that might not be such a great idea, Bob. First, Stan may be a little ticked off if you were suggesting he might be doing something unethical. It could blow the relations between our companies. Second, suppose he does say that the material is going to be used for scaffolding. We would no longer be able to say we didn't know what it was going to be used for, and our best legal defense is out the window. I'd advise against calling him."

Bob thought about discussing the situation with John White, but White was out of town. Also, White prided himself on giving his traders a great deal of autonomy. Going to White too often for answers to questions was perceived as showing a lack of initiative and responsibility.

Against Mike's earlier warnings, Bob called Stan after lunch and discovered to his dismay that the material was going to be used as scaffold plank.

"Listen, Bob, I've been trying to sell this account for three months and this is the first inquiry that I've had a chance on. This is really important to me personally and to my superiors here at Quality. With this sale, we could land this account."

"But, Stan, we both know that our material doesn't meet the specs for scaffold plank."

"I know, I know," said Stan, "but I'm not selling it to the customer as scaffold plank. It's just regular construction lumber as far as we are both con-

cerned. That's how I've sold it, and that's what will show on the invoices. We're completely protected. Now just between you and me, the foreman on the job kinda winked at me and told me it was going to be scaffolding, but they're interested in keeping their costs down too. Also, they need this lumber by Friday, and there just isn't any scaffold plank in the local market."

"It just doesn't seem right to me," replied Bob.

"Look, I don't particularly like it, either. The actual specifications call for 2-inch thick material, but since it isn't actually scaffold plank, I'm going to order 3-inch planks. That is an extra inch of strength, and we both know that the load factors given in the engineering tables are too conservative to begin with. There's no chance that the material could fail in use. I happen to know that Haney Lumber is quoting a non-scaffold grade in a 2-inch material. If we don't grab this, someone else will and the material will be a lot worse than what we are going to supply."

When Bob continued to express hesitation, Stan said, "I won't hear about the status of the order until tomorrow, but we both know that your material will do this job OK—scaffold plank or not. The next year or two in this business are going to be lean for everyone, and our job—yours and mine—is putting lumber on job sites, not debating how many angels can dance on the head of a pin. Now if Quality can't count on you doing your job as a supplier, there are plenty of other wholesalers calling here every day who want our business. You better decide if you are going to be one of the survivors or not! I'll talk to you in the morning, Bob."

The next morning, Bob found a note on his desk telling him to see John White ASAP. Bob entered John's oak-paneled office and described the conversation with Stan yesterday. John slid a company sales order across the desk, and Bob saw it was a sales order for the 3 × 12s to Quality Lumber. In the space for the salesman's name, Bob saw that John had filled in "Bob Hopkins." Barely able to control his anger, Bob said, "I don't want anything to do with this order. I thought White Lumber was an ethical company, and here we are doing the same thing that all the fly-by-nighters do," sputtered Bob in concluding his argument.

John White looked at Bob and calmly puffed on his pipe. "The first thing you better do, Bob, is to calm down and put away your righteous superiority for a moment. You can't make or understand a good decision when you are as lathered up as you are. You are beginning to sound like a religious nut. What makes you think that you have the monopoly on ethical behavior? You've been out of college for four or five years, while I've been making these decisions for forty years. If you go into the industry or the community and compare your reputation with mine, you'll find out that you aren't even in the same league."

Bob knew John White was right. He had, perhaps, overstated his case, and in doing so, sounded like a zealot. When he relaxed and felt as though he was once again capable of rational thought, he said, "We both know that this lumber is going to be used for a purpose for which it is probably not suitable. Granted, there is only a very small chance that it will fail, but I don't see how we can take that chance."

"Look, Bob, I've been in this business for a long time, and I've seen practices that would curl your hair. Undershipping (shipping 290 pieces when the order calls for 300), shipping material a grade below what was ordered, bribing building inspectors and receiving clerks, and so on. We don't do those things at my company."

"Don't we have a responsibility to our customers, though?" asked Bob.

"Of course we do, Bob, but we aren't policemen, either. Our job is to sell lumber that is up to specification. I can't and won't be responsible for how the lumber is used after it leaves our yard. Between the forest and the final user, lumber may pass through a dozen transactions before it reaches the ultimate user. If we are to assume responsibility for every one of those transactions, we would probably have time to sell about four boards a year. We have to assume, just like every other business, that our suppliers and our customers are knowledgeable and will also act ethically. But whether they do or don't, it is not possible for us to be their keepers."

Bob interjected, "But we have reason to believe that this material will be used as scaffolding. I think we have an obligation to follow up on that information."

"Hold on, just a second, Bob. I told you once we are not the police. We don't even know who the final user is, so how are we going to follow up on this? If Stan is jerking us around, he certainly won't tell us. And even if we did know, what would we do? If we are going to do this consistently, that means we would have to ask every customer who the final end user is. Most of our customers would

interpret that as us trying to bypass them in the distribution channel. They won't tell us, and I can't blame them. If we carry your argument to its final conclusion, we'll have to start taking depositions on every invoice we sell.

"In the Quality Lumber instance, we are selling material to the customer as specified by the customer, Stan at Quality Lumber. The invoice will be marked, 'This material is not suitable for use as scaffold plank.' Although I'm not a lawyer, I believe that we have fulfilled our legal obligation. We have a signed purchase order and are supplying lumber that meets the specifications. I know we have followed the practices that are customary in the industry. Finally, I believe that our material will be better than anything else that could conceivably go on the job. Right now, there is no 2-inch dense 171 scaffold plank in this market, so it is not as though a better grade could be supplied in the time allotted. I would argue that we are ethically obligated to supply this lumber. If anyone is ethically at fault, it is probably the purchasing agent who specified a material that is not available."

When Bob still appeared to be unconvinced, John White asked him, "What about the other people here at the company? You're acting as though you are the only person who has a stake in this. It may be easy for you to turn this order down—you've got a college degree and a lot of career options. But I have to worry about all of the people at this company. Steve out there on the forklift never finished high school. He's worked here thirty years and if he loses this job, he'll probably never find another one. Janet over in bookkeeping has a disabled husband. While I can't afford to pay her very much, our health insurance plan keeps their family together. With the bills her husband accumulates in a year, she could never get him on another group insurance plan if she lost this job.

"Bob, I'm not saying that we should do anything and then try to justify it, but business ethics in the real world is not the same thing you studied in the classroom. There it is easy to say, 'Oh, there is an ethical problem here. We better not do that.' In the classroom, you have nothing to lose by taking the morally superior ground. Out here, companies close, people lose their jobs, lives can be destroyed. To always say, 'No, we won't do that' is no better than having no ethics at all. Ethics involves making tough choices, weighing costs and benefits. There are no hard-and-fast answers in these cases. We just have to approach each situation individually."

As Bob left John's office, he was more confused than ever. When he first entered his office, he had every intention of quitting in moral indignation, but John's argument had made a lot of sense to him, and he both trusted and respected John. After all, John White had a great deal more experience than he did and was highly respected in both the community and the lumber industry. Yet he was still uncomfortable with the decision. Was selling lumber to Quality merely a necessary adjustment of his ivory tower ethics to the real world of business? Or was it the first fork in the road to a destination he did not want to reach?

CASE 7

Royal Dutch Shell and the Execution of Ken Saro-Wiwa

This case was prepared by Charles W. L. Hill of the University of Washington.

INTRODUCTION

In 1995, a Nigerian military tribunal, in what most observers decried as a "sham trial," ordered the execution of noted author and playwright Ken Saro-Wiwa and eight other members of the Movement for the Survival of the Ogoni People. The Ogoni are a 500,000-member ethnic group of farmers and fishermen who live in an area of Nigeria's coastal plain. For several years, the Ogoni had been waging a vigorous political campaign against Nigeria's military rulers and the giant oil company, Royal Dutch Shell. They had been seeking greater self-determination, rights to the revenue stemming from oil exploration on traditional Ogoni lands, and compensation for the environmental degradation to their land caused by frequent oil spills from fractured pipelines. Shell had been pumping oil from Ogoni lands since the late 1950s. In 1994, four Ogoni chiefs who advocated cooperation rather than confrontation with Nigeria's military government were lynched by a mob of Ogoni youth. Though he was not present, Saro-Wiwa, a leader of the protest movement, was arrested and subsequently sentenced to death along with eight other Ogoni activists.

Despite intensive international pressure that included appeals to Shell to use its influence in the country to gain clemency for the convicted, the executions went ahead as scheduled on November 10, 1995. In the aftermath of the executions, Shell was roundly criticized in the Western media for its apparent unwillingness to bring pressure to bear on Nigeria's totalitarian regime. The incident started some soul-searching at Shell about the social and environmental responsibility of a multinational corporation in societies such as Nigeria that fall short of Western standards for the protection of human rights and the environment.

BACKGROUND

In 1961, the African nation of Nigeria won independence from Britain. At that time, many believed that Nigeria had the potential to become one of the engines of economic growth in Africa. The country was blessed with abundant natural resources, particularly oil and gas, was a net exporter of food stuffs, and had a large population that, by African standards, was well educated. (Today, Nigeria has the largest population in Africa—more than 110 million people.) By the mid 1990s, it was clear that much of that potential was still to be realized. Thirty-five years after winning independence, Nigeria still depended heavily on the oil sector. Oil production accounted for 30 percent of GDP, 95 percent of foreign exchange earnings, and about 80 percent of the government's budget revenues. The largely subsistence agricultural sector had failed to keep up with rapid population growth, and Nigeria, once a large net exporter of food, now had to import food. GDP per capita was a paltry $230, one quarter of what it had been in 1981, and the country was creaking under $40 billion of external debt. Nigeria had been unable to garner financial assistance from institutions such as the International Monetary Fund because of an unwillingness on the part of the government to account for how it used the revenues from oil taxes.

Political problems partly explained Nigeria's economic malaise. The country has suffered from internal strife between some of the more than 250 ethnic groups that constitute the nation. In the 1960s, the country was racked by a particularly nasty civil war. In December 1983, the civilian government of the country was replaced in a coup by a military regime, which proceeded to rule by decree. In 1993, democratic elections were held, but the military government nullified the results, declaring that there had been widespread ballot fraud.

Royal Dutch Shell is the main foreign oil producer operating in Nigeria. The company was formed at the turn of the century when Holland's Royal Dutch Company, which had substantial oil operations in Indonesia, merged with Britain's Shell Transport and Trading to create one of the world's first multinational oil companies. Shell is now the world's largest oil company, with annual revenues exceeding $130 billion. The company has been operating in Nigeria since 1937 and by the mid 1990s was pumping about half of Nigeria's oil. Nigerian oil accounts for about 11 to 12 percent of the company's global output and generates net income for Shell of around $200 million per annum.

PROBLEMS IN THE OGONI REGION

In 1958, Royal Dutch Shell struck oil on Ogoni lands. By some estimates, the company has extracted some $30 billion worth of oil from the region since then. Despite this, the Ogoni remain desperately poor. Most live in palm-roofed mud huts and practice subsistence agriculture. Of Shell's 5,000 employees in Nigeria, in 1995 only 85 were Ogoni. Because they are a powerless minority among Nigeria's 110 million people, the Ogoni are often overlooked when it comes to the allocation of jobs either in government or in the private sector.

Starting in 1982, the Nigerian government supposedly directed 1.5 percent of the oil revenue it received back to the communities where the oil was produced. In 1992, that percentage was increased to 3 percent. The Ogoni, however, claim that they have seen virtually none of this money. Most appears to

have been spent in the tribal lands of the ruling majority or has vanished in corrupt deals. Although there were ninety-six oil wells, two refineries, a petrochemical complex and a fertilizer plant in the Ogoni region in 1994, the lone hospital was an unfinished concrete husk, and the government schools, unable to pay teachers, were rarely open.

In addition to the lack of returns from oil production in their region, the Ogoni claim that their lands have suffered from environmental degradation, much of which could be laid at the feet of Shell. Ogoni activists claim that Shell's poor environmental safeguards have resulted in numerous oil spills and widespread contamination of the soil and ground water. A Shell spokesman, interviewed in 1994, seemed to acknowledge that there might be some basis to these complaints. He stated that "Some of the facilities installed during the last 30 years, while acceptable at the time, aren't as we would build them today. Given the age of some of these lines [oil pipelines], regrettably oil spills have occurred from time to time."[1] However, the same spokesman also blamed many of the more recent leaks in the Ogoni region on deliberate sabotage. The sabotage, he stated, had one of two motives— to back up claims for compensation or to support claims of environmental degradation.

On hearing of these claims, Ken Saro-Wiwa called them "preposterous." Saro-Wiwa argued that although uneducated youths, frustrated and angry, may have damaged some Shell installations in one or two incidents, "the people would never deliberately spill oil on their land because they know the so-called compensation is paltry and the land is never restored."[2] To support his position, Saro-Wiwa pointed to a spill from the 1960s near a settlement called Ebubu that still had not been cleaned up. In response, Shell stated that the spill occurred during the civil war in the 1960s, and cleanup work was completed in 1990. Subsequently, sunken oil reappeared at the surface, but Shell claims that it was unable to do anything about this because of threats made against its employees in the region. Indeed, in January 1993, out of concern for their safety, Shell barred its employees from entering the region.

In April 1993, the Ogoni organized their first protests against Shell and the government. Ogoni farmers stood in front of earthmoving equipment that was laying a pipeline for Shell through croplands. Although Shell stated that the land had been acquired by legal means and that full compensation had been paid to the farmers and local community, some of the locals remained unhappy about what they viewed as continuing exploitation of their land. Seeing a threat to the continuity of its oil operations, Shell informed the Nigerian government about the protest. Units from the Nigerian military soon arrived, and shots were fired into the crowd of protesters, killing one Ogoni man and wounding several others.

Subsequently, in a series of murky incidents, Nigerian soldiers stormed Ogoni villages, saying that they were quelling unrest between neighboring Ogoni tribes. For their part, the Ogoni claimed that the raids were punishment for obstructing Shell. They stated that the military had orders to use minor land disputes, which had long been settled with little violence, as an excuse to lay waste entire villages. A feared unit of the Mobile Police with the nickname "Kill and Go" conducted some of the raids. Although details are sketchy, it has been reported that hundreds of people lost their lives in the violence. In any event, the cycle of violence ultimately culminated in the killing of the Ogoni chiefs who argued for compromise with the Nigerian government. In turn, this provided the government with the justification it needed to arrest Ken Saro-Wiwa and eight associates in the Movement for the Survival of the Ogoni People.

NIGERIA AND SHELL UNDER PRESSURE

Saro-Wiwa's arrest achieved the goal that the protests and bloodshed had not; it focused international attention on the plight of the Ogoni, the heavy-handed policies of the Nigerian government, and Shell's activities in Nigeria. Several human rights organizations immediately pressured Shell to use its influence to gain the release of Saro-Wiwa. They also urged Shell to put on hold plans to start work on a $3.5 billion liquefied natural gas project in Nigeria. The project was structured as a joint venture with the Nigerian government. Shell's central role in the project gave it considerable influence over the government, or so human rights activists believed.

For its part, Shell stated that it deplored the heavy-handed approach taken by the Nigerian government toward the Ogoni, and regretted pain and loss suffered by Ogoni communities. The company

also indicated that it was using "discreet diplomacy" to try and bring influence to bear on the Nigerian government. Nigeria's military leadership, however, was in no mood to listen to discreet diplomacy from Shell or anyone else. After a trial by a military tribunal that was derided as nothing more than a "kangaroo court," Saro-Wiwa and his associates were sentenced to death by hanging. The sentence was carried out shortly after sunrise on November 10, 1995.

AFTERMATH

In the wake of Saro-Wiwa's hanging, a storm of protest erupted around the world. The heads of state of the fifty-two nation British Commonwealth, meeting in New Zealand at the time of Saro-Wiwa's execution, suspended Nigeria and stated that they would expel the country if it did not return to democratic rule within two years. U.S. President Bill Clinton recalled the U.S. ambassador to Nigeria and banned the sale of military equipment, on top of aid cuts made in protest at Saro-Wiwa's arrest. British Prime Minister John Major banned arms sales to Nigeria and called for the widest possible embargo. Ambassadors from the fifteen nation European Union were recalled, and the EU suspended all aid to Nigeria.

On the other hand, no country halted purchases of Nigerian oil or sales of oil service equipment to Nigeria. The United States, which imports 40 percent of Nigeria's daily output of 2 million barrels, was silent on the question of an oil embargo. Similarly, no Western country—many of which had national companies working in the Nigerian oil industry—indicated that it would impose an embargo on sales to, or purchase from, the Nigerian oil industry. Alone among major public figures, South African President Nelson Mandela called for a ban on Shell. The call was echoed by several environment groups, including Greenpeace and Friends of the Earth, both of which urged their supporters to boycott Shell products. However, South Africa never did enact a formal ban, and the boycott calls met with only limited success.

For its part, Shell indicated that it would go ahead with its plans for a liquefied natural gas operation in Nigeria in partnership with the Nigerian government. In a public notice published in British newspapers, Shell stated that "it has been suggested that Shell should pull out of Nigeria's liquefied natural gas project. But if we do so now, the project will collapse. Maybe forever. So let's be clear who gets hurt if the project gets cancelled. A cancellation would certainly hurt the thousands of Nigerians who will be working on the project, and the tens of thousand benefiting in the local economy."[3]

In November 1996, the Center for Constitutional Rights filed a federal lawsuit in the U.S. District Court in Manhattan on behalf of relatives of Saro-Wiwa who now resided in the United States. The lawsuit accused Royal Dutch Shell of being part of a conspiracy that led to Saro-Wiwa's hanging. Shell denied the allegations and stated that they would be refuted in court.

In May 1997, at the annual general meeting of Shell Transport and Trading in London, a group of eighteen institutional investors tabled a resolution that would have required Shell to establish an independent external body to monitor its environmental and human rights policies. John Jennings, the outgoing chairman of the company, told reporters after the meeting that proxy votes from shareholders were running 10 to 1 against the resolution.

One reason for the defeat of the shareholder resolution was that the company had already indicated that it was taking steps to reform its culture and improve its own monitoring of environmental and human rights policies. Indeed, prior to the shareholder meeting, the company issued its own report on its policies in Nigeria, in which the company did admit that it needed to improve its monitoring of environmental and human rights policies. Under the leadership of its new head, Mark Moody-Stuart, Shell subsequently stated that it expected its companies to express support for fundamental human rights, in line with the legitimate role of business, and to give proper regard to health, safety, and the environment consistent with its commitment to sustainable development. The company also embraced the U.N. Universal Declaration of Human Rights, and pledged to set up socially responsible management systems and to develop training procedures to help management deal with human rights dilemmas.

Commenting on these steps, a spokesman for Human Rights Watch stated: "I'm prepared to give them some credit that they realized they had to look at what their own operations were and how to respond. They acknowledged that big companies have social responsibility, and that's a pretty big step for the multinational corporations."[4]

Endnotes

1. G. Brooks, "Slick Alliance," *Wall Street Journal*, May 6, 1994, p. A1.
2. G. Brooks, "Slick Alliance," *Wall Street Journal*, May 6, 1994, p. A1.
3. P. Beckett, "Shell Boldly Defends Its Role in Nigeria," *Wall Street Journal*, November 27, 1995, p. A9.
4. M. Hamilton, "Shell's New Worldview," *The Washington Post*, August 2, 1998, p. H1. Additional sources used in the preparation of this case are "Multinationals and Their Morals," *Economist,* December 2, 1995; R. Corzine, "Shell Discovers Time and Tide Wait for No Man," *Financial Times*, March 10, 1998, p. 17; R. Corzine, and Boulton, "Shell Defends Its Ethics on Eve of General Meeting," *Financial Times*, May 14, 1997, p. 29; J. Hoagland, "Shell's Game in Nigeria," *Washington Post*, November 5, 1995, p. C7; R. Hudson and M. Rose, "Shell Is Pressured to Scrap Its Plans for a New Plant in Nigeria Amid Protests," *Wall Street Journal*, November 14, 1995, p. A11; T. Kamm, "Executions Raise Sanction Threat," *Wall Street Journal*, November 13, 1995, p. A10.

B

Business Level: Domestic and Global Cases

America Online and the Internet (A)

This case was prepared by Charles W. L. Hill of the University of Washington.

Content, context, community, commerce and connectivity at a low cost.

—*Steve Case, CEO of America Online*

INTRODUCTION

As of June 1996, America Online (AOL) was the world's leading provider of commercial on-line services. Since its initial public offering in 1992, AOL had grown from an obscure on-line service with fewer than 200,000 subscribers and revenues of just $27 million into a titan in the fast-evolving world of cyberspace, with 6.2 million subscribers, revenues in excess of $1 billion, and strategic alliances with a slew of Internet software and service providers, including AT&T, Microsoft, and Netscape. Once seen as a distant third to its well-funded rivals, Prodigy and CompuServe, AOL was now clearly *the* major force in the commercial on-line market. Reflecting this, the stock had soared more than 100-fold since its initial public offering, hitting a peak of $71 per share in May 1996. At that price, AOL had a market capitalization of more than $6.4 billion! (See the financial data shown in Table 1.)

However, in the rapidly changing world of high technology, competitive advantage is often a fleeting thing. By the fall of 1996 there were wolves baying at AOL's door. One perennial problem cited by skeptics was AOL's high churn rate. (Churn rate refers to the number of subscribers who leave the service within a defined period of time, normally one year.) Estimates suggested that 30 to 40 per-

This case is intended to be used as a basis for class discussion rather than as an illustration of either effective or ineffective handling of the situation. This case was prepared by Charles W. L. Hill, University of Washington. Used by permission.

cent of subscribers quit the service within one, year of signing on. The reasons given to explain this high churn rate typically included uninspiring content and connection problems that frustrated subscribers. Another problem concerned a slow-down in the rate of subscriber growth, which became evident during the summer of 1996. AOL claimed that this slowdown reflected "normal" seasonal trends, but critical observers weren't so sure. There were also repeated allegations that AOL used questionable accounting practices, which understated the cost of acquiring new subscribers and overstated its operating profit. AOL was also facing increased price competition from Internet access providers and other on-line commercial services. To cap it all, many technophiles saw AOL's real competition as the World Wide Web, which they characterized as an ocean of content and information in comparison to AOL, which they dismissed as nothing more than a pond. Why on earth, they wondered, would consumers want to sign on with AOL, when for a flat fee of less than $20 per month they can sign on with any one of a growing number of Internet access providers and surf the Web at will using a Web browser downloaded for free from Netscape or Microsoft? Reflecting these concerns, AOL's stock price fell sharply from its May 1996 highs, hitting $24 per share by early October, a loss of more than 60 percent in less than four months. The investment community clearly had doubts about the ability of AOL to establish itself as a viable enterprise. How would AOL respond?

TABLE I

America Online Financial Data: 1991–1995

Per Share Data ($) (Year ended June 30)	1995	1994	1993	1992	1991
Tangible book value	$ 1.08	$ 1.70	0.51	0.43	–0.65
Cash flow	$ 0.57	$ 0.11	0.07	0.06	0.03
Earnings	$–0.50	$ 0.10	0.06	0.05	0.00
Dividends	Nil	Nil	Nil	Nil	Nil
Payout ratio	Nil	Nil	Nil	Nil	Nil
Prices—high	$ 44¼	$ 14⅝	$ 8¾	$ 3⅝	NA
—low	$ 12⅜	$ 6	$ 2¼	$ 1⅜	NA
P/E Ratio—high	NM	NM	NM	73	NA
—low	NM	NM	NM	27	NA
Income Statement Analysis (million $)					
Revenues	$ 394	$ 104	$40.0	$27.0	$21.0
Operating income	$ 103	$ 9.3	$ 5.1	$ 3.8	$ 2.0
Depreciation	$ 72.1	$ 1.3	$ 0.6	$ 0.5	$ 0.5
Interest expense	$ 1.0	NA	NA	NA	NA
Pretax income	$–18.5	$ 10.0	$ 5.0	$ 3.6	$ 1.5
Effective tax rate	NM	38%	38%	38%	38%
Net income	$–33.6	$ 6.2	$ 3.1	$ 2.2	$ 0.9
Balance Sheet & Other Financial Data (million $)					
Cash	$ 64.1	$ 67.7	$14.3	$14.0	$ 1.0
Current assets	$ 133	$ 105	$25.0	$19.0	$ 4.0
Total assets	$ 406	$ 148	$32.0	$24.0	$ 8.0
Current liability	$ 133	$ 40.4	$ 8.6	$ 4.4	$ 3.8
Long-term debt	$ 19.5	$ 5.8	Nil	Nil	$ 0.2
Common equity	$ 218	$ 99	$23.8	$18.9	$–6.0
Total capital	$ 273	$ 108	$24.0	$19.0	$ 4.0
Capital expense	$ 57.8	$ 17.5	$ 1.8	$ 0.7	$ 0.1
Cash flow	$ 38.4	$ 7.5	$ 3.7	$ 2.7	$ 0.5
Current ratio	1.0	2.6	3.0	4.4	1.0
% Long-term of capitalization	7.1%	5.4%	Nil	Nil	4.8%
% Net income of revenues	NM	5.9%	7.7%	8.3%	4.4%
% Return on assets	NM	6.6%	10.7%	7.4%	NA
% Return on equity	NM	9.7%	13.9%	NM	NA

Source: Company accounts.

CYBERSPACE

Cyberspace—that vast, hip, cool, creative, anarchic, digitally constructed visual and audio reality that is diffused throughout and embedded within the growing World Wide Web of interconnected computers—owes its origins to, of all things, cold war paranoia. The Internet, or the skeleton on which the flesh of cyberspace hangs, started its life

in 1969 in a military laboratory under the sponsorship of the Pentagon's Advanced Research Projects Agency. The Internet was conceived as a means of allowing scientists working on military contracts all over America to share expensive computers and other resources. As an afterthought, a few of the original designers also came up with a way of sending messages between computers, and E-mail was born.

The design of the Internet displays its military origins.[1] At its most basic, the Internet is nothing more than a collection of computers linked to a network of high-speed telephone lines and switches (see Figure 1). To ensure easy connectivity, the Internet is based on a communications protocol known as TCP/IP, which is in the public domain (it is an open standard). Data traveling along the Internet are split into tiny packets of information; an Internet address is assigned to each packet; and, given their common addresses, the packets can take different routes to their destination. This makes it hard for anyone to eavesdrop on messages—an important source of comfort to the paranoid warriors of the cold war. Moreover, a "packet-switched" network can resist large-scale destruction. If one route is knocked out for some reason (for example, by a nuclear bomb), packets will simply travel along a route that remains intact.

Until the early 1980s, the Internet was tiny and very obscure, consisting of fewer than 500 "host" computers. However, academics were starting to take notice. They found the Internet to be a useful conduit for sharing information with their colleagues. Because the Internet utilized open standards, it was easy to hook into, and because the U.S. government had subsidized the building of much of the early infrastructure, it was inexpensive to use. Soon universities and research laboratories around the world were connecting their own internal networks of computers to the Internet, transforming it into a globally dispersed "network of networks," and by 1987 approximately 28,000 host computers were attached. The Internet, however, was still a very dry place, lacking in color, sound, and images. To become of interest to a wider audience, it needed to change.

The World Wide Web

The change, when it came, was accidental and explosive. In the late 1980s, Tim Bernes Lee, a physicist at the CERN research institute for particle physics in Switzerland, developed a method of organizing on-line scientific information. His insight was that documents stored in digital form could be cross-referenced, or linked, by using "hypertext." Associated with the hypertext would be an Internet address. Users could select a hypertext term in a document they were reading on-line, and they would be linked electronically to a document associated with that term. For example, a physicist at CERN who was using her computer to read a research paper that cited a study undertaken by scientists in Los Alamos would simply have to click on the cite with her computer's mouse—assuming that it was formatted in hypertext—and she would be linked with the source document, which might be stored on a computer at Los Alamos, or for that matter, on any other computer linked to the Internet. Bernes Lee developed a simple computer code, known as hypertext markup language, or HTML, for formatting documents containing hypertext. Within HTML he also embedded instructions that could be used to display graphics files connected with a document on a computer screen. Without really knowing it, Bernes Lee had invented the World Wide Web (WWW).

In 1993, a young computer programmer at the University of Illinois, Mark Andreessen, masterminded the development of a browser that could be used to surf the Internet, read documents that had been formatted with HTML, and display the associated text and graphics on a personal computer screen. In 1994, he left Illinois to help establish Netscape, a software company that produced an improved version of the HTML browser he had developed at Illinois, Netscape Navigator. Netscape also produced Web server software that could be placed on the computer servers, which were the nodes of the rapidly developing WWW, to manage Web files and handle traffic.

Facilitated by the wide availability of browsers and Web server software and powered by the sudden rush of nontechnical users to get on-line, the growth of the WWW was nothing short of stunning. In 1990, less than 1 million users were connected to the Internet. By late 1995, largely as a result of the popularity of the WWW, the figure was approaching 80 million. Projections suggest there will be 160 million users by 1998, and perhaps as many as 500 million by early in the next century.[2]

A related development was the invention of the Java computer programming language at Sun Microsystems, one of the leading suppliers of computer workstations and servers. A program written in Java can be stored anywhere on the WWW and accessed by anyone with a Web browser on his or her personal computer that contains a Java inter-preter. (The new versions of most Web browsers such as Netscape's Navigator and Microsoft's Internet Explorer include a Java interpreter.) Java is indifferent to the operating system of the personal computer on which a Web browser resides. Therefore, in theory, someone using a current version of Netscape Navigator can access a word processing program placed somewhere on the Web as and when it is needed. Instead of purchasing the program outright for hundreds of dollars, all the user needs to do is pay a few cents for the run time during which the program is used. To date, the main use of Java has been to run simple visual applications on downloaded Web pages.[3]

The Infrastructure of the Internet

The infrastructure of the Internet is composed of five key elements: a backbone, digital switches, dedicated computers known as servers, Points of Presence (POPs), and the computers of connected users (see Figure 2).[4] The backbone of the net is a system of fiber-optic telecommunications lines that can transfer 40 million bits of data per second between two nodes in the system at the speed of light. (In comparison, using "slow" telephone lines, the average modem transfers data at 28,800 bits per second.) Most backbone lines are owned by the telephone companies (AT&T, MCI, Sprint), which lease capacity wholesale to Internet users, Digital ATM switches are found at the nodes of the system, of which there are tens of thousands. These ATM switches, which are nothing more than specialized computers, direct the packets of data that flow along the Internet.

From the ATM switches, fiber-optic lines branch off to connect large users, such as universities and corporations. These larger users have their own internal networks (local area networks known as LANs), complete with local switches. Users within the organization can connect to the Internet from their personal computers by utilizing networking software such as Windows NT or Novell Netware. Most larger users also maintain servers where they store data that can be accessed by anyone connected to the Internet (for example, HTML documents such as WWW home pages).

Other lines branch off from ATM switches to connect smaller organizations and individuals to the Internet. These users must first dial a telephone number to connect to a POP, which is simply another switch connected to the ATM switch. (Anyone who uses AOL's service first has to dial a telephone number to connect to a POP before accessing the service.) From the POP, lines branch off to home users who connect through analog modems and ISDN lines. (An ISDN telephone line uses digital rather than analog signals to transmit data, which significantly increases transmission speed.) The local area networks of smaller organizations may also be connected to the Internet through a POP. Many of these smaller organizations also maintain their own Web servers.

Internet Service Providers

During the early 1990s, personal computers penetrated small businesses and the home market in record numbers. (By 1995, an estimated 30 percent of U.S. households owned a personal computer.) The rapid diffusion of PCs among the households and small businesses, when coupled with the development of HTML and Web browsers, created consumer demand for access to the World Wide Web. The initial demand was largely from academicians and students, who were using it to access the Web through various university networks and wanted similar access at home. Soon, however, demand mushroomed to include small businesses, many of which wanted to experiment with selling goods and services via the WWW, and individuals from a wide range of backgrounds.

Internet service providers (ISPs) emerged to serve this demand. There are literally hundreds of ISPs operating today in the United States, but they are increasingly dominated by a handful of big names, including all three major long-distance carriers (AT&T, MCI, and Sprint), along with some less familiar names (UUNet, Netcom Online, PSI Net, AGIS-Net99, BBN, and GNN—an ISP owned by AOL). Some of the Internet service providers have invested heavily in building the infrastructure of the Internet (UUNet and Sprint, for example), installing fiber-optic backbone lines, ATM switches, servers, and POPs. These ISPs often lease their surplus capacity to other ISPs. Most ISPs license Web browsers from Microsoft and/or Netscape, providing these for free to their customers.

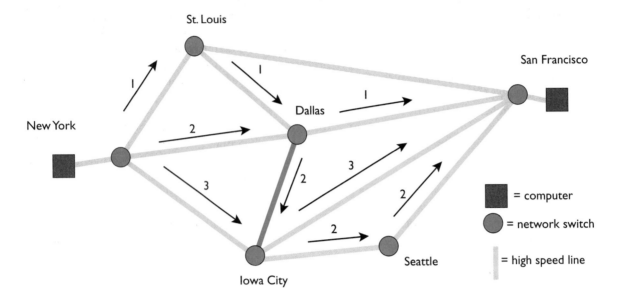

FIGURE I

How the
Internet Works

The emergence of ISPs is a relatively recent phenomenon. By early 1996, there were about 600,000 direct ISP subscribers in the United States, compared with 10.5 million subscribers for various proprietary on-line services such as AOL, Prodigy, MSN, and CompuServe.[5] However, the entry of companies such as AT&T into this business and the growing familiarity of users with the Web point toward a potentially dramatic increase in the number of ISPs over the next few years. Some observers speculate that over the next few years subscriber growth will be increasingly oriented toward ISPs, as opposed to the established on-line service.

By 1996, two trends were evident among ISPs—consolidation and intensifying price competition. The most dramatic example of consolidation was the acquisition for $2 billion of UUNet by MSF Communications, a competitive-access telephone service company with operations in the United States and Europe. According to the CEO of MSF Communications, "The combination of our fiber-optic network and UUNet's Internet services are a match made in heaven."[6] For UUNet, the great advantage of the acquisition was that it would reduce

UUNet's costs. ISPs normally have to pay substantial fees to local and long-distance telephone companies in order to access their networks. In 1995, more than 40 percent of UUNet's network expenses were for local communications service.[7] The acquisition would reduce these, putting UUNet on a level footing with the likes of AT&T and MCI.

By 1995, most ISPs were charging a basic monthly fee for access (usually in the $10-per-month range) plus an hourly rate that would kick in after the first five to ten hours of usage in a month (for example, $2.95 after the first five hours of access time). Under this pricing structure, it was not uncommon for active subscribers to run up bills in excess of $50 per month. By 1996, however, the pricing trend among ISPs seemed to be headed toward a flat rate monthly fee for a basic service. This development was driven by the entry of large telephone companies into the ISP business. In early 1996, AT&T entered the ISP business with the introduction of its WorldNet service. AT&T announced that it would provide its long-distance customers with five free hours of Internet access a month and charge $2.50 per hour for additional ac-

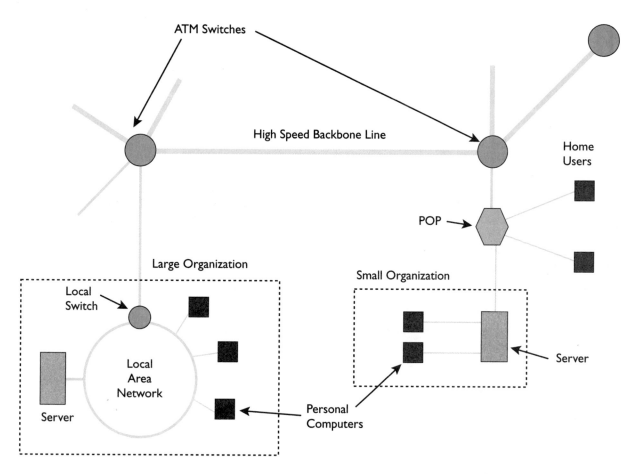

FIGURE 2

Internet Infrastructure

cess. It also offered unlimited Internet access for $19.95 per month. AT&T's announcement resulted in 212,000 customers signing up for the service by the time it went live on March 14, 1996. So strong was the demand that AT&T found itself without the network capacity (POPs and switches) and software to service the demand, and by mid-1996 there was a two-month waiting list before customers could connect to the service.[8]

MCI responded to AT&T's entry with a similar pricing structure, including the flat rate charge of $19.95 per month for unlimited access. MCI also announced that it would triple the capacity of its Internet access network and offer its customers high-speed ISDN Internet access. In announcing

this move, a senior vice president at MCI noted that "MCI's pioneering efforts in the Internet market have resulted in a $100 million business that we expect to grow to $2 billion by 2000."[9]

Proprietary On-Line Services

Long before the ISPs had a notable presence, there were the proprietary on-line service providers (OSPs). The OSPs differ from the ISPs in that an OSP allows a fee-paying subscriber access to a private, closed network that contains exclusive content. ISPs simply grant access to the World Wide Web, but OSPs bundle exclusive content for their subscribers. Currently, subscribers have to use a proprietary interface to access these on-line services. In addition, OSP subscribers can use the service as a gateway to the WWW. An AOL subscriber, for example, can browse the Web using AOL's Web browser, Netscape Navigator, or Microsoft's Internet Explorer.

As of mid 1996, there were four major OSPs in the United States: America Online, CompuServe, Prodigy, and the Microsoft Network (MSN). AOL is discussed in detail later in this case. Prodigy is the oldest and smallest of these services, with around 1 million subscribers. Prodigy was established in 1984 as a joint venture between Sears, IBM, and CBS. IBM was to provide the technology, Sears wanted to experiment with on-line commerce, and CBS was to provide news and advertising. CBS pulled out after a short time, but IBM and Sears stuck with it until May 1996, pouring $1.2 billion into Prodigy. By that point it was clear that Prodigy was losing out to other OSPs, so IBM and Sears sold the service for $250 million to International Wireless, a Boston-based investment group. When discussing Prodigy's failure to grow, analysts often cited its clunky interface, poorly organized and uninspiring content, failure to embrace chat rooms and E-mail, and unimaginative distribution strategy.[10]

With 4.7 million subscribers, CompuServe is second only to AOL in the OSP market, although until two years ago it was substantially larger than AOL. CompuServe was established by H&R Block in an effort to diversify H&R Block's core tax return business (which has a pronounced seasonal fluctuation in revenues) and to provide an on-line conduit for Block's financial services business. In April 1996, H&R Block took the first step in the process of spinning off CompuServe to independent investors, selling 16 million shares, or a 17.7 percent stake in the service, for an average price of $30 per share, raising $454 million in the process.[11]

During 1995, CompuServe added new subscribers at the rate of about 100,000 per month, substantially less than AOL's subscriber acquisition rate of 400,000 per month.[12] CompuServe's inability to match AOL has been variously attributed to a confusing pricing scheme, poor marketing, and an interface that was less intuitive and appealing than that employed by AOL.

In August 1995, CompuServe took a number of steps that were designed to correct these prob-

lems. The pricing structure, which charged subscribers a different price for different aspects of the service, was revamped and replaced with a flat monthly fee of $9.95 for the first five hours and $2.95 for each subsequent hour. CompuServe also announced plans to introduce a new low-cost service aimed at Internet novices and children in an attempt to strengthen its network infrastructure by increasing the number of access points from 50,000 to 105,000 and to triple its spending on marketing to $115 million.[13]

CompuServe's new service, WOW, was introduced in the spring of 1996.[14] WOW was designed to challenge AOL on both price and child safety. Although WOW is produced by CompuServe, it is a completely different service. For a flat fee of $18 per month, WOW offers unlimited access to a mix of proprietary content and features, as well as to the Internet's World Wide Web and E-mail. WOW utilizes Microsoft's Internet Explorer as its Web browser. WOW was explicitly designed with features to protect children from accessing undesirable content on the Web (that is, pornography), and to give children a gateway to the on-line world. When a subscriber first signs onto WOW, a master account is set up for a parent and up to five subaccounts for other family members. If any of these accounts is designated as a children's account, it will see only a special kid's version of WOW, with child-oriented designs and features. It remains to be seen whether this new service can help break the lock that AOL apparently has on new-subscriber growth.

In August 1995, Microsoft launched its own proprietary on-line service, the Microsoft Network, or MSN. At the time, many thought that MSN would rapidly capture market share from the three established OSPs, partly because an icon that enabled PC users to connect with MSN was one of the first things people saw when they booted up Windows 95, Microsoft's new operating system. However, things turned out rather differently.

Although MSN did build up its subscriber base at a rapid rate (more than 1.6 million subscribers had signed up by October 1996, making MSN the world's largest on-line service), Microsoft abruptly changed its strategy in December 1995. The catalyst for the change in strategy was the growing popularity of Netscape and Java. The shift from desktop-centered to Web-centered computing promised by the fusion of Netscape and Java was perceived by many as a threat to Microsoft's core operating system and applications business.[15] In response, Microsoft changed its Internet strategy to embrace the Web and set itself up as a direct competitor to Netscape.

As one element of this strategy, MSN was to be recast as a Web site that would be built according to the Internet's software standards (including HTML and Java) as opposed to a proprietary software standard developed by Microsoft. Parts of the Web site were to be accessible for free by anyone with a Web browser. The free part of the site was to include MSNBC, a joint venture with NBC that offered a twenty-four-hour cable TV news service to compete with CNN and a regularly updated text-based news content on the MSN Web site. By October 1996, MSNBC could be accessed by 17 million cable TV viewers and anyone with a browser and access to the Web. Fee-paying MSN subscribers could also gain access to additional service offerings that would be closed to nonsubscribers.[16]

On October 10, 1996, Microsoft formally unveiled the new Web-based MSN. In addition to providing access to the Web like any ISP, MSN provided subscribers with a number of proprietary services, including a news and entertainment area; E-mail; chat rooms; bulletin boards; an Internet navigator to help MSN subscribers find useful content on the Web; and various other reference materials, such as an on-line version of Encarta, Microsoft's best-selling multimedia encyclopedia. MSN offered subscribers a choice of pricing structure. One scheme was based on $6.95 per month for five hours, with additional hours being priced at $2.50. The other scheme, aimed at heavy users, offered unlimited access for $19.95 per month.[17]

A final proprietary on-line service of some note was e*World, the on-line service offered by Apple to users of its computers. It turned out to be one of Apple Computer's spectacular failures, just like its personal digital assistant, the Newton. Apple pinned its hopes for e*World on interactive games. This strategy did little to whet the appetite of the world's 15 million or so Macintosh users, and subscriptions topped out at 100,000 in 1995 before heading downhill. In 1996, Apple announced that it would close down e*World. Why did e*World fail to garner more support? Reasons given for the failure of the service include poor marketing, high prices, the lack of a free trial period (most on-line services

offer new subscribers one month of free access), narrow content, and a failure to open up e*World to the non-Macintosh computer owner.[18]

The Commercialization of Cyberspace

Many believe that the Internet will soon become a huge conduit for electronic commerce. The Web is a place where buyers and sellers can find each other and trade at a much lower cost than in the material world. For example, consider Lands' End, which sells casual clothing through mail-order catalogs. Two of the largest items in the cost structure of Lands' End are the cost of catalogs and postage. The extent to which the customers of Lands' End can be encouraged to browse for clothes at Lands' End's own Internet store (www.landsend.com) may ultimately limit the need for Lands' End to send out catalogs, significantly reducing the company's cost structure.

Another example is Amazon.com, which promotes itself as the world's largest bookstore. Established in the summer of 1995, Amazon.com sells more than 1.1 million titles (five times the inventory of the largest book superstore), yet it does not have a material retail presence. All of its business is conducted through the Web. This means that Amazon.com has a substantially lower cost structure than book retailers that operate physical stores, which in turn supports discounts of 10 to 30 percent on a wide range of books. Amazon.com will deliver popular books in two to three days, although more obscure titles can take three weeks.[19]

The software industry is perhaps the industry in which the migration to the Web is most natural. After all, software is nothing more than bits of information, and software programs can be easily downloaded over the Web. Among other things, this new channel of distribution might ultimately put traditional software retailers, such as Egghead Software, out of business.

According to International Data Corporation, as of early 1996 there were more than 100,000 retailers on the Web, although total revenues in 1995 amounted to just $324 million.[20] However, the volume of business is expected to grow exponentially. AT&T, for example, estimated that merchants would sell some $518 million worth of goods over the Internet in 1996 and that this figure would rise to $6.6 billion by the year 2000.[21] Other forecasts see slower growth. Price Waterhouse, for example, sees Internet sales of $1.4 billion by 1998.[22] By comparison, according to Forrester Research Inc., the mail catalog industry generated $53 billion in sales in 1995.[23]

On-line financial services, including on-line banking and on-line stock trading, are emerging as another potentially large segment of on-line commerce. A growing number of banks—among them giants such as Wells Fargo, Citicorp, and Chase—are embracing the concept of on-line banking, and many are working with software companies such as Microsoft and Intuit to develop an on-line presence. Stockbrokerage firms are also moving onto the Web. As of mid 1996, around 800,000 individual investors were trading stocks electronically, although many were still using proprietary software offered by institutions with a material retail presence such as Charles Schwab and Fidelity. However, a number of electronic brokerage firms, such as E*Trade, have recently set up operations on the Web, and the possibility exists that these firms might experience substantial growth in the future. The great attraction of on-line banking and stock brokering is that it reduces the need for maintaining a costly physical presence in the marketplace, including physical facilities and employees (such as bank tellers and stockbrokers).[24]

One of the great impediments to the growth of Internet commerce is doubt among consumers about the security of transactions executed over the Internet. There is a fear that computer hackers might be able to access credit card numbers transmitted over the Internet and use those numbers to run up large debts. To combat this problem, a number of software companies, such as CyberCash and Veri-Fone, have developed encryption technology that provides for more secure electronic transactions executed via the Web. Growing confidence in the security offered by encryption technology could significantly help to boost Internet commerce.[25]

Electronic Bottlenecks

Issues of security aside, a number of other factors are currently holding back the development of the Internet. An August 1996 survey of Internet users by *BusinessWeek* and Louis Harris & Associates reported that 73 percent found slow access to be a minor or major problem, 56 percent said that the high cost of access was a problem, 66 percent said

that the difficulty of locating useful information was a problem, 61 percent cited difficult connections as a problem, and 36 percent cited uninteresting content as a problem.[26]

Concerns about slow access point toward a major problem with the Internet—a lack of bandwidth. Bandwidth is related to the speed of data transmission. Many users have only low bandwidth and hence low speed links to the Internet (for instance, modems that transfer data at 14,400 bps or 28,800 bps). With these slow links, it can take a long time to download graphic-intensive Web pages. However, much faster modems are being developed. ISDN modems are already available that allow access to the Web at speeds of 128 bps. Cable modems that offer access speeds 1,000 times faster than conventional modems are currently being tested in the market and should be widely available by the year 2000. (Cable modems utilize the coaxial cable feeds that are currently used for cable TV.)

However, even with significantly faster modems, bandwidth problems will still persist on the Internet because of the vast volume of traffic now flowing through the infrastructure. Ultimately, large investments in infrastructure, including backbone fiber-optic links and ATM switches, as well as the development of data compression techniques, will be required to overcome the Internet's bandwidth problems. If the Internet develops into an economic force, however, these investments should be forthcoming.

AOL

The history of AOL is interwoven with that of the company's thirty-eight-year-old CEO, Steve Case. After a brief spell in marketing at Procter & Gamble and Pizza Hut, Case joined Control Video, the forerunner of AOL, in 1983 as a marketing assistant. At the time, Control Video was a gaming service for Atari computer owners. Case was introduced to the founders of Control Video by his older brother, Dan, who was then an associate with the San Francisco investment bank Hambrecht & Quist and represented the bank on the company's board. (Dan Case is now CEO of Hambrecht & Quist.)

Soon after Steve Case was hired, Control Video ran out of money. The board promptly fired the existing management team and brought in as CEO Jim Kimsey, an entrepreneur who had been working part-time at Control Video. Under Kimsey's direction Control Video was reborn in 1985 as Quantum Computer Services, an on-line service for owners of Commodore computers.

Right from the beginning, Kimsey groomed Case to succeed him. Case played a role in raising $5 million in venture capital for Quantum, and he was the prime mover in expanding Quantum's business. By the early 1990s, Quantum, which changed its name to America Online in 1991, was gunning for a share of the still small, but rapidly growing commercial on-line service business. The two market leaders at the time were Prodigy and CompuServe. In need of capital to expand its service, in 1992 AOL undertook an initial public offering, which raised $66 million. At the time, AOL had $27 million in annual revenues, 200,000 subscribers, and 250 employees.

Case's strategy for AOL has had three main elements: extensive marketing to generate rapid subscriber growth, the acquisition of desirable content to keep those subscribers interested in the service, and investment in a high-speed network infrastructure that will guarantee subscribers rapid access to AOL. Judged by subscriber and revenue growth, the strategy seems to have worked. Between 1994 and late 1996, AOL added 5 million customers, propelling AOL past Prodigy and CompuServe into the number one spot in the on-line industry. As of June 1996, AOL had more than 6.2 million customers (up from only 3 million a year earlier), annualized revenues in excess of $1.1 billion, and more than 4,500 employees. Moreover, with only 11 percent of households in the United States subscribing to on-line services as of 1996, the potential for further growth looked bright.[27]

The Service

When they sign on to AOL, subscribers are greeted with an attractively designed interface that allows them to access a wide range of services through twenty "channels." For example, someone interested in investing in stocks can click on the "personal finance" channel. Within this channel they can access a vast amount of useful investment information, including company stock reports, analysts' estimates of future corporate earnings, stock market quotes that are updated every fifteen minutes, industry and company news, investment advice from proprietary content providers such as the Motley Fool, stock bulletin boards where sub-

scribers post their thoughts on the prospects for individual companies, investment chat rooms, and much more.

Other channels allow subscribers to read on-line versions of many popular newspapers (for example, the *New York Times, Investors Business Daily*) and magazines (for example, *BusinessWeek, Scientific American, PC World, Time*); to access and download a vast library of computer software; to play interactive games on-line with other subscribers; to get regularly updated local, national, and international news and to discuss that news with other interested subscribers in dedicated chat rooms; to keep up with developments in their favorite sport; to browse through a wide array of entertainment offerings including on-line versions of Viacom's cable TV channels, MTV, Nickelodeon, and VH1; and to plan vacations and purchase airline tickets. AOL also has a "person to person" feature that contains a large number of chat rooms, each of which can accommodate more than thirty-nine users at any one time and which are devoted to topics that range from the general and mundane to the bizarre and strange (one popular chat room with the title "raiding the fridge" seems devoted to discussing the merits—culinary and otherwise—of SPAM). It is also possible for subscribers to create their own "private" chat room to converse with friends or family. Subscribers can send E-mail over the Internet, and they can use AOL's Web browser to access and surf the World Wide Web. (They can also use Microsoft's Internet Explorer and Netscape's Navigator if they so wish.)

According to AOL data, as of early 1996 the breakdown of an average subscriber's use of on-line time was as follows: 15 percent spent surfing the World Wide Web; 25 percent spent in chat rooms; 20 percent spent writing or reading E-mail; 30 percent spent viewing content on AOL; and 10 percent spent on other activities, such as interactive games.[28]

Content Providers

AOL has contracts with more than 1,000 content providers, including some of the biggest names in the media business (for example, Viacom, Time Warner, Capital Cities/ABC). AOL tracks the amount of time that individual subscribers spend visiting different content areas, assigns a dollar amount to that time, and offers content providers a percentage share of revenues generated during a subscriber's visit. So, for example, if a subscriber spends an hour in Viacom's MTV area at a rate of $2.95 per hour, AOL might keep 50 percent of that revenue and pass the remaining percent on to Viacom. The actual percentage revenue split varies significantly from provider to provider.

Initially, AOL adopted something of a laissez-faire attitude toward the presentation of content, letting providers make content and presentation decisions. More recently, the company has come to the realization that this approach often resulted in dull and uninspiring content. For example, having *Time* magazine repackage its print product for on-line consumers was not creating the desired excitement among subscribers. To try to improve the quality of content on AOL, the company developed two different models for working with content providers—cooperative joint ventures and the Greenhouse.[29]

The joint venture model explicitly recognizes that AOL will work cooperatively with well-established content providers to develop on-line content. Underlying this approach is a presumption that AOL can increase the value of a content offering by bringing its own experience to bear on the development of that offering. Some examples of the results of such partnerings include an expanded health channel jointly developed with Time Warner; fashion and lifestyles sites developed in collaboration with Capital Cities/ABC; and the MTV and Nickelodeon sites developed in cooperation with Viacom.

The Greenhouse takes entrepreneurial companies that would otherwise not have the capital, marketing, or distribution to function on their own and gives them a low-cost loan to start their business, a place on the AOL network, and the benefit of AOL's experience. The idea is to help create new content providers that are specifically geared to take advantage of the unique features and power of the on-line medium. In return for this backing, AOL reserves the right to purchase a portion of the equity of a Greenhouse partner if it so desires. One of the most successful products of the Greenhouse system has been the Motley Fool, an on-line investment forum run by two brothers, Tom and David Gardner. Located in AOL's personal finance channel, the Fool has expanded to become one of AOL's

top ten content providers, and one of the most renowned of the new media companies to be found in cyberspace.

Infrastructure

Difficulty connecting to the service, the slow speed of data transmission, and frequent service breakdowns were among the biggest sources of dissatisfaction voiced by AOL subscribers during the 1993–1995 period. To a large degree, these problems were a result of AOL's subscriber growth outstripping the growth in its network capacity. In response, AOL has been investing heavily in network infrastructure.

In February 1995, AOL acquired Advanced Network Services (ANS) for $35 million. ANS has years of experience in building high-speed infrastructure for the Internet. With the help of ANS, in mid 1995 AOL launched AOLnet, a high-speed network that adheres to the Internet's TCP/IP communications standard and is wholly owned and operated by AOL. With the establishment of AOLnet, AOL now has access to one of the fastest TCP/IP backbones in the world, along with 500 Points of Presence (POPs). By owning many of its own POPs rather than leasing them from the likes of Sprint or MCI, AOL can guarantee access to subscribers and avoid the variable costs associated with leasing POPs.

By March 1996, around 50 percent of AOL's network traffic was funneled through AOLnet, and by mid 1997 the figure should be around 85 percent.[30] Apart from improving access, one of the advantages of a proprietary network is that over time it should allow AOL to shift from a variable-cost to a fixed-cost model for data communications, while the overall per-hour cost of providing data communications should decrease. The impact of AOLnet was evident in the last quarter of fiscal 1996 (ended June 30), when AOL's gross margin rose to 46.6 percent from 42.2 percent in the prior year. According to AOL, the improvement in gross margin was a direct result of more traffic being handled by AOLnet.[31] The buildup of AOLnet continues to require a substantial investment in telecommunications equipment, much of which AOL is financing through leasing.[32]

Despite its investments in infrastructure, AOL still does experience some connection problems. In August 1996, AOL's entire network was shut down for seventeen hours due to what the company called a "coincidental series of events that are unlikely to occur again." Whatever the cause, the shutdown was a major inconvenience, particularly for those business users who relied on AOL for E-mail and other data transmission services.[33]

In addition to network infrastructure, AOL has invested in data compression software in an attempt to push back some of the constraints on access speed in a world where most subscribers connect with modems that operate at the "slow" speed of 28,800 bps or less. In February 1996, AOL acquired Johnson-Grace, a software company known for its data-compression technology. Using high-speed data-compression technology, AOL has been able to reduce significantly the time it takes to download graphics onto a personal computer. As a result, according to Steve Case,

> We can provide a virtual broadband service to people with slow modems.... This displaces the need for high bandwidth connectivity. The bandwidth gap—the bandwidth haves and the bandwidth havenots—plays right into the hands of AOL. We're optimizing the service in recognition of the fact that consumers have slow modems and that the Internet was designed for people with high speed connectivity.[34]

Pricing, Marketing, and Churn

Through December 31, 1994, the standard monthly membership fee for AOL was $9.95 for five hours of access and $3.50 per hour thereafter. In January 1995, AOL reduced the per hour fee to $2.95, although it left the base fee unchanged. In May 1996, AOL announced an additional pricing plan for heavy users of the service. This included twenty hours of service for $19.95 per month and an hourly fee of $2.95 for use in excess of that. As of November 1996, the company was said to be considering a move toward a flat-rate fee for unlimited use of the service.

To get people to try out its service, AOL spends heavily on marketing. The company gives away the interface and connection software for free and frequently runs mass-mail promotions, sending out tens of thousands of AOL software disks at a time to potential subscribers in an attempt to lure them onto the service. All new subscribers get a one-month free trial period. In September 1996, Case announced

that AOL would spend $100 million on a fall quarter print-and-television-media campaign aimed at attracting new users. The company's goal called for 10.5 million AOL subscribers by June 1997.

Aggressive marketing does not come cheaply. For the nine months ending in March 31, 1996, AOL's marketing expenses were $145.9 million, an increase of 205 percent compared with the nine-month period ending March 31, 1995. Moreover, AOL's subscriber acquisition costs have been on an even steeper incline. Subscriber acquisition costs add other costs, such as the costs of software disks and postage for direct-mail campaigns, to marketing costs. For the nine months ending March 31, 1996, AOL's subscriber acquisition costs were $306.7 million, an increase of 368 percent over the $65.5 million spent in the nine-month period ending March 31, 1995. Estimates of AOL's cost of acquiring customers in the financial year ending June 1996 ranged from $40 to $110 per customer. Steve Case claims that the true cost is toward the low end of this range. In an interview given in September 1996, he noted that "right now we are spending $45 to get someone new on the system."[35] There is, however, some confusion as to exactly how the company calculates these figures, since there is a difference between getting people onto the system for a one-month free trial period and getting them to stay on the system as fee-paying subscribers. Some analysts claim that AOL's estimates of subscriber acquisition costs are calculated on the basis of those who try out the system and include those who don't stay after the first month. This approach understates the true cost of acquiring fee-paying subscribers. In any event, AOL does admit that the cost of acquiring new subscribers will increase to $50 to $60 per subscriber in fiscal 1997 as a result of an intensive marketing campaign to attract new subscribers.[36]

Whatever the true cost of acquiring customers, there is certainly controversy over how AOL has chosen to account for these costs. For accounting purposes, AOL has treated many of the costs of acquiring new subscribers as capital investment rather than as a current expense. These costs have then been amortized against earnings over twenty-four months. The effect has been to increase AOL's current earnings, but at the price of an increase in the level of deferred subscriber acquisition costs on AOL's balance sheet. (For the year ending June

TABLE 2

AOL's Income Under Different Accounting Assumptions ($millions)[37]

	1993	1994	1995
Total revenues	$52.4	$117.5	$397.3
Deferred subscriber acquisition expenses	$ 3.6	$ 19.5	$ 50.8
Total expenses reported	$52	$114.9	$431
Total income reported	$ 0.4	$ 2.6	−$ 33.6
Total expenses revised	$55.6	$134.4	$481.8
Net income revised	−$ 3.2	−$ 7.0	−$ 84.5

1996, deferred subscriber acquisition costs rose to $314 million, up from $50.8 million in the year ending June 1995.) Table 2 summarizes the results of a study, commissioned by *BusinessWeek,* which restated AOL's earnings using more conventional accounting practices. The table suggests that in 1995 AOL's loss would have more than doubled had it used more conventional accounting practices. (AOL's financial statements are given in Table 1.)

Part of the reason for AOL's high subscriber acquisition costs is the high churn rate associated with its service. It is difficult to pin down AOL's churn rate, and the company is less than forthcoming with estimates. However, most analyst estimates suggest that somewhere between 30 and 40 percent of AOL's fee-paying customers leave the service within the first year of signing on, a figure that Case does not dispute. (These figures exclude those who try the service for a free one-month trial period and drop off before receiving their first bill.)[38] In the quarter that ended June 1996 *BusinessWeek* reported that while AOL signed up about 1.8 million new members, 1.5 million dropped the service (many before receiving their first bill) for a net gain of 300,000.[39] A more detailed analysis of AOL's churn rate in the quarter that ended March 31, 1996, suggests that of the 1.1 million subscribers that dropped the service, 450,000 left before their first bill (they were never really subscribers), 300,000 left during the next three months, and 100,000 old subscribers departed.[40] Tom Gardner, cofounder of AOL's successful Motley Fool investment service, has speculated that the reasons for the high churn rate, in order of importance, are connection problems, uninspiring content, price, and customer service.[41]

Revenue Sources

For the year ending June 30, 1996, AOL earned revenues of $1,093 million compared with $394 million in the year ending June 30, 1995. Most of these revenues (around 91 percent) are generated from subscriber fees. Over the years, there has been a steady increase in the average monthly fee per subscriber, from about $15 per month in 1994, to $17 per month in 1995, and $19 per month by June 1996.[42] This average figure, however, hides wide variation. Some analysts believe that the top 15 percent of AOL's subscribers generate around 50 percent of the subscription revenue. In mid 1996, these on-line addicts had an average monthly bill of $63.[43]

AOL's other revenues are generated from the sale of merchandise, data network services (primarily to businesses), on-line transactions, and advertising. For the nine months ending March 31, 1996, these revenues totaled $70.9 million, an increase of 126 percent from the same period a year earlier.

Diversifying Revenue Sources

Although AOL aimed to have 10.5 million subscribers by June 1997, it also wanted to reduce its dependence on fees from subscribers by diversifying its revenue sources. Initiatives currently under way to attain this objective include attempts to increase advertising revenues, establish Enterprise AOL as a valuable service for large organizations, expand internationally, and enter the fast-growing ISP market.

Advertising   In 1996, Steve Case announced plans aimed at dramatically increasing the revenues generated from advertising and on-line merchandise sales. In early 1996, AOL hired an ex-advertising agency executive and gave him a staff of thirty-five dedicated people to sell ad space on AOL. AOL has 102 "screens" on which it is selling ad space. A screen lists a set of choices within a channel. For example, within AOL's personal finance channel, there is a screen that allows users to pull up stock quotes, check the current value of their portfolio, check market news, or utilize various company and market research options. Advertisements typically appear as banners on a screen. AOL is pricing the ad space on its screens on the basis of the number of impressions, or hits, a screen gets. The pricing is generally within the range of $30 to $60 per 1,000 impressions, although some deals are apparently being done above that price point. AOL anticipates generating annual advertising revenues of $500,000 to $3 million per screen.[44]

AOL envisions the on-line advertising market growing to about $1.5 billion to $2.0 billion by the year 2000. The company is aiming to get a 20 percent share of this market. AOL claims that advertisements on AOL have a conversion rate of 12.5 percent, compared with a normal direct mail conversion rate of 3 percent, meaning that AOL is better at targeting potential purchasers of an advertiser's goods or services. In mid 1996, AOL's 6.2 million subscribers had an average income of $68,000, making them a highly desirable audience for many advertisers.[45]

Enterprise AOL   Enterprise AOL, a division of AOL, focuses on selling private on-line services, known as PAOLs, to large users. Early clients of this service include Century 21 (the nationwide real estate company), Harvard Business School, and PIP Printing. PAOLs are best suited to large organizations that lack dedicated networks and franchise organizations that need to get a lot of information out to their franchisees. As of mid 1996, AOL had contracts to establish ten PAOLs.

International Services   In November 1995, AOL announced a joint venture with Bertelsmann, the large German publishing and media company, to establish on-line services in Europe, starting with Germany, France, and Britain. These services were to be localized and written in the dominant local tongue. AOL is something of a late entrant into this market. CompuServe, for example, has been running an on-line service in Germany for seven years and has 250,000 German subscribers. In addition,

there are a number of other local on-line services in Europe. By June 1996, AOL had 100,000 European customers, the majority in Germany.[46]

ISP Market   GNN, or Global Network Navigator, is an Internet service provider that AOL acquired in June 1995 for $11 million. AOL relaunched GNN as an ISP in October 1995, and by June 1996 the service had around 300,000 subscribers. GNN subscribers cannot access AOL's proprietary service, but for a flat fee they can use a standard browser (Microsoft's Explorer or Netscape's Navigator) to surf the Web. Unlike many other ISPs, GNN will have the advantage of a dedicated network infrastructure in AOLnet.

AOL's decision to establish GNN seems to indicate that the company might be hedging its bets with regard to the rapid rise of the World Wide Web as a potential alternative to AOL. Some of the thinking behind this move was contained in a confidential internal AOL memo that found its way into the hands of the press. According to the memo, AOL conducted a market trial of 260 people who accessed AOL and the Internet using high-speed cable modems. Of the 260, 170 elected to keep some form of on-line access and pay for it. Of the 170, about 11 percent chose to utilize just AOL's service, 29 percent chose to access both the Internet and AOL, and 60 percent chose the Internet without AOL.[47]

CONCLUSION

Much of 1996 was full of contradictions for AOL. On the one hand, AOL emerged as the dominant on-line service in the world, with 6.2 million subscribers and annual revenues in excess of $1 billion. On the other, critics of the company charged that the combination of high churn rate, questionable accounting practices, market saturation, and a real threat from low-priced Internet service providers left AOL increasingly vulnerable. Reflecting growing uncertainty about AOL's viability, the stock price had fallen from more than $71 per share in May 1996 to $24 in October of the same year.

In contrast, in an interview given in late 1996, Steve Case claimed that AOL's churn rate (with somewhere less than 40 percent of subscribers leaving before the end of their first year of paid-up subscription) was comparable with magazine publishing norms and nothing to be too concerned about. He also pointed out that with only 11 percent of U.S. homes hooked into an on-line service, there was still enormous room for growth at AOL. As for the Internet and World Wide Web, Case sees this not as a threat, but as an opportunity.

> The threat [of the Web] is more perception than reality. Certainly we run scared. If it weren't for that threat, we'd be pretty cocky and arrogant right now. We're responding to them [ISPs], but the vision for the company hasn't changed that much. . . . We haven't buried our heads in the sand and said the Web is irrelevant. We started providing Internet access a few years ago. . . . Let's imagine that AOL didn't exist, and the Net did. The Internet basically is this broken up world. Consumers would hook up with service providers and subscribe to services they want on an à la carte basis. Which is probably fine for a technologically astute early adopter but seems awfully complicated for the consumer market. If you want to reach a mainstream audience, you have to make it more plug and play. One stop shopping. One disk to install. One price to pay. One customer service number to call. Building web sites and hoping people will find them is a significant leap of faith.[48]

Endnotes

1. "The Accidental Superhighway: A Survey of the Internet," *Economist*, July 1, 1995, p. 7.
2. Raul Taylor, "Internet Users Likely to Reach 500 Million by 2000," *Financial Times*, May 13, 1996, p. 4.
3. George Gilder, "Telecoms: The Coming Software Shift," *Forbes ASAP*, August 1995, pp. 146–162.
4. Randy Befumo, "The Digital World," A Motley Fool Investment Report, March 1996.
5. Ibid.
6. Louise Kehoe, "Group Pays $2 Billion for Internet Service Provider," *Financial Times*, May 1, 1996, p. 1.
7. Ibid.
8. Alan Cane, "MCI Price Move Intensifies Internet Wars," *Financial Times*, March 19, 1996, p. 17.
9. Ibid.
10. Roger Lowenstein, "Being There First Isn't Good Enough," *Wall Street Journal*, May 16, 1996, p. C1.
11. Thomas Weber, "CompuServe Corp. Offering Is Priced at $30 a Share," *Wall Street Journal*, April 19, 1996, p. B6.
12. Befumo, "Digital World."
13. Jared Sandberg, "CompuServe to Revamp Service, Change Prices, Before Rival Microsoft Launch," *Wall Street Journal*, August 2, 1996, p. B3.
14. Walter Mossberg, "Cheaper, Kid Friendly On Line Service Will WOW PC Users," *Wall Street Journal*, March 21, 1996, p. B1.
15. George Gilder, "Telecoms: The Coming Software Shift."
16. Don Clark, "New Internet Model Leaves Some Content Providers Without Much of a Home," *Wall Street Journal*, April 12, 1996, p. A3.
17. Microsoft press release, "New Web Based Version of the Microsoft Network Debuts," October 10, 1996.
18. Befumo, "Digital World."
19. G. Bruce Knecht, "How a Wall Street Whiz Found a Niche Selling Books on the Internet," *Wall Street Journal*, May 16, 1996, p. A1.
20. Ibid.
21. AT&T home page, "Commerce on the Web" (http://www.att.com).
22. Alan Cane, "Net's Rivals Feel the Squeeze," *Financial Times*, February 26, 1996, p. 13.
23. Joan Rigdon, "Netscape and GE Join to Develop Internet Business Software for Internet Use," *Wall Street Journal*, April 10, 1996, p. B6.
24. Vanessa O'Connell, "Let the Buying Begin," *Wall Street Journal*, June 17, 1996, p. A8.
25. Don Clark, "Verifone Sets Internet Payment System for Banks to Sell, Lowering Web Barriers," *Wall Street Journal*, June 18, 1996, p. B4.
26. *Business Week*/Harris Poll, "Internet Travelers Aren't Fed Up—Yet," *BusinessWeek*, August 26, 1996, p. 66.
27. Amy Cortese et al. "The Online World of Steve Case," *BusinessWeek*, April 15, 1996, pp. 78–87; Gene Koprowski, "AOL CEO Steve Case," *Forbes ASAP*, October 7, 1996, pp. 94–95.
28. Befumo, "Digital World."
29. Ibid.
30. Randy Befumo, "The Lunchtime News," Motley Fool, August 9, 1996.
31. America Online press release, August 8, 1996.
32. America Online 10K report, June 1996.
33. Thomas Weber, "AOL's Blackout and Loss of Subscribers Eclipse Jump in Fourth Quarter Profits," *Wall Street Journal*, August 9, 1996, p. B3.
34. Koprowski, "AOL CEO Steve Case," p. 96.
35. Ibid.
36. Befumo, "The Lunchtime News."
37. Koprowski, "AOL CEO Steve Case."
38. Amy Cortese et al., "The Online World of Steve Case."
39. Amy Barrett and Paul Eng, "AOL Downloads a New Growth Plan," *BusinessWeek*, October 14, 1996, pp. 85–86.
40. Tom Gardner, "How Do We Value America Online?" Motley Fool Online Forum, June 8, 1996.
41. Ibid.
42. America Online 10-K reports for 1996 and 1995.
43. Thomas Weber, "America Online May Face Long Hot Summer as Stock Wilts 10% on Some Bearish Reports," *Wall Street Journal*, June 6, 1996, p. C2.
44. Randy Befumo, "America Online Blitzed Analysts," The Evening News: Motley Fool Online Forum, June 14, 1996.
45. Ibid.
46. Douglas Lavin, "America Online Enters a Crowded Europe," *Wall Street Journal*, November 28, 1995, p. B6; Befumo, "America Online Blitzed Analysts."
47. Jared Sandberg, "America Online Agrees to Licensing Pact with AOL," *Wall Street Journal*, March 12, 1996, p. B5.
48. Koprowski, "AOL CEO Steve Case," pp. 94–96.

CASE 9

America Online (B)

This case was prepared by Charles W. L. Hill of the University of Washington.

INTRODUCTION

Nineteen hundred and ninety-six was a pivotal year for America Online (AOL). After four years of break-neck growth, AOL was now a major player in cyberspace. Subscribers had increased from 200,000 to more than 6 million. In June 1996, annual revenues passed the $1 billion mark. AOL was handling more than 11 million E-mail messages a day. It hosted 7,000 chat rooms nightly and featured more than 1,100 proprietary content sites on 21 "channels." An astounding one out of every three users on the Internet used AOL.[1] But for all its success, the on-line service provider was suddenly beset by problems from all sides.

The Internet was becoming increasingly well organized, leading some critics to question the need for a proprietary on-line service like AOL. Internet service providers (ISPs) from small mom-and-pop operations to telecommunications giants like AT&T and MCI had started offering unlimited access to the Internet for $19.95 a month. AOL's pricing plan charged users a fee of $9.95 per month plus $2.95 per hour, which meant that heaviest users could run up bills anywhere from $50 to $300 per month. Partly as a result, AOL's subscriber churn rate was unacceptably high. Estimates that by mid 1996 the monthly churn rate would be around 6 percent, implied that more than 70 percent of AOL's customers would leave the service within one year of joining![2] Increasingly, the customers who were leaving were long-time heavy users who were AOL's biggest spenders. Although

This case is intended to be used as the basis for class discussion rather than as an illustration of either effective or ineffective handling of the situation. This case was prepared by Charles W. L. Hill, University of Washington. Used by permission.

representing only one-third of the subscriber base, these heavy users were accounting for two-thirds of AOL's revenues.

To complicate matters, marketing costs associated with acquiring new customers were spiraling out of control, with many households receiving multiple packages of promotional material containing AOL software disks. Moreover, critics on Wall Street were blasting the company for its practice of amortizing the costs of acquiring new customers against earnings over twenty-four months, rather than treating them as a current expense—a practice that inflated AOL's current earnings. By June 1996, AOL had some $314 million in deferred costs on its balance sheet—enough to bury the $30 million pretax profit for fiscal 1996 under a sea of red ink. Shortly after the fiscal 1996 figures were released in June 1996, Bill Razzouck, AOL's president, resigned. Only four months previously, Razzouck had joined the company from Federal Express. His brief had been to bring order to AOL's operations. Wall Street interpreted his sudden departure as a sign that things at AOL were out of control. Reflecting these problems, AOL's stock price had tumbled from the $70 range to the $20 range by June 1996. Many now wondered if the service could survive.

SUMMER 1996

Throughout the summer of 1996, AOL's management team tried to grapple with these seemingly intractable problems. Solving the pricing and churn problems was at the top of their agenda. The big concern was that if the company adopted a flat-rate pricing scheme similar to that used by ISPs, the loss of revenue would be devastating (at the time, AOL was garnering 85 percent of its revenues from user fees). ISPs offered no more than access and a browser, which enabled them to operate with a low-cost structure. In comparison, as a proprietary service, AOL had to cover its overhead costs related to content, marketing, and personnel. Could AOL with its high-cost structure afford to move to a flat-rate pricing scheme?

In May 1996, AOL had announced its first response to the ISP threat, a new "20/20" pricing plan, which charged users a flat fee of $19.95 for the first twenty hours of use and $2.95 per hour thereafter. The plan did little to slow down customer defection rates. Moreover, the plan upset many of AOL's content providers, who depended on the $2.95 hourly fee for their income. (Most content providers received a cut of the dollar value of the time a user spent at their site on AOL.)

Throughout the summer, the internal debate within AOL continued. The primary issue was how to protect revenues if the switch to flat-rate pricing was adopted. The company was already pursuing a host of options, including increasing revenues from selling advertising space on the service, selling AOL merchandise, and taking a cut of on-line transactions executed over AOL. Among the other options considered was offering an "adult only" channel that would carry a surcharge.[3] The idea was to connect AOL users to an aggregation of adult content culled from the World Wide Web, restrict access to those over twenty-one, and charge a premium price for this option. The option was pulled after focus groups suggested that the inclusion of such a channel would outrage some users and might damage AOL's brand image.

One thing was clear—under any scenario AOL had to continue to grow, and it had to make its brand more compelling. If it did not, there was no way that the company would be able to command a high price for advertising space or offer businesses the opportunity to sell directly to AOL users through its service. For CEO Steve Case, a critical issue was identifying the right person to help build AOL's brand. By late summer, he seemed to have found a solution in the person of Bob Pittman.

Then forty-two years old, Pittman had already left his mark on global pop culture. A one-time radio disk jockey, in 1981, together with John Lack, Pittman started an all-music cable television channel called Music Television, or MTV. Charismatic,

photogenic and charming, Pittman was in many ways the ultimate marketing wunderkind. In addition to MTV, Pittman also had a hand in the creation of VH1 and the Nick at Nite cable TV channels.[4] Pittman had left MTV in 1985 and spent several years running Time Warner Enterprises, the business development unit of Time Warner. While there, he oversaw the purchase of the struggling Six Flags theme park chain. Pittman became CEO of Six Flags, masterminded its turnaround, and then sold 51 percent of the division to Boston Venture Partners for $1 billion (Pittman reportedly made $40 million on the deal).[5] In 1995, Pittman left Time Warner to run Century 21, a nationwide residential real estate chain. It was at this point that Steve Case began to court Pittman, sensing that he was the right person to build AOL's brand. Pittman joined AOL's board in October 1995, but Case was looking for closer involvement.

After Razzouck's departure in June 1996, Case stepped up his courting of Pittman. In early August, Pittman took a vacation to think things over. Then disaster hit AOL. On August 7, during a routine overhaul of some equipment at AOL's data center, the system inexplicably shut down. It took nineteen hours to get AOL back on line. The media was all over the story. The AOL blackout was the lead on CNN's *Headline News* that evening, ahead of a segment that signs of life had been detected in rocks from Mars. The next morning, the AOL blackout garnered front-page headlines in most newspapers. The media detailed stories of the inconvenience suffered by those who could not access their E-mail or surf the Internet, and noted the thousands of dollars in revenues lost by businesses that depended on AOL traffic. One story relayed the woes of the flower delivery service, 1–800-FLOWERS, which received a significant share of its orders over the Internet and which estimated that it lost $40,000 to $50,000 as a result of the blackout. Critics claimed that AOL's blackout was due to a failure to upgrade its infrastructure to keep pace with subscriber growth.[6] AOL claimed that the blackout occurred due to a highly unlikely series of event that were unlikely to ever occur again. Following the blackout, many investors turned sour on the already struggling company, and AOL's stock sunk further. Bob Pittman drew a different conclusion from these events. To Pittman, the media frenzy proved that AOL had become a mainstream company providing a valuable service. He formally joined AOL's management team in late October 1996.

FALL 1996

In September 1996, AOL held a pep rally for its 1,500 northern Virginia employees at a local convention center. The occasion was a $300 million marketing blitz intended to "relaunch" AOL. There were roller dancers and satellite hookups, theme songs, and a cheering crowd. Case, wearing jeans, sunglasses, and a leather jacket, addressed the crowd. Ted Leonsis, head of AOL's studio system, came out and shouted, "We can be like Coca-Cola! We can become like Disney, like Nike, like MTV!"[7]

On October 10, 1996, Microsoft's MSN announced that it would henceforth base its site on HTML—hypertext markup language—open up part of its site to anyone browsing the Web, and adopt a flat-rate pricing scheme of $19.95 per month for unlimited access to MSN's "proprietary content" and the Web. The move forced AOL's hand. On October 29, AOL responded with a number of announcements.[8]

First, Pittman was formally introduced as a member of AOL's management team. To better focus the enterprise and accommodate Pittman, Case split AOL into three operating divisions. These were ANS Communications, which would handle the access infrastructure under the leadership of Bruce Bind; AOL Studios, which would develop content under the leadership of Ted Leonsis; and AOL Networks, the flagship on-line service, which Pittman would run. In his remarks to the press, Pittman compared the on-line business with the cable TV industry he helped to create. Like the cable TV business in the 1980s, Pittman stated, "you have to convince people it's a real business. . . . but it's destined to be part of the American landscape. . . . I've seen this movie before, I've been here."[9]

Second, AOL announced that starting December 1, it too would offer unlimited access for $19.95 per month. Many of AOL's content providers greeted this announcement with trepidation. They were upset that AOL had not given them any warning that this was coming and were concerned about the implications of the move for their revenue stream. Until now, many content providers

had earned money from their share of AOL's hourly fees. (Content providers would typically receive a share of the hourly revenue generated while users were at their AOL site.) Now the hourly fees were going away, which indicated that revenues would have to come from advertising and transactions. The shift to flat-rate pricing also meant that controlling costs became an immediate issue. AOL announced that it would lay off 300 employees—the first layoffs in its history—and shut down its GNN Internet access division. The value of GNN, which was AOL's own Internet service provider, had been effectively obviated by the move to flat-rate pricing.

Third, AOL bit another bullet when Case announced that AOL would take a charge of $353.7 million against earnings to write off deferred subscriber acquisition costs. Henceforth, subscriber acquisition costs would be treated as an expense and accounted for when they were incurred, rather than amortized against earnings over twenty-four months. The write-off wiped out all of the profit that AOL had made up to this point and resulted in a loss of $3.80 per share in the first quarter of fiscal 1997. To the critics, this provided more proof that AOL was nothing more than a game of smoke and mirrors. To the company's supporters, it showed a new atmosphere of realism at the company.

TOO MUCH OF A GOOD THING

Anticipating increased usage after the December 1 introduction of unlimited access, AOL entered into an agreement with BBN Corporation under which BBN was to build out AOL's TCP/IP dial-up network, AOLNet, to ensure that AOL could handle the expected increase in demand for its service. Under the four-year, $340 million contract, AOL would add 70,000 modems per year to AOLNet. At the time, AOLNet had 170,000 modems, so the increase in capacity amounted to 40 percent per year. It wasn't enough. On December 1, usage surged to 2.5 million hours—up from an average of 1.6 million hours per day in October. Members trying to log on were frequently greeted with busy signals. On December 2, AOL responded by announcing that it would accelerate the buildout of its dial-up network, spending an additional $250 million by mid 1997.

After the announcement of the move to flat-rate pricing and unlimited access, AOL's membership surged. The service added more than half a million new members in December alone. By early January, close to 8 million people were using the service, exceeding both the company's expectations and the capacity of its network. By mid January, mail had doubled in three months to 24 million pieces a day and usage had increased to 4.5 million hours per day. Hundreds of thousands of new members were joining the service. The busy signals continued. Complaints from irritated members were overwhelming the capacity of AOL's customer service operation. On January 16, Case responded by announcing that AOL would invest an additional $100 million in its dial-up network over the next few months. The company also pledged to reduce its marketing expenditures and pull its TV ad campaign until the capacity of its network had been upgraded. The busy signals continued. A number of state attorneys general banded together and announced that they would sue AOL for deceptive selling practices, false advertising, and even fraud. By the end of January, Case agreed to give a refund to any member who requested it as compensation for the inability to access the network. In return, the states agreed to drop their lawsuit.[10]

RETHINKING AOL

While Case was busy trying to cope with the consequences of the unexpected surge in demand for AOL's service, Pittman was rethinking AOL's business model. It was clear to Pittman that AOL was a terrific brand. Despite all the gaffes over the last year, the service continued to grow at breakneck speed. With revenue growth from subscribers now constrained by flat-rate pricing, Pittman knew that it was time to leverage the brand in order to maximize revenues from advertising and e-commerce—and that AOL had to move quickly. Although AOL had already embarked on this road a year ago, Pittman gave the strategy a new impetus. Moreover, he sharpened the focus of the strategy. Prior to his arrival, AOL had been considering entering all sorts of businesses itself, from selling books to long-distance telephone service. Under Pittman's leadership, the emphasis changed to helping other organizations sell their goods and services to AOL members.

On February 25, 1997, Pittman announced the first of what was to become a steady stream of deals. Under this deal, Tel-Save Holdings, a long-distance telephone service reseller, paid AOL $100 million for the privilege of being able to sell long-distance services to AOL's members. Prior to the deal, Tel-Save had 500,000 customers. The $100 million was an advance on future commission payments that would be due to AOL for members Tel-Save signed up. For Tel-Save, the deal had two big attractions. It was a cost effective way of reaching 8 million potential customers, and AOL would bill Tel-Save customers electronically and charge their credit cards for calls made using Tel-Save. Tel-Save estimated that electronic billing and credit card payments would reduce its unit costs by 30 percent, enabling it to offer customers long-distance rates 20 percent below those offered by rivals.[11] By March 1998, AOL and Tel-Save announced that the long-distance reseller had added 500,000 customers from AOL.[12]

On March 4, 1997, AOL opened to advertisers its 14,000 chat rooms, which logged 1 million hours daily. On June 10, CUC International agreed to pay AOL an advance of $50 million against future commissions in order to market its range of discount services directly to AOL subscribers. CUC expected to generate more than 1 million new interactive memberships per year from its AOL connection.[13] On July 7, Amazon.com, the Internet bookseller, agreed to pay AOL at least $19 million over three years in advances on commissions to be the featured bookseller on AOL's Web site, aol.com. If Amazon.com sales through AOL exceeded targets, this figure would be increased. Barnes & Noble paid a similar amount (later increased to $40 million) to be the bookseller on AOL's proprietary service. Also in July 1997, 1–800-FLOWERS agreed to pay AOL at least $25 million in advances on commissions over four years to sell on the service. The flower company expected the deal to produce $250 million in sales over four years.[14]

Around the same time, AOL began to charge retailers "rents" of at least $250,000 per year for their spots on AOL, in addition to commissions. This represented a shift from AOL's old practice of simply taking a cut of the revenues generated from sales over AOL. Revenues from this source had been disappointing, but Pittman felt that the change in incentive structure implied by the imposition of rents would yield significant dividends down the road.

In addition to taking a cut out of e-commerce transactions, during this period, AOL also began to change its relationship with content providers. Under the old pricing scheme, AOL *paid* content providers a fee based on the time members spent at their sites. With the hourly fee now gone, AOL had no incentive to pay content providers. Instead, the company started requiring content providers to pay it a fee in exchange for the privilege of being able to offer content through AOL. In one of the first deals, announced in July 1997, AOL stated that it had signed CBS Sportsline to serve as an "anchor tenant" for the service's sports channel.[15]

In addition to demanding fees, AOL started to weed out weak content providers, refusing to renew their contracts when they came due. For example, in August 1997, AOL refused to renew the contract for MetaCreations Inc., an on-line game company that created MetaSquares, a checkerslike game that could be played on-line at AOL. Prior to the new pricing regime, MetaCreations received 20 percent of the hourly fees generated for AOL while members were playing MetaSquares. When the contract came up for renewal, AOL sought to do away with the royalty arrangement, although the company did offer to buy the game outright. MetaCreations claimed the offer was too low and refused to sell. Aside from the game, MetaCreations had other content on AOL, including technical support sessions for people who used its software. That content was also removed, because MetaCreations refused to pay the $50,000 annual fee demand by AOL.[16]

The fruits of this change in strategy started to become apparent by 1998. In fiscal 1995, AOL generated some $6 million in revenues from advertising and commercial fees. This increased to $100.2 million in 1996, $180 million in 1997, and $511 million in 1998. The figure for 1999 seemed likely to exceed $1 billion out of total AOL revenues of more than $4 billion. Moreover, there was no sign of a slowdown in the flow of deals bringing cash into AOL's coffers. In early 1999, AOL entered into a five-year agreement valued at $500 million with First USA under which First USA became the exclusive marketer of credit card products and service on AOL. Similarly, in July 1999 drkoop.com, an Internet-based health care site established by Dr. Everett Koop, the former surgeon general of the United States, agreed to pay AOL $89 million over four years. This was an advance on commissions for the chance to sell to AOL's members, which by then exceeded 19 million.[17] As of March 31, 1999, AOL's *backlog* of advertising and commerce rev-

enues exceeded $1.3 billion (the *backlog* refers to future revenues guaranteed to AOL under the terms of agreements with content providers and on-line retailers).[18]

THE STUDIO SYSTEM

In October 1996, AOL established AOL Studios under the leadership of Ted Leonsis. The goal of AOL Studios was to turn AOL into a major producer of original on-line content that would generate direct revenues of $50 million to $100 million by 2000, and significantly more in indirect revenues from advertising on sites created by AOL Studios. Prior to AOL Studios, AOL attempted to develop compelling on-line content through the medium of its Greenhouse unit, which invested $50 million between 1994 and 1996 in start-up providers on on-line content. Other than that effort, however, AOL was primarily a distributor of other people's content.

With the establishment of AOL Studios, AOL seemed to be signaling that it wanted to get more involved in the creation of proprietary content. To Leonsis, the initiative made sense given that by 1997, on any night, as many people logged on to AOL as were watching MTV or CNN. At the same time, Leonsis had no illusions that AOL Studios would be able to do it all on its own, and he actively solicited proposals in search of ventures to seed, license, or buy outright. AOL Studios also posted its content on the Web, in addition to AOL's proprietary network.

In its first full year, AOL Studios invested in or created about fifty on-line properties, some of which were proprietary to AOL and some of which were Web based.[19] They included Digital Cities (a Web-based local content service, which can be accessed at http://home.digitalcity.com), Electra (an arena aimed at women's issues), Entertainment Asylum (a site for film, TV, and music fans), Real Fans Sports Network (a site for sports fans), and Xtream Games (an AOL channel for on-line gaming that charges a premium price of $1.99 per hour).

Critics charged that AOL Studios would have a tough time competing against established content providers in the areas it had targeted—entertainment, women, sports, and games. In the sports area for example, Disney's ESPN Sports-Zone and CBS's SportsLine both had a strong Web presence.[20] Moreover, other on-line providers were also moving into the same space, most notably Microsoft, whose MSN Network offers a similar range of content.

In practice, like any other content creator, AOL Studios seems likely to have its share of successes and failures. Real Fans Sports, for example, was pulled in favor of CBS's SportsLine. On the other hand, a Studios creation, Love@AOL, quickly evolved into one of the most popular destinations on the network, with 50 million or more hits (page views) per month. The area includes 50,000 personal ads, often accompanied by photographs, places to chat with guest star sex symbols and "Party Games." The area needs only about twelve AOL employees to keep it running, costs $2 million per year, but generates significantly more than that in advertising revenues from brand sponsors.[21] Digital Cities, Electra, and Entertainment Asylum have also turned out to be hits.

COMPUSERVE GOES AOL

While AOL continued to grow its member base, even through the troubled summer of 1996, its rivals continued to lag far behind. By 1997, Prodigy was almost extinct, CompuServe seemed stuck at 2.6 million customers and was losing money, and MSN was still far behind AOL with 2.3 million members. In September 1997, AOL took another big step toward establishing a sustainable position in cyberspace when in a three-way transaction with telecommunications provider WorldCom and CompuServe's parent, H&R Block, AOL acquired CompuServe's on-line network.[22]

Under the deal, WorldCom announced that it would buy CompuServe from H&R Block in a $1.3 billion stock swap. The deal, however, was engineered by AOL, which had been eyeing CompuServe's subscriber base for some time. WorldCom transferred CompuServe's 2.6 million subscribers, software, data centers, and content to AOL, while holding on to CompuServe's Internet infrastructure. In return for this and $175 million, AOL transferred its network infrastructure unit, ANS, to WorldCom. AOL also agreed to purchase its network services from WorldCom for at least five years. The price, agreed to in advance, was reported to be little more than what AOL was paying ANS in-house. As a result of the deal, AOL effectively exited the network services business, while increasing its membership roll to 11.6 million. Af-

ter the deal, AOL commanded a 54 percent share of the U.S. on-line service market. [23]

After completing this acquisition, on February 8, 1998, AOL announced another reorganization of the company. In the new structure, Pittman was appointed president and chief operating officer of AOL, solidifying his position as number two at the company. Three divisions were put under Pittman—AOL Networks, CompuServe, and AOL Studios (implying that Leonsis, AOL's long-time number two, would now report to Pittman). AOL elected to continue running CompuServe as a separate service. The three divisions would share the same sales and marketing, customer service, and backroom functions.

On the same date, AOL also announced that it would be increasing its monthly fee for unlimited access by $2, to $21.95. The company's stock surged to an all-time high of $115 7/16 on February 11, 1998, whereas it had been in the $20 range during the summer of 1996. On February 12, AOL reported its earnings for the three months ending December 31, 1997: $20.8 million on record revenues of $592 million. AOL's balance sheet was also much improved. As a result of various deals, the company now had $750 million in cash. After having been written off by many commentators during 1996, AOL was rapidly evolving into the first blue chip Internet company.

ICQ

Although AOL remains primarily a proprietary on-line service, the company has been steadily moving offerings onto the Web. AOL has had a Web presence for several years at http//www.aol.com, its Internet gateway, or portal, that can be accessed either from the proprietary service or from the Web by anyone with a browser and Internet access, AOL member or not. Some of the offerings of AOL Studios, such as Digital Cities, are also Web based. In June 1998, AOL took another step in this direction when it acquired Mirabilis, an Israeli software company, for $287 million. The primary asset of Mirabilis was a little-known software package called ICQ (http://www.icq.com).

ICQ (which stands for "I seek you") is a sophisticated instant message system that can link individual users in real-time dialogue via the Internet. Anyone can subscribe to ICQ and download the software for free. ICQ can alert a subscriber when designated friends are on-line and let a user chat, transfer files, or play games, all while other applications are running on the user's computer. ICQ is a persistent program—it becomes active as soon as a subscriber turns on the computer and is the first thing to appear on a subscriber's screen, even before the user reaches an Internet portal site or activates a browser. The small rectangular ICQ screen stays on a user's monitor until the computer is turned off, running in the background whenever a user is on-line. Pop-up messages alert an ICQ subscriber to an incoming message or chat request.

Despite its low profile, at the time of the Mirabilis acquisition, 13 million people subscribed to ICQ—as many as subscribed to AOL's proprietary service.[24] The big difference between the two is that while most of AOL's members are located in North America, ICQ subscribers are scattered around the world. After the acquisition, AOL announced that it would continue to offer ICQ for free, and would let ICQ operate as a separate entity within AOL. By March 31, 1999, ICQ subscribers had grown to more than 32 million, 13 million of whom had used the service within the last thirty days. More than 7 million people used ICQ every day.[25] While AOL did not at this time rent out advertising space on ICQ's screen, the company was reportedly considering the option.[26] With the acquisition of ICQ, Bob Pittman began referring to AOL as a company with four brands—AOL, CompuServe, Digital Cities, and ICQ.[27]

AOL, NETSCAPE, AND SUN

AOL's acquisition spree continued in November of 1998 when the company announced that it had agreed to acquire Netscape in a stock swap valued at $4.3 billion. Netscape was one of the first Internet companies, and despite inroads from Microsoft's Internet Explorer, its browser, Netscape Navigator, was still the most widely used. Netscape also had a popular Web portal, Netscape Netcenter, but its most valuable asset was its e-commerce software, which was sold to businesses to help them manage on-line transactions and accounted for 70 percent of Netscape's revenues at the time of the purchase.[28]

Simultaneously, AOL reached a three-year agreement with Sun Microsystems, which manufactures computer workstations and servers, and has developed a popular version of the UNIX operating sys-

tem and two software languages geared toward the Web, Java and Jini. Under the agreement, Sun will market Netscape's business software and help develop versions of AOL for digital devices. In addition, AOL and Sun will jointly sell electronic commerce packages to businesses that want to market their wares on-line. AOL also committed to buying Sun computers and services valued at $500 million. For its part, Sun will pay AOL more than $350 million in licensing, marketing, and advertising fees.

According to a statement by Steve Case, the AOL-Netscape-Sun combination will facilitate the growth of electronic commerce by offering "end-to-end" solutions for those businesses that want to get into e-commerce, a market that Forester Research estimates will be worth $35 billion by 2002.[29] Companies that want to build stores in cyberspace could start with Sun's servers and operating system. Then they would add Netscape's software programs for building a virtual store and handling transaction processing. Finally, they could turn to AOL to market the stores to millions of consumers through AOL's service, Digital Cities, Netscape's Netcenter portal, and perhaps ICQ. Sun also brings its 7,000-person sales force to the table, and it can be used to sell Netscape's software and AOL's storefront locations in cyberspace.

As critics have been quick to point out, however, this deal takes AOL into new territory. Up to this point, AOL has been a consumer mass-market company, but the deal adds businesses to the mix. Moreover, the deal brings the AOL-Netscape-Sun troika into direct competition with a couple of very powerful companies that have already a strong hold on selling e-commerce solutions to businesses—Microsoft and IBM. Microsoft in particular, offers a compelling alternative, given the rapid market acceptance of its Windows NT operating system, transaction processing and back-office software. Moreover, despite AOL's success, there are plenty of other outlets for businesses in cyberspace, including Microsoft's MSN Network, and popular portals such as Yahoo! and Lycos.[30]

The Netscape acquisition closed in mid March 1999. Shortly afterward, AOL announced that it would be laying off 350 to 500 employees at Netscape and as many as 500 at AOL. The layoffs were presented as the consequence of greater efficiencies achieved by combining the two organizations. Simultaneously, AOL stated that it would split the company into four product groups: The Interactive Services Group, which includes the flagship AOL service, along with Netscape's Netcenter portal; the Netscape Enterprise Group, which will handle Netscape's corporate software offering; AOL Studios, which now includes ICQ; and AOL International.[31]

THE QUEST FOR BANDWIDTH

Pittman has frequently stated that in cyberspace "location, location, location" is the key. So far, he has been proved correct, but as 1999 progressed, it became increasingly clear that besides location AOL needed to be able to offer its members greater bandwidth. Bandwidth refers to the rate at which digital data can be transferred between two points. Currently, most consumers have only relatively low bandwidth connections to the Internet over standard telephone lines (a typical computer modem can transmit and receive data at 56 kilobits per second). Case has long argued that greater bandwidth connections would allow high-resolution video and audio data to be transmitted effectively to consumers over the Internet. In turn, this would dramatically expand the range of interactive service that consumers could access over the Internet, which could drive forward the growth in demand for AOL's various offerings.

There are various ways of delivering high bandwidth connections to the home, all of which are in the early stages of being rolled out. [32] One way utilizes DSL (digital subscriber line) technology to increase the bandwidth of standard copper telephone lines. DSL technology typically moves data at between 128K and 1.5 megabits per second, with 640K being the norm. This is the solution favored by telephone companies. By mid 1999, there were about 180,000 DSL subscribers in the United States. But DSL signals degrade with distance and typically will not work more than 3 miles from a phone switch.

Another solution involves adapting the coaxial cable used to transmit cable TV signals to carry two-way Internet traffic. Consumers with cable modems attached to their PCs would then be able to access the Internet at speeds up to 500 times faster than with a standard 56K telephone modem. TV cables run past 95 percent of homes in the United States. By mid 1999, 750,000 people in the United States were using services based on cable modems.

A third solution is to use digital satellite technology to beam down data at very high bandwidth rates. The problem with this solution right now is that the consumers can not beam data back at similar rates. Rather, they have to communicate requests for data through conventional telephone lines operating at 56K. This might change in a few years when new satellite systems, such as Teledesic, go into operation. Microsoft's Bill Gates and his Seattle neighbor, Craig McCaw, who owns Nextel, a large wireless company, are funding Teledesic. The service aims to put about 300 satellites in low earth orbit that can handle high bandwidth two-way communication. Consumers will not need a cable link or telephone line to communicate with a Teledesic satellite, just an antenna on their roof. By mid 1999, some 25,000 consumers were using satellite services to connect to the Internet.

Case is not the only one who believes that high bandwidth connectivity is the key to expanding demand for interactive services over the Internet. Gates also believes that high bandwidth connectivity is crucial, and sees high bandwidth driving forward demand for Microsoft software and services, including AOL rival, MSN.[33] In 1998, Microsoft began to invest in cable TV companies as part of a strategy to create incentives for the cable companies to speed up their moves to upgrade their coaxial cable networks so that they could carry Internet traffic.

Microsoft started the ball rolling with a $5 billion investment in Comcast, a nationwide cable operator. Soon afterward, AT&T jumped into the fray when it acquired the number one cable operator in the United States, TCI, for $75 billion. AT&T announced that it intended to provide phone service and Internet access over cable. Along with TCI came @Home, in which TCI had a controlling ownership stake and which was a leader in offering access to the Internet over coaxial cable. Then on May 10, 1999, AT&T acquired another major cable company, MediaOne, for $60 billion. MediaOne happened to be part-owner of Roadrunner, which was a major competitor to @Home. As part of the AT&T–MediaOne deal, Microsoft agreed to invest $5 billion in AT&T and to purchase a 30 percent stake in MediaOne's European cable TV operating subsidiary, TeleWest (at one point, Microsoft was rumored to be preparing a rival bid for MediaOne). In return for Microsoft's investment, AT&T agreed to put Microsoft's Windows CE operating system into the set-top boxes that will be used to pipe the Internet into existing TV sets. Some observers also wondered whether this meant that Microsoft's MSN portal would be the first thing to pop up on an Internet-enabled TV set.[34]

This flurry of deals led to speculation that AOL might be shut out of high bandwidth access to the Internet via cable. So far cable networks have been closed to AOL because federal regulators have ruled that cable operators have the exclusive right to market data services to their own subscribers. AOL has challenged this ruling but initially met with little success. As an alternative, in early 1999 AOL entered into strategic alliances with two of America's telephone giants, Bell Atlantic and SBC Communications, to use DSL technology to make available a high-speed upgrade connection to AOL subscribers starting in the summer of 1999. By the end of 1999, AOL planned to offer a high-speed broadband upgrade in areas covering nearly 16 million homes in 21 states. The company was rumored to be contemplating charging consumers a higher fee for broadband services.

The deals with the telephone companies were followed by a May 12 announcement that AOL would make a record $1.5-billion investment in Hughes Electronics and jointly introduce new consumer offerings with the Hughes DirecTV satellite service.[35] The proposed offerings include AOL-Plus, which will provide high-speed Internet connection over satellite, and AOL TV for such television-based functions as interactive shopping, Web surfing, E-mail and electronic chat, more commonly performed over the Internet. A set-top box, which the partners are developing jointly, will allow TV viewers to chat with friends, check their E-mail and engage in e-commerce. While this deal put AOL back in the broadband race, and positioned the company to enter the interactive TV market, the shortcomings of current satellite systems still leave AOL at a potential disadvantage.

NEXT MOVES?

For the three months ending March 31, 1999, AOL announced strong financial results. Revenues increased 66 percent over the same period a year earlier, to a record $1.3 billion. These results suggested that the company was likely to record revenues in excess of $4.5 billion in fiscal year 1999, which ended in June. After-tax profits increased to

$117 million for the quarter, up from $39 million for the same period a year earlier (these results exclude any contribution from the Netscape acquisition, which closed on March 17, 1999). Advertising and commerce revenues were $275 million, up 94 percent from a year earlier. Some 16.9 million people now subscribed to AOL's flagship service, and another 2 million to CompuServe. Some 3 million of these subscribers were outside North America—mostly in Europe, where AOL had a successful joint venture with the large German publishing company, Bertelsmann. ICQ had 32 million registered users, and Netscape's Netcenter portal, 15 million registered users. By early July, AOL's stock had surged to $130 a share, up from $17 a share in October 1998. At this price, AOL had a market value of $140 billion, making the company the twentieth most valuable enterprise on the planet. By comparison, General Motors had a market value of around $44 billion.

In many ways, AOL had never been stronger, and yet uncertainties still swirled around the company and its market space. The Internet continued to get more organized. Portals such as Yahoo!, Lycos, and MSN were increasingly becoming gateways of choice for consumers accessing the Web. AOL's proprietary service was also a gateway, but questions remained as to how valuable a portal it would be as Web users became increasingly sophisticated, particularly since some of AOL's strongest features, such as E-mail and chat, could now be found on the Web. Of course, AOL was also participating in this space with its ICQ chat and messaging service and its own Web-based portals, aol.com and Netcenter. Still, some questioned the long-term growth prospects of the proprietary service, particularly in view if the $140 billion valuation that investors had assigned to AOL.

This concern was heightened by signs that, after their initial enthusiasm, at least some advertisers had become disenchanted with the Web, casting doubt on the ability of AOL and others to grow revenues from Web advertising at the anticipated rates. For example, Levi Strauss pulled its Web advertising in 1999 after an internal analysis showed that it did not generate the traffic required to cover costs. According to a company spokesman, Levi Strauss was spending anywhere from $56 to $120 per paying customer in Web-based advertising fees to get customers to visit its Web site, but once they were there, spending did not even come close to covering the costs.[36] Part of the problem seems to

FIGURE 1

AOL's Financial Data

Year ended June 30, Total Revenues Dollars in millions		1998		1997		1996
Online service revenues	$	2,161	$	1,429	$	992
Advertising, commerce and other revenues		439		256		102
Total revenues	$	2,600	$	1,685	$	1,094
Operations						
Worldwide members		14,605,000		8,636,000		6,196,000
Employees		8,546		7,371		5,338
Average hours per AOL member per month (Q4 average)		22.1		18.5		6.4
Maximum AOL simultaneous users		692,000		384,000		120,000

Source: AOL 1998 Annual Report.

be that while television viewers are used to passively watching ads, Web surfers consider ads a distraction and tend to ignore them.

AOL's defenders point out that the elegant and intuitive design of the proprietary service's interface and the well-thought-out programming continued to give the service a big advantage over competing portals such as MSN and Yahoo!, which were far more intimidating to the on-line neophyte. Moreover, AOL still had huge growth prospects, both in its core North American market, where some 60 percent of homes were still not connected to the Internet, and internationally, where on-line usage lagged that in North America by several years. As for the sustainability of growth rates in on-line advertising revenue, it should be noted that while advertising spending on the Internet reached a record $1.9 billion in 1998, that was still only 5 percent of the figure spent on television advertising. Surely, there was room for growth here, many argued, particularly when high bandwidth connections make streaming audio and video more viable, which could change the form of much Web-based advertising.

Going forward, part of AOL's game plan is to offer AOL on a wide range of digital devices that can access the Internet, including hand-held devices, smart phones, and television sets equipped with set-top boxes. AOL hopes that this "AOL Anywhere" strategy will dramatically expand the company's role as a premier information mediator. Another AOL strategy is to turn tasks traditionally performed by personal computer software into services delivered on-line. Early efforts have focused on delivering E-mail without the need for E-mail software to reside on a personal computer. AOL members can now read and send E-mail from any Web browser. The next wave will focus on personal information applications, such as address books and calendars. In support of this strategy, in April 1999 AOL spent $150 million to acquire a small company, When.com, which provides calendar services over the Internet. The system operates much like the appointment book built into Microsoft's Outlook personal information manager, but with a twist—each time a user enters an appointment, the information travels across the Internet and gets stored on a server computer. This means that users can check and update their calendars from any Web-connected digital device, anywhere, anytime.[37]

Endnotes

1. F. Rose, "Keyword: Context," *Wired*, Release 4.12, December 1996.
2. K. Swisher, *AOL.COM: How Steve Case Beat Bill Gates, Nailed the Netheads, and Made Millions in the War for the Web* (New York: Random House, 1998).
3. Ibid.
4. D. Hilzenrath, "Turnaround Task at AOL," *Washington Post*, October 31, 1996, p. E1.
5. F. Rose, "Keyword."
6. R. Chandrasekaran and D. Hilzenrath, "Routine Maintenance Turned AOL Off," *Washington Post*, August 9, 1996, p. F1.
7. F. Rose, "Keyword."
8. D. Hilzenrath, "Emergency Overhaul for AOL," *Washington Post*, October 30, 1996, p. A1.
9. D. Hilzenrath, "Turnaround Task."
10. K. Swisher, *AOL.COM: How Steve Case Beat Bill Gates.*
11. J. Sandberg, "Firm Pays AOL $100 Million in Phone Pact," *Wall Street Journal*, February 26, 1997, pp. B4, B6.
12. "AOL and Tel-Save Approach Half a Million Long Distance Lines," AOL press release, March 25, 1998.
13. "AOL and CUC Announce Online Partnership," AOL press release, June 10, 1997.
14. J. Sandberg, "Retailers Pay Big for Internet Space," *Houston Chronicle*, July 13, 1997, 2 STAR Edition, p. 8.
15. "AOL/SportsLine Deal," *New Media Age*, July 10, 1997, p. 6.
16. G. Miller, "Heard on the Beat," *Los Angeles Times*, August 18, 1997, p. 3.
17. P. Tolme, "AOL, Koop in $89 Million Alliance," *Associated Press*, July 8, 1999.
18. "America Online Reports FY99 Third Quarter Income," AOL press release, April 27, 1999.
19. J. Sandberg, "Inside AOL's Bid to Develop Its Own Hot Sites," *Wall Street Journal*, November 21, 1997, p. B1.
20. C. Yang, "A Major Studio Named AOL?" *Business Week*, December 1, 1997, p. 173.
21. J. Sandberg, "Inside AOL's Bid."
22. "Opportunity Knocks," *Economist*, September 13, 1997, p. 63.
23. C. Yang, "Answered Prayers at America Online," *Business Week*, September 22, 1997, p. 30.
24. V. Baldwin Hick, "Passionate Members of ICQ Fear a Link with America Online," *St. Louis Post Dispatch*, June 15, 1998, p. 1.
25. "America Online Reports FY99 Third Quarter Income."
26. T. E. Weber, "America Online's Next Frontier: All AOL, All the Time," *Wall Street Journal*, March 19, 1999, p. B1.
27. C. Dubow, "AOL Beats Estimates, Adds 1.8 Million Subscribers," *Forbes Digital Tool*, www.forbes.com, (April 28, 1999).
28. T. E. Weber, "AOL Sets Accord to Purchase Netscape in a Stock Transaction for $4.3 Billion," *Wall Street Journal*, November 25, 1998, p. A3.
29. "Internet Riders," *Economist*, November 28, 1998, p. 63.
30. H. Green, "Not So Odd a Couple After All," *Business Week*, December 21, 1998, p. 77.
31. T. E. Weber, "AOL Unveils Job Cuts, Reorganization," *Wall Street Journal*, March 25, 1999, p. B4.
32. A. Reinhardt, "As the Web Spins," *Business Week*, May 24, 1999, p. 30.
33. Bill Gates interview with Charles W. L. Hill, June 1998.
34. A. Sloan, "AT&T-MediaOne Soap Opera Has Just About Everything," *Business Week*, May 11, 1999, p. 3.
35. S. Hofmeister, "AOL, Hughes Link Up to Challenge Cable," *Los Angeles Times*, June 22, 1999, p. 1.
36. J. Gaw, "Some Log Off the Web," *Seattle Times*, July 11, 1999, p. F1.
37. T. E. Weber, "Power Tools," *Wall Street Journal*, June 21, 1999, p. R23.

CASE 10

Amazon.com: Expanding Beyond Books

This case was prepared by Suresh Kotha of the University of Washington.

Jeff Bezos, the CEO of Amazon.com, was pleased that his three year-old on-line start-up, www. amazon.com, had gone from being an underground sensation for book lovers on the World Wide Web (WWW) to one of the most admired Internet retailers on Wall Street. To date, his attempts to transform the traditional book-retailing format through technology that taps the interactive nature of the Internet has been very successful. Although his company garnered rave reviews from respected Wall Street analysts, Bezos clearly understood that this was not the moment to dwell on the past. In the fast-moving world of the Internet, he and his firm continued to face many formidable challenges.

This case describes how Bezos has managed to build a rapidly growing retail business on the Internet and the challenges he and his top management face as other industry giants such as Barnes & Noble, and Bertelsmann, the German publishing conglomerate, attempt to imitate his model of competition.

COMPANY BACKGROUND

In 1994, Jeffrey Bezos, a computer science and electrical-engineering graduate from Princeton University, was the youngest senior vice president in the history of D. E. Shaw, a Wall Street–based investment bank. During the summer of 1994, one important statistic about the Internet caught his attention, and imagination—Internet usage was

growing at 2,300 percent a year. His reaction: "Anything that's growing that fast is going to be ubiquitous very quickly. It was my wake-up call."

He left his job at D. E. Shaw and drew up a list of twenty possible products that could be sold on the Internet. He quickly narrowed his prospects to music and books. Both shared a potential advantage for on-line sale: far too many titles for a single store to stock. He chose books.

> There are so many of them! There are 1.5 million English-language books in print, 3 million books in all languages worldwide. This volume defined the opportunity. Consumers keep demonstrating that they value authoritative selection. The biggest phenomenon in retailing is the big-format store—the "category killer"— whether it's selling books, toys, or music. But the largest physical bookstore in the world has only 175,000 titles.... With some 4,200 US publishers and the two biggest booksellers, Barnes & Noble and Borders Group Inc., accounting for less than 12% of total sales, there aren't any 800-pound gorillas in book selling.[1]

In contrast, the music industry had only six major record companies, which controlled the distribution of records and CDs sold in the United States. With such control, these firms had the potential to lock out a new business threatening the traditional record store format.

To start his new venture, Bezos left New York City to move west—to Boulder, Seattle, or Portland. As he drove west, he refined and fine-tuned his thoughts as well as his business plan. In doing so, he concluded that Seattle was his final destination. He recalls:

It sounds counterintuitive, but physical location is very important for the success of a virtual business. We could have started Amazon.com anywhere. We chose Seattle because it met a rigorous set of criteria. It had to be a place with lots of technical talent. It had to be near a place with large numbers of books. It had to be a nice place to live—great people won't work in places they don't want to live. Finally, it had to be in a small state. In the mail-order business, you have to charge sales tax to customers who live in any state where you have a business presence. It made no sense for us to be in California or New York.... Obviously Seattle has a great programming culture. And it's close to Roseburg, Oregon, which has one of the biggest book warehouses in the world.[2]

Renting a house in Bellevue, a Seattle suburb, Bezos started working out of his garage. Ironically, he held meetings with prospective employees and suppliers at a nearby Barnes & Noble superstore. Bezos also raised several million dollars from private investors. Operating from a 400-square-foot office in Bellevue, he launched his venture, Amazon.com, on the Internet in July 1995.

As word about his new venture spread quickly across the Internet, sales picked up rapidly. Six weeks after opening, Bezos moved his new firm to a 2,000-square-foot warehouse. Six months later, he moved once again, this time to a 17,000-square-foot building in an industrial neighborhood in Seattle. To fund further expansion, Bezos attracted $8 million from Kleiner, Perkins, Caufield & Byers, a venture-capital firm based in the Silicon Valley that has funded firms such as Sun Microsystems and Netscape.

By the end of 1996, his firm was one of the most successful Web retailers, with revenues reaching $15.6 million. (Revenues for a large Barnes & Noble superstore amount to about $5 million on average per year.) With revenues surging quarter after quarter, Bezos decided to take his company public. However, just days before the firm's initial public offering (IPO) of 3 million shares, Barnes & Noble—the nation's largest book retailer—launched its on-line store and sued Amazon.com for claiming to be the world's largest bookstore. To entice customers to visit its Web store, Barnes & Noble offered deeper discounts. Bezos retaliated with a counter lawsuit.[3]

On May 14, 1997, Bezos took Amazon.com public. The *Wall Street Journal* noted that "Amazon's May 1997 debut on the Nasdaq Stock Market came with no small amount of hype. On the first day of trading, investors bid the price of shares up to $23.50 from their offering price of $18. But the shares then fell, and within three weeks of the IPO they were below their offering price." Despite this, customers have continued to flock to Amazon.com's Web site. By October 1997, Amazon.com served its millionth "unique" customer. To keep pace with such growth, the firm expanded its Seattle warehouse and built a second 200,000-square-foot state-of-the-art distribution center in New Castle, Delaware. With these additions Amazon.com successfully increased its stocking and shipping capabilities to nearly six times its 1996 levels.

As the firm continued to expand its customer base, sales revenues have surged. The firm's revenues increased from $15.7 million in 1996 to $147 million in 1997 (see Tables 1 and 2 for the firm's balance sheet and income statements). They were expected to top $550 million for fiscal 1998. In response to this revenue growth, the company's stock and market capitalization have risen as well. As of July 1998, the capitalization was around $6.4 billion, a number that represents the combined value of the nation's two largest retailers, Barnes & Noble and Borders Books & Music, whose combined sales are about ten times those of Amazon.com.

THE BOOK PUBLISHING INDUSTRY

The United States is the world's largest market for books, with retail book sales accounting for $20.76 billion in 1997. Comprising more than 2,500 publishers, the U.S. book publishing industry is one of the oldest and most fragmented industries.[4] Figure 1 shows its structure.

The Sellers and the Buyers

The industry sells a variety of books, including trade, professional, mass-market, El-hi (elementary-high school) and college textbooks, and others, and each of these categories varies in terms of sales, competition, profitability, and volatility (see Tables 3 and 4).

Publishers   Publishers sell books on a consignment basis and assume all the risk in this industry. They also accept returns on unsold books, guaranteeing their distributors a 100 percent refund on

TABLE I

Amazon.com—Consolidated Balance Sheets, Unaudited
(in thousands, except share and per share data)

	June 30, 1998	December 31, 1997
Assets		
Current assets:		
Cash	$ 2,523	$ 1,567
Marketable securities	337,396	123,499
Inventories	17,035	8,971
Prepaid expenses and other	12,487	3,298
Total current assets	369,441	137,335
Fixed assets, net	14,014	9,265
Deposits and other	284	166
Goodwill and other purchased intangibles, net	52,398	—
Deferred charges	7,622	2,240
Total assets	$ 443,759	$ 149,006
Liabilities and Stockholders' Equity		
Current liabilities:		
Accounts payable	$ 47,556	$ 32,697
Accrued advertising	9,971	3,454
Other liabilities and accrued expenses	13,713	6,167
Current portion of long-term debt	684	1,500
Total current liabilities	71,924	43,818
Long-term portion of debt	332,225	76,521
Long-term portion of capital lease obligation	181	181
Stockholders' equity:		
Preferred stock, $0.01 par value:		
Authorized shares—10,000,000; issued and outstanding shares—none		
Common stock, $0.01 par value:		
Authorized shares—300,000,000 issued and outstanding shares—49,669,601 and 47,874,338 shares, resp	497	479
Additional paid-in capital	104,368	63,552
Deferred compensation	(1,301)	(1,930)
Other gains (losses)	(35)	—
Accumulated deficit	(64,100)	(33,615)
Total stockholders' equity	39,429	28,486
Total liabilities and stockholders' equity	$ 443,759	$ 149,006

TABLE 2

Amazon.com— Consolidated Statements of Operations, Unaudited
(in thousands, except per share data)

	Quarter Ended June 30		Six Months Ended June 30	
	1998	1997	1998	1997
Net sales	$ 115,977	$ 27,855	$ 203,352	$ 3,860
Cost of sales	89,786	22,633	157,840	35,117
Gross profit	26,191	5,222	45,512	8,743
Operating expenses:				
Marketing and sales	26,452	7,773	45,955	11,679
Product development	8,060	2,808	14,789	4,383
General and administrative	3,262	1,708	5,225	2,850
Amortization of goodwill and other purchased intangibles	5,413	—	5,413	—
Total operating expenses	43,187	12,289	71,382	18,912
Loss from operations	(16,996)	(7,067)	(25,870)	(10,169)
Interest income	3,334	366	4,974	430
Interest expense	(7,564)	(4)	(9,589)	(4)
Net interest income (expense)	(4,230)	362	(4,615)	426
Net loss	$ (21,226)	$ (6,705)	$ (30,485)	$ (9,743)
Basic and diluted loss per share	$ (0.44)	$ (0.16)	$ (0.64)	$ (0.24)
Shares used in computation of basic and diluted loss per share	47,977	42,634	47,299	40,719

them. They provide money and contracts to prospective authors and decide how many copies of a book to print. Typically, a first-run printing for a book varies from 5,000 to 50,000 copies. However, best-selling authors' first-run printings are generally set at around 300,000 copies.

In practice, however, trade (adult and juvenile books) and paperback publishers print far more copies than will be sold. About 25 percent of all books distributed to wholesalers are returned, and at times these percentages run as high as 40 percent for mass-market paperbacks. According to industry experts, 20 to 30 percent for hardcover book returns is judged acceptable and 30 to 50 percent is generally considered high. Anything above

50 percent is viewed as disastrous. In a process known as remaindering (offering books to discount stores, jobbers, and other vendors), publishers drastically reduce the price after a certain period. Apart from the material cost of returns and the lost revenue they represent, publishers spend millions of dollars each year transporting books back and forth. In this industry, profit margins are driven by book volume, which in turn hinges on the size of each print run. Generally about 10 percent of titles make a profit, with 90 percent barely breaking even. Table 5 indicates the margins on a typical hardcover book.

The "big three"—publishers Warner Books, Simon & Schuster, and Pearson—accounted for 21

FIGURE 1

Book Publishing Market
Structure

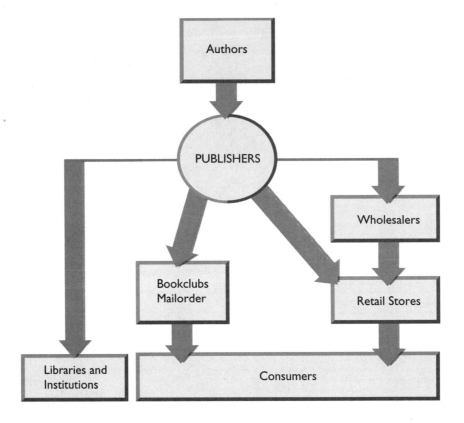

percent of sales in 1995. The twenty largest book-publishing companies in the United States command more than 60 percent of all retail sales. Warner Books, a subsidiary of Time Warner, the U. S. entertainment giant, was the largest publisher in 1995, with sales of $3.7 billion. Simon & Schuster, a division of Viacom Corporation, ranked second, with sales reaching $2.17 billion, and Pearson, a group that owns the *Financial Times*, ranked third, with revenues of $1.75 billion.

Wholesalers. Wholesalers distribute books. They take orders from independent booksellers and chains, and consolidate them into lot-orders for publishers. Publishers supply wholesalers, who in turn supply the thousands of retail bookstores located throughout the country. Wholesalers accounted for almost 30 percent of publishers' sales in 1996. Unlike publishing and retailing, wholesaling is highly concentrated, with firms like Ingram Book Co. and Baker and Taylor commanding more than 80 percent of the market.

Competition in wholesaling revolves around the speed of delivery and the number of titles

stocked. Ingram, for instance, receives more than 70 percent of its orders electronically and offers one-day delivery to about 82 percent of its U.S. customers. In 1994, the average net profit per book for wholesalers was less than 1.5 percent. This figure was down from the traditional margins of about 2 percent a few years earlier.[5]

Technological advances have made warehouse operations more efficient, which in turn has made it possible for wholesalers to provide attractive discounts to retailers. Also, the types of books wholesalers are supplying to retailers are changing. Bookstores are increasingly relying on wholesalers for fast-selling titles and less-popular backlist books.[6] However, with the emergence of superstores, such large retailers as Barnes & Noble and Borders Books & Music are no longer using wholesalers for initial orders of major titles. For example, Borders Books & Music buys more than 90 percent of its titles directly from publishers.

Retail Bookstores Bookstore chains and independent and general retailers accounted for between 35 and 40 percent of industry revenues in 1994

TABLE 3

The Various Product Categories

Trade Books.

This segment includes general interest hardcover and paperback books sold to adults and juveniles. Trade books accounted for almost 25 percent of book revenues in 1997. According to industry reports, books sold to adults increased by more than 30 percent between 1991 and 1995. Juvenile book sales, showed a double-digit growth rate in the late 1980s and early 1990s. However, juvenile hardcover book sales represented a 2.3 percent increase in 1997 over the previous year, and juvenile paperback book sales fell by as much as 18.6 percent during the same period. This slow growth was attributed to a decline in the number of popular titles and increased spending by children on toys and games.

Random House, Bantam Doubleday Dell, Simon & Schuster, HarperCollins, and Penguin are some of the leading firms that competed in this product category.

Professional Books.

More than 165 million profession books were sold in 1997, accounting for $4.15 billion, Since 1991, professional book sales have grown at a compound annual rate of 3.0 percent (in units). Legal publishing was the largest segment of the professional-books category, with the scientific and technical category coming in second place. The long-term outlook for this category was good because employment in the medical, legal, scientific, and business profession was expected to grow strongly.

Thomson Crops was the largest professional-books publisher, with sales of $1.99 billion. Professional book revenues made up 31 percent of Thomson's total revenues. Reed Elsevier ranked second with 1994 sales of $1.63 billion, and was followed by Wolters Kluwer and Times Mirror with $1.07 billion and $775 million in sales, respectively.

Mass-Market Books.

A large proportion of these books are sold through magazine wholesalers and outlets such as newsstands and drugstores. This category includes bestsellers that have shelf lives of about three to six weeks, and in 1997 they accounted for about 7 percent of all books sold. Although the cost of acquiring the paperback rights to a best-selling hardcover title can cost millions of dollars, the per-unit fixed costs for printing are small because print runs were as large as 500,000. However, when return rates, which typically exceed 40 percent, are factored in, profit margins tend to be less than 12 percent.

The largest publishers are Random House, Bantam Doubleday Dell, Simon & Schuster, and HarperCollins.

El-Hi Textbooks.

El-hi, or elementary–high school, books accounted for 14 percent of all books sold in 1997, (they used to represent 30 percent of all books sold in 1994). Sales in this segment rose nearly 14 percent in 1997, and forecasts suggest that are likely to increase by 4.8 percent in 1998. El-hi is driven by state adoption and enrollment levels, and the books are sold to school systems on a contract basis. The development of materials for schools is a capital-intensive process that typically takes up to five years for most new programs. Per pupil expenditures, as well as the number of students, are expected to grow through the year 2000, implying moderate growth (3 to 4 percent) for this segment.

The big publishers are owned by media conglomerates such as News Corp., Times Mirror, and Paramount. The largest el-hi publisher is McGraw-Hill, followed by Paramount (the parent company of Prentice-Hall and Silver Burdett), Harcourt Brace, and Houghton Mifflin.

College Textbooks.

College publishing is the most profitable category. The cost of producing a college text is lower than in the el-hi market, because the texts are typically prepared by university faculty members and used individually. However, the unit sales tend to be small and used textbook sales generally accounted for 20 to 40 percent of total sales. College textbook sales represented 12.8 percent of all book sales in 1997. Sales are estimated to increase 6.9 percent, to $2.85 billion, in 1998.

Prentice-Hall (owned by Paramount) is the largest college publisher, followed by HB College (owned by Harcourt General), International Thomson, McGraw-Hill, and Irwin (a division of Times Mirror).

TABLE 4

Unit Sales (in millions) and Dollar Sales (in millions) by Product Category

Product Category	1997 Units	1997 ($mill)	1998* Units	1998* ($mill)	Profit Margins in 1993
Trade books					
Adults (hardcover and paperbacks)	441.8	$4095.2	438.9	$4160.0	13.7%**
Juvenile (hardcover and paperbacks)	343.8	1358.0	355.9	1437.6	7.7%
Mass market	473.2	1433.8	472.3	1480.3	3.1%
Book clubs	137.7	1145.3	141.3	1207.2	
Mail order	85.7	521.0	81.8	504.7	
Religious	166.6	1132.7	170.3	1178.0	12.4%
Professional (business, medical, scientific, and technical)	165.2	4156.4	169.6	4404.6	8.0%
University press	17.8	367.8	18.0	382.1	
El-hi (elementary–high school)	286.5	2959.6	282.8	3102.4	14.9%
College (textbook and materials)	168.2	2669.7	173.7	2852.8	15.8%
Standard tests	—	191.4	—	204.3	
Subject reference	1.2	736.5	1.2	766.9	
Total	2287.7	$20,767.4	2305.8	$21,680.9	

*Projected sales.
**For hardcover books.
Source: Book Industry Study Group Trends, 1998.

TABLE 5

Profit Margins for a "Typical" Book

Book List Price	$19.95	
Revenue to publisher (i.e., price paid by wholesaler or bookstore)	$10.37	48% discount off suggested retail price
Manufacturing cost	$ 2.00	Printing, binding, jacket design, composition, typesetting, paper, ink
Publisher overhead	$ 3.00	Marketing, fulfillment
Returns and allowances	$ 3.00	
Author's royalties	$ 2.00	
Total publishing costs	$10.00	
Publisher's operating profit	$ 0.37	Returns amount for 3.7%

TABLE 6

Book Sales in 1994 by Various Distribution Channels

Channel	% of Total sales
Bookstore chains, independents and general retailers	35%–40%
Mail order and book clubs	21%
Sales to college book stores	17%
Schools	15%
Libraries and other institutions	10%

(see Table 6). From 1975 to 1995, the number of bookstores in the United States increased from 11,990 to 17,340. According to industry sources, the total sales for the nation's four largest bookstore chains—Barnes & Noble, Borders Books & Music, Books-A-Million, and Crown Books—rose 14.3 percent, to $5.68 billion, for the fiscal year ending in January 1998 (see Table 7). This figure represented about 24 percent of all book sales. Industry analysts point out that from 1992 through 1995, superstore bookstore sales grew at a com-

TABLE 7

Bookstore Chain Sales ($millions)

Chain	1998*	1997	% Change
Barnes & Noble	$2,797.0	$2448.0	14.2%
Borders Group	2,266.0	1,958.8	15.7
Books-A-Million	324.8	278.6	16.5
Crown Books	297.5	287.7	3.4
Total	$5685.3	$4,973.1	14.3%

*Estimates
Source: Publishers Weekly, March 23, 1998, p.17.

pounded rate of 71 percent while non-superstore sales grew at a rate of 4 percent.

With the increasing growth of these superstores, experts cautioned that in smaller markets a shakeout was inevitable.[7] Also, 1995 marked the first year in which bookstore chains sold more books than independents.[8] A spokesperson for the American Booksellers Association, noted that "In the three years from 1993 to 1995, 150 to 200 independent-owned bookstores went out of business—50 to 60 in 1996 alone.... By contrast in the same period, approximately 450 retail superstore outlets opened, led by Barnes & Noble and the Borders Group, with 348 openings."[9]

Independent booksellers believed, however, that the growth of superstores might be reaching a saturation point. Still, even as Barnes & Noble and Borders entered city after city, as many as 142 U.S. metropolitan markets did not have a book superstore. According to Amy Ryan, a Prudential Securities analyst, the current rate of expansion could continue at least through the year 2000, for the country could support about 1,500 such stores.

Institutions and Libraries   There are more than 29,000 private, public, and academic libraries in the United States.[10] This market is crucial to publishers because of its stability and size. Since libraries order only what they want, this lowers the overhead costs associated with inventory and return processing, making this segment a relatively profitable one for publishers. Moreover, as hardcover trade books have become relatively expensive, many readers now borrow them from libraries instead of buying them. Industry experts observed that about 95 percent of general titles published in any year sold less than 20,000 copies; of that number, about 55 percent were purchased by libraries. Libraries also frequently repurchase titles to replace worn-out and stolen books. By doing so, they keep the backlist sales healthy.

Mail Order and Book Clubs   The industry has witnessed a significant drop in the mail-order book business. This drop in sales was attributed to the growth of large discount-sale retailers. Publishers' book club sales on the other hand have risen steadily, gaining 9 percent in 1994 and in early 1995. This growth was attributed to the increasing popularity of specialized book clubs, which focus on favorite baby-boomer interests such as gardening and computers.

The Buying Public   A survey commissioned by American Booksellers Association found that some 106 million adults purchased about 456.9 million books in any given quarter. The survey, which looked at book-buying habits of consumers during the calendar year 1994, revealed that six in ten American adults say they purchased at least one book in the last three months. Annually, that corresponds to 1.8 billion books sold, an average of seventeen books per book-buying consumer a year. The average amount paid for the three most recent books purchased by consumers in the last thirty days was about $15. According to another report, by the Book Industry Study Group, "1996 was a year of major transition and flux in the publishing industry with buyer and seller alike reexamining standard operating procedures to work together in order to adapt to recent changes including growth of retail space and the impact of the Internet."

The Growing Presence of Virtual Bookstores

In its two hardest challenges—physically distributing the right number of books to bookstores and getting the word about serious books out to potential readers—bookselling is getting a more than trivial assist from the new on-line technologies. The rapid growth of the on-line businesses is spreading to book publishing and retailing. According to Larry Daniels, director of information technologies for the National Association of College Stores, "Booksellers' concern revolves around the potential for publishers to deal directly with consumers and the media on the Internet. . . . The phenomenon could mean the elimination of middlemen such as bookstores."[11] Daniels also notes the potential for publishers to be "disintermediated," because computer-literate writers can now publish and distribute their own works on-line. However, the leading publishing houses are skeptical of electronic book-publishing capabilities and remain uncertain about the Internet's future with regard to physical books.

Despite industry skepticism and concern, the Internet has a plethora of virtual bookstores selling books. A cursory search on an Internet search-engine such as Yahoo! produced a listing of 475 on-line bookstores operating on the World Wide Web as of August 1998. A search on Buyers Index (www.buyersindex.com), a mail-order buyers' search engine, yielded more than 234 on-line bookstores. Many of these firms are relatively unknown compared with such on-line retailers as Amazon.com and Barnes & Noble. These two firms in particular have been growing at the self-reported double-digit rates and are fast becoming a formidable presence on the Web. Book and music sales on-line accounted for $156 million in 1997. Although this amount represented a small percentage of the overall retail book sales in 1997, it is projected to reach about $1.1 billion in 2001.

COMPETING ON THE WORLD WIDE WEB

Operating a Virtual Bookstore

Unlike traditional bookstores, Amazon.com has no bookshelves for browsing. All contact with the company is either through its Web site [www.amazon.com] or by E-mail. At the firm's Web site, customers can search for a specific book, topic, or author, or they can browse their way through a book catalog featuring numerous subjects. Visitors can also read book reviews from other customers, the *New York Times,* the *Atlantic Monthly*, and Amazon.com's staff. Customers can browse, fill up a virtual shopping basket, and then complete the sale by entering their credit card information or by placing their order on-line and then phoning in their credit card information. Customer orders are processed immediately. Books in stock (mostly bestsellers) are packaged and mailed the same day. When their order has been shipped, customers are notified by E-mail. Amazon.com places orders for non-bestsellers with the appropriate book publisher immediately.

Shunning the elaborate graphics that clutter many Web sites on the Internet, the firm instead loads up its customers with information. For many featured books, it offers capsule descriptions, snippets of reviews and "self-administered" interviews posted by authors. The firm has found a way to use the technology to offer services that a traditional store or catalog can't match. As Bezos notes,

> An Amazon customer can romp through a database of 1.1 million titles (five times the largest superstore's inventory), searching by subject or name. When you select a book, Amazon is programmed to flash other related titles you may also want to buy. If you tell Amazon about favorite authors and topics, it will send you by

electronic mail a constant stream of recommendations. You want to know when a book comes out in paperback? Amazon will E-mail that too.[12]

Additionally, the firm offers space for readers to post their own reviews and then steps out of the way and lets its customers sell to each other. Bezos points out the advantages of cyberspace for book customers:

> There are so many things we can do on-line that can't be done in the real world. We want customers who enter Amazon.com to indicate whether they want to be "visible" or "invisible." If they choose "visible," then when they're in the science fiction section, other people will know they're there. People can ask for recommendations— 'read any good books lately?'—or recommend books to others. I'm an outgoing person, but I'd never go into a bookstore and ask a complete stranger to recommend a book. The semi-anonymity of the on-line environment makes people less inhibited.[13]

Value Propositions and Customer Service

When asked why people come to his site, Bezos responds:

> Bill Gates laid it out in a magazine interview. He said, "I buy all my books at Amazon.com because I'm busy and it's convenient. They have a big selection, and they've been reliable." Those are three of our four core value propositions: convenience, selection, service. The only one he left out is price: we are the broadest discounters in the world in any product category. . . . These value propositions are interrelated, and they all relate to the Web.[14]

At Amazon.com, almost all books are discounted. Bestsellers are sold at a 30 to 40 percent discount and the other books at a 10 percent discount. Bezos explains that "We discount because we have a lower cost structure than physical stores do and we turn our inventory 150 times a year. That's like selling bread in a supermarket. Physical bookstores turn their inventory only 3 or 4 times a year."

The firm's Seattle and Delaware warehouses are used to stock popular books items, and to consolidate and repack customer orders. Moreover, only after the firm receives a paid customer order does it

TABLE 8

Amazon.com's Customer Bill of Rights

Amazon.com specifies these rights for its customers:

1. No obligation.
Eyes & Editors Personal Notification Services are provided free of charge, and you are under no obligation to buy anything.

2. Unsubscribing.
You can unsubscribe or change your subscriptions at any time.

3. Privacy.
We do not sell or rent information about our customers. If you would like to make sure we never sell or rent information about you to third parties, just send a blank E-mail message to never@amazon.com.

request the appropriate publisher to ship the book to Amazon.com. The firm then ships the book to the customer.[15] It owns little expensive retail real estate and its operations are largely automated. Its distribution center in Delaware, for example, uses state-of-the-art technology to consolidate and package books for shipment.

To keep customers interested in Amazon.com, the firm offers two forms of E-mail-based service to its registered customers. "Eyes" is a personal notification service, in which customers can register their interests in a particular author or topic. Once customers register with Amazon.com, they receive information about new books published by their favorite author. "Editor's service" provides editorial comments about featured books via E-mail. Three full-time editors read book reviews, pore over customer orders, and survey current events to select the featured books. These, and other freelance editors employed by the firm, provide registered users with E-mail updates on the latest and greatest books they've been reading. These services are automated and are available free of charge, and customers subscribing to these services have certain guaranteed rights (see Table 8 for "Customer Bill of Rights"). According to Bezos, such services are vital for success on the Internet:

Customer service is a critical success factor for on-line merchants. If you make customers unhappy in the physical world, they might each tell a few friends. If you make customers unhappy on the Internet, they can each tell thousands of friends with one message to a newsgroup. If you make them really happy, they can tell thousands of people about that. I want every customer to become an evangelist for us. About 63 percent of the book orders come from repeat customers.

The firm's employees also compile a weekly list of the twenty most obscure titles on order, and Bezos awards a prize for the most amusing. Amazon.com drums up all these orders through a mix of state-of-the-art software and old-fashioned salesmanship. When asked to differentiate his firm from potential rivals, Bezos stresses the challenges of electronic marketing:

People who just scratch the surface of Amazon.com say—"oh, you sell books on the Web"—don't understand how hard it is to actually be an electronic merchant. We're not just putting up a Web site. We do 90 percent of our customer service by E-mail rather than by telephone.... There are very few off-the-shelf tools that help do what we're doing. We've had to develop lots of our own technologies. There are no companies selling software to manage email centers. So we had to develop our own tools. In a way this is good news. There are lots of barriers to entry.[16]

Culture and Philosophy

Amazon.com had 800 employees in August 1998. A significant portion of the firm's employees manage "content" on the firm's Web site, including such tasks as Web page updating and formatting book reviews for display. The firm also employs a large number of people to develop software tools for operating on the Internet, and a large group of employees do nothing but answer E-mails from customers. At Amazon.com, "ingenuity and problem-solving" are key, says Bezos

Almost nothing is off-the-shelf at Amazon.com: Our software engineers are developing programs that are the first of their kind; our editors create original content; our site team designs features that can't be found anywhere else....

Also, we have some of the best programmers, and the best servers in the world.

According to Amazon.com insiders, "This is a very driven place. Hours are typically 8 to 8 and many people work weekends. Jeff spends every waking hour on this business." Bezos confirms that

Everyone at Amazon.com works hard, long, and smart. We act like owners because we are owners—stock options give each of us an equity stake in the company. We are passionate about what we're doing. Because of that, we have fun at work, and it makes it easy for us to work hard. What we're building is unprecedented. We're not aspiring to a corporate model—we are creating the model. This to me is the most compelling reason for people to come to work here.

As for his workers, Bezos points out that "There is no Amazon.com 'type.'"

There are Amazon.com employees who have three master's degrees and some who speak five languages. We have people who worked at Procter & Gamble and Microsoft, and people who worked at *Rolling Stone* and the *Village Voice*. We have a professional figure skater, two race-car drivers, a Rhodes scholar, a set of twins, a husband and wife, and their dog. We wear jeans to work, have meetings in the hallway, and we get excited about HTML-enabled E-mail.

He describes his firm's corporate philosophy as follows:

The Amazon.com corporate philosophy is simple: If it's good for our customers, it's worth doing. Our company mission is to leverage technology and expertise to provide the best buying experience on the Internet. Put another way, we want people to come to Amazon.com, find whatever they want, discover things they didn't know they wanted, and leave feeling they have a new favorite place to shop.

Operating Philosophy

The firm's operating philosophy is unlike that of traditional bookstores. At Amazon.com there are no salespeople. The firm is open for business twenty-four hours a day and has a global presence. More than 3 million customers from 160 countries have purchased books from the firm. The firm is devoid of expensive furnishings, and money is spent sparingly. "We made the first four desks we have here ourselves," Bezos recalls, adding that "all our desks are made out of doors and four-by-fours. . . . My monitor stand is a bunch of old phone books. We spend money on the things that matter to our customers and we don't spend money on anything else."[17]

Amazon.com spends a substantial amount on Web advertising and marketing. According to Jupiter Communications, the firm spent more than $340,000 in the first half of the 1996 and ranked thirty-fourth in Web ad spending. Since then, however, these expenses have gone up significantly. This is partly because Amazon.com has entered into multiyear advertising agreements with Internet aggregators, such as Yahoo!, Excite, and AOL. For the quarter ending June 1998, the firm spent $26.5 million on marketing, equivalent to 23 percent of sales.

Since Amazon.com is an Internet-only retailer, Web advertising gives it a unique opportunity to track the success of an ad by the number of click-throughs to the store's Web site and the number of Internet surfers who actually purchase something. Industry analysts estimate that between 2 and 3 percent of people who see an ad on the Web will actually click-through to see more.

The firm advertises mainly in such large-circulation newspapers as the *Wall Street Journal*, *New York Times*, and *San Jose Mercury News*, and on Internet search-engine sites such as Yahoo!, Lycos, the Microsoft Network (MSN), and Microsoft's *Slate* magazine. Amazon.com keeps its banner ads simple, with just a few words and a Web address. Recently, the firm has started advertising on radio and television (for example, CNN). It also hands out discount coupons in several cities to entice customers to use its services.

The decision to locate Amazon.com in Seattle appears to be paying off. The firm has been able to attract some Microsoft veterans and many highly qualified executives. Figure 2 illustrates how the firm is organized and the Appendix provides a brief description of the firm's top management.

Growth Through Micro-Franchising

Amazon.com has been growing at a rapid pace each quarter. Part of the reason for this fast growth is the firm's Associates Program. The program was designed to increase traffic to Amazon.com by creating a referral service from other Web sites to Amazon.com's 2.5-million book catalog. An associates Web site, such as Starchefs—which features cookbook authors—recommends books and makes a link from its Web page to Amazon.com's catalog page for the books. The associated Web site then earns referral fees for sales generated by these links. Partners receive weekly referral fee statements and a check for the referral fees earned in that quarter. More than 90,000 sites have already signed up for this program and earn a commission sometimes up to 15 percent of the value of books bought by the referred customer. The "Web technology," says Bezos, "has made it possible to set up micro-franchises, and with zero overhead."[18]

Since July 1995, Amazon.com has doubled in size every 2.4 months.[19] By August 1996, sales were growing at 34 percent a month. The firm posted revenues of $147.8 million for 1997, an 838 percent increase over the previous year. However,

FIGURE 2

Amazon.com's Organizational Structure

the net loss for fiscal 1997 was 27.6 million, compared with a net loss in fiscal 1996 of $5.8 million. When the company was founded in 1995, the plan was to be profitable in five years. The firm claims to have exceeded expectations and has made its business plan more aggressive. Despite continuing losses, Wall Street's interest in the new venture has remained strong. Furthermore, based on cybershare (and revenues), the firm is acknowledged to be the largest on-line bookstore on the Web.

Bezos is focused on expanding Amazon.com. "In the year 2000, our goal is to be one of the world's leading bookstores," he says. "We believe we're expanding the market for books. With this new way of selling books on the Web we can expose people to far more books than before. People buy books from us that they won't find in bookstores. And we're growing rapidly in this stagnant market."

CHALLENGES FACING AMAZON.COM

Although Bezos is pleased that Amazon.com is well regarded by analysts on Wall Street, he acknowledges that many strategic challenges remain. Three in particular demand his immediate attention: finding creative ways to fend off formidable new competitors; leveraging the firm's brand name to expand beyond just books; and integrating the new acquisitions made by the firm.

Fending Off Formidable Competitors

Competition between on-line book merchants is likely to become even more intense, with a growing number of publishers and retailers going on-line. For example, Ingram and other large publishers have begun experimenting with the World Wide Web. As the *Wall Street Journal* has reported, "In addition to Amazon and Barnes & Noble, publisher Random House Inc. sells books on-line and Viacom Inc.'s Simon & Schuster unit launched an Internet book-selling site grandly called 'The SuperStore.'"[20]

Barnes & Noble, the largest U.S. book retailer, launched its on-line store in May 1997, a little less than two years after Amazon.com opened for business. Although Barnes & Noble finds itself in the unusual position of trailing a competitor, it claims that it holds the unique distinction of operating in four different channels—retail stores, the Internet, 1-800-THE-BOOK, and mail order. Stephen Riggio,

vice chairman of Barnes & Noble, who is presiding over the new on-line venture, sees a rosy future: "How big is it [on-line sales] going to get? We're looking at $100 million in sales this year [1998]. We're not being speculative about that range. We're going to be there. It's going to be bigger than a billion dollar business." Barnes & Noble on-line sales for the year ending in 1997 amounted to $14 million, a small fraction of the firm's overall retail book sales. However, according to a report in *Business Week*, Leonard Riggio, CEO of Barnes & Noble, is dead serious about the on-line segment:

> Riggio plans to spend $40 million to ballyhoo the service in 1998. . . . Riggio is already thinking ahead of how to integrate this technology into the shelves of Barnes & Noble. In the bookstore of the future, he says, customers could tap into millions of titles and print any part from these works on the spot. He talks about software programs that could point customers to specific lines in various books, threaded by a single topic, or ones that could ferret out and print obscure texts that never made it into book form. In short, Riggio envisions modifying what constitutes a published work.[21]

In July 1998, Borders Group Inc. (the parent corporation of Borders Books & Music) entered the fray with Borders.com, a newly formed subsidiary. At the Borders Web site, customers can purchase books, music CDs, and videos. The firm's Web site described Borders' late entry as follows:

> We're not content with being just another on-line bookseller. We want to do it right. Anyone who's been to a Borders store knows that selling books, music, and videos isn't just a business, it's a passion. . . . At Borders.com, we aim to provide the same high level of expertise and vast selection customers have come to associate with the Borders name. No other on-line bookseller can offer 10 million books, CDs, and videos—in stock and available now.

In late 1997, Ingram, the largest U.S. distributor of books, started experimenting with on-line retailing. It began testing an experimental service to create new on-line retailers. According to a report in *Business Week*, "All the would-be retailers had to do was lure the shoppers. Ingram handled everything else, from maintaining the Web site to taking orders, processing credit-card billings, and shipping the books. In effect the virtual bookshops became little more than a retail façade of Ingram. However, after six months of test-marketing, Ingram quietly pulled the plug in early October."[22]

Undaunted by Ingram's failure, Bertelsmann, the German media conglomerate, announced in February 1998 that it planned to open an on-line store (tentatively called BooksOn-line) that will sell books in English, French, Spanish, German, and Dutch.[23] Bertelsmann hoped to ship books to customers in Europe and the United States through its extensive distribution in both countries. In October 1998, however, the firm announced it was buying a 50 percent share in Barnesandnoble.com for $200 million, and both Bertelsmann and Barnes & Noble are expected to spend another $100 million each to strengthen their joint operation. Furthermore, Bertelsmann will abandon the U.S. rollout of its BooksOn-line service. Maria Latour-Kadison, an on-line retail analyst at *Forrester Research*, calls the linking-up of the two firms a "real powerhouse combination: the retail power of Barnes & Noble and the fulfillment power of Bertelsmann.... They already have what Amazon is spending millions to acquire [a brand name and infrastructure]. There's a very steep learning curve associated with doing on-line retailing well, and Bertelsmann will be able to leapfrog some of it because of Barnesandnoble.com's experience.[24]

Bezos acknowledges that "Bertelsmann can be a formidable competitor. They have 50 percent stake in AOL's German operations, over 35 million active book and music club members and significant warehousing and book distribution assets spread out internationally." He points out, however, that Amazon.com is

> ... not competitor focused but customer focused. Figuring out what the customer wants is a never ending process. We differentiate along the following dimensions: selection (we are still the largest); ease of use; price; and discovery. Scale is important in e-commerce and so is 'ease of use.' Our innovations like '1-Click shopping' continue to make our Web site far more attractive than competitors. We are working with interesting features such as "book matcher," using the latest collaborative filtering technology that we acquired from Net Perceptions. We believe such things greatly enhance the customer experience at our store. Discovery means under-

standing customers as individuals and finding ways to accelerate their discovery process while they are at the store. We are working on software that increases the odds that customers will find the right book that they are looking for when searching in our store. Discovery is powerful for customers.

Consequently, Bezos's immediate concern centers on finding innovative ways to stay ahead of his competitors, and he acknowledges that this will remain a continuing challenge.

Leveraging the Amazon.com Brand Name

In June 1998, Amazon.com expanded its product line to include music. The music store offers more than 125,000 titles—ten times the CD selection of the typical music store—and everyday savings of up to 40 percent. The new music store features expert and customer reviews, interviews, an essentials lists, a list of the hottest CDs from around the country and the world, music news, and recommendations. Music fans can search for their favorite music by CD title, artist, song title, or label. Bezos describes the new venture as follows:

> You can browse through nearly 300 styles ranging from Alternative to Zydeco (everything but Classical, which is on the way) or use "Essentials" (my favorite feature) to learn about the best CDs to help you start or build a collection in a particular style. And you can reduce guesswork by listening to some of our 225,000 song clips.... It's a music discovery machine. Using the power of technology and the Internet, we're enriching the music experience for everyone, from casual to devoted listeners alike.

Customers, he adds, had a large part in the store's creation:

> The music store was designed with the help of more than 20,000 customers who responded to our invitation to "build the music store of your dreams." Many of the features in our new music store are the direct result of these suggestions. Our customers told us they wanted a site that is as rich in musical selection and content as the Amazon.com bookstore—with the same great prices, features, and customer service.

The launch of Amazon.com's music store was accompanied by a major update of the firm's Web site, and Bezos sums up the changes:

> We didn't focus only on music. We've also redesigned our store to make it even easier to find the books you want.... The new store design permits customers to move easily between the book and music areas, making it fast and simple to find what they are looking for and to discover new titles. We now provide an integrated shopping cart, 1-Click ordering, and consolidated shipping across both books and music.

Unlike book retailers, many on-line music stores such as cdnow.com (www.cdnow.com) and n2k.com (www.n2k.com) have been in operations for more than a few years. For example, cdnow.com claims that it is the world's leading on-line music store by offering more than 250,000 music related items, and n2k.com operates many music sites (called channels), including Music Boulevard on the World Wide Web (see Table 9 for a partial listing of on-line music stores). In response to Amazon.com's entry into the music business, Cdnow and N2K signed an agreement in October to merge their two companies. Bezos, however, says that "We don't really view existing on-line music stores as our direct competitors. We are more focused on parties that already have a large portion of music sales." Some analysts, though, take a skeptical view of Amazon.com's efforts to compete in music business, as a report in the *Wall Street Journal* illustrates:

> But the move [to offer music CDs] is risky too; Cyberspace is increasingly crowded with online superstores set up by Amazon's physical-world counterparts, companies with more marketing clout and track records of profitability. And Amazon could lose cachet with bibliophiles if its forays into other media dilute its reputation as a destination for booklovers.... [M]ail-order giants Columbia House, a joint venture of Time Warner Inc. and Sony Corp., and Bertelsmann AG's BMG Entertainment have made Internet selling a top priority. Columbia House is taking orders from music-club members on one site; on a separate super-store site, Total E, it's moving straight into Amazon territory with plans to add books and CD-ROMs to its existing catalogue of videos and CDs.[25]

Analysts have also pointed out that the music business is "somewhere between a no-margin and a low-margin business" and hence have questioned the firm's move into the music field. Bezos sees the situation differently:

> Amazon.com brand has to stand for something. For us the brand name means price, convenience, customer service, and a great selection. There is a huge advantage in expanding to other product categories. The customer acquisition costs are significantly lower and so are the costs related to the life time value of that customer. If we can successfully expand the brand, as we think we can, then there are significant economic benefits to expansion.... We recognize that the music business is a different environment than books. About half-a-dozen players control the entire distribution of music in this country and the likely implication of such control is lower margins. However, we like to emphasize the incremental dollar value of music sales to our existing customers.

Integrating New Acquisitions

Capitalizing on increased market value, Amazon.com acquired three companies, Bookpages, Telebook, and Internet Movie Database in April 1998. Bezos assesses the value of these additions as follows:

> With these we have accelerated our expansion into European e-commerce and acquired a foundation for a best-of-breed video store. These acquisitions will enable Amazon.com to offer a new set of consumers the same combination of selection, service and value that we now provide our U.S. book customers. Fortunately, we were able to build an international brand name as a by product of operating on the Internet. People in Japan, Germany, and UK are very familiar with the Amazon.com name (about 22 percent of the firm's sales come from outside the United States currently).

Although Bezos remains quiet about his intentions regarding Internet Movie Database, analysts speculate that *The Internet Movie Database* is likely to form the key underpinning for Amazon.com's eventual entry into on-line video sales.

TABLE 9

A Partial Listing of On-line Music Stores

Cdnow*
The idea for this store was conceived in the summer of 1994, and it was started by twin brothers Jason and Matt Olim in their parents' basement in 1994. In 1997, the firm posted sales of $15 million. It reported averages of about 18 percent in operating margins.

Music Boulevard (www.musicboulevard.com).
Owned by n2k, Music Boulevard operates transaction sites in English, French, German, Japanese, and Spanish. Started in September 1996, n2k.com bills itself as "the premier on-line music entertainment company and the Internet's only complete source for music content, community and comment." In 1997 it reported revenues of $11.7 million.

Musicspot (www.musicspot.com).
According to a recent 10,000-household PC-Meter survey, CUC's musicspot ranked top among the top "Hot Storefronts."

Tunes.com (www.tunes.com).
Tunes.com, based in Berkeley, California, was launched in November 1996. It features 200,000 thirty-second music clips backed by collaborative filter, which matches visitors' music interests to profiles created by people with similar tastes. The company plans to have 1 million samples on-line by mid 1998, which will make it the largest music sampling source on-line.

Records Clubs.
Record clubs are shaping up to be the Web's most powerful retailers. An estimated 16.5 million customers belong to record clubs in the United States. Columbia House and BMG both debuted Web sites in 1995. Their sites now handle all club chores, including administration, buying, status checking, and the commendable job of cyber-retailing.

*Cdnow and Music Boulevard signed an agreement on October 8, 1998, to merge their two companies.

In July 1998, Amazon.com signed agreements to acquire two additional firms. They include Junglee Corp and PlanetAll. PlanetAll, is a Cambridge, Massachusetts, firm that provides a unique Web-based address book, calendar, and reminder service. Junglee Corp., based in Sunnyvale, California, is a leading provider of advanced Web-based virtual database (VDB) technology that can help shoppers find millions of products on the Internet (see Table 10). Discussing his firm's intention to acquire these two firms, Bezos stressed their importance:

PlanetAll is the most innovative use of the Internet I've seen. It's simply a breakthrough in doing something as fundamental and important as staying in touch. The reason PlanetAll has over 1.5 million members—and is growing even faster than the Internet—is simple: it creates extraordinary value for its users. I believe PlanetAll

will prove to be one of the most important online applications. . . . Junglee has assembled an extraordinary team of people. Together we'll empower customers to find and discover the products they want to buy.

Commenting on the recent expansion and acquisitions, Bezos described his company's way of proceeding and the criteria it uses:

Our product extension and geographic expansion is better late than early. Why better late than early? We had to first focus on the book business and grow that until we were comfortable with it. There are always numerous opportunities to expand. We try to err on the side of being slow. Fortunately, we are not capital constrained, but we are definitely people constrained. We only pursue opportunities when

TABLE 10

Recent Acquisitions by Amazon.com

Bookpages (www.bookpages.co.uk).
As one of the largest on-line bookstores in the United Kingdom, the firm provides access to all 1.2 million UK books in print.*

Telebook (www.telebuch.de).
This firm, operating through its ABC Bücherdienst subsidiary, is Germany's number one on-line bookstore, with a catalog of nearly 400,000 German-language titles.

Internet Movie Database (www.imdb.com).
Originally launched in 1990, Internet Movie Database is a comprehensive repository for movie and television information on the Internet and is an excellent example of genuine community on the Internet.

PlanetAll.com (www.PlanetAll.com).
The firm launched in November 1996 reportedly has 1.5 million members and reports that thousands of new members are joining each day to use the secure, free service to organize and automatically update information about friends, business associates, relatives, and alumni. Users accessing PlanetAll service have complete control over their own contact information and decide what information they want to share with others on a person-by-person basis. Moreover, PlanetAll's service is compatible with personal information managers (PIMs) and personal digital assistants (PDAs), such as Microsoft Outlook and 3Com PalmPilot. Also, it has integrated its service within the sites of a number of Internet leaders, including Lycos and GeoCities, as well as numerous universities and professional associations. Amazon.com intends to operate PlanetAll as a wholly owned subsidiary located in Cambridge. Savage and the two cofounders will remain with the company.**

Junglee Corp (www.junglee.com).
The firm was founded in June 1996. The firm's breakthrough virtual database (VDB) technology derives from the founders' doctoral research carried out at Stanford University. Junglee's first deployment was CareerPost.com, the Washington Post Company's on-line recruitment site, in January 1997. Junglee carries more than 15 million items in the Junglee Shopping Guide and over 90,000 job listings in its Job Canopy. Junglee has developed break-through database technology that can dramatically enhance customers' ability to discover and choose from among millions of products on-line. To date, two of the markets it has targeted have been on-line retailing and on-line recruitment. Junglee's customers and partners in these markets include Yahoo!, Compaq, Snap!, six of the top seven newspaper companies, and many other new-media companies. All founders of Junglee are expected to remain with the company.

*Each of these three acquisitions, Bookpages, Telebook, and Internet Movie Database, will be accounted for under the purchase method of accounting. The company will incur total charges of approximately $55 million in connection with all three transactions. Consideration comprised of cash and common stock, and the company anticipates issuing an aggregate of approximately 540,000 shares of common stock as a result of these transactions.
**Amazon.com will acquire 100 percent of the outstanding shares and assume all outstanding options of Junglee and PlanetAll in exchange for equity having an aggregate value of approximately $280 million. Amazon.com will issue approximately 800,000 shares and assume all outstanding options in connection with the acquisition of PlanetAll; it anticipates accounting for this transaction as a pooling of interests. Amazon.com will issue approximately 1.6 million shares and assume all outstanding options in connection with the acquisition of Junglee and anticipates accounting for this transaction under the purchase method of accounting.

the people bandwidth is not constrained. . . . The single most important criterion that we use to acquire a new company is this: Who are the people behind this venture, and what is the people bandwidth of the acquired company going to be? We are looking for business athletes indoctrinated in this space and companies that have a culture that is common with ours.

The *Wall Street Journal*, however, casts some doubt on the company's prospects for success:

In the end, though, neither specialization nor branding may determine who succeeds in the on-line sales game. In the physical world, hard-core-comparison shopping has been left to a highly motivated faction of consumers willing to trudge between stores. But on the Web, it's become almost effortless. Today, a user can enter a title of a book on Yahoo! Inc.'s Visa Shopping Guide site which then queries multiple booksellers for prices and displays the result in a table. Hyperlink next to book prices lets users order the cheapest one at the click of a mouse. With comparison services proliferating elsewhere on the Web—and for dozens of other products—it's unclear whether a sterling brand like Amazon's will ultimately sway consumers when rock-bottom prices are so easy to spot.[26]

Bezos concedes that many challenges still confront him and his top-management team as they ponder the future moves by his firm:

> It is hard to provide great customer service and experience for the customer. It is hard to grow the business. But when you combine these two, the complexity of operating increases exponentially. We are expanding our product line and broadening our geographic reach simultaneously, and there is a lot of execution risk when you try to do this. Moreover, many of our new initiatives will continue to require aggressive investment and entail significant execution challenges. However, that is the nature of this business.

APPENDIX: AMAZON.COM'S TOP-MANAGEMENT TEAM

Jeffrey P. Bezos, *Founder and Chief Executive Officer,* Jeff Bezos has always been interested in anything that can be revolutionized by computers. Intrigued by the amazing growth in the use of the Internet, Jeff created a business model that leveraged the Internet's unique ability to deliver huge amounts of information rapidly and efficiently. In 1994, he founded Amazon.com, Inc., an Internet retailer of books and other information-based products that offers what traditional retailers cannot: lower prices, authoritative selection, and a wealth of product information. Before heading west to start Amazon.com, Jeff worked at the intersection of computer science and finance, leading the development of computer systems that helped manage more than $250 billion in assets for Bankers Trust Company. He also helped build one of the most technically sophisticated quantitative hedge funds

on Wall Street for D. E. Shaw & Co. Jeff received a degree in electrical engineering and computer science, summa cum laude, from Princeton University in 1986. He is a member of Phi Beta Kappa.

George T. Aposporos, *Vice President, Business Development* George Aposporos joined Amazon.com in May 1997 as vice president of business development and is responsible for identifying and negotiating key strategic relationships for the company. Prior to joining Amazon.com, George was founder and president of Digital Brands, a strategic consulting and interactive marketing firm that has served clients such as Starbucks Coffee, Sybase, American Express, and BMG Entertainment. While at Digital Brands, he placed Starbucks in the first campaign to use animated advertising on America On-line. From March 1994 to August 1995, George was vice president of I.C.E., a Toronto-based multimedia developer and corporate communications firm, where he spearheaded involvement in interactive media, including development of the company's interactive television and Internet capabilities. From 1989 to 1994, he was an independent producer in a variety of media, including television, video, and CD-ROMs. George was an Olin Scholar at Wesleyan University.

Rick Ayre, *Vice President and Executive Editor* Rick Ayre joined Amazon.com in September 1996 as vice president and executive editor and is responsible for the editorial content and design of the Amazon.com Web site. Rick comes to Amazon.com from *PC Magazine,* the popular Ziff-Davis publication, where he served as executive editor for technology. Rick launched *PC Magazine* on the World Wide Web in March 1995. He was responsible for the print coverage of on-line technology, and he ran *PC Magazine*'s on-line services, including the *PC Magazine* on-line Web site and PC MagNet, part of ZD Net on Compuserve. During his five years at *PC Magazine,* Rick also held positions as the magazine's executive editor for software and as technical director for software in its labs, where he supervised all software product testing. Before joining the magazine, Rick served as chief of information resources management at the Highland Drive VAMC, a 750-bed hospital in Pittsburgh. He began his technology career while a Ph.D. candidate in psychiatric epidemiology at the University of Pittsburgh in the early 1980s. There he learned to program in Fortran to manipulate large data sets on an early DEC time-sharing system.

When the IBM PC was born, he quickly adopted one and taught himself to program in Pascal and to use dBASE. He was soon logging on to local BBS systems, and he's been working on-line ever since.

Joy D. Covey, *Chief Financial Officer* Joy Covey joined Amazon.com in December 1996 as chief financial officer and vice president of finance and administration. She is responsible for financial and management systems and reporting, and she also manages planning and analysis, legal, administrative, and investor relations, and human relations activities. Before joining Amazon.com, Joy was vice president of business development and vice president of operations, broadcast division, of Avid Technology, a leader in the digital media industry. From 1991 to 1995, she was the CFO of Digidesign, where she managed a successful IPO and eventual merger with Avid Technology. During her tenure, Digidesign achieved an annual growth of more than 50 percent and strong and consistent profitability and cash flow, and it strengthened its dominant position in the digital audio production systems market. Before she worked at Digidesign, Joy was a mergers and acquisitions associate at the investment bank of Wasserstein Perella & Co. and a certified public accountant with Arthur Young & Co. (currently Ernst & Young). She holds both a J.D. and an M.B.A. from Harvard, where she was a Baker Scholar, and a B.S. in business administration, summa cum laude, from California State University, Fresno.

Richard L. Dalzell, *Chief Information Officer* Richard Dalzell joined Amazon.com in August 1997 as chief information officer and is responsible for all Amazon.com information systems, including corporate networks, logistics, electronic buying, accounting, and data warehousing. Before joining Amazon.com, Rick was vice president of information systems for Wal-Mart Stores. He managed all merchandising and logistics systems, led the development of world-class supply chain systems, set the standard for international retailing and merchandising systems, and was instrumental in establishing the world's largest commercial decision-support and data-mining systems. From 1990 to 1994, Rick held several management positions within the information systems division at Wal-Mart. Prior to that, he spent three years as the business development manager for E-Systems and seven years as a teleprocessing officer in the U.S. Army. Rick re-

ceived a B.S. in engineering from the U.S. Military Academy, West Point, in 1979.

Mary Engstrom Morouse, *Vice President, Merchandising* Mary Engstrom Morouse joined Amazon.com in February 1997 as vice president of publisher affairs and became vice president of merchandising in April 1998. She is responsible for managing supplier relationships and direct purchasing. Before joining Amazon.com, Mary served as general manager of the security business unit and vice president of product marketing at Symantec Corporation, a developer of information management and productivity enhancement software. In these roles, she managed the development, production, testing, manufacturing, distribution, and marketing of Symantec's line of antivirus and security products, including the Norton AntiVirus line. From July 1989 to September 1994, she held several management positions at Microsoft Corporation, including group product manager for Microsoft Access, group product manager for Microsoft Project, and director of marketing in strategic relations. She received her B.A. in economics from the University of California, Berkeley, in 1984 and her M.B.A. from the Anderson Graduate School of Management at the University of California, Los Angeles, in 1989.

Sheldon J. Kaphan, *Chief Technology Officer* Shel Kaphan has served as Amazon.com's vice president and chief technology officer since March 1997. In this role, Shel is responsible for technical architecture and directing technical efforts. From October 1994 to March 1997, he was vice president of research and development for the company and was responsible for developing Amazon.com's core software and maintaining the company's Web site. Shel brings more than twenty years of experience in designing hardware and software systems and services to Amazon.com. Before joining the company, he held senior engineering positions at Kaleida Labs, Frox, and Lucid. He received a B.A. in mathematics, cum laude, from the University of California, Santa Cruz, in 1980.

John David Risher, *Senior Vice President, Product Development* David Risher joined Amazon.com in February 1997 as vice president of product development, responsible for developing new products and services. He was promoted to senior vice president of product development in December 1997 and now has overall responsibility for product development, marketing, editorial, and content licensing. Before joining Amazon.com, David was founder of and product unit manager for Microsoft Investor, Microsoft Corporation's Web site for personal investment. From 1991 to 1995, he held a variety of marketing and project management positions within the Microsoft Access product team, including Microsoft Access team manager. In this role, he managed all aspects of the product development team, including design, development, branding, advertising, and customer research, to produce Microsoft Access 95. From 1987 to 1989, David was an associate at the LEK Partnership, a corporate management consulting firm. He holds a B.A. in comparative literature, magna cum laude, from Princeton University and an M.B.A. from Harvard Business School.

Joel R. Spiegel, *Vice President, Engineering* Joel Spiegel joined Amazon.com in March 1997 as vice president of engineering and is responsible for all Web site software. From March 1995 to March 1997, Joel held several positions with Microsoft Corporation, including Windows 95 Multimedia development manager, Windows Multimedia group manager, and product unit manager for information retrieval. From June 1986 to March 1995, he held a variety of positions at Apple Computer, most recently as senior manager, and was responsible for new product development in the Apple Business Systems Division. Prior to that, he held software product development positions at a number of companies, including Hewlett-Packard and VisiCorp. During his career, Joel has had a hand in the development and delivery of a wide range of software products, including Windows 95 Multimedia, DirectX, Macintosh System 7 File Sharing, several versions of MacDraw, AppleSearch, Smalltalk–80 for the Macintosh, and VisiON. Joel holds a B.A. in biology, with honors, from Grinnell College.

Jimmy Wright, *Chief Logistics Officer* Jimmy Wright joined Amazon.com in July 1998 as vice president and chief logistics officer. He is responsible for all global supply chain activities, including managing the company's distribution centers, product purchasing, distribution, and shipping. Jimmy comes to Amazon.com with more than twenty-six years of experience in logistics management. He was recognized as one of the key logistics leaders within Wal-Mart Stores, the world's largest retailer

and a company globally known for its logistics excellence. He joined Wal-Mart in 1985 and served as vice president of distribution from 1990 until his retirement in 1998. During that time he was responsible for more than thirty regional and specialty distribution centers, which accounted for 38 million square feet of retail distribution space, staffed by more than 32,000 employees. Jimmy's career in logistics management began at the Fina Oil and Chemical Company, a branch of Petrofina S.A., based in Brussels. From 1972 to 1985, he held a variety of positions, including general manager of distribution. He received a B.B.A. in personnel management from the University of Texas in 1976.

Endnotes

1. "Who's Writing the Book on Web Business?" *Fast Company* (October–November 1996), 132–133.
2. Ibid.
3. In October 1997, Barnes & Noble and Amazon.com settled their respective lawsuits by saying that they would prefer to get back to business and compete in the marketplace rather than in the courtroom.
4. Much of the information discussed in this section, and the section that follows, is drawn from "Amazon.com," a Washington University Business School case, by Suresh Kotha and Emer Dooley, 1997.
5. *Publishers Weekly*, January 1, 1996.
6. Although the bestselling books get the bulk of the attention and marketing dollars, backlist books are considered the bread and butter of the industry. A backlist is the publishing company's catalog of books that have already appeared in print. Estimates indicated that as much as 25 to 30 percent of a publisher's revenues come from this source. Backlisted books have predictable sales, with occasional bumps, such as when a subject matter loses favor with consumers or when an author dies. Since these books require no editing and little promotion, they are generally profitable. Moreover, print runs are easier to predict, resulting in fewer returns to publishers.
7. *Publishers Weekly*, March 11, 1996. Superstores, originally confined to big metropolitan areas, were increasingly entering markets with populations of 150,000 or less. Industry estimates indicated that superstores had to make around $200 a square foot to turn a profit. For example, a typical Barnes & Noble superstore needed $3 million to $4 million in sales revenues to break even. Some industry observers questioned whether such cities can support these mammoth stores and whether superstores in these locations could sell enough books to turn a profit.
8. *Philadelphia Business Journal*, September 27, 1996.
9. "A Nonchain Bookstore Bucks the Tide," *New York Times*, September 8, 1996.
10. *Standard and Poor's Industry Surveys*, July 20, 1995.
11. *Christian Science Monitor*, September 18, 1996.

12. *Wall Street Journal,* May 16, 1996.
13. *Fast Company* (October–November 1996).
14. Ibid.
15. Industry observers note that although Amazon discounts most books, it levies a $3 service charge per order, plus 95 cents per book. Furthermore, it can take Amazon a week to deliver a book that isn't a bestseller, and even longer for the most esoteric titles. Also, some people don't like providing their credit card number over the Internet.
16. *Fast Company* (October–November 1996).
17. *Upside* (October 1996).
18. "Amazon.com forges new sales channel," *Web Week*, August 19, 1996.
19. *Financial Times*, October 7, 1996.
20. *Wall Street Journal*, October 21, 1997.
21. "The Baron of Books," *Business Week*, June 29, 1998.
22. Ingram's experimental foray into on-line retailing floundered because many of the new on-line entrants were unable to attract enough customers. Notes *Business Week*, "Ingram stirred a backlash among its existing clientele, who were clearly not happy with the prospect of having to compete with other low-cost clones."
23. Bertelsmann AG is the world's third largest media conglomerate, with $14 billion in sales in 1997. In July 1998, Bertelsmann acquired U.S.-based Random House Publishing. This single largest publisher of English-language books owns Doubleday, Bantam Books, Dell Publishing, and several other publishing companies.
24. *Internet World*, October 12, 1998.
25. "In Looking to Branch Out, Amazon Goes Out on a Limb," *Wall Street Journal*, May 12, 1998.
26. *Wall Street Journal*, May 12, 1998.

CASE 11

RealNetworks

This case was prepared by Margaret Johnston and Suresh Kotha of the University of Washington.

RealNetworks is a streaming-media software firm located in Seattle, Washington. The firm's streaming software products enable multimedia content developers and others to stream both audio and video content over the Internet and intranets to end-users.[1] End users, in turn, can view this content with the firm's "player" software, know as RealPlayer. Within three years of its founding, the firm has managed to create a strong demand for its streaming server software products and become a leader in this important segment. Many aspects of its business model are being imitated by competitors.

The firm permits users to download its Real-Player software for free at its Web site (http://www.real.com). With more than 40,000 downloads a day, the firm claims that more than 18 million RealPlayers have been distributed globally. Recently, the firm signed an exclusive licensing agreement with Microsoft, the world's dominant PC software firm, to bundle RealPlayer with every copy of the Internet Explorer that Microsoft distributes. Microsoft's Internet Explorer is the world's second most popular Internet browser software, after Netscape's Navigator. However, despite the rapid growth and well-entrenched position of RealNetworks, its top management faces a host of challenges.

This case discusses the genesis of RealNetworks, its rapid growth, and its approach to competition in audio and video streaming in the Internet and intranet markets. It highlights the issues that confront the firm as its top management formulates a strategy for continued rapid growth despite various uncertainties and challenges.

COMPANY BACKGROUND

Founded in April 1994 as Progressive Networks, the firm quickly established itself as a pioneer and industry leader in the delivery of real-time audio and video content over the Internet. The firm was the brainchild of Rob Glaser, a former Microsoft executive. Early in 1994, Glaser was toying with the idea of using interactive multimedia technology to create a "cable channel focused on politics and culture." Robert Reid, who has chronicled the early growth of the Web and Glaser's contributing role in its evolution, points out that

> The notion of interactive television (ITV) was by then [early 1994] all the rage. Many smug pundits were even viewing the PC as downright dowdy. For his part, Rob was at first agnostic about whether to use ITV or the PC as the medium for his half-formed vision. Then he encountered Mosaic—a 'total epiphany,' he remembers. He almost immediately concluded that 'interactive TV was going to be stillborn,' and that 'the whole mechanism that Mosaic had used to bootstrap itself, A, was a big deal in its own right, and B, once established, itself could be used as a bootstrapping mechanism for other stuff.' That *other stuff*, or rather some of it, turned out to be RealAudio.[2]

According to a report in the *Wall Street Journal,* "Mr. Glaser sank about $1 million of his own money into a start-up that would first produce software for compressing and transmitting sound. With additional funding from friends such as Lotus founder Mitch Kapor, RealAudio 1.0 quickly made its debut in April 1995."[3] That was exactly one year since Glaser founded the firm.

Despite some disdain from the Internet elite because of the tinny sound, which created an unsatisfying experience, RealAudio 1.0 broke the Web's sound barrier. Soon the product began to win industry favor. Notes Reid:

> RealAudio debuted on the Web on April 10, 1995, along with content from ABC News, National Public Radio (NPR), and others. Tiny Progressive was soon covered by such publications as the *New York Times*, the *Wall Street Journal*, and the *Economist*. *USA Today* characterized RealAudio as 'The technology of the '20s meeting the technology of the '90s,' while *Time* [magazine] meanwhile assured the image-conscious that 'Glaser's system is not just for geeks.'[4]

Within a month, Netscape, the world's largest browser software firm, began shipping RealAudio as part of its Navigator browser software. By August of that year, Progressive Networks had sold its server products to several large Internet media companies, including Starwave, Ziff-Davis, and ABC News.

Just a couple of months later, in October 1995, the firm released a newer and more advanced version of its server and player (RealAudio 2.0) products. Its player software won the *Internet World* magazine's "Outstanding Software Product of the Year" award in April 1996. By September 1996, Progressive Networks released yet another version, RealAudio 3.0. Shortly thereafter Prodigy, a leading on-line service provider, began bundling the firm's player software with its custom browser. Although a handful of other firms provided audio-streaming solutions, none matched the rapid growth of RealNetworks.

Having established itself as a leading provider of audio-streaming software, Progressive Networks turned its attention to video streaming. According to a report in *Wired,*

> In December 1995, while attempting to vacation in Hawaii, Glaser got some email from a two-person San Francisco company, FreeVu, which had an Internet videoconferencing tool under development. Glaser took a look, was impressed, and persuaded FreeVu's principals to sign on as Progressive employees. RealVideo's development effort had begun.[5]

In February 1997, the firm released a product that combined video and audio streaming, RealPlayer 4.0. By then, however, several video-streaming providers—for instance, Xing Technologies, VDOnet, Vosaic, and VXtreme—were already marketing products on the World Wide Web. Recognizing this, Glaser signed an exclusive licensing agreement with Microsoft to bundle RealPlayer with Internet Explorer. With such an agreement, the firm has had little difficulty in achieving a dominant position in video streaming on the Internet.

In September 1997, the firm changed its name from Progressive Networks to RealNetworks and filed for an initial public offering (IPO). The IPO was undertaken to raise capital to continue funding product development. During this period, the firm also introduced the fifth major upgrade of its server (RealSystem) and player (RealPlayer) software.[6] On October 3, 1997, RealNetworks went public on the NASDAQ Stock Exchange with a 3.5 million share offering. The stock opened at $12.50 per share and then moved to $19 per share before settling around $16. Net proceeds for the offering were approximately $38.5 million. The stock has remained healthy throughout the fall of 1997, despite the slump in over-the-counter stocks of other Internet companies. Within a three-month time period, Glaser had successfully partnered with Microsoft, launched a major upgrade of the product system, and had taken RealNetworks public.

With frequent product upgrades, RealNetworks has garnered widespread support and won many industry awards. For example, writing about its latest product upgrade, Allen Weiner, an analyst with Dataquest, notes that the firm has demonstrated superiority in all areas of streaming:

> With the release of RealSystem 5.0, RealNetworks is taking the streaming media market by storm. . . . RealNetworks' emphasis on innovation, coupled with its cross-platform architecture, incredible brand recognition and majority market share, continues to place it at the forefront of the streaming media market."[7]

Most importantly, RealNetworks has managed to compile an impressive list of companies that use its server software to transmit multimedia content over the Internet. This list includes all three major U.S. television networks (NBC, ABC, and CBS), two major long-distance telephone carriers, the U.S. Senate, and many of the biggest companies in the music industry, including Sony. In just four years since its founding, RealNetworks had produced more than eight product varieties and grown to more than 350 employees. For 1997, the firm as a whole reported total revenue of $32.7 million, an increase of 134 percent from $14.0 million in 1996. However, the net loss was $11.2 million for 1997, compared with $3.8 million for the previous year (see Table 1).

PRODUCTS, MARKETS, AND COMPETITION

RealNetworks competes in two different markets—the Internet and the intranet markets. The potential Internet customers include the Web site creators and the end users that access those Web sites. The potential intranet customers include all businesses with internal networks that connect employees.

TABLE I

Summary Consolidated Financial Data

	Period from February 9, 1994 (inception) to December 31, 1994	Year Ended December 31, 1995	Year Ended December 31, 1996	Nine Months Ended September 30, 1996	Nine Months Ended September 30, 1997
			(in thousands, except per share data)		
Statement of Operations Data:					
Total net revenues	$ —	$ 1,812	$14,012	$ 8,274	$22,417
Total cost of revenues	—	62	2,185	969	4,609
Gross profit	—	1,750	11,827	7,305	17,808
Operating loss	(545)	(1,595)	(4,016)	(2,475)	(9,759)
Net loss	(545)	(1,501)	(3,789)	(2,315)	(8,575)
Pro forma net loss per share[1]			$ (0.14)		$ (0.32)
Shares used to compute pro forma net loss per share(1)			27,779		28,315

	December 31, 1996	September 30, 1997 Actual	September 30, 1997 As Adjusted[2]
		(in thousands)	
Balance Sheet Data:			
Cash, cash equivalents and short-term investments	$ 19,595	$ 67,648	$108,529
Working capital	16,893	50,762	91,643
Total assets	26,468	84,372	125,253
Redeemable, convertible preferred stock	23,153	49,278	—
Shareholders' equity (deficit)	(3,320)	(8,089)	82,070

1. For an explanation of pro forma net loss per share and the number of shares used to compute pro forma net loss per share, see Note 1 of Notes to Consolidated Financial Statements.

2. As adjusted to give effect to the (i) conversion of all outstanding shares of Series A Common Stock, Series B Common Stock, Series C Common Stock, Series A Preferred Stock, Series B Preferred Stock, Series C Preferred Stock and Series D Preferred Stock into Common Stock and Series E Preferred Stock into Special Common Stock, in each case on closing of the offering; (ii) sale by the Company of the 3,000,000 shares of Common Stock offered hereby at the initial public offering price of $12.50 per share; (iii) application of the estimated net proceeds of the offering; and (iv) issuance of 998,058 shares of Common Stock upon exercise of outstanding warrants at an average exercise price of $6.97 per share (for an aggregate of $6,956,000). Excludes up to 3,709,305 shares of Special Common Stock (representing additional cash and shareholders' equity of up to $50,001,431) issuable on exercise of the Series E Warrant.

Source: RealNetworks Prospectus, November 21, 1997.

TABLE 2

Major Features of RealSystem 5.0.

The RealSystem 5.0 software includes these major features:

- **Animation.** In addition to streaming videos and audio messages, customers could stream animation clips, such as cartoons and computer aided drawing (CAD) sequences. Animation sequences can be synchronized with RealAudio.

- **Ad Insertion and Rotation.** Moving advertisements can appear along with any video or animation sequence. If viewers use their mouse to click on the advertisement, they could be sent to the advertiser's Web site.

- **User Registration and Tracking.** For Web site creators who wish to offer video and audio streams to select viewers only, the server software can detect who is making the request and track usage. This is particularly useful to Web site developers who wish to charge a fee for viewing content.

- **Fast-Modem Optimization.** The 5.0 RealVideo system is designed for optimal use with the fast 56.6 Kbps modems that have appeared on the market.

The RealSystem 5.0-server software is priced from $700 to $21,000 depending on how many streams can be sent at one time. The lower-priced products target customers who want to make audio and video available on their Web site. The more expensive line of professional server products targets ISPs, commercial Web developers and content providers. The firm also offers a free trial version of the server software that streams to sixty viewers at one time. This free software can be downloaded directly from the firm's Web site.

The Internet Market

Core Products The firm's core products include the RealPlayer and RealSystem server software. The RealSystem server software allows developers to display, or "stream," video content to viewers via the Internet. The RealPlayer software enables individuals to view a video clip being "streamed" from a server. The player software can be downloaded for free directly from the firm's Web site. The firm also offers RealPlayer Plus, an enhanced version, for $29. This version offers several easy to use features including memory buttons that are not included in the free version. It can be purchased separately in a retail software store or purchased bundled with products such as modems. It can also be downloaded and paid for directly from RealNetworks.

When using the RealSystem product, customers have the choice of either streaming video "live" or "on-demand." In order to stream video on-demand to Internet end users (viewers), customers or developers must take three steps. First, using the Real-Publisher tool that is included with the RealSystem software they convert the video content into a digital-video file. Special video-editing equipment, not included with the RealSystem software, is needed for this process. Second, this file must be uploaded onto a server computer that end users can reach. When end users link to the server by means of a browser with RealPlayer software (a plug-in) properly installed, the player software will automatically begin streaming the video from the server onto the viewer's computer.[8]

As noted earlier, the most recent product release from RealNetworks is RealSystem 5.0. This version includes capabilities that were not part of earlier products (see Table 2). Since its release in the fourth quarter of 1997, the number of Web pages using streaming media has grown by 50 percent. According to industry experts, about 80 percent of those Web pages now use RealAudio, RealVideo, or RealFlash content.

Despite the growing popularity of video streaming, however, the quality of the video streamed over the Internet does not compare with that of broadcast TV.[9] Although the quality of the streaming video has improved with each new product release, the video images still look jerky when customers use a 28.8 Kbps modem to access such content. But for customers who use higher-bandwidth access lines such as an ISDN connection, the video quality is markedly better.

Other Products and Services   In addition to selling software products, RealNetworks offers a range of consulting services, which include training sessions on setting up and administering the firm's server software and on creating RealAudio and RealVideo content. For large customer installations, the RealNetworks consulting staff often assist in redesigning the customer's information systems to best adapt and incorporate its streaming technology. Although some of the consulting services offered by the firm are free, many are fee based, and charges for such services vary with individual client requirements.

An additional source of revenue for the firm is its content aggregation and hosting business on the Internet. On the firm's Web site, customers can view different types of content (audio or video) assembled on many different Web properties. Although many are managed by RealNetworks, some of them are owned and maintained by others. But all of these sites are hosted by RealNetworks (see Table 3 for a detailed list). By combining different sites, the firm hopes to demonstrate the capability and superior quality of its streaming technology solutions (relative to its competitors), provide exclusive access to interesting multimedia content to Web surfers, and generate revenues from advertisement sales based on the site's ability to attract traffic. Finally, the firm operates a virtual store called RealStore, where customers can purchase products such as content-creation utilities, training videos, modems, and other software products.

Competitive factors in this market include the quality and reliability of software; features provided for creating, editing and adapting multimedia content; the ease of use and interactive user features provided as part of the system; issues pertaining to scalability and cost per user; and compatibility with the user's existing network components and software systems.

Customers   The firm's Internet customers can be broadly segmented into two groups: server and player customers. These two segments can be further divided by customer requirements. For the player segment, there are three basic types of customers: beginner/light users, experienced/light

users, and advanced users. Beginner/light users are interested in a viewing solution that is easy to install and use. These customers are likely to choose the $29 RealPlayer Plus product over the free version distributed by the firm. This is because this Plus version includes a manual that provides installation and setup instructions. The more experienced/light users are likely to choose the free version of the RealPlayer product. Finally, the advanced users may or may not choose the Plus product depending on how much they value the extra features offered by that version relative to competitor products.

The Internet server customers can be divided into five specific segments:

- *Media companies* such as the *Wall Street Journal*, CBS, Fox News, and Warner Brothers, which create content and fund parts of the infrastructure for delivering that content.

- *Commercial Web site developers*, or businesses with Web sites used for revenue generation, such as Yahoo!, Lands' End, and numerous others. Some of these sites generate revenue through transactions, whereas others focus on generating advertising revenues based on the traffic attracted to the sites.

- *Noncommercial Web site developers*, or firms that operate Web sites to distribute information. Examples include government agencies, schools, and private clubs that could potentially include streaming content on their sites.

- *Internet service providers (ISPs)*, or businesses that sell access to the Internet and also frequently offer Web site development and management services to their customers. These types of businesses may wish to offer their customers streaming capabilities and thus purchase streaming server products directly from RealNetworks.

- *Streaming service providers*, or businesses that exist solely to develop and manage sites with streaming content. US-West Enterprise Networking and Digital Nation are examples of "hosting" service businesses.

As of December 1997, the estimated number of Internet users in the world was 40 million. According to NetRatings, a market research firm, by the year

TABLE 3

Content Offerings at RealNetworks

RealNetwork's offerings include the following:

- **Timecast,** a guide to RealAudio and RealVideo content and programming information. The site provides links to more than 2,500 Web sites, including more than 500 radio and television stations where customers can view multimedia content created using RealNetworks' software products.

- **MusicNet,** a preview site featuring more than 1,000 songs from nearly 400 artists. The site is organized in ten categories.

- **Daily Briefing,** the Internet's first personalized, on-demand audio and video newscast. It allows customers to design their own custom streaming media newscasts from more than thirty-five short programs in the areas of news, sports, entertainment, weather, and business/technology, and to receive custom newscasts daily. Daily Briefing providers include NBC News, The Weather Channel, CBS/SportsLine, and Warner Bros.

- **Film.com,** the leading source of professional movie reviews on the Internet, with more than sixty critics. The site provides in-depth information about, and streaming media clips of, movies, including reviews and previews.

- **LiveConcerts.com,** a Web site operated in cooperation with House of Blues. It offers live streamed music concerts, album previews, and archives containing streaming music. It also provides up-to-date concert schedules.

- **Web Active,** a Web site that focuses on giving a voice to progressive political and social opinion, news, and activism on the Internet.

- **Real Planet,** an international guide to RealAudio and RealVideo content. It has ongoing features of events from around the globe.

2000 this number should grow to 200 million. In January 1998, a little more than 21 percent of all U.S. households had access to the Internet. Of these, about a quarter had signed up only in the preceding six months. Hence, the size of the potential consumer market for the firm's products is growing rapidly, but so is the competition.

Competition The market for software and services for the Internet (and intranet) is relatively new, constantly evolving, and becoming intensely competitive. In a broad sense, audio and video streaming technology faces competition from traditional media such as TV and radio broadcasting, and storage devices such as VCRs and CD-ROMs. A major limitation of current streaming technology is its inability to deliver the video quality similar to that of broadcast TV. Consequently, these existing alternatives limit the immediate market potential for streaming products. However, the appeal of

streaming media is its potential to deliver multimedia content directly to users *on demand*.

RealNetworks' direct competitors include companies such as Microsoft, VDOnet, Xing Technology, VivoActive Software, and Vosaic. All these companies offer products and services similar to those of RealNetworks (see Table 4 for third-party reviews of the products). Additionally, a large number of potential competitors such as media companies and browser developers may aggressively pursue this market.

A competitive threat to RealNetworks is the likely integration of streaming software with other widely used applications. Although Microsoft currently ships its Internet Explorer browser software with a RealNetworks' media player, it has announced that future versions of its operating systems will include a built-in streaming-viewer product. For example, a product labeled "Windows Media Player" is expected to be included in the

TABLE 4

Streaming Software Competitors

Company	Streaming Video Product	Server Price	Excerpts from Product Reviews
RealNetworks	RealVideo 5.0	$650 and up	"With RealSystem 5.0, RealNetworks continues the pattern of innovation started in 1994 when the company introduced multimedia to the Internet with RealAudio. RealSystem 5.0 features creative advanced functionality that will soon prove invaluable to high-volume video producers. At the same time, Real, facing competitive pressure from Microsoft's free product, NetShow, is offering free streaming audio and video to lower-volume producers who don't need the special features offered by RealSystem 5.0." (*PC Magazine*, October 10, 1997)
Microsoft	NetShow 2.0	Free	"It's very much a work in progress, offering average-quality video, a server with network-utilization safeguards, and a well-featured but slightly irritating player. It's all free, too." (*PC Magazine*, October 7, 1997)
VDOnet	VDOLive 2.1	$299 and up	"If you're looking for a stable, server-based technology for your intranet, consider VDOnet's VDOLive 2.1. This veteran of the nascent streaming-video market offers high-quality video and a wide array of configuration options, including the ability to limit network use by user number or stream count. Only the higher quality of RealVideo's and VivoActive's video and the better functionality of RealVideo make those products stand out above VDOLive. And if you're on a budget, you'll be pleased with VDOLive's price." (*PC Magazine*, October 7, 1997)
VivoActive Software	VivoActive 2.0	$695	"For users who don't want to worry about server maintenance, VivoActive Software's VivoActive 2.0 is an inexpensive, high-quality, serverless technology that emphasizes ease of use and simplicity over a mass of features. VivoActive 2.0 has no server component, so VivoActive can't protect network utilization by limiting users or video-transfer bandwidth. With a total implementation cost of $695 for an unlimited number of streams, VivoActive is an ideal, inexpensive choice for smaller companies." (*PC Magazine*, October 7, 1997)
Vosaic	MediaSuite 1.04	$150 and up	"Although a promising entry in the streaming-video market and particularly adept at high-motion video, Vosaic MediaSuite 1.04 ultimately can't compete with such products as RealVideo or VDOLive on most intranet applications. Vosaic ranked near the bottom on our talking-head tests, and though the server, player, and encoder are functional, they're not as polished or feature-rich as those of other systems. You don't have to pay for the server, but at $150 per stream, Vosaic's technology is still relatively expensive." (*PC Magazine*, October 7, 1997)
Xing Technology	StreamWorks 3.0	$3000 and up	"StreamWorks 3.0.252 produces high-quality video at high bandwidths but doesn't scale down well, resulting in last-place finishes on our jury tests. The $3,000 price for 50 seats is reasonable, but you probably shouldn't consider StreamWorks unless you transmit the bulk of your videos at bandwidths of 256 Kbps or higher." (*PC Magazine*, October 7, 1997)

forthcoming Windows '98. Furthermore, Microsoft has also announced plans to release a server product for video and audio streaming, known as Site-Server. It intends to provide its player and server products for free. Although some Web browsers already include a "media player" component, industry observers predict that all Web browsers will include a streaming-media viewer in the near future.

RealNetworks' products also compete, to a lesser degree, with nonstreaming audio- and video-delivery technologies such as AVI and QuickTime, and indirectly with delivery systems such as Flash, marketed by Macromedia, a leading producer of animation and multimedia authoring software. Flash is a product used for delivering text-based training content on the Internet.

The Intranet Market

Products   There are two basic products targeted at intranet customers: the server, and player products. Businesses interested in streaming video and audio content can purchase both the server and player as a bundle. Such bundles are available in five configurations. The low-end solution bundle is free, offering the ability to stream 10 video clips at one time. This product is called the Intranet Solution RealServer 5.0. The second bundle, the RealSystem Intranet Solution IS100, allows 100 simultaneous streams and is priced around $5,000. It offers features not available in the free version. The third bundle, the IS600, is priced at $25,000 and supports 600 streams. The two largest bundles, the IS2500 and the IS7500, support 2,500 and 7,500 streams and cost $50,000 and $100,000, respectively. These prices are for annual licensing fees. In addition to the licensing fees, customers have the option to purchase support and upgrade contracts ranging from $2,000 to $40,000, depending on the bundle purchased initially.

Customers   Although there are many types of businesses buying solutions from RealNetworks, the firm targets companies with an intranet. Intranets are private computer networks that use Internet technology to connect employees within the firm. Specifically, RealNetworks focuses on businesses that can afford a $50,000 solution and frequently create multimedia content for company-wide dissemination. Many businesses recognize the benefits of streaming multimedia content to em-

ployees in many different locations nationally and globally. RealNetworks promotes two streaming video applications for such firms:

- *Corporate Communications.* Businesses can use RealVideo and RealAudio to distribute companywide information. For example, Boeing uses RealVideo to provide employees with the latest information on their company, products, and industry. Boeing estimates that it saved nearly $1 million in 1997 on replication and distribution costs of multimedia content alone.

- *Training.* Businesses can use RealVideo to stream training material to employees. Such video training modules can be viewed on demand by employees in different locations. For example, General Electric uses RealVideo to create video-based interactive product training programs for new employees. Such programs are distributed over the firm's intranets.

RealNetworks sells RealSystem Intranet Solution products directly to customers. For large customers, RealNetworks has outside account executives and consultants available to visit the customers on site. These account executives and consultants study the customers' requirements before making a recommendation.

Competition   VDOnet, Xing Technologies, and Microsoft compete with RealNetworks in the intranet market. All three competitors have streaming-video products targeted at businesses with corporate networks. The technologies offered by VDOnet and Xing Technologies are designed specifically for higher-speed networks and thus are more of a threat to RealNetworks in the intranet market than in the Internet market.[10]

APPROACH TO COMPETITION

Glaser's objective is to build RealNetworks into a "leading media streaming company, providing software and services that enable the delivery of a broad range of multimedia content over the Internet and Intranet, thereby facilitating the evolution of the Internet into a mass communications and commerce medium." He and his top-management team plan to achieve this objective by (1) making the "Real" brand name ubiquitous on the Internet and corporate intranets; (2) developing and fostering alliances and partnerships to promote multimedia streaming; (3) shaping industry standards for streaming; and (4) funding innovation in streaming technology to stay ahead of the competition.

Brand Ubiquity

From its inception, RealNetworks has chosen to offer its RealPlayer software to individuals free of charge. RealNetworks has done so to promote the widespread adoption of its client (player) software and to speed up the acceptance of the Internet as a mass-communications medium for streaming multimedia content. Any person with a PC and an Internet connection could download a free copy of the firm's player software to view and listen to video and audio clips. "Our belief has always been that we benefit tremendously by pursuing the most rapid and broadest paths to growing the streaming-media market," Glaser says. "You can expect us to continue to be oriented towards ubiquity."[11] Glaser adds that he "was really struck by the fact that if you look at the long-term survivors against Microsoft—Novell, Oracle, even Intuit . . . they didn't try to make all their money on initial-use client software. They made their money on a mix of things."[12]

Reid offers an additional insight regarding the giveaways:

> The genesis of Rob's decision to give away his client software lay in his decade . . . [of experience at] Microsoft. There he learned that if you make your business beholden to making money from the initial-use client software, the result could be easily that Microsoft would just sort of suck away your core business, either by putting a feature in Windows, or by aggregating a set of things like with Office.[13]

According to Reid, although Glaser's business model appears similar to that pioneered by Netscape, it was in no way inspired by it. Indeed, Glaser settled on this model months before Netscape shipped the Navigator.[14]

To encourage free RealPlayer downloads and RealPlayer Plus sales, RealNetworks advertises heavily on the Internet and also promotes its brand name with many public relations activities. As mentioned earlier, it has managed to attract the attention of many mainstream journalists from newspapers and magazines including the *New York Times*, the *Wall Street Journal*, *USA Today*, *Time*, and *Wired*. Also, the firm's products have garnered many awards at industry trade shows, thus increasing its visibility. It is not surprising, therefore, that Glaser confidently calls the "Real" brand "one of the most widely recognized brands on the Internet."

Alliances and Partnerships

Under Glaser's leadership, RealNetworks has formed numerous partnerships and alliances. It has signed development partnerships with others to ensure that its products work well when integrated with their technologies. When using a streaming media solution, server customers in particular are mixing this technology with hardware and software products bought from others. For example, the firm partnered with Microsoft to ensure that the RealPlayer and RealSystem products work in Windows 95 and Windows NT environments. RealNetworks has also partnered with Sun Microsystems, the makers of the Solaris operating systems to ensure that its products would operate smoothly in a Unix environment. The firm also makes its products compatible with machines that use the Macintosh operating system. Additionally, the firm has agreements with Macromedia, the largest provider of animation-editing software, to transmit animated material over the Internet.

RealNetworks also partners with technology companies to create combined services. In August of 1997, for example, it signed a joint-venture agreement with MCI and launched the *Real Broadcast Network*. This pilot service, created by combining the RealSystem technology with MCI's worldwide Internet network infrastructure, offers broadcasting services for content developers to deliver tens of thousands of video streams simultaneously on the Internet. MCI, which owns a significant portion of the Internet infrastructure (or backbone), has upgraded its infrastructure to facilitate rapid streaming. This was done by strategically placing RealNetworks splitter and multicast technology throughout its network. Such devices eliminate bottlenecks by allowing computer users to access a video/audio feed from the closest of MCI's nine U.S. locations. RealNetworks and MCI are targeting media companies and *Fortune* 1000 companies that might use this service for internal employee training or to post new product announcements on the Web. ABC News' on-line service, for example, used the service to broadcast audio and video clips accompanying a text story of the 1997 UPS strike. Other customers include Atlantic Records, ESPN, and Home & Garden Television.[15] The service costs up to $8,500 a month. The cost is much higher for continuous broadcasting.

Shaping Evolving Industry Standards

The firm's efforts have also focused on shaping industry standards regarding streaming technology and protocols. An aspect of the firm's rapidly evolving marketplace is the trend toward open standards and protocols for streaming software. Until recently, only users with a RealNetworks viewer could watch video and audio clips streamed from the firm's server products. RealNetworks has also joined other important industry players (for example, Microsoft and Sun Microsystems) in their efforts to set protocol, transmission, and compression standards. RealNetworks and Microsoft, for instance, have taken special pains to define the industry standards for streaming products. Their goal is to ensure that any server software can send streams (audio and video) to any player. Emphasizing the need for common standards, Microsoft's soon-to-be-released Windows Media Player will be able to play streams from RealNetworks' server software. At that time, the NetShow, a Microsoft server product, will play video streaming from RealNetworks' server products. Similarly, RealPlayers could play video streaming from Microsoft's Net-Show server.

On July 21, 1997, Microsoft acquired a 10 percent nonvoting minority stake in RealNetworks for $30 million. However, Microsoft's new NetShow product is a direct competitor to RealVideo, Real-Networks' video-streaming software. The two companies declared that the partnership was necessary if an industry standard was going to be formed. According to Glaser,

> We see a real pathway forward to turn the Internet into a mass medium. We have worked successfully with Microsoft in the past, and this agreement brings our relationship to a new level. The ultimate goal is for Microsoft's and Progressive's streaming formats to become fully compatible, allowing all on-line audio and video

broadcasts to be interpreted by both companies' players.

As Rich Tong, a Microsoft vice president points out: "The user only wants it to work. . . . So it is good business to work with RealNetworks to set standards for compatibility and expand the market for all of us."[16]

Several of the streaming technologies that Real-Networks has developed have been submitted to Internet standards committees for review. Although none of these standards have been fully accepted by the players in the industry so far, many are highly favored.[17] The firm aggressively pursues the acceptance of these standards in order to gain more industry recognition as well as more market share. However, because of RealNetworks' 80 percent market share, its approach to streaming has become the de facto industry standard.

Technological Innovation

Whenever a competitor releases a new product, the industry observers quickly rush to compare it with those of RealNetworks. Therefore, to stay ahead of competition, the firm must make frequent product upgrades and improvements. It devotes a substantial portion of its resources to developing new products and product features, expanding and improving its fundamental streaming technology, and strengthening its technological expertise. For example, during the fiscal year that ended December 31, 1996, and the six months that ended June 30, 1997, RealNetworks spent 34 percent and 41 percent of its total net revenues on research and development activities. As of August 1997, it had 90 employees, or 32 percent of its work force, engaged in research and development activities. RealNetworks' executives say that the firm must hire additional skilled software engineers to further its research and development efforts. Given its small size, such efforts are increasingly straining the firm's resources and capabilities.

Part of RealNetworks' R&D strategy is to hire the brightest, most experienced developers and executives in the world (see Appendix A for list of executives hired to assist Glaser in managing RealNetworks). Glaser sees this strategy as essential, for, he says, "In an industry where intellectual capital is the primary asset of the firm, the people you hire can make or break the firm. Developers must be constantly nurtured and trained in order to turn out new technology at the speed of light."

CHALLENGES IN GOING FORWARD

As the top management of RealNetworks looks to the future, it confronts several new challenges.

Bandwidth Constraints

The growth of the streaming-video market is hampered by bandwidth constraints of the Internet and World Wide Web. Most home users access the WWW with 28.8 kbps or slower modems. At these low-transmission speeds, users cannot play video without distortion. However, industry experts predict that this situation is likely to change as Internet service providers and telecommunications firms such as MCI and AT&T upgrade their infrastructure to provide customers with technologies that provide greater bandwidth to WWW surfers. Also, the increasing use of technologies such as ISDN telephone lines, cable modems, and direct-broadcast satellite services may help alleviate the current bandwidth constraints.

More troubling, however, is the fact that a majority of Web surfers are unwilling to pay for content (print, video or audio) offered on the Internet. Although a few exceptions such as the *Wall Street Journal Interactive* exist, most of the content providers have been unable to convert traffic on their Web sites into paying members.

Balancing Competition and Cooperation

Despite its large market share, RealNetworks still faces significant threats from Microsoft and others. When Microsoft acquired a minority stake in RealNetworks, a surprising aspect of this agreement was that Microsoft also licensed the RealAudio and RealVideo 4.0 programming code for an additional $30 million (see Appendix B for details of this agreement). Such a close relationship between RealNetworks and Microsoft has left many industry analysts wondering whether the firm might end up in the situation of trying to make money on technology that Microsoft gives away for free. Glaser offered this view of the situation:

> If we don't execute well, it could turn out to be a bad deal. . . . But face it—if we don't execute well, we would have been in just as much trouble without the deal. And if we do execute—if we keep driving our standards forward independently and remain at the forefront of the market and the technology—it'll turn out to be an amazing deal. There are pitfalls. But if you want a sure thing, you should take a job at the post office, right?[18]

On August 5, 1997, just fifteen days after the Microsoft-RealNetworks partnership announcement, Microsoft purchased VXtreme, one of RealNetworks' biggest competitors on the Internet. Microsoft plans to use the acquired technology to further develop its products in this segment. For example, Microsoft is expected to release NetShow, its streaming server product later this year. Earlier in November of 1997, Microsoft had announced that it would include its streaming server software for free with all Microsoft NT server product.

The Department of Justice, along with several industry analysts, has expressed concerns about such tactics. It has been suggested that Microsoft is effectively trying to drive its streaming competitors out of the server business. Alan Weiner, an analyst with Dataquest, states that "Microsoft is taking dead aim at RealNetworks in terms of the dominance of the streaming video market. As the pipes get fatter, streaming media servers will be the backbone to serve all kinds of content in the future. It's important to establish dominance now."[19] To many analysts it is unclear whether RealNetworks can compete successfully with Microsoft's free and heavily marketed NetShow product. However, according to a *Wall Street Journal* report in early 1998, Microsoft "may decide to charge for the latest version of NetShow coming out this year, which would be good for RealNetworks. Microsoft will also continue to bundle RealNetworks' player software with Microsoft browser, which is good for RealNetworks. And the day after RealNetworks' Sun deal, Microsoft announced an agreement with RealNetworks' server software, also good for RealNetworks."[20]

Continuing to Innovate

It is in this uncertain environment that RealNetworks has begun planning yet another upgrade of its player and server software. The firm hopes that by incorporating new capabilities, such as animation, ad insertion, and pay-per-view features, it can maintain its dominant position for streaming software. However, such product enhancements cost money, which leads to the firm's most important challenge: improving its profitability to ensure acceptable financial returns for its new stockholders.

Despite rapid growth, RealNetworks remains unprofitable. The firm posted a $12 million deficit for 1997 and is unlikely to show a profit until the end of 1999."[21] With continuous losses, it is unclear whether the firm can continue to fund the future product developments. Compounding this issue is the ever-increasing cost of developing new upgrades to its existing software. Furthermore, finding sophisticated talent in an increasingly tight labor market is expensive.

As the novelty of the Internet wears off, customers may start demanding better-quality video streaming. The cost of funding new product developments to further advance streaming technology and add features is becoming expensive. In such an environment, management must decide whether a focus on winning market share can continue to be a viable strategy. Some at RealNetworks concede that the firm may have to look for partners to undertake joint-product development efforts in the future.

In light of these uncertainties facing the firm, Rob Glaser and his top-management team have to decide whether a shift in strategy is necessary.

APPENDIX A: REALNETWORKS' TOP-MANAGEMENT TEAM

Rob Glaser, chairman and CEO, is the founder of RealNetworks (Nasdaq: RNWK), the leader in streaming media products and services for the Internet. Since 1995, RealNetworks has played a pioneering and leadership role in media delivery over the Internet through its RealAudio, RealVideo, RealPlayer, and RealSystem products. Glaser is a member of several nonprofit boards and committees, including, most recently, his appointment by President Clinton to the Advisory Committee on Public Interest Obligations of Digital Television Broadcasters. Before founding RealNetworks, Glaser spent ten years at Microsoft, most recently attaining the position of vice president of multimedia and consumer systems and bringing to market successful pioneering products in the areas of multimedia, computer networking, and desktop applications.

Bruce Jacobsen has served as president and chief operating officer since February 1996 and as a director since August 1997. From April 1995 to February 1996, he was chief operating officer of Dreamworks Interactive, a joint venture between Microsoft and Dreamworks SKG, a partnership among Steven Spielberg, Jeffery Katzenberg and David Geffen. From August 1986 to April 1995, Jacobsen was employed at Microsoft in a number of capacities, including general manager of the Kids/Games business unit. He graduated summa cum laude with honors from Yale University and holds an M.B.A. from Stanford University.

Mark Klebanoff has served as chief financial officer since June 1996. From May 1992 to June 1996, he was vice president of finance and operations of Industrial Systems, a client/server process information management software vendor, which merged with Aspen Technology in 1995. From 1989 to 1992, Klebanoff worked in a number of general management capacities for the Japanese trading company Itochu. He has a B.A. from Yale University and a master's degree from the Yale School of Management.

Len Jordan has served as senior vice president, media systems since January 1997. From November 1993 to November 1996, he worked in a number of capacities at Creative Multimedia, a developer and publisher of CD-ROM/Internet products, and became its president. From September 1989 to November 1993, Jordan was employed at Central Point Software, a utility software publisher. Jordan graduated magna cum laude from Eccles School of Business at the University of Utah with B.S. degrees in finance and economics.

Phillip Barrett has served as senior vice president, media systems, since January 1997, and from November 1994 to January 1997, had been vice president, software development. From March 1986 to October 1994, Barrett was a development group manager at Microsoft, where he led development efforts for Windows 386, Windows 3.0, and Windows 3.1. He has an A.B. in mathematics from Rutgers University and an M.S. in computer sciences from the University of Wisconsin, Madison.

Maria Cantwell has served as senior vice president, consumer and e-commerce, since July 1997. From April 1995 to July 1997, she served as vice president, marketing of the company. From February 1995 to April 1995, Cantwell was a consultant to the company. Before that, she was a member of the 103rd Congress. She has a B.A. in public administration from Miami University.

James Higa has served as vice president, Asia/ROW, since September 1996. From January

1989 to August 1996, he was the director for Asia/Pacific for NeXT Software. From 1986 to 1989, Higa served as director of product marketing at Apple Japan. He has a B.A. in political science from Stanford University.

John Atcheson has served as vice president, media publishing, since January 1997. From March 1990 to May 1996, he was president and chief executive officer of MNI Interactive, a developer and distributor of consumer interactive services. Atcheson has a B.A. from Brown University and an M.B.A. from the Stanford Graduate School of Business.

Kelly Jo MacArthur has served as vice president and general counsel since October 1996. From January 1995 to March 1996, she was general counsel and director of business affairs for Compton's NewMedia, which was acquired by Learning Co. in 1996. From July 1989 to December 1994, MacArthur was an attorney at Sidley & Austin. She graduated summa cum laude from the University of Illinois at Champaign-Urbana and has a J.D. from Harvard Law School.

Erik Moris has served as vice president, marketing, since August 1997 and from April 1997 until then had been product manager. From September 1996 to April 1997, Moris was a consultant to the company. From May 1995 to August 1996, he was employed at Microsoft, where he managed advertising for the Windows 95 launch and was group manager for the Internet Platform and Tools Division. From 1985 to 1994, Moris was a senior vice president at McCann-Erickson Advertising. He has a B.A. in communications and business from Western Washington University.

Jeff Lehman has served as vice president, advertising sales, since October 1997. From September 1985 to September 1997, he was employed by Ziff-Davis/Softbank in a number of publishing positions, including those of vice president and director. He graduated cum laude from the University of Central Florida with a B.S.B.A. and an M.B.A. with honors.

Philip Rosedale has served as vice president, media systems, since October 1997. From February 1996 to October 1997, he had been the firm's general manager, software development. From June 1986 to February 1996, Rosedale was chief executive officer of Automated Management Systems, a developer and marketer of software applications, which he had founded. Rosedale graduated cum laude from the University of California, San Diego, with a B.S. in physics.

APPENDIX B: DETAILS OF REALNETWORKS' RELATIONSHIP AGREEMENT WITH MICROSOFT

In June 1997, RealNetworks entered into a strategic agreement with Microsoft, according to which RealNetworks granted Microsoft a nonexclusive license to substantial elements of the source code of the firm's RealAudio/RealVideo Version 4.0 technology, including its basic RealPlayer and elements of its EasyStart Server products, and related trademarks.

Under the agreement, Microsoft may sublicense its rights to the RealAudio and RealVideo Version 4.0 technology to third parties under certain circumstances. The agreement also provides for substantial refunds to Microsoft under prescribed circumstances that are solely within the firm's control. The amount of these refunds diminishes over time. The firm may not assign its obligations under the agreement without Microsoft's consent. Microsoft is obligated to distribute the firm's RealPlayer Version 4.0 for a defined term as long as the firm's player supports certain Microsoft architectures.

RealNetworks also agreed to work with Microsoft and several other companies to author and promote ASF as a standard file format for streaming media. The agreement also requires the firm to provide Microsoft with engineering consultation services, certain error corrections, and certain technical support over a defined term.

In connection with the agreement, Microsoft also purchased a minority interest in the firm. Microsoft currently offers its own streaming media product, NetShow. Additionally, Microsoft recently acquired VXtreme, a direct competitor of the firm in the market for streaming media software. Microsoft also owns a minority interest in VDOnet, a direct competitor of the firm in the market for streaming video software.

Endnotes

1. Streaming technology enables the transmission and playback of continuous "streams" of multimedia content, such as audio and video, over the Internet and intranets and represents a significant advancement over earlier technologies.
2. R. Reid, *Architects of the Web* (New York: Wiley, 19), p. 77.
3. "A Web Pioneer Does a Delicate Dance with Microsoft," *Wall Street Journal*, February 12, 1998.
4. Reid, *Architects*, p. 79.

5. R. Reid, "Real Revolution," *Wired* (October 1997).
6. When the firm releases a new product, it releases both the server and player versions simultaneously. For example, the most recent product released by the firm is the RealSystem 5.0. Customers can acquire either the server or the player version of the new software. The new RealVideo servers are always backward compatible with older server products and can stream audio only, or video *and* audio content.
7. "RealSystem 5.0 Experiences Rapid Market Adaptation," RealNetworks press release, December 1997.
8. The approach used for streaming media live is similar. The difference between live streaming and on-demand streaming is that the content is converted to streaming format as it is being created. For example, a customer could stream a live video of a conference speaker. To view the speech, a person would have to be at his or her computer at the time of the actual presentation. Live streaming media content can be recorded for on-demand viewing at a later time.
9. Television video (using NTSC standards) has a basic rate of roughly 100 megabits per second. Encoding this signal at 100 Kbs implies a compression ratio of 1000:1. By comparison, audio is typically compressed at a rate of roughly 15:1. Clearly, the process of video compression is challenging. Solutions typically involve dramatically reducing (subsampling) the size and frame rate of the images. However, such tactics induce visual artifacts in the reconstructed images. Artifacts are noticeable differences between the original images and the encoded images that can be identified and characterized.
10. One major difference between intranet and Internet customers is the speed of transmission. The transmission between an intranet server and a player is usually much faster. This is because businesses have network connections for their employees' computers that are faster than the modems typically used by home computer users. Faster transmission of data means that video clips are less distorted.
11. G. Welz and J. Carl, "Progressive Networks' CEO Talks About RealVideo," *Web Week*, March 17, 1997.
12. Reid, *Architects,* p. 80.
13. R. Reid, *Architects*, p. 79.
14. R. Reid, "Real Revolution."
15. "MCI and Progressive Team Up; Microsoft to Acquire VXtreme," *Wall Street Journal Interactive Edition*, August 10, 1997.
16. *Wall Street Journal*, February 12, 1998.
17. The firm has adopted RTSP (Real Transport streaming protocol), a proposed protocol for standardizing the control and delivery of streaming media over the Internet. The firm claims that RTSP is a unified standard for a broad range of media data types and is intended to promote a greater level of interoperability among various streaming media solutions. RTSP is built on top of a number of other Internet standard protocols such as HTTP, TCP/IP, and Real Transport protocol, and is complementary with ASF, a file format for streaming media that does not specify a method of client-server interaction. RTSP provides the client-server specification necessary to stream ASF and other file types. According to RealNetworks, its proposed RTSP was submitted to the IETF in October 1996 and this protocol was supported by more than forty companies.
18. R. Reid, "Real Revolution," *Wired* (October 1997), on-line version.
19. A. Orr, "Microsoft, Sun ride down stream," *ZDNet News Channel On-line*, January 26, 1998.
20. *Wall Street Journal*, February 12, 1998.
21. "RealNetworks Beats Estimates, but Investors Send Stock Lower," *Wall Street Journal*, January 30, 1998.

CASE 12

Microsoft's Windows CE: Digital Devices and the Next Computing Paradigm

This case was prepared by Charles W. L. Hill of the University of Washington.

INTRODUCTION

"Whisper it quietly, the personal computer—the machine of the 1990s—will be entering its twilight years by the beginning of the new millennium."[1] So claimed the influential newsmagazine, the *Economist*, in a recent article. Nor is the *Economist* alone in making this prediction. IDC, a forecaster of computing trends, recently issued a report entitled "The end of the PC-centric era." Similarly, Forrester Research, a consulting firm that focuses on high-technology businesses, has argued that the PC era may be "winding down." What these various visions of the future are depicting is a paradigm shift of potentially enormous dimensions. Ground zero of this shift is a concept known as ubiquitous computing.

Credit to coining the concept of ubiquitous computing is normally given to Mark Weiser, chief technologist at Xerox's Palo Alto research center.[2] Weiser argues that we are about to enter the third era in the evolution of computing.[3] The first era was the mainframe era. In this era, computers were rare and expensive, and we serviced them. The second era, in which we are still deeply immersed, is the personal computing era. The PC is a relatively inexpensive and commonplace general-purpose appliance. Our relationship to the personal computer is, well, personal. PCs are increasingly indispensable in our lives. They are also, according to Weiser (and a host of other critics) unwieldy, noisy, unreliable, and unfriendly machines that lack the elegance, simplicity, and performance of specialized appli-

ances. Some go as far as to argue that we are psychologically addicted to our PCs, and because of this, we put up with inefficiencies and inelegance that would not be tolerated in any other product.[4] Despite the limitations of the PC, Weiser argues that this second wave of computing will grow larger still, before it has its energy sapped on the shores of the third era of computing.

The third era, according to Weiser, will be the era of ubiquitous computing. This era will be characterized by a profusion of inexpensive computers that we will interact with on an almost constant basis. Computers, in the form of special-purpose embedded processors, can already be found in watches, ovens, cars, wallets, and cell phones. Inevitably, these computers will become more pervasive, will talk to one another, and will form the invisible computational infrastructure of our lives. So ultimately, says Weiser, "If your refrigerator watches you take the milk carton in and out every day, and if your refrigerator could talk to your wallet, then when you went to the store the wallet could tell the milk cartons that you need milk. And the milk cartons could then say to you, 'Hey buy me, you're out of milk.' "[5]

Although Weiser believes that his vision is still six to ten years off, the harbingers of the third era of computing are already with us. Small digital devices are proliferating, from palm devices and PC companions to smart phones, set-top boxes, digital cameras, and auto PCs. By using the communications protocols of the World Wide Web, these intelligent devices are being empowered with the ability to talk to each other across high-speed wireline and wireless networks.[6] In 1997, 96 percent of the devices hooked into the Internet were PCs, but according to recent predications by IDC, within four years close to half of the total will be non-PC devices, including palm tops, set-top boxes, cell phones, and video game terminals. By 2002, IDC estimates that non-PC devices with Web capability will total 41 million units, up from 3.6 million in 1998.[7]

Where will Microsoft be in the era of ubiquitous computing? If some of the company's competitors have their way, nowhere to be seen. One vision of the future of computing depicts a world in which digital devices based on non-Microsoft operating systems "grow up" to replace the PC. These devices will run Java applications, be interconnected using Jini-networks built around Sun servers, access data from Oracle databases, and receive their service from AOL.

Leading Microsoft's charge against this potential reality is the latest component of the company's embrace-and-extend strategy, Windows CE. CE is Microsoft's operating system for digital devices. However, in attempting to get Windows CE established as the de facto standard for digital devices, Microsoft faces significant challenges. To drive forward adoptions, it must get the product attributes and the strategy right. It must out-maneuver competitors who are themselves becoming increasingly sophisticated with regard to standard building strategies. And it must validate the implicit assumption that the same basic business model that worked so spectacularly for PCs, also applies to the more fragmented world of digital devices.

DIGITAL DEVICES

The term *digital devices* refers to a bewildering array of products that perform a wide variety of applications. For purposes of taxonomy, they can be segmented into four main groups: hand-held devices, smart phones, vertical application devices, and other devices (see Table 1). This segmentation is very rough since there is a significant degree of blurring across boundaries.

Hand-held Devices

Hand-held devices are normally defined to include palm-sized devices—for example, 3Com's popular PalmPilot and Palm III personal information organizers; "Clamshell" PC companions such as Hewlett-Packard's 660LX; and larger "Mondo" PC companions that use Microsoft's "Jupiter" Windows CE 2.11 operating system such as HP's Jornada 820. These devices range in price from $300 to $1,000. The initial growth in demand for such devices was driven by the spectacular success of the PalmPilot. Within eighteen months of its launch in April 1996, more than 1 million PalmPilots were shipped, making for a faster product ramp-up than occurred with the first cell phones and pagers. By late 1998, more than 2 million units had been sold.

Hand-helds are used for personal information management (scheduling, address books, and so forth), note taking, E-mail, word processing, and expense tracking. According to Sherwood Research, the five most popular hand-held applications of "mobile professionals" who used both a hand-held and a notebook PC are personal information management (87 percent), note taking (42 percent), E-mail (31 percent), word processing (28 percent), and expense tracking (23 percent).[8]

Estimates from Sherwood Research of the market segmentation and near term growth prospects in the *United States* for certain hand-held devices are given in Table 2.[9]

Another market research group, IDC, expects the total *worldwide* hand-held companion market

TABLE 1

A Simple Taxonomy of Digital Devices

Hand-helds	Smart Phones	Vertical Application Devices	Other Devices
Palm devices		Pen tablet	Set-top Boxes
PC companions		Pen notepad	Auto PCs
PDAs		Keypad hand-held	Game terminal
			Digital cameras
			Digital books
			Point of sale terminals

TABLE 2

Growth Forecasts for Hand-held Devices

	1998	1999	2000
Palm	1,433,000	2,054,000	2,724,000
Clamshell	523,000	628,000	756,000
Mondo (Jupiter)	54,000	295,000	869,000
Total	2,010,000	2,977,000	4,349,000

to grow from 3.1 million units in 1997, to 13.1 million units in 2001, a compound annual growth rate of around 44 percent.[10] IDC notes, however, that customer confusion over the price and benefits of hand-held devices may inhibit adoption of the technology. Moreover, the multiplicity of choices with regard to form factors and operating systems may further confuse consumers and slow down adoption rates. Competition from low-priced/low-weight notebooks may also cut into growth in the hand-held device market.

Smart Phones

Smart phones represent a fusion of the attributes of digital cell phones and hand-held devices. Smart phones can handle data as well as voice traffic. They function both as a cell phone and as a personal digital assistant, thereby limiting the number of devices that people have to carry. The Nokia 9110 Communicator—which has a flip-up screen and is capable of composing and sending faxes, E-mail and Web browsing—is at the leading edge of smart phone technology.

According to Dataquest, global sales of mobile phones will rise from 100 million in 1997 to around 360 million in 2002. Of these, Dataquest estimates that 15 to 20 percent will be smart phones. A more conservative view of likely diffusion of smart phone technology comes from IDC. IDC believes that adoption of smart phone technology will take off first in the European and Japanese markets, primarily because they have a critical complement in place: a universal wireless communications infrastructure (for example, GSM in Europe).[11] Alternatively, the lack of a universal

wireless standard in the United States will slow down adoption rates.

IDC believes that smart phone technology is still in the early adopter growth phase. Growth is being held back by high price and lack of customer education. Consumers are confused as to the difference between smart phones and advanced digital cell phones. IDC estimates that 0.437 million smart phones were shipped worldwide in 1997. The research group forecasts that the market will expand to 5.898 million units by 2001 as demand for the device begins to take off. The European Union and Japan are forecasted to account for 1.65 million units and 1.32 million units, respectively, while the United States will account for 0.899 million units.[12]

Vertical Application Devices

Vertical application devices (VADs) are hand-held pen- or keypad-based devices used to gather data from the field or in other mobile situations and transmit it to a central point. Familiar examples include the keypad-based handsets used by FedEx delivery and pickup drivers to collect tracking data for packages. Other uses of VADs include collecting inventory information from a warehouse, and bedside accessing of a patient's records in a hospital setting.

IDC estimates that the VAD market amounted to 2 million units in 1998 and forecasts that it will grow to 3.5 million by 2001.[13] IDC believes that small pen-based notepads using a Windows CE operating system will present themselves as inexpensive alternatives to traditional devices and start to gain share. Connectivity with corporate data systems that run on Windows NT servers may facilitate this trend.

Other Devices

The "other device" category represents a diverse grab bag of digital devices including set-top boxes, auto PCs, and game terminals.

Set-Top Boxes Set-top boxes add functionality to cable service (for instance, movies on demand or additional information linked to programming). They also bring Web browsing capabilities to the TV, and promise to transform TVs into interactive communication devices (for example, E-mail, home shopping). The potential market for set-top boxes is huge. There are 250 million TV sets in the United States alone ready for upgrade. Then again, sales of *WebTV* have been slow, and it is unclear at this point how interested consumers are in using the TV to access the Web.

In the United States, the Telecom Act of 1996 mandated that by July 1, 2000, consumer premise equipment (such as set-top boxes) must be available to consumers from sources other than their cable operator or the vendor from whom the service is obtained. In other words, the FCC has ruled that all set-top boxes must be made available for retail sale. The ruling requires manufacturers to build set-top boxes based on standards that allow the devices to connect with any number of headends (servers) and be compatible with any cable system. This implies that all new set-top boxes must be interoperable. Device manufacturers and cable operators alike are moving aggressively in order to deliver affordable devices that act like a cable converter box, cable modem, and network computer all rolled into one.

A number of companies are developing or already marketing set-top box operating systems. Microsoft is in the market with its Windows CE product. Others include Sun (Java), Apple, Oracle, Sony, and Psion, which is preparing to license its EPOC operating system to set-top box device manufacturers and cable operators.[14]

AutoPCs   In December 1998, Clarion started to sell its AutoPC, an in-dashboard personal computer and audio system with voice control.[15] The AutoPC utilizes a Windows CE operating system. It follows voice commands and has the capability to talk back, reading E-mail that can be received via a special radio broadcast. It can also use its address book to dial an in-car cell phone. The basic system retails for about $1,300 and fits into the space of a traditional car radio. The voice recognition software homes in on syllables rather than complete words and responds only to a limited range of commands, which improves accuracy.

For consumers, the promised benefits of a voice-controlled auto PC are convenience and safety. Instead of having to fumble to dial an in-car cell phone, figure out how to turn down the air conditioner, or change the track on a CD, the words "phone dial 555–1212," "temperature 70 degrees," or "play disk two, track three" should suffice.

Ford will begin to incorporate the AutoPC in its top of the line Jaguar car range in Spring 1999. Although it will probably be several years before the technology penetrates the mass market, the potential market is clearly immense. There are 15 million automobiles sold each year in the United States alone, and 50 million worldwide.

Game Terminals   As of late 1998, the video game terminal market was dominated by hardware from Sony and Nintendo. There are now more than 20 million Sony PlayStations and Nintendo 64 consoles in U.S. homes and more than 50 million worldwide.[16] Sony reportedly has 70 percent of the market and Nintendo 30 percent.[17] If the history of the industry is any guide, however, there could be a sea change in market share when the next generation of more powerful game machines debuts.

The first of the next generation machines, Sega's Dreamcast, was introduced in Japan in November 1998 and was scheduled for U.S. introduction in late 1999. This was to be followed by a new Sony machine in 2000, and the next generation Nintendo machine in 2001. All three of these machines are expected to come with Internet capability, allowing for multiplayer games over the Web.

Sega led the video game industry with its 16-bit system Sega Genesis in the early 1990s. However, Sega disappeared almost completely from the market when the 32-bit Sega Saturn failed to gain consumer acceptance in the face of strong competition from Sony. Sega hopes that the Dreamcast will reverse its humiliation. The new machine is based on a 128-bit processor, boasts leading-edge 3D graphics capabilities, comes equipped with Internet capability, and utilizes a version of Microsoft's Windows CE operating system.

Sega's decision to go with CE was based on a calculation that the choice will make it easier for Sega to win back game developers, who now focus on developing games for the Sony and Nintendo systems or for the PC game market. Because of the commonalities between Windows and Windows CE, developers who write games for the PC based on Windows operating system protocols will have an easier time adapting their games to Sega's Windows CE system than to a proprietary operating system.

Additional Products   Set-top boxes, auto PCs, and game terminals represent just three examples of the wide range of intelligent devices that will increasingly populate our world. Other examples include digital cameras, Web phones, digital books, car navigation systems, DVD players, digital wallets, home thermostats that can be monitored and adjusted from remote locations, and perhaps one day, even Weiser's intelligent refrigerator. Indeed, it is in the nature of technological progress that many of the future applications of embedded microprocessors cannot yet be foreseen. When these unforeseen applications do emerge, however, the question remains, "What operating system will they use?"

MICROSOFT'S STRATEGY: WINDOWS CE

At the forefront of Microsoft's strategy for ubiquitous computing is an attempt to extend its Windows franchise into the world of digital devices. Leading the charge is the Windows CE 2.0 operating system, which the company is trying to license to as many device manufacturers as possible. The goal is to get CE established as the de facto standard for digital devices. In theory, standardization on a single operating system, by expanding the market for applications written to that operating system, lowers the risk and increases the potential payoff associated with developing applications, thereby increasing the supply of applications. Standardization, in other word, sets up a self-reinforcing virtuous cycle, in which lower development risk leads to increased supply of applications, which increases the demand for digital devices and drives further expansions of supply and demand. By such a process, standardization can help to create the market.

So far, Microsoft has registered some significant wins for CE. Versions of Windows CE 2.0 have been licensed to manufacturers of hand-held PCs and palm PCs such as Hewlett-Packard, Sharp, NEC, Casio, and Philips. CE has been licensed to TCI for use in its set-top boxes, to Samsung for use in smart phones, to Clarion as the OS for its AutoPC, and to Sega for its Dreamcast video game player. Moreover, Windows CE seems likely to move into new devices. Hewlett-Packard is studying CE to see if it can be used in HP printers. Atlanta based Radiant Systems plans to sell Windows CE point-of-sale devices to fast-food restaurants (customers press buttons on a screen to select the food and drinks they want). Intermec, a leader in bar code technology, is developing a Windows CE vertical application device for data collection that is designed for use in inventory-tracking applications.[18] Microsoft has also entered into a joint venture with Qualcomm to develop wireless devices and services based on CE and Qualcomm's CDMA digital cellular technology.[19]

Windows CE 2.0 runs on a number of central processing units, including the MIPS R3000 and R4000, Motorola PowerPC, Hitachi SH3, Intel X86, and ARM chips. CE resides in read-only memory chips, not random access memory, which reduces the likelihood of a crash. As would be expected for a digital device operating system, CE requires relatively little memory and can be stored in 4.0 megabytes of ROM.

Windows CE is modular and can be customized to suit needs of customers, thereby enabling CE to function as the operating system on a wide variety of divergent devices. Modularity means that device manufacturers can pick the elements of CE that they need to use. A manufacturer can choose among 120 options, mixing and matching features as needed. For example, if the device has no display, there is no need for the display code. Thus, for embedded-type applications without a display, a customer might choose to use just the kernel, which takes up less space than the complete operating system. Or a manufacturer could use the kernel and one or more Windows CE components for applications such as set-top boxes. The next version of CE, code-named Cedar, will include modular components that will enable OEMs to create a true Windows CE–based cellular phone OS.[20]

Windows CE communicates effortlessly with standard Microsoft applications, making data sharing and synchronization with desktop PCs easy. Hand-held PCs have pocket versions of Microsoft's Office suite programs, which can be quickly swapped with a PC, as well as a pocket version of Internet Explorer and a pocket Outlook. Synchronization with a desktop computer or server is accomplished using Windows CE Services 2.1, which is included with each Windows CE hand-held product and runs only on Windows 95/98 or NT systems.

An attraction of CE is that developers can use Microsoft Windows development tools and Win 32 APIs to write applications. This leverages the skill base of the large Windows development community. It is estimated that some 5 million developers around the world are currently writing software for Windows 95 and NT, so in theory there is a huge reservoir of talent out there ready to write software for Windows CE, and programs for other systems can be quickly modified for CE.[21]

On October 8, 1998, Microsoft introduced Windows CE 2.11 Hand-held PC Professional Edition. This version of CE is aimed at larger-form-factor PC companion hardware, known as the H/PC Pro platform (formally known as Jupiter). The format has a larger keyboard and LCD screen than other hand-held PCs. These devices are targeted at corporate users who are mobile and need "Windows lite" functionality. The device is a PC companion, however, and not a PC, in that it lacks the functionality of desktops, such as support for off-the-shelf Windows applications, CD-ROM drives, and so forth. Twelve vendors have announced that they are supporting the H/PC Pro platform. IDC believes that the product suffers from poor market positioning.[22] There is some concern that ultimately this platform will cannibalize low-end notebook sales.[23]

A clear advantage of Windows CE is that it leverages Microsoft's existing brand recognition amongst end users. Adopters of hand-held devices, such as PC companions and palm PCs, find it intuitively appealing to use an interface that has so many commonalities with the familiar desktop environment. This preference for the familiar, and for a device that is easy to synchronize with desktop PCs, might be expected to produce a presumption in favor of Windows CE. This presumption seemed to be confirmed in a recent IDC market survey, which asked potential and actual corporate adopters what operating system should run on a hand-held device they selected. The results, which are given in Table 3, suggest that Windows CE has significant appeal.

While the worldwide market for digital devices running Windows CE could clearly be immense—within a few years outnumbering by a factor of five to ten the number of PCs sold per year—the licensing revenue per unit will probably be significantly less than that derived from a PC.[25] Still, it is important to understand that the diffusion of Windows CE could drive demand for Windows NT data bases, electronic commerce, and transaction servers, thereby enabling Microsoft to gain substantial indirect revenue contributions from CE.

To this end, Microsoft is positioning Windows CE as part of a total solution strategy. The company is creating bundles that allow service providers to easily link Windows CE devices with NT-based services. As an example, Microsoft is reportedly working with CableData to sell NT-based billing and customer service products that let cable customers with Windows CE set-top boxes order movies or check account balances via their remote control units.[26] Thus, the diffusion of CE will help Microsoft sell complementary products such as NT, on which it earns larger margins.

DOUBTS ABOUT CE

Despite Microsoft's dominance in the desktop world, and its deep pockets, many industry participants and observers are skeptical about the company's ability to dominate the digital device arena in the same way that it has dominated the PC arena.

A frequently heard argument is that the digital device arena lacks the same compelling need for standardization that Microsoft exploited in the PC arena.[27] The world of digital devices is far more fragmented than that of PCs, so the argument goes, hence standards are naturally less important. This

TABLE 3

Operating System Preferences for Hand-held Devices[24]

Operating System	Super PC Companion (H/PC Pro)	PC Companion	Personal Companion
Windows CE	71.9%	64.8%	38.7%
Palm OS	4.3%	6.8%	33.8%
Java	12%	19.3%	16.7%

view is reflected in the following quote from Jerry Fidler, CEO of Wind River Systems, whose VxWorks operating system kernel for embedded processors competes in some of the same space as Windows CE. Fidler has suggested that "It's going to be tough for Microsoft. This isn't a one size fits all market. Applications are specific, not standard like they are in the PC world. This world is chaos."[28] Similarly, Forrester Research has argued that operating system conformity isn't as important in the digital device arena because, unlike PCs, most devices do not have to run thousands of applications. More than 90 percent of 3Com's PalmPilot users, for example, rely entirely on a handful of embedded applications such as the contact list and calendar.[29]

A big driver for standardization in the PC world is the need to ensure that data flows easily between software applications, and between the PC and a wide range of peripherals. In the digital device arena, however, it has been argued that Internet connectivity and standard data formats such as HTML and the emerging Web access protocol will provide the lingua franca for devices. Moreover, synchronization tools from companies such as Puma Technologies and Starfish software will tap into PCs and Internet resident databases to ensure that phone lists and preferences on smart appliances are kept in sync, regardless of the underlying operating system.

Other critics have focused more on the shortcomings of Windows CE than on any actual or perceived flaws in Microsoft's strategy. A big issue with Windows CE is that it currently does not offer strong real time operating system (RTOS) capabilities. With its response time of 250 microseconds, CE is just too slow to be used for applications that must be choreographed to the microsecond, such as the motion of a print head on an ink-jet printer, factory floor automation systems, or precision robotics, all of which require thread latencies of below 50 microseconds.[30] RTOS capabilities are also required for many wireless applications. However, Windows CE should have RTOS capabilities by the fall of 1999. This should help Windows CE to penetrate the embedded systems market.

Another issue is related to the reported size of the RTOS for Windows CE. Major RTOS vendors, such as Wind River Systems and Integrated Systems, offer scalable systems that start with kernels of around 1 kilobyte. Frugal use of memory is a key requirement for many embedded system designs.

However, current reports suggest that Windows CE RTOS will need at least 2 megabytes of ROM to hold the CE operating system. This is far more memory allocation than developers for embedded systems normally have to account for. If true, many potential users will be repelled by the need to squander so much memory.[31]

COMPETITORS

As might be expected, competitors offer a significant threat to market acceptance of Windows CE. This threat is enhanced by the fact that many important suppliers of complements, such as TCI in the set-top box arena, have a vested interest in ensuring that the market for digital device operating systems remains fragmented. (TCI licensed Windows CE for 5 million of the 12 million set-top boxes it is planning to build. At the same time, TCI has licensed Personal-Java from Sun for all its boxes). One of the biggest fears of device manufacturers and suppliers of complement services, such as cable, is that Microsoft will dominate the digital device world in much the same way as it has dominated the PC world. If this were to occur, Microsoft could conceivably capture much of the economic value in the marketplace, leaving device manufacturers and service providers to compete with each other in a commodity world. In the words of TCI president, Leo Hinderly, many device manufacturers and complement suppliers "don't want to be a Bill Gates download."[32] This fear adds momentum to any offering that helps to keep Microsoft's ambitions in check. In other words, there is something of a presumption in favor of non-Microsoft solutions on the part of many other participants in the digital device value chain.

There is certainly an abundance of non-Microsoft solutions, including 3Com's Palm OS, Psion's EPOC, Sun Microsystems' Java OS, and Wind River System's VxWorks (see Table 4). Several of these alternatives are discussed in detail below.

3Com's PalmPilot and Palm OS

The PalmPilot was the brain child of Jeff Hawkins and Donna Dubinsky. Their vision was to produce a simple electronic device that would have four basic functions: a calendar, an address book, a to-do list, and memo writing function. They believed that

TABLE 4

OS Competitors for Digital Devices[33]

Vendor	OS	Comments
3Com	Palm OS	Used in Palm Computing devices sold by 3Com and its licensees; also targeting smart phones
Integrated Systems	PSOS	Ships in car navigation systems, digital cameras, phones, and Sony's satellite set-top box
Lucent	Inferno	Focuses on phones and network devices like firewalls and routers.
Microsoft	Windows CE	Currently targeting set-top boxes, DVD players, game consoles, phones, and hand-held devices
Power TV	Power TV OS	Aimed at set-top boxes, TVs, network computers, and DVD players; used in Scientific Atlanta's digital set top
Psion	EPOC	Targeting hand-held devices, smart phones, and set-top boxes
QNX	QNX Software	Targeting set-top boxes, DVD players, VCRs and phones.
Sun Micro	Java OS	Built by coupling real time OS and Java virtual machine; dependent on new Java applications; licensed for use in TCI set-top boxes
Wind River Systems	VxWorks	Ships in satellite set tops and digital cameras; targeting DVD and wireless phones

the main competitor for the Pilot would not be computers, but paper. Accordingly, they tried hard to make the Pilot a model of simplicity. For example, looking up the day schedule is no more difficult than opening a date book: one push of a button and there it is.

This was not a vision that sold easily in Silicon Valley. Dubinsky and Hawkins repeatedly tried to raise venture capital money but kept running up against objections that the device was too simple and lacked important attributes, such as a PC card, or functions, such as a spreadsheet. After eighteen months of their effort, U.S. Robotics, a Midwest company, emerged as the "angel" backer (U.S. Robotics later merged with 3Com).[34]

The PalmPilot was launched in April 1996. An electronic address book and calendar/date book that recognizes handwriting and communicates with any PC, it retailed for $200–$400. For the first four months sales were painfully slow; then demand started to increase exponentially as the Pilot suddenly became a "hip" device for busy execu-

tives. Within eighteen months of the initial launch, more than 1 million PalmPilots were shipped, making for a faster demand ramp-up than the first cell phones and pagers. By the end of 1998, more than 2 million units had been sold.

Benefiting from early mover advantages, 3Com built a large community of developers that now offer applications for the PalmPilot and its successor, the Palm III (the Palm III incorporates a larger screen and built-in infrared beam to share data—such as electronic business cards—with other users). There are now more than 5,000 developers making add-on products for the Palm devices, such as PilotMail and PilotClock. By late 1998, there were some 1,600 applications for the PalmPilot and Palm III, versus 300 for Windows CE hand-held devices. An abundance of shareware and freeware is helping to drive market acceptance of the PalmPilot. Sales for applications are also being driven by alternative distribution channels, such as the Web.

As with any successful new product, competitors soon imitated the Pilot's form and functions.

The most notable imitator was Microsoft's "Palm PC," with its Windows CE operating system. Several other companies have licensed Windows CE to produce Palm PC devices, including Casio and Philips. Windows CE Palm PC devices have more built-in features than 3Com's PalmPilot and Palm III, but they take longer to load data and consume battery power more rapidly.

In 1998, IDC calculated that the PalmPilot accounted for 78 percent of the $980 million a year hand-held market. Trying to build installed base, 3Com is licensing the Palm OS as fast as it can to companies such as IBM and Qualcomm. Qualcomm is adapting the Palm OS for use in a smart phone, the pdQ, which is scheduled to ship in 1999.

IDC expects that the global market for palm devices will grow from 1.2 million units in 1997 to 8.2 million units in 2001.[35] Sherwood Research estimates that U.S. sales of palm computing devices utilizing 3Com's Palm OS will hit 1.433 million in 1998, and grow to 2.724 million by 2000. Sherwood's sales forecasts appear in Table 5.

Some observers doubt that the Palm OS can survive over the long term in the corporate area, primarily because the keyboards on hand-held PCs are better input devices for most corporate users. Moreover, some argue that the PalmPilot, which uses an aging 16-bit processor, suffers from a lack of standardized programming tools. They predict that the major portion of the back-end enterprise market will eventually connect to CE devices because they run the most commonly used 32-bit code.[37]

Sherwood Research believes that "3Com will continue to dominate the palm-sized market, and by default the entire handheld PC market. The form factor and functionality, combined with a powerful set of developer applications, means that 3Com really only faces competition from itself as it cannibalizes its own product line with the introduction of new products that incorporate enhanced or new features."[38]

Support for this position can be found in the fact that major corporate applications providers, such as SAP, Oracle, Sybase, and Computer Associates, are all working on ways to deliver their enterprise resource planning, database, and management software to Palm OS platforms. For example, SAP's mobile R/3, introduced in mid 1998, runs on a version of the 3Com PalmPilot sold by Symbol, as well as on 3Com's PalmPilot and IBM's WorkPad version of the PalmPilot.[39] Similarly, Oracle is planning to enter the mobile database market. In mid 1998, Oracle announced a partnership with 3Com to integrate a 150-kilobyte version of the Oracle Lite client database into Palm OS units. Oracle states that this integration will let Palm OS applications and data be replicated, synchronized, and shared with Oracle8 databases. However, the company also plans to run Oracle Lite betas on Windows CE. Indeed, most applications companies are hedging their bets by developing applications for *both* the Palm OS and Windows CE platforms.

Psion and EPOC

Psion is a British company that was an early leader in the market for hand-held computers. Its Series 5 machine was introduced in mid 1997, a full six months before similar devices utilizing Windows CE. The Series 5 was greeted with critical and popular acclaim, especially in Europe. The Series 5, which is a derivative of Psion's popular Series 3 machine, uses Psion's EPOC operating system, and a novel and highly usable keyboard, which offers far more than the tiny-buttoned keyboards usually associated with hand-held computers. The Psion Series 5 comes with a set of built-in applications, which share data formats with popular Microsoft desktop applications. These include a Word-compatible word processor. Psion provides excellent desktop connectivity with Windows through its PsiWin product.[40]

Despite beating Windows CE hand-held devices to the market by some time, Psion had been facing an uphill struggle as CE gained momentum. Indeed,

TABLE 5

Sales Forecasts for Palm Devices[36]

Type	1998	1999	2000
Palm OS	995,000	1,435,000	1,780,000
Palm size PCs/CE	344,000	547,000	654,000
Other	94,000	72,000	290,000
Total	1,433,000	2,054,000	2,724,000

many were ready to write the company off—that is until Psion pulled an ace out of the hole in the form of Symbia. Symbia is a joint venture with cellular telephone giants Ericsson, Nokia, and Motorola. The objective of the venture is to adopt Psion's EPOC operating system as the OS for the next generation of "smart cellular phones." According to Dataquest, by 2002 roughly 50 million smart phones will be sold every year—equivalent to the number of PCs sold today. Psion's partners in Symbia account for more than 70 percent of the sales of mobile phones. If their share holds and smart phone sales grow as predicted, Psion's EPOC could still emerge as a significant competitor to Windows CE.[41]

Symbia will license EPOC to all comers for a fee of around $5 to $10 per phone, which compares favorably with the $25 per unit that Microsoft reportedly charges to license CE.[42] Psion claims that EPOC is better suited than CE to cell phones, where long battery life and efficient use of memory are more important than links to a PC desktop. Be that as it may, EPOC has another attribute that attracts Psion's partners and any potential licensees—it is not a Microsoft product. Psion's founder, David Potter, underscored this point as he outlined the thinking behind Symbia: "We looked at the cellular industry, an industry selling 100 million units a year, and asked: 'Are these guys really going to allow the mighty Bill to come in and take their businesses?' It's absolutely obvious that there is no way they are going to do that. We looked at their needs and said, let's make these guys secure."[43] Building on this success, Potter has announced his intentions to license EPOC to other electronic hardware manufacturers, such as set-top box manufacturers.

Wind River Systems

Wind River Systems is a long-time participant in the market for embedded system operating systems with its VxWorks real-time operating system and its set of Tornado development tools for embedded system applications. As of 1998, Wind River controls about 33 percent of the market for third-party RTOS for embedded processors. Wind River has been involved in more than 10,000 customer products and projects, from Cisco routers to Kodak digital cameras. VxWorks is considered so reliable that NASA used it on the Mars Pathfinder.[44]

Wind River does not intend to go head-to-head with Microsoft. Indeed, the company seems to be de-emphasizing embedded markets, such as hand-held

PCs, where Microsoft has already established a strong position. Rather, Wind River intends to compete by finding new uses for its technology, such as GUIs and Internet connections on a wide range of products, including camcorders, copiers, printers and retail kiosks. Toward that end, the company has made a number of acquisitions designed to boost its graphic interface and Internet capabilities.[45] Despite Wind River's attempts to avoid head-to-head competition with Microsoft, adding GUI and Internet functionality to VxWork seems likely to bring the company into conflict with Microsoft at some point.

Sun Micro: Dreams of Java and Jini

Sun Microsystems is trying to position Java as a threat to Windows CE in all of its markets. The great strength claimed for Java is its platform independence—the same compiled Java code will run on any processor or operating system with a compatible Java Virtual Machine (JVM). The Java concept of "write once run anywhere" is obviously very attractive to developers—and if it works it will reduce the imperative for standardizing on a single operating system. Sun is also pushing its own Java operating system for embedded applications, JavaOS.

Java has certainly made some inroads into the digital device world. For example, Hitachi and TCI have both licensed Java for use in their respective set-top boxes. A wide range of other companies are offering Java support for embedded system applications. Wind River Systems offers a version of its own operating systems for embedded processors, VxWorks, that runs Java. Other competitors in the embedded system space, including Integrated Systems, Mentor Graphics, and Cygnus Solutions, also offer embedded system tools for Java.[46]

Jini is the latest addition to Sun's Java vision. What Java aims to do for software, Jini hopes to do for the machines that run it: provide an overarching universal platform—a distributed operating system, in effect, in which devices of every description can meet. Jini is about trying to create an architecture, a universal language, a set of super protocols—to knit together the emerging global computer and communications network, and make everything work with and make it accessible by everything else.[47]

The basic point of Jini is to simplify user interaction with the network. The key to Jini is Java's platform independence and its own innate ability to work over existing network software and protocols. As an extension of Java code, along with the federation of Java Virtual Machines (JVMs), Jini becomes the universal language for disparate devices. The core of Jini's architecture lies in a "lookup service," known as JavaSpace. The lookup service acts as an electronic bulletin board that monitors the devices attached to a network. So the combination of Java's ability to run on different computers and the ability of Jini-enabled devices to send their own software code to the lookup service and receive instructions from other devices is what gives a Jini network its potential magic.[48]

To consumers this means the ability to connect, power, and control through the network any appliance with an embedded processor, including hand-held devices, smart phones, set-top boxes, and home thermostats. Once connected, the device announces itself to the network, indicates what it is there to do, and then carries out its task.

On a corporate scale, Jini has potential for altering the way networks operate, without changing the underlying structure. Computing power would be distributed among devices connected to the computer, letting them share each other's resources. If Jini works, you will be able to sit with your laptop, it will be able to reach out across the network, and for the moments that you need the power, it will become the largest supercomputer in the world.[49] Instead of a platform designed to provide all capabilities in all cases, Jini provides only what is needed. And by using Java as the standard platform, interoperability is achieved. Basically, any device with a link to the network and a programmable ROM can be a network device with Jini.[50]

Sun is trying to position the Java/Jini combination as the offering that will make Weiser's vision of ubiquitous computing a reality. To this end, Sun is reportedly going to license Jini for free to diffuse the technology as rapidly as possible. If successful, Sun's vision will lead to a world in which a myriad of digital devices running Java connect and communicate with each other via Jini networks. In this vision of the future of computing, there is no imperative for standardization on a particular operating system, and the dominance of Microsoft will evaporate.

The problem with this vision is that so far it has promised far more than has been delivered. The Java/Jini combination may make for great press, but while it is widely supported, there is little evidence of overwhelming momentum in favor of Java in the digital device arena. Meanwhile, Jini remains a re-

search project. One Microsoft spokesman claimed that Jini does little more than reinvent the kinds of network services—such as file and print—that are already in widespread use in non-Java environments. Sun needs Jini, so the argument goes, because Java does not provide any services of this kind, and Java-only devices, therefore, have no way of connecting to network services.[51]

Even Windows CE skeptics, such as Forrester Research, believe that a dearth of Java applications and Microsoft's existing tools and developer community will make CE rather than Java the leader in the high-end "net visible" space, which includes set-top boxes and hand-held PC companions. Like CE, Java is also too slow for many embedded system applications that require real time capabilities.[52]

Perhaps more troubling for Sun, there are signs that the Java community is beginning to fragment, raising the specter that Java may go the way of UNIX, which fragmented into a set of partly incompatible versions. Hewlett-Packard has developed its own clone of Java, Chai, that HP claims is a better alternative to "real" Java in many embedded system applications. Elsewhere, much to Sun's chagrin, a breakaway group of companies has banded together to form a version of Java that is suitable for real time applications.[53]

KEY STRATEGIC ISSUES

The competitive situation in the digital device arena is still unfolding daily. Huge uncertainties abound as to the future direction of the market. How will the technology evolve? Will Weiser's vision of ubiquitous computing come to pass? What are the attributes of the technology required to facilitate this development? Will standards be important in the digital device arena, or in segments of that arena? What kind of products will be demanded by mass-market consumers, as opposed to technophiles? Where will the growth be? What product attributes in terms of form factors and functions will be required to drive forward expansions of demand? What is the correct technological, product development and competitive strategy for Microsoft to pursue in order for the company to help grow the market and to position itself to profit from that growth, irrespective of how critical uncertainties resolve themselves? How can Microsoft gain a major share in a market where not only competitors, but also suppliers of important complements, have a vested interest in seeing the company's market share bounded?

Endnotes

1. "After the PC," *Economist,* September 12, 1998, p. 79.
2. E. Wasserman, "Electronics Guru Predicts Ubiquitous Computing," *Arizona Republic,* January 19, 1998, p. E1.
3. M. Weiser, "The Future of Ubiquitous Computing on Campus," *Communications of the ACM,* 4 (January 1998), 41.
4. T. K. Landauer, *The Trouble with Computers* (MIT Press, 1995).
5. Wasserman, "Electronics Guru," p. E1.
6. J. Markoff, "Taking a Step Towards Converting the Home into a Supercomputer," *New York Times,* July 15, 1998, p. 1.
7. E. W. Desmond and J. Hodges, "Microsoft's Big Bet on Small Machines," *Fortune,* July 20, 1998, p. 86.
8. Sherwood Research, "Effects Handhelds Will Have on Notebook PCs," February 16, 1998.
9. Sherwood Research, "Handheld Forecast Update: Breakout of the Palm Sized Market," September 14, 1998.
10. IDC, "Boom or Bust? Worldwide Smart Handheld Devices Market Review and Forecast Update," 1997–2001, 1998.
11. Ibid.
12. Ibid.
13. Ibid.
14. Sherwood Research, "Consumer CE-Based Appliances, Set Top Boxes," August 31, 1998.
15. G. L. White, "Cars That Listen Promise a New Direction in Driving," *Wall Street Journal,* December 28, 1998, p. B1; S. Manes, "Compute While You Are Driving," *Forbes,* January 11, 1999, p. 112–114.
16. N. Weinberg, "Sega's New Dimension," *Forbes,* September 7, 1998, p. 206–208.
17. D. Takahashi, "Video Game Makers See Soaring Sales Now—and Lots of Trouble Ahead," *Wall Street Journal,* June 15, 1998, p. A10.
18. J. G. Spooner, "Windows CE Goes Vertical," *PC Week,* November 9, 1998, p. 39.
19. J. G. Spooner, "Alliance to Bolster CE," *PC Week,* November 9, 1998, p. 16.
20. A. Fiebus, "WinCE: Your Next OS?" *Information Week,* November 16, 1998, p. 127.
21. J. Jurvis, "Business Support Grows for Windows CE," *Information Week,* March 2, 1998.
22. IDC, "Smart Hand-held Devices: Jupiter—Not for Many Moons," October 1998.
23. Sherwood Research, "Effects Handhelds Will Have on Notebook PCs," February 16, 1998.
24. IDC, "U.S. Customer Directions and Buying Behavior: The 1998 Smart Handheld Devices Survey," 1998, Table 14.
25. The estimate of five to ten times as many CE digital devices and Windows PCs was given by Craig Mundie in a recent *Fortune* article, E.W. Desmond and J. Hodges, "Microsoft's Big Bet on Small Machines," *Fortune,* July 20, 1998, p. 86.
26. "Windows CE Falls Short."
27. Ibid.
28. Desmond and Hodges, "Microsoft's Big Bet."
29. "Windows CE Falls Short."
30. T. Foremski, "Microsoft Gets Real," *Electronics Weekly,* May 6, 1998, p. 34.
31. Ibid.
32. S. Hamm, "Microsoft's Future: A Band of Powerful Foes Is Determined to Slow the Gates Juggernaut," *Business Week,* January 19, 1998, p. 58.
33. Compiled from various sources, including "Windows CE Falls Short," *Forrester Report,* 5 (May 1998).
34. D. S. Jackson, "Palm-to-Palm Combat," *Time Magazine,* March 16, 1998, p. 42.
35. IDC, "Boom or Bust?"
36. Sherwood Research, "Handheld Forecast Update."
37. R. Levin and T. Davey, "Handhelds—Mobile Evolution," *Information Week,* June 15, 1998, p. 20.
38. Sherwood Research, "Handheld Forecast Update."
39. Levin and Davey, "Handhelds."
40. N. Clayton and S. Vogel, "Palmistry," *Scotsman,* September 9, 1998, p. 8.
41. Wallace, "The Man Bill Gates Fears Most," *Fortune,* November 23, 1998, p. 257.
42. D. Gillmor, "Formidable Force Aims at Microsoft," *San Jose Mercury News,* July 7, 1998, p. E1.
43. Wallace, "The Man Bill Gates Fears Most."
44. D. Diamond, "Lord of the Toasters," *Wired* (September 1998).
45. P. Coffee, "Wind River, Zinc to Duel Win CE," *PC Week,* July 6, 1998, p. 16.
46. "Major Embedded Tool Companies Turn Towards Java," *Java World* (January 1998).
47. K. Kelly and S. Reiss, "One Huge Computer," *Wired* (August 1998).
48. "Net Watch: Sun Microsystems and Jini Architecture," *Izarek Shopper* (October 1998).
49. Ibid.
50. A. Goldberg, "I Dream of Jini, and So Should You," *PC Week,* August 3, 1998.
51. "Microsoft Says Jini Is Old Hat," Computergram International, July 17, 1998.
52. "Windows CE Falls Short."
53. D. Lyons, "Java in Jeopardy," *Forbes,* January 11, 1999, p. 110–111.

Sun Microsystems, Inc.

This case was prepared by Irene Hagenbuch and Alan N. Hoffman of Bentley College.

The Network is the computer's means to make all the systems work together like one big resource. Sun has always seen our customers' computing needs answered by a variety of computing resources in a heterogeneous network.

—Scott G. McNealy, CEO, April 1987

COMPANY BACKGROUND

John Doerr, of Klein Perkins, has described Sun Microsystems with world headquarters in Palo Alto, California, as "the last standing, fully integrated computing company adding its own value at the chip, OS and systems level."

The company's history started in 1982, when Andreas Bechtolsheim, Bill Joy, Vinod Khosla, and Scott McNealy founded Sun Microsystems for Stanford University Network. Within a month after the introduction of the business plan, which Bechtolsheim, an electrical engineering whiz, had built it for Stanford's computer network. The same year, the first Sun system, the Sun-1, a high-performance computer based on readily available, inexpensive components and UNIX, was produced. After a rocky two-year start, McNealy, who started out as vice president for manufacturing and operations, was appointed president in 1984 when Khosla left the company. Today, Sun has emerged as a global *Fortune* 500 leader in enterprise network computing, with operations in 150 countries and more than $8 billion in revenues.

The company's philosophy is to enable customers to create breakaway business strategies by using their network computing products, solutions, and services. Sun further states that in an age

This case is intended to be used as the basis for class discussion rather than as an illustration of either effective or ineffective handling of the situation. This case was prepared by Irene Hagenbuch and Alan N. Hoffman, Bentley College. Used by permission.

where information is power it provides the technology, innovation, and partnerships that enable individuals or entire organizations to access information from anywhere to anything on any device allowing users to better differentiate and more effectively create breakaway business products and services.

Supporting and enforcing their philosophy where everything they bring to the market is predicated upon the existence of the network, where Java is on every client and every server, Sun has a vision statement. It says that its "vision is for a networked computing future driven by the needs and choices of the customer. It is a vision in which every man, woman and child has access to the collective planetary wisdom that resides on the network." Sun further explains that the Internet represents the first environment through which the company's vision can actually start to be achieved. They see their role as one of making the most of the opportunity, by delivering open, affordable and useful products to help as many people as possible share in the power of the network around the world.

COMPETITION

Sun's competitors in the technical and scientific markets are primarily Hewlett-Packard (HP), International Business Machines Corporation (IBM), Compaq Computer (CPQ) and Silicon Graphics, Inc. (SGI).

The information technology industry, the market for Sun's services and products, is extremely competitive. The industry is characterized by rapid, continuous change, frequent product performance improvements, short product life cycles and price reductions. This environment forces Sun to rapidly and continuously develop, introduce, and deliver in quantity new systems, software, and service products, in addition to new microprocessor technologies, to offer its customers improved performance at competitive prices. The company has begun to improve, change, and implement a number of new business practices, processes, and a series of related information systems. Jim Moore from GeoPartners Research in Cambridge, Massachusetts, compares Sun with IBM in its glorious days, when customers viewed it as the repository of wisdom and competence: "Sun has suddenly become a thought leader for the whole industry."

Compared with previous years, Sun has become increasingly dependent on the ability of its suppliers. Their competence in designing, manufacturing, and delivering advanced components required for the timely introduction of new products is crucial to Sun's future competitiveness. The failure of any of these suppliers to deliver components on time or in sufficient quantities or the failure of any of Sun's own designers to develop innovative products on a timely basis could also have a serious impact on the company's operating results. To prevent any adverse effect on its net revenues and operating results, Sun frequently makes advanced payments to specific suppliers and often enters into non-cancelable purchase contracts with vendors early in the design process. The commitments help secure components for the development, production, and introduction of new products. The distribution of the computer systems sold by Sun is accomplished through the company's own systems. No customer accounted for more than 10 percent of Sun's revenues in fiscal 1997, 1996, or 1995. Sun's vision and strategy have stayed constant. With more market opportunities, an increasing number of companies are realizing the benefits of open network computing.

After Sun observed that sharing data between computers was crucial to key business tasks, McNealy worked extensively to transform Sun's product line in order to capitalize on networking. Today, its main products can be divided into six categories: servers and workstations, Solaris and Sol-stice, SunSpectrum, WorkShop and NEO, UltraSparc and Java processors, and Java software (see Table 1). This wide variety of products is used to implement the McNealy philosophy: "The network is the computer." Sun was refiguring its UNIX operating system for workstations, called Solaris, to run servers that coordinate work and store data on networks.

The year 1994 was marked as a big year in the computer industry. Sun faced the dramatic expansion of the Internet's World Wide Web. Millions of users came to believe that the network was indeed the computer. Since this statement has been accepted by Sun for a long time, the company had been faster in making the transition compared with its UNIX rivals IBM and Hewlett-Packard. This led to many customers turning to Sun for their workstations. According to Computer Intelligence, a research firm located in La Jolla, California, 26 percent of all Web servers in use in the United States were made by Sun—that is more than by any other company.

By 1998, Sun was the leading provider of UNIX-based servers. Java has helped increase sales, even though the language does nothing yet to make Sun's servers better than any of its competitors. Using Java to sell servers is a necessity, since the workstation, the computer Sun was built on, is going the way of the minicomputer. The more expensive machines made by Sun and others are being replaced by PCs incorporating cheaper Intel microprocessors. While companies are having inexpensive Windows NT servers handle their simpler networking tasks, they still rely on UNIX for their most critical applications since Solaris servers crash a lot less than NT servers. Nonetheless, the PCs that run Microsoft's Windows NT operating system, Compaq, Dell and others will soon take over the market for workstations priced under $10,000.

In January 1998, however, Sun announced sweeping innovations made to its award-winning power desktop line. This move, designed to capture new growth within the $19 billion market for high-end personal computers and powerful workstations, allows the company to grow market share at both the low end (less than $5,000) and high end (more than $15,000) of the workstation market. Putting its expertise in high-performance system design has enabled the company to bring down the price of advanced workstations and graphics technologies. Sun's announcement of new graphics capabilities, as well as of the fastest workstation, the

TABLE I

Sun Microsystems Products

- *Servers and Workstations.* The company offers a full line of Ultra Enterprise servers to support an immense database and mission-critical business applications. With its Netra server family, Sun delivers preconfigured solutions for intranet and Internet publishing. Its Ultra workstation series combines accelerated graphics, high-bandwidth networking, and fast processing to provide outstanding performance for technical applications.

- *Solaris and Solstice.* With Sun's installed base of more than 2 million systems, Solaris software is the leading operating environment for open client-server networks. The Solstice products consist of a highly scalable and comprehensive suite of Intranet management software, helping organizations securely access, administer, and manage rapidly changing Intranet computing environments.

- *SunSpectrum.* This newly developed portfolio of enterprisewide support services connects Sun's customers to a highly responsive organization that supports more than half a million systems worldwide. That combination of hardware, system software, and application support with premium account-level services maximizes both system availability and customer satisfaction.

- *Workshop and NEO.* The Workshop family, which includes the new Java WorkShop solution, delivers visual development tools that quickly and easily create multiplatform applications for the Internet, intranets, and enterprise networks. NEO delivers system administration tools, object-oriented development tools, and transparent networking in order to reduce the cost of creating, customizing, and maintaining applications.

- *UltraSPARC and Java Processors.* Well-developed UltraSPARC microprocessors accelerate multimedia and networking applications with their innovative architecture and VIS media instruction set through powering networked systems from routers to supercomputers. The planned JavaChip microprocessor family will be optimized for Java-powered applications.

- *Java Software.* It is the first software platform planned from the start for the Internet and corporate intranets that will run on any computer.

Source: (Form-10k)

Ultra 60 multiprocessing system, ideally positioned the company to take market share from competitors such as Hewlett-Packard, IBM, DEC, and Silicon Graphics at the high end of the market. Sun is pushing Silicon Graphics' technology to the limits with its new price/performance levels and intends to overtake SGI's market share in the $25,000+ workstation market, which was approximately $3 billion in 1996. These new workstations allowed the users to run the most popular Microsoft Windows 95 applications alongside the Solaris applications. This meant that users could run the more than 12,000 Solaris applications, which offered proven UNIX reliability/uptime, handled larger data sets and delivered faster real-world modeling capabilities than the NT environment, in addition to the PC applications like Microsoft office.

The new Darwin line was designed to appeal to the growing base of desktop users who were demanding more reliability and power. When the Darwin systems are coupled with new accelerated graphics, it allows Sun to focus more on the needs of the rapidly growing base of digital contents creators. This desktop line sets a new low-price point for workstation functionality, enabling Sun to grasp market share from Compaq and other PC vendors at the lower end of the market. Part of this move into the desktop markets was the announcement of a worldwide trade-in program designed to ensure investment protection for existing Sun customers and to attract new customers currently using other PCs and workstations that compete with the Sun platform. To specifically draw the attention of Silicon Graphics, Apple Computer, and

Compaq customers, as well as those of other PC vendors, toward the performance and speedy graphics advantages of Sun systems, Sun designed its "Jurassic-Back," "Mac-Back," and "Paq-Back" trade-in promotions.

FINANCIAL PERFORMANCE

Even though Sun's industry is fast changing and highly competitive, the company has managed to have at least 10 percent sales growth over the last several years across its product line. Its net revenue in fiscal 1998 increased to $9.7 billion, or 13 percent compared with $8.6 billion in fiscal 1997 (see Table 2). Net income was flat for 1998—at $762 million for fiscal 1998, the same as for fiscal 1997. However, the product's gross margin was 53.8 percent for fiscal 1998, compared with 51.1 percent for fiscal 1997. Research and development expenses increased by $188 million, or 22.7 percent,

TABLE 2

Sun Microsystems' Consolidated Statements of Income
(In thousands, except per share amounts)

	Years ended June 30		
	1998	*1997*	*1996*
Net avenues:			
Products	$8,603,259	$7,747,115	$6,392,358
Services	1,187,581	851,231	702,393
Total net revenues	9,790,840	8,598,346	7,094,751
Costs and expenses:			
Cost of sales—products	3,972,283	3,790,284	3,468,416
Cost of sales—services	721,053	530,176	452,812
Research and development	1,013,782	825,968	653,044
Selling, general and administrative	2,777,264	2,402,442	1,787,567
Purchased in-process research and development	176,384	22,958	57,900
Total costs and expenses	8,660,766	7,571,828	6,419,739
Operating income	1,130,074	1,026,518	675,012
Gain on sale of equity investment	—	62,245	—
Interest income	47,663	39,899	42,976
Interest expense	(1,571)	(7,455)	(9,114)
Income before income taxes	1,176,166	1,121,207	708,874
Provision for income taxes	413,304	358,787	232,486
Net income	$ 762,862	$ 762,420	$ 476,388
Net income per common share—basic	$ 2.04	$ 2.07	$ 1.28
Net income per common share—diluted	$ 1.93	$ 1.96	$ 1.21
Shares used in the calculation of net income per common share—basic	373,728	368,426	371,134
Shares used in the calculation of net income per common share—diluted	394,274	388,967	393,380

in fiscal 1998. Sun has one of the strongest balance sheets in the industry, with $822 million in cash in the bank (see Table 3.) Having been the world leader in workstation sales (with 39 percent in unit sales and 35 percent in revenues, per Dataquest), the company is successfully transforming itself into an enterprise-computing firm with a focus on global network computing. This was a necessary move as Sun's workstation sales started to slip and its server sales to gain.

Over the last ten years, the company's revenues have grown an average of 34.1 percent annually as the demand for its open network computing products and services has risen. The revenues by geography are well balanced. Approximately 49 percent of the total revenue is generated from outside the United States. The company's net income has grown 41 percent annually on average over the same time period.

CORPORATE GOVERNANCE

Scott G. McNealy

The life story of Sun's current chairman of the board, president, and chief executive officer, Scott G. McNealy, is not very typical for a Silicon Valley entrepreneur. He didn't drop out of college to realize his idea for the PC business, nor did he work his way up through engineering. His background in manufacturing makes McNealy a fierce competitor who knows his business fundamentals, always keeps score, and has good moves. He is smart, complex, and fiercely ambitious. Over the many years at Sun, McNealy has become one of the industry's most respected managers. Lawrence J. Ellison, CEO of Oracle says, "There are two things I think about Scott. One is passionate leadership, and the other is his rigorous financial management. And that's uncommon to find in one person" (*Fortune,* October 13, 1997). Those talents, along with his competitive instinct and nonstop drive, have kept Sun rolling through a decade of tremendous change in the computer industry.

McNealy grew up in a house where hard work and a fast-paced environment were part of everyday life. As a child, McNealy learned a great deal about manufacturing. His curiosity about his father's work (his father was vice chairman of American Motors) led the gradeschooler to look into his dad's briefcase at night to inspect its contents.

Many Saturdays, he went along to the plant and snooped around while his father caught up on paperwork. By the time he reached his teenage years, McNealy was spending evenings with his father reading over memos and playing golf with industry leaders such as Lee A. Iacocca.

Graduating from Harvard University in economics, McNealy took a job for two years as a foreman at a Rockwell International Corp. plant in Ashtabula, Ohio, which made body panels for semi tractors. In 1978, he enrolled in Stanford University's business school, where he focused on manufacturing at a time when finance and information technologies were the ways to the top. While many of his classmates wanted to launch a Digital Age business, McNealy signed on as a manufacturing trainee for FMC Corp. The company assigned him to a factory in Silicon Valley where it was building Bradley fighting vehicles for the U.S. Army.

McNealy's career in the computer world started in 1981, when his mentor from Harvard asked him for help in the troubled production department of a workstation company called Onyx Systems. After only ten months at Onyx, he was contacted by a former Stanford classmate, Vinod Khosla, and asked to join him and Bechtolsheim in starting Sun. In 1982, he joined Sun to head its manufacturing and operations. His manufacturing skills enabled the new company to keep up with the high demand as sales went from $9 million in 1983 to $39 million in 1984. Nonetheless, the high amount of new orders surpassed the cash available for expansion. McNealy then asked their customer Eastman Kodak to invest $20 million. As a condition of the investment, Kodak insisted that McNealy take over as president. In 1984, he was officially named CEO of the company.

McNealy showed his ability as a CEO over the coming years. After the company went public in 1986, it took two years for Sun to outgrow its production capacities, which led to the company's first quarterly loss. Its troubled production facilities were reason enough for McNealy to move from Sun's executive suite to the floor of Sun's biggest factory and revamp the company's manufacturing. In the months after production was rolling again, he showed skills nobody expected. He deliberately pruned the product line, sharpening Sun's focus to workstations built around a high-powered processor of its own design. The realization that fixing problems on the factory floor was no job for the

TABLE 3

Sun Microsystems' Consolidated Balance Sheets

(In thousands, except share and per share amounts)

	At June 30	
	1998	1997
Assets		
Current assets:		
Cash and cash equivalents	$ 822,267	$ 660,170
Short-term investments	476,185	452,590
Accounts receivable, net of allowances of $235,563 in 1998 and $196,091 in 1997	1,845,765	1,666,523
Inventories	346,446	437,978
Deferred tax assets	371,841	286,720
Other current assets	285,021	224,469
Total current assets	4,147,525	3,728,450
Property, plant and equipment:		
Machinery and equipment	1,251,660	1,057,239
Furniture and fixtures	113,636	93,078
Leasehold improvements	256,233	166,745
Land and buildings	635,699	341,279
	2,257,228	1,658,341
Accumulated depreciation and amortization	(956,616)	(858,448)
	1,300,612	799,893
Other assets, net	262,925	168,931
	$5,711,062	$4,697,274
Liabilities and Stockholders' Equity		
Current liabilities:		
Short-term borrowings	$ 7,169	$ 100,930
Accounts payable	495,603	468,912
Accrued payroll-related liabilities	315,929	337,412
Accrued liabilities and other	810,562	625,600
Deferred service revenues	264,967	197,616
Income taxes payable	188,641	118,568
Note payable	40,000	———
Total current liabilities	2,122,871	1,849,038
Deferred income taxes and other obligations	74,563	106,299
Commitments and contingencies		
Stockholders' equity:		
Preferred stock, $0.001 par value, 10,000,000 shares authorized; no shares issued and outstanding	—	—
Common stock, $0.00067 par value, 950,000,000 shares authorized; issued: 430,311,441 shares in 1998 and 430,535,886 shares in 1997	288	288
Additional paid-in capital	1,345,508	1,229,797
Retained earnings	3,150,935	2,409,850
Treasury stock, at cost: 54,007,866 shares in 1998 and 60,050,380 shares in 1997	(1,003,191)	(915,426)
Currency translation adjustment and other	20,088	17,428
Total stockholders' equity	3,513,628	2,741,937
	$5,711,062	$4,697,274

CEO of a company of Sun's size led McNealy to reorganize the company's structure. He pushed profit-and-loss responsibility down to individual product organizations, called planets, which let them feel the troubles if things went wrong.

At Sun's headquarters, McNealy, having an image in the industry of being brash, was building a corporate culture based on his own motto: "Kick butt and have fun." Soon after that, the company became known for its aggressive marketing, featuring Network, McNealy's Greater Swiss Mountain dog, and various juvenile behavior taking place within Sun's headquarters.

This humor had an important effect on the culture. During these competitive times in the computer industry when good positions and good workers were hard to find, it helped employees live with their demanding jobs and bound the company. Both Carol A. Bartz, former sales vice president of Sun, and Thomas J. Meredith, former Sun treasurer, agree that McNealy has a special gift. Using humor and a tremendous amount of energy, McNealy has the ability to raise employees enthusiastically to their feet.

Sun does not consist of McNealy alone, however. According to Ellison, McNealy has complemented his leadership with very capable people. "You don't find Scott surrounded by dummies. You find Scott surrounded by real smart people, like Bill Joy and Eric Schmidt [chief technology officer] and others who do wonderful work."

JAVA—THE PROGRAMMING LANGUAGE

Java originated in a 1990 programming language, code-named Oak, that would enable all computerized devices to run simple programs distributed to them over a network. At one point, Oak was part of the effort to develop a two-way interactive cable TV system (which Sun lost out to Silicon Graphics). By the end of 1994, Oak seemed to be going nowhere. During one last presentation of Oak, McNealy recognized the potential of the programming language—how to reach his ultimate goal of harnessing the Internet to stop Microsoft from swallowing all of them—and became its biggest supporter. Soon after that, the language was renamed Java, a colloquial word for "coffee." The fact that the name was informal and generic compared with previous programming language names which were obscure and

somewhat daunting, implied that normal people should also care about Java, whether they knew what it did or not. By May 1995, McNealy informed the public about the new concept, but at that point the public did not know what to make of it. On January 12, 1996, Sun officially released Java, its new network software, and Sun entered a new era with a tremendous amount of public exposure and a heightened interest in the company.

The brand name Java refers both to a programming language and to a set of components and tools. It was originally viewed as a language that would jazz up Web pages with graphic animations—dancing icons, for example. To Microsoft's dismay, Java has evolved to trick people into thinking it is a computing platform. What makes Java a self-sufficient computing system is the Java Virtual Machine, or JVM—a piece of software that imitates all the functions of the computing device. This gives Java the possibility to run on any machine with a JVM, insensitive to the underlying operating system (Windows, Macintosh, UNIX, and so forth), and allows applications written in Java to run on all machines without being changed. The Java digital language is the first universal software that would allow all computerized devices to share programs and communicate over a network. It makes possible the rapid development of versatile programs for communicating and collaborating on the Internet.

Compared with ordinary software applications, Java applications, or "applets," are little programs that reside on the network in centralized servers. The network delivers the programs to the user's machine when needed. Because the applets are so much smaller, they require comparably less time to download. In other words, Java lets programmers write small applications that can zip across the World Wide Web. Without leaving the browser, the user will then be able to print out attractive text and charts. The user always gets the latest version of the applets. As the software is stored in only one place, corporations can keep it updated more easily. Java's designers believed that in this new environment, the program's speed would be measured by how fast a program ran on a network and not by how fast a program ran on an individual computer. In this sense, being object oriented versus speed oriented makes programs run faster, or at least appear to. Java was developed to have its objects move quickly into and out of different machines and merge with other Java objects on the network, even when these objects appeared unexpectedly.

With the immense growth of the World Wide Web, Java's introduction was one of those magic moments where place and time seemed perfect. It appeared to be the language best suited for Internet computing. Besides applying to all PCs, Java is inherently virus-proof, because the language was designed so that applets cannot alter data in the user's computer's files or on its hard disk. Silicon Graphics and Macromedia partnered with Sun to jointly define a new set of open multimedia formats and application programming interfaces (APIs) to extend Sun's Java. The companies believe that these new API formats will enhance Java's capabilities for providing animation and interactivity, especially in the area of 3D rendering and multimedia over the Internet or corporate networks.

With the increasing importance of the Internet, McNealy once more is convinced that Java will alter the dynamics of the business. "Java opens up a whole new world for Sun," he says. It can be said that a part of the new world has already come into view. Java is well on its way to becoming the Internet software standard, which would put Sun as the leader in Internet computing. Millions of personal computer owners already have access to Java because the software was built into the 1996 release of Netscape's Web browser. As the "intelligent network" starts to include mobile phones, smart pagers, and hand-held electronic assistants, along with the traditional computers, Java is set to become a standard language for these far-flung devices.

Although Sun is planning eventually to donate the software language to the computer world through publicizing all the specifications and letting anybody use them, Java should continue to spur profitable growth for the company. According to management, Java will increase Sun's sale of Internet servers, priced at $25,000, and starts its new line of JavaStation network computers. Java will also raise the demand for Sun's software development tools and for special Sun chips, which other computer makers can incorporate into their machines to run Java faster.

McNealy's view of the future is not shared universally, however. It is very unlikely that Java will change computing so soon. The programming language is still at a fairly immature stage and its programs run considerably more slowly than programs written specifically for a particular computer oper-

ating system. Furthermore, there have been security issues raised by a system of distributing software on the Net.

The Java Controversy

By the first week of December 1995, many of the top names in computing—from Netscape, Oracle, and Apple to BulletProof, Wind River Systems, Toshiba, and IBM—had endorsed Java. IBM had 2,500 programmers working to improve Java because it saw Java as the glue that can finally link its many lines of computers seamlessly. Because Java programs run on any hardware or operating system, Java could bypass, and therefore break, Microsoft's cash cow, Microsoft Office. So that Java might be on further PCs, Sun tried to persuade Microsoft to incorporate a Java interpreter right into the Windows operating systems. After four months of negotiations, Sun received a fax from Microsoft in March 1996 agreeing to license Java on Sun's terms. Microsoft had changed its strategy of writing its own software for any interface or function (unless customers demanded that Microsoft adopt another) because of a software language. In its many years of business, Microsoft had rarely adopted anyone else's software or hardware standards. The company had agreed to license a product from Sun because it did not have a lot of choices.

On October 7, 1997, however, Sun Microsystems announced that the company had filed a lawsuit in U.S. District Court, Northern District of California, San Jose Division, against Microsoft Corporation for breaching its contractual obligation to deliver a compatible implementation of Java technology on its products. The complaint also charged Microsoft with trademark infringement, false advertising, unfair competition, interference with prospective economic advantage, and inducing breach of contract. Sun claimed that Microsoft has deliberately violated its licensing agreement in an attempt to reduce the cross-platform compatibility made possible by the Java technology and deliver a version of the technology that worked only with Microsoft's products. Additionally, Sun charged that Microsoft illegally placed Sun's software code on its World Wide Web site. Sun asked for $35 million in damages over that one issue.

Even though there have been threats about revoking Microsoft's Java licensing agreement, Sun did not plan to cancel Microsoft's license. The company's goal was to pressure Microsoft to fulfill the obligations created in that license. Sun was seeking a court order to prevent Microsoft from improperly using the Java Compatible logo and deceiving the marketplace. The logo appeared in different locations in and on Microsoft's consumer packaging and promotional materials. Sun was further seeking to prevent Microsoft from misleading Java developers and from delivering anything but fully compatible Java technology implementations. Sun felt it had the responsibility to defend the integrity of Java. Michael Morris, Sun's vice president and general counsel, stated that "nowhere is the sanctity of a trademark more important than in the field of computer software. Our customers rely on the reputation and the goodwill of the trademark to make informed, efficient decisions about the technology they are using."

One of any of Java licensee's most significant contractual obligations is to pass the Java compatibility tests. These tests determine if a licensee's technology conforms to the Java specifications and APIs. In Microsoft's case, the products that failed were the new Internet Explorer 4.0 browser and the Software Development Kit for Java (SDKJ). The new technology did not pass Sun's compatibility tests because of an improper modification of the products by Microsoft. Hence, applications written using Microsoft's development tools do not run on all machines without some necessary adjustments.

For the two companies the stakes are high. McNealy is convinced that Sun can win a lawsuit against Microsoft, the most powerful software company in the world, by having a court that looks at the case, and not at the companies involved. Winning the suit would enable Sun to live up to the CEO's idea behind his drive to develop Java: to free the world of the duopolistic grip of Microsoft and Intel, or so-called Wintel. It would open the market for Sun and other computer companies. As Microsoft is fully aware of McNealy's concept, its strategy is to encourage developers to write Java programs that are tied to Windows. This would block Sun's efforts to expand the language into a possibly full-blown operating system.

Sun and its CEO are very confident that the court will see the merits of the complaint and move to a speedy resolution. Sun seems to ignore, however, that Microsoft, Intel, Digital Equipment, and Compaq Computer have all signed an open letter on September 11, 1997, urging Sun to turn control of Java over to the International Standards Organization (ISO). This demand would put the Java logo in the public domain. Sun seems to have missed the point that this suit is not solely about Microsoft. It is about whether Sun can respond to the standards body. If Sun loses, its previously forwarded plan where the ISO would have some oversight over Java might not get accepted and Sun would have to give up control of the key components of Java and the Java brand. This, in turn, would lead to a huge future loss in revenue and a decline in investments by many trustworthy companies such as IBM, which have partnered with Sun in the development of Java. Furthermore, it would enable Microsoft to establish a Windows-only variant of Java—one that would benefit just Wintel (PCs based on Intel's microprocessor using the Windows operating system) machine users—as a competing standard that would block Sun from creating a uniform Java that can run equally well on any type of computer.

The Feud with Microsoft

The suit had developed into a public fight between Sun Microsystems and Microsoft, two extremely successful companies. This sniping between Sun and Microsoft is more about who controls the future of computing than the surface spat over the Java Internet programming language. Microsoft has brought its weight into play to slow Sun down further. Microsoft is using its power, market visibility and market presence to try to reposition Java as "just another programming language."

The rivalry between the two companies has become so shrill that Aaron Goldberg, of Computer Intelligence in La Jolla, California, calls it a "urinary Olympics." After winning out over Apple, Lotus, and WordPerfect, Microsoft is convinced that it is on its way to win the browser war as well. Although Netscape is still growing and finding new customers, it may lose out to Microsoft as well. Thinking that Sun will succeed where others have failed is probably irrational.

At the same time, it has to be said that it may be smart to be perceived as the one company that is attacking Microsoft. Many CIOs have started to worry about the increasing costs of information technology systems and software and their dependence on Microsoft and Intel. The incredibly high sums spent on equipment and maintenance increased the CIOs' willingness to support new alternatives. In addition to the CIOs, customers have always liked to apply pressure to the market leaders in the hope of driving down prices. Consumers like the concept that no user of Java needs to buy the software in a retail store or from an electronic catalogue; it is part of the economic transaction. There is also a willingness and availability of money in the industry to help anyone who might loosen Microsoft's control over the way things will be in the future. This is why there has been so much support for Java, even more than McNealy originally expected.

McNealy soon will have to decide if this almost personal vendetta against Microsoft to break its power in the computer industry is in the best interest of Sun's shareholders and if it is a healthy path for Sun in the future. He could have considered cooperating with Microsoft. This would have opened up Java to the masses and could have helped Sun sell even more highly profitable servers and workstations. Stating Sun's point of view that Java does not have to make money for the company as long as it helps the company break Microsoft's business model shows McNealy's intent. Sadly enough, this might really not be in the public's best interest. McNealy is convinced that "if Java catches on big, the software lock-in of the Microsoft Windows/Intel design will end. Then, computer and software companies will once again be able to differentiate their products. Indeed, they will have to." If Java does not catch on or especially, if Sun loses the suit, no one, including McNealy, will know what Sun's future will look like in the computer technology industry—especially if one considers that the lawsuit, as well as Java itself, does not affect Microsoft as much as originally thought. The fact that many people like Java does not change how customers want to use those computers on their desks. They still want to calculate spreadsheets, process words, hold presentations, and manage personal information by using software that allows them to do all of it as conveniently as possible. It does not seem to make a difference that the new programmers will use Java to create new software. Many of the present programmers will continue using conventional languages to develop commercial software as all the new languages will end up running on Windows machines anyway, because these are the machines the majority of the users already have.

Sun Microsystems Faces Revolt over Java Control

On November 3, 1998, the *Financial Times* proclaimed in a front-page article:

> Sun Microsystems is facing an industry revolt against its control of Java, the computer language which allows programs to run on any system. On November 2, 1998, 14 companies, including Hewlett-Packard, Microsoft, Siemens and Rockwell, announced they would start setting their own standards for creating Java programs which control devices such as cellphones and printers. The move follows several months of negotiations with Sun over industry complaints that it was being too slow at developing new software standards and was charging too much in licensing fees.
>
> Joe Beyers, general manager of Internet Software at Hewlett-Packard, said, "We are trying to respond to customer needs but Sun has been unwilling to relinquish control of Java. If they want to go in a different direction they can, but I hope they can join us."
>
> Sun has focused on developing Java for mainstream computer programming to the frustration of companies wishing to develop other uses. Sun has yet to start selling its own system for running Java programs on embedded processors.
>
> Hewlett-Packard this year broke Sun's grip on Java by developing its own system for operating Java programs called Chai, which does not require a license from Sun.
>
> Mr. Beyers says several other companies are developing similar systems.

On November 24, 1998, America Online announced that it was purchasing Netscape Communications for $4.2 billion and entering into a multi-layered strategic partnership with Sun Microsystems to develop new Internet access devices.

References

Alsop, S. "Warning to Scott McNealy: Don't Moon the Ogre." *Fortune.* October 13, 1997.
———. "Sun's Java: What's Hype, What's Real." *Fortune.* July 7, 1997.
Bank, D. "Sun Lawsuit Is Latest Shot at Microsoft." *Wall Street Journal.* October 9, 1997.
———. "Sun Suit Says Microsoft Disrupts Java." *Wall Street Journal.* October 10, 1997.

Fitzgerald, Michael. "Sun's Threat: Microsoft Could Lose Java License." *ZDNet.* September 23, 1997.

Gomes, L. "Sun Microsystems 1st-Period Net, Sales Miss Expectations Due to Currency Rates." *Wall Street Journal.* October 17, 1997.

———. "Profits at Sun Microsystems Increases 56%." *Wall Street Journal.* April 16, 1997.

Gomes, L., and D. Clark. "Java Is Finding Niches But Isn't Yet Living Up to Its Early Promises." *Wall Street Journal,* August 27, 1997.

Hamm, S., with R. Hof. "Operation Sunblock: Microsoft Goes to War." *Business Week,* October 27, 1997.

Hof, R. D., with P. Burrows and K. Rebello. "Scott McNealy's Rising Sun." *BusinessWeek,* January 22, 1996.

Hof, Robert D., with J. Verity. "Now, Sun Has to Keep Java Perking." *BusinessWeek,* January 22, 1996.

Indiana Rigdon, J. "Sun Microsystems' Earnings Soar 41% Due to Strength at Top of Product Line." *Wall Street Journal,* January 16, 1997.

Kirkpatrick, D. "Meanwhile, Back At Headquarters. . . ." *Fortune,* October 13, 1997.

Mitchell, R. "Extreme Fighting, Silicon Valley Style." *U.S. News & World Report,* October 20, 1997.

Schlender, B. "The Adventures of Scott McNealy." *Fortune,* October 13, 1997.

———. "Sun's Java: The Threat to Microsoft Is Real." *Fortune,* November 11, 1996.

Seminerio, M. "Java Jive: Microsoft vs. Sun Draws No Blood—Yet." *ZDNet,* September 23, 1997.

Sun Microsystems, Inc., home page (www.sun.com).

"Sun Microsystems, Silicon Graphics and Macomecia Intend to Define a New Set of Open 3D and Multimedia Interfaces for Java and the Web," from Sun Microsystems, Inc., home page (www.sun.com).

Sun Microsystems, Inc., Annual Report 1996.

Sun Microsystems, Inc., Annual Report 1997.

"Wind River System's Tornado for Java Passes Sun Microsystems' Java Compatibility Tests," biz.yahoo.com/prnews/980121/ca_wind_ri_1.html. (January 21, 1998)

"BulletProof Releases JdesignerPro 2.32—Advanced RAD Application Development System for Java," biz.yahoo.com/prnews/980120/ca_bulletp_1 html. (January 20, 1998).

"Sun Unveils Plans to Grow Desktop Market at Expense of Compaq, H-P and SGI," www.sun.dom/smi/Press/sunflash/9801/sunflash.980113.3.html. (January 13, 1998).

"Sun Sues Microsoft for Breach of Java Contract": www.sun.com/smi/Press.sunflash/9710/sunflash/.971007.10.html (October 7, 1997).

"Sun Microsystems Seeks to Bar Microsoft from Unauthorized Use of 'Java Compatible' Logo," www.java.sun.com/pr/1997/nov/sun.pr97118.html. (November 18, 1997).

CASE 14

ATL: Strategic Positioning

This case was prepared by Charles W. L. Hill of the University of Washington.

INTRODUCTION

In early July 1998, the top-management team of ATL Ultrasound, a leader in the medical ultrasound business, gathered in the bucolic surroundings of the Columbia Winery in Washington State for its annual two-day strategic planning retreat. Its task was to discuss several key strategic issues that had been confronting the company for some time and had yet to be resolved to anyone's satisfaction.

ATL was established in 1969 in order to commercialize technology developed at the University of Washington's health sciences complex. The company was one of the early pioneers in the market for medical ultrasound equipment. Over the next quarter of a century, it established a reputation for technological leadership. This reputation was solidified in 1988, when ATL introduced the world's first digital ultrasound equipment. By 1997, ATL had established itself as one of the top four ultrasound manufacturers in the world, along with Acuson, Hewlett-Packard, and Toshiba. Each of these companies had about 15 percent to 17 percent of the global market. In 1997, ATL generated record revenues of $431 million and near record net profits of $21.2 million. Almost half of its revenues were booked outside the United States.

In November 1997, the company had launched its latest product, the HDI 5000, a high-end digital ultrasound unit priced around $250,000. The HDI 5000 represented ATL's fifth generation of all-digital

technology and, in something of a public relations coup, was selected by NASA for use by astronauts to perform sophisticated medical diagnostics aboard the international space station when it is launched in 2001. Essentially a specialized computer, the HDI 5000 can perform more than 14 billion operations per second. It incorporates a range of advanced diagnostic features, including a patented new Doppler blood flow imaging technology and adaptive system intelligence. The product garnered strong reviews from radiologists and gained rapid market acceptance. By July 1998, it was apparent that the HDI 5000 would sell more than 1,000 units in its first year alone, exceeding the company's prelaunch goal.

Despite the success of the HDI 5000, as ATL's top managers gathered at the Columbia Winery, they knew they faced some major challenges. There was significant disagreement within the company about the appropriate strategic focus. ATL offered a broad product line, spanning all major clinical applications of ultrasound technology, from the premium- to mid-price range. Some questioned the wisdom of such a broad market strategy; they believed that ATL lacked the technical and financial resources to pursue it successfully. In their view, the company would be better served by focusing its development efforts on premium machines targeted at the radiology or general imaging market. Others embraced the goal of offering a broad product line aimed at the premium and mid-range price segments, but believed that ATL had yet to identify and clearly articulate the appropriate strategy for attaining this goal.

To complicate matters, in recent years General Electric and Siemens had moved aggressively into the medical ultrasound market. These companies already had a strong position in medical diagnostic imaging equipment, selling everything from x-ray machines and computed tomography (CT) scanners to magnetic resonance imaging (MRI) machines. Both GE and Siemens seemed intent on adding ultrasound equipment to their product portfolio. To this end, in early 1988 General Electric Medical Systems (GEMS) purchased a second-tier ultrasound company, Diasonics. This purchase, when combined with GE's existing ultrasound sales, gave GE potential 1998 revenues in the $460 million range. In 1997, Siemens had worldwide ultrasound revenues of $267 million, and it, too, was reportedly on the lookout for acquisition candidates. ATL's managers had to decide how best to respond to this new competitive threat. A particular cause for concern was that by bundling together a diverse range of imaging products and offering deep price discounts to hospitals and multihospital systems that purchase the entire bundle, multimodality firms such as GE and Siemens might be able to capture share from dedicated ultrasound companies such as ATL.

Although the worldwide market for medical ultrasound equipment was projected to grow, some worried that these new competitors might accelerate the erosion in average selling price that ATL and its competitors had experienced. During the first half of the 1990s, average retail prices for ultrasound equipment had fallen by around 10 percent to 15 percent per annum. Since 1997, the decline had been reversed by the introduction of new "super-premium" machines such as ATL's HDI 5000 and Acuson's Sequoia. However, ATL was forecasting some weakening of average retail prices after 2000 as these products aged. To maintain gross margins against the background of falling prices, ATL would have to find ways to drive down its cost structure.

MEDICAL IMAGING

Medical imaging is a critical step in the diagnosis of many ailments. For eighty years, the business of taking pictures of the inside of the body was routine: send x-rays through the body and record an image on film. Over the last quarter of a century, however, a number of different imaging technologies have made their way into the medical mainstream. Where once there were only x-rays, now there are CT scanners, MRI machines, and ultrasound. Each

of these techniques is transforming diagnosis of disease, and each has its strengths and weaknesses. Competition among these different imaging techniques is growing.

Computed tomography is closest to x-rays. It uses a series of x-ray pictures taken by a camera orbiting the body. A computer combines these to form a detailed cross-sectional image. A problem with x-rays is that they distinguish between body areas of different density—though that makes them useful for studying the skeleton, for example. A problem with the CT scan is that it produces much more radiation than an x-ray. That is not considered dangerous, but receiving hundreds of CT scans may be inadvisable. Both these problems are dealt with by magnetic resonance imaging, which takes a picture of where water is in the body without using x-rays. It distinguishes clearly between skin, fat, and muscle. The technology is based on the fact that water molecules can behave like tiny magnets. An MRI scanner bathes the body in a powerful magnetic field and the water molecules in the body line up. The molecules are jarred by a radio wave pulse, and as they realign with the magnetic field, they emit their own radio pulse. The pattern of that return pulse is turned into a cross section of the body by a computer. But MRI has three drawbacks: the machinery required costs about $2 million and fills a room (a CT scanner costs about $1 million); the powerful magnets wipe magnetic storage media such as credit cards and floppy disks and may harm patients with heart pacemakers; and, like CT, all it provides are snapshots.

This is where ultrasound imaging comes in. A noninvasive procedure, ultrasound uses the reflection of high frequency sound waves to create images of the body's soft tissue, organs, and blood flow in real time on a television monitor. The principle is very similar to the echo sonar by which dolphins, bats, and submarines navigate. Ultrasound systems include three major components: a scanhead, which transmits sound waves into the body of a patient, receives returning echoes from the patient, and converts the echoes into electrical signals; a computer processing unit, which processes the electrical echo signals into images or measurements of physiological conditions within the patient's body; and a monitor, which displays the resulting images or measurement information. The scanhead is held by the ultrasound operator and passed over the area being imaged. Because of the real-time capability of ultrasound, one can, for example, watch a heart beat or a fetus move in a woman's womb.

In the hands of a skilled operator, an ultrasound image may be as clear as a CT scan or an x-ray, but in general, the image quality is inferior. The best images are of structures near the surface of the body, up to a depth of about 10 centimeters. The images show a smaller area than MRI or CT scans. However, increases in the clarity and power of ultrasound equipment is enabling ultrasound operators to distinguish between different types of tissue and, therefore, do some of the work previously allocated to CT and MRI specialists. Radiologists are also increasingly making use of contrast agents in ultrasound to increase image precision and show various structures within the body more clearly.

A cost-effective procedure, ultrasound can eliminate the need for more invasive and expensive procedures. Ultrasound machinery is small enough to be wheeled about on a trolley and costs between $250,000 and $30,000, depending on the sophistication of the machine. Although the image quality is lesser than that produced by CT or MRI, the lower cost of ultrasound equipment is facilitating market adoption, particularly in countries where MRI and CT machines are viewed as prohibitively expensive.

Recent advances in ultrasound have emphasized enhancing the diagnostic properties of the technology. Among the areas of intense research are tissue harmonic imaging, contrast imaging, and three-dimensional imaging. Tissue harmonic imaging involves using broadbeam scanheads to detect and image echoes that are reflected off tissue at a higher frequency than those originally transmitted. The shifting from one frequency to another is called harmonics. Tissue harmonic imaging enables a dramatic reduction in image artifacts, reduces haze and clutter, and significantly increases contrast resolution. Contrast imaging involves using contrast agents, microbubbles of which reflect ultrasound waves at a different frequency than the surrounding tissue. When used in conjunction with harmonic imaging, contrast agents enable the physician to gain a clearer image of specific soft tissue. Three-dimensional imaging—such as a 3D view of a beating heart—can provide more information for a diagnostic decision.

Scanhead technology represents another area of research in ultrasound. As mentioned earlier, scanheads are held by the ultrasound operator over the area to be imaged, and they transmit and receive sound waves. In addition to having broadbeam capability, so that they can transmit and receive signals of a different frequency (necessary for harmonic imaging), modern scanheads come in a wide range of specialized design for different diagnostic tasks.

THE MEDICAL ULTRASOUND MARKET

In 1997, more than $8 billion was spent on medical imaging equipment worldwide. Diagnostic ultrasound products, upgrades, and accessories sold for use in hospitals, clinics, and physicians' offices accounted for an estimated $2.8 billion of this total, a 5.5 percent increase over the prior year. Ultrasound sales booked in the United States totaled around $853 million. Western Europe accounted for another $765 million, Japan for $400 million, the rest of Asia for $330 million, and Latin America for $225 million. After several slow years, the ultrasound market was predicted to grow steadily over the next few years, particularly in the United States, where new product introductions were projected to drive growth. Most industry sources forecast growth of 6 to 8 percent between 1997 and 2002; they see the global market for ultrasound closing in on around $3.5 billion by 2002, and expect the U.S. market to exceed $1.2 billion.

The medical ultrasound business is divided into different market segments based on medical specialty and price. The main medical segments, in order of importance, are radiology, cardiology, obstetrics-gynecology, and vascular surgery. Figure 1 summarizes the 1997 market segment data in the United States and Figure 2 summarizes the 1997 international data. The definitions of market segments differ slightly since in the international market, general imaging is taken to include both radiology *and* internal medicine. In radiology, ultrasound is used to obtain diagnostic information on organs and soft tissue, particularly in the abdominal area. It is also used to ascertain fetal development, guide tissue biopsies, and visualize blood flow. In cardiology, ultrasound is used to capture real-time images of the heart and its valves. Referred to as echocardiography, these images help the physician assess heart function, as well as congenital and valvular disease. Echocardiography is a useful tool for the detection and assessment of coronary

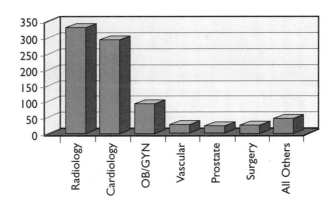

artery disease. In ob-gyn, ultrasound is the preferred imaging technique for the assessment of fetal development, because it is noninvasive and involves no ionizing radiation. Ultrasound is also used for general gynecological and infertility examinations. In vascular surgery, ultrasound is used to identify plaque deposits and their characteristics, clots, and valve competence in blood vessels. In the United States, the number of radiology exams using ultrasound grew from 25.8 million in 1996 to 27.5 million in 1997. The ultrasound exam figures for cardiology were 13.4 million in 1996 and 14.8 million in 1997. For ob-gyn, they increased from 10.8 million exams to 11.4 million.

Customers in each segment demand machines that have diagnostic features appropriate for their specialty. Cardiologists, for example, are more interested in 3D imaging capabilities and advanced quantitative data output than radiologists. It should be noted, however, that a substantial proportion of the radiology market also requires machines that have cardiac imaging capabilities. Often referred to

as the shared service market, many community or smaller hospitals in the United States fall into this category.

The ultrasound market can be segmented not only according to medical specialty, but also on the basis of price (see Figure 3). Its four main price segments are premium-performance, high-performance, mid-range, and low-end machines. Premium-performance machines make up about 18 percent of the world market and cost more than $160,000, with the super-premium machines fetching as much as $250,000. These powerful systems provide the physician with superior color definition of subtle tissue characteristics and incorporate an array of advanced features, such as tissue harmonic imaging and 3D imaging capability. They also come equipped with a wide variety of specialized scanheads for specific imaging tasks. High-performance machines, which are priced between $100,000 and $160,000 and constitute about 30 percent of the world market, also include many advanced color-imaging capabilities and a variety of scanheads.

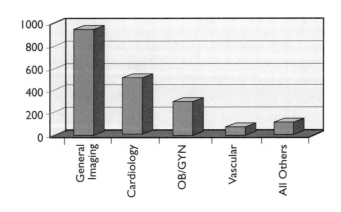

FIGURE 3

Ultrasound Price
Segments in 1997

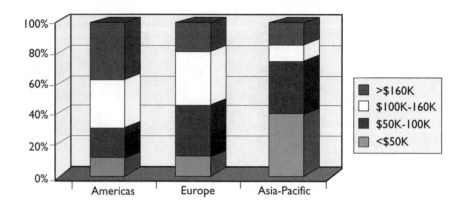

Generally, however, they lack cutting-edge diagnostic technology, such as tissue harmonic imaging. Mid-range ultrasound systems sell for between $50,000 and $100,000 and make up about 28 percent of the world ultrasound market. These systems produce a basic low-resolution color image and utilize a limited number of scanheads. Low-end machines sell for under $50,000 and constitute 24 percent of the world market. This market segment is characterized by basic black-and-white imaging systems, and a limited selection of scanheads. These machines provide limited diagnostic information.

What is clear from Figure 3 is that the international markets are far more price sensitive than the U.S. market. Some 62 percent of all units sold in 1997 in the Americas—the bulk of them in the United States—were priced at more than $100,000, whereas 77 percent of all units sold in the Asian Pacific region were priced at under $100,000. These differences reflect not only differences in the wealth of a region, but also societal differences in the proportion of resources devoted to health care. The international market is primarily a mid-range and low-end market.

Toshiba is the largest manufacturer of ultrasound equipment in the world, with 14.7 percent of the global market as measured by combined product and service revenues in 1997 (see Figure 4). However, Toshiba's position reflects its dominance in Japan and parts of Asia. Elsewhere, it is a relatively weak player. GE, after its early 1988 acquisition of Diasonics, has catapulted into second place, followed closely by HP, Acuson, and ATL. In the important U.S. market, which is the lead market for new generation ultrasound products, Acuson, HP, ATL, and GE/Diasonics dominate. (See Figure 5,

which shows market share data based on revenues from equipment sales and upgrades; service revenues are excluded.) The relative ranking of the three companies has historically been driven by the age of their product offerings. In 1996, HP led the market, but Acuson captured the lead in 1997 due to strong sales of its new generation premium product, the Sequoia. ATL had a relatively weak year in 1997 because its lead product, the HDI 3000, had been introduced in October 1994 and was now aging. ATL was expected to come on strong in 1998 following the successful launch of its latest product, the HDI 5000.

Although HP is number two in the U.S. market, its strong showing is primarily due to a dominant position in the cardiology market—a market HP pioneered—where it held a 55 percent share of equipment sales and upgrades in 1997. Acuson was second with a 22 percent share, and ATL third with 12 percent. In the U.S. radiology market, Acuson led the way with a 41.5 percent share of equipment sales and upgrades, followed by ATL (20.2 percent), and GE (14.3 percent). HP had only a 3.2 percent share of this market.

The ultrasound market is a high-technology business with relatively short product life cycles and continuing pressures to develop new products that incorporate new or improved diagnostic features. Competition between the major players is intense and based on technological features, price, and service support. Hospitals are the major customers, accounting for 71 percent of unit shipments by value in the United States in 1997. Demand for equipment in the private sector (clinics and doctors' offices) is, however, growing somewhat faster than demand from hospitals.

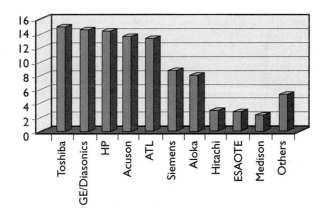

Within the United States, most large companies sell directly, while smaller companies typically turn over distribution to multiproduct distributors. According to industry data, Acuson had a seventy-person sales force in 1997, of which twenty-eight were dedicated to the cardiology market. ATL had a seventy-seven person sales force, with twenty-three dedicated to cardiology and fourteen to women's health. HP had a fifty-eight person sales force, fifty of whom were dedicated to cardiology. Internationally a mix of direct sales and distributors is used. ATL, for example, uses direct sales in fifteen major foreign markets but utilizes distributors elsewhere. The large companies also maintain their own customer support and service operations in those countries where they have a direct-sales presence. Dealers provide service and support in other markets.

The whole industry was characterized by low profitability in the mid 1990s as companies struggled with a combination of aging products, slowing demand growth, falling prices, and intense competition. An emphasis on health care cost containment in the United States also had a negative impact on market demand and prices for ultrasound equipment during the mid 1990s. Acuson lost $10.6 million in 1997, but made $22.4 million in 1997 as sales for its new Sequoia and Aspen products began to take off. ATL reported record net income of $21.2 million in 1997, but its profit margin was only 5 percent. HP's ultrasound business was estimated to be profitable but suffering from margin pressure. Both GE and Diasonics probably did no better than break even in 1997. Toshiba's ultrasound business was reportedly

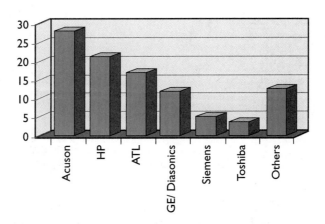

barely profitable, while the ultrasound operations of Siemens were unprofitable. There was some hope that prices and margins might improve in 1998–2000 as additional new products such as ATL's HDI 5000 gained market acceptance.

ATL

Since its establishment in 1969, ATL has consistently been among the leading companies in the medical ultrasound business. Located just north of Seattle, ATL had 1997 sales of $431 million, profits of $21.2 million, and 2,700 employees. Some 49 percent of its revenues were generated outside of the United States. (See Table 1 for financial statements.) The company has direct sales and service subsidiaries in fourteen nations, including Australia, Canada, China, France, Germany, India, Italy, Sweden, the United Kingdom, and Singapore. The Chinese subsidiary, the most recent, was established in May 1997. In other parts of the world, ATL has a presence through an extensive network of independent distributors.

In 1980, ATL was acquired by Squibb, a large pharmaceutical and medical equipment enterprise. In 1986, Squibb spun off its medical equipment op-

erations under a separate company, Westmark Holdings. Denis Fell moved from Squibb to head Westmark. In 1992, Westmark split itself into two entities, ATL and Spacelabs, a manufacturer of patient-monitoring systems. Fell became ATL's CEO. Throughout this period, ATL retained its own separate identity, first within Squibb and then within Westmark.

Always a technology-driven company with a strong core of scientific talent, back in 1988 ATL led the industry in the development of digital ultrasound when it introduced the first digital ultrasound product. Similarly, in the 1990s ATL pioneered harmonic imaging technology, introducing, in 1996, the first machine with harmonic imaging capability, a version of the HDI 3000. Reflecting its focus on technological leadership, traditionally ATL's strongest position has been in the premium and high-end segments of the market. Nevertheless, given that half of the world market is for units priced under $100,000, ATL has long looked for a way to compete effectively in the mid-range. To this end, in May 1994 ATL acquired Interspec, a smaller Pennsylvania-based ultrasound company that had a presence in the mid range and cardiology market segments.

TABLE 1

ATL's Financial Data
(in thousands, except per share data)

	1997	1996	1995
Results of Operations			
Revenues	$431,244	$419,157	$399,446
Gross profit	213,819	204,982	184,525
Selling, general and administrative expenses	128,739	122,990	119,955
Research and development expenses	59,710	53,969	50,255
Net income (loss)	$ 21,171	$ (828)	$ 12,002
Net income, excluding nonrecurring items	$ 21,171	$ 21,829	$ 10,617
Net income (loss) per share—diluted	$ 1.41	$ (0.06)	$ 0.88
Net income per share, excluding nonrecurring items—diluted	$ 1.41	$ 1.47	$ 0.78
Balance Sheet			
Cash and short-term investments	$ 30,821	$ 63,262	$ 35,654
Total assets	361,810	380,201	353,448
Long-term debt	12,307	12,936	14,837
Shareholders' equity	229,721	211,250	210,923
Common Shares Outstanding	14,413	14,023	13,610

Current Product Offerings

In mid 1998, ATL offered four main products: the HDI 5000, targeted at the premium price segment of the market; the older HDI 3000, targeted at the high-performance price segment; the HDI 1000, targeted at the mid-range price segment; and the Ultramark 400, targeted at the mid- to low-end price segment.

HDI 5000 The HDI 5000 was ATL's fifth generation digital ultrasound machine. First sold in November 1997, the HDI 5000 is a state-of-the-art system that incorporates a wide range of advanced diagnostic features and can be equipped with a wide range of high-performance ATL broadband scanheads, three of which are new to this model. In addition, the HDI 5000 comes with networking capability, which will allow physicians to share ultrasound images with each other via the Web. A variant of the HDI 5000, the HDI 5000cv, is targeted at the cardiology marketplace and comes equipped with the diagnostic features and scanheads demanded by cardiologists. Priced as high as $250,000 depending on features, the HDI 5000 seemed to be garnering significant market acceptance and was on track to sell more than 1,000 units in under twelve months. With the sales boost provided by the HDI 5000, in May 1998 ATL announced that it had shipped more than 10,000 all-digital HDI ultrasound systems since the product family was first introduced in 1988. ATL estimated that the worldwide installed base of all-digital systems numbered 14,000 by mid 1998, giving ATL a market share of more than 70 percent. To improve market acceptance of the HDI 5000, ATL offered the product both as a new system, and as an on-site upgrade to the older HDI 3000 system. This was made possible by the fact that the two products shared the same basic platform. The HDI 5000 could also make use of scanheads designed for the HDI 3000.

Despite the success of the HDI 5000, some within the company noted that the HDI 5000cv lacked the detailed quantification data capabilities that came with Hewlett-Packard's SONOS 5500 and SONOS 2500 dedicated cardiology ultrasound products. Quantification data were viewed by cardiologists as an important diagnostic tool. According to one manager, HP was about a year ahead of ATL with regard to quantification features. On the other hand, the harmonic imaging and contrast agent features of the HDI 5000 were at the forefront of ultrasound technology. Still, others noted that while ATL remains a leader in digital ultrasound technology and the beam-forming required for harmonic imaging, the company's principal competitors had narrowed the performance gap and were fast catching up. Yet another view was offered by one executive, who feared that the current push to add additional cardiology features to the HDI 5000cv might divert scarce scientific talent away from radiology and general imaging. This executive noted that "around 80 percent of the new features planned for the HDI 5000 and 3000 focus on cardiology applications such as quantification and 3D imaging—we are not paying sufficient attention to our core general imaging market. We lack the depth of scientific talent to focus on all of these market opportunities. We need to prioritize better."

HDI 3000 The HDI 3000 was ATL's fourth generation digital machine, and had been sold since October 1994. Originally sold as a premium machine, the product had been repositioned toward the high-performance price segment. Although this machine lacked the raw processing power of the HDI 5000, ATL had continued adding advanced features to it—such as tissue harmonic imaging, which was added in March 1997. A variant of the HDI 3000, the HDI 3000cv, was targeted at the cardiology marketplace.

HDI 1000 In early 1997, ATL introduced the HDI 1000, a product that was conceived as ATL's internally developed and produced digital offering for the mid-range marketplace. This was a market segment in which ATL had long struggled to develop a strong product offering. Although the mid-range market accounted for 28 percent of global ultrasound sales by value, ATL accounted for less than 10 percent of all sales to this segment. Some felt that if ATL was to meet Wall Street's growth expectations, the company needed to develop a viable mid-range offering. ATL's previous offering, the Apogee 800, which was introduced in October 1994, was acquired as part of the 1994 Interspec acquisition. The Apogee system had not lived up to expectations.

The HDI 1000 began as a controversial development project within ATL. Some internal critics believed that the HDI 1000 demonstrated all too well the long standing problem that the company was having not only in developing a viable mid-range offering, but also in making the difficult choice about what to focus on. A key problem ATL faced was how to design and produce an ultrasound system that built on ATL's strengths in digital ultrasound technology, but could be produced at a cost that would make it a profitable product offering in the mid range. The HDI 1000 was based on a revolutionary design philosophy. The design concept, as first articulated in the early 1990s, was to take advantage of the increasing power and falling cost of computer processing in order to replace many hardware components within ultrasound machines with software. The thinking was that by replacing specialized hardware with software, the unit cost of manufacturing the HDI 1000 could be driven down, enabling ATL to cost-effectively produce a powerful all-digital mid-range unit. Fell, the company's CEO, referred to the HDI 1000 design concept as a second inflection point in the ultrasound market, comparable in importance to the introduction of the first digital system back in 1988 (the first inflection point).

At the time the HDI 1000 project was launched, some voiced concern that the project would divert scarce engineering resources from ATL's core product offerings, and dedicate them to a complex project with a low probability of success. Moreover, they argued that the project was driven by a technological vision, as opposed to market needs. Despite such reservations, the promoters of the project had some important allies on the board, including the founder of the company and the current CEO, so the project was given the go-ahead.

Developing the HDI 1000 turned out to be a daunting task. The engineering problems inherent in replacing custom hardware with software had been underestimated, and ATL lacked the engineers required to work out the problems in an expeditious manner. Despite these constraints, ATL did manage to replace more than fifty percent of the hardware components in a conventional ultrasound machine with software, which in the HDI 1000 performs more than 70 percent of the functions of the ultrasound system. At the heart of this software-intensive system is a proprietary multitasking software management technology, developed by the HDI 1000 team, which utilizes object-oriented software architecture to perform self-contained software tasks that replace conventional hardware.

When the HDI 1000 was eventually introduced in 1997, the project was already two years over schedule, it cost more to manufacture than initially planned, and it suffered from some software reliability problems. Moreover, the product lacked several critical shared-service features, particularly those required by cardiologists. Although development continued and a new version of the HDI 1000 scheduled for release in January 1999 included an expanded feature set, initial sales were below expectations. The product did find a niche, but it was as an ob-gyn machine in the United States market. As of June 1998, the HDI 1000 had not given ATL the presence in the global mid-range market that the company had been looking for.

Ultramark 400   The failure of the HDI 1000 to match ATL's expectations in the global mid-range market was the catalyst behind a strategic partnership, announced in May 1998, between ATL and Medison, a South Korean ultrasound company. Medison had been building a reputation as a highly competitive manufacturer of basic ultrasound products in the $30,000 to $50,000 price range. Under the deal announced, ATL agreed to start marketing Medison's basic black-and-white digital ultrasound system throughout its global direct sales and distribution network. The product, referred to as the Ultramark 400, is to be manufactured for ATL by Medison in South Korea. In the U.S. market, ATL indicated that it would target the Ultramark 400 system at the office-based ob-gyn market, while continuing to sell the more sophisticated HDI 1000 color imaging system to the ob-gyn departments in hospitals and larger clinics.

The announcement of the Medison deal caught many of ATL's own managers by surprise. They wondered whether the deal signaled a shift in the strategic thinking of top management at ATL away from the philosophy of developing mid-range offerings in house, or whether the deal was nothing more than a temporary solution to a problem caused by the failure of the HDI 1000 to live up to its initial promise.

HDI 1500   The Ultramark 400 marketing deal was conceived as the first step in a deeper collaboration between ATL and Medison. The next step involves codevelopment of a new product, based on ATL technology, that will be aimed at the mid-range market, manufactured by Medison in South Korea, and sold through ATL's global network. Referred to as the HDI 1500, this all-digital color system is scheduled for introduction in late 1998 and seems likely to replace the HDI 1000 and Ultramark 400 as ATL's primary mid-range offering. The HDI 1500 will have the advantage of sharing common platform features with the HDI 5000 and HDI 3000 and of being able to utilize most HDI broadband scanheads.

The Product Development Process

At ATL, product development is the responsibility of the product generation function (engineering). The product generation function is organized as a conventional matrix, with basic engineering functions on one side and projects on the other (see Figure 6). Two committees play an important role in driving the activities of the product generation organization: the senior technology staff and the product generation council.

The senior technology staff is a committee of fifteen engineers, selected by their peers, who are responsible for developing the technology strategy of ATL. The fifteen engineers elect a chief, and for two years this individual is accorded VP status and serves on both the product generation council and the executive management committee of ATL. The product generation council is responsible for product strategy. Its members include the heads of the various engineering functions and projects, along with key marketing and manufacturing personnel. The council is responsible for the new product generation strategy at ATL and for the integration of cross-functional requirements within the product generation organization.

Technology Strategy At ATL, technology strategy is concerned with identifying, understanding, and developing technologies that are essential to the development of diagnostic ultrasound. ATL divides technology into two broad categories: (1) ultrasound-specific technologies, including the physics and engineering knowledge used in ultrasound and a basic understanding of its clinical application, and (2) supporting technologies, which are not necessarily specific to diagnostic ultrasound. Examples of the former technologies include the physics of harmonic imaging and the use of contrast agents and 3D imaging in diagnostic ultrasound. Examples of the latter include software and hardware architectural issues, communications technologies, and issues related to manufacturing.

ATL's goals in developing its technology strategy are to differentiate its products on the basis of superior proprietary diagnostic ultrasound technology, to bring reliable products to market in a reasonable time span, and to do so in a manner that does not increase manufacturing costs. An ideal goal is to bring product to market two to three years ahead of competitors, or when there is a competitive release, to be able to respond within a year. Five guiding principles govern all areas of technical strategy: (1) leveraging commonality across products so as to reduce time to market and system costs (the HDI 5000 and 3000 machines, for example, share the same basic hardware platform and many software features); (2) influencing and embracing broad industry standards; (3) using commercially available technology wherever appropriate; (4) developing and maintaining key ultrasound tools where commercial tools are not available; and (5) maintaining awareness of progress in key technological areas through contacts with academic institutions, research publications, academic conferences, and the like.

An example of technology strategy at work at ATL is the company's evolving competence in harmonic contrast imaging. Contrast agents are used to highlight certain tissue structures. ATL was the first to demonstrate that the microbubbles in different contrast agents reflect sound waves at different frequencies, and that in conjunction with broadband scanners this feature could be used to enhance image quality and diagnostic value. ATL is continuing to pursue microbubble physics research and is working closely with the manufacturers of contrast agents. The knowledge gained should enable ATL to optimize ultrasound images for specific contrast agents. ATL is also devoting considerable effort to developing a good quantification package for echocardiogram applications.

New Product Strategy New product generation strategy is developed by the product generation council and implemented through the product generation organization. ATL's top executives had committed the company to the goal of becoming the global market share leader in the ultrasound business, with products that served all major price segments. The product development strategy of the company called for the development of a family of digital ultrasound products aimed at the premium

FIGURE 6

ATL's Product
Generation Organization

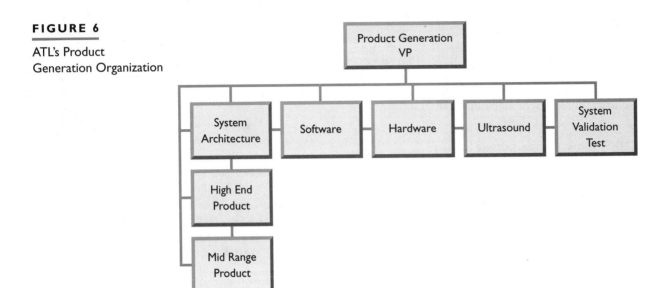

to mid-range price segments of the market and containing the feature sets appropriate for radiology, cardiology, ob-gyn, and vascular surgery. The family of products, which would be based on a common platform to reduce manufacturing costs, was scheduled for market introduction between late 2000 and early 2001. It was not clear whether the mid-range offerings in this family would be manufactured by ATL, or by a partner such as Medison.

Commenting on this strategy, one insider noted that "It's typical ATL. Once again we are trying to be all things to all people. We need to prioritize better. We do not have the resource to simultaneously pursue all of these product opportunities." Fell disagreed. "I know people say these things," he commented, "but we really have no choice. We cannot achieve our growth objective and boost our stock price unless we participate in the major segments of the market, and that includes the mid range. Anyway, part of my job is to push people to achieve goals that they do not think are possible."

The product generation council uses a number of mechanisms to control and drive the product development process. To begin with, the council has developed an aggregate product plan, which describes all development activities, including the resources needed, estimated development costs, and time lines. This plan is reviewed by the council on a quarterly basis. The council is responsible for prioritizing the development activities listed in the plan. To become part of the aggregate plan, a proj-

ect charter and contract must be reviewed and approved by the council. The project charter contains a brief description of the project and identifies the core team members and the project sponsor. The project contract—which is a contract between the council, core team members, and the project sponsor—contains detailed goals and objectives, and estimates development costs and the development schedule, including important calendar milestones. Once the contract is agreed on, any change must be reviewed and approved by the council. Once allocated to a development team, core team members are 100 percent accountable to the project, not to their function. There is also an incentive program, which links the bonus pay of core team members to development team results.

After the project is initiated, ATL utilizes a phase gate process to review and control its development (see Figure 7). This process contains a limited number of gates, which are either decision points or review points; some of them are optional, depending on the nature of the product being developed. For example, new platform projects have to go through a more rigorous process than simple derivative projects. The criteria for moving on to the next stage of development also vary, depending on the nature of the project.

FDA Regulations   Because ATL produces medical equipment, its product development processes are closely monitored and regulated by the Federal

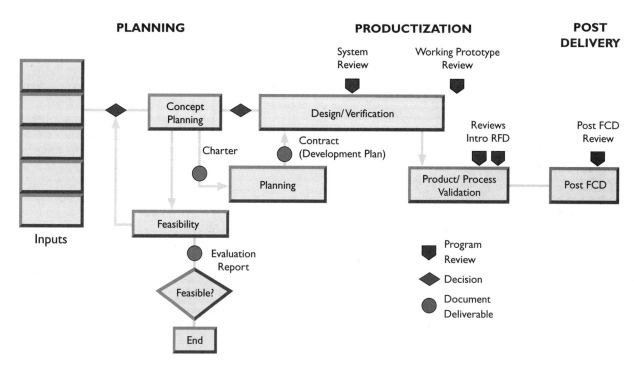

FIGURE 7

ATL's Stage Gate
Process

Drug Administration. The FDA must approve all new products and major modifications before marketing can begin. FDA regulations now also embrace monitoring and approval of manufacturing and service activities. Product design processes, too, are open to rigorous FDA inspection and critique. The FDA requires that all medical devices introduced into the market be preceded either by a premarket notification clearance order (referred to as a 510k), or an approved premarket application (PMA). An approved PMA application indicates that the FDA has determined that the device has been proven, through the submission of clinical trial data and manufacturing quality assurance information, to be safe and effective for its labeled indications. The process of obtaining a 510k typically takes six to nine months, whereas a PMA approval typically takes more than one year.

Manufacturing

ATL manufactures both ultrasound systems and scanheads. The exceptions are the Ultramark 400 and upcoming HDI 1500, which are manufactured by Medison. Since the early 1990s, ATL has aggressively implemented a number of improvements in its internal manufacturing processes in order to drive down system costs, increase quality, and reduce build time. For example, build time for ultrasound systems has been reduced from 140 days in 1988 to just 15 days in 1997, enabling ATL to implement a "build to order" strategy, which minimizes inventory. Build time for scanheads has been reduced from 25 days in 1988 to 16 days in 1997. ATL builds scanheads utilizing a "make to stock" strategy, putting items into finished goods inventory.

Materials account for the largest portion of system and scanhead costs (about 70 percent and 50 percent, respectively), followed by labor (5 percent and 12 percent, respectively), and overhead (20 percent and 38 percent, respectively). Materials costs are driven down each year by focusing on design cost reductions (design for manufacturing) and by negotiating aggressively with suppliers for volume discounts. Until 1990, ATL purchased finished circuit boards for its systems from external vendors. Dissatisfied with the costs it had to pay, in the early 1990s ATL began to move surface mount technology in-house (surface mount technology refers to the process of mounting electronic components onto circuit boards). At the time, ATL was paying as much as 21.5 cents per placement to purchase circuit boards from external manufacturers. By optimizing capacity utilization through better production scheduling, ATL has driven per placement costs from 17.5 cents in 1990, when it first started to finish circuit boards in-house, to just more than 5 cents per placement in 1997. As a result of moving production in-house, ATL now builds and assembles as much as 90 percent of the major modules within its ultrasound systems and scanheads. This level of in-house production is unusual among high-technology companies.

Organization and Management

The bulk of ATL employees are to be found in one of three main functions: product generation (engineering), worldwide sales and marketing, and operations. Three smaller functions—finance, human resources, and legal affairs—perform important support roles. Overall management of ATL is provided by an executive committee composed of the vice presidents of these functions, along with Fell, the CEO. The worldwide marketing and sales organization is divided into three main geographical regions—the Americas, Asia/Pacific, and Europe. Sales and marketing also has a unit dedicated to the U.S. cardiology business. There is no formal crossfunctional matrix structure, although as discussed earlier, product generation is organized as a matrix.

In interviews with this case writer, several managers within ATL voiced concerns about the general organization and management of the company. Internal critics believed that ATL has been too technology driven. The failure of the HDI 1000 was repeatedly mentioned as an example of this phenomenon. The critics believed that ATL's three core functions—product generation, operations, and sales and marketing—were silos that did not communicate sufficiently with each other. They expressed concern that the personalities of some of the key players in the company made matters worse. Fell was nearing seventy, and although he was unquestionably a strong advocate for the com-

pany on Wall Street and had led ATL well, some felt that it was time for him to step down and pass on the reins of leadership. They noted that Fell delegated significant decision-making authority to the executive committee, but the executive committee itself seemed reluctant to make difficult choices, to set overall strategic direction, or to effectively prioritize between competing claims on resources. In the words of one manager, "Failure to focus and prioritize is a real problem within the company. We do not ask whether a dollar spent here yields a greater return than a dollar spent elsewhere. Top management needs to do a better job of communicating priorities." Moreover, the vice president for worldwide sales and marketing was viewed by some of his colleagues on the executive committee as being overly protective of his turf and not enough of a team player. This helped to stymie any attempts by the executive committee to make difficult choices. As a result, according to one internal critic, "This is a company run by the middle management. The executive committee doesn't drive the workings of the company."

At the same time, most managers interviewed acknowledged that the company did have strong technical skills, perhaps stronger than most of its competitors, and that its employees were both excellent and loyal. To quote one, "This is a company with a strong employee base. There is a lot of intellectual horsepower at ATL. People stay here. The employee turnover is low." Another notable feature of the company was the cosmopolitan nature of its management. For example, Fell was English, as was the head of the technology staff, and the executive team included a Frenchman and a Spaniard.

Key Strategic Issues Going Forward

As senior managers met for the 1998 strategic planning review, a number of issues had made their way to the top of the agenda. A key issue was the appropriate strategic focus for ATL. Specifically, should the company continue to participate in the cardiology and mid-range market segments, particularly given its limited resources, and if so, what should the appropriate strategy be? There were some within the company who felt that focusing on the cardiology and mid-range segments pulled scarce resources away from the company's core premium and high-end radiology franchise. Others believed that if the company was to grow, it needed to find some way to participate successfully in these important segments.

The question surrounding the mid-range strategy had been thrown into sharp relief by the failure if the HDI 1000 system to meet its original expectations and by the recent, and to many surprising, deal with Medison. Several managers wondered whether the Medison deal marked a new strategic departure for ATL, or whether it was simply an opportunistic way of maintaining a position in the mid-range market while ATL again tried to develop its own product offering for this segment.

Also high in people's minds was the question of how to respond to the emergence of multimodality competitors in the medical imaging space, such as GE and Siemens, both of which could bundle ultrasound products with other imaging and medical products in their efforts to make purchases more attractive to hospitals. How big a threat would GE prove to be, and how should ATL respond to this threat?

CASE 15

Cooper Tire & Rubber Company, 1998

This case was prepared by Javad Kargar of North Carolina Central University.

INTRODUCTION

Cooper Tire & Rubber Company is one of only a few companies to achieve both consistent and high growth and strong returns for more than a decade. It's future looks bright as well, although top managers must confront threats from the increased competition in the replacement tire market and the recent major changes in the new products, such as run-flats, and production systems announced by the big three tire companies. In addition, foreign low-cost production and sales opportunities have been created with the passage of the North American Free Trade Agreement (NAFTA) and the conclusion of the General Agreement on Tariffs and Trade (GATT).

The Early Years: Rubber Meets Road

Cooper was founded in 1914 as a manufacturer of patches, cement, and repair kits for tires. By 1920, Ira J. Cooper had broadened the scope of the firm, repositioning it as a tire manufacturer. At that time, Cooper had more than 130 domestic competitors, 40 in Ohio alone. The corporation's founder emphasized three principles: good merchandise, fair play, and a square deal. This so-called "Cooper Creed" remains a well-known corporate doctrine.[1]

In 1930, the Cooper Corporation and Giant Tire & Rubber merged with the Falls Rubber Company to form the Master Tire & Rubber Company. Within

This case is intended to be used as the basis for class discussion rather than as an illustration of either effective or ineffective handling of the situation. This case was prepared by Javad Kargar of North Carolina Central University. Used by permission.

a year, the combined production of the three plants totaled 2,850 tires per day. In 1946, the firm's name was changed to Cooper Tire & Rubber Company, in recognition of Ira J. Cooper's contribution.[2]

The Middle Years: Pumping Up Production

Several converging growth factors made the postwar era one of expansion for the tire industry. More disposable income enabled more Americans to own cars. The expansion of the interstate highway system and the trend toward suburbanization meant more wear and tear on tires and an increasing demand for replacement tires. Furthermore, buses, taxis, and trucks were rapidly supplanting the rail system for local and long-distance transportation. Cooper's expansion included the 1956 acquisition and refurbishment of a plant from the Dismuke Tire and Rubber Company in Clarksdale, Mississippi, which enabled Cooper to meet the growing demand for inner tubes and tread rubber. In addition, between 1947 and 1964, Cooper Tire developed its own national wholesaling system. The company attracted private-label customers and earned retailer loyalty by pledging not to open its own sales outlets—a strategy that also allowed it to avoid the headaches of the retail market.[3]

In 1960, the company went public with a listing on the New York Stock Exchange, and its distribution of shares facilitated another decade of growth. That year Cooper also acquired a plant in Auburn, Indiana, where all its automotive and custom-engineered rubber parts were produced. In 1964, an industrial rubber products division was established, and production was expanded with the acquisition of a second industrial product plant near

El Dorado, Arkansas. Other capital improvements at Cooper's corporate headquarters during the 1960s included a new warehouse at the Findlay, Ohio, plant and a research and engineering building to accommodate testing, laboratory, tire design, engineering, and sales training operations. Before the decade had ended, Cooper had completed a new tire plant in Texarkana, Arkansas.

By 1973, Cooper had completed research and development of its own radial tire building equipment and in-house product testing. Full-scale production of steel-belted radial passenger tires at the Findlay and Texarkana plants began the following year. A plant in Bowling Green, Ohio, was purchased in 1977 to manufacture reinforced hose and extruded rubber products.

The 1980s and 1990s: Wheeling and Dealing

The 1980s were years of significant change for Cooper. The company's strong financial condition has enabled it to expand tire production capacity while most of the industry has been contracting. Research and development at Cooper were enhanced by several capital investments during the 1980s. By mid decade, its warehousing capacity had increased to accommodate 3.2 million units of tires. In 1983, Cooper made the *Fortune* 500 list of America's largest industrial companies. In the following year, its net sales exceeded $500 million, and its net income was more than $24 million. In 1985, Cooper made its first foreign acquisition—a manufacturer of inner tubes in Mexico. That same year, Cooper was named one of the *101 Best Performing Companies in America*. In 1988, the Findlay plant and the Moraine distribution center were granted foreign trade subzone status by the U.S. Department of Commerce, which reduced and deferred the company's duty payments on imported raw materials.

As Cooper celebrated its seventy-fifty anniversary in 1989, the company's emphasis on the replacement tire market was rewarded. In the same year, the Tupelo, Mississippi, plant's tire-finishing operations were automated, reducing production costs, and a new building was added to the Bowling Green plant for warehousing. Warranty coverage on Cooper's premium radial was also expanded that year to include treadwear protection. In 1990, Cooper purchased its fourth tire-manufacturing facility, a 1.8-million-square-foot plant in Albany, Geor-

gia. Other expansions of existing plants were made in 1991 and 1992. Cooper acquired British-based Avon Tyres in early 1997. Cooper's capital investment has continued to grow during the 1990s, reaching $194.89 million in 1995, $193.69 million in 1996, and $107.52 million in 1997.

OVERVIEW OF THE TIRE INDUSTRY

Tire manufacturing became an important industry in the first half of the twentieth century as motor vehicles became the dominant mode of transportation. Tire industry comprises two major market segments: (1) the original equipment (OE) market, and (2) the replacement market. Both markets include passenger car tires; light, medium, and heavy truck tires; and farm vehicle tires.

The demand for OE tires is directly related to the number of new vehicles produced. However, demand for replacement tires depends on such factors as the average age of a car, the durability of tire tread, the number of cars in circulation, the average number of miles driven, and gasoline prices. Any reduction in new car sales is considered good news in the replacement market because it means that drivers are hanging on to their cars longer. Even in a strong economy, used car sales rise along with those of new cars, and motorists also spend more time on the road, further increasing the demand for replacement tires. Over the past four years, worldwide production of motor vehicles has remained steady at around 48 million units per year. However, the demand for OE passenger-car tires rose about 10 percent in 1996, to about 57.1 million units, and this demand is expected to continue to rise, reaching 58.1 million in 1998.[4]

The Original Equipment Market Segment

Auto manufacturers buy all of their tires directly from tire manufacturers. No auto producers have integrated backward into tire manufacturing as they have into other component vehicle parts.[5] Competition among the tire manufacturers to supply tires to the auto manufacturers has been fierce. Since tires are such a small cost item in the overall price of new vehicles, changes in OE tire prices have virtually zero effect on total OE tire demand.[6] However, the demand for OE tires, is highly elastic to the ease with which motor vehicle manufacturers could switch to other tire manufacturers' brands. All the major tire manufacturers were eager to have new vehicles equipped with their own brands in order to enhance replacement tire sales. The sale of OE tires was thus seen as strategically important, not only as a way to strengthen sales in the more profitable replacement segment but also to achieve economies of scale in manufacturing.

Vehicle manufacturers set detailed tire specifications for each of their vehicle models, and tire producers must meet those specifications if their tires are to be considered original equipment. It was typical for auto/truck manufacturers to establish higher quality standards for the OE tires they purchased than was the case for replacement tires. The automobile companies buy tires in large quantities and, since the number of buyers is low, they can usually negotiate low prices. Using this leverage over the years, the automakers have managed to negotiate an average price for an OE tire that was several dollars below what wholesale distributors paid tire manufacturers for a replacement tire of somewhat lower quality. In effect, the auto companies bought OE tires for roughly half the retail price commanded by replacement tires. As a result, the original equipment market has become a low-margin one relative to the replacement tire market.

According to the latest forecast by the Tire Market Analysis Committee (TMAC) of the Rubber Manufacturers Association, demand for OE passenger tires is expected to increase a modest 1.2 percent in 1998, rising to 58.1 million units, compared with 57.4 million units predicted in 1997. But OE shipments of light truck tires will remain relatively flat—at or below the 1997 shipment level of 6 million tires, the TMAC predicted.[7]

The Replacement Tire Market Segment

Demand for replacement tires during the 1970s and early 1980s was weak, partly because of the higher gasoline prices, which reduced the average number of miles driven annually per vehicles. In the United States, the average number of miles driven annually per vehicle dropped from 10,800 before the gasoline shortage era to 9,500 miles in 1993.[8] Recently, stable gasoline prices had contributed to a rise in the annual mileage rate per vehicle. Every 100-mile change in the average number of miles traveled per vehicle produced a 1-million unit change in replacement tire production.[9] Since 1991, unit shipments of replacement tires have increased every year (see Table 1 for volume trends in the United States by segment). In 1996, the replacement tire market in the passenger car and light truck in the United States was three times larger than the original equipment market, with a projected 2 percent annual growth rate.[10] During its useful life, a vehicle may require between two and six sets of replacement tires.

Tire manufacturers produce a large variety of grades and lines of tires for distribution under both

TABLE 1

Trends in U.S. Tire Shipments, 1993–1998 (in millions of units)

Type of Tire	1993	1994	1995	1996	1997	1998
Passenger car:						
Replacement	165.2	170.0	171.0	175.3	178.5	180.0
OE	52.2	58.5	55.0	57.1	57.4	58.1
Retread	6.6	5.9	5.0	4.2	3.5	3.1
Light truck, truck, bus:						
Replacement	34.4	37.8	36.6	39.2	41.5	42.8
OE	8.5	10.8	11.6	10.2	10.9	10.9
Retread	22.8	23.3	23.0	23.5	24.2	24.8

Source: Tire Business, December 8, 1997, p. 14.

manufacturers' brand names and private labels. Branded replacement tires are manufactured to the tire producer's own specifications, which are usually below those required by auto manufacturers for OE tires. Some private-label tires supplied to wholesale distributors and large chain retailers are manufactured to the buyer's specifications rather than to the manufacturer's standards. There are often subtle differences in trade depth, grades of rubber, and component construction such that many replacement tires on the market are not equal to the quality and durability of OE tires.[11] As a consequence, replacement tires have a somewhat shorter life span than OE tires. By 1992, most tire manufacturers provided a guaranteed mileage warranty to the buyers of replacement tires. Moreover, nearly all branded replacement tires now carry lifetime warranties against manufacturing defects.

The major tire producers often use network TV campaigns to promote their brands, introduce new types of tires, and pull customers to their retail dealer outlets. Their network TV ad budgets commonly run from $10 million to $30 million a year, and their budgets for cooperative ads with dealers run from $20 million to $100 million a year. Several tire companies also sponsor auto racing events to promote the performance capabilities of their tires.

Replacement tires are marketed to vehicle owners through a variety of retail channels, including independent tire dealers, service stations, manufacturer-owned retail stores, major department stores with auto centers, retail chains, automobile dealerships, and warehouse clubs. Independent tire dealers usually carry the brands of several different major manufacturers as well as a discount-priced private-label brand, providing replacement buyers with a full assortment of brands with varying tread design, widths, durability, quality, and price attributes. Over the years, independent tire dealers handled about 66 percent of replacement tire segments. Surveys have shown that dealers were able to influence a car owner's choice of replacement tires, both as to brand and as to type of tire. Studies have also shown that most replacement tire buyers do not have strong tire brand preferences, making it easy for tire salespeople to switch customers to tire brands and grades with the highest dealer margins.[12] Dealers normally push their private-label tires because their profit margins on them are higher than they are on the name-brand tires of major manufacturers. Dealer margins on re-

placement tires are typically in the 35 to 40 percent range. Independent tire dealers frequently run price promotion ads in the local newspapers, making it easy for price-sensitive buyers to watch for sales and buy at off-list prices.

Service stations stock one or two manufacturers' brand tires and maybe a private-label brand. Retail tire outlets owned and franchised by the tire manufacturers carry only the manufacturer's name brands and perhaps a private-label made by the manufacturer. Department stores and the major retail chains usually market their own private-label brands, but occasionally carry also manufacturers' label tires.

In the past, retread tires have been widely used, and retreaded tire buyers were very price conscious. Retreaded tires were made from tires with worn treads. In 1996, the retreaded tire segment was very small and declining partly because buyers could purchase a new, more reliable set of tires for about $100 more than the cost of retreads. The size of the U.S. passenger car retread market dropped from 6.6 million units in 1993 to about 3.1 million units in 1996 (see also Table 1).

According to TMAC, dealers can look forward during 1998 to continued market growth in the wake of the previous year's expected record of 178.5 million passenger tires and 29 million light truck units. It is forecasting replacement shipments of 12.6 million tires in 1998, up less than 1 percent from 1997's anticipated 12.5 million units.[13]

Securities analyst Harry Millis of Fundamental Research in Willoughby, Ohio, also is upbeat about the industry's prospects in 1998. His forecast calls for slightly higher shipments to the replacement market—182.2 million units of passenger tires and 30.4 million light truck tires. He expects replacement shipments of medium truck tires to reach 13.4 million units during 1998, up 6.3 percent from his last year's estimate. Overall, Millis looks for OE and replacement shipments of all tires to rise about 1.9 percent in 1998 to 293.8 million units.[14]

Raw Material Supplies

More than 200 raw materials are used in manufacturing tires. The most important are natural rubber, synthetic rubber, fabric and fabric cord, polyvinyl alcohol, sulfur, crude oil, carbon black, and high-carbon steel bead wire. Crude oil is the largest raw

TABLE 2

North American Market Leaders 1996

Company/Plant Location	Year Opened	Unionized	Employees	Estimated Capacity
Goodyear				
Medicine Hat, Alberta	1960	Yes	230	8,200 units/day
Napanee, Ontario	1990	No	550	17,000 units/day
Valleyfield, Quebec	1964	Yes	1,300	26,000 units/day
Akron, Ohio	1983	Yes	600	2,000 units/day
Danville, VA	1966	Yes	2,300	13,000 units/day
Gadsden, AL	1929	Yes	2,300	33,000 units/day
Lawton, OK	1978	No	2,300	59,000 units/day
Topeka, KA	1944	Yes	2,000	8,100 units/day
Union City, TN	1968	Yes	3,000	53,100 units/day
Kelly-Springfield Tire, Fayetteville, NC	1969	Yes	2,900	62,000 units/day
Kelly-Springfield Tire, Freeport, III, IL	1964	Yes	1,700	30,000 units/day
Tyler, TX	1962	Yes	1,500	37,500 units/day
Compania Hulera Goodyear	1941	Yes	2,150	18,000 units/day
			22,830	366,900 units/day
Michelin				
Granton, Nova Scotia	1971	No	1,300	9,000 units/day
Waterville, Nova Scotia	1982	No	900	2,000 units/day
Bridgewater, Nova Scotia	1973	No	1,200	11,000 units/day
Uniroyal Goodrich, Kitchene, Ontario	1962	Yes	1,050	17,000 units/day
Michelin Aircraft Tire, Norwood, NC	1989	No	455	12,500 units/day
Dothan, AL	1979	No	700	4,500 units/day
Greenville, SC	1975	No	2,000	23,000 units/day
Lexington, SC	1981	No	1,300	15,000 units/day
Spartanburg, SC	1978	No	1,500	5,000 units/day
Uniroyal Goodrich, Opelika, AL	1963	Yes	1,625	26,000 units/day
Uniroyal Goodrich, Ardmore, OK	1969	No	1,975	32,000 units/day

material cost; the manufacture of an average-size passenger car radial tire consumes about 10 gallons of crude oil. Raw material costs for a typical passenger car radial were about $16, about half of a tire manufacturing cost in 1993.[15]

All of the raw materials are commodities, available in bulk from a variety of sources on world markets.[16] Several manufacturers had integrated backward into rubber manufacturing and tire fabrics, and supply all or part of their production needs for these materials. However, there is no evidence that these manufacturers have gained a meaningful cost advantage or have better ability to differentiate their products on the basis of quality.[17]

The overall price of tire materials has climbed about 8 percent in 1993.[18] Most notable is the rise in the cost of natural rubber, resulting from supply shortages at Asian producers. Those shortages caused an increase in the use of other materials, but that situation has subsequently worsened because of production snags and some facilities going off-line temporarily. Natural rubber will likely remain in short supply for some time, since increasing production is a relatively slow process. Synthetic material prices, however, may decline because the shortage is more a function of production capacity than material availability.[19]

Labor Costs

Although tire manufacturing is relatively capital intensive, there is significant labor content. Labor

TABLE 2 *(continued)*

Company/Plant Location	Year Opened	Unionized	Employees	Estimated Capacity
Uniroyal Goodrich, Fort Wayne, IN	1961	Yes	1,500	29,000 units/day
Uniroyal Goodrich, Tuscaloosa, AL	1945	Yes	2,000	30,000 units/day
			17,505	216,000 units/day
Bridgestone				
Bridgestone/Firestone, Joliette, Quebec	1965	Yes	880	12,500 units/day
Bridgestone/Firestone, Bloomington, Ill	1965	Yes	515	300 units/day
Bridgestone/Firestone, Decature, Ill, IL	1963	Yes	1,945	24,000 units/day
Bridgestone/Firestone, Des Moines, IOWA	1945	Yes	1,741	12,100 units/day
Bridgestone/Firestone, Oklahoma City	1969	Yes	1,032	34,500 units/day
Bridgestone/Firestone, Warren County, TN	1990	Yes	851	5,500 units/day
Bridgestone/Firestone, Wilson, NC	1973	No	2,181	41,000 units/day
			9,145	129,900 units/day
Cooper Tire & Rubber				
Albany, GA	1991	No	900	22,000 units/day
Findlay, Ohio	1919	Yes	1,000	26,000 units/day
Texarkana, Ark	1964	Yes	1,300	39,000 units/day
Tupelo, Miss.	No	No	1,100	39,000 units/day
			4,300	126,000 units/day
Continental/General Tire				
Bryan, Ohio	1967	Yes	350	300 units/day
Charlotte, NC	1967	Yes	1,848	29,000 units/day
Mayfield, KY	1960	Yes	350	5,000 units/day
Mount Vernon, Ill	1974	No	1,961	27,000 units/day
			4,509	87,600 units/day

Source: Tire Business, December 8, 1997, p.15

costs run from about 15 to 40 percent of total costs, depending on wage rates and labor productivity.[20] Industry observers are predicting greater worldwide sourcing of tires from countries having the lowest labor costs, with Korea, Mexico, and Brazil becoming increasingly attractive production locations.[21] Several major tire manufacturers were said to be considering plant locations in low-wage countries. Shipping costs for tires made in foreign countries and then marketed in the United States were approximately $1 per tire in 1992.[22]

Efforts to reduce labor costs at U.S. plants focused mainly on unionized plants and generally took the form of boosting worker productivity through both automation and the elimination of costly work rules.[23] Tire producers' relations with the United Rubber Workers Union (URW) had historically been stormy. URW over the years had won, sometimes after long strikes, an excellent wage and fringe benefit package.[24] Each local union had also negotiated plant work rules that in many cases held down labor productivity. The URW in the past has struck several foreign-owned facilities located in the United States, and the negotiation process appears to be increasingly acrimonious. Herein lies an opportunity for the other tire manufacturers, since demand for OE and replacement tires is already strong.[25] Table 2 shows the North American plants of the various tire producers, their unionized status, and their production capacities.

COMPETITION IN THE REPLACEMENT TIRE MARKET

In recent years, competition in the replacement tire market has centered mainly on price and tire performance. The recession and the uncertainty about job security had forced many consumers to become more price conscious and less brand loyal. Furthermore, since the demand for cars declined between 1988 and 1995, the market for OE tires has shrunk, making competition fiercer in the replacement market. Thus, many tire producers have dumped entire inventories into the replacement market, lowering prices and making profit margins even leaner. Many of the vehicles on the road are old—the average age of the U.S. vehicle fleet is now more than eight years. While these cars and trucks are maintained, the owners often do not want to spend a lot of money on them because there is a new car in the future. This mentality, fostered by the prevailing economical climate, plays right into the hands of the low-cost tire producers.

Tire producers had long emphasized performance characteristics such as traction, handling, and braking. Overall, tire quality and performance were on the upswing. The longer tread life of OE and replacement tires threatened to radically reduce the number of sets of replacement tires needed per vehicle in service.

Cooper's Competitors

Even with sales more than $1.8 billion, Cooper is still relatively small in an industry dominated by a few giant firms. Over the last few years, Cooper's major competitors in the replacement tire market have been Goodyear, Michelin, Bridgestone, and Continental/General Tire. As can be seen in Table 3, the five largest tire manufacturers collectively accounted for approximately 83 percent of the North American's $19.9 billion tire sales in 1996.

Goodyear Goodyear Tire Company, headquartered in Akron, is the largest rubber producer in the world, with about 91,750 employees. Together with its subsidiary, Kelly-Springfield Tire Company, Goodyear can produce in its North American plants approximately 489,300 units of tires a day, which represents more than 35 percent of the North American tire production capacity (see

TABLE 3

Tire Market Leaders, 1996 (in thousands)

Company	Sales	Market Share (%)
Goodyear	$5,815	29.2%
Michelin	4,200	21.1%
Bridgestone	3,900	19.6%
Cooper	1,300	6.3%
Continental	1,250	6.5%
Others	3,435	17.3%
	$19,900	100%

Source: *Tire Business*, December 8, 1997, p. 14.

Table 4). It leads both the North American tire market and Latin American, but ranks second in the world tire market (see Table 5). Its market share accounted for 29.2 percent of North American's $19.9 billion tire sales in 1996.

Goodyear's reputation for tire quality has been considered strong, generally on a par with Michelin and slightly ahead of Bridgestone. Goodyear has had the broadest line of tire products of any manufacturer. Over the years, Goodyear has been among the top fifty national advertisers, promoting its tires. Its distinctive blimps are among the best-known advertising symbols in the United States. Goodyear's R&D expenditures for 1996 were about

TABLE 4

World Top Tire Producers

Company	Units (millions)	Average Price/Unit
Goodyear	178.6	$66
Michelin	171.3	76
Bridgestone	169.0	73
Continental	76.1	61
Sumitomo	61.5	65
Pirelli	48.0	65
Yokohama	21.0	n.a.
Cooper	37.0	43

Source: National Tire Dealers Retreaders Association.

TABLE 5

Tire Market Profitability, 1996 *(in millions)*

Company	Sales	Net Earnings	% of Sales
Bridgestone	$17,993	$646.3	3.6
Goodyear	13,110	101.7	0.78
Michelin	13,943	609.0	4.4
Continental	6,952	128.3	1.8
Sumitomo	5,353	43.0	0.8
Yokohama	3,700	34.5	0.93
Pirelli	6,636	300.0	4.5
Toyo	2,417	9.8	0.41
Cooper	1,615	107.9	6.7
Kumho	1,517	7.7	0.51
Hankook	1,267	12.6	1.0
Ohtsu	944	2.8	0.3

Source: Tire Business, December 8, 1997, p. 14.

$375 million, with a capital investment of more than $618 million (see Table 6).

The company's problems have been aggravated by heavy interest payments (more than $1 million per year) on debts incurred for fending off a hostile takeover in 1986 and by continuing losses on its "All American" oil transport unit. In early 1991, Goodyear reported a $38 million loss on its 1990 operations, the company's first money-losing year since the De-

pression. In June 1991, Goodyear's board of directors hired S.G. Gault as the company's new CEO. Gault immediately made Goodyear's program to become a low-cost producer a high priority, with the goal of reducing costs by $350 million within three years. In addition, Gault set up programs to boost sales by introducing new types of tires. Goodyear became very active in purchasing multi-outlet retailers, while its sales force attempted to convert independent tire dealers to Goodyear brands and to win new accounts for Kelly-Springfield and Lee Tires.

Goodyear's strategy in acquiring large-volume independent dealerships that carried three or four brands was to increase the share of Goodyear tires being sold in these outlets. Later in 1991, Wal-Mart agreed to market Douglas brand radial car and light-truck tires made by Goodyear's Kelly-Springfield subsidiary. Goodyear also recruited Sears to sell seven lines of its tires at Sears's 850 auto centers after research showed that some 2 million Goodyear tires a year were being replaced by tires bought at Sears. In early 1992, Goodyear introduced its Aqua-tred line, with a tread design that prevented hydroplaning, and a new Invicta tire designed to produce less friction and to boost fuel economy by 4 percent. Goodyear made an impressive turnaround, with earnings of $97 million in 1991.

In 1993, tires and tubes represented about 83 percent of Goodyear's 11.60 billion in sales. The company's total profitability that year was $1.16

TABLE 6

R&D and Capital Expenditures in 1996 (in millions)

Company	R & D Expenditures	% of Sales	Capital Investment	% of Sales
Michelin	$697	5.0	$802	5.8
Goodyear	375	2.9	618	4.7
Bridgestone	336	1.9	1,169	6.5
Continental	278	4.0	368	5.3
Pirelli	204	3.1	351	5.3
Sumitomo	161	3.0	423	7.9
Yokohama	123	3.3	na	na
Toyo	76	3.1	163	6.7
Hankook	55	4.3	55	8.3
Cooper	20	1.2	194	12

Source: Tire Business, December 8, 1997, p. 17.

billion. Foreign sales accounted for about 42 percent of its revenues. The OE tire market accounted for approximately 40 percent of Goodyear's tire sales, with the remaining 60 percent made in the replacement market.

In the last decade, Goodyear and its subsidiaries have increased their share of the U.S. replacement tire market from about 15.5 percent to about 29 percent. Goodyear's North American market share in the passenger car replacement market was 17 percent in 1996. In the original equipment tire market, where Goodyear is a major supplier to auto manufacturers, its share has grown from about 27 percent to 36 percent.[26]

Goodyear will likely suffer less of the impact of the supply shortages than other companies because it grows most of its own natural rubber. In 1994, Goodyear led the year's second round of price hikes with 2 to 4 percent increases in October. Other companies followed the higher rates.[27] The company's strategy was to position its more expensive product at a better relative value to attract more interest in the replacement market.[28]

There is no question as to who's in charge at Goodyear in 1998. Sam Gibara continues to hold all three of the company's top jobs—chairman, CEO, and president. He says that's not because he wants to be all-powerful, but because he feels obligated to directly oversee implementation of Goodyear's strategic plan. Gibara was assigned the key role in mapping Goodyear's strategy by Stan Gault, his predecessor, while Gault helped Goodyear survive the financial devastation caused by raider James Goldsmith's hostile attempt to take over the company. Calling on his experience with Goodyear in many parts of the world, Gibara has truly globalized the company and emphasized growth overseas. He has placed heavy emphasis on technology. This is evidenced by the hiring of some 200 scientists and technicians and by the company's development of all-steel ultra-tensile steel (UTS) tire construction and run-flat extended mobility tire (EMT) and by the introduction of its automated IMPACT tire-building system.

The introduction of EMT in July 1997 and UTS technology for tire construction and automated IMPACT tire-production system in February 1998 certainly indicate the company's commitment to providing its dealers and their customers with the very best products available. According to Gibara,

EMT and run-flat tires are top of the line tires that are relatively expensive. He expects that by the end of 1999 about 15 percent of total Goodyear tire production will be run-flat tires and that by the year 2003 it will be 70 percent. Meanwhile, a significant portion of the company's capital budget for 1999 will be devoted to expansion and implementation of the IMPACT system. It takes up to twenty-four months to install the system and to train people to operate it, but the company expects that by 2003, about 15 percent of its tires will be produced by IMPACT.

Goodyear plans to reduce the number of tires it produces, reversing a trend among tire makers of expanding the lines and sizes offered. Over the next three years, Goodyear will introduce at least twenty-one new tires, Marco Molinnari, vice president of sales and marketing, told dealers attending the company's national dealer conference in Nashville, on February 9–12, 1998. But, during that same period, Goodyear will cut the number of lines it offers by 38 percent. Reducing the number of lines will simplify the selling proposition. Fewer lines will also improve the inventory mix and cash flow.

Celebrating its 100th year in business, Goodyear told dealers about two technological innovations that will lead the company into its second century of business: a new low-cost, highly efficient manufacturing process; and a new steel wire cord that is 40 percent stronger than conventional tire reinforcement.

Management at Goodyear also believes in product differentiation. In its centennial year, the Akron-based tire maker has introduced four innovative tires designed to keep it and its dealers ahead of the pack in the competitive North American tire marketplace: (1) Wrangler RF-A (rotation-free aquatred), a 60,000-mile light truck tire package that eliminates the need for tire rotation; (2) Eagle F1 Steel ultra light performance tire; (3) Eagle Aquasteel EMT run-flat performance tire; and (4) Integrity, an OE tire now being offered to the replacement market.[29]

Groupe Michelin Groupe Michelin, a French tire producer, is the acknowledged leader in radial tire technology. The company has about 120,000 employees, and its plants are reputed to be among the most highly automated in the industry. Michelin operates seventy tire plants in fifteen countries in Europe, the U.S., Africa, and Asia. In North America,

Michelin has thirteen tire plants with a total production capacity of 216,000 units per day; eight plants (all nonunion) make Michelin brand tires, while five plants (one nonunion) produce Uniroyal and Goodrich brand tires (see Table 2).

With its 1989 acquisition of Uniroyal-Goodrich, Groupe Michelin became the global market share leader. The company ranked second, behind Goodyear, in market share throughout the North American market. In 1993, its total market share accounted for over 21 percent of North America's tire sales. However, its North American market share in the passenger replacement tire market was 15 percent in the same year. The B.F. Goodrich brand is being positioned to focus on performance and targets the light-truck sector of the U.S. replacement tire market. But the Uniroyal brand is being aimed at the OE sector and at the middle of the replacement tire sector, targeting vehicle owners seeking a medium-grade tire at a medium or average price.

Michelin is represented by nearly 8,000 dealers operating in most cities and many towns. Its Michelin brand tires appeal mainly to quality-sensitive buyers who drive relatively expensive cars. The tire's high performance has permitted the company to claim that children are safer riding on Michelins and, because of this reputation, it can charge top dollar. In 1992, Michelin introduced its XH4 line of tires, guaranteed to deliver 80,000 miles of treadwear. According to one company official, "if new vehicles come equipped with 80,000-mile tires, by the time the owner replaces the OE tires, he won't be planning to keep the car much longer, and he won't be looking at first-line replacement tires."

It has always been Michelin's mission to be a leader in finding new solutions with new tire products. For example, Michelin recently developed a new concept and PAX technology. It is a major step in tire technology because the PAX provides outstanding zero-pressure (run-flat) performance without sacrificing anything in its operation while fully inflated. Present run-flat tires are heavier than standard tires. With heavier side walls capable of supporting the weight of the vehicle, you have a higher rolling resistance that reduces fuel economy. Even with a hole in it with the size of a golf ball, the Michelin Zero Pressure tire will take you up to 50 miles at 55 mph. Recently, Michelin said it would introduce its MXV4 ZP—a broad-market, run-flat passenger tire—to the aftermarket.

Like any totally new concept, the PAX will require changes not only in technology, but also in thinking. Vehicles have carried a spare tire for 100 years and the present tire and rim design has not changed in 40 years. According to Edouard Michelin, there has been tremendous interest in PAX technology from new-vehicle manufacturers. At present the company has about fifty projects worldwide in which it is working with OE automakers on possible PAX applications. Michelin is open to the idea of licensing PAX technology for use by others. The PAX clearly sets a whole new performance standard, which can not be duplicated with the present tire/wheel system and, therefore, will not face the same marketing problem. Over time and with mass production, it is believed that the PAX system will not add cost to the vehicle, specifically since it will require only four tires instead of five by eliminating the spare. It is also believed that this system will be fully successful. However, there is always a risk with any new concept.

Michelin plans to increase its supply of tires for North America by 10 million units per year over the next eighteen months, by increasing both production in North American plants and exports. Overall, its plan is to increase sales by 3 to 5 percent in the next three to five years.

Michelin has always maintained a great deal of secrecy about the C3M automated tire-making facilities. The C3M process results in excellent products with a great degree of uniformity. In addition, the flexibility of this process is outstanding. The C3M can be set up in two or three days. A single machine replaces twenty to thirty machines required in a normal tire-making process, and tire lines can be switched quickly to meet the company's needs. Michelin has eight C3M facilities—one in Sweden, two in the United States, four in France, and one in Brazil. Recently, Michelin announced that it had begun producing tires at a plant in Greenville, S.C., using its new C3M advanced manufacturing process. The highly flexible manufacturing process uses one-third the energy and needs much less factory space than traditional tire plants.

Michelin's Reno plant in the United States is right next to its tire distribution center. The company can switch tire lines being produced to quickly replace tires shipped from inventory, as needed to efficiently maintain its supplies on hand.

For the first half of 1998, Michelin's net earnings fell 11.8 percent, to $290.4 million, while operating profits went down 8.5 percent, to $453.2 million. The company expects the numbers to rebound in the second half of 1998 because of several factors, including recent price increases in North America and Europe, greater truck tire manufacturing capacity across Europe, and productivity gains.

The company's capital spending in the first half of 1998 rose 16 percent, to $526 million, putting it on a pace to exceed the full year expenditures record set last year at $1.05 billion. Among new projects is a medium truck tire plant in China, built adjacent to the existing Michelin Shen Yang Tire Co. Ltd. car and light truck tire plant.

Bridgestone   Bridgestone was the first Japanese tire company to produce tires in the United States. It began manufacturing truck tires in the United States in 1984, when it acquired a truck tire plant from Firestone. Between 1984 and 1988, Bridgestone worked hard to expand its network of retail dealers in order to enhance its U.S. replacement tire market share. In 1988, Bridgestone bought what remained of Firestone for $2.6 billion. The Bridgestone/Firestone subsidiary gave the Japanese tire manufacturer a seven-plant production base and a network of more than 4,000 retail tire outlets and MasterCare auto service centers in North America.

Nevertheless, its acquisition of Firestone has been costly for Bridgestone. Having failed to survey Firestone's plants prior to the purchase, Bridgestone has spent more than anticipated on upgrading its tire plants. The company's president, Akira Yeiri, has installed a new management at the money-losing Bridgestone/Firestone subsidiary, and the new team seems to have made a lot of changes. Bridgestone dominated the Japanese tire market, ranked third in the U.S. market, and was the second top tire producer worldwide in 1993, with sales of $14.4 billion. The company's total profitability in that year was $1.15 billion.[30] Of the 20.5 percent of its North American market share in 1993, about 12 percent was in the replacement tire market. The company's R&D budget for 1996 was $336 million, with a capital investment of more than $1.1 billion. Bridgestone employed more than 9,000 people in its seven North American plants in 1996.[31]

Continental AG   Continental is Germany's largest tire producer and the second largest company in Europe (behind Michelin). Its acquisition of General Tire in 1987 made it the world's fourth largest producer. Immediately after the acquisition of General Tire, Continental launched a five-year, $670 million program to modernize General's U.S. and Canadian plants. Continental supplies OE tires to Mercedes-Benz, BMW, Audi, Volkswagen, Porsche, and Volvo.[32] In 1996, Continental had twenty-four tire plants in sixteen countries. Continental is committed to product development and research. In 1996, Continental spent $278 million in R&D, which represents about 4 percent of its total sales. Its tires are viewed as premium quality and offer independent tire dealers attractive profit margins.

In 1991, Continental merged its sales force for the Continental and General brands under General Tire management at the subsidiary's Akron headquarters.[33] The plan was to position General tires in the mainstream portion of the market, target Continental brands for the upscale segments, and offer dealers more models to better cover the price-quality spectrum. This program also offered dealers the advantages of combined delivery, common purchase terms, and more economical cooperative advertising packages.

The management at Continental believes that the best way to gain market share is by acquiring more dealers rather than through a merger of producers. For this reason, in recent years, Continental had strengthened its access to the replacement tire market by buying a 400-unit retail chain in Great Britain and buying a minority interest in 400 additional retail outlets in Germany, Scotland, Canada, and the United States.[34]

According to Frangengerg, the company's CEO, cost reduction and dealer development have been two of the four pillars of the company's strategy. The others are advancement of innovation and technology and improving the motivation of employees.[35]

COOPER OPERATIONS

Corporate Structure and Top Management

The early 1970s were very troubled times at Cooper; its very survival was in question.[36] In 1972, certified public account Ivan W. Gorr was an employee of Arthur Young & Co. assigned to the Cooper account, and Cooper was looking for a corporate controller. Gorr was offered the job. For Gorr, the decision to join Cooper in the face of adversity was a challenge. He became president and chief operating officer of the company in 1982 and chairman and chief executive officer in 1989.[37]

According to Gorr, "The company turned itself around by embracing one of the fundamental tenets of modern quality management: Listen to your employees. The company had a lot of highly capable people at that time, and top management gave them a chance to stand up and say what the company should be doing and what they could do to help it get there."[38] Moreover, Gorr says: "The cornerstone of Cooper's *customer need* orientation and the driving force behind its goals and objectives is the company's corporate philosophy: to produce value and quality, as defined by the customer. To leverage its core competencies in product quality, efficient production methods, and outstanding service to the distribution channel, Cooper has charted a more aggressive strategic plan, entitled "Cooper 21,"[39] with these key elements:

1. Commitment to rapid global expansion
2. Increased awareness of the Cooper brand
3. Acceleration of already successful cost reduction efforts
4. Greater emphasis on product innovation

A high level of free-flowing communication has been developed among all employees concerning company strategies and objectives. Top management deeply believes that the success of the organization is based on the success of its individual members, and vice versa. Cooper emphasizes a strong commitment to customer service and to quality, both of which demand a high degree of loyalty and an integrated effort among all employees.[40] To foster this integration, Cooper maintains very short lines in the organization of its staffing. Information needed for decision making is accessed quickly, without unnecessary bureaucratic protocols, and communications are direct. The company's stated goals and objectives are well communicated all the way down the line. The bureaucratic layering is said to be so thin that it is difficult to find anyone who bears the title of *assistant*.

Production

Cooper specializes in the manufacturing and marketing of rubber products for consumers and for industrial uses. These products include automobile and truck tires, inner tubes, vibration control products, hose and tubing, and automotive body sealing products. Production takes place in two divisions: the tire division and the engineered rubber products division.[41] Tire products represent about 85 percent of the company's production and sales. Cooper runs its tire plants at 100 percent capacity, while others operate at around 80 percent capacity.[42] In a capital-intensive industry, that creates a lot of leverage.

Cooper's engineered products division (which accounted for about 16 percent of revenues) manufactures a variety of products primarily for the original equipment automotive market. Engineered products division is a relatively fractured area, with competition spread widely among both rubber and plastics companies. Since improving profitability in the tire industry is becoming increasingly difficult, many companies are turning to engineered products.[43] Automakers, in their own efforts to reduce costs, have been pushing suppliers to lower prices. This is creating opportunities for those companies that have the economies of scale needed to manufacture products cheaply and still remain profitable. Cooper, with its low-cost production know-how, will be in a good position to grab a lot of new contracts. According to Cooper's management, the company has received high service ratings from customers for its engineered products and is planning to take full advantage of these opportunities. Cooper is constantly introducing several new tire product lines each year.

In July 1993, Cooper opened a purchasing office in Singapore for raw materials, such as crude rubber. According to management, this move put Cooper closer to the suppliers for better control of the quality and consistency of materials. Cooper's inventory-control policies and procedures are believed to be very efficient—buying ahead on occasion to get the best deals, but no hedging on raw materials.

Cooper's tire operations position it as North America's fourth largest replacement tire maker, and ninth worldwide. With a mix equally divided between proprietary house brand and private customers, Cooper markets its tires in more than 100 countries around the globe.

Cooper's engineered products operations serve virtually every North American light vehicle manufacturer, as well as an expanding number of European-based original equipment manufacturers. With more than 1,800 specific parts, primary product categories for the engineered products operation include vibration control systems to help minimize vehicle vibrations; automotive sealing products to help seal the vehicle from outside elements; and hoses and assemblies to transport fluids, fuels, and gases.

Spurred by trends such as outsourcing and source consolidation, Cooper has steadily strengthened its position as a partner with major OEMs in vehicle design and system problem solving. All six engineered products manufacturing facilities have earned the QS–9000 certification as required by the Big Three automakers. Reflecting the commitment to world-class manufacturing, Cooper's plants have received numerous quality awards, including the Gold Pentastar from Chrysler, the Certified Supplier Award from Eaton Yale Suspension Division, and the Q1 award from Ford Motor. Cooper also received the Source Award as the top supplier in the automotive division.[44]

Historically, Cooper has generated the highest operating margins in the U.S. industry. A key element of the "Cooper 21" plan is to achieve efficiencies across all operating areas. Based on results today, management expects to exceed its 1998 cost savings target of $30 million, and has set a goal of $40 million in cost savings for 1999.[45]

Market Positioning

One factor in Cooper's success is its confining itself to the replacement tire market. Although Cooper is a midget among the world's tire makers, it is the only major U.S. producer that steers clear of the low-margin business of making OE tires for new cars. Instead, it concentrates on the replacement tire market, which is about four times larger than the OE market, and growing faster because the owners of today's highly durable cars are keeping them longer.[46] Although the major competitors control 57 percent of the replacement market, Cooper doubled its share of the balance between 1986 and 1993 to 23 percent. In fact, Cooper made about 8 percent of the 230 million replacement tires sold in North America in 1996.

Research and Development

The second resoundingly correct decision involves R&D. While other tire makers incur high R&D expenses to capture a share of the OE tire market segment, Cooper has been able to produce tires with a proven track record and sell them to value-oriented

customers. Instead of pioneering its own designs, the company often waits to see what sells well as original equipment. Gorr says, "All we have to do is produce the winners."[47] Original tires on new cars normally last up to four years. Therefore, the company has been able to reduce speculative research and development expenditures and has had ample time to produce its own versions. It does not just copy others' designs, however; it has very active R&D departments in both its tire and its engineered rubber products divisions. There is very good communication between the R&D departments and other organizational units. Engineers in R&D are crossed-trained in manufacturing procedures and spend a lot of time on the floor so that they will not be working in isolation. In 1996, Cooper spent $20 million on R&D, more than the $15.1 million spent in 1993. This represents about 1.2 percent of 1996 sales, compared with about 2.9 percent for Goodyear, 1.9 percent for Bridgestone, 4 percent for Continental, and 5 percent for Michelin.

Cooper continues to make progress in the efficiency and productivity of its manufacturing process. According to the management, the major thrust in Cooper has been to reduce the time it takes to develop and produce tires. Speed to market is, and will continue to be, very important to the customers. In early 1998, Cooper expanded its research and engineering capabilities, including a 73,500-square-feet addition to its facility in Findlay, Ohio, and a 900-acre test site near San Antonio.

Computer technology is used in product design and development, machine design, and mold design. Cooper's innovative application of advanced computer technology provides the company with a competitive advantage in bringing new, high-quality products to market quickly. Data collection devices on a wide range of equipment throughout the production process provide accurate information on the components being made. Comparing the component data with product orders from customers ensures that the proper tires are scheduled for production.[48]

A state-of-the-art material handling system to transport materials between the component production and tire assembly areas was introduced at the Tupelo plant in 1992. Automating "high handling" functions has improved efficiency and safety.

Cooper's equipment design engineers continually work to improve existing production equipment or to design custom machines when commercial models are unavailable or are inadequate for the company's requirements. Current projects include developing total systems for tire assembly and component production, as well as collateral equipment and machine modifications to increase efficiency and productivity.[49] Employee teams, comprising production, technical, and marketing employees, are often involved in machine design and process improvements.

In 1995, Cooper entered into an agreement with the ContiTech group of Hanover, Germany, to share technologies in the design and development of original equipment products for the world car market.

Pampering Employees

Much of the credit for Cooper Tire's success, says Alec Reinhardt, the company's chief financial officer, should go to a work force motivated in a way that fits nicely with management's unending search for new ways to hold down costs.[50] Under the direction of Gorr, the company has made great strides in developing a participative, cooperative, and less hierarchical work climate. Cooper's management has long recognized that the performance of dedicated employees can make a difference in a market where one or more competitors sell products with very little difference among them. Therefore, Cooper is always seeking motivated employees who are team players and good communicators and who have the right attitude toward their jobs. Employees become involved at all levels of the organization, especially in the areas of productivity, quality assurance, and customer service. Monthly meetings are held in each department to update workers on new developments and to solicit their suggestions and information about problems. Gorr has recently cited employee recommendations in the key areas of business positioning, product distribution, dealer relations, and quality assurance as the cornerstones on which Cooper's current success rest.[51]

Cooper's employee recruiting process operates by examining applicants through a series of screening procedures. Those applicants who pass the initial screening are motivated people—team players and good communicators—with the right attitude and personality to fit the job for which they have applied. Then they take two pencil-and-paper tests, one of which is keyed to a video tape, followed by a one-on-one behavioral-type interview with a su-

pervisor. Those who make it through the preliminary screening are placed in groups, where *teams* work on problem solving in situations involving some stress.

All new Cooper employees undergo a basic, two-week training and orientation course. Each new employee's spouse is also asked to come in to learn what it means to work for Cooper and why the company considers an employee's spouse to be part of the team. Training courses are designed to meet the specific needs of each employee. After the two weeks' basic course, an employee's training can continue for anywhere from three days to over a year. Cooper's management schedules working hours and shifts so as to allow employees ample days off for participating in community activities and to develop a family atmosphere at the plants.

Incentive is a driving force for Cooper's employees. Cooper's innovative compensation system, in which the earnings of everyone from the CEO to line workers rise and fall with the individual performance and contribution to productivity, instills loyalty. In fact, although incentive programs are offered to every Cooper employee, none of them is based on market share. According to Reinhardt, "Market share is not something that drives our company at all. We are very oriented to return on assets."[52] Executives' compensation provides for cuts as well as raises of up to 30 percent. Profit-sharing opportunities and paid incentives also augment paychecks of Cooper's blue-collar and clerical workers. Hourly workers get paid extra for producing more, and salaried employees can earn bonuses of up to 7.5 percent on the return on assets they handle.

Employee turnover is discouraged by Cooper's stock option plan. Cooper has a very low (3.1 percent) turnover rate, and absenteeism is at one-tenth of 1 percent.[53] For staff and management alike, a long tenure with the company is the norm. At the age of sixty-three, Gorr himself ranked as a newcomer because of having put in only twenty-one years with the company. President Patrick W. Rooney has been with Cooper for forty-one years, and even Reinhardt—the most junior member of the top-management team—joined the company almost twenty-two years ago. The company feels that all jobs are important, and its management has good relations with the workers. According to Gorr, "Dedicated workers help. We grow our talent and we motivate them with ownership, identity, and pride. The non-performed leaves us very quick."[54] All of Cooper's managers are substantial stockholders, as are many workers. Reinhardt estimates that employees hold 20 percent of Cooper's stock. Cooper's stock purchase program has been very rewarding for many employees. If the company's matching contributions are included, those workers who began faithfully investing 6 percent of their salary in Cooper stock when Gorr joined Cooper would have an equity share of well over $1 million.[55]

About 15 percent of Cooper's employees are unionized, a figure considerably lower than that of its rivals. The company had a new contract at one of its two unionized plants in 1994, and the other plant's contracts were reviewed in 1995. According to management, this facility has not posed a serious threat to output. Also, union health care issues were resolved in 1990. Furthermore, a strike probably would not materially affect Cooper's earnings since the company can shift production to nonunionized facilities.

Choosing a Location

Another possible factor in Cooper's superior performance lies in its small-town locations. Cooper wastes no money on frills, not even on utilization of its headquarters in the small town of Findlay, Ohio. When Cooper wants to expand its capacity, it does so cheaply by buying old plants and refurbishing them. This has been made possible by the fact that more than thirty-five tire plants have been shut down since the 1970s.[56] Cooper has a good engineering department, which designs and builds the company's own production equipment, as well as adapts and modifies other equipment to meet its own needs and specifications. This engineering team also continually monitors advances in new technology for possible incorporation in Cooper's manufacturing processes.[57]

Cooper's tire plants are in places such as Tupelo, Mississippi, and Texarkana, Arkansas, where the company is a master employee and where people have a strong work ethic. In these small towns, Cooper employees at all levels and their families constantly interact in community churches and organizations. A feeling seems to develop that everyone has a stake in the future of the company. Analysts say that Cooper's small-town locations permit it to pay lower salaries and to reap other savings over companies in urban sites. Most Cooper employees grew up in and around the rural areas where the company's four tire plants are located. Employees drawn from these smaller communities tend to make a more long-term commitment to the firm and to exhibit a stronger work ethic than employees from larger and more mobile communities. According to Reinhardt, "There's a different work ethic in smaller communities."[58]

Quality Control

Cooper's quality control policies and procedures are managed by specific staff, but a great deal of the responsibility for quality rests with the individual worker, who is trained to do his own quality-assurance checks. Cooper's employee-centered organization results in high product quality. Employees receive as many as 900 hours of training, and signs bearing such slogans as "Quantity is Important, but Quality is MORE Important" hang from factory walls. To symbolize a personal commitment to quality, each tire carries not only a brand name, but also a sticker identifying the worker who built it. This helps foster pride in workmanship among Cooper's employees and the company hopes, creates a bond with the consumers buying the tires.[59]

According to an industry analyst, Cooper is far ahead of the curve in emphasizing quality products and services. Quality has become such a big part of Cooper's culture that it is not talked about anymore.[60] As a leader of the 215,000-member U.S. Chamber of Commerce, Gorr plans to travel frequently, carrying the message that there is no substitute for producing quality products and being sensitive to customer needs in today's competitive global marketplace. He will be able to point to the difference in performance that adopting this culture has made in his own company.[61]

Distribution and Marketing

Cooper markets its products nationally and internationally through well-established channels of distribution. Among its customers are automotive manufacturing companies, independent tire dealers and wholesale distributors, and large retail chains. Independent dealers and distributors remain crucial to the company's success. Rather than selling through its own retail chains as Goodyear and Bridgestone/Firestone do, Cooper continues to sell about half of its production as private labels to the store chains, mass merchants, and discounters. Private-label customers include Sears, TBC, Hercules, Pep Boys, Del-Nat, Parrish, and Nokian. The other half of the production is primarily sold under the company's Cooper, Mastercraft, Starfire, and Roadmaster house brand through independent tire dealers, which, according to *Modern Tire Dealer*, as a distribution channel represented 71 percent of all passenger tires sold in 1997.[62] According to industry research, customers buy the tires recommended by the dealer more than 50 percent of the time.[63] And according to the tire trade press, dealers love Cooper because it provides them with the highest gross margins in the industry and does not have company retail stores that compete against them. Says Gorr, "Our aim is to assist our dealers, who are our valued customers, not compete against them."[64] Cooper's ten largest customers accounted for approximately 90 percent of its total 1996 sales. Net sales in 1996 reached more than $1.6 billion, increasing 8.4 percent over the prior year's sales.

Product shipments to customers are directed through a strategic, nationwide network of distribution centers, which ensures timely deliveries to customers. A new management information system was introduced to further streamline inventory and order-processing operations and to provide even better service to customers.

Cooper focuses its relatively modest marketing budget on supporting its independent dealers, mainly by providing superior service and delivery and by offering a value-priced product on which the dealers generally make larger profits. Cooper advertising programs assist dealers and distributors with promotional materials in their local markets. Cooperative advertising allowances are based on annual dealer purchases and are applicable to all types of media.[65] Cooper's 1993 marketing and general administrative expenses were about 5 percent of sales, compared with Goodyear's 17 percent. The "American-Owned, American-Made" theme, introduced during 1992, gained much publicity for the company. A variation of this theme was used in 1993: "Put your trust in American hands." Cooper has no active advertising or promotion for its engineered products because these are targeted to industrial users (auto manufacturers), who comprise a small market.

Cooper's house brands are growing a little faster than its private-label business. To broaden brand awareness among customers, at the beginning of 1997 Cooper signed Arnold Palmer as company spokesman and stepped up its media advertising expenditures. It is believed that these moves are beginning to pay off, with all four house brands showing healthy sales increases and the Cooper brand making the strongest showing.

Over the past few years, price pressure on private-label tires has increased, squeezing the price differential between major brands and private-labels. But Cooper management believes that private-label tires still play a very important role in the replacement tire market. Private-label tires are an excellent value and provide independent tire dealers with the ability to call their marketing shots and maintain product control in their local markets. The strong private brands with distributors and dealers who provide good service will continue to prosper.[66]

Cooper has expanded exports for its products over the past several years. Its new acquisition of British-based Avon Tyres has added $169 million to annual sales, increasing Cooper's international sales exposure from its 8 percent preacquisition level and providing a strong base for future global expansion. Management has set a goal of achieving 25 to 30 percent of total sales from international operations within five years, with the growth planned to come from tires and engineered products.[67]

In 1997 and 1998, Cooper was honored by private brand customer Sears and also received high marks from independent dealers. The Company received the Sears Partners in Progress Award out of more than 10,000 vendors vying for this recognition. Additionally, Cooper and Mastercraft house brands were ranked at the top of a national survey of tire dealers conducted by *Tire Review*, with dealers ranking Mastercraft first and Cooper second.[68]

Financial Performance

Over the past decade, Cooper has demonstrated that a company does not have to lead its industry to generate enormous wealth for its owners. The company has posted impressive profits over the years as other tire makers have struggled to regain profitability. Its average return on equity between 1988 and 1994 was more than 22 percent. In 1997, the company's net income reached $122.4 million, up 13.5 percent from net income in 1996 of $107.9 million. Net income for 1995 reached 112.8 million, down about 14 percent from 1994. Return on stockholders' equity was about 14.7 percent in

1997 and averaged 19.5 percent over the past five years. Cooper's stock price increased dramatically in the last decade, rising by 3,800 percent. Stock reached a high of $28.44 versus a low of $15.75 during 1997. Cooper's financial statements are shown in Tables 7 and 8.

Cooper's strong operating cash flows provided funds for investment in capacity expansion and technological advances and contributed to growing financial strength. The company's capital expenditures during 1997 amounted to $107.5 million, compared with $193.7 million in 1996, and $194.9 million in 1995. The cash flow from operations after capital spending has been very good, and Cooper has been able to reduce its debt over several years. Its long-term debt-to-equity ratio was about 1 to 4 in 1997, up from 1 to 20 in 1994.

Toward the Future

There are a number of issues to be considered. Cooper has always operated under a *price umbrella* created by the OE tire manufacturers; therefore, as that umbrella rises, so does Cooper's profitability. However, the industry is becoming extremely competitive as major tire makers recognize the attractiveness of the replacement tire market. Cooper will not have the luxury of watching how a tire performs for two or three years before deciding whether to copy it. Furthermore, Cooper's competitors have recently narrowed the gap on this low-cost producer, and the closer rivalry is likely to cause the company's margins to rise more slowly than in the past years. This may signal the beginning of heightened price competition. More tire manufacturers have started providing guaranteed longer mileage warranties to the buyers of replacement tires, and the longer warranties of 60,000 to 80,000 miles are likely to create an intermediate-term demand problem. Therefore, Cooper may find it difficult to maintain its growth rate. Finally, with the passage of NAFTA and the conclusion of GATT, foreign sales opportunities appear to be increasingly meaningful.

What should Cooper do to ensure its continued growth? Some managers suggest that Cooper should develop new-model tires and aggressively expand capacity in its OE manufacturing business in the United States and Mexico. Few managers believe that Cooper's performance could be made stronger by increased output. They argue that the expansion recently completed should enable the

TABLE 7

Consolidated Statements of Income (dollars in thousands, except per share)

	Year Ended December 31			
	1997	1996	1995	1994
Net sales	$ 1,813,005	$ 1,619,345	$ 1,493,622	$ 1,403,243
Cost of goods sold	1,403,968	1,289,729	1,179,582	1,070,375
Gross income	314,573	252,796	250,727	277,265
Selling, Admin. and GE	105,532	79,874	73,796	68,748
Depreciation and amort.	94,464	76,820	63,313	55,603
Operating income	209,041	172,922	176,931	208,517
Other income (expenses)	1,406	824	3,836	2,282
Interest expenses	17,283	5,969	4,212	3,850
Pretax income	194,792	172,092	180,070	208,119
Income taxes	72,381	64,208	67,250	79,600
Net income	122,411	107,884	112,820	128,519
Net income per share	1.55	1.30	1.35	1.54
Average shares outstanding	77,442,158	81,581,768	83,510,732	83,623,000

Source: Cooper Tire & Rubber Company, 1997, Annual Report.

TABLE 8

Consolidated Balance Sheet (in thousands)

	1997	*1996*	*1995*	*1994*
Assets				
Current assets:				
Cash and cash equivalents	$ 52,910	$ 19,459	$ 23,187	$ 103,285
Accounts receivable	292,416	267,149	257,049	221,237
Inventories	191,684	141,618	137,964	116,523
Prepaid expenses	17,602	15,399	12,384	13,666
Total current assets	$ 554,612	$ 443,625	$ 430,584	$ 454,711
Properties and plants, net	860,448	792,419	678,876	549,601
Other assets	80,896	36,965	34,241	35,419
Total assets	$1,495,959	$1,273,009	$1,143,701	$1,039,731
Liabilities and Shareholders' Equity				
Current liabilities				
Accounts payable—trade	$ 100,135	$81,571	$ 78,823	$83,864
Notes payable and current long-term debt	11,273	37,081	5,035	5,112
Accrued payables	40,311	32,299	29,422	58,324
Income taxes payable	6,477	3,116	10,834	6,049
Total current liabilities	$ 200,331	$ 187,495	$ 158,368	$ 151,608
Long-term debt	205,525	69,489	28,574	33,614
Provision risks/charges	144,566	139,070	132,963	127,347
Deferred taxes	73,608	52,768	36,656	29,737
Other long-term liabilities	38,351	37,575	38,341	35,348
Shareholders' equity	833,575	786,612	748,799	662,077
Total liabilities and equity	$1,495,956	$1,273,009	$1,143,701	$1,039,731

Source: Cooper Tire & Rubber Company, 1997 Annual Report.

company to boost annual sales of $2.5 billion, while more than doubling profits within five years. However, some other managers want to challenge such projections. They argue that the company could not handle such rapid expansion and strongly believe that the key success factor for Cooper is to achieve more efficiencies across all the existing operations. Some even suggest that the company stop growing. They argue that the tire industry is mature and that currently North America has 16 percent more capacity for making car tires. Some managers also argue that the company's product identifiability should be aggressively im-

proved. In light of these arguments, it is left to management to find concrete answers to these and other strategic question.

Endnotes

1. Cooper Tire & Rubber Company, "Our History," 1997.
2. Ibid.
3. Ibid.
4. *Tire Business,* December 8, 1997. A Crain publication.
5. A. A. Thompson, Jr., "Competition in the World Tire Industry, 1993," *Strategic Management,* 7th ed., (Irwin, 1993), pp. 581–614
6. Ibid.

7. *Tire Business,* December 8, 1997
8. Thompson, "Competition in the World Tire Industry."
9. Ibid.
10. *Tire Business,* December 8, 1997.
11. Thompson, "Competition in the World Tire Industry."
12. Ibid.
13. *Tire Business,* January 5, 1998. A Crain publication.
14. Ibid.
15. Thompson, "Competition in the World Tire Industry."
16. Ibid.
17. Ibid.
18. E. B. Lusk, "Tire & Rubber Industry," *Value Line,* September 16, 1994.
19. Ibid.
20. Thompson, "Competition in the World Tire Industry."
21. Ibid.
22. Ibid.
23. Ibid.
24. Ibid.
25. Lusk, "Tire & Rubber Industry."
26. *Tire Business,* December 8, 1997.
27. Lusk, "Tire & Rubber Industry."
28. Ibid.
29. *Tire Business,* December 8, 1997.
30. Ibid.
31. Ibid.
32. Thompson, "Competition in the World Tire Industry."
33. *Tire Business,* November 4, 1991, p. 12. A Crain publication.
34. Thompson, "Competition in the World Tire Industry."
35. *Modern Tire Dealer* (August 1998), 79, A Bill publication.
36. A. G. Holzinger, "A Successful Competition," *Nation's Business* (April 1993).
37. Ibid.
38. Ibid.
39. Cooper's home page (http://www.coopertire.com/profilepage2.htm).
40. Holzinger, "A Successful Competition."
41. Cooper Tire & Rubber Company, 1993 Annual Report, February 1993.
42. A. Taylor, "Cooper Tire & Rubber: Now Hear This Jack Welch!" *Fortune,* April 6, 1992.
43. Lusk, "Tire & Rubber Industry."
44. Cooper's home page.
45. Ibid.
46. Holzinger, "A Successful Competition."
47. Taylor, "Cooper Tire & Rubber."
48. Holzinger, "A Successful Competition."
49. Cooper Tire & Rubber Company, 1993 Annual Report, February 1993.
50. *Tire Business,* December 8, 1997.
51. Holzinger, "A Successful Competition."
52. Taylor, "Cooper Tire & Rubber."
53. Holzinger, "A Successful Competition."
54. Ibid.
55. H. Byrne, "Cooper Tire and Rubber: Ready to Accelerate," *Barron's,* March 21, 1994.
56. Ibid.
57. Holzinger, "A Successful Competition."
58. Ibid.
59. Byrne, "Cooper Tire and Rubber."
60. Ibid.
61. Holzinger, "A Successful Competition."
62. *Modern Tire Dealer.*
63. Holzinger, "A Successful Competition."
64. Thompson, "Competition in the World Tire Industry."
65. Holzinger, "A Successful Competition."
66. Cooper's home page.
67. Ibid.
68. Ibid.

The Home Video Game Industry: From *Pong* to Dreamcast

This case was prepared by Charles W. L. Hill of the University of Washington.

AN INDUSTRY IS BORN

In 1968, Nolan Bushnell, the twenty-four-year-old son of a Utah cement contractor, graduated from the University of Utah with a degree in engineering.[1] After graduation, he moved to California, where he briefly worked in the computer graphics division of Ampex. At home, Bushnell turned his daughter's bedroom into a laboratory (the little girl was expelled to the living room couch). There he created a simpler version of *Space War*, a computer game that had been invented in 1962 by an MIT graduate student, Steve Russell. Bushnell's version of Russell's game, which he called *Computer Space*, was made of integrated circuits connected to a 19-inch black-and-white television screen. Unlike a computer, Bushnell's invention could do nothing but play the game, but that also meant that unlike a computer, it could be produced cheaply.

Bushnell envisioned video games like his standing next to pinball machines in arcades. With hopes of having his invention put into production, Bushnell left Ampex for a small pinball company that manufactured 1,500 copies of his video game. The game never sold, primarily because players had to read a full page of directions before they could play the game—far too complex for an arcade game. Bushnell left the pinball company and, together with a friend, Ted Dabney, put in $500 to start a company that would develop a simpler video game. They wanted to call the company Syzygy, but the name was already taken, so they set-

tled on Atari, a Japanese word that was the equivalent of *check* in the *go*.

In his home laboratory, Bushnell built the simplest game he could think of. People knew the rules immediately, and it could be played with one hand, which, according to Bushnell, had the virtue of enabling a player to hold a beer in the other. In the game, which was modeled on table tennis, a ball was batted back and forth by paddles that could be moved up and down sides of a court by twisting knobs. He named the game *Pong* after the sonarlike sound that was emitted every time the ball connected with a paddle.

In the fall of 1972, Bushnell installed his prototype for *Pong* in Andy Capp's tavern in Sunnyvale, California. The only instructions were "avoid missing the ball for a high score." In its first week, 1,200 quarters were deposited in the casserole dish that served for a coin box in Bushnell's prototype. Bushnell was ecstatic; his simple game had brought in $300 in a week. The pinball machine that stood next to it averaged $35 a week.

Lacking the capital to mass-produce the game himself, Bushnell approached established amusement game companies, only to be repeatedly shown the door. Down but hardly out, Bushnell cut his hair, put on a suit, and talked his way into a $50,000 line of credit from a local bank. With this, he set up a production line in an abandoned roller skating rink. He hired a motley collection of long-haired geeks and put them to work assembling machines while Led Zeppelin and the Rolling Stones were played at full volume over the speaker system of the rink. Among his first batch of employees was a skinny seventeen-year-old named Steve Jobs, who would later found a few companies of his own,

This case is intended to be used as the basis for class discussion rather than as an illustration of either effective or ineffective handling of the situation. This case was prepared by Charles W. L. Hill, University of Washington. Used by permission.

including Apple Computer, NeXT, and Pixar. Like others, Jobs had been attracted by a help wanted ad that read: "Have Fun and Make Money."

In no time at all, Bushnell was selling all of the machines that his small staff could make—about ten per day—but to really grow, he needed additional capital. While the ambiance at the rink, with its mix of freaks, rock music, and marijuana fumes, put off most potential investors, Don Valentine, one of the country's most astute and credible venture capitalists, was impressed with the growth story. Armed with Valentine's money, Atari began to ramp up production and expand its range of games. New games included *Tank* and *Breakout*—the latter designed by Jobs and a friend of his, Steve Wozniak, who had left Hewlett-Packard to work at Atari.

By 1974, 100,000 *Pong*-like games were sold worldwide. Although only 10 percent of those were manufactured by Atari, the company still made $3.2 million that year. With the *Pong* clones coming on strong, Bushnell decided to make a *Pong* system for the home. In fact, Magnavox had been marketing a *Pong*-type game for the home since 1972, although sales had been modest.[2] Bushnell's team managed to compress Atari's coin-operated *Pong* game down to a few inexpensive circuits, which were contained in the game console. Atari's *Pong* had a sharper picture and more sensitive controllers than the Magnavox machine; it also cost less. Bushnell then went on a road show, demonstrating *Pong* to toy store buyers, but met with an indifferent response and no sales. Dejected, he returned to Atari with no idea of what to do next. Then the buyer for the sports goods department at Sears came to see Bushnell, reviewed the machine, and offered to buy every home *Pong* game Atari could make. With the backing of Sears, Bushnell boosted production. Sears ran a major television ad campaign to sell home *Pong*, and Atari's sales soared, hitting $450 million in 1975. The home video game had arrived.

BOOM AND BUST

Nothing attracts competitors like success, and by 1976 some twenty different companies were crowding into the home video game market, including National Semiconductor, RCA, Coleco, and Fairchild. It was the last of these companies that was to revolutionize the industry. Recognizing the limitations of existing home video game designs, in 1976 Fairchild came out with a home video game system capable of playing multiple games. The Fairchild system consisted of three components—a console, controllers, and cartridges. The console was a small computer optimized for graphics processing capabilities. It was designed to receive information from the controllers, process it, and send signals to a TV monitor. The controllers were handheld devices used to direct on-screen action. The cartridges contained chips encoding the instructions for a game. They were designed to be inserted into the console.

In 1976, Bushnell sold Atari to Warner Communications for $28 million. Bushnell stayed on to run Atari. Backed by Warner's capital, in 1977 Atari developed and bought out its own cartridge-based system, the Atari 2600. The 2600 system was sold for $200, and associated cartridges retailed for $25 to $30. Sales surged during the 1977 Christmas season. However, a lack of manufacturing capacity on the part of market leader Atari and a very cautious approach to inventory by Fairchild led to shortages and kept sales significantly below what they could have been. Fairchild's cautious approach was the result of prior experience in consumer electronics. A year earlier, it had ramped up demand for its digital watches, only to get severely burnt by a buildup of excess inventory that had caused the company to take a $24.5 million write-off.[3]

Coming out of the 1977 Christmas season, Atari claimed to have sold around 400,000 units of the 2600 VCA, about 50 percent of all cartridge-based systems in American homes. Atari had also racked up more than $100 million in sales of game cartridges. By this point, second-place Fairchild sold around 250,000 units of its system. Cartridge sales for the year totaled about 1.2 million units, with an average selling price of around $20. Fresh from this success, and fortified by market forecasts predicting sales of 33 million cartridges and an installed base of 16 million machines by 1980, Bushnell committed Atari to manufacturing 1 million units of the 2600 for the 1978 Christmas season. Atari estimated that total demand would reach 2 million units. Bushnell was also encouraged by signals from Fairchild that it would again be limiting production to around 200,000 units. At this point, Atari had a library of around nine games. Fairchild had seventeen.[4]

Atari was not the only company to get excited by the growth forecasts. In 1978, a host of other companies entered the market with incompatible cartridge-based home systems. They included Coleco, National Semiconductor, Magnavox, General Instrument, and around a dozen others. However, the multitude of choices did not seem to entice consumers, and the 1978 Christmas season brought unexpectedly low sales. An industry shake-out followed in which only Atari and Coleco survived. Atari lost Bushnell, who was ousted by Warner executives (Bushnell went on to start Chuck E. Cheese Pizza Time Theater, a restaurant chain that had 278 outlets by 1981). Bushnell later stated that part of the problem was a disagreement over strategy. Bushnell wanted Atari to price the 2600 at cost and make money on sales of software; Warner wanted to continue making profits on hardware sales.[5]

Several important developments occurred in 1979. Several game producers and programmers defected from Atari to set up their own firm, Activision, to make games compatible with the Atari 2600. Their success encouraged others to follow suit. Second, Coleco developed an expansion module that allowed its machine to play Atari games. Atari and Mattel (which entered in 1979) did likewise. Third, 1979 saw the introduction of three new games into the home market—*Space Invaders*, *Asteroids*, and *Pac-Man*. All three were adapted from popular arcade games and all three helped drive demand for players.

Demand recovered strongly in late 1979 and kept growing for the next three years. In 1981, U.S. sales of home video games and cartridges hit $1 billion. In 1982, they surged to $3 billion, with Atari accounting for half of this amount. It seemed as if Atari could do no wrong. The 2600 was everywhere. Some 20 million units were sold, and by late 1982, there were now hundreds of games available for it. A large number of independent companies were now producing games for the 2600, including Activision, Imagic, and Epyx. Second-place Coleco was also doing well, partly based on a highly popular arcade game, *Donkey Kong*, that it had licensed from a Japanese company called Nintendo.

Atari was also in contact with Nintendo. In 1982, the company very nearly licensed the rights to Nintendo's Famicom, a cartridge-based video game system machine that was a big hit in Japan. Atari's successor to the 2600, the 5200, was not

selling well and the Famicom seemed like a good substitute. However, the negotiations broke down when Atari discovered that Nintendo had extended its *Donkey Kong* license to Coleco. This allowed Coleco to port a version of the game to its home computer, which was a direct competitor to Atari's 800 home computer.[6]

Coming off a strong 1982, the industry hoped for continued growth in 1983. Then the bottom dropped out of the market. Sales of home video games plunged to $100 million. Atari lost $500 million in the first nine months of the year, causing the stock of the parent company, Warner Communications, to drop in half. Part of the blame for the collapse was laid at the feet of an enormous inventory overhang of unsold games. Some 15 to 20 million surplus game cartridges were left over from the 1982 Christmas season (in 1981 there were none). On top of this, around 500 new games hit the market in 1993. The average price of a cartridge plunged from $30 in 1979 to $16 in 1982, and then $4 in 1983. As sales slowed, retailers cut back on the shelf space allocated to video games. It proved difficult for new games to make a splash in a crowded market. Atari had to bulldoze 6 million *ET: The Extraterrestrial* games. Meanwhile, big hits from previous years, such as *Pac-Man*, were bundled with game players and given away free to try to encourage system sales.[7]

Surveying the rubble, commentators claimed that the video game industry was dead. The era of dedicated game machines was over, they said. Personal computers were taking their place.[8] It seemed to be true. Mattel sold off its game business, Fairchild moved on to other things, Coleco folded, and Warner decided to break up Atari and sell its constituent pieces—at least those for which it could find a buyer. No one in America seemed to want to have anything to do with the home video game business—no one except Minoru Arakawa, the head of Nintendo's U.S. subsidiary, Nintendo of America (NOA). Picking through the rubble of the industry, Arakawa noticed that there was one group of people who seemed to be oblivious to the obituaries. Video arcades were still packed, bringing in $7 billion a year—more money than the entire movie industry. Perhaps it was not a lack of interest in home video games that had killed off the industry. Perhaps it was bad business practice.

THE NINTENDO MONOPOLY

Nintendo was a century-old Japanese company that had built up a profitable business making playing cards before diversifying into the video game business. Based in Kyoto and still run by the founding Yamauchi family, in the late 1970s the company started to diversify into the video game business. The first step was to license video game technology from Magnavox. In 1977, Nintendo introduced a home video game system in Japan based on this technology that played a variation of *Pong*. In 1978, the company began to sell coin-operated video games. It had its first hit with *Donkey Kong*, designed by Sigeru Miyamoto.

The Famicom

In the early 1980s, the company's boss, Hiroshi Yamauchi, decided that Nintendo had to develop its own video game machine. He pushed the company's engineers to develop a machine that combined superior graphics-processing capabilities with a low price. Yamauchi wanted a machine that could sell for $75, less than half the price of competing machines at the time. He dubbed the machine the "Family Computer," or Famicom. The machine his engineers designed was based on the controller, console, and plug-in cartridge format pioneered by Fairchild. It contained two custom chips: an 8-bit central processing unit and a graphics-processing unit. Both chips had been scaled down to perform only essential functions. A 16-bit processor was available at the time, but to keep costs down, Yamauchi refused to use it.

Nintendo approached Ricoh, the electronics giant, which had spare semiconductor capacity. The chips, they said, had to cost no more that 2,000 yen. Ricoh thought that the 2,000 yen price point was absurd. Yamauchi's response was to guarantee Ricoh a 3-million-chip order within two years. Since the leading companies in Japan were selling at most 30,000 video games per year at the time, many within the company viewed this as an outrageous commitment, but Ricoh went for it.[9]

Another feature of the machine was its memory; 2,000 bytes of RAM (random access memory) as opposed to the 256 bytes of RAM in the Atari machine. The result was a machine with superior graphics-processing capabilities and faster action that could handle far more complex games than

Atari games. Nintendo's engineers also built a new set of chips into the game cartridges. In addition to chips that held the game program, Nintendo developed memory map controller (MMC) chips, which took over some of the graphics-processing work from the chips in the console and enabled the system to handle more complex games. With the addition of the MMC chips, the potential for more sophisticated and complex games had arrived. Over time, Nintendo's engineers developed more powerful MMC chips, enabling the basic 8-bit system to do things that originally seemed out of reach. The engineers also figured out a way to include a battery backup system in cartridges, which allowed some games to store information independently—to keep track of where a player had left off or to track high scores.

The Games

Yamauchi recognized that great hardware would not sell itself. The key to the market, he reasoned, was great games. When developing the hardware, Yamauchi had instructed the engineers to make sure that "it was appreciated by software engineers." Moreover, Nintendo decided that Nintendo would become a haven for game designers. "An ordinary man," he said, "cannot develop good games no matter how hard he tries. A handful of people in this world can develop games that everyone wants. Those are the people we want at Nintendo."[10]

Here Yamauchi had an ace in the hole in the person of Sigeru Miyamoto. Miyamoto, a graduate of Kanazawa Munici College of Industrial Arts, had joined Nintendo at the age of twenty-four. Yamauchi had hired Miyamoto as a favor to his father, an old friend, although he had little idea what he would do with an artist. For three years, Miyamoto worked as Nintendo's staff artist. Then in 1980, Yamauchi called Miyamoto into his office. Nintendo had started selling coin-operated video games, but one of the new games, *Radarscope*, was a disaster. Could Miyamoto come up with a new game? Miyamoto was delighted. He had always spent a lot of time drawing cartoons, and as a student, he had played video games constantly. Miyamoto believed that video games could be used to bring cartoons to life.[11]

The game Miyamoto developed was nothing short of a revelation. At a time when most coin-operated video games lacked characters or depth,

Miyamoto created a game around a story that had both. At a time when most games involved battles with space invaders or heroes shooting lasers at aliens, Miyamoto's game did neither. Based loosely on *Beauty and the Beast* and *King Kong*, Miyamoto's game has a pet ape run off with his master's beautiful girlfriend. His master is an ordinary carpenter, called Mario. Neither handsome nor heroic, Mario has a bulbous nose, a bushy mustache, a pair of large, pathetic eyes, and a red cap (which Miyamoto added because he was not good at hairstyles). He does not carry a laser gun. The ape runs off with the girl to get back at his master, who was not especially nice to the beast. The man, of course, has to get the girl back. To do that, the little man has to run up ramps, climb ladders, jump off elevators, and the like, while the ape throws objects at the hapless carpenter. Since the main character is an ape, Miyamoto called him *Kong*, and because he was as stubborn as a donkey, he called the game *Donkey Kong*.

Released in 1981, *Donkey Kong* was a sensation in the world of coin-operated video arcades and a smash hit for Nintendo. In 1984, Yamauchi again summoned Miyamoto to his office. He needed more games, this time for the Famicom. Miyamoto was made the head of a new R&D group. He was told to come up with the most imaginative video games ever.

Miyamoto began with Mario from *Donkey Kong*. A colleague had told him that Mario looked more like a plumber than a carpenter, so a plumber he became. Miyamoto gave Mario a brother, Luigi, who was as tall and thin as Mario was short and fat. They became the *Super Mario Brothers*. Since plumbers spend their time working on pipes, large green sewer pipes became obstacles and doorways into secret worlds. Mario and Luigi's task was to search for the captive Princess Toadstool. Mario and Luigi are endearing bumblers, unequal to their task yet surviving. They shoot, squash, or evade their enemies—a potpourri of Dr. Seuss–like inventions that include flying turtles and stinging fish, man-eating flowers and fire-breathing dragons—while they collect gold coins, blow air bubbles, and climb vines into smiling clouds.[12]

Super Mario Brothers was introduced in 1985. For Miyamoto, this was just the beginning. Between 1985 and 1991, he produced eight *Mario* games. Some 60 to 70 million were sold worldwide, making Miyamoto the most successful game designer in

the world. After adapting *Donkey Kong* for the Famicom, he went on to create other top-selling games, including another classic, *The Legend of Zelda*. While Miyamoto drew freely on folklore, literature, and pop culture, the main source for his ideas was his own experience. The memory of being lost among a maze of sliding doors in his family's home was recreated in the labyrinths of the *Zelda* games. The dog that attacked him when he was a child attacks Mario in *Super Mario*. As a child, Miyamoto had once climbed a tree to catch a view of far-off mountains and got stuck. Mario gets himself into a similar fix. Once Miyamoto went hiking without a map and was surprised to stumble across a lake. In the *Legend of Zelda*, part of the adventure is to walk into new places without a map and be confronted by surprises.

Nintendo in Japan

Nintendo introduced the Famicom into the Japanese market in May 1983. The Famicom was priced at $100, more than Yamauchi wanted, but significantly less than the products of competitors. When he introduced the machine, Yamauchi urged retailers to forgo profits on the hardware because it was just a tool to sell software, and that is where they would make their money. Backed by an extensive advertising campaign, 500,000 units of the Famicom were sold in the first two months. Within a year, the figure stood at a million, and sales were still expanding at a rapid clip. With the hardware rapidly finding its way into Japanese homes, Nintendo was besieged by calls from desperate retailers frantically demanding more games.

It was at this point that Yamauchi told Miyamoto to come up with the most imaginative games ever. However, Yamauchi also realized that Nintendo alone could not satisfy the growing thirst for new games, and so he initiated a licensing program. To become a Nintendo licensee, companies had to agree to an unprecedented series of restrictions. Licensees could issue only five Nintendo games per year, and they could not write those titles for other platforms. The licensing fee was set at 20 percent of the wholesale price of each cartridge sold (game cartridges wholesaled for around $30). It typically cost $500,000 to develop a game and took around six months. Nintendo insisted that games did not contain any excessively violent or sexually suggestive material and reviewed every game before allowing it to be produced.[13]

Despite these restrictions, six companies agreed to become Nintendo licensees, not least because millions of customers were now clamoring for games. They were Bandai, Capcom, Konami, Namco, Taito, and Hudson. Bandai was Japan's largest toy company. The others already made either coin-operated video games or computer software games. Because of these licensing agreements, they saw their sales and earnings surge. For example, Konami's earnings went from $10 million in 1987 to $300 million in 1991.

After the six licensees began selling games, reports of defective games began to reach Yamauchi. The original six licensees were allowed to manufacture their own game cartridges. Realizing that he had given away the ability to control the quality of the cartridges, Yamauchi decided to change the contract for future licensees. Future licensees were required to submit all manufacturing orders for cartridges to Nintendo. Nintendo charged licensees $14 per cartridge, required that they place a minimum order for 10,000 units, and insisted on cash payment in full when the order was placed (later the minimum order was raised to 30,000). Nintendo outsourced all manufacturing to other companies, using the volume of its orders to get rock-bottom prices. The cartridges were estimated to cost Nintendo between $6 and $8 each. The licensees then picked up the cartridges from Nintendo's loading dock and were responsible for distribution. In 1985, there were seventeen licensees; by 1987, there were fifty. At this point, 90 percent of the home video game systems sold in Japan were Nintendo systems.

Nintendo in America

In 1980, Nintendo established a subsidiary in America to sell its coin-operated video games. The subsidiary was headed by Yamauchi's American-educated son-in-law, Minoru Arakawa. All of the other essential employees were Americans, including Ron Judy and Al Stone. Based originally in Seattle, for its first two years Nintendo of America (NOA) struggled to sell second-rate games such as *Radarscope*. The subsidiary seemed on the brink of closing. NOA could not even make the rent payment on the warehouse. Then they received a large shipment from Japan: 2,000 units of a new coin-operated video game. Opening the box, they dis-

covered *Donkey Kong*. After briefly playing the game, Judy exclaimed that is was a disaster. Stone walked out of the building, declaring that "its over."[14] The managers were appalled. They could not imagine a game less likely to sell in video arcades. The only promising sign was that a twenty-year employee, Howard Philips, rapidly became glued to the machine. They had to pry him off.

Arakawa, however, knew he had little choice but to try to sell the game. Judy persuaded the owner of the Spot Tavern near Nintendo's office to take one of the game on a trial basis. After one night, Judy discovered there was $30 in the coin box, a phenomenal amount. The next night there was $35, and $36 the night after that. NOA had a hit on its hands.

By the end of 1982, NOA had sold more than 60,000 copies of *Donkey Kong* and booked sales in excess of $100 million. Having outgrown its Seattle location, the subsidiary moved to a new site in Redmond, a Seattle suburb, where it located next to a small but fast-growing software company run by an old school acquaintance of Howard Philips, one Bill Gates.

By 1984, NOA was riding a wave of success in the coin-operated video-game market. Arakawa, however, was interested in the possibilities of selling Nintendo's new Famicom system in the United States. Throughout 1984, Arakawa, Judy, and Stone met with numerous toy and department store representatives to discuss the possibilities, only to be repeatedly rebuffed. Still smarting from the 1983 debacle, they wanted nothing to do with the home video-game business. They also met with former managers from Atari and Coleco to gain their insights. The most common responses they received was that the market collapsed because the last generation of games "sucked."

Arakawa and his team decided that if they were going to sell the Famicom in the United States, they would have to find a new distribution channel. The obvious choice was consumer electronics stores. Thus, Arakawa asked the R&D team back in Kyoto to redesign the Famicom for the U.S. market so that it looked less like a toy (the Famicom was encased in red and white plastic), and more like a consumer electronics device. The redesigned machine was renamed the Nintendo Entertainment System (NES).

Another major issue was how to avoid the "suck factor" with games. Arakawa's big fear was that illegal, low-quality, Taiwanese games would flood the U.S. market if the NES was successful. To stop counterfeit games being played on the NES, Arakawa asked Nintendo's Japanese engineers to design some kind of security system into the U.S. version of the Famicom, so that only Nintendo-approved games could be played on the NES. The Japanese engineers responded by designing a security chip that was to be embedded in the game cartridges. The NES would not work unless the security chips in the cartridges connected with a chip in the NES. Since the code embedded in the security chip was proprietary, the implication of this system was that no one could manufacture games for the NES without Nintendo's specific approval.

To overcome the skepticism and reluctance of retailers to stock a home video-game system, in late 1985 Arakawa decided to make an extraordinary commitment. Nintendo would stock stores and set up displays and windows. Retailers would not have to pay for anything they stocked for ninety days. After that, retailers could pay Nintendo for what they sold and return the rest. The NES was bundled with Nintendo's best-selling game in Japan, *Super Mario Brothers*. It was essentially a risk free proposition for retailers, but even with this, most were skeptical. Ultimately, thirty Nintendo personnel descended on the New York area. Referred to as the Nintendo SWAT team, after an extraordinary blitz that involved eighteen-hour days, they persuaded some stores to stock the NES. To support the New York product launch, Nintendo also committed itself to a $5 million advertising campaign, heavily concentrated at the seven- to fourteen-year-old boys, who seemed to be Nintendo's likely core audience.

By December 1985, between 500 and 600 stores in the New York area were stocking Nintendo systems. Sales were moderate—about half of the 100,000 NES machines shipped from Japan were sold—but it was enough to justify going forward. The SWAT team then moved on—first Los Angeles, then Chicago, and then Dallas. As in New York, sales started at a moderate pace, but by late 1986 they were starting to accelerate rapidly, and Nintendo went national with the NES.

In 1986, around 1 million NES units sold in the United States. In 1987, the figure increased to 3 million. In 1988, it jumped to more than 7 million. In the same year, 33 million game cartridges were sold. Nintendo mania had arrived in the United States. To expand the supply of games, Nintendo licensed the rights to produce up to five games per year to thirty-one American software companies. Nintendo continued to use a restrictive licensing

agreement that gave it exclusive rights to any games, required licensees to place their orders through Nintendo, and insisted on a 30,000-unit minimum order.[15]

By 1990, the home video-game market was worth $5 billion worldwide. Nintendo dominated the industry with a 90 percent share of the market for game equipment. The parent company was now deemed by some to be the most profitable company in Japan. By 1992, it was netting more than $1 billion in gross profit annually, or more than $1.5 million for each employee in Japan. The company's stock market value exceeded that of Sony, Japan's premier consumer electronics firm. Indeed, the company's net profit exceeded that of all the American movie studios combined. Nintendo games, it seemed, were bigger than the movies.

As of 1991, there were more than 100 licensees for Nintendo, and more than 450 titles were available for the NES. In the United States, Nintendo products were distributed through toy stores (30 percent of volume), mass merchandisers (40 percent of volume), and department stores (10 percent). Nintendo tightly controlled the number of game titles and games that could be sold, quickly withdrawing titles as soon as interest appeared to be declining. In 1988, retailers requested 110 million cartridges from Nintendo. Market surveys suggested that perhaps 45 million could have been sold, but Nintendo only allowed 33 million to be shipped.[16] Nintendo claimed that the shortage of games was in part due to a worldwide shortage of semiconductor chips.

A number of companies had tried to reverse-engineer the code embedded in Nintendo's security chip, which competitors characterized as a "lock-out" chip. Nintendo successfully sued them. The most notable was Atari Games, one of the successors of the original Atari, which in 1987 sued Nintendo of America for anticompetitive behavior. Atari claimed that the purpose of the security chip was to monopolize the market. At the same time, Atari announced that it had found a way around Nintendo's security chip and would begin to sell unlicensed games.[17] NOA responded with a countersuit. In a March 1991 ruling, Atari was found to have obtained Nintendo's security code illegally and ordered to stop selling NES-compatible games. However, Nintendo did not always have it all its own way. In 1990, under pressure from Congress, the Department of Justice, and a number of other lawsuits, Nintendo rescinded its exclusivity requirements, freeing up developers to write games for other platforms. However, developers faced a problem: what platform could they write for?

SEGA'S SONIC BOOM

Back in 1954, David Rosen, a twenty-year-old American, left the U.S. Air Force after a tour of duty in Tokyo.[18] Rosen had noticed that Japanese people needed lots of photographs for ID cards, but that local photo studios were slow and expensive. He formed a company, Rosen Enterprises, and went into the photo-booth business. The booths were a big success, and by 1957 Rosen had established a successful nationwide chain. At this point, the Japanese economy was booming so Rosen decided it was time to get into another business—entertainment. As his vehicle, he chose arcade games, which were unknown in Japan at the time. He picked up used games on the cheap from America and set up arcades in the same Japanese department stores and theaters that typically housed his photo booths. Within a few years, Rosen had 200 arcades nationwide. His only competition came from another American-owned firm, Service Games (or SeGa), whose original business was jukeboxes and fruit machines.

By the early 1960s, the Japanese arcade market had caught up with the U.S. market. The problem was that game makers had run out of exciting new games to offer. Rosen decided that he would have to get into the business of designing and manufacturing games, but to do that he needed manufacturing facilities. SeGa manufactured its own games, so in 1965 Rosen approached the company and suggested a merger. The result was Sega Enterprise, a Japanese company that had Rosen as the CEO.

Rosen himself designed Sega's first game, *Periscope*, in which the objective was to sink chain-mounted cardboard ships by firing torpedoes, represented by lines of colored lights. *Periscope* was a big success not only in Japan, but also in the United States and Europe, and allowed Sega to build up a respectable export business. Over the years, the company continued to invest heavily in game development, always using the latest electronic technology.

Gulf and Western, a U.S. conglomerate, acquired Sega in 1969, with Rosen running the subsidiary. In 1975, Gulf & Western took Sega public in the United States, but left Sega Japan as a G&W subsidiary. Hayao Nakayama, a former Sega distributor, was drafted as president. In the early 1980s, Nakayama pushed G&W to invest more in Sega Japan, so that the company could enter the then booming home video-game market. When G&W refused, Nakayama suggested a management buyout. G&W agreed, and in 1984, for the price of just $38 million, Sega became a Japanese company once more (Sega's Japanese revenues were around $700 million, but by now the company was barely profitable).

Sega was caught off guard by the huge success of Nintendo's Famicom. Although it released its own 8-bit system in 1986, the machine never commanded more than 5 percent of the Japanese market. Nakayama, however, was not about to give up. From years in the arcade business, he understood that great games drove sales. Nevertheless, he also understood that more powerful technology gave game developers the tools to design games that are more appealing. This philosophy underlay Nakayama's decision to develop a 16-bit game system, the Genesis.

To do this, Sega took the design of its 16-bit arcade machine and adapted it for the Genesis. Compared with Nintendo's 8-bit machine, the 16-bit machine was able to boast an array of superior technological features. These included high-definition graphics and animation, a full spectrum of colors, two independent scrolling backgrounds that created an impressive depth of field, and near CD-quality sound. The design strategy also made it easy to port Sega's catalog of arcade hits over to the Genesis.

The Genesis was launched in Japan in 1989, and in the United States in 1990. In the United States, the machine was priced at $199. The company hoped that sales would be increased by the popularity of its arcade games, such as the graphically violent *Altered Beast*. Sega also licensed other companies to develop games for the Genesis platform. In an effort to recruit licensees, Sega asked for lower royalty rates than Nintendo, and it gave licensees the right to manufacture their own cartridges. However, independent game developers were slow to climb on board, while the $200 price tag for the player held back sales.

One of the first independent game developers to sign up with Sega was Electronic Arts. Established by Trip Hawkins, Electronic Arts had focused on designing games for personal computers, and consequently, had missed the Nintendo 8-bit era.

Now Hawkins was determined to get a presence in the home video-game market, and hitching his company's wagon to Sega seemed to be the best option. The Nintendo playing field was already excessively crowded, and besides, Sega was offering a far less restrictive licensing deal than Nintendo. Electronic Arts subsequently wrote a number of big-selling games for the Genesis, including *John Madden Football*, and several gory combat-type games.[19]

Nintendo had not been ignoring the potential of the 16-bit system. Nintendo's own 16-bit system, the Super NES, was ready for market introduction in 1989—at the same time as Sega's Genesis. Nintendo did introduce the Super NES in Japan in 1990, where it quickly established a strong market presence and beat out Sega's Genesis. However, in the United States the company decided to hold back longer in order to reap the full benefits of the dominance it enjoyed with the 8-bit NES system. Yamauchi was also worried about the lack of backward compatibility between Nintendo's 8-bit and 16-bit systems. (The company had tried to make the 16-bit system able to play 8-bit games but concluded that the cost of doing so was prohibitive.) These concerns may have led the company to delay market introduction until the 8-bit market was saturated.

Meanwhile, in the United States, the Sega bandwagon was beginning to gain momentum. One development that gave the Genesis a push was the introduction of a new Sega game, *Sonic the Hedgehog*. Developed by an independent team contracted to Sega, the game featured a cute hedgehog that impatiently tapped his paw when the player took too long to act. Impatience was Sonic's central feature—he had places to go, and quickly. He zipped along, collecting brass rings when he could find them, before rolling into a ball and flying down slides with loops and through underground tunnels. Sonic was Sega's Mario.

In mid 1991, in an attempt to jump-start slow sales, Tom Kalinske, head of Sega's American subsidiary, decided to bundle *Sonic the Hedgehog* with the game player. He also reduced the price for the bundled unit to $150, and relaunched the system with an aggressive advertising campaign aimed at teenagers. The campaign was built around the slogan "Genesis does what Nintendon't." The shift in strategy worked, and sales accelerated sharply.

Sega's success prompted Nintendo to launch its own 16-bit system. Nintendo's Super NES was intro-

duced at a $200 price point. However, Sega now had a two-year head start in games. By the end of 1991, about 125 game titles were available for the Genesis, compared with 25 for the Super NES. In May 1992, Nintendo reduced the price of the Super NES to $150. At this time, Sega was claiming a 63 percent share of the 16-bit market in the United States, and Nintendo a 60 percent share. By now, Sega was cool. As it became cool, Sega took more chances with mass media–defined morality. When Acclaim Entertainment released its bloody *Mortal Kombat* game in September 1992, the Sega version let players rip off heads and tear out hearts. Reflecting Nintendo's image of its core market, the Nintendo version was sanitized. Sega version outsold Nintendo's two to one.[20] Therefore, the momentum continued to run in Sega's favor. By January 1993, there were 320 titles available for the Sega Genesis, and 130 for the Super NES. In early 1994, independent estimates suggested that Sega had 60 percent of the U.S. market and Nintendo 40 percent. Nintendo disputed this.

3DO TRIES TO DO IT

Trip Hawkins, whose first big success was Electronic Arts, founded 3DO in 1991.[21] His vision for 3DO was to shift the home video-game business from the existing cartridge-based format toward a CD-ROM-based platform. The original partners in 3DO were Electronic Arts, Matsushita, Time Warner, AT&T, and the venture capital firm Kleiner Perkins. Collectively, they invested more than $17 million in 3DO, making it the best-capitalized start-up in the history of the home video-game industry. In May 1993, 3DO went public at $15 per share. By October of that year, the stock had risen to $48 per share, valuing 3DO at $1 billion—not bad for a company that had yet to generate a single dollar in revenues.

The basis for 3DO's $1 billion market cap was patented computer system architecture and copyrighted operating system that allowed for much richer graphics and audio capabilities. The system was built around a 32-bit RISC microprocessor and proprietary graphics processor chips. The 3DO system stored games on a CD-ROM instead of a cartridge. It could hold up to 600 megabytes of content, sharply up from the 10 megabytes of content found in the typical game cartridge of the time. The slower access time of a CD-ROM compared with that of a cartridge was finessed somewhat by using a double-speed CD-ROM drive.[22]

The belief at 3DO—a belief apparently shared by many investors—was that the superior storage and graphics-processing capabilities of the 3DO system would prove very attractive to game developers, allowing them to be far more creative. In turn, better games would rapidly attract customers away from Nintendo and Sega. Developing games to take advantage of the capabilities of a CD-ROM system altered the economics of game development. Estimates suggested that it would cost approximately $2 million to produce a game for the 3DO system and could take as long as twenty-four months to develop the game. However, at $2 per disk, a CD-ROM cost substantially less to produce than a cartridge.

The centerpiece of 3DO's strategy was to license its hardware technology for free. Game developers paid a royalty of $3 per disk for access to the 3DO operating code. Disks typically retailed for $40 each.

Matsushita introduced the first 3DO machine into the U.S. market in October 1993. Priced at $700, the machine was sold through electronic retailers that carried Panasonic high-end electronics products. Commenting on the machine, Sega's Kalinske noted that "It's a noble effort. Some people will buy 3DO, and they'll have a wonderful experience. It's impressive, but it's a niche. We've done the research. It does not become a large market until you go below $500. At $300, it starts to get interesting. We make no money on hardware. It's a cutthroat business. I hope Matsushita understands that."[23] CD-ROM disks for the 3DO machine retailed for around $75. The machine came bundled with *Crash n Burn*, a high-speed combat racing game. However, only 18 titles for the 3DO were available by the crucial Christmas period, although reports suggested that 150 titles were being developed.[24]

Sales of the hardware were slow, reaching only 30,000 by January 1994.[25] In the same month, AT&T and Sanyo both announced that they would begin to manufacture the 3DO machine. In March, faced with continuing sluggish sales, 3DO announced that it would give hardware manufacturers two shares of 3DO stock for every unit sold at or below a certain retail price. Matsushita dropped the price of its machine to $500. About the same time, Toshiba, LG, and Samsung all announced that they would start to produce 3DO machines.

By June 1994, cumulative sales of 3DO machines in the United States stood at 40,000 units. Matsushita announced plans to expand distribution beyond its 3,500 outlets to include the toy and mass merchandise channels. Hawkins and his partners announced that they would invest another $37 million in 3DO. By July, there were 750 licensees of 3DO software, but only forty titles were available for the format. Sales continued at a very sluggish pace and the supply of new software titles started to dry up.[26]

In September 1996, 3DO announced that it would either sell its hardware system business or move it into a joint venture.[27] It also announced that about 150 people, or one-third of the work force, would probably lose their jobs in the restructuring. According to Hawkins, 3DO would now focus on developing software for on-line gaming. Hawkins stated that the Internet, and Internet entertainment, constituted a huge opportunity for 3DO. The stock dropped $1.375, to $6.75, on the news.

SEGA'S SATURN

Both Sega and Sony also introduced CD-ROM–based systems in the mid 1990s. Sega had in fact beaten 3DO to the market with its November 1992 introduction of the Sega CD, a $300 CD-ROM add-on to the 16-bit Genesis. Sega sold 100,000 units in its first month alone. However, sales then slowed down, and by December 1993 were standing at just 250,000 units. One reason for the slowdown, according to critics, was a lack of strong games. Sega was also working on a 32-bit CD-ROM system, the Saturn, which was targeted for a mid 1995 introduction in the United States. In January 1994, Sega announced that Microsoft would supply the operating system for the Saturn.[28]

In March 1994, Sega announced the Genesis Super 32X, a $150 add-on cartridge, designed to increase the performance of Genesis cartridge and CD-ROM games. The 32X contained the 32-bit Hitachi microprocessor that was to be used in the Saturn. Sega called the 32X "the poor man's 32-bit machine" because it sold for a mere $149. Introduced in the fall of 1994, the 32X never lived up to its expectations. Most users appeared willing to wait for the real thing, the Sega Saturn, promised for release the following year.

In early 1995, Sega informed the press and retailers that it would release the Saturn on "Sega

Saturn Saturday, Sept 2nd." Actually, Sega released the 32-bit Saturn in May 1995. It was priced at $400 per unit and accompanied by the introduction of just ten games. Sega apparently believed that the world would be delighted by the May release of the Saturn. However, the Saturn was released without the industry fanfare that normally greets a new game machine. Moreover, only four retail chains received the Saturn in May, while the rest were told they would have to wait until September. This move alienated retailers, who responded by dropping Sega products from their stores.[29] Sega, it appeared, had made a marketing blunder.[30]

SONY'S PLAYSTATION

In the fall of 1995, Sony entered the fray with the introduction of the Sony PlayStation.[31] The PlayStation used a 32-bit RISC microprocessor running at 33 MHz and a double-speed CD-ROM drive. The PlayStation cost an estimated $500 million to develop. The machine had actually been in development since 1991, when Sony decided that the home video-game industry was getting too big to ignore. Initially, Sony was in an alliance with Nintendo to develop the machine, but when Nintendo walked away from the alliance in 1992 after a disagreement over who owned the rights to any future CD-ROM games, Sony went it alone.[32]

Right from the start, Sony felt that it would be able to leverage its presence in the film and music business to build a strong position in the home video-game industry. A consumer electronics giant with a position in the Hollywood movie business and the music industry (Sony owned Columbia Pictures and the Columbia record label), Sony believed that it had access to significant intellectual property that could form the basis of many popular games.

In 1991, Sony established a division in New York, Sony Electronic Publishing, that was to serve as an umbrella organization for Sony's multimedia offerings. Headed by Iceland native Olaf Olafsson, then just twenty-eight years old, this organization ultimately took the lead role in both the market launch of the PlayStation, and in developing game titles.[33] In 1993, as part of this effort, Sony purchased a well-respected British game developer, Psygnosis. By fall 1995 launch, this unit had twenty games ready to complement the PlayStation. These included *The Haldeman Diaries*, *Mickey Mania* (developed in collaboration with Disney), and

Johnny Mnemonic, based on William Gibson's short story. To entice independent game developers such as Electronic Arts, Namco, and Acclaim Entertainment, Olafsson used the promise of low royalty rates. The standard royalty rate was set at $9 per disk, although those that signed on early enough were given a lower royalty rate. Sony also provided some 4,000 game development tools to licensees in an effort to help them speed games to market.[34]

To distribute the PlayStation, Sony set up a retail channel separate from Sony's consumer electronics sales force and marketed the PlayStation as a hip and powerful alternative to the outdated Nintendo and Sega cartridge-based systems. Sony worked closely with retailers before the launch to find out how it could help them sell the PlayStation. To jump start demand, Sony set up in-store displays to allow potential consumers to try the equipment. Just before the launch, Sony had lined up an impressive 12,000 retail outlets in the United States.[35]

Sony targeted its advertising for the PlayStation at males in the eighteen to thirty-five age range. The targeting was evident in the content of many of the games. One of the big hits for the PlayStation was *Tomb Raider*, whose central character, Lara Croft, combined sex appeal with savviness and helped to recruit an older generation to the PlayStation.[36] The PlayStation was initially priced at $299, and games retailed for as much as $60. Sony's Tokyo-based executives had reportedly been insisting on a $350-$400 price for the PlayStation, but Olafsson pushed hard for the lower price. Because of the fallout from this internal battle, in January 1996 Olafsson resigned from Sony. By then, however, Sony was following his script.[37]

Sony's prelaunch work was rewarded with strong early sales. By January 1996, more than 800,000 PlayStations, as well as 4 million games, had been sold in the United States. In May 1996, with 1.2 million PlayStations shipped, Sony reduced the price of the PlayStation to $199. Sega responded with a similar price cut for its Saturn. The prices on some of Sony's initial games were also reduced to $29.99. The weekend after the price cuts, retailers reported that PlayStation sales were up by between 350 and 1,000 percent over the prior week.[38] The sales surge continued through 1996. By the end of the year, sales of the PlayStation and associated software amounted to $1.3 billion, out of total U.S. sales of $2.2 billion for all video-game hardware and software. In March 1997, Sony cut the price of the PlayStation again, this time to $149. It also reduced its suggested retail price for games by $10, to $49.99. By this point, Sony had sold 3.4 million units of the PlayStation in the United States, compared with Saturn's 1.6 million units.[39] Worldwide, the PlayStation had outsold the Saturn 13 million to 7.8 million units, and Saturn sales were slowing.[40] The momentum was clearly running in Sony's favor, but the company now had a new challenge to deal with: Nintendo's latest generation game machine, the N64.

NINTENDO STRIKES BACK

In July 1996, Nintendo launched the Nintendo 64 (N64) in the Japanese market. This was followed by a late fall introduction in the United States. The N64 is a 64-bit machine developed in conjunction with Silicon Graphics. Originally targeted for introduction a year earlier, the N64 had been in development since 1993. The machine used a plug-in cartridge format rather than a CD-ROM drive. According to Nintendo, cartridges allow for faster access time and are far sturdier than CD-ROMs (an important consideration with children).[41]

The most striking feature of the N64 machine, however, was its 3D graphics capability. The N64 provides fully rounded figures that can turn on their heels, rotating through 180 degrees. Advanced ray tracing techniques borrowed from military simulators and engineering workstations added to the sense of realism by providing proper highlighting, reflections, and shadows.

The N64 was targeted at children and young teenagers, priced at $200, and launched with just four games. Despite the lack of games, initial sales were very robust. Indeed, 1997 turned out to be a strong year for both Sony and Nintendo. The overall U.S. market was robust, with sales of hardware and software combined reaching a record $5.5 billion. According to estimates, the PlayStation accounted for 49 percent of machines and games by value. The N64 captured a 41 percent share, leaving Sega trailing badly with less than 10 percent of the market. During the year, the average price for game machines had fallen to $150. By year-end, there were 300 titles available for the PlayStation compared with 40 for the N64. Games for the PlayStation retailed for $40, on average, compared with more than $60 for the N64.[42]

By late 1998, there were signs that the PlayStation was widening its lead over the N64. In the crucial North American market, the PlayStation was reported to be outselling the N64 by a 2 to 1 margin, although Nintendo retained a lead in the under-twelve age category. At this point, there were 115 games available for the N64, against 431 for the PlayStation.[43] Worldwide, Sony had now sold close to 55 million PlayStations. The success of the PlayStation had a major impact on Sony's bottom line. In fiscal 1998, the PlayStation business generated revenues of $5.5 billion for Sony, 10 percent of its worldwide revenues, but accounted for $886 million, or 22.5 percent, of the company's operating income.[44]

THE NEXT GENERATION

After almost vanishing from the marketplace in 1998, Sega made a bold attempt to retake a leadership position with the late 1998 Japanese introduction of its Dreamcast home video game machine. The Dreamcast is the most powerful home video-game machine yet with the capability to display advanced 3D graphics. The Dreamcast runs on a 128-bit microprocessor that runs at 200 MHz and uses a Microsoft Windows CE operating system. The games are stored on a CD-ROM, and the machine comes equipped with a 56K modem to facilitate multiplayer on-line game playing. Priced at $240, and launched with only a handful of games, the Dreamcast still sold more than 1 million units in its first few months on the Japanese market.

Sega has scheduled a September 1999 date for the U.S. launch of the Dreamcast. The machine will be priced at $199. Up to 12 games will be available at launch, including a new version of *Sonic the Hedgehog,* which cost an estimated $30 million to produce. By Christmas 1999, there should be 30 games, and 100 by mid 2000. Sega has licensed some 100 independent developers to work on Dreamcast games. The company has plans to spend some $100 million on advertising to launch the system in the United States. Sega has already struck distribution agreements with some of the largest chains in the United States, including Toys "R" Us, Wal-Mart, and Sears. Some 20,000 stores should be carrying the Dreamcast. As of the spring of 1999, advanced orders for the Dreamcast stood at 300,000.[45]

Sony also has plans to launch a 128-bit machine, dubbed the PlayStation II, in 2000. Reportedly, the company is investing $1 billion in the development of the PlayStation II. The machine is expected to have graphics capabilities 200 times faster than the original PlayStation and will utilize a DVD disk for storage. In an attempt to leverage its huge global installed base, Sony plans to make its new machine backward compatible with the original PlayStation.[46] Nintendo is also reportedly working on a 128-bit machine, although details are sketchy.

Going forward, the great unknown is the threat that the personal computer poses to the video-game industry. The threat has been discussed for years, but until recently general purpose PCs have lacked the capabilities of specialized game machines. This may now be changing. Microsoft has provided a direct interface between Windows applications and three-dimensional graphics technology with a variation on its Active X technology, Direct X. According to game developers, the combination of Direct X, fast Pentium microprocessors, faster CD-ROM drives, and graphics accelerator chips has made the PC a much more appealing platform for which to write games. Another attraction of writing for the PC is that game developers do not have to pay royalties to PC manufacturers for the privilege of supplying compatible games.

Since early 1997, most new PCs have been sold with 3D graphics capability. Moreover, with prices dropping to under $1,000 for high powered entry-level PCs, industry estimates suggest that more than 100 million PCs may be sold in 1998, all of them with a high enough specification to run advanced games. Indeed, game software may be the only application that really stretches the modern PC.[47]

Endnotes

1. A good account of early history of Bushnell and Atari can be found in S. Cohen, *Zap! The Rise and Fall of Atari* (New York: McGraw-Hill, 1984).
2. R. Isaacs, "Video Games Race to Catch a Changing Market," *Business Week*, December 26, 1977, p. 44B.
3. P. Pagnano, "Atari's Game Plan to Overwhelm Its Competitors," *Business Week,* May 8, 1978, p. 50F.
4. Isaacs, "Video Games."
5. P. Pagnano, "Atari's Game Plan"; D. Sheff, *Game Over* (New York: Random House, 1993).
6. Cohen, *Zap!*
7. L. Kehoe, "Atari Seeks Way Out of Video Game Woes," *Financial Times*, December 14, 1983, p. 23.
8. M. Schrage, "The High-Tech Dinosaurs: Video Games, Once Ascendant, Are Making Way," *Washington Post*, July 31, 1983, p. F1.
9. Sheff, *Game Over.*
10. Quoted in Sheff, *Game Over.*
11. Sheff, *Game Over.*
12. D. Golden, "In Search of Princess Toadstool," *Boston Globe*, November 20, 1988, p. 18.
13. N. Gross, and G. Lewis, "Here Comes the *Super Mario Bros,*" *Business Week*, November 9, 1987, p. 138.
14. Sheff, *Game Over.*
15. Golden, "In Search of Princess Toadstool."
16. "Marketer of the Year," *Adweek*, November 27, 1989, p. 15.
17. C. Lazzareschi, "No Mere Child's Play," *Los Angeles Times*, December 16, 1988, p. 1.
18. For a good summary of the early history of Sega, see J. Battle and B. Johnstone, "The Next Level: Sega's Plans for World Domination," *Wired*, release 1.06, December 1993.
19. Sheff, *Game Over.*
20. Battle and Johnstone, "The Next Level."
21. For background details, see J. Flower, "3DO: Hip or Hype?" *Wired,* release 1.02, May/June 1993.
22. R. Brandt, "3DO's New Game Player: Awesome or Another Betamax?" *Business Week*, January 11, 1993, p. 38.
23. Flower, "3DO: Hip or Hype?"
24. S. Jacobs, "Third Time's a Charm (They Hope)," *Wired*, release 2.01, January 1994.
25. A. Dunkin, "Video Games: The Next Generation," *Business Week,* January 31, 1994, p. 80.
26. J. Greenstein, "No Clear Winners, Though Some Losers: The Video Game Industry in 1995," *Business Week*, December 22, 1995, p. 42.
27. "3DO Says 'I Do' on Major Shift of its Game Strategy," *Los Angeles Times*, September 17, 1996, p. 2.
28. Battle and Johnstone, "The Next Level."
29. Greenstein, "No Clear Winners."
30. D. P. Hamilton, "Sega Suddenly Finds Itself Embattled," *Wall Street Journal*, March 31, 1997, p. A10.
31. S. Taves, "Meet Your New Playmate," *Wired*, release 3.09, September 1995.
32. I. Kunni, "The Games Sony Plays," *Business Week*, June 15, 1998, p. 128.
33. C. Platt, "WordNerd," *Wired*, release 3.10, October 1995.
34. Kunni, "The Games Sony Plays."
35. J. A. Trachtenberg, "Race Quits Sony Just Before U.S. Rollout of Its PlayStation Video-Game System," *Wall Street Journal*, August 8, 1995, p. B3.
36. S. Beenstock, "Market Raider: How Sony Won the Console Game," *Marketing*, September 10, 1998, p. 26.
37. J. A. Trachtenberg, "Olafsson Calls It Quits as Chairman of Sony's Technology Strategy Group," *Wall Street Journal*, January 23, 1996, p. B6.
38. J. Greenstein, "Price Cuts Boost Saturn, PlayStation Hardware Sales," *Video Business*, May 31, 1996, p. 1.
39. J. Greenstein, "Sony Cuts Prices of PlayStation Hardware," *Video Business*, March 10, 1997, p. 1.
40. Hamilton, "Sega Suddenly Finds Itself Embattled."
41. "Nintendo Wakes Up," *Economist*, August 3, 1996, p. 55–56.
42. D. Takahashi, "Game Plan: Video Game Makers See Soaring Sales Now—and Lots of Trouble Ahead," *Wall Street Journal*, June 15, 1998, p. R10.
43. D. Takahashi, "Sony and Nintendo Battle for Kids Under 13," *Wall Street Journal*, September 24, 1998, p. B4.
44. Kunni, "The Games Sony Plays."
45. D. Takahashi, "Sega Is Pricing Game Machine on the Low Side," *Wall Street Journal*, April 16, 1999, p. B6.
46. J. Paradise, "Sony to Launch New PlayStation in Coming Year," *Wall Street Journal*, March 3, 1999, p. B1.
47. B. Fitzgerald, "Pieces of the Puzzle—Closer to Reality," *Wall Street Journal*, November 16, 1998, p. R33.

CASE 17

Carnival Corporation, 1998

This case was prepared by Mike Keeffe, John K. Ross III, and Bill Middlebrook of the Southwest Texas State University.

In terms of passengers carried, revenues generated, and available capacity, Carnival Corporation is the largest cruise line in the world and considered the leader and innovator in the cruise travel industry. Though its beginnings were inauspicious, Carnival has grown from two converted ocean liners to an organization with two cruise divisions (and a joint venture to operate a third cruise line), as well as a chain of Alaskan hotels and tour coaches. Corporate revenues for fiscal 1997 reached $2.4 billion, with net income of $666 million from operations. The growth continues, with May 1998 revenues up $100 million over the same quarter in 1997—to $1.219 billion. Carnival has several firsts in the cruise industry including these two: more than 1 million passengers carried in a single year, and being the first cruise line to carry 5 million total passengers by fiscal 1994. Currently, their market share of the cruise travel industry stands at approximately 26 percent overall.

Carnival Corporation's CEO and Chairman, Micky Arison, and Carnival Cruise Lines' President, Bob Dickinson, are prepared to maintain their reputation as the leader and innovator in the industry. They have assembled one of the newest fleets catering to cruisers and introduced several superliners built specifically for the Caribbean and Alaskan cruise markets. By the year 2002, the company expects to invest more than $3 billion in new ships. The company has also expanded its Holland America Lines fleet to cater to more established cruisers

and plans to add three of the new ships to its fleet in the premium cruise segment. Strategically, Carnival Corporation seems to have made the right moves at the right time, sometimes in direct contradiction to industry analysts and cruise trends.

Cruise Lines International Association (CLIA), an industry trade group, has tracked the growth of the cruise industry for more than twenty-five years. In 1970, approximately 500,000 passengers took cruises for three consecutive nights or more, reaching a peak of 5 million passengers in 1997—an average annual compound growth rate of approximately 8.9 percent. (This growth rate has declined to approximately 2 percent per year over the period from 1991 to 1995.) At the end of 1997, the industry had 136 ships in service, with an aggregate berth capacity of 119,000. CLIA estimates that the number of passengers carried in North America increased from 4.6 million in 1996 to 5 million in 1997, or approximately 8.7 percent. CLIA expects the number of cruise passengers to increase to 5.3 million in 1998; and with new ships to be delivered, the North American market will have roughly 144 vessels, with an aggregate capacity of 132,000 berths.

Carnival has exceeded the recent industry trends, and its growth rate in the number of passengers carried was 11.2 percent per year over the 1992–1996 period. The company's passenger capacity in 1991 was 17,973 berths and had increased to 31,078 at the end of fiscal 1997. More capacity will be added with the delivery of several new cruise ships already on order, such as the *Elation,* which went into service in early 1998, adding 2,040 to the passenger capacity.

Even with the growth in the cruise industry, the company believes that cruises represent only 2 per-

This case is intended to be used as the basis for class discussion rather than as an illustration of either effective or ineffective handling of the situation. This case was prepared by Dr. Mike Keeffe, Dr. John K. Ross III, and Dr. Bill Middlebrook, Southwest Texas State University. Used by permission.

cent of the applicable North American vacation market, defined as persons who travel for leisure purposes on trips of three nights or longer, involving at least one night's stay in a hotel. The Boston Consulting group, in a 1989 study, estimated that only 5 percent of the people in the North American target market have taken a cruise for leisure purposes and that the market potential was in excess of $50 billion. Carnival Corporation (1996) believes that only 7 percent of the North American population has ever cruised. Various cruise operators, including Carnival Corporation, have based their expansion and capital spending programs on the possibility of capturing part of the 93 to 95 percent of the North American population who have yet to take a cruise vacation.

THE EVOLUTION OF CRUISING

The replacement of ocean liners by aircraft in the 1960s as the primary means of transoceanic travel created the opportunity for developing the modern cruise industry. No longer needed to ferry passengers from destination to destination, ships became available to investors with visions of a new vacation alternative to complement the increasing affluence of Americans. Cruising, once available mainly to the rich and the leisure class, was targeted to the middle class, with service and amenities similar to the grand days of first-class ocean travel.

According to Robert Meyers, editor and publisher of *Cruise Travel* magazine, the increasing popularity of taking a cruise as a vacation can be traced to two serendipitously timed events. First, television's *Love Boat* series dispelled many myths associated with cruising and depicted people of all ages and backgrounds enjoying the cruise experience. This show was among the top ten shows on television for many years, according to Nielsen ratings, and provided extensive publicity for cruise operators. Second, the increasing affluence of Americans and the increased participation of women in the work force gave couples and families more disposable income for discretionary purposes, especially vacations. As the myths were dispelled and disposable income grew, cruising attracted younger couples and families as a vacation alternative, creating a large new target market for the cruise product which accelerated the growth in the number of Americans taking cruises as a vacation.

CARNIVAL HISTORY

In 1972, Ted Arison, backed by American Travel Services, Inc. (AITS), purchased an aging ocean liner from Canadian Pacific Empress Lines for $6.5 million. The new AITS subsidiary, Carnival Cruise Line, refurbished the vessel from bow to stern and renamed it the *Mardi Gras* to capture the party spirit. (Also included in the deal was another ship later renamed the *Carnivale*.) The company's start was not promising, however, as on the first voyage the *Mardi Gras*, with more than 300 invited travel agents aboard, ran aground in Miami Harbor. The ship was slow and guzzled expensive fuel, limiting the number of ports of call and lengthening the minimum stay of passengers on the ship to break even. Arison then bought another old ocean vessel from Union Castle Lines to complement the *Mardi Gras* and the *Carnivale* and named it the *Festivale*. To attract customers, he began adding diversions on board such as planned activities, a casino, nightclubs, discos, and other forms of entertainment designed to enhance the shipboard experience.

Carnival lost money for the next three years, and in late 1974 Arison bought out the Carnival Cruise subsidiary of AITS, Inc., for $1 cash and the assumption of $5 million in debt. One month later, the *Mardi Gras* began showing a profit and through the remainder of 1975 operated at more than 100 percent capacity. (Normal ship capacity is determined by the number of fixed berths available. Ships, like hotels, can operate beyond this fixed capacity by using rollaway beds, pullmans, and upper bunks.) Arison (then chairman), along with Bob Dickinson (who was then vice president of sales and marketing) and his son Micky Arison (then president of Carnival), began to alter the approach to cruise vacations. Carnival went after first-time and younger cruisers with a moderately priced vacation package that included airfare to the port of embarkation and home after the cruise. Per diem rates were very competitive with other vacation packages and Carnival offered passage to multiple exotic Caribbean ports, several meals provided daily with premier restaurant service, and all forms of entertainment and activities included in the base fare. The only things not included in the fare were items of a personal nature, liquor purchases, gambling, and tips for the cabin steward, table waiter, and busboy. Carnival continued to enhance the shipboard experience with a greater variety of activities, nightclubs, and other forms of entertainment, and varied ports of call to increase its attractiveness to potential customers. It was the first modern cruise operator to use multimedia advertising promotions, and it established the theme of "fun ship" cruises, primarily promoting the ship as the destination and ports of call as secondary. Carnival told the public that it was throwing a shipboard party and everyone was invited. The "fun ship" theme still permeates all Carnival Cruise ships.

Throughout the 1980s, Carnival was able to maintain a growth rate of approximately 30 percent, about three times that of the industry as a whole, and between 1982 and 1988 its ships sailed with an average of 104 percent capacity (currently, they operate at 104 to 105 percent capacity, depending on the season). Targeting younger, first-time passengers by promoting the ship as a destination proved to be extremely successful. Carnival's 1987 customer profile showed that 30 percent of the passengers were between the ages of twenty-five and thirty-nine, with household incomes of $25,000 to $50,000.

In 1987, Ted Arison sold 20 percent of his shares in Carnival Cruise Lines and immediately generated more than $400 million for further expansion. In 1988, Carnival acquired the Holland America Lines, which had four cruise ships with 4,500 berths. Holland America was positioned to the higher-income travelers, with cruise prices averaging 25 to 35 percent more than similar Carnival cruises. The deal also included two Holland America subsidiaries, Windstar Sail Cruises and Holland America Westours. This success, and the foresight of management, allowed Carnival to begin an aggressive "superliner" building campaign for their core subsidiary. By 1989, the cruise segments of Carnival Corporation carried more than 750,000 passengers in one year, a first in the cruise industry.

Arison relinquished the role of chairman to his son Micky in 1990, a time when the explosive growth of the 1980s began to subside. Higher fuel prices and increased airline costs began to affect the industry as a whole, and the Persian Gulf War caused many cruise operators to divert ships from European and Indian ports to the Caribbean area of operations, increasing the number of ships competing directly with Carnival. Carnival's stock price fell from $25 in June 1990 to $13 late in the year. The company also incurred a $25.5 million loss during fiscal 1990 for the operation of the Crystal Palace

Resort and Casino. In 1991, Carnival reached a settlement with the Bahamian government (effective March 1, 1992) to surrender the 672-room Riveria Towers to the Hotel Corporation of the Bahamas in exchange for the cancellation of some debt incurred in constructing and developing the resort. The corporation took a $135 million write-down on the Crystal Palace for that year.

The early 1990s, even with industrywide demand slowing, were still a very exciting time. Carnival took delivery of its first two superliners: the *Fantasy* (1990) and the *Ecstasy* (1991), which were to further penetrate the three- and four-day cruise market and supplement the seven-day market. In early 1991, Carnival took delivery of the third superliner, the *Sensation* (inaugural sailing November 1, 1993) and later in the year contracted for the fourth one, to be named the *Fascination* (inaugural sailing 1994).

In 1991, Carnival attempted to acquire Premier Cruise Lines, which was then the official cruise line for Disney World in Orlando, Florida, for approximately $372 million. The deal was never consummated since the parties involved could not agree on price. In 1992, Carnival acquired 50 percent of Seabourn, gaining the cruise operations of K/S Seabourn Cruise Lines, and formed a partnership with Atle Byrnestad. Seabourn serves the ultraluxury market with destinations in South America, the Mediterranean, Southeast Asia, and the Baltic area.

The 1993–1995 period saw the addition of the superliner *Imagination* for Carnival Cruise Lines and the *Ryndam* for Holland America Lines. In 1994, the company discontinued operations of Fiestamarina Lines, which had attempted to serve a Spanish-speaking clientele. Fiestamarina was beset with marketing and operational problems and never achieved continuous operations. Many industry analysts and observers were surprised at the failure of Carnival to successfully develop this market. In 1995, Carnival sold a 49 percent interest in the Epirotiki Line, a Greek cruise operation, for $25 million and purchased $101 million (face amount) of senior secured notes of Kloster Cruise Limited, the parent of competitor Norwegian Cruise Lines, for $81 million. Kloster was having financial difficulties and Carnival could not obtain common stock of the company in a negotiated agreement. If Kloster were to fail, Carnival Corporation would be in a good position to acquire some of the assets of Kloster.

Carnival Corporation is expanding through internally generated growth as evidenced by the

TABLE I

Carnival and Holland America Ships Under Construction

Vessel	Expected Delivery	Shipyard	Passenger Capacity*	Cost (millions)
Carnival Cruise Lines				
Elation	03/98	Masa-Yards	2,040	$300
Paradise	12/98	Masa-Yards	2,040	300
Carnival *Triumph*	07/99	Fincantieri	2,640	400
Carnival *Victory*	08/00	Fincantieri	2,640	430
CCL newbuild	12/00	Masa-Yards	2,100	375
CCL newbuild	2001	Masa-Yards	2,100	375
CCL newbuild	2002	Masa-Yards	2,100	375
Total Carnival Cruise Lines			15,912	$2,437
Holland America Lines				
Volendam	6/99	Fincantieri	1,440	274
Zaandam	12/99	Fincantieri	1,440	286
HAL newbuild	9/00	Fincantieri	1,440	300
Total Holland America Lines			4,260	$860
Windstar Cruises				
Wind Surf	5/98	Purchase	312	40
Total for all Vessel's			20,484	$3,337

*In accordance with industry practice, all capacities indicated here are calculated based on two passengers per cabin, even though some cabins can accommodate three or four passengers. 10Q–5/31/98.

number of new ships on order (see Table 1). Additionally, Carnival seems to be willing to continue with its external expansion through acquisitions if the right opportunity arises.

In June 1997, Royal Caribbean made a bid to buy Celebrity Cruise Lines for $500 million and assumption of $800 million in debt. Within a week, Carnival had responded by submitting a counter offer to Celebrity for $510 million and the assumption of debt, then two days later raising the bid to $525 million. However, Royal Caribbean seems to have had the inside track and announced on June 30, 1997, the final merger arrangements with Celebrity. The resulting company would have seventeen ships with approximately 30,000 berths.

However, not to be thwarted in its attempts at continued expansion, Carnival announced in June 1997 the purchase of Costa, an Italian cruise company and the largest European cruise line, for $141 million. External expansion continued when on May 28, 1998, Carnival announced the acquisition

of Cunard Line for $500 million from Kvaerner ASA. Cunard was then merged with Seabourn Cruise Line (50 percent owned by Carnival), with Carnival owning 68 percent of the resulting Cunard Line Limited.

THE CRUISE PRODUCT

Ted and Mickey Arison envisioned a product where the classical cruise elegance along with modern convenience could be had at a price comparable to land-based vacation packages sold by travel agents. Carnival's all-inclusive package, when compared with resorts or a theme park such as Disney World, often is priced below these destinations—especially when the array of activities, entertainment, and meals is considered.

A typical vacation on a Carnival cruise ship starts when the bags are tagged for the ship at the airport. Upon arriving at the port of embarkation, passengers are ferried by air-conditioned buses to the ship for boarding, and luggage is delivered by the cruise ship staff to the passenger's cabin. Waiters dot the ship offering tropical drinks to the backdrop of a Caribbean rhythm, while the cruise staff orients passengers to the various decks, cabins, and public rooms. In a few hours (most ships sail in the early evening), dinner is served in the main dining rooms, where wine selection rivals the finest restaurants and the variety of main dishes is designed to suit every palate. Diners can always order double portions if they decide not to save room for desserts and after-dinner treats.

After dinner, cruisers can choose between many forms of entertainment, including live music, dancing, nightclubs (most ships have five or more distinct nightclubs), and a selection of movies; or they can sleep through the midnight buffet until breakfast. During the night, a daily program of activities arrives at the passengers' cabins. The biggest decisions to be made for the rest of the vacation will be what to do (or not to do), what to eat and when (usually eight separate serving times, not including the twenty-four-hour room service), and when to sleep. Service in all areas, from dining to housekeeping, is upscale and immediate. The service is so good that a common shipboard joke says that if you leave your bed during the night to visit the head (sea talk for bathroom), your cabin steward will have made the bed and placed chocolates on the pillow by the time you return.

After the cruise, passengers are transported back to the airport in air-conditioned buses for the flight home. Representatives of the cruise line are on hand at the airport to help cruisers in meeting their scheduled flights. When all amenities are considered, most vacation packages would be hard-pressed to match Carnival's per diem prices, which range from $125 to $250 per person, depending on accommodations. (Holland America and Seabourn are higher, averaging $300 per person/per day.) Occasional specials offer even lower prices, and special suite accommodations can be had for an additional payment.

CARNIVAL OPERATIONS

Carnival Corporation, headquartered in Miami, is composed of Carnival Cruise Lines, Holland America Lines which includes Windstar Sail Cruises as a subsidiary, Holland America Westours, Westmark Hotels, Airtours, and the newly created Cunard Line Limited. Carnival Cruise Lines, Inc., is a Panamanian corporation, and its subsidiaries are incorporated in Panama, the Netherlands Antilles, the British Virgin Islands, Liberia, and the Bahamas. The ships are subject to inspection by the U.S. Coast Guard for compliance with the Convention for the Safety of Life at Sea (SOLAS), which mandates specific structural requirements for safety of passengers at sea, and by the U.S. Public Health Service for sanitary standards. The company is also regulated in some aspects by the Federal Maritime Commission.

At its helm, Carnival Corporation has Micky Arison, the CEO and chairman of the board and Bob Dickinson, the president and COO of Carnival Cruise Lines. A. Kirk Lanterman is the president and CEO of the Holland America cruise division, which includes Holland America Westours and Windstar Sail Cruises. (A list of the corporate officers appears in Figure 1.)

The company's product positioning stems from its belief that the cruise market actually comprises three primary segments with different passenger demographics, passenger characteristics, and growth requirements: the contemporary, premium, and luxury segments. The contemporary segment is served by Carnival ships for cruises that last seven days or less and feature a casual ambiance. The premium segment, served by Holland America, offers seven-day and longer cruises and appeals to the more affluent consumers. The luxury segment, while considerably smaller than the others, caters to experienced cruisers for seven-day and longer sailings and is served by Seabourn. Specialty sailing cruises are provided by Windstar Sail Cruises, a subsidiary of Holland America.

The corporate structure is built around the "profit center" concept and is updated periodically, as needed for control and coordination. Carnival's cruise subsidiaries give it a presence in most of the major cruise segments and make possible worldwide operations.

Carnival has always placed a high priority on marketing in an attempt to promote cruises as an alternative to land-based vacations. It wants customers to know that the ship in itself is the destination and the ports of call are important, but secondary, to the cruise experience. Education and the creation of awareness are critical to corporate marketing efforts. Carnival was the first cruise line

FIGURE I

Corporate Officers of Carnival Corporation

Micky Arison, chairman of the board and CEO, Carnival Corporation

Howard S. Frank, vice chairman and COO, Carnival Corporation

Gerald R. Cahill, senior vice president, finance, and CFO, Carnival Corporation

Roderick K. McLeod, senior vice president, marketing, Carnival Corporation

Lowell Zemnick, vice president and treasurer, Carnival Corporation

Robert H. Dickinson, president and COO, Carnival Cruise Lines

Meshulam Zonis, senior vice president, operations, Carnival Cruise Lines

A. Kirk Lanterman, chairman of the board and CEO, Holland America Lines

Peter T. McHugh, president and COO, Holland America Lines

Source: Carnival Corporation, 1998

to successfully break away from traditional print media and use television to reach a broader market. Even though other lines have followed Carnival's lead in selecting promotional media and are near in total advertising expenditures, the organization still leads all cruise competitors in advertising and marketing expenditures.

Carnival wants to remain the leader and innovator in the cruise industry and intends to do this through sophisticated promotional efforts and by gaining the loyalty of former cruisers, refurbishing ships, varying activities and ports of call, and being innovative in all aspects of ship operations. Given the company's historical success with this promotional effort, management intends to build on the theme of the ship as a destination. The company capitalizes and amortizes direct-response advertising and expenses other advertising costs as incurred. Advertising expenses totaled $112 million in 1997; $109 million in 1996; $98 million in 1995; and $85 million in 1994.

FINANCIAL PERFORMANCE

Carnival retains Price Waterhouse as independent accountants, the Barnett Bank Trust Company–North America as the registrar and stock transfer agent, and its Class A common stock trades on the New York Stock Exchange under the symbol CCL. In December 1996, Carnival amended the terms of its revolving credit facility primarily to combine two facilities into a single $1 billion unsecured revolving credit facility due 2001. The borrowing rate on the One Billion Dollar Revolver is a maximum of LIBOR* plus fourteen basis points and the facility fee is six basis points.

In October 1996, Carnival initiated a commercial paper program which is supported by the One Billion Dollar Revolver. As of November 30, 1996, the Company had $307 million outstanding under its commercial paper program and $693 million

*"LIBOR Rate" means, for an Interest Period for each LIBOR (London Interbank Offer Rate) Rate Advance comprising part of the same Borrowing, the rate determined by the Agent to be the rate of interest per annum (i) rounded upward to the nearest whole multiple of 1/100 of 1% per annum, appearing on Telerate screen 3750 at 11:00 A.M. (London time) two Business Days before the first day of such Interest Period for a term equal to such Interest Period and in an amount substantially equal to such portion of the Loan, or if the Agent cannot so determine the LIBOR Rate by reference to Telerate screen 3750, then (ii) equal to the average (rounded upward to the nearest whole multiple of 1/100 of 1% per annum, if such average is not such a multiple) of the rate per annum at which deposits in United States Dollars are offered by the principal office of each of the Reference Lenders in London, England, to prime banks in the London interbank market at 11:00 A.M. (London time) two Business Days before the first day of such Interest Period for a term equal to such Interest Period and in an amount substantially equal to such portion of the Loan. In the latter case, the LIBOR Rate for an Interest Period shall be determined by the Agent on the basis of applicable rates furnished to and received by the Agent from the Reference Lenders two Business Days before the first day of such Interest Period, subject, however, to the provisions of Section 2.05. If at any time the Agent shall determine that by reason of circumstances affecting the London interbank market (i) adequate and reasonable means do not exist for ascertaining the LIBOR Rate for the succeeding Interest Period or (ii) the making or continuance of any Loan at the LIBOR Rate has become impracticable as a result of a contingency occurring after the date of this Agreement which materially and adversely affects the London interbank market, the Agent shall so notify the Lenders and the Borrower. Failing the availability of the LIBOR Rate, the LIBOR Rate shall mean the Base Rate thereafter in effect from time to time until such time as a LIBOR Rate may be determined by reference to the London interbank market.

TABLE 2

Carnival Corporation, Consolidated Statements of Operations (in thousands)

	Six-Month Comparison	
	May 31, 1998	May 31, 1997
Revenues	$1,219,196	$1,117,696
Costs and expenses:		
Operating expense	669,951	634,622
Selling and administrative	163,784	156,219
Depreciation and amortization	89,266	82,658
	923,000	493,564
Operating income before affiliated	296,195	244,197
Income from affiliated	(13,034)	11,694
Operating income	283,161	232,503
Other income (expense):		
Interest income	5,885	3,382
Interest expense, net of capitalized interest	(24,735)	(31,536)
Other income (expense)	(662)	2,105
Income tax expense	6,861	6,353
	(12,651)	(19,696)
Income before extraordinary item	270,510	212,807
Extraordinary item		
Loss on early extinguishment of debt		
Discontinued operations		
Hotel casino operating loss		
Loss on disposal of hotel casino		
Net income	$270,510	$212,807

available for borrowing under the One Billion Dollar Revolver.

The consolidated financial statements for Carnival Cruise Lines, Inc., are shown in Tables 2 and 3, and selected financial data are presented in Table 4.

Customer cruise deposits, which represent unearned revenue, are included in the balance sheet when received and recognized as cruise revenues on completion of the voyage. Customers are required to pay the full cruise fare (minus deposit) sixty days in advance, with the fares being recognized as cruise revenue on completion of the voyage.

Property and equipment on the financial statements are listed at cost. Depreciation and amortiza-

tion are calculated using the straight-line method over the following estimated useful lives: vessels twenty-five to thirty years, buildings twenty to forty years, equipment two to twenty years, and leasehold improvements at the "term of lease" or "related asset life," whichever is shorter. Goodwill of $275 million resulting from the acquisition of HAL Antillen, N.V. (Holland America Lines) is being amortized using the straight line-method over forty years.

During 1995, Carnival received $40 million from the settlement of litigation with Metra Oy, the former parent company of Wartsila Marine Industries, related to losses suffered in connection with

			Years Ended November 30			
1997	*1996*	*1995*	*1994*	*1993*	*1992*	*1991*
$2,447,468	$2,212,572	$1,998,150	$1,806,016	$1,556,919	$1,473,614	$1,404,704
1,322,669	1,241,269	1,131,113	1,028,475	907,925	865,587	810,317
296,533	274,855	248,566	223,272	207,995	194,298	193,316
167,287	144,987	128,433	110,595	93,333	88,833	85,166
1,786,489	1,661,111	1,508,112	1,362,342	1,209,253	1,148,718	1,088,799
660,979	551,461					
53,091	45,967					
714,070	597,428	490,038	443,674	347,666	324,896	315,905
8,675	18,597	14,403	8,668	11,527	16,946	10,596
(55,898)	(64,092)	(63,080)	(51,378)	(34,325)	(53,325)	(65,428)
5,436	23,414	19,104	(9,146)	(1,201)	2,731	1,746
(6,233)	(9,045)	(9,374)	(10,053)	(5,497)	(9,008)	(8,995)
(48,020)	(31,126)	(38,947)	(61,909)	(29,496)	(43,123)	(62,081)
666,050	566,302	451,091	381,765	318,170	281,773	253,824
					(5,189)	
						(33,173)
						(135,463)
$666,050	$566,302	$451,091	$381,765	$318,170	$276,584	$84,998

the construction of three cruise ships. (Wartsila had declared bankruptcy in late 1994.) Of this amount, $14.4 million was recorded as "other income," with the remainder used to pay legal fees and reduce the cost basis of the three ships.

On June 25, 1996, Carnival reached an agreement with the trustees of Wartsila and creditors for the bankruptcy; it resulted in a cash payment of approximately $80 million. Of the $80 million received, $5 million was used to pay certain costs, $32 million was recorded as other income and $43 million was used to reduce the cost basis of certain ships that had been affected by the bankruptcy.

By May 31, 1998, Carnival had outstanding long-term debt of $1.55 billion, with the current portion being $58.45 million. This debt consists primarily of $306.8 million in commercial paper and a number of unsecured debentures and notes of less than $200 million, each at rates ranging from 5.65 to 7.7 percent.

According to the Internal Revenue Code of 1986, Carnival is considered a "controlled foreign corporation (CFC)" since 50 percent of its stock is held by individuals who are residents of foreign countries and its countries of incorporation exempt shipping operations of U.S. persons from income tax. Because of CFC status, Carnival expects

TABLE 3

Carnival Corporation, Consolidated Balance Sheets
(in thousands)

		Years Ended November 30		
	May 31, 1998	1997	1996	1995
Assets				
Current assets:				
Cash and cash equivalents	$120,600	$139,989	$111,629	$53,365
Short-term investments	9,414	9,738	12,486	50,395
Accounts receivable	66,503	57,090	38,109	33,080
Consumable inventories (average cost)	76,226	54,970	53,281	48,820
Prepaid expenses and other	102,754	74,238	75,428	70,718
Total current assets	375,497	336,025	290,933	256,378
Property and equipment (at cost)				
Less accumulated depreciation and amortization	5,469,814	4,327,413	4,099,038	3,414,823
Other assets				
Goodwill (less accumulated amortization)	403,077	212,607	219,589	226,571
Long-term notes receivable				78,907
Investment in affiliates and other assets	425,715	479,329	430,330	128,808
Net assets of discontinued operations	37,733	71,401	61,998	
	6,711,836		5,101,888	$4,105,487
Liabilities and shareholders' equity:				
Current liabilities:				
Current portion of long-term debt	58,457	59,620	66,369	$72,752
Accounts payable	187,897	106,783	84,748	90,237
Accrued liabilities	169,048	154,253	126,511	113,483
Customer deposits	755,890	420,908	352,698	292,606
Dividends payable	44,619	44,578	32,416	25,632
Reserve for discontinued operations				
Total current liabilities	121,911	786,142	662,742	594,710
Long-term debt	1,557,016	1,015,294	1,277,529	1,035,031
Convertible notes			39,103	115,000
Other long-term liabilities	23,907	20,241	91,630	15,873
Shareholders' equity:				
Class A common stock (1 vote share)	5,949	2,972	2,397	2,298
Class B common stock (5 votes share)			550	550
Paid in capital	871,676	866,097	819,610	594,811
Retained earnings	2,912,499	2,731,213	2,207,781	1,752,140
Other	1,799	4,816	546	(4,926
Total shareholders' equity	3,791,923	3,605,098	3,030,884	2,344,873
	$6,711,836	$5,426,775	$5,101,888	$4,105,487

Source: 1997 and 1998 10k and 10Qs.

	Years Ended November 30		
	1994	*1993*	*1992*
Assets			
Current assets:			
Cash and cash equivalents	$54,105	$60,243	$115,014
Short-term investments	70,115	88,677	111,048
Accounts receivable	20,789	19,310	21,624
Consumable inventories (average cost)	45,122	37,245	31,618
Prepaid expenses and other	50,318	48,323	32,120
Total current assets	240,449	253,798	311,424
Property and equipment (at cost)			
Less accumulated depreciation and amortization	3,071,431	2,588,009	1,961,402
Other assets			
Goodwill (less accumulated amortization)	233,553	237,327	244,789
Long-term notes receivable	76,876	29,136	
Investment in affiliates and other assets	47,514	21,097	38,439
Net assets of discontinued operations		89,553	89,553
	$3,669,823	$3,218,920	$2,645,607
Liabilities and shareholders' equity:			
Current liabilities:			
Current portion of long-term debt	$84,644	$91,621	$97,931
Accounts payable	86,750	81,374	71,473
Accrued liabilities	114,868	94,830	69,919
Customer deposits	257,505	228,153	178,945
Dividends payable	21,190	19,763	19,750
Reserve for discontinued operations		34,253	36,763
Total current liabilities	564,957	549,994	474,781
Long-term debt	1,046,904	916,221	776,600
Convertible notes	115,000	115,000	
Other long-term liabilities	14,028	10,499	9,381
Shareholders' equity:			
Class A common stock (1 vote share)	2,276	2,274	1,136
Class B common stock (5 votes share)	550	550	275
Paid in capital	544,947	541,194	539,622
Retained earnings	1,390,589	1,089,323	850,193
Other	(9,428)	(6,135)	(6,381)
Total shareholders' equity	1,928,934	1,627,206	1,384,845
	$3,669,823	$3,218,920	$2,645,607

TABLE 4

Carnival Corporation, Selected Financial Data by Segment
(in thousands)

	Years Ended November 30					
	1997	*1996*	*1995*	*1994*	*1993*	*1992*
Revenues						
Cruise	$2,257,567	$2,003,458	$1,800,775	$1,623,069	$1,381,473	$1,292,587
Tour	242,646	263,356	241,909	227,613	214,382	215,194
Intersegment revenues	(52,745)	(54,242)	(44,534)	(44,666)	(38,936)	(34,167)
	2,447,468	2,212,572	1,998,150	1,806,016	1,556,919	1,473,614
Gross Operating Profit						
Cruise	1,072,758	913,880	810,736	726,808	598,642	552,669
Tour	52,041	57,423	56,301	50,733	50,352	55,358
	1,124,799	971,303	867,037	777,541	648,994	608,027
Depreciation and Amortization						
Cruise	157,454	135,694	120,304	101,146	84,228	79,743
Tour	8,862	8,317	8,129	9,449	9,105	9,090
Corporate	971	976				
	167,287	144,987	128,433	110,595	93,333	88,833
Operating Income						
Cruise	656,009	535,814	465,870	425,590	333,392	310,845
Tour	13,262	21,252	24,168	18,084	14,274	23,051
Corporate	44,799	40,362				
	714,070	597,428	490,038	443,674	347,666	333,896
Identifiable Assets						
Cruise	4,744,140	4,514,675	3,967,174	3,531,727	2,995,221	2,415,547
Tour	163,941	150,851	138,313	138,096	134,146	140,507
Discontinued resort and casino	518,694				89,553	89,553
Corporate	5,426,775	436,362				
		5,101,888	4,105,487	3,669,823	3,218,920	2,645,607
Capital Expenditures						
Cruise	414,963	841,871	456,920	587,249	705,196	111,766
Tour	42,507	14,964	8,747	9,963	10,281	11,400
Corporate	40,187	1,810				
	$497,657	$858,645	$465,667	$597,212	$715,477	$123,166

Source: 1997 and 1998 10k and 10Qs.

that all of its income (with the exception of U.S. source income from the transportation, hotel, and tour businesses of Holland America) will be exempt from U.S. federal income taxes at the corporate level.

The primary financial consideration of importance to Carnival management involves the control of costs, both fixed and variable, for the maintenance of a healthy profit margin. Carnival has the lowest break-even point of any organization in the cruise industry (ships break even at approximately 60 percent of capacity) due to operational experience and economies of scale. However, fixed costs, including depreciation, fuel, insurance, port charges, and crew costs, which represent more than 33 percent of the company's operating expenses, cannot be significantly reduced in relation to decreases in passenger loads and aggregate passenger ticket revenue. (Major expense items are airfares (25–30 percent), travel agent fees (10 percent), and labor (13–15 percent) Increases in these costs could negatively affect the profitability of the organization.

PRINCIPAL SUBSIDIARIES

Carnival Cruise Line

At the end of fiscal 1996, Carnival operated eleven ships with a total berth capacity of 20,332. Carnival operates principally in the Caribbean and has an assortment of ships and ports of call serving the three-, four-, and seven-day cruise markets (see Table 5).

Each ship is a floating resort, including a full maritime staff, shopkeepers and casino operators, entertainers, and complete hotel staff. Approximately 14 percent of corporate revenue is generated from shipboard activities such as casino operations, liquor sales, and gift shop items. At various ports of call, passengers can also take advantage of tours, shore excursions, and duty-free shopping at their own expense.

Shipboard operations are designed to provide maximum entertainment, activities, and service. The size of the company and the similarity in design of the new cruise ships have allowed Carnival to achieve various economies of scale, and management is very cost-conscious.

Although the Carnival Cruise Lines division is increasing its presence in the shorter cruise markets, its general marketing strategy is to use three-, four-, or seven-day moderately priced cruises to fit the time and budget constraints of the middle class. Shorter cruises can cost less than $500 per person (depending on accommodations), up to roughly $3,000 per person in a luxury suite on a seven-day cruise, including port charges. (Per diem rates for shorter cruises are slightly higher, on average, than per diem rates for seven-day cruises.) Average rates per day are approximately $180, excluding gambling, liquor and soft drinks, and items of a personal nature. Guests are expected to tip their cabin steward and waiter at a suggested rate of $3 per person/per day, and the bus boy at $1.50 per person/per day.

Around 99 percent of all Carnival cruises are sold through travel agents, who receive a standard commission of 10 percent (15 percent in Florida). Carnival works extensively with travel agents to help promote cruises as an alternative to a Disney or European vacation. In addition to training travel agents from nonaffiliated travel and vacation firms to sell cruises, a special group of employees regularly visit travel agents posing as prospective clients. If the agent recommends a cruise before another vacation option, he or she receives $100. If the travel agent specifies a Carnival cruise before other options, the reward is $1,000 on the spot. During fiscal 1995, Carnival took reservations from about 29,000 of the approximately 45,000 travel agencies in the U.S. and Canada, and no one travel agency accounted for more than two percent of Carnival revenues.

On-board service is labor intensive. Carnival employs help from some fifty-one nations—mostly Third World countries—with reasonable returns to employees. For example, waiters on the *Jubilee* can earn approximately $18,000 to $27,000 per year (base salary and tips)—significantly more than could be earned in their home country for similar employment. Waiters typically work ten hours per day, with approximately one day off per week for a specified contract period (usually three to nine months). Carnival records show that employees remain with the company for approximately eight years and that applicants exceed the demand for all cruise positions. Nonetheless, the American Maritime Union has cited Carnival (and other cruise operators) several times for exploitation of its crew.

Holland America Lines

On January 17, 1989, Carnival acquired all the outstanding stock of HAL Antillen N.V. from Holland

TABLE 5

The Ships of Carnival Corporation

	Registry	Built	First in company	Service cap*	Gross tons	Length/ Width	Areas of operation
Carnival Cruise Lines							
Carnival Destiny	Panama	1996	1997	2,642	101,000	893/116	Caribbean
Inspiration	Panama	1996	1996	2,040	70,367	855/104	Caribbean
Imagination	Panama	1995	1995	2,040	70,367	855/104	Caribbean
Fascination	Panama	1994	1994	2,040	70,367	855/104	Caribbean
Sensation	Panama	1993	1993	2,040	70,367	855/104	Caribbean
Ecstasy	Liberia	1991	1991	2,040	70,367	855/104	Caribbean
Fantasy	Liberia	1990	1990	2,044	70,367	855/104	Bahamas
Celebration	Liberia	1987	1987	1,486	47,262	738/92	Caribbean
Jubilee	Panama	1986	1986	1,486	47,262	738/92	Mexican Riviera
Holiday	Panama	1985	1985	1,452	46,052	727/92	Mexican Riviera
Tropicale	Liberia	1982	1982	1,022	36,674	660/85	Alaska, Caribbean
Total Carnival ships' capacity: 20,332							
Holland America Line							
Veendam	Bahamas	1996	1996	1,266	55,451	720/101	Alaska, Caribbean
Ryndam	Netherlands	1994	1994	1,266	55,451	720/101	Alaska, Caribbean
Maasdam	Netherlands	1993	1993	1,266	55,451	720/101	Europe, Caribbean
Statendam	Netherlands	1993	1993	1,266	55,451	720/101	Alaska, Caribbean
Westerdam	Netherlands	1986	1988	1,494	53,872	798/95	Canada, Caribbean
Noordam	Netherlands	1984	1984	1,214	33,930	704/89	Alaska, Caribbean
Nieuw Amsterdam	Netherlands	1983	1983	1,214	33,930	704/89	Alaska, Caribbean
Rotterdam IV	Netherlands	1997	1997	1,316	62,000	780/106	Alaska, Worldwide
Total HAL ships' capacity: 10,302							
Windstar Cruises							
Wind Spirit	Bahamas	1988	1988	148	5,736	440/52	Caribbean, Mediterranean
Wind Song	Bahamas	1987	1987	148	5,703	440/52	Costa Rica, Tahita
Wind Star	Bahamas	1986	1986	148	5,703	440/52	Caribbean, Mediterranean
Total Windstar ships' capacity: 444							
Total capacity: 31,078							

*In accordance with industry practice, passenger capacity is calculated based on two passengers per cabin even though some cabins can accommodate three or four passengers.

America Lines N.V. for $625 million in cash. Carnival financed the purchase through $250 million in retained earnings (cash account) and borrowed the other $375 million from banks at 0.25 percent over the prime rate. Carnival received the assets and operations of the Holland America Lines, Westours, Westmark Hotels, and Windstar Sail Cruises. Holland America has seven cruise ships, with a capac-

ity of 8,795 berths, and new ships are to be delivered in the future.

Founded in 1873, Holland America Lines is an upscale line (it charges an average of 25 percent more than similar Carnival cruises), with principal destinations in Alaska during the summer months and the Caribbean during the fall and winter. It also offers some worldwide cruises of up to ninety-eight days. Holland America targets an older, more sophisticated cruiser and has fewer youth-oriented activities. On its ships, passengers can dance to the sounds of the Big Band era and avoid the discos of Carnival ships. Passengers on Holland America ships enjoy more service (a higher staff-to-passenger ratio than Carnival offers) and have more cabin and public space per person; in addition, there is a "no tipping" shipboard policy. Although Holland America has not experienced the spectacular growth of Carnival cruise ships, it has had constant growth over the decade of the 1980s and early 1990s, with high occupancy. The operation of these ships and the structure of the crew resemble the Carnival cruise ship model, and the acquisition of the line gave the Carnival Corporation a presence in the Alaskan market, where it had none before.

Holland America Westours is the largest tour operator in Alaska and the Canadian Rockies and provides vacation synergy with Holland America cruises. The transportation division of Westours includes more than 290 motor coaches, consisting of the Gray Line of Alaska, the Gray Line of Seattle, Westours motorcoaches, the McKinley Explorer railroad coaches, and three day boats for tours to glaciers and other points of interest. Carnival management believes that Alaskan cruises and tours should increase in the future due to a number of factors, such as the aging population wanting relaxing vacations with scenic beauty and Alaska being a U.S. destination.

Westmark Hotels comprises sixteen hotels in Alaska and the Yukon Territory, and also provide synergy with cruise operations and Westours. Westmark is the largest group of hotels in the region, offering moderately priced rooms for the vacationer.

Windstar Sail Cruises was acquired by Holland America Lines in 1988 and consists of three computer-controlled sailing vessels, with a berth capacity of 444. Windstar is very upscale and offers an alternative to traditional cruise liners with a more intimate, activity-oriented cruise. The ships operate primarily in the Mediterranean and the South Pacific, visiting ports not accessible to large cruise ships. Although catering to a small segment of the cruise vacation industry, Windstar helps fulfill Carnival's commitment to participate in all segments of the cruise industry.

Seabourn Cruise Lines

In April 1992, the company acquired 25 percent of the capital stock of Seabourn. As part of the trans-

action, the company also made a subordinated secured ten-year loan of $15 million and a $10 million convertible loan to Seabourn. In December 1995, the $10 million convertible loan was converted by the company into an additional 25 percent equity interest in Seabourn.

Seabourn targets the luxury market with three vessels, providing 200 passengers per ship with all-suite accommodations. Seabourn is considered the "Rolls-Royce" of the cruise industry and in 1992 was named the "World's Best Cruise Line" by the prestigious Condé Nast Traveler's Fifth Annual Readers Choice poll. Seabourn cruises the Americas, Europe and the Mediterranean, and the Far East.

Airtours

In April 1996, the company acquired a 29.5 percent interest in Airtours for approximately $307 million. Airtours, along with its subsidiaries, is the largest air-inclusive tour operator in the world and is publicly traded on the London Stock Exchange. Airtours provides air-inclusive packaged holidays to the British, Scandinavian, and North American markets. It serves approximately 5 million people per year and owns or operates thirty-two hotels, two cruise ships, and thirty-one aircraft.

Airtours operates eighteen aircraft (one additional aircraft is scheduled to enter service in the spring of 1997) exclusively for its U.K. tour operators, meeting a large proportion of their flying requirements. In addition, Airtours' subsidiary Premiair operates a fleet of thirteen aircraft (one additional aircraft is also scheduled to enter service with Premier in the spring of 1997), which meets most of the flying requirements for Airtours' Scandinavian tour operators.

Airtours owns or operates thirty-two hotels (6,500 rooms), which provide rooms to Airtours' tour operators principally in the Mediterranean and the Canary Islands. In addition, Airtours has a 50 percent interest in Tenerife Sol, a joint venture with Sol Hotels Group of Spain, which owns and operates three additional hotels in the Canary Islands, providing 1,300 rooms.

Through its subsidiary Sun Cruises, Airtours owns and operates two cruise ships. Both the 800-berth MS *Seawing* and the 1,062-berth MS *Carousel* commenced operations in 1995. Recently, Airtours acquired a third ship, the MS *Sundream*, which is the sister ship of the MS *Carousel*. The MS *Sundream* is expected to commence operations in

May 1997. The ships operate in the Mediterranean, the Caribbean, and around the Canary Islands and are booked exclusively by Airtours' tour operators.

Costa Crociere S.p.A.

In June 1997, Carnival and Airtours purchased the equity securities of Costa from the Costa family at a cost of approximately $141 million. Costa is headquartered in Italy and is considered Europe's largest cruise line, with seven ships and 7,710 passenger capacity. Costa operates primarily in the Mediterranean, Northern Europe, the Caribbean, and South America. The major market for Costa is southern Europe, mainly Italy, Spain, and France. In January 1998, Costa signed an agreement to construct an eighth ship, with a capacity of approximately 2,100 passengers.

Cunard Line

Carnival's most recent acquisition has been the Cunard Line, announced on May 28, 1998. Comprising five ships, the Cunard Line is considered a luxury line with strong brand name recognition. Carnival purchased 50 percent of Cunard for an estimated $255 million, with the other 50 percent being owned by Atle Brynestad. Cunard was immediately merged with Seabourn, and the resulting Cunard Cruise Line Limited (68 percent owned by Carnival), with its now eight ships, will be headed by the former president of Seabourn, Larry Pimentel.

Joint Venture with Hyundai Merchant Marine Co. Ltd.

In September 1996, Carnival and Hyundai Merchant Marine Co. Ltd. (HMM) signed an agreement to form a 50/50 joint venture to develop the Asian cruise vacation market. Each has contributed $4.8 million as the initial capital of the joint venture. In addition, in November 1996, Carnival sold the cruise ship *Tropicale* to the joint venture for approximately $95.5 million cash. Carnival then chartered the vessel from the joint venture until the joint venture is ready to begin cruise operations in the Asian market, targeting a start date in or around the spring of 1998. The joint venture borrowed the $95.5 million purchase price from a financial institution and Carnival and HMM each guaranteed 50 percent of the borrowed funds.

This arrangement was, however, short-lived as in September 1997 the joint venture was dissolved and Carnival repurchased the *Tropicale* for $93 million.

FUTURE CONSIDERATIONS

Carnival's management will have to continue monitoring several strategic factors and issues for the next few years. The industry itself should see further consolidation through mergers and buyouts, and the expansion of the industry could negatively affect the profitability of various cruise operators. Another factor of concern to management is how to reach the large North American market, of which only 5 to 7 percent have ever taken a cruise.

With the industry maturing, cruise competitors have become more sophisticated in their marketing efforts, and price competition is the norm in most cruise segments. (For a partial listing of major industry competitors, see Appendix A.) Royal Caribbean Cruise Lines has also instituted a major shipbuilding program and is successfully challenging Carnival Cruise Lines in the contemporary segment. The announcement of the Walt Disney Company that it would enter the cruise market with two 80,000-ton cruise liners by 1998 should significantly affect the family cruise vacation segment.

With competition intensifying, industry observers believe the wave of failures, mergers, buyouts and strategic alliances will swell. Regency Cruises ceased operations on October 29, 1995, and has filed for Chapter 11 bankruptcy. American Family Cruises, a spinoff from Costa Cruise Lines, failed to reach the family market, and Carnival's Fiestamarina failed to reach the Spanish-speaking market. EffJohn International sold its Commodore Cruise subsidiary to a group of Miami-based investors, which then chartered one of its two ships to World Explorer Cruises/Semester at Sea. Sun Cruise Lines merged with Epirotiki Cruise Line under the name of Royal Olympic Cruises, and Cunard bought the Royal Viking Line and its name from Kloster Cruise Ltd., with one ship of its fleet being transferred to Kloster's Royal Cruise Line. All of these failures, mergers, and buyouts occurred in 1995, which was not an unusual year for changes in the cruise line industry.

The increasing industry capacity is also a source of concern to cruise operators. The slow growth in industry demand is occurring during a period when industry berth capacity continues to grow. The entry of Disney and the ships already on order by current operators will increase industry berth capacity by more than 10,000 per year for the next three years—a significant increase. (See Appendix B for new ships under construction.) The danger lies in cruise operators using the price weapon in their marketing campaigns to fill cabins. If cruise operators cannot make a reasonable return on investment, they will have to reduce operating costs to remain profitable, and that will affect the quality of service. In these circumstances, further industry acquisitions, mergers, and consolidations would become more likely. The worst-case scenario would be the financial failure of weaker lines.

Still, Carnival's management believes that demand should increase during the remainder of the 1990s. Considering that only 5 to 7 percent of the North American market has taken a cruise vacation, reaching more of the North American target market would improve industry profitability. Industry analysts point out, however, that an assessment of market potential is only an educated guess. What will happen if the current demand figures foreshadow the future?

APPENDIX A:
MAJOR INDUSTRY COMPETITORS

Celebrity Cruises, 5200 Blue Lagoon Drive, Miami, FL 33126
Celebrity Cruises operates four modern cruise ships on four-, seven-, and ten-day cruises to Bermuda, the Caribbean, the Panama Canal, and Alaska. Celebrity attracts first-time as well as seasoned cruisers. Purchased by Royal Caribbean on July 30, 1997.

Norwegian Cruise Lines, 95 Merrick Way., Coral Gables, FL 33134
Norwegian Cruise Lines (NCL), formerly Norwegian Caribbean Lines, was the first to base a modern fleet of cruise ships in the Port of Miami. It operates ten modern cruise liners on three-, four-, and seven-day eastern and western Caribbean cruises and cruises to Bermuda. A wide variety of activities and entertainment attracts a diverse array of customers. NCL has just completed reconstruction of two ships and is building the *Norwegian Sky*, a 2,000-passenger ship to be delivered in the summer of 1999.

Disney Cruise Line, 500 South Buena Vista Street, Burbank, CA 91521

Disney has just recently entered the cruise market with the introduction of the *Disney Magic* and *Disney Wonder*. Both ships will cater to both children and adults and will feature 875 staterooms each. Each cruise will include a visit to Disney's private island, Castaway Cay. Although Disney currently has only two ships and the cruise portion of Disney is small, the company's potential for future growth is substantial. It had more than more than $22 billion in revenues and $1.9 billion net profits in 1997.

Princess Cruises, 10100 Santa Monica Boulevard, Los Angeles, CA 90067
Princess Cruises, with its fleet of nine "Love Boats," offers seven-day and extended cruises to the Caribbean, Alaska, Canada, Africa, the Far East, South America, and Europe. Its primary market is the upscale fifty-plus experienced traveler, according to Mike Hannan, senior vice president for marketing services. Princess ships have an ambiance best described as casual elegance and are famous for their Italian-style dining rooms and onboard entertainment.

Royal Caribbean Cruise Lines, 1050 Caribbean Way, Miami, FL 33132
The nine ships have consistently been given high marks by passengers and travel agents over the past twenty-one years. The ships are built for the contemporary market, are large and modern, and offer three-, four-, and seven-day, as well as extended, cruises. The company prides itself on service and exceptional cuisine. With the purchase of Celebrity, RCCL becomes the largest cruise line in the world, with seventeen ships and a passenger capacity of more than 31,100. Plans include the introduction of six additional ships by 2002. In 1997, RCCL had a net income of $175 million on revenues of $1.93 billion.

Other Industry Competitors (Partial List)

American Hawaii Cruises, two ships—Hawaiian Islands
Club Med, two ships—Europe, Caribbean
Commodore Cruise Line, one ship—Caribbean
Cunard Line, eight ships—Caribbean, worldwide
Dolphin Cruise Line, three ships—Caribbean, Bermuda
Radisson Seven Seas Cruises, three ships—worldwide
Royal Olympic Cruises, six ships—Caribbean, worldwide

Royal Cruise Line, four ships—Caribbean, Alaska, worldwide

Source: Cruise Line International Association, 1996, and company 10k's and annual reports.

APPENDIX B:
CURRENT AND FUTURE LINERS

Liners Completed and Placed in Service During the Past Three Years

Carrier and Vessel (Year), Number of Passengers
Carnival Cruise Lines, *Elation* (1998), 2040
Carnival Cruise Lines, *Destiny* (1997), 2642
Carnival Cruise Lines, *Inspiration* (1996), 2040
Celebrity Cruises, *Mercury* (1997), 1870
Celebrity Cruises, *Galaxy* (1996), 1870
Costa Cruises, *Costa Victoria* (1996), 1950
Holland America Line, *Veendam* (1996), 1266
Holland America Line, *Rotterdam VI* (1997), 1316
Princess Cruises, *Dawn Princess* (1997), 1950
Princess Cruises, *Grand Princess* (1998), 2600
Radisson Seven Seas Cruises, *Paul Gaugin* (1997), 320
Royal Caribbean Cruises, *Rhapsody of the Seas* (1997), 2000
Royal Caribbean Cruises, *Enchantment of the Seas* (1997), 1950
Royal Caribbean Cruises, *Splendour of the Seas* (1996), 1800
Royal Caribbean Cruises, *Grandeur of the Seas* (1996), 1850
Royal Caribbean Cruises, *Vision of the Seas* (1998), 2000

Future Liners Now Under Construction

Carrier and Vessel (Expected Launch), Number of Passengers
Disney Cruise Line, *Disney Magic* (1998), 1740
Carnival Cruise Lines, *Paradise* (1998–99), 2040
Disney Cruise Line, *Disney Wonder* (1998–99), 1740
Carnival Cruises Lines, *Triumph* (1999), 2758
Holland America Line, *Volendam* (1999), 1440

Holland America Line, *Zaandam* (1999), 1440
Norwegian Cruise Line, *Norwegian Sky* (1999), 2000
Princess Cruises, *Sea Princess* (1999), 1950
Princess Cruises, *Ocean Princess* (1999), 2022
Radisson Seven Seas, unnamed (1999), 490
Renaissance Cruises, *R3* (1999), 684
Renaissance Cruises, *R4* (1999), 684
Royal Caribbean Cruises, *Voyager of the Seas* (1999), 3114
Carnival Cruise Lines, *Victory* (2000), 2642
Carnival Cruise Lines, unnamed (2000), 2100
Costa Cruises, unnamed (2000), 1950
Celebrity Cruises, unnamed (2000), 1950
Delta Queen Steamboat Co., unnamed (2000), 225
Holland America Line, unnamed (2000), 1380
P & O Cruises, unnamed (2000), 1840
Royal Caribbean Cruises, *Project Eagle* (2000), 3114
Silversea Cruises, unnamed (2000), 396
Celebrity Cruises, unnamed (2001), 1950
Princess Cruises, unnamed (2001), 2600
Princess Cruises, unnamed (2001), 2600
Royal Caribbean Cruises, unnamed (2001), 2000
Silversea Cruises, unnamed (2000), 396
Royal Caribbean Cruises, unnamed (2002), 3114
American Hawaii Cruises, 2 unnamed, undetermined
Source: Cruise News @http://www.cruise-news.com/.

References

Cruise Lines International Association (CLIA) 1996–1998 (www.cruising.com).
Carnival Corporation (www.carnival.com).
Carnival Corporation Annual Reports, 1996–1998.
Carnival Corporation 1997 and 1998 10k, retrieved from EDGAR database (http://www.sec.gov/edaux/formlynx.htm).
Carnival Corporation 1997 and 1998 10Qs, retrieved from EDGAR database (http://www.sec.gov/edaux/formlynx.htm).
Celebrity Cruises (www.celebrit-cruises.com).
Celebrity Cruises 1997 and 1998 10k, retrieved from EDGAR database (http://www.sec.gov/edaux/formlynx.htm).
Celebrity Cruises 1997 and 1998 10Qs, retrieved from EDGAR database (http://www.sec.gov/edaux/formlynx.htm).
Disney Cruise Line (www.disney.go.com/DisneyCruise).
Norwegian Cruise Lines (www.ncl.com).
Princess Cruises (www.princess.com).
Royal Caribbean Cruise Lines (www.rccl.com).

CASE 18

Circus Circus Enterprises, Inc., 1998

This case was prepared by John K. Ross III, Mike Keeffe, and Bill Middlebrook of the Southwest Texas State University.

We possess the resources to accomplish the big projects: the know-how, the financial power and the places to invest. The renovation of our existing projects will soon be behind us, which last year represented the broadest scope of construction ever taken on by a gaming company. Now we are well-positioned to originate new projects. Getting big projects right is the route to future wealth in gaming; big successful projects tend to prove long staying power in our business. When the counting is over, we think our customers and investors will hold the winning hand.

Circus Circus Annual Report, 1997

INTRODUCTION[1]

Big projects and a winning hand—Circus Circus does seem to have both. And big projects they are, with huge pink-and-white-striped concrete circus tents, a 600-foot-long riverboat replica, a giant castle, and a great pyramid. Its latest project, Mandalay Bay, will include a 3,700-room hotel/casino, an 11-acre aquatic environment with beaches, a snorkeling reef, and a swim-up shark exhibit.

Circus Circus Enterprises, Inc.—hereafter Circus—describes itself as in the business of entertainment and has been one of the innovators in the theme resort concept popular in casino gaming. Its areas of operation are the glitzy vacation and convention meccas of Las Vegas, Reno, and Laughlin, Nevada, as well as other locations in the United

This case is intended to be used as the basis for class discussion rather than as an illustration of either effective or ineffective handling of the situation. This case was prepared by Dr. John K. Ross III, Dr. Mike Keeffe, and Dr. Bill Middlebrook of the Southwest Texas State University. Used by permission.

States and abroad. Historically, Circus's marketing of its products has been called "right out of the bargain basement," and has catered to low rollers. Circus has continued to broaden its market and now aims more at the middle-income gambler and family-oriented vacationers, as well as the more upscale traveler and player.

Circus was purchased in 1974 for $50,000 as a small and unprofitable casino operation by partners William G. Bennett, an aggressive cost-cutter who ran furniture stores before entering the gaming industry in 1965, and William N. Pennington. The partners were able to rejuvenate Circus with fresh marketing, went public with a stock offering in October 1983, and experienced rapid growth and high profitability over time. Within the period 1993–1997, the average return on invested capital was 16.5 percent and Circus had generated more than $1 billion in free cash flow. Circus has become one of the major players in the Las Vegas, Laughlin, and Reno markets in terms of square footage of casino space and number of hotel rooms—despite the incredible growth in both markets. In 1997, for the first time in the company's history, casino gaming operations provided slightly less than one half of total revenues, and that trend continued into 1998 (see Table 1). On January 31, 1998, Circus reported a net income of approximately $89.9 million on revenues of $1.35 billion. This was down slightly from the 1997 net income of more than $100 million on revenues of $1.3 billion. During that same year Circus invested more than $585.8 million in capital expenditures and another $663.3 million was invested in fiscal year 1998.

CIRCUS CIRCUS OPERATIONS

Circus defines entertainment as pure play and fun, and it goes out of the way to see that customers have plenty of opportunities for both. Each Circus location has a distinctive ambiance. Circus Circus–Las Vegas is the world of the big top, where live circus acts are performed free every thirty minutes. Kids may cluster around video games while the adults migrate to nickel slot machines and dollar game tables. Located at the north end of the Vegas strip, Circus Circus–Las Vegas sits on 69 acres of land with 3,744 hotel rooms, shopping areas, two specialty restaurants, a buffet with seating for 1,200, fast-food shops, cocktail lounges, video arcades, and 109,000 square feet of casino space. It also includes the Grand Slam Canyon, a 5-acre glass-enclosed theme park with a four-loop roller coaster. Approximately 384 guests may also stay at nearby Circusland RV Park. The company had invested $126.7 million in this property for new rooms and remodeling in the year ending January 31, 1997, and another $35.2 million in fiscal year 1998.

The Luxor, hotel and casino complex with an Egyptian theme, opened on October 15, 1993, when 10,000 people entered to play the 2,245 slot and video poker games and 110 table games in the 120,000-square-foot casino in the hotel atrium (reported to be the world's largest). By the end of the opening weekend, 40,000 people per day were visiting the thirty-story bronze pyramid that encases the hotel and entertainment facilities.

Besides the pyramid, the Luxor features two new twenty-two-story hotel towers containing 492 suites and is connected to Excalibur—a giant, colorful medieval castle—by a climate-controlled skyway with moving walkways. Situated at the south end of the Las Vegas strip on a 64-acre site adjacent to the Excalibur, the Luxor features a food and entertainment area on three different levels beneath the hotel atrium. The pyramid's hotel rooms can be reached from the four corners of the building by state-of-the-art "inclinators" which travel at a 39-degree angle. Parking is available for nearly 3,200 vehicles; approximately 1,800 of those spaces are in a covered garage.

Luxor underwent major renovations, costing $323.3 million during fiscal 1997 and another $116.5 million in fiscal 1998. The resulting complex contains 4,425 hotel rooms, extensively renovated casino space, an additional 20,000 square feet of convention area, an 800-seat buffet, a series of IMAX attractions, five theme restaurants, seven cocktail lounges, and a variety of specialty shops. Circus expects to draw significant walk-in traffic to the newly refurbished Luxor and is one of the principal components of the Masterplan Mile.

Located next to Luxor, Excalibur is one of the first sights travelers see as they exit Interstate 15 (management was confident that the castle would make a lasting impression on mainstream tourists and vacationing families arriving in Las Vegas). Guests cross a drawbridge over a moat, onto a cobblestone walkway where multicolored spires, turrets, and battlements rise above them. The castle walls are four twenty-eight story hotel towers containing a total of 4,008 rooms. Inside is a medieval world containing a Fantasy Faire filled with strolling jugglers, fire eaters, and acrobats, as well as a Royal Village complete with peasants, serfs, and ladies-in-waiting around medieval theme shops. The 110,000-square-foot casino encompasses 2,442 slot machines, more than 89 game tables, a sports book, and a poker and keno area. There are twelve restaurants, capable of feeding more than 20,000 people daily, and a 1,000-seat amphitheater. Excalibur, which opened in June 1990, was built for $294 million and primarily financed with internally generated funds. In the year ending January 31, 1997, it contributed 23 percent of the organization's revenues, down from 33 percent in 1993. Yet 1997 was a record year, generating the company's highest margins and more than $100 million in operating cash flow. In fiscal 1998, Excalibur underwent $25.1 million in renovations and was connected to the Luxor by enclosed, moving walkways.

Situated between the two anchors on the Las Vegas strip are two smaller casinos owned and operated by Circus. The Silver City Casino and Slots-A-Fun primarily depend on the foot traffic along the strip for their gambling patrons. Combined, they offer more than 1,202 slot machines and 46 gaming tables on 34,900 square feet of casino floor.

Circus owns and operates ten properties in Nevada and one in Mississippi. It also has a 50 percent ownership in three others (see Table 2).

All of the Circus operations do well in the city of Las Vegas. However, Circus Circus 1997 operational earnings for the Luxor and Circus Circus–Las Vegas were off 38 percent from the previous year. Management blames the disruption in services due to renovations for this decline. However, Circus's combined hotel-room occupancy rates had remained above 90 percent, partly because of low room rates ($45 to $69 at Circus Circus–Las Vegas) and popular buffets. Each of the major properties contains large, inexpensive buffets that management believe make staying with Circus more attractive. Recently results, though, show a room occupancy rate of 87.5 percent, partly because of the building boom in Las Vegas.

The company's other big-top facility is Circus Circus–Reno. With the addition of Skyway Tower in 1985, this big top now offers a total of 1,605 hotel rooms, 60,600 square feet of casino, a buffet which can seat 700 people, shops, video arcades, cocktail lounges, midway games, and circus acts. Circus Circus–Reno had several marginal years, but has become one of the leaders in the Reno market. Circus anticipates that recent remodeling, at a cost of $25.6 million, will increase this property's revenue-generating potential.

The Colorado Belle and The Edgewater Hotel are located on the banks of the Colorado River, in Laughlin, Nevada, a city 90 miles south of Las Vegas. The Colorado Belle, opened in 1987, features a huge paddle-wheel riverboat replica, buffet, cocktail lounges, and shops. The Edgewater, acquired in 1983, has a southwestern motif, a 57,000-square-foot casino, a bowling center, buffet, and cocktail lounges. Combined, these two properties contain 2,700 rooms and more than 120,000 square feet of casino. The two operations contributed 12 percent of the company's revenues in the year ended January 31, 1997, and again in 1998—down from 21 percent in 1994. The extensive proliferation of casinos throughout the region, primarily on Indian land, and the development of mega-resorts in Las Vegas have seriously eroded outlying markets such as Laughlin.

Three properties purchased in 1995 and located in Jean and Henderson, Nevada, represent continuing investments by Circus in outlying markets. The Gold Strike and Nevada Landing service the I-15 market between Las Vegas and southern California. These properties have more than 73,000 square feet of casino space, 2,140 slot machines and 42 gaming tables combined. Each has limited hotel space (1,116 rooms total) and depends heavily on I-15 traffic. The Railroad Pass is considered a local casino and is dependent on Henderson residents as its market. This smaller casino contains only 395 slot machines and 11 gaming tables.

Gold Strike–Tunica (formerly Circus Circus–Tunica) is a dockside casino in Tunica, Mississippi, opened in 1994 on 24 acres of land along the Mississippi River, approximately 20 miles south of Memphis. In 1997, its operating income declined by more than 50 percent due to the increase in competition and lack of hotel rooms. Circus decided to renovate this property and add a 1,200 room tower hotel. Total cost for all the remodeling was $119.8 million.

Joint Ventures

Circus is engaged in three joint ventures through the wholly owned subsidiary Circus Participant. In Las Vegas, Circus joined with Mirage Resorts to build and operate the Monte Carlo, a hotel-casino with 3,002 rooms designed along the lines of the grand casinos of the Mediterranean. It is located on 46 acres (with 600 feet on the Las Vegas strip) between the New York–New York casino and the soon to be completed Bellagio, with all three casinos to be connected by monorail. The Monte Carlo features a 90,000-square-foot casino containing 2,221 slot machines and 95 gaming tables, along with a 550-seat bingo parlor, high-tech arcade rides, restaurants and buffets, a microbrewery, approximately 15,000 square feet of meeting and convention space, and a 1,200-seat theater. Opened on June 21, 1996, the Monte Carlo generated $14.6 million as Circus's share in operating income for the first seven months of operation.

In Elgin, Illinois, Circus is in a 50 percent partnership with Hyatt Development Corporation in The Grand Victoria. Styled to resemble a Victorian riverboat, this floating casino and land-based entertainment complex includes some 36,000 square feet of casino space, containing 977 slot machines and 56 gaming tables. The adjacent land-based complex contains two movie theaters, a 240-seat buffet, restaurants and parking for approximately 2,000 vehicles. Built for a total of $112 million, The Grand Victoria returned to Circus $44 million in operating income in 1996.

TABLE 1

Circus Circus Enterprises, Inc.
Sources of Revenues as a Percentage of Net Revenues

	1998	1997	1996	1995
Casinos	46.7%	49.2%	51.2%	52.3%
Food and beverage	15.9	15.8	15.5	16.2
Hotel	24.4	22.0	21.4	19.9
Other	10.5	11.0	12.2	14.2
Unconsolidated	7.3	6.5	3.5	.5
Less: complimentary allowances	4.8	4.5	3.8	3.1

Source: Circus Circus 10-K, January 31, 1995–1998

The third joint venture is a 50 percent partnership with Eldorado Limited in the Silver Legacy. Opened in 1995, this casino is located between Circus Circus–Reno and the Eldorado Hotel and Casino on two city blocks in downtown Reno, Nevada. The Silver Legacy has 1,711 hotel rooms, 85,000 square feet of casino, 2,275 slot machines and 89 gaming tables. Management seems to believe that the Silver Legacy holds promise; however, the Reno market is suffering, and the opening of the Silver Legacy has cannibalized the Circus Circus–Reno market.

Circus was engaged in a fourth joint venture to penetrate the Canadian market, but on January 23, 1997, announced it had been bought out by Hilton Hotels Corporation, one of three partners in the venture.

Circus has achieved success through an aggressive growth strategy and a corporate structure designed to enhance that growth. A strong cash position, innovative ideas, and attention to cost control have allowed Circus to satisfy the bottom line during a period when competitors were typically taking on large debt obligations to finance new projects (see Tables 3 through 6). Yet the market is changing. Gambling of all kinds has spread across the country. No longer does the average individual need to go to Las Vegas or New Jersey; instead, gambling can be found as close as the local quick market (lottery), bingo hall, many Indian reservations, the Mississippi River, and other places. There are now almost 300 casinos in Las Vegas alone, 60 in Colorado, and 160 in California. In order to maintain a competitive edge, Circus has con-tinued to invest heavily in renovation of existing properties (a strategy common to the entertainment/amusement industry) and continues to develop new projects.

New Ventures

Circus has three new projects planned for opening in the near future. The largest project, Mandalay Bay, is scheduled for completion in the first quarter of 1999, and its cost is estimated at $950 million (excluding land). Circus owns a contiguous mile of the southern end of the Las Vegas strip, which it calls its Masterplan Mile and which currently contains the Excalibur and Luxor resorts. Located next to the Luxor, Mandalay Bay will aim for the upscale traveler and player and will be styled as a South Seas adventure. The resort will contain a forty-three story hotel-casino with more than 3,700 rooms and an 11-acre aquatic environment. The aquatic environment will have a surfing beach, swim-up shark tank, and snorkeling reef. A Four Seasons Hotel with some 400 rooms will complement the remainder of Mandalay Bay. Circus anticipates that the rest of the Masterplan Mile will eventually comprise at least one additional casino resort and a number of stand-alone hotels and amusement centers.

Circus also plans three other casino projects, provided all the necessary licenses and agreements can be obtained. In Detroit, Michigan, Circus has combined with the Atwater Casino Group in a joint venture to build a $600 million project. Negotiations with the city to develop the project have been completed; however, the rest of the appropri-

TABLE 2

Circus Circus Enterprises, Inc.
Properties and Percent of Total Revenues

	Percent of Revenues			
Properties	*1998*	*1997*	*1996*	*1995*
Las Vegas, Nevada				
Circus Circus–Las Vegas	25[1]	24[1]	27[1]	29[1]
Excalibur	21	23	23	25
Luxor	23	17	20	24
Slots-A-Fun and Silver City				
Reno, Nevada				
Circus Circus–Reno				
Laughlin, Nevada				
Colorado Belle	12[2]	12[2]	13[2]	16[2]
Edgewater				
Jean, Nevada				
Gold Strike	6[3]	6[3]	4[3]	NA
Nevada Landing				
Henderson, Nevada				
Railroad Pass				
Tunica, Mississippi				
Gold Strike	4	4	5	3
50% ownership:				
Silver Legacy, Reno, Nevada	7.3	6.5[4]	3.5[4]	.5[4]
Monte Carlo, Las Vegas, Nevada				
Grand Victoria Riverboat Casino, Elgin, Illinois				

[1] Combined with revenues from Circus Circus-Reno.
[2] Colorado Belle and Edgewater have been combined.
[3] Gold Strike and Nevada Landing have been combined.
[4] Revenues of unconsolidated affiliates have been combined.
Revenues from Slots-A-Fun and Silver City, management fees, and other income were not separately reported.

ate licenses will need to be obtained before construction begins.

Along the Mississippi Gulf, at the north end of the Bay of St. Louis, Circus plans to construct a casino resort containing 1,500 rooms at an estimated cost of $225 million. Circus has received all necessary permits to begin construction, but these approvals have been challenged in court, delaying the project.

In Atlantic City, Circus has entered into an agreement with Mirage Resorts to develop a 181-acre site in the Marina District. Land title has been transferred to Mirage, but Mirage has purported to cancel its agreement with Circus. Circus has filed suit against Mirage seeking to enforce the contract, while others have filed suit to stop all development in the area.

Most of Circus's projects are being tailored to attract mainstream tourists and family vacationers. However the addition of several joint ventures and the completion of the Masterplan Mile will also attract the more upscale customer.

TABLE 3

Circus Circus Selected Financial Information

	FY98	FY97	FY96	FY95	FY94	FY93	FY92	FY91
Earnings Per Share	0.40	0.99	1.33	1.59	1.34	2.05	1.84	1.39
Current Ratio	.85	1.17	1.30	1.35	.95	.90	1.14	.88
Total Liabilities/ Total Assets	.65	.62	.44	.54	.57	.48	.58	.77
Operating Profit Margin	17.4%	17%	19%	22%	21%	24.4%	24.9%	22.9%

Sources: Circus Circus Annual Reports and 10-Ks, 1991–1998.

THE GAMING INDUSTRY

By 1997 the gaming industry had captured a large amount of the vacation and leisure-time dollars spent in the United States. Gamblers lost more than $44.3 billion on legal wagering in 1995 (up from $29.9 billion in 1992), including wagers at racetracks, bingo parlors, lotteries, and casinos. This figure does not include dollars spent on lodging, food, transportation, and other expenditures associated with visits to gaming facilities. Casino gambling accounts for 76 percent of all legal gambling expenditures, far ahead of second-place Indian reservation gambling at 8.9 percent, and lotteries at 7.1 percent. The popularity of casino gambling may be credited to a more frequent and somewhat higher payout as compared with lotteries and racetracks; however, as winnings are recycled, the multiplier effect restores a high return to casino operators.

Geographic expansion has slowed considerably as no additional states have approved casino-type gambling since 1993. Growth has occurred in developed locations, with Las Vegas, Nevada, and Atlantic City, New Jersey, leading the way.

Las Vegas remains the largest U.S. gaming market and one of the largest convention markets, with more than 100,000 hotel rooms hosting more than 29.6 million visitors in 1996, up 2.2 percent over 1995. Casino operators are building to take advantage of this continued growth. Recent projects include the Monte Carlo ($350 million), New York–New York ($350 million), Bellagio ($1.4 billion), Hilton Hotels ($750 million), and Project Paradise ($800 million). Additionally, Harrah's is adding a 989-room tower and remodeling 500 current rooms, and Caesar's Palace has expansion plans to add 2,000 rooms. Las Vegas hotel and casino capacity is expected to continue to expand, with some 12,500 rooms opening within a year, beginning in the fall of 1998. According to the Las Vegas Convention and Visitor Authority, Las Vegas is a destination market, with most visitors planning their trip more than a week in advance (81 percent), arriving by car (47 percent) or airplane (42 percent), and stay-

TABLE 4

Circus Circus Twelve-Year Summary of Revenues and Net Income

FY	Revenues (in thousands)	Net Income (in thousands)
98	$1,354,487	$89,908
97	1,334,250	100,733
96	1,299,596	128,898
95	1,170,182	136,286
94	954,923	116,189
93	843,025	117,322
92	806,023	103,348
91	692,052	76,292
90	522,376	76,064
89	511,960	81,714
88	458,856	55,900
87	373,967	28,198
86	306,993	37,375

Sources: Circus Circus Annual Reports and 10-Ks, 1986–1998.

TABLE 5

Circus Circus Enterprises Inc., Annual Income (in thousands)

	Year Ended January 31				
	1998	*1997*	*1996*	*1995*	*1994*
Revenues					
Casino	$ 632,122	$ 655,902	$ 664,772	$ 612,115	$538,813
Rooms	330,644	294,241	278,807	232,346	176,001
Food and beverage	215,584	210,384	201,385	189,664	152,469
Other	142,407	146,554	158,534	166,295	117,501
Earnings of unconsolidated affiliates	98,977	86,646	45,485	5,459	—
	1,419,734	1,393,727	1,348,983	1,205,879	984,784
Less complimentary allowances	(65,247)	(59,477)	(49,387)	(35,697)	(29,861)
Net revenue	1,354,487	1,334,250	1,299,596	1,170,182	954,923
Costs and expenses					
Casino	316,902	302,096	275,680	246,416	209,402
Rooms	122,934	116,508	110,362	94,257	78,932
Food and beverage	199,955	200,722	188,712	177,136	149,267
Other operating expenses	90,187	90,601	92,631	107,297	72,802
General and administrative	232,536	227,348	215,083	183,175	152,104
Depreciation and amortization	117,474	95,414	93,938	81,109	58,105
Preopening expense	3,447	—	—	3,012	16,506
Abandonment loss		48,309	45,148	—	—
	1,083,435	1,080,998	1,021,554	892,402	737,118
Operating profit before corporate expense	271,052	223,252	278,042	277,780	217,805
Corporate expense	34,552	31,083	26,669	21,773	16,744
Income from operations	236,500	222,169	251,373	256,007	201,061
Other income (expense)					
Interest, dividends and other income (loss)	9,779	5,077	4,022	225	(683)
Interest income and guarantee fees from unconsolidated affiliate	6,041	6,865	7,517	992	—
Interest expense	(88,847)	(54,681)	(51,537)	(42,734)	(17,770)
Interest expense from unconsolidated affiliate	(15,551)	(15,567)	(5,616)	—	—
	(88,578)	(58,306)	(45,614)	(41,517)	(18,453)
Income before provision for income tax	147,922	163,863	205,759	214,490	182,608
Provision for income tax	58,014	63,130	76,861	78,204	66,419
Income before extraordinary loss			—	—	116,189
Extraordinary loss	—	—	—	—	—
Net income	$ 89,908	$ 100,733	$ 128,898	$ 136,286	$116,189
Earnings per share					
Income before extraordinary loss	.95	.99	1.33	1.59	1.34
Extraordinary loss	—	—	—	—	—
Net income per share	$ .94	$ .99	$ 1.33	$ 1.59	$ 1.34

Sources: Circus Circus Annual Reports and 10-Ks, 1994–1998.

TABLE 6

Circus Circus Enterprises, Inc., Consolidated Balance Sheets (in thousands)

	Year Ended January 31				
	1998	1997	1996	1995	1994
Assets					
Current assets:					
Cash and cash equivalents	$ 58,631	$ 69,516	$ 62,704	$ 53,764	$ 39,110
Receivables	33,640	34,434	16,527	8,931	8,673
Inventories	22,440	19,371	20,459	22,660	20,057
Prepaid expenses	20,281	19,951	19,418	20,103	20,062
Deferred income tax	7,871	8,577	7,272	5,463	
Total current	142,863	151,849	124,380	110,921	87,902
Property, equipment	2,466,848	1,920,032	1,474,684	1,239,062	1,183,164
Other assets					
Excess of purchase price over fair market value	375,375	385,583	394,518	9,836	10,200
Notes receivable	1,075	36,443	27,508	68,083	
Investments in unconsolidated affiliates	255,392	214,123	173,270	74,840	
Deferred charges and other assets	21,995	21,081	17,533	9,806	16,658
Total other	653,837	657,230	612,829	162,565	26,858
Total assets	$3,263,548	$2,729,111	$2,213,503	$1,512,548	$1,297,924
Liabilities and Stockholders' Equity					
Current liabilities:					
Current portion of long-term debt	3,071	379	863	106	169
Accounts and contracts payable					
Trade	22,103	22,658	16,824	12,102	14,804
Construction	40,670	21,144	—	1,101	13,844
Accrued liabilities					
Salaries, wages and vacations	36,107	31,847	30,866	24,946	19,650
Progressive Jackpots	7,511	6,799	8,151	7,447	4,881
Advance room deposits	6,217	7,383	7,517	8,701	6,981
Interest payable	17,828	9,004	3,169	2,331	2,278
Other	33,451	30,554	28,142	25,274	25,648
Income tax payable					3,806
Total current liabilities	166,958	129,768	95,532	82,008	92,061
Long-term debt	1,788,818	1,405,897	715,214	632,652	567,345
Other liabilities					
Deferred income tax	175,934	152,635	148,096	110,776	77,153
Other long-term liabilities	8,089	6,439	9,319	988	1,415
Total other liabilities	184,023	159,074	157,415	111,764	78,568
Total liabilities	2,139,799	1,694,739	968,161	826,424	737,974
Redeemable preferred stock		17,631	18,530		
Temporary equity		44,950			
Commitments and contingent liabilities					
Stockholders' equity					
Common stock	1,893	1,880	1,880	1,607	1,603
Preferred stock					
Additional paid-in capital	558,658	498,893	527,205	124,960	120,135
Retained earnings	1,074,271	984,363	883,630	754,732	618,446
Treasury stock	(511,073)	(513,345)	(185,903)	(195,175)	(180,234)
Total stockholders' equity	1,123,749	971,791	1,226,812	686,124	559,950
Total liabilities and stockholders' equity	$3,263,548	$2,729,111	$2,213,503	$1,512,548	$1,297,924

Sources: Circus Circus Annual Reports and 10-Ks, 1994–1998.

ing in a hotel (72 percent). Gamblers are typically return visitors (77 percent), who like playing the slots (65 percent) and average 2.2 trips per year.

The primary difference between the Las Vegas market and that of Atlantic City is the type of consumer frequenting these markets. While Las Vegas attracts overnight resort-seeking vacationers, Atlantic City's clientele comprises predominantly day-trippers traveling by automobile or bus. Gaming revenues are expected to continue to grow, perhaps to $4 billion in 1997 split between ten casino/hotels currently operating. Growth in the Atlantic City area will be concentrated in the Marina section of town, where Mirage Resorts has entered into an agreement with the city to develop 150 acres of the Marina as a destination resort. This development will include a resort wholly owned by Mirage, a casino/hotel developed by Circus, and a complex developed by a joint venture with Mirage and Boyd Corp. Currently in Atlantic City, Donald Trump's gaming empire holds the largest market share—30 percent—with Trump's Castle, Trump Plaza, and the Taj Mahal. The next closest in market share is Caesar's (10.3 percent), Tropicana and Bally's (9.2 percent each), and Showboat (9 percent).

A number of smaller markets exist around the United States, primarily in Mississippi, Louisiana, Illinois, Missouri, and Indiana. Each state has imposed various restrictions on the development of casino operations within it. In some cases—for example, in Illinois, where there are only ten gaming licenses available—the restrictions have limited the growth opportunities and hurt revenues. But in Mississippi and Louisiana, revenues are up 8 percent and 15 percent, respectively, in riverboat operations. Native American casinos continue to be developed on federally controlled Indian land. These casinos are not publicly held but do tend to be managed by publicly held corporations. Overall, these other locations present a mix of opportunities and generally constitute only a small portion of total gaming revenues.

MAJOR INDUSTRY PLAYERS

Over the past several years, mergers and acquisitions have reshaped the gaming industry. As of the end of 1996, the industry was a combination of corporations ranging from those engaged solely in gaming to multinational conglomerates. The largest competitors, in terms of revenues, combined multiple industries to generate both large revenues and substantial profits (see Table 7). However, those engaged primarily in gaming could also be extremely profitable.

In 1996, Hilton began a hostile acquisition attempt of ITT Corporation. As a result of this attempt, ITT has merged with Starwood Lodging Corporation and Starwood Lodging Trust. The resulting corporation is one of the world's largest hotel and gaming companies, owning the Sheraton, The Luxury Collection, the Four Points Hotels, and Caesar's, as well as communications and educational services. In 1996, ITT hosted approximately 50 million customer nights in locations worldwide. Gaming operations are located in Las Vegas, Atlantic City, Halifax and Sydney (Nova Scotia), as well as elsewhere in Canada, Lake Tahoe, Tunica (Mississippi), Lima (Peru), Cairo (Egypt), and Australia. In 1996, ITT's net income was $249 million on revenues of $6.579 billion. In June 1996, the company had announced plans to join with Planet Hollywood to develop casino/hotels with the Planet Hollywood theme in both Las Vegas and Atlantic City. However, these plans may be deferred as ITT becomes fully integrated into Starwood and management has the opportunity to refocus on the operations of the company.

Hilton Hotels owned (as of February 1, 1998) or leased and operated 25 hotels and managed 34 hotels partially or wholly owned by others, along with 180 franchised hotels. Eleven of the hotels are also casinos, 6 of which are located in Nevada, 2 in Atlantic City, and the other 3 in Australia, and Uruguay. In 1997, Hilton had net income of $250 million on $5.31 billion in revenues. Hilton received some 38 percent of total operating revenues from gaming operations and continued to expand in the market. Recent expansions included the Wild Wild West theme hotel casino in Atlantic City, the completed acquisition of all the assets of Bally's, and construction of a 2,900-room Paris Casino resort located next to Bally's in Las Vegas.

Harrah's Entertainment, Inc., is primarily engaged in the gaming industry with casino/hotels in Reno, Lake Tahoe, Las Vegas, and Laughlin, Nevada, as well as Atlantic City, New Jersey; riverboats in Joliet, Illinois, and Vicksburg and Tunica, Mississippi, Shreveport, Louisiana, and Kansas City,

TABLE 7

Major U.S. Gaming, Lottery and Pari-mutuel Companies
1996 Revenues and Net Income (in millions)

	1997 Revenues	*1997 Income*	*1996 Revenues*	*1996 Net Income*
Starwood/ITT			$6597.0	$249.0
Hilton Hotels	$5316.0	$250.0	3940.0	82.0
Harrah's Entertainment	1619.0	99.3	1586.0	98.9
Mirage Resorts	1546.0	207	1358.3	206.0
Circus Circus	1354.4	89.9	1247.0	100.7
Trump Hotel and Casino, Inc.	1399.3	−42.1	976.3	−4.9
MGM Grand	827.5	111.0	804.8	74.5
Aztar	782.3	4.4	777.5	20.6
Int. Game Technology	743.9	137.2	733.5	118.0

Sources: Individual companies' annual reports and 10-Ks, 1996.

Kansas; two Indian casinos; and a casino in Auckland, New Zealand. In 1997, it operated a total of approximately 774,500 square feet of casino space, with 19,835 slot machines and 934 table games. From this and some 8,197 hotel rooms, the company had a net income of $99.3 million on $1.619 billion in revenues.

All of the Mirage Resorts gaming operations are currently located in Nevada. The company owns and operates the Golden Nugget–Downtown, Las Vegas, the Mirage on the strip in Las Vegas, Treasure Island, and the Golden Nugget–Laughlin. Additionally, it is a 50 percent owner of the Monte Carlo with Circus Circus. Net income for Mirage Resorts in 1997 was $207 million on revenues of $1.546 billion. Current expansion plans include the development of the Bellagio in Las Vegas ($1.6 billion estimated cost) and the Beau Rivage in Biloxi, Mississippi ($600 million estimated cost). These two properties would add a total of 265,900 square feet of casino space to the current Mirage inventory and an additional 252 gaming tables and 4,746 slot machines. Still another project is the development of the Marina area in Atlantic City, New Jersey, in partnership with Boyd Gaming.

MGM Grand Hotel and Casino is located on approximately 114 acres at the northeast corner of Las Vegas Boulevard, across the street from the New York–New York Hotel and Casino. The casino covers approximately 171,500 square feet, and is one of the largest casinos in the world. It has 3,669

slot machines and 157 table games. Current plans call for extensive renovation, costing $700 million. Through a wholly owned subsidiary, MGM owns and operates the MGM Grand Diamond Beach Hotel and a hotel/casino resort in Darwin, Australia. Additionally, MGM and Primadonna Resorts, Inc., each own 50 percent of the New York–New York Hotel and Casino, a $460 million architecturally distinctive themed destination resort, which opened on January 3, 1997. MGM also intends to construct and operate a destination resort hotel/casino—an entertainment and retail facility in Atlantic City on approximately 35 acres of land on the Atlantic City Boardwalk.

THE LEGAL ENVIRONMENT

Within the gaming industry, all current operators must consider compliance with extensive gaming regulations as a primary concern. Each state or country has its own specific regulations and regulatory boards and extensive reporting and licensing requirements. For example, in Las Vegas, Nevada, gambling operations are subject to regulatory control by the Nevada State Gaming Control Board, by the Clark County Nevada Gaming and Liquor Licensing Board, and by city government regulations. The laws, regulations and supervisory procedures of virtually all gaming authorities are based on public policy primarily concerned with preventing unsavory or unsuitable persons from having a direct or indirect involvement with gaming at any time or in any capacity and the establishment and maintenance of responsible accounting practices. Additional regulations typically cover the following: maintenance of effective controls over the financial practices of licensees, including the establishment of minimum procedures for internal fiscal affairs and the safeguarding of assets and revenues; providing reliable record keeping and requiring the filing of periodic reports; prevention of cheating and fraudulent practices; and providing a source of state and local revenues through taxation and licensing fees. Changes in such laws, regulations, and procedures could have an adverse effect on any gaming operation. All gaming companies must submit detailed operating and financial reports to authorities. Nearly all financial transactions, including loans, leases, and the sale of securities must be reported. Some financial activities are subject to approval by regulatory agencies. As Circus moves into other locations outside of Nevada, it will need to adhere to local regulations.

FUTURE CONSIDERATION

According to Circus Circus, it is "in the business of entertainment, with . . . core strength in casino gaming," and it intends to focus its efforts in Las Vegas, Atlantic City, and Mississippi. The company also believes that the "future product in gaming . . . is the entertainment resort" (Circus Circus 1997 Annual Report).

Circus was one of the innovators of the gaming resort concept and has continued to be a leader in that field. However, the mega-entertainment resort industry operates differently than the traditional casino gaming industry. In the past consumers would visit a casino to experience the thrill of gambling. Now they not only gamble, but expect to be dazzled by enormous entertainment complexes that are costing billions of dollars to build. The competition has continued to increase at the same time that growth rates have been slowing.

For years, analysts have questioned the ability of the gaming industry to continue high growth in established markets as the industry matures. Through the 1970s and 1980s the gaming industry experienced rapid growth. Through the 1990s, the industry began to experience a shakeout of marginal competitors and consolidation phase. Circus Circus

has been successful through this turmoil but now faces the task of maintaining high growth in a more mature industry.

APPENDIX A: CIRCUS CIRCUS ENTERPRISES, INC., TOP MANAGEMENT

Board of Directors

Clyde T. Turner, 59, chairman of the board and CEO

Michael S. Ensign, 59, vice chairman of the board and COO

Glenn Schaeffer, 43, president and CFO

William A. Richardson, 50, vice chairman of the board and executive vice president

Richard P. Banis, 52, former president and COO

Arthur H. Bilger, 44, former president and COO of New World Communications Group International

Richard A. Etter, 58, former chairman and CEO of Bank of America–Nevada

William E. Bannen, M.D., 48, vice president/chief medical officer of Blue Cross Blue Shield of Nevada

Donna B. More, 40, partner in the law firm of Freeborn & Peters

Michael D. McKee, 51, executive vice president of The Irving Company

Officers

Clyde T. Turner, chairman of the board and CEO

Michael S. Ensign, vice chairman of the board and COO

Glenn Schaeffer, president, CFO, and treasurer

William A. Richardson, vice chairman of the board and executive vice president

Tony Alamo, senior vice president, operations

Gregg Solomon, senior vice president, operations

Kurt D. Sullivan, senior vice president, operations

Steve Greathouse, senior vice president, operations

Yvett Landau, vice president, general counsel, and secretary

Les Martin, vice president and chief accounting officer

Sources: Annual Report 1998; Proxy Statement May 1, 1998.

References

Anderson, "Economic Impacts of Casino Gaming in the United States." American Gaming Association, May 1997.

Aztar Corp., 1997 and 1998 10-K. Retrieved from EDGAR database (http://www.sec.gov/Archives/edgar/data/).

"Circus Circus Announces Promotion." *PR Newswire*, June 10, 1997.

Circus Circus Enterprises, Inc. Annual Report to Shareholders, January 31, 1989, January 31, 1990, January 31, 1993, January 31, 1994, January 31, 1995, January 31, 1996, January 31, 1997, and January 31, 1998.

Corning, Blair. "Luxor: Egypt Opens in Vegas." *San Antonio Express News*, October 24, 1993.

Harrah's Entertainment, Inc., 1997 and 1998 10-K. Retrieved from EDGAR database (http://www.sec.gov/Archives/edgar/data/).

"Harrah's Survey of Casino Entertainment." Harrah's Entertainment, Inc., 1996.

Hilton Hotels Corp., 1997 and 1998 10-K. Retrieved from EDGAR database (http://www.sec.gov/Archives/edgar/data/).

"ITT Board Rejects Hilton's Offer as Inadequate, Reaffirms Belief That ITT's Comprehensive Plan Is in the Best Interest of ITT Shareholders." Press release, August 14, 1997.

ITT Corp., 1997 10-K. Retrieved from EDGAR database (http://www.sec.gov/Archives/edgar/data/).

Lalli, Sergio. "Excalibur Awaiteth." *Hotel and Motel Management*, June 11, 1990.

Mirage Resorts, Inc., 1997 and 1998 10-K. Retrieved from EDGAR database (http://www.sec.gov/Archives/edgar/data/).

MGM Grand, Inc., 1997 and 1998 10-K. Retrieved from EDGAR database (http://www.sec.gov/Archives/edgar/data/).

Standard & Poor's. "Casinos Move into New Areas." *Industry Surveys*, March 11, 1993, pp. L35–L41.

——— "Industry Surveys—Lodging and Gaming," *Industry Surveys*, June 19, 1997.

CASE 19

The Evolution of the Air Express Industry

The case was prepared by Charles W.L. Hill of the University of Washington.

INTRODUCTION

The air express industry is that segment of the broader air cargo industry that specializes in rapid (normally overnight) delivery of small packages. It is generally agreed that the air express industry in the United States began with Fred Smith's vision for Federal Express Company, which started operations in 1973. Federal Express transformed the structure of the existing air cargo industry and paved the way for rapid growth in the overnight package segment of that industry. A further impetus to the industry's development was the 1977 deregulation of the U.S. air cargo industry. For the first time this allowed Federal Express (and its emerging competitors) to buy large jets. The story of the industry during the 1980s was one of rapid growth and new entry. Between 1982 and 1989, air express cargo shipments in the United States grew at an annual average rate of 31 percent. In contrast, shipments of air freight and air mail grew at an annual rate of only 2.7 percent.[1] This rapid growth attracted new entrants such as United Parcel Service (UPS) and Airborne Freight (which operates under the name Airborne Express). The entry of UPS triggered severe price cutting, which ultimately drove some of the weaker competitors out of the market and touched off a wave of consolidation in the industry.

By the mid 1990s, the industry structure had stabilized, with three firms—Federal Express, UPS, and Airborne Express—accounting for around 70 percent of U.S. air express shipments. (See Table 1 for a comparison of the three companies.)[2] During

This case is intended to be used as a basis for class discussion rather than as an illustration of either effective or ineffective handling of the situation. This case was prepared by Charles W. L. Hill, University of Washington. Used by permission.

the first half of the 1990s, the air express industry continued to grow at a healthy rate, with express shipments expanding from 4,404 million ton miles in 1990 to 7,042 million ton miles in 1994, an annual growth rate of slightly more than 16 percent (see Figure 1).[3] Despite this growth, the industry was hit by repeated rounds of price cutting as the three biggest firms battled to capture major accounts. In addition to price cutting, the big three also competed vigorously on the basis of technology, service offerings, and the global reach of their operations.

THE INDUSTRY IN 1973

In 1973, roughly 1.5 billion tons of freight were shipped annually in the United States. Most of this was carried by surface transport, with airfreight accounting for less than 2 percent of the total.[4] While shipment by airfreight was often quicker than shipment by surface freight, the high cost of airfreight had kept down demand. The typical users of airfreight at this time were suppliers of time-sensitive, high-priced goods, such as computer parts and medical instruments, which were needed at dispersed locations but which were too expensive for their customers to hold as inventory.

The main cargo carriers in 1973 were major passenger airlines, which operated a number of all-cargo planes and carried additional cargo in the bellies of their passenger planes. There was also a handful of all-cargo airlines, such as Flying Tiger. From 1973 onward, the passenger airlines moved steadily away from all-cargo planes and began to concentrate cargo freight in the bellies of passenger planes. This was a response to increases in fuel

TABLE 1

Main U.S. Air Express Operators, 1995

	Federal Express	*UPS*	*Airborne Express*
U.S. Market Share*	35%	26%	9%
Revenues	$10.3 billion	$21 billion	$2.2 billion
Aircraft fleet	559	184	109
Employees	122,000	335,000	19,000
Delivery vehicles	36,000	65,000	12,800

*Market share figures refer to share of U.S. domestic airfreight and express mail delivery. Figures for just express mail delivery are higher.
Source: All of the data come from the company Web sites with the exception of market share data, which are from Standard & Poor's, "Aerospace and Air Transport," *Industry Surveys* (February 1996).

costs, which made the operation of many older cargo jets uneconomical.

With regard to distribution of cargo to and from airports, in 1973 about 20 percent of all airfreight was delivered to airports by the shipper and/or picked up by the consignee. The bulk of the remaining 80 percent was accounted for by three major intermediaries: (1) Air Cargo Incorporated, (2) freight forwarders, and (3) the U.S. Postal Service. Air Cargo Incorporated was a trucking service, wholly owned by twenty-six airlines, which performed pickup and delivery service for the airlines' direct customers. Freight forwarders were trucking carriers that consolidated cargo going to the airlines. They purchased cargo space from the airlines and retailed this in small amounts. They dealt primarily with small customers, providing pickup and delivery services in most cities, either in their own trucks or through contract agents. The U.S. Postal Service used air service for transportation of long-distance letter mail and air parcel post.[5]

FIGURE 1

Volume Growth of the U.S. Air Express Market, 1985–1994 (millions of air cargo ton miles)

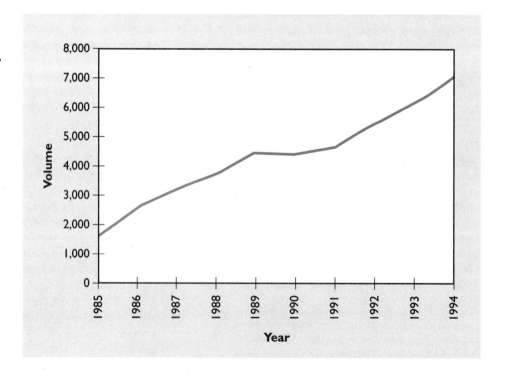

THE FEDERAL EXPRESS CONCEPT

Federal Express, founded by Fred Smith, Jr., was incorporated in 1971 and began operations in 1973. At that time, a significant proportion of small package airfreight flew on commercial passenger flights. Smith believed that there were major differences between packages and passengers, and he was convinced that the two had to be treated differently. Most passengers moved between major cities and wanted the convenience of daytime flights. Cargo shippers preferred nighttime service to coincide with late-afternoon pickups and next-day delivery. Because small package airfreight was subservient to the requirements of passengers' flight schedules, it was often difficult for the major airlines to achieve next-day delivery of airfreight.

Smith's aim was to build a system that could achieve next-day delivery of small package airfreight (less than 70 pounds). He set up Federal Express with his $8 million family inheritance and $90 million in venture capital. Federal Express established what was at that time a unique hub-and-spoke route system. The hub of the system was Memphis, chosen for its good weather conditions, central location, and the fact that it was Smith's hometown. The spokes were regular routes between Memphis and shipping facilities at public airports in the cities serviced by Federal Express. Every weeknight, aircraft would leave their home cities with a load of packages and fly down the "spokes" to Memphis (often with one or two stops on the way). At Memphis, all packages were unloaded, sorted by destination, and reloaded. The aircraft then returned to their home cities in the early hours of the morning. Packages were ferried to and from airports by Federal Express couriers driving the company's vans and working to a tight schedule. Thus, from door to door the package was in Federal Express's hands. This system guaranteed that a package picked up from a customer in New York at 5 P.M. would reach its final destination in Los Angeles (or any other major city) by noon the following day. It enabled Federal Express to realize economies in sorting and to utilize its air cargo capacity efficiently. Federal Express also pioneered the use of standard packaging, with an upper weight limit of 70 pounds and a maximum length plus girth of 108 inches. This helped Federal Express to gain further efficiencies from mechanized sorting at its Memphis hub. Later entrants into the industry copied Federal Express's package standards and hub-and-spoke operating system.

To accomplish overnight delivery, Federal Express had to operate its own planes. However, restrictive regulations enforced by the Civil Aeronautics Board (CAB) prohibited the company from buying large jet aircraft. To get around this restriction, Federal Express bought a fleet of twin-engine executive jets, which it converted to minifreighters. These planes had a cargo capacity of 6,200 pounds, which enabled Federal Express to get a license as an air taxi operator.

After 1973, Federal Express quickly built up volume. By 1976, it had an average daily volume of 19,000 packages, a fleet of 32 aircraft, 500 delivery vans, and 2,000 employees, and it had initiated service in seventy-five cities. Moreover, after three loss-making years, the company turned in a profit of $3.7 million on revenues of $75 million.[6] However, volume had grown to the point at which Federal Express desperately needed to use larger planes to maintain operating efficiencies. As a result, Smith's voice was added to those calling for Congress to deregulate the airline industry and allow greater competition.

DEREGULATION AND ITS AFTERMATH

In November 1977, Congress relaxed regulations controlling competition in the air cargo industry, one year before passenger services were deregulated. This involved a drastic loosening of standards for entry into the industry. The old CAB authority to name the carriers that could operate on the various routes was changed to the relatively simple authority to decide which among candidate carriers was fit, willing, and able to operate an all-cargo route. In addition, CAB controls over pricing were significantly reduced. The immediate effect was an increase in rates for certain types of shipments, particularly minimum- and high-weight categories, suggesting that prices had been held artificially low by regulation. As a result, the average yield (revenue per ton mile) on domestic airfreight increased 10.6 percent in 1978 and 11.3 percent in 1979.[7]

Freed from the constraints of regulation, Federal Express immediately began to purchase larger jets and quickly established itself as a major carrier of small-package airfreight. However, despite the increase in yields, new entry into the air cargo industry was limited, at least initially. This was mainly due to the high capital requirements involved in establishing an all-cargo carrier. Indeed, by the end of 1978, there were only four major all-cargo carriers serving the domestic market: Airlift International, Federal Express, Flying Tiger, and Seaboard World Airlines. While all of these had increased their route structure following deregulation, only Federal Express specialized in next-day delivery for small packages. Demand for a next-day delivery service continued to boom. Industry estimates suggest that the small-package priority market had grown to about 82 million pieces in 1979, up from 43 million in 1974.[8]

At the same time, in response to increasing competition from the all-cargo carriers, the passenger airlines continued their retreat from the all-cargo business (originally begun in 1973 as a response to high fuel prices). Between 1973 and 1978, there was a 45 percent decline in the mileage of all-cargo flights by the airlines. This was followed by a 14 percent decline between 1978 and 1979. Instead of all-cargo flights, the airlines concentrated their attentions on carrying cargo in the bellies of passenger flights. This practice hurt the freight forwarders badly. The freight forwarders had long relied on the all-cargo flights of major airlines to achieve next-day delivery. Now the freight forwarders were being squeezed out of this segment by a lack of available lift at the time needed to ensure next-day delivery.

It was this problem that led to one of the major postderegulation developments in the industry: the acquisition and operation by freight forwarders of their own fleets of aircraft. Between 1979 and 1981, five of the six largest freight forwarders became involved in this activity. The two largest of these were Emery Air Freight and Airborne Express. Emery operated a fleet of sixty-six aircraft at the end of 1979, the majority of which were leased from other carriers. In mid 1980 this fleet was providing service to approximately 129 cities, carrying both large-volume shipments and small-package express.

Airborne Express acquired its own fleet of aircraft in April 1980 with the purchase of Midwest Charter Express, an Ohio-based all-cargo airline. Then, in 1981, Airborne opened a new hub in Ohio, which became the center of its small-package express operation. This enabled Airborne to provide next-day delivery for small packages to 125 cities in the United States.[9] Other freight forwarders that moved into the overnight mail market included Purolator Courier and Gelco, both of which offered overnight delivery by air on a limited geographic scale.

INDUSTRY EVOLUTION, 1980–1986

New Products and Industry Growth

In 1981, Federal Express expanded its role in the overnight market with the introduction of an overnight letter service, with a limit of 2 ounces. This guaranteed overnight delivery service was set up in direct competition with the U.S. Postal Service's Priority Mail. The demand for such a service was illustrated by its expansion to about 17,000 letters per day within its first three months of operation.

More generally, the focus of the air express industry was changing from being predominantly a conduit for goods to being a distributor of information—particularly company documents, letters, contracts, drawings, and the like. As a result of the growth in demand for information distribution, new product offerings such as the overnight letter, and Federal Express's own marketing efforts, the air express industry enjoyed high growth during the early 1980s, averaging more than 20 percent per annum.[10] Indeed, many observers attribute most of the growth in the overnight delivery business at this time to Federal Express's marketing efforts. According to one industry participant, "Federal Express pulled off one of the greatest marketing scams in the industry by making people believe they absolutely, positively, had to have something right away."[11]

Increasing Price Competition

Despite rapid growth in demand, competitive intensity in the industry increased sharply in 1982 following the entry of UPS into the overnight-delivery market. UPS was already by far the largest private package transporter in the United States, with an enormous ground-oriented distribution network and revenues in excess of $4 billion per annum. In addition, UPS had for a long time offered a second-day air service for priority packages, primarily by using the planes of all-cargo and passenger airlines. In 1982, UPS acquired a fleet of twenty-four used Boeing 727-100s and added four DC-8 freighters from Flying Tiger, enabling it to introduce next-day air service in September of that year—at roughly half the price Federal Express was charging at the time.[12]

Federal Express countered almost immediately by announcing that it would institute 10:30 A.M. priority overnight delivery (at a cost to the company of $18 million). However, none of the other carriers followed suit, reasoning that most of their customers are usually busy or in meetings in the morning hours, so delivery before noon was not really that important. Instead, by March of 1983 most of the major carriers in the market were offering their high-volume customers contract rates that matched the UPS price structure (including Federal Express). Then three new services introduced by Purolator, Emery, and Gelco Courier pushed prices even lower.

What followed was something of a competitive free-for-all, with constant price changes and volume discounts being offered by all industry participants. Not surprisingly, these developments began to hit the profit margins of the express carriers. Between 1983 and 1984, Federal Express saw its average revenue per pack fall nearly 14 percent, while Emery saw a 15 percent decline in its yield on small shipments.[13]

A further factor driving price down at this time was the growing tendency of customers to group together and negotiate for lower prices. For example, Xerox set up accounts with Purolator and Emery that covered not only Xerox's express packages but also those of fifty other companies, including Mayflower Corp., the moving company, and the Chicago Board of Trade. By negotiating as a group, these companies were able to achieve prices as much as 60 percent lower than those they could get on their own.[14]

The main beneficiary of the price war was UPS, which by 1985 had gained the number two spot in the industry, with 15 percent of the market. Federal Express, meanwhile, had seen its market share slip back to 37 percent from around 45 percent two years earlier. The other four major players in the industry at this time were Emery Air Freight (with 14 percent of market share), Purolator (with 10 percent of market share), Airborne Express (with 8 percent of market share), and the U.S. Postal Service (with 8 percent of market share).[15] The survival of all four of these carriers in the air express business was in question by 1986. Emery, Purolator, and the U.S. Postal Service were all reporting losses on their air express business, while Airborne had seen its profits slump 66 percent in the first quarter of 1986 and now had razor-thin margins.

The Specter of Fax

To make matters worse, by the mid 1980s there were increasing concerns that electronic mail would take much of the information distribution business away from the air express operators. In particular, as the speed and quality of facsimile machines improved and the price of the equipment fell, fax emerged as a very real threat to the volume of document traffic handled by the air express carriers.

Federal Express responded to this perceived threat by its 1984 entry into the electronic mail business with its ZAPMAIL product. The company established fax equipment in its retail outlets, as well as in some of its trucks. Federal's existing courier service would pick up documents and then transmit them by fax to a Federal Express receiver. The document would then be delivered to its destination by the courier service. The aim was to provide door-to-door service within two hours. Unfortunately for Federal Express, fax technology developed rapidly, making it cost effective for corporate clients to buy their own equipment, rather than use Federal's. In 1986, after two years of large losses, Federal Express admitted its mistake and abandoned ZAPMAIL.

The growth of facsimile continued to be a threat, however, and undoubtedly squeezed the growth rate in the document traffic. Federal Express's experience in this category is illuminating. During 1986, its year-to-year gains in monthly overnight document traffic were in the 50 to 60 percent range. By late 1988, the gains were down in the 9 to 10 percent range.[16] However, a 1988 study by Airborne Express of the impact of fax machines puts this threat in some perspective. Eighty-one percent of executives contacted for a study by Airborne said that their use of fax had increased over the past year. However, those same executives said that fax is having a limited impact on air express; approximately 77 percent said that their use of air express had either remained constant or increased during the same period.[17]

INDUSTRY EVOLUTION, 1987–1996

Industry Consolidation

A slowdown in the growth rate of the air express business due to increasing geographic saturation and inroads made by electronic transmission stimulated further price discounting in 1987 and early

1988. Predictably, this created problems for the weakest companies in the industry. The first to go was Purolator Courier, which had lost $65 million during 1985 and 1986. Purolator's problems stemmed from a failure to install an adequate computer system. The company was unable to track shipments, a crucial asset in this industry, and its best corporate customers were billed 120 days late.[18] In 1987 Purolator agreed to be acquired by Emery. The latter was unable to effect a satisfactory integration of Purolator and itself sustained large losses in 1988 and early 1989.

In April 1989, Consolidated Freightways, a major trucking company and parent of CF Air Freight, the third largest heavy shipment specialist in the United States, acquired Emery for $478 million. However, CF Air Freight soon found itself struggling to cope with Emery's problems. In its first eleven months with CF, Emery lost $100 million. One of the main problems was Emery's billing and tracking system, described as a "rat's nest" of conflicting tariff schedules, which caused overbillings of customers and made tracking packages en route a major chore. In addition, CF enraged corporate customers by trying to add a "fuel surcharge" of 4 to 7 percent to prices in early 1989. Competitors held the line on prices and picked up business from CF/Emery.[19]

As a result of the decline of the CF/Emery/Purolator combination, the other firms in the industry were able to pick up market share. By 1994, the industry's estimates suggested that Federal Express accounted for 35 percent of domestic airfreight and air express industry revenues; UPS had 26 percent, Airborne Express was third with 9 percent; and Emery, DHL (a large Brussels-based international air express carrier), and the U.S. Postal Service each held on to 4 percent of the market. The remainder of the market was split between numerous small cargo carriers and several combination carriers, such as Evergreen International and Atlas Air. (Combination carriers specialize mostly in heavy freight but do carry some express mail.)[20]

The other major acquisition in the industry during this time was the purchase of Flying Tiger by Federal Express for $880 million in December 1988. Although Flying Tiger had some air express operations in the United States, its primary strength was as a heavy cargo carrier with a global route structure. The acquisition was part of Federal Express's goal of becoming a major player in the in-

ternational air express market (more of this later). However, the acquisition was not without its problems. For one thing, many of Flying Tiger's biggest customers, including UPS and Airborne Express, are Federal's competitors in the domestic market. These companies have long paid Tiger to carry packages to those countries where they have no landing rights. It seemed unlikely that these companies would continue to push international business to their biggest domestic competitor. Further problems arose in the process of trying to integrate the two operations. These included the scheduling of aircraft and pilots, the servicing of Tiger's fleet, and the merging of Federal's nonunionized pilots with Tiger's unionized pilots.[21]

During the late 1980s and early 1990s, there were also hints of further consolidations. TNT Ltd., a large Australian-based air cargo operation with a global network, made an unsuccessful attempt to acquire Airborne Express in 1986. TNT's bid was frustrated by opposition from Airborne and by the difficulties inherent in getting around U.S. law, which currently limits foreign firms from having more than a 25 percent stake in U.S. airlines. In addition, DHL Airways, the U.S. subsidiary of DHL International, was reportedly attempting to enlarge its presence in the United States and was on the lookout for an acquisition.[22]

Pricing Trends

In October 1988, UPS offered new discounts to high-volume customers in domestic markets. For the first time since 1983, competitors declined to match the cuts. Then in January 1989, UPS announced a price increase of 5 percent for next-day air service, its first price increase in nearly six years. Federal Express, Airborne, and Consolidated Freightways all followed suit with moderate increases. Further rate increases of 5.9 percent on next-day air letters were announced by UPS in February 1990. Federal Express followed suit in April, and Airborne also implemented selective price hikes on noncontract business of 5 percent or 50 cents a package on packages up to 20 pounds.[23]

However, just as prices were beginning to stabilize, along came the 1990–1991 recession. For the first time in the history of the U.S. air express industry, there was a decline in year-on-year shipments, with express freight falling from 4,455 million ton miles in 1989 to 4,403 million ton miles in 1990. This decline triggered another round of competitive price cuts, and yields plummeted. Although demand rebounded strongly, repeated attempts to raise prices in 1992, 1993, and 1994 simply did not stick.[24] Much of the price cutting was focused on large corporate accounts, which by this time were generating 75 percent by volume of express mail shipments. For example, as a result of deep price discounting in 1994, UPS was able to lure home shopping programmer QVC and computer mail-order company Gateway 2000 away from Federal Express. However, at about the same time, Federal Express used discounting to capture retailer Williams-Sonoma away from UPS.[25] This prolonged period of price discounting depressed profit margins and contributed to losses at all three major carriers during the early 1990s. Bolstered by a strong economy, prices finally began to stabilize during late 1995, when price increases announced by UPS were followed by those at Federal Express and Airborne.[26]

Product Trends

Second-Day Delivery   Having seen a slowdown in the growth rate of the next day document delivery business during the early 1990s, the major operators in the air express business began to look for new product opportunities to sustain their growth and margins. One trend has been to move into the second-day delivery market, or deferred services as it is called in the industry.[27] The move toward second-day delivery was started by Airborne Express in 1991, and it was soon imitated by its major competitors. Second-day delivery commands a substantially lower price point than first-day delivery. In 1994, for example, Federal Express made an average of $9.23 on second-day deliveries, compared with $16.37 on priority overnight service.

The express mail operators see deferred services as a way to utilize excess capacity at the margin, thereby boosting revenues and profits. Since many second-day packages can be shipped on the ground, the cost of second-day delivery can more than compensate for the lower price. Still, in some ways the service has been almost too successful. During the mid 1990s the growth rate for deferred services was significantly higher than for priority overnight mail, as many corporations came to the realization that they could live with a second-day service. At Airborne Express, for example, second-

day delivery accounted for 42 percent of total volume in 1996, up from 37 percent in 1995.[28]

Premium Services   Another development has been a move toward a premium service. In 1994, UPS introduced its Early AM service, which guaranteed delivery of packages and letters by 8:30 A.M. in select cities. UPS aimed Early AM at a range of businesses that need documents or materials before the start of the business day. These include hospitals, which are expected to use the service to ship critical drugs and medical devices; architects who need to have their blueprints sent to a construction site; and salespeople. Although demand for the service is predicted to be light, the premium price makes for high profit margins. In 1994, UPS's price for a letter delivered at 10:30 A.M. was $10.75, while it charge $40 for an equivalent Early AM delivery. UPS believes that it can provide the service at little extra cost because most of its planes arrive in their destination cities by 7:30 A.M. Federal Express and Airborne initially declined to follow UPS's lead.[29]

Logistics Services   A further development of some note has been the move by all major operators into third-party logistics services. Since the later half of the 1980s, more and more companies have been relying on air express operations as part of their just-in-time inventory control systems. As a result, the content of packages carried by air express operators has been moving away from letters and documents and toward high-value, low-weight products. By 1994, less than 20 percent of Federal Express's revenues came from documents.[30] To take advantage of this trend, all of the major operators have been moving into logistics services that are designed to assist business customers in their warehousing, distribution, and assembly operations. The emphasis of this business is on helping customers reduce the time involved in their production cycles and gain distribution efficiencies.

In the late 1980s, Federal Express set up a business logistics services (BLS) division. The new division evolved from Federal Express's Parts Bank. The Parts Bank stores critical inventory for clients, most of whom are based in the high-tech electronics and medical industries. On request, Federal Express will ship this inventory to its client's customers. The service saves clients from having to invest in their own distribution systems; it also allows them to achieve economies of scale by making large production runs and then storing the inventory at the Parts Bank.

The BLS division has expanded this service to include some assembly operations and customs brokerage and to assist in achieving just-in-time manufacturing. Thus, for example, one U.S. computer company relies on BLS to deliver electronic subassemblies from the Far East as a key part of its just-in-time system. Federal Express brings the products in on its aircraft, clears them through customs with the help of a broker, and manages truck transportation to the customer's dock.[31]

UPS moved into the logistics business in 1993 when it established UPS Worldwide Logistics, which it positioned as a third-party provider of global supply chain management solutions, including transportation management, warehouse operations, inventory management, documentation for import and export, network optimization, and reverse logistics. UPS's logistics business is based at its Louisville, Kentucky, hub. In 1995 the company announced that it would invest $75 million to expand the scope of this facility, bringing total employment in the facility to 2,200 by the end of 1988.[32]

Airborne Express has also made a significant push into this end of the business. A number of Airborne's corporate accounts utilize a warehousing service called Stock Exchange. As with Federal Express's Parts Bank, clients warehouse critical inventory at Airborne's hub in Wilmington, Ohio, and then ship those items on request to their customers. In addition, Airborne has set up a commerce park on 1,000 acres around its Wilmington hub. The park is aimed at companies that want to outsource logistics to Airborne and can gain special advantages by locating at the company's hub. Not the least of these is the ability to make shipping decisions as late as 2 A.M. Eastern time.

Information Systems

Since the late 1980s, the three major U.S. air express carriers have devoted ever more attention to competing on the basis of information technology. The ability to track a package as it moves through an operator's delivery network has always been an important aspect of competition in an industry where reliability is so highly valued. Given this, all of the major players in the industry have invested heavily in bar code technology, scanners, and computerized tracking systems. More recently, UPS, Federal Express, and Airborne have all invested in Internet-based technology that allows customers to order pickups, print shipping labels, and track deliveries on-line.

Globalization

Perhaps the most important development for the long-run future of the industry has been the increasing globalization of the airfreight industry. The combination of a healthy U.S. economy, strong and expanding East Asian economies, and the move toward ever closer economic integration in Western Europe all offer opportunities for growth in the international air cargo business. Moreover, the increasing globalization of companies in a whole range of industries, from electronics to autos and from fast food to clothing, is beginning to dictate that the air express operators follow suit.

Global manufacturers want to keep inventories at a minimum and deliver just-in-time as a way of keeping down costs and fine-tuning production, which requires speedy supply routes. Thus, some electronics companies will manufacture key components in one location, ship them by air to another for final assembly, and then deliver them by air to a third location for sale. This is particularly true among industries producing small high-value items (for example, electronics, medical equipment, and computer software) that can be economically transported by air—industries for which just-in-time inventory systems are crucial for keeping down costs. It is also true in the fashion industry, where timing is all important. For example, the clothing chain The Limited manufactures clothes in Hong Kong and then ships them by air to the United States to keep from missing out on fashion trends.[33] In addition, an increasing number of wholesalers are beginning to turn to international air express as a way of meeting delivery deadlines.

The emergence of integrated global corporations is also increasing the demand for the global shipment of contracts, confidential papers, computer printouts, and other documents that are far too bulky for fax machines to handle. Major U.S. corporations are increasingly demanding the same kind of service that they receive from air express operators within the United States for their far-flung global operations.

As a consequence of these trends, rapid growth is predicted in the global arena. According to recent forecasts, the market for international air express is expected to grow at around 18 percent annually from 1996 through to 2016.[34] Faced with an increasingly mature market at home, the race is on among the major air cargo operators to build global air and ground transportation networks that will enable them to deliver goods and documents between any two points on the globe within forty-eight hours.

Currently, the company with the most extensive international operations is DHL. As of 1995 DHL enjoyed a 44 percent share of the worldwide market for international air express services (see Table 2).[35] Started in California in 1969 and now based in Brussels, DHL is smaller than many of its rivals, but it has managed to capture as much as an 80 percent share in some markets, such as documents leaving Japan, by concentrating solely on international air express. The strength of DHL was enhanced in mid 1992 when Lufthansa, Japan Airlines, and the Japanese trading company, Nisho Iwai, announced that they intended to invest as much as $500 million for a 57.5 percent stake in DHL. Although Lufthansa and Japan Airlines are primarily known for their passenger flights, they also are among the top five airfreight haulers in the world, both because they carry cargo in the holds of their passenger flights and because they each have a fleet of all-cargo aircraft.[36]

TNT Ltd., a $6 billion Australian conglomerate, is another big player in the international air express market, with courier services from 184 countries as well as package express and mail services. In 1995, its share of the international air express market was 12 percent, down from 18 percent in 1990.[37]

TABLE 2

International Air Express Market, Market Share—1995

Company	Market Share
DHL International	44%
Federal Express	21%
UPS	12%
TNT	12%
Others	11%

Source: Standard & Poor's, "Aerospace and Air Transport," *Industry Surveys,* February 1996.

Among U.S. carriers, Federal Express was first off the blocks in the race to build up a global air express network. Between 1984 and 1989, Federal Express purchased seventeen other companies worldwide in an attempt to build up its global distribution capabilities, culminating in the $880 million purchase of Flying Tiger. The main asset of Flying Tiger was not so much its aircraft, as its landing rights overseas. The Flying Tiger acquisition gave Federal Express service to 103 countries, a combined fleet of 328 aircraft, and revenues of $5.2 billion in fiscal 1989.[38]

However, Federal Express has had to suffer through years of losses in its international operations. Start-up costs were heavy, due in part to the enormous capital investments required to build an integrated air and ground network worldwide. Between 1985 and 1992, Federal Express spent $2.5 billion to build an international presence. In addition, faced with heavy competition, Federal Express found it difficult to generate the international volume required to fly its planes at above break-even capacity on many international routes. Since the demand for outbound service from the United States is greater than the demand for inbound service, planes that would leave New York full often returned half-empty.

Moreover, trade barriers have also proved very damaging to the bottom line. Customs regulations require a great deal of expensive and time-consuming labor, such as checking paperwork and rating package contents for duties. This obviously inhibits the ability of international air cargo carriers to effect express delivery. Federal Express has been particularly irritated by Japanese requirements that each inbound envelope be opened and searched for pornography, a practice that seems to be designed to slow down the company's growth rate in the Japanese market.

Federal Express has also found it extremely difficult to get landing rights in many markets. For example, it took three years to get permission from Japan to make four flights per week from Memphis to Tokyo, a key link in the overseas system. Then in 1988, just three days before the service was due to begin, the Japanese notified Federal that no packages weighing more than 70 pounds could pass through Tokyo. To make matters worse, until 1995 Japan limited Federal's ability to fly on from Tokyo and Osaka to other locations in Asia. The Japanese claimed, with some justification, that due to government regulations, the U.S. air traffic market is difficult for foreign carriers to enter, so they see no urgency to help Federal build a market presence in Japan and elsewhere in Asia.[39]

After heavy financial losses, in 1992 Federal abruptly shifted its international strategy, selling off its expensive European ground network to local carriers in order to concentrate on intercontinental deliveries. Under the new strategy, Federal will rely on a network of local partners to deliver its packages. Also, Federal entered into an alliance with TNT to share space on Federal's daily transatlantic flights. Under the agreement, TNT will fly packages from its hub in Cologne Germany, to Britain, where they will be loaded onto Federal's daily New York flight.[40]

UPS has also moved to build up an international presence. In 1988, UPS bought eight smaller European airfreight companies and Hong Kong's Asian Courier Service, and it announced air service and ground delivery in 175 countries and territories. However, it has not been all smooth sailing for UPS either. UPS had been using Flying Tiger for its Pacific shipments. The acquisition of Flying Tiger by Federal Express left UPS in the difficult situation of shipping its parcels on a competitor's plane. UPS was concerned that it could get its shipments pushed to the back of the aircraft. Since there were few alternative carriers, UPS pushed for authority to run an all-cargo route to Tokyo, but approval was slow in coming. Moreover, "beyond rights" to carry cargo from Tokyo to further destinations (such as Singapore and Hong Kong) were also difficult to gain.

In March 1996, UPS sidestepped years of frustrations associated with building an Asian hub in Tokyo by announcing that it would invest $400 million in a Taiwan hub, which would henceforth be the central node in its Asian network. The decision to invest in an Asian hub followed close on the heels of a 1995 decision by UPS to invest $1.1 billion to build a ground network in Europe. In September 1996, UPS went one step further toward building an international air express service when it announced that it would start a Pan-European next-day delivery service for small packages. UPS hopes that its recent moves will finally push its international operations into the black after eight years of losses.[41]

The other U.S. carrier that is making a determined push overseas is Airborne Express. However, right from the start Airborne's strategy differs from that of Federal Express and UPS insofar as it decided not to invest in its own international air-

fleet and ground operations. Airborne's strategy has two aspects. First, it will continue to fly its own planes in the United States but book space on other air carriers for shipments going overseas. Second, it has been looking for strategic alliances with foreign companies that would give it market access and ground operations overseas. In 1989, the company announced an alliance with Mitsui & Co., a $125 billion-a-year Japanese trading and finance firm, and Tonami Transportation Co., operators of a ground-based express delivery service in Japan called Panther Express. The deal calls for Mitsui to purchase $40 million worth of Airborne's stock and to provide $100 million in aircraft financing over the next five years and for the partners to collaborate in building volume in the lucrative Japan-U.S. air express market. Non-Japanese firms currently only handle 15 percent of the air shipments going in and out of Japan, but now that Mitsui owns part of Airborne, the Seattle-based company is counting on getting the inside track on the other 85 percent of the market.[42]

Endnotes

1. Standard & Poor's, "Aerospace and Air Transport," *Industry Surveys* (February 1996).
2. Ibid.
3. Ibid.
4. C. H. Lovelock, "Federal Express (B)," *Harvard Business School Case* No. 579-040, 1978.
5. Standard & Poor's, "Aerospace and Air Transport," *Industry Surveys* (January 1981).
6. Lovelock, "Federal Express (B)."
7. Standard & Poor's, "Aerospace and Air Transport," *Industry Surveys* (January 1981).
8. Ibid.
9. Ibid.
10. Standard & Poor's, "Aerospace and Air Transport," *Industry Surveys* (January 1984).
11. C. Hall, "High Fliers," *Marketing and Media Decisions,* August 1986, p. 138.
12. Standard & Poor's, "Aerospace and Air Transport," *Industry Surveys* (January 1984).
13. Standard & Poor's, "Aerospace and Air Transport," *Industry Surveys* (December 1984).
14. B. Dumaine, "Turbulence Hits the Air Couriers," *Fortune,* July 21, 1986, pp. 101–106.
15. Ibid.
16. Standard & Poor's, "Aerospace and Air Transport," *Industry Surveys* (May 1989).
17. "Are Faxes Putting the Whammy on Air Express? This Study Says No," *Distribution* (January 1989), 22.
18. C. Hawkins, "Purolator: Still No Overnight Success," *Business Week,* June 16, 1986, pp. 76–78.
19. J. O'C. Hamilton, "Emery Is One Heavy Load for Consolidated Freightways," *Business Week,* March 26, 1990, pp. 62–64.

20. Standard & Poor's "Aerospace and Air Transport," *Industry Surveys* (February 1996).

21. "Hold That Tiger: FedEx Is Now World Heavyweight," *Purchasing,* September 14, 1989, pp. 41–42.

22. Standard & Poor's, "Aerospace and Air Transport," *Industry Surveys* (April 1988).

23. R. G. Blumenthal, "UPS Move to Lift Rates Could Spur Increases by Rivals," *Wall Street Journal,* February 13, 1990, pp. B1, B4.

24. Standard & Poor's, "Aerospace and Air Transport," *Industry Surveys* (February 1996).

25. David Greising, "Watch Out for Flying Packages," *Business Week,* November 1994, p. 40.

26. "UPS to Raise Its Rates for Packages," *Wall Street Journal,* January 9, 1995, p. C22.

27. R. Frank, "Federal Express Grapples with Changes in U.S. Market," *Wall Street Journal,* July 5, 1994, p. B6.

28. M. Royce, "Airborne Freight," *Value Line Investment Survey,* September 20, 1996.

29. R. Frank, "UPS Planning Earlier Delivery," *Wall Street Journal,* September 29, 1994, p. A4.

30. Frank, "Federal Express Grapples with Changes in U.S. Market."

31. P. Bradley, "Good Things Come in Small Packages," *Purchasing,* November 9, 1989, pp. 58–64.

32. Company press releases (http://www.ups.com/news/).

33. J. M. Feldman, "The Coming of Age of International Air Freight," *Air Transport World,* June 1989, pp. 31–33.

34. Standard & Poor's, "Aerospace and Air Transport," *Industry Surveys* (February 1996).

35. Ibid.

36. P. Greiff, "Lufthansa, JAL, and a Trading Firm Acquire a Majority Stake in DHL," *Wall Street Journal,* August 24, 1992, p. A5.

37. Standard & Poor's, "Aerospace and Air Transport," *Industry Surveys* (February 1996).

38. "Hold That Tiger."

39. D. Blackmon, "FedEx Swings from Confidence Abroad to a Tightrope," *Wall Street Journal,* March 15, 1996, p. B4.

40. D. Pearl, "Federal Express Plans to Trim Assets in Europe," *Wall Street Journal,* March 17, 1992, p. A3.

41. Company press releases (http://www.ups.com/news/).

42. Byron Acohido, "Expansion Express," *Seattle Times,* June 30, 1990, pp. E1, E6.

CASE 20

Airborne Express

This case was prepared by Charles W. L. Hill of the University of Washington.

INTRODUCTION

Airborne Freight, which operates under the name Airborne Express, is an integrated air express transportation company, providing next-morning delivery of small packages (less than 70 pounds) and documents throughout the United States. The company owns and operates an airline and a fleet of ground-transportation vehicles to provide complete door-to-door service. It is also an airfreight forwarder, moving shipments of any size on a worldwide basis. As of 1996 Airborne Express held third place in the U.S. air express industry, with 9 percent of the market. Its main domestic competitors are Federal Express, which has 35 percent of the market; United Parcel Service (UPS), which has 24 percent of the market; and Consolidated Freightways (CF) and the U.S. Postal Service, each of which holds a 4 percent market share.[1]

The evolution of the air express industry and the state of competition in the industry are discussed in the preceding case, "The Evolution of the Air Express Industry." This case focuses on the operating structure, competitive strategy, organizational structure, and cultures of Airborne Express.

HISTORY OF AIRBORNE EXPRESS

Airborne Express was originally known as Pacific Air Freight when it was founded in Seattle at the close of World War II by Holt W. Webster, a former

Army Air Corps officer. (See Table 1 for a listing of major milestones in the history of Airborne Express.) The company was merged with Airborne Freight Corporation of California in 1968, taking the name of the California company but retaining management direction by the former officers of Pacific Air Freight. Airborne was initially an exclusive airfreight forwarder. Freight forwarders such as Airborne arrange for the transportation of air cargo between any two destinations. They purchase cargo space from the airlines and retail this in small amounts. They deal primarily with small customers, providing pickup and delivery services in most cities, either in their own trucks or through contract agents.

Following the 1977 deregulation of the airline industry, Airborne entered the air express industry by leasing the airplanes and pilots of Midwest Charter, a small airline operating out of its own airport in Wilmington, Ohio. However, Airborne quickly became dissatisfied with the limited amount of control it was able to exercise over Midwest, which made it very difficult to achieve the kind of tight coordination and control of logistics that was necessary to become a successful air express operator. Instead of continuing to lease Midwest's planes and facility, in 1980 Airborne decided to buy "the entire bucket of slop; company, planes, pilots, airport and all."

Among other things, the Midwest acquisition put Airborne in the position of being the only industry participant to own an airport. Airborne immediately began the job of developing a hub-and-spoke system capable of supporting a nationwide distribution system. An efficient sorting facility was established at the Wilmington hub. Airborne upgraded Midwest's fleet of prop and propjet aircraft, building a modern fleet of DC-8s, DC-9s, and YS-11

TABLE I

Fifty Years of Airborne Express

1946	Airborne Flower Traffic Association of California founded to fly fresh flowers from Hawaii to the mainland.
1968	Airborne of California and Pacific Air Freight of Seattle merge to form Airborne Freight Corporation, with headquarters in Seattle, Washington.
1979–1981	Airborne Express is born. Airborne purchases Midwest Air Charter and then purchases Clinton County Air Force Base in Wilmington, Ohio, becoming the only carrier to own and operate an airport. The package sort center opens, creating the hub for the hub-and-spoke system.
1984–1986	Airborne is first carrier to establish a privately operated Foreign Trade Zone in an air industrial park.
1987	Airborne opens the Airborne Stock Exchange, a third-party inventory management and distribution service. New service provided to and from more than 8,000 Canadian locations.
1988	Airborne is first air express carrier to provide same-day delivery through the purchase of Sky Courier.
1990	Airborne named at the International Cargo Forum and Exposition as the carrier with the most outstanding integrated cargo system over the previous two years.
1991	Airborne is first transportation company to receive Volvo-Flying Motors' Excellent Performance Award. Ranked "most effective user of information systems in the U.S. transportation industry" by Computerworld. Receives "Spread the Word!" electronic data interchange (EDI) award for the largest number of EDI users worldwide in the air express and freight-forwarding industry.
1992	Airborne introduces the first prepurchased Express Letters and Packs with Flight-Ready SM.
1993	Airborne introduces Advanced Logistics Services (ALS), a new subsidiary providing outsourced warehousing and distribution services. IBM consolidates its international shipping operation with Airborne.
1994	Airborne is first express carrier to introduce ocean-shipping services with opening of Ocean Service Division. Advanced Logistics services (ALS) establishes the first new film distribution program for the movie industry in fifty years. Airborne is the first to provide on-line communication to Vietnam.
1995	Airborne Alliance Group, a consortium of transportation, logistics, third-party customer service operations, and high-tech companies providing value-added services, is formed. Airborne opens a second runway at its hub, the largest privately owned airport in the United States. Expanded fleet with acquisition of Boeing 767-200 aircraft.
1996	Airborne Express celebrates fifty years of providing distribution solutions to businesses.

aircraft. These planes left major cities every evening, flying down the spokes carrying letters and packages to the central sort facility in Wilmington, Ohio. There the letters and packages were unloaded, sorted according to their final destination, and then reloaded and flown to their final destination for delivery before noon the next day.

During the late 1970s and early 1980s, dramatic growth in the industry attracted many competitors. (See Figure 1 for data on Airborne's domestic shipment growth.) As a consequence, despite a high-growth rate, price competition became intense, forcing a number of companies to the sidelines by the late 1980s. (See Figure 2 for data on revenues per shipment.) Airborne was able to survive this period by pursuing a number of strategies that increased productivity and drove costs down to the

lowest levels in the industry. (See Figure 3 data on operating costs per shipment.) As a consequence, by the late 1980s Airborne had pulled away from a pack of struggling competitors to become one of the top three companies in the industry, a position it still held in the mid 1990s.

AIR EXPRESS OPERATIONS

The Domestic Delivery Network

As of 1996, Airborne Express had 265 ground stations within the United States. The stations are essentially the ends of the spokes in Airborne's hub-and-spoke system (the hub being Wilmington, Ohio—see Figure 4). In each station there are about 50 to 55 or so drivers plus staff. About 80

FIGURE 1

Shipment Growth,
1984–1995

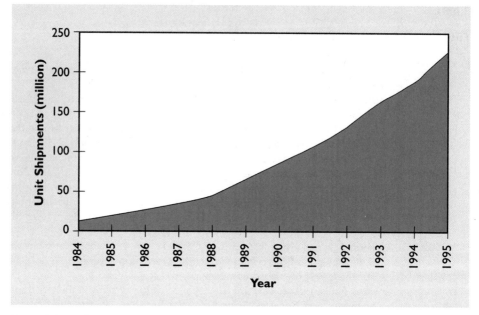

Source: Airborne Express

FIGURE 2

Unit Revenues per
Domestic Shipment,
1984–1995

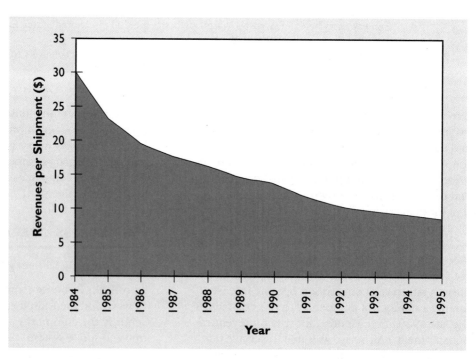

Source: Airborne Express

FIGURE 3

Operating Costs per Shipment

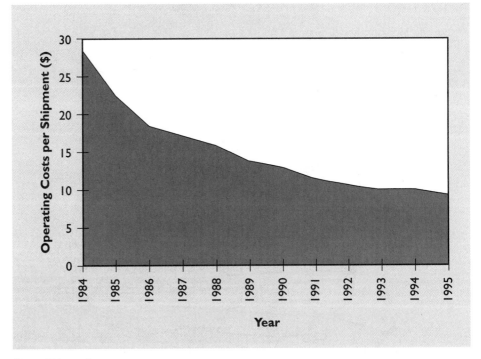

Source: Airborne Express

percent of Airborne's 19,500 full-time and part-time employees are found at this level. The stations are the basic units in Airborne's delivery organization. Their primary task is to ferry packages between clients and the local air terminal. Airborne utilizes approximately 12,800 radio-dispatch delivery vans and trucks to transport packages, of which 4,500 are owned by the company. Independent contractors under contract with the company provide the balance of the company's pickup and delivery services.

Airborne's drivers make their last round of major clients at 5 P.M. The drivers either collect packages directly from clients or from one of the company's 9,800 plus drop boxes. The drop boxes are placed at strategic locations, such as in the lobbies of major commercial buildings. To give clients a little more time, in most major cities there are also a few central drop boxes that are not emptied until 6 P.M. If a client needs still more time, so long as the package can be delivered to the airport by 7 P.M., it will make the evening flight.

When a driver picks up a package, he or she will read a bar code that is attached to the package with a hand-held scanner. This information is then

fed directly into Airborne's proprietary FOCUS (Freight, On-Line Control and Update System) computer system. The FOCUS system, which has global coverage, records shipment status at key points in the life cycle of a shipment. Thus, a customer can call Airborne on a twenty-four-hour basis to find out where in Airborne's system a package is. FOCUS also allows a customer direct access to shipment information through the Internet. All a customer needs to do is access Airborne's Web site and key the code number assigned to a package, and the FOCUS system will tell the customer where in Airborne's system the package is currently.

When the driver has completed the pickup route, she or he takes the load to Airborne's loading docks at the local airport. (Airborne serves all ninety-nine major metropolitan airports in the United States.) There the packages are loaded into C-containers (discussed later in this case study). Several C-containers are then towed by hand or by tractor to a waiting aircraft, where they are loaded onto a conveyer belt and in turn pass through the passenger door of the aircraft. Before long, the aircraft is loaded and takes off. It will either fly directly to the company's hub at Wilmington, or it

FIGURE 4

Airborne's Hub-and-Spoke System

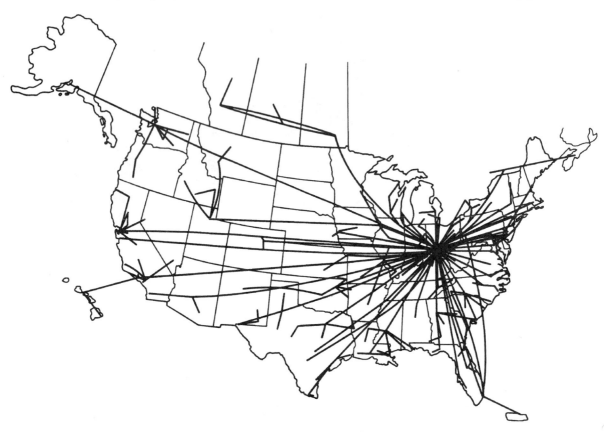

may make one or two stops along the way to pick up more packages.

Sometime between midnight and 2 A.M., most of the aircraft will have landed at Wilmington. An old strategic air command base, Wilmington lies within a 600-mile radius (an overnight drive or one-hour flying time) of 60 percent of the U.S. population. Wilmington has the advantage of a good-weather record. In all the years that Airborne has operated at Wilmington, air operations have been "fogged out" on only a handful of days. In 1995, Airborne opened a second runway at Wilmington. Developed at a cost of $60 million, the second runway makes Wilmington the largest privately owned airport in the country. The runway expansion was part of a $120 million upgrade of the Wilmington sorting facility.

After arrival at Wilmington, the plane taxis down the runway and parks alongside a group of

aircraft that are already disgorging their load of C-containers. Within minutes the C-containers are un-loaded from the plane down a conveyer belt and towed to the sort facility by a tractor. The sort facility has the capacity to handle 980,000 packages per night. During 1995, the facility handled an average of 835,000 packages a night. The bar codes on the packages are read, and then the packages are directed through a labyrinth of conveyer belts and sorted according to final destination. The sorting is partly done by hand and partly automated. At the end of this process, packages are grouped together by final destination and loaded into a C-container. An aircraft bound for the final destination is then loaded with C-containers, and by 5 A.M. most aircraft have taken off.

Upon arrival at the final destination, the plane is unloaded and the packages sorted according to their delivery points within the surrounding area.

Airborne couriers then take the packages on the final leg of their journey. Packages have a 75 percent probability of being delivered to clients by 10:30 A.M., and a 98 percent probability of being delivered by noon.

Regional Trucking Hubs

Although about 75 percent of packages are transported by air and pass through Wilmington, Airborne has also established ten regional trucking hubs that deal with the remaining 25 percent of the company's domestic volume. These hubs sort shipments that originate and have a destination within approximately a 300-mile radius. The first one opened was in Allentown, Pennsylvania, which is centrally located on the East Coast. This hub handles packages that are being transported between points within the Washington, D.C., to Boston area. Instead of transporting packages by air, packages to be transported within this area are sorted by the drivers at pickup and delivered from the driver's home station by scheduled truck runs to the Allentown hub. There they are sorted according to destination and taken to the appropriate station on another scheduled truck run for final delivery.

One advantage of ground-based transportation through trucking hubs is that operating costs are much lower than for air transportation. The average cost of a package transported by air is more than five times greater than the cost of a package transported on the ground. However, this cost differential is transparent to the customer, who assumes that all packages are flown. Thus, Airborne can charge the same price for ground-transported packages as for air-transported packages, but the former yields a much higher return. The trucking hubs also have the advantage of taking some of the load off the Wilmington sorting facility, which is currently operating at about 90 percent capacity.

International Operations

In addition to its domestic express operations, Airborne is also an international company, providing service to more than 200 companies worldwide. International operations currently account for about 16 percent of total revenues, although this share is expected to increase with the forecasted growth in the international air express industry. (See "The Evolution of the Air Express Industry, 1973–1996," Case 19.)

Airborne offers two international products: freight products and express products. Freight products are commercial-sized, larger-unit shipments. This service provides door-to-airport service. Goods are picked up domestically from the customer and then shipped to the destination airport. A consignee or an agent of the consignee gets the paperwork and must clear the shipment through customs. Express packages are small packages, documents, and letters. This is a door-to-door service, and all shipments are cleared through customs by Airborne.

Airborne does not fly any of its own aircraft overseas. Rather, it contracts for space on all-cargo airlines or in the cargo holds of passenger airlines. Airborne owns facilities overseas in Japan, Taiwan, Hong Kong, Singapore, Australia, New Zealand, and London. These function in a manner similar to Airborne's domestic stations. (That is, they have their own trucks and drivers and are hooked into the FOCUS tracking system.) The majority of foreign distribution, however, is carried out by foreign agents. Foreign agents are large, local, well-established surface delivery companies. Airborne has entered into a number of exclusive strategic alliances with large foreign agents. These include alliances with Purolator (Canada) and Mitsui (Japan). The rationale for entering strategic alliances, along with Airborne's approach to global expansion, is discussed in greater detail later in this case.

Another aspect of Airborne's international operations has been the creation at its Wilmington hub of the only privately certified Foreign Trade Zone (FTZ) in the United States. While in an FTZ, merchandise is tax free and no customs duty is paid on it until it leaves. Thus, a foreign-based company may store critical inventory in the FTZ and have Airborne deliver it just-in-time to U.S. customers. This allows the foreign company to hold inventory in the United States without having to pay customs duty on it until the need arises.

Aircraft Purchase and Maintenance

As of 1996, Airborne Express owned a fleet of 105 aircraft, including 33 DC-8s, 61 DC-9s, and 11 YS-11 turboprop aircraft. In addition, approximately 70 smaller aircraft are chartered nightly to connect smaller cities with company aircraft that then operate to and from the Wilmington hub. To keep down capital expenditures, Airborne has traditionally purchased only used planes. Airborne converts the planes to suit its specifications at a maintenance facility based at its Wilmington hub. Once it gets a plane, Airborne typically guts the interior and installs state-of-the-art electronics and avionics equipment. The company's philosophy is to get all of the upgrades that it can into an aircraft. Although this can cost a lot up front, there is a payback in terms of increased aircraft reliability and a reduction in service downtime. Airborne also standardizes cockpits as much as possible. This makes it easier for crews to switch from one aircraft to another if the need arises. According to the company, the total purchase and modification of a secondhand DC-9 costs about $10 million, compared with an equivalent new plane cost of $40 million. An additional factor reducing operating costs is that Airborne's DC-9 and YS-11 aircraft require only a two-person cockpit crew, as opposed to the three-person crews required in most Federal Express and UPS aircraft.

After conversion, Airborne strives to keep aircraft maintenance costs down by carrying out virtually all of its own fleet repairs. (It is the only all-cargo carrier to do so.) The Wilmington maintenance facility can handle everything except major engine repairs and has the capability to machine critical aircraft parts if needed. The company sees this in-house facility as a major source of cost savings. It estimates that maintenance labor costs run $16 per hour versus an industry standard of $65 per hour for subcontracted labor.

In December 1995, Airborne announced a deal to purchase twelve used Boeing 767-200 aircraft between the years 1997 and 2000, and it announced plans to purchase a further ten to fifteen used 767-200s between the years 2000 and 2004. These will be the first wide-bodied aircraft in Airborne's fleet. The cost of introducing the first twelve aircraft will be about $290 million, and the additional aircraft will cost a further $360 million. The shift to wide-bodied aircraft was prompted by an internal study, which concluded that with growing volume, wide-bodied aircraft would lead to greater operating efficiencies.

C-Containers

C-containers are uniquely shaped 60-cubic-foot containers, developed by Airborne Express in 1985 at a cost of $3.5 million. They are designed to fit through the passenger doors of DC-8 and DC-9 aircraft. They replaced the much larger A-containers,

widely used in the air cargo business. At six times the size of a C-container, A-containers can be loaded only through specially built cargo doors and require specialized loading equipment. The loading equipment required for C-containers is a modified belt loader, similar to that used for loading baggage onto a plane, and about 80 percent less expensive than the equipment needed to load A-containers. The use of C-containers also means that Airborne does not have to bear the $1 million per plane cost required to install cargo doors that will take A-containers. The C-containers are shaped to allow maximum utilization of the planes' interior loading space. Fifty of the containers fit into a converted DC-9, and about 83 fit into a DC-8-62. Moreover, a C-container filled with packages can be moved by a single person, making them easy to load and unload. Airborne Express has taken out a patent on the design of the C-containers.

Information Systems

Airborne utilizes three information systems to help it boost productivity and improve customer service. The first of these systems is referred to as the LIBRA II system. LIBRA II equipment, which includes a metering device and PC computer software, is installed in the mailroom of clients. With minimum data entry, the metering device weighs the package, calculates the shipping charges, generates the shipping labels, and provides a daily shipping report. As of early 1996, the system was in use at approximately 8,200 domestic customer locations. Its use not only benefits the customers but also lowers Airborne's operating costs since LIBRA II shipment data are transferred into Airborne's FOCUS shipment tracking system automatically, thereby avoiding duplicate data entry.

FOCUS is the second of Airborne's three main information systems. As discussed earlier, the FOCUS system is essentially a worldwide tracking system. The bar codes on each package are read at various points (for example, at pickup, at sorting in Wilmington, at arrival, and so forth) using handheld scanners, and this information is fed into Airborne's computer system. Using FOCUS, Airborne can track the progress of a shipment through its national and international logistics system. The major benefit is in terms of customer service. Through an Internet link, Airborne's customers can track their own shipment through Airborne's system on a twenty-four-hour basis.

For its highest-volume corporate customers, Airborne has developed Customer Linkage, an electronic data interchange (EDI) program and the third information system. The EDI system is designed to eliminate the flow of paperwork between Airborne and its major clients. The EDI system allows customers to create shipping documentation at the same time they are entering orders for their goods. At the end of each day, shipping activities are transmitted electronically to Airborne's FOCUS system, where they are captured for shipment tracking and billing. Customer Linkage benefits the customer by eliminating repetitive data entry and paperwork. It also lowers the company's operating costs by eliminating manual data entry. (In essence, both LIBRA II and Customer Linkage push off a lot of the data-entry work into the hands of customers.) The EDI system includes electronic invoicing and payment remittance processing. Airborne also offers its customers a program known as Quicklink, which significantly reduces the programming time required by customers to take advantage of linkage benefits.

Logistics Services

Although small-package express mail remains Airborne's main business, through its Advanced Logistics Services Corp. (ALS) subsidiary the company is increasingly promoting a range of third-party logistics services. These services provide customers with the ability to maintain inventories in a 1-million-square-foot "stock exchange" facility located at Airborne's Wilmington hub or at sixty smaller "stock exchange" facilities around the country. The inventory can be managed either by the company or by the customer's personnel. Inventory stored at Wilmington can be delivered utilizing either Airborne's airline system or, if required, commercial airlines on a next-flight-out basis. ALS's central print computer program allows information on inventories to be sent electronically to customers' computers located at Wilmington, where Airborne's personnel monitor printed output and ship inventories according to customers' instructions.

For example, consider the case of Data Products Corp., a producer of computer printers. Data Products takes advantage of low labor costs to carry out significant assembly operations in Hong Kong. Many of the primary component parts for its printers, however, such as microprocessors, are manufactured in the United States and have to be shipped to Hong Kong. The finished product is then shipped back to the United States for sale. In setting up a global manufacturing system, Data Products had a decision to make: either consolidate the parts from its hundreds of suppliers in-house and then arrange for shipment to Hong Kong, or contract out to someone who could handle the whole logistics process. Data Products decided to contract out, and they picked Airborne Express to consolidate the component parts and arrange for shipments.

Airborne controls the consolidation and movement of component parts from the component part suppliers through to the Hong Kong assembly operation in such a way as to minimize inventory-holding costs. The key feature of Airborne's service is that all of Data Products' materials are collected at Airborne's facility at Los Angeles International Airport. Data Products' Hong Kong assembly plants can then tell Airborne what parts to ship by air as and when they are needed. Airborne is thus able to provide inventory control for Data Products. In addition, by scheduling deliveries so that year-round traffic between Los Angeles and Hong Kong can be guaranteed, Airborne is able to negotiate a better air rate from Japan Air Lines (JAL) for the transportation of component parts.

STRATEGY

Positioning Strategy

In the early 1980s Airborne Express tried hard to compete head-to-head with Federal Express. This included an attempt to establish broad market coverage, including both frequent and infrequent users. Frequent users are those that generate more than $20,000 of business per month, or more than 1,000 shipments per month. Infrequent users generate less than $20,000 per month, or less than 1,000 shipments per month.

To build broad market coverage, Airborne followed Federal Express's lead of funding a television advertising campaign designed to build consumer awareness. However, by the mid 1980s Airborne decided that this was an expensive way of building market share. The advertising campaign bought recognition but little penetration. One of the principal problems was that it was expensive to serve infrequent users. Infrequent users demanded the same level of service as frequent users, but Airborne would typically only get one shipment per pickup with an infrequent user, compared with ten or more shipments per pickup with a frequent user, so far more pickups were required to generate the same volume of business. Given the extremely competitive nature of the industry at this time, such an inefficient utilization of capacity was of great concern to Airborne.

Consequently, in the mid 1980s Airborne decided to become a niche player in the industry and focused on serving the needs of high-volume corporate accounts. The company slashed its advertising expenditure, pulling the plug on its TV ad campaign, and invested more resources in building a direct sales force, which is now 300 strong. By focusing upon high-volume corporate accounts, Airborne was able to establish scheduled pickup routes and use its ground capacity more efficiently. This enabled the company to achieve significant reductions in its unit cost structure. Partly due to this factor, Airborne executives reckon that their cost structure is as much as $3 per shipment less than that of their primary competitor, Federal Express.

Of course, there is a downside to this strategy. High-volume corporate customers have a great deal more bargaining power than infrequent users, so they can and do demand substantial discounts. For example, in March 1987 Airborne achieved a major coup when it won an exclusive three-year contract to handle all of IBM's express packages weighing less than 150 pounds. However, to win the IBM account, Airborne had to offer rates up to 84 percent below Federal Express's list prices. Nevertheless, so far the strategy seems to have worked for Airborne. As of 1995, approximately 80 percent of Airborne's revenues have come from corporate accounts, most of them secured through competitive bidding. The concentrated volume that this business represents has helped Airborne to drive down costs.

Delivery Time, Reliability, and Flexibility

A further feature of Airborne's strategy was the decision not to try to compete with Federal Express on delivery time. Federal Express and UPS currently guarantee delivery by 10:30 A.M. Airborne guarantees delivery by midday, although it offers a 10:30 guarantee to some very large corporate customers. Guaranteeing delivery by 10:30 A.M. would mean stretching Airborne's already tight scheduling system to the limit. To meet its 10:30 A.M. deadline, Federal Express has to operate with a deadline for the previous day's pickups of 6:30 P.M. Airborne can

afford to be a little more flexible and can arrange pickups at 6:00 P.M. if that suits a corporate client's particular needs. Later pickups clearly benefit the shipper, who is, after all, the paying party.

In addition, Airborne executives feel that a guaranteed 10:30 A.M. delivery is unnecessary. The extra hour and a half does not make a great deal of difference to most clients, and they are willing to accept the extra time in exchange for lower prices. In addition, Airborne stresses the reliability of its delivery schedules. As one executive put it, "a package delivered consistently at 11:15 A.M. is as good as delivery at 10:30 A.M." This reliability is enhanced by Airborne's ability to provide shipment tracking through its FOCUS system.

Deferred Services

With a slowdown in the growth rate of the express mail market toward the end of the 1980s, in 1990 Airborne decided to enter the deferred-delivery business with its Select Delivery Service (SDS) product. The SDS service provides for next-afternoon or second-day delivery. Packages weighing 5 pounds or less are generally delivered on a next-afternoon basis, with packages of more than 5 pounds being delivered on a second-day basis. SDS shipment comprised approximately 42 percent of total domestic shipments in 1995. They are priced lower than overnight express products, reflecting the less time-sensitive nature of these deliveries. The company utilizes any spare capacity on its express flights to carry SDS shipments. In addition, Airborne uses other carriers, such as passenger carriers with spare cargo capacity in the bellies of their planes, to carry less urgent SDS shipments.

Early in 1996, Airborne began to phase in two new services to replace its SDS service. Next Afternoon Service is available for shipments weighing 5 pounds or less, and Second Day Service is offered for shipments of all weights.

International Strategy

One of the major strategic challenges currently facing Airborne (along with the other express mail carriers) is how best to establish an international service that is comparable to its domestic service. Many of Airborne's major corporate clients are becoming ever more global in their own strategic orientation. As this occurs, they are increasingly demanding a compatible express mail service. In addition, the rise of companies with globally dispersed manufacturing operations that rely on just-in-time delivery systems to keep their inventory holding costs down has created a demand for a global air express service that can transport critical inventory between operations located in different parts of the world. (Consider the example of Data Products discussed earlier in this case study.)

The initial response of Federal Express and UPS to this challenge was to undertake massive capital investment to establish international airlift capability and international ground operations based on the U.S. model. (For details, see "The Evolution of the Air Express Industry," Case 19). Their rationale was that a wholly owned global delivery network was necessary to establish the tight control, coordination, and scheduling required for a successful air express operation. More recently, however, Federal Express pulled out of its European ground operations, while continuing to fly its own aircraft overseas.

Airborne has decided on a quite different strategy. In part born of financial necessity (Airborne lacks the capital necessary to imitate Federal Express and UPS), Airborne has decided to pursue what it refers to as a *variable cost strategy*. This involves two main elements: (1) the utilization of international airlift on existing air cargo operators and passenger aircraft to get its packages overseas, and (2) entry into strategic alliances with foreign companies that already have established ground delivery networks. In these two ways, Airborne hopes to be able to establish global coverage without having to undertake the kind of capital investments that Federal Express and UPS have made.

Airborne executives defend their decision to continue to purchase space on international flights rather than fly their own aircraft overseas by making a number of points. First, they point out that Airborne's international business is currently 70 percent outbound and 30 percent inbound. If Airborne were to fly its own aircraft overseas, this would mean flying them back half-empty. Second, on many routes Airborne simply doesn't yet have the volume necessary to justify flying its own planes. Third, currently national air carriers are giving Airborne good prices. If Airborne began to fly directly overseas, the company would be seen as a competitor and might no longer be given price breaks. Fourth, getting international airlift space is currently not a problem. While space can be limited in the third and fourth quarters of the year, Airborne is such a big customer that it usually has few problems getting lift.

On the other hand, the long-term viability of this strategy is questionable, given the rapid evolution in the international air express business. Flying Tiger was once one of Airborne's major providers of international lift. However, following the purchase of Flying Tiger by Federal Express, Airborne has reduced its business with Flying Tiger. (The business Airborne gave to Flying Tiger dropped from $27 million in 1988 to $14 million in 1989.) Apart from concerns about giving business to a competitor, Airborne fears that its packages will be "pushed to the back of the plane" whenever Flying Tiger has problems of capacity overload.

A further, potentially adverse, development occurred in June 1990, when the trio of JAL, Lufthansa, and the Japanese trading company Nisho Iwai purchased a 57.5 percent stake in DHL, a major international delivery operator with an extensive ground network in many industrialized nations, and announced intentions to invest $500 million in DHL. Since JAL has been a major carrier of Airborne's packages around the Pacific Rim, this could have negative implications for the company.

With regard to strategic alliances, Airborne currently has major alliances with Purolator (Canada) and Mitsui (Japan). The Purolator alliance dates back to October 1987. Purolator is primarily a ground service with 2,200 delivery vehicles, 5,600 employees, and delivery to 8,000 points within Canada. Airborne flies directly to a number of Canadian destinations, while Purolator handles the ground deliveries.

The alliance with Mitsui was announced in December 1989. Mitsui is one of the world's leading trading companies. Together with Tonami Transportation Co., Mitsui owns Panther Express, one of the top five express carriers in Japan and a company with a substantial ground network. The deal calls for the establishment of a joint venture between Airborne, Mitsui, and Tonami. To be known as Airborne Express Japan, the joint venture will combine Airborne's existing Japanese operations with Panther Express. Airborne will handle all of the shipments to and from Japan. The joint venture will be owned 40 percent by Airborne, 40 percent by Mitsui, and 20 percent by Tonami. The agreement specifies that board decisions must be made by consensus between the three partners. A majority of two cannot outvote the third. In addition, the deal calls for Mitsui to invest $40 million in Airborne Express through the purchase of a new issue of nonvoting 6.9 percent cumulative convertible preferred stock and a commitment to Airborne from Mitsui of up to $100 million for aircraft financing. There is no doubt that Airborne executives see the Mitsui deal as a major coup, both financially and in terms of market penetration into the huge Japanese market. The primary advantage claimed by Airborne executives for expanding via strategic alliances is that the company gets an established ground-based delivery network overseas without having to make capital investments.

ORGANIZATION

The Top-Management Team

The organizational structure of Airborne Express is flat (to keep lines of communication short) and is arranged on a functional basis. The top level is shown in Figure 5. Robert Cline, the CEO, and

Robert Brazier, the president and COO, have been with the company since the early 1960s. Carl Donaway bears primary responsibility for the ABX Air, Inc., subsidiary. He specializes in airline operations, which includes managing the Wilmington hub, the package sorting facility, and all aircraft and flight maintenance operations. Working under him are 2,800 employees—300 pilots, and 2,500 airport, aircraft maintenance, and sorting workers.

Roy Liljebeck's responsibilities center on the finance and administrative functions. His departments include treasurer, controller, accounting, purchasing, information systems, data processing, and archiving. Of the approximately 1,100 people working at headquarters, 700 to 800 fall within these areas.

Richard Goodwin handles all human resource functions. Since there are no field personnel officers (except at Wilmington), everything related to employment is handled through the Seattle head office.

FIGURE 5

Airborne's Organizational Structure

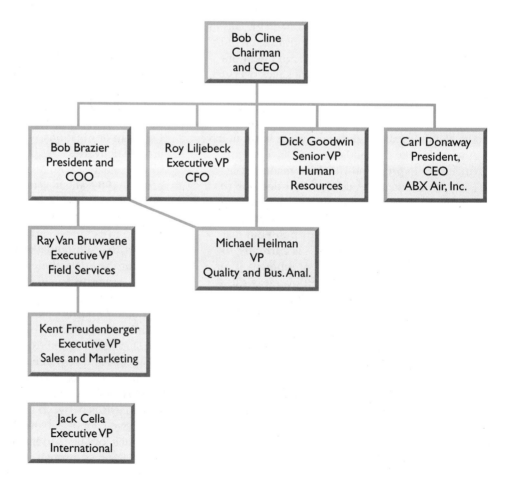

This includes recruiting, hiring, compensation and benefits, training, and employee communications.

The following three senior managers report directly to Brazier: Kent Freudenberger, executive vice president for marketing and sales; Ray van Bruwaene, executive vice president for field services; and Jack Cella, executive vice president for international.

Freudenberg's concern is marketing the express product (not freight), both nationally and internationally, and making direct pricing decisions. The 300-person direct sales force is responsible to Freudenberger.

Van Bruwaene deals with operations, that is, the service that Airborne sells. This includes picking up the package, getting it to Wilmington, and delivery to the final destination. He is responsible for managing the delivery network and for the associated functions such as customer service and data entry in the field. The stations, along with the drivers and station staff, are under Van Bruwaene's control.

Cella deals with international issues such as joint venture agreements, marketing agreements, agent and broker relations, pricing decisions, and so forth.

A striking feature of this top-management team is its longevity of service. The most recent arrival has been with Airborne for twenty-one years, while many of the top officers have spent their entire careers with the company. Despite their long service, several of the senior managers still have five to ten years to go before retirement. The advantage of a long-serving top-management team is that the members know each other well, having established a solid working relationship over a long number of years. Among other things, this consistency means that many of the interpersonal and communications difficulties that can plague top-management teams have been worked out long ago. One potential disadvantage is that the top-management team could become somewhat inbred and myopic. Another is that several promising younger managers have been frustrated by the lack of promotion opportunities at Airborne and have moved on to other organizations.

Decision Making, Control, and Culture

The philosophy at Airborne is to keep the organizational structure as flat as possible, to shorten lines of communication and allow for a free flow of ideas within the managerial hierarchy. The top managers generally feel that they are open to ideas suggested by lower-level managers. At the same time, the decision-making process is fairly centralized. The view is that interdependence between functions makes centralized decision making necessary. To quote one executive, "Coordination is the essence of this business. We need centralized decision making in order to achieve this."

Control at Airborne Express is geared toward boosting productivity, lowering costs, and maintaining a reliable high-quality service. This is achieved through a combination of budgetary controls, pay-for-performance incentive systems, and a corporate culture that continually stresses key values.

For example, consider the procedure used to control stations (which contain about 80 percent of all employees). Station operations are reviewed on a quarterly basis using a budgetary process. Control and evaluation of station effectiveness stress four categories. The first is service, measured by the time between pickup and delivery. The goal is to achieve 95 to 97 percent of all deliveries before noon. The second category is productivity, measured by total shipments per employee hour. The third category is controllable cost, and the fourth is station profitability. Goals for each of these categories are determined each quarter in a bottom-up procedure that involves station managers in the goal-setting process. These goals are then linked to an incentive pay system whereby station managers can earn up to 10 percent of their quarterly salary just by meeting their goals, with no maximum on the upside if they go over the goals.

The direct-sales force also has an incentive pay system. The target pay structure for the sales organization is 70 percent base pay and a 30 percent commission. There is, however, no cap on the commissions for salespeople. So in theory, there is no limit to what a salesperson can earn. There are also contests that are designed to boost performance. For example, there is a so-called Top Gun competition for the sales force, in which the top salesperson for each quarter wins a $20,000 prize.

Incentive pay systems apart, however, Airborne is not known as a high payer. The company's approach is not to be the compensation leader. Rather, the company tries to set its salary structure to position it in the middle of the labor market. Thus, according to Dick Goodwin, "We target our pay philosophy (total package—compensation plus benefits) to be right at the 50th percentile plus or minus 5 percent."

A degree of self-control is also achieved by trying to establish a corporate culture that focuses employees' attention on the key values required to maintain a competitive edge in the air express industry. The values continually stressed by top managers at Airborne, and communicated throughout the organization by the company's newspaper and a quarterly video, emphasize serving customers' needs, maintaining quality, doing it right the first time around, and excellent service. There is also a companywide emphasis on productivity and cost control. One executive, when describing the company's attitude to expenditures, said, "We challenge everything. . . . We're the toughest sons of bitches on the block." Another noted that "among managers I feel that there is a universal agreement on the need to control costs. This is a very tough business, and our people are aware of that. Airborne has an underdog mentality—a desire to be a survivor."

FINANCIAL STRATEGY

A summary of Airborne's financial situation is given in Table 2. Airborne's principal source of liquidity for capital expenditures has been through internally generated cash flows. Management has set a self-imposed limit of senior debt to total capital of 40 percent and total long-term debt to capital of 50 percent. Airborne issues new equity shares as debt

TABLE 2

Selected Financial Data
(in thousands)

	1995	1994	1993	1992
Operating Results				
Revenues				
Domestic	$1,871,163	$1,660,003	$1,484,787	$1,259,792
International	368,188	310,756	235,194	224,524
Total	2,239,351	1,970,759	1,719,981	1,484,316
Operating Expenses	2,170,370	1,881,821	1,636,861	1,456,450
Earnings from Operations	68,981	88,938	83,120	27,866
Interest, Net	29,347	24,663	24,093	18,779
Earnings Before Taxes	39,634	64,275	59,027	9,087
Income Taxes	15,814	25,440	23,738	3,930
Net Earnings Before Changes in Accounting	23,820	38,835	35,289	5,157
Cumulative Effect of Changes in Accounting	———	———	3,828	———
Net Earnings	23,820	38,835	39,117	5,157
Preferred Stock Dividends	276	894	2,760	2,760
Net Earnings Available to Common Shareholders	$ 23,544	$ 37,941	$ 36,357	$ 2,397
Financial Structure				
Working Capital	$ 91,599	$ 66,871	$ 56,521	$ 50,276
Property and Equipment	842,703	766,346	733,963	730,937
Total Assets	1,217,384	1,078,506	1,002,866	964,739
Long-Term Debt	364,621	279,422	269,250	303,335
Subordinated Debt	115,000	118,580	122,150	125,720
Redeemable Preferred Stock	3,948	5,000	40,000	40,000
Shareholders' Equity	406,315	387,398	318,824	285,639

levels reach these limits. Its last equity issue was in July 1990. Other sources of financing for Airborne are sales and leasebacks of aircraft and the joint venture with Mitsui (which provided $40 million and a commitment of $100 million in aircraft financing). During 1989 Airborne sold and leased back nine planes. This reduced the company's debt and generated $83 million in cash. Airborne wants to continue to lease back 20 to 30 percent of their aircraft.

AN INTERVIEW WITH ROBERT CLINE

Robert Cline is the CEO of Airborne Freight, the parent company of Airborne Express. Below are selections from an interview with Cline conducted by Charles Hill in 1990.

Hill: The margins in this business are often described as razor thin. Airborne is already an efficient operation. Do you see any hope of margins widening in the future?

Cline: I do see hope. The industry is consolidating, which is resulting in much greater price stability. Instead of ten viable players, in our portion of the industry there are now really just three. Last year we saw the most stable pricing environment in a decade, and I think it's going to continue. The reason I say this is that we are seeing UPS raise rates, and there is a very good chance from all we hear that Federal Express will follow. So that with price stability and our continued ability to bring down costs, it should lead to continued margin improvement.

Hill: Do you ever fear being squeezed out in a price war between Federal Express and UPS? While Airborne has the lowest cost structure, does the company still lack the financial resources to compete head-to-head with Federal Express and UPS in a price war?

Cline: That's always been a concern that we have had … that the two elephants will wrestle around in the grass and accidentally roll over us. Our best guess is that won't happen. One, because at this point in time UPS has not decided to discount. They are not really bidding for corporate accounts. Now, will they eventually get into it? It's a difficult one to say. We take the position that we don't think they will, but we'd better be prepared for it. But you know, if UPS does get into discounting in the air, they'd better be prepared to do it on the ground as well.

As for FedEx, you never now; they might. I would feel more comfortable against FedEx, quite honestly, than I would against UPS because of their size, and they have this surface element to subsidize air. Our costs are definitely lower than FedEx's. Sure, if they went to an all-out price war, it would be difficult to match them, but their balance sheet is not that strong.

Hill: Why do you think FedEx is losing money internationally?

Cline: I think it's a tough nut to crack. They are flying their planes over there, and they don't have enough volume to justify it. The volume just isn't there, especially the backhaul. I'm sure it's killing them. They have built this enormous overhead, and now the volume has to catch up with it. Because of their international problems, it wouldn't make much sense for them to get into a domestic price war and erode the only good margins they have.

Hill: How do you see the global market for express mail developing over the next decade?

Cline: It's in its infancy. It's where the U.S. market was eight to ten years ago. There will be very rapid growth, I think, especially in the smaller package business. Who the players will be has yet to be decided. UPS and Federal have got the resources and have leapt in with direct service, flying their aircraft and operating stations. Then you have the guys who aren't flying planes: ourselves; DHL, who probably has the biggest franchise going right now; and TNT, the Australian firm that owns 15 percent of us is also a very big player, especially in Europe.

We will remain an indirect carrier. We are not flying. We don't intend to fly—we don't really need to fly—there are all kinds of capacity available. Take Europe. UPS goes into Cologne and Federal goes into Brussels. We use scheduled airlines, so we have a choice. If it's to Paris, we go direct. If it's to London, we go direct. Whereas they have to go into a hub and redistribute. So actually, in many cases we have a service advantage over them. The only advantage they are going to have over us is if they can fill their aircraft with high-yielding freight— then their cost structure will be lower.

Hill: Fred Smith [CEO of Federal Express] says that to succeed internationally you have to fly your own planes and build your own ground network to get tight control over distribution.

Cline: That was his whole theory in the U.S., and he was right because we didn't have the service. But I don't know if that's necessary internationally. I mean, there are so many flights, a lot of capacity. Now once we develop enough volume both ways on a consistent basis we might fly. The only problem with flying the scheduled airlines is that you are subject to their pricing schedules, and their prices do go up and down.

Hill: Where would you like Airborne to be in the global market by the year 2000?

Cline: Our global program is to develop strategic alliances. Our deal with Mitsui is a major step in that direction. The advantage is what they can bring to the table in the way of business, their knowledge of the area [Japan], their ability to get into markets that we as an American company cannot. Federal Express is kidding themselves if they think they are ever really going to make a dent in the Japanese market.

Hill: It's often said that the prime motive that Japanese companies have for entering into joint ventures is that they want to learn from their U.S. partners, and once they have learned what they want to learn they often quit. Do you think there is any danger of this occurring?

Cline: I doubt it. I don't think Mitsui could ever develop its own U.S. airline system due to the foreign ownership problem [foreign ownership of U.S. airlines is limited to 25 percent]. We have a unique franchise, and there is really nobody else they can go to. So I don't worry about that too much. Besides, we did get a commitment from them for $140 million. If they walk away from this thing, they also walk away from a pretty big investment.

Hill: What is the current state of your relationship with TNT? Are they likely to try another takeover bid?

Cline: It's an uneasy relationship. We actually do work together in certain areas of the world ... but those are arm's-length transactions. I know that TNT would like a stronger relationship with Airborne, but we do not see any economic advantage in a closer relationship. I think that TNT has backed away from any future takeover bid, primarily due to the foreign ownership rule.

Hill: What is the impact on your margins of rising fuel costs?

Cline: Fuel costs amount to 4 percent of our total costs, so it's not a major impact. On the other hand, if fuel costs go up by 50 percent, it will knock down our margins by 2.5 percent. And since our margins are only 5 percent, it does have an effect.

CONCLUSION

As Airborne Express approaches the year 2000, a number of key strategic opportunities and emerging threats confront the company. These include (1) the rapid globalization of the air express industry; (2) the development of logistics services based on rapid air transportation; (3) the growth potential for a second-day air service; (4) capacity constraints (Airborne is currently utilizing 90 percent of its airlift capacity, which leaves little margin for error should aircraft need repairs); (5) an economic recession in the United States; and (6) the increase in fuel costs that seems sure to follow a worldwide surge in oil prices during 1996 (oil prices rose from $18 a barrel in mid 1995 to $25 a barrel in late 1996). The company must decide how to position itself with regard to each of these opportunities and threats.

Endnote

1. Standard & Poor's "Aerospace and Air Transport," *Industry Surveys* (February 1996).

CASE 21

Wal-Mart Stores: Strategies for Continued Market Dominance

This case was prepared by James W. Camerius of Northern Michigan University.

David Glass assumed the role of president and chief executive officer at Wal-Mart, the position previously held by Sam Walton. Known for his hard-driving managerial style, Glass gained his experience in retailing at a small supermarket chain in Springfield, Missouri. He joined Wal-Mart as executive vice president for finance in 1976 and was named president and chief operating officer in 1984. In 1998, as he reflected on growth strategies of the firm, he offered this comment: "Seldom can you count on everything coming together as well as it did this year. We believe we could always do better, but we improved more this year than I can ever remember in the past. If Wal-Mart had been content to be just an Arkansas retailer in the early days, we probably would not be where we are today."

A MATURING ORGANIZATION

In 1998, Wal-Mart Stores, Inc., Bentonville, Arkansas, operated mass-merchandising retail stores under a variety of names and retail formats, including the following: Wal-Mart discount department stores; Sam's Wholesale Clubs, wholesale/retail membership warehouses; and Wal-Mart Supercenters, large combination grocery and general merchandise stores in all fifty states. Its international division operated in Canada, Mexico, Ar-

This case is intended to be used as a basis for class discussion rather than to illustrate either effective or ineffective handling of the situation. This case was prepared by James W. Camerius of Northern Michigan University. Used by permission.

gentina, Brazil, Germany, and Puerto Rico, and through joint ventures in China. It was not only the nation's largest discount department store chain, but had surpassed the retail division of Sears, Roebuck, and Co. in sales volume as the largest retail firm in the United States. The McLane Company, a support division with over 36,000 customers, was the nation's largest distributor of food and merchandise to convenience stores and served selected Wal-Marts, Sam's Clubs, and Supercenters. Wal-Mart also continued to operate a small number of discount department stores called Bud's Discount City. A financial summary of Wal-Mart Stores, Inc., for the fiscal years ended January 31, 1997 and 1998 appears in Table 1.

THE SAM WALTON SPIRIT

Much of the success of Wal-Mart was attributed to the entrepreneurial spirit of its founder and chairman of the board, Samuel Moore Walton (1918–1992). Many considered him one of the most influential retailers of the century.

Sam Walton, or "Mr. Sam" as some referred to him, traced his down-to-earth, old-fashioned, home-spun, evangelical ways to growing up in rural Oklahoma, Missouri, and Arkansas. Although he was remarkably blasé about his roots, some suggested that it was the simple belief in hard work and ambition that had "unlocked countless doors and showered upon him, his customers, and his employees . . . the fruits of . . . years of labor in building [this] highly successful company."

TABLE I

Wal-Mart Stores, Inc., Financial Summary

Consolidated Statements of Income (in millions except per share data)			
	Fiscal Years Ended January 31		
	1998	1997	1996
Revenues:			
Net sales	$117,958	$104,859	$93,627
Other income—net	1,341	1,319	1,146
	119,299	106,178	94,773
Costs and expenses:			
Cost of sales	93,438	83,510	74,505
Operating, selling and general and administrative expenses	19,358	16,946	15,021
Interest costs:			
Debt	555	629	692
Capital leases	229	216	196
	113,580	101,301	90,414
Income before income taxes, minority interest and equity in unconsolidated subsidiaries	5,719	4,877	4,359
Provision for income taxes			
Current	2,095	1,974	1,530
Deferred	20	(180)	76
	2,115	1,794	1,606
Income before minority interest and equity in unconsolidated subsidiaries	3,604	3,083	2,753
Minority interest and equity in unconsolidated subsidiaries	(78)	(27)	(13)
Net income	$3,526	$3,056	$2,740
Net income per share—basic and dilutive	$1.56	$1.33	$1.19

Consolidated Balance Sheets (in millions)		
	January 31, 1998	January 31, 1997
Assets		
Current assets:		
Cash and cash equivalents	$1,447	$883
Receivables	976	845
Inventories		
At replacement cost	16,845	16,193
Less LIFO reserve	348	296
Inventories at LIFO cost	16,497	15,897
Prepaid expenses and other	432	368
Total current assets	19,352	17,993
Property, plant and equipment, at cost:		
Land	4,691	3,689
Building and improvements	14,646	12,724
Fixtures and equipment	7,636	6,390
Transportation equipment	403	379
	27,376	23,182
Less accumulated depreciation	5,907	4,849
Net property, plant and equipment	21,469	18,333

Consolidated Balance Sheets (in millions)		
	January 31, 1998	**January 31, 1997**
Property under capital lease:		
Property under capital lease	3,040	2,782
Less accumulated amortization	903	791
Net property under capital leases	2,137	1,991
Other assets and deferred charges	2,426	1,287
Total assets	$45,384	$39,604
Liabilities and Shareholders' Equity		
Current liabilities:		
Accounts payable	$9,126	$7,628
Accrued liabilities	3,628	2,413
Accrued income taxes	565	298
Long-term debt due within one year	1,039	523
Obligations under capital leases due within one year	102	95
Total current liabilities	14,460	10,957
Long-term debt	7,191	7,709
Long-term obligations under capital leases	2,483	2,307
Deferred income taxes and other	809	463
Minority interest	1,938	1,025
Shareholders' equity		
Preferred stock ($.10 par value; 100 shares authorized, none issued)		
Common stock ($.10 par value; 5,500 shares authorized, 2,241 and 2,285 issued and outstanding in 1998 and 1997, respectively)	224	228
Capital in excess of par value	585	547
Retained earnings	18,167	16,768
Foreign currency translation adjustment	(473)	(400)
Total shareholders' equity	18,503	17,143
Total liabilities and shareholders' equity	$45,384	$39,604

Source: Company Annual Reports.

"Our goal has always been in our business to be the very best," Sam Walton said in an interview, "and ... we believe that in order to do that, you've got to make a good situation and put the interests of your associates first. If we really do that consistently, they in turn will cause ... our business to be successful, which is what we've talked about and espoused and practiced." "The reason for our success," he said, "is our people and the way that they're treated and the way they feel about their company." Many have suggested that this "people first" philosophy, which guided the company through the challenges and setbacks of its early years, has allowed it to maintain its consistent record of growth and expansion in later years.

There was little about Sam Walton's background that foretokened his amazing success. He was born in Kingfisher, Oklahoma, on March 29, 1918, to Thomas and Nancy Walton. Thomas Wal-

ton was a banker at the time and later entered the farm mortgage business and moved to Missouri. Growing up in rural Missouri in the depths of the Great Depression, Sam Walton discovered early on that he "had a fair amount of ambition and enjoyed working," he once noted. He completed high school at Columbia, Missouri, and received a bachelor of arts degree in economics from the University of Missouri in 1940. "I really had no idea what I would be," he said, adding as an afterthought, "at one point in time, I thought I wanted to become president of the United States."

An enthusiastic and positive individual, Sam Walton was "just your basic home-spun billionaire," a columnist once suggested, noting that "Mr. Sam is a life-long small-town resident who didn't change much as he got richer than his neighbors." Walton had tremendous energy, enjoyed bird hunting with his dogs, and flew a corporate plane. When the company was much smaller, he could boast that he personally visited every Wal-Mart store at least once a year. A store visit usually included Walton leading Wal-Mart cheers that began, "Give me a W, give me an A. . . ." To many employees he had the air of a fiery Baptist preacher. Paul R. Carter, a Wal-Mart executive vice president, was quoted as saying, "Mr. Walton has a calling." He became the richest man in America, and by 1991 had created a personal fortune for his family in excess of $21 billion.

Sam Walton's success was widely chronicled. He was selected by the investment publication *Financial World* in 1989 as the CEO of the Decade. He had honorary degrees from the University of the Ozarks, the University of Arkansas, and the University of Missouri. He also received many of the most distinguished professional awards of the industry such as Man of the Year, Discounter of the Year, and Chief Executive Officer of the Year, and was the second retailer to be inducted into the Discounting Hall of Fame. In 1984, he received the Horatio Alger Award and in December 1989 was acknowledged by *Discount Stores News* as Retailer of the Decade. "Walton does a remarkable job of instilling near-religious fervor in his people," said analyst Robert Buchanan of A. G. Edwards. "I think that speaks to the heart of his success." In late 1989, Sam Walton was diagnosed as having multiple myeloma, or cancer of the bone marrow. He planned to remain active in the company as chairman of the board of directors.

THE MARKETING CONCEPT

Genesis of an Idea

Sam Walton started his retail career in 1940 as a management trainee with the J. C. Penney Company in Des Moines, Iowa. He was impressed with the Penney method of doing business and later modeled the Wal-Mart chain on "The Penney Idea" (see Table 2). The Penney Company found strength in calling employees "associates" rather than clerks. Penney's, founded in Kemerer, Wyoming, in 1902, located stores on the main streets of small towns and cities throughout the United States.

Following service in the U.S. Army during World War II, Sam Walton acquired a Ben Franklin variety store franchise in Newport, Arkansas. He operated this store successfully with his brother, James L. "Bud" Walton (1921–1995), until losing the

TABLE 2

The Penney Idea, 1913

1. To serve the public, as nearly as we can, to its complete satisfaction.

2. To expect for the service we render a fair remuneration and not all the profit the traffic will bear.

3. To do all in our power to pack the customer's dollar full of value, quality, and satisfaction.

4. To continue to train ourselves and our associates so that the service we give will be more and more intelligently performed.

5. To improve constantly the human factor in our business.

6. To reward men and women in our organization through participation in what the business produces.

7. To test our every policy, method, and act in this wise: "Does it square with what is right and just?"

Source: Vance H. Trimble, *Sam Walton: The Inside Story of America's Richest Man* (New York: Dutton, 1990).

lease in 1950. When Wal-Mart was incorporated in 1962, the firm was operating a chain of fifteen stores. Bud Walton became a senior vice president of the firm and concentrated on finding suitable store locations, acquiring real estate, and directing store construction.

The early retail stores owned by Sam Walton in Newport and Bentonville, Arkansas, and later in other small towns in adjoining southern states, were variety store operations. Relatively small (6,000 square feet), they were located on the main street and displayed merchandise on plain wooden tables and counters. Bearing the Ben Franklin name and supplied by Butler Brothers of Chicago and Saint Louis, they were characterized by a limited price line, low gross margins, high merchandise turnover, and concentration on return on investment. The firm, operating under the Walton 5 & 10 name, was the largest Ben Franklin franchisee in the country in 1962. The variety stores were phased out by 1976 to allow the company to concentrate on the growth of Wal-Mart discount department stores.

Foundations of Growth

The original Wal-Mart discount concept was not a unique idea. Sam Walton became convinced in the late 1950s that discounting would transform retailing. He traveled extensively in New England, the cradle of off-pricing. After he had visited just about every discounter in the United States, he tried to interest Butler Brothers executives in Chicago in the discount store concept. The first Kmart—described as a "conveniently located one-stop shopping unit where customers could buy a wide variety of quality merchandise at discount prices"—had just opened in Garden City, Michigan. Walton's theory was to operate a similar discount store in a small community, and in that setting he would offer name brand merchandise at low prices and would add friendly service. Butler Brothers executives rejected the idea. The first Wal-Mart Discount City opened in late 1962 in Rogers, Arkansas.

Wal-Mart stores would sell nationally advertised, well-known brand merchandise at low prices in austere surroundings. As corporate policy, they would cheerfully give refunds, credits, and rain checks. Management conceived the firm as a "discount department store chain offering a wide variety of general merchandise to the customer." It sought opportunistic purchases of merchandise from whatever sources were available, and strongly emphasized health and beauty aids in the product line, as well as the "stacking it high" way of presenting merchandise. By the end of 1979, there were 276 Wal-Mart stores located in eleven states.

The firm developed an aggressive expansion strategy. New stores were located primarily in towns with a population of 5,000 to 25,000. The stores ranged in size from 30,000 to 60,000 square feet, with 45,000 as the average. The firm also expanded by locating stores in contiguous areas, town by town, state by state. When its discount operations came to dominate a market area, it moved to an adjoining area. While other retailers built warehouses to serve existing outlets, Wal-Mart built the distribution center first and then spotted stores all around it, pooling advertising and distribution overhead. Most stores were less than a six-hour drive from one of the company's warehouses. The first major distribution center, a 390,000 square-foot facility, opened in Searcy, Arkansas, outside Bentonville, in 1978.

National Perspectives

At the beginning of 1991, the firm had 1,573 Wal-Mart stores in thirty-five states, with expansion planned for adjacent states. Wal-Mart became the largest retailer and the largest discount department store in the United States.

As a national discount department store chain, Wal-Mart Stores, Inc., offered a wide variety of general merchandise to the customer. The stores were designed to offer one-stop shopping in thirty-six departments, which included family apparel, health and beauty aids, household needs, electronics, toys, fabric and crafts, automotive supplies, lawn and patio supplies and furnishings, jewelry, and shoes. In addition, at certain store locations, the company also operated a pharmacy, an automotive supply and service center, a garden center, or a snack bar. Instead of stressing special promotions, which called for multiple newspaper advertising circulars, Wal-Mart prided itself on its "everyday low price." It also expected its stores to "provide the customer with a clean, pleasant, and friendly shopping experience."

Although Wal-Mart carried much the same merchandise as the competition, offered similar prices, and operated stores that resembled those of its rivals, there were many differences. In the typical Wal-Mart store, employees wore blue vests to identify themselves, aisles were wide, apparel departments were carpeted in warm colors, a store employee followed customers to their cars to pick up their shopping carts, and the customer was welcomed at the door by a "people greeter," who gave directions and struck up conversations. In some cases, merchandise was bagged in brown paper sacks rather than plastic bags because customers seemed to prefer them. A simple Wal-Mart logo in white letters on a brown background on the front of the store served to identify the firm. In consumer studies, it was determined that the chain was particularly adept at striking the delicate balance needed to convince customers that its prices were low without making people feel that its stores were too cheap. In many ways, competitors such as Kmart sought to emulate Wal-Mart by introducing people greeters, upgrading interiors, developing new logos and signage, and introducing new inventory response systems.

A "satisfaction guaranteed" refund and exchange policy was introduced to make customers trust Wal-Mart's merchandise and quality. Technological advancements such as scanner cash registers, hand-held computers for ordering of merchandise, and computer linkages of stores with the general office and distribution centers improved communications and merchandise replenishment. Each store was encouraged to initiate programs that would make it an integral part of the community in which it operated. Associates were encouraged to "maintain the highest standards of honesty, morality, and business ethics in dealing with the public."

THE EXTERNAL ENVIRONMENT

Industry analysts labeled the 1980s and early 1990s as eras of economic uncertainty for retailers. Many retailers were negatively affected by increased competitive pressures, sluggish consumer spending, slower-than-anticipated economic growth in North America, and recessions abroad. In 1995, Wal-Mart management felt that the high consumer debt level caused many shoppers to reduce or defer spending on anything other than essentials and that the lack of exciting new products or apparel trends reduced discretionary spending. Fierce competition resulted in lower margins, and the lack of inflation stalled productivity increases. By 1998, the country had returned to prosperity. Unemployment was low, total income was relatively high, and interest rates were stable. Combined with a low inflation rate, buying power was perceived to be high and consumers were generally willing to buy.

Many retail enterprises confronted heavy competitive pressure by restructuring. Sears, Roebuck and Co., based in Chicago, became a more focused retailer by divesting itself of Allstate Insurance Company and its real estate subsidiaries. In 1993, the company announced it would close 118 unprofitable stores and discontinue the unprofitable Sears general merchandise catalog. It eliminated 50,000 jobs and began a $4 billion, five-year remodeling plan for its remaining multiline department stores. After unsuccessfully experimenting with an "everyday low price" strategy, management chose to realign its merchandise strategy to meet the needs of middle-market customers, who were primarily women, by focusing on product lines in apparel, home, and automotive. The new focus on apparel was supported with the advertising campaign "The Softer Side of Sears." A later company-wide campaign broadened the appeal: "The many sides of Sears fit the many sides of your life." Sears completed its return to its retailing roots by selling off its ownership in Dean Witter Financial Services, Discovery Card, Coldwell Banker Real Estate, and Sears mortgage banking operations.

By the early 1990s, the discount department store industry had changed in a number of ways and many analysts thought it had reached maturity. Several formerly successful firms, such as E. J. Korvette, W. T. Grant, Atlantic Mills, Arlans, Federals, Zayre, Heck's, and Ames, had declared bankruptcy and as a result either liquidated or reorganized. Venture announced liquidation in early 1998. Regional firms such as Target Stores and Shopko Stores began carrying more fashionable merchandise in more attractive facilities and shifted their emphasis to national markets. Specialty retailers such as Toys 'R' Us, Pier 1 Imports and Oshmans were making big inroads in toys, home furnishing, and sporting goods. The "superstores" of drug and food chains were rapidly discounting increasing amounts of general merchandise. Some firms, such as May Department Stores Company, with Caldor and Venture, and Woolworth Corporation, with Woolco, had withdrawn from the field by either selling their discount divisions or closing them down entirely. The firm's remaining 122 Woolco stores in Canada were sold to Wal-Mart in 1994. All remaining Woolworth variety stores in the United States were closed in 1997.

Several new retail formats had emerged in the marketplace to challenge the traditional discount department store format. The superstore, a 100,000–300,000-square-foot operation, combined a large supermarket with a discount general-merchandise store. Originally a European retailing concept, these outlets were known as "malls without walls." Kmart's Super Kmart Centers, American Fare, and Wal-Mart's Supercenter Store were examples of this trend toward large operations. Warehouse retailing, which involved some combination of warehouse and showroom facilities, used warehouse principles to reduce operating expenses and thereby offer discount prices as a primary customer appeal. Home Depot combined the traditional hardware store and lumber yard with a self-service home improvement center to become the largest home center operator in the nation.

Some retailers responded to changes in the marketplace by selling goods at price levels (20 to 60 percent) below regular retail prices. These off-price operations appeared as two general types: (1) factory outlet stores such as Burlington Coat Factory Warehouse, Bass Shoes, and Manhattan's Brand Name Fashion Outlet, and (2) independents such as Loehmann's, T. J. Maxx, Marshall's, and Clothestime which bought seconds, overages, closeouts or left-over goods. Other retailers chose to dominate a product classification. Some super specialists, such as Sock Appeal, Little Piggie, and Sock Market, offered a single narrowly defined classification of merchandise with an extensive assortment of brands, colors, and sizes. Others, as niche specialists, such as Kids Mart, a division of Woolworth Corporation, and McKids, a division of Sears, targeted an identified market with carefully selected merchandise and appropriately designed stores. Certain retailers, such as Silk Greenhouse (silk plants and flowers), Office Club (office supplies and equipment), and Toys 'R' Us (toys) were called "category killers" because they had achieved merchandise dominance in their respective product categories. Stores such as The Limited, Limited Express, Victoria's Secret, and The Banana Republic became minidepartment specialists by showcasing new lines and accessories alongside traditional merchandise lines.

Kmart Corporation, headquartered in Troy, Michigan, became the industry's third largest retailer after Sears, Roebuck and second largest discount department store chain in the United States in the 1990s. It had 2,136 stores and $32,183 million in sales at the beginning of 1998. The firm was perceived by many industry analysts and consumers in several independent studies as a laggard. It had been the industry sales leader for a number of years and had recently announced a turnaround in profitability. In the same studies, Wal-Mart was perceived as the industry leader even though, according to the *Wall Street Journal*, "they carry much the same merchandise, offer prices that are pennies apart and operate stores that look almost exactly alike." "Even their names are similar," the newspaper pointed out. The original Kmart concept of a "conveniently located, one-stop shopping

unit where customers could buy a wide variety of quality merchandise at discount prices" had lost its competitive edge in a changing market. As one analyst noted in an industry newsletter, "They had done so well for the past 20 years without paying attention to market changes, now they have to." Kmart acquired a new chairman, president and chief executive officer in 1995. Wal-Mart and Kmart sales growth over the period 1987–1997 is summarized in Table 3, and a competitive analysis of four major retail firms is presented in Table 4.

Some retailers, such as Kmart, had initially focused on appealing to professional, middle-class consumers who lived in suburban areas and who were likely to be price sensitive. Other firms, such as Target (Dayton Hudson), which had adopted the discount concept early, generally attempted to go after an upscale consumer who had an annual household income of $25,000 to $44,000. Still other firms, such as Fleet Farm and Menard's, served the rural consumer, while those like Chicago's Goldblatt's Department Stores and Ames Discount Department Stores chose to serve blacks and Hispanics in the inner city.

In rural communities, Wal-Mart's success often came at the expense of established local merchants and units of regional discount store chains. Hardware stores, family department stores, building supply outlets, and stores featuring fabrics, sporting goods and shoes were among the first either to close or to relocate elsewhere. Regional discount retailers in the Sunbelt states—for instance, Roses, Howard's, T.G.&Y., and Duckwall-ALCO, which once enjoyed solid sales and earnings—were forced to reposition themselves by renovating stores, opening bigger and more modern units, re-merchandising assortments, and offering lower prices. In many cases, stores such as Coast-to-Coast, Pamida, and Ben Franklin closed upon a Wal-Mart announcement that it was planning to build in a specific community. As a local newspaper editor put it, "Just the word that Wal-Mart was coming made some stores close up."

CORPORATE STRATEGIES

The corporate and marketing strategies that emerged at Wal-Mart were based on a set of two main objectives that had guided the firm through its growth years. The first objective featured the

TABLE 3

Competitive Sales and Store Comparison, 1987–1997
(in $ millions)

	Kmart			Wal-Mart	
Year	Sales	Stores[1]		Sales	Stores[1]
1997	$32,183,000	2,136		117,958,000	3,406
1996	31,437,000	2,261		104,859,000	3,054
1995	34,389,000	2,161		93,627,000	2,943
1994	34,025,000	2,481		82,494,000	2,684
1993	34,156,000	2,486		67,344,000	2,400
1992	37,724,000	2,435		55,484,000	2,136
1991	34,580,000	2,391		43,886,900	1,928
1990	32,070,000	2,350		32,601,594	1,721
1989	29,533,000	2,361		25,810,656	1,525
1988	27,301,000	2,307		20,649,001	1,364
1987	25,627,000	2,273		15,959,255	1,198

[1]Number of general merchandise stores.

customer: "customers would be provided what they want, when they want it, all at a value." The second objective emphasized team spirit: "treating each other as we would hope to be treated, acknowledging our total dependency on our Associate-partners to sustain our success." The strategies included aggressive plans for new store openings; expansion to additional states; upgrading, relocation, refurbishing and remodeling of existing stores; and opening new distribution centers. The plan was to not have a single operating unit that had not been updated in the past seven years. For Wal-Mart management, the 1990s became "A new era for Wal-Mart; an era in which we plan to grow into a truly nationwide retailer, and should we continue to perform, our sales and earnings will also grow beyond where most could have envisioned at the dawn of the 80s."

In the decade of the 1980s, Wal-Mart had developed a number of new retail formats. The first SAM's Club opened in Oklahoma City, Oklahoma, in 1983. The wholesale club was an idea which had been developed by other firms earlier but which found its greatest success and growth in acceptability at Wal-Mart. SAM's Clubs featured a vast array of product categories with limited selection of brand and model, cash-and-carry business with limited hours, large (100,000-square-foot), bare-bones facilities, rock-bottom wholesale prices, and minimal promotion. The limited-membership plan permitted not only wholesale members who bought membership to shop there, but also nonmembers, who usually paid a percentage above the ticket price of the merchandise. At the beginning of 1998, there were 483 SAM's Clubs in operation. A revision in merchandising strategy resulted in fewer items in the inventory mix, with more emphasis on lower prices.

Wal-Mart supercenters were large combination stores. They were first opened in 1988 as Hypermarket*USA, a 222,000-square-foot superstore that combined a discount store with a large grocery store, a food court of restaurants, and other service businesses such as banks or video tape rental stores. A scaled-down version of Hypermarket*USA was called the Wal-Mart SuperCenter—similar in merchandise offerings, but with about half the square footage of hypermarts. These expanded-store concepts also included convenience stores and gasoline distribution outlets to "enhance shopping convenience." The company proceeded slowly with these plans and later suspended its plans for building any more hypermarkets in favor of the smaller supercenter. In 1998, Wal-Mart operated 502 supercenters. It also announced plans to build

TABLE 4

An Industry Comparative Analysis, 1997

	Wal-Mart	Sears[1]	Kmart	Target
Sales (in millions)	$117,958	$36,371	$32,183	$20,368
Net income (in thousands)	$ 3,526	$ 1,188	$ 249	$ 1,287
Net income per share	$ 1.56	$ 3.03	$ .51	$ n/a
Dividends per share	$ .27	$ n/a	$ n/a	$ n/a
Percent of sales change	12.0 percent	8.0 percent	2.4 percent	14 percent

Number of stores
   Wal-Mart and subsidiaries
      Wal-Mart stores: 2,421
      SAM's Clubs: 483
      Supercenters: 502

   Kmart Corporation
      General merchandise: 2,136

   Dayton Hudson Corporation
      Target: 796
      Mervyn's: 269
      Department stores: 65

   Sears, Roebuck (all divisions)[1]
   Sears Merchandise Group
      Department stores: 833
      Hardware stores: 255
      Furniture stores: 129
      Sears dealer stores: 576
      Auto/tire stores: 780
      Auto parts stores
         Western Auto: 39
         Parts America: 576
      Western Auto dealer stores: 800

Source: Corporate Annual Reports.

several full-fledged supermarkets called Wal-Mart Food and Drug Express, with a drive-through option, as "laboratories" to test how the concept would work and what changes would be required before making a decision to proceed with additional units.

In 1991, Wal-Mart acquired The McLane Company, a provider of retail and grocery distribution services for retail stores. It was not considered a major segment of the total Wal-Mart operation.

On the international level, Wal-Mart management had a goal to be the dominant retailer in each country it entered. With the acquisition of 122 former Woolco stores in Canada, the company exceeded expectations in sales growth, market share, and profitability. With a tender offer for shares and mergers of joint ventures in Mexico, the company had a controlling interest in Cifra, Mexico's largest retailer. Cifra operated stores with a variety of con-

cepts in every region of Mexico, ranging from the nation's largest chain of sit-down restaurants to a softline department store. Plans were also proceeding with start-up operations in Argentina and Brazil as well as China. The acquisition of 21 hypermarkets in Germany at the end of 1997 marked the company's first entry into Europe, which management considered "one of the best consumer markets in the world." These large stores offered one-stop shopping facilities similar to Wal-Mart Supercenters. The international expansion accelerated management's plans for the development of Wal-Mart as a global brand along the lines of Coca-Cola, Disney, and McDonald's. "We are a global brand name," said Bobby Martin, president of the international division of Wal-Mart. "To customers everywhere it means low cost, best value, greatest selection of quality merchandise and highest standards of customer service." Some changes were mandated in Wal-Mart's international operations to meet local tastes and intense competitive conditions. "We're building companies out there," said Martin. "That's like starting Wal-Mart all over again in South America or Indonesia or China." Although stores in different international markets would coordinate purchasing to gain leverage with suppliers, developing new technology and planning overall strategy would be done from Wal-Mart headquarters in Bentonville, Arkansas. At the beginning of 1998, Wal-Mart's international division operated 500 discount stores, 61 supercenters, and 40 SAM'S Clubs.

The company launched several programs to "highlight" popular social causes. The "Buy American" program was a Wal-Mart retail program initiated in 1985. The theme was "Bring It Home To The USA" and its purpose was to communicate Wal-Mart's support for American manufacturing. The company exerted substantial influence to encourage manufacturers to produce goods in the United States rather than import them. Vendors were attracted into the program by encouraging manufacturers to initiate the process by contacting the company directly with proposals to sell goods that were made in the United States. Buyers also targeted specific import items in their assortments on a state-by-state basis to encourage domestic manufacturing. According to Haim Dabah, president of Gitano Group, Inc., a maker of fashion discount clothing, which imported 95 percent of its clothing and now makes about 20 percent of its products here, "Wal-Mart let it be known loud and clear that if you're going to grow with them, you sure better have some products made in the U.S.A." Farris Fashion, Inc. (flannel shirts), Roadmaster Corporation (exercise bicycles), Flanders Industries, Inc. (lawn chairs), and Magic Chef (microwave ovens) were among the vendors that chose to participate in the program.

From the Wal-Mart standpoint, the "Buy American" program centered on value—producing and selling quality merchandise at a competitive price. The promotion included television advertisements featuring factory workers, a soaring American eagle, and the slogan: "We buy American whenever we can, so you can too." Prominent in-store signage and store circulars were also included. One store poster read: "Success Stories—These items formerly imported, are now being purchased by Wal-Mart in the U.S.A."

Wal-Mart was one of the first retailers to embrace the concept of "green" marketing. The program offered shoppers the option of purchasing products that were better for the environment in three respects: manufacturing, use, and disposal. It was introduced through full-page advertisements in the *Wall Street Journal* and *USA Today*. In-store signage identified those products that were environmentally safe. As Wal-Mart executives saw it, "customers are concerned about the quality of land, air, and water, and would like the opportunity to do something positive." To initiate the program, Wal-Mart notified 7,000 vendors that it had a corporate concern for the environment and was seeking their support. Wal-Mart television advertising showed children on swings, fields of grain blowing in the wind, and roses. Green-and-white store signs, printed on recycled paper, marked products or packaging that had been developed or redesigned to be more environmentally sound.

Wal-Mart had become the channel commander in the distribution of many brand name items. As the nation's largest retailer and, in many geographic areas, the dominant distributor, it exerted considerable influence in negotiation for the best price, delivery terms, promotion allowances, and continuity of supply. Many of these benefits could be passed on to consumers in the form of quality name brand items available at lower than competitive prices. As a matter of corporate policy, management often insisted on doing business only with a producer's top sales executives rather than going through a manufacturer's representative. Wal-Mart had been accused of threatening to buy from other producers if firms refused to sell to it directly. In the ensuing power struggle, Wal-Mart executives refused to talk about the controversial policy or admit that it existed. As a member of an industry association representing a group of sales agencies suggested, "In the Southwest, Wal-Mart's the only show in town." An industry analyst added, "They're extremely aggressive. Their approach has always been to give the customer the benefit of a corporate saving. That builds up customer loyalty and market share."

Another key factor in the mix was an inventory-control system that was recognized as the most sophisticated in retailing. A high-speed computer system linked virtually all the stores to headquarters and the company's distribution centers. It electronically logged every item sold at the checkout counter, automatically kept the warehouses informed of merchandise to be ordered, and directed the flow of goods to the stores and even to the proper shelves. Most important for management, it helped detect sales trends quickly and speeded up market reaction time substantially. According to Bob Connolly, executive vice president of merchandising, "Wal-Mart has used the data gathered by technology to make more inventory available in the key items that customers want most, while reducing inventories overall."

DECISION MAKING IN A MARKET-ORIENTED FIRM

One principle that distinguished Wal-Mart was the unusual depth of employee involvement in company affairs. Corporate strategies emphasized human resource management. Wal-Mart employees became associates, a term borrowed from Sam Walton's early association with J.C. Penney. Input was encouraged at meetings at the store and corporate level. The firm hired employees locally and provided training programs. In addition, through a "Letter to the President" program, management encouraged employees to ask questions and made words such as "we," "us," and "our" part of the corporate language. A number of special award programs recognized individual, department, and division achievement. Stock-ownership and profit-sharing programs were introduced as part of a "partnership" concept.

The corporate culture was acknowledged by the editors of the trade publication *Mass Market Retailers* when it recognized all 275,000 associates collectively as the Mass Market Retailers of the Year. "The Wal-Mart associate," the editors noted, "in this decade that term has come to symbolize all that is right with the American worker, particularly in the retailing environment and most particularly at Wal-Mart." The "store within a store" concept, as a Wal-Mart corporate policy, trained individuals to be merchants by being responsible for the performance of their own departments as if they were running their own businesses. Seminars and training programs afforded them opportunities to grow within the company. "People development, not just a good 'program' for any growing company but a must to secure our future," is how Suzanne Allford, vice president of the Wal-Mart people division explained the firm's decentralized approach to retail management development.

"The Wal-Mart Way," was a phase that was used by management to summarize the firm's unconventional approach to business and the development of the corporate culture. As noted in a report referring to a recent development program, "We stepped outside our retailing world to examine the best managed companies in the United States in an effort to determine the fundamentals of their success and to 'benchmark' our own performances. The name Total Quality Management (TQM) was used to identify this vehicle for proliferating the very best things we do while incorporating the new ideas our people have that will assure our future."

THE GROWTH CHALLENGE

And what of Wal-Mart without Mr. Sam? "There's no transition to make," said Glass, "because the principles and the basic values he used in founding this company were so sound and so universally accepted." "As for the future," he suggested,

> There's more opportunity ahead of us than behind us. We're good students of retailing and we've studied the mistakes that others have made. We'll make our own mistakes, but we won't repeat theirs. The only thing constant at Wal-Mart is change. We'll be fine as long as we never lose our responsiveness to the customer.

Management identified four key legacies of Sam Walton to guide the company's "quest for value" in the future: (1) everyday low prices, (2) customer service, (3) leadership, and (4) change.

For more than twenty-five years, the company experienced tremendous growth and, as one analyst put it, "has been consistently on the cutting edge of low-markup mass merchandising." Much of the forward momentum had come from the entrepreneurial spirit of Samuel Moore Walton. The company announced on Monday, April 6, 1992, following Walton's death, that his son, S. Robson Walton, vice chairman of Wal-Mart, would succeed his father as chairman of the board. Glass would remain president and CEO. The Wal-Mart board of directors and executive officers in 1998 are listed in the appendix.

A new management team was in place. Management felt that it had positioned the firm as an industry leader. However, a number of new challenges had to be met. It had been predicted as early as 1993 that Wal-Mart's same-store growth would likely slip into the 7 to 8 percent range in the near future. Analysts were also concerned about the increased competition in the warehouse club business and the company's move from its roots in southern and midwestern small towns to the more competitive and costly markets of the Northeast. Wal-Mart supercenters faced more resilient rivals in the grocery field. Unions representing supermarket workers delayed and in some cases killed expansion opportunities. Some analysts said: "the company is simply suffering from the high expectations its stellar performance over the years has created." In early 1996, management acknowledged that 1995 had not been a "Wal-Mart year." After ninety-nine consecutive quarters of earnings growth, Wal-Mart management said profit for the fiscal fourth quarter, ending January 31, would decline as much as 11 percent from the year before. Much of the company's sales growth in 1996 and 1997 was attributed to the opening of new stores in an expansion program. Same-store sales growth in 1996 and 1997 was 5 percent and 6 percent, respectively, when compared with the previous year's sales performance.

APPENDIX: WAL-MART STORES, INC., BOARD OF DIRECTORS AND CORPORATE OFFICERS, 1998

Directors: Jeronimo Arango, Paul R. Carter, John A. Cooper, Jr., Stephen Friedman, Stanley C. Gault, David D. Glass, Frederick S. Humphries, E. Stanley Kroenke, Elizabeth A. Sanders, Jack C. Shewmaker, Donald G. Soderquist, Dr. Paula Stern, John T. Walton, S. Robson Walton; *Chairman of the Board:* S. Robson Walton; *CEO, President:* David D. Glass; *Vice Chairman, COO:* Donald G. Soderquist; *Executive VP, President-Wal-Mart Realty:* Paul R. Carter; *Executive VP Merchandising:* Bob Connolly; *Executive VP, COO-Operations, Wal-Mart Stores Division:* Thomas M. Coughlin; *Executive VP-Specialty Division:* David Dible; *Executive VP, President-Sam's Club Division:* Mark Hansen; *Executive VP, President-International Division:* Bob L. Martin; *Executive VP, CFO:* John B. Menzer; *Executive VP, President-Wal-Mart Stores Division:* H. Lee Scott; *Executive VP-Supercenter:* Nick White; *Senior VP, Secretary-General Counsel:* Robert K. Rhoads; *Senior VP, Finance-Treasurer:* J. J. Fitzsimmons

References

"A Supercenter Comes to Town." *Chain Store Age Executive*, December 1989, 23–30.

Barrier, Michael. "Walton's Mountain." *Nation's Business*, April 1988, 18–20.

Bergman, Joan. "Saga of Sam Walton." *Stores*, January 1988, 129–130.

Blumenthal, Karen. "Marketing with Emotion: Wal-Mart Shows the Way." *Wall Street Journal*, November 20, 1989, B3.

Bragg, Arthur. "Wal-Mart's War on Reps." *Sales & Marketing Management*, March 1987, 41–43.

Brauer, Molly. "Sam's: Setting a Fast Pace." *Chain Store Age Executive*, August 1983, 20–21.

Corwin, Pat, Jay L. Johnson, and Renee M. Rouland. "Made in U.S.A." *Discount Merchandiser*, November 1989, 48–52.

"David Glass's Biggest Job Is Filling Sam's Shoes." *Business Month*, December 1988, 42.

Fisher, Christy, and Patricia Sternad. "Wal-Mart Pulls Back on Hypermart Plans." *Advertising Age*, February 19, 1990, 49.

Fisher, Christy, and Judith Graham. "Wal-Mart Throws 'Green' Gauntlet." *Advertising Age*, August 21, 1989, 1.

Friedland, Johnathan, and Louise Lee. "The Wal-Mart Way Sometimes Gets Lost in Translation Overseas." *Wall Street Journal*, October 8, 1997, A1, A12.

"Glass Is CEO at Wal-Mart." *Discount Merchandiser*, March 1988, 6.

Helliker, Kevin. "Wal-Mart's Store of the Future Blends Discount Prices, Department-Store Feel." *Wall Street Journal*, May 17, 1991, B1, B8.

Helliker, Kevin, and Bob Ortega. "Falling Profit Marks End of Era at Wal-Mart." *Wall Street Journal*, January 18, 1996, B1.

Huey, John. "America's Most Successful Merchant." *Fortune*, September 23, 1991, 46–48.

Johnson, Jay L. "Are We Ready for Big Changes?" *Discount Merchandiser*, August 1989, 48, 53–54.

——— "Hypermarts and Supercenters—Where Are They Heading?" *Discount Merchandiser*, November 1989, 60.

——— "Internal Communication: A Key To Wal-Mart's Success." *Discount Merchandiser*, November 1989, 68.

——— "The Supercenter Challenge." *Discount Merchandiser*, August 1989, 70.

Kelly, Kevin. "Sam Walton Chooses a Chip Off the Old CEO." *Business Week*, February 15, 1988, 29.

Kerr, Dick. "Wal-Mart Steps Up 'Buy American.'" *Housewares*, March 7–13, 1986, 1.

Lee, Louise. "Discounter Wal-Mart Is Catering to Affluent to Maintain Growth." *Wall Street Journal*, February 7, 1996, A1.

Lee, Louise, and Joel Millman. "Wal-Mart to Buy Majority Stake in Cifra." *Wall Street Journal*, June 4, 1997, A3.

"Management Style: Sam Moore Walton." *Business Month*, May 1989, 38.

Marsch, Barbara. "The Challenge: Merchants Mobilize to Battle Wal-Mart in a Small Community." *Wall Street Journal*, June 5, 1991, A1, A4.

Mason, Todd. "Sam Walton of Wal-Mart: Just Your Basic Homespun Billionaire." *Business Week*, October 14, 1985, 142–143.

Nelson, Emily. "Wal-Mart to Build a Test Supermarket in Bid to Boost Grocery-Industry Share." *Wall Street Journal*, June 19, 1998, A4.

"Our People Make the Difference: The History of Wal-Mart." Bentonville, Ark.: Wal-Mart Video Productions, 1991. Video cassette.

Peters, Tom J., and Nancy Austin, *A Passion for Excellence*. New York: Random House, 266–267.

Rawn, Cynthia Dunn. "Wal-Mart vs. Main Street." *American Demographics*, June 1990, 58–59.

Reier, Sharon. "CEO of the Decade: Sam M. Walton." *Financial World*, April 4, 1989, 56–57.

"Retailer Completes Purchase of Wertkauf of Germany." *Wall Street Journal*, December 31, 1997, B3.

Rudnitsky, Howard. "How Sam Walton Does It." *Forbes*, August 16, 1982, 42–44.

—— "Play It Again, Sam." *Forbes*, August 10, 1987, 48.

"Sam Moore Walton." *Business Month*, May 1989, 38.

Schwadel, Francine. "Little Touches Spur Wal-Mart's Rise." *Wall Street Journal*, September 22, 1989, B1.

Sheets, Kenneth R. "How Wal-Mart Hits Main St." *U.S. News & World Report*, March 13, 1989, 53–55.

Smith, Sarah. "America's Most Admired Corporations." *Fortune*, January 29, 1990, 56.

Sprout, Alison L. "America's Most Admired Corporations." *Fortune*, February 11, 1991, 52.

"The Early Days: Walton Kept Adding 'a Few More' Stores." *Discount Store News*, December 9, 1985, 61.

Thurmond, Shannon. "Sam Speaks Volumes About New Formats." *Advertising Age*, May 9, 1988, S26.

Trimble, Vance H. *Sam Walton: The Inside Story of America's Richest Man*. New York: Dutton, 1990.

"Wal-Mart Spoken Here." *Business Week*, June 23, 1997, 138.

Wal-Mart Stores, Inc. Annual Reports, 1996, 1997, and 1998.

"Wal-Mart's 'Green' Campaign to Emphasize Recycling Next." *Adweek's Marketing Week*, February 12, 1990, 60–61.

"Wal-Mart Rolls Out Its Supercenters." *Chain Store Age Executive*, December 1988, 18–19.

"Wal-Mart: The Model Discounter." *Dun's Business Month*, December 1982, 60–61.

"Wal-Mart to Acquire McLane, Distributor to Retail Industry." *Wall Street Journal*, October 2, 1990, A8.

"Wholesale Clubs." *Discount Merchandiser*, November 1987, 26.

"Work, Ambition—Sam Walton." press release, Wal-Mart Stores, Inc.

Zweig, Jason. "Expand It Again, Sam." *Forbes*, July 9, 1990, 106.

Kmart: A Corporate Strategy Dilemma

This case was prepared by James W. Camerius of Northern Michigan University.

Floyd Hall, chairman, president, and chief executive officer of Kmart Corporation since June 1995, was pleased with Kmart's financial results reported in the first quarter of fiscal 1998. Earnings had more than tripled from the previous year's levels. Net income for the quarter ended April 29 rose to $47 million from $14 million a year earlier. Hall was very optimistic about the company's future. The financial information convinced him that a new corporate strategy that he had introduced recently would revitalize Kmart's core business, its 2,136 discount stores, and put the company on the road to recovery. Industry analysts had noted that Kmart, once an industry leader, had posted eleven straight quarters of disappointing earnings and had been dogged by persistent bankruptcy rumors. Analysts cautioned that much of Kmart's growth reflected the strength of the consumer economy and that the company's future in a period of slower economic growth still looked uncertain.

Kmart was one of the world's largest mass-merchandise retailers. After several years of restructuring, it comprised mainly general merchandise businesses in the form of traditional Kmart discount department stores and Big Kmart (consumables and convenience) stores, as well as Super Kmart Centers (food and general merchandise). It operated in all fifty states and in Puerto Rico, Guam, and the U.S. Virgin Islands. It also had equity

This case is intended to be used as a basis for class discussion rather than to illustrate either effective or ineffective handling of the situation. This case was prepared by James W. Camerius of Northern Michigan University. Used by permission.

interests in Meldisco subsidiaries of Melville Corporation, which operated Kmart footwear departments. Measured in sales volume, Kmart was the third largest retailer and the second largest discount department store chain in the United States.

The discount department store industry was perceived to have reached maturity. Kmart, as part of that industry, had a retail management strategy that was developed in the late 1950s and revised in the early 1990s. The company was in a dilemma regarding its corporate strategy. The problem was how to stop Kmart's financial decline and provide a new direction that would reposition the company in a fiercely competitive environment.

THE EARLY YEARS

Kmart grew out of an organization founded in 1899 in Detroit by Sebastian S. Kresge. The first S. S. Kresge store represented a new type of retailing: it featured low-priced merchandise for cash in low-budget, relatively small buildings (4,000 to 6,000 square feet) with sparse furnishings. The adoption of the "5¢ and 10¢" or "variety store" concept, pioneered by F. W. Woolworth Company in 1879, led to rapid and profitable development of what was then the S. S. Kresge Company.

Kresge believed it could substantially increase its retail business through centralized buying and control, the development of standardized store operating procedures, and expansion in heavy traffic areas by opening new stores there. When the firm was incorporated in 1912, in Delaware, it had eighty-five stores, with sales of $10,325,000, and, next to Woolworth's, was the largest variety chain in the world. In 1916, it was reincorporated in Michigan. Over the next forty years, it experimented with mail-order catalogues, full-line department stores, self-service, a number of price lines, and the opening of stores in planned shopping centers. However, it continued to emphasize variety stores.

By 1957, corporate management became aware that the development of supermarkets and the expansion of drugstore chains into general merchandise lines had made inroads into market categories previously dominated by variety stores. It also became clear that a new form of store with a discount merchandising strategy was emerging.

THE CUNNINGHAM CONNECTION

In 1957, in an effort to save the company and make it competitive again, Frank Williams, the then president of Kresge, nominated Harry B. Cunningham as general vice president. He did so to free Cunningham, who had worked his way up the ranks in the organization, from operating responsibility. Cunningham was being groomed for the presidency and was given the assignment to study existing retailing businesses and recommend marketing changes.

In his visits to Kresge stores, and those of the competition, Cunningham became interested in discounting—particularly in a new operation in Garden City, Long Island. Eugene Ferkauf had recently opened large discount department stores called E. J. Korvette. The stores emphasized discount mass merchandising and featured low prices and margins, high turnover, large free-standing departmentalized units, and ample parking space. Typically, they were located in the suburbs.

Cunningham was impressed with the discount concept, but he knew he had first to convince the Kresge board of directors, whose support would be necessary for any new strategy to succeed. He studied the company for two years and presented it with the following recommendation:

> We can't beat the discounters operating under the physical constraints and the self-imposed merchandise limitations of variety stores. We can join them—and not only join them, but with our people, procedures, and organization, we can become a leader in the discount industry.

In a speech delivered at the University of Michigan, Cunningham made his management approach clear by concluding with an admonition from the British author, Sir Hugh Walpole: "Don't play for safety, it's the most dangerous game in the world."

The board of directors had a difficult job. Change is never easy, especially when the company has established procedures in place and a proud heritage. Before the first presentation to the board could be made, rumors were circulating that one shocked senior executive had said:

> We have been in the variety business for 60 years—we know everything there is to know about it, and we're not doing very well in that, and you want to get us into a business we don't know anything about.

Nevertheless, the board accepted Cunningham's recommendations. When Williams retired, Cunningham became the new president and chief executive officer and was directed to proceed with his recommendations.

THE BIRTH OF KMART

Management conceived the original Kmart as a conveniently located one-stop shopping unit where customers could buy a wide variety of quality merchandise at discount prices. The typical Kmart had 75,000 square feet, all on one floor. It generally stood by itself in a high-traffic, suburban area, with plenty of parking space. All stores had a similar floor plan.

The company made an $80 million commitment in leases and merchandise for thirty-three stores before the first Kmart opened in 1962 in Garden City, Michigan. As part of this strategy, management decided to rely on the strengths and abilities of its own people to make decisions rather than employing outside experts for advice.

The original Kresge 5 & 10 variety store operation was characterized by low gross margins, high turnover, and concentration on return on investment. The main difference in the Kmart strategy would be the offering of a much wider merchandise mix.

The company had the knowledge and ability to merchandise 50 percent of the departments in the planned Kmart merchandise mix and contracted for operation of the remaining departments. In the following years, Kmart took over most of those departments originally contracted to licensees. Eventually, all departments, except shoes, were operated by Kmart.

By 1987, the twenty-fifth anniversary of the opening of the first Kmart store in America, sales and earnings of Kmart Corporation were at an all-time high. The company was the world's largest discount retailer, with sales of $25,627 million, and operated 3,934 general merchandise and specialty stores.

On April 6, 1987, Kmart Corporation announced that it agreed to sell most of its remaining Kresge variety stores in the United States to McCrory Corporation, a unit of the closely held Rapid American Corporation of New York.

THE NATURE OF THE COMPETITIVE ENVIRONMENT

A Changing Marketplace

The retail sector of the United States economy went through a number of dramatic and turbulent changes during the 1980s and early 1990s. Retail analysts concluded that many retail firms were negatively affected by increased competitive pressures, sluggish consumer spending, slower-than-anticipated economic growth in North America, and recessions abroad. As one retail consultant noted,

> The structure of distribution in advanced economies is currently undergoing a series of changes that are as profound in their impact and as pervasive in their influence as those that occurred in manufacturing during the 19th century.

This changing environment affected the discount department store industry. Nearly a dozen firms, including E. J. Korvette, W. T. Grant, Arlans, Atlantic Mills, and Ames, passed into bankruptcy or reorganization. Some firms, such as Woolworth (Woolco Division), withdrew from the field entirely after years of disappointment. Saint Louis–based May Department Stores sold its Caldor and Venture discount divisions, each with annual sales of more than $1 billion. Venture announced liquidation in early 1998.

As senior management at Kmart saw it, most of the firms facing difficulties in the industry had this situation in common: they had been very successful five or ten years ago but had not changed and, therefore, had become somewhat dated. Management that had a historically successful formula, particularly in retailing, found it hard to adapt to change, especially at the peak of success, and would wait too long when faced with threats in the environment. Then they were forced to scramble to regain competitiveness.

Wal-Mart Stores, Inc., based in Bentonville, Arkansas, was an exception. Growth-oriented, it had emerged in 1991 as the nation's largest retailer and retained that position through 1997. It was also the largest discount department store chain in sales volume. Operating under a variety of names and formats, nationally and internationally, the company included Wal-Mart stores, Wal-Mart Supercenters, and SAM's Warehouse Clubs. The firm found early strength in cultivating rural markets, merchandise restocking programs, "everyday low pricing," and the control of operations through companywide computer programs that linked cash registers to corporate headquarters.

Among other companies, Sears, Roebuck, and Co., in a state of stagnated growth for several years, completed a return to its retailing roots by spinning off to shareholders its $9 billion controlling stake in its Allstate Corporation insurance unit and by the divestment of financial services. After unsuccessfully experimenting with an "everyday low-price" strategy, management chose to refine its merchandising program to meet the needs of middle-market customers, who were primarily women, by focusing on apparel, home, and automotive product lines.

Many retailers such, as Target (Dayton Hudson), which adopted the discount concept, attempted to go after the upscale customer—that is, someone with an annual household income of $25,000 to $44,000. Other pockets of population were served by firms such as Zayre, which had focused on consumers in the inner city before being acquired by Ames Department Stores, and Wal-Mart, which initially served the needs of the more rural consumer in secondary markets.

Kmart executives found that discount department stores were being challenged by several retail formats. Some retailers were assortment oriented, offering a much greater depth of assortment within a given product category. For example, Toys 'R' Us operated 20,000-square-foot toy supermarkets. Its prices were very competitive within an industry that was very competitive. When consumers entered a Toys 'R' Us facility, they usually had no doubt that if the product wasn't there, no one else had it. In 1997, however, Toys 'R' Us was challenged by industry leader Wal-Mart and other firms that offered a higher level of service and had more aggressive pricing practices.

Some retailers were experimenting with the "off price" apparel concept—that is, selling name brands and designer goods at 20 to 70 percent discounts. Others, such as Home Depot and Menard's, operated home improvement centers that were warehouse-style stores with a wide range of hardline merchandise for both do-it-yourselfers and professionals. Still others opened drug supermarkets that offered a wide variety of high-turnover merchandise in a convenient location. In these cases, competition was becoming more risk oriented by putting $3 million or $4 million in merchandise at retail value in an 80,000-square-foot facility and offering genuinely low prices. Jewel-Osco stores in the Midwest, Rite Aid, and a series of independents exemplified the organizations that employed an entirely new concept of the drug supermarket.

Thus, competition was offering something that was new and different in terms of depth of assortment, competitive price image, and format. Kmart management perceived the changes as a threat because these were viable businesses and they were hindering it in its ability to improve and maintain market share in specific merchandise categories. An industry competitive analysis is shown in Table 1.

EXPANSION AND CONTRACTION

When Joseph E. Antonini was appointed chairman of Kmart Corporation in October, 1987, he was charged with the responsibility of maintaining and eventually

TABLE I

An Industry Competitive Analysis, 1997

	Kmart	**Wal-Mart**	**Sears**	**Dayton Hudson**
Sales (in millions)	$32,183	$117,958	$41,296	$27,757
Net income (in millions)	$249	$3,526	$1,188	$751
Sales growth	2.4%	12%	8%	9%
Profit margin	.8%	2.9%	2.9%	2.7%
Sales/sq.ft	211	N/A	318	226
Return/equity	5%	19.8%	20%	16.8%

Number of Stores

Kmart Corporation
    Kmart traditional discount stores: 2,037
    Super Kmart centers: 99

Wal-Mart Stores, Inc. (includes international)
    Wal-Mart discount stores: 2,421
    Supercenters: 502
    SAM'S Clubs: 483

Sears, Roebuck and Company
    Full-line stores: 833
    Hardware stores: 255
    Homelife furniture stores: 129

Sears dealer stores: 576
Sears tire group
    Sears Auto Centers: 780
    National Tire & Battery stores: 326
Sears Parts Group
    Parts America stores: 576
    Western Auto stores: 39
    Western Auto (locally owned): 800

Dayton Hudson Corporation
    Target: 796
    Mervyn's: 269
    Department store division: 65

Source: Company Annual Reports.

accelerating the chain's record of growth, despite a mature retail marketplace. He moved to link experimental formats into profitable chains. As he noted, it was essential to embrace change:

> Our vision calls for the constant and never-ceasing exploration of new modes of retailing, so that our core business of U.S. Kmart stores can be constantly renewed and reinvigorated by what we learn from our other businesses.

In the mid 1970s and throughout the 1980s, Kmart became involved in the acquisition or development of several smaller new operations. For instance, Kmart Insurance Services, Inc., acquired as Planned Marketing Associates in 1974, offered a full line of life, health, and accident insurance at centers located in twenty-seven Kmart stores, primarily in the South and Southwest.

In 1982, Kmart initiated its own off-price specialty apparel concept, called Designer Depot. That year it opened twenty-eight Designer Depot stores to appeal to customers who wanted quality upscale clothing at a budget price. A variation of this concept, called Garment Rack, was opened to sell apparel that normally would not be sold in Designer Depot. A distribution center was added in 1983, to supplement them. Neither venture proved successful.

Kmart also attempted a joint venture with the Hechinger Company of Washington, D.C., a warehouse home center retailer. However, after much deliberation, Kmart chose instead to acquire, in 1984, Home Centers of America of San Antonio, Texas, which operated 80,000-square-foot warehouse home centers. The new division, renamed Builders Square, had grown to 167 units by 1996. It capitalized on Kmart's real estate, construction, and management expertise and Home Centers of America's merchandising expertise. Builders Square was sold in 1997.

Waldenbooks, a chain of 877 bookstores, was acquired from Carter, Hawley Hale, Inc., in 1984. Part of Kmart's strategy was to capture a greater share of the market with a product category that it already had in its stores. Kmart had been interested in the book business for some time and took advantage of an opportunity in the marketplace to build on its common knowledge base. Borders Books and Music, an operator of 50 large-format superstores,

became part of Kmart in 1992 to form the Borders Group, a division that would include Waldenbooks. The Borders Group, Inc., was sold in 1995.

The Bruno's, Inc., joint venture in 1987 formed a partnership to develop large combination grocery and general merchandise stores, or "hypermarkets," called American Fare. The giant one-stop-shopping facilities of 225,000 square feet traded on the grocery expertise of Bruno's and the general merchandise of Kmart to offer a wide selection of products and services at discount prices. A similar venture, called Super Kmart Center, represented later thinking on combination stores with a smaller size and format. In 1998, Kmart operated ninety-nine Super Kmart Centers, all in the United States.

In 1988, the company acquired a controlling interest in Makro, Inc., a Cincinnati-based operator of warehouse club stores. Makro, with annual sales of about $300 million, operated member-only stores, which were stocked with low-priced fresh and frozen groceries, apparel, and durable goods in suburbs of Atlanta, Cincinnati, Washington, and Philadelphia. PACE Membership Warehouse, Inc., a similar operation, was acquired in 1989. The "club" stores were sold in 1994.

PayLess Drug Stores, which operated super-drugstores in a number of western states, was sold in 1994 to Thrifty PayLess Holdings, Inc., an entity in which Kmart maintained a significant investment. Interests in The Sport Authority, an operator of large-format sporting goods stores, which Kmart acquired in 1990, were disposed of during 1995.

On the international level, an interest in Coles Myer, Ltd, Australia's largest retailer, was sold in November 1994. At the beginning of 1996, interests in thirteen Kmart general merchandise stores in the Czech and Slovak Republics were sold to Tesco PLC, one of the United Kingdom's largest retailers. In February 1998, Kmart stores in Canada were sold to Hudson's Bay Co., a Canadian chain of historic full-service department stores. The interest in Kmart Mexico, S.A.de C.V., was disposed of in fiscal year 1997.

Founded in 1988, OfficeMax, with 328 stores, was one of the largest operators of high-volume, deep discount office products superstores in the United States. In 1991, it became a Kmart unit in which Kmart had ownership of more than 90 percent. Kmart sold its interest in OfficeMax in 1995.

In 1998, Kmart maintained an equity interest in Meldisco subsidiaries of Melville Corporation, operators of Kmart footwear departments.

THE MATURATION OF KMART

Early corporate research revealed that 80 percent of the population found it convenient to shop at Kmart. One study concluded that one out of every two adults in the United States shopped at a Kmart at least once a month. Despite this popular appeal, strategies that had allowed the firm to have something for everybody were no longer felt to be appropriate for the 1990s. Kmart found that it had a broad customer base because it operated on a national basis. Its strategies had assumed that the company was serving everyone in the markets where it was established.

Kmart was often perceived as aiming at the low-income consumer. The financial community believed that Kmart catered to the blue-collar, low-income and upper-lower-class customers. Actually, though, Kmart was serving the professional and middle-class market because its stores were initially in suburban communities, where that population lived.

In more recent years, Kmart has made a major commitment to secondary or rural markets, but these were areas it had not previously cultivated. When developing its initial strategies, the firm perceived the rural consumer as different from the urban or suburban customer. In re-addressing the situation, it discovered that its assortments in rural areas were too limited and that there were too many preconceived notions regarding what the Nebraska farmer really wanted. Kmart discovered that the rural consumer didn't always shop for bib overalls and shovels but was looking for microwave ovens and the same things everyone else shopped for.

Kmart's goal was not to attract more customers but to get customers to spend more. Customers were thought of as categories demonstrating divergent tastes and needs. The upper-income consumer would buy more health and beauty aids, cameras, and sporting goods, whereas the lower-income consumer would buy toys and clothing.

As it sought to capture a larger share of the market and get people to spend more, Kmart began to recognize a market that was more upscale. When consumer research was conducted and management examined the profile of the trade area and

the profile of the person who shopped at Kmart in the previous month, they were found to be identical. Kmart was predominately serving the suburban consumer in suburban locations. In 1997, Kmart's primary target customers were women between the ages of twenty-five and forty-five, with children at home and with annual household incomes of $20,000 to $50,000. The core Kmart shopper averaged 4.3 visits to a Kmart store per month. The purchase amount per visit was $40, and the purchase rate during a store visit was 95 percent. The firm estimated that 180 million people shopped at Kmart in an average year.

Through research on lifestyle in the markets it served, Kmart determined that there were more two-income families, that families were having fewer children, that there were more working wives, and that customers tended to be homeowners. Customers were very careful how they spent their money and were perceived as seeking quality. This was a distinct contrast to the 1960s and early 1970s, which tended to have the orientation of a throw-away society. Now the customer said, "What we want is products that will last longer. We'll have to pay more for them but we'll still want them and at the lowest price possible." Thus, prices had to be competitive, but the insistence on better quality was the new element. According to a Kmart Annual Report, "Consumers today are well educated and informed. They want good value and they know it when they see it. Price remains a key consideration, but the consumers' new definition of value includes quality as well as price."

Corporate management at Kmart considered the discount department store to be a mature idea. Although maturity was sometimes looked on with disfavor, Kmart executives did not think that maturity had to mean a lack of profitability or a lack of opportunity to increase sales. The industry was perceived as being "reborn." It was in this context, in 1990, that a series of new retailing strategies were developed with the aim of upgrading the Kmart image.

THE RENEWAL PROGRAM

The strategies that emerged to confront a changing environment resulted from an overall reexamination of existing corporate strategies. The new program included the following: accelerated store expansion and refurbishing; capitalizing on dominant lifestyle departments; centralized merchandising; more capital investment in retail automation; aggressive and focused advertising; and continued growth through new specialty retail formats.

This five-year, $2.3 billion program involved virtually all Kmart discount stores. There would be approximately 250 new full-size Kmart stores, 620 enlargements, 280 relocations and 30 closings. In addition 1,260 stores would be refurbished to bring their layout and fixtures up to new store standards.

Product displays received a good deal of attention early on, for they needed improvement. The traditional Kmart layout was by product category, and the locations for specific departments were often holdovers from the variety store. Many departments would not give up prime locations. As part of its new marketing strategy, the company introduced the shop concept. The concept resulted in a variety of new departments such as Soft Goods for the Home, Kitchen Korners, and Home Electronic Centers. They carried goods that were complementary—to entice shoppers to buy several interrelated products rather than just one item. The goal of each of these "do-it-yourself" departments, as management called them, was to sell a lifestyle-oriented approach to consumers.

Kmart's five-year program also focused on utilizing and revitalizing the space that the company already had under its control. The remodeling and updating of existing properties gave virtually all U.S. Kmart discount stores a new look: a broad poppy-red-and-gold band around interior walls as a "horizon," and new round, square, and honeycomb racks that displayed the full garment. Other changes included the relocation of jewelry and women's apparel to areas closer to the entrance, and the redesigning of counters to make them look more upscale and hold more merchandise.

Name brands were added in soft and hard goods as management recognized that the customer transferred the product quality of branded goods to perceptions of private-label merchandise. "If you sell Wrangler, there is good quality. Then the private label must be good quality"—that, in the view of Kmart management, would be the customer's way of thinking. Consequently, the company increased its emphasis on trusted national brands such as Rubbermaid, Procter & Gamble, and Kodak and stressed major strategic vendor relationships. In addition, it began to enhance its private-label brands such as Kathy Ireland, Jaclyn Smith, Route 66, and Sesame Street in apparel. Additional private-label merchandise included K Gro in home gardening, American Fare in grocery and consumables, White-Westinghouse in appliances, and Penske Auto Centers in automotive services. Some private labels were discontinued after a review.

The goal of creating a quality image received a great deal of attention. Pro golfer Fuzzy Zoeller was engaged to promote golf equipment and other associated products. Mario Andretti, who raced in the Championship Auto Racing Teams' Indy car series, agreed to the cosponsorship of his car with associated promotion.

Kmart hired Martha Stewart, an upscale Connecticut author of lavish best-selling books on cooking and home entertaining, as its "life-style spokesperson and consultant." She was featured as a corporate symbol for housewares and associated products in advertising and in store displays. Management visualized her as the next Betty Crocker (a fictional character created some years ago by General Mills) and a representative of its interest in lifestyle trends. The "Martha Stewart Everyday" home fashion product line was introduced successfully in 1995 and expanded in 1996 and 1997. The company established a separate division to manage strategy for all Martha Stewart–label goods and programs.

The redesigned once-a-week Kmart newspaper circular featuring merchandise also carried the advertising theme: "The quality you need, the price you want."

To maintain "price leadership across America," the company reduced several thousand prices. As management noted, "it is absolutely essential that we provide our customers with good value—quality products at low prices." Although lower prices hurt margins and contributed significantly to a decline in earnings, management concluded that unit turnover of items with lowered prices increased sufficiently to "enable Kmart to maintain its pricing leadership that will have a most positive impact on our business in the years ahead."

A "centralized merchandising system" was introduced to improve communication. A computerized, highly automated replenishment system tracked how quickly merchandise sold, and just as quickly put fast-moving items back on the shelves. Satellite capability and a point-of-sale (POS) scanning system were introduced as part of the program. Regular, live satellite communication from Kmart headquarters to the stores would allow senior management to stay in touch with store managers and ask and answer questions. The POS scanning system made possible the recording of every sale and transmission of the data to headquarters. This enabled Kmart to respond quickly to what was new, what was in demand, and what would keep customers coming back.

A new corporate logo was designed to signify the changes taking place inside the stores. It featured a big red *K* with the word *mart* written in smaller white script inside the *K*.

The company opened its first Super Kmart Center in 1992. The format combined general merchandise and food. The centers ranged in size from 135,000 to 190,000 square feet and stressed customer service and convenience. The typical Super Kmart operated seven days a week, twenty-four-hours a day, and generated high traffic and sales volume. The centers also had wider shopping aisles, appealing displays, and pleasant lighting intended to enrich the shopping experience. Super Kmarts featured in-house bakeries, USDA fresh meats, fresh seafood, delicatessens, cookie kiosks, cappuccino bars, in-store eateries, food courts, and salad bars. In many locations, the centers provided customer services such as video rental, dry cleaning, shoe repair, beauty salons, optical shops, and express shipping services, as well as a full line of traditional Kmart merchandise. To enhance the appeal of the merchandise assortment, the centers emphasized "cross merchandising." For example, toasters stood above the fresh baked breads, kitchen gadgets hung across the aisle from produce, and baby centers offered everything from baby food to toys.

By 1998, the company operated ninety-nine Super Kmart Centers and served twenty-one states with this regionally based combination store format.

THE PLANNING FUNCTION

Corporate planning at Kmart was the result of executives, primarily the senior executive, recognizing change. The senior executive's role was to make others see that nothing is good forever. "Good planning" was perceived as the result of those who recognized that at some point they would have to get involved. "Poor planning" was done by those who didn't recognize the need for it. When they did, it was too late to survive. Good planning, if done on a regular and timely basis, was assumed to result in improved performance. Kmart's Michael Wellman, then director of planning and research, contended that

> . . . planning, as we like to stress, is making decisions now to improve performance tomorrow. Everyone looks at what may happen tomorrow, but the planners are the ones who make decisions today. That's where I think too many firms go wrong. They think they are planning because they are writing reports and are aware of changes. They don't say, 'because of this, we must decide today to spend this money to do this to accomplish this goal in the future.'

In the view of Kmart management, the firm had been very successful in the area of strategic planning. "When it became necessary to make significant changes in the way we were doing business," Wellman said, "that was accomplished on a fairly timely basis." When the organization made the change in the 1960s, it recognized that there was a very powerful investment opportunity and capitalized on it—far beyond what anyone else would have done. "We just opened stores," Wellman continued, "at a great, great pace. Management, when confronted with a crisis, would state, 'It's the economy, or it's this, or that, but it's not the essential way we are doing business.'" But he noted that, "suddenly management would recognize that the economy may stay like this forever," and it would decide to take action. Strategic planning was thought to arise out of some difficult times for the company.

Planning at Kmart was organized in a fairly formal way. It involved a constant evaluation of what was happening in the marketplace, what the competition was doing, and what kinds of opportunities were available. Management saw the need to diversify because a company would not be viable unless it was growing, and the Kmart format was unlikely to stimulate growth forever. It needed growth and opportunity, particularly for a company that was able to open 200 stores on a regular basis. Wellman recognized that "Given a corporate culture that was accustomed to challenges, management would have to find ways to expend that energy." "A corporation that is successful," he argued, "has to continue to be successful. It has to have a basic understanding of corporate needs and be augmented by a much more rigorous effort to be aware of what's going on in the external environment."

A planning group at Kmart represented a number of functional areas of the organization. Management described it as an "in-house consulting group" with some independence. Its members came from financial planning, economic and consumer analysis, and operations research. The CEO was identified as the primary planner.

REORGANIZATION AND RESTRUCTURING

Kmart financial performance for 1993 was clearly disappointing. The company announced a loss of $974 million on sales of $34,156,000 for the fiscal year ended January 26, 1994. Noting the deficit, the chairman, Joseph Antonini, concluded that it occurred primarily because of lower margins in the U.S. Kmart stores division. "Margin erosion," he said, "stemmed in part from intense industry-wide pricing pressure throughout 1993." He was confident, however, that Kmart was on track with its renewal program to make the more than 2,350 U.S. Kmart stores more "competitive, on-trend, and cutting merchandisers." Tactical Retail Solutions, Inc., estimated that during Antonini's seven-year tenure with the company, Kmart's market share in the discount arena fell to 23 percent, from 35 percent. Other retail experts suggested that because the company had struggled for so long to have the right merchandise in the stores at the right time, it had lost customers to competitors. An aging customer base was also cited.

In early 1995, following the posting of Kmart's eighth consecutive quarter of disappointing earnings, the company's board of directors announced that Joseph Antonini would be replaced as chairman. It named Donald S. Perkins, former chairman of Jewel Companies, Inc., and a Kmart director, to the position. Antonini relinquished his position as president and CEO in March. After a nationwide search, Floyd Hall, aged fifty-seven, a former chairman and CEO of the Target discount store division of Dayton-Hudson Corporation, was appointed chairman, president, and chief executive officer of Kmart in June of 1995.

In 1996, Kmart announced a restructuring of its merchandising organization aimed at improving product assortments, category management, customer focus, sales, and profitability. The company

had also concluded the disposition of many non-core assets, including the sale of the Borders Group, OfficeMax, the Sports Authority, and Coles Myer. It had closed 214 underperforming stores in the United States, and cleared out $700 million in aged and discontinued inventory in the remaining Kmart stores.

The corporate mission was "to become the discount store of choice for middle-income families with children by satisfying their routine and seasonal shopping needs as well as or better than the competition." Management believed that the actions taken by the new president would have a dramatic impact on how customers perceived Kmart, how frequently they shopped in the stores, and how much they would buy on each visit. Increasing the frequency of customers' visits and the amount purchased on each visit were viewed as crucial to the effort to increase the company's profitability.

In 1996, Kmart converted 152 of its traditional stores to feature a new design that was referred to as the high-frequency format. These stores were named Big Kmart. The stores emphasized those departments that were deemed the most important to core customers and offered an increased mix of high frequency, everyday basics and consumables in the pantry area located at the front of each store. These items were typically priced at a 1 to 3 percentage differential from the leading competitors in each market and served to increase inventory turnover and gross margin dollars. In addition to the pantry area, Big Kmart stores featured improved lighting, new signage that was easier to see and read, and adjacencies that created a smoother traffic flow.

Floyd Hall felt Kmart's financial results for 1997 and early 1998 reflected the major financial restructuring that was underway at the company. Since he joined the company, his top priority had been to build a management team with "a 'can-do' attitude that would permeate all of our interaction with customers, vendors, shareholders, and one another." Major changes were made to the management team. Of the company's thirty-seven corporate officers, twenty-three were new to the company's team since 1995. The most dramatic restructuring had taken place in the merchandising organization where all four of the general merchandise managers responsible for buying organizations joined Kmart since 1995. In addition, fifteen new divisional vice presidents joined Kmart during

1997. Significant changes also were made in the board of directors: of the fifteen directors, nine were new to the company since 1995. (See Appendix for the board of directors and corporate officers at the beginning of 1998.) Hall argued that the company had turned a corner and that it was "finally and firmly on the road to recovery."

APPENDIX: KMART CORPORATION

Executive Directors
1997

The name, age, position and a description of the business experience for each of the executive officers of the company is listed below as of August 31, 1997. The business experience for each of the executive officers described below includes the principal positions held by them since 1992.

Floyd Hall (58)
Chairman of the board, president and chief executive officer since June 1995. Previously, he served concurrently as chairman and chief executive officer ofd the Museum Company, Alva Reproduction, Inc. And Glass Masters, Inc. From 1989 to 1995.

Warren Flick (53)
Director, president and chief operating officer, U.S. Kmart Stores since November 1996.

Laurence L. Anderson (55)
Executive vice president and president, Super Kmart since August 1997.

Warren Cooper (52)
Executive vice president, human resources & administration since March 1996.

Donald W. Keeble (48)
Executive vice president, store operations since February 1995.

Anthony N. Palizzi (54)
Executive vice president, general counsel since 1992.

Marvin P. Rich (52)
Executive vice president, strategic planning, finance and administration since 1994.

William N. Anderson (50)
Senior vice president and general merchandise manager, hardlines since September 1996.

Andrew A. Giancamilli (47)
Senior vice president, general merchandise manager, home and consumables since June 1997.

Ernest L. Heether (51)
Senior vice president, merchandise operations planning and replenishment since April 1996.

Paul J. Hueber (49)
Senior vice president, store operations since 1994.

Donald E. Norman (60)
Senior vice president, chief information officer since December 1995.

William D. Underwood (56)
Senior vice president, global sourcing since 1994.

Martin E. Welch III (49)
Senior vice president and chief financial officer since 1995.

Jerome J. Kuske (45)
Senior vice president, general merchandise manager, health and beauty care/pharmacy since June 1997.

James P. Mixon (53)
Senior vice president, logistics since June 1997.

E. Jackson Smailes (54)
Senior vice president, general merchandise manager, apparel since August 1997.

Board of Directors

James B. Adamson[4]#
Chairman and Chief Executive Officer
Flagstar Companies Inc.

Lilyan H. Affinito [1*,3,5,]
Former Vice Chairman of the Board
Maxxam Group Inc.

Stephen F. Bollenbach [4] #
President and Chief Executive Officer
Hilton Hotels Corporation

Joseph A. Califano, Jr. [4]
Chairman and President
The National Center on Addiction and Substance Abuse at Columbia University

Richard G. Cline [2*,3,5,]#
Chairman
Hawthorne Investors Inc., Former Chairman and Chief Executive Officer
NICOR Inc.

Willie D. Davis [2]
President
All Pro Broadcasting, Inc.

Enrique C. Falla [1]
Senior Vice President
The Dow Chemical Company

TABLE 2

Kmart Corporation, Consolidated Balance Sheets and Operating Statements, 1996–1997 (in millions, except per share data)

	Years Ended January 28, 1998, January 29, 1997, and January 31, 1996		
	1997	1996	1995
Sales	$32,183	$31,437	$31,713
Cost of sales, buying, and occupancy	25,152	24,390	24,675
Gross margin	7,031	7,047	7,038
Selling, general and administrative expenses	6,136	6,274	6,876
Voluntary early retirement program	114	—	—
Other (gains) losses	—	(10)	41
Continuing income before interest, income taxes and dividends on convertible preferred securities of subsidiary	781	783	121
Interest expense, net	363	453	434
Income tax provision (credit)	120	68	(83)
Dividends on convertible preferred securities of subsidiary, net of income taxes of $26 and $16	49	31	—
Net income (loss) from continuing operations before extraordinary item	249	231	(230)
Loss from discontinued operations, net of income taxes of $(3) and $(139)	—	(5)	(260)
Loss on disposal of discontinued operations, net of income taxes of $(240) and $88	—	(446)	(30)
Extraordinary loss, net of income taxes of $(27)	—	—	(51)
Net income (loss)	$ 249	$ (220)	$ (571)
Basic/diluted income (loss) per common share			
Continuing operations	$.51	$.48	$(.51)
Discontinued operations	—	(.01)	(.57)
Loss on disposal of discontinued operations	—	(.92)	(.06)
Extraordinary item	—	—	(.11)
Net income(loss)	$ .51	$ (.45)	$ (1.25)
Basic weighted average shares (in millions)	487.1	483.6	459.8
Dilute weighted average shares (in millions)	491.7	486.1	459.9

Joseph P. Flannery [3,4*,5]
Chairman of the Board, President and Chief Executive Officer
Uniroyal Holding Inc.

Warren Flick[#]
President and Chief Operating Officer, U.S. Kmart Stores
Kmart Corporation

Floyd Hall [3*] [#]
Chairman of the Board, President and Chief Executive Officer
Kmart Corporation

Robert D. Kennedy [4] [#]
Former Chairman and Chief Executive Officer
Union Carbide Corporation

J. Richard Munro [2,3,5*]

	As of January 28, 1998, and January 29, 1997	
	1997	1996
Current assets:		
Cash and cash equivalents	$498	$406
Merchandise inventories	6,367	6,354
Other current assets	611	973
Total current assets	7,476	7,733
Property and equipment, net	5,472	5,740
Property held for sale or financing	271	200
Other assets and deferred charges	339	613
Total assets	$13,558	$14,286
Current liabilities:		
Long-term debt due within one year	$78	$156
Trade accounts payable	1,923	2,009
Accrued payroll and other liabilities	1,064	1,298
Taxes other than income taxes	209	139
Total current liabilities	3,274	3,602
Long-term debt and notes payable	1,725	2,121
Capital lease obligations	1,179	1,478
Other long-term liabilities	965	1,013
Company obligated mandatorily redeemable convertible preferred securities of a subsidiary trust holding solely 7¾% convertible junior subordinated debentures of Kmart (redemption value of $1,000)	981	980
Common stock, $1 par value, 1,500,000,000 shares authorized; 488,811,271 and 486,996,145 shares issued, respectively	489	486
Capital in excess of par value	1,620	1,608
Retained earnings	3,343	3,105
Treasury shares and restricted stock	(15)	(37)
Foreign currency translation adjustment	(3)	(70)
Total liabilities and shareholders' equity	$13,558	$14,286

Source: Company Annual Reports.

Chairman of the Board
Gene tech, Inc.

Robin B. Smith#
Chairman and Chief Executive Officer
Publishers Clearing House

William P. Weber [1] #
Vice Chairman
Texas Instruments Incorporated

James O. Welch, Jr. [2] #
Former Vice Chairman
RJR Nabisco and Chairman
Nabisco Brands, Inc.

Committees:

1=Audit
2=Compensation & Incentives

TABLE 3

Kmart Corporation, Financial Performance 1988–1997
(in $ millions)

Year	Sales	Assets	Net Income*	Net Worth
1988	$27,301,000	$12,126,000	$803,000	$5,009,000
1989	29,533,000	13,145,000	323,000	4,972,000
1990	32,070,000	13,899,000	756,000	5,384,000
1991	34,580,000	15,999,000	859,000	6,891,000
1992	37,724,000	18,931,000	941,000	7,536,000
1993	34,156,000	17,504,000	(974,000)	6,093,000
1994	34,025,000	17,029,000	296,000	6,032,000
1995	31,713,000	15,033,000	(571,000)	5,280,000
1997	32,183,000	13,558,000	249,000	6,445,000

*After taxes and extraordinary credit or charges.
Data from 1995, 1996 and 1997 reflect disposition of subsidiaries.
Source: Fortune financial analysis and Kmart Annual Reports.

TABLE 4

Wal-Mart Stores, Inc., Financial Performance 1988–1997
(in $ millions)

Year	Sales	Assets	Net Income	Net Worth
1988	$ 20,649,001	$ 6,359,668	$ 837,221	$ 3,007,909
1989	25,810,656	8,198,484	1,075,900	3,965,561
1990	32,601,594	11,388,915	1,291,024	5,365,524
1991	43,886,900	15,443,400	1,608,500	6,989,700
1992	55,484,000	20,565,000	1,995,000	8,759,000
1993	67,344,000	26,441,000	2,333,000	10,753,000
1994	82,494,000	32,819,000	2,681,000	12,726,000
1995	93,627,000	37,541,000	2,740,000	14,756,000
1996	104,859,000	39,604,000	3,056,000	17,143,000
1997	117,958,000	45,384,000	3,526,000	18,503,000

Source: Wal-Mart Annual Reports and *Fortune* financial analysis.

3=Executive
4=Finance
5=Nominating
*=Committee Chair
#=Joined Board since 1995

References

Berner, Robert. "Kmart's Earnings More Than Tripled in First Quarter." *Wall Street Journal*, May 14, 1998, A13.

Brauer, Molly. "Kmart in Black 'in 6 Months.'" *Detroit Free Press*, January 26, 1996, E1.

Bussey, John. "Kmart Is Set to Sell Many of Its Roots to Rapid-American Corp's McCrory." *Wall Street Journal*, April 6, 1987, 24.

Carruth, Eleanore. "Kmart Has to Open Some New Doors on the Future." *Fortune*, July 1977, 143-150, 153-154.

Chakravarty, Subrata N. "A Tale of Two Companies." *Forbes*, May 27, 1991, 86-96.

Dewar, Robert E. "The Kresge Company and the Retail Revolution." *University of Michigan Business Review*, July 2, 1975, 2.

Duff, Christina, and Joann S. Lubin. "Kmart Board Ousts Antonini as Chairman." *Wall Street Journal*, January 18, 1995, A3.

Elmer, Vickie, and Joann Muller. "Retailer Needs Leader, Vision." *Detroit Free Press*, March 22, 1995, 1A, 9A.

Guiles, Melinda G. "Attention, Shoppers: Stop That Browsing and Get Aggressive." *Wall Street Journal*, June 16, 1987, 1, 21.

———. "Kmart, Bruno's Join to Develop 'Hypermarkets.'" *Wall Street Journal*, September 8, 1987, 17.

Ingrassia, Paul. "Attention Non Kmart Shoppers: A Blue-Light Special Just for You." *Wall Street Journal*, October 6, 1987, 42.

"It's Kresge . . . Again." *Chain Store Executive*, November 1975, 16.

Key, Janet. "Kmart Plan: Diversify, Conquer: Second Largest Retailer Out to Woo Big Spenders." *Chicago Tribune*, November 11, 1984, 1-2.

Kmart Corporation, Annual Reports, 1990, 1995, 1996, and 1997.

———. *Kmart Fact Book*, 1997.

"Kmart Looks to New Logo to Signify Changes." *Wall Street Journal*, September 13, 1990, 10.

"Kmart Will Expand Line With Purchase of Warehouse Club." *Wall Street Journal*, December 14, 1990, 4.

Main, Jerry. "Kmart's Plan to Be Born Again." *Fortune*, September 21, 1981, 74-77, 84-85.

Mitchell, Russell. "How They're Knocking the Rust Off Two Old Chains." *Business Week*, September 8, 1986, 44-48.

Rice, Faye. "Why Kmart Has Stalled." *Fortune*, October 9, 1989, 79.

Saporito, Bill. "Is Wal-Mart Unstoppable?" *Fortune*, May 6, 1991, 50-59.

Schwadel, Francine. "Attention Kmart Shoppers: Style Coming to This Aisle." *Wall Street Journal*, August 9, 1988, 6.

———. "Kmart to Speed Store Openings, Renovations." *Wall Street Journal*, February 27, 1990, 3.

Sellers, Patricia. "Attention, Kmart Shoppers." *Fortune*, January 2, 1989, 41.

Stavro, Barry. "Mass Appeal." *Forbes*, May 5, 1986, 128, 130.

Sternad, Patricia. "Kmart's Antonini Moves Far Beyond Retail 'Junk' Image." *Advertising Age*, July 25, 1988, 1, 67.

Wellman, Michael. Interview with Michael Wellman, director of planning and research, Kmart Corporation, August 6, 1984.

"Where Kmart Goes Next Now That It's No. 2." *Business Week*, June 2, 1980, 109-110, 114.

"Why Chains Enter New Areas." *Chain Store Executive*, December 1976, 22, 24.

Woodruff, David. "Will Kmart Ever Be a Silk Purse?" *Business Week*, January 22, 1990, 46.

CASE 23

The Cat Recovers: Caterpillar, Inc., in the Late 1990s

This case was prepared by M. Edgar Barrett of Thunderbird—The American Graduate School of International Management.

In early 1998, Donald V. Fites had reason to be more than just satisfied with the performance of Caterpillar, Inc. (Cat), under his leadership. Named chief executive officer in 1990, he had presided over a tumultuous—but highly successful—period in Cat's history. Sales had increased by approximately 85 percent between 1991 and 1997, with annual net income moving from a negative $404 million to a positive $1,665 million during the same period.

Nonetheless, he was concerned about the firm's likely future. The construction equipment industry was in the process of being both redefined and restructured, new competitors were emerging, and the rate of change seemed to be accelerating.

INDUSTRY BACKGROUND

The heavy construction equipment industry, with worldwide sales of $71 billion for 1996, was expected to continue its growth at about four percent per annum for the next four years.[1] Heavy construction equipment, ranging from the 240-ton off-highway trucks to mini-excavators, was being used all over the world for commercial and industrial construction, mining, transportation, forestry, road building, and many other applications. Five main categories made up the heavy construction equip-

ment industry: earthmoving equipment (loaders, scrapers, graders, rollers, and compactors); off-highway trucks; construction cranes; mixers, pavers, and related equipment; and parts and attachments (hoes, dragline buckets, winches, and so forth).

The construction equipment industry had experienced numerous changes over the last three decades. Rapid demand growth in the early 1970s was soon interrupted by world recessionary conditions caused by rising oil prices. After almost a decade of sluggish demand, construction equipment sales picked up. Demand growth in developing countries was expected to exhibit an above average rate as they set out to build basic infrastructure (see Tables 1 and 2). Developed nations, especially the United States, were expected to continue to show stable growth throughout the next decade.

These new conditions had created new challenges for construction equipment manufacturing firms. Growing Third World economies, primarily needing equipment for road building, housing, and mining, were expected to prefer used equipment coming from developed nations as they often lacked credit worthiness and were greatly concerned about investment costs. On the other hand, developed nations with fully developed infrastructures were expected to exhibit an increased level of demand for construction equipment for use in repairs and smaller construction projects. These combined effects were seen as resulting in strong growth for compact equipment within the developed world and larger machines for the developing nations.

Compact equipment generally had lower margins and faced stronger competition from regional

TABLE 1

Construction Equipment Industry: Supply and Demand by Region (in millions of U.S. $)

	Construction Equipment Demand				
	1987	*1992*	*1996*	*2001*	*2006*
North America	$10,950	$11,215	$19,660	$20,610	$24,680
Central and South America	2,500	2,605	3,660	5,050	6,600
Europe	17,320	17,945	17,935	22,230	26,700
Africa and Middle East	1,900	2,240	2,680	3,400	4,270
Asia and Oceania	10,010	18,390	27,340	35,330	45,730
Total	**$42,680**	**$52,395**	**$71,275**	**$86,620**	**$107,980**

	Construction Equipment Production				
	1987	*1992*	*1996*	*2001*	*2006*
North America	$10,240	$12,380	$19,755	$21,850	$27,800
Central and South America	1,415	1,419	1,923	2,710	3,610
Europe	19,890	20,027	21,017	26,275	31,940
Africa and Middle East	100	125	175	220	280
Asia and Oceania	10,565	16,179	26,955	34,145	43,160
Total	**$42,210**	**$50,130**	**$69,825**	**$85,200**	**$106,790**

Source: The Freedonia Group, Inc., July 1997.

construction equipment manufacturers. More than 200 participants were active in the mature U.S. market, although only a handful possessed extensive product lines and strong market share. The earth-moving business, although expected to grow at a slightly lower rate than the other segments, contributed almost half of industry sales. As shown in Table 2, demand for off-highway trucks, mixers, pavers, and related equipment was expected to climb at a faster rate than the other three categories.

Full-range suppliers such as Caterpillar and Komatsu offered a broad line of equipment for the construction industry around the world. In 1996, they commanded a 17.1 percent and 8.1 percent worldwide market share, respectively, of the heavy construction equipment industry. The next ten competitors, which included Case, Deere, Hitachi, Ingersoll-Rand, Liebherr, and Volvo, held 24.8 percent of the market.[2]

High rates of production volume were viewed as critical for construction equipment manufacturers as they allowed the spreading of high fixed overhead and research and development expenses across a larger number of units. Successful manufacturers had been implementing extensive cost-cutting measures and rationalization of production facilities to retain profitability in this increasingly competitive industry. A general trend toward outsourcing could also be seen throughout the industry, allowing equipment makers to focus on design and final assembly. In addition, manufacturers were reducing the number of suppliers in order to simplify supplier networks and promote cooperation.

Over the last decade, cooperative agreements had also become common. Collaboration took place either through joint ventures designed to share production facilities or through technology-sharing agreements. Joint ventures, such as the Caterpillar-Mitsubishi one in Japan, were being used to produce specific models for regional or worldwide sales. Examples of technology-sharing arrangements included Komatsu's 50/50 joint venture with Cummins Engine for the manufacture of diesel engines.

Historically, a strong dealer network has also been key in helping the company remain competi-

TABLE 2

Construction Equipment Industry: Demand for Specific Product Categories (in millions of U.S. $)

Demand for Earthmoving Equipment*

	1987	1992	1996	2001	2006
North America	$5,255	$4,970	$9,848	$10,090	$12,070
Central and South America	1,279	1,308	1,768	2,495	3,290
Europe	8,964	9,203	9,031	11,125	13,290
Africa and Middle East	895	1,115	1,375	1,650	2,080
Asia and Oceania	4,609	8,941	13,459	17,140	22,070
Total	**$21,002**	**$25,537**	**$35,481**	**$42,500**	**$52,800**

Demand for Off-Highway Trucks

	1987	1992	1996	2001	2006
North America	$526	$973	$1,519	$1,635	$1,935
Central and South America	331	410	550	745	985
Europe	747	719	671	830	1,015
Africa and Middle East	291	260	370	470	590
Asia and Oceania	1,091	1,702	2,607	3,540	4,655
Total	**$2,986**	**$4,064**	**$5,717**	**$7,220**	**$9,180**

Demand for Cranes

	1987	1992	1996	2001	2006
North America	$961	$1,259	$2,372	$2,480	$3,035
Central and South America	139	134	224	275	350
Europe	1,905	1,996	2,083	2,620	3,160
Africa and Middle East	191	260	280	360	460
Asia and Oceania	764	1,531	2,291	2,955	3,795
Total	**$3,960**	**$5,180**	**$7,250**	**$8,690**	**$10,800**

Demand for Mixers, Pavers, and Related Equipment

	1987	1992	1996	2001	2006
North America	$691	$666	$1,171	$1,285	$1,520
Central and South America	139	149	206	295	385
Europe	1,067	1,143	1,185	1,510	1,860
Africa and Middle East	81	95	120	155	200
Asia and Oceania	629	1,269	1,971	2,615	3,475
Total	**$2,607**	**$3,322**	**$4,653**	**$5,860**	**$7,440**

Demand for Parts and Attachments

	1987	1992	1996	2001	2006
North America	$3,517	$3,347	$4,750	$5,120	$6,120
Central and South America	612	604	912	1,240	1,590
Europe	4,637	4,884	4,965	6,145	7,375
Africa and Middle East	442	510	535	765	940
Asia and Oceania	2,917	4,947	7,012	9,080	11,735
Total	**$12,125**	**$14,292**	**$18,174**	**$22,350**	**$27,760**

Source: The Freedonia Group, Inc., July 1997.
*Except off-highway trucks.

tive. Parts supply and equipment service are critical for customers due to high construction downtime costs. In turn, the sale of parts and attachments represented about one-fourth of industry sales. This highly profitable portion of the business generated important revenues for companies with a large installed base of construction equipment scattered throughout the globe. A strong service network could also be used to support the marketing effort of the equipment maker and provide it with valuable market information.

Most large and medium-size construction equipment makers offered both wholesale and retail financing. Wholesale financing is designed to allow distributors and dealers to maintain an adequate inventory of products and parts. Retail financing is used to assist end users with the purchase of equipment. This could be an important purchase variable for large construction projects or in cash-strapped, emerging markets.

The sale of heavy construction equipment often requires a substantial effort by dealers as well as by equipment makers. Relationships with large contractors and government officials are often critical, especially in developing nations, where large infrastructure projects are common. Large construction and engineering firms, as well as mine operators, frequently seek to limit the number of brands in their fleets in order to reduce training and maintenance costs at construction sites.

The retail price of heavy construction equipment had remained practically flat throughout the world during the last decade. Several reasons seemed to have produced this trend. Competition in medium- and small-sized equipment had dramatically increased. This was primarily due to the increasing number of equipment makers offering quality products. As the reliability of products from different equipment makers converged, brand loyalty decreased, especially for smaller projects, where each purchase could result in a reevaluation of the alternative sources of new equipment. New equipment also had to compete with longer-lasting used machinery that often sold at a 30 to 60 percent price discount. However, overall prices were expected to rise as equipment demand in developing countries outpaced the supply of used equipment coming from developed nations. The demand for new equipment was also likely to be affected positively as new credit, leasing, and renting options became available in the emerging world.

Equipment makers were constantly working on improving the quality of their products as a means of differentiation from both competitors and old machines. Onboard electronics provided continuous monitoring, thus optimizing performance and reducing repair costs. Features to enhance operator efficiency and comfort had also been added. These new features offered such benefits as improved maneuverability, quieter machines, reduced vibrations, and automatic transmissions.

CATERPILLAR: AN ENDURING LEADER

Caterpillar Incorporated, headquartered in Peoria, Illinois, had been the heavy construction industry leader since the mid 1920s. Its three main lines of business (machinery, engines, and financial products) all contributed to its $18.9 billion in sales for 1997 (see Table 3 for additional financial data). Caterpillar designed, manufactured, and marketed equipment for construction, earthmoving, mining, and agriculture. It was also a major manufacturer of forklifts, container handlers, and warehouse equipment. Cat engines were used to power on-highway trucks, ships and boats, locomotives, and other construction, mining, and agricultural equipment. Other power generating systems manufactured by Cat were commonly utilized as prime or standby sources of power for applications that ranged from off-shore drilling rigs to emergency power for factories and airports. Caterpillar's financial products complemented its manufacturing operations by offering a wide variety of financing options and insurance, both for its customers and for its worldwide network of distributors and dealers. (See Table 4 for data on the size and margins of the different business segments.)

Caterpillar, under the Caterpillar, Cat, Barber-Green, and Mak brand names, sold $18.1 billion worth of machinery and engines in 1997. Its full line of earthmovers included tractors, loaders, excavators, trucks, scrapers, paving products, motor graders, mining shovels, pipelayers, log skidders, log loaders, and related parts. As shown in Table 4, Cat's end users ranged from the energy industry and commercial and industrial construction to mining and transportation applications.

Engines and turbines provided Caterpillar with additional revenue growth that, in 1997, accounted for a quarter of Cat's net revenues. Additionally, the

TABLE 3

Caterpillar: Financial Highlights (millions of dollars unless indicated otherwise)

	1982	1983	1984	1985	1986	1987
(Year ended December 31)						
Sales and revenues	6,472	5,429	6,597	6,760	7,380	8,294
Sales of machinery and engines	6,469	5,424	6,576	6,725	7,321	8,180
Percent inside the United States	43%	54%	58%	58%	54%	52%
Percent outside the United States	57%	46%	42%	42%	46%	48%
Revenues of financial products	3	5	21	35	59	114
Profit (loss)	(180)	(345)	(428)	198	76	350
As a percent of sales and revenues	(2.8%)	(6.4%)	(6.5%)	2.9%	1.0%	4.2%
Profit (loss) per share of common stock	(2.04)	(3.74)	(4.47)	2.02	0.39	1.76
Dividends declared per share of common stock	2.40	1.50	1.25	0.50	0.31	0.28
Return on average common stock equity	(4.9%)	(10.1%)	(13.8%)	6.7%	2.4%	10.4%
Capital expenditures:						
Land, buildings, machinery and equipment	532	313	234	228	290	463
Equipment leased to others	3	14	23	55	41	30
Depreciation and amortization	505	507	497	485	453	425
Research and engineering expenses	376	340	345	326	308	298
As a percent of sales and revenues	5.8%	6.3%	5.2%	4.8%	4.2%	3.6%
Provision (credit) for income taxes	(303)	(264)	(115)	25	21	118
Wages, salaries, and employee benefits	2,474	2,142	2,426	2,173	2,184	2,284
Average number of employees	73,249	58,402	61,189	55,815	54,024	53,770
December 31						
Total receivables:						
Trade and other	965	1,451	1,133	1,296	1,755	2,044
Finance	64	74	66	117	466	795
Inventories	1,801	1,193	1,246	1,139	1,211	1,323
Total assets:						
Machinery and engines	7,153	6,849	6,084	5,951	6,134	6,647
Financial products	68	96	169	235	627	984
Long-term debt:						
Machinery and engines	2,389	1,894	1,384	1,177	963	900
Financial products	——	5	4	87	171	387
Total debt:						
Machinery and engines	2,612	2,247	1,861	1,404	1,582	1,484
Financial products	1	7	26	130	370	712
Ratios, excluding financial products						
Current assets to current liabilities	2.81	2.07	1.43	1.69	1.50	1.55
Percentage of total debt to total debt and stockholders' equity	42.8%	40.2%	39.5%	31.4%	33.4%	29.4%

Source: Caterpillar, Inc., Annual Reports.

machinery business benefited from advances in the power generation business, for Cat was seen as being in the forefront in efficiency and power in the engines and turbine businesses.

Caterpillar employed 59,860 people in manufacturing facilities around the world and in its nu-merous distribution centers. (See Table 5 for a list of manufacturing plant locations and employees.) Historically, one of Caterpillar's competitive advantages had been its strong international focus, which had contributed, over the last decade, to approximately 50 percent of total sales. Recent sales trends

1988	1989	1990	1991	1992	1993	1994	1995	1996	1997
10,435	11,126	11,436	10,182	10,194	11,615	14,238	16,072	16,522	18,925
10,255	10,882	11,103	9,838	9,840	11,235	13,863	15,451	15,814	18,110
50%	47%	45%	41%	45%	51%	51%	48%	49%	49%
50%	53%	55%	59%	55%	49%	49%	52%	51%	51%
180	244	333	344	354	380	465	621	708	815
616	497	210	(404)	(2,435)	652	955	1,136	1,361	1,665
5.9%	4.5%	1.8%	(4.0%)	(23.9%)	5.6%	6.7%	7.1%	8.2%	8.8%
3.04	2.45	1.04	(2.00)	(12.06)	3.21	4.70	5.72	7.07	4.44
0.43	0.60	0.60	0.53	0.30	0.30	0.63	1.30	1.55	4.37
16.0%	11.6%	4.7%	(9.4%)	(86.7%)	34.6%	37.4%	36.1%	36.3%	37.9%
732	984	926	653	515	417	501	464	506	824
61	105	113	121	125	215	193	215	265	282
434	471	533	602	654	668	683	682	696	738
334	387	420	441	446	455	435	532	570	700
3.2%	3.5%	3.7%	4.3%	4.4%	3.9%	3.0%	3.3%	3.4%	3.7%
262	162	78	(152)	(114)	42	354	501	613	796
2,643	2,888	3,032	3,051	2,795	3,038	3,146	2,919	3,437	3,773
57,954	60,784	59,662	55,950	52,340	50,443	52,778	54,263	54,968	58,366
2,349	2,353	2,361	2,133	2,330	2,769	3,096	2,657	3,084	3,465
1,222	1,498	1,891	2,145	2,525	3,140	3,988	4,820	5,646	6,541
1,986	2,120	2,105	1,921	1,675	1,525	1,835	1,921	2,222	2,603
8,226	9,100	9,626	9,346	10,979	11,131	11,582	11,238	12,156	13,001
1,460	1,826	2,325	2,696	2,956	3,676	4,668	5,592	6,572	7,755
1,428	1,797	2,101	2,676	2,753	2,030	1,934	2,049	2,018	2,367
525	491	789	1,216	1,366	1,865	2,336	1,915	2,514	4,575
2,116	2,561	2,873	3,136	3,271	2,387	2,037	2,219	2,176	2,474
1,144	1,433	1,848	2,111	2,401	3,041	3,866	4,181	5,283	4,575
1.76	1.78	1.67	1.74	1.57	1.53	1.62	1.78	1.68	1.62
34.0%	36.4%	38.8%	43.7%	67.5%	52.1%	41.2%	39.6%	34.6%	34.6%

(see Table 6) illustrated the relative growth of emerging regions of the world such as Asia-Pacific and Latin America, and a slowdown of business in Europe.

An extensive dealer network had led the company into its leadership position. The network of close to 200 dealers, 137 of which were located outside the United States, was unmatched by any other equipment maker. This allowed Cat to remain the market leader in every country in which it does business, with the exception of Japan. Cat's rival Komatsu led the industry in Japan.

TABLE 4

Caterpillar: Sales and Profit Composition by Segment (millions of U.S. $ unless indicated otherwise)

	1982	*1983*	*1984*	*1985*	*1986*	*1987*
Sales by Segment						
Machinery	4,795	4,211	5,053	5,208	5,761	6,529
Engines	1,674	1,213	1,523	1,517	1,560	1,651
Financial products	—	—	—	—	—	—
Total sales and revenues	6,469	5,424	6,576	6,725	7,321	8,810
Operating Profit by Segment						
Machinery	(78)	(29)	(52)	376	281	588
Engines	85	(64)	(74)	68	97	155
Financial products	—	—	—	—	—	—
Total operating profit	7	(93)	(126)	444	378	743
Profit Margin by Segment						
Machinery	(1.6%)	(0.7%)	(1.0%)	7.2%	4.9%	9.0%
Engines	5.1%	(5.3%)	(4.9%)	4.5%	6.2%	9.4%
Financial products	n.a.	n.a.	n.a.	n.a.	n.a.	n.a.
Weighted profit margin	0.1%	(1.7%)	(1.9%)	6.6%	5.2%	9.1%
New Machine Sales by End User						
Energy	22%	19%	20%	21%	18%	15%
Transportation	30%	28%	26%	29%	31%	27%
Housing and forest	17%	20%	22%	12%	13%	15%
Commercial and industrial construction	0%	0%	0%	9%	10%	13%
Mining	9%	11%	10%	10%	11%	11%
Food and water	6%	6%	6%	4%	4%	4%
Other	16%	16%	16%	15%	13%	15%

Source: Caterpillar, Inc., Annual Reports.

Profits for 1997 were at an all-time high, with a net profit margin of 8.8 percent. Years of investments in automation and cost reduction were instrumental in achieving these results. Cat's stock price reflected these financial results, showing an increase of nearly 300 percent from December 1992 to December 1997. But management was worried that changing consumer trends, labor disputes, and the increasing power of competitors might collectively serve to undermine the firm's achievements.

The Origins

Now the largest manufacturer of construction equipment in the world, Caterpillar was formed by the merger of Holt Manufacturing and C. L. Best Tractor companies in 1925. By the 1940s, Caterpillar had a product line that included track-type tractors, motor graders, blade graders, elevated graders, and terracers. Sales began to climb during World War II when track-type tractors were demanded by the Allies for pulling artillery and supply wagons through tough terrain. World War II also brought with it greater demand for construction equipment, resulting in a large number of pieces of Caterpillar equipment being dispersed throughout the world. Caterpillar quickly came to dominate the marketplace, commanding 50 percent of the earthmoving equipment market.

The 1980s

After a boom period in the 1970s, the world recession of the early 1980s severely affected Caterpillar's bottom line. The effects of the strong dollar

1988	1989	1990	1991	1992	1993	1994	1995	1996	1997
8,206	8,478	8,735	7,397	7,209	8,132	10,164	11,336	11,862	13,350
2,049	2,404	2,368	2,441	2,631	3,103	3,699	4,115	3,952	4,760
180	244	344	344	354	380	465	621	708	815
10,435	11,126	11,447	10,182	10,194	11,615	14,328	16,072	16,522	18,925
932	733	273	(281)	(107)	436	1,099	1,210	1,562	1,889
243	235	84	(10)	79	226	348	462	395	497
15	27	37	37	35	47	64	88	114	142
1,190	995	394	(254)	7	709	1,511	1,760	2,071	2,528
11.4%	8.6%	3.1%	(3.8%)	(1.5%)	5.4%	10.8%	10.7%	13.2%	14.1%
11.9%	9.8%	3.5%	(0.4%)	3.0%	7.3%	9.4%	11.2%	10.0%	10.4%
8.3%	11.1%	10.8%	10.8%	9.9%	12.4%	13.8%	14.2%	16.1%	17.4%
11.4%	8.9%	3.4%	(2.5%)	0.1%	6.1%	10.5%	11.0%	12.5%	13.4%
15%	16%	18%	20%	22%	19%	22%	12%	14%	13%
25%	25%	24%	25%	27%	28%	28%	23%	22%	24%
16%	15%	15%	14%	13%	15%	15%	15%	15%	15%
13%	11%	10%	9%	8%	9%	7%	12%	15%	15%
13%	13%	13%	13%	13%	12%	12%	20%	18%	17%
4%	4%	4%	5%	5%	5%	4%	6%	6%	6%
14%	16%	16%	14%	12%	12%	12%	12%	10%	10%

and depressed worldwide demand began to surface in 1982, when sales figures fell 29 percent compared with the previous year. The company registered a $180 million loss that same year, the second since its incorporation in 1925. (Caterpillar had registered a loss of $1.6 million in 1932.)

Caterpillar tried to alleviate the pressure on its cost structure by laying off 13,000 of its 47,000 U.S. hourly workers. Salaries for top management and other employees were cut by 10 percent and a range of 3 to 9 percent, respectively, affecting 13,800 employees. Additionally, salaries of 9,600 secretaries and technicians were frozen indefinitely. Capital expenditures were trimmed by 36 percent from the previous year's investment of $836 million. Debt soared to $2.6 billion, compared with $1.8 billion in 1981.

The United Auto Workers, representing about 13,000 employees in Caterpillar's U.S. plants, went out on strike in the second half of 1982 after talks broke down over new contract negotiations. The UAW asked for a continuation of the previous contract, while Caterpillar demanded wage freezes and a reduction in the cost-of-living adjustments (COLA) in light of the tough times. The strong dollar had produced huge wage differentials between Caterpillar and Japanese rival Komatsu, whose workers earned roughly half the pay of Cat's workers when expressed in dollar terms.

The strike ended in April 1983, after seven months of talks. Because Caterpillar had anticipated the strike and had expanded inventory levels, it was able to weather the long strike, although by April inventory levels were almost completely

TABLE 5

Caterpillar: Plant Locations and Employees

Plant Locations					
Inside the United States			**Outside the United States**		

Manufacturing

California	Peoria	*North Carolina*	*Australia*	Peterlee	*Italy*
Gardena	Pontiac	Clayton	Burnie*	Skinningrove	Bazzano
San Diego	Sterling	Franklin	Cowell*	Stockton	Jesi
Florida	*Indiana*	Leland	Melbourne	Wolverhampton	Milan*
Jacksonville	Lafayette	Morganton	Perth	*France*	*Japan*
Georgia	*Kansas*	Sanford	*Belgium*	Grenoble	Akashi*
Jefferson	Wamego	*Oregon*	Gosselies	Rantigny	Sagamihara*
LaGrange	*Kentucky*	Dallas	*Brazil*	*Germany*	*Mexico*
Illinois	Danville	*Pennsylvania*	Piracicaba	Kiel	Monterrey
Aurora	*Michigan*	York	*Canada*	Wackersdorf	Tijuana
Champaign*	Menominee	*South Carolina*	Montreal	Zweibrucken	*Northern Ireland*
Decatur	*Minnesota*	Greenville	*China*	*Hungary*	Larne*
DeKalb	Minneapolis	Sumter	Guangzhuo*	Godollo**	*Poland*
Dixon	New Ulm	*Tennessee*	ErLiBan*	*India*	Janow Lubelski**
East Peoria	*Mississippi*	Dyersburg	Tianjin**	Bangalore*	*Russia*
Joliet	Oxford	Rockwood	Xuzhou**	Mumbai*	St. Petersburg
Mapleton	*Missouri*	*Texas*	*England*	*Indonesia*	*Sweden*
Mossville	Boonville	Houston	Leicester	Jakarta**	Soderhamn

Remanufacturing and Overhaul

Mississippi			*Australia*	*Indonesia*
Corinth			Melbourne	Bandung
Prentiss County			*Belgium*	*Malaysia*
Texas			Gosselies	Kuala Lumpur
De Soto			*Canada*	*Mexico*
Mabank			Edmonton	Nuevo Laredo

Full-Time Employees at Year-End						
	1992	*1993*	*1994*	*1995*	*1996*	*1997*
Inside the United States	37,311	38,103	39,749	39,978	38,571	39,722
Europe	8,011	7,999	8,146	8,413	11,953	12,627
Latin America	4,088	3,735	4,500	4,104	4,540	5,340
Asia-Pacific	1,155	1,235	1,383	1,630	1,746	1,843
Canada	97	91	117	121	127	219
Other	87	87	91	106	89	112
Outside the United States	13,438	13,147	14,237	14,374	18,455	20,141
Total	50,749	51,250	53,986	54,352	57,026	59,863

*Facility of affiliated company (50% or less owned).
**Facility of partially-owned subsidiary (greater than 50%, less than 100%).
Source: Caterpillar, Inc., Annual Reports and Form 10-K, 1997.

TABLE 6

Caterpillar: Sales Composition by Region (millions of dollars unless otherwise stated)

	1988	1989	1990	1991	1992	1993	1994	1995	1996	1997
Sales by Region										
United States	5,077	5,132	5,023	4,058	4,421	5,710	7,008	7,422	7,676	8,926
Asia-Pacific	1,113	1,472	1,595	1,411	1,309	1,612	1,964	2,290	2,560	2,474
Europe	1,875	1,939	2,049	1,780	1,785	1,578	2,078	2,686	2,366	2,619
Latin America	729	829	842	873	908	849	1,151	1,183	1,238	1,702
Africa and Middle East	720	732	922	1,148	892	802	753	914	1,151	1,183
Canada	741	778	672	568	525	684	909	956	823	1,206
Total Sales	10,255	10,882	11,103	9,838	9,840	11,235	13,863	15,451	15,814	18,110
Exports from the United States										
Asia-Pacific	781	1,002	1,130	1,023	948	1,191	1,359	1,527	1,753	1,693
Europe	684	693	833	739	698	745	973	1,176	1,240	1,331
Latin America	420	447	484	659	666	605	852	927	993	1,288
Africa and Middle East	439	488	630	781	606	577	522	644	767	757
Canada	606	661	608	503	416	625	806	852	748	1,049
Total Exports	2,930	3,291	3,685	3,705	3,334	3,743	4,512	5,126	5,501	6,118
Imports as Percent of Sales										
Asia-Pacific	70.2%	68.1%	70.8%	72.5%	72.4%	73.9%	69.2%	66.7%	68.5%	68.4%
Europe	36.5%	35.7%	40.7%	41.5%	39.1%	47.2%	46.8%	43.8%	52.4%	50.8%
Latin America	57.6%	53.9%	57.5%	75.5%	73.3%	71.3%	74.0%	78.4%	80.2%	75.7%
Africa and Middle East	61.0%	66.7%	68.3%	68.0%	67.9%	71.9%	69.3%	70.5%	66.6%	64.0%
Canada	81.8%	85.0%	90.5%	88.6%	79.2%	91.4%	88.7%	89.1%	90.9%	87.0%
U.S. Exports as Percent of Sales Abroad	56.6%	57.2%	60.6%	64.1%	61.5%	67.7%	65.8%	63.8%	67.6%	66.6%

					Growth Rates					
	1989	1990	1991	1992	1993	1994	1995	1996	1997	Comp. Annual
Sales by Region										
United States	1.1%	(2.1%)	(19.2%)	8.9%	29.2%	22.7%	5.9%	3.4%	16.3%	6.5%
Asia-Pacific	32.3%	8.4%	(11.5%)	(7.2%)	23.1%	21.8%	16.6%	11.8%	(3.4%)	9.3%
Europe	3.4%	5.7%	(13.1%)	0.3%	(11.6%)	31.7%	29.3%	(11.9%)	10.7%	3.8%
Latin America	13.7%	1.6%	3.7%	4.0%	(6.5%)	35.6%	2.8%	4.6%	37.5%	9.9%
Africa and Middle East	1.7%	26.0%	24.5%	(22.3%)	(10.1%)	(6.1%)	21.4%	25.9%	2.8%	5.7%
Canada	5.0%	(13.6%)	(15.5%)	(7.6%)	30.3%	32.9%	5.2%	(13.9%)	46.5%	5.6%
Total sales	6.1%	2.0%	(11.4%)	0.0%	14.2%	23.4%	11.5%	2.3%	14.5%	6.5%
Exports from the United States										
Asia-Pacific	28.3%	12.8%	(9.5%)	(7.3%)	25.6%	14.1%	12.4%	14.8%	(3.4%)	9.0%
Europe	1.3%	20.2%	(11.3%)	(5.5%)	6.7%	30.6%	20.9%	5.4%	7.3%	7.7%
Latin America	6.4%	8.3%	36.2%	1.1%	(9.2%)	40.8%	8.8%	7.1%	29.7%	13.3%
Africa and Middle East	11.2%	29.1%	24.0%	(22.4%)	(4.8%)	(9.5%)	23.4%	19.1%	(1.3%)	6.2%
Canada	9.1%	(8.0%)	(17.3%)	(17.3%)	50.2%	29.0%	5.7%	(12.2%)	40.2%	6.3%
Total exports	12.3%	12.0%	0.5%	(10.0%)	12.3%	20.5%	13.6%	7.3%	11.2%	8.5%

Source: Caterpillar, Inc., Annual Reports.

depleted. The parties agreed to wage freezes and reduction of bonus pay, maintaining COLA payments and pension and medical benefits. This lengthy strike was only the beginning of years plagued by disputes with the UAW.

In 1984, the U.S. market started to show signs of recovery, but demand abroad remained sluggish. Soft oil and gas prices severely affected petroleum-dependent emerging economies, hindering their infrastructure growth. Given its cash-strapped customers, Caterpillar set out to barter machinery for other products. Dealers in those regions were battling to keep inventory levels at an appropriate level. That same year, Cat created its financial products division in order to help these dealers and to provide financing for the equipment end buyers.

Miscalculating the length and effect of the world recession, Caterpillar, in 1984, found that it had 75 percent more capacity than in 1973, but only 25 percent more production. The strong dollar eroded overseas earnings and enabled foreign competitors, such as Komatsu and Italy's Fiatallis Europe, to wage a price war in the United States. At that time, PaineWebber estimated that each percentage-point fall in the yen-dollar exchange rate would result in a $0.10 reduction in Cat's earnings per share. In only eight months, from March to November 1984, the stock price fell from $52 to $31.

Caterpillar's CEO, George Schaefer, was clearly worried about Cat's condition. He outlined a series of initiatives designed to bring the company out of the hole. Caterpillar was to cut annual costs by 22 percent, or $2 billion, by the end of 1986. The plans included the shutting down of six plants and a job cut of 4 percent, on top of a 15 percent reduction since 1982. Schaefer also called for reducing the number of suppliers and seeking low-cost overseas sources. Capital expenditures were to be shaved an additional 26 percent, to $260 million. The company was to move away from competing in the area of advanced, large-sized machines sold at premium prices and pursue instead the often rejected smaller customers that demanded smaller, lower-priced earthmovers. That same year, Caterpillar signed an agreement with CMI Corp. in the United States and Franz Eder Maschinenfabrik in Germany to build small equipment to complement Cat's product line. Additionally, Caterpillar set out to develop new products to compete in the farm equipment market, a highly competitive, slow-growing industry led by Deere & Co.

At the same time, Cat's rival Komatsu was worried about possible U.S. protectionism and exchange rate swings. It responded by building its first U.S. assembly plant, Komatsu America Manufacturing Corp. Komatsu's weakest link in America was its distribution system. Komatsu, in the mid 1980s, garnered only 5 percent of the U.S. market, far behind Cat's leading position.

By 1985, Schaefer's plans were well under way. Caterpillar reached its cost-cutting goals one year ahead of schedule. It also reduced its work force and developed foreign sourcing agreements. Debt was trimmed to $1 billion, from $2.6 billion in 1982. Moreover, after three straight years of losses, the company regained its profitability.

Caterpillar developed a new backhoe loader and grouped it under the Century Line, targeting the same equipment market. This new product, built in a small lift-truck plant in Leicester, England, became an almost instant success after its 1985 introduction. Original sales were well above internally derived projections.

However promising the new line of products appeared, Cat was to directly compete with Case, which at the time held 50 percent of the backhoe loader market in the United States and had twice the number of sales outlets. Furthermore, this was a very price-sensitive market and offered substantially lower margins. Komatsu also jumped on the bandwagon and signed an agreement with Clark Equipment to market its line of mini-excavators under the Bobcat trademark.

Meanwhile, Caterpillar's sales to Asia were growing rapidly, accounting for one-tenth of total machinery sales in 1987. The Japanese market, however, was difficult to crack due to the strong position of Komatsu. Cat, nonetheless, announced an expansion of its joint venture with Mitsubishi Heavy Industries Ltd. Under the amended terms of the agreement, the Cat-Mitsubishi JV would make excavator equipment for Japan, as well as light construction equipment for the United States, and a broad line of products for the entire Pacific Rim.

Caterpillar continued to cut costs aggressively. By 1987, the work force had already been trimmed to 60 percent of the 1982 level, and nine manufacturing facilities had been closed. At the same time, Cat's product line had more than doubled from 150 products in 1984 and had grabbed 11 percent of the backhoe loader market. Cat products were still selling, however, at a 10 to 15 percent price premium over competitors. The recovering yen also benefited Caterpillar's position, as Komatsu was forced to increase prices in U.S. dollar terms. By 1988, Komatsu's dollar prices were 20 percent higher than in 1981, compared with Caterpillar's increase of only 9.5 percent during the same period.

In February 1988, Komatsu announced a 50/50 joint venture with Dresser Industries. The companies were to combine their construction equipment manufacturing and engineering facilities in the Americas. The joint venture appeared to be a sound opportunity for both Komatsu and Dresser. Komatsu could avoid building up facilities from scratch, while Dresser could utilize some of its 50 percent idle manufacturing capacity. Komatsu also acquired a 25 percent stake in Hanomag AG of Germany. At that time, Hanomag had a 30 percent share of market in Europe. This was to greatly benefit Komatsu's position in Europe.

Fearful of future exchange rate difficulties and impelled by Komatsu's success in automation of manufacturing facilities in Japan, Cat's CEO, Schaefer, announced an ambitious modernization program that would affect the majority of its thirty factories around the world. The new project, dubbed "Plant with a Future" (PWAF),[3] called for an investment of $1.8 billion and was to be completed by 1992.

Despite an overall success with the cost-cutting measures, Schaefer was still worried about Cat's future in this highly cyclical industry. Caterpillar's boom came after World War II, when its equipment was used to help rebuild Europe, roll out the United States interstate highway system, and build giant dams in the Third World. In the 1970s, rising oil prices sparked demand for Cat's oil field equipment and launched numerous massive construction projects in oil-rich economies. But in the 1980s, high interest rates and cheap oil prices had slowed the construction industry; housing development in the United States was stagnant; and construction and repair of the highway system was crimped by government budget cuts. In light of all this, Schaefer formed a committee of eight executives to study Caterpillar's position and consider diversification options.

CHANGING RULES OF THE GAME

Plant with a Future (PWAF)

Between 1982 and 1985, Caterpillar accumulated losses of almost $1 billion. Six plants were closed and employment was cut severely—44 percent among hourly workers and 26 percent among salaried staff. Komatsu enjoyed lower labor costs because of the weaker yen. It had also engaged in an automation effort that further enhanced its competitive position.

The industry was expected to continue to suffer from excess capacity, making it imperative for Cat to have the ability to face Komatsu head-on. Furthermore, Cat's product line expansions toward the growing, low-margin, smaller-machine segment placed even heavier financial pressure on its manufacturing facilities.

In 1986, Schaefer launched a daring, factorywide plant modernization program termed "Plant with a Future," or "PWAF."[3] Initial forecasts estimated capital expenditures of $1 billion, which were later revised to $1.8 billion, spread between 1986 and 1992. The objective was to shift from traditional mass manufacturing to forms of advanced, flexible production through the use of just-in-time inventory techniques and sophisticated factory automation, resulting in estimated savings on manufacturing costs of 20 percent by late 1992. That would mean about $1.5 billion a year in savings. The long-standing "functional" arrangement of people and machines on the factory floor was to be dismantled. Instead, all manufacturing work was to be arranged in product and subproduct dedicated "cells," or modules.

As expressed by Pierre Guerindon, manufacturing executive vice president, in a meeting with stock analysts in 1988, "There are four basic elements of PWAF. First, we *consolidate* manufacturing space worldwide. Then we *simplify* product designs, manufacturing processes, and operating procedures. At the same time, we *automate* many machining and materials handling processes. And finally, we *integrate* the engineering, logistics, and shop floor functions into one single information system."[4] However, computer integration would be a long-term goal designed to gain an advantage over competitors. The benefits of cost reduction and customer responsiveness were to be realized within the earlier phases.

Donald V. Fites

Donald V. Fites, born on a farm in Tippecanoe, Indiana, was appointed CEO in 1990, succeeding Schaefer. His career at Caterpillar dated back to 1956. Straight out of Indiana's Valparaiso University, Don Fites started in Caterpillar as a district sales representative in South Africa, where he met and married his wife. He was later transferred to Germany and again to Switzerland. Fites returned to the United States in 1970 and was sent to MIT for a graduate degree in management. His thesis topic, "Japan Inc.: Can U.S. Industry Compete," reflected his fascination with Japan's industrial success. This, in turn, earned him a job as marketing director of Caterpillar's construction equipment joint venture with Mitsubishi in Tokyo, where he spent four and a half years.[5]

Fites's overseas experiences were a strong influence for the rest of his career. According to Fites, his first job as a sales representative taught him how stifling a large bureaucracy can be. He was impressed by the way unionized workers in Japan would sacrifice their interests for those of the company. He also admired the way Japanese companies rotated their managers through manufacturing, engineering, and sales to create better-rounded leaders.

Upon his return to Peoria in 1975, Fites applied Japanese-style management to Caterpillar's product development process by creating cross-functional teams including marketing, design, and manufacturing people. Results were impressive as development time was cut in half.

Recalling his frustrating experience with the central office when he worked overseas, Fites continued his reforms with Cat's worldwide marketing structure. After becoming executive vice president in 1985, he put more marketing staffers into the field and turned the authority for market-sensitive decisions, such as pricing, over to district offices. Additionally, he eliminated 100 management jobs that he considered to be redundant.

When he was elected CEO in 1990, Fites launched a three-point campaign. This campaign called for: decentralizing Caterpillar's top-down organizational structure and empowering lower management; setting clear return-on-assets targets, tied to incentive compensation plans; and trying to avoid massive layoffs. This ambitious program created tension within the ranks, but Fites was driven by the idea that "if you're not competitive everywhere, you're not competitive anywhere."[6]

In an effort to slash Cat's $2.2 billion in annual overhead costs, Fites reorganized the company into thirteen functionally independent profit centers and four service divisions (now seventeen and five), each of which would have its own budget and a before-tax return-on-assets target of 15 percent. Service operations and component supply segments would compete at market prices. Results were very favorable. In only four years, time to market of products was cut in half, to less than three years. Manufacturing process time for parts was cut from twenty-five days to six between 1987 and 1993. No official layoffs were announced during this time period. Caterpillar was able to make a profit in 1993 after two years of negative earnings.

But the true challenge for Fites appeared to be with the United Auto Workers.

United Auto Workers: Troubles Continue

By the early 1990s, Caterpillar had greatly improved its manufacturing processes, realigned its organizational structure, and was regaining market share lost in the 1980s to Komatsu. An important issue, however, remained unresolved. High labor costs and the relative lack of flexibility of union workers positioned Cat at a disadvantage relative to Japan's Komatsu. Cat's wages and benefits for an average hourly worker in 1991 of $31.74 were roughly the same as Komatsu's due to the weakening of the dollar. Fites, however, was worried that exchange rate fluctuations could quickly alter this (see Table 7). Almost 60 percent of Cat's sales of machinery and engines came from abroad in 1991. And 64 percent of those sales were exported from the United States.

With the UAW contract expiring on September 30, 1991, Fites pushed for a cut in health care costs. Cat's health care costs, including expenses for retirees, ran at about $9,000 per active employee per year. Health care costs had risen 14 percent the previous year and were expected to jump 75 percent by 1994 if the current contract was maintained. Fites also wanted to create a two-tier system, where new hires were locked into a lower pay scale. Furthermore, he wanted to eliminate companywide contract negotiations, allowing each profit center to use whatever work arrangements were best for its particular needs.

Caterpillar's contract negotiation problems stemmed from the fact that it wanted to tailor contracts for the company, while the UAW demanded a contract similar to those negotiated with the American automakers. Cat's position was further affected after Deere & Co. accepted the UAW's package later that same year—a package that included an immediate 3 percent wage hike, continued COLA adjustments, and improved health care benefits. But Fites,

TABLE 7

Yen/Dollar Exchange Rates, December 31

1971	1972	1973	1974	1975	1976	1977	1978	1979	1980
320	301	280	300	306	295	241	196	240	209
1981	1982	1983	1984	1985	1986	1987	1988	1989	1990
219	242	234	248	203	162	128	124	143	134
1991	1992	1993	1994	1995	1996	1997			
128	124	110	100	102	114	130			

Source: Federal Reserve Bank of St. Louis.

expecting a strike, had built up enough inventory to survive a six-month stretch. In November 1991, the UAW placed 2,400 members on strike in hopes of pressuring Cat. Cat retaliated by locking out 6,000 more workers and laying off 500.

Caterpillar's average worker at the time was forty-six years old, and more than 60 percent of the workers would be eligible for retirement within six years. The UAW appeared to be afraid that Cat would shrink its work force through retirement and, perhaps, fill some vacant positions with nonunion workers.

After enduring a five-month strike, Cat's management announced on April 1, 1992, that striking workers had to return to work by April 6 or risk losing their jobs to (permanent) replacement workers. Cat's human resources department estimated that it could interview no more than several hundred applicants per week and that it would take about two months to train new hires. So far throughout the strike, about 5,000 managers and office employees had replaced the striking workers in Cat's U.S.-based manufacturing facilities.

Eight days after the April 6 deadline, the UAW sent the strikers back to work. It did not, however, agree to sign the contract on Cat's terms. The union appeared to be worried that workers would cross picket lines once the new replacement workers arrived. It wasn't certain that the UAW workers would risk their $47,000-a-year jobs for $100-a-week strike pay. Cat's offer included a wage in-crease limited to 13 percent over the life of the contract, as opposed to the 26 percent demanded by the UAW. This would save the company some $150 million over the life of the new contract, a figure that would merely compensate for the costs resulting from the five-and-a-half-month strike.

Workers stayed on the job without a contract for the next two years, only to walk out again on June 21, 1994. Over the two intervening years, Cat experienced several local walkouts after disciplining and firing workers for wearing T-shirts that disparaged the company, some with the slogan "Permanently Replace Fites." These continuing, low-level labor problems resulted in the National Labor Relations Board filing some 140 complaints against Cat, the largest number of complaints that had ever been issued to any one company.

For Caterpillar's management, the most important issue appeared to be its desire to avoid signing an agreement that would contain elements similar to the UAW's contracts with the American automobile manufacturers and other construction and agricultural equipment makers, such as Deere & Co. Fites argued that Caterpillar was different from both the auto companies and from Deere, which derived almost 70 percent of its revenue from sales in the United States and did not compete directly with strong Japanese equipment makers such as Komatsu. Cat's management also found it to be unacceptable that it could not make outsourcing decisions without consulting the union, which demanded that the number of jobs be guaranteed. Furthermore, Cat's UAW workers were paid an average of $19.60 per hour, plus overtime, compared with the national average manufacturing wage of $12.73 per hour.

Fites saw the union demands as constraining the company's ability to stay competitive and keep from collapsing in the next economic downturn. "What it is," said Fites, "is not so much a battle about economics as it is a battle of who's going to run the company. It's worth it. You know what you're doing is right for the company. What scares me is not being competitive in today's world."[7]

The UAW members returned to work in December 1995, after an eighteen-month strike. However, they refused to ratify Caterpillar's contract. It was a clear victory for the company. Thanks to Fites's organizational skills, the use of temporary workers, and the one-third of the Cat UAW workers that had crossed the UAW picket lines, Cat sales increased 23 percent in 1994 and 11 percent in 1995 despite the ongoing strike. Earnings rose 46 percent and 19 percent in the same time period.

After almost six and a half years without a contract, the UAW ratified a new six-year agreement with Caterpillar in March 1998, effective through April 1, 2004, covering approximately 12,000 Cat employees. In this new specially tailored contract, Caterpillar agreed to an immediate wage increase ranging from 2 to 4 percent depending on the worker's experience level. The agreement also provided for three lump-sum payments of 3 percent of earnings in 1999, 2001, and 2003. The cost-of-living allowance (COLA) was to be maintained for all workers, except for entry-level employees. Pensions were also revised to $38.50 per month per year of certified service. Decisions on where to source components and products remained solely with the company, and there was no set level of guaranteed employment.

Dealer Network

Caterpillar's management believed that it had enjoyed the benefits of engineering excellence, manufacturing efficiency, and quality products. But according to Fites, "the biggest reason for Caterpillar's success has been our system of distribution and product support and the close customer relationships it fosters."[8] With a backbone of 197 worldwide dealers, 132 of them outside the United States, Caterpillar had been able to maintain a close relationship with its customers and gain market insight and feedback on its products and services. Together, the 197 dealers owned 1,217 branch stores and employed about 79,900 people, or almost 20,000 more than Cat. The average dealer had annual revenues of $150 million. The combined net worth of the dealer network was about $5.68 billion in 1997.

Despite its overall good quality and reliability, construction equipment eventually wears out. Earthmovers have an operating life of up to thirty years. However, the equipment will most likely need to be repaired several times throughout its life, as a result of the tough operating environment and the regular wear and tear on its components. Caterpillar's manufacturing and distribution systems were designed so that any part, anywhere in the world, could be replaced in a maximum of forty-eight hours. Eighty percent of the time, however, parts were provided immediately from dealers' inventory.

Over the past decade, Caterpillar had also invested in an ambitious project to maximize equipment uptime and minimize customers' cost of service and repairs through the use of information technology. The system uses onboard sensors on each of Caterpillar's machines around the world that will automatically send an electronic alert to the local dealer's technicians when a problem is identified. The technician will connect to the Caterpillar machine via a laptop computer and use diagnostic software to identify the problem, without having to visit the customer and spend hours examining the machine. Once the problem is diagnosed and the needed parts are identified, a parts request will be generated through the system and an automatic search sequence based on proximity (starting with the dealer's inventory and the dealer's branch stores, and searching through Caterpillar's worldwide inventory, if necessary) will be triggered. This order will go into the system of factories or warehouses that can supply the parts, activating the printing of an order ticket and automatically setting into motion an automated crane that retrieves the parts from the storage rack. The parts will be immediately shipped to the dealer's pickup site (99.7 percent of the parts ordered from Caterpillar or the dealer were already being shipped the same business day).

By early 1998, most of the system was already in place: the onboard sensors; computers that diagnose problems and instruct on repairs; and the information system that links together Caterpillar's factories, distribution centers, and most of the 197 dealers. The two pieces still missing were the remote monitoring system and the worldwide sharing of inventories by Caterpillar and its dealers and suppliers. The company expected to spend about $250 million in completing the system. It hoped, however, to reduce both customer downtime and Cat's $2 billion parts inventory.

The extensive dealer network also provided Caterpillar with timely market intelligence and data about its products. Information about changing trends of the overall construction industry and of product use could be gathered through extensive communication with the dealer network. Dealers were also actively involved in programs of product quality and cost reduction with design engineers from Cat. This process was developed to more promptly respond to problems encountered by customers, making adjustments in the design and specifications of new machines.

Although all of their dealers were independent, Caterpillar tended to treat them as part of the family. Cat frequently helped dealers finance purchases by their own customers and offered advice on inventory management, logistics, equipment management, and maintenance programs. Financing had been especially important for dealers operating in emerging markets, where occasional economic crises had impaired the health of many construction equipment dealers. All five dealers operating in Mexico during a recent economic downturn survived a period when the construction industry practically came to a halt. In contrast, competitors' dealers struggled and many failed. These kinds of relationships had resulted in extremely low dealer turnover; the average dealer remained with Caterpillar for more than fifty years, with several predating the 1925 merger that created the company.

Cooperative Agreements and Joint Ventures

In 1963, Caterpillar and Mitsubishi Heavy Industries Ltd. formed one of the first joint ventures in Japan to feature partial U.S. ownership. Operations started in 1965 from a new plant in Sagamihara, 28 miles from Tokyo. The 50/50 joint venture was re-named Shin Caterpillar Mitsubishi Ltd. after the original agreement was expanded in 1987. By early 1998, primary production facilities were located in Kanagawa, Akashi, and Saitama. This permitted Cat to compete with Komatsu on its home ground with a Japanese product, although Komatsu continued to maintain its majority share of the market. In 1997, Cat entered an additional joint venture with Mitsubishi Heavy Industries Ltd. for the production of forklifts in Europe.

One of Caterpillar's primary market regions was Europe, which contributed about 15 percent of sales in 1997. Caterpillar expanded its European presence in the mid 1990s through various acquisitions. In 1995, it acquired Brown Group Holdings in the United Kingdom, a producer of heavy trucks. In 1996, Cat purchased Mak Maschinenbau GmbH, a diesel engine producer from Germany. Also in Germany, Cat formed a joint venture in 1997 with Claas KGaA for the sale and manufacturing of harvesters and rubber-belted agricultural tractors in North America and Europe. In February 1997, Caterpillar announced an agreement to acquire a majority share of Skogsjan AB, a Swedish manufacturer of "cut-to-length" forestry machines and equipment, including forwarders, wheel harvesters, and harvester heads. Cat entered into an agreement with Emerson Electric Company in 1995 for the production of diesel generator sets, acquiring a stake in Emerson FG Wilson Limited (UK) subsidiary.

Other cooperative agreements for the production of construction equipment included Caterpillar Xuzhou Limited, a joint venture formed in 1995 that produces hydraulic excavators for the Chinese market; and an 80/20. Caterpillar–PT Natra Raya (India) joint venture designed to produce crawler bulldozers, wheel loaders, and hydraulic excavators for the Asia-Pacific region.

Caterpillar also engaged in a series of cooperative agreements, acquisitions, and joint ventures for the design, production, and supply of engines. In January 1995, it announced a joint venture with Empresa Nacional Bazan Motores (Spain), for the production of a new, higher-powered, lightweight version of the Caterpillar 3600 family of engines. Caterpillar had been producing engines in India through its joint venture with Hindustan Powerplus Limited since 1989, although it did not start selling engines under Cat's brand until its ISO 9001 certification in 1996. A new venture in north cen-

TABLE 8

Komatsu, Ltd.: Financial Highlights (millions of yen unless otherwise stated)

	1984*	1985*	1986*	1987*	1988*
Net sales equipment and industrial machinery**					
Finance and interest income	27,692	28,698	31,517	33,217	5,907
Other income	713,472	796,235	788,726	740,599	174,599
Net sales	741,164	824,933	820,243	773,816	180,513
Cost of goods sold	502,813	582,362	591,478	555,146	128,866
Income before accounting changes	22,642	21,917	14,701	9,504	3,107
(Year ended March 31)*					
Cash and equivalents	24,365	26,436	33,738	42,779	43,668
Receivables	312,688	333,810	364,132	344,919	342,672
Inventories	172,488	175,044	155,383	152,998	164,395
Property, plant and equipment	20,693	21,414	156,908	156,714	157,211
Other current and noncurrent assets	413,572	446,856	273,521	330,065	325,770
Total assets	943,806	1,003,560	983,682	1,027,475	1,033,716
Short-term loans	228,811	262,182	246,395	274,600	277,431
Accounts payable	167,221	180,129	161,349	170,624	170,109
Long-term debt	80,722	73,143	65,182	61,676	61,507
Total liabilities	588,430	629,240	601,713	628,866	632,916
Stockholders' equity	355,376	374,320	381,969	398,609	400,800
Total liabilities and stockholders' equity	943,806	1,003,560	983,682	1,027,475	1,033,716
Cash flows from operations				35,981	5,147
Cash flows from investing activities				(71,042)	(3,236)
Cash flows from financing activities				44,318	(1,016)
Net increase (decrease) in cash***				9,041	889

*From 1960 to 1987, Komatsu ended its fiscal year December 31. Beginning in 1988, Komatsu ended its fiscal year in March 31. Figures for 1988 represent the transition period of January 1988 to March 1988.
**Prior to 1989, sales of equipment and industrial machinery are included in other income.
***Includes the effects of exchange rates on cash.

tral China, Shanxi International Castings, Co., Ltd., was to manufacture engine-related castings for medium- and heavy-duty diesel engines. In December 1997, Caterpillar announced the acquisition of Perkins Engine, LucasVarity's diesel engine subsidiary, for $1.3 billion. Perkins engine, a leading manufacturer of small to medium-sized diesel engines (<200 hp) had sales of approximately $1.1 billion in the year ended January 31, 1997. The addition of Perkins offered Cat a position in smaller engines, both for powering Cat's products, as small and compact construction equipment became increasingly important, and for sale to OEM and end-user customers.

KOMATSU

Komatsu was the second largest player in the construction equipment industry, with a worldwide market share of 8.1 percent for 1996. (Financial data for Komatsu Ltd. is shown in Table 8.) It derived 65 percent of its sales from construction and mining equipment, which included the sale of hydraulic excavators, bulldozers, wheel loaders, dump trucks, cranes, road equipment, underground machinery, and other equipment. (See Table 9 for data on regional and industry segments sales.) The remaining 35 percent was derived from its business in civil engineering and construction (general civil

1989	1990	1991	1992	1993	1994	1995	1996	1997
592,541	657,380	747,132	667,243	603,908	586,593	647,607	772,718	860,595
27,129	31,936	39,633	54,606	43,133	29,141	35,911	31,710	18,919
200,268	229,728	241,765	252,510	266,020	259,260	271,303	226,609	238,321
819,938	919,044	1,028,530	974,359	913,061	874,994	954,821	1,031,037	1,117,835
590,550	657,554	718,714	689,039	662,408	649,512	702,416	763,045	827,665
20,833	27,282	31,258	10,898	3,037	1,303	10,225	14,291	18,160
59,770	37,520	28,593	24,635	21,504	22,192	27,285	82,553	87,827
364,060	412,357	457,284	407,053	370,833	419,013	418,564	442,104	463,001
132,292	152,895	184,483	171,051	155,524	176,888	181,899	188,054	193,798
149,801	178,494	217,896	261,211	260,999	260,720	257,219	264,842	299,098
423,034	449,370	430,933	588,868	515,100	497,153	657,005	615,450	469,006
1,128,957	1,230,636	1,319,189	1,452,818	1,323,960	1,375,966	1,541,972	1,593,003	1,512,730
213,026	209,410	213,886	306,310	244,628	307,410	348,887	305,855	281,743
203,700	252,511	247,206	194,523	176,496	179,039	199,990	220,731	234,306
127,640	109,900	171,899	222,088	207,027	142,578	140,550	140,208	163,590
683,982	740,040	794,399	929,431	807,551	870,095	966,438	986,559	970,797
444,975	490,596	524,790	523,387	516,409	505,871	575,534	606,444	541,933
1,128,957	1,230,636	1,319,189	1,452,818	1,323,960	1,375,966	1,541,972	1,593,003	1,512,730
61,960	63,808	(24,596)	55,144	65,675	70,545	54,210	55,424	67,919
(112,952)	(53,878)	(55,555)	(21,063)	13,315	(55,851)	(38,183)	71,083	(14,871)
67,202	(32,840)	71,361	(37,964)	(82,024)	(13,652)	(10,743)	(71,424)	(47,190)
16,102	(22,250)	(8,927)	(3,958)	(3,131)	688	5,093	55,268	5,274

engineering, prefabricated structures for commercial use, and real estate sales and leasing); electronics operations (for example, electronic control equipment, information equipment, and silicon wafers); industrial machinery (such as sheet-metal presses, industrial robots, and machine tools); and, other operations, including diesel engines, compressors, generator sets, and forklift trucks.

History in Brief

Komatsu Ltd. was established in 1921, resulting from the separation of Komatsu Ironworks and Takeuichi Mining Co. The company started producing sheet metal presses and, in 1931, introduced the first crawler-type farm tractor. This was the first Japanese agricultural tractor. In 1947, Komatsu began production of bulldozers and produced its first diesel engine the next year. By the early 1960s, Komatsu was already producing forklifts, motor graders, dump trucks, shovel loaders, and wheel loaders. Sales of 28 billion yen in 1960 were mostly confined to Japan. In 1961, Komatsu signed a diesel engine technology sharing agreement with Cummins Engine Co., Inc. (USA), with the objective of improving the quality of its products by ensuring access to the latest engine technology in a cost-effective way. Looking for expansion into global

TABLE 9

Komatsu, Ltd.: Sales Composition by Region and Segment (in millions of yen unless otherwise indicated)

	1993	1994	1995	1996	1997
Sales by Region					
Japan			608,187	660,948	687,459
The Americas			149,573	148,630	170,683
Asia-Pacific			76,423	104,724	126,812
Europe			72,741	70,378	87,047
Africa and Middle East			11,986	14,647	26,915
Total sales			918,910	999,327	1,098,916
Sales by Segment					
Construction equipment	549,198	536,294	619,113	642,804	716,932
Civil eng. and construction	100,076	101,266	104,123	114,821	99,801
Electronics	50,165	53,598	62,080	75,637	90,553
Industrial machinery	64,710	50,299	28,494	36,151	47,967
Others	105,779	104,396	105,100	129,914	143,663
Total sales and revenues	869,928	845,853	918,910	999,327	1,098,916

Source: Komatsu, Ltd.; *Fact Book 1997.*

markets, Komatsu opened its first operation abroad in 1967: Komatsu Europe S.A. in Belgium. By 1970, sales had shot up to 264 billion yen, or $734 million. However, Komatsu was still very far behind Cat's worldwide revenue in that same year. The quality of its products was also lagging, having a durability just over half that of Cat.

Komatsu's management focus at that time was both to improve the quality of its product and to expand internationally in order to achieve the economies of scale necessary to be able to compete with Cat. Shoji Nogawa, the president of Komatsu, referred respectfully to Caterpillar as "sendatsu," a Japanese word meaning pioneer or guide. But the rivalry between the number one and number two heavy construction equipment manufacturers was fierce.

Komatsu negotiated licensing arrangements with International Harvester Company and Bucyrus Erie to sell wheel loaders and excavators built from these firms' designs in Japan. After the agreements expired in 1982, Komatsu deepened its commitment to the U.S. market; it invested an estimated $200 million in a manufacturing facility in Chattanooga, Tennessee, and established Komatsu

America Manufacturing Corp., now Komatsu America International Company. This facility was to produce bulldozers, hydraulic excavators, and off-highway dump trucks to go head-to-head with Caterpillar on its home turf. As Nogawa acknowledged, "The United States is still the largest market in the world. We are not so strong there now, but we think we can increase our market share."[9] Despite sacrificing lower Japanese labor costs, Nogawa saw the move as insulation from possible U.S. protectionist policies and from future currency swings.

In 1984, Komatsu's U.S. market share was estimated at 5 percent, compared with Cat's 50 percent. Experts considered its dealer network as its weakest link. Komatsu had fifty U.S. dealers, compared with Cat's eighty-four. Furthermore, Komatsu's dealers were financially weaker than Cat's, and only a few carried Komatsu's equipment exclusively. As dealers heavily depend on parts and service revenues, they preferred to represent companies that sell the most machines.

At the same time, Komatsu was carrying out a massive automation effort, including computer-driven flexible manufacturing, to improve cost competitiveness. An estimated $80 million was destined for this effort, which was to result in further cost advantages over Caterpillar. At the time, Caterpillar had 40 percent higher labor costs, lower employee productivity, and lower inventory turnover.

Komatsu-Dresser

In 1988, Komatsu established a 50/50 joint venture with Dresser Industries, an energy-related firm that had moved into the construction equipment business by acquiring International Harvester's construction equipment business in 1983. Dresser's products included crawler dozers, crawler loaders, scrapers, and a complete line of underground mining equipment. The new venture was to combine the companies' manufacturing and engineering facilities in construction equipment in the Americas for the manufacture and marketing of crawler tractors, crawler loaders, hydraulic excavators, cranes, off-highway trucks, and electric-wheel mining trucks. Operating at 50 percent of capacity due to deteriorating sales, the Dresser JV would allow Komatsu to expand its U.S. presence without having to invest in building manufacturing facilities from scratch. Komatsu was to pour $300 million into the venture in an attempt to renovate Dresser's outdated and inefficient facilities. Initially, the venture was to be headed by a Dresser executive and the two firms were to maintain separate dealer networks. At the time, this represented a complete departure from Komatsu's traditional expansion policies of wholly owned subsidiaries and Japanese management leading the various operations.

The joint venture produced disastrous results, with aggregate losses of $125 million over the first four years of operation. The problems included a depressed construction machinery market, a costly reorganization of production lines, cumbersome distribution and dealer operations, and cultural misunderstandings between Japanese and American executives. However, sales of Komatsu-Dresser started to increase in 1993 as a result of the sharp rise in the overall U.S. construction equipment industry.

In 1993, Komatsu expanded its ownership position to 81 percent and in September 1994 bought the remaining 19 percent. At the time, North American facilities operated by Komatsu included Peoria, Illinois; Chattanooga, Tennessee; Galion, Ohio; and Quebec, Canada. In 1996, Komatsu Dresser Company was renamed Komatsu America International Company.

Komatsu's Position

Throughout the early and mid 1990s, Komatsu was unable to match the growth rate of its main competitor, Caterpillar. From 1990 to 1997, Komatsu managed a 21 percent growth rate in yen (or 55 percent in dollar terms), behind Cat's 63 percent increase. Despite continued diversification efforts, Komatsu remained heavily exposed to downturns in the Japanese economy, which represented 63 percent of its 1997 construction equipment sales revenues. Furthermore, its other divisions, with the exception of its electronics business, had shown unexciting growth and equally unexciting geographic diversification figures.

Nonetheless, Komatsu had slowly increased its presence in other areas of the world—in Europe, Asia, and North and South America. In 1996, Komatsu America generated revenues of $1.4 billion, making it one of the largest suppliers of construction equipment in the area. With a wide variety of products sold under the Komatsu, Dresser, Galion, and Haulpak brand names, Komatsu had been able to amass 20 percent of the hydraulic excavator and 13 percent of the wheel loader markets in the United States as of 1997.

KMS in Vernon Hills, Illinois, was established by Komatsu in April 1997. It is the second largest supplier of mining equipment in North America, manufacturing and marketing various mining products, including large-sized wheel loaders and large-sized dump trucks. Also in 1997, Komatsu agreed to extend its alliance with Cummins Engine, the largest producer of diesel engines above 200 horsepower, and form a third 50/50 joint venture company. The new venture, headquartered in Tochigi Prefecture, Japan, was to engage in engine development for construction equipment markets worldwide. The technologies developed were to be used by the two companies in their own manufacturing facilities. The increasing demand in the diesel engine industry, driven by increased customer expectations and new environmental standards, had motivated the two companies to cooperate in the past. This third joint venture would further benefit Komatsu's development effort relative to engine for construction equipment. Additionally, it had the potential to expand Komatsu's revenue base.

TABLE 10

Deere & Company: Financial Highlights* (in millions of U.S. $ unless otherwise indicated)

	1986	1987	1988	1989
Net sales of equipment	3,516	4,135	5,365	6,234
Finance and interest income	89	96	66	101
Other income	20	23	24	15
Net sales	3,625	4,253	5,454	6,350
Cost of goods sold	3,214	3,634	4,356	5,036
Income before accounting changes	(229)	(99)	287	380
(Year ended December 31)				
Cash and equivalents	182	116	49	57
Receivables	2,297	2,156	2,355	2,790
Inventories	483	465	708	711
Property, plant and equipment	951	982	944	982
Other current and noncurrent assets	1,062	1,040	1,189	1,372
Total assets	4,974	4,760	5,245	5,913
Short-term loans	396	356	477	640
Accounts payable	1,014	1,052	1,149	1,217
Long-term debt	1,280	1,052	805	824
Total liabilities	2,975	2,840	2,789	3,132
Stockholders' equity	1,999	1,920	2,456	2,780
Total liabilities and stockholders equity	4,974	4,760	5,245	5,913
Cash flows from operations				
Cash flows from investing activities				
Cash flows from financing activities				
Net increase (decrease) in cash**				

*Deere & Company Operations with Financial Services on the equity basis.
**Includes the effects of exchange rates on cash.
Source: Deere & Company, Annual Reports.

Komatsu also increased its commitment in Europe. In November 1995, Komatsu entered into a 50/50 joint venture with Mannesmann Demag (Germany) for the development, manufacture, and marketing of large and super-large hydraulic excavators. Furthermore, in June 1996, Komatsu increased its stake in Komatsu Hanomag AG to 98 percent from the 25 percent stake it had taken when it first invested in the corporation. High restructuring costs on top of weak demand in Europe, however, damaged Hanomag's profitability, resulting in losses of 4 billion yen in 1996 and forcing it to cut staff by nearly 30 percent. Other European operations included Komatsu UK Limited, FKI-FAI Komatsu Industries SpA (Italy), Moxy Trucks AS (Norway), and Unex (Czech Republic).

Despite the slowdown, Asia was probably the most promising area because of its lack of infrastructure and perceived future potential growth. Komatsu, through joint ventures or wholly owned subsidiaries, operated manufacturing facilities in China, Thailand, Indonesia, India, Singapore, and Vietnam. Lower wage costs and proximity to markets were expected to favor future profit potential for Komatsu.

In an effort to catch up with Caterpillar's impressive systems infrastructure, in October 1997 Komatsu announced plans to standardize all its global affiliates on software developed by The Baan

1990	1991	1992	1993	1994	1995	1996	1997
6,779	5,848	5,723	6,479	7,663	8,830	9,640	11,082
112	116	99	84	81	105	121	115
19	21	23	23	24	28	29	48
6,910	5,985	5,845	6,587	7,768	8,964	9,789	11,244
5,430	4,904	4,902	5,381	6,033	6,944	7,486	8,499
411	(20)	37	184	604	706	817	960
26	99	40	72	104	531	625	411
3,281	3,242	3,187	3,436	3,267	3,437	3,418	3,477
678	538	525	464	698	721	829	1,073
1,135	1,220	1,287	1,216	1,282	1,295	1,301	1,479
1,652	1,831	1,870	2,431	2,359	2,481	2,595	3,045
6,771	6,930	6,908	7,618	7,710	8,464	8,768	9,484
850	881	856	476	54	396	224	171
1,297	1,334	1,319	1,533	1,617	1,860	1,975	2,134
804	1,018	1,234	1,069	1,019	703	626	540
3,764	4,091	4,258	5,533	5,153	5,379	5,211	5,337
3,008	2,836	2,650	2,085	2,558	3,085	3,557	4,147
6,771	6,927	6,908	7,618	7,710	8,464	8,768	9,484
		148	702	677	715	1,213	1,006
		(253)	(226)	(339)	(293)	(384)	(553)
		47	(443)	(308)	4	(735)	(664)
		(59)	31	32	427	94	(214)

Company, providing an infrastructure for managing the company's supplier network, production facilities, and distribution system. By 2000, Komatsu planned to implement a standard across its global network based on a fully integrated ERP system in an effort to be in a better position to respond to changing global market conditions.

Komatsu was also investing large sums of money in research and development in an attempt to improve the quality and features of its existing equipment and the design of new construction equipment. The company was expanding into growing lines of business such as machines for underground work, environmental preservation (for instance, trash crushers), and building demolition. Komatsu's R&D expense ratio of over 4 percent of sales was the highest in the industry.

OTHER IMPORTANT COMPETITORS

Deere & Company

Deere & Company, originally known as John Deere, was founded in 1837 in Grand Detour, Illinois, by a thirty-three-year-old blacksmith. Since then, it had grown to be the biggest agricultural equipment manufacturer in the world, with $11 billion in sales for 1997. (See Table 10 for financial highlights on the firm.) Deere historically competed with Caterpillar in several product lines, although its main focus had always been on agricultural equipment.

Over the past decade, Deere had increased its construction equipment business, which produced $2.3 billion in revenues and $216 million in operating profits in 1997, contributing 20 percent of Deere's total revenues. Construction equipment

TABLE 11

Deere & Company: Sales Composition by Region and Segment (in millions of U.S. $)

	1986	1987	1988	1989
Sales by Region				
United States	2,268	2,790	3,643	4,332
Canada	365	323	429	481
Europe, Africa, and Middle East	727	818	1,030	1,074
Latin America	122	106	134	159
Asia-Pacific	34	98	129	188
Total sales	3,516	4,135	5,365	6,234
Sales by Segment				
Agricultural equipment	2,648	3,224	4,203	4,110
Industrial equipment*	868	911	1,162	1,310
Commercial and consumer equipment**	—	—	—	814
Total sales and revenues	3,516	4,135	5,365	6,234

*Primarily construction equipment.
**Prior to 1989, commercial and consumer equipment is included in industrial equipment.
Source: Deere & Company Annual Reports; *Fact Book 1997.*

sold included crawler loaders, excavators, motor graders, scrapers, and backhoe loaders. In 1995, Deere started a four-year product development program that introduced thirty-nine new construction equipment products by 1997. Deere also competed with Caterpillar in the sale of diesel and natural gas engines. (See Table 11 for Deere sales by both geographic region and industry segment.)

As it was primarily focused on agricultural equipment, Deere faced less competition from large foreign rivals such as Komatsu, reducing its exposure to foreign exchange fluctuations. Deere sales were highly concentrated in the United States (65 percent) and in Europe (18 percent), although the company was slowly increasing its presence in Asia. By the end of 1997, Deere's dealer network in the United States included 1,700 dealers employing 25,000 people.

Deere had also teamed up with Hitachi Construction Machinery Co., Ltd. (Japan), to improve its position in Asia. They began the collaboration in 1988 by investing $58.8 million in a facility to produce hydraulic excavators in the United States, and the relationship contributed to more than a doubling of Deere's sales in Asia between 1993 and 1997. The partnership combined Deere's reliability and productivity with Hitachi's Asian market knowledge. Deere-designed four-wheel-drive loaders and other Deere-designed construction equip-

ment were also being manufactured and marketed by the Deere-Hitachi Construction Machinery Corporation for sale in the Far East.

Case Corporation

Case Corporation, with revenues of $6 billion in 1997, was also a leading manufacturer of agricultural and construction equipment. Construction equipment constituted approximately one-third of total sales for Case. Case was one of the world's largest manufacturers and distributors of light- to medium-sized construction equipment, marketed under the Case and Case Poclain brand names. The Case Poclain brand was the result of Case's acquisition of Poclain, the French firm, which was the largest manufacturer of hydraulic excavators in the world in the early 1970s. It derived 60 percent of its construction equipment sales from North America, 31 percent from Europe, 6 percent from Latin America, and 3 percent from Asia-Pacific. However, sales in Latin America climbed 19 percent in 1996, and the company had engaged in a joint venture in China (Liuzhou Case Liugong Construction Equipment Company) to further its growth in emerging markets.

In the early 1990s, Case was seen as inefficient, had excess capacity, was said to be building too many components in-house, and kept making un-

1990	1991	1992	1993	1994	1995	1996	1997
4,777	3,968	3,768	4,431	5,266	6,016	6,211	7,167
381	379	379	503	594	632	675	851
1,158	1,148	1,147	1,126	1,253	1,608	1,993	2,021
149	171	251	212	279	241	351	529
247	180	178	207	271	333	410	514
6,779	5,848	5,723	6,479	7,663	8,830	9,640	11,082
4,519	4,054	3,759	4,078	4,718	5,277	6,097	7,048
1,348	1,014	1,068	1,348	1,640	1,875	1,919	2,262
912	780	896	1,053	1,305	1,678	1,624	1,772
6,779	5,848	5,723	6,479	7,663	8,830	9,640	11,082

popular lines. In 1991, Case's parent corporation, Tenneco Inc., hired turnaround expert Michael H. Walsh as CEO. He, in turn brought in Dana G. Mead as CEO of Case. By 1993, Mead had moved Case into the black, up from a $1.3 billion loss in 1992. The firm's payroll was cut by 35 percent, 250 wholly owned dealers were sold, more than $2 billion in excess inventory was eliminated, and $920 million worth of fixed assets were written down. Between 1991 and 1995, G & A expense had fallen to 13 percent from 23 percent of sales, and gross margins had increased to 23 percent from 9 percent of sales.

Case also sent engineers and marketing managers to talk to 150 key customers and users of rival machines. With this information, it built a new family of backhoe loaders around a common platform where 75 percent of the parts were shared, up from 30 percent. By early 1998, Case was widely seen as being able to compete head-on with Caterpillar on both price and quality in the product categories where they overlapped.

FUTURE CHALLENGES FOR CATERPILLAR

While pleased with how well Caterpillar had been able to reposition itself as a firm over the last ten to fifteen years, Fites and the company's other senior managers clearly had reason to be concerned. The rate of change in this and other industries had clearly accelerated. Several of Cat's major competitors had become better focused, better managed, and more financially robust. Furthermore, the exact shape and size of the industry segments in which they competed were very hard to project. Competing in the new world economy did not look like it would be an easy process.

Endnotes

1. Forecasts presented are based on information provided by The Freedonia Group Incorporated, a leading international industry study/database company, in its report titled "World Heavy Construction Equipment to 2001," July 1997.
2. Freedonia Group, "World Heavy Construction Equipment Market Share, 1996" (July 1997).
3. This was almost immediately dubbed "Peoria Without a Factory," and several other less pleasant terms, by disgruntled workers in the Greater Peoria region.
4. P. Miller and T. O'Leary, "Accounting, 'Economic Citizenship' and the Spatial Reordering of Manufacture," *Accounting, Organizations and Society,* 19. No. 1 (1994), 15–43.
5. K. Kelly, A. Bernstein, and R. Neff, "Caterpillar's Don Fites: Why He Didn't Blink," *Business Week,* August 10, 1992.
6. J. Reingold, "CEO of the Year," *Financial World,* March 28, 1995.
7. Ibid.
8. D. V. Fites, "Make Your Dealers Your Partners," *Harvard Business Review* (March–April 1996), 83–95.
9. "Komatsu Digs Deeper into the U.S.," *Business Week,* October 1, 1984.

CASE 24

Komatsu Ltd.: Project G's Globalization

This case was prepared by Christopher A. Bartlett of Harvard Business School.

On a breezy spring day in 1991, passers-by on the bustling street in front of Komatsu's world headquarters stopped, pointed, and stared at the spectacle atop the building. Ten stories above, workers were dismantling one of central Tokyo's most notable landmarks—a giant, yellow Komatsu bulldozer precariously perched on a tall pole. For twenty-five years, this corporate icon had symbolized Komatsu's overriding strategic aim to surpass Caterpillar (Cat) and become the world's premiere construction equipment manufacturer.

President Tetsuya Katada had carefully timed the removal of this corporate symbol to mark recent changes in the company in preparation for Komatsu's spring celebration of its seventieth anniversary. Soon, a new electronic beacon would flash a new logo and a new corporate slogan ("The Earth Company, Unlimited"), confirming the changes in strategy and management practices that Katada and his management had started to implement. The new company president explained:

> Pulling down the bulldozer is just one example showing the strong determination of the president to outsiders and, more importantly, employees that we can't single-mindedly pursue production of the bulldozer. . . . Instead, we have challenged the organization with a new slogan, "Growth, Global, Groupwide"—or "the Three G's" for short. It's a much more abstract challenge than one focused on catching and beating Cat, but I hope it will stimulate people to think and discuss creatively what Komatsu can be.

This case is intended to be used as a basis for class discussion rather than as an illustration of either effective or ineffective handling of the situation. This case was prepared by Christopher A. Bartlett of Harvard Business School.

Katada's Three G's slogan challenged managers in all parts of Komatsu to reignite growth through a renewed commitment to global expansion, and an increase in groupwide leveraging of resources. For the core construction equipment business, it implied nothing less than a revolution. After three decades of focusing on the goal "to catch up and surpass Cat," this group was now being told to broaden its perspective and define the business on its own terms. In particular, Katada's challenge would require even further expansion of the company's three regionally based operations in the Americas, Europe, and Asia-Pacific. Furthermore, although several parts of this organization were new and untried, management felt it must try to integrate these operations more into a worldwide network of resources. Finally, those in Tokyo recognized that unless they began to elicit the ideas and leverage the expertise of these international operations, Project G would be little more than rhetoric.

KOMATSU COMPANY AND MANAGEMENT HISTORY

Established in 1921 as a specialized producer of mining equipment, Komatsu expanded into agricultural machinery during the 1930s and, during the Second World War, into the production of military equipment. The heavy-machinery expertise the company developed positioned it well to expand into earthmoving equipment needed for postwar reconstruction. Soon, construction equipment dominated Komatsu's sales.

In the high-demand and capital-constrained Japanese environment, Komatsu held a market share of more than 50 percent despite the low quality of its equipment at that time. This comfortable situation changed in 1963 when, after the government decided to open the industry to foreign investors, Cat announced it would enter the market in partnership with Mitsubishi. At this time, Komatsu had sales of $168 million and a product line well below world standards. Local analysts predicted three years of struggle before Cat bankrupted the puny, local company.

Emergence and Expansion: The Kawai Era (1964–1982)[1]

It was in this context that Ryoichi Kawai assumed the presidency of Komatsu from his father in 1964. The older man had prepared the company by initiating a Total Quality Control (TQC) program in 1961. Building on this base, Ryoichi Kawai's strategy for the company was straightforward—to acquire and develop advanced technology, to raise quality, and to increase efficiency to the level necessary to "catch up with and surpass Cat." To galvanize the company around his challenge and to focus management on his strategic priorities, Kawai introduced a style of management which he called "management by policy." Kawai explained the philosophy behind his strongly focused and directive approach:

> Personally, I believe that a company must always be innovative. To this end, the basic policy and value of the target must be clarified so that all the staff members can fully understand what the company is aiming for in a specific time period. This is the purpose of the management-by-policy system.

Under the umbrella of the TQC philosophy that was now deeply ingrained in Komatsu, management by policy began with Kawai's statement of an overriding, focused priority for the company. Launched the year after Cat announced its entry into the Japanese market, his first policy, "Project A," sought to raise the quality of Komatsu's middle-sized bulldozers to Cat's level. To support this goal, Kawai began an aggressive program to license technology from leading companies such as Cummins, International Harvester, and Bucyrus-Erie. As he implemented his "management-by-policy" approach, the young CEO instituted a new system of control, the "Plan, Do, Check, Act" (PDCA) cycle. Once Kawai announced the projects and priorities at the beginning of the year, the continuous PDCA cycle concentrated efforts within the company on attaining the broad policy objective until it was fully implemented (see Figure 1).

Kawai's new management approach, as reflected in Project A, was an immediate and outstanding success. Project A enabled Komatsu to double its warranty period within two years while cutting claim rates by two-thirds. And, in the face of Cat's entry into Japan, it triggered an increase in sales that raised Komatsu's market share from 50 to 65 percent by 1970, thereby confounding the experts' forecasts of an early demise.

An avalanche of policies followed, steering Komatsu through the turbulent environment. In response to the economic stagnation that hit Japan in 1965, Kawai targeted a "cost down" program at slashing costs. In 1966, his five-year "World A" campaign sought to make Komatsu internationally competitive in cost and quality, thus reducing Komatsu's potentially dangerous reliance on domestic sales. And, in rapid succession, Kuwai launched Projects B, C, and D to improve reliability and durability in large bulldozers and shovels, payloaders, and hydraulic excavators, respectively. Throughout the 1970s, not a year went by without a major project, campaign, or program aimed at catching and surpassing Cat.

By the early 1980s, Komatsu had emerged as the major challenger in the construction equipment industry, putting Cat clearly on the defensive (see Table 1). Nowhere were Cat's concerns clearer than in its 1982 annual report, which opened with a picture of a Komatsu bulldozer and a stern warning that Cat would not be able to compete against its Japanese rival at prevailing exchange and wage rates.

Struggle and Turmoil: The Nogawa Era (1982–1987)

Having guided the organization through an eighteen-year period of extraordinary growth, Ryoichi Kawai handed over operating leadership to Shoji Nogawa in 1982. Unfortunately for Nogawa, this date also marked the beginning of an era of falling demand, worldwide price wars, a rapidly appreciating yen, and heightened trade frictions throughout the industry.

Nogawa was an engineer who had risen through the manufacturing side of the construction equipment division. A reputed strong-willed, hands-on manager, he had high expectations of his managers, and drove them hard to meet those expectations. In spite of the growing challenges facing the industry, Nogawa was initially reluctant

FIGURE I

Company Description of "Plan, Do, Check, Act" Control Cycle

	Stage	Actual Activities
What is control? The term "control" is explained in the concept of a plan-do-check-act circle. Please understand that the concept of control is practice. In short, control means the plan-do-check-act circle.	**Plan (P)**	• **In a work shop: arranging daily operation, preparing operation standards, equipment, jigs and tools, and planning for cost reduction.** • **In a technical department: planning for research and establishing design policy.** • **In a sales department: preparation of daily or monthly sales and visiting plans according to a given target.** • **Working out countermeasures for any defects or debts.** • **Understanding the problem through facts.** One must grasp the facts of the matter in order to know the problem. Never adopt false data. **To grasp the facts** • **See the place where the problem exists.** • **Observe the job and operation.** • **Investigate the actual problem.** • **Examine the data.** • **Listen to people.** • **Priority principle** Treat the gathered facts and problem points on a priority principle, stressing those which are more important in view of expected effects. The Pareto diagram described later will be very helpful. -Maximum effect with minimum labor- 70% of the problem is solved if the planning is properly done.
	Do (D)	Put the plan into practice and operate according to the rules and standards. This includes training on rules and standards.
	Check (C)	• It is your responsibility to check your own work. (Self inspection as well as error checks for drawings, documents, and business forms produce quality products.) Do not hand trouble on to the next person. • Check the result in comparison with the plan.
	Act (A)	• If a result deviates from the standard, correct it. • If any abnormality is found, investigate and remove the cause, and take action to prevent its reoccurrence. (Emergency and preventive measures are necessary.)

Source: Company records

to change Komatsu's traditional policies, including the company's reliance on its highly efficient, centralized, global production facilities. As conditions worsened and external pressures increased (see Table 2), the new president seemed to focus more on cost-cutting and aggressive pricing than on shifting production overseas or reducing Komatsu's dependence on the stagnating construction industry. As the company implemented its aggressive sales strategy worldwide, political pressure mounted. Faced with several antidumping suits, Nogawa introduced new strategic goals in 1984, including faster product introduction and expansion of non-construction industrial machinery businesses.

The situation reached a crisis pitch in 1985 and 1986, when the value of the yen surged alarmingly. (See Table 2.) With domestic markets in turmoil, a 25 percent rise in the value of the yen in nine months exposed Komatsu's foreign exchange vulnerability, putting Nogawa under pressure to internationalize production more rapidly. His short-term strategy included raising prices abroad, expanding overseas parts procurement, and cutting production costs. His medium-term strategy called for developing more marketable construction equipment products through increased R&D spending and capital investments in manufacturing facilities. In the long-term, he told shareholders, "Komatsu is gearing itself toward new business areas of high-growth potential."

In addition, in 1985 he responded to the growing internal and external pressures for internationalization, approving the establishment of two important overseas plants—one in Chattanooga, Tennessee, and the other in a closed Cat facility in Birtley, United Kingdom. "As a drastic means of efficiently managing the sensitive trade friction and volatile foreign exchange environments," he told shareholders, "we have secured manufacturing bases in the world's major markets." Even after the plants were established, however, Nogawa seemed reluctant to embrace them fully into Komatsu's strategy. For example, when U.S. distributors began lobbying the head office to move additional production overseas, he rejected their proposals outright, finally relenting only when the yen appreciated even further, to ¥140 per dollar.

The rising tide of problems, rapidly deteriorating results, Nogawa's apparent resistance to faster and more dramatic change, and the deleterious influence of his unpopular autocratic management style eventually resulted in his replacement. Chairman Kawai explained: "With this serious appreciation of the yen . . . we have no time to lose. We need to have a complete change in people's attitudes so that we can build a new organization, aiming at progress in the 1990s and the twenty-first century."

Steadying the Ship: The Tanaka Transition (1987–1989)

In June 1987, Ryoichi Kawai chose Masao Tanaka to replace Nogawa as president. A former general manager of the domestic sales division and, more recently, three-year general manager of the overseas division, Tanaka responded quickly to the competitive crisis in the domestic market. Chosen, in part, for his diplomatic skills, Tanaka demonstrated his conciliatory approach by emphasizing the need to end price discounting and high-pressure sales practices. In one of his many public statements on the topic, he argued:

> Market share is certainly a source of profit, but there can be no such thing as market share that ignores long-term profitability. We are trying to establish a situation where we can recoup the money spent on development and investment. If Komatsu cannot do this, there is no other company in Japan that can. If business conditions become worse, we should cover this not by carrying out a price war, but by reducing production.

Slowly, the industry responded and Tanaka's efforts culminated in a spate of collective OEM supply agreements within the industry and the creation of the Japan Construction Equipment Manufacturers Association in March 1990. More important from Komatsu's perspective, restoring market order improved the bottom line. In the hydraulic excavator market segment alone, for example, while Komatsu's market share fell from 35 to 31 percent, overall profits rose.

Tanaka's pricing and sales policies were controversial within the company. When Komatsu developed the first mini-excavator that used advanced microelectronic controls, for example, some managers contended that with its traditional lower prices and aggressive sales methods, the company could capture a 50 percent market share. But Tanaka's philosophy prevailed, and the product was introduced at a 10 percent premium to existing prices.

TABLE I

Selected Data on Komatsu, Caterpillar, and Assorted Other Competitors
($ millions; fiscal year ends December 31 unless noted)

	1991	1990	1989	1988	1987	1986
Komatsu[a]						
Company sales	6,915	7,013	5,615	5,961	6,121	4,992
Construction equipment sales	4,356	4,685	3,824	4,131	4,389	3,592
Net income	82	222	173	157	79	93
Percent of sales outside Japan	30%	30%	31%	31%	39%	47%
Percent of sales from construction equipment	63%	67%	68%	69%	72%	72%
Caterpillar						
Sales (companywide)	9,838	11,103	10,882	10,255	8,180	7,321
Net income	(404)	21	497	616	350	76
Percent of sales from outside the United States	59%	55%	53%	50%	48%	46%
Sales of Other Major Construction and Agricultural Equipment Manufacturers						
Clark Equipment	1,190	1,445	1,392	1,278	1,055	954
Deere[b] (FY Oct. 31)	5,060	6,780	6,234	5,365	4,135	3,516
Hitachi Construction Machinery (FY Mar. 31)	1,812	1,780	1,777	1,725	1,195	824
Ingersoll-Rand[c]	1,363	1,445	1,328	1,140	969	865
International Harvester[b,d]						
J I Case (Division of Tenneco)	4,449	5,396	5,069	4,309	3,676	3,369
Shin-Caterpillar Mitsubishi (FY Mar. 31)	1,519	1,810	1,728			

Sources: Annual reports, Yamaichi Research Institute, company records, forms 10-K, Moody's Industrial Manuals, various years.
"NR" means business segment data not reported.
[a]Komatsu fiscal year ended on Mar. 31 between 1989 and 1991 and on Dec. 31 between 1975 and 1987. Data from 1988 are for the period April to March and correspond with January to December of other companies.
[b]Construction and agricultural machinery segments only.
[c]Standard machinery segment only. Includes some nonconstruction and agricultural equipment.
[d]J I Case acquired agricultural equipment division of International Harvester in 1985. Komatsu data are converted from yen-denominated data at fiscal year-end exchange rates.

Tanaka also pursued internationalization much more aggressively than his predecessor. More than internationalizing sales or market exposure, Tanaka wished to establish autonomous bases with regional capabilities in manufacturing, sales, and finance in the three core markets—Japan, the United States, and Europe. Explained Tanaka:"On the assumption that the yen will further appreciate to, let's say, ¥100 per U.S. dollar, I believe any extension of conventional measures such as management and production rationalization will no longer be effective." Extending its conservative domestic pricing strategy, in 1988 the company raised U.S. prices 7 percent, the seventh mark-up since September 1985. (Collectively, these represented a 40 percent aggregate price increase.)

Much of the driving force behind this emerging strategy came from Tanaka's director for corporate planning, Tetsuya Katada. Concerned about Komatsu's dwindling growth prospects in construction equipment and its dangerous reliance on domestic production, Katada pushed the company toward regionalizing production in Europe and the United States.

In Europe, Komatsu pursued a number of initiatives to reduce its yen exposure, respond to political pressure, and flesh out its product line. In response to an antidumping suit, the company

1985	1984	1983	1982	1981	1980	1979	1978	1977	1976	1975
3,581	2,831	3,235	3,434	3,199	2,944	2,736	1,999	2,118	1,680	1,506
3,023	2,177	2,585	2,733	2,488	2,338	2,214	1,597	1,655	1,252	1,137
110	90	113	138	141	126	116	82	66	63	60
49%	46%	54%	58%	49%	43%	37%	38%	42%	41%	45%
76%	77%	80%	80%	81%	79%	81%	80%	76%	75%	75%
6,725	6,576	5,424	6,469	9,154	8,598	7,613	7,219	5,849	5,042	4,964
198	428	345	180	578	564	491	566	445	383	399
44%	42%	46%	57%	57%	57%	54%	48%	51%	58%	57%
964	878	702	824	1,077	1,534	1,732	1,503	1,309	1,261	1,425
4,061	4,399	3,968	4,608	5,447	5,470	4,933	4,155	3,604	3,134	2,995
602										
929	876	771	988	1,292	772	686	676	676	615	529
	NR	NR	NR	NR	NR	4,069	3,200	3,065	2,930	2,992
2,697	1,741	1,752	NR	NR	NR	NR	1,386	1,149	1,054	964

began producing wheel loaders in its U.K. plant. It began sourcing mini-excavators for the European market—the subject of another antidumping suit—from the Italian company, FAI, using engines made by Perkins, a British diesel manufacturer. And it began sourcing articulated dump trucks from Brown (U.K.) and vibratory rollers from ABG Werke (Germany), marketing them around the world under its own name. It even imported backhoe loaders from FAI into Japan.

In the United States, the company's moves were even bolder. In September 1988, Komatsu's U.S. company entered into a 50/50 joint venture with Dresser, the American oil services company that had acquired International Harvester's construction equipment business in 1983. The new $1.4 bil-lion company (Komatsu Dresser Corp., or KDC) combined the U.S.-based finance, engineering, and manufacturing operations for both companies, while maintaining separate sales and marketing organizations in KDC. Using all four of the two parent companies' plants in the United States and Brazil, the joint venture produced most major construction products, including hydraulic excavators, bulldozers, wheel loaders, and dump trucks.

The joint venture was controversial within Komatsu, partly because many within the company had heard the industry speculation that Dresser entered the joint venture as a means of exiting this money-losing business segment in which it had a neglected product line, lagging quality, and out-of-date plants. Furthermore, it represented a radical de-

TABLE 2

Conditions for Komatsu and the Japanese Construction Industry, 1966–1990

	1990^b	1989^b	1987	1986	1985	1984	1983	1982	1980	1970	1966
Average exchange rate (¥/$)	158	133	121	158	200	252	232	236	204	360	360
Domestic construction investment expenditures											
• ¥ trillion	72.6	67.4	61.5	53.6	50.0	48.5	47.6	50.2			
• % of GNP	17.7	17.4	17.3	15.8	15.4	15.9	16.6	18.3			
Komatsu construction equipment (CE)											
• CE segment sales (¥ billion)	603.9	549.5	531.1	567.5	604.5	548.7	546.6	646.6	505.3	183.2	64.5
• Overseas CE production (% total CE)	30.2	12.2	8.9	2.4	3.2						
• Overseas share of CE sales (%)	40.9	38.9	47.9	55.4	58.5	54.3	62.8	67.0	43.3	13.9	10.2
• Japanese CE industry, export ratio	27.2	27.8	36.2	44.2	52.3	49.9	55.1	57.0	36.8	10.6	7.6
Global unit demand (excl. Japan) for selected types of CE^a											
• Bulldozers	18,000	22,000	25,000	22,000	21,000	21,000	22,000	20,000			
• yearly % change	−18	−4	+14	+5	0	−5	+10				
• Hydraulic excavators	39,000	40,000	33,000	29,000	29,000	24,000	23,000	20,000			
• yearly % change	−3	+8	+14	0	+21	+4	+15				
Global unit demand (excl. Japan) all types of CE	110,500	121,000	112,000	104,000	107,000	98,000	96,000	86,000			
• yearly % change	−9	+3	+8	−3	+9	+2	+12				
Komatsu results:											
Sales (¥ billion)	887	793	741	789	796	713	751	810	648	264	28
Income (¥ billion)	27	21	10	15	22	23	26	33	28	13	2
Income (% of sales)	3.0	2.6	1.3	1.9	2.8	3.2	3.5	4.1	4.3	4.9	7.1

Sources: MITI, company records, *Komatsu Fact Book* (various years), Yamaichi Research Institute of Securities and Economics.

^a Bulldozers are large pieces of equipment used primarily in road construction, earth moving, agricultural engineering, forestry, mining and waste management. Hydraulic excavators are lighter machinery used in these areas as well as river maintenance, building and demolition, water and sewer main construction, landscaping, and cargo-handling.

^b Komatsu's results are for year ending December 31 up to 1987, and year ending March 31 from 1989 on.

TABLE 3

Komatsu Financial Highlights, 1982–1989 (consolidated, ¥ million)

	Fiscal Year Ended March 31			Fiscal Year Ended December 31					
	1991	1990	1989	1987	1986	1985	1984	1983	1982
Net sales	988,897	887,108	792,809	740,599	788,726	796,235	713,472	750,530	810,379
Net income	31,258	27,282	20,833	9,504	14,701	21,915	22,642	26,265	32,639
Net income per share	31.20	27.54	22.71	11.02	17.68	26.49	27.76	32.40	40.78
Total assets	1,319,189	1,230,636	1,128,957	1,027,475	938,682	1,003,560	943,806	894,549	930,685
Shareholders' equity	524,790	490,596	444,975	398,609	381,969	374,320	355,376	337,084	315,701
As a percentage of total assets (%)	39.8	39.9	39.4	38.8	38.8	37.3	37.7	37.7	33.9
Number of consolidated subsidiaries	51	43	37	37	35	36	35	33	30
Number of companies included in account	34	33	28	25	25	24	27	26	26
CE sales (as % total sales)	63.6	68.1	69.3	71.7	71.9	75.9	76.9	72.8	79.8

Source: Komatsu, Fact Book, 1992

TABLE 4

Global Trends in Construction Equipment Demand by Region and Type of Equipment

Region	1991 Number of Units	1991 Growth Rate	1990 Number of Units	1990 Growth Rate	1989 Number of Units	1989 Growth Rate
The Americas	28,000	−30%	40,000	−22%	51,000	−6%
Europe	42,000	−7	45,000	−4	47,000	4
Middle East and Africa	9,000	0	9,000	29	7,000	0
Asia and Oceania	13,000	−24	17,000	6	16,000	33
Total	92,000	−17	111,000	−8	121,000	3

Equipment Type	1991 Number of Units	1991 Growth Rate	1990 Number of Units	1990 Growth Rate	1989 Number of Units	1989 Growth Rate
Bulldozers	14,000	−22%	18,000	−18%	22,000	−4%
Dozer shovels	2,000	−33	3,000	−40	5,000	−17
Wheel loaders	35,000	−10	39,000	−7	42,000	2
Hydraulic excavators	32,000	−20	40,000	0	40,000	8
Motor graders	7,000	−13	8,000	0	8,000	4
Dump trucks	2,000	−33	3,000	0	3,000	0
Motor scrapers	0	0	0	0	1,000	0
Total	92,000	−17	111,000	−8	121,000	3

Source: Komatsu, *Fact Book,* 1992.

Note: Figures in both tables exclude those for the Japanese market and show totals for bulldozers, dozer shovels, wheel loaders, hydraulic excavators, motor graders, dump trucks, and motor scrapers only.

parture from several of Komatsu's closely held strategic maxims and traditional management policies: centralized production, total control over product development, whole ownership of subsidiaries, and Japanese management throughout the Komatsu group. In this way, the KDC deal served notice that the company was committed to a major change in the way it managed its international operations

ENTERING THE 1990s

New Leadership: Tetsuya Katada

In June 1989, Masao Tanaka stepped down as president and was replaced by his internationally oriented vice president of corporate planning, Tetsuya Katada. With a degree from Kyoto University of Law, Katada had risen through Komatsu's ranks in

personnel, labor relations, and corporate planning. After thirty-six years in the company, Katada was well known. Colleagues saw him as a "quiet and cool-headed commander," who spoke freely and honestly with superiors and subordinates alike. His introduction in the press signaled that he intended to take bold action. In response to questions about yet another change in Komatsu's leadership, the new president differentiated his strategy and style from his predecessor's:

> Mr. Tanaka placed defense above anything else in his management policy. [Defense] was necessary because of the persistent high-yen environment. I, however, will be on the offensive in my own management policy.

When pressed on his relationship with Ryoichi Kawai, Mr. Katada added: "I have never hesitated to talk straight with my superiors.... [Chairman] Kawai

1988		1987		1986	1985	1984	1983	1982
Number of Units	Growth Rate	Number of Units	Growth Rate	Number of Units	Number of Units	Number of Units	Number of Units	Number of Units
54,000	-2%	55,000	10%	50,000	50,000	45,000	35,000	23,000
45,000	15	39,000	11	35,000	33,000	30,000	30,000	28,000
7,000	-13	8,000	-20	10,000	13,000	13,000	21,000	23,000
12,000	33	10,000	11	9,000	10,000	9,000	9,000	12,000
118,000	5	112,000	8	104,000	106,000	97,000	95,000	86,000

1988		1987		1986	1985	1984	1983	1982
Number of Units	Growth Rate	Number of Units	Growth Rate	Number of Units	Number of Units	Number of Units	Number of Units	Number of Units
23,000	-8%	25,000	14%	22,000	21,000	21,000	22,000	20,000
6,000	-14	7,000	0	7,000	6,000	6,000	6,000	5,000
41,000	14	36,000	6	34,000	37,000	34,000	34,000	31,000
37,000	12	33,000	14	29,000	28,000	24,000	22,000	19,000
7,000	-13	8,000	-11	9,000	10,000	8,000	8,000	7,000
3,000	50	2,000	0	2,000	3,000	3,000	2,000	3,000
1,000	0	1,000	0	1,000	1,000	1,000	1,000	1,000
118,000	5	112,000	8	104,000	106,000	97,000	95,000	86,000

is indispensable at Komatsu. He is, however, nothing more or nothing less than an important advisor."

Questioning the Past

The situation Katada inherited was anything but promising. Despite Komatsu's recent yet belated internationalization, sales were virtually unchanged from their level seven years prior, and profits were only half those of 1982 (see Table 3). This stagnation was made all the more painful by the incredible growth taking place all around Komatsu. In the same 1982 to 1989 period, while Komatsu's profits plunged, Japan's GNP grew 43 percent. Although the worldwide demand for construction equipment had rebounded since the 1982–1983 downturn, a simultaneous shift toward smaller, lighter, and therefore less expensive, equipment such as the hydraulic excavator and

the mini-excavator had dampened the impact of the recovery (see Table 4).

Worse still, worldwide industry demand was expected to dip again, at least over the next few years (see Exhibits 2 and 5). With the global political economy in the midst of a major upheaval and large-scale development projects on the wane, Katada was concerned about the suitability of a strategy tightly focused on this declining sector:

There are doubts about the future demand for construction equipment. Central and South America and Africa are having problems with accumulated debt; the Soviet Union and China also have their problems; and the price of oil is [depressing demand for construction equipment.] In the places where there is latent demand, the market is dormant. As a result, 90% of our demand is in America, Japan, and Europe....

We cannot hope for growth by relying simply on construction equipment. We need to take an objective look at the world economic situation and to discuss future moves within the company. In other words, I want everyone to stop concentrating simply on catching up with Caterpillar.

This call to abandon Komatsu's long-established competitive slogan surprised many observers. But Katada went even further. He openly challenged many of the company's deeply ingrained organizational processes and even much of the management philosophy that had made Komatsu the textbook example of management by "strategic intent."[2] The new president expressed his views openly:

The company is now stagnating. It has become stereotyped and bureaucratic. The spirit of enterprise and challenge has been lost.... When Mr. Kawai was president, the time and our situation allowed him to employ a top-down approach to lead the company. But times have changed.... First, the world economy is more and more borderless, and companies must play an important role in developing international harmony. Also, the values of the young people in Japan are changing, and increasingly they question narrow, top-down directions.

A New Culture; A New Direction

Managers at Komatsu confirmed that Katada was less autocratic than prior leaders. Said one colleague, "Mr. Katada believes that one can't manage from the top down, and that any important idea or concept should be fully understood by everyone before a campaign proceeds.... His style of free discussion is new in Komatsu."

In keeping with his participatory style, Katada encouraged debate about the company's future direction. In off-site meetings and other forums, he invited a broad spectrum of managers to help shape Komatsu's new mission. During a June 1989 off-site meeting (billed as a "directors' free-discussion camp-out"), Katada proposed a new slogan to help crystallize the nascent consensus of the company's new strategic thrusts: "Growth, Global, Groupwide," or the "Three G's." Katada explained:

Top-down management by policy is becoming obsolete. Although it is still useful, we can no longer have TQC at the center of the management process. The future outlook for the indus-

try is not bright. Managers can no longer operate within the confines of a defined objective. They need to go out and see the needs and opportunities, and operate in a creative and innovative way, always encouraging initiative from below....

Although the "three G" slogan is something I came up with when I became president, there's nothing new or unusual about it given the economic conditions we were in—stagnant sales and a bureaucratic and rigidly structured company. These three simple words were intended to promote discussions, directions and policies at the board level and throughout the organization. The slogan may seem abstract, but it was this abstract nature that stimulated people to ask what they could do, and respond creatively.

Stimulating New Initiatives

Stimulated by the new open organizational forums, and encouraged by Katada's participative and challenging management style, Komatsu executives struggled to give meaning and definition to the "Three G's" slogan in a series of meetings that cascaded down the organization from September 1989 to March 1990. By this time, Katada and his top team were ready to formally adopt the new slogan and operationalize it in a long-term strategic plan, known as "Project G."

The most basic element of Project G was that the organization committed itself to return to growth, the first of the three Gs. Following the months of intensive negotiation and debate during 1989–1990, Katada announced that the company would aim at achieving a sales level of ¥1,400 billion by the mid-1990s—a level almost double its 1989 revenue level.

The core task in achieving this objective was to begin to grow construction equipment sales that had been stagnating (as reported in yen) since the early 1980s. This was to be the company's major globalization task—the second G—and Katada predicted that by the year 2000, the overseas operations of this business would manufacture over half of Komatsu's total output. To signal his continued commitment to this core business, Katada announced plans to triple the company's capital investment in construction equipment to ¥50 billion per annum, and challenged his managers to develop the proposals to justify that commitment.

Beyond revitalizing construction equipment, the third major element in Project G was a belief that Komatsu had to reduce its dependence on its traditional business through the groupwide leveraging of existing assets and resources to apply them to new product and business opportunities. Katada planned to encourage his organization to grow business such as electronics, robotics and plastics, so that by the mid 1990s the nonconstruction part of Komatsu would account for 50 percent of its sales. (For a representation of Komatsu's diverse business holdings, see Figure 2).

To communicate this new vision, Katada began referring to the company not as a construction equipment manufacturer (and certainly not as one that defined itself in terms of its old rival Caterpillar), but rather as "a total technology enterprise." And the old Japan-centered, engineering-dominated organization was now redefined in futuristic terms as "a globally integrated high-tech organization that integrates hardware and software as systems."

GLOBALIZING CONSTRUCTION EQUIPMENT

The implications of Project G for Komatsu's core construction equipment business were profound. It implied a commitment to globalization that would build on and expand the thrust that had begun in the late 1980s under Katada's urging when he was director for corporate planning. Mr. Aoyama, Katada's new director for corporate planning, commented on the business's new long-term strategic objectives outside Japan:

> We don't want our strategic position to depend just on exchange rate fluctuations or the latest trade frictions. We want a stable, perpetual system of being in the construction equipment business around the world in a more integrated way, starting from development through marketing and sales.

Katada wanted to change the way the construction equipment business was managed, loosening the traditional company policy of whole ownership and control over subsidiaries to allow much more flexibility and local participation. Under his guidance, Komatsu Dresser Corporation (KDC) had not only been structured as a 50/50 joint venture, but was managed jointly. Indeed, despite the fact that it contributed half of the joint venture's equity, Komatsu asked for only two seats on KDC's twelve-person board—and it asked Dresser to provide the

CEO. (It did, however, still maintain equal management representation on KDC's six-person management committee that oversaw operations and decided the basic policy for the joint venture.) Katada explained the change in thinking behind the new organization:

> We have begun to doubt whether it is possible to become a "localized and international enterprise" using only the capital, management, and engineers of Komatsu. I consider the joint venture to be a combination of Japanese technology with American management and marketing. Of course, Japanese also have pride and confidence in their administrative and marketing skills, but these cannot be fully effective in an American environment. At the same time, Dresser is behind in development and capital investment, so we plan to combine Komatsu's design and development technology with American management and marketing to achieve localization.

With a major presence in North America, attention next focused on Europe. In July 1989, one month after Katada became president, Komatsu acquired an interest in the 154-year-old German niche producer of construction equipment, Hanomag. In addition, the company finalized a supply arrangement with FAI spa, the Italian producer of mini-excavators. Over the next three years, Komatsu signed no fewer than eighteen agreements establishing various partnerships and alliances with local firms. Again, the objective was to obtain a local marketing and management capability.

To oversee the growing number of operations, Katada agreed to the proposal to form Komatsu Europe International SA (KEISA) in November 1989 to develop a more integrated group of European operations, and to coordinate the "mutual supply" of parts and increasingly specialized products. Under KEISA's guidance, for example, Hanomag took over Komatsu U.K.'s (KUK) production of wheel loaders. This arrangement capitalized both on Hanomag's 20 percent share of the German market for wheel loaders and its 100-outlet-strong distribution network in Europe. It also freed KUK to specialize in hydraulic excavators. Extending the specialized sourcing network, Italian licensee FAI supplied mini-excavators to all European markets. Table 5 shows the resulting regionalization and specialization that emerged.

FIGURE 2

The Komatsu Group

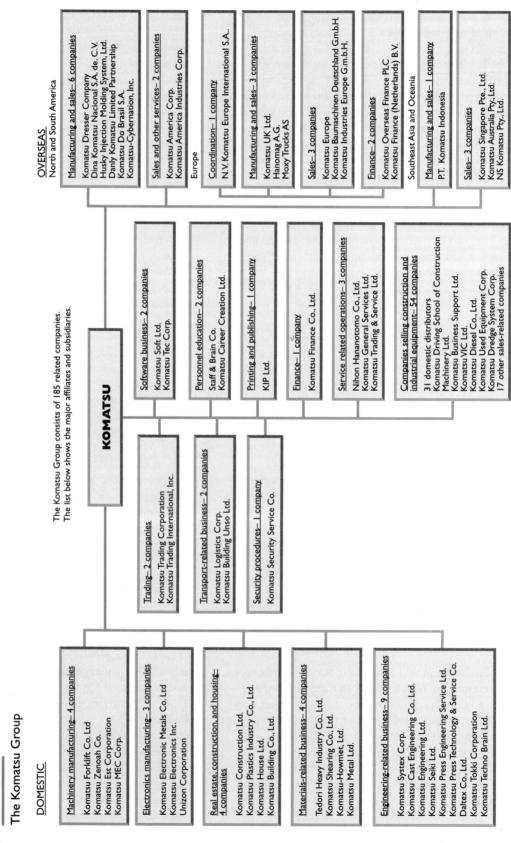

The Komatsu Group consists of 185 related companies.
The list below shows the major affiliates and subsidiaries.

DOMESTIC

KOMATSU

OVERSEAS
North and South America

Machinery manufacturing— 4 companies

Komatsu Forklift Co. Ltd
Komatsu Zenoah Co.
Komatsu Est Corporation
Komatsu MEC Corp.

Electronics manufacturing— 3 companies

Komatsu Electronic Metals Co. Ltd
Komatsu Electronics Inc.
Unizon Corporation

Real estate, construction, and housing—
4 companies

Komatsu Construction Ltd.
Komatsu Plastics Industry Co., Ltd.
Komatsu House Ltd.
Komatsu Building Co., Ltd.

Materials-related business— 4 companies

Tedori Heavy Industry Co., Ltd.
Komatsu Shearing Co., Ltd.
Komatsu-Howmet, Ltd.
Komatsu Metal Ltd.

Engineering-related business— 9 companies

Komatsu Systex Corp.
Komatsu Cast Engineering Co., Ltd.
Komatsu Engineering Ltd.
Komatsu Seiki Ltd.
Komatsu Press Engineering Service Ltd.
Komatsu Press Technology & Service Co.
Daltex Co., Ltd.
Komatsu Tokki Corporation
Komatsu Techno Brain Ltd.

Trading— 2 companies

Komatsu Trading Corporation
Komatsu Trading International, Inc.

Transport-related business— 2 companies

Komatsu Logistics Corp.
Komatsu Building Unso Ltd.

Security procedures— 1 company

Komatsu Security Service Co.

Software business— 2 companies

Komatsu Soft Ltd.
Komatsu Tec Corp.

Personnel education— 2 companies

Staff & Brain Co.
Komatsu Career Creation Ltd.

Printing and publishing— 1 company

KIP Ltd.

Finance— 1 company

Komatsu Finance Co., Ltd.

Service related operations— 3 companies

Nihon Hananotomo Co., Ltd.
Komatsu General Services Ltd.
Komatsu Trading & Service Ltd.

Companies selling construction and
industrial equipment— 54 companies

31 domestic distributors
Komatsu Driving School of Construction
    Machinery Ltd.
Komatsu Business Support Ltd.
Komatsu VIC Ltd.
Komatsu Diesel Co., Ltd.
Komatsu Used Equipment Corp.
Komatsu Dredge System Corp.
17 other sales-related companies

Manufacturing and sales— 6 companies

Komatsu Dresser Company
Dina Komatsu Nacional S.A. de. C.V.
Husky Injection Molding System, Ltd.
Danly Komatsu Limited Partnership
Komatsu Do Brasil S.A.
Komatsu-Cybernation, Inc.

Sales and other services— 2 companies

Komatsu America Corp.
Komatsu America Industries Corp.

Europe

Coordination— 1 company

N.V. Komatsu Europe International S.A...

Manufacturing and sales— 3 companies

Komatsu UK Ltd.
Hanomag A.G.
Moxy Trucks AS

Sales— 3 companies

Komatsu Europe
Komatsu Baumaschinen Deutschland G.m.b.H.
Komatsu Industries Europe G.m.b.H.

Finance— 2 companies

Komatsu Overseas Finance PLC
Komatsu Finance (Netherlands) B.V.

Southeast Asia and Oceania

Manufacturing and sales— 1 company

P.T. Komatsu Indonesia

Sales— 3 companies

Komatsu Singapore Pte., Ltd.
Komatsu Australia Pty, Ltd.
NS Komatsu Pty., Ltd.

TABLE 5

Specialization of Manufacturing Operations by Region and by Plant, 1992

Plant Komatsu Share (year stake taken)	Komatsu Ownership %	Number of Employees (= Japanese Expatriates)	Main Product	Local Content	Regions Supplied
Europe:					
Komatsu UK (1985)	100%	370 (10)[a]	Hydraulic excavators	70–75%	Europe, North Africa
Hanomag, Germany (1988)	64.1	1,600 (5)[a]	Wheel loaders	60–65	Europe, North Africa
FAI, spa, Italy (1991)	10	600	Mini-excavators	85	Europe, North Africa
Asia (non-Japan):					
Indonesia (1982)	50	530 (24)[a]	Bulldozers, wheel loaders	15–25	Indonesia, SE Asia, cast metal for Japan
			Hydraulic excavators, motor graders, casting and forging products, sheet metal (for Japan)		
Americas:					
Komatsu Dresser Corp. (1988)[b]	50	2779	Wheel loaders, hydraulic excavators, dump trucks, motor graders	50–65	U.S., Canada
Mexico (1974)	68.4	190 (15)[b]	Small pressers, sheet metal to USA	NA	Small presses to U.S.; sheet metal
Brazil (1973)	100	1,010 (10)[a] (10)[a]	Hydraulic excavators, bulldozers, wheel loaders, motor graders	8–95	South America, U.S., Indonesia

Source: Company records; Komatsu *Fact Book,* 1992.

[a]Number of Japanese employees as of year-end 1991.

[b]Includes companies in Peoria (1,020 employees), Chattanooga (261), Gallon (330), Candiac, Canada (110)

TABLE 6

Construction Equipment: Overseas Production (¥ million)

Overseas Production Subsidiaries	1986	1987	1988	1989	1990	1991	1992
Komatsu Dresser Co.					¥182,000[b]	¥199,000	¥136,000
Komatsu America Mfg. Corp.	NM[a]	¥600	¥17,100	¥25,400	NM	NM	NM
Komatsu Do Brasil SA	¥7,100	7,000	11,700	9,200	NM	NM	1,100[c]
Komatsu UK Ltd.	NM[a]	100	4,400	12,600	19,000	19,200	18,600
Dina Komatsu Nacional							
SA de CV	6,400	1,600	1,900	1,800	2,200	NM	NM
PT Komatsu Indonesia	3,100	2,400	6,400	5,500	8,600	11,600	9,300
Hanomag AG	NM	NM	NM	NM	NM	26,700	26,300
Overseas production	16,600	11,700	41,500	54,500	211,800	256,500	191,600
Domestic production	500,800	475,500	427,500	447,600	489,400	533,200	437,200
Overseas production as percentage of total production	3.2	2.4	8.9	12.2	30.2	32.5	30.5

Source: Company records.

"NM" = not meaningful (see notes below).

[a]Production began in the United States and the United Kingdom at the end of 1986.

[b]After 1989, Komatsu America Mfg. Corp. and Komatsu Brasil SA were reported as part of the Komatsu Dresser joint venture.

[c]In October 1991, Komatsu Brasil SA was again separated from Komatsu Dresser.

As a result of the aggressive expansion of offshore operations, the company's overseas production of construction equipment rose from ¥11.7 billion, or 2.4 percent of total production in 1987, to ¥256.5 billion, or 32.5 percent of the total in 1991 (see Table 6). This growth in offshore production, together with an overall slowdown in the market, led to a major decline in the importance of parent company export sales. Accounting for 67 percent of sales at its peak in 1982 Komatsu Limited's export ratio had fallen to 37.7 percent by 1992. Nonetheless, exports still remained an important part of Komatsu's sales to all three global regions (see Table 7).

Expanding Overseas Responsibilities

Beyond developing its resource base abroad, the construction equipment management group also began to expand the roles and responsibilities of these offshore operations. With an overall vision of building a three-party, regional geographic structure, these overseas units began to develop not only manufacturing and sales functions, but also purchasing and development capabilities.

In the late 1980s, international production facilities mushroomed from a handful of offshore assembly plants to a worldwide network of sophisticated manufacturing facilities as described briefly above. Much more gradual was the shift in responsibilities for product design and development. The company's traditionally centralized development and applications policies were challenged when Hanomag's operations were found to have excellent engineering and development capabilities. The company decided to build on this asset by delegating clear development responsibility to the German company, and eliminating some duplication of effort with Tokyo. For example, management gave Hanomag full responsibility to develop all small wheel loaders for Europe, and a joint-development role with Tokyo on larger models.

In its U.K. company, however, the decision was a more basic one. Up until 1988, KUK had a three-person product engineering office headed by a Japanese manager, whose main task was to make minor modifications to Japanese drawings. Gradually, however, Komatsu began transferring responsibility for the redevelopment of the PW170 wheel excavator to a new development facility in KUK, expanding the department to include twenty-seven design engineers and twelve test engineers by 1992.

Such responsibility transfer had considerable immediate and tangible benefits. Starting with an

TABLE 7

Komatsu Financial Highlights, 1982–1989 (consolidated, ¥million)

	The Americas			Europe, Middle East, and Asia			Asia and Oceania			Total		
	Net Sales		Company	Net Sales		Company	Net Sales		Company	Net Sales		Exchange
	Yen in billions	U.S. $ In millions	Export Share (%)	Yen in billions	U.S. $ in millions	Export Share (%)	Yen in billions	U.S. $ in millions	Export Share (%)	Yen in billions	U.S. $ in millions	Rate (Yen/Dollar)
1979	¥49	$205	26.8	¥88	$367	48.0	¥46	$192	25.2	¥183	$764	240
1980	51	248	21.8	128	628	55.3	53	260	22.9	232	1,136	204
1981	57	261	18.7	203	920	66.0	47	214	15.3	307	1,396	220
1982	31	131	7.4	274	1,163	65.9	111	471	26.7	416	1,753	236
1983	41	177	10.9	268	1,157	71.3	67	288	17.7	376	1,621	232
1984	107	423	34.1	149	591	47.6	57	227	18.3	313	1,240	252
1985	103	517	31.8	145	723	44.4	78	388	23.8	325	1,627	200
1986	94	594	29.2	180	1,140	56.1	47	299	14.7	321	2,032	158
1987	87	718	36.3	98	812	41.1	54	445	22.6	239	1,976	121
1989	67	505	33.6	80	605	40.2	53	395	26.2	200	1,505	133
1990	61	385	28.1	81	513	37.4	75	472	34.5	216	1,370	158
1991	50	354	21.6	94	667	40.7	87	617	37.7	231	1,638	141
1992	38	282	19.2	97	728	49.7	61	456	31.1	195	1,466	133

Source: Company records.

Note: The exchange rate for each year reflects the Federal Reserve Bank of New York fiscal year-end average. This table excludes the three-month fiscal period ended March 31, 1988, because it represented an extraordinary term caused by the change in the fiscal period.

existing undercarriage from Europe, KUK engineers designed and modified a wheel excavator to satisfy European safety regulations and new work range requirements. Aware of strict local standards on braking and steering performance, these British engineers reduced the engine size and thus maximum speed, avoiding a far more costly redesign of the braking system. German engineers at Hanomag, too, modified basic product dimensions of a different vehicle to meet European roadwidth standards, creating a model better suited to local conditions than Tokyo's. Generally, local engineers were also able to simplify the manufacturing process design and bring the new product to market far faster than if it had been engineered in Tokyo. By operating according to centrally mandated standards covering parts and serviceability concepts, designers ensured that parts for the locally designed product were compatible with others in its product line. Said one former KUK manager:

> Before, if manufacturing had a concern about a drawing, they had no way to complain. Three engineers could not solve the problem. Information had to be transferred to Tokyo asking for a solution from the Osaka test center. Now, locals can decide on design changes as long as they meet commonality requirements.

KUK's recently opened test center, and its newly assigned responsibility for two additional projects, pointed to a continually expanding role for the group. The impact on local morale was immediate and visible.

Localizing Management

To have enduring value, it was clear to Komatsu's top management—and constantly emphasized by Katada—that this transfer of responsibility had to be accompanied by an equally strong commitment to the recruitment, development, and promotion of local managers. This strong belief was formalized in a July 1989 human resources policy that required a substantial increase in the number of foreign nationals in management positions. Komatsu Europe, for example, reduced the number of Japanese managers from 26 out of 180 employees in 1986 to 13 out of 260 by 1992, and planned to reduce that number to 6 within two years.

Despite the transfer of responsibilities and the replacement of expatriates with locals, Komatsu

managers expressed surprise at how long the transition was taking. For example, their strong belief that "bottom-up problem solving" was an essential ingredient of the spirit of Komatsu led to frustration at the lack of initiative at the local level as responsibility was expanded. When one senior executive routinely began to answer employee reports of problems with the question, "How do you propose we fix it?" he was disappointed to find that typically the employees were surprised—and without answer. Other managers commented on fundamental differences in attitudes toward core values such as quality and customer service, and how long it took for such values to take deep root in Komatsu subsidiaries.

Those running the business found several causes of these problems and several areas where they needed to take action. Part of the challenge of localizing management entailed changing the way headquarters communicated with the subsidiaries. Mr. Suketomo, a director and former president of KUK, explained his difficulty in motivating non-Japanese employees in an environment where all high-level documents were written in Japanese:

> When I became KUK's president, there was a real difficulty with the language problem because all important communication with Tokyo was in Japanese. So my first job was to send a letter to Tokyo explaining that *all* communication from Tokyo would be in English, or I would ignore it! Soon, all official letters to me were in English. It not only allowed me to distribute copies to local managers, but more importantly, it forced expatriate staff to improve their English skills.

The other major problem was that many of the local nationals recruited in the earlier era were not strong managers. The main need prior to the late 1980s was for loyal implementers—"yes men," as one Japanese executive described them. As a result, many were not equal to the new challenges being given to them, and overseas units had to undertake major efforts to upgrade their personnel. In 1987, for example, Komatsu Europe had recruited only one university graduate; by 1991, it had recruited twenty-three, including its first two MBAs.

Localization created another unforeseen problem. As the number of Japanese nationals in the overseas operations decreased, the local entities' ability to coordinate their activities with the parent company—and even with each other—began to deteriorate noticeably. Numerous examples of miscommunication began to surface regularly, on issues ranging from market forecasts to product specifications. Said one observer:

> Just at the time they need more coordination than ever, they are reducing the number of Japanese managers abroad. For many Japanese companies, the most difficult task for local nationals has been to operate effectively in a linkage or coordinative role due to the high language and cultural barriers within the organization. As they increase their global integration, the intensity of such a role is going to increase dramatically.

Despite these difficulties in adjusting, in 1992 some managers believed that Japanese and Western management practices were converging, with each group learning from the other. Said one manager who spent four years in KDC:

> Our partner's style is very different from ours. The Komatsu style represents the typical Japanese emphasis on growth potential and market share for long-term survival. Dresser puts the highest priority on ROI and profit measures. Because of these differences, we encountered some friction at first. Recently, Komatsu managers have learned the importance of ROI; and those in Dresser came to understand that they must think beyond the short-term. In the future, I think we can expect a hybrid system of management.

Management also began to recognize that its localization program was only one step on a long road to fully internationalizing the management process. As Katada told the Japanese press in November 1990,

> Our goal is to transfer management from Tokyo to overseas outlets run by local nationals. As far as nationalities are concerned, this has already been accomplished in such key units as Komatsu Dresser and Hanomag. . . . But this is not enough for doing business. In this regard, what we really need to do is internationalize our headquarters in Tokyo.

Two full years later, Suketomo felt pride in the achievements, but echoed Katada's concerns:

> We have been successful increasing the local management of KUK, but there is a danger here in our thinking. If you ask, "Could the top of KUK or KDC become top of the home office in Japan, I would have to express my doubt. That reflects a limitation on our part, and I think we should see that as a challenge.

Achievements and Challenges

After three years of growth, Komatsu's construction equipment business experienced a sharp downturn in 1992. Overseas sales fell 10.6 percent to ¥246 billion, while domestic sales in this segment slipped even further, falling 13.5 percent to ¥334 billion. Worse, its operating income from construction equipment plummeted 60 percent.

Management attributed the setback to the downturn in industry demand associated with a recession that seemed to be deepening worldwide in 1992. To some industry observers, however, the continued performance problems also hinted at deeper problems with Komatsu's overall globalization strategy. Said one:

> There are clear risks in basing international expansion so heavily on joint ventures with and acquisitions of local and regional players each of which has different products, capabilities, and approaches. It's going to be hard for them to achieve the same product quality, efficiency, and strategic focus as they had a decade ago. The task is made all the more difficult if we continue to withdraw experienced Japanese expatriates from our overseas operations in the name of localization.

Nonetheless, Katada remained confident. In response to the downturn, he confirmed that Komatsu would continue its long-term globalization investments and its commitment to localization. In the short term, he was preparing a major new sales drive for hydraulic excavators, wheel loaders, and dump trucks in all three regional markets. He was clearly prepared to stay the course.

Endnotes

1. For a detailed description of the Kawai era, see "Komatsu: Ryoichi Kawai's Leadership," *Harvard Business School Case* No. 390-037.
2. See G. Hamel and C. K. Prahalad, "Strategic Intent," *Harvard Business Review* (May–June 1989), 63.

CASE 25

Kentucky Fried Chicken and the Global Fast-Food Industry

This case was prepared by Jeffrey A. Krug of the University of Illinois at Urbana–Champaign.

Kentucky Fried Chicken Corporation (KFC) was the world's largest chicken restaurant chain and third largest fast-food chain. KFC held more than 55 percent of the U.S. market in terms of sales and operated more than 10,200 restaurants worldwide in 1998. It opened 376 new restaurants in 1997 (more than one restaurant a day) and operated in seventy-nine countries. One of the first fast-food chains to go international during the late 1960s, KFC has developed one of the world's most recognizable brands.

Japan, Australia, and the United Kingdom accounted for the greatest share of KFC's international expansion during the 1970s and 1980s. During the 1990s, KFC turned its attention to other international markets that offered significant opportunities for growth. China, with a population of more than 1 billion, and Europe, with a population roughly equal to that of the United States, offered such opportunities. Latin America also offered a unique opportunity because of the size of its markets, its common language and culture, and its geographical proximity to the United States. Mexico was of particular interest because of the North American Free Trade Agreement (NAFTA), a free trade zone between Canada, the United States, and Mexico that went into effect in 1994.

Prior to 1990, KFC expanded into Latin America primarily through company-owned restaurants in Mexico and Puerto Rico. Company-owned restaurants gave KFC greater control over its operations than franchised or licensed restaurants. By 1995, KFC had also established company-owned restaurants in Venezuela and Brazil. In addition, it had established franchised units in several Caribbean countries. During the early 1990s, KFC shifted to a two-tier strategy in Latin America. First, it established twenty-nine franchised restaurants in Mexico following enactment of Mexico's new franchise law in 1990. This allowed KFC to expand outside of its company restaurant base in Mexico City, Guadalajara, and Monterrey. KFC was only one of many U.S. fast-food, retail, and hotel chains to begin franchising in Mexico following the new franchise law. Second, KFC began an aggressive franchise-building program in South America. By 1998, it was operating franchised restaurants in thirty-two Latin American countries. Much of this growth was in Brazil, Chile, Colombia, Ecuador, and Peru.

COMPANY HISTORY

Fast-food franchising was still in its infancy in 1952 when Harland Sanders began his travels across the United States to speak with prospective franchisees about his "Colonel Sanders Recipe Kentucky Fried Chicken." By 1960, "Colonel" Sanders had granted KFC franchises to more than 200 take-home retail outlets and restaurants across the United States. He had also succeeded in establishing a number of franchises in Canada. By 1963, the number of KFC franchises had risen to more than 300 and revenues had reached $500 million.

By 1964, at the age of seventy-four, the Colonel

This case is intended to be used as the basis for class discussion rather than as an illustration of effective or ineffective handling of the situation. This case was prepared by Jeffrey A. Krug, University of Illinois at Urbana–Champaign. Used by permission.

had tired of running the day-to-day operations of his business and was eager to concentrate on public relations issues. Therefore, he sought out potential buyers, eventually deciding to sell the business to two Louisville businessmen—Jack Massey and John Young Brown Jr.—for $2 million. The Colonel stayed on as a public relations man and goodwill ambassador for the company.

During the next five years, Massey and Brown concentrated on growing KFC's franchise system across the United States. In 1966, they took KFC public and the company was listed on the New York Stock Exchange. By the late 1960s, a strong foothold had been established in the United States, and Massey and Brown turned their attention to international markets. In 1969, a joint venture was signed with Mitsuoishi Shoji Kaisha, Ltd., in Japan, and the rights to operate 14 existing KFC franchises in England were acquired. Subsidiaries were also established in Hong Kong, South Africa, Australia, New Zealand, and Mexico. By 1971, KFC had 2,450 franchises and 600 company-owned restaurants worldwide, and was operating in forty-eight countries.

Heublein, Inc.

In 1971, KFC entered negotiations with Heublein, Inc., to discuss a possible merger. The decision to seek a merger candidate was partially driven by Brown's desire to pursue other interests, including a political career (Brown was elected governor of Kentucky in 1977). Several months later, Heublein acquired KFC. Heublein was in the business of producing vodka, mixed cocktails, dry gin, cordials, beer, and other alcoholic beverages. However, Heublein had little experience in the restaurant business. Conflicts quickly erupted between Sanders, who continued to act in a public relations capacity, and Heublein management. Sanders became increasingly distraught over quality-control issues and restaurant cleanliness. By 1977, new restaurant openings had slowed to about twenty per year. Few restaurants were being remodeled and service quality had declined.

In 1977, Heublein sent in a new management team to redirect KFC's strategy. A "back-to-the-basics" strategy was immediately implemented. New unit construction was discontinued until existing restaurants could be upgraded and operating problems eliminated. Restaurants were refurbished, an emphasis was placed on cleanliness and service,

marginal products were eliminated, and product consistency was reestablished. By 1982, KFC had succeeded in establishing a successful strategic focus and was again aggressively building new units.

R.J. Reynolds Industries, Inc.

In 1982, R.J. Reynolds Industries, Inc. (RJR), merged Heublein into a wholly owned subsidiary. The merger with Heublein represented part of RJR's overall corporate strategy of diversifying into unrelated businesses, including energy, transportation, food, and restaurants. RJR's objective was to reduce its dependence on the tobacco industry, which had driven RJR sales since its founding in North Carolina in 1875. Sales of cigarettes and tobacco products, while profitable, were declining because of reduced consumption in the United States. This was mainly the result of an increased awareness among Americans about the negative health consequences of smoking.

RJR had no more experience in the restaurant business than did Heublein. However, it decided to take a hands-off approach to managing KFC. Whereas Heublein had installed its own top management at KFC headquarters, RJR left KFC management largely intact, believing that existing KFC managers were better qualified to operate KFC's businesses than were its own managers. In doing so, RJR avoided many of the operating problems that plagued Heublein. This strategy paid off for RJR as KFC continued to expand aggressively and profitably under RJR ownership. In 1985, RJR acquired Nabisco Corporation for $4.9 billion. Nabisco sold a variety of well-known cookies, crackers, cereals, confectioneries, snacks, and other grocery products. The merger with Nabisco represented a decision by RJR to concentrate its diversification efforts on the consumer foods industry. It subsequently divested many of its nonconsumer food businesses. RJR sold KFC to PepsiCo, Inc. one year later.

PEPSICO

Corporate Strategy

PepsiCo, Inc., was formed in 1965 with the merger of the Pepsi-Cola Co. and Frito-Lay Inc. The merger of these companies created one of the largest consumer products companies in the United States. Pepsi-Cola's traditional business was the sale of soft drink concentrates to licensed independent and company-owned bottlers that manufactured, sold, and distributed Pepsi-Cola soft drinks. Pepsi-Cola's best known trademarks were Pepsi-Cola, Diet Pepsi, Mountain Dew, and Slice. Frito-Lay manufactured and sold a variety of snack foods, including Fritos Corn Chips, Lay's Potato Chips, Ruffles Potato Chips, Doritos, Tostitos Tortilla Chips, and Chee-tos Cheese Flavored Snacks. PepsiCo quickly embarked on an aggressive acquisition program similar to that pursued by RJR during the 1980s, buying a number of companies in areas unrelated to its major businesses. Its acquisitions included North American Van Lines, Wilson Sporting Goods, and Lee Way Motor Freight. However, these businesses did not prove as successful as the company had expected, mainly because PepsiCo lacked the expertise required to operate them.

Poor performance in these businesses led the then chairman and chief executive officer Don Kendall to restructure PepsiCo's operations in 1984. First, businesses that did not support PepsiCo's consumer product orientation, such as North American Van Lines, Wilson Sporting Goods, and Lee Way Motor Freight were divested. Second, the company sold its foreign bottling operations to local businesspeople, who better understood the culture and business environment in their respective countries. Third, Kendall reorganized PepsiCo along three lines: soft drinks, snack foods, and restaurants.

Restaurant Business and Acquisition of Kentucky Fried Chicken

PepsiCo first entered the restaurant business in 1977 when it acquired Pizza Hut's 3,200-unit restaurant system. Taco Bell was merged into a division of PepsiCo in 1978. The restaurant business complemented PepsiCo's consumer product orientation. The marketing of fast food followed many of the same patterns as the marketing of soft drinks and snack foods. Therefore, PepsiCo believed that its management skills could be easily transferred among its three business segments. This was compatible with the company's practice of frequently moving managers among its business units as a way of developing future top executives. PepsiCo's restaurant chains also provided an additional outlet for the sale of Pepsi soft drinks. Pepsi-Cola soft drinks and fast-food products could be marketed together in the same television and radio segments,

thereby providing higher returns for each advertising dollar. To complete its diversification into the restaurant segment, PepsiCo acquired Kentucky Fried Chicken Corporation from RJR-Nabisco for $841 million in 1986. The acquisition of KFC gave PepsiCo the leading market share in chicken (KFC), pizza (Pizza Hut), and Mexican food (Taco Bell), three of the four largest and fastest-growing segments within the U.S. fast-food industry.

Management

Following the acquisition by PepsiCo, KFC's relationship with its parent company underwent dramatic changes. RJR had operated KFC as a semiautonomous unit, satisfied that KFC management understood the fast-food business better than it did. In contrast, PepsiCo acquired KFC in order to complement its already strong presence in the fast-food market. Rather than allowing KFC to operate autonomously, PepsiCo undertook sweeping changes. These changes included negotiating a new franchise contract to give PepsiCo more control over its franchisees, reducing staff in order to cut costs, and replacing KFC managers with its own. In 1987, a rumor spread through KFC's headquarters in Louisville that the new personnel manager, who had just relocated from PepsiCo's headquarters in New York, was overheard saying that "There will be no more home grown tomatoes in this organization."

Such statements by PepsiCo personnel, uncertainties caused by several restructurings that led to layoffs throughout the KFC organization, the replacement of KFC personnel with PepsiCo managers, and conflicts between KFC and PepsiCo's corporate cultures created a morale problem within KFC. KFC's culture was built largely on Sanders's laid-back approach to management. Employees enjoyed relatively good employment stability and security. Over the years, a strong loyalty had been created between KFC employees and franchisees, mainly because of Sanders's efforts to provide for his employees' benefits, pension, and other non-income needs. In addition, the southern environment of Louisville resulted in a friendly, relaxed atmosphere at KFC's corporate offices. This corporate culture was left essentially unchanged during the Heublein and RJR years.

In stark contrast to KFC, PepsiCo's culture was characterized by a strong emphasis on performance. Top performers expected to move up through the ranks quickly. PepsiCo used its KFC, Pizza Hut, Taco Bell, Frito Lay, and Pepsi-Cola divisions as training grounds for its top managers, rotating its best managers through its five divisions on average every two years. This practice created immense pressure on managers to continuously demonstrate their managerial prowess within short periods, in order to maximize their potential for promotion. It also made many KFC managers feel that they had few career opportunities with the new company. One PepsiCo manager commented that "You may have performed well last year, but if you don't perform well this year, you're gone, and there are 100 ambitious guys with Ivy League MBAs at PepsiCo who would love to take your position." An unwanted effect of this performance-driven culture was that employee loyalty was often lost and turnover tended to be higher than in other companies.

When Kyle Craig, president of KFC's U.S. operations, was asked about KFC's relationship with its corporate parent, he commented as follows:

> The KFC culture is an interesting one because I think it was dominated by a lot of KFC folks, many of whom have been around since the days of the Colonel. Many of those people were very intimidated by the PepsiCo culture which is a very high performance, high accountability, highly driven culture. People were concerned about whether they would succeed in the new culture. Like many companies, we have had a couple of downsizings which further made people nervous. Today, there are fewer old KFC people around and I think to some degree people have seen that the PepsiCo culture can drive some pretty positive results. I also think the PepsiCo people who have worked with KFC have modified their cultural values somewhat and they can see that there were a lot of benefits in the old KFC culture.

PepsiCo pushes their companies to perform strongly, but whenever there is a slip in performance, it increases the culture gap between PepsiCo and KFC. I have been involved in two downsizings over which I have been the chief architect. They have been probably the two most gut-wrenching experiences of my career. Because you know you're dealing with people's lives and their families, these changes can be emotional if you care about the people in your organization.

> However, I do fundamentally believe that your first obligation is to the entire organization.

A second problem for PepsiCo was its poor relationship with KFC franchisees. A month after becoming president and chief executive officer in 1989, John Cranor addressed KFC's franchisees in Louisville, in order to explain the details of the new franchise contract. This was the first contract change in thirteen years. It gave PepsiCo greater power to take over weak franchises, relocate restaurants, and make changes in existing restaurants. In addition, restaurants would no longer be protected from competition from new KFC units, and PepsiCo would have the right to raise royalty fees on existing restaurants as contracts came up for renewal. After Cranor finished his address, there was an uproar among the attending franchisees, who jumped to their feet to protest the changes. The franchisees had long been accustomed to relatively little interference from management in their day-to-day operations (a tradition begun by Sanders). This type of interference, of course, was a strong part of PepsiCo's philosophy of demanding change. KFC's franchise association later sued PepsiCo over the new contract. The issue remained unresolved until 1996, when the most objectionable parts of the contract were removed by KFC's new president and CEO, David Novak. A new contract was ratified by KFC's franchisees in 1997.

PepsiCo's Divestiture of KFC, Pizza Hut, and Taco Bell

PepsiCo's strategy of diversifying into three distinct but related markets—soft drinks, snack foods, and fast-food restaurants—created one of the world's largest consumer products companies and a portfolio of some of the world's most recognizable brands. Between 1990 and 1996, PepsiCo grew at an annual rate of more than 10 percent, surpassing $31 billion in sales in 1996. However, the company's sale growth masked troubles in its fast-food businesses. Operating margins (profit as a percent of sales) at Pepsi-Cola and Frito Lay averaged 12 and 17 percent between 1990 and 1996, respectively. During the same period, margins at KFC, Pizza Hut, and Taco Bell fell from an average of more than 8 percent in 1990 to a little more than 4 percent in 1996. Declining margins in the fast-food chains reflected increasing maturity in the U.S. fast-food industry, more intense competition among U.S. fast-food companies, and the aging of the KFC and Pizza Hut restaurant base. As a result, PepsiCo's restaurant chains absorbed nearly one-half of PepsiCo's annual capital spending during the 1990s. However, they generated less than one-third of PepsiCo's cash flows. Therefore, cash was diverted from PepsiCo's soft drink and snack food businesses to its restaurant businesses. This reduced PepsiCo's return on assets, made it more difficult to compete effectively with Coca-Cola, and hurt its stock price. In 1997, PepsiCo spun off its restaurant businesses into a new company, called Tricon Global Restaurants, Inc. (see Figure 1). The new company was based in KFC's headquarters in Louisville, Kentucky. PepsiCo's objective was to reposition itself as a packaged goods company, to strengthen its balance sheet, and to create more consistent earning growth. PepsiCo received a one-time distribution from Tricon of $4.7 billion, $3.7 billion of which was used to pay off short-term debt. The balance was earmarked for stock repurchases.

FAST-FOOD INDUSTRY

According to the National Restaurant Association (NRA), food-service sales topped $320 billion in 1997 for the approximately 500,000 restaurants and other food outlets making up the U.S. restaurant industry. The NRA estimated that sales in the fast-food segment of the food service industry grew 5.2 percent, to $104 billion, in 1997, up from $98 billion in 1996. This marked the fourth consecutive year that fast-food sales had either matched or exceeded sales in full-service restaurants, which grew 4.1 percent, to $104 billion, in 1997. The growth in fast-food sales reflected the long, gradual change in the restaurant industry from an industry once dominated by independently operated sit-down restaurants to an industry fast becoming dominated by fast-food restaurant chains. The U.S. restaurant industry as a whole grew by approximately 4.2 percent in 1997.

Major Fast-Food Segments

Six major business segments made up the fast-food segment of the food service industry. Sales data for the leading restaurant chains in each segment are shown in Table 1. Most striking is the dominance of McDonald's, which had sales of more than $16 billion in 1996. This represented 16.6 percent of U.S. fast-food sales, or nearly 22 percent of sales among the nation's top thirty fast-food chains. Sales at McDonald's restaurants averaged $1.3 million per year, compared with about $820,000 for the average U.S. fast-food restaurant. Tricon Global Restaurants (KFC, Pizza Hut, and Taco Bell) had U.S. sales of $13.4 billion in 1996. This represented 13.6 percent of U.S. fast-food sales and 17.9 percent of the top thirty fast-food chains.

Sandwich chains made up the largest segment of the fast-food market. McDonald's controlled 35

FIGURE I

Tricon Global
Restaurants'
Organizational Chart
(1998)

Tricon Global Restaurants, Inc.
Corporate Offices
(Louisville, Kentucky)
Andrall Pearson, chairman and CEO
David Novak, vice chairman and president

Kentucky Fried Chicken Corporate
(Louisville, Kentucky)
Jeffrey Moody, chief concept officer
Charles Rawley, chief operating officer

Pizza Hut, U.S.A.
(Dallas, Texas)
Michael Rawlings, president and CCO
Aylwin Lewis, chief operating officer

Taco Bell Corp.
(Irvine, California)
Peter Waller, president and CCO
Thomas Davin, chief operating officer

Tricon Restaurants International
(Dallas, Texas)
Peter Bassi, president

TABLE 1

Leading U.S. Fast-Food Chains Ranked by 1996 Sales (in $ thousands)

Sandwich Chains	Sales	Share (%)	Family Restaurants	Sales	Share (%)
McDonald's	$16,370	35.0	Denny's	$1,850	21.2
Burger King	7,300	15.6	Shoney's	1,220	14.0
Taco Bell	4,575	9.8	Big Boy	945	10.8
Wendy's	4,360	9.3	Int'l House of Pancakes	797	9.1
Hardee's	3,055	6.5	Cracker Barrel	734	8.4
Subway	2,700	5.8	Perkins	678	7.8
Arby's	1,867	4.0	Friendly's	597	6.8
Dairy Queen	1,225	2.6	Bob Evans	575	6.6
Jack in the Box	1,207	2.6	Waffle House	525	6.0
Sonic Drive-In	985	2.1	Coco's	278	3.2
Carl's Jr.	648	1.4	Steak 'n Shake	275	3.2
Other Chains	2,454	5.2	Village Inn	246	2.8
Total	$46,745	100.0	Total	$8,719	100.0

Dinner Houses	Sales	Share (%)	Pizza Chains	Sales	Share (%)
Red Lobster	$1,810	15.7	Pizza Hut	4,927	46.4
Applebee's	1,523	13.2	Domino's Pizza	2,300	21.7
Olive Garden	1,280	11.1	Little Caesars	1,425	13.4
Chile's	1,242	10.7	Papa John's	619	5.8
Outback Steakhouse	1,017	8.8	Sbarros	400	3.8
T.G.I. Friday's	935	8.1	Round Table Pizza	385	3.6
Ruby Tuesday	545	4.7	Chuck E. Cheese's	293	2.8
Lone Star Steakhouse	460	4.0	Godfather's Pizza	266	2.5
Bennigan's	458	4.0	Total	$10,614	100.0
Romano's Macaroni Grill	344	3.0			
Other Dinner Houses	1,942	16.8			
Total	$11,557	100.0			

Chicken Chains	Sales	Share (%)
KFC	$3,900	57.1
Boston Market	1,167	17.1
Popeye's Chicken	666	9.7
Chick-fil-A	570	8.3
Church's Chicken	529	7.7
Total	$6,832	100.0

Grilled Buffet Chains	Sales	Share (%)
Golden Corral	$711	22.8
Ponderosa	680	21.8
Ryan's	604	19.4
Sizzler	540	17.3
Western Sizzlin'	332	10.3
Quincy's	259	8.3
Total	$3,116	100.0

Source: Nation's Restaurant News.

percent of the sandwich segment, while Burger King ran a distant second with a 15.6 percent market share. Competition had grown particularly intense within the sandwich segment as the U.S. fast-food market became more saturated. To increase sales, chains sought to win customers away from other sandwich chains by offering new products, introduced products traditionally offered by non-sandwich chains (such as pizzas, fried chicken, and tacos), streamlined their menus, and upgraded product quality. Burger King introduced its Big King, a direct clone of the Big Mac. McDonald's quickly retaliated by introducing its Big 'n Tasty, a direct clone of the Whopper. Wendy's introduced chicken pita sandwiches and Taco Bell introduced sandwiches called "wraps"—breads stuffed with various fillings. Hardee's successfully introduced fried chicken in most of its restaurants. Besides turning out new products, chains lowered prices, improved customer service, cobranded with other fast-food chains, and established restaurants in non-traditional locations (for instance, McDonald's installed restaurants in Wal-Mart stores across the country) to beef up sales.

The second largest fast-food segment was dinner houses, dominated by Red Lobster, Applebee's, Olive Garden, and Chili's. Between 1988 and 1996, dinner houses increased their share of the fast-food market from 8 to more than 13 percent. This increase came mainly at the expense of grilled-buffet chains, such as Ponderosa, Sizzler, and Western Sizzlin'. The market share of steak houses fell from 6 percent in 1988 to less than 4 percent in 1996. The rise of dinner houses during the 1990s was partly the result of an aging and wealthier population, which increasingly demanded higher-quality food in more upscale settings. However, rapid construction of new restaurants, especially among relative newcomers, such as Romano's Macaroni Grill, Lone Star Steakhouse, and Outback Steakhouse, resulted in overcapacity within the dinner house segment. This reduced per restaurant sales and further intensified competition. Eight of the sixteen largest dinner houses posted growth rates of 10 percent or more in 1996: Romano's Macaroni Grill, 82 percent; Lone Star Steakhouse, 41 percent; Chili's, 32 percent; Outback Steakhouse, 27 percent; Applebee's, 23 percent; Red Robin, 14 percent; Fuddruckers, 11 percent; and Ruby Tuesday, 10 percent.

The third largest fast-food segment was pizza, long dominated by Pizza Hut. While Pizza Hut controlled more than 46 percent of the pizza segment in 1996, its market share had slowly eroded because of intense competition and its aging restaurant base. Domino's Pizza and Papa John's Pizza have been particularly successful. Little Caesars is the only pizza chain to remain predominately a takeout chain, though it recently began home delivery. However, its policy of charging customers $1 per delivery damaged consumers' perception of it as a high value pizza chain. Home delivery, successfully introduced by Domino's and Pizza Hut, was a driving force for success among the market leaders

during the 1970s and 1980s. However, the success of home delivery drove competitors to look for new methods of increasing their customer bases. Pizza chains diversified into non-pizza items (for example, chicken wings at Domino's, Italian cheese bread at Little Caesars, and stuffed crust pizza at Pizza Hut), developed nontraditional units (such as airport kiosks and college campuses), offered special promotions, and brought out new pizza variations with an emphasis on high-quality ingredients (for instance, Roma Herb and Garlic Crunch pizza at Domino's and Buffalo Chicken Pizza at Round Table Pizza).

Chicken Segment

KFC continued to dominate the chicken segment, with 1997 sales of $4 billion (see Table 2). Its nearest competitor, Boston Market, was second with sales of $1.2 billion. In 1998, KFC operated 5,120 restaurants in the United States, 8 fewer restaurants than in 1993. Rather than building new restaurants in the already saturated U.S. market, KFC focused on building restaurants abroad. In the United States, KFC focused on closing unprofitable restaurants, upgrading existing restaurants with new exterior signage, and improving product quality. The strategy has paid off. While overall U.S. sales during the last ten years remained flat, annual sales per unit increased steadily in eight of the last nine years.

Despite KFC's continued dominance within the chicken segment, it has lost market share to Boston Market, a new restaurant chain emphasizing roasted rather than fried chicken. Boston Market has successfully created the image of an upscale deli offering healthy, "home-style" alternatives to fried chicken and other fast-foods. It has broadened its menu beyond rotisserie chicken to include ham, turkey, meat loaf, chicken pot pie, and deli sandwiches. In order to minimize its image as a fast-food place, it has refused to put drive-throughs in its restaurants and has established most of its units in outside shopping malls rather than in freestanding units at intersections so characteristic of other fast-food restaurants.

In 1993, KFC introduced its own rotisserie chicken, called Rotisserie Gold, to combat Boston Market. However, it quickly learned that its customer base was considerably different from that of Boston Market's. KFC's customers liked KFC chicken despite the fact that it was fried. In addi-

TABLE 2

Top U.S. Chicken Chains

	Sales (in $ millions)						
	1992	*1993*	*1994*	*1995*	*1996*	*1997*	*Growth Rate(%)*
KFC	$3,400	$3,400	$3,500	$3,700	$3,900	$4,000	3.3
Boston Market	43	147	371	754	1,100	1,197	94.5
Popeye's	545	569	614	660	677	727	5.9
Chick-fil-A	356	396	451	502	570	671	11.9
Church's	414	440	465	501	526	574	6.8
Total	$4,758	$4,952	$5,401	$6,118	$6,772	$7,170	8.5
	Number of U.S. Restaurants						
KFC	5,089	5,128	5,149	5,142	5,108	5,120	0.1
Boston Market	83	217	534	829	1,087	1,166	69.6
Popeye's	769	769	853	889	894	949	4.3
Chick-fil-A	487	545	534	825	717	762	9.0
Church's	944	932	937	953	9,890	1,070	2.5
Total	7,372	7,591	8,007	8,638	8,795	9,067	4.2
	Sales per Unit (in $ thousands)						
KFC	$668	$663	$680	$720	$764	$781	3.2
Boston Market	518	677	695	910	1,012	1,027	14.7
Popeye's	709	740	720	743	757	767	1.6
Chick-fil-A	731	727	845	608	795	881	3.8
Church's	439	472	496	526	531	537	4.1
Total	$645	$782	$782	$782	$782	$782	3.9

Source: Tricon Global Restaurants, Inc., 1997 Annual Report; Boston Chicken, Inc., 1997 Annual Report; Chick-fil-A, corporate headquarters, Atlanta; AFC Enterprises, Inc., 1997 Annual Report.

tion, customers did not respond well to the concept of buying whole chickens for takeout. They preferred to buy chicken by the piece. KFC withdrew its rotisserie chicken in 1996 and introduced a new line of roasted chicken called "Tender Roast," which could be sold by the piece and mixed with its Original Recipe and Extra Crispy Chicken.

Other major competitors within the chicken segment included Popeye's Famous Fried Chicken and Church's Chicken (both subsidiaries of AFC Enterprises in Atlanta), Chick-fil-A, Bojangle's, El Pollo Loco, Grandy's, Kenny Rogers Roasters, Mrs. Winner's, and Pudgie's. Both Church's and Popeye's had similar strategies—to compete head-on with other "fried chicken" chains. Unlike KFC, neither chain offered rotisserie chicken, and nonfried chicken products were limited. Chick-fil-A focused exclusively on pressure-cooked and char-grilled skinless chicken breast sandwiches, which it served to customers in sit-down restaurants located predominately in shopping malls. As many malls added food courts, often consisting of up to fifteen fast-food units competing side by side, shopping malls became less enthusiastic about allocating separate store space to food chains. Therefore, in order to complement its existing restaurant base in shopping malls, Chick-fil-A began to open smaller units in shopping mall food courts, hospitals, and colleges. It also opened freestanding units in selected locations.

Demographic Trends

A number of demographic and societal trends contributed to increased demand for food prepared away from home. Because of the high divorce rate in the United States and the fact that people married later in life, single-person households represented about 25 percent of all U.S. households, up from 17 percent in 1970. This increased the number of individuals choosing to eat out rather than eat at home. The number of married women working outside of the home also increased dramatically during the last quarter of the twentieth century, with about 59 percent of all married women having careers. According to the Conference Board, 64 percent of all married households will be double-income families by 2000. About 80 percent of households headed by individuals between the ages of twenty-five and forty-four (both married and unmarried) will be double-income. Greater numbers of working women increased family incomes. According to *Restaurants & Institutions* magazine, more than one-third of all households had incomes of at least $50,000 in 1996. About 8 percent of all households had annual incomes over $100,000. The combination of higher numbers of dual-career families and rising incomes meant that fewer families had time to prepare food at home. According to Standard & Poor's *Industry Surveys*, Americans spent 55 percent of their food dollars at restaurants in 1995, up from 34 percent in 1970.

Fast-food restaurant chains met these demographic and societal changes by expanding their restaurant bases. However, by the early 1990s, the growth of traditional freestanding restaurants slowed as the U.S. market became saturated. The major exception was dinner houses, which continued to proliferate in response to Americans' increased passion for beef. Since 1990, the U.S. population has grown at an average annual rate of about 1 percent and reached 270 million people in 1997. Rising immigration since 1990 dramatically altered the ethnic makeup of the U.S. population. According to the Bureau of the Census, Americans born outside of the United States made up 10 percent of the population in 1997. About 40 percent were Hispanic, while 24 percent were Asian. Nearly 30 percent of Americans born outside of the United States arrived since 1990. As a result of these trends, restaurant chains expanded their menus to appeal to the different ethnic tastes of consumers, expanded into nontraditional locations such as department stores and airports, and made food more available through home delivery and takeout service.

INDUSTRY CONSOLIDATION AND MERGERS AND ACQUISITIONS

Lower growth in the U.S. fast-food market intensified competition for market share between restaurant chains and led to consolidation, primarily through mergers and acquisitions, during the mid 1990s. Many restaurant chains found that market share could be increased more quickly and cheaply by acquiring an existing company than by building new units. In addition, fixed costs could be spread across a larger number of restaurants. This raised operating margins and gave companies an opportunity to build market share by lowering prices. An expanded restaurant base also gave companies greater purchasing power over suppliers. In 1990, Grand Metropolitan, a British company, purchased Pillsbury Co. for $5.7 billion. Included in the purchase was Pillsbury's Burger King chain. Grand Met strengthened the franchise by upgrading existing restaurants and eliminated several levels of management in order to cut costs. This gave Burger King a long-needed boost in improving its position against McDonald's, its largest competitor. In 1988, Grand Met had purchased Wienerwald, a West German chicken chain, and the Spaghetti Factory, a Swiss chain.

Perhaps most important to KFC was Hardee's acquisition of 600 Roy Rogers restaurants from Marriott Corporation in 1990. Hardee's converted a large number of these restaurants to Hardee's units and introduced "Roy Rogers" fried chicken into its menu. By 1993, Hardee's had introduced fried chicken into most of its U.S. restaurants. Hardee's was unlikely to destroy the customer loyalty that KFC long enjoyed. However, it did cut into KFC's sales, because it was able to offer consumers a widened menu selection that appealed to a variety of family eating preferences. In 1997, Hardee's parent company, Imasco Ltd., sold Hardee's to CKE Restaurants, Inc. CKE owned Carl's Jr., Rally's Hamburgers, and Checker's Drive-In. That same year, Boston Chicken, Inc., acquired Harry's Farmers Market, an Atlanta grocer that sold fresh quality prepared meals. The acquisition was designed to help Boston Chicken develop distribution beyond its Boston Market restaurants. Also in 1997, AFC Enterprises, which operated Popeye's and Church's, acquired Chesapeake Bagel Bakery of McLean, Virginia, in order to diversify away from fried chicken and to strengthen its balance sheet.

The effect of these and other recent mergers and acquisitions on the industry was powerful. The top ten restaurant companies controlled almost 60 percent of fast-food sales in the United States. The consolidation of a number of fast-food chains within larger, financially more powerful parent companies gave restaurant chains strong financial and managerial resources that could be used to compete against smaller chains in the industry.

International Quick-Service Market

Because of the aggressive pace of new restaurant construction in the United States during the 1970s and 1980s, opportunities to expand domestically through new restaurant construction in the 1990s were limited. Restaurant chains that did build new restaurants found that the higher cost of purchasing prime locations resulted in immense pressure to increase annual per restaurant sales, in order to cover higher initial investment costs. Many restaurants began to expand into international markets as an alternative to the United States. In contrast to the U.S. market, international markets offered large customer bases with comparatively little competition. However, only a few U.S. restaurant chains had defined aggressive strategies for penetrating international markets by 1998.

Three restaurant chains that had established aggressive international strategies were McDonald's, KFC, and Pizza Hut. McDonald's operated the largest number of restaurants. In 1998, it operated 23,132 restaurants in 109 countries (10,409 restaurants were located outside of the United States). In comparison, KFC, Pizza Hut, and Taco Bell together operated 29,712 restaurants in 79, 88, and 17 countries, respectively (9,126 restaurants were located outside of the United States). Of these four chains, KFC operated the greatest percentage of its restaurants (50 percent) outside of the United States. McDonald's, Pizza Hut, and Taco Bell operated 45, 31, and 2 percent of their units abroad. KFC opened its first restaurant outside of the United States in the late 1950s. By the time PepsiCo acquired KFC in 1986, KFC was already operating restaurants in 55

countries. KFC's early expansion abroad, its strong brand name, and managerial experience in international markets gave it a strong competitive advantage vis-à-vis other fast-food chains that were investing abroad for the first time.

Table 3 shows *Hotels*' 1994 list of the world's thirty largest fast-food restaurant chains (*Hotels* discontinued reporting these data after 1994). The seventeen largest restaurant chains of the thirty (ranked by number of units) were headquartered in the United States. The relative scarcity of fast-food restaurant chains outside of the United States had a number of possible explanations. First, the United States represented the largest consumer market in the world, accounting for more than one-fifth of the world's gross domestic product (GDP). Therefore, the United States was the strategic focus of the largest restaurant chains. Second, Americans were quicker to accept the fast-food concept. Many other cultures had strong culinary traditions that were difficult to break down. Europeans, for example, had a history of frequenting more mid-scale restaurants, where they spent several hours in a formal setting enjoying native dishes and beverages. While KFC was again building restaurants in West Germany by the late 1980s, it previously failed to penetrate the German market because Germans were not accustomed to takeout food or to ordering food over the counter. McDonald's had greater success penetrating the German market because it made a number of changes in its menu and operating procedures, in order to better appeal to German culture. For example, German beer was served in all of McDonald's German restaurants. KFC had more success in Asia and Latin America, where chicken was a traditional dish.

Aside from cultural factors, international business carried risks not present in the U.S. market. Long distances between headquarters and foreign franchises often made it difficult to control the quality of individual restaurants. Large distances also caused servicing and support problems. Transportation and other resource costs were higher than in the domestic market. In addition, time, cultural, and language differences increased communication and operational problems. Therefore, it was reasonable to expect U.S. restaurant chains to expand domestically as long as they achieved corporate profit and growth objectives. As the U.S. market became saturated, and companies gained

TABLE 3

The World's Thirty Largest Fast-Food Chains, Ranked by Number of Countries

		For the Year Ended December 31, 1993		
Rank	Franchise	Headquarters Location	Units	Countries
1	Pizza Hut	Dallas, Texas	10,433	80
2	McDonald's	Oakbrook, Illinois	23,132	70
3	KFC	Louisville, Kentucky	9,033	68
4	Burger King	Miami, Florida	7,121	50
5	Baskin Robbins	Glendale, California	3,557	49
6	Wendy's	Dublin, Ohio	4,168	38
7	Domino's Pizza	Ann Arbor, Michigan	5,238	36
8	TCBY	Little Rock, Arkansas	7,474	22
9	Dairy Queen	Minneapolis, Minnesota	5,471	21
10	Dunkin' Donuts	Randolph, Massachusetts	3,691	21
11	Taco Bell	Irvine, California	4,921	20
12	Arby's	Fort Lauderdale, Florida	2,670	18
13	Subway Sandwiches	Milford, Connecticut	8,477	15
14	Sizzler International	Los Angeles, California	681	14
15	Hardee's	Rocky Mount, North Carolina	4,060	12
16	Little Caesar's	Detroit, Michigan	4,600	12
17	Popeye's Chicken	Atlanta, Georgia	813	12
18	Denny's	Spartanburg, South Carolina	1,515	10
19	A&W Restaurants	Livonia, Michigan	707	9
20	T.G.I. Friday's	Minneapolis, Minnesota	273	8
21	Orange Julius	Minneapolis, Minnesota	480	7
22	Church's Fried Chicken	Atlanta, Georgia	1,079	6
23	Long John Silver's	Lexington, Kentucky	1,464	5
24	Carl's Jr.	Anaheim, California	649	4
25	Loterria	Tokyo, Japan	795	4
26	Mos Burger	Tokyo, Japan	1,263	4
27	Skylark	Tokyo, Japan	1,000	4
28	Jack-in-the-Box	San Diego, California	1,172	3
29	Quick Restaurants	Berchem, Belgium	876	3
30	Taco Time	Eugene, Oregon	300	3

Source: Hotels (May 1994); PepsiCo, Inc., 1994 Annual Report.

expertise in international markets, more companies turned to profitable international markets as a means of expanding restaurant bases and increasing sales, profits, and market share.

KENTUCKY FRIED CHICKEN CORPORATION

KFC's worldwide sales, which included sales of both company-owned and franchised restaurants, grew to $8.0 billion in 1997. U.S. sales grew 2.6 percent over 1996 and accounted for about one-half of KFC's sales worldwide. KFC's U.S. share of the chicken segment fell 1.8 points, to 55.8 percent, in 1997 (see Table 4). This marked the sixth consecutive year that KFC sustained a decline in market share. Market share fell from 72.1 percent of the market in 1988 to 55.8 percent in 1997, a total market share loss of 16.3 points. Boston Market, which established its first restaurant in 1992, increased its market share from zero to 16.7 percent

TABLE 4

Top U.S. Chicken Chains—Market Share (%)

	KFC	Boston Market	Popeye's	Chick-fil-A	Church's	Total
1988	72.1	0.0	12.0	5.8	10.1	100.0
1989	70.8	0.0	12.0	6.2	11.0	100.0
1990	71.3	0.0	12.3	6.6	9.8	100.0
1991	72.7	0.0	11.4	7.0	8.9	100.0
1992	71.5	0.9	11.4	7.5	8.7	100.0
1993	68.7	3.0	11.4	8.0	8.9	100.0
1994	64.8	6.9	11.3	8.4	8.6	100.0
1995	60.5	12.3	10.8	8.2	8.2	100.0
1996	57.6	16.2	10.0	8.4	7.8	100.0
1997	55.8	16.7	10.1	9.4	8.0	100.0
Change	−16.3	16.7	−1.9	3.6	−2.1	0.0

Source: Nation's Restaurant News.

over the same period. On the surface, it might appear that it did so by taking customers away from KFC. However, KFC's sales growth remained fairly stable and constant over the last ten years. Boston Market's success was largely a function of its appeal to consumers who did not regularly patronize KFC or other chicken chains that sold fried chicken. By appealing to a market niche that was previously unsatisfied, Boston Market was able to expand the existing consumer base within the chicken segment of the fast-food industry.

Refranchising Strategy

The relatively low growth rate in sales in KFC's domestic restaurants during the 1992–1997 period was largely the result of KFC's decision in 1993 to begin selling company-owned restaurants to franchisees. When Colonel Sanders began to expand the Kentucky Fried Chicken system in the late 1950s, he established KFC as a system of independent franchisees. This was done in order to minimize his involvement in the operations of individual restaurants and to concentrate on the things he enjoyed the most—cooking, product development, and public relations. This resulted in a fiercely loyal and independent group of franchises. PepsiCo's strategy when it acquired KFC in 1986 was to integrate KFC's operations into the PepsiCo

system in order to take advantage of operational, financial, and marketing synergies. However, such a strategy demanded that PepsiCo become more involved in decisions over franchise operations, menu offerings, restaurant management, finance, and marketing. This was met with resistance by KFC franchises, who fiercely opposed increased control by the corporate parent. One method for PepsiCo to deal with the conflict with KFC franchises was to expand through company-owned restaurants rather than through franchising and to use strong PepsiCo cash flows to buy back unprofitable franchised restaurants, which could then be converted into company-owned restaurants. In 1986, company-owned restaurants made up 26 percent of KFC's U.S. restaurant base. By 1993, they made up about 40 percent of the total (see Table 5).

While company-owned restaurants were relatively easier to control compared with franchises, they also required higher levels of investment. This meant that high levels of cash were diverted from PepsiCo's soft drink and snack food businesses into its restaurant businesses. However, the fast-food industry delivered lower returns than the soft-drink and snack foods industries. Consequently, increased investment in KFC, Pizza Hut, and Taco Bell had a negative effect on PepsiCo's consolidated return on assets. By 1993, investors became concerned that

TABLE 5

KFC Restaurants in the United States

	Company-Owned	%Total	Franchised/Licensed	%Total	Total
1986	1,246	26.4	3,474	73.6	4,720
1987	1,250	26.0	3,564	74.0	4,814
1988	1,262	25.8	3,637	74.2	4,899
1989	1,364	27.5	3,597	72.5	4,961
1990	1,389	27.7	3,617	72.3	5,006
1991	1,836	36.6	3,186	63.4	5,022
1992	1,960	38.8	3,095	61.2	5,055
1993	2,014	39.5	3,080	60.5	5,094
1994	2,005	39.2	3,110	60.8	5,115
1995	2,026	39.4	3,111	60.6	5,137
1996	1,932	37.8	3,176	62.2	5,108
1997	1,850	36.1	3,270	63.9	5,120
1986–1993 Compounded Annual Growth Rate					
	7.1%		−1.7%		1.1%
1993–1997 Compounded Annual Growth Rate					
	−2.1%		1.5%		0.1%

Source: Tricon Global Restaurants, Inc., 1997 Annual Report; PepsiCo, Inc., Annual Reports for 1994, 1995, 1996, and 1997.

PepsiCo's return on assets failed to match returns delivered by Coca-Cola. In order to shore up its return on assets, PepsiCo decided to reduce the number of company-owned restaurants by selling them back to franchisees. This strategy lowered overall company sales, but it also lowered the amount of cash tied up in fixed assets, provided PepsiCo with one-time cash flow benefits from initial fees charged to franchisees, and generated an annual stream of franchise royalties. Tricon Global continued this strategy after the spinoff in 1997.

Marketing Strategy

During the 1980s, consumers began to demand healthier foods, greater variety, and service in nontraditional locations such as grocery stores, restaurants, airports, and outdoor events. This forced fast-food chains to expand menu offerings and to investigate nontraditional distribution channels and restaurant designs. Families also demanded greater

value in the food they bought away from home. This increased pressure on fast-food chains to reduce prices and to lower operating costs in order to maintain profit margins.

Many of KFC's problems during the late 1980s stemmed from its limited menu and its inability to quickly bring new products to market. The popularity of its Original Recipe Chicken allowed KFC to expand through the 1980s without significant competition. As a result, new product introductions were never an important element of KFC's overall strategy. One of the most serious setbacks suffered by the company came in 1989 as it prepared to add a chicken sandwich to its menu. While KFC was still experimenting with its chicken sandwich, McDonald's test-marketed its McChicken sandwich in the Louisville market. Shortly thereafter, it rolled out the McChicken sandwich nationally. By beating KFC to the market, McDonald's was able to develop strong consumer awareness for its sandwich. This significantly increased KFC's cost of developing awareness for its own sandwich, which KFC introduced several months later. KFC eventually withdrew its sandwich because of low sales.

In 1991, KFC changed its logo in the United States from Kentucky Fried Chicken to KFC, in order to reduce its image as a fried chicken chain. It continued to use the Kentucky Fried Chicken name internationally. It then responded to consumer demands for greater variety by introducing several products that would serve as alternatives to its Original Recipe Chicken. These included Oriental Wings, Popcorn Chicken, and Honey BBQ Chicken. It also introduced a desert menu that included a variety of pies and cookies. In 1993, it rolled out Rotisserie Chicken and began to promote its lunch and dinner buffet. The buffet, comprising thirty items, was introduced into almost 1,600 KFC restaurants in twenty-seven states by year-end. In 1998, KFC sold three types of chicken—Original Recipe and Extra Crispy (fried chicken) and Tender Roast (roasted chicken).

One of KFC's most aggressive strategies was the introduction of its Neighborhood Program. By mid 1993, almost 500 company-owned restaurants in New York, Chicago, Philadelphia, Washington, D.C., St. Louis, Los Angeles, Houston, and Dallas had been outfitted with special menu offerings to appeal exclusively to the black community. Menus were expanded with side dishes such as greens, macaroni and cheese, peach cobbler, sweet-potato pie, and red beans and rice. In addition, restaurant employees wore African-inspired uniforms. The introduction of the Neighborhood Program increased sales by 5 to 30 percent in restaurants appealing directly to blacks. KFC then tested Hispanic-oriented restaurants in the Miami area, offering side dishes such as fried plantains, flan, and tres leches.

One of KFC's most significant problems in the U.S. market was that overcapacity made expansion of freestanding restaurants difficult. Fewer sites were available for new construction and those sites, because of their increased cost, were driving profit margins down. Therefore, KFC initiated a new, three-pronged distribution strategy. First, it focused on building smaller restaurants in nontraditional outlets such as airports, shopping malls, universities, and hospitals. Second, it experimented with home delivery. Home delivery was introduced in the Nashville and Albuquerque markets in 1994. By 1998, home delivery was offered in 365 U.S. restaurants. Other nontraditional distribution outlets being tested included units offering drive-through and carryout service only, snack shops in cafeterias, scaled-down outlets for supermarkets, and mobile units that could be transported to outdoor concerts and fairs.

A third focus of KFC's distribution strategy was restaurant cobranding, primarily with its sister chain, Taco Bell. By 1997, 349 KFC restaurants had added Taco Bell to their menus and displayed both the KFC and Taco Bell logos outside their restaurants. Cobranding gave KFC the opportunity to expand its business dayparts. While about two-thirds of KFC's business was dinner, Taco Bell's primary business occurred at lunch. Combining the two concepts in the same unit could increase sales at individual restaurants significantly. KFC believed that there were opportunities to sell the Taco Bell concept in more than 3,900 of its U.S. restaurants.

Operating Efficiencies

As pressure continued to build on fast-food chains to limit price increases, restaurant chains searched for ways to reduce overhead and other operating costs in order to improve profit margins. In 1989, KFC reorganized its U.S. operations, to eliminate overhead costs and increase efficiency. This reorganization included a revision of KFC's crew-training programs and operating standards. The company renewed its emphasis on improving customer service, cleaner restaurants, faster and friendlier service, and continued high-quality products. In 1992, KFC reorganized its middle-management ranks, eliminating 250 of the 1,500 management positions at the corporate headquarters. More responsibility was assigned to restaurant franchisees and marketing managers and pay was more closely aligned with customer service and restaurant performance. In 1997, Tricon Global signed a five-year agreement with PepsiCo Food Systems (which was later sold by PepsiCo to AmeriServe Food Distributors) to distribute food and supplies to Tricon's 29,712 KFC, Pizza Hut, and Taco Bell units. This provided KFC with significant opportunities to benefit from economies of scale in distribution.

INTERNATIONAL OPERATIONS

The top ten fast-food chains owed much of their success to aggressive building strategies. Chains were able to discourage competition by building in low-population areas that could support only a single fast-food chain. McDonald's was particularly successful as it was able to expand quickly into small towns across the United States, preempting other fast-food chains. It was equally important to beat a competitor into more densely populated areas, where location was of prime importance. KFC's early entry into international markets placed it in a strong position to benefit from international expansion as the U.S. market became saturated. In 1997, 50 percent of KFC's restaurants were located outside of the United States. While 364 new restaurants were opened outside of the United States, only 12 new restaurants were added to the U.S. system in 1997. Most of KFC's international expansion was through franchises, though some restaurants were licensed to operators or jointly operated with a local partner. Expansion through franchising was an important strategy for penetrating international markets because franchises were owned and operated by local entrepreneurs with a deeper understanding of local language, culture, and customs, as well as local law, financial markets, and marketing characteristics. Franchising was particularly important for expansion into smaller countries such as the Dominican Republic, Grenada, Bermuda, and Suriname, which could support only one restaurant. Costs were prohibitively high for KFC to operate company-owned restaurants in these smaller markets. Of the 5,117 KFC restaurants located outside of the United States in 1997, 68 percent were franchised, while 22 percent were company-owned, and 10 percent were licensed restaurants or joint ventures.

In larger markets such as Japan, China, and Mexico, there was a stronger emphasis on building company-owned restaurants. By coordinating purchasing, recruiting and training, financing, and advertising, fixed costs could be spread over a large number of restaurants and lower prices on products and services could be negotiated. KFC was also better able to control product and service quality. In order to take advantage of economies of scale, Tricon Global Restaurants managed all of the international units of its KFC, Pizza Hut, and Taco Bell chains through its Tricon International division, located in Dallas, Texas. This enabled Tricon Global Restaurants to leverage its strong advertising expertise, international experience, and restaurant management experience across all its KFC, Pizza Hut, and Taco Bell chains.

Latin American Strategy

KFC's primary market presence in Latin America during the 1980s was in Mexico, Puerto Rico, and the Caribbean. KFC established subsidiaries in Mexico and Puerto Rico, from which it coordinated the construction and operation of company-owned restaurants. A third subsidiary, in Venezuela, was closed because of the high fixed costs associated with running the small subsidiary. Franchises were used to penetrate other countries in the Caribbean whose market size prevented KFC from profitably operating company restaurants. KFC relied exclusively on the operation of company-owned restaurants in Mexico through 1989. While franchising was popular in the United States, it was virtually unknown in Mexico until 1990, mainly because of the absence of a law protecting patents, information, and technology transferred to the Mexican franchise. In addition, royalties were limited. As a result, most fast-food chains opted to invest in Mexico using company-owned units.

In 1990, Mexico enacted a new law that provided for the protection of technology transferred into Mexico. Under this legislation, the franchiser and franchisee were free to set their own terms. The new law also allowed royalties. Royalties were taxed at 15 percent on technology assistance and know-how and at 35 percent on other royalty categories. The new franchise law resulted in an explosion of franchises in fast-food, services, hotels, and retail outlets. In 1992, franchises had an estimated $750 million in sales in more than 1,200 outlets throughout Mexico. Before the law was passed, KFC had limited its Mexican operations primarily to Mexico City, Guadalajara, and Monterrey. This enabled KFC to better coordinate operations and minimize costs of distribution to individual restaurants. The new franchise law gave KFC and other fast-food chains the opportunity to expand their restaurant bases more quickly to more rural regions of Mexico, where responsibility for management could be handled by local franchisees.

After 1990, KFC altered its Latin American strategy in a number of ways. First, it opened 29 franchises in Mexico to complement its company-owned restaurant base. Then it expanded its company-owned restaurants into the Virgin Islands, reestablished a subsidiary in Venezuela, and it expanded its franchise operations into South America. In 1990, a franchise opened in Chile, and in 1993 in Brazil. Subsequently, franchises were established in Colombia, Ecuador, Panama, and Peru, among other South American countries. A fourth subsidiary was established in Brazil, in order to develop company-owned restaurants. Brazil was Latin America's largest economy and McDonald's primary Latin American investment location. By June 1998, KFC operated 438 restaurants in thirty-two Latin American countries. By comparison, McDonald's operated 1,091 restaurants in twenty-eight countries.

Table 6 gives a count of KFC's and McDonald's Latin American operations. KFC's early entry into Latin America during the 1970s gave it a leadership position in Mexico and the Caribbean. It had also gained an edge in Ecuador and Peru, countries

where McDonald's had not yet developed a strong presence. McDonald's focused its Latin American investment in Brazil, Argentina, and Uruguay, countries where KFC had little or no presence. McDonald's was also strong in Venezuela. Both KFC and McDonald's were strong in Chile, Colombia, Panama, and Puerto Rico.

Economic Environment and the Mexican Market

Mexico was KFC's strongest market in Latin America. Although McDonald's had aggressively established restaurants in Mexico since 1990, KFC retained the leading market share. Because of its proximity to the United States, Mexico was an attractive location for U.S. trade and investment. Mexico's population of 98 million was approximately one-third as large as that of the United States and represented a large market for U.S. companies. In comparison, Canada's population of 30.3 million people was only one-third as large as Mexico's.

TABLE 6

KFC and McDonald's Restaurants in Latin America (as of December 31, 1997)

	KFC			
	Company Restaurants	Franchised Restaurants	Total Restaurants	McDonald's
Argentina	—	—	—	131
Bahamas	—	10	10	3
Barbados	—	7	7	—
Brazil	6	2	8	480
Chile	—	29	29	27
Colombia	—	19	19	18
Costa Rica	—	5	5	19
Ecuador	—	18	18	2
Jamaica	—	17	17	7
Mexico	128	29	157	131
Panama	—	21	21	20
Peru	—	17	17	5
Puerto Rico and Virgin Islands	67	—	67	115
Trinidad and Tobago	—	27	27	3
Uruguay	—	—	—	18
Venezuela	6	—	6	53
Other	—	30	30	59
Total	207	231	438	1,091

Source: Tricon Global Restaurants, Inc.; McDonald's, 1997 Annual Report.

Because Mexico neighbors the United States, transportation between the two countries cost much less than shipments to and from Europe or Asia. This increased the competitiveness of U.S. goods in comparison with European and Asian goods; indeed, the United States was Mexico's largest trading partner. More than 75 percent of Mexico's imports came from the United States, while 84 percent of its exports went there (see Table 7). Many U.S. firms invested in Mexico in order to take advantage of lower wage rates. Produced in Mexico, U.S. goods could be shipped into the United States for sale or shipped to third markets at lower cost.

While the U.S. market was critically important to Mexico, Mexico still represented only a small percentage of overall U.S. trade and investment. Since the early 1900s, the portion of U.S. exports to Latin America had declined. Instead, U.S. exports to Canada and Asia, where economic growth outpaced growth in Mexico, increased more quickly. Canada was the largest importer of U.S. goods. Japan was the largest exporter of goods to the United States, with Canada a close second. U.S. investment in Mexico had also been small, mainly because of government restrictions on foreign investment. Most U.S. foreign investment was in Europe, Canada, and Asia.

The lack of U.S. investment in and trade with Mexico during this century was mainly due to Mexico's long history of restricting trade and foreign direct investment. The Institutional Revolutionary Party (PRI), which came to power in Mexico during the 1930s, had historically pursued protectionist economic policies, in order to shield Mexico's economy from foreign competition. Many industries were government-owned or controlled and many Mexican companies focused on producing goods for the domestic market without much attention to building export markets. High tariffs and other trade barriers restricted imports into Mexico, and foreign ownership of assets in Mexico was largely prohibited or heavily restricted.

Additionally, a dictatorial and entrenched government bureaucracy, corrupt labor unions, and a long tradition of anti-Americanism among many government officials and intellectuals reduced the motivation of U.S. firms for investing in Mexico. The nationalization of Mexico's banks in 1982 led to higher real interest rates and lower investor confidence. Afterward, the Mexican government battled high inflation, high interest rates, and labor unrest and lost consumer purchasing power. Investor confidence in Mexico, however, improved after 1988, when Carlos Salinas de Gortari was elected president and began an ambitious restructuring of the Mexican economy. He initiated policies to strengthen the free market components of the economy, lowered top marginal tax rates to 36 percent

TABLE 7

Mexico's Major Trading Partners (% of total exports and imports)

	1992 Exports	1992 Imports	1994 Exports	1994 Imports	1996 Exports	1996 Imports
U.S.A	81.1	71.3	85.3	71.8	84.0	75.6
Japan	1.7	4.9	1.6	4.8	1.4	4.4
Germany	1.1	4.0	0.6	3.9	0.7	3.5
Canada	2.2	1.7	2.4	2.0	1.2	1.9
Italy	0.3	1.6	0.1	1.3	1.2	1.1
Brazil	0.9	1.8	0.6	1.5	0.9	0.8
Spain	2.7	1.4	1.4	1.7	1.0	0.7
Other	10.0	13.3	8.0	13.0	9.6	12.0
% Total	100.0	100.0	100.0	100.0	100.0	100.0
Value ($M)	46,196	62,129	60,882	79,346	95,991	89,464

Source: International Monetary Fund, *Direction of Trade Statistics Yearbook* (1997).

(down from 60 percent in 1986), and eliminated many restrictions on foreign investment. Foreign firms can now buy up to 100 percent of the equity in many Mexico firms. Previously, foreign ownership of Mexican firms was limited to 49 percent.

Privatization

The privatization of government-owned companies came to symbolize the restructuring of Mexico's economy. In 1990, legislation was passed to privatize all government-run banks. By the end of 1992, more than 800 of some 1,200 government-owned companies had been sold, including Mexicana and AeroMexico, the two largest airline companies in Mexico, and Mexico's 18 major banks. However, more than 350 companies remained under government ownership. These represented a significant portion of the assets owned by the state at the start of 1988. Therefore, the sale of government-owned companies, in terms of asset value, was moderate. Government-run companies controlled a large percentage of the remaining government-owned assets in certain strategic industries such as steel, electricity, and petroleum. These industries had long been protected by government ownership. As a result, until 1993 additional privatization of government-owned enterprises was limited. That year, however, President Salinas opened up the electricity sector to independent power producers, and Petroleos Mexicanos (Pemex), the state-run petrochemical monopoly, initiated a program to sell off many of its nonstrategic assets to private and foreign buyers.

North American Free Trade Agreement (NAFTA)

Before 1989, Mexico levied high tariffs on most imported goods. In addition, many other goods were subjected to quotas, licensing requirements, and other non-tariff trade barriers. In 1986, Mexico joined the General Agreement on Tariffs and Trade (GATT), a world trade organization designed to eliminate barriers to trade among member nations. As a member of GATT, Mexico was obligated to apply its system of tariffs to all member nations equally; consequently, it dropped tariff rates on a variety of imported goods. It also dropped import license requirements for all but 300 imported items. During the Salinas administration, tariffs were reduced from an average of 100 percent on most items to an average of 11 percent.

On January 1, 1994, the North American Free Trade Agreement (NAFTA) went into effect. The passage of NAFTA, which included Canada, the United States, and Mexico, created a trading bloc with a larger population and gross domestic product than the European Union (see Table 8). All tariffs on goods traded among the three countries were scheduled to be phased out. NAFTA was expected to be particularly beneficial for Mexican exporters because reduced tariffs made their goods more competitive in the United States compared with goods exported to the United States from other countries. In 1995, one year after NAFTA went into effect, Mexico posted its first balance of trade surplus in six years. Part of this surplus was attributed to reduced tariffs resulting from the NAFTA agreement. However, the peso crisis of 1995, which lowered the value of the peso against the dollar, increased the price of goods imported into Mexico and lowered the price of Mexican products exported to the United States. Therefore, it was still too early to assess the full effects of the NAFTA agreement.

Foreign Exchange and the Mexican Peso Crisis of 1995

Between 1982 and 1991, a two-tiered exchange rate system was in force in Mexico. The system consisted of a controlled rate and a free market rate. The controlled rate was used for imports, foreign debt payments, and conversion of export proceeds; it covered an estimated 70 percent of all foreign transactions. The free market rate was used for other transactions. In 1989, President Salinas instituted a policy of allowing the peso to depreciate against the dollar by one peso per day. The result was a grossly overvalued peso. This lowered the price of imports and led to an increase in imports of more than 23 percent in 1989. At the same time, Mexican exports became less competitive on world markets.

In 1991, the controlled rate was abolished and replaced with an official free rate. To limit the range of fluctuations in the value of the peso, the government fixed the rate at which it would buy or sell pesos. A floor (the maximum price at which pesos could be purchased) was established at Ps 3,056.20 and remained fixed. A ceiling (the maximum price at which the peso could be sold) was established at Ps 3,056.40 and allowed to move up-

TABLE 8

Selected Economic Data for Canada, the United States, and Mexico

	Percent of Annual Change				
	1993	*1994*	*1995*	*1996*	*1997*
GDP Growth					
Canada	3.3%	4.8%	5.5%	4.1%	—
United States	4.9	5.8	4.8	5.1	5.9
Mexico	21.4	13.3	29.4	38.2	—
Real GDP Growth					
Canada	2.2	4.1	2.3	1.2	—
United States	2.2	3.5	2.0	2.8	3.8
Mexico	2.0	4.5	–6.2	5.1	—
Inflation					
Canada	1.9	0.2	2.2	1.5	1.6
United States	3.0	2.5	2.8	2.9	2.4
Mexico	9.7	6.9	35.0	34.4	20.6
Depreciation Against $U.S.					
Canada (C$)	4.2	6.0	–2.7	0.3	4.3
Mexico (NP)	–0.3	71.4	43.5	2.7	3.6

Source: International Monetary Fund, *International Financial Statistics,* 1998.

ward by Ps 0.20 per day. This was later revised to Ps 0.40 per day. In 1993, a new currency, called the new peso, was issued with three fewer zeros. The new currency was designed to simplify transactions and to reduce the cost of printing currency.

When Ernesto Zedillo became Mexico's president in December 1994, one of his objectives was to maintain the stability of prices, wages, and exchange rates achieved by Salinas during his five years as president. However, Salinas had achieved stability largely on the basis of price, wage, and foreign exchange controls. While giving the appearance of stability, an over-valued peso continued to encourage imports which exacerbated Mexico's balance of trade deficit. Mexico's government continued to use foreign reserves to finance its balance of trade deficits. According to the Banco de Mexico, foreign currency reserves fell from $24 billion in January 1994 to $5.5 billion in January 1995. Anticipating a devaluation of the peso, investors began to move capital into U.S. dollar investments. To relieve pressure on the peso, Zedillo announced on December 19, 1994, that the peso would be allowed to depreciate by an additional 15 percent per year against the dollar compared with the maximum allowable depreciation of 4 percent per year

established during the Salinas administration. Within two days, continued pressure on the peso forced Zedillo to allow the peso to float freely against the dollar. By mid January 1995, the peso had lost 35 percent of its value against the dollar and the Mexican stock market plunged 20 percent. By November 1995, the peso had depreciated from 3.1 pesos to the dollar to 7.3 pesos to the dollar.

The continued devaluation of the peso resulted in higher import prices, higher inflation, destabilization within the stock market, and higher interest rates. Mexico struggled to pay its dollar-based debts. To thwart a possible default by Mexico, the U.S. government, International Monetary Fund, and World Bank pledged $24.9 billion in emergency loans. Zedillo then announced an emergency economic package called the "pacto," which included reduced government spending, increased sales of government-run businesses, and a freeze on wage increases.

Labor Problems

One of KFC's primary concerns in Mexico was the stability of the labor markets. While labor was relatively plentiful and wages were low, much of the work force was relatively unskilled. KFC benefited from lower labor costs, but labor unrest, low job retention, high absenteeism, and poor punctuality were significant problems. Absenteeism and punctuality were partially cultural. However, problems with worker retention and labor unrest stemmed primarily from workers' frustration over the loss of their purchasing power due to inflation and government controls on wage increases. Absenteeism remained high—at approximately 8 to 14 percent of the labor force—though it was declining because of job security fears. Turnover continued to be a problem and ran at between 5 and 12 percent per month. Therefore, employee screening and internal training were important issues for firms investing in Mexico.

Higher inflation and the government's freeze on wage increases led to a dramatic decline in disposable income after 1994. Furthermore, a slowdown in business activity, brought about by higher interest rates and lower government spending, led many businesses to lay off workers. By the end of 1995, an estimated 1 million jobs had been lost as a result of the economic crisis sparked by the peso devaluation. Industry groups within Mexico called for new labor laws that would give them more freedom to hire and fire employees and increased flexibility to hire part-time rather than full-time workers.

RISKS AND OPPORTUNITIES

The peso crisis of 1995 and the resulting recession in Mexico left KFC managers with a great deal of uncertainty regarding Mexico's economic and political future. KFC had benefited from economic stability between 1988 and 1994. Inflation had been brought down, the peso was relatively stable, there was little labor unrest, and Mexico's new franchise law had enabled KFC to expand into rural areas through franchises rather than company-owned restaurants. By the end of 1995, KFC had built twenty-nine franchises in Mexico. The foreign exchange crisis of 1995, however, had severe implications for U.S. firms operating in Mexico. The devaluation of the peso resulted in higher inflation and capital flight out of Mexico. Capital flight reduced the supply of capital and led to higher interest rates. To reduce inflation, Mexico's government instituted an austerity program that resulted in lower disposable income, higher unemployment, and lower demand for products and services.

Another problem was Mexico's failure to reduce restrictions on U.S. and Canadian investment in a timely fashion. Many U.S. firms experienced problems in getting required approvals for new ventures from the Mexican government. A good example was United Parcel Service (UPS), which sought government approval to use large trucks for deliveries in Mexico. Approvals were delayed, forcing UPS to use smaller trucks. This put UPS at a competitive disadvantage vis-à-vis Mexican companies. In many cases, UPS was forced to subcontract delivery work to Mexican companies that were allowed to use larger, more cost-efficient trucks. Other U.S. companies such as Bell Atlantic and TRW faced similar problems. TRW, which signed a joint venture agreement with a Mexican partner, had to wait fifteen months longer than anticipated before the Mexican government released rules on how it could receive credit data from banks. TRW claimed that the Mexican government slowed the approval process in order to placate several large Mexican banks.

A final area of concern for KFC was increased political turmoil in Mexico during the last several years. On January 1, 1994, the day NAFTA went into effect, rebels (descendants of the Mayans) rioted in the southern Mexican province of Chiapas, on the Guatemalan border. After four days of fighting, Mexican troops had driven the rebels out of several towns that the rebels had seized. Around 150 people—mostly rebels—were killed. The uprising symbolized many of the fears of the poor in Mexico. While Salinas's economic programs had increased economic growth and wealth in Mexico, many of Mexico's poorest felt that they had not benefited. Many of Mexico's farmers, faced with lower tariffs on imported agricultural goods from the United States, felt that they might be driven out of business because of lower priced imports. Therefore, social unrest among Mexico's Indians, farmers, and the poor could potentially unravel much of the economic success achieved in Mexico during the previous five years.

Moreover, Salinas's hand-picked successor for president was assassinated in early 1994 while campaigning in Tijuana. The assassin was a twenty-three-year-old mechanic and migrant worker believed to have been affiliated with a dissident group upset with the PRI's economic reforms. The possible existence of a dissident group raised fears of political violence in the future. The PRI quickly named Ernesto Zedillo, a forty-two-year-old economist with little political experience, as its new presidential candidate, and as mentioned earlier, he was elected president in December 1994.

Political unrest was not limited to Mexican officials and companies. In October 1994, between thirty and forty masked men attacked a McDonald's restaurant in the tourist section of Mexico City to show their opposition to California's Proposition 187, which would have curtailed benefits to illegal aliens (primarily from Mexico). The men threw cash registers to the floor, cracked them open, smashed windows, overturned tables, and spray-painted slogans on the walls such as "No to Fascism" and "Yankee Go Home."

KFC was still facing a variety of issues in Mexico and Latin America in 1998. Prior to 1995, few restaurants had been opened in South America.

However, KFC was now aggressively building new restaurants in the region. It had halted openings of franchised restaurants in Mexico, and all restaurants opened since 1995 were company-owned. KFC was more aggressively building restaurants in South America, which remained largely unpenetrated by KFC through 1995. Of greatest importance was Brazil, where McDonald's had already established a strong market share position. Brazil was Latin America's largest economy and a largely untapped market for KFC. However, the danger in ignoring Mexico was that a conservative investment strategy could jeopardize KFC's market share lead over McDonald's in a large market where KFC long enjoyed enormous popularity.

CASE 26

Outback Goes International

This case was prepared by Marilyn L. Taylor of the University of Missouri at Kansas City, George M. Puia of the Indiana State University, Krishnan Ramaya of the University of Southern Indiana, and Madelyn Gengelbach of the University of Missouri at Kansas City.

In early 1995, Outback Steakhouse enjoyed the position as one of the most successful restaurant chains in the United States. Entrepreneurs Chris Sullivan, Bob Basham, and Tim Gannon, each with more than twenty years experience in the restaurant industry, started Outback Steakhouse with just two stores in 1988. In 1995, the company was the fastest-growing U.S. steakhouse chain, with more than 200 stores throughout the United States.

Outback achieved its phenomenal success in an industry that was widely considered as one of the most competitive in the United States. Fully 75 percent of entrants into the restaurant industry failed within the first year. Outback's strategy was driven by a unique combination of factors atypical of the food service industry. As Chairman Chris Sullivan put it, "Outback is all about a lot of different experiences that have been recognized as entrepreneurship." Within six years of commencing operations, Outback was voted the best steakhouse chain in the country. The company also took top honors along with Olive Garden as America's favorite restaurant. In December 1994, Outback was awarded *Inc's* prestigious Entrepreneur of the Year award. In 1994 and early 1995, the business press hailed the company as one of the biggest success stories in corporate America in recent years.

In late 1994, Hugh Connerty was appointed president of Outback International. In early 1995,

This case is intended to be used as the basis for class discussion rather than as an illustration of effective or ineffective handling of the situation. This case was prepared by prepared by Marilyn L. Taylor of the University of Missouri at Kansas City, George M. Puia of the Indiana State University, Krishnan Ramaya of the University of Southern Indiana, and Madelyn Gengelbach of the University of Missouri at Kansas City. Used by permission.

Connerty, a highly successful franchisee for Outback, explained the international opportunities facing Outback Steakhouse as it considered its strategy for expansion abroad:

> We have had hundreds of franchise requests from all over the world. [So] it took about two seconds for me to make that decision [to become President of Outback International] . . . I've met with and talked to other executives who have international divisions. All of them have the same story. At some point in time the light goes off and they say, "Gee we have a great product. Where do we start?" I have traveled quite a bit on holiday. The world is not as big as you think it is. Most companies who have gone global have not used any set strategy.

Despite his optimism, Connerty knew that the choice of targeted markets would be critical. Connerty wondered what strategic and operational changes the company would have to make to assure success in those markets.

HISTORY OF OUTBACK STEAKHOUSE, INC.

Chris Sullivan, Bob Basham, and Tim Gannon met in the early 1970s shortly after they graduated from college. The three joined Steak & Ale, a Pillsbury subsidiary and restaurant chain, as management trainees—their first post-college career positions. During the 1980s, Sullivan and Basham became successful franchisees of seventeen Chili's restaurants in Florida and Georgia with franchise headquarters in Tampa, Florida.[1] Meanwhile, Tim Gannon played significant roles in several New Orleans restaurant chains. Sullivan and Basham sold their Chili's franchises in 1987 and used the proceeds to fund Outback, their start-from-scratch entrepreneurial venture. They invited Gannon to join them in Tampa in the fall of 1987. The trio opened their first two restaurants in Tampa in 1988.

The three entrepreneurs recognized that in-home consumption of meat, especially beef, had declined.[2] Nonetheless, upscale and budget steakhouses were extremely popular. The three concluded that people were cutting in-home red meat consumption but were still very interested in going out to a restaurant for a good steak. They saw an untapped opportunity between high-priced and budget steakhouses to serve quality steaks at an affordable price.

Using an Australian theme associated with the outdoors and adventure, Outback positioned itself as a place providing not only excellent food but also a cheerful, fun, and comfortable experience. The company's Statement of Principles and Beliefs referred to employees as "Outbackers" and highlighted the importance of hospitality, sharing, quality, fun, and courage.

Catering primarily to the dinner crowd,[3] Outback offered a menu that featured specially seasoned steaks and prime rib. The menu also included chicken, ribs, fish, and pasta entrees, in addition to the company's innovative appetizers.[4] CFO Bob Merritt cited Outback's food as a prime reason for the company's success. As he put it,

> One of the important reasons for our success is that we took basic American meat and potatoes and enhanced the flavor profile so that it fit with the aging population. . . . Just look at what McDonalds and Burger King did in their market segment. They [have] tried to add things to their menu that were more flavorful [for example] McDonald's put the Big Mac on the menu. . . . as people age, they want more flavor. . . . higher flavor profiles. It's not happenstance. It's a science. There's too much money at risk in this business not to know what's going on with customer taste preferences.

The company viewed suppliers as "partners" in the company's success and was committed to work with suppliers to develop and maintain long-term relationships. Purchasing was dedicated to obtaining the highest quality ingredients and supplies. Indeed, the company was almost fanatical about quality. As Tim Gannon, vice president and the company's chief chef, said, "We won't tolerate less than the best." One example of the company's quality emphasis was its croutons. Restaurant kitchen staff made the croutons daily on site. The croutons had seventeen different seasonings, including fresh garlic and butter, and they were cut by hand into irregular shapes so that customers would recognize they were handmade. At about 40 percent of total costs, Outback had one of the highest food costs in the industry. On Friday and Saturday nights, customers waited up to two hours for a table. Most felt that Outback provided exceptional value for the average entree price of $15 to $16.

Outback focused not only on the productivity and efficiency of Outbackers but also on their long-term well-being. Executives referred to the company's employee commitment as "tough on results, but kind with people." A typical Outback restaurant staff consisted of a general manager, an assistant manager, and a kitchen manager, as well as fifty to seventy mostly part-time hourly employees. The company used aptitude tests, psychological profiles, and interviews as part of the employee selection process. Every applicant was interviewed by two managers. The company sought to create an entrepreneurial climate where learning and personal growth were strongly emphasized. Sullivan explained:

> I was given the opportunity to make a lot of mistakes and learn, and we try to do that today. We try to give our people a lot of opportunity to make some mistakes, learn, and go on.

To make operations easier for employees, the company chose a restaurant design that gave 45 percent of the floor space to the kitchen area. Wait staff were assigned only three tables at a time. Most Outback restaurants were open only from 4:30 to 11:30 p.m. daily. Outback's wait staff enjoyed higher income from tips than the staff in restaurants that also served lunch. Restaurant management staff worked fifty to fifty-five hours per week, in contrast to the seventy or more common in the industry. Company executives felt that the dinner-only concept had led to effective utilization of systems, staff, and management. Outbackers reported that they were less worn out working at Outback and that they had more fun than when they worked at other restaurant companies.

Outback executives were proud of their "B-locations" (with) "A-demographics" location strategy.

They deliberately steered clear of high-traffic sites targeted by companies that served a lunch crowd. Until the early 1990s, most of the restaurants were leased locations—retrofits of another restaurant location. The company tried to choose locations where Outback's target customer would be in the evening. The overall strategy payoff was clear. In an industry where a sales-to-investment ratio of 1.2 to 1 was considered strong, Outback's restaurants generated $2.10 for every $1 invested in the facility. The average Outback restaurant unit generated $3.4 million in sales.

In 1995, management remained informal. Headquarters were located on the second floor of an unpretentious building near the Tampa airport. There was no middle management—top management selected the joint venture partners and franchisees, who reported directly to the president. Franchisees and joint venture partners in turn hired the general managers at each restaurant.

Outback provided ownership opportunities at three levels of the organization: at the individual restaurant level; through multiple store arrangements (joint venture and franchise opportunities); and through a stock ownership plan for every employee. Health insurance was also available to all employees, a benefit not universally granted to restaurant industry workers. Outback's employment and ownership opportunities for restaurant-level general managers were atypical in the industry. A restaurant general manager invested $25,000 for a 10 percent ownership stake in the restaurant, a contract for five years in the same location, a 10 percent share of the cash flow from the restaurant as a yearly bonus, opportunity for stock options, and a 10 percent buyout arrangement at the end of the five years. Outback store managers typically earned an annual salary and bonus of more than $100,000, compared with the industry average of about $60,000–70,000. Outback's management turnover of 5.4 percent was one of the lowest in its industry in which the average was 30–40 percent.

Community involvement was strongly encouraged throughout the organization. The corporate office was involved in several nonprofit activities in the Tampa area and also sponsored major national events, such as the Outback Bowl and charity golf tournaments. Each store was involved in community participation and service. For example, the entire proceeds of an open house held just prior to every restaurant opening went to a charity of the store manager's choice.

Early in its history, the company had been unable to afford any advertising. Instead, Outback's founders relied on their strong relationships with local media to generate public relations and promotional efforts. One early relationship developed with Nancy Schneid, who had extensive experience in advertising and radio. Schneid later became Outback's first vice president of marketing. Under her direction, the company developed a full-scale national media program, which concentrated on television advertising and local billboards. The company avoided couponing, and its only printed advertising typically came as part of a package offered by a charity or sports event.

Early financing for growth had come from limited partnership investments by family members, close friends, and associates. The three founders' original plan did not call for extensive expansion or franchising. However, in 1990 some friends, disappointed in the performance of several of their Kentucky-based restaurants asked to franchise the Outback concept. The converted Kentucky stores enjoyed swift success. Additional opportunities with other individuals experienced in the restaurant industry arose in various parts of the country. These multistore arrangements were in the form of franchises or joint ventures. Later in 1990, the company turned to a venture capital firm for financing for a $2.5 million package. About the same time, Bob Merritt joined the company as CFO. Merritt's previous IPO[5] experience helped the company undertake a quick succession of three highly successful public equity offerings. During 1994, the price of the company's stock ranged from $22.63 to a high of $32.00. The company's income statements, balance sheets, and a summary of the stock price performance appear as Tables 1, 2, and 3 respectively.

OUTBACK'S INTERNATIONAL ROLLOUT

Outback's management believed that the U.S. market could accommodate at least 550 to 600 Outback steakhouse restaurants. At the rate the company was growing (70 stores annually), Outback would near the U.S. market's saturation within four to five years. Outback's plans for longer-term growth hinged on a multipronged strategy. The company planned to roll out an additional 300 to

TABLE 1

Outback Steakhouse, Inc., Consolidated Statements of Income

	Years Ended December 31		
	1994	*1993*	*1992*
Revenues	$451,916,000	$309,749,000	$189,217,000
Costs and expenses			
Costs of revenues	175,618,000	121,290,000	73,475,000
Labor and other related expenses	95,476,000	65,047,000	37,087,000
Other restaurant operating expenses	93,265,000	64,603,000	43,370,000
General & administrative expenses	16,744,000	12,225,000	9,176,000
(Income) from oper. of unconsol. affl.	(1,269,000)	(333,000)	
	379,834,000	262,832,000	163,108,000
Income from operations	72,082,000	46,917,000	26,109,000
Non-operating income (expense)			
Interest income	512,000	1,544,000	1,428,000
Interest expense	(424,000)	(369,000)	(360,000)
	88,000	1,175,000	1,068,000
Income before elimination			
Minority partners' interest and income taxes	72,170,000	48,092,000	27,177,000
Elimination of minority partners' interest	11,276,000	7,378,000	4,094,000
Income before provision for income taxes	60,894,000	40,714,000	23,083,000
Provision for income taxes	21,602,000	13,922,000	6,802,000
Net income	$39,292,000	$26,792,000	$16,281,000
Earnings per common share	$0.89	$0.61	$0.39
Weighted average number of			
common shares outstanding	43,997,000	43,738,000	41,504,000
Pro forma:			
Provision for income taxes	22,286,000	15,472,000	8,245,000
Net income	$38,608,000	$25,242,000	$14,838,000
Earnings per common share	$0.88	$0.58	$0.36

350 Outback stores, expand into the lucrative Italian dining segment through its joint venture with the successful Houston-based Carrabbas Italian Grill, and develop new dining themes.

At year-end 1994, Outback had 164 restaurants in which the company had direct ownership interest. The company had six restaurants that it operated through joint ventures, in which the company had a 45 percent interest. Franchisees operated another 44 restaurants. Outback operated the company-owned restaurants as partnerships in which the company was general partner. The company owned between 81 and 90 percent, and the remainder was owned by

the restaurant managers and joint venture partners. The six restaurants operated as joint ventures were also organized as partnerships in which the company owned 50 percent. The company was responsible for 50 percent of the costs of these restaurants.

Outback organized the joint venture with Carrabbas in early 1993. It was responsible for 100 percent of the costs of the new Carrabba's Italian Grills, although it owned a 50 percent share. As of year-end 1994, the joint venture operated ten Carrabba's restaurants.

The franchised restaurants generated 0.8 percent of the company's 1994 revenues as franchise

TABLE 2

Outback Steakhouse, Inc., Consolidated Balance Sheets

	December 31				
	1994	**1993**	**1992**	**1991**	**1990**
Assets					
Current assets:					
Cash and cash equivalents	$18,758,000	$24,996,000	$60,538,000	17,000,700	2,983,000
Short-term municipal securities	4,829,000	6,632,000	1,316,600		
Inventories	4,539,000	3,849,000	2,166,500	1,020,800	319,200
Other current assets	11,376,000	4,658,000	2,095,200	794,900	224,100
Total current assets	39,502,000	40,135,000	66,116,700	18,816,400	3,526,300
Long-term municipal securities	1,226,000	8,903,000	7,071,200		
Property, fixtures and equipment, net	162,323,000	101,010,000	41,764,500	15,479,000	6,553,200
Investments in and advances					
to unconsolidated affiliates	14,244,000	1,000,000			
Other assets	11,236,000	8,151,000	2,691,300	2,380,700	1,539,600
	$228,531,000	$159,199,000	$117,643,700	36,676,100	11,619,100
Liabilities and Stockholders' equity					
Current liabilities					
Accounts payable	$10,184,000	$1,053,000	$3,560,200	643,800	666,900
Sales taxes payable	3,173,000	2,062,000	1,289,500	516,800	208,600
Accrued expenses	14,961,000	10,435,000	8,092,300	2,832,300	954,800
Unearned revenue	11,862,000	6,174,000	2,761,900	752,800	219,400
Current portion of long-term debt	918,000	1,119,000	326,600	257,000	339,900
Income taxes payable			369,800	1,873,200	390,000
Total current liabilities	41,098,000	20,843,000	16,400,300	6,875,900	2,779,600
Deferred income taxes	568,000	897,000	856,400	300,000	260,000
Long-term debt	12,310,000	5,687,000	1,823,700	823,600	1,060,700
Interest of minority partners in					
consolidated partnerships	2,255,000	1,347,000	1,737,500	754,200	273,000
Total liabilities	56,231,000	28,774,000	20,817,900	8,753,700	4,373,300
Stockholders' equity					
Common stock, $0.01 par value,					
100,000,000 shares authorized for 1994 and 1993;					
50,000,000 authorized for 1992					
42,931,344 and 42,442,800 shares issues and					
outstanding as of December 31, 1994 and					
1993, respectively. 39,645,995 shares					
issued and outstanding as of					
December 31, 1992.	429,000	425,000	396,500	219,000	86,300
Additional paid-in capital	83,756,000	79,429,000	74,024,500	20,296,400	4,461,100
Retained earnings	88,115,000	50,571,000	22,404,800	7,407,000	2,698,400
Total stockholders' equity	172,300,000	130,425,000	96,825,800	27,922,400	7,245,800
	$228,531,000	$159,199,000	$117,643,700	36,676,100	11,619,100

TABLE 3

Outback Steakhouse, Inc., Selected Financial and Stock Data

Year	Systemwide Sales	Company Revenues	Net Income	EPS	Company Stores	Franchises & JVS	Total
1988	2,731	2,731	47	0.01	2	0	2
1989	13,328	13,328	920	0.04	9	0	9
1990	34,193	34,193	2,260	0.08	23	0	23
1991	91,000	91,000	6,064	0.17	49	0	49
1992	195,508	189,217	14,838	0.36	81	4	85
1993	347,553	309,749	25,242	0.58	124	24	148
1994	548,945	451,916	38,608	0.88	164	50	214

Outback Stock Data					
	High	Low		High	Low
1991			**1993**		
Second quarter	$4.67	$4.27	First quarter	22.00	15.50
Third quarter	6.22	4.44	Second quarter	26.16	16.66
Fourth quarter	10.08	5.5	Third quarter	24.59	19.00
			Fourth quarter	25.66	21.16
1992			**1994**		
First quarter	13.00	9.17	First quarter	29.50	23.33
Second quarter	11.41	8.37	Second quarter	28.75	22.75
Third quarter	16.25	10.13	Third quarter	30.88	23.75
Fourth quarter	19.59	14.25	Fourth quarter	32.00	22.63

fees. The portion of income attributable to restaurant managers and joint venture partners amounted to $11.3 million of the company's $72.2 million 1994 income.

By late 1994, Outback's management had also begun to consider the potential of non-U.S. markets for the Outback concept. Sullivan concluded that

we can do 500–600 (Outback) restaurants, and possibly more over the next five years. . . . [However,] the world is becoming one big market, and we want to be in place so we don't miss that opportunity. There are some problems, some challenges with it, but at this point there have been some casual restaurant chains that have gone (outside the United States) and their average unit sales are way, way above the sales level they enjoyed in the United States. So the

potential is there. Obviously, there are some distribution issues to work out, things like that. But we are real excited about the future internationally. That will give us some potential outside the United States to continue to grow as well.

In late 1994 the company began its international venture by appointing Hugh Connerty president of Outback International. Connerty, like Outback's three founders, had extensive experience in the restaurant industry. Before joining Outback, he developed a chain of successful Hooter's restaurants in Georgia. He used the proceeds from the sale of these franchises to fund the development of his franchise of Outback restaurants in northern Florida and southern Georgia. Connerty's success as a franchisee was well recognized. Indeed, in 1993 Outback began to award a large crystal trophy with the designation "Connerty Franchisee of the Year" to the company's outstanding franchisee.

Much of Outback's growth and expansion were generated through joint venture partnerships and franchising agreements. Connerty commented on Outback's franchise system:

Every one of the franchisees lives in their areas. I lived in the area I franchised. I had relationships that helped with getting permits. That isn't any different than the rest of the world. The loyalties of individuals that live in their respective areas [will be important]. We will do the franchises one by one. The biggest decision we have to make is how we pick that franchise partner. . . . That is what we will concentrate on. We are going to select a person who has synergy with us, who thinks like us, who believes in the principles and beliefs.

Outback developed relationships very carefully. "The trust between (Outback) and the individual franchisees is not to be violated," Connerty said "The company grants franchises one at a time. It takes a lot of trust to invest millions of dollars without any assurance that you will be able to build another one."[6]

However, Connerty recognized that expanding abroad would present challenges. He described how Outback would approach its international expansion:

There are some principles and beliefs we live by. It almost sounds cultish. We want international to be an opportunity for our suppliers. We feel strongly about the relationships with our suppliers. We have never changed suppliers. We have an undying commitment to them and in exchange we want them to have an undying commitment to us. They have to prove they can build plants [abroad].

He added that

it would be foolish of us to think that we are going to go around the world buying property and understanding the laws in every country, the culture in every single country. So the approach that we are going to take is that we will franchise the international operation with company-owned stores here and franchises there so that will allow us to focus on what I believe is our pure strength, a support operation.

U.S. RESTAURANTS IN THE INTERNATIONAL DINING MARKET

Prospects for international entry for U.S. restaurant companies in the early 1990s appeared promising. Between 1992 and 1993 alone, international sales for the top fifty restaurant franchisers increased from U.S. $15.9 billion to U.S. $17.5 billion. Franchising was the most popular means for rapid expansion. Table 4 provides an overview of the top U.S. restaurant franchisers, including their domestic and international revenues and number of units in 1993 and 1994.

International expansion was an important source of revenues for a significant number of players in the industry. International growth and expansion in the U.S. restaurant industry over the 1980s and into the 1990s was largely driven by major fast-food restaurant chains. Some of these companies, for example, McDonald's, Wendy's, Dairy Queen, and Domino's Pizza, were public and freestanding. Others, such as Subway and Little Caesars, remained private and freestanding. Some of the largest players in international markets were subsidiaries of major consumer products firms such as PepsiCo and Grand Metropolitan PLC.[7] In spite of the success enjoyed by fast-food operators in non-U.S. markets, casual dining operators were slower about entering the international markets. (See Appendix A for brief overviews of the publicly available data on the top ten franchisers and casual dining chains that had ventured abroad as of early 1995.)

One of the major forces driving the expansion of the U.S. food service industry was changing demographics. In the United States, prepared foods had become a fastest-growing category because they relieved the cooking burdens on working parents. By the early 1990s, U.S. consumers were spending almost as much on restaurant fare as for prepared and nonprepared grocery store food. U.S. food themes were very popular abroad. U.S. food themes were common throughout Canada as well as Western Europe and East Asia. As a result of the opening of previously inaccessible markets such as Eastern Europe, the former Soviet Union, China, India, and Latin America, the potential for growth in U.S. food establishments abroad was enormous.

In 1992 alone, there were more than 3,000 franchisers in the U.S. operating about 540,000 franchised outlets—a new outlet of some sort

TABLE 4

Top Fifty U. S. Restaurant Franchises (ranked by sales in $ millions)

Rank	Firm	Total Sales		International Sales		Total Stores		International Stores	
		1994	1993	1994	1993	1994	1993	1994	1993
1	McDonald's	25,986	23,587	11,046	9,401	15,205	13,993	5,461	4,710
2	Burger King	7,500	6,700	1,400	1,240	7,684	6,990	1,357	1,125
3	KFC	7,100	7,100	3,600	3,700	9,407	9,033	4,258	3,905
4	Taco Bell	4,290	3,817	130	100	5,615	4,634	162	112
5	Wendy's	4,277	3,924	390	258	4,411	4,168	413	377
6	Hardee's	3,491	3,425	63	56	3,516	3,435	72	63
7	Dairy Queen	3,170	2,581	300	290	3,516	3,435	628	611
8	Domino's	2,500	2,413	415	275	5,079	5,009	840	550
9	Subway	2,500	2,201	265	179	9,893	8,450	944	637
10	Little Caesars	2,000	2,000	70	70	4,855	4,754	155	145
	Average of firms 11–20	1,222	1,223	99	144	2,030	1,915	163	251
	Average of firms 21–30	647	594	51	26	717	730	37	36
	Average of firms 31–40	382	358	7	9	502	495	26	20
	Average of firms 41–50	270	257	17	23	345	363	26	43

Non-Fast-Food Restaurants in Top Fifty

Rank	Firm	Total Sales		International Sales		Total Stores		International Stores	
		1994	1993	1994	1993	1994	1993	1994	1993
11	Denny's	1,779	1,769	63	70	1,548	1,515	58	63
13	Dunkin' Donuts	1,413	1,285	226	209	3,453	3,047	831	705
14	Shoney's	1,346	1,318	0	0	922	915	0	0
15	Big Boy	1,130	1,202	100	0	940	930	90	78
17	Baskin-Robbins	1,008	910	387	368	3,765	3,562	1,300	1,278
19	T.G.I.Friday's	897	1,068	114	293	314	NA	37	NA
20	Applebee's	889	609	1	0	507	361	2	0
21	Sizzler	858	922	230	218	600	666	119	116
23	Ponderosa	690	743	40	38	380	750	40	38
24	Int'l House of Pancakes	632	560	32	29	657	561	37	35
25	Perkins	626	588	12	10	432	425	8	6
29	Outback Steakhouse	549	348	0	0	NA	NA	NA	NA
30	Golden Corral	548	515	1	0	425	425	2	1
32	TCBY Yogurt	388	337	22	15	2,801	2,474	141	80
37	Showbiz/Chuck E. Cheese	370	373	7	8	332	NA	8	NA
39	Round Table Pizza	357	340	15	12	576	597	29	22
40	Western Sizzlin	337	351	3	6	281	NA	2	NA
41	Ground Round	321	310	0	0	NA	NA	NA	NA
42	Papa John's	297	NA	0	NA	632	NA	0	NA
44	Godfather's Pizza	270	268	0	0	515	531	0	0
45	Bonanza	267	327	32	47	264	NA	30	NA
46	Village Inn	266	264	0	0	NA	NA	NA	NA
47	Red Robin	259	235	27	28	NA	NA	NA	NA
48	Tony Roma's	254	245	41	36	NA	NA	NA	NA
49	Marie Callender	251	248	0	0	NA	NA	NA	NA

NA: Not ranked in the top 50 for that category

Source: "Top 50 Franchises," *Restaurant Business*, November 1, 1995, pp. 35–41).

opened about every sixteen minutes. In 1992, franchised business sales totaled $757.8 billion, about 35 percent of all retail sales. Franchising was used as a growth vehicle by a variety of businesses, including automobiles, petroleum, cosmetics, convenience stores, computers, and financial services. However, food service constituted the franchising industry's largest single group. Franchised restaurants generally performed better than freestanding units. For example, in 1991 franchised restaurants experienced per-store sales growth of 6.2 percent versus an overall restaurant industry growth rate of 3.0 percent. However, despite generally favorable sales and profits, franchiser-franchisee relationships were often difficult.

Abroad, franchisers operated an estimated 31,000 restaurant units. The significant increase in restaurant franchising abroad was driven by universal cultural trends, rising incomes, improved international transportation and communication, rising educational levels, increasing number of women entering the work force, demographic concentrations of people in urban areas, and the willingness of younger generations to try new products.[8] However, there were substantial differences in these changes between the United States and other countries and from country to country.

FACTORS AFFECTING SELECTION OF COUNTRY

Although Outback had not yet formed a firm plan for its international rollout, Connerty indicated the preliminary choice of markets targeted for entry as Canada, Hawaii, South America, and Asia for the first year. "At the second year," he said, "we'll begin a relationship in Great Britain and from there a natural progression throughout Europe. But we view it as a very long-term project. I have learned that people think very different than Americans." U.S. restaurant chains had to take into account numerous considerations when determining which non-U.S. markets to enter. Some of these factors are summarized in Table 5, and issues regarding infrastructure and demographics are discussed in the next section—including some of the difficulties that U.S. restaurant companies encountered in various countries. Profiles of Canada, South Korea, Japan, Germany Mexico, and Great Britain appear in Appendix B.

Infrastructure

A supportive infrastructure in the target country is essential. Proper means of transportation, communication, basic utilities such as power and water, and locally available supplies are crucial elements in the decision to introduce a particular restaurant concept. A restaurant must have the ability to get resources to its location. Raw materials for food preparation, equipment for manufacture of food served, employees, and customers must be able to enter and leave the establishment. The network that brings these resources to a firm is commonly called a supply chain.

The level of economic development is closely linked to the development of a supportive infrastructure. According to the U.S. International Trade Commission,

> Economic conditions, cultural disparities, and physical limitations can have substantial impact on the viability of foreign markets for a franchise concept. In terms of economics, the level of infrastructure development is a significant factor. A weak infrastructure may cause problems in transportation, communication, or even the provision of basic utilities such as electricity. . . . International franchisers frequently encounter problems finding supplies in sufficient quantity, of consistent quality, and at stable prices. . . . Physical distance also can adversely affect a franchise concept and arrangement. Long distances create communication and transportation problems, which may complicate the process of sourcing supplies, overseeing operations, or providing quality management services to franchisees.[9]

Some food can be sourced locally, some regionally or nationally, and some must be imported. A country's transportation and distribution capabilities may become a factor in the decision on the country's suitability for a particular restaurant concept.

Sometimes supply chain issues require firms to make difficult decisions that affect the costs associated with the foreign enterprise. Family Restaurants Inc. encountered problems providing brown gravy for its CoCo's restaurants in South Korea. "If you want brown gravy in South Korea," said Barry Krantz, company president, "you can do one of two things. Bring it over, which is very costly. Or, you can make it yourself. So we figure out the flavor

TABLE 5

Factors Affecting Companies' Entry into International Markets

External Factors

Country Market Factors
Size of target market, competitive structure—atomistic, oligopolistic to monopolistic, local marketing infrastructure (distribution etc.).

Country Production Factors
Quality, quantity and cost of raw materials, labor, energy, and other productive agents in the target country, as well as the quality and cost of the economic infrastructure (transportation, communications, port facilities and similar considerations).

Country Environmental Factors
Political, economic and sociocultural character of the target country—government policies and regulations pertaining to international business.
Geographic distance—impact on transportation costs.
Size of the economy, absolute level of performance (GDP per capita), relative importance of economic sectors—closely related to the market size for a company's product in the target country.
Dynamics including rate of investment, growth in GDP, personal income, changes in employment. Dynamic economies may justify entry modes with a high break-even point even when the current market size is below the break-even point.
Sociocultural factors—cultural distance between home country and target country societies. The smaller the cultural distance, the quicker the entry into these markets (e.g., Canada).

Home Country Factors
Big domestic market allows a company to grow to a large size before it turns to foreign markets. Competitive structure. Firms in oligopolistic industries tend to imitate the actions of rival domestic firms that threaten to upset competitive equilibrium. Hence, when one firm invests abroad, rival firms commonly follow the lead. High production costs in the home country are an important factor.

Internal Factors

Company Product Factors
Products that are highly differentiated with distinct advantages over competitive products give sellers a significant degree of pricing discretion.
Products that require an array of pre- and post-purchase services make it difficult for a company to market the products at a distance.
Products that require considerable adaptation.

Company Resource/Commitment Factors
The more abundant a company's resources in management, capital, technology, production skills, and marketing skills, the more numerous its entry mode options. Conversely, a company with limited resources is constrained to use entry modes that call for only a small resource commitment. Size is therefore a critical factor in the choice of an entry mode. Although resources are an influencing factor, it must be joined with a willingness to commit them to foreign market development. A high degree of commitment means that managers will select the entry mode for a target from a wider range of alternative modes than managers with a low commitment.

The degree of a company's commitment to international business is revealed by the role accorded to foreign markets in corporate strategy, the status of the international organization, and the attitudes of managers.

Source: Franklin Root, *Entry Strategies for International Markets* (Lexington, Mass.: Heath, 1987).

profile, and make it in the kitchen." Krantz concedes that a commissary is "an expensive proposition but the lesser of two evils."[10]

In certain instances, a country may be so attractive for long-term growth that a firm dedicates itself to creating a supply chain for its restaurants. An excellent illustration is McDonald's expansion into Russia in the late 1980s:

> ...supply procurement has proved to be a major hurdle, as it has for all foreign companies operating in Russia. The problem has several causes: the rigid bureaucratic system, supply shortages caused by distribution and production problems, available supplies not meeting McDonald's quality standards....To handle these problems, McDonald's scoured the country for supplies, contracting for such items as milk, cheddar cheese, and beef. To help ensure ample supplies of the quality products it needed, it undertook to educate Soviet farmers and cattle ranchers on how to grow and raise those products. In addition, it built a $40 million food-processing center about 45 minutes from its first Moscow restaurant. And because distribution was [and still is] as much a cause of shortages as production was, McDonald's carried supplies on its own trucks.[11]

Changing from one supply chain to another can affect not only the availability of quality provisions, but also the equipment used to make the food that is served. For example,

> Wendy's nearly had its Korean market debut delayed by the belatedly discovered problem of thrice-frozen hamburger. After being thawed and frozen at each step of Korea's cumbersome three-company distribution channel, ground beef there takes on added water weight that threw off Wendy's patty specifications, forcing a hasty stateside retooling of the standard meat patty die used to mass-produce its burgers.[12]

Looking at statistics such as the number of ports, airports, quantity of paved roads, and transportation equipment as a percentage of capital stock per worker can give a bird's-eye view of the level of infrastructure development.

Demographics

Just as in the domestic market, restaurants in a foreign market need to know who their customers will be. Different countries will have different strata in age distribution, religion, and cultural heritage. These factors can influence the location, operations, and menus of restaurants in a country.

A popular example is India, where eating beef is contrary to the beliefs of the 80 percent of the population that is Hindu.[13] Considering India's population is nearly one billion people, companies find it hard to ignore this market even if beef is a central component of the firm's traditional menu. "We're looking at serving mutton patties," says Ann Connolly, a McDonald's spokeswoman.[14]

Another area where religion plays a part in affecting the operation of a restaurant is the middle east. Dairy Queen expanded to the region and found that during the Islamic religious observance of Ramadan no business was conducted; indeed, the windows of shops were boarded up.[15]

Age distribution can affect who should be the target market. "The company [McDonald's in Japan] also made modifications [not long after entering the market], such as targeting all advertising to younger people, because the eating habits of older Japanese are very difficult to change."[16] Age distribution can also impact the pool of labor available. In some countries over 30 percent of the population is under fifteen years old; in other countries over 15 percent is sixty-five or older. These varying demographics could create a change in the profile for potential employees in the new market.

Educational level may be an influence on both the buying public and the employee base. Literacy rates vary, and once again this can change the profile of an employee as well as who comprises the buying public.

Statistics can help compare countries using demographic components like literacy rates, total population and age distribution, and religious affiliations.

Income

Buying power is another demographic that can provide clues to how the restaurant might fare in the target country, as well as how the marketing program should position the company's products or services. Depending on the country and its economic development, the firm may have to attract a different segment than in the domestic market. For example, in Mexico,

> major U.S. firms have only recently begun targeting the country's sizable and apparently burgeoning middle class. For its part, McDonald's

has changed tactics from when it first entered Mexico as a prestige brand aimed almost exclusively at the upper class, which accounts for about 5 percent of Mexico's population of some 93 million. With the development of its own distribution systems and improved economies of scale McDonald's lately has been slashing prices to aid its penetration into working-class population strongholds. "I'd say McDonald's pricing now in Mexico is 30 percent lower, in constant dollar terms, than when we opened in '85," says Moreno [Fernando Moreno, now international director of Peter Piper Pizza], who was part of the chain's inaugural management team there.[17]

There are instances where low disposable income does not translate to a disinterest in dining out in a Western-style restaurant. While Americans dine at a fast-food establishment such as McDonald's one or two times per week, lower incomes in the foreign markets make eating at McDonald's a special, once-a-month occurrence. "These people are not very wealthy, so eating out at a place like McDonald's is a dining experience."[18] China provides another example:

at one Beijing KFC last summer, [the store] notched the volume equivalent of nine U.S. KFC branches in a single day during a $1.99 promotion of a two-piece meal with a baseball cap. Observers chalk up that blockbuster business largely to China's ubiquitous "spoiled-brat syndrome" and the apparent willingness of indulgent parents to spend one or two months' salaries on splurges for the only child the government allows them to rear.[19]

Statistics outlining the various indexes describing the country's gross domestic product, consumer spending on food, consumption and investment rates, and price levels can assist in evaluating target countries.

Trade Law

Trade policies can be friend or foe to a restaurant chain interested in expanding to other countries. Trade agreements such as the North American Free Trade Agreement (NAFTA) and the General Agreement on Tariffs and Trade (GATT) could help allevi-

ate the ills of international expansion if they achieve their aims of

reducing or eliminating tariffs, reducing non-tariff barriers to trade, liberalizing investment and foreign exchange policies, and improving intellectual property protection.... The recently signed Uruguay Round Agreements [of GATT] include the General Agreement on Trade in Services (GATS), the first multilateral, legally enforceable agreement covering trade and investment in the services sector. The GATS is designed to liberalize trade in services by reducing or eliminating governmental measures that prevent services from being freely provided across national borders or that discriminate against firms with foreign ownership.[20]

Franchising, one of the most popular modes for entering foreign markets, scored a win in the GATS agreement. For the first time, franchising was addressed directly in international trade talks. However, most countries have not elected to make their restrictions on franchising publicly known. The U.S. International Trade Commission has pointed out that

Specific commitments that delineate barriers are presented in Schedules of Commitments (Schedules). As of this writing, Schedules from approximately 90 countries are publicly available. Only 30 of these countries specifically include franchising in their Schedules ... The remaining two-thirds of the countries did not schedule commitments on franchising. This means that existing restrictions are not presented in a transparent manner and additional, more severe restrictions may be imposed at a later date.... Among the 30 countries that addressed franchising in the Schedules, 25 countries, including the United States, have committed themselves to maintain no limitations on franchising except for restrictions on the presence of foreign nationals within their respective countries.[21]

Despite progress, current international restaurant chains have encountered a myriad of challenges because of restrictive trade policies. Some countries make the import of restaurant equipment into their country difficult and expensive. The Asian region possesses "steep tariffs and [a] patchwork of inconsistent regulations that impede imports of commodities and equipment."[22]

OUTBACK'S GROWTH CHALLENGE

Connerty was well aware that there was no mention of international opportunities in Outback's 1994 Annual Report. The company distributed that Annual Report to shareholders at the April 1995 meeting. More than 300 shareholders packed the meeting to standing room only. During the question-and-answer period, a shareholder had closely questioned the company's executives as to why the company did not pay a dividend. The shareholder pointed out that the company made a considerable profit in 1994. Sullivan responded that the company needed to reinvest the cash that might be used as dividends in order to achieve the targeted growth. His response was a public and very visible commitment to continue the company's fast-paced growth. Connerty knew that international expansion had the potential to play a critical role in that growth. His job was to help craft a strategy that would assure Outback's continuing success as it took on the new and diverse markets abroad.

APPENDIX A: PROFILES OF CASUAL DINING AND FAST-FOOD CHAINS[1]

This appendix provides summaries of the 1995 publicly available data on (1) the two casual dining chains represented among the top fifty franchisers that had operations abroad (Applebee's and T.G.I. Friday's/Carlson Companies, Inc.) and (2) the top ten franchisers in the restaurant industry, all of which are fast-food chains (Burger King, Domino's, Hardee's, International Dairy Queen, Inc., Little Caesar's, McDonald's, Pepsico including KFC, Taco Bell and Pizza Hut, Subway, and Wendy's).

CASUAL DINING CHAINS WITH OPERATIONS ABROAD

Applebee's

Applebee's was one of the largest casual dining chains in the United States. It ranked twentieth in sales and thirty-sixth in stores for 1994. Like that of

---

1. Unless otherwise noted the information in this appendix was drawn from "Top 50 Franchisers," *Restaurant Business,* November 1, 1995. pp. 35–41; Hoover's Company profile Database, 1996, The Reference Press, Inc., Austin, Texas (from American Online Service); and various company listings.

most other casual dining operators, much of the company's growth had been fueled by domestic expansion. Opening in 1986, the company experienced rapid growth and by 1994 had 507 stores. The mode of growth was franchising, but in 1992 management began a program of opening more company-owned sites and buying restaurants from franchisees. The company positioned itself as a neighborhood bar and grill and offered a moderately priced menu, including burgers, chicken, and salads.

In 1995, Applebee's continued a steady program of expansion. Chairman and CEO Abe Gustin set a target of 1,200 U.S. restaurants and had also begun a slow push into international markets. In 1994, the company franchised restaurants in Canada and Curaçao and signed an agreement to franchise twenty restaurants in Belgium, Luxembourg, and the Netherlands.

Applebee's

Year	1989	1990	1991
Sales*	29.9	38.2	45.1
Net income*	0.0	1.8	3.1
EPS ($)	(0.10)	0.13	0.23
Stock Price Close($)	4.34	2.42	4.84
Dividends ($)	0.00	0.00	0.01
# Employees	1,149	1,956	1,714
Year	1992	1993	1994
Sales*	56.5	117.1	208.5
Net income*	5.1	9.5	16.9
EPS ($)	0.27	0.44	0.62
Stock Price Close($)	9.17	232.34	13.38
Dividends ($)	0.02	0.03	0.04
# Employees	2,400	46,600	8,700

*$m.   **1994: Debt ratio 20.1%; ROE 19.2; Cash $17.2M; Current ratio 1.13; LTD $23.7.

T.G.I. Friday's/Carlson Companies, Inc.

T.G.I. Friday's was owned by Carlson Companies, Inc., a large, privately held conglomerate that had interests in travel (65 percent of 1994 sales), hospitality (30 percent), plus marketing, employee training, and incentives (5 percent). Carlson also owned 345 Radisson Hotels and Country Inns plus 240 units of Country Kitchen International, a chain of family restaurants.

T.G.I. Friday's

Year	1985	1986	1987	1988	1989
Sales*	0.9	1.3	1.5	1.8	2.0
Year	1990	1991	1992	1993	1994
Sales*	2.2	2.3	2.9	2.3	2.3

*$b; no data available on income; excludes franchisee sales.

Most of Carlson's revenues came from its travel group. The company experienced a surprise in 1995 when U.S. airlines announced that they would put a cap on the commissions they would pay to book U.S. flights. Because of this change, Carlson decided to change its service to a fee-based arrangement and expected sales to drop by $100 million in 1995. To make up for this deficit, Carlson began to focus on building its hospitality group of restaurants and hotels through expansion in the United States and overseas. The company experienced significant senior management turnover in the early 1990s, and founder Curtis Carlson, aged eighty, had announced his intention to retire at the end of 1996. His daughter was announced as next head of the company.

T.G.I. Friday's grew 15.7 percent in revenue and 19.4 percent in stores in 1994. With 37 restaurants overseas, international sales were 12.7 percent of sales and 11.8 percent of stores systemwide. Carlson operated a total of 550 restaurants in seventeen countries. About one-third of overall sales came from activities outside the United States.

THE TOP TEN FRANCHISERS IN THE RESTAURANT INDUSTRY

Burger King

In 1994, Burger King was number two in sales and number four in stores among the fast-food competitors. Burger King did not have the same presence in the global market as McDonald's and KFC. For example, McDonald's and KFC had been in Japan since the 1970s. Burger King opened its first Japanese locations in 1993. By that time, McDonald's already had over 1,000 outlets there. In 1994 Burger King had 1,357 non-U.S. stores (17.7 percent of systemwide total) in fifty countries, and overseas sales (18.7 percent) totaled $1.4 billion.

Burger King was owned by the British food and spirits conglomerate Grand Metropolitan PLC. Among the company's top brands were Pillsbury, Green Giant, and Haagen-Dazs. Grand Met's situation had not been bright during the 1990s, with the loss of major distribution contracts like Absolut vodka and Grand Marnier liqueur, as well as sluggish sales for its spirits in major markets. Burger King was not a stellar performer, either, and undertook a major restructuring in 1993 to turn the tide, including reemphasis on the basic menu, cuts in prices, and reduced overhead. After quick success, BK's CEO James Adamson left his post in early 1995 to head competitor Flasgston Corporation.

Domino's

Domino's Pizza was eighth in sales and seventh in stores in 1994. Sales and store unit growth had leveled off; from 1993 to 1994 sales grew 3.6 percent, and units only 1.4 percent. The privately held company registered poor performance in 1993, with a

Burger King

Year	1985	1986	1987	1988	1989	1990	1991	1992	1993	1994
Sales*	5,590	5,291	4,706	6,029	9,298	9.394	8.748	7,913	8,120	7,780
Net Income*	272	261	461	702	1,068	1,069	432	616	412	450
EPS($)	14	16	19	24	28	32	33	28	30	32
Stock Price—Close($)	199	228	215	314	329	328	441	465	476	407
Dividend/Share($)	5.0	5.1	6.0	7.5	8.9	10.2	11.4	12.3	13.0	14.0
Employees(K)	137	131	129	90	137	138	122	102	87	64

*Millions of sterling; 1994: debt ratio 47.3%; ROE. 12.4%; cash (Ster.) 986M; LTD (Ster.) 2,322M.
1994 Segments sales (profit): North America: 62% (69%); U.K. and Ireland 10% (10%); Africa and Middle East 2% (1%); other Europe: 21% (18%); other countries: 5% (2%).
Segment sales (profits) by operating division: drinks 43% (51%); food 42% (26%); retailing 14% (22%); other 1% (1%).

Domino's

Year	1985	1986	1987	1988	1989
Sales ($ millions)	1,100	1,430	2,000	2,300	2,500
Stores	2,841	3,610	4,279	4,858	5,185
Employees (K)	na	na	na	na	na

Year	1990	1991	1992	1993	1994
Sales ($ millions)	2,600	2,400	2,450	2,200	2,500
Stores	5,342	5,571	5,264	5,369	5,079
Employees (K)	100	na	na	na	115

0.6 percent sales decline from 1992. Observers suggested that resistance to menu innovations contributed to the share decline. In the early 1990s the company did add deep-dish pizza and buffalo wings.

Flat company performances and expensive hobbies were hard on the owner and founder, Thomas Monaghan. He attempted to sell the company in 1989 but could not find a buyer. He then replaced top management and retired from business to pursue a growing interest in religious activities. Company performance began to slide, and the founder emerged from retirement to retake the helm in the early 1990s. Through extravagant purchases of the Detroit Tigers, Frank Lloyd Wright pieces, and antique cars, Monaghan put the company on the edge of financial ruin. He sold off many of his holdings (some at a loss), reinvested the funds to stimulate the firm, and once again reorganized management.

Despite all its problems, Domino's had seen consistent growth in the international market. The company opened its first foreign store in 1983 in Canada. Primary overseas expansion areas were eastern Europe and India. By 1994 Domino's had 5,079 stores with 823 of these in thirty-seven major international markets. International brought in 17 percent of 1994 sales. Over the next ten to fifteen years, the company had contracts for 4,000 additional international units.[2] These units would give Domino's more international than domestic units. International sales were 16.6 percent of total, and international stores were 16.5 percent of total in 1994.

Hardee's

Hardee's was number six in sales and eleven in stores for 1994. In 1981 the large diversified Canadian company Imasco purchased the chain. Imasco also owned Imperial Tobacco (Player's and du Maurier, Canada's top two sellers), Burger Chef, two drugstore chains, the development company Genstar, and CT Financial.

Hardee's had pursued growth primarily in the United States. Of all the burger chains in the top ten franchises, Hardee's had the smallest international presence, with seventy-two stores generating $63 million (1.8 percent and 2.0 percent of sales and stores, respectively) in 1994.

Hardee's sales grew by about 2 percent annually for 1993 and 1994. A failed attempt by Imasco to merge their Roy Roger's restaurants into the Hardee's chain forced the parent company to maintain both brands. Hardee's attempted to differentiate from the other burger chains by offering an upscale burger menu, which got a lukewarm reception by consumers.

2. "Big News Over There!" *Restaurants and Institutions,* July 1, 1994.

Hardee's

Year	1985	1986	1987	1988	1989	1990	1991	1992	1993	1994
Sales*	3,376	5,522	6,788	7,311	8,480	9,647	9,870	9,957	9,681	9,385
Net income*	262	184	283	314	366	205	332	380	409	506
EPS ($)	1.20	0.78	1.12	1.26	1.44	1.13	0.64	0.68	0.74	0.78
Stock Price—Close ($)	13.94	16.25	12.94	14.00	18.88	13.81	18.25	20.63	20.06	19.88
Dividends ($)	0.36	0.42	0.48	0.52	0.56	0.64	0.64	0.68	0.74	0.78
Employees (K)	na	na	na	na	190	190	180	na	200	200

* $M— all $ in Canadian; 1994: Debt ratio: 38.4%; ROE. 16.1%; Current ratio: 1.37; LTD(M): $1,927;
1994 Segment Sales (Operating Income): CT Financial Services 47% (28%); Hardees 32% (11%); Imperial Tobacco 16% (20%); Shoppers Drug Mart 2% (9%); Genstar Development 1% (2%).

International Dairy Queen, Inc.

Year	1985	1986	1987	1988	1989	1990	1991	1992	1993	1994
Sales*	158	182	210	254	282	287	287	296	311	341
Net income*	10	12	15	20	23	27	28	29	30	31
EPS ($)	0.33	0.42	0.51	0.70	0.83	0.97	1.05	1.12	1.79	1.30
Stock Price—Close ($)	5.20	7.75	8.00	11.50	14.75	16.58	21.00	20.00	18.00	16.25
Dividends($)	-0-	-0-	-0-	-0-	-0-	-0-	-0-	-0-	-0-	-0-
Employees (K)	430	459	503	520	549	584	592	672	538	564

*$M; 1994: Debt ratio 15.3%; R.O.E. 24.4%; Current ratio 3.04; LTD $23M.
1994 Restaurants: U.S. 87%; Canada 9%; Other 4%; Restaurants by type: DQ's: franchised by company: 62%; franchised by territorial operators 27%; foreign 3%; Orange Julius: 7%; Karmelkorn 1%, Golden Skillet less than 1%); Sales by Source: Good supplies & equipment to franchises 78%; service fees 16%; franchise sales & other fees 3%; real-estate finance & rental income 3%.

International Dairy Queen, Inc.

Dairy Queen was one of the oldest fast-food franchises in the United States: the first store was opened in Joliet, Illinois, in 1940. By 1950, there were more than 1,100 stores, and by 1960 Dairy Queen had locations in twelve countries. Initial franchise agreements focused on the right to use the DQ freezers, an innovation that kept ice cream at the constant 23 degrees (Fahrenheit) necessary to maintain the soft consistency. In 1970, a group of investors bought the franchise organization; but the group has been only partly successful in standardizing the fast-food chain. In 1994 a group of franchisees filed an antitrust suit in an attempt to get the company to loosen its control on food supply prices and sources. DQ franchises cost $30,000 initially plus continuing payments of 4 percent of sales.

The company's menu consisted of ice cream, yogurt, and brazier items (hamburgers and other fast food). Menu innovations had included Blizzard (candy and other flavors mixed in the ice cream). The company had also acquired several other companies, including the Golden Skillet (1981), Karmelkorn (1986), and Orange Julius (1987).

In 1994, Dairy Queen ranked number seven in sales and six in stores. By that same year the company had expanded its presence into nineteen countries with 628 stores and $300 million in international sales. The year was an excellent one for DQ: sales were up 22.8 percent over 1993. This dramatic change (1993 scored an anemic 3.0 percent gain) was fueled by technology improvements for franchisees and international expansion. In 1992 Dairy Queen opened company-owned outlets in Austria, China, Slovenia, and Spain. DQ announced in 1995 that it had a plan to open twenty stores in Puerto Rico over a four-year period.

Little Caesar's

Little Caesar's ranked tenth in sales and eighth in stores for 1994. Sales growth had stopped: the 1992–1993 increase of 12.2 percent evaporated into no increase for 1993–1994. These numbers were achieved without a significant overseas presence. Of the top ten franchises, only Hardee's had a smaller number of stores in foreign lands. Little Caesar's received 3.5 percent of sales from foreign stores. Only 3.2 percent of the company's stores were in non-U.S. locations, namely, Canada, Czech and Slovak Republics, Guam, Puerto Rico, and the United Kingdom.

Little Caesar's

Year	1985	1986	1987	1988	1989	1990	1991	1992	1993	1994
Sales*	340	520	725	908	1,130	1,400	1,725	2,050	2,150	2,000
Number of stores	900	1,000	1,820	2,000	2,700	3,173	3,650	4,300	5,609	4.700
Employees	18,000	26,160	36,400	43,600	54,000	63,460	73,000	86,000	92,000	95,000

McDonald's

Year	1985	1986	1987	1988	1989	1990	1991	1992	1993	1994
Sales*	3,695	4,144	4,894	5,566	6,142	6,640	6,695	7,133	7,408	8,321
Net income*	433	480	549	656	727	802	860	959	1,083	1,224
EPS($)	0.56	0.63	0.73	0.86	0.98	1.10	1.18	1.30	1.46	1.68
Stock Price—Close($)	9.00	10.16	11.00	12.03	17.25	14.56	19.00	24.38	28.50	29.25
Dividends($)	0.10	0.11	0.12	0.14	0.16	0.17	0.18	0.20	0.21	0.23
Employees (K)	148	159	159	169	176	174	168	166	169	183

*$M; 1994: Debt ratio 41.2%; ROE.: 20.7%; Cash: $180M; Current ratio: 0.31: LTD $2.9M; Market Value: $20B

McDonald's

At the top in 1994 international sales and units, McDonald's Inc. was the most profitable retailer in the United States during the 1980s and into the 1990s. The company opened its first store in California in 1948, went public in 1965, and by 1994 had over 20 percent of the U.S. fast-food business. McDonald's opened its first international store in Canada in 1967. Growing domestic competition in the 1980s gave impetus to the company's international expansion. By 1994 there were over 15,000 restaurants under the golden arches in seventy-nine countries. The non-U.S. stores provided about one-third of total revenues and half of the company's profits. McDonald's planned to open 1,200–1,500 new restaurants in 1995—most outside the United States. International markets had grown into an attractive venue for the burger giant because there was "less competition, lighter market saturation, and high name recognition" in international markets.

The company's growth was fueled by aggressive franchising. In the early 1990s two-thirds of the McDonald's locations were franchised units, and franchisees remained with the company an average of twenty years. McDonald's used heavy advertising ($1.4 billion in 1994) and frequent menu changes and other innovations (1963: Filet-O-Fish sandwich and Ronald McDonald; 1968 Big Mac and first TV ads; 1972: Quarter Pounder, Egg McMuffin (breakfast); 1974: Ronald McDonald House; 1975: drive through; 1979: Happy Meals; 1983: Chicken McNuggets; 1986: provided customers with list of products' ingredients; 1987: salads; 1980s "value menus"; 1991: McLean DeLuxe, a low-fat hamburger—not successful—and experimentation with decor and new menu items at the local level; 1993: first restaurants inside another store, Wal-Mart). The company planned to open its first restaurants in India in 1996 with menus featuring chicken, fish sandwiches, and vegetable nuggets. There would be no beef items.

From 1993 to 1994, McDonald's grew 10.2 percent in sales and 8.7 percent in stores. Because of its extensive experience in international markets, international sales had grown to 42.5 percent of their total revenues and half its profits. Indeed, McDonald's was bigger than the twenty-five largest full-service chains put together.

PepsiCo: KFC and Taco Bell (Also Includes Pizza Hut which Is Not in the Top Fifty)

PepsiCo owned powerful brand names such as Pepsi-Cola and Frito-Lay and was also the world's

Pepsico

Year	1985	1986	1987	1988	1989	1990	1991	1992	1993	1994
Sales*	8,057	9,291	11,485	13,007	15,242	17,803	19,608	21,970	25,021	28,474
Net income*	544	458	595	762	901	1,077	1,080	1,302	1,588	1,784
EPS($)	0.65	0.58	0.76	0.97	1.13	1.35	1.35	1.61	1.96	2.22
Stock Price—Close($)	8.06	8.66	11.11	13.15	21.31	26.00	22.88	31.40	40.88	36.25
Dividends/Share($)	0.15	0.21	0.22	0.25	0.31	0.37	0.44	0.50	0.58	0.68
Employees (K)	150	214	225	235	266	308	338	372	423	471

*$M; 1994: Debt ratio 48.1%; ROE.: 27.0%; Cash: $1,488M; Current ratio: 0.96: LTD(M) $8,841.
1994 Segment Sales (Operating Income): Restaurants: 37% (22%); Beverages 34% (37%); Snack foods 29% (41%).

number one fast-food chain with its ownership of KFC, Taco Bell, and Pizza Hut.

KFC was third in sales and stores of the top fifty franchises in 1994. Active in the international arena since the late 1960s, KFC had been a major McDonald's competitor in non-U.S. markets. In 1994, the company had $3.6 billion in sales and 4,258 stores in other countries. McDonald's had been commonly number one in each country it entered, but KFC had been number two in international sales and had the number one sales spot in Indonesia. In 1994, KFC international revenues were 50.7 percent of sales with 45.3 percent of stores in international locations.

Taco Bell was fourth in sales and fifth in stores of the top fifty franchises in 1994. This ranking had been achieved with minimal international business to date. Taco Bell had $130 million in sales and 162 stores internationally. The company attempted to enter the Mexican market in 1992 with a kiosk and cart strategy in Mexico City. The venture did not fare well, and Taco Bell soon pulled out of Mexico.[3] In 1994, international revenues were 3.0 percent of sales and 2.9 percent of stores were international locations.

Subway

Founded more than twenty-nine years ago, Subway remained privately held in 1994.[4] The company had experienced explosive growth during the 1990s. It ranked ninth in sales and second in stores for 1994. Sales grew 13.6 percent from 1993 to 1994, and 26 percent from 1992 to 1993. Stores grew 17.1 percent from 1993 to 1994, and 15.3 percent from 1992 to 1993. In 1994, Subway overtook KFC as the number two chain in number of stores behind

McDonald's. The company attributed its growth at least partially to an exceptionally low-priced and well-structured franchise program. In addition, store sizes of 500–1500 square feet were small. Thus, the investment for a Subway franchise was modest.

The company's growth involved a deliberate strategy. The formula involved no cooking on site, except for the baking of bread. The company promoted the "efficiency and simplicity" of its franchise and advertised its food as "healthy, delicious, (and) fast." The company advertised regularly on TV with a $25M budget and planned to increase that significantly. All stores contributed 2.5 percent of gross sales to the corporate advertising budget. Subway's goal was "to equal or exceed the number of outlets operated by the largest fast-food company in every market that it entered." In most cases, the firm's benchmark was burger giant McDonald's.

International markets played an emerging role in Subway's expansion. In 1994, international sales were 10.6 percent of sales, compared to 8.9 percent the previous year. International stores were 9.5 percent of total in 1994, and 7.5 percent in 1993. Subway boasted a total of 9,893 stores in all fifty states and nineteen countries.[5]

Wendy's

Wendy's was number five in sales and number nine in stores for 1994. In 1994, after twenty-five years of operation, Wendy's had grown to 4,411 stores. This growth had been almost exclusively domestic until 1979, when Wendy's ventured out of the United States and Canada to open its first outlets in Puerto Rico, Switzerland, and West Germany. Wendy's granted JC Penney the franchise rights to France, Belgium, and Holland, and had one store opened in Belgium by 1980.

3. "US Operators Flock to Latin America," *Nation's Restaurant News,* November 17, 1994.
4. There is thus no publicly available financial data on Subway.

5. Subway's site on the Internet, accessed March 24, 1996.

Wendy's

Year	1985	1986	1987	1988	1989	1990	1991	1992	1993	1994
Sales*	1,126	1,140	1,059	1,063	1,070	1,011	1,060	1,239	1,320	1,398
Net income*	76	(5)	4	29	24	39	52	65	79	97
EPS($)	0.82	(0.05)	0.04	0.30	0.25	0.40	0.52	0.63	0.76	0.91
Stock price—close($)	13.41	10.25	5.63	5.75	4.63	6.25	9.88	12.63	17.38	14.38
Div/share($)	0.17	0.21	0.24	0.24	0.24	0.24	0.24	0.24	0.24	0.24
Employees(K)	40	40	45	42	39	35	39	42	43	44

*$M; 1994: Debt ratio 36.6%; ROE. 5.2%; Current ratio 0.98; LTD(M) $145

Wendy's still saw opportunities for growth in the United States. Industry surveys had consistently ranked Wendy's burgers number one in quality, but poor in convenience (Wendy's had one store for every 65,000 people while McDonald's, in contrast, had one for every 25,000). Growth was driven primarily by franchising. In 1994, 71 percent of the stores were operated by franchisees and 29 percent by the company. Company restaurants provided 90 percent of total sales while franchise fees provided 8 percent. The company had made menu and strategic changes at various points in its history. For example, in 1977 it first began TV advertising; in 1979 it introduced its salad bar; in 1985 it experimented with breakfast; in 1986 and 1987 it introduced Big Classic and SuperBar buffet (neither very successful); in 1990 it introduced grilled chicken sandwich and 99 cent Super Value Menu items; and in 1992, packaged salads.

Wendy's planned to add about 150 restaurants each year in foreign markets. With a presence of 236 stores in thirty-three countries in 1994, international was 9.1 percent of sales and 9.4 percent of stores that year.

APPENDIX B
COUNTRY SUMMARIES[1]

Canada

In the 1990s, Canada was considered an ideal first stop for U.S. business seeking to begin exporting. Per capita output, patterns of production, market economy, and business practices were similar to those in the United States. U.S. goods and services were well received in Canada: 70 percent of all Canadian imports were from the United States. Canada's market conditions were stable, and U.S. companies continued to see Canada as an attractive option for expansion.

Canada had one of the highest real growth rates among the OECD during the 1980s, averaging about 3.2 percent. The Canadian economy softened during the 1990s, but Canadian imports of U.S. goods and services were expected to increase about 5 percent in fiscal year 1996.

Although Canada sometimes mirrored the United States, there are significant cultural and linguistic differences between it and the United States and between the regional markets in Canada. These differences were evident in the mounting friction between the English- and French-speaking areas of Canada. The conflict had the potential of slicing Canada into two separate countries, and the prospect of such an outcome left foreign investors tense.

Germany

In the mid 1990s, Germany was the largest economy in Europe and the fifth largest overall importer of U.S. goods and services. Since reunification in 1990, the eastern part of Germany had continued to receive extensive infusions of aid from western Germany, and these funds were only just beginning to show an impact. The highly urbanized and skilled western German population enjoyed a very high standard of living, with abundant leisure time. In 1994, Germany emerged from a recession and scored a GDP of $2 trillion.

A unique feature of Germany was the unusually even distribution of both industry and population—there was no single business center for the country. This was a challenge for U.S. firms. They had to establish distribution networks that adequately covered all areas of the country. In Germany, there was little opportunity for regional concentration around major population centers as in the United States.

The country was a good market for innovative high-tech goods and high-quality food products. Germans expected high-quality goods and would reject a less expensive product if quality and support were not in abundance. The strongest competition for U.S. firms were the German domestic firms, not only because of their home-grown familiarity with the market, but also because of the consumers' widely held perception that German products were "simply the best."

A recurring complaint from Germans was the prevalent "here today, gone tomorrow" business approach of American firms. Germans viewed business as a long-term commitment to support growth in markets and did not always receive the level and length of attention necessary from U.S. companies to satisfy them.

Conditions in the former East Germany were not the doomsday picture often painted, nor were they as rosy as the German government depicts. It

---

1. The material in this appendix is adapted from the Department of Commerce Country Commercial Guides and the *CIA World Fact Book.*

would take ten to fifteen years for the eastern region of the country to catch up to the western region in terms of per capita income, standard of living, and productivity.

Japan

Japan had the second largest economy in the world. Overall economic growth in Japan over the past thirty-five years had been incredible: 10 percent average annual growth during the 1960s, and 5 percent in the 1970s and 1980s. Growth ground to a halt during the 1990s due to tight fiscal policy. The government tightened fiscal constraints in order to correct the significant devaluation of the real estate markets. The economy posted a 0.6 percent growth in 1994 largely due to consumer demand. The overall economic outlook remained cloudy, but the outlook for exports to Japan remained positive.

Japan is a highly homogeneous society, with business practices characterized by long-standing close relationships among individuals and firms. It took time for Japanese businessmen to develop relationships, and for non-Japanese businesspeople the task of relationship building in Japan was formidable. It was well known that Japan's market was not as open as that of the United States, but the U.S. government had mounted multifaceted efforts to help U.S. businesspeople "open doors." While these efforts were helpful, most of the responsibility in opening the Japanese market to U.S. goods or services remained with the individual firm. Entering Japan was expensive and generally required four things: (1) financial and management capabilities and a Japanese-speaking staff residing within the country; (2) modification of products to suit Japanese consumers; (3) a long-term approach to maximizing market share and achieving reasonable profit levels; and (4) careful monitoring of Japanese demand, distribution, competitors, and government. Despite the challenges of market entry, Japan ranked as the second largest importer of U.S. goods and services.

Historically, Japanese consumers were conservative and brand conscious, although the recession during the 1990s nurtured opportunities for "value" entrants. Traditional conformist buying patterns were still prominent, but more individualistic habits were developing in the younger Japanese, aged eighteen to twenty-one. This age cohort had a population of 8 million and boasted a disposable income of more than $35 billion.

Japanese consumers were willing to pay a high price for quality goods. However, they had a well-earned reputation for having unusually high expectations for quality. U.S. firms with high quality and competitive products had to be able to undertake the high cost of initial market entry. For those that could and were willing to do so, Japan could provide respectable market share and attractive profit levels.

Mexico

Mexico had experienced a dramatic increase in imports from the United States since the late 1980s. During 1994, the country experienced 20 percent growth over 1993. In 1994, Mexico's peso experienced a massive devaluation brought on by investor anxiety and capital flight. Although the Mexican government implemented tight fiscal measures to stabilize the peso, its efforts could not stop the country from plunging into a serious recession.

Inflation rose as a result of the austerity policies, and it was expected to be between 42 and 54 percent in 1995. Negative economic growth was anticipated in 1995 as well. The U.S. financial assistance package (primarily loans) provided Mexico with nearly $50 billion and restored stability to the financial markets by mid 1995. The government was taking measures to improve the country's infrastructure. Mexico's problems mask the fact that its government had, on the whole, practiced sound economic fundamentals.

Mexico was still committed to political reform despite the economic challenges. After ruling the country uninterrupted for sixty years, the PRI party had begun to lose some seats to other political parties. Mexico was slowly evolving into a multiparty democracy.

Despite the economic misfortunes of the 1990s, Mexico remained the United States' third largest trading partner. Mexico still held opportunities for U.S. firms able to compete in the price-sensitive recessionary market. Mexico had not wavered on the NAFTA agreement since its ratification, and in the mid 1990s 60 percent of U.S. exports to Mexico entered duty free.

South Korea

South Korea had been identified as one of the U.S. Department of Commerce's ten "Big Emerging Markets." Its economy overcame tremendous obstacles after the Korean War in the 1950s left the country in ruins. The driving force behind South Korea's growth was export-led development and energetic emphasis on entrepreneurship. Annual real GDP growth from 1986 to 1991 was over 10 percent. This blistering pace created inflation, tight labor markets, and a rising current account deficit. Fiscal policy in 1992 focused on curbing inflation and reducing the deficit. Annual growth, reduced to a still enviable 5 percent in 1992, rose to 6.3 percent in 1993. Fueled by exports, the 1994 growth was a heady 8.3 percent. South Korea's GDP was larger than that of Russia, Australia, or Mexico.

The American media had highlighted such issues as student demonstrations, construction accidents, and North Korean nuclear problem and trade disputes. Investors needed to closely monitor developments related to North Korea. However, the political landscape in South Korea had been stable enough over the 1980s to fuel tremendous economic expansion. The country was undertaking significant infrastructure improvements. Overall, South Korea was a democratic republic with an open society and a free press. It was a modern, cosmopolitan, fast-paced, and dynamic country, with abundant business opportunities for savvy American businesses.

There had been a staggering development of U.S. exports to South Korea: $21.6 billion in 1994 and more than $30 billion expected in 1995. While South Korea was twenty-two times smaller than China in terms of population, it imported twice as many U.S. goods and services than China in 1994.

Although South Korea ranked as the United States' sixth largest export market, obstacles for U.S. firms still remained. Despite the country's participation in the Uruguay Round of GATT and related trade agreements, customs clearance procedures and regulations for labeling, sanitary standards, and quarantine often served as significant non-tariff barriers.

The United Kingdom (or Great Britain)

The United Kingdom was the United States' fourth largest trading partner and the largest market for U.S. exports in Europe. Common language, legal heritage, and business practices facilitated U.S. entry into the British market.

The United Kingdom had made significant changes in its taxation, regulation, and privatization policies, which altered the structure of the British economy and increased its overall efficiency. The reward for this disciplined economic

approach had been a sustained, modest growth during the 1980s and early 1990s. The GDP grew 4.2 percent in 1994—the highest level in six years. The United Kingdom trimmed its deficit from $75 billion in fiscal 1994 to $50 billion in fiscal 1995.

The country had no restrictions on foreign ownership and movement of capital. There was a high degree of labor flexibility. Efficiencies had soared, and in the mid 1990s the country boasted the lowest real per-unit labor cost of the Group of Seven (G7) industrialized countries.

The United Kingdom's shared cultural heritage and warm relationship with the United States translated into the British finding U.S. goods and services to be attractive purchases. These reasons, coupled with a policy emphasizing free enterprise and open competition, made Britain the destination of 40 percent of all U.S. investment in the European Union.

The U.K. market was based on a commitment to the principles of free enterprise and open competition. Demand for U.S. goods and services was growing. The abolition of many internal trade barriers within the European Common market enabled European-based firms to operate relatively freely. As a result, U.S. companies used the United Kingdom as a gateway to the rest of the European Union. Of the top 500 British companies, one in eight was a U.S. affiliate. Excellent physical and communications infrastructure, combined with a friendly political and commercial climate, was expected to keep the United Kingdom as a primary target for U.S. firms for years to come.

Pizza Hut and Kentucky Fried Chicken, which had operations in more than sixty countries, and Taco Bell, which had operations in eleven countries, are owned by Pepsico.

Endnotes

1. All three Outback founders credited casual dining chain legend and mentor Norman Brinker with his strong mentoring role in their careers. Brinker played a key role in all of the restaurant chains Sullivan and Basham were associated with prior to Outback.

2. American consumption of meat declined from the mid 1970s to the early 1990s primarily as a result of health concerns about red meat. In 1976, Americans consumed 131.6 pounds of beef and veal, 58.7 pounds of pork, and 12.9 pounds of fish. In 1990, the figures had declined to 64.9 pounds of beef and veal, and 46.3 of pork, but rose to 15.5 of fish. The dramatic decrease in the consumption of beef and veal was attributed to consumer attitudes toward a low-fat, healthier diet. Menu items that gained in popularity

were premium baked goods, coffees, vegetarian menu items, fruits, salsa, sauces, chicken dishes, salads, and spicy dishes. George Thomas Kurian, *Datapedia of the United States 1790-10000* (Md: Bernan Press, 1994), p. 113.

3. Outback's original Henderson Boulevard Restaurant in Tampa, Florida was one of the few open for lunch. By 1995, the chain had also begun to open in some locations for Sunday lunch or for special occasions such as Mother's Day lunch.

4. Outback's signature trademark was its best-selling "Aussie-Tizer," the "Bloomin' Onion." The company expected to serve 9 million "Bloomin' Onions" in 1995.

5. Merritt had worked as CFO for another company, which had come to the financial markets with its IPO (initial public offering).

6. Outback did not grant exclusive territorial franchises. Thus, if an Outback franchisee did not perform, the company could bring additional franchisees into the area. Through 1994 Outback had not had territorial disputes between franchisees.

7. Pepsico owned Kentucky Fried Chicken, Taco Bell, and Pizza Hut; Grand Met owned Burger King.

8. Ref. AME 76 (KR).

9. "Industry and Trade Summary: Franchising," (Washington, D.C., U.S. International Trade Commission, 1995), pp. 15–16.

10. "World Hunger," *Restaurant Hospitality* (November 1994), p.97.

11. *International Business Environments and Operations*, 7th ed., (1995), pp. 117–119.

12. "U.S. Restaurant Chains Tackle Challenges of Asian Expansion," *Nation's Restaurant News*, February 14, 1994, p.36.

13. "India," *CIA World Factbook*, 1995.

14. "Big McMuttons," *Forbes*, July 17, 1995, p.18.

15. Interview with Cheryl Babcock, professor at the University of St. Thomas, October 23, 1995.

16. "Franchise Management in East Asia," *Academy of Management Executive*, 4, No. 2 (1990), p.79.

17. "U.S. Operators Flock to Latin America," *Nation's Restaurant News*, October 17, 1994, p. 47.

18. Interview with Cheryl Babcock.

19. "U.S. Restaurant Chains Tackle Challenges of Asian Expansion," p.36.

20. "Industry and Trade Summary: Franchising," p.30.

21. Ibid.

22. "U.S. Restaurant Chains Tackle Challenges of Asian Expansion," p.36.

C

Corporate Level: Domestic and Global Cases

CASE 27

Nucor

This case was prepared by Frank C. Barnes of the University of North Carolina, Charlotte.

INTRODUCTION

Nuclear Corporation of America had been near bankruptcy in 1965, when a fourth reorganization put a thirty-nine-year-old division manager, Ken Iverson, into the president's role. Iverson began a process that resulted in Nucor, a steel mini-mill and joist manufacturer, which rated national attention and reaped high praise.

In a 1981 article subtitled "Lean living and mini-mill technology have led a one-time loser to steel's promised land," *Fortune* stated:

> Although Nucor didn't build his first mill until 1969, it turned out 1.1 million tons of steel last year, enough to rank among the top 20 U.S. producers. Not only has Nucor been making a lot of steel, it's been making money making steel—and a lot of that as well. Since 1969, earnings have grown 31% a year, compounded, reaching $45 million in 1980 on sales of $482 million. Return on average equity in recent years has consistently exceeded 28%, excellent even by Silicon Valley's standards and almost unheard of in steel. The nine-fold increase in the value of Nucor's stock over the last five years—it was selling recently at about $70 a share—has given shareholders plenty of cause for thanksgiving.[1]

The *Wall Street Journal* commented, "The ways in which management style combines with technology to benefit the mini-mill industry is obvious at Nucor Corp., one of the most successful of the

forty or more mini-mill operators."[2] Ken Iverson was featured in an NBC special, "If Japan Can, Why Can't We?" for his management approach. As the *Wall Street Journal* commented, "You thought steel companies are only a bunch of losers, with stodgy management, outmoded plants and poor profits?" Well, Nucor and Iverson were different.

However, the challenges hadn't stopped. The economy made the 1980s a horrible time for the steel industry. All companies reported sales declines, most lost profitability and some, in both major and mini-mill operations, closed or restructured. Nucor's 30 percent plus return on equity hit 9 percent. Iverson, however, was one of fifty-two recipients of the bronze model from *Financial World* in 1983 for holding on to profitability; it kept costs down but not at the expense of laying off its people—a near-religious commitment at Nucor.

By 1990, Nucor was the ninth largest steel producer in the United States and number 323 on the *Fortune* 500 list. But the easy gains scored by the new mini-mill operations over the integrated mills were over. The historical steel companies were awakening from their twenty-year slumber, adding modern technology, renegotiating with their equally aged unions, and closing some mills. They were determined to fight back. Mini-mill was fighting mini-mill, as well as imports, and a number had closed. Thus the industry faced a picture of excess capacity which would be the backdrop in the battle for survival and success over the next years.

Iverson and Nucor knew how to fight the battle. They invested $325 million in new processes in 1988. They went from $185 million in idle cash in 1986 to $180 million in debt by 1988. They had opened the first new fastener plant in the United States in decades, completed a joint venture with the Japanese to build a plant to make structural steel products, and built the first mini-mill in the world to make flat-rolled steel, the largest market and major business of the integrated producers. They had broken away from the other mini-mills and had at least a three-year headstart in taking a share of this market from the integrated mills. Iverson believed with their new products they should double sales, and probably earnings, by 1991. Analysts predicted a jump to seventh largest among mills and doubling or tripling share price in the immediate future.

BACKGROUND

Nucor was the descendant of a company that manufactured the first Oldsmobile in 1897. After seven years of success, R. E. Olds sold his first company and founded a new one to manufacture the Reo. Reo ran into difficulties and filed for voluntary reorganization in 1938. Sales grew fifty times over the next ten years, based on defense business, but declined steadily after World War II. The motor division was sold and then resold in 1957 to the White Motor Corporation, where it operates as the Diamond Reo division. Reo Motors' management planned to liquidate the firm, but before it could do so, a new company gained control through a proxy fight. A merger was arranged with Nuclear Consultants, Inc., and the stock of Nuclear Corporation of America was first traded in 1955. Nuclear acquired a number of companies in high-tech fields but continued to lose money until 1960, when an investment banker in New York acquired control. New management proceeded with a series of acquisitions and dispositions: they purchased U.S. Semi-Conductor Products, Inc.; Valley Sheet Metal Company, an air conditioner contractor in Arizona; and Vulcraft Corporation, a Florence, South Carolina, steel joist manufacturer. Over the next four years, sales increased five times, but losses increased seven times. In 1965, a New York investor purchased a controlling interest and installed the fourth management team. The new president was Ken Iverson, who had been in charge of the Vulcraft division.

Ken Iverson had joined the Navy upon graduation from a Chicago-area high school in 1943. The Navy first sent him to Northwestern University for an officer training program but then decided it needed aeronautical engineers and transferred him

to Cornell. This had been "fine" with Iverson, because he enjoyed engineering. Upon receiving his bachelor's degree in 1945 at age twenty, he served in the Navy for six months, completing his four-year tour.

He wasn't too excited about an aeronautical engineering career because of the eight years of drafting required for success. Metals and their problems in aircraft design had intrigued him, so he considered a master's degree in metallurgy. An uncle had attended Purdue, so he chose that school. He married during this time, gave up teaching geometry so he could finish the program in one year, and turned down an offer of assistance toward a Ph.D. to "get to work."

At Purdue he had worked with the new electron microscope. International Harvester's research physics department had just acquired one and hired Iverson as assistant to the chief research physicist. Iverson stayed there five years and felt he was "set for life." He had great respect for his boss, who would discuss with him the directions businesses took and their opportunities. One day the chief physicist asked if that job was what he really wanted to do all his life. There was only one job ahead for Iverson at International Harvester and he felt more ambition than to end his career in that position. At his boss's urging, he considered smaller companies.

Iverson joined Illium Corporation, 120 miles from Chicago, as chief engineer (metallurgist). Illium was a sixty-person division of a major company but functioned like an independent company. Iverson was close to the young president and was impressed by his good business skill; this man knew how to manage and had the discipline to run a tight ship, to go in the right direction with no excess manpower. The two of them proposed an expansion, which the parent company insisted they delay three to four years until they could handle it without going into debt.

After two years at Illium, Iverson joined Indiana Steel products as assistant to the vice president of manufacturing, for the sole purpose of setting up a spectrographic lab. After completing this job within one year, he could see no other opportunity for himself in the company, because it was small and he could get no real responsibility. A year and a half later, Iverson left to join Cannon Muskegon as chief metallurgist.

The next seven years were "fascinating." This small ($5–6 million in sales and sixty-to-seventy people) family company made castings from special metals that were used in every aircraft made in the United States. The company was one of the first to get into "vacuum melting," and Iverson, because of his technical ability, was put in charge of this activity. Iverson then asked for and got responsibility for all company sales. He wasn't dissatisfied but realized that if he was to be really successful he needed broader managerial experience.

Cannon Muskegon sold materials to Coast Metals, a small, private company in New Jersey which cast and machined special alloys for the aircraft industry. The president of Coast got to know Iverson and realized his technical expertise would be an asset. In 1960 he joined Coast as executive vice president, with responsibility for running the whole company.

Nuclear Corporation of America wished to buy Coast; however, Coast wasn't interested. Nuclear's president then asked Iverson to act as a consultant to find metal businesses Nuclear could buy. Over the next year, mostly on weekends, he looked at potential acquisitions. He recommended buying a joist business in North Carolina. Nuclear said it would, if he would run it. Coast was having disputes among its owners and Iverson's future there was clouded. He ended his two years there and joined Nuclear in 1962 as a vice president, Nuclear's usual title, in charge of a 200-person joist division.

By late 1963, he had built a second plant in Nebraska and was running the only division making a profit. The president asked him to become a group vice president, adding the research chemicals (metals) and contracting businesses, and to move to the home office in Phoenix. In mid 1965 the company defaulted on two loans and the president resigned. During the summer Nuclear sought some direction out of its difficulty. Iverson knew what could be done, put together a pro-forma statement, and pushed for these actions. It was not a unanimous decision when he was made president in September 1965.

The new management immediately abolished some divisions and went to work building Nucor. According to Iverson, the vice presidents of the divisions designed Nucor in hard-working, almost T-group-type meetings. Iverson was only another participant and took charge only when the group couldn't settle an issue. This process identified Nucor's strengths and set the path for Nucor.

By 1966, Nuclear consisted of the two joist plants, the research chemicals division, and the nuclear division. During 1967, a building in Fort Payne, Alabama, was purchased for conversion into another joist plant. "We got into the steel business because we wanted to be able to build a mill that could make steel as cheaply as we were buying it from foreign importers or from offshore mills." In 1968 Nucor opened a steel mill in Darlington, South Carolina, and a joist plant in Texas. Another joist plant was added in Indiana in 1972. Steel plant openings followed in Nebraska in 1977 and in Texas in 1975. The Nuclear division was divested in 1976. A fourth steel plant was opened in Utah in 1981 and a joist plant was opened in Utah in 1982. By 1984, Nucor consisted of six joist plants, four steel mills, and a research chemicals division.

In 1983, in testimony before the Congress, Iverson warned of the hazards of trade barriers, that they would cause steel to cost more and that manufacturers would move overseas to use the cheaper steel shipped back into this country. He commented, "We have seen serious problems in the wire industry and the fastener industry." *Link* magazine reported that in the last four years, forty domestic fastener plants had closed and that imports had over 90 percent of the market.

In 1986, Nucor began construction of a $25 million plant in Indiana to manufacture steel fasteners. Iverson told the *Atlanta Journal,* "We are going to bring that business back."[3] He told *Inc.* magazine, "We've studied for a year now, and we decided that we can make bolts as cheaply as foreign producers and make a profit at it."[4] He explained that in the old operation two people, one simply required by the union, made one hundred bolts a minute. "But at Nucor, we'll have an automated machine which will manufacture 400 bolts a minute. The automation will allow an operator to manage four machines." Hans Mueller, a steel industry consultant at East Tennessee State University, told the *Journal,* "I must confess that I was surprised that Iverson would be willing to dive into that snake pit. But he must believe that he can do it because he is not reckless."[5]

Before making the decision, a Nucor task force of four people traveled the world to examine the latest technology. The management group was headed by a plant manager who joined Nucor after several years' experience as general manager of a bolt company in Toronto. The manager of manufacturing was previously plant manager of a 40,000-ton melt-shop for Ervin Industries. The sales manager was a veteran of sales, distribution, and manufacturing in the fastener industry. The plant's engineering manager transferred from Nucor R & D in Nebraska. The Touche-Ross accountant who worked on the Nucor account joined the company as controller. The first crew of production employees received three months of in-depth training on the bolt-making machines, with extensive cross-training in tool making, maintenance, and other operations. By 1988, the new plant was operating close to its capacity of 45,000 tons.

In what the *New York Times* called their "most ambitious project yet," Nucor signed an agreement in January 1987 to form a joint venture with Yamato Kogyo, Ltd., a small Japanese steel maker, to build a steel mill on the Mississippi River with a 600,000 ton per year capacity."[6] The $200 million dollar plant would make very large structural products, up to 24 inches. Structural steel products are those used in large buildings and bridges. Iverson noted, "These are now only made by the Big Three integrated steel companies." The Japanese company, which would own 49 percent of the stock, had expertise in continuous-casting in which Nucor was interested. Their 1985 sales totaled $400 million, with approximately 900 workers. They would provide the continuous-casting technology while Nucor would provide the melting technology and management style. The mill was completed in 1988 at a cost of $220 million for 650,000 tons of capacity. By the end of 1988, the plant was operating at 50 percent of capacity.

In August 1986, Iverson told Cable News Network, "We are talking about within the next two years perhaps building a steel mill to make flat roll products; that would be the first time a mini-mill has been in this area."[7] It was expected that approximately $10 million would be needed to develop this process. The thin-slab would also produce feed stock for Vulcraft's 250,000 tons per year steel deck operation. Although the project was considered pure research at the time and projected for "late 1988," the Division Manager stated, "The more we look into it, the more we feel we'll be able to successfully cast those slabs." This process would be the most significant development in the steel industry in decades and would open up the auto and appliance businesses to the mini-mills. Then in January 1987 plans were announced to build the $200 million, 800,000 ton mill for the production of high-grade flat rolled steel by the first half of 1989. They stated, "We've tested numerous approaches . . . this one is commercially feasible. It's been tested and it can do the job."[8]

The flat rolled steel was the largest market for steel products at 40 million tons in 1988 and 52 percent of the U.S. market. This is the thin sheet steel used in car bodies, refrigerators, and countless products. Making flat rolled steel required casting a slab rather than a billet and had not been achieved in the mini-mill. Nucor had invested several million in research on a process but in 1986 chose to go with a technology developed by SMS, a West Germany company. SMS had a small pilot plant using the new technology and Nucor would be the first mini-mill in the world to manufacture flat rolled steel commercially.

The plant would be built in Crawfordsville, Indiana, with an April 1988 start-up. It was expected that labor hours per ton would be half the integrated manufacturer's 3.0, yielding a savings of $50 to $75 on a $400 a ton selling price. If the project were completed successfully, Nucor planned to have three plants in operation before others could build. Investment advisers anticipated Nucor's stock could increase to double or triple by the mid 1990s. In July 1989, when Nucor announced a 14 percent drop in 2nd quarter earnings due to start-up costs, its stock went up $1.62, to $63. Iverson stated, "We hope this will map out the future of the company for the next decade."

However, it would not be as easy as earlier ventures. In April 1989, *Forbes* commented "if any mini-mill can meet the challenge, it's Nucor. But expect the going to be tougher this time around."[9] The flat-rolled market was the last bastion of the integrated manufacturers and they had been seriously modernizing their plants throughout the '80s.

In December 1986, Nucor announced its first major acquisition, Genbearco, a steel bearings manufacturer. At a cost of more than $10 million, it would add $25 million in sales and 250 employees. Iverson called it "a good fit with our business, our policies, and our people." It was without a union and tied pay to performance.

In October 1988, Nucor agreed to sell its Chemicals Division to a New York company for a $38 million gain.

Nucor's innovation was not limited to manufacturing. In the steel industry, it was normal to price an order based on the quantity ordered. In 1984, Nucor broke that pattern. As Iverson stated, "Some time ago we began to realize that with computer order entry and billing, the extra charge for smaller orders was not cost justified. We found the cost of servicing a 20 ton order compared with a 60 ton order was about 35 cents a ton and most of that was related to credit and collection. We did agonize over the decision, but over the long run we are confident that the best competitive position is one that has a strong price to cost relationship." He noted that this policy would give Nucor another advantage over foreign suppliers in that users could maintain lower inventories and order more often. "If we are going to successfully compete against foreign suppliers, we must use the most economical methods for both manufacturing and distribution."

THE STEEL INDUSTRY

The early 1980s had been the worst years in decades for the steel industry. Data from the American Iron and Steel Institute showed shipments falling from 100.2 million tons in 1979 to the mid-80 levels in 1980 and 1981. Slackening in the economy, particularly in auto sales, led the decline. In 1986, when industry capacity was at 130 million tons, the outlook was for a continued decline in per capita consumption and movement toward capacity in the 90–100 million ton range. The chairman of Armco saw "millions of tons chasing a market that's not there; excess capacity that must be eliminated."

The large, integrated steel firms, such as U.S. Steel and Armco, which made up the major part of the industry, were the hardest hit. The *Wall Street Journal* stated, "The decline has resulted from such problems as high labor and energy costs in mining and processing iron ore, a lack of profits and capital to modernize plants, and conservative management that has hesitated to take risks."[10]

These companies produced a wide range of steels, primarily from ore processed in blast furnaces. They had found it difficult to compete with imports, usually from Japan, and had given up market share to imports. They sought the protection of import quotas. Imported steel accounted for 20 percent of the U.S. steel consumption, up from 12 percent in the early 1970s. The U.S. share of world production of raw steel declined from 19 percent to 14 percent over the period. Imports of light bar products accounted for less than 9 percent of U.S. consumption of those products in 1981, according to the U.S. Commerce Department, while imports of wire rod totaled 23 percent of U.S. consump-

tion. "Wire rod is a very competitive product in the world market because it's very easy to make," Ralph Thompson, the Commerce Department's steel analyst, told the *Charlotte Observer.*[11]

Iron Age stated that that exports, as a percent of shipments in 1985, were 34 percent for Nippon, 26 percent for British Steel, 30 percent for Krupp, 49 percent for USINOR of France, and less than 1 percent for every American producer on the list. The consensus of steel experts was that imports would average 23 percent of the market in the last half of the 1980s.[12]

Iverson was one of very few in the steel industry to oppose import restrictions. He saw an outdated U.S. steel industry which had to change.

> About 12% of the steel in the U.S. is still produced by the old open hearth furnace. The Japanese shut down their last open hearth furnace about five years ago. . . . The U.S. produces about 16% of its steel by the continuous casting process. In Japan over 50% of the steel is continuously cast. . . . We Americans have been conditioned to believe in our technical superiority. For many generations a continuing stream of new inventions and manufacturing techniques allowed us to far outpace the rest of the world in both volume and efficiency of production. In many areas this is no longer true and particularly in the steel industry. In the last three decades, almost all the major developments in steel making were made outside the U.S. There were 18 continuous casting units in the world before there was one in this country. I would be negligent if I did not recognize the significant contribution that the government has made toward the technological deterioration of the steel industry. Unrealistic depreciation schedules, high corporate taxes, excessive regulation and jaw-boning for lower steel prices have made it difficult for the steel industry to borrow or generate the huge quantities of capital required for modernization.

By the mid 1980s the integrated mills were moving fast to get back into the game; they were restructuring, cutting capacity, dropping unprofitable lines, focusing products, and trying to become responsive to the market. The president of USX explained: "Steel executives, in trying to act as prudent businessmen, are seeking the lowest-cost solutions to provide what the market wants." Karlis Kirsis, director of World Steel Dynamics at PaineWebber, told *Purchasing Magazine,* "The industry as we knew it five years ago is no more; the industry as we knew it a year ago is gone."[13]

Purchasing believed that buyers would be seeing a pronounced industry segmentation. There would be integrated producers making mostly flat-rolled and structural grades, reorganized steel companies making a limited range of products, mini-mills dominating the bar and light structural product areas, specialty steel firms seeking niches, and foreign producers. There would be accelerated shutdowns of older plants, elimination of products by some firms, and the installation of new product lines with new technologies by others. There would also be corporate facelifts as executives diversified from steel to generate profits and entice investment dollars. They saw the high-tonnage mills restructuring to handle sheets, plates, structurals, high quality bars, and large pipe and tubular products which would allow for a resurgence of specialized mills: cold-finished bar manufacturers, independent strip mills and mini-mills.[14]

Wheeling-Pittsburgh illustrated the change under way in the industry. Through Chapter 11 reorganization, it had cut costs by more than $85 per ton. It divided into profit centers, negotiated the lowest hourly wage rate ($18 per hour) among unionized integrated steel plants, renegotiated supply contracts, closed pipe and tube mills, and shut 1.6 million tons of blast furnace capacity in favor of an electric furnace with continuous casting.

PaineWebber pointed out the importance of "reconstituted mills," which it called the "People Express" of the industry. These were companies that had reorganized and refocused their resources, usually under Chapter 11. They included Kaiser Steel, the Weirton Works, Jones and Laughlin, Republic, Youngstown, Wheeling, LTV, and others.

Joint Ventures had arisen to produce steel for a specific market or region. The chairman of USX called them "an important new wrinkle in steel's fight for survival" and stated, "If there had been more joint ventures like these two decades ago, the U.S. steel industry might have built only half of the dozen or so hot-strip mills it put up in that time and avoided today's overcapacity." *Purchasing* observed, "The fact is that these combined operations are the result of a laissez-faire attitude within the Justice Department under the Reagan administration following the furor when government restrictions killed the planned USS takeover of National Steel (which later sold 50 percent interest to a Japanese steelmaker)."[15]

However, the road ahead for the integrated mills would not be easy. While it was estimated they would need $10 billion to improve their facilities, the industry had lost over $7 billion since 1982. *Purchasing* pointed out that tax laws and accounting rules are slowing the closing of inefficient plants. Shutting down a 10,000-person plant could require a firm to hold a cash reserve of $100 million to fund health, pension, and insurance liabilities. The chairman of Armco commented: "Liabilities associated with a plant shutdown are so large that they can quickly devastate a company's balance sheet."[16]

The American Iron and Steel Institute (AISI) reported steel production in 1988 of 99.3 million tons, up from 89.2 in 1987, and the highest in seven years. As a result of modernization programs, 60.9 percent of production was from continuous casters. Exports of steel were increasing, 2 million tons in 1988 and forecast to 3 in 1989, and imports were falling, expected to be less than 20 percent in 1989. Some steel experts believed the United States was now cost competitive with Japan. Several countries did not fill their quotas allowed under the five-year-old voluntary restraint agreements, which would expire in September 1989. The role of service centers in the distribution of steel continued with its fifth consecutive record year in 1988 of 23.4 million tons.

"If 1988 is remembered as the year of steel prosperity despite economic uncertainties, then 1989 is just as likely to go down as the year of 'waiting for the other shoe to drop,'" according to *Metal Center News* in January 1989.[17] The fears and the expectation of a somewhat weaker year arose from concerns about a recession, expiration of the voluntary import restraints, and labor negotiations schedules in several companies. Declines in car production and consumer goods were expected to hit flat-rolled hard. Service centers were also expected to be cutting back on inventories. AUJ Consultants told *MCN,* "The U.S. steel market has peaked. Steel consumption is tending down. By 1990, we expect total domestic demand to dip under 90 million tons."[18] Iverson expected 1989 to be mediocre compared with 1988.

THE MINI-MILL

A new type of mill, the "mini-mill," emerged in the United States during the 1970s to compete with the integrated mill. The mini-mill used electric arc furnaces to manufacture a narrow product line from scrap steel. In 1981, the *New York Times* reported:

> The truncated steel mill is to the integrated steel mill what the Volkswagen was to the American auto industry in the 1960's: smaller, cheaper, less complex and more efficient. Although mini-mills cannot produce such products as sheet steel [flat rolled] and heavy construction items, some industry analysts say it is only a matter of time before technological breakthroughs make this possible.[19]

Since mini-mills came into being in the 1970s, the integrated mills' market share has fallen from about 90 percent to about 60 percent, with the loss equally divided between mini-mills and foreign imports. While the integrated steel companies averaged a 7 percent return on equity, the mini-mills averaged 14 percent, and some, such as Nucor, achieved about 25 percent.

The leading mini-mills were Nucor, Florida Steel, Georgetown Steel (Korf Industries), North Star Steel, and Chaparral. Nucor produced "light bar" products: bars, angles, channels, flats, smooth round, and forging billets. It was beginning to make more alloy steels. Florida Steel made mostly reinforcing bar for construction (rebar) and dominated the Florida market. Korf Industries had two mini-mill subsidiaries, which used modern equipment to manufacture wire-rod.

The mini-mills were not immune to the economic slump in the early 1980s. Korf Industries, which owned Georgetown Steel, found its interest charges too large a burden and sought reorganization in 1983. In March 1983, Georgetown followed the historic wage cutting contract between the United Steel Workers of America and the major steel companies and asked its union to accept reductions and to defer automatic wage increases. In 1982, Nucor froze wages and executives took a 5 percent pay cut. Plants went to a four-day schedule in which workers would receive only base rate if they chose to work a fifth day doing cleanup.

Florida Steel, with two-thirds of its sales in Florida, also felt the impact. At its headquarters in Tampa, a staff of over 100 handled accounting, payroll, sales entry, and almost all other services for all its facilities. Their division managers did not have sales responsibilities. Florida Steel experienced a sales decline for 1982 of 22 percent and an earnings drop from $3.37 per share to a loss of $1.40. The next year was also a year of losses.

Florida Steel employees had faced periodic layoffs during the recession. The firm was non-union (although the Charlotte plant lost an election in 1973) and pay was based on productivity. A small facility at Indian Town, near West Palm Beach, never became productive, even with personnel changes, and had to be closed. A new mini-mill in Tennessee was completed in late 1983.

Mini-mills had tripled their output in the last decade to capture 17 percent of domestic shipments. PaineWebber predicted the big integrated mills' share of the market would fall to 40 percent, the mini-mills' share would rise to 23 percent, "reconstituted" mills would increase from 11 percent to 28 percent, and specialized mills would increase their share from 1 percent to 7 percent. Iverson stated mini-mills could not go beyond a 35 percent to 40 percent share due to technical limitations; mini-mills could not produce the flat rolled sheet steel used in cars and appliances.

Iverson told *Metal Center News* in 1983: "We are very interested in the development of a thin slab, which would then allow mini-mills to produce plate and other flat rolled products . . . actually, the thinnest slab that can now be produced is about 6 inches thick. . . . (That results in a plant that is too large.) There are a number of people working to develop the process. . . . We have done some work, but our primary efforts at the moment are in connection with other people who are working on it. . . . The likelihood is it would be developed by a foreign company. There are more efforts by foreign steel companies in that direction than in the United States. . . . I'd say probably a minimum of three to five years, or it could take as much as 10 to achieve this."[20]

In 1983, Iverson described the new generation of mini-mills he foresaw: "If you go way back, mini-mills got started by rolling reinforcing bar. With the advent of continuous casting and improvements in rolling mills, mini-mills gradually got into shapes. Now they have moved in two other directions: one being to larger sizes, and the other being a growing metallurgical expertise for improved product quality and production of special bar quality in alloys.

Both of these represent expansion of markets for mini-mills."

By 1986, the new competitive environment was apparent. Four mini-mills had closed their doors within the year and Iverson saw that more shutdowns were ahead. The overcapacity of steel bar products and the stagnant market had made it difficult for some companies to generate the cash needed to modernize and expand their product lines. "The mini-mills are going through the same kind of restructuring and rethinking as the integrated mill. They know the problem of overcapacity isn't going to go away quickly. And, for some of the remaining firms to survive, they will have to move into more sophisticated products like special quality and clean-steel bars and heavier structurals and, once the technology is perfected, flat-rolled products. You won't see the market growth by the mini-mills the way it was in the past until the overcapacity issue is resolved and the mills begin entering new product areas."

ORGANIZATION

Nucor, with its eighteen-person corporate office located in Charlotte, North Carolina, had divisions spread across the United States. The 15 divisions, one for every plant, each had a general manager, who was also a vice-president of the corporation, directly responsible to Iverson and Aycock. (See Figure 1.) The divisions were of two basic types, joist plants and steel mills. The corporate staff consisted of single specialists in personnel and planning and a four-person financial function under Sam Siegel. Iverson, in the beginning, had chosen Charlotte "as the new home base for what he had envisioned as a small cadre of executives who would guide a decentralized operation with liberal authority delegated to managers in the field," according to *South Magazine*.[21]

Iverson gave his views on organization:

> You can tell a lot about a company by looking at its organization chart. . . . If you see a lot of staff, you can bet it is not a very efficient organization. . . . Secondly, don't have assistants. We do not have that title and prohibit it in our company. . . . In this organization nobody reports to the corporate office; the division managers report directly to me. . . . And one of the most important things is to resist as much as possible the number of management layers. . . . I've often

thought that when a company builds a fancy corporate office, it's on its way down.

> Each division is a profit center and the division manager has control over the day-to-day decisions that make that particular division profitable or not profitable. We expect the division to provide contribution, which is earnings before corporate expenses. We do not allocate our corporate expenses, because we do not think there is any way to do this reasonably and fairly. We do focus on earnings. And we expect a division to earn 25 percent return on total assets employed, before corporate expenses, taxes, interest or profit sharing. And we have a saying in the company—if a manager doesn't provide that for a number of years, we are either going to get rid of the division or get rid of the general manager, and it's generally the division manager.

A joist division manager commented:

> I've been a division manager four years now and at times I'm still awed by it: the opportunity I was given to be a Fortune 500 vice-president. . . . I think we are successful because it is our style to pay more attention to our business than our competitors. . . . We are kind of a "no nonsense" company. That is not to say we don't have time to play, but we work hard when we work and the company is first and foremost in our minds. . . . I think another one of the successes of our company has been the fact that we have a very minimum number of management levels. We've been careful to avoid getting topheavy and so consequently we put a great deal of responsibility on each individual at each level. It has often been said, jokingly, that if you are the janitor at Vulcraft and you get the right promotions, about four promotions would take you to the top of the company.

> Mr. Iverson's style of management is to allow the division manager all the latitude in the world. His involvement with the managers is quite limited. As we've grown, he no longer has the time to visit with the managers more than one or twice a year. . . . Whereas in many large companies the corporate office makes the major decisions and the people at the operating level sit back to wait for their marching orders, that's not the case at Nucor. . . . In a way I feel like I run my own company because I really don't get any marching orders from Mr. Iverson.

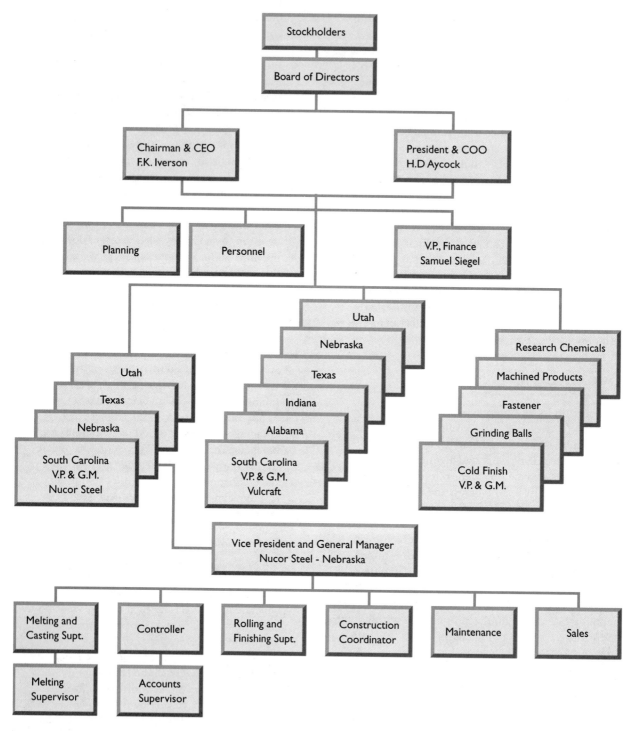

FIGURE I

Nucor Organizational Chart

He lets you run the division the way you see fit and the only way he will step in is if he sees something he doesn't like, particularly bad profits, high costs or whatever. But in the years I've worked with him I don't believe he has ever issued one single instruction to me to do something differently. I can't recall a single instance.

The divisions did their own manufacturing, selling, accounting, engineering, and personnel management. A steel division manager, when questioned about Florida Steel, which had a large plant 90 miles away, commented, "I really don't know anything about Florida Steel. . . . I expect they do have more of the hierarchy. I think they have central purchasing, centralized sales, centralized credit collections, centralized engineering, and most of the major functions." He didn't feel greater centralization would be good for Nucor. "The purchasing activity, for example, removed from the field tends to become rather insensitive to the needs of the field and does not feel the pressures of responsibility. And the division they are buying for has no control over what they pay. . . . Likewise centralized sales would not be sensitive to the needs of their divisions."[22]

South Magazine observed that Iverson had established a characteristic organizational style described as "stripped down" and "no nonsense." "Jack Benny would like this company," observed Roland Underhill, an analyst with Crowell, Weedon and Co. of Los Angeles; "so would Peter Drucker." Underhill pointed out that Nucor's thriftiness doesn't end with its "spartan" office staff or modest offices. "There are no corporate perquisites," he recited. "No company planes. No country club memberships. No company cars."[23]

Fortune reported, "Iverson takes the subway when he is in New York, a Wall Street analyst reports in a voice that suggests both admiration and amazement."[24] The general managers reflected this style in the operation of their individual divisions. Their offices were more like plant offices or the offices of private companies built around manufacturing rather than for public appeal. They were simple, routine, and businesslike.

In 1983, one of Iverson's concerns had been that as Nucor continued to grow they would have to add another layer of management to their lean structure. In June 1984 he named Dave Aycock president and chief operating officer, while he became chairman and chief executive officer—they

would share one management level. Aycock had most recently been Division Manager of the steel mill at Darlington. But he had been with the company longer than Iverson, having joined Vulcraft in 1955, and had long been recognized as a particularly valued and close adviser to Iverson.

Iverson explained: "The company got to the size that I just wasn't doing the job that I thought should be done by this office. I couldn't talk to the analysts and everyone else I have to talk to, put the efforts into research and development I wanted to, and get to all the units as frequently as I should. That's why I brought Dave in. And, of course, he has been with the company forever." In a February 1985 letter, he told stockholders: "These changes are to provide additional emphasis on the expansion of the company's businesses."

"Dave is a very analytical person and very thorough in his thought process," another division manager told *33 Metal Producing,* a McGraw-Hill publication. "And Ken, to use an overworked word, is an entrepreneurial type. So, they complement each other. They're both very aggressive men, and make one hell of a good team."[25] Aycock stated: "I am responsible for the operations of all our divisions. To decide where we are going, with what technologies; what are our purposes. And what is our thrust. I help Ken shape where we are going and with what technologies. . . . I've been quite aggressive my whole career at updating, adapting, and developing new technology and new ideas in production and marketing. "Dave's the fellow who now handles most of the day-to-day operations," Iverson commented. "And he handles most of the employees who write to us"—about 10 to 15 percent of his time.[26]

DIVISION MANAGERS

The general managers met three times a year. In late October, they presented preliminary budgets and capital requests. In late February, they met to finalize budgets and treat miscellaneous matters. Then, at a meeting in May, they handled personnel matters, such as wage increases and changes of policies or benefits. The general managers as a group considered the raises for the department heads, the next lower level of management. As one of the managers described it,[27]

In May of each year, all the general managers get together and review all the department heads throughout the company. We have kind of an informal evaluation process. It's an intangible thing, a judgment as to how dedicated an individual is and how well he performs compared to the same position at another plant. Sometimes the numbers don't come out the way a general manager wants to see them, but it's a fair evaluation. The final number is picked by Mr. Iverson. Occasionally there are some additional discussions with Mr. Iverson. He always has an open mind and might be willing to consider a little more for one individual. We consider the group of, say, joist production managers at one time. The six managers are rated for performance. We assign a number, such as +3 to a real crackerjack performer or a –2 to someone who needs improvement. These ratings become a part of the final pay increase granted.

The corporate personnel manager described management relations as informal, trusting, and not "bureaucratic." He felt that there was a minimum of paperwork, that a phone call was more common and that no confirming memo was thought to be necessary. Iverson himself stated:

Management is not a popularity contest. If everybody agrees with the organization, something is wrong with the organization. You don't expect people in the company to put their arms around each other, and you don't interfere with every conflict. Out of conflict often comes the best answer to a particular problem. So don't worry about it. You are always going to have some conflict in an organization. You will always have differences of opinion, and that's healthy. Don't create problems where there are none.

A Vulcraft manager commented: "We have what I would call a very friendly spirit of competition from one plant to the next. And of course all of the vice presidents and general managers share the same bonus systems so we are in this together as a team even though we operate our divisions individually." The general managers are paid a bonus based on a total corporate profit rather than their own divisions' profits. A steel mill manager explained:

I think it's very important for the general managers to be concerned with contributing to the overall accomplishment of the company. There is a lot of interplay between the divisions with a flow of services, products, and ideas between divisions. Even though we are reasonably autonomous, we are not isolated.... We don't like the division managers to make decisions that would take that division away from where we want the whole company to go. But we certainly want the divisions to try new things. We are good copiers; if one division finds something that works, then we will all try it. I think that's one of our strengths. We have a lot of diverse people looking at ways to do things better.

Iverson revealed his view of management in his disdain for consultants:

They must have a specific job to do because they can't make your decisions.... The fellow on the line has to make decisions.... First he has to communicate and then he has to have the intestinal fortitude and the personal strength to make the decisions, sometimes under very difficult conditions.... A good manager is adaptable and he is sensitive to cultural, geographical, environmental, and business climates. Most important of all, he communicates.... You never know if someone is a good manager until he manages. And that's why we take people as young as we possibly can, throw responsibility at them, and they either work or they don't. In a sense it's survival of the fittest. But don't kid yourself; that's what industry is all about.

A steel division manager commented in comparing the Nucor manager with the typical manager of a large corporation:

We would probably tend to have managers who have confidence in their abilities and, very importantly, have confidence in other people in their division. And people who are very sensitive to the employees of their division.... But I think if you saw four or five different division managers, you'd have four or five different decision-making styles.

A Vulcraft general manager in his early forties who had been promoted to the division manager level nine years earlier said:

The step from department manager to division manager is a big one. I can't think of an instance when a general manager job has been offered to an individual that it has been passed up. Often it means moving from one part of the country to another. There are five department heads in six joist plants, which means there are 30 people who are considered for division manager slots at a joist plant. Mr. Iverson selects the division managers.

His own experience was enlightening:

When I came to this plant four years ago, we had too many people, too much overhead. We had 410 people at the plant and I could see, because I knew how many people we had in the Nebraska plant, we had many more than we needed. That was my yardstick and we set about to reduce those numbers by attrition.... We have made a few equipment changes that made it easier for the men, giving them an opportunity to make better bonuses. Of course the changes were very subtle in any given case but overall in four years we have probably helped the men tremendously. With 55 fewer men, perhaps 40 to 45 fewer in the production area, we are still capable of producing the same number of tons as four years ago.

The divisions managed their act with the corporate staff. Each day disbursements were reported to Siegel's office. Payments flowed into regional lock boxes. On a weekly basis, joist divisions reported total quotes, sales cancellations, backlog, and production. Steel mills reported tons-rolled, outside shipments, orders, cancellations, and backlog. Iverson graphed the data. He might talk to the division about every two weeks. On the other hand, Iverson was known to bounce ideas off the steel division manager in Darlington with whom he had worked since joining the company.

The Vulcraft manager commented on the communications with the corporate office: "It's kind of a steady pipeline. I might talk to the corporate office once a day or it might be once a week. But it generally involves, I would not say trivial information, just mundane things. Occasionally I hear from Sam or Ken about serious matters."

Each month the divisions completed a two-page (11 by 17 inches) "Operations Analysis" which was sent to all the managers. Its three main purposes were (1) financial consolidation, (2) sharing information among the divisions, and (3) Iverson's examination. The summarized information and the performance statistics for all the divisions were then returned to the managers.

VULCRAFT—THE JOIST DIVISIONS

Half of Nucor's business was the manufacture and sale of open web steel joists and joist girders at six Vulcraft divisions located in Florence, South Carolina; Norfolk, Nebraska; Ft. Payne, Alabama; Grapeland, Texas; St. Joe, Indiana; and Brigham City, Utah. Open web joists, in contrast to solid joists, were made of steel angle iron separated by round bars or smaller angle iron (see Figure 2).

These joists were costless and of lower greater strength for many applications and were used primarily as the roof support systems in larger buildings, such as warehouses and stores.

The joist industry was characterized by high competition among many manufacturers for many small customers. The Vulcraft divisions had over 3,000 customers, none of whom dominated the business. With an estimated 25 percent of the market, Nucor was the largest supplier in the United States. It utilized national advertising campaigns and prepared competitive bids on 80 percent to 90 percent of buildings using joists. Competition was based on price and delivery performance. Nucor had developed computer programs to prepare designs for customers and to compute bids based on current prices and labor standards. In addition, each Vulcraft plant maintained its own engineering department to help customers with design problems or specifications. The Florence manager commented, "Here on the East Coast we have six or seven major competitors; of course none of them are as large as we are. The competition for any order will be heavy, and we will see six or seven different prices."[28] He added, "I think we have a strong selling force in the marketplace. It has been said to us by some of our competitors that in this particular industry we have the finest selling organization in the country."

Nucor aggressively sought to be the lowest-cost producer in the industry. Materials and freight were two important elements of cost. Nucor maintained its own fleet of almost 100 trucks to ensure on-time delivery to all of the states, although most business was regional because of transportation costs. Plants were located in rural areas near the markets they served.

The Florence manager stated:

I don't feel there's a joist producer in the country that can match our cost.... We are sticklers

FIGURE 2

Illustration of Joists

(a)   (b)

about cutting out unnecessary overhead. Because we put so much responsibility on our people and because we have what I think is an excellent incentive program, our people are willing to work harder to accomplish these profitable goals.

Production

On the basic assembly line used at Nucor, three or four of which might make up any one plant, about 6 tons per hour would be assembled. In the first stage, eight people cut the angles to the right lengths or bent the round bars to desired form. These were moved on a roller conveyer to six-man assembly stations, where the component parts would be tacked together for the next stage, welding. Drilling and miscellaneous work were done by three people between the lines. The nine-man welding station completed the welds before passing the joists on roller conveyers to two-man inspection teams. The last step before shipment was the painting.

The workers had control over and responsibility for quality. There was an independent quality control inspector who had authority to reject the run of joists and cause them to be reworked. The quality control people were not under the incentive system and reported to the engineering department.

Daily production might vary widely, since each joist was made for a specific job. The wide range of joists made control of the workload at each station difficult; bottlenecks might arise anywhere along

the line. Each workstation was responsible for identifying such bottlenecks so that the foreman could reassign people promptly to maintain productivity. Since workers knew most of the jobs on the line, including the more skilled welding job, they could be shifted as needed. Work on the line was described by one general manager as "not machine type but mostly physical labor." He said the important thing was to avoid bottlenecks.

There were four lines of about twenty-eight people each on two shifts at the Florence division. The jobs on the line were rated on responsibility and assigned a base wage, from $6 to $8 per hour. In addition, a weekly bonus was paid on the total output of each line. Each worker received the same percent bonus on his base wage.

The amount of time required to make a joist had been established as a result of experience; the general manager had seen no time studies in his fifteen years with the company. As a job was bid, the cost of each joist was determined through the computer program. The time required depended on the length, number of panels, and depth of the joist.

At the time of production, the labor value of production, the standard, was determined in a similar manner. The general manager stated, "In the last nine or ten years we have not changed a standard." The standards list in use was over ten years old. Previously, they adjusted the standard if the bonus was too high. He said the technological improvements over the last few years had been small. The general manager reported that the bonus had increased from about 60 percent nine years earlier to

TABLE 1

Tons per Manhour, Fifty-two-Week Moving Average

1977	.163
1978	.179
1979	.192
1980	.195
1981	.194
1982	.208
1983	.215
1984	.214
1985	.228
1986	.225
1987	.218

about 100 percent in 1982 and had stabilized at that point. Tables 1 and 2 show data typically computed on performance and used by the manager. He said the difference in performance on the line resulted from the different abilities of the crews:

> We don't have an industrial engineering staff. Our Engineering Department's work is limited to the design and the preparation of the paperwork prior to the actual fabrication process. Now, that is not to say that we don't have any involvement in fabrication. But the efficiency of the plant is entirely up to the manufacturing department.... When we had our first group in a joist plant, we produced 3½ tons an hour. We thought that if we ever got to 4 tons, that would

TABLE 2

A Sample of Percentage Performance, July 1982

		Line			
		1	2	3	4
Shift	1st	117	97	82	89
	2nd	98	102	94	107

be the Millennium. Well, today we don't have anybody who produces less than 6½ tons an hour. This is largely due to improvements that the groups have suggested.

Management

In discussing his philosophy for dealing with the work force, the Florence manager stated:[29]

> I believe very strongly in the incentive system we have. We are a non-union shop and we all feel that the way to stay so is to take care of our people and show them we care. I think that's easily done because of our fewer layers of management.... I spend a good part of my time in the plant, maybe an hour or so a day. If a man wants to know anything, for example, an insurance question, I'm there and they walk right up to me and ask me questions which I'll answer the best I know how.... You can always tell when people are basically happy. If they haven't called for a meeting themselves or they are not hostile in any way, you can take it they understand the company's situation and accept it.... We do listen to our people.... For instance last fall I got a call from a couple of workers saying that people in our Shipping and Receiving area felt they were not being paid properly in relation to production people. So we met with them, discussed the situation and committed ourselves to reviewing the rates of other plants. We assured them that we would get back to them with an answer by the first of the year. Which we did. And there were a few minor changes.

The manager reported none of the plants had any particular labor problems, although there had been some in the past.

> In 1976, two years before I came here, there was a union election at this plant which arose out of racial problems. The company actually lost the election to the U.S. Steelworkers. When it came time to begin negotiating the contract, the workers felt, or came to see, that they had little to gain from being in the union. The union was not going to be able to do anything more for them than they were already doing. So slowly the union activity died out and the union quietly withdrew.

He discussed formal systems for consulting with the workers before changes were made:

> In the economic slump of 1982, we scheduled our line for four days, but the men were allowed to come in the fifth day for maintenance work at base pay. The men in the plant on an average running bonus might make $13 an hour. If their base pay is half that, on Friday they would only get $6–$7 an hour. Surprisingly, many of the men did not want to come in on Friday. They felt comfortable with just working four days a week. They are happy to have that extra day off. Of course we're cautioned by our labor counsel to maintain an open pipeline to our employees. We post all changes, company earnings, changes in the medical plan, anything that might affect an employee's job. Mr. Iverson has another philosophy, which is, "Either tell your people everything or tell them nothing." We choose to tell them everything. We don't have any regularly scheduled meetings. We meet whenever there's a need. The most recent examples were a meeting last month to discuss the results of an employee survey and three months before was held our annual dinner meetings off site.
>
> We don't lay our people off and we make a point of telling our people this.

Recently the economic trouble in Texas had hurt business considerably. Both plants had been on decreased schedules for several months. About 20 percent of the people took the fifth day at base rate, but still no one had been laid off.

In April 1982, the executive committee decided, in view of economic conditions, that a pay freeze was necessary. The employees normally received an increase in their base pay the first of June. The decision was made at that time to freeze wages. The officers of the company, as a show of good faith, accepted a 5 percent pay cut. In addition to announcing this to the workers with a stuffer in their pay envelopes, meetings were held. Each production line, or incentive group of workers, met in the plant conference room with all supervision—foreman, plant production manager, and division manager. The economic crisis was explained to the employees by the production manager and all questions were answered.

STEEL DIVISIONS

Nucor had steel mils in five locations: Indiana, Nebraska, South Carolina, Texas, and Utah. The mills were modern mini-mills, all built within the last twenty years to convert scrap steel into standard angles, flats, rounds, and channels using the latest technology. Sales in 1988 were 1.44 tons, a 10 percent increase over those of 1987. This figure represented about 70 percent of the mills' output, the remainder being used by other Nucor divisions. In recent years, Nucor has broadened its product line to include a wider range of steel chemistries, sizes, and special shapes. The total capacity of the mills reached 2.8 tons in 1988.

A case writer from Harvard recounted the development of the steel divisions:

> By 1967 about 60% of each Vulcraft sales dollar was spent on materials, primarily steel. Thus, the goal of keeping costs low made it imperative to obtain steel economically. In addition, in 1967 Vulcraft bought about 60% of its steel from foreign sources. As the Vulcraft Division grew, Nucor became concerned about its ability to obtain an adequate economical supply of steel and in 1968 began construction of its first steel mill in Darlington, South Carolina. By 1972 the Florence, South Carolina, joist plant was purchasing over 90% of its steel from this mill. The Fort Payne plant bought about 50% of its steel from Florence. The other joist plants in Nebraska, Indiana and Texas found transportation costs prohibitive and continued to buy their steel from other steel companies, both foreign and domestic. Since the mill had excess capacity, Nucor began to market its steel products to outside customers. In 1972, 75% of the shipments of Nucor steel was to Vulcraft and 25% was to other customers.[30]

Iverson explained in 1984:

> In constructing these mills we have experimented with new processes and new manufacturing techniques. We serve as our own general contractor and design and build much of our own equipment. In one or more of our mills we have built our own continuous casting unit, reheat furnaces, cooling beds and in Utah even our own mill stands. All of these to date have

cost under $125 per ton of annual capacity—compared with projected costs for large integrated mills of $1,200–1,500 per ton of annual capacity, ten times our cost. Our mills have high productivity. We currently use less than four man hours to produce a ton of steel. This includes everyone in the operation: maintenance, clerical, accounting, and sales and management. On the basis of our production workers alone, it is less than three man hours per ton. Our total employment costs are less than $60 per ton compared with the average employment costs of the seven largest U.S. steel companies of close to $130 per ton. Our total labor costs are less than 20% of our sales price.

In contrast to Nucor's less than four man hours, similar Japanese mills were said to require more than five hours and comparable U.S. mills over six hours. Nucor's average yield from molten metal to finished products was over 90 percent compared with an average U.S. steel industry yield of about 74 percent, giving energy costs of about $39 per ton compared with their $75 a ton. Nucor ranked 46th on *Iron Age's* annual survey of world steel producers. It was second on the list of top ten producers of steel worldwide based on tons per employee, at 981 tons. At the head of the list was Tokyo Steel at 1,485. U.S. Steel was seventh at 479. Some other results were: Nippon Steel, 453; British Steel, 213; Bethlehem Steel, 329; Kruppstahl, 195; Weirton Steel, 317; and Northstar Steel, 936. Nucor also ranked seventh on the list ranking growth of raw steel production. U.S. Steel was fifth on the same list. U.S. Steel topped the list based on improvement in tons-per-employee, at 56 percent; Nucor was seventh with a 12 percent improvement.[31]

THE STEEL-MAKING PROCESS

A steel mill's work is divided into two phases, preparation of steel of the proper "chemistry" and the forming of the steel into the desired products. The typical mini-mill utilized scrap steel, such as junk auto parts, instead of the iron ore that would be used in larger, integrated steel mills. The typical mini-mill had an annual capacity of 200–600 thousand tons, compared with the 7 million tons of Bethlehem Steel's Sparrow's Point, Maryland, integrated plant.

A charging bucket fed loads of scrap steel into electric arc furnaces. The melted load, called a heat, was poured into a ladle to be carried by an overhead crane to the casting machine. In the casting machine, the liquid steel was extruded as a continuous red-hot solid bar of steel and cut into lengths weighing some 900 pounds, called "billets." In the typical plant, the billet, about 4 inches in cross section and about 20 feet long, was held temporarily in a pit where it cooled to normal temperatures. Periodically, billets were carried to the rolling mill and placed in a reheat oven to bring them up to 2000°F, at which temperature they would be malleable. In the rolling mill, presses and dies progressively converted the billet into the desired round bars, angles, channels, flats, and other products. After being cut to standard lengths, they were moved to the warehouse.

Nucor's first steel mill, employing more than 500 people, was located in Darlington, South Carolina. The mill, with its three electric arc furnaces, operated twenty-four hours per day, five and a half days per week. Nucor had made a number of improvements in the melting and casting operations. The former general manager of the Darlington plant had developed a system that involved preheating the ladles, allowing for the faster flow of steel into the caster and resulting in better control of the steel characteristics. Less time and lower capital investment were required. The casting machines were "continuous casters," as opposed to the old batch method. The objective in the "front" of the mill was to keep the casters working. At the time of the Harvard study at Nucor each strand was in operation 90 percent of the time, while a competitor had announced a "record rate" of 75 percent, which it had been able to sustain for a week.

Nucor was also perhaps the only mill in the country that regularly avoided the reheating of billets. This saved $10–12 per ton in fuel usage and losses due to oxidation of the steel. The cost of developing this process had been $12 million. All research projects had not been successful. The company spent approximately $2 million in an unsuccessful effort to utilize resistance-heating. They lost even more on an effort at induction melting. As Iverson told *33 Metal Producing,* "That cost us a lot of money. Timewise it was very expensive. But you have got to make mistakes and we've had lots of failures."[32] In the rolling mill, the first machine was a roughing mill by Morgarshammar, the first of its kind in the Western Hemisphere. This Swedish machine had been chosen because of it lower cost, higher productivity, and the flexibility. Passing through another five to nine finishing mills converted the billet into the desired finished product. The yield from the billet to finished product was about 93 percent.

The Darlington design became the basis for plants in Nebraska, Texas, and Utah. The Texas plant had cost under $80 per ton of annual capacity. Whereas the typical mini-mill cost approximately $250 per ton, the average cost of all four of Nucor's mills was under $135. An integrated mill was expected to cost between $1,200 and $1,500 per ton.

The Darlington plant was organized into twelve natural groups for the purpose of incentive pay: two mills, each had two shifts with three groups—melting and casting, rolling mill, and finishing. In melting and casting there were three or four different standards, depending on the material, established by the department manager years ago based on historical performance. The general manager stated, "We don't change the standards." The caster, the key to the operation, was used at a 92 percent level—one greater than the claims of the manufacturer. For every good ton of billet above the standard hourly rate for the week, workers in the group received a 4 percent bonus. For example, with a common standard of 10 tons per run hour and an actual rate for the week of 28 tons per hour, the workers would receive a bonus of 72 percent of their base rate in the week's paycheck.

In the rolling mill there were more than 100 products, each with a different historical standard. Workers received a 4 percent to 6 percent bonus for every good ton sheared per hour for the week over the computed standard. The Darlington general manager said that the standard would be changed only if there was a major machinery change and that a standard had not been changed since the initial development period for the plant. He commented that in exceeding the standard the worker wouldn't work harder but would cooperate to avoid problems and move more quickly if a problem developed: "If there is a way to improve output, they will tell us." Another manager added: "Meltshop employees don't ask me how much it costs Chaparral or LTV to make a billet. They want to know what it costs Darlington, Norfolk, Jewitt to

put a billet on the ground—scrap costs, alloy costs, electrical costs, refractory, gas, etc. Everybody from Charlotte to Plymouth watches the nickels and dimes."[33]

The Darlington manager, who became COO in 1984, stated:

> The key to making a profit when selling a product with no aesthetic value, or a product that you really can't differentiate from your competitors, is cost. I don't look at us as a fantastic marketing organization, even though I think we are pretty good; but we don't try to overcome unreasonable costs by mass marketing. We maintain low costs by keeping the employee force at the level it should be, not doing things that aren't necessary to achieve our goals, and allowing people to function on their own and by judging them on their results.
>
> To keep a cooperative and productive workforce you need, number one, to be completely honest about everything; number two, to allow each employee as much as possible to make decisions about that employee's work, to find easier and more productive ways to perform duties; and number three, to be as fair as possible to all employees. Most of the changes we make in work procedures and in equipment come from the employees. They really know the problems of their jobs better than anyone else. We don't have any industrial engineers, nor do we ever intend to, because that's a type of specialist who tends to take responsibility off the top division management and give them a crutch.
>
> To communicate with my employees, I try to spend time in the plant and at intervals have meetings with the employees. Usually if they have a question they just visit me. Recently a small group visited me in my office to discuss our vacation policy. They had some suggestions and, after listening to them, I had to agree that the ideas were good.[34]

THE INCENTIVE SYSTEM

The foremost characteristic of Nucor's personnel system was its incentive plan. Another major personnel policy was providing job security. Also all employees at Nucor received the same fringe benefits. There was only one group insurance plan. Holidays and vacations did not differ by job. The company had no executive dining rooms or restrooms, no fishing lodges, no company cars, or reserved parking places.

Absenteeism and tardiness were not problems at Nucor. Each employee had four days of absence before pay was reduced. In addition to these, missing work was allowed for jury duty, military leave, or the death of close relatives. After this, a day's absence cost them bonus pay for that week and lateness of more than a half hour meant the loss of bonus for that day.

Employees were kept informed about the company. Charts showing the division's results in return-on-assets and bonus payoff were posted in prominent places in the plant. The personnel manager commented that as he traveled around to all the plants, he found everyone in the company could tell him the level of profits in their division. The general managers held dinners at least twice a year with their employees. The dinners were held with fifty or sixty employees at a time. After introductory remarks, the floor was open for discussion of any work-related problems. The company also had a formal grievance procedure. The Darlington manager couldn't recall the last grievance he had processed.

There was a new employee orientation program and an employee handbook, which contained personnel policies and rules. The corporate office sent all news releases to each division where they were posted on bulletin boards. Each employee in the company also received a copy of the Annual Report. For the last several years the cover of the Annual Report had contained the names of all Nucor employees. Every child of every Nucor employee received up to $1,200 a year for four years if he or she chose to go on to higher education, including technical schools.

The average hourly worker's pay was $31,000, compared with the average earnings in manufacturing in that state of slightly more than $13,000. The personnel manager believed that pay was not the only thing the workers liked about Nucor. He said that an NBC interviewer, working on the documentary "If Japan Can, Why Can't We," often heard, "I enjoy working for Nucor because Nucor is the best, the most productive, and the most profitable company that I know of."[35]

"I honestly feel that if someone performs well, they should share in the company and if they are going to share in the success, they should also share in the failures," Iverson stated.[36] There were four incentive programs at Nucor, one each for production workers, department heads, staff people such as accountants, secretaries, or engineers, and senior management, which included the division managers. All of these programs were on a group basis.

Within the production program, groups ranged in size from twenty-five to thirty people and had definable and measurable operations. The company believed that a program should be simple and that bonuses should be paid promptly. "We don't have any discretionary bonuses—zero. It is all based on performance. Now we don't want anyone to sit in judgment, because it never is fair . . .," said Iverson. The personnel manager stated: "Their bonus is based on roughly 90 percent of historical time it takes to make a particular joist. If during a week they make joists at 60 percent less than the standard time, they received a 60 percent bonus." This was paid with the regular pay the following week. The complete pay check amount, including overtime, was multiplied by the bonus factor. Bonus was not paid when equipment was not operating: "We have the philosophy that when equipment is not operating everybody suffers and the bonus for downtime is zero."[37] The foremen are also part of the group and received the same bonus as the employees they supervised.

The second incentive program was for department heads in the various divisions. The incentive pay here was based on division contribution, defined as the division earnings before corporate expenses and profit sharing are determined. Bonuses were reported to run as high as 51 percent of a person's base salary in the division and 30 percent for corporate positions.

Officers of the company were under a single profit sharing plan. Their base salaries were approximately 75 percent of comparable positions in industry. Once return on equity reached 9 percent, slightly below the average for manufacturing firms, 5 percent of net earnings before taxes went into a pool that was divided among the officers based on their salaries. "Now if return-on-equity for the company reaches, say 20 percent, which it has, then we can wind up with as much as 190 percent of our base salaries and 115 percent on top of that in stock. We get both."[38] In 1982 the return was 9 percent and the executives received no bonus. Iverson's pay in 1981 was approximately $300,000 but dropped the next year to $110,000. "I think that ranked by total compensation I was the lowest paid CEO in the *Fortune* 500. I was kind of proud of that, too."[39] In 1986, Iverson's stock was worth over $10 million. The young Vulcraft manager was likewise a millionaire.

There was a third plan for people who were neither production workers nor department managers. Their bonus was based on either the division return on assets or the corporate return on assets.

The fourth program was for the senior officers. The senior officers had no employment contracts, pension or retirement plans, or other normal perquisites. Their base salaries were set at about 70 percent of what an individual doing similar work in other companies would receive. More than half of the officers' compensation was reported to be based directly on the company's earnings. Ten percent of pretax earnings over a preestablished level, based on a 12 percent return on stockholders' equity, was set aside and allocated to the senior officers according to their base salary. Half the bonus was paid in cash and half was deferred.

In lieu of a retirement plan, the company had a profit sharing plan with a deferred trust. Each year 10 percent of pretax earnings was put into profit sharing. Fifteen percent of this was set aside to be paid to employees the following March as a cash bonus and the remainder was put into trust for each employee on the basis of percent of their earnings as a percent of total wages paid within the corporation. The employee was vested 20 percent after the first year and gained an additional 10 percent vesting each year thereafter. Employees received a quarterly statement of their balance in profit sharing.

The company had an Employer Monthly Stock Investment Plan to which Nucor added 10 percent to the amount the employee contributed and paid the commission on the purchase of any Nucor stock. After each five years of service with the company, the employee received a service award consisting of five shares of Nucor stock. Additionally, if profits were good, extraordinary bonus payments would be made to the employees. In December 1988, each employee received a $500 payment.

According to Iverson:

I think the first obligation of the company is to the stockholder and to its employees. I find in this country too many cases where employees are underpaid and corporate management is making huge social donations for self-fulfillment. We regularly give donations, but we have a very interesting corporate policy. First, we give donations where our employees are. Second, we give donations which will benefit our employees, such as the YMCA. It is a difficult area and it requires a lot of thought. There is certainly a strong social responsibility for a company, but it cannot be at the expense of the employees or the stockholders.[40]

Nucor had no trouble finding people to staff its plants. When the mill in Jewett, Texas, was built in 1975, there were over 5,000 applications for the 400 jobs—many coming from people in Houston and Dallas. Yet everyone did not find work at Nucor what they wanted. In 1975, a Harvard team found high turnover among new production workers after start-up. The cause appeared to be pressure from fellow workers in the group incentive situation. A survival-of-the-fittest situation was found in which those who didn't like to work seldom stuck around. "Productivity increased and turnover declined dramatically once these people left," the Harvard team concluded. Iverson commented: "A lot of people aren't goal-oriented. A lot of them don't want to work that hard, so initially we have a lot of turnover in a plant but then it's so low we don't even measure after that."[41]

The *Wall Street Journal* reported in 1981:

Harry Pigg, a sub-director for the USW in South Carolina, sees a darker side in Nucor's incentive plan. He contends that Nucor unfairly penalizes workers by taking away big bonus payments for absence or tardiness, regardless of the reason. Workers who are ill, he says, try to work because they can't afford to give up the bonus payment. "Nucor whips them into line," he adds. He acknowledges, though, that high salaries are the major barrier to unionizing the company.[42]

Having welcomed a parade of visitors over the years, Iverson had become concerned with the pattern: "They only do one or two of the things we do. It's not just incentives or the scholarship program;

it's all those things put together that results in a unified philosophy for the company."

Looking ahead, Iverson had said: "The next decade will be an exciting one for steel producers. It will tax our abilities to keep pace with technological changes we can see now on the horizon." Imports didn't have to dominate the U.S. economy. He believed the steel industry would continue to play a pivotal role in the growth of American industry. He pointed out comparative advantages of the U.S. steel industry: an abundance of resources, relatively low energy costs, lower transportation costs, and the change in the government's attitude toward business.

The excitement he had predicted had occurred. Imports were a challenge for steel, just as for textiles, shoes, machine tools, and computers. The old steel companies were flexing their muscle and getting back into the game. Overcapacity hadn't left the mini-mill immune; there was no safe haven for anyone. Nucor was no longer a small company, David, with free shots at Goliath.

The honeymoon appeared over. Wall Street worried about what Nucor should do. Cable News Network posed the position of some on Wall Street: "They say basically you guys are selling to the construction companies; you are selling to some fairly depressed industries. They also say, Nucor, they were a specialized little niche company. They did what they did very well; but now all of a sudden, they are going out, building these big mills to make huge pieces of steel and they are talking casted cold, all that stuff. They're worried that you may be getting into deals that are a little too complicated from what they perceive you as being able to do well."[43]

The *New York Times* pointed out that expansion would certainly hurt earnings for the next several years. They quoted a steel consultant: "It is hard to do all that they are trying to do and keep profits up. With the industry in the shape it's in, this is not the time to expand beyond the niche they've established."[44]

When they were sitting with $185 million in cash, Iverson told *Inc.*: "It (going private) has been mentioned to us by a number of brokerage firms and investment houses, but we wouldn't even consider it. It wouldn't be fair to employees, and I don't know whether it would be fair to the stockholders.... You're going to restrict the growth op-portunities.... You either grow or die.... Opportunities wouldn't be created for people within the company."[45]

Iverson told CNN: "We've decided that really we want to stay in that niche (steel). We don't want to buy any banks.... All of the growth of the company has been internally generated. We think there are opportunities in the steel industry today. ... There are ample opportunities, although they are somewhat harder to find than they used to be."[46]

"Another of my strengths is the ability to stick to my knitting. The reason executives make a lot of mistakes is that sometimes they get bored—they think the grass is greener on the other side so they go out and buy a bank or an oil company or they go into business where they have no expertise.... I have never gotten bored with this company. I've done this job so long that I think I have some insight into the needs and the capabilities of the company. I'm not misled into thinking we can do something that we can't."[47]

An economics professor and steel consultant at Middle Tennessee State University told the *Times,* "You're not going to see any growth in the steel market, so the only way to make money is to reduce costs and have new technology to penetrate other company's business."[48]

The *New York Times* stated: "Critics question whether it is wise to continue expanding production capabilities, as Nucor is doing, when there is already overcapacity in the steel industry and intense competition already exists between the mini-mills." Iverson insisted the strategy would pay off in the long-term. He told the *Times,* "The company's strategy makes sense for us. To gain a larger share in an ever-shrinking market, you've got to take something from someone else."[49]

They had sold the chemicals division, gotten into the structural steel components business, into the fastener industry, and should soon be ready to go head-to-head with the major integrated producers for the lucrative flat-rolled market. Sales and earnings were projected to double in the next two years, as the stock price doubled or tripled.

Iverson's position was clear: "We're going to stay in steel and steel products. The way we look at it, this company does only two things well, builds plants economically and runs them efficiently. That is the whole company. We don't have any financial expertise, we're not entrepreneurs, we're not into acquisitions. Steel may not be the best business in the world, but it's what we know how to do and we do it well."

Endnotes

1. Richard I. Kirkland, Jr., "Pilgrims' Profits at Nucor," *Fortune,* April 6, 1981, pp. 43–46.
2. Douglas R. Sease, "Mini-Mill Steelmakers, No Longer Very Small, Outperform Big Ones," *Wall Street Journal,* January 12, 1981, pp. 1, 19.
3. Chris Burritt, "Foreign Steel Doesn't Scare Nucor's CEO," *Atlanta Journal,* August 24, 1986, pp. 1M, 5M.
4. "Steel Man Ken Iverson," *Inc.* (April 1986), 41–48.
5. Burritt, "Foreign Steel Doesn't Scare Nucor's CEO," pp. 1M, 5M.
6. "Nucor's Ambitious Expansion," *New York Times,* June 30, 1986, pp. D1, D3.
7. "Inside Business," interview with Ken Iverson, Cable News Network, August 17, 1986.
8. Jo Isenberg-O'Loughlin and Joseph J. Innace, "Full Steam Ahead on the Nucor Unlimited," *33 Metal Producing* (January 1986), 35–50.
9. R. Simon, "Nucor's Boldest Gamble," *Forbes,* April 3, 1989, p. 122.
10. Sease, "Mini-Mill Steelmakers," pp. 1, 19.
11. The *Charlotte Observer,* various issues.
12. "1985 Top 50 World Steel Producers," *Iron Age,* May 2, 1986, p. 48B1.
13. "Metals Report: Steel 1986," *Purchasing,* September 25, 1986, pp. 52–65.
14. Ibid.
15. Ibid.
16. Ibid.
17. *Metal Center News* (January 1989).
18. Ibid.
19. "The Rise of Mini-Steel Mills," *New York Times,* September 23, 1981, pp. D1, D6.
20. "Iverson Alloys Usher in New Era," *Metal Center News* (August 1987), 29.
21. Don Bedwell, "Nucor's Lean, Mean Management Team," *South Magazine* (August 1980), 50.
22. Interviews conducted by Frank C. Barnes.
23. Bedwell, "Nucor's Lean, Mean Management Team," p. 55.
24. "Pilgrims' Profits at Nucor," *Fortune,* April 6, 1981.
25. Isenberg-O'Loughlin and Innace, "Full Steam Ahead on the Nucor Unlimited," pp. 35–50.
26. "Ken Iverson," *33 Metal Producing,* 4.
27. All quotes are either from Ken Iverson or from interviews with Nucor managers conducted by Frank C. Barnes.
28. Interviews conducted by Frank C. Barnes.
29. Ibid.
30. Harvard Intercollegiate Case Clearing House, Harvard Business School.
31. "1985 Top 50 World Steel Producers," *Iron Age,* May 2, 1986, p. 48B1.
32. Isenberg-O'Loughlin and Innace, "Full Steam Ahead on the Nucor Unlimited," pp. 35–50.
33. Interview conducted by Frank C. Barnes.
34. Ibid.
35. Ibid.
36. "Nucor's Ken Iverson on Productivity and Pay," *Personnel Administrator* (October 1986), 46–108.
37. Ibid.
38. Ibid.
39. Ibid.
40. Ibid.
41. "A Calm Hand in an Industry Under the Gun," *The Business Journal,* September 5, 1986, p. 9.
42. Sease, "Mini-Mill Steelmakers," pp. 1, 19.
43. "Inside Business," Interview with Ken Iverson, Cable News Network, August 17, 1986.
44. "Nucor's Ambitious Expansion," *New York Times,* June 30, 1986.
45. "Steel Man Ken Iverson," p. 48.
46. "Inside Business."
47. "A Calm Hand," p. 9.
48. "Nucor's Ambitious Expansion."
49. Ibid.

CASE 28

Ups and Downs at Kodak

This case was prepared by Gareth R. Jones of Texas A & M University.

It was time to prepare the 1990 Annual Report, and Kay Whitmore, the new chief executive officer of the Eastman Kodak Company, was reflecting on Kodak's situation. His predecessor, Colby Chandler, to lessen Kodak's dependence on the photographic products industry and to counter competition from other imaging techniques, had engaged in an ambitious program of diversification. Moreover, Chandler had taken steps to strengthen Kodak's position in its core business. This strategy had seemed to be working, for Kodak's sagging performance had picked up in 1987 and 1988, and optimism in the company had been high. However, 1989 had been a disastrous year, with profits falling dramatically; and although things were looking a little better in 1990 after the latest round of cost containment efforts and restructuring, it was unclear whether this improvement was a short-term phenomenon or a sign of good times ahead. Was Kodak's new strategy working, Whitmore wondered, and what could be done? If a turn-around did not happen soon, the prospect of corporate raiders dismantling the company (which was valued at a far higher figure than its stock price) would increase. Whitmore wondered how he could solve Kodak's problems.

KODAK'S HISTORY

Eastman Kodak Company was incorporated in New Jersey on October 24, 1901, as successor to the Eastman Dry Plate Company, the business originally established by George Eastman in September

This case is intended to be used as a basis for class discussion rather than as an illustration of either effective or ineffective handling of the situation. This case was prepared by Gareth R. Jones, Texas A & M University. Used by permission.

1880.[1] The Dry Plate Company had been formed to develop a dry photographic plate that was more portable and easier to use than other plates in the rapidly developing photography field. To mass-produce the dry plates uniformly, Eastman patented a plate-coating machine and began to manufacture the plates commercially. Eastman's continuing interest in the infant photographic industry led to his development in 1884 of silver halide paper-based photographic roll film. Eastman capped this invention with his introduction of the first portable camera in 1888. This camera used his own patented film, which was developed using his own proprietary method. Thus, Eastman had gained control of all the stages of the photographic process. His breakthroughs made possible the development of photography as a mass leisure activity. The popularity of the "recorded images" business was immediate, and sales boomed. Eastman's inventions revolutionized the photographic industry, and his company was uniquely placed to lead the world in the development of photographic technology.

From the beginning, Kodak focused on four objectives to guide the growth of its business: (1) mass production to lower production costs, (2) maintaining the lead in technological developments, (3) extensive product advertising, and (4) the development of a multinational business to exploit the world market. Although common now, those goals were revolutionary at the time. In due course, Kodak's yellow boxes could be found in every country in the world. Preeminent in world markets, Kodak operated research, manufacturing, and distribution networks throughout Europe and the rest of the world. Kodak's leadership in the development of advanced color film for simple, easy-to-use cameras and in quality film processing was maintained by constant research and development in its many research laboratories. Its huge volume of production allowed it to obtain economies of scale. Kodak was also its own supplier of the plastics and chemicals needed to produce film, and it made most of the component parts for its cameras.

Kodak became one of the most profitable American corporations, and its return on shareholders' equity averaged 18 percent for many years. To maintain its competitive advantage, it continued to invest heavily in research and development in silver halide photography, remaining principally in the photographic business. In this business, as the company used its resources to expand sales and become a multinational enterprise, the name Kodak became a household word signifying unmatched quality. By 1990, approximately 40 percent of Kodak's revenues came from sales outside the United States.

Starting in the early 1970s, however, and especially in the 1980s, Kodak ran into major problems, reflected in the drop in return on equity. Its preeminence has been increasingly threatened as the photographic industry and industry competition have changed. Major changes have taken place within the photography business, and new methods of recording images and memories beyond silver halide technology have emerged.

THE NEW INDUSTRY ENVIRONMENT

In the 1970s, Kodak began to face an uncertain environment in all its product markets. First, the color film and paper market from which Kodak made 75 percent of its profits experienced growing competition from the Japanese when, led by Fuji Photo Film Co., they entered the market. Fuji invested in huge, low-cost manufacturing plants, using the latest technology to mass-produce film in large volume. Fuji's low production costs and aggressive, competitive price cutting squeezed Kodak's profit margin. Finding no apparent differences in quality and obtaining more vivid colors with the Japanese product, consumers began to switch to the cheaper Japanese film, and this shift drastically reduced Kodak's market share.

Besides greater industry competition, another liability for Kodak was that it had done little internally to improve productivity to counteract rising costs. Supremacy in the marketplace had made Kodak complacent, and it had been slow to introduce productivity and quality improvements. Further-

more, Kodak (unlike Fuji in Japan) produced film in many different countries in the world, rather than in a single country, and this also gave Kodak a cost disadvantage. Thus, the combination of Fuji's efficient production and Kodak's own management style allowed the Japanese to become the cost leaders—to charge lower prices and still maintain profit margins.[2]

Kodak was also facing competition on other product fronts. Its cameras had an advantage because of their ease of use as compared with complex 35mm single-lens reflex models. They were also inexpensive. However, the quality of their prints could not compare with those of 35mm cameras. In 1970 Kodak had toyed with the idea of producing a simple-to-use 35mm camera but had abandoned it. In the late 1970s, however, the Japanese did develop an easy-to-use 35mm pocket camera featuring such innovations as auto flash, focus, and rewind. The quality of the prints produced by these cameras was far superior to the grainy prints produced by the smaller Instamatic and disc cameras, and consumers began to switch to these products in large numbers. This shift led to the need for new kinds of film, which Kodak was slow to introduce, thus adding to its product problems.

Shrinking market share due to increased competition from the Japanese was not Kodak's only problem. In the early 1980s, Kodak introduced several less-than-successful products. In 1982 Kodak introduced a new disk camera as a replacement for the pocket Instamatic. The disk camera used a negative even smaller than the negative of the Instamatic and was smaller and easier to use. Four and a half million units were shipped to the domestic market by Christmas, but almost a million of the units still remained on retailers' shelves in the new year. The disk cameras had been outsold by pocket 35mm cameras, which produced higher-quality pictures.[3] The disk camera also sold poorly in the European and Japanese markets. Yet Kodak's research showed that 90 percent of disk camera users were satisfied with the camera and especially liked its high "yield rate" of 93 percent printable pictures, compared with 75 percent for the pocket Instamatic.

A final blow on the camera front came when Kodak lost its patent suit with Polaroid Corp. Kodak had foregone the instant photography business in the 1940s when it turned down Edwin Land's offer to develop his instant photography process. Polaroid developed it, and instant photography was wildly successful, capturing a significant share of the photographic market. In response, Kodak set out in the 1960s to develop its own instant camera to compete with Polaroid's. According to testimony in the patent trial, Kodak spent $94 million perfecting its system, only to scrub it when Polaroid introduced the new SX-70 camera in 1972. Kodak then rushed to produce a competing instant camera, hoping to capitalize on the $6.5 billion in sales of instant cameras. However, on January 9, 1986, a federal judge ordered Kodak out of the instant photography business for violating seven of Polaroid's patents in its rush to produce an instant camera. The estimated cost to Kodak for closing its instant photography operation and exchanging the 16.5 million cameras sold to consumers was expected to reach $800 million. In 1985 Kodak reported that it had exited the industry at a cost of $494 million.[4] However, the total costs of this misadventure were finally realized on July 15, 1991, when Kodak agreed to pay Polaroid a sum of $925 million to settle out of court a suit that Polaroid had brought against Kodak for patent infringement.[5]

On its third product front, photographic processing, Kodak also experienced problems. It faced stiff competition from foreign manufacturers of photographic paper and from new competitors in the film-processing market. Increasingly, film processors were turning to cheaper sources of paper to reduce the costs of film processing. Once again the Japanese had developed cheaper sources of paper and were eroding Kodak's market share. At the same time many new independent film-processing companies had emerged and were printing film at far lower rates than Kodak's own official developers. These independent laboratories had opened to serve the needs of drugstores and supermarkets, and many of them offered twenty-four-hour service. They used the less expensive paper to maintain their cost advantage and were willing to accept lower profit margins in return for a higher volume of sales. As a result, Kodak lost markets for its chemical and paper products—products that had contributed significantly to its revenues and profits.

The photographic industry surrounding Kodak had changed dramatically. Competition had increased in all product areas, and Kodak, while still the largest producer, faced increasing threats to its profitability as it was forced to reduce prices to match the competition. To cap the problem, by 1980 the market was all but saturated: 95 percent of all U.S. households owned at least one camera. Facing increased competition in a mature market was not an enviable position for a company used to high profitability and growth.

The second major problem that Kodak had to confront was due not to increased competition in existing product markets but to the emergence of new industries that provided alternative means for producing and recording images. The introduction of videotape recorders, and later video cameras, gave consumers an alternative way to use their dollars to produce images, particularly moving images. Video basically destroyed the old, film-based home movie business on which Kodak had a virtual monopoly. Since Sony's introduction of the Betamax machine in 1975, a video industry has grown into a multibillion-dollar business.[6] VCRs and 16mm video cameras are increasingly hot-selling items as their prices fall with the growth in demand and the standardization of technology. More recently, 8mm video cameras have been emerging—obviously much smaller than the 16mm version. The introduction of laser and compact disks has also been a significant development. The vast amount of data that can be recorded on these disks gives them a great advantage in reproducing images through electronic means, and it may be only a matter of time before compact disk cameras become available. It increasingly appears as though the whole nature of the recording industry is changing from chemical methods of reproduction to electronic methods. This transformation, of course, will undermine Kodak's edge in the market because its technical preeminence is based on silver halide photography.

Changes in the competitive environment have caused enormous difficulties for Kodak. Between 1972 and 1982 profit margins from sales declined from 15.7 percent to 10.7 percent.[7] Kodak's glossy image lost its luster. It was in this declining situation that Colby Chandler took over as chairman in July 1983.

KODAK'S NEW STRATEGY

Chandler saw the need for dramatic changes in Kodak's businesses and quickly pioneered four changes in strategy: (1) he strove to increase Kodak's control of its existing chemical-based imaging businesses; (2) he aimed to make Kodak the leader in electronic imaging; (3) he spearheaded attempts by Kodak to diversify into new businesses to create value; and (4) he embarked on major efforts to reduce costs and improve productivity. To achieve the first three objectives, he embarked on a huge program of acquisitions, realizing that Kodak did not have the time to venture new activities internally. Because Kodak was cash rich and had low debt, financing these acquisitions was easy.

For the next six years, Chandler acquired businesses in four main areas, and by 1989 Kodak had been restructured into four main operating groups: imaging, information systems, health, and chemicals. In a statement to shareholders at the annual meeting in 1988, Chandler announced that with the recent acquisition of Sterling Drug for $5 billion, the company had achieved its objective: "With a sharp focus on these four sectors, we are serving diversified markets from a unified base of science and manufacturing technology. The logical synergy of the Kodak growth strategy means that we are neither diversified as a conglomerate nor a company with a one-product family."[8]

Table 1 summarizes the four groups and their activities. The way these operating groups emerged over time is described below.

The Imaging Group

Imaging contains Kodak's original businesses, including consumer products, motion picture and audiovisual products, photofinishing, and consumer electronics. The unit is responsible for strengthening Kodak's position in its existing businesses. Kodak's strategy in its photographic imaging business has been to fill gaps in its product line by introducing new products either made by Kodak or bought from Japanese manufacturers and sold under the Kodak name. For example, in attempting to maintain market share in the camera business, Kodak introduced a new line of disk cameras to replace the Instamatic lines. However, in addition, Kodak entered into an agreement with Chinon of Japan to produce a range of 35mm automatic cameras under the Kodak name. This arrangement would capitalize on the Kodak name and give Kodak a presence in this market to maintain its camera and film sales. That venture succeeded; Kodak sold 500,000 cameras and had 15 percent of the market.

In addition, Kodak had developed a whole new range of "DX" coded film to match the new 35mm camera market—film that possesses the vivid color

qualities of Fuji film. Kodak had not developed vivid film color earlier because of its belief that consumers wanted "realistic" color.

Kodak also entered the electronic imaging industry through a joint venture with Matsushita. Matsushita produced a range of 8mm video cameras under the Kodak name. However, sales of these cameras never took off (some blame the outdated design of the camera), and in 1987 Kodak announced that it was withdrawing from the market.

Kodak has made major moves to solidify its hold on the film-processing market. It has attempted to stem the inflow of foreign photographic paper by gaining control over the processing market. In 1986 it acquired Texas-based Fox Photo Inc. for $96 million, becoming the largest wholesale photograph finisher. In 1987, it acquired the laboratories of American Photographic Group. In 1989, it solidified its hold on the photofinishing market by forming a joint venture between its operations and the photofinishing operations of Fuqua Industries. The new company, Qualex Inc., has ninety-four laboratories nationwide. These acquisitions provide Kodak with a large, stable "captive" customer for its chemical and paper products as well as control over the photofinishing market. Also, in 1986 Kodak introduced new, improved one-hour film-processing labs to compete with other photographic developers. To accompany the new labs, Kodak popularized the Kodak "color watch system," which requires these labs to use only Kodak paper and chemicals.[9] Kodak hoped that this would stem the flow of business to one-hour mini-labs and also establish the quality standards of processing.

As a result of these moves, Kodak gained strong control over the processing end of the market and made inroads into the film and camera end as well. In 1988, Kodak earnings were helped by the decline in value of the dollar, which forced Fuji Photo, its main competitor, to raise its prices. Consequently, Kodak was able to increase its prices. All these measures increased Kodak's visibility in the market and allowed it to regain strength in its existing businesses.

New and improved film products, including Kodak Gold Label film and Ektachrome film, were announced during 1988. Similarly, new types of 35mm cameras, some of which Kodak intended to make in its Rochester plant, were announced. Kodak also formed a battery venture with Matsushita. Matsushita produces a range of alkaline batteries for Kodak, and a gold-top battery is being exten-

TABLE I

Kodak's Product Groups

Imaging	Chemicals	Health	Information Systems
Photographic products group Consumer imaging division Consumer services division Motion picture and television products division Professional photography division	**Eastman Chemical Company** Chemicals Plastics Fibers	Sterling Drug Inc. Health Sciences Division Clinical Products Lehn & Fink	**Commercial systems group** Copy products division Customer equipment service division Graphics imaging systems division Kodak apparatus division **Imaging information systems group** Business imaging systems division Federal systems division Image acquisition products division Integration and systems products division Mass memory division Printer products division

Source: Eastman Kodak Company, Annual Report, 1989.

sively advertised in opposition to Duracell's copper-top battery. In 1988, Kodak announced the introduction of new and improved Kodak Supralife and Ultralife batteries to be produced in a joint venture with Matsushita at a new battery-manufacturing facility built in Georgia, where production began in 1989. Moreover, Kodak internally ventured a new lithium battery, which lasts six times as long as conventional batteries. This was an opportunity for future growth because of the extensive use of the battery in cameras.

Kodak also engaged in a massive cost-cutting effort to improve the efficiency of the photographic products group. For the last six years it has introduced more and more stringent efficiency targets aimed at reducing waste while increasing productivity. In 1986, it established a baseline for measuring the total cost of waste incurred in the manufacture of film and paper throughout its worldwide operations. By 1987 it had cut that waste by 15 percent, and by 1989 it announced total cost savings worth $500 million annually.

Despite these strategic moves, the net earnings of Kodak's photographic business dropped dramat-

ically in 1989. Although Kodak's volume and sales of its products were up, profit margins were down. Polaroid with its new One Film product was advertising aggressively to capture market share. Fuji, realizing the strong threat posed by Kodak's reassertion of industry control, responded with an intense competitive push. Both Fuji and Kodak were spending massive amounts to advertise their products in order to increase market share. Kodak had 80 percent of the $7 billion film market in 1989 and Fuji had 11 percent, but Fuji increased its advertising budget by 65 percent in 1989 to increase its market share and simultaneously offered discount coupons on its film products. Moreover, Fuji announced plans for a major new film-making plant in Europe—a plant the size of its Japanese plant, which by itself can produce film for one quarter of the world market. The result has been a huge amount of excess capacity in film production, which raises costs and encourages competition. Fighting back, Kodak announced a fifteen-year agreement with the Walt Disney Company to use Disney characters in its advertising. Kodak also announced new multipacks and discounts on its products. However, these moves were very expensive for Kodak and cut into profits. They offset some of the prospective benefits from Kodak's cost-cutting efforts and led to the poor earnings results. Thus, growth in Kodak's photographic imaging business has been slow.

It was because of this slow industry growth that Chandler saw the need for diversification. Because sales increased only 5 percent a year and Kodak already had 80 percent of the market, it was tied to the fortunes of one industry. This fact, plus the increase in the use of other imaging techniques, led to Chandler's second strategic thrust: an immediate policy of acquisition and diversification into the electronic imaging business with the stated goal of being "first in both industries."[10]

The Information Systems Group

In 1988, when Sony introduced an electronic camera that could take still pictures and then transmit them back to a television screen, it became increasingly obvious that the threat to Kodak from new electronic imaging techniques would continue to increase. Although the pictures could not match the quality achieved with chemical reproduction with video film, the advent of compact disks offered the prospect of an imaging medium that could meet such standards in the future. To survive and prosper in the imaging business, Kodak realized that it required expertise in a broad range of technologies to satisfy customers' recording and imaging needs. Furthermore, it saw the electronic imaging business increasing and a large number of different types of markets emerging, including business and industrial customers. Electronic imaging had become important in the medical sciences and in all business, technical, and research activities, especially since the advent of the computer. Thus, Kodak began targeting electronics, communications, computer science, and various hard-copy-output technologies as being increasingly important to its future imaging products. To buy time until it could produce its own products, Kodak marketed the products of others under its own famous brand name—for instance, an electronic publishing system for corporate documents and an automated microfilm-imaging system.

Kodak's goal of reinvesting profits to build and extend its businesses could be seen in its move toward acquisitions and joint ventures. Growth of the Information Systems group has been due to several acquisitions, including Atex Inc., Eikonix Corp., and Disconix Inc. Atex, acquired in 1981, makes newspaper and magazine publishing systems.[11] It sells versatile electronic publishing and text-editing systems to newspapers and magazines worldwide as well as to government agencies and law firms. Its list of customers include leading newspapers in such cities as Boston, Chicago, Dallas, Houston, Miami, New York, and Philadelphia; national magazines such as *Time, Newsweek, U.S. News & World Report, Forbes, Reader's Digest,* and *National Geographic;* and government customers such as the U.S. Supreme Court and the U.S. Government Printing Office.

Eikonix Corp. is a leader in the design, development, and production of precision digital imaging systems. Included in its range of commercial products are devices that scan and convert images into digital form and equipment to edit and manipulate color photographs and transparencies to produce color separations for printing and graphic arts applications. The Eikonix Designmaster 8000 allows users to proceed directly from artwork to printing plates with unmatched quality and flexibility.

Further growth within the Information Systems group came with the development of the Ektaprint line of copier-duplicators. The copiers achieved good sales growth and reached new standards for quality, reliability, and productivity in the very competitive high-volume segment of the copier marketplace. In 1988, Kodak announced another major move into the copier service business. It purchased IBM's copier service business and copier sales agreements in the United States. Kodak also announced that it would market copiers manufactured by IBM while continuing to market its own Ektaprint copiers. This service agreement was eventually extended to sixteen countries outside the United States.[12]

Kodak further enhanced its position in imaging with the announcement of two new image management packages: the Kodak Ektaprint Electronic Publishing System (KEEPS) and the Kodak Imaging Management System (KIMS). KIMS electronically scans, digitizes, and stores film images and transmits image information electronically. The system enables users with large, active databases to view and manipulate information stored on microfilm and magnetic or optical disks.[13] Presently, KIMS is being marketed by Digital Equipment Corporation in a joint venture. KEEPS is designed for use where there is a need for high-quality documents formed from text, graphics, and other images. The documents are reproduced by software designed specifically for electronic publishing. KEEPS has the ability to edit, print, and update text and graphics for publications. The computer comes from Sun Microsystems Inc. The software, enhanced by Kodak, is produced by Interleaf Inc., and the printer is manufactured by Canon (one of Kodak's Japanese competitors).[14] Kodak has also announced a new $500,000 imaging system that locates microfilm and scans it for computer use. This product is directed at the banking and insurance company markets. In 1988, Kodak announced that it would begin marketing a "VY-P1" printer developed in a joint venture with Hitachi. This printer can make high-quality still images from VCRs and camcorders.

With these moves, Kodak extended its activities into the electronic areas of artificial intelligence, computer systems, consumer electronics, peripherals, telecommunications, and test and measuring equipment. Kodak hoped to gain a strong foothold in these businesses to make up for losses in its traditional business. Kodak purchased companies that made products as diverse as computer workstations and floppy disks. It aggressively acquired companies to fill in its product lines and obtain technical expertise in information systems. After taking more than a decade to make its first four acquisitions, Kodak completed seven acquisitions in 1985 and more than ten in 1986. Among the 1985 acquisitions—for $175 million—was Verbatim Corporation, a major producer of floppy disks. This acquisition made Kodak one of the three big producers in the floppy disk industry.

Entry into the information systems market, like the expansion in its core photographic products business, produced new competitive problems for Kodak. In entering office information systems, Kodak entered areas where it faced strong competition from established companies such as Digital and IBM.[15] The Verbatim acquisition brought Kodak into direct competition with 3M. Entering the copier market brought Kodak into direct competition with Japanese firms such as Canon, which competitively market their own lines of advanced, low-cost products. Kodak was entering new businesses where it had little expertise, where it was unfamiliar with the competitive problems, and where there was already strong competition.

Kodak was forced to retreat from some of these markets. In 1990, it announced that it would sell Verbatim to Mitsubishi. (Mitsubishi was immedi-ately criticized by Japanese investors for buying a company with an old, outdated product line.) Kodak has withdrawn from many other areas of business by selling assets or closing operations and taking a write-off. For example, to reduce costs, it sold Sayett Technology, Kodak Video programs and videocassettes, and Aquidneck Data Corporation. The decline in the performance of the Information Systems group, attributed to increased competition, a flat office systems market, and delays in bringing out new products, reduced earnings from operations from a profit of $311 million in 1988 to a loss of $360 million in 1989.

The Health Group

Kodak's interest in health products emerged from its involvement in the design and production of film for medical and dental x-rays. The growth of imaging in medical sciences offered Kodak an opportunity to apply its skills in new areas, and it began to develop such products as Kodak Ektachem—clinical blood analyzers. It developed other products—Ektascan laser imaging films, printers, and accessories—for improving the display, storage, processing, and retrieval of diagnostic images. However, Kodak did not confine its interests in medical and health matters to imaging-based products

In 1984, it established within the health group a life sciences division to develop and commercialize new products deriving from Kodak's distinctive competencies in chemistry and biotechnology. One of the division's objectives was to focus on product opportunities in markets with relatively few competitors and high profit potential—products such as nutritional supplements that can be delivered orally or intravenously, as well as nutrition products for sale over the counter to consumers. Another objective was to develop innovative ways to control the absorption of pharmaceutical drugs into the body so that a drug remains therapeutically effective for the optimum amount of time. A third objective involved developing new applications for existing products and processes. Kodak has in its files about 500,000 chemical formulations on which it can base new products.

Within life sciences was the bio-products division, which engaged in joint research with biotechnology companies such as Cetus Corporation, Amgen, and Immunex. Bio-Products pursued an aggressive strategy to scale up and commercialize products based on biotechnology derived from in-house as well as outside contract research. Ventures entered into by the bio-products division included an agreement with Advanced Genetic Sciences for the commercial production of SNOW-MAX, a product useful in making artificial snow for ski areas.[16]

Kodak began to enter into joint ventures in the biotechnical industry, both to build its business and to enter new businesses. In April 1985 Kodak and ICN Pharmaceuticals jointly announced the formation of a research institute that would explore new biomedical compounds aimed at stopping the spread of viral infections and slowing the aging process. Kodak and ICN were to invest $45 million over six years to form and operate the Nucleic Acid Research Institute, a joint venture located at ICN's Costa Mesa, California, facility. The institute would dedicate much of its research exclusively to preclinical studies of new antiviral and anti-aging substances.

However, these advances into biotechnology proved expensive, and the uncertainty of the industry caused Kodak to question the wisdom of entering this highly volatile area. In 1988, to reduce the costs of operating the bio-products division, a joint venture incorporating bio-products was formed between Kodak and Cultor Ltd. of Finland, and Kodak essentially left the market. The remaining parts of the life sciences division were then folded into the health group in 1988, when Chandler completed Kodak's biggest acquisition, the purchase of Sterling Drug for more than $5 billion.

The Sterling acquisition once again totally altered Kodak's strategy for the health group. Sterling Drug is a worldwide manufacturer and marketer of prescription drugs, over-the-counter medicine, and consumer products. It has such familiar brand names as Bayer aspirin, Phillips' milk of magnesia, and Panadol. Chandler thought this merger would provide Kodak with the marketing infrastructure and international drug registration that it needed to become a major player in the pharmaceuticals industry. With this acquisition Kodak's health group became pharmaceutically oriented, its mission being to develop a full pipeline of major prescription drugs and a world-class portfolio of over-the-counter medicine.[17]

Analysts, however, questioned the acquisition. Once again Chandler was taking Kodak into an industry where competition was intense and the in-dustry itself was consolidating because of the massive cost of drug development. Kodak had no expertise in this area, despite its forays into biotechnology, and the acquisition was unrelated to the other activities of the health group. Some analysts claimed that the acquisition was aimed at deterring a possible takeover of Kodak and that it was too expensive.

The acquisition of Sterling dramatically increased the sales of the health group but dampened Kodak's earnings and helped lead to a reversal in profits in 1989. Moreover, by purchasing Sterling, Kodak had obtained Sterling's Lehn & Fink products division, which produced products as diverse as Lysol and Minwax wood-care products. Far from wishing to sell this division, Kodak believed that this acquisition would lead to long-term profits. Analysts asked whether this was growth without profitability.

The Chemicals Group

Established more than sixty-five years ago as a supplier of raw materials for Kodak's film and processing businesses, the Eastman Chemical Company has been responsible for developing many of the chemicals and plastics that have made Kodak the leader in the photographic industry. The company has also been a major supplier of chemicals, fibers, and plastics to thousands of customers worldwide. Kodak has been enjoying increased growth in its plastic material and resins unit because of outstanding performance and enthusiastic customer acceptance of Kodak PET (polyethylene terephthalate), a polymer used in soft-drink bottles and other food and beverage containers. The growth in popularity of 16-ounce PET bottles spurred a record year for both revenue and volume in 1985. Kodak announced the opening of a major new PET facility in England in 1988. In 1986, three new businesses were established within the chemicals group: specialty printing inks, performance plastics, and animal nutrition supplements. They all share the common objective of enabling the chemicals group to move quickly into profitable new market segments where there is the potential for growth.[18]

In its chemical business, too, Kodak has run into the same kinds of problems experienced by its other operating groups. There is intense competition in the plastics industry, not only from U.S. firms like Du Pont but also from large Japanese and European firms like Imperial Chemical Industries PLC and Hoech, which compete directly with Kodak for sales. In specialty plastics and PET, for example, volume increased but Kodak was forced to reduce prices by 5 percent to compete with other firms in the industry. This squeeze in profit margins also contributed to the reversal in earnings in 1989.

Logical Synergies?

With the huge profit reversal in 1989 after all the years of acquisition and internal development, analysts were questioning the existence of the "logical synergy" that Chandler, in his 1988 address to shareholders, claimed for Kodak's businesses. Certainly, the relative contributions of the various operating groups to Kodak's total sales differed from the past, and Kodak was somewhat less dependent on the photographic industry. But was Kodak positioned to compete successfully in the 1990s? What was the rationale for Kodak's entry into different businesses; what were the synergies that Chandler was talking about? Wasn't the improvement on profits in 1990 due to corporate restructuring to reduce costs?

CORPORATE RESTRUCTURING AND COST REDUCTION

As Chandler tackled changes in strategy, he also directed his efforts at reshaping Kodak's management style and organizational structure to (1) reduce costs and (2) make the organization more flexible and attuned to the competitive environment. Because of its dominance in the industry, in the past Kodak had not worried about outside competition. As a result, the organizational culture at Kodak emphasized traditional, conservative values rather than entrepreneurial values. Kodak was often described as a conservative, plodding monolith because all decision making had been centralized at the top of the organization among a clique of senior managers. Furthermore, the company had been operating along functional lines. Research, production, and sales and marketing had operated separately in different divisions. The result of all these factors was a lack of communication and slow, inflexible decision making that led to delays in making new product decisions. When the company attempted to transfer resources between divi-

sions, the separate functional operations also led to poor interdivisional relations, for managers protected their own turf at the expense of corporate goals. Moreover, there was a lack of attention to the bottom line, and management failed to institute measures to control waste.

Another factor encouraging Kodak's conservative orientation was its promotion policy. Seniority and loyalty to "mother Kodak" counted nearly as much as ability when it came to promotions. The company had been led by only twelve presidents since its beginnings in the 1880s.[19] Long after George Eastman's suicide in 1932, the company followed his cautious ways: "If George didn't do it, his successors didn't either."[20]

Kodak's technical orientation also contributed to its problems. Traditionally, its engineers and scientists had dominated decision making, and marketing had been neglected. The engineers and scientists were perfectionists who spent enormous amounts of time developing, analyzing, testing, assessing, and retesting new products. Little time, however, was spent determining whether the products satisfied consumer needs. As a result of this technical orientation, management passed up the invention of xerography, leaving the new technology to be developed by a small Rochester firm named Haloid Company (later Xerox). Similarly, Kodak had passed up the instant camera business. Kodak's lack of a marketing orientation allowed competitors to overtake it in several areas that were natural extensions of the photography business, such as 35mm cameras and video recorders.

Kodak's early management style, while profitable throughout the 1960s because of the company's privileged competitive position, was thus creating difficulties. With its monopoly in the photographic film and paper industry gone, Kodak was in trouble. Chandler had to alter Kodak's management orientation. He began with some radical changes in the company's culture and structure.

Firmly committed to cost cutting, Chandler orchestrated a massive downsizing of the work force to eliminate the fat that had accumulated during Kodak's prosperous past. Traditionally, Kodak had prided itself on being one of the most "Japanese" of all U.S. companies, hiring college graduates and giving them a permanent career. Now it had to go against one of its founding principles and reduce its work force. Kodak's policy of lifetime employment was swept out the door when declining profitability led to a large employee layoff.[21] Chandler instituted a special early retirement program, froze pay raises, and ordered the company's first layoffs in more than a decade. By 1985, the "yellow box factory" had dropped 12,600 of its original 136,000 employees. To further reduce costs in 1986, divisions were required to cut employment by an additional 10 percent and to cut budgetary expenditures by 5 percent. These measures helped, but because of Kodak's deteriorating performance, new rounds of cost cutting came in 1988 and 1989. Additional 5 percent reductions in employment aimed at saving $1 billion. The effect of these huge cuts was seen in 1990 when profits rebounded; however, it was not clear whether their effect on earnings would be short run or long run.

Although these measures had an effect on Kodak's culture, Chandler still needed to reshape Kodak's structure. In 1985 he began by shedding the old, stratified corporate structure for what he called an "entrepreneurial" approach. The first step was to reorganize the imaging group into seventeen operating units. Each of the seventeen line-of-business units now contains all the functions necessary for the success of the enterprise, including marketing, financial, planning, product development, and manufacturing. Each unit is treated as an independent profit center and managed by a young executive with authority over everything from design to production. All units have a common goal of improving quality and efficiency and eliminating problems in the transfer of resources and technology among operating groups. The purpose behind this change was to eliminate the old divisional orientation, which had led to competition and reduced integration within the company. Chandler hoped that the changes in organizational control and structure would promote innovation, speed reaction time, and establish clear profit goals.[22] With this restructuring, Chandler also reduced Kodak's top-heavy management in order to decentralize decision making to lower levels in the hierarchy. This reorganization was a sign that the company was at last shedding its paternalistic approach to management.[23]

In further attempts to bring costs more into line with those of foreign competitors who benefit from lower wage rates, favored government treatment, and currency advantages, Kodak instituted new control systems. In February 1986, operating groups were directed to reduce operating and expense budgets. In the move to maintain quality while keeping costs low, manufacturing plants have introduced stringent specifications that have improved both quality and efficiency. To compete effectively in a global marketplace, Kodak uses quality as the yardstick to measure its success.[24]

Relying on its new risk-taking attitude, Kodak also attempted to create a structure and culture to encourage internal venturing. It formed a "venture board" to help underwrite small projects and make conventional venture capital investments. In addition, the company created an "office of submitted ideas" to screen outside projects. Kodak received more than 3,000 proposals, although only 30 survived the screening process.[25] This aggressive research program led to a breakthrough in tubular silver halide grains, which improve the light-gathering capability of film. The discovery resulted in the new line of 35mm products.

However, Kodak's attempts to intrapreneurship have generally been unsuccessful. Of the fourteen ventures that Kodak created, six have been shut down, three have been sold, and four have been merged into the company; only one still operates independently.[26] One reason for this failure was that Kodak did not give managers an equity stake in the new ventures, so they felt that they had no stake in the ventures' success.

Having learned its lesson, Kodak announced that throughout the company pay would be more closely related to performance. For example, in 1989 as much as 40 percent of a manager's annual compensation was to be based on corporate performance. Even at the middle-manager level, 15 percent of compensation was to be linked to company results. Finally, at the level of wages, Kodak announced that it would link dividends paid to ordinary workers to the company's return on assets. It hopes by these measures to make the company more entrepreneurial and to move it along the cost reduction path. However, cost cutting will not be enough to turn Kodak around if its businesses do not generate increased revenues and achieve their profit potential.

Kodak also reorganized its worldwide facilities to reduce costs. International divisions were turning out identical products at higher cost than their counterparts in the United States. In a plan to coordinate worldwide production to increase productivity and lower costs, Kodak streamlined European production by closing duplicate manufacturing facilities and centralizing production and marketing operations, and it also brought some foreign manufacturing home. As a result, Kodak gained $55 million in productivity savings. However, the rise of the dollar boosted the cost of export products to foreign customers; thus, export expenses offset most of the gains.[27] Now that the dollar has fallen, these problems have been reversed, and profits from foreign operations are helping Kodak's earning figures as Kodak's international operations have regained their profitability. However, Fuji's new European facility will pose a severe challenge. Starting from scratch and employing production techniques learned from low-cost Japanese operations, Fuji will squeeze Kodak's profit margins and cause further changes in its European operations. In 1989, Kodak moved its international headquarters to London to decentralize authority to managers on the spot.

KODAK'S FUTURE

Whether Kodak has succeeded in its efforts to reorganize its strategy and structure has yet to be seen. Some analysts, pointing to the recent upswing in profits, are confident that the changes already made will restore Kodak's profitability. Others think that Kodak has done too little too late, that it has not achieved a clear rationale for its pattern of acquisitions, and that it still has many problems to deal with. They claim that Kay Whitmore needs to take a close look at Kodak's acquisitions and decide whether mistakes have been made and, if necessary, to divest acquisitions. On the other hand, given the investment in Sterling Drug and in other product lines, Whitmore needs to consider whether Kodak should make additional acquisitions to strengthen its stake in these new businesses so that it can deal with the fierce competition in the new product markets. Are there synergies to be achieved between operating groups? If there are, is the right structure in place to achieve them?

Kodak faces challenges in managing its new businesses. Given the failure of its intrapreneurship program, managing these ventures with a new entrepreneurial style rather than through the centralized, conservative approach of the past will not be easy. Already, difficulties have crept in. One example is Kodak's managing of Atex Inc., the manufacturer of desk-top publishing systems that Kodak bought in 1981. Because of Kodak's overbearing management style, the top executives and employees of Atex resigned, creating serious management problems for Kodak. The Atex executives claimed that Kodak executives were hard working but bureaucratic and did not understand the competitive nature of computer technology. Kodak managers should have been reacting to the computer marketplace weekly. They did not, and Atex executives could not handle Kodak's slow pace.[28]

What effects the reorganization of Kodak into four operating groups will have on performance remains to be seen. Even with reorganization, however, Kodak has moved into some uncertain environments in which the company has little experience and faces formidable rivals. Kodak faces competition from RCA and GE in consumer electronics, IBM and DEC in office systems. It must combat foreign competition from Fuji, Konica, Nikon, Canon, and Minolta in still cameras and copiers. It has already lost the battle with Matsushita, Sony, and Toshiba in video cameras and recorders and videotapes. Kodak also has the problem that entry into new businesses means lower profit margins. Ventures such as electronic imaging, magnetic tape, and floppy disks were in highly competitive industries that traditionally have lower profit margins than does chemical photography. Besides, new businesses are very expensive to enter, and Kodak's long-term earnings are heavily dependent on the future growth of these industries and on its ability to profit from this growth.

Venturing into the volatile biotechnology, pharmaceuticals, and office information systems business was obviously a gamble. However, Kodak had little choice because its existing business in mature and amateur and professional photography was a saturated market. Nevertheless, some analysts claim that Kodak should have stayed inside the imaging business and kept its activities closely aligned to its core skills. They argue that Kodak is still a one-business company and that its recent activities only disguise that fact. Indeed, they view the whole acquisition process over the last ten years as a way of fending off takeover attempts by companies competing for Kodak's huge cash flow. In 1990, they pointed to Kodak's creation of "tin parachutes" as yet one more way in which the company is fighting to maintain its independence. In the event of a takeover, Kodak has guaranteed all its employees large severance pay and other benefits. This plan makes Kodak a very expensive takeover target. Whether a takeover will occur depends on the outcome of the litigation with Polaroid. The amount of the settlement has yet to be announced. As soon as it is, analysts claim that takeover is a distinct possibility. Already a friendly takeover of Kodak by the Walt Disney Company has been suggested because of their fifteen-year marketing agreement. Would this add value to Kodak or to Disney? What should be done?

Can Kodak learn to play a different and tougher competitive game, or will it be taken over? The market has changed, and Kodak must play in businesses where it is no longer a worldwide leader and where it has neither a technological advantage nor a significant cost advantage. The question now is whether Kodak's moves under Whitmore can make Chandler's acquisition strategy bear fruit and whether Kodak can manage its new strategy and structure to fight off a takeover attempt. Financially, Kodak is still one of the top twenty-five U.S. companies. It is financially sound, with total assets of $25 billion. Kodak's brand name is also a major asset: it is one of the most recognized in the world. Can Kodak utilize these assets in the new competitive environment, or is it too late?

Endnotes

1. "Eastman Kodak Co.," *Moody's Industrial Manual,* 1 (1986), 3016.
2. Thomas Moore, "Embattled Kodak Enters the Electronic age," *Fortune,* August 22, 1983, pp. 120–128.
3. "Kodak's New Lean and Hungry Look," *Business Week,* May 30, 1983, p. 33.
4. Charles K. Ryan, *Eastman Kodak, Company Outline,* Merrill Lynch, Pierce, Fenner & Smith Incorporated, May 7, 1986.
5. Press release, Eastman Kodak Company, July 15, 1991.
6. John Greenwald, "Aiming for a Brighter Picture," *Time,* January 9, 1984, p. 49.
7. Barbara Buell, "Kodak Is Trying to Break Out of Its Shell," *Business Week,* June 10, 1985, pp. 92–95.
8. Eastman Kodak Company, *Kodak Highlights, First Quarter,* 1988, p. 7.
9. Taylor, "Kodak Scrambles," pp. 34–38.
10. Eastman Kodak Company, Annual Report, 1989.
11. Taylor, "Kodak Scrambles," pp. 34–38.
12. Eastman Kodak Company, *Kodak Highlights, Third Quarter,* 1988, p. 9.
13. Eastman Kodak Company, Annual Report, 1985, p. 5.
14. Barbara Buell, "Kodak Scrambles to Fill the Gap," *Business Week,* February 8, 1986, p. 30.
15. "Kodak's New Image: Electronic Imaging," *Electron Business,* January 1986, 38–43.
16. Eastman Kodak Company, Annual Report, 1986, p. 24.
17. Eastman Kodak Company, *Kodak Highlights, Third Quarter,* 1988, p. 5.
18. Eastman Kodak Company, Annual Report, 1986, p. 19.
19. Barbara Buell, "A Gust of Fresh Air for the Stodgy Giant of Rochester," *Business Week,* June 10, 1985, p. 93.
20. Moore, "Embattled Kodak," p. 120.
21. Buell, "A Gust of Fresh Air," p. 93.
22. Ibid.
23. "Yellow at the Edges," *Economist,* December 7, 1984, p. 90.
24. Eastman Kodak Company, Annual Report, 1985, p. 12.
25. Taylor, "Kodak Scrambles," pp. 34–38.
26. James S. Hirsch, "Kodak Effort at 'Intrapreneurship' Fails," *Wall Street Journal,* August 17, 1990, p. 32.
27. Eastman Kodak Company, Annual Report, 1985.
28. Moore, "Embattled Kodak," pp. 120–128.

CASE 29

Hanson PLC (A): The Acquisition Machine

This case was prepared by Charles W. L. Hill of the University of Washington.

INTRODUCTION

Hanson PLC is one of the ten biggest companies in Britain, and its U.S. arm, Hanson Industries, is one of America's sixty largest industrial concerns. A conglomerate with more than 150 different businesses in its portfolio, Hanson PLC has grown primarily by making acquisitions. By the end of 1989, the company had recorded twenty-six years of uninterrupted profit growth, cumulating in 1989 operating income of $1.61 billion on revenues of $11.3 billion and assets of $12.03 billion. The company's shareholders have been major beneficiaries of this growth. Between 1974 and 1989, the price of the company's shares on the London Stock Exchange increased eightyfold, compared with an average increase of fifteenfold for all companies quoted on the London Stock Exchange during this period.[1] Along the way, Hanson has gained a reputation for being one of the most successful takeover machines in the world. Its acquisitions during the 1980s included three American conglomerates (U.S. Industries, SCM Corporation, and Kidde) and three major British companies (London Brick, the Imperial Group, and Consolidated Gold Fields). So high is Hanson's profile that Oliver Stone, in his film *Wall Street,* reportedly used Sir Gordon White, head of Hanson Industries, as the model for the British corporate raider (the one who outmaneuvered the evil Gordon Gekko).

This case is intended to be used as a basis for class discussion rather than as an illustration of either effective or ineffective handling of the situation. This case was prepared by Charles W. L. Hill, University of Washington. Used by permission.

Despite this impressive track record, as Hanson enters the 1990s analysts increasingly wonder about the strategy of the company. There is speculation that the company may be on the verge of breaking itself up and returning the gains to shareholders. The age of the company's founders is fueling this speculation. The two men who built and still run the conglomerate, Lord Hanson and Sir Gordon White, are in their late sixties, and both have promised to consider retiring when they are seventy. As one insider put it, "The guys that started it off will finish it off."[2] Another factor is that Hanson is now so big that it would take some spectacular deals to continue its historic growth rate. According to many, including Harvard Business School strategy guru Michael Porter, there simply are not that many obvious companies for Hanson to buy. Thus, "even Hanson will be faced with poorer and poorer odds of maintaining its record."[3] On the other hand, at the end of 1989 Hanson had $8.5 billion in cash on its balance sheet. That, along with the billions it could borrow if need be (the company reportedly has a borrowing capacity of $20 billion), suggests that if Hanson and White should so wish, they could undertake an acquisition that would rival the RJR-Nabisco deal in size.

Other commentators question the long-term viability of the company. Some claim that Hanson PLC is little more than an asset stripper that in the long run will drive the companies it manages into the ground. According to one investment banker, "I'm not convinced that Hanson runs companies any better than anyone else. But I certainly know it squeezes them for cash, sucking the life from them."[4] Similarly, one former executive noted that "some of the incentive programs that they write for managers actually keep the company from growing. . . . They become so concerned with profit today that they don't re-invest for tomorrow."[5] The company disagrees. Sir Gordon White clearly sees Hanson PLC as reducing inefficiencies in the companies it acquires, not stripping assets. If anything is stripped away from acquisitions, according to White, it is unnecessary corporate bureaucracy, overstaffed head offices, and top-management perks, not assets. He steadfastly maintains that the company treats all acquired businesses as if it were going to keep them.[6]

With these issues in mind, in this case we consider the growth and development of Hanson PLC. We review the administrative systems that the company uses to manage its ongoing businesses, and we look at two acquisitions and their aftermath in depth: the 1987 acquisitions of SCM Corporation and the Imperial Group.

HISTORY

The origins of Hanson PLC go back to the port city of Hull in Yorkshire, England, in the 1950s.[7] At that time, James Hanson was learning his family's transportation business (the family operated a fleet of passenger coaches), and Gordon White was selling advertising for Welbecson Limited, a magazine printing company owned by his father. James Hanson's brother, Bill, was White's closest friend, and when Bill died of cancer at twenty-nine, James and Gordon became close friends. In the late 1950s, Hanson and White decided to team up in business. They formed Hanson White Ltd., a greeting card company. Although the company did well, the two soon became bored with the limited challenges and potential that the greeting card business offered, and in 1963 they sold out and began to look for acquisition opportunities.

Their first buy was Oswald Tillotson Ltd., a vehicle distribution company. This company was subsequently acquired by Wiles Group Ltd., a Yorkshire-based manufacturer of agricultural sacks and fertilizers. As part of the takeover deal, Hanson and White were given a substantial ownership position in the Wiles Group. Hanson and White soon gained management control of the Wiles Group, and in 1969, after deciding that James Hanson's name had a nicer ring to it than Gordon White's, they changed the name to Hanson Trust. Because of a series of small acquisitions, by the end of 1973 Hanson Trust owned twenty-four companies with combined sales of $120 million.

By 1973, however, the British economy was in deep trouble. The stock market had collapsed; the country was paralyzed by labor disputes; inflation was increasing rapidly, as was unemployment; and Prime Minister Edward Heath of the supposedly probusiness Conservative party had blasted conglomerate companies such as Hanson Trust as representing "the unacceptable face of capitalism." All of this prompted Gordon White to rethink his future. As White put it,

> I was disgusted with England at the time. Disgusted with socialism and unions and excessive, antibusiness government, disgusted with the way initiative was being taxed out of existence. . . . I'd done a lot of thinking. I told James (Hanson) that maybe we should just call it a day. I thought I'd try America.[8]

Hanson replied that there was no need to split up, and they agreed that Hanson would run the British operations while White tried to build operations in America.

White arrived in New York in the fall of 1973 in possession of a round-trip ticket, a one-year work visa, and $3,000 in traveler's checks, which was the most that British currency controls permitted a U.K. citizen to take abroad at that time. Moreover, because of British exchange controls, White could not gain access to Hanson's ample treasury without substantial penalties, and he had to struggle to convince banks that he was creditworthy. Despite this, in 1974 White managed to borrow $32 million from Chemical Bank to finance his first major U.S. acquisition, a friendly takeover of J. Howard Smith Company, a New Jersey-based processor of edible oils and animal feed that was later renamed Seacoast Products. The CEO of J. Howard Smith was David Clarke, whose family business it was. Clarke subsequently became White's right-hand man. He is now president of Hanson Industries and the most senior executive in the United States after White.

Over the next ten years, White made another six major U.S. acquisitions, all of them friendly (see Table 1). Then, in 1984, White was ready for his first hostile takeover, the $532-million purchase of U.S. Industries (USI). USI was a conglomerate that had grown by acquisitions during the 1960s and 1970s.

TABLE I

U.S. Acquisitions, 1974–1990

Date	Acquisition	Cost (millions)	Businesses
1974	Seacost	$ 32	Fish processing, pet food
1975	Carisbrook	36	Textile manufacturing
1976	Hygrade	32	Castings and casing units
1977	Old Salt Seafood	2	Prepared foods
1978	Interstate United	30	Food service management
1978	Templon	7	Textile manufacturing
1981	McDonough	185	Cement, concrete
1984	U.S. Industries	532	33-company conglomerate
1986	SCM	930	22-company conglomerate
1987	Kaiser Cement	250	Cement plants
1988	Kidde	1,700	108-company conglomerate
1990	Peabody	1,230	Coal mining

Source: Adapted from Gordon White, "How I Turned $3,000 into $10 Billion," *Fortune,* November 7, 1988, pp. 80–89; and "Hanson PLC," *Value Line,* July 20, 1990, p. 832.

White became interested in the company when he read in a newspaper that management was putting together a leveraged buyout at $20 a share for a total purchase price of $445 million. He suspected that the company was worth more than that and quickly worked out how big a loan Hanson Industries could handle, using USI's projected cash flow to cover interest charges. To USI's pretax earnings of $67 million he added $40 million generated by depreciation and $24 million in savings that he thought Hanson could effect by removing USI's corporate headquarters. That yielded a total cash flow of $131 million, or more than $70 million after taxes. With interest rates running at 13 percent, White figured that Hanson Industries could afford a loan of $544 million. In what was to become standard White thinking, he also reckoned that even with a worst-case scenario, he could recoup his investment by selling off the disparate pieces of the company.

Hanson Industries began to buy USI shares and by April 1984 held 5 percent of the company. Hanson then made a $19 per share bid for the company, which was quickly rebuffed by USI management. Three days later White increased Hanson's bid to $22 per share. USI's management, which had yet to raise the financing for its own proposed leveraged buyout, responded by increasing the purchase price to $24 per share. Hanson responded by initiating a tender offer of $23 per share in cash. For stockholders, cash in hand at $23 per share was far more attractive than management's promise of $24 per share if financing could be arranged, and Hanson's bid quickly won the day.

After the acquisition was completed, Hanson Industries President David Clarke spent six months at USI's corporate headquarters reviewing operations. At the end of this period USI's corporate headquarters was closed down, the staff was laid off, and financial control was centralized at Hanson Industries' small headquarters. However, most of the operating managers in charge of USI's constituent companies stayed on, lured by Hanson's incentive pay scheme and the promise that they could run their own shows. In what was also typical Hanson fashion, nine of USI's operating companies were subsequently sold off to outside investors for a price of $225 million.

The acquisition of USI was followed by three other hostile takeover bids in the United States: for SCM Corporation, Kaiser Cement, and Kidde. Of these, the SCM bid was by far the most acrimonious. SCM took a poison pill and tried to protect

TABLE 2

U.K. Acquisitions During the 1980s

Date	Acquisition	Cost (millions)	Businesses
1981	Ever Ready	£95	Dry cell batteries
1983	UDS	£250	Retail operations
1984	London Brick	£247	Brick manufacturer
1984	Powell Duffryn	£150	Engineering, shipping, fuel
1986	Imperial Group	£2,500	Tobacco, brewing, food
1989	Consolidated Gold Fields	£3,610	Gold mining, building aggregates

Source: Various press reports.

its position through the law courts before Hanson finally won control over the company. (The SCM takeover is discussed in detail later in this case.)

While White was making these U.S. acquisitions, Hanson was not sitting idle in Britain. During the 1980s the company made a series of acquisitions in the United Kingdom. These are summarized in Table 2. The most notable were the 1983 acquisition of London Brick, Britain's largest brick manufacturer, against vigorous opposition from London Brick's incumbent management; the £2.36-billion acquisition of Imperial, the largest tobacco company in Britain and the third largest in the world; and the £3.61-billion acquisition of Consolidated Gold Fields, the second largest gold-mining business in the world. The acquisitions of Imperial and Consolidated Gold Fields were the two largest takeovers ever undertaken in Britain. (The Imperial takeover is discussed in detail later in this case.)

ACQUISITIONS PHILOSOPHY

Hanson PLC's acquisitions on both sides of the Atlantic are primarily overseen by Sir Gordon White. Lord Hanson is primarily responsible for the ongoing administration of the company. As Lord Hanson says of White, "He's the one with the gift for takeovers."[9] In turn, White says of Hanson, "James is a brilliant administrator and really knows how to run

a company."[10] White claims that many of his acquisition ideas, including the USI deal, come from the newspapers. Others are suggested to him by contacts in the investment banking community, particularly Bob Pirie, president of the Rothschild investment bank, with whom White has lunch once a week.

Whenever possible, White avoids working at the office, opting instead to work from one of his four houses. Unlike corporate raiders such as Saul Steinberg and Carl Icahn, White rarely reads annual reports or detailed stock reports on a target company, claiming that he can get all of the financial information that he needs from Standard & Poor's two-page summaries. In addition, his three-person takeover staff distills reams of financial data on a target and provides him with a short memo on the target company. Says White, "I'm like Churchill, tell me everything you can tell me. On one page."[11]

Under White's leadership, one of the things that has distinguished Hanson PLC from many other acquisitive conglomerates is its distinctive acquisitions philosophy (which is, in essence, White's philosophy). This philosophy appears to be based on a number of consistent factors that are found to underlie most of Hanson's acquisitions.[12]

1. *Target characteristics.* Hanson looks for companies based in mature, low-technology industries that have a less-than-inspiring record but show potential for improving performance.

Normally, the objective has been to identify a poorly performing target where the incumbent management team has gone some way toward improving the underlying performance but whose efforts have not yet been reflected in either the profit-and-loss account or, more importantly, the target's stock price.

2. *Research.* Although White claims that he does little reading on takeover targets, his takeover staff does undertake detailed research into the potential of target companies before any bid is made. The staff routinely investigates companies undertaking leveraged buyouts.

3. *Risk assessment.* One of White's most often quoted edicts is "watch the downside." What this means is that instead of considering the potential benefits of a deal, give consideration to what can go wrong and the likely consequences of a worst-case scenario. White will purchase a company only if he thinks that in a worst-case scenario he will be able to recover the purchase price by breaking the target up and selling off its constituent parts.

4. *Funding.* White was one of the early pioneers of the highly leveraged takeover deal. All of the U.S. acquisitions have been financed by nonrecourse debt, secured on the assets of the target. This enabled White to engineer substantial acquisitions when Hanson Industries itself had a very small capital base. The British acquisitions have been funded by a mix of cash, equity, convertible securities, and loan stock.

5. *Disposals to reduce debt.* After an acquisition has been completed, Hanson sends some of its own managers along with a group of external accountants to go through and audit the acquired businesses. After a thorough review, Hanson typically sells off the parts of the acquired company that cannot reach Hanson's stringent profitability targets. In the process, Hanson is able to reduce the debt taken on to fund the acquisition. The most outstanding example followed the purchase of SCM for $930 million. After the takeover, Hanson sold off SCM's real estate, pulp and paper, and food holdings for a price of $964 million while holding on to SCM's typewriter and chemicals business, which in effect had been acquired for nothing. Thus, within six months of the takeover's being completed, Hanson was able to eliminate the debt taken on to finance the SCM acquisition. Similar, although less spectacular, disposals have characterized almost all of Hanson's major acquisitions on both sides of the Atlantic.

6. *Elimination of excess overhead.* Another objective of Hanson's housecleaning of acquired companies is to eliminate any excess overhead. This typically involves closing down the corporate headquarters of the acquired company, eliminating some of the staff, and sending other staff down to the operating level. Before Hanson took over, SCM had 230 people in its corporate office, USI had 180, Kidde had 200, and Hanson itself had 30. Today the total headquarters staff for all four is 120.

Hanson also disposes of any management perks found either at the corporate or the operating level of an acquired company. For example, one of Kidde's operating companies had a collection of art and antiques, a hunting lodge, and three corporate jets. Hanson kept one jet and disposed of the rest, including the man at the top who had spent the money.

7. *The creation of incentives.* Hanson tries to create strong incentives for the management of acquired operating companies to improve performance. This is achieved by (a) decentralization designed to give operating managers full autonomy for the running of their businesses, (b) motivating operating managers by setting profit targets that, if achieved, will result in significant profit enhancements, and (c) motivating managers by giving them large pay bonuses if they hit or exceed Hanson's profit targets.

ORGANIZATION AND MANAGEMENT PHILOSOPHY

In addition to its acquisitions philosophy, Hanson is also renowned for its ongoing management of operating companies, of which there are more than 150 in the corporate portfolio. Although Hanson does have some interests elsewhere, the strategic development of the group has centered on the United States and Britain, where a broad balance has tended to exist in recent years. Hanson PLC looks after the British operations, and Hanson Industries, the U.S. subsidiary, manages the U.S. operations. Each of these two units is operated on an entirely autonomous basis. Only one director sits on the board of both companies. Hanson PLC is headed by Hanson; Hanson Industries is headed by White.[13]

There are two corporate headquarters, one in the United States and one in Britain. At both locations there is a small central staff responsible for monitoring the performance of operating companies, selecting and motivating operating management, the treasury function (including acting as a central bank for the operating units), acquisitions and disposals, and professional services such as legal and taxation.

Below each headquarters are a number of divisions (see Figure 1). These are not operating companies. Rather, they are groupings of operating companies. In 1988 there were four U.S. divisions (consumer, building products, industrial, and food) and four British divisions (again, consumer, building

products, industrial, and food). There are no personnel at the divisional level with the exception of a divisional CEO. Below the divisions are the operating companies. Each operating company has its own CEO who reports to the divisional CEO. The divisional CEOs in Britain are responsible to Lord Hanson; those in the United States are responsible to David Clarke, White's right-hand man. White himself is primarily concerned with acquisitions and leaves most issues of control to David Clarke. Indeed, White claims that he has never visited Hanson Industries' U.S. corporate headquarters and as a matter of policy never visits operating companies.[14]

The following principles seem to characterize Hanson's management philosophy.

- *Decentralization.* All day-to-day operating decisions are decentralized to operating company

FIGURE I

Hanson PLC Organizational Structure

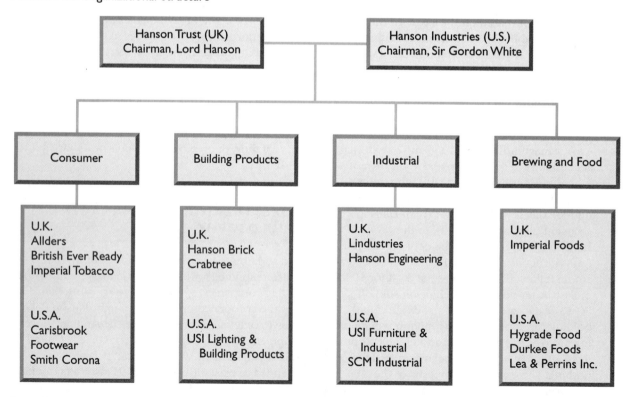

Source: Hanson Industries, Annual Report, 1986.

managers. The corporate center does not offer suggestions about how to manufacture or market a product. Thus, within the limits set by centrally approved operating budgets and capital expenditures, operating management has unlimited autonomy. As a consequence, operating managers are responsible for the return on capital that they employ.

■ *Tight financial control.* Financial control is achieved through two devices: (1) operating budgets and (2) capital expenditure policies. In a bottom-up process, operating budgets are submitted annually to the corporate center by operating company managers. The budgets include detailed performance targets, particularly with regard to return on capital employed (ROK). Corporate staff reviews the budgets and, after consultation with operating management, approves a budget for the coming year. Once agreed upon, the operating budget becomes gospel. The performance of an operating company is compared against budget on a monthly basis, and any variance is investigated by the corporate center. If an operating company betters its projected ROK, the figure used as the base for the next year's budget is the actual ROK, not the budgeted figure.

Any cash generated by an operating company is viewed as belonging to the corporate center, not to the operating company. Capital expenditures are extremely closely monitored. All cash expenditures in excess of $3,000 (£1,000 in Britain) have to be agreed upon by corporate headquarters. Capital expenditure requests are frequently challenged by headquarters staff. For example, a manager who contends that an investment in more efficient machinery will cut labor costs must even provide the names of the employees that he or she expects to lay off to achieve the savings. According to company insiders, when justifying a request for capital expenditure, a manager must explain every possibility. In general, Hanson looks for a pretax payback on expenditures of three years. The quicker the payback, the more likely it is that an expenditure will be approved.

■ *Incentive systems.* A major element of the pay of operating managers is linked directly to operating company performance. A manager can earn up to 60 percent of his or her base salary if the operating company exceeds the ROK tar-

get detailed in its annual budget. Bonuses are based strictly on bottom-line performance. As White puts it, "There are no bonuses for being a nice chap."[15] In addition, there is a share option scheme for the most senior operating company and corporate managers. More than 600 managers are members of the option scheme. The options are not exercisable for at least three years after they have been granted.

■ *Board structure.* No operating company managers are ever appointed to the board of either Hanson PLC or Hanson Industries. The idea is to eliminate any conflicts of interest that might arise over budgets and capital expenditures.

■ *De-emphasizing operating synergy.* In contrast to many diversified companies, Hanson has no interest in trying to realize operating synergy. For example, two of Hanson PLC's subsidiaries, Imperial Tobacco and Elizabeth Shaw (a chocolate firm), are based in Bristol, England, and both deliver goods to news agents and corner shops around Britain. However, Hanson prohibits them from sharing distribution because it reckons that any economies of scale that result would be outweighed by the inefficiencies that would arise if each operating company could blame the other for distribution problems.

THE SCM ACQUISITION

SCM was a diversified manufacturer of consumer and industrial products. SCM had twenty-two operating companies based in five industries: chemicals, coatings and resins, paper and pulp, foods, and typewriters.[16] Among other things, SCM was the world's leading manufacturer of portable typewriters (Smith-Corona typewriters), the world's third largest producer of titanium dioxide (a white inorganic pigment widely used in the manufacture of paint, paper, plastic, and rubber products), the sixth largest paint manufacturer in the world through its Glidden Paints subsidiary, and a major force in the U.S. food industry through its Durkee Famous Foods group (see Table 3).

Attractions to Hanson

The SCM group was first brought to White's attention by Bob Pirie, president of Rothschild Inc. in New York. Pirie thought, and Hanson's research

TABLE 3

SCM Divisional Results for the Year Ended June 1985

Division	Revenues		Profits	
	$m	Percentage of Change from 1984	$m	Percentage of Change from 1984
Chemicals	$539.0	+49%	$73.7	−100%
Coatings and resins	687.0	+5%	49.9	−3%
Paper and pulp	362.0	+3%	23.1	+10%
Foods	422.0	+7%	23.0	+35%
Typewriters	176.0	−11%	(47.4)*	−200%

*Loss after a $35 million charge for restructuring.
Source: Data from Hanson Industries, Annual Report, 1986.

team soon confirmed, that SCM had a number of characteristics that made it a perfect Hanson buy.

1. *Poor financial performance.* Summary financial data for SCM are given in Table 4. Pretax profit had declined from a peak of $83.2 million in 1980 to $54.1 million in 1985. The 1985 return on equity of 7.7 percent was very poor by Hanson's standards, and earnings per share had declined by 19 percent since 1980.
2. *Beginnings of a turnaround.* There were signs that incumbent management was coming to grips with SCM's problems, particularly in the troubled typewriter operation, where the

1985 loss was due to a one-time charge of $39 million for restructuring. Financial performance had improved since the low point in 1983, but the benefits of this improvement were not yet reflected in the company's stock price.
3. *Mature businesses.* SCM's presence in mature, proven markets that were technologically stable fit White's preferences.
4. *Low risk.* Some 50 percent of SCM's turnover covered products well known to the U.S. consumer (for example, Smith-Corona typewriters, Glidden paint, Durkee foods). White felt that there would be a ready market for such highly

TABLE 4

Financial Data for SCM

	1980	1981	1982	1983	1984	1985
Net sales ($m)	$1,745.0	$1,761.0	$1,703.0	$1,663.0	$1,963.0	$2,175.0
Pretax profits ($m)	83.2	72.6	35.3	37.8	64.8	54.1
Earnings per share ($)—fully diluted	$4.76	$5.01	$3.20	$2.63	$4.05	$3.85
Return on equity	12.40%	12.00%	5.80%	4.90%	8.00%	7.70%

Source: Data from Hanson Industries, Annual Report, 1986.

branded businesses if Hanson decided to dispose of any companies that did not meet its stringent ROK requirements.

5. *Titanium dioxide.* Titanium dioxide was dominated by a global oligopoly. Hanson was aware of two favorable trends in the industry that made high returns likely: (a) worldwide demand was forecasted to exceed supply for the next few years, and (b) input costs were declining because of the currency weakness of the major raw material source, Australia.

6. *Corporate overhead.* A corporate staff of 230 indicated to White that SCM was "a lumbering old top-heavy conglomerate with a huge corporate overhead that was draining earnings."[17] He envisioned substantial savings from the elimination of this overhead.

The Takeover Battle

After reviewing the situation, in early August White decided to acquire SCM. He began to buy stock, and on August 21 Hanson Industries formally made a $60 per share tender offer for SCM, valuing the company at $740 million. SCM's top management team responded on August 30 with its own offer to shareholders in the form of a proposed leveraged buyout of SCM. SCM's management had arranged financing from its investment banker Merrill Lynch and offered shareholders $70 per share. On September 4 White responded by raising Hanson's offer to $72 per share.

SCM's management responded to White's second offer by increasing its own offer to $74 per share. To discourage White from making another bid, SCM's management gave Merrill Lynch a "lock-up" option to buy Durkee Famous Foods and SCM Chemicals (the titanium dioxide division) at a substantial discount should Hanson or another outsider gain control. In effect, SCM's management had agreed to give its crown jewels to Merrill Lynch for less than their market value if Hanson won the bidding war.

White's next move was to apparently throw in the towel by announcing withdrawal of Hanson's tender offer. However, in contrast to normal practice on Wall Street, White went into the market and quickly purchased some 25 percent of SCM's stock at a fixed price of $73.5 per share, taking Hanson's stake to 27 percent. Furious at this break with convention, SCM's lawyers drafted a lawsuit against Hanson charging that White's tactics violated ten-

der-offer regulations and demanding a restraining order prohibiting Hanson from making any further market purchases. Hanson quickly filed a countersuit, claiming that Merrill Lynch's lock-up option to buy the two SCM divisions illegally prevented the shareholders from getting the best price.

Hanson lost both suits in federal court in New York. White immediately appealed and on September 30 a U.S. court of appeals ruled in Hanson's favor. This, however, was not to be the end of the matter. On October 7 Hanson spent another $40 million to increase its stake in SCM to 33 percent, thereby effectively stalling the leveraged buyout plan, which needed approval by two-thirds of the shareholders. The following day Hanson revised its tender offer to an all-cash $75 per share offer, subject to SCM's dropping the "lock-up" option because the option had been triggered by Hanson's acquiring 33 percent of SCM.

Hanson's next move, on October 10, was to file a suit to prevent Merrill Lynch from exercising the right to buy SCM's crown jewels. On October 15 it followed this with a second suit against Merrill Lynch for conspiracy. A U.S. district court ruled on November 26 that the lock-up was legal and that Hanson had triggered its exercise by the size of its stake. Once again Hanson appealed to a higher court. On January 6, 1986, a U.S. court of appeals overturned the lower court ruling, granting to Hanson an injunction that prevented SCM from exercising the lock-up option. The following day Hanson Industries won control over SCM after further market purchases. The final purchase price was $930 million, which represented a price/earnings multiple of 11.5.

After the Acquisition

Having gained control of SCM, Hanson immediately set about trying to realize SCM's potential. Within three months, 250 employees were laid off, mostly headquarters staff, and the former SCM headquarters in New York was sold for $36 million in cash. At the same time, White and his team were using their new position as owners to thoroughly audit the affairs of SCM's operating companies. Their objective was to identify those businesses whose returns were adequate or could be improved upon and those businesses for which the outlook was such that they were unlikely to achieve Hanson's stringent ROK requirements.

At the end of this process, four businesses were sold off in as many months for a total amount that recouped for Hanson the original purchase price and left Hanson with the two best businesses in SCM's portfolio: Smith-Corona typewriters and the titanium dioxide business. In May 1986, SCM's paper and pulp operations were sold to Boise Cascade for $160 million in cash, a price that represented a price/earnings multiple of 29 and was 3 times book value. Hanson felt that the outlook for those operations was not good because of a depression in paper and pulp prices. Boise Cascade obviously thought otherwise. Shortly afterward, Sylvachem, part of SCM's chemicals division, was sold for $30 million, representing a price/earnings multiple of 18.5.

In August 1986 Glidden Paints was sold to the British chemical giant and Europe's largest paint manufacturer, Imperial Chemical Industries PLC (ICI) for $580 million. This represented a price/earnings multiple of 17.5 and was 2.5 times book value. The purchase of this operation enabled ICI to become the world's largest paint manufacturer. A few days later Durkee Famous Foods was sold to another British firm, Reckitt & Colman PLC, for $120 million in cash and the assumption of $20 million in debt. This represented a price/earnings multiple of 17 and was 3 times book value. This disposal served to withdraw Hanson from an area that was subject to uncontrollable and volatile commodity price movements. For Reckitt & Colman, however, which was already one of the largest manufacturers of branded food products outside the United States, it represented an important strategic addition.

The four disposals amounted to $926 million and were accomplished at an average price/earnings multiple of 19.5. Having recovered 100 percent of the purchase price paid for SCM within eight months, Hanson had effectively acquired for nothing a number of businesses that were projected to contribute around $140 million to net pretax profit for their first full year under Hanson's control.

Hanson retained the titanium dioxide business for two main reasons. First, with the industry operating at close to 100 percent capacity and with projections indicating an increase in demand through to 1989, prices and margins were expected to increase substantially. Although several companies had plans to expand global capacity, given the three- to four-year time lag in bringing new capacity on stream, this sellers' market was likely to persist for a while. Nor did it look as if the additional capacity would outstrip the projected rise in demand. Second, two-thirds of world production of titanium dioxide is in the hands of global producers. SCM's business is ranked third with 12 percent of world capacity, behind Du Pont and Tioxide PLC. Given this oligopoly, orderly pricing in world markets seemed likely to continue.

Hanson also decided to retain SCM's typewriter business, despite the fact that in recent years it had been the worst-performing unit in SCM's portfolio. Hanson quickly realized that SCM management had in effect just completed a drastic overhaul of the typewriter businesses and that a dramatic turnaround was likely. In the two years prior to Hanson's acquisition, SCM's management had undertaken the following steps:

1. A new line of electronic typewriters had been introduced to match the increasingly sophisticated Japanese models.
2. Capacity had been reduced by 50 percent, and six U.S. production facilities had been consolidated into a single assembly plant and distribution center in New York to manufacture all electronic models.
3. As a result of automation, economies of scale, and labor agreements, productivity at the New York plant had increased fourfold since 1984, and unit labor costs had declined by 60 percent.
4. The manufacture of electric models had been moved offshore to a low-cost facility in Singapore.
5. Smith-Corona had just introduced the first personal word processor for use with a portable electronic typewriter, and it retailed at slightly less than $500.

As a result of these improvements, the Smith-Corona business seemed ready to become a major profit producer. Hanson forecasted profits of $30 million for this business during 1986–1987, compared with an operating loss of $47.4 million in financial year 1985.

THE IMPERIAL ACQUISITION

On December 6, 1985, while still engaged in the SCM acquisition, Hanson opened another takeover battle in Britain by announcing an offer of £1.5 billion for Imperial Group PLC.[18] Imperial Group was one of the ten largest firms in Britain. Imperial was

TABLE 5

Imperial Divisional Results for the Year Ended October 1985

Division	Revenues £m	Revenues Percentage of Change from 1984	Profits £m	Profits Percentage of Change from 1984
Tobacco	£2,641	+7%	£123.1	+11%
Brewing and leisure	974	+8%	97.0	+20%
Foods	719	+4%	33.0	+5%
Howard Johnson	617	+11%	11.1	−40%

Source: Data from Hanson Industries, Annual Report, 1986.

Britain's leading tobacco manufacturer and the third largest tobacco company in the world. Its Courage Brewing subsidiary was one of the "big six" beer companies in Britain. Its leisure operations included 1,371 public houses (taverns), 120-plus restaurants, and more than 750 specialized retail shops. Imperial manufactured more than 1,000 branded food products. (See Table 5 for a breakdown of Imperial's divisional results.) In September 1985 Imperial had sold its fourth business, the U.S. motel chain Howard Johnson, to Marriott. Howard Johnson had been purchased in 1980 and was widely regarded as one of the worst acquisitions ever made by a major British company.

Attractions to Hanson

Hanson's interest in Imperial was prompted by the news on December 2, 1985, of a planned merger between Imperial and United Biscuits PLC, a major

manufacturer of branded food products. The financial press perceived this measure as a defensive move by Imperial. However, despite its well-documented problems with Howard Johnson, Imperial's financial performance was reasonably strong (see Table 6). What factors made Imperial an attractive takeover target to Hanson? The following seem to have been important.

- *Mature business.* Like SCM's businesses, most of Imperial's businesses were based in mature, low-technology industries. There is little prospect of radically changing fashions or technological change in the tobacco, brewing, and food industries.

- *Low risk.* Most of Imperial's products had a high brand recognition within Britain. Thus, Hanson could easily dispose of those that did not stand up to Hanson's demanding ROK targets.

TABLE 6

Financial Data for Imperial

	1981	1982	1983	1984	1985
Revenues (£m)	£4,526	£4,614	£4,381	£4,593	£4,918
Pretax profits (£m)	106	154	195	221	236
Earnings per share (pence)	12.8	16.4	18.0	20.3	22.4
Return on capital (%)	12.7%	17.9%	20.4%	21.1%	18.1%

Source: Data from Hanson Industries, Annual Report, 1986.

- *Tobacco cash flow.* Imperial's tobacco business was a classic cash cow. The company had 45 percent of the tobacco market and seven of the ten best-selling brands in 1985. Although tobacco sales are declining in Britain because of a combination of health concerns and punitive taxation, the decline has been gradual, amounting to 29 percent since the peak year of 1973. Given Hanson's emphasis on ROK and cash flow, this made Imperial particularly attractive to Hanson. Imperial had arguably squandered much of this cash flow by using it to underwrite unprofitable growth opportunities, particularly Howard Johnson.

- *Failure of Imperial's diversification strategy.* Imperial's recent track record with respect to diversification was poor. In 1978 it bought a construction company, J. B. Eastward, for £40 million. After four years of trading losses, Eastward was sold in 1982 for a total loss of £54 million. In 1979 Imperial paid $640 million for Howard Johnson, the U.S. motel and restaurant chain. In 1985, after six years of declining profits, this business was sold for $341 million. These losses suggested a fundamental weakness in Imperial's top management in an area in which Hanson was strong: diversification strategy. Moreover, the failure of Imperial's diversification strategy probably resulted in Imperial's shares being discounted by the stock market.

- *Inadequate returns in brewing and leisure.* Imperial's brewing and leisure operations earned an ROK of 9 percent in 1985. This return was considered very low for the brewing industry, which was characterized by strong demand and was dominated by a mature oligopoly that had engineered high prices and margins. Hanson thought that this return could be significantly improved.

The Takeover Battle

The planned merger between Imperial and United Biscuits PLC (UB), announced on December 2, 1985, gave rise to considerable concern among Imperial's already disgruntled shareholders. Under the terms of the proposed merger, UB, although contributing just 21 percent of net assets, would end up with a 42 percent interest in the enlarged group. The implication was that Imperial's shareholders would experience significant earnings dilution. In addition, it was proposed that the corporate management of the enlarged group would primarily come from UB personnel. These factors prompted a reverse takeover by UB of the much larger Imperial group. See Table 7.

Hanson's interest was sparked by this controversy. Hanson's corporate staff had been tracking Imperial for some time, so when the for-sale sign was raised over Imperial, Hanson was able to move quickly. On December 6, 1985, Hanson made a 250-pence per share offer for Imperial, valuing the group at £1.9 billion. This offer was rejected out of hand by Imperial's management.

The next major development came on February 12, 1986, when the British secretary of state of trade and industry referred the proposed Imperial/UB merger to the Monopolies and Mergers Commission for consideration. Britain's Monopolies and Mergers Commission has the authority to prohibit any merger that might create a monopoly. The referral was due to the recognition that an Imperial/UB group would command more than 40 percent of the British snack-food market.

On February 17, Hanson took advantage of the uncertainty created by the referral to unveil a revised offer 24 percent higher than its original offer, valuing Imperial at £2.35 billion. On the same day, UB announced a bid of £2.5 billion for Imperial and indicated that, if the offer was successful, Imperial's snack-food businesses would be sold, thus eliminating the need for a Monopolies and Mergers Commission investigation. Imperial's board duly recommended the UB offer to shareholders for acceptance.

Many of Imperial's shareholders, however, were in no mood to accept Imperial's recommendation. Under British stock market regulations, once the Imperial board accepted UB's offer, Imperial's shareholders had two months in which to indicate their acceptance or rejection of it. If the offer was rejected, then the shareholders were free to consider the hostile bid from Hanson. What followed was an increasingly acrimonious war of words between Hanson and Imperial. Hanson charged Imperial with mismanagement. Imperial responded by trying to depict Hanson as an asset stripper with no real interest in generating internal growth from the companies it owned. In the words of one Imperial executive during this period, Lord Hanson "buys and sells companies well, but he manages

TABLE 7

Hanson PLC—Financial Data

				Income Data (million $)*							
Year Ended Sept. 30	Revs.	Oper. Inc.	% Oper. Inc. of Revs.	Cap. Exp.	Depr.	Int. Exp.	Net Bef. Taxes	Eff. Tax Rate	Net‡ Inc.	% Net Inc. of Revs.
1989§	$11,302	$1,609	14.2%	$2,141	$200	$533	$1,718†	23.6%	1,313	11.6%
1988§	12,507	1,561	12.5%	724	215	485	1,488†	23.2%	1,143	9.1%
1987‖	10,975	1,230	11.2%	522	172	493	1,217†	22.8%	939	8.6%
1986‖	6,196	713	11.5%	848	105	359	667	22.5%	517	8.3%
1985	3,771	477	12.7%	84	74	172	356	23.5%	272	7.2%
1984	2,930	303	10.3%	61	55	119	208	25.7%	154	5.3%
1983	2,226	207	9.3%	59	47	81	137	30.2%	94	4.2%
1982	1,952	NA	NA	NA	NA	NA	NA	NA	72	3.7%
1981	1,549	NA	NA	NA	NA	NA	NA	NA	62	4.0%

					Balance sheet data (million $)*						
Sept. 30	Cash	Assets	Curr. Liab.	Ratio	Total Assets	% Ret. on Assets	Long-Term Debt	Common Equity	Total Inv. Capital	% LT Debt. of Cap.	% Ret. on Equity
1989	$8,574	$12,038	$5,278	2.3	$17,482	8.5%	$8,028	$1,689	$10,683	75.1%	47.6%
1988	6,527	10,413	4,165	2.5	13,210	9.4%	3,592	3,707	7,878	45.6%	33.5%
1987	5,025	8,236	3,422	2.4	10,471	9.3%	2,837	2,841	6,151	46.1%	37.5%
1986	2,509	7.977	3,572	2.2	9,577	7.6%	2,834	2,068	5,252	54.0%	29.1%
1985	1,659	2,908	1,277	2.3	4,021	7.7%	903	1,376	2,563	35.2%	27.7%
1984	641	1,775	925	1.9	2,638	9.0%	981	505	1,540	63.7%	36.7%

*Data as originally reported; prior to 1986 data as reported in the 1985 Annual Report (prior to 1984, data are from the listing application of November 3, 1986), conversion to U.S. dollars at year-end exchange rates. †Includes equity in earnings of nonconsolidated subsidiaries. ‡Before specific item(s) in 1989, 1988, 1986. §Excludes discount operations and reflects merger or acquisition. ‖Reflects merger or acquisition.
Source: Standard & Poor's, *Standard & Poor's NYSE Stock Reports,* Vol. 57, No. 54, Sec. 12, p. 1096. Reprinted by permission of Standard & Poor's, a division of The McGraw-Hill Companies, Inc.

them jolly badly. He buys, squeezes and goes on to the next one. The only way to grow is by bigger and bigger acquisitions. Like all great conglomerate builders of the past, he's over the hill."[19]

Imperial's management failed to win the war of words. By April 17, UB had secured acceptances for only 34 percent of Imperial's shares, including 14.9 percent held by UB associates. The UB offer lapsed, leaving the way clear for Hanson. On April 18 Hanson secured acceptances for more than 50 percent of Imperial's shares, and its offer went uncondi-

tional. At £2.5 billion, the takeover was the largest in British history; it implied a price/earnings multiple of 12.3 on Imperial's prospective earnings.

After the Acquisition

After the acquisition Hanson moved quickly to realize potential from Imperial. Of the 300 staff at Imperial's headquarters, 260 were laid off, and most of the remainder were sent back to the operating level. In July Imperial's hotels and restaurants were sold to Trusthouse Forte for £190 million in cash, representing a price/earnings multiple of 24 on prospective earnings and amounting to 1.7 times book value. That sale was followed in September 1986 by the sale of the Courage Brewing operations, along with a wine and spirits wholesaler and an "off-license" chain (liquor stores) to Elders IXL, an Australian brewing company, for £1.4 billion in cash. The price/earnings multiple for that deal amounted to 17.5 times prospective earnings and represented a premium of £150 million over book value. It was quickly followed by the sale of Imperial's Golden Wonder snack-food business to Dalgety PLC, a British food concern, for £87 million in cash, representing a price/earnings multiple of 13.5 over prospective earnings.

As a result of these moves, by the autumn of 1986 Hanson had raised £1.7 billion from the sale of Imperial's businesses. Effectively, Hanson recouped 66 percent of the total cost of its acquisition by selling companies that contributed slightly more than 45 percent of Imperial's net profit forecasted for the year to October 1986. The net cost of Imperial on this basis had fallen to £850 million, with a consequent decline in the price/earnings multiple on prospective earnings from 12.3 to 7.6.

This was followed in 1988 by the sale of Imperial's food businesses for £534 million, along with the sale of various other smaller interests for £56 million. By the end of 1988, therefore, Hanson had raised £2.26 billion from the sale of Imperial's assets. It still retained Imperial Tobacco, by far the largest business in Imperial's portfolio, which it had in effect gained for a net cost of £240 million—this for a business that in 1988 generated £150 million in operating profit.

LATER DEVELOPMENTS

Following the SCM and Imperial acquisitions, in 1987 Hanson acquired Kidde, a 108-company U.S. conglomerate, for $1.7 billion. Kidde seemed set for the "Hanson treatment." Its headquarters was closed within three months of the takeover, and a series of disposals was arranged. These were followed in 1988 by continuing disposals of operations acquired in the Imperial and Kidde acquisitions. In total, they amounted to $1.5 billion.

In mid 1989 Hanson embarked on its biggest takeover ever, the £3.61 billion ($4.8 billion) acqui-

sition of Consolidated Gold Field PLC (CGF). In addition to being the second largest gold-mining operation in the world, CGF also owns a large stone and gravel operation, ARC Ltd., with major holdings in Britain. CGF came to Hanson's attention following an abortive takeover bid for the company from South African-controlled Minorco.

Hanson bought Minorco's 29.9 percent minority stake in CGF and launched its own takeover bid in July 1989. After raising its bid, Hanson won control of CGF in August. CGF also seemed set to be broken up. About half of CGF's value consists of minority stakes in publicly quoted mining companies in the United States, South Africa, and Australia. These stakes range from 38 to 49 percent, enough to hold the key to control in many of the companies. Thus, Hanson should be able to extract a premium price for them. Initial estimates suggest that Hanson should be able to raise $2.5 billion from the sale of CGF's minority holdings.[20] Indeed, by February 1990 Hanson had reportedly recouped about one-third of the purchase price of CGF through disposals and was looking to sell additional operations while gold prices remained high.[21]

The CGF deal led directly to the June 1990 acquisition of Peabody Holdings Co., the largest U.S. coal producer, for a total cost of $1.23 billion in cash. CGF had a 49 percent stake in Newmont Mining Corp., the biggest U.S. gold-mining concern. In turn, Newmont owned 55 percent of Peabody. In April 1990 Hanson purchased the 45 percent of Peabody not owned by Newmont from three minority owners. Then in June it outbid AMAX Corporation for Newmont's stake in Peabody.

The attraction of Peabody to Hanson lies in two factors: (1) the company owns large deposits of low-sulfur coal, which is increasingly in demand because of environmental concerns; (2) the company has recently invested heavily to upgrade its plant. As a result, in the past four years labor productivity has increased 50 percent.[22] In addition, analysts speculate that the deals, by improving Newmont's financial position (Newmont has used the cash to reduce its debt), may make it possible for Hanson to sell off its 49 percent stake in Newmont for a reasonable premium.

Endnotes

1. "The Conglomerate as Antique Dealer," *Economist,* March 11, 1989, pp. 71–73.
2. Quoted in ibid.

3. Quoted in John Byrne and Mark Maremont, "Hanson: The Dangers of Living by Takeover Alone," *BusinessWeek,* August 15, 1988, pp. 62–64.
4. Quoted in Andrew Marton, "The Buccaneer from Britain," *Mergers and Acquisitions* (February 1987), pp. 141–146.
5. Quoted in Byrne and Maremont, "Hanson: The Dangers."
6. Gordon White, "How I Turned $3,000 into $10 Billion," *Fortune,* November 7, 1988, pp. 80–89.
7. The material in this section is based on the following sources: White, "How I Turned," pp. 80–89; Marton, "The Buccaneer from Britain," pp. 141–146; and Hope Lampert, "Britons on the Prowl," *New York Times Magazine,* November 29, 1987, pp. 22–24, 36, 38, 42.
8. White, "How I Turned," p. 81.
9. Quoted in Lampert, "Britons on the Prowl," p. 36.
10. Quoted in White, "How I Turned," p. 81.
11. Quoted in Lampert, "Britons on the Prowl," p. 24.
12. The material in this section is based on the following sources: White, "How I Turned," pp. 80–89; Lampert, "Britons on the Prowl," pp. 22–24, 36, 38, 42; and Mark Cusack, *Hanson Trust: A Review of the Company and Its Prospects* (London: Hoare Govett Limited, 1987).
13. The material in this section is based on the following sources: Cusack, *Hanson Trust;* "The Conglomerate as Antique Dealer," pp. 71–73; Byrne and Maremont, "Hanson: The Dangers," pp. 62–64; and Gordon White, "Nothing Hurts More Than a Bogus Bonus," *Wall Street Journal,* July 20, 1987, p. 18.
14. White, "How I Turned," p. 81.
15. White, "Nothing Hurts More," p. 18.
16. Most of the detail in this section is drawn from two sources: Cusack, *Hanson Trust;* and Lampert, "Britons on the Prowl," pp. 22–24, 36, 38, 42.
17. White, "How I Turned," p. 84.
18. The material in this section is based on the following sources: Cusack, *Hanson Trust;* and Lampert, "Britons on the Prowl," pp. 22–24, 36, 38, 42.
19. Quoted in Philip Revzin, "U.K.'s Hanson Trust Aims for Big Leagues in Takeovers," *Wall Street Journal,* February 25, 1986, p. 30.
20. Mark Maremont and Chuck Hawkins, "Is Consgold Just an Appetizer for Hanson?" *BusinessWeek,* July 10, 1989, pp. 41–42.
21. Joann Lubin, "Hanson to Buy Peabody Stake for $504 Million," *Wall Street Journal,* February 16, 1990, p. A4.
22. "Hanson PLC," *Value Line,* July 20, 1990, p. 832.

CASE 30

Hanson PLC (B): Breaking It Up

This case was prepared by Charles W. L. Hill of the University of Washington.

INTRODUCTION

During the 1970s and 1980s, Hanson PLC put together one of the most impressive growth stories of any industrial company in the world. Under the leadership of James Hanson and Gordon White, Hanson PLC made its name by acquiring poorly run conglomerate companies in both Britain and America at prices that were often below their book value. In quick order Hanson would then change the senior management of the acquired company, sell many of the company's assets to other enterprises, typically for a considerable profit, and impose tight financial controls on what remained in order to maximize profitability and cash flow. The locus classicus was Hanson's 1986 acquisition of the Imperial Group, a diversified British tobacco, brewing, and food conglomerate, where some £2.4 billion of the £2.5 billion purchase price was recouped from asset disposals, leaving Hanson with the cash-generating tobacco business intact. The results of this strategy were nothing short of stunning. Between 1973 and 1991, Hanson put together twenty-nine years of uninterrupted profit growth to build a diversified company with revenues of £7.69 billion ($12.3 billion) and operating income of £1.33 billion ($2.13 billion). Hanson's stock price appreciation was also spectacular, increasing more than a hundredfold between 1973 and 1991.

However, 1991 may have been the high-water mark of Hanson's growth story. In 1990 Hanson took a 2.9 percent stake in the British chemical and

This case is intended to be used as a basis for class discussion rather than as an illustration of either effective or ineffective handling of the situation. This case was prepared by Charles W. L. Hill, University of Washington. Used by permission.

pharmaceutical company, Imperial Chemical Industries (ICI). Many saw this as a prelude to yet another Hanson acquisition, but ICI was not about to be taken over. After a bitter public relations battle during which ICI characterized Hanson's management as having a short-term orientation and criticized them for failure to add value to the companies they acquired, Hanson sold its stake in May 1991. While the stake was sold for a profit of £45 million ($70 million), the public relations battle damaged Hanson's image. A year later Hanson was outbid for a British food company, RHM, by a smaller conglomerate run by a former Hanson manager. These two failures raised questions as to whether Hanson's two founders, who were now both in their seventies, were still up to the rough game of hostile takeovers. To compound matters further, for the year ending in September 1993, with many of its cyclical businesses suffering from the effects of a recession in both Britain and America, Hanson reported a 33 percent decline in after-tax profits to $1.5 billion, the first such decline in its history. Reflecting these problems, Hanson's stock price peaked in early 1991 and remained flat over the next few years, while the equity markets in Britain and America boomed.

A NEW DIRECTION?

In 1992 the leadership mantle at Hanson started to pass from the company's charismatic founders, the now ennobled (Lord) Hanson and White, to Derek Bonham and David Clarke, who were then forty-eight and fifty, respectively. Bonham took over as CEO with primary responsibilities for Hanson's

British-based operations, while Clarke succeeded White as president of Hanson's substantial American operations. Lord Hanson remained on in the chairman's role, while White continued as the company's senior person in charge of mergers and acquisitions. (White died in 1995.)

Although both long-time Hanson employees, Bonham and Clarke clearly lacked the predatory thirst that had driven Hanson and White. Early in his tenure Bonham admitted that Hanson had become "too much of a mishmash" and stated that he hoped to correct that by focusing management's attention on improving the performance of its core businesses in building materials, chemicals, tobacco, and natural resources (primarily timber and coal). While this might require "bolt on acquisitions," Bonham seemed to be signaling that the swashbuckling days of hostile acquisitions and quick asset disposals to pay down debt were over.[1]

Another signal of a shift in management's philosophy came in May 1994, when Hanson announced that it would lengthen the payback period required of new capital investments from three or four years to five or six years. The company stated that it had lengthened the required payback period to take advantage of low interest rates and continuing low inflation. However, many also saw the shift as an attempt to allay fears in the financial community that Hanson's management style was too focused on the short term. Moreover, the move seemed to be consistent with Bonham's stated goal of increasing internal investments as a way of generating growth.[2] The growth that Bonham was talking about, however, was a far cry from the 20 percent annual rate achieved under the leadership of Hanson and White. According to Bonham, "The reality is that we are living in a low growth, low inflation climate. To suggest that you can continue to grow by 20 percent is out of line."[3]

Both Bonham and Clarke repeatedly stated that they saw Hanson growing at about twice the rate of inflation during the 1990s, which suggested a growth rate of around 6 percent, given British and American inflation rates.

Acquiring Quantum

The first significant strategic move under Bonham occurred on June 31, 1993, when Hanson an-

nounced that it had reached an agreement to purchase Quantum Chemical Corp., the largest U.S. producer of polyethylene plastics, in a stock swap that valued Quantum at $20 per share, or $720 million. The purchase price represented a premium of 60 percent over Quantum's closing price of $12.50 on June 30. Hanson also stated that it would assume all of Quantum's $2.5 billion in debt. The acquisition added to Hanson's U.S. chemical operations, which included SCM Chemicals, the world's third largest producer of titanium dioxide.

According to observers, the acquisition represented a strategic bet by Hanson that a protracted cyclical downturn in the polyethylene business was nearing an end. At the peak of the last plastics cycle in 1988, Quantum earned $760 million. However, Quantum had saddled itself with the $2.5 billion debt load in a 1989 restructuring, undertaken while plastics prices were at their previous cyclical peak. Massive debt service requirements and a slump in polyethylene prices had left Quantum with a 1992 loss before accounting charges of $118.4 million, or $3.98 per share. One immediate financial benefit of the acquisition was that Hanson was able to use its superior credit rating to refinance Quantum's debt (much of which was in the form of junk bonds with an average yield of more than 10 percent) at rates closer to Hanson's 5 percent borrowing costs. This move alone cut Quantum's $240 million annual interest bill in half.[4]

In retrospect the Quantum acquisition turned out to be particularly well timed. Prices for low density polyethylene bottomed out in the summer of 1993 at $28 per gallon. By the end of 1994 they had risen to $33 per gallon.[5] Quantum's profits turned out to be highly leveraged to prices. As a result of this leverage and lower interest payments, Quantum's chemical operations earned almost $200 million in fiscal 1994, more than $300 million ahead of its 1992 results. Quantum's results helped Hanson to rebound from its poor showing in 1993. For 1994 it reported a 32 percent rise in pretax profits and a record operating profit of £1.23 billion ($1.92 billion).[6]

1993–1994 Disposals

Throughout 1993 and 1994, Hanson proceeded with a series of relatively minor asset disposals. The objectives of these disposals were twofold: first, to focus the company on its core businesses and, second, to help pay down Hanson's enormous debt load, the legacy of its acquisitions including Quantum. In fiscal 1993 Hanson's long-term debt stood at £7.22 billion ($11.5 billion), and its debt to equity ratio was 1.83 (see Table 1). This debt load was beginning to trouble the financial community, who were starting to question the ability of Hanson to maintain its historically high dividend. In a previous era Hanson had quickly paid down debt from

acquisitions by raising cash through asset disposals, but there had been little movement in this direction since the late 1980s.

Between January 1993 and August 1994, Hanson sold more than fifteen companies for a total of £815 million ($1.3 billion). These disposals included its Beazer home building operations in both the United States and the United Kingdom; an office supply business; and Axelson, an oil industry equipment group.[7]

TABLE 1

Hanson PLC—Financial Data

Income Data (million £)*

Year Ended Sept. 30	($) Per Pound[†]	Revs.	Oper. Inc.	% Oper. Inc. of Revs.	Cap. Exp.	Depr.	Int. Exp.	Net Bef. Taxes	Eff. Tax Rate	Net Inc.[‖]	% Net Inc. of Revs.	Cash Flow
1994	1.509	11,199	1,633	14.6	293	401	545	1,346	20.9%	1,065	9.5	1,466
1993	1.523	9,760	1,288	13.2	301	310	600	1,016	27.8%	734	7.5	1,044
1992	1.822	8,798	1,322	15.0	279	254	777	1,286	15.3%	1,089	12.4	1,343
1991‡	1.820	7,691	1,327	17.3	266	216	741	1,319	21.5%	1,035	13.5	1,251
1990‡	1.700	7,153	1,236	17.3	247	180	638	1,285	24.4%	971	13.6	NA
1989‡	1.690	6,998	996	14.2	192	124	330	1,064	23.6%	813	11.6	NA
1988‡	1.770	7,396	923	12.5	198	127	287	880	23.2%	676	9.1	NA
1987§	1.560	6,682	749	11.2	151	105	300	741	22.8%	572	8.6	NA

Balance Sheet Data (million £)*

Sept. 30	($) Per Pound[†]	Cash	Curr. Assets	Curr. Liab.	Ratio	Total Assets	% Ret. on Assets	Long-Term Debt	Common Equity	Total Inv. Cap.	% LT Debt of Cap.	% Ret. on Equity
1994	1.566	6,815	9,933	6,704	1.5	21,536	4.7	5,038	4,598	9,768	51.6	24.9
1993	1.525	8,067	11,636	7,065	1.6	24,057	3.3	7,221	3,953	11,266	64.1	18.0
1992	1.779	8,445	11,204	6,386	1.8	20,541	5.9	5,069	4,224	9,430	53.8	28.9
1991	1.750	7,771	9,955	4,751	2.1	16,583	6.6	4,880	3,325	8,351	58.4	33.6
1990	1.870	6,883	8,993	4,226	2.1	14,754	7.6	4,258	2,834	7,222	59.0	50.1
1989	1.620	5,309	7,454	3,269	2.3	10,825	8.7	4,971	1,046	6,133	81.1	50.1
1988	1.690	3,860	6,158	2,463	2.5	7,812	9.5	2,124	2,192	4,659	45.6	34.1
1987	1.630	3,059	5,014	2,083	2.4	6,375	8.8	1,727	1,730	3,745	46.1	35.5

*Data as originally reported; prior to 1988 as reported in 1987 Annual Report. Based on UK GAAP.
†Average exchange rates for income data; fiscal year-end exchange rates for balance sheet.
‡Excludes discretionary operations and reflects merger or acquisition.
§Reflects merger or acquisition.
‖Before special items.

Spinning off U.S. Industries

The next big strategic move occurred in February 1995, when Hanson announced that it would spin off thirty-four of its smaller American-based companies into a new entity called U.S. Industries under the leadership of David Clarke. Hanson would retain ownership over several of its larger U.S. operations, including Quantum Chemical and Peabody Coal. The new company was to include such well-known brand names as Jacuzzi whirlpools, Farberware cookware, Ames garden tools, Rexair vacuum cleaners, and Tommy Armour golf clubs. In 1994 the thirty-four companies had sales of $3 billion and operating profits of $252 million. The company was to be responsible for $1.4 billion of Hanson's debt. According to one analyst,

> For Hanson, it achieves a one shot divestiture of a number of companies they may have struggled to sell independently, not because the individual assets are unattractive, but because it's messy to sell so many of them. They are able to divest in a tax efficient way and at the same time take a lot of cash out, leaving them with the ability to buy something else.[8]

The spinoff was completed on June 1, 1995. At the time, David Clarke stated that the new company's first objective would be to reduce its debt load, primarily by selling off a number of companies valued at $600 million.[9]

Acquiring Eastern Group

On July 31, 1995, Hanson announced that it would acquire Eastern Group, one of Britain's major electric utilities, for £2 billion ($3.2 billion). Eastern, which was privatized in 1990, has a customer base of 3 million and is responsible for 15 percent of the electricity produced in Britain, primarily for natural gas-fired generating facilities. Eastern is also the seventh largest natural gas supplier in the country. In the year ending March 31, 1995, Eastern's earnings were up 15 percent to £203 million ($324 billion) on revenues of £2.06 billion ($3.2 billion).[10]

Hanson stated that it was attracted to Eastern by its steady earnings growth. However, critics noted that the deal yet again stretched Hanson's balance sheet, which once more had begun to look solid after the U.S. Industries spinoff. The debt-financed purchase of Eastern caused Hanson's debt-to-equity ratio to shoot up from 37 percent to 130 percent, once more raising concerns that Hanson might not be able to service its historically high dividends. A partial response to these concerns came in December 1995, when the company announced plans to dispose of two additional U.S. subsidiaries—Suburban Propane and Cavenham Forest Industries—for £1.5 billion ($2.4 billion). The proceeds were to be used to pay down Hanson's debt load. Analysts calculated that the cash raised from these spinoffs would reduce Hanson's debt-to-equity ratio to around 90 percent.[11]

THE DEMERGER

By late 1995 it was becoming increasingly clear within Hanson's senior management team that drastic action would be required to boost the company's lagging share price.[12] As the British and American economies continued in their long recovery from recession, Hanson's cyclical business staged a significant performance improvement, with operating profits increasing by 44 percent for the fiscal year that ended in September 1995. Despite this performance, the company's share price had been essentially flat since the early 1990s (see Figure 1). Over the same period both the London and New York stock markets had increased substantially. By the end of 1995 the price-to-earnings ratio of Hanson's shares was 30 percent below that of the average stock on the London exchange, while Hanson's dividend yield at over 6.5 percent was among the highest offered by any company. It seemed that nothing could move the stock price, not the strong profit performance, not the spinoff of U.S. Industries, not the Eastern acquisition, and not the recently announced disposals.

It was against this background that Hanson stunned both London and Wall Street with its January 29 announcement that it would divide the company up into four independent businesses, effectively dismantling the conglomerate assembled by Hanson and White. Hanson stated that it would split into a chemicals business, an energy company, a tobacco company, and a building materials enterprise. Imperial Tobacco would be the

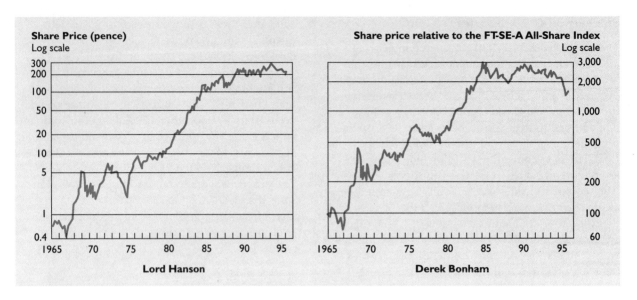

FIGURE I

Hanson PLC

largest company, with sales of £3.57 billion ($5.37 billion). The energy business, which would include Hanson's coal and electric businesses, would have sales of £3.5 billion ($5.27 billion). The chemicals business would have sales of £2 billion ($3.04 billion), while the building materials group would have sales of £2.3 billion ($3.48 billion).[13] Bonham was to run the energy business, while Hanson was to take over the building materials group until his retirement. The company estimated that the demerger would be completed by early 1997.

Hanson's stock price initially surged 7 percent on the news, but it fell later the same day and ended up less than 0.5 percent. The lack of a sustained positive reaction from the stock markets on both sides of the Atlantic puzzled Hanson's managers. Over the last few years, a number of diversified companies had announced demergers—including ITT, AT&T, and Sears—and their stock prices had almost always responded in a very positive fashion. In Hanson's case, however, this did not occur.

One possible explanation for the lack of a favorable reaction came from Moody's Investor Service, which put Hanson's debt under review for a possi-

ble downgrade one day after the breakup was announced. Moody's noted that "this is a highly complex sequence of transactions which are at an early stage and which will require various approvals."[14] Among the concerns expressed were that the demerger might raise Hanson's borrowing costs. The tax consequences of the demerger were also not immediately apparent, although there were some indications that there might be some one-time capital gains tax charges. Moreover, several stock analysts commented that the demerged Hanson units might not be able or willing to maintain Hanson's historically high level of dividends. One influential London-based stock analyst also noted that unlike most conglomerates that were demerging, there were few if any hidden assets at Hanson. This analyst calculated that Hanson's constituent parts should be valued at 194 pence, which was below the 212 pence price that Hanson's stock closed at on January 30, 1996.[15]

As a further prelude to the demerger, in March 1996 Hanson announced the sale of its remaining U.S. timberland operations to Willamette Industries for $1.59 billion. This sale followed Hanson's disposal of Cavenham Forest Industries in December

1995, and it completed Hanson's exit from the timber business. The cash generated from the sale was to be used to pay down Hanson's debt.[16]

Endnotes

1. R. A. Melcher, "Can This Predator Change Its Stripes?" *BusinessWeek,* June 22, 1992, p. 38; J. Guyon, "Hanson Crosses the Atlantic to Woo Investors," *Wall Street Journal,* December 6, 1983, p. 7D.
2. R. Rudd, "Hanson Increases Investment Payback Time," *Financial Times,* May 16, 1994, p. 15.
3. P. Dwyer and J. Weber, "Hanson Looks for a Hat Trick," *BusinessWeek,* March 14, 1994, pp. 68–69.
4. S. McMurray, "UK's Hanson to Buy Maker of Polyethylene," *Wall Street Journal,* July 1, 1993, p. A3.
5. D. Wighton, "Conglomerate's $3.2 Billion Gamble Pays Off," *Financial Times,* December 2, 1994, p. 23.
6. "Hanson Posts 32% Rise in Pre Tax Profits," *Wall Street Journal,* December 2, 1994, p. B3.
7. P. Taylor, "Hanson Lifted by Quantum Chemical," *Financial Times,* August 17, 1994, p. 13.
8. R. W. Stevenson, "Hanson Plans to Spin Off 34 U.S. Companies," *New York Times,* February 23, 1995, p. C1.
9. L. L. Brownless and J. R. Dorfman, "Birth of U.S. Industries Isn't Without Complications," *Wall Street Journal,* May 18, 1995, p. B4.
10. D. Wighton, "Hanson Plugs into New Current," *Financial Times,* July 31, 1995, p. 15.
11. D. Wighton, "Hanson Seeks £1.5 Billion from U.S. Disposals," *Financial Times,* December 21, 1995, p. 13.
12. "Widow Hanson's Children Leave Home," *Economist,* February 3, 1996, pp. 51–52.
13. R. Bonte-Friedheim and J. Guyon, "Hanson to Divide into Four Businesses," *Wall Street Journal,* January 31, 1996, p. A3.
14. Bonte-Friedheim and Guyon, "Hanson to Divide into Four Businesses."
15. D. Wighton, "Centrifugal Forces That Pulled Hanson Apart," *Financial Times,* January 31, 1996, p. 18.
16. "Hanson to Sell Mills," *Wall Street Journal: Money & Investing Update,* March 12, 1996.

CASE 31

First Greyhound, Then Greyhound Dial, Then Dial, Now What?

This case was prepared by Gareth R. Jones of Texas A & M University.

It was July 1996, and John Teets, the chairman, president, and chief executive officer of the Dial Corporation, was under increasing attack from Michael Price, president of Heine Securities Corp. Price was the adviser to the Mutual Series Funds, a large mutual fund company that owned 9.9 percent of Dial's stock. Teets had announced in February 1996 that he had decided to break Dial up into two companies to try to increase the company's earnings and boost its lackluster performance. Price, along with other analysts, however, argued that this move would reduce, not increase, value for shareholders and that what Teets should do was to divest Dial's many different businesses and return the proceeds to shareholders. Who is correct? To try to answer this question, it is necessary to understand the way that Dial's strategy has evolved over time under a succession of different CEOs.

GREYHOUND'S EARLY HISTORY AND GROWTH

Greyhound was founded in Hibbing, Minnesota, in 1914. Its first business was providing bus transportation to carry miners to work at the Mesabi Iron Range. Because Greyhound was the sole provider of bus service for these workers, it was immediately successful. In its very first year, the new corporation started expanding its routes and

acquiring interests in bus companies operating near Chicago. For the next sixteen years, the young company continued purchasing interests in bus companies, extending its route structure from New York to Kansas City. In 1930, the name *Greyhound Corporation* was adopted, and the now-familiar running-dog logo was painted on the buses.[1]

For the next twenty-seven years, Greyhound continued to acquire bus interests in order to consolidate its routes and link its various bus operations. Growth proceeded sometimes by purchase, sometimes by stock swaps, and sometimes by merger. However, the result was always the same to the traveling public: it saw more and more of the familiar running dog. By 1960, Greyhound had substantially achieved its objective of operating a bus system that could carry passengers to most destinations in the continental United States and Canada.

By 1962, however, Greyhound was facing the prospect of increasingly limited opportunities to expand its route system. In the company's favor was the fact that bus operations were generating large sums of excess cash, which could fund expansion into new businesses. So Greyhound's board of directors decided to diversify into operations outside of the bus transportation industry.

In that same year, Greyhound began the program of acquisition that turned it into a conglomerate. It solidified its bus-manufacturing operations into Motor Coach Industries, which became the foundation of Greyhound Dial's transportation manufacturing operating division. Also in 1962, the corporation acquired Boothe Leasing Company, an enterprise that specialized in equipment leasing. Boothe Leasing was renamed Greyhound Leasing and became the core business around which Greyhound's financial services division was to be built. Thus, by the end of 1963, Greyhound Corporation was operating in three major businesses: bus transportation, bus manufacturing, and financial services. Bus manufacturing supplied buses to bus transportation as well as to other bus companies.

ACQUISITIONS BETWEEN 1966 AND 1970

Gerry Trautman was appointed CEO in 1966, and he wasted no time in accelerating Greyhound's new strategy for expansion and growth.[2] From Trautman's installation as CEO until 1970, Greyhound acquired more than thirty widely different companies and formed a new operating division, services: it specialized in managing transportation-related businesses, such as Border Brokerage Company, which operated two duty-free shops at the Canadian border, and Florida Export Group, which also handled duty-free commerce. In addition, the services division included Manncraft Exhibitors, a company that specialized in building displays for major exhibitions; Nassau Air Dispatch, a Caribbean shipping company; and Freeport Flight Services, a Bahamian aircraft-servicing business. Trautman also brought in a line of cruise ships in the Caribbean, the Bahama Cruise Line Company.[3] Then he added companies as diverse as Ford Van Lines of Lincoln, Nebraska, a company specializing in furniture moving; Red Top Sedan Service, a Florida limousine service; two regional intercity bus lines; Washington Airport Transport, a commuter carrier from the Washington, D.C., suburbs to Dulles Airport; and Gray Line New York Tours Corporation, a sightseeing bus line. Furthermore, he added Hausman Bus Parts to the bus-manufacturing unit.[4]

Not all the companies that Trautman acquired proved to be as profitable or as manageable as he had hoped. What he was looking for was value as well as some synergy with Greyhound's existing transportation activities. However, as the acquisition process continued, synergy became a secondary objective. When Trautman became dissatisfied with an acquisition, he would divest it as quickly as he had acquired it, and many companies were spun off. Near the end of his tenure as CEO, Trautman would boast that Greyhound had achieved "diversification within diversification."[5]

What he meant was that in his view the operating groups had become diversified, so that each individually was recession-proof and all were enhancing the financial strength of the holding company.

Trautman's boldest maneuver and biggest acquisition came in 1970. He acquired Armour & Co., another large conglomerate that had many diverse business interests in food and consumer products. Trautman paid $400 million in cash, notes, and stock to take over Armour, which was primarily a large meat-packing company with more than $2 billion of sales in marginally profitable businesses. However, Armour also had interests in pharmaceuticals, cosmetics, and consumer products, such as soap, through its very profitable Dial division.

Trautman knew that it appeared as though he had overpaid for Armour–Dial. However, he soon reduced the price of the acquisition by selling off, for some $225 million, a number of Armour's divisions that he considered to be peripheral to Armour's core food and consumer businesses. In 1977, he sold off Armour's pharmaceutical division for $87 million, reducing Greyhound's net investment to $88 million.[6] What remained after the divestitures were Armour's food operations and Armour's Dial division, from which would emerge Greyhound Dial's consumer products operating division.

Trautman hoped that his new acquisition would be more recession-proof than the bus business, if not countercyclical to it. However, the Armour acquisition brought to Greyhound new businesses that had management problems of their own—in areas in which Greyhound had no experience, such as the price of pork bellies, cycles for meat packers' contracts, and foreign competition.

TRAUTMAN'S ACQUISITIONS AND DIVESTITURES BETWEEN 1970 AND 1978

For the next eight years, Greyhound under Trautman continued buying businesses and increasing the size of the operating divisions in its corporate portfolio. By 1978, Greyhound's holding company consisted of five operating divisions: transportation, bus manufacturing, food and consumer products, financial, and services/food service. Each of these operating divisions acquired many new businesses, so Greyhound was still undergoing "diversification within diversification." Many of the new acquisitions, however, were failures. Businesses as diverse as a chicken hatchery, a European acquisition to expand the financial services group, and various transportation businesses (Caribbean Gray Cruise Line, Ltd., VAVO Greyhound N.V. of Schoonhoven, Netherlands, Shannon-Greyhound Coaches, and Hausman Bus Parts) proved unprofitable.[7]

Greyhound's portfolio of businesses kept changing during this period, and Trautman continued to feel that he was shaping a diversified company that would have a powerful base in many lines of business. He was willing to take the risk of acquiring some companies that would be failures as long as the overall health of the company was strengthened. However, Greyhound became more and more distant from its core business—bus transportation.

In April 1978, Trautman engineered another major acquisition by acquiring 97 percent of the stock of Verex Corporation, the largest private insurer of residential mortgages in the United States. The Verex acquisition was intended to strengthen the operations of Greyhound's financial operating division. Verex insured first mortgages on residential real estate generally having loan-to-value ratios in excess of 80 percent.

By 1978, Greyhound had grown nearly as large as it would grow under Trautman's leadership. The collection of businesses that he had assembled—some by acquisition, some by internal growth, and some by selling off pieces of larger businesses—was designed to make Greyhound more resistant to economic downturns. The activities of Greyhound's five major operating divisions are summarized below.

■ *Transportation.* This operating division comprised the intercity services division and the travel services division. Transportation operated regularly scheduled passenger bus service between most metropolitan areas in North America and engaged in related operations, such as package shipping, sightseeing services, airport ground transportation, and deluxe tour and charter bus services.

■ *Bus manufacturing.* The largest maker of intercity buses in North America, the bus-manufacturing division had operations that were vertically integrated to fabricate bus shells of in-

tercity design, assemble buses, and manufacture bus parts for final assembly. In addition, this operating division warehoused and distributed replacement parts to meet its own requirements and the larger requirements of the bus industry. Greyhound bus manufacturing was the principal U.S. supplier of buses to charter operators and sightseeing companies.

■ *Food and consumer products.* The companies in this operating group manufactured and marketed products to independent retailers under private-label arrangements and distributed several products under their own trademarks. These trademarks included Dial, Tone, and Pure & Natural soaps, Armour Star and Armour Tree canned meat and meat food products, Dial antiperspirants and shampoos, Appian Way pizza mixes, Parsons' ammonia, Bruce floor care products, Magic sizing and prewash, and Malina handknitting yarns and needle products.

■ *Services/food service.* Companies in this operating division provided a broad range of services directed primarily to business markets, although duty-free shops located at airports and on cruise ships were targeted toward the consumer market. Greyhound convention services (GCS) specialized in designing, fabricating, warehousing, shipping, and setting up exhibits for trade shows, conventions, and exhibitions. GCS also served as a decorating contractor at conventions and trade show sites. The Food Service division, generally known as Greyhound food management (GFM), served approximately 400 locations in industrial plants, bus terminals, airports, office buildings, schools, colleges, and other facilities.

■ *Financial.* This operating division consisted of Greyhound Computer Corporation, a company specializing in computer leasing and sales in the United States, Canada, Mexico, and Europe; Greyhound Leasing and Financial Corporation, a company specializing in worldwide industrial equipment leasing; Pine Top Insurance, an entity that reinsured commercial property and provided excess casualty insurance for large policyholders; and Verex Corporation, the leading private insurer of highly leveraged residential mortgages for primary lenders. Travelers Express Company, Inc., another company in the financial division, specialized in providing traveler's checks and check-cashing services in 32,000 retail establishments and financial institutions in the mainland United States and Puerto Rico.

Together, those five operating divisions were generating combined revenues of nearly $4.5 billion. Trautman had accomplished his objective of using profits from the bus operations to move Greyhound into other businesses.

TRAUTMAN SELECTS TEETS TO TAKE OVER GREYHOUND

Serious problems became apparent at Armour when the food and consumer products operating division went from a profit of $22 million in 1979 to a loss of $1.7 million in 1980. Armour's problems came at a very inconvenient time for Trautman because he had planned to retire in 1980. Trautman wanted to solve Armour's difficulties while he kept business rolling at Greyhound's other groups and prepared a successor to take over the collection of companies that he had assembled. That successor was to be John Teets.

Teets was very different from Trautman. His background did not include Harvard Business School or law practice. Instead, Teets had learned to be an effective hands-on manager by staying as close to the action as possible. He had worked for his father's construction company but decided that he wanted to operate a restaurant. He borrowed money, started his own restaurant, and quickly made it successful. However, soon after he had paid back his loan money and his restaurant was earning a profit, it burned to the ground. In search of a new business opportunity, Teets answered a newspaper advertisement about a position managing a Greyhound food service concession stand at the New York World's Fair in 1964.

After joining the services/food service operating group, Teets quickly distinguished himself as a tight-fisted cost cutter who could make money on a miserly budget. He seemed to have a talent for squeezing every last penny out of everything he managed. Teets moved up quickly, gaining a reputation as an extremely effective manager. By 1975, he was put in charge of the food service group, which primarily operated a conglomeration of marginally profitable, obscure, franchised restaurants. His aggressive management style produced quick results, and in 1980 he was named the outstanding execu-

tive in the food industry. Also in 1980, in addition to Teets' responsibilities as CEO of the food service group, Trautman named Teets to head Armour and turn around the division's performance.

In 1981, Armour's major problem, as Teets saw it, was its paying from 30 to 50 percent more in wages and fringe benefits than its competitors. Teets asked Armour's unions for immediate wage concessions. He told the unions that if he failed to get the concessions, he would have to start closing plants. After a bitter strike, wage concessions in excess of 15 percent were obtained. Given these concessions, the cost cutting from plant closings, and more efficient operating procedures, it looked as though Armour had bought itself some time.

With Armour running more efficiently, the bus business cruising along on excess profits because of the recession and energy crunch in 1979–1980, and high profits in its financial operating division generated by high interest rates in the early 1980s, it looked as though the stage was set for Trautman's retirement. In fact, all that remained to be done was to formally select a successor. It was not difficult for Trautman to make up his mind about who should be his successor. He was impressed with Teet's successes in managing the services/food service group and also with the way in which Teets had dominated Armour's labor unions.

TEETS SEEKS SOLUTIONS

In 1981, John Teets succeeded Gerry Trautman as the chief executive officer of the Greyhound Corporation. The challenge facing Teets was to manage Greyhound's diverse businesses so that he would be able to achieve at least a 15 percent return on equity. However, many problems on the horizon might hinder the achievement of this goal. Some were the direct consequence of Trautman's ambitious expansion and diversification efforts. Others resulted from changes in environmental factors and consumer preferences. Still others stemmed from internal inefficiencies that Teets hoped he would be able to remedy.[8]

Two challenges in particular caused Teets to feel uneasy about the corporation's overall profit picture. The first problem was Armour's high production costs, which made it a weak competitor. The second was the challenge faced by Greyhound Bus Lines: the need to compete in a newly deregulated bus transportation market. He knew that if he did not find solutions for these two problems, they would seriously diminish the Greyhound Corporation's earnings. The contribution of each operating division to Greyhound's total sales revenues in 1981 is presented in Figure 1.

Dealing with Armour's High Production Costs

Having been president of Armour, Teets was very familiar with the division's problems: its high production costs, the reluctance of union leadership and rank-and-file workers to agree with Greyhound's assessment of Armour's problems, and its utter inability to successfully change its marketing orientation in order to compete effectively. In addition, Teets was concerned about Armour's inefficient plants and volatility of hog and pork-belly prices, which cyclically depressed Armour's 1981 profit of $9 million and represented a profit margin of less than 0.39 percent on sales of more than $2.3 billion.[9] Teets sensed that it was not going to be easy to make Armour a low-cost leader. Thus, he decided to divest Armour.

In preparation for the sale, he separated the Armour Food Company from Armour-Dial. On December 18, 1983, the food company was sold to ConAgra, Inc., for $166 million. With the Armour sale, Teets was chopping off nearly half of Greyhound's business. Nevertheless, even with Greyhound's revenues dropping from $5 billion in 1982 to less than $3 billion in 1984 without Armour, the sale gave Teets the opportunity to put Greyhound in better shape than it had been in years.

The Bus Line Divestiture

Teets was also concerned about the 1981 passage of House bill H.R. 3663, which deregulated the intercity bus business. Greyhound Bus Lines had based its route system on the competitive conditions that had existed in the earlier business environment. Teets, however, sensed that future success in the bus business would be based not on the extensiveness of Greyhound's route system or its fifty years of experience in operating in a regulated industry but on its ability to make money by charging competitive fares.

With the beginning of deregulated competition in the intercity bus business and declining passenger revenues resulting from the end of the energy crunch, Greyhound found itself paying wages and benefits that were from 30 to 50 percent higher than those paid by its competitors. Furthermore, its chief competitor, Trailways, having negotiated signif-

FIGURE 1

Greyhound in 1981

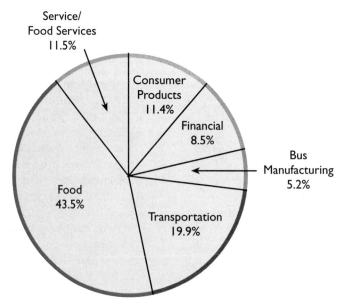

Total Revenues: $5.16 Billion

Source: Data from Greyhound Dial Corporation, Annual Report, 1990.

icant wage concessions from the Amalgamated Transit Union, had immediately passed the savings on to customers in the form of lower fares. Trailways' action was a frontal assault on Greyhound's most lucrative routes in an attempt to gain market share. Greyhound's response was to match every one of Trailways' price cuts. Although Greyhound preserved its market share, it lost millions of dollars.

For Greyhound Bus Lines, the legacy of deregulation was a total inability to be a low-cost provider of bus transportation. Deregulation had brought about the emergence of lower-cost competitors in regional markets, competitors that were able to be responsive and flexible in pricing and in reacting to Greyhound's actions. As a result, Greyhound lost its competitive edge.[10] In 1986, in an effort to save the bus lines, Teets converted 120 company-owned terminals to commission agencies, trimming a huge overhead burden. He also created four stand-alone regional bus companies and a new travel and charter company. Finally, he franchised several of Greyhound's least profitable routes to independent operators, licensing them to use the Greyhound logo and trademark.

However, the one factor that Teets could not control was winning a new labor contract. In February 1986, an offer to freeze wages was rejected by the union. In October, in a deteriorating market, a second offer involving concessions was presented with the understanding that its rejection would prompt the sale of the company. The offer was subsequently rejected, and fifteen days later Teets announced the sale of Greyhound Bus Lines for approximately $350 million to an investor group headquartered in Dallas. Teets claimed that the actions taken by management in an effort to salvage the bus business were exactly the ones that made it an attractive acquisition for the Currey Group in Dallas.

The sale of Greyhound Bus Lines brought in $290 million in cash and equivalents, including a 22.5 percent interest in a new holding company established by the Dallas investor group.[11]

Divestitures in the Financial Operating Division

Besides selling Greyhound Bus Lines in 1987, Teets also sold Greyhound Capital Corporation (GCC). The decision to sell GCC reportedly reflected Teets's conviction that "some businesses just fit better into Greyhound's plans than others."[12] What this statement really meant was that GCC had become an underperformer in the face of lowered interest rates and changes in the tax laws that disallowed investment tax credits. GCC was sold for $140 million, realizing a one-time gain of $79.7 million for Greyhound.

In early 1987, Greyhound announced its intention to sell Verex. The timing of the acquisition had been a disaster, given the recession in the real estate market caused by the oil bust in the early 1980s. Verex suffered huge losses generated by insurance claims from business generated before 1985. These claims were originating in states where severe downturns in farming, auto production, and oil drilling had led to a widespread inability to keep up with mortgage payments.

Not surprisingly, Teets could not find a buyer for Verex. In January 1988, Greyhound announced that it had stopped taking applications for new mortgage insurance and that it was discontinuing its mortgage insurance business. It also announced that 1987 results would reflect a one-time after-tax charge of $45 million as a result of reclassifying Verex as a discontinued operation; then Greyhound would manage Verex's existing portfolio to minimize continuing losses from the company's operations. Management hoped the remnants of Verex would not be a drain on corporate resources.

With the sale of Greyhound Bus Lines, Greyhound Capital Corporation, and Armour, and with the discontinuation of Verex, Teets announced that he was near the end of his mammoth task of restructuring Greyhound and shedding businesses that seemed to lack sufficient growth potential. By late 1987, Greyhound Corporation was primarily a consumer products and services company. Figure 2 summarizes the contribution of the different operating groups to total revenues in 1988. Compare the Greyhound Corporation that Teets structured (Figure 2) with the corporation he inherited in 1982 (Figure 1).

TEETS'S NEW MOVES

With the restructuring in place, Wall Street looked for an improvement in Greyhound's performance. However, it soon became obvious that the stack of businesses created by Teets was not proving much

FIGURE 2

Greyhound 1988

Total Revenues: 3.3 Billion

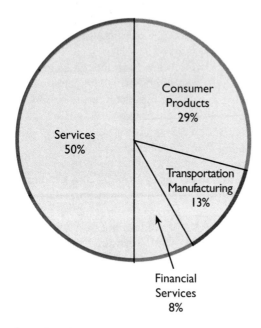

Source: Data from Greyhound Dial Corporation, Annual Report, 1990.

more profitable than the ones he had divested. There was only an 8.8 percent return on equity in 1987, and net income after nonrecurring losses was $25.1 million, the lowest for many years. Revenue was $2.5 billion. Teets maintained that the problems with Greyhound's various divisions could not have been foreseen as the restructuring was taking place but that Greyhound was set for "substantial profits in the future." Teets began a program of acquisitions and new product developments to strengthen Greyhound's presence in the four business areas identified in Figure 2 and begin the turnaround process.

Consumer Products

In the midst of the divestiture of Armour and Greyhound Bus Lines, Teets had made one major acquisition. On February 21, 1985, Teets an-

nounced the purchase of Purex Industries and its thirty household cleaning products for $264 million. Teets's aim with this acquisition was to boost profits in Greyhound's Consumer Products operating division (principally composed of the old Dial division) by using the Dial sales force and marketing expertise to sell Purex products— Purex bleach, Brillo soap pads, Old Dutch cleanser, and Sweetheart and Fels-Naptha soap, among others.

The Purex acquisition drew mixed reviews from Wall Street. It did not meet Teets's goal of a 15 percent return, but Teets believed that it would by 1988. Analysts were also unimpressed with the purchase because Greyhound had not been successful in managing Armour. Teets responded that Dial was capable of marketing consumer products, although it had not been successful at developing its own lines. He cited as evidence the fact that Dial was marketing the number one deodorant soap in its Dial brand. Analysts did concede that Teets should be able to realize increased profitability by using the same sales force to sell Purex and Dial products. Along with Purex's household cleaners, Greyhound also got Elio's Pizza as part of the Purex acquisition. Teets was enthusiastic about expanding this frozen pizza business nationwide from its East Coast base. This was to be done by means of the Dial sales force.[13]

The Dial operating division, as it was now known, became the center of Teets's attention and the flagship of the Greyhound Corporation. In the past Dial had not had much success in launching new products, but Teets was determined to change the situation, recognizing that growth in revenue had to come from the manufacture and marketing of new products. The first product introduced by the Dial division was Lunch Buckets, a range of microwavable meals with a stable shelf life of two years. This was a new market segment. Previously all microwavable meals had been frozen. Lunch Buckets meals were very successful and surpassed early expectations by a wide margin. By 1988, they had national distribution. By 1990, they had seized a 30 percent market share, becoming the market leader. In 1990, Dial announced new low-calorie Lunch Buckets.

Another new product introduced in 1987 was Liquid Dial antibacterial soap. This product, too, was very successful, and by 1990 it had achieved a

20 percent market share and was the second best-selling liquid soap in the market, after Procter & Gamble's Ivory liquid. Another successful new product was Mountain Fresh Dial, a highly scented version of Dial's deodorant soap. Additional developments were liquid Purex detergent and other cleaning products.

In 1988, Teets acquired the household products and industrial specialties businesses of the 20 Mule Team division of United States Borax and Chemical Corporation. Teets announced a new advertising campaign to reestablish the market presence of Borax bleaches and cleaning powders. Teets's formula for increasing the Dial division's market share called for

> further extensions of the Dial brand, further extensions of the Purex brand name, Parsons' ammonia working in those various regional markets. Finding new products that fit in those product niches that will augment the major shares that we have already, that will have a high enough dollar price on them to add to our income.[14]

The Emergence of Greyhound Dial

On June 4, 1990, Teets learned that Greyhound Bus Lines, the bus transportation company that he had sold in 1987, had declared bankruptcy and Greyhound's stake was now valueless. To distance his "new" company from Greyhound, he changed the company's name to Greyhound Dial in February 1990. The name change also marked the company's new focus on its consumer products division. However, the price of Greyhound Dial's stock, which had been more or less unchanged for the last six years, started to plunge in 1990 after Greyhound Dial reported a loss. Analysts wondered whether Teets would ever be able to improve the company's profitability.

In September 1990, another consumer products acquisition was announced: Breck hair care products. Breck had 1989 revenues of $60 million. Teets announced that integrating Breck into Dial would result in annual sales of more than $1 billion for the Dial division. Teets said that "Breck has been a household name for 60 years. It's a perfect fit with our other Dial products and under Dial management the power of the Breck name will flourish."[15] Under its previous owners, Breck had languished.

Teets hoped to turn the product around by applying Dial's marketing skills.

From the changes he had orchestrated, Teets was hoping for sizable revenue growth and profit from the Dial division, and in March 1991, as an indication of the company's future strategy, the company's name was again changed, to the Dial Corporation.

Services

By 1987, Greyhound's restaurant food services division was contributing the most to total revenues. It was natural, therefore, that Teets should seek to strengthen food operations. In 1987, Greyhound purchased the nation's second biggest airline catering and airline retailing business. The new operation had three units: Dobbs International Services, the nation's second largest provider of in-flight meals for airlines; Dobbs Houses, the operator of restaurants at many airports; and Carson International, which operated the food and beverage concession at Chicago's O'Hare Airport. In 1990, Teets announced that Dobbs had had a record year—the company had served sixty scheduled airlines in forty cities. Moreover, it had added five new accounts, including Houston International Airport.

Teets commented about Greyhound's food service businesses as follows:

> I see major changes in the food service business. We are exiting the service businesses that require a great deal of marketing, i.e., pizza and hamburger businesses. And, Greyhound is now primarily in the contract feeding business, be it Dobbs Houses or Restaura, our in-house catering business. Our operations in airports are primarily captive audiences. We also perform contract feeding for General Motors, IBM, office buildings, and banks.[16]

Teets strengthened Greyhound Dial's Travelers Express money order business with the purchase of Republic Money Orders, Inc., of Dallas. This acquisition made Greyhound Dial the leader in the money order business, ahead of the U.S. Postal Service. Teets had returned to the cruise-ship industry in 1984 with the takeover of Premier Cruise Lines. In 1986, he negotiated an agreement with the Walt

Disney Company that made Premier Disney's exclusive cruise-ship line, with three- and four-day sailing to the Bahamas from Cape Canaveral in Florida. The cruise-lines business enjoyed record sales, and in 1989 another line was added.

THE NEW LOOK OF THE DIAL CORPORATION

The new look of Dial's businesses after the acquisitions and divestitures is shown in Table 1. Teets acknowledged the wide diversity of businesses in the company's portfolio. However, he contended that the businesses did fit together. In his words, "We are a multiservice business. We operate in niches and were number one or two in most of these niches. From a recession standpoint, I think we're going to feel it less than most major companies."[17] Teets argued that Greyhound Dial was making acquisitions to strengthen its presence in existing niches. By concentrating on a niche, the corporation avoided going head-to-head with major competitors. Moreover, the niches were recession-proof, small-ticket items such as Lunch Buckets and

TABLE I

Greyhound's Businesses

Consumer Products	Services	Transportation Manufacturing	Financial Services
The Dial Corporation	Brewster Transport Company, Ltd.	Motor Coach Industries (MCI)	Greyhound Financial Corporation
Food	Consultants and Designers, Inc.	Transportation Manufacturing Corporation (TMC)	Greyhound Financial and Leasing
Personal care	Carson International, Inc.	• Custom Coach	Greyhound Financial Services, Ltd.
Laundry and household	Dobbs Houses, Inc.		Greyhound Bank PLC
	Dobbs International Services, Inc.		

Greyhound Airport Services Companies	Greyhound International Travel, Inc. (GITI)
Greyhound Exhibitgroup, Inc.	Greyhound Leisure Services, Inc. (GLSI)
Greyhound Exposition Services, Inc.	• Florida Export Warehouse
Greyhound Food Management, Inc.	• International Cruise Shops
• Faber Enterprises, Inc.	• Greyhound Leisure Services Duty-Free Shops
• Glacier Park, Inc.	• Premier Cruise Lines, Ltd.
• GFM Engineering and Design Group	Greyhound Lines of Canada, Ltd.
• GFM Fast Food Division	Travelers Express Company, Inc.
• GFM Public Service Division	• Republic Money Orders, Inc.
• GFM Truckstop Systems	Universal Coach Parts, Inc.
• Restaura	
• Restaura, S.A.	

Source: Greyhound Dial Corporation, Annual Report, 1990.

TABLE 2

The Dial Corporation: Consolidated Balance Sheet
(000 omitted, except per share data)

	Year ended December 31		
	1995	**1994**	**1993**
Revenues	$3,575,070	$3,546,847	$3,000,342
Costs and expenses			
Costs of sales and services	3,271,151	3,216,627	2,725,049
Restructuring charges and asset write-downs	191,100		
Unallocated corporate expense and other items, net	43,194	43,938	42,734
Interest expense	75,994	61,195	57,292
Minority interests	4,346	3,392	3,618
	3,585,785	3,325,152	2,828,693
Income (loss) before income taxes	(10,715)	221,695	171,649
Income taxes (benefit)	(11,852)	81,384	61,376
Income from Continuing Operations	1,137	140,311	110,273
Income from discontinued operations			32,120
Income before extraordinary charge and cumulative effect of change in accounting principle	1,137	140,311	142,393
Extraordinary charge for early retirement of debt, net of tax benefit of $11,833			(21,908)
Cumulative effect, net of tax benefit of $7,544, to January 1, 1995, of initial application of SFAS No. 121,"Accounting for the Impairment of Long-Lived Assets and for Long-Lived Assets to Be Disposed Of"	(17,696)		
Net income (loss)	$ (16,559)	$ 140,311	$ 120,485
Income (Loss) per Common Share			
Continuing operations	$0.00	$1.61	$1.28
Discontinued operations			0.38
Income before extraordinary charge and cumulative effect of change in accounting principle	0.00	1.61	1.66
Extraordinary charge			(0.26)
Cumulative effect, to January 1, 1995, of initial application of SFAS No. 121	(0.20)		
Net income (loss) per common share	$ (0.20)	$ 1.61	$ 1.40

soap, not refrigerators and cars. Teets argued that Greyhound Dial was positioned for growth and that management expected revenues to increase steadily over the next few years. See Table 2.

Some analysts, however, felt that the organization was still a hodgepodge of different businesses in need of rationalization. They pointed to the lack of fit between a cruise-ship line and hotel operations in Glacier National Park and contract cater-ing, saying that Greyhound Dial was still a collection of companies with no real connection. They also argued that Greyhound Dial's breakup value was more than $60 a share, while its stock price had been in the range of $25 to $35 for years. Teets agreed that some minor divestitures were necessary, but he believed that the best way to proceed was to stay in the same niches and manage the existing businesses more efficiently.

Dial in the 1990s

In 1991, it appeared that, at last, things were going Dial's way. Dial's share price, which had plummeted to less than $10 a share at the end of 1990, rose to almost $25 a share by the end of 1992. This turnaround occurred for several reasons. First, Dial had finally spun off its loss-making financial services group to stockholders so that the liabilities of the new "Finova" Company no longer affected its balance sheet. Second, its consumer products group, and in particular the Dial soap division, was performing strongly. Dial had become the number one selling deodorant soap in the United States, with more than 20 percent of the market. Third, Teets had orchestrated a major downsizing, or what he had called "rightsizing," reducing the number of corporate managers from 400 to 300. Also, all of Dial's different businesses were subjected to close scrutiny to try to reduce costs, and employment was reduced across the board, even in the successful Dial division. Teets also reduced corporate debt from a high of $850 million to $550 million by the sales of certain assets such as Dobbs House, its airport catering company. Analysts hoped that all these events were the first signs of a turnaround in the company's performance.

These hopes were doomed, however, by a series of problems that emerged in Dial's various businesses. In the 1990s, businesses in Dial's transportation manufacturing unit began to perform poorly, draining the company's profits. In 1993, Teets decided to dispose of it. Also, its washing Purex bleach business was doing poorly and losing money. It began to seem that just when Dial was making strides in one of its businesses, problems in another were wiping out the effects of the improvement. Investors began to wonder again about Teets's claims for his recession-proof niche strategy.

By 1995, major problems were affecting many areas of the company, including the pivotal Dial division. Teets, desperate to increase the company's return on equity and stock price, which had been flat since its high in 1992, began again to slash costs. One way he slashed costs was by reducing the advertising budget for Dial soap products from $8.7 million to $4.9 million. However, this was something that no niche player could afford to do when battling such industry giants as Procter & Gamble and Unilever, whose new soap Lever 2000 made major inroads into sales of Dial soap. Dial soap's market share dropped to 17.6 percent from 19.7 percent of the market in 1995, which was a severe blow to the Dial Corporation's most important product line and a disaster for the company.

The Purex division also was not performing well. The Purex bleach line was phased out in 1995 because of mounting losses. Purex detergents, the low-priced detergent that had been selling well, came under intense pressure from Procter & Gamble, which introduced a competing low-priced brand, Ultra Bonus, that was aimed directly at Purex late in 1995. Dial was forced to slash the price of Purex by 10 percent to compete, further cutting into the company's profits. Furthermore, Dial's successful Lunch Buckets, the line of microwave products, had generated a host of imitators from major food companies that quickly introduced their own competing products. Having lost this niche and no longer able to compete, Dial phased out Lunch Buckets in 1995. It began to seem to Dial's managers that even when they found a winning strategy their larger competitors just stole the idea away from them.

Dial's other businesses were also suffering problems. Its cruise-ship line, Premier Cruise Lines, which had formed an agreement with the Walt Disney Company to operate Disney's theme cruises in the Big Red Boat, lost its license in 1995 when Disney decided that it would launch its own cruise line. With four aging ships, and lacking any differentiated appeal in the increasingly competitive cruise-ship industry in the 1990s, the company put its ships up for sale and withdrew from the cruise-ship business—one more recession-proof niche gone.

Then, Dial's airline food business began to suffer in the 1990s when, to cut down on costs in an increasingly competitive airline industry, the major airlines cut back on the quality of the food they offered their customers. Airlines that had offered full meals began to offer snacks, and airlines such as Southwest offered passengers nothing. In airports, too, there had been a move to allow fast-food chains to set up their franchises on-site to increase the variety of foods offered to customers. All this hurt Dial's catering businesses.

It was becoming increasingly obvious to industry analysts that Dial was nothing more than a hodgepodge of different businesses that had nothing in common, were not recession proof, and did not even have a secure niche.

NOW WHAT?

With its profits flat or eroding and no turnaround in sight, the question became how to create new value from Dial's different businesses. The movement of many diversified companies to break up their operations and let individual businesses go it alone in the early 1990s gave Teets his answer. He would split apart Dial's consumer products and services operations—thus dismantling the empire he had built since 1984—into two different companies. One, which will still be known as the Dial Corp., would consist of all its consumer products interests and have revenues of about $1.3 billion. The other, to be called Viad Corp., would manage its remaining financial, catering, and exhibition businesses and have revenues of about $2.2 billion.

Initially, analysts thought that the breakup would allow the two new companies to realize more value. For example, by operating separately, a downturn in the business of one division would no longer hurt the performance of the other. Moreover, after the breakup managers would be able to make decisions that could promote their own businesses, not corporate interests. However, analysts later came to realize that in the future there would be two sets of managers who would have to be paid to manage the two companies and two sets of overhead costs. Moreover, the question arose as to whether there was any value to be created by the breakups because all of Dial's businesses were under threats from more efficient and aggressive competitors.

Analysts came to believe increasingly that more value could be made for shareholders if the company dismantled itself and sold off its assets to the highest bidder. A bidder could then merge a particular Dial business into its own operations and thus reduce manufacturing, distribution, or marketing costs or even use its skills to increase the division's differentiation advantage. Of course, the selloff would mean that many of Dial's managers might find themselves out of well-paying jobs, including Teets who had earned many millions of dollars over the years. On the other hand, these managers had not created much value for their shareholders.

In 1996, Teets answered his critics with half-page ads in the *Wall Street Journal* arguing that his strategy was a "strategy for empowered growth" that would allow each of the two new companies to "aggressively pursue acquisition opportunities without worry about upsetting the balance in Dial's existing mix of business." However, he did not explain how new value would be created by the two companies or how the proposed acquisitions might create value. Since Teets's acquisition strategy has met little success for the last twelve years, what reason would shareholders have to suppose it would improve in the future?

In July 1996, Michael Price, seeking to prevent the split-off by arguing that it was not in the best interests of shareholders, filed a claim with the Securities and Exchange Commission. A Dial spokesperson immediately responded that Dial felt that a delay was not in the best interest of Dial's shareholders and that the company still planned to go ahead with the split-off, which was scheduled for sometime in the fall of 1996.

Endnotes

1. *Moody's Transportation Manual,* 1987.
2. A. Stuart, "Greyhound Gets Ready for a New Driver," *Fortune,* March 3, 1966, pp. 34–38.
3. Greyhound Corporation, Annual Reports, 1966–1970.
4. Ibid.
5. Greyhound Corporation, Annual Report, 1980.
6. "Greyhound: A Big Sell-off Leaves It Built for Better Speed," *BusinessWeek,* July 25, 1983, pp. 88–90.
7. Greyhound Corporation, Annual Reports, 1970–1978.
8. "Greyhound's New Strategy: Slimmed Down and Decentralized, It's After More Market Share, 15% on Equity," *Dun's Business Month* (February 1984), 66–68.
9. "Greyhound: A Big Sell-off."
10. "Greyhound's New Strategy."
11. Greyhound Corporation, Annual Report, 1986.
12. Ibid.
13. S. Toy and J. H. Dobrzynski, "Will More Soap Help Greyhound Shine?" *BusinessWeek,* March 11, 1985, pp. 73–78.
14. "The Greyhound Corporation," *Wall Street Journal Transcript,* February 5, 1990, pp. 96, 204.
15. Greyhound Dial News Release, September 10, 1990.
16. "The Greyhound Corporation," pp. 96, 204.
17. Ibid.

CASE 32

Enron International in India

This case was prepared by Charles W. L. Hill of the University of Washington.

INTRODUCTION

Back in 1990, Enron, a Houston-based independent power company, established a subsidiary, Enron International, and gave it the mission of building and running power generation projects in the developing world. Enron's chairman appointed one of his protégés, Rebecca Mark, then only thirty-six years old, as CEO of the new unit. By 1997, the outspoken and photogenic Mark, who was fast gaining a reputation as one of the most dynamic businesswomen in America, had built Enron International into a global operation with sales of $1.1 billion, annual profits of $220 million, and a backlog of international energy projects worth more than $20 billion. The potential jewel in Enron International's crown was a growing presence in India. By the end of 1997, Enron International had plans to invest $20 billion in India. Getting to this point, however, had severely tested Mark's diplomatic skills and political acumen.

ENRON'S INDIA STRATEGY

Enron's interests in India date back to 1991, when the country's former prime minister, Narasimha Rao, visited the United States to seek help with India's economic development. Rao asked Enron if it was interested in independent power projects in the country. This request signaled a shift of policy in India. Since independence from Britain in 1947, political opinion in India had by and large been op-

This case is intended to be used as the basis for class discussion rather than to illustrate either effective or ineffective handling of the situation. This case was prepared by Charles W. L. Hill of the University of Washington. Used by permission.

posed to significant foreign direct investment on anything other than terms that were highly favorable to the host country. Indeed, for almost half a century, Indian politics had been strongly influenced by Gandhi's doctrine of *swadeshi*, or self-reliance. This had been translated into a presumption against foreign investment and a desire to see India build its own domestic industries under the protection of restrictions on foreign investment and high import tariffs.

However, by the 1990s the winds of ideological change were blowing through India. The national government seemed to be embracing a free market approach, which included substantial deregulation and the loosening of rules on foreign direct investment. Consistent with this, in October 1991 Rao's government liberalized India's domestic power-producing sector, allowing private developers, both Indian and foreign, to build and operate independent power projects with no restrictions on foreign equity ownership.

India's need for power was obvious. A plentiful supply of electric power is a key requirement for economic development, but India was suffering from chronic power shortages. At peak periods, demand for electricity often exceeded available power supply by more than 20 percent. Moreover, the installed capacity in the early 1990s, which amounted to around 80,000 megawatts, was working at only about 60 percent efficiency. Forecasts suggested that an extra 140,000 megawatts of capacity would be needed by 2005, but public money to finance such massive investments in infrastructure was scarce. In the mid 1990s, around 70 percent of India's electricity supply was being produced by state-owned electricity generation and distribution boards, which collectively were running up losses of more than $2 billion per year. Clearly, they could not afford to fund the required expansions in capacity.

Mark jumped on Rao's offer but quickly discovered that India's energy problems involved more than a simple lack of generating capacity. The country also lacked adequate supplies of fuel. To help solve these problems, Mark articulated a strategic vision that was audacious in scope. The vision called for Enron to invest up to $20 billion to become the largest distributor and consumer of liquefied natural gas (LNG) in India by 2010. Under the plan, Enron would set up two LNG terminals and regassification units in India, one at Dabhol in the state of Maharashtra, and one at Ennore in the state of Tamil Nadu. The company would construct two gas-based power-generating plants near the terminals. Enron would also build a network of pipelines to pipe the gas to its LNG terminals from oil and gas fields near Bombay, and then onward to its own and other power plants around the country. The Bombay fields, however, were not large enough to supply India's projected LNG needs, so the company also planned to import LNG from a facility that it was building in the Gulf State of Qatar. The Qatar facility would cost $4 billion to complete, and was being funded by a group of investors including the state-owned Qatar Gas & Pipeline Co., Enron International's parent company, and Royal Dutch Shell. Enron International had promised investors in the Qatar facility a 15 percent annual growth in shareholders' income. Achieving this goal, however, depended on the success of Mark's India strategy. Without India, Enron might lack sufficient customers to absorb the LNG output from its Qatar facility.

THE DABHOL PROJECT

By mid 1992, Mark was moving forward with the first stage of her plan. She was deep in negotiations with the Indian federal government and the government of the state of Maharashtra where Enron's Dabhol power plant was to be constructed. The Dabhol project was bold; Enron was to develop a 2,015-megawatt power plant that would be fired by LNG. The total cost for the project was well over $2 billion, making the Dabhol project the single largest foreign investment ever committed to India and the biggest independent power project in the world.

The choice of Dabhol for Enron's first investment in India was dictated by a number of factors. Located on India's western seaboard, the state of Maharashtra and its capital, Bombay, were enjoying a sustained period of political stability and economic growth. This had enabled the state to attract industry from other areas of India, such as the traditional industrial heartlands of Calcutta and eastern India. Economic growth in these regions had suffered under successive Communist governments at the state level. The Western seaboard was also closer to the Gulf States, and Qatar in particular, which would lower the costs of shipping LNG. Moreover, the state of Maharashtra was at that time governed by the Congress Party, the same party that governed the nation. Mark reasoned that Prime Minister Rao would be able to pressure the local state government to approve the project.

Mark was alert to the basic political realities in India. While the federal government in Delhi might in principle approve the project, she realized that Enron would also have to win approval from the Maharashtra state government and cultivate the approval of key players in India's extensive civil service. To get the Dabhol project approved, the company needed to get 170 different state and federal permits, to sort through fifty complicated legal questions, and to deal with a complex web of state and federal taxes. Reflecting on this process, Mark reported that

> I've had tea with every bureaucrat in India.... People (foreigners) don't understand how to get things done in India. Politicians lay out a plan, but that's different from working through the system. There's only one political level approval—that of the foreign investment board. But then there are all sorts of channels and procedures needed. Politicians will never intervene and force a bureaucrat to make a decision when an issue of process is at stake. This is where companies mess up and are confused.[1]

By early 1995, Enron had received full approval for the project and was proceeding with the initial construction. However, storm clouds were gathering on the political horizon of Maharashtra, and they spelled trouble for Enron. Throughout the negotiations, Maharashtra had been controlled by the Congress Party. Its local leader, Sharad Pawar, was a big supporter of Enron's Dabhol project. Unfortunately, during 1994 and early 1995 the popularity of the Congress Party started to decline. In 1994, a series of ethnic riots swept through Bombay. Anti-Muslim hysteria had been whipped up by Shiv Sena, a local militant Hindu nationalist party. The party was led by Bal Thackery, a former political cartoonist and an admirer of Adolf Hitler. To fight upcoming state elections in February 1995, Shiv Sena formed an alliance with a less extreme Hindu nationalist party, the BJP. In the event that the alliance won the state elections, Shiv Sena would control the local administration in Maharashtra, while the BJP would occupy any seats won by the alliance in the national parliament.

During the election campaign, Shiv Sena seized on the Dabhol project and used it to attack the Congress Party and its leader, Sharad Pawer. Shiv Sena claimed that Pawer had been bribed by Enron to support the Dabhol project. This played well in the court of public opinion in India, where in the words of one observer, "the popular belief is that any dealings with foreigners are bound to be either crooked or disadvantageous. Maybe 9 times out of 10 this is correct."[2] The BJP also warmed to this theme as the election campaign progressed, and began to champion the Gandhi doctrine of *swadeshi*. Both the BJP and Shiv Sena successfully contrasted their defense of Indian rights and Indian self-reliance with what they depicted as the corrupt machinations of Enron, Pawer, and the Congress Party.

Fuel was added to this fire when an Enron official, in testimony before a committee of the U.S. Congress that was dealing with foreign aid allocations, revealed that Enron had spent $20 million to educate Indians about the benefits of its various power projects in the country. (The Enron official made the apparently innocent suggestion that the U.S. government might want to use its foreign aid help with such educational campaigns). Elements of the Indian press, in concert with Shiv Sena, seized on this "revelation" to claim that the $20 million had been used primarily to "educate" corrupt officials such as Pawer in order to win approval for the Dabhol project—in other words, that much of the $20 million had been in the form of bribes. In the heat of the election campaign, it apparently mattered little that there was no evidence whatsoever that Enron had bribed anyone. Mud sticks, and the charges proved to be powerful ammunition. As a result, in February 1995 Pawer and the Congress Party were swept from power in the state of Maharashtra to be replaced by Shiv Sena and its new chief minister, Manohar Joshi.

After the election, the new government set up a committee, under the leadership of Gopinath Munde, the BJP deputy minister in the coalition, to review the Dabhol project. The committee was to review the charges of corruption and abuse that had been leveled at Enron during the election campaign. However, Rebecca Mark felt she was on solid ground. Enron had not done anything wrong, contracts had been signed, construction work on the project was under way, India clearly needed the power, and the agreements protected Enron from any unilateral breach of contract. If the state canceled the project, it would be hit with a $200 million cancellation fee.

In mid 1995, the state government committee reviewing the Dabhol project finished its report. The report was never published, although excerpts were leaked to the press and in them Enron was accused of deception and cost padding. Enron vigorously denied these charges. On the cost padding charges, Rebecca Mark later noted that "In India you are supposed to have a 20 percent import duty on equipment. But when it comes right down to it, very common in a project is that it doesn't end up being 20 percent but whatever the customs inspector wants it to be on the day you get there. So you have to price that risk in."[3] The implication was that a risk premium had been built into Enron's contract with the state of Maharashtra.

The report also criticized the previous administration for not putting the Dabhol project out to competitive bid. Privately, Enron officials noted that this was an absurd charge. After all, Enron had been invited to the country by Prime Minister Rao, it was Enron that had first suggested the Dabhol project, and Enron was the only foreign power producer apparently willing to shoulder the risk associated with such a large investment in the country. Reflecting this, Bob Pender, an independent lawyer who specializes in financing energy projects, noted that the lack of competitive bidding "was the opportunity cost of getting a company to come and create an industry."[4]

Significantly though, the committee was not able to uncover any evidence of corruption on the part of either Enron or Indian political officials. However, after having made such an issue of the project during the election, the Shiv Sena/BJP coalition was not yet ready to back down. On August 3, 1995, the state government issued a work stoppage order on the deal, after Enron had already spent $100 million.

Two days later, Enron served the state government with legal notice that it would pursue arbitration in London. The Maharashtra state government was now facing damages of at least $300 million, with the possibility of another $500 million on top of that. On August 12, Little & Co, which had acted as the lawyers for the Maharashtra state government for the previous twenty years, resigned and stated off the record that the state's position was indefensible. Top civil servants in the state also reportedly told Munde and Joshi that the government's position was untenable.

Simultaneously, Enron mounted a public relations campaign of its own. Enron ran full-page advertisements in Indian newspapers publicizing the benefits to India of its Dabhol project. It also prevailed on U.S. president Bill Clinton to call the Indian premier to try and get the project started again. By September, public opinion polls showed that 80 percent of the people in Maharashtra and 60 percent of those in India wanted the project restarted.

Despite rising pressure to restart the project, the Shiv Sena/BJP coalition government was unwilling to back off without getting something in return. By this point, however, it was clear that the best interests of all parties would be served by a compromise. Enron wanted to get the project back on track. It still had big plans for India, and then there was that plant in Qatar whose output was projected for India. The Maharashtra government, for its part, was facing the potential of heavy damages, and was rapidly losing support for its position. At the same time, the government needed evidence that its efforts had not been for naught; it needed to save face.

That fall Mark returned to the bargaining table, and a settlement was worked out. Enron agreed to cut the price it charged for power generated by the Dabhol project by 22.6 percent. In return, Enron walked away with a deal for a 2,450-megawatt plant, 450 megawatts bigger than the initial plant. According to Enron, the larger plant would realize much greater scale economies and allow Enron to maintain its projected rate of return on investment while simultaneously cutting prices.

AFTERMATH

Reflecting on her Indian experience, Mark suggests that the key to Enron's success was its intention to help India solve a problem and to stay engaged in the country for the long term. She and her colleagues have spent six years coming to India, meeting with the same people, talking about the same projects. Says Mark, "I don't think that anyone who works with us doubts our intentions, goodwill, or long term commitment to India. We've earned a place on the list of friendlies."[5] Mark also believes that Enron's appeal to the people of India ultimately served the company well. She concludes that "Our experience tells us that India's a good environment for foreign investment, and a market where foreign investors are seen as necessary. If anything, our experience proves the strength of the system in India to withstand a lot of assaults from different places. Even though the political system is shaky, the judiciary and the business system work."[6]

In February 1997, Enron reaffirmed its commitment to India when it submitted a proposal to build five to seven more power plants in the country at a total cost of $10 billion. As for the Dabhol plant, the first phase of the project, which will generate 740 megawatts of power, was completed in December 1998, three months ahead of schedule.

For India's part, there is little doubt that Enron's experience with the Dabhol project was something of a public relations setback. Although ultimately the outcome reaffirmed the country's commitment to encouraging foreign direct investment, the perception has been created that the shifting political landscape, bureaucratic rules, and the crosscurrents between national and state governments, make India a difficult place in which to invest. As noted by a former U.S. ambassador to India, William Clark, the Dabhol incident "Sends the right signals, but unfortunately it sent off the wrong signals for a while. Just like a retraction in a newspaper, it will take a long time for people to notice."[7]

Endnotes

1. From C. Hill, "How Rebecca Mark Solved India," *Institutional Investor* (January 1998), 28G.
2. B. Edwards and M. Shukla, "The Mugging of Enron," *Euromoney* (October 1995), 28–33.
3. P. Sibbald, "You Have to Be Pushy and Aggressive," *Business Week*, February 24, 1997, p. 56.
4. Edwards and Shukla, "The Mugging of Enron."
5. Hill, "How Rebecca Mark Solved India."
6. "It's a Done Deal," *Journal of Commerce*, December 20, 1996, p. 7B.
7. Ibid. The following sources were also used in the preparation of this case: T. Mack, "High Finance with a Touch of Theater," *Forbes*, May 18, 1998, p. 140–154; G. McWilliams, "More Power to India," *Business Week*, January 22, 1996, p. 62; and M. Nicholson, "Dabhol Plant Finally Gets Green Light," *Financial Times*, January 9, 1996, p. 6

CASE 33

Nestlé: Global Strategy

This case was prepared by Charles W. L. Hill of the University of Washington.

INTRODUCTION

Nestlé is one of the oldest of all multinational businesses. The company was founded in Switzerland in 1866 by Heinrich Nestlé, who established Nestlé to distribute "milk food"—a type of infant food that he had invented that was made from powered milk, baked food, and sugar. From its very early days, the company looked to other countries for growth opportunities, establishing its first foreign offices in London in 1868. In 1905, the company merged with the Anglo-Swiss Condensed Milk, thereby broadening its product line to include both condensed milk and infant formulas. Forced by Switzerland's small size to look outside for growth opportunities, Nestlé established condensed milk and infant food processing plants in the United States and Britain in the late nineteenth century, and in Australia, South America, Africa and Asia in the first three decades of the twentieth century.

In 1929, Nestlé moved into the chocolate business when it acquired the activities of a Swiss chocolate maker. This was followed in 1938 by the development of Nestlé's most revolutionary product, Nescafé, the world's first soluble coffee drink. In the period after the second world war Nestlé continued to expand into other areas of the food business, primarily through a series of acquisitions that included Maggi (1947), Cross & Blackwell (1960), Findus (1962), Libby's (1970), Stouffer's (1973), Carnation (1985), Rowntree (1988), and Perrier (1992).

This case is intended to be used as the basis for class discussion rather than as an illustration of either effective or ineffective handling of the situation. This case was prepared by Charles W. L. Hill, University of Washington. Used by permission.

As a result of this growth strategy, by the late 1990s Nestlé had 500 factories in 76 countries and sold its products in a staggering 193 nations—just about every country in the world. In 1998, the company generated sales of close to CHF 72 billion ($51 billion), only 1 percent of which were made in its home country. Similarly, only 3 percent of its 210,000 employees were located in Switzerland. Nestlé was the world's biggest maker of infant formula, powdered milk, chocolates, instant coffee, soups, and mineral waters. It was number two in ice cream, breakfast cereals, and pet food. Roughly 38 percent of its food sales were made in Europe, 32 percent in the Americas, and 20 percent in Africa and Asia.

A GROWTH STRATEGY FOR THE TWENTY-FIRST CENTURY CHALLENGES TO GROWTH

Despite its undisputed success, by the early 1990s Nestlé realized that it faced significant challenges in maintaining its growth rate. The large western European and North American markets were now mature. In several countries, population growth had stagnated, and in some there had been a small decline in food consumption. Moreover, the retail environment in many Western nations had become increasingly challenging, and the balance of power was shifting away from the large scale manufacturers of branded foods and beverages and toward nationwide supermarket and discount chains.

Increasingly, retailers found themselves in the unfamiliar position of being able to play off manufacturers of branded foods against each other, bargaining down prices in the process. Particularly in Europe, this trend was enhanced by the successful

C462

introduction of private label brands by several of Europe's leading supermarket chains. The results included increased price competition in several key segments of the food and beverage market, such as cereals, coffee, and soft drinks.

At Nestlé, one response to these developments has been to look toward emerging markets in eastern Europe, Asia, and Latin America for growth possibilities. The logic is simple and obvious—a combination of economic and population growth, when coupled with the widespread adoption of market-oriented economic policies by the governments of many developing nations, makes for attractive growth opportunities. Many of these countries are still relatively poor, but their economies are growing rapidly. For example, if current economic growth forecasts come to pass, by 2010 there will be 700 million people in China and India that have income levels approaching those of Spain in the mid 1990s. As income levels rise, it is increasingly likely that consumers in these nations will start to substitute branded food products for basic foodstuffs, thereby creating a large market opportunity for companies such as Nestlé.

In general, the company's strategy has been to try and enter emerging markets early—hopefully before competitors—and build up a substantial position by selling basic food items that appeal to the local population base, such as infant formula, condensed milk, noodles, and tofu. By narrowing its initial market focus to just a handful of strategic brands, Nestlé claims it can simplify life, reduce risk, and concentrate its marketing resources and managerial effort on a limited number of key niches. The goal is to build a commanding market position in each of these niches. By pursuing such a strategy, Nestlé has taken as much as 85 percent of the market for instant coffee in Mexico, 66 percent of the market for powdered milk in the Philippines, and 70 percent of the market for soups in Chile. As income levels rise, the company progressively moves out from these niches, introducing more upscale items, such as mineral water, chocolate, cookies, and prepared foodstuffs.

Although the company is known worldwide for several key brands, such as Nescafé, it uses local brands in a wide range of local markets. Indeed, although it owns 8,500 brands, only 750 of them are registered in more than one country, and only 80 are registered in more than ten countries. While Nestlé will use the same "global brands" in multiple developed markets, in the developing world it focuses more effort on trying to optimize ingredients and processing technology to local conditions, and then using a brand name that resonates locally. Customization rather than globalization, therefore, is the key to its strategy in emerging markets.

EXECUTING THE STRATEGY

Successful execution of the strategy for developing markets requires a degree of flexibility, an ability to adapt in often unforeseen ways to local conditions, and a long-term perspective that puts building a sustainable business before short-term profitability. In Nigeria, for example, a crumbling road system, aging trucks, and the danger of violence forced the company to rethink its traditional distribution methods. Instead of operating a central warehouse, as is its preference in most nations, it has built a network of small warehouses around the country. For safety reasons, trucks carrying Nestlé goods are allowed to travel only during the day, and frequently under armed guard. Marketing also poses challenges in Nigeria. With little opportunity for typical Western style advertising on television or billboards, the company has resorted to hiring local singers to go to towns and villages offering a mix of entertainment and product demonstrations.

China provides another interesting example of local adaptation and a long-term focus. After thirteen years of talks, Nestlé was formally invited into China in 1987 by the government of Heilongjiang province. Nestlé opened a plant to produce powdered milk and infant formula there in 1990 but quickly realized that the local rail and road infrastructure was totally inadequate and inhibited the collection of milk and delivery of finished products. Rather than try and make do with the local infrastructure, Nestlé embarked an ambitious plan to establish its own distribution network, known as "milk roads," between twenty-seven villages in the region and factory collection points, called "chilling centers." Farmers brought their milk—often on bicycles or carts—to the centers, where it was weighed and analyzed. Unlike the government, Nestlé paid the farmers promptly. Suddenly, the farmers had an incentive to produce milk, and many bought a second cow, increasing the cow population in the district by 3,000 to 9,000 in eighteen months. Area managers then organized a delivery system that used dedicated vans to deliver the milk to Nestlé's factory.

Although at first glance this might seem to be a very costly solution, Nestlé calculated that the long-term benefits would be substantial. Indeed, Nestlé's strategy is similar to that undertaken by many European and American companies during the first waves of industrialization in those countries. There, too, companies often had to invest in infrastructure that we now take for granted in order to get production off the ground. Sure enough, once the infrastructure was in place, production took off. In 1990, 316 tons of powdered milk and infant formula was produced. By 1994, the output exceeded 10,000 tons, and the company decided to triple capacity. Based on this experience, Nestlé has decided to build another two powdered milk factories in China and is aiming to generate sales of $700 million by 2000.

Nestlé is pursuing a similar long-term bet in the Middle East—an area that most multinational food companies have little presence in. Collectively, the Middle East accounts for only about 2 percent of Nestlé's worldwide sales, and the individual markets are very small. However, Nestlé's long-term strategy is based on the assumption that regional conflicts will subside and intraregional trade will expand as trade barriers between countries in the area come down. Once that happens, Nestlé's factories in the Middle East should be able to sell throughout the region, thereby realizing scale economies. In anticipation of this development, Nestlé has established a network of factories in five countries in hopes that each will someday supply the entire region with different products. The company currently makes ice cream in Dubai, soups and cereals in Saudi Arabia, yogurt and bouillon in Egypt, chocolate in Turkey, and ketchup and instant noodles in Syria. For the present, Nestlé can survive in these markets by using local materials and focusing on local demand. The Syrian factory, for example, relies on products that use tomatoes, a major local agricultural product. Syria also produces wheat, which is the main ingredient in instant noodles. Even if trade barriers don't come down anytime soon, Nestlé has indicated that it will remain committed to the region. By using local inputs and focusing on local consumer needs, it has been able to earn a good rate of return in the region, even though the individual markets are small.

Despite its successes in places such as China and parts of the Middle East, not all of Nestlé's

moves have worked out so well. Like several other Western companies, Nestlé has had its problems in Japan, where a failure to adapt its coffee brand to local conditions meant the loss of a significant market opportunity to another Western company, Coca-Cola. For years, Nestlé's instant coffee brand was the dominant coffee product in Japan. In the 1960s, cold canned coffee (which can be purchased from soda vending machines) started to gain a following in Japan. Nestlé dismissed the product as just a coffee-flavored drink, rather than the real thing, and declined to enter the market. Nestlé's local partner at the time, Kirin Beer, was so incensed at Nestlé's refusal to enter the canned coffee market that it broke off its relationship with the company. In contrast, Coca-Cola entered the market with a product developed specifically for this segment of the Japanese market, Georgia. By leveraging its existing distribution channel, Coca-Cola was able to capture a 40 percent share of the $4-billion-a-year market for canned coffee in Japan. Nestlé, which failed to enter the market until the 1980s, has only a 4 percent share.

While Nestlé has built businesses from the ground up in many emerging markets, such as Nigeria and China, in others it will purchase local companies if suitable candidates can be found. The company pursued just such a strategy in Poland, which it entered in 1994 by purchasing Goplana, the country's second largest chocolate manufacturer. With the collapse of communism and the opening up of the Polish market, income levels in Poland have started to rise, and so has chocolate consumption. Once chocolate was a scarce item, but the market grew by 8 percent per annum throughout the 1990s. To take advantage of this opportunity, Nestlé has pursued a strategy of evolution, rather than revolution. It has kept the top management of the company staffed with locals— as it does in most of its operations around the world—and carefully adjusted Goplana's product line to better match local opportunities. At the same time, it has pumped money into Goplana's marketing, which has enabled the unit to gain share from several other chocolate makers in the country. Still, competition in the market is intense. Eight companies, including several foreign-owned enterprises, such as the market leader, Wedel, which is owned by PepsiCo, are vying for market share, and this has depressed prices and profit margins, despite the healthy volume growth.

MANAGEMENT STRUCTURE

Nestlé is a decentralized organization. Responsibility for operating decisions is pushed down to local units, which typically enjoy a high degree of autonomy with regard to decisions involving pricing, distribution, marketing, human resources, and so on. At the same time, the company is organized into seven worldwide strategic business units (SBUs) that have responsibility for high-level strategic decisions and business development. There is, for example, a strategic business unit that focuses on coffee and beverages. Another one focuses on confectionery and ice cream. These SBUs engage in overall strategy development, including acquisitions and market entry strategy. In recent years, two-thirds of Nestlé's growth has come from acquisitions, so this is a critical function. Running in parallel to this structure is a regional organization that divides the world into five major geographical zones, such as Europe, North America, and Asia. The regional organizations assist in the overall strategy development process and are responsible for developing regional strategies (an example would be Nestlé's strategy in the Middle East, which was discussed earlier). Neither the SBU nor regional managers, however, get involved in local operating or strategic decisions on anything other than an exceptional basis.

Although Nestlé makes intensive use of local managers, to knit its diverse worldwide operations together the company relies on its "expatriate army." This is a cadre of managers who spend the bulk of their careers on foreign assignments, moving from one country to the next. There are around 700 individuals in this group. Selected primarily on the basis of their ability, drive, and willingness to live a quasi-nomadic lifestyle, these individuals often work in half a dozen different nations during the course of their career. Nestlé also uses management development programs as a strategic tool for bringing together managers and creating an *esprit de corps*. At Rive-Reine, the company's international training center in Switzerland, the company brings together managers from around the world, at different stages in their careers, for specially targeted development programs of two to three weeks' duration. The objective of these programs is to give the managers a better understanding of Nestlé's culture and strategy, and to give them access to the company's top management.

The Research and Development operation has a special place within Nestlé, which is perhaps not surprising for a company that was established to commercialize innovative foodstuffs. The R&D function comprises eighteen different groups, which operate in eleven countries throughout the world. Nestlé spends approximately 1 percent of its annual sales revenue on R&D and has 3,100 employees dedicated to the function. Around 70 percent of the R&D budget is spent on development initiatives. These initiatives focus on developing products and processes that fulfill market needs, as identified by the SBUs, in concert with regional and local managers. So, for example, Nestlé instant noodle products were originally developed by the R&D group in response to the perceived needs of local operating companies through the region. The company also has longer-term development projects, which focus on new technological platforms, such as non-animal protein sources or agricultural biotechnology products.

References

Hall, W. "Strength of Brands Is Key to Success." *Financial Times*, November 30, 1998, p. 2.

"How to Conquer China (and the World) with Instant Noodles." *Economist*, June 17, 1995.

Lorenz, C. "Sugar Daddy." *Financial Times*, April 20, 1994, p. 19.

Michaels, D. "Chocolate Giants Worldwide Find Themselves Sweet on Polish Market." *Wall Street Journal*, December 12, 1997.

Nestlé. Key Facts and History (www.nestle.com).

Rapoport, C. "Nestlé's Brand-Building Machine." *Fortune*, September 19, 1994, p. 147.

Steinmetz, G. and T. Parker-Rope. "All over the Map." *Wall Street Journal*, September 26, 1996, p. R4.

Sullivan, M. "Nestlé Is Looking to Coffee Market in Russia for Sales." *Wall Street Journal*, August 7, 1998, p. B7.

Pharmacia & Upjohn

This case was prepared by Gareth R. Jones of Texas A & M University.

In September 1995 the Upjohn Company, one of the largest pharmaceutical companies in the United States, announced that it was merging with Pharmacia, the largest Swedish pharmaceutical company. With Upjohn's annual sales of $3.3 billion and Pharmacia's of $3.6 billion, the merger created the ninth largest pharmaceutical company in the world, Pharmacia & Upjohn. What prompted Upjohn's management to seek a merger that would change the future of the company forever? To answer this question, it is necessary to study Upjohn's history and its performance in the turbulent pharmaceutical industry of the last decade.

HISTORY

For the first seventy-three years of its existence, the Upjohn Company was a family-owned and -operated, domestic pharmaceutical company. In 1885, W. E. Upjohn was granted a patent on a manufacturing process that produced a "friable" pill. The new pill disintegrated rapidly in the body to speed the release of medication. This friability contrasted with the hardness of many of the mass-produced pills of the day, which often passed through the body without releasing their contents. This manufacturing process and the secrecy that surrounded it fueled the early growth of the company and made it difficult for other companies to imitate the popular product. The founder speeded the company's growth with a policy of selling his pills at

This case is intended to be used as a basis for class discussion rather than as an illustration of either effective or ineffective handling of the situation. This case was prepared by Gareth R. Jones, Texas A & M University. Used by permission.

about half the price of the old-style, mass-produced pills, generating considerable hostility from competitors in doing so. The company expanded its product line quickly, offering 500 products by 1892 and 2,000 by 1900.

By 1900, the new technology of compressed tablets superseded the friable pill, and Upjohn had to imitate the innovations of other companies and produce the new tablets. Tablets that disintegrated rapidly in the body were much easier to mass-produce. The company began featuring tablets and created a tablet department to speed product development.

From its beginnings, Upjohn was strongly aware of the need to develop marketing strengths to complement the company's research and development and manufacturing skills. Realizing early that the profit potential from mass-produced tablets would be low, Upjohn emphasized the need to develop and market quality-based, high-price drug products that would give higher profit margins. Perceiving the company as operating in a luxury market, he had the insight to switch its focus from pills to tablets and to emphasize product characteristics. For example, he pioneered the development of pleasantly flavored drugs to suit consumers' tastes. One result was an important innovation called phenolax, a sweetly flavored laxative. It proved to be a big seller for more than forty years.

In the next two decades, Upjohn added a number of promising research areas. In 1912, bacterial vaccines became part of the company's product line. Research was begun in endocrinology and digitalis extracts for heart failure in 1914. A pleasant-tasting alkalizer called Citrocarbonate was introduced in 1921 and reached $1 million in annual sales by 1926, the first Upjohn product to do so. This product and the intensive sales effort that accompanied it marked the emergence of the company as a first-class pharmaceutical house. A succession of other introductions followed, including new flavored versions of cough syrup, cod liver oil, and Kaopectate, still a best-selling antidiarrhea product. Each of these research efforts was stimulated by a perceived need to respond to the demands of the medical community for improved drug products.

Upjohn was always sensitive to the needs of its main "distributor," the doctors who prescribed its products. An aggressive sales push directed toward pharmacists and doctors helped the company to grow through the tough 1930s and into the years of World War II. The medical department was created in 1937 by a member of the founding family, Gifford Upjohn, to upgrade the company's contacts with physicians. This focus became a hallmark of sales efforts at Upjohn. Through the decades that followed, the company continued to differentiate its products and match its sales strategy to the changing composition of the medical profession.

Much of the company's growth through the 1930s and 1940s was tied to vitamins. In 1929, Upjohn was the first to produce a standardized combination of vitamins A and D in the United States. Vitamins accounted for half of the $40 million in sales in 1945 and marked the company as a leader in nutritional supplements. Other products critical to Upjohn's growth included Kaopectate, estrogenic hormone products introduced in the 1930s, antibiotics, and an antidiabetic drug brought out in the 1940s and 1950s.

By 1952, the research department had 421 employees, who viewed their research output as second in quality only to that of Merck & Co. among domestic pharmaceutical companies. The department began to establish broad research areas, which are still important to the company today: antibiotics, steroids, antidiabetes agents, nonsteroidal anti-inflammatory drugs, and central nervous system agents.

The progress of the company's research efforts led to increasing demand for specialty chemicals to manufacture new drug introductions. The company had purchased standardized chemicals in the past, but the growing need for unique materials led to the establishment of the fine chemicals manufacturing division in 1949 to supply the company with its own products. The division expanded into external sales, and by 1984, 40 percent of its production was for other companies.

After World War II, the Upjohn Company continued a modest export program, sending most of its foreign sales representatives to Central and South America. The creation of the export division in 1952 was the first strong corporate signal that management was committed to competing globally. The division was formed in reaction to the globalization strategies of the leading domestic drug companies, which recognized the potential in developing a worldwide market for their products.

In 1958, the twenty-member board of directors, eleven of whom were related directly or by marriage to the founder, voted to recommend public ownership. The following year, the Upjohn Company was formally accepted for listing and trading on the New York Stock Exchange. The decision to go public did not end the involvement of the extended family of the founder, W. E. Upjohn, but it did give the company the additional financial resources it needed to become a stronger force in the global pharmaceutical market.

The company continued to expand its international scope quickly to include sales subsidiaries in Canada, England, and Australia. Through the 1960s and 1970s, it added more subsidiaries and sales offices and built two major production facilities outside the continental United States: one in Belgium in 1963 and the other in Puerto Rico in 1974. By the mid 1980s these plants, in combination with the principal facility in Kalamazoo, Michigan, produced pharmaceuticals for sale in more than 150 countries.

Upjohn's first large venture out of pharmaceuticals came via its entry into animal health products in the late 1940s, when it repackaged several human products, such as antibiotics, for animal use. New products specifically for animals began flowing in 1952, and a sales force targeting veterinarians was established, growing from 1 person in 1956 to 20 in 1957. The sales force gradually increased to 130 by the mid 1980s.

Other agricultural products were added over time. After deciding against entry into fertilizers, the company acquired its core seed company, Asgrow Seed Company, in 1968 to develop new, improved strains of seeds. It added another top-ten domestic seed company, O's Gold, in 1983. The latter was chosen because its sales force and products complemented Asgrow's. In 1974, Upjohn acquired Cobb Breeding Corporation, a producer of chicken broiler breeders, to continue its expansion into animal drugs. In 1986, the company formed a joint venture with Tyson Foods, Inc., to further expand its broiler operations.

Nonagricultural diversification began in the 1960s. The company started manufacturing polymer chemical products in 1962, with the purchase of the Carwin Company, which was combined with the fine chemicals manufacturing operations. The company entered cosmetics in 1964, when several other pharmaceutical companies were doing likewise. In 1969, it entered home nursing services when it purchased Homemakers, Inc.

The chemicals business was profitable for many years. After profits peaked in 1979, however, rapid decline set in because of a down cycle in the principal markets for chemicals. The polymer chemicals operation was sold in 1985, but the fine chemicals manufacturing division was retained. The cosmetics business never proved very profitable and was liquidated in 1974. The home nursing service business was renamed Upjohn Healthcare Services. It quickly added new locations and became the market leader in 1974.

By the mid 1980s, Upjohn had become a global, research-based manufacturer and marketer of pharmaceuticals, chemicals, agricultural seeds and specialties, and health services. In 1987, it had research, manufacturing, sales, and distribution facilities in more than 200 locations worldwide. The company generated almost $2.3 billion in sales in 1986, its centennial year, from two broad industrial segments. First, Upjohn's World-wide Human Health Care Businesses, which concentrates on the development, manufacture, and marketing of drug products globally, accounted for almost 82 percent of total sales in 1986. Second, the agricultural division, which develops and supplies seeds and drugs for use in agriculture and animal production, accounted for slightly more than 18 percent of the company's sales.

Globally, in 1986, 67 percent of Upjohn's sales revenues were generated in the United States, 15 percent in Europe, and 18 percent were scattered elsewhere across the world. By 1986, Upjohn's share of the worldwide pharmaceutical market was 1.5 percent, and top management's ambition was to achieve a minimum of 2 percent of the market by 1990. The realization of this goal would move Upjohn from among the top-fifteen to among the top-ten drug companies globally.

The middle to late 1980s proved to be a turning point in Upjohn's history, however, as a result of changes in both the domestic and global pharmaceutical industry and because of a series of internal problems that became evident in the company at this time. These problems were to plague Upjohn for the next decade, and it was the attempt to resolve them that led Upjohn's management to seek the merger with Pharmacia in 1995.

THE PHARMACEUTICAL INDUSTRY ENVIRONMENT

By the late 1970s and early 1980s, important changes were reshaping competition in the domestic and global pharmaceutical markets. First, more countries were imposing greater regulation on the drug approval process. In the United States, the Kefauver-Harris amendment of 1962 placed major new constraints on pharmaceutical manufacturers. They required that companies set forth substantial proof that a drug was safe and effective before the FDA could allow it on the market. As a result of this legislation, the new-drug introduction process became considerably longer and more expensive, which was viewed by many as the single most important nonscientific event to affect the industry since World War II.

The Kefauver-Harris amendment marked the beginning of substantially increased regulation of the domestic pharmaceutical industry. As drug approval time lengthened, valuable years of patent protection were being eroded. The Waxman-Hatch Act of 1984 reflected the tremendous growth in domestic political influence of the Generic Pharmaceutical Industry Association (GPIA).

Another major thrust of the bill was to speed the introduction of generic drugs after patent expiration in order to reduce their price. This put increasing pressure on the profits of the company that developed a new drug. Development costs were estimated to approach $100 million for each new drug introduced in 1986, and they are $150 million today. To placate the large drug companies, the bill guaranteed several drug companies, including Upjohn, the exclusive rights for five years beyond normal patent length to market four major drugs each. These patent extensions were to compensate for the FDA's slow handling of drug registrations over the previous few years.

However, by 1990 approvals for generic copies of patent-expired drugs were being issued at a very rapid pace, and the large drug companies were experiencing price competition on many fronts. Large pharmaceutical companies, including Upjohn, came under intense pressure during the 1990s. In the early 1990s, for example, Upjohn faced the prospect of a loss of patent protection on four of its major revenue-generating drugs: Xanax, an antidepressant; Halcion, a sleeping pill; Micronase, a treatment for diabetes; and Ansaid, an anti-inflammatory agent. Upjohn lost more than $400 million in annual revenues as generic drug companies began producing their own versions of these drugs. In fact, Upjohn avoided losing more money only because it began to produce a generic version of its own drug, Xanax, allowing it to keep 80 percent of prescriptions of the drug. This marked a major move for Upjohn into the production of low-priced generic drugs and over-the-counter drugs sold under its own brand name.

Similar legislative pressures to reduce drug prices were mounting in many other countries. Between 1981 and 1984, the Japanese government ordered price reductions on drugs averaging 40.1 percent. Such legislation marked an industry trend toward, as Upjohn's president and chief operating officer, Lawrence C. Hoff, put it, a "two-tier industry with innovators in one group and a large number of generic manufacturers in the other segment, competing fiercely on the sole basis of price." In the 1990s, many drug companies such as Upjohn have been fighting to gain a foothold in both markets to increase their revenues in a more competitive marketplace.

Many countries also had begun protectionist campaigns, restricting drug marketing to products manufactured by the domestic industry. Furthermore, many foreign companies benefited from development support from their respective governments, allowing them to avoid the full cost of their research efforts. Since regulatory procedures, processes, and time orientations differ considerably from one country to another, domestic companies often experienced difficulty in obtaining information on how drugs move through foreign regulatory agencies. Although an attempt to achieve standardization of clinical procedures and disseminate intelligence on postmarketing response of users through an international information network was under way in the 1980s, it never came to fruition.

With increasing competition in research and increasing difficulty and costs in achieving regulatory approval, drug companies began concentrating their research in specific fields of medicine in order to reduce the cost of developing new drugs. To maintain their profitability, companies began specializing in the world's three most lucrative markets for new drugs: heart disease, anti-inflammatory agents and analgesics, and antibiotics. This concentration of resources by major companies in a few specific areas was suggested by an Upjohn spokesperson to be the cause of the scarcity of new drugs classified as breakthrough developments by the FDA in recent years. However, the slowdown in drug innovation seems to be on the verge of reversal. The advent of biotechnology has fueled a surge in new global pharmaceutical products as cures and medications for major diseases begin to appear, albeit at a slower pace than expected.

Another major environmental threat to Upjohn arose from the changing U.S. pharmaceutical environment in the 1990s. In the early 1990s, the new Clinton administration championed the introduction of a national health care system and also proposed that in the future drug companies should be strictly regulated in the amount they could charge for new and existing drugs. Because this would obviously eat into the profits of the large drug companies, their stock price declined.

Although these proposals eventually came to nothing, another major trend was developing in the 1990s: the emergence of managed health care by health maintenance organizations (HMOs). HMOs are national chains of medical and health centers that employ doctors and buy drugs in huge quantities from major pharmaceutical companies. Because they buy in such bulk, HMOs can bargain with pharmaceutical companies for lower prices, and this occurred during the 1990s and squeezed the profit margins of these companies. Moreover, besides pressures from HMOs, mail-order drug companies, such as Medco, sprang up. By virtue of their national customer base and huge buying power, they were also able to bargain with the large drug companies for lower prices by threatening to switch suppliers.

Finally, global competition became intense in the 1990s as the increasing costs of developing drugs, combined with reduced patent protection and competition from generic drug makers, put pressure on pharmaceutical makers to recoup their investments on a global level. In the 1990s, drug companies could only hope to be as profitable as they have been in the past if they could successfully market a drug on a global level.

Thus, pharmaceutical companies have experienced significant environmental challenges in the last decade, challenges that are still becoming stronger. First, there has been increasing price competition in the health care industry from the rapid growth of generic drug companies. Second, there has been an increase in legislative pressures on new drug development, both at home and abroad. Third, there has been an increase in global competition as drug companies vie with each other on a worldwide basis.

In response to all these pressures, a wave of merger activity occurred in the pharmaceutical industry in the 1990s. Merck bought Medco, the national mail-order drug supply company mentioned earlier, for $6.6 billion in 1993; American Home Products bought American Cyanamid for $9.6 billion in 1994; Eli Lilly bought PCS Health Systems, another mail-order drug company, for $4 billion; and Wellcome bought Glaxo Holdings in 1995 for $14.2 billion. The increasing consolidation of the global pharmaceutical industry is still continuing as companies fight to position themselves for the events in the next century. Clearly, the problem facing Upjohn's management was how to maintain its growth in the domestic and international markets in the face of this increasing industry competition and regulatory pressure. Upjohn, with its very small share of the global market, realized it had to find a global partner if it was to stay in the big league.

UPJOHN'S NEW CORPORATE STRATEGY

In 1990, Upjohn stated that its pharmaceutical business strategy to the year 2000 was to ensure that it delivered the greatest volume of quality pharmaceuticals to the greatest number of people globally and, at the same time, maintained an appropriate return on investment to ensure its continued growth. Three goals were particularly stressed: (1) sales growth (with concurrent market share growth); (2) a continuing growth in return on investment; and (3) competition based on high quality rather than low price.

The aggressive nature of this approach was indicated by Upjohn's quest to become one of the top ten drug companies by the mid 1990s. During the early 1990s, however, it became clear that achieving these goals would be difficult because of a number of internal problems that had arisen at this time.

One of its first problems was that the number of new promising drugs waiting in its product-development pipeline for FDA approval dropped off precipitously in the 1990s. Its previous blockbuster drugs, such as Xanax and Halcion, were losing their patent protection, and these drugs had not been followed by new blockbusters. As a result, during the early 1990s, Upjohn faced the prospect of flat revenues, which would not help it to achieve its ambitious goals.

The lack of new drugs in the pipeline was not the result of a lack of investment in research and development. Upjohn continued to invest heavily in R&D. For example, Upjohn invested heavily in biotechnology as a way of promoting new product development. Dr. Ralph E. Christofferson, a long-time consultant, was hired by the company, assigned a budget, given a custom-constructed facility, and instructed to hire the best people in the field. The 150-person staff began working with research professionals in Upjohn's other businesses to show them how the new technology could help applied-research efforts in both human health services and agriculture. However, the pace of new product development was disappointing, and costs were rising. Under any circumstances, the development of new drugs is a very uncertain and risky process, and it has been estimated that only one out of ten to fifteen drugs that start the development process come to the market—hence, the high prices that drug companies are forced to charge.

Besides the lack of new products in the pipeline, Upjohn's previous strategies of vertical integration and diversification were causing problems. Vertical integration had been a part of Upjohn's strategy since its inception. Upjohn pursued backward integration into the production of fine chemicals so that it could maintain quality control from initial chemical manufacture to the final packaging of its products in order to protect the quality of its drugs. Upjohn's production unit purchased most of its bulk chemicals from Upjohn's chemicals unit. In the 1990s, however, vertical integration was proving an expensive strategy that raised costs and did little to increase the bottom line. It had become clear that in many cases it was now cheaper to buy rather than make many of the chemicals that the company needed, so that the costs of vertical integration were now outweighing the benefits.

Similarly, Upjohn's diversification efforts had not produced the gains that had been expected. Its Asgrow seeds division, while profitable, was far removed from its core pharmaceutical business, and few synergies had been obtained. Its home health care business was similarly far removed from the company's core activities. The costs associated with managing all these different businesses were rising, sucking up a lot of top management's time, and did not seem to promise much of a return.

In the early 1990s, Upjohn's top management began to realize that its diversification efforts were not helping the company and were unlikely to help it achieve its central mission of becoming a top-ten global pharmaceutical company. So it sold off various of its chemicals businesses and its home health care business. However, the turning point for Upjohn came in 1994, when Theodore Cooper, Upjohn's long-time CEO, died and was replaced by John L. Zabriskie, one of Merck's former top managers. Zabriskie took a long, hard look at Upjohn's current strategy, and he immediately decided that Upjohn's strategy of using acquisitions to achieve its objectives of diversification and expansion in health and agriculture was not working. Zabriskie decided that he needed to restructure Upjohn, and he moved quickly to do so.

In early 1994, Zabriskie sold off what were now regarded as noncore assets, such as Asgrow Seeds and the chicken-breeding venture with Tyson Foods, among others, getting the company out of the agricultural business. He also eliminated 1,400 managerial jobs by restructuring and consolidating Upjohn's manufacturing and sales and marketing operations. For example, he decreased the number of Upjohn's global manufacturing sites to reduce excess capacity and operating costs in the years ahead. Then, he restructured its U.S. pharmaceutical sales and marketing efforts to focus solely on large customers such as health care systems, HMOs, and insurance providers. Because of Upjohn's new strategy, sales for 1994 reached $3.3 billion, slightly below 1993 sales, but net earnings jumped by 25 percent as costs fell.

Zabriskie then turned his attention to the company's research and development operations. He realized that it was here, in the development of important new pharmaceutical products, that the company's future lay. He decided to refocus the company's R&D efforts on developing thirty major products aimed at product markets that seemed to offer the greatest prospects for future new-product development. Many other R&D programs were terminated to save money. Then, Zabriskie pumped more money into R&D to promote these thirty new products. The company spent more than $600 million in 1994, which represented more than 18 percent of sales and was above the industry average, to speed the development of new products to the marketplace.

In the process of refocusing Upjohn's efforts, however, Zabriskie realized that, at best, all that these remedies offered was a short-term fix for the company's problems. It had became clear to him that, especially in view of the wave of mergers taking place within the industry, Upjohn was increasingly becoming a prospective takeover target for another pharmaceutical company seeking a quick way to become a major player. Zabriskie had to find a means of raising Upjohn's global presence and speeding the new-product development process. So even before he had finished with these major restructuring efforts, he convened a meeting of the company's top twenty executives in the summer of 1994 to develop a plan to take Upjohn into the next century as one of the top ten global pharmaceutical companies.

It became clear from this meeting that none of these executives thought that Upjohn could become a major global player on its own and that the company could not wait for its next generation of drugs to be approved for sale over the next five to ten years if it was to avoid being taken over. Zabriskie and his managers decided that Upjohn must seek a merger partner, one that could remedy Upjohn's weaknesses with its strengths. Accordingly, Zabriskie began to analyze the global pharmaceutical companies that had not yet been taken over to find a potential partner.

Enter Pharmacia

Jan Ekberg, chief executive of Pharmacia, was also very aware of the merger movement proceeding in the pharmaceutical industry. Since 1992, when the previously state-owned company had been privatized, he had been approached by several other European pharmaceutical companies about a possible merger. These companies had realized the potential of Pharmacia, because it had a very strong product-development process, with several promising new drugs in the pipeline. Ekberg was not tempted by these merger opportunities because he saw that Pharmacia's major weakness was its lack of developed sales and marketing channels in the United States, the world's biggest drug market. He realized that to become a global player, Pharmacia would need a strong presence in the U.S. market and that the way to do this was to search for a U.S. partner.

When Zabriskie took over at Upjohn, Ekberg saw an opportunity for a distribution deal between the two companies. He saw that Pharmacia's well-developed sales and marketing operations in Europe could efficiently handle the sales of Upjohn's products in Europe, and he saw that Upjohn's U.S. sales and marketing network would provide an avenue to distribute Pharmacia's new drugs in the United States. Ekberg called Zabriskie to discuss the distribution agreement, but Zabriskie, on the lookout for a merger partner, was thinking along different lines.

Like Ekberg, he saw that a combined distribution operation between Pharmacia and Upjohn would allow both companies to offer a much wider product line to HMOs and national drug-supply companies throughout the United States and Europe. Combined distribution operations and a larger presence would give them a better bargaining position and an opportunity to increase global sales volume. However, Zabriskie also saw that, in the short run, the many new drugs in Pharmacia's drug pipeline would compensate for the lack of new drugs in Upjohn's and remedy Upjohn's major weakness in this area. Given his recent cost-cutting efforts, he also saw that there might be many other areas in which a combined Pharmacia and Upjohn could reduce costs. Pharmacia began to look like the ideal merger partner.

Zabriskie proposed a meeting in Washington, D.C., which quickly led to a whole string of meetings across Europe as a surprised Ekberg began to warm up to the idea of a formal merger rather than just a strategic alliance through a distribution agreement. After some negotiations, both men bought into the idea and began the process of convincing their major stockholders to agree to the merger. They pointed out that after a merger a combined Pharmacia and Upjohn would allow major cost savings in marketing and sales, manufacturing, and research and development. Each of these activities could be sourced on a global level to the country where factor skills or costs were most fa-

vorable, for example, and they announced that they expected to be able to reduce staff by 4,000 people, or 12 percent of the work force. Alongside this, of course, they expected sales revenues to increase because of the combined company's ability to serve the global marketplace better, so that they saw big profits ahead.

Moreover, the two CEOs also pointed out that the continuing wave of merger activity implied that if they did not agree to a merger now, both companies might be the object of unfriendly takeover attempts. A combined Pharmacia and Upjohn, and a new place as the ninth largest pharmaceutical company in the world, would better position the company and make it a global player by the year 2000.

In August 1995, the two companies announced a tax-free stock swap that would result in a merger of equals. The new company would have its headquarters in London. Zabriskie would be the new CEO, and Ekberg would be the nonexecutive chairman. The company would have an R&D budget of more than $1 billion a year, equal to any major global pharmaceutical company.

In 1996, it was not clear what the future would hold for Pharmacia & Upjohn. Would the new company be able to combine the strengths of both companies, eliminate their weaknesses, and develop a sustainable pipeline of important new drugs so that the company becomes a truly global player? Alternatively, would Upjohn's new research and development efforts come to nothing so that the short-term boost to revenues brought about by Pharmacia's new drug pipeline would fizzle out? If this happens, the combined company may itself become a takeover target in the next few years, as the global pharmaceutical industry continues to consolidate. Zabriskie clearly does not believe in this latter scenario. In a public announcement, he claimed that

> This is a merger that truly constitutes far more than the sum of the parts. The new company will be able to take full advantage of uniquely complementary geographic reach, product portfolio, pipeline, and R&D strengths. As a result of the merger, Pharmacia & Upjohn will have extensive financial and operating resources, market scope, and earnings potential. Consequently, we fully expect the new company to achieve additional growth in expected 1996 earnings per share (EPS) as well as acceleration of future earnings growth.

CASE 35

Monsanto: Building a Life Sciences Company

This case was prepared by Charles W. L. Hill of the University of Washington.

INTRODUCTION

As Monsanto approached the new millennium, Bob Shapiro, Monsanto's CEO, reflected on how much the company had changed during the last quarter of a century, and the vast opportunities and daunting challenges now confronting the enterprise. Monsanto was established in 1901 when John Queeny, a chemicals salesman, invested $5,000 in manufacturing facilities to produce saccharin, a synthetic sweetener. Over the next half a century, Monsanto moved into raw materials production, becoming an integrated chemical manufacturer. By the early 1970s, Saint Louis–based Monsanto was one of the world's largest producers of high-volume, commodity chemical products. Then the first OPEC oil shock hit and Monsanto saw its margins drastically compressed by rising raw material prices and plunging demand.

It was at this point that Monsanto started on a journey that was to transform the company into a life sciences behemoth. From small beginnings, the company had grown to become one of the world's leading producers of agricultural and animal biotechnology products. Along the way, the company had acquired G. D. Searle, a second-tier pharmaceutical firm, thereby adding human life sciences to its animal and agricultural life science businesses. By the late 1990s, twenty years of investment in life sciences seemed to be paying off. Monsanto had introduced genetically altered cotton, potatoes, corn, and soybean seeds. These seeds were engineered to produce natural herbicides

This case is intended to be used as the basis for class discussion rather than as an illustration of either effective or ineffective handling of the situation. This case was prepared by Charles W. L. Hill, University of Washington. Used by permission.

and/or to resist damage from Roundup, Monsanto's best selling chemical herbicide; their sales were growing rapidly as farmers recognized their potential to boost crop yields. Furthermore, Monsanto had plans to roll out forty new genetically altered seed products during the 1999–2002 period.[1] Meanwhile, under Monsanto's tutelage, Searle had assembled one of the best new product pipelines in the pharmaceutical industry, and expected to launch more than two dozen new products between 1999 and 2002, led by Celebrex, the first in a class of new painkillers.[2] To complete the transformation of Monsanto from a chemical to a life sciences company, in September 1997 Monsanto spun off its chemical operations as an independent company, Solutia. What remained was a company with sales of more than $9 billion that analysts thought could grow its earnings at an annual compound rate of 20 percent for years to come.

Despite the growth potential of the new Monsanto, however, Shapiro had more than a few worries. Getting Monsanto to this position had been an expensive endeavor that had left the company straining under an $8.2 billion debt load and a debt to equity ratio of 1.25 and a $360 million annual interest bill. Given its debt, some analysts questioned whether Monsanto had the financial resources, and the marketing and sales muscle, to maximize the potential of its pharmaceutical and agricultural biotechnology pipelines. To address these concerns, in June 1998 Monsanto announced an agreement to merge with American Home Products. Many saw the potential merger as an ideal marriage of complementary assets, with AHP's financial resources and strengths in pharmaceutical distribution being a good match for Monsanto's bulging new product pipeline. However, in October 1998 the merger talks broke down, reportedly due to disagreements between senior executives at the two companies over operations and strategy. Now Shapiro had to devise an alternative strategy to maximize the value of Monsanto's pipeline.

If this were not enough, in September 2000 Monsanto's U.S. patent on glyphosate, the key ingredient in Roundup, would expire. Roundup was Monsanto's best-selling product, accounting for over $1.5 billion of its $4 billion in 1998 sales to agricultural markets. In countries outside of the United States where the patent had already expired, prices for Roundup had been cut in half. Many analysts believed that the same was about to occur in the United States. Of course, Shapiro's hope was that the slack would be taken up by the increased sales of Roundup-ready seeds, which should also boost demand for Roundup. Here, too, however, there was a problem, for there was growing opposition to genetically engineered foodstuffs among the environmental community, which referred to transgenic crops as a form of "genetic pollution."[3] The resistance was strongest in Europe, where in response to public disquiet, the European Union had considered blocking imports of genetically altered agricultural products.[4]

BUILDING LIFE SCIENCES AT MONSANTO

The life science business at Monsanto was constructed over a quarter of a century during the tenure of three CEOs: John Hanley, Richard Mahoney, and Robert Shapiro. At the outset of this twenty-five-year odyssey, Monsanto was a major chemical company with substantial sales from low-margin, capital-intensive, commodity chemical operations that produced fibers, plastics, and agricultural chemicals. The main raw material input for these products was petrochemicals, leaving Monsanto highly vulnerable to fluctuations in the price of oil. Pushed by the OPEC oil price hikes of 1973 and 1979, both Hanley and Mahoney repeatedly emphasized the need for Monsanto to migrate its revenues away from low-margin commodity business toward proprietary, high-margin businesses. In the words of Richard Mahoney in a 1989 article,

> Our current strategy at Monsanto began to emerge in the mid 1970s, undertaken because we realized that, after 30 years of growth, many

of our traditional chemical markets were maturing. In addition, oil companies and oil producing nations were crowding into these markets. Not wanting to become a me-too player, we began to evaluate potential new directions. That decision liberated us to look at other technologies. Underlying that search was a determination to find technologies that would present whole new families of opportunities to exploit. We dedicated ourselves to becoming one of the truly great industrial enterprises by the early 1990s. In financial terms that means a 20% return on equity consistently, year after year.[5]

Hanley, who ran Monsanto from 1972 to 1983, made the first moves into biotechnology. Mahoney, his successor, built on this over the next ten years, and in addition, steered the company toward human pharmaceuticals with the 1985 acquisition of G. D. Searle. Shapiro, who succeeded Mahoney in 1993, completed the process.

Establishing Competencies in Biotechnology

The genesis of life sciences at Monsanto can be traced to a 1973 decision to fund a small biotechnology skunkworks to carry out cellular research.[6] The skunkworks was the brainchild of Ernie Jaworski, a senior research scientist at Monsanto. Jaworski had been following developments in plant genetics among the academic community. Like many other scientists, he had been stunned by the news in early 1973 that two California scientists, Stanley Cohn and Herbert Boyer, had managed to isolate fragments of a gene from one bacterium and insert them into another to create a bit of living cellular material that had never before existed.[7] Jaworski reasoned that it might be possible to use the Cohn-Boyer method—referred to as recombinant DNA technology—to genetically alter crop seeds to make them resistant to herbicides. The herbicides could then be used to kill the weeds around the crops as they were growing, without fear of harming the crops. This would help boost demand for one of Monsanto's newest products, the herbicide Roundup. Approved for market introduction in 1974, Roundup was a proprietary, environmentally friendly herbicide developed by Monsanto. At the time, Roundup could only be applied before crop growth since it failed to discriminate between weeds and crops. Another possibility might be to genetically alter crops so that they expressed proteins that functioned as "natural" insecticides, repelling harmful pests. An example would be the cotton bollworm, which ate cotton plants and forced cotton farmers to spend significant sums on insecticides.

Jaworski proposed his idea to Hanley, Monsanto's new CEO who joined Monsanto from Procter & Gamble in 1972. Hanley agreed to fund the establishment of the skunkworks, and Jaworski set up the operation with a staff of thirty-five scientists. The main focus of Jaworski's skunkworks was on understanding cell biology with a view to creating crops with innate herbicide resistance. At the same time, Jaworski was cognizant of the opportunities that might exist if animal proteins could be produced using recombinant DNA technology. Back in the 1930s, Russian scientists had extracted growth hormone from the pituitary glands of slaughtered pigs and cows. They found when injected into live animals, the hormone could accelerate growth and, in the case of cows, increase milk production. However, the process was too expensive, and the technology required to mass-produce growth hormone proteins did not exist at that point in time, so for decades growth hormone remained little more than a scientific curiosity.[8] Now Jaworski realized that recombinant DNA technology might be used to mass-produce animal growth hormones, so he authorized research into growth hormones, but progress was hindered by a lack of resources.

In 1976, Jaworski tried to persuade Monsanto to invest in Genentech, one of the first biotechnology start-ups. Herbert Boyer, one of the inventors of recombinant DNA technology, was one of the two founders of the company. At the time, Genentech was seeking initial venture capital to finance basic research aimed at producing human proteins using recombinant DNA technology. Jaworski believed that Genentech might be an interesting way for Monsanto to get a foothold in this emerging field. However, Monsanto's top management was enamoured of the growth possibilities that might be had producing silicon for semiconductors, and expressed no interest in Jaworski's proposal. In retrospect, this proved to be a mistake.

In 1978, Genentech produced the first human protein (somatostatin) in a microorganism (*E. coli* bacterium). Also in 1978, it succeeded in cloning human insulin using the same technology. The method involved using recombinant DNA technology to insert the piece of human DNA that carries instructions for producing the desired human protein (for example, the gene to produce insulin) into the DNA of a microorganism (usually *E. coli* bacterium or some form of yeast). Because it now contains the gene for making the human protein, the microorganism will express (produce) this protein. Cultures of the microorganism are then placed in fermentation tanks where they multiply and produce more of the desired protein. The microorganism is then harvested, and the desired protein is removed and converted into a drug, such as human insulin, that can then be injected into people who lack the protein (diabetics, in the case of insulin).[9] In 1979, Genentech used this technology to engineer microorganisms to produce human growth hormone. The company went public in 1980 with an offering that leapt from $35 a share to a high of $88 after less than an hour on the market. At the time, this was one the largest stock run-ups ever.[10]

Against the background of rising interest in biotechnology, in 1979 Hanley hired Howard Schneiderman to head Monsanto's R&D efforts. At the time he was hired, Schneiderman was the dean of biological sciences at the University of California, Irvine. As a member of the National Academy of Science and a recognized expert in the techniques of genetic engineering, Schneiderman struck Hanley as the ideal person to oversee Monsanto's biotechnology efforts. As Schneiderman later recalled it, Hanley posed a question to Schneiderman: "We spent $170 million on research in 1978. We probably should have spent $275 million. Do you have any good ideas?"[11] Schneiderman was instantly sold. "If you are a red-blooded American who has chosen research as a career, and a guy comes along and says 'Do you have any good ideas for $100 million worth of research?' it's a fantastic temptation."[12] At Irvine, Schneiderman had administered an $8 million budget.[13] Hanley made Schneiderman senior vice president for research and development and gave him the charter to make Monsanto a "significant world force in molecular biology."[14]

Schneiderman moved quickly. Jaworski's group was transferred into central R&D under Schneiderman's direction. Jaworski was made the director of biological sciences within the corporate R&D staff, and given free rein to go on a hiring spree to attract brilliant young researchers. It wasn't easy; a surge of new biotechnology start-ups offering attractive stock options contracts to scientists competed with Monsanto for scarce talent. Monsanto had an advantage, however. Its financial resources offered scientists the opportunity to engage in long-term research projects, free from financial worries. Schneiderman's reputation also helped, and the company hired 135 Ph.D.'s in the first three years of his tenure. What also helped was the company's decision to invest $165 million to build a life sciences research center on a 210-acre campus 25 miles west of downtown Saint Louis. Referred to within Monsanto as "the house that Howard built," the research center was a powerful symbol of Monsanto's commitment to basic biotechnology research. By 1990, the facility had 250 laboratories and 900 research scientists, making it one of the most powerful concentrations of life science research effort anywhere in the world.[15]

Research Alliances

Despite Monsanto's aggressive investment in R&D, Schneiderman was the first to admit that Monsanto could not do it all alone. Within three months of joining the company. Schneiderman entered into an alliance with Genentech. By this time, Genentech had already figured out how to use recombinant DNA technology to mass-produce human growth hormone. Monsanto was interested in using the same technology to mass-produce animal growth hormones. In return for the rights to the bovine somatotropin growth hormone (BST), Monsanto paid Genentech $990,000, agreed to make several subsequent milestone payments, and promised royalties on future sales of BST. Genentech delivered the first 600 milligrams of BST in December 1981, and initial tests showed that the product worked like natural BST.[16]

In 1982, Monsanto forged an alliance with nearby Washington University in order to get access to leading-edge academic research on molecular biology. This was Monsanto's second big involvement with a university. Back in 1974, the company had entered into a twelve-year, $23-million agreement with Harvard Medical School for research on the molecular basis of organ development. However, Monsanto was not satisfied with this arrangement. A major problem had been that the Harvard researchers refused to give Monsanto access to research findings until they had

been published in academic journals. Moreover, the company had found it was unable to direct or influence the course of research at Harvard.[17]

This time, Monsanto structured the agreement to give it greater access to research results and a greater ability to direct the research process. The agreement called for Monsanto to invest $23.5 million over five years for biomedical research into teins and peptides, small proteins that modify the behavior of cells. About one-third of the effort was to be directed toward basic research, and the rest toward new pharmaceutical products aimed at treating a variety of ailments, including allergies. The contract specified that faculty members participating in projects funded by Monsanto would be free to publish all results of their findings and that Washington University would hold any resulting patents. Monsanto, on the other hand, would have exclusive marketing rights to such patents. Projects to receive funding would be selected by a committee that included four university and four Monsanto scientists. Monsanto scientists would be able to work side by side with university researchers in university labs, and vice versa.

This agreement raised concerns in some quarters that it might violate fundamental principles of academic research and freedom. Albert Gore Jr., then a Democratic representative from Tennessee and chairman of the Investigation and Oversight Subcommittee of the House Committee on Science and Technology commented that "You don't have to know algebra to figure out how that committee works. No research can be done unless the company gives permission."[18] In reply, Schneiderman insisted that "everything is carefully designed to enable the university to be true to its fundamental purpose."[19]

The Washington University deal was followed by a series of other research deals structured along similar lines. These included a $5-million, five-year agreement with Oxford University in the United Kingdom to sequence the structure of certain plant proteins and a $4-million, five-year agreement with Rockefeller University to investigate the structure and regulation of plant genes involved in photosynthesis. Smaller agreements were also signed with the California Institute of Technology, the University of California (San Francisco), and Harvard University. In 1985, the Washington University agreement was extended to cover eight and a half years, and the total funds committed increased to

$62 million, making it the largest collaborative agreement of its kind.[20] According to Schneiderman, such contracts provide "a powerful insight into the future," fund research that is "more likely to make a leap," keep Monsanto researchers "in the front line of academic research," and "can be a magnet for attracting good people to Monsanto."[21]

Acquiring Searle

As Monsanto embarked on its journey into the life sciences business, it was not altogether clear exactly what the focus of the company would ultimately be. Jaworski's skunkworks, and many of the scientists hired after Schneiderman arrived, focused primarily on applying the principles of molecular biology to plants. This made good sense, given Monsanto's strong position in agricultural herbicides—a position that was getting stronger all the time due to the success of Roundup. In the early 1980s, this herbicide was generating more than $500 million a year in sales and was Monsanto's most profitable product.[22] On the other hand, the alliance with Genentech signaled an interest in animal proteins, and the agreement with Washington University was in large part directed at producing human pharmaceuticals.

Within Monsanto, the debate was not so much about whether the company should leverage its growing life science expertise to enter the human pharmaceutical business as it was about how best to achieve this. By 1983, Monsanto, in collaboration with its university partners, was beginning to identify some interesting candidates for clinical investigation. An example was atrial peptide, a human protein that had been isolated from the atrium of the heart by researchers at Washington University. The protein dilates the vascular system, and Monsanto believed that it might have value as a drug for controlling blood pressure.[23] However, Monsanto lacked both the regulatory experience with the FDA and the distribution network required to maximize the potential of such pharmaceuticals.

The slow pace of Monsanto's move away from its low-margin commodity chemicals business added urgency. By 1984, the company was still generating 60 percent of its sales from its traditional chemical operations, even though 65 percent of its operating profits came from agricultural chemicals, and most of those could be attributed to just two products, Roundup and another herbicide, Lasso

(the patent on Lasso was set to expire in 1988). Monsanto's new CEO, Richard Mahoney, wanted to accelerate the shift away from commodity chemicals, and simultaneously gain a pharmaceutical distribution network. To further the attainment of these objectives, in 1983 Monsanto hired the investment banker Goldman, Sachs & Co. to identify acquisition candidates in the pharmaceutical business. In 1984, Monsanto acquired a small Belgian drug company, Continental Pharma, but a large acquisition candidate eluded it. G.D. Searle was on the list compiled by Goldman, Sachs, but the company was 34 percent owned by the Searle family, and it seemed unlikely to sell. This changed in 1984 when the Searle family indicated that it wanted to sell its stake, effectively putting Searle on the block. Searle's pharmaceutical business had been a lackluster performer in recent years. The company had not introduced a significant new drug for eight years. It did, however, have a powerful anti-ulcer drug, Cytotec, in late-stage clinical trials. There were also a number of interesting drug candidates farther down the product development pipeline. Searle also had aspartame (NutraSweet), the artificial sweetener that generated $600 million in annual sales—roughly half of Searle's total revenues. However, the patent on aspartame was due to expire in 1992. Initially, Monsanto wanted to purchase Searle's pharmaceutical business, leaving Searle with NutraSweet, but Searle refused to deal and negotiations broke down.

In 1985, Monsanto approached Searle again, this time with an offer to buy the entire company. The change in Monsanto's position was in part due to a reassessment of the value of NutraSweet. Searle had just won regulatory approval to use 100 percent NutraSweet in diet soda. Mahoney believed that this would expand sales for NutraSweet to close to $1 billion before the patent expired, throwing off significant free cash flow in the process. In Mahoney's words, "NutraSweet brings a very interesting earnings stream in the time between now and when our biotechnology begins to pay off."[24]

In July 1985, Monsanto announced that it had agreed to purchase Searle for $2.7 billion, or about seventeen times Searle's estimated 1985 earnings. While many analysts commented that the acquisition was too expensive and that Monsanto was paying a hefty premium for a mediocre drug company, which had not introduced any significant new products for some time, Monsanto seemed pleased with its purchase. One business development executive in the company noted that "Searle's marketing and distribution operations will be the vehicle by which we can go forward and commercialize new products worldwide. Now Monsanto has the infrastructure to realize the benefits of biotechnology."[25] Mahoney also noted that "Searle has done a very good job of finding product leads of its own. We are engaged in a long term strategic move to have Searle's and Monsanto's strengths melded together."[26] In fact, by mid 1986, Searle had twenty-one new chemical or biological entities in various stages of clinical development—one of the best pipelines in the pharmaceutical industry. These included cardiovascular drugs for hypertension and irregular heartbeat; central nervous system drugs for depression, epilepsy, and pain; immuno-inflammatory drugs for arthritis; and an ulcer medication.[27] However, most of these products were still in the early stages of clinical testing, there was no guarantee that they would show the desired combination of efficacy and manageable side effects in clinical trials, and even if they did, they were years from market introduction.

DEVELOPING PRODUCTS

With the 1985 acquisition of Searle, Monsanto had assembled the main building blocks required to embark on the transformation from a major chemical company into a life sciences concern. At the time, Jaworski commented that "by 1990 Monsanto will be the greatest biotechnology company in the world."[28] Executives in other biotechnology firms characterized such comments as "absolutely ridiculous" and an "extraordinary boast."[29] They noted that it was small entrepreneurial biotechnology enterprises such as Amgen, Genentech, and Biogen that had succeeded in moving biotechnology products to market, not large corporations like Monsanto. Large companies, the critics noted, lacked the required sense of urgency, drive, and creativity of smaller biotechnology enterprises. In 1986, only two biotechnology products were on the market, insulin and human growth hormone. Genentech, not a large pharmaceutical firm, produced both of these. Moreover, all five biotechnology products then in phase III (final stage) clinical trials belonged to entrepreneurial biotechnology companies, not large pharma-

ceutical enterprises. More than anything else, the critics felt that Monsanto was underestimating the problems involved in developing biotechnology products and bringing them to market.

Ps–3732

By 1986, Monsanto was already beginning to get a taste of the problems involved in developing biotechnology products. On May 20 of that year, the Environmental Protection Agency turned down an application from Monsanto to field-test its first genetically altered microbe, dealing a body blow to one of the company's most advanced agricultural biotechnology research projects.[30] The microbe in question was a genetically engineered bacterium that produced a protein that functioned as a natural insecticide and was capable of killing insects that fed on corn. In denying the company's request to proceed with field testing, the EPA was bowing to pressure from environmental activists, who had criticized Monsanto's testing procedures and questioned the safety of releasing genetically altered organisms into the environment.

The research project that produced the bacterium was begun in 1980 when a twenty-person team of scientists, led by thirty-two-year-old Robert Kaufman, received approval for research to develop microbes that produced "natural" insecticides. The thinking was straightforward; farmers around the world were spending about $7 billion on chemical pesticides, but these pesticides also killed animals, polluted ground water and rivers, and showed up in traces in foods. Surely, Monsanto executives believed, farmers would buy a genetically engineered product that was cheaper, easier to use, and did not harm the environment or human health.

By late 1982, after collecting and analyzing hundred of bacteria that colonized the roots of corn, Dr. Kaufman and his team isolated a single microbe, dubbed Ps–3732, capable of mass reproduction and able to compete with other microorganisms for space around the roots of corn plants. The team had also identified a natural toxin capable of killing caterpillar-type pests and generated by one of the 3,000 to 5,000 genes in the chromosomes in another common bacterium, Bacillus thuringiensis. By the end of 1983, the team had isolated the gene and succeed in inserting it into the chromosomes of Ps–3732 using recombinant DNA technology.

The team now believed that it had a means to deliver a natural insecticide. The plan was to sell corn seeds coated with the genetically modified bacteria. After the farmer planted the seeds, the bacteria would multiply in the soil and form a barrier around the roots of the corn, preventing damage from cutworms, a common pest. Before field-testing the bacteria, Kaufman's team undertook seventeen safety studies, designed to establish the environmental impact of the genetically modified Ps–3732. The bacteria were fed to mice, quail, and fish, and bees and a wide variety of plants were exposed to it. No adverse effects were observed. Armed with this data, Monsanto submitted a request to the EPA to move forward with a field test.

At this point, Jeremy Rifkin entered the picture. A well-known radical activist, Rifkin was president of the Foundation for Economic Trends, a policy study group largely funded from sales of Rifkin's own books. Rifkin had already established a reputation as a vocal and effective critic of the imperialism of modern science in general, and biotechnology in particular. In Monsanto's request, he saw an opportunity to nip the emerging agricultural biotechnology movement in the bud.

Rifkin's attack on Monsanto had two thrusts. First, he argued that once released into the environment, genetically altered bacteria could spread uncontrollably. Such "genetic pollution" might cause problems that had not yet been identified. Second, he requested from the EPA access to all of Monsanto's data on safety studies. He then had these data reviewed and critiqued by several ecologists and microbiologists that he had worked with for several years. These experts criticized Monsanto's safety studies as poorly conducted and scientifically inconclusive. Armed with this finding, Rifkin formally petitioned the EPA to deny Monsanto a permit to field-test Ps–3732.

The EPA subsequently issued a report on Monsanto's safety study tests. Written by microbiologists on the EPA's staff, the report stated that thirteen of the seventeen studies were either inconclusive or scientifically flawed. Kaufman acknowledged that some of the safety studies were scanty, but argued that Monsanto was breaking new ground, that many of the tests were the first of their kind, and that the EPA ignored a lot of good data and instead simply focused on those tests where there was some question about the sample design. Kaufman subsequently met with the EPA's advisory panel—which was composed of independent academic advisers—after which the panel indicated that it would "reverse" the staff evaluation and recommend that the EPA allow Monsanto to proceed with the experiment. In reaching its decision, the panel acknowledged that some of Monsanto's safety studies were poorly designed but added that it had enough data from other sources to know that if Monsanto's microbe were released into the environment, it would not be a hazard.

Unfortunately for Monsanto, the panel's advice is not binding, although reversal of the panel's recommendation is a rare event. Alerted by EPA insiders as to what the panel recommendation would be, Rifkin continued to put pressure on the EPA, indicating that he would sue the agency if it approved the field test. This put Dr. John Moore, the head of the EPA, in a difficult position. Although privately he acknowledged that Monsanto's microbe was in all probability not harmful, he recognized that a lawsuit would give Rifkin the opportunity to probe Monsanto and the EPA in public. Cognizant of Rifkin's eloquence and his influence among certain members of Congress and aware of the holes in some of Monsanto's studies, Moore decided to deny the request, although he urged the company to undertake several safety studies and resubmit the request. In a short letter to the company, Moore wrote, "I believe that it is in the best interests of Monsanto and the EPA that the general public develop a feeling of trust and confidence that all decisions to permit experiments of this sort be based on expert evaluation of reliable data." Later, Moore pointed out that "we do not have the knowledge to completely understand the interactions of organisms in the environment. I think caution is absolutely justified."[31] Commenting on the decision, Rifkin stated that "we owe it to ourselves and the next generation to raise these issues and ask these questions. We are talking about the ability to change the genetic code of life, and that's ominous power. We ought to have a thorough, reasonable, and well thought out public debate. It ought not to be left in the hands of Monsanto."[32]

In the aftermath of the EPA's decision, Kaufman resigned from Monsanto to join a start-up biotechnology company, his team was reassigned, and

Monsanto decided to shelve the project and pursue other avenues in the agricultural biotechnology research arena.

Genetically Altering Plants

One of the other avenues that the company was pursuing was the genetic manipulation of plant DNA. Unknowingly, human beings have been manipulating plant DNA since the dawn of the agricultural revolution thousands of years ago, but they have done it through the slow and highly imprecise methods of selective breeding and hybridization. By harnessing biotechnology, Monsanto hoped to dramatically reduce the time required to produce new varieties of crops, and to design crops that had specific desirable traits. To this end, in 1981 a twenty-eight-year-old scientist within Monsanto, Robert Fraley, was put in charge of the plant molecular biology group and given the task of developing better crops through genetic engineering.[33]

Fraley's group first had to confront the problem of how to alter a plant's DNA. They settled on the novel approach of harnessing bacteria that have the natural ability to invade plant cells without destroying the cells. The bacterium they chose, *Agrobacterium tumefaciens*, invades a plant's cell and produces tumorous crown galls on infected species. The utility of this bacterium as a gene transfer system was first recognized when it was demonstrated that the crown galls were actually produced as a result of the transfer and integration of genes from the bacterium into the genome of the plant cells. The scientists theorized that if they could disable the disease causing genes in *Agrobacterium*, it would prove to be a useful vector for transporting foreign genes into the DNA of a plant.[34]

It took two years to disassemble *Agrobacterium*'s genetic code and remove the regions of DNA that produced crown gall. They then took another bacterium, *E. coli*, and isolated the gene that made *E. coli* resistant to an antibiotic called kanamycin. They cut the kanamycin-resistant gene out of the *E. coli* and spliced it into the DNA of the *Agrobacterium*. They then infected cells from a petunia plant with the modified *Agrobacterium*. The significance of this is that kanamycin is normally lethal to petunias. When they exposed *Agrobacterium*-infected petunia cells to kanamycin, however, the petunia cells continued to divide. In 1983, Fraley announced that Monsanto

had produced a kanamycin-resistant petunia that was the world's first genetically engineered plant.[35] Subsequent experiments found that traits introduced into the DNA of host plants were stable over multiple generations during crossbreeding.[36]

Fraley then used the same methodology for more elaborate, and commercially important, plant transformations. The first successful gene-altering experiment with a staple crop came in 1987, when Fraley's group succeeded in modifying soybeans to resist damage from glyphosate, the active ingredient the company's best-selling herbicide, Roundup. The glyphosate gene had been isolated from bacteria and then inserted into the cells' genetic structure of soybeans using recombinant DNA technology.

While Monsanto claimed Roundup-resistant plants would boost yields, critics in the environmental community opposed Monsanto's attempt to create crops resistant to Roundup. Because Roundup does not discriminate between weeds and crops, farmers must use it with extreme care and avoid it altogether in soybean, corn, and cotton fields. The development of Roundup-resistant crops, however, allows farmers to spray the herbicide freely—a fact that troubled environmentalists. As one put it, "Monsanto's rhetoric is low or no pesticide agriculture, but in fact what they are delivering is a whole new generation of herbicide tolerant plants that will shackle us to chemicals for the foreseeable future."[37] For its part, Monsanto pointed out that Roundup is an environmentally friendly herbicide. Glyphosate becomes inert on contact with the soil, breaking down into nitrogen and other nontoxic elements that are naturally found in the soil.

A series of other crop modifications followed the creation of Roundup-resistant soybeans. These included the engineering of an array of crops—tomatoes, potatoes, alfalfa, tobacco, and cucumbers—that were resistant to viral infections. By 1990, the company had also succeeded in engineering transgenic cotton, tomato, and potato plants that contain genes from bacteria that produce proteins fatal to budworms, bollworms, and other common farm pests.[38] The insect-resistant crops were based on genes from a family of bacteria called *Bacillus thuringiensis*, commonly referred to as *Bt*. The *Bt* genes are a code for assembling proteins that can kill certain pests while having no effect on beneficial insects and animals. *Bt*'s have been used in sprays for decades, mostly by organic farmers who forgo the use of manmade chemicals. But the sprays were not effective enough to make much of a dent in the chemical-pesticides market. Monsanto wanted to change that, in the process saving farmers millions of dollars per year in spending on insecticides. Once more, however, the environmental community protested loudly. A big concern is that over time common pests will develop resistance to the *Bt* protein. In particular, environmentalists worry that insects and weeds will quickly build up resistance to the transgenic plants and the herbicides used in conjunction with them, possibly leaving farmers worse off than before after a short burst of extra productivity.[39]

BST

Monsanto licensed the rights to bovine somatotropin growth hormone (BST) from Genentech in 1981 and received the first batch of BST in December of that year. Monsanto planned to perfect BST so that it could be used to boost milk production in dairy cattle (subsequently, studies at universities and at dairy farms have found that the drug increases milk production 10 to 20 percent in well-managed herds). It took twelve years and an estimated $300 million in R&D before the company finally won approval to sell BST in the marketplace.[40]

Monsanto's product is made by inserting the BST gene from cows into *E. coli* bacteria, which are then multiplied in fermentation tanks. The bacteria are then harvested, the BST protein is removed, purified, and converted into the drug that can be injected into cows. This process might sound straightforward, but it is not. It took several years for Monsanto's scientists to find the ideal environment in fermentation vats for the care and feeding of the BST-producing *E. coli*. *E. coli* turned out to be difficult to mass-produce, requiring just the right amount of oxygen and nutrients and the correct temperature. If any one of these variables was not right, other bacteria could swamp *E. coli*, dramatically lowering BST yields from the fermentation process. Then researchers ran into problems when they tried to kill the bacteria and "crack open" the organisms. Cracking open bacteria involves submitting the organisms to very high pressure, and then releasing that pressure. The sudden drop in pressure causes the bacteria to pop open and release their contents. Monsanto found that the BST-laden bacteria quickly wore down the stainless steel

valves on pressure equipment. The reason was that BST protein particles have the consistency of superhard grains of sand. As a result, the pressure equipment was breaking down constantly. Solving the problem required the invention of ceramic valves that could withstand the wear and tear from BST. After cracking, Monsanto found that it needed to conduct a further seven purification steps to separate the BST molecules from thousands of other proteins, fats, and carbohydrates in the *E. coli* mix. To perfect the purification process, Monsanto had to develop special filters that prevented BST from becoming contaminated.

Another problem was finding the correct formulation of the drug. Early BST tests required scientists to inject cows every day, but Monsanto concluded that such a regime would be too expensive and cumbersome for farmers, and it developed a formulation that only needed to be injected weekly. Then there was also the issue of where to produce BST. United States regulations prohibit the export of drugs that have not been approved for marketing by the Federal Drug Administration (FDA) in the United States. Monsanto reasoned that it might get approval to market BST from foreign regulators before it received FDA approval (correctly as it turned out), so the company decided to locate the manufacturing facilities in Austria.

Difficult as they were, however, solving all of these production problems was a minor matter compared with the political and regulatory problems that Monsanto had to solve before BST could be marketed. The problems started in 1985, when researchers at Cornell University reported the results of early field trials that found the drug increased milk production by as much as 40 percent. The widely publicized results dismayed dairy farmers in New York, Wisconsin, Minnesota, and other milk-producing states. They came at a time when large dairy surpluses were pushing prices down, forcing family farms out of business. Thousands of farmers in the Upper Middle West joined with Jeremy Rifkin in a grassroots campaign that in 1990 succeeded in persuading the state legislatures of Wisconsin and Minnesota to enact temporary moratoriums on the use of the drug in the event it was approved. The moratoriums expired in 1991. In the same year, an unprecedented review by a panel of experts convened by the National Institutes of Health declared the drug safe.

In November 1993, the FDA got its turn. After extensive testing and review, the FDA approved Monsanto's BST. This was the first time that the government was allowing food to be produced using a genetically engineered drug. The decision was made by Dr. David A. Kessler, the commissioner of food and drugs, who noted that "There is virtually no difference in milk from treated and untreated cows. In fact, it's not possible using current scientific techniques to tell them apart. We have looked carefully at every single question raised, and we are confident this product is safe for consumers, for cows and for the environment." Jeremy Rifkin was defiant in his response: "We have said since 1986 that if the F.D.A. ever approved this drug that the final battleground would be the grocery stores, restaurants and convenience stores. This is the beginning of food politics in this country. If Monsanto succeeds with this product, they open the floodgates on the biotechnology age. If we succeed, it will send a chilling message through the agricultural business that people don't want genetically engineered foods."[41]

COX–2 Inhibitor

In 1999, Monsanto's Searle unit introduced Celebrex, the first in a new class of pain treatments for arthritis that offers the same benefit as existing pain relief medications for arthritis (such as aspirin), but with a sharp reduction in the harmful, and often dangerous, side effects of stomach irritation, ulcers, and internal bleeding. The product was the result of a fifteen-year quest by Philip Needleman to understand the role of cyclo-oxygenase (COX) enzymes in the regulation of prostaglandins, hormone-like fatty acids that are crucial to the body's maintenance.[42] As a researcher in the medical school at Washington University, Needleman studied complex chemicals that act as on and off switches in the body. Needleman and a colleague discovered a chemical inhibitor that affects prostaglandins. He learned more from an English researcher, who discovered that aspirin and aspirin-like drugs block the production of prostaglandins and thus reduce pain. But too much blocking is dangerous. Prostaglandins help regulate blood flow through the kidneys and aid in blood clotting. Without prostaglandins producing a protective coating, the stomach would eat itself due to the acid it secretes during digestion. As a result of this effect, patients taking drugs that block COX enzymes, such as aspirin, can suffer from serious stomach lesions. The resulting internal bleeding contributed to the death of some 16,000 people a year in the United States alone.

Needleman found that there are two COX enzymes: COX-1 handles the body's housekeeping; injury or disease triggers COX-2. Aspirin and other similar painkillers, referred to as nonsteroidal anti-inflammatory drugs (NSAIDs), block both enzymes—hence the side effects. Needleman wanted to block just COX-2. If that could be achieved, it would be possible to develop a pain medicine that lacked the side effect profile of NSAIDs. By the late 1980s, Needleman was convinced that this was possible, but he did not have the resources to do much about it. At this point he was also chair of the department of pharmacology at Washington University. In this role, he had helped negotiate the original Monsanto–Washington University research agreement and now helped the company allocate funds to Washington University researchers. The company was looking for a successor to Schneiderman and was favorably disposed toward hiring another academic. Needleman had the combination of scientific credentials and leadership skills that Monsanto was looking for, and he was also a known quantity to the company. Like Schneiderman before him, Needleman found the possibilities enticing; "I became enthralled with the idea of what it's like to have all of the people and resources to attack a problem."[43] In 1989, he joined the company as chief scientist.

At Monsanto's Searle division, Needleman found a company that had a long history of household-name products, but the new product pipeline seemed relatively bare to him, and he found the research effort to be diffused. Moreover, Needleman was aware of the costs and risks involved in bringing a new drug to market. Producing human pharmaceuticals is, if anything, a more expensive and risky business than producing transgenic crops. On average, it can take twelve years and cost $300 million to take a drug from the laboratory to the marketplace. To make matters worse, some 80 percent of products that enter clinical trials fail to make it to the market. A drug candidate must go through three sets of increasingly expensive clinical trials to test for safety, dosage, and efficacy (referred to as phase I, II, and III trials). The drug then faces a rigorous review by the FDA. On average, 70 percent of drug candidates that enter into phase I trials make it through to phase II, 47 percent entering phase II make it to phase III, and

82 percent entering phase III make it to the FDA, where 74 percent are approved.[44]

Realizing that Searle lacked the resources of its larger pharmaceutical industry rivals, Needleman developed a two-pronged strategy for Searle's R&D.[45] First, he directed research effort toward three main therapeutic areas: arthritis, oncology, and cardiovascular problems. By concentrating resources, Searle could match or exceed the dollars spent per therapeutic area by larger rivals. In 1998, for example, Searle spent $280 million per therapeutic area, compared with $250 million at Pfizer and $200 million at Merck.[46] Second, Needleman developed the discipline of ending drug development projects early if they didn't survive what he characterizes as "killer experiments."

As part of this strategy, Needleman "exploded the budget for COX–2." The search for a COX–2 inhibitor became the biggest project Searle had ever undertaken. For three years, a team of thirty chemists and thirty biologists examined 2,000 chemical compounds in the quest to find a COX–2 inhibitor. Urgency was added to the quest by the fact that Merck was also racing to develop a COX–2 inhibitor. When the Searle team found the compound that that eventually became Celebrex, they submitted it to a "killer experiment" while it was being tested in phase I trials as an arthritis treatment. The killer experiment was to discover whether the drug relieved severe tooth pain. Needleman reasoned that if the drug alleviated dental pain, it would also ease the pain of arthritis. Celebrex survived the experiment, and the phase I and II trials suggested that the drug not only relieved pain, but also had none of the dangerous side effects associated with other treatments. After an 8,000-patient phase III trial produced favorable results, Searle, in August 1998, filed for FDA approval to market the drug. Because the drug was the first COX–2 inhibitor to come up for review, the FDA granted Celebrex a proprietary review, which meant that it would announce a decision within six months (normally, FDA approval can take as long as twelve months). Approval was granted in December 1998, and Celebrex was launched in mid January 1999, the first in a new class of "super aspirin" painkillers.

PRODUCT LAUNCHES

Monsanto launched BST in February 1994. It was to be the first in a series of new product launches over the next five years that was to finally generate significant revenues for the company—almost a quarter of a century after Jaworski's skunkworks started Monsanto down the biotechnology road.

BST

By early 1999, BST, which Monsanto sold under the brand name Posilac, was being regularly injected in some 30 percent of dairy herds in the United States. Follow-up data showed that BST boosted milk production by about 10 percent on average. Robust demand for milk and milk products in the United States has meant that the supply glut feared by dairy farmers had not materialized. Monsanto and the FDA continued to monitor BST for possible adverse effects. As of 1999, the FDA continued to state that milk from BST-treated cows poses no health risks. The American Medical Association, the World Health Organization, and the National Institutes of Health have issued similar findings. According to Monsanto, BST has enjoyed robust sales gains, and in 1998 passed 100 million doses—at $5.80 per dose.[47]

Despite its success in the United States, however, Monsanto has still not been able to get the product approved for sale in either Canada or the European Union. In early 1999, Health Canada, the Canadian version of the FDA, rejected Monsanto's application to market BST. While a review of existing data by Canadian scientists found no significant risk to human beings who ingest products from animals treated with BST, they noted that short-term tests on lab rats suggest that further study is needed. Health Canada concluded that there was sufficient concern to warrant not approving the drug.[48]

In 1989, the European Union imposed a moratorium on the use of animal growth hormones and the sale of products produced by those hormones, on the grounds that European farmers were already producing too much milk and beef and there was no need for greater production. The moratorium was extended in 1996 and 1997. The current version is due to expire at the end of 1999. In early 1999, the animal health and welfare committee of the European Union concluded that BST should not be injected into cattle. Its report cites increased likelihood of mastitis, foot problems, and injection site reactions, which would also lead to welfare problems besides human health risks. In contrast, another European Union committee, the committee for veterinary medicinal products, had ruled in 1998 that BST was perfectly safe.[49] More generally, public opinion in the European Union seemed to be strongly against not just BST, but genetically modified foods in general. In the United States, the Clinton administration was considering appealing to the World Trade Organization on the grounds that the European Union ban on BST represented an unfair restraint of trade that was at variance with WTO rules, of which the European Union was a signatory.

Genetically Modified Crops

Following regulatory approval, in 1996 Monsanto introduced the first wave of its genetically modified crops; Roundup-ready soybeans, Bollgard insect-protected cotton, and New Leaf insect-protected potatoes. Getting to this point had required sixteen years of research and according to various estimates, cost between $300 million and $500 million in R&D spending. A series of other products were scheduled to follow over the next few years, including Roundup-ready canola, cotton and rape seed, Yield Guard insect-protected corn, insect-protected tomatoes, corn rootworm-protected cotton, and Roundup-ready insect-protected soybeans (which adds *Bt* to Roundup-ready soybeans to provide both insect resistance and herbicide tolerance).

Although it was acknowledged as a technology leader and the first to bring a substantial number of products to market, Monsanto did not have the field entirely to itself. Monsanto faced the prospect of competition from several large companies, including Du Pont and Swiss-based Novartis. Du Pont had developed soybeans that tolerated the company's powerful Synchrony herbicide. Novartis had genetically altered corn seed so that it produced a protein that killed a common pest, the European corn borer. Both companies also had active research programs that promised to produce a range of genetically modified crops over the next decade.

Several smaller agricultural biotechnology companies had also been developing genetically altered crops, including DeKalb Genetics and Calgene. Calgene had introduced the first genetically engineered crop the previous year, a tomato that ripened more slowly and would stay fresh longer on supermarket shelves. Calgene was also developing a variety of soybean that was resistant to glyphosate, the active ingredient in Roundup. Simi-

larly, DeKalb was developing corn seed that was resistant to glyphosate. Monsanto purchased Calgene in April 1997 for $240 million.

Distribution Agreements   The delivery vehicle for all of Monsanto's genetic improvements was seed. However, the company had not traditionally been a strong player in the seed business. Thus, to produce and deliver genetically modified seed to farmers, Monsanto needed to find a way to participate in the seed industry. Companies in this industry grow seeds and then distribute them to farmers. The issue was further complicated by the fact that the genes that Monsanto created provided only one specific trait to the farmer. It was crucial that Monsanto's genes be incorporated in the best germplasm available, necessitating that Monsanto find some way to cooperate with leading seed companies. In its 1998 Annual Report, the company explained the issue as follows:

> Seed is the delivery vehicle for biotechnology traits. Integrating seed into our life sciences system will accelerate the development of new traits and their introduction into new varieties. The combination of breeding and genomics will accelerate the development of new varieties with better quality. Germplasm, the basic genetic structure of a plant, determines the characteristics of that variety, such as yield potential or drought resistance. Germplasm is crucial to grower acceptance; our traits must be available in the varieties that growers prefer. While we license our technology for use in other companies' germplasm—and that's an integral part of our overall strategy—we need to be involved from the start in developing new varieties that include the best traits.

The seed industry itself was highly concentrated, with a small number of players dominating the market. Different seed companies also focused on different product and vertical segments of the seed market. For example, Delta and Pine Land had a 55 percent share of the U.S. market for cotton seeds, but a zero percent share of the market for corn seeds, and only 1 percent of the market for soybean seeds. In contrast, Pioneer Hi-Bred had a 44 percent share of the market for corn seeds, a 19 percent share of the soybean market, and no position in the market for corn seeds. Other large seed companies included DeKalb Genetics, Northrup

King (owned by Sandoz), Cargill, Ciba Seeds (owned by Ciba-Geigy), Asgrow (owned by ELM of Mexico), and Holden's Foundation Seeds. DeKalb Genetics and Holden's were among the companies that focused on producing seeds, which they then sold to distributors.

Monsanto's initial approach was to explore a variety of relationships with seed companies. It decided to license its Roundup-ready soybean technology to a broad range of seed companies. In contrast, it entered into an exclusive licensing agreement with Delta Pine & Land to produce and market Bollgard cotton. In early 1996, the company acquired a minority position in DeKalb, which would produce Monsanto's Yield Guard corn. Independently of Monsanto, DeKalb Genetics had developed a strain of corn that was resistant to glyphosate. This was followed in September 1996, when Monsanto acquired one of its Roundup-ready soybean technology licensees, Asgrow, for $240 million. At the time of the acquisition, Asgrow ranked second among U.S. soybean seed companies, with an 18 percent market share for licensed and proprietary products. Monsanto stated that it would continue to license its technology to other soybean seed companies

In January 1997, Monsanto acquired Holden's Foundation Seeds and Corn States Hybrid Service and Corn States International, which marketed Holden's products worldwide, for around $1 billion. Like DeKalb, Holden's specializes in developing corn germ plasma, the genetic foundation for seed corn varieties. It licenses the germ plasma to independent companies, which in turn create corn hybrids for commercial use. Although Holden's doesn't sell seeds directly to farmers, it supplies one-third of the corn seed parent stock planted in the United States every year. Along with DeKalb and leading corn seed seller Pioneer Hi-Bred International, Holden's owns one of the three largest pools of corn genetics in the world. It is stored in the form of millions of kernels in cooled storage rooms. According to Monsanto's CEO, Holden's would give Monsanto "an excellent delivery mechanism for our biotechnology innovations in corn. These acquisitions mean the latest technological advances will be made available to the greatest possible number of seed companies of all sizes with unparalleled speed."[50] Holden's had been the subject of acquisition rumors for months before the Monsanto takeover. The company reportedly got

bids or inquiries from several multinational companies that were moving into agricultural biotechnology, including DuPont, Dow-Elanco, AgrEvo and Novartis.[51]

The acquisition spree continued in 1998 when Monsanto purchased DeKalb Genetics outright for $2.3 billion, Delta and Pine Land for $1.3 billion, wheat seed company AgriPro, and the international seed business of Cargill. As a result of these acquisitions, Monsanto controlled an estimated 86 percent of the U.S. cotton seed market and nearly 50 percent of the corn and soybean seed markets.[52] To finance these acquisitions, Monsanto offered about $1.5 billion in common and preferred stock, and took on $2.5 billion in long-term debt, adding significant leverage to its balance sheet.[53] Monsanto's view of the industry value chain in early 1999, and its position in it, is summarized in Figure 1. The companies listed under the "seed" box in Figure 1 are biotechnology companies with which Monsanto had research alliances in 1999.

Monsanto was not alone is buying its way into the seed business. In May 1997, Du Pont invested $1.7 billion to acquire a 20 percent stake in Pioneer High Breeds, the largest seed producer in the United States. Like Monsanto, Du Pont made the purchase in order to speed up the process of commercializing its discoveries in agricultural biotechnology, and bring genetically altered seeds to market more rapidly. Many independent observers worried that in their race to become the Coke and Pepsi of agricultural biotechnology, Monsanto and Du Pont were fast creating an oligopolistic situation in the seed business.[54] Their fears intensified in March 1999, when Du Pont offered $ 7.7 billion to purchase all of Pioneer. If regulators approve the Du Pont–Pioneer deal, three companies—Du Pont, Monsanto, and Novartis—will control two-thirds of the North American seed corn market and 45 percent of the soybean seed market, and 85 percent of the U.S. cotton seed market.[55]

Pricing Strategy   A big issue for Monsanto was how to price genetically altered seeds to capture the value implied by its proprietary position, and years of heavy investment in R&D. With regard to Bollgard cotton, which was distributed by Delta and Pine Land, Monsanto decided to price the seed at market rates but to tack on a separate technology fee of $32 per acre, which the farmers had to

FIGURE I

The Value Chain for
Transgenic Crops

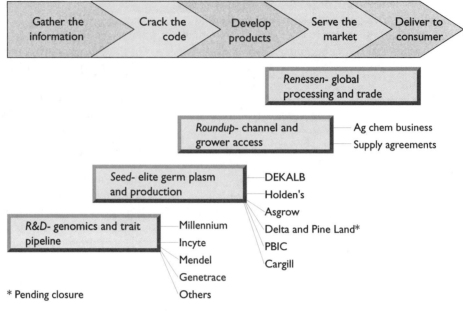

GLOBAL PLATFORM SPANS VALUE CHAIN

Source: Monsanto Investment Conference, May 3, 1999.

pay directly to Monsanto. The pricing strategy presented farmers with something of a gamble: would it cost more to fight pests using traditional methods, or should they pay the fee to Monsanto? And would the cotton survive if they didn't use Bollgard? Depending on the year, most farmers estimate that they spend anywhere from $20 to $100 per acre spraying against pests. While some of this cost is saved if they plant Bollgard cotton, they might still have to use some sprays to fight other pests.[56]

According to Monsanto, in its first full year, 1996, more than 5,700 U.S. farmers purchased Bollgard cotton and planted 1.8 million acres, or 13 percent of the total cotton acres in the United States. Approximately 60 percent of Bollgard users were able to totally eliminate insecticides, saving the average grower $33 per acre on land planted with Bollgard. Crop yields from fields planted with *Bt* cotton increased by 8 to 10 percent. Four out of five users said they were either satisfied or very satisfied with the cotton's overall performance. Only 2 percent said that they would not use it again.[57]

With regard to Roundup-ready soybeans, Monsanto decided to charge a technology fee of $5 per 50-pound bag of seed. A 50-pound bag of soybean

seeds was selling for between $13 and $15 in 1996. Roundup-ready soybeans cost between $18 and $20 per bag, depending on the seed company (Monsanto did not control the retail price; distributors did). Monsanto also required farmers to sign an agreement promising not to reuse the patented seed—which annoyed many farmers who were in the habit of doing so. Furthermore, the farmers had to agree to use Roundup, and not any competing glyphosate-based herbicide. In addition, the contract also allowed Monsanto to visit their farms for three years to make sure they kept their promise. In response to numerous complaints, Monsanto later dropped the requirement that farmers allow the company to inspect their operations but raised the technology fee to $6.50 per bag in 1998.[58]

Monsanto's marketing pitch for Roundup-ready soybeans emphasized two things. First, the company extolled the virtues of being able to use the environmentally friendly broad-spectrum Roundup herbicide to control weeds *after* crops began to sprout, rather than more expensive crop-specific herbicides. The company estimated that this would save farmers $12 to $16 per acre in reduced weed control costs, which of course had to be offset against the $5 technology fee. Second, Monsanto emphasized that if farmers made greater use of Roundup, they could reduce their use of traditional deep tillage weed control methods. This would have a long-term benefit in terms of reduced soil erosion. Put differently, it would facilitate the adoption of conservation tillage methods.

Roundup Strategy If Monsanto's push into Roundup-ready crops generated the sales that the company hoped for, the result would be a substantial surge in demand for Roundup that should succeed in expanding sales past the expiration of its U.S. patent on glyphosate in September 2000. By 1996, Roundup was generating more than $1 billion in annual sales for Monsanto. To ensure that revenue growth was not held back by volume constraints, in 1996 Monsanto embarked on a $200-million project to expand production capacity for Roundup over three years. To help protect its proprietary position, the company developed a new formulation of Roundup, Roundup Ultra, and applied for a patent on Ultra. Roundup Ultra contained surfactants and additives that that improved the herbicides absorption by weeds. This means that Ultra has less chance of being washed away by rain—it is absorbed by weeds in one to two hours, whereas basic Roundup takes six hours. The company estimated that 90 percent of Roundup users would switch to Ultra by 1997, primarily because of the convenience (prior to Ultra, they had to purchase surfactants and additives separately and add them to Roundup).[59]

At the same time, Monsanto continued a move begun ten years previously to price Roundup aggressively. Between 1992 and 1998, Monsanto reduced the price of Roundup by 9 percent in the U.S. market. This, coupled with the tie-in to sales of Monsanto's genetically altered crops, produced a 201 percent increase in the volume of Roundup sales. Even larger volume increases were observed in other nations where Monsanto's patent had already expired. In Brazil, for example, Monsanto cut the price of Roundup by 45 percent between 1992 and 1998 and was rewarded by a 685 percent surge in volume. In Canada, a 34 percent reduction in price over the same time period led to a 310 percent increase in Roundup volume.[60]

In 1998 and 1999, Monsanto took additional steps to deal with the increased threat of competition after the U.S. patent on glyphosate expired. The catalyst was an attempt by Zeneca, to test its own brand of glyphosate-based herbicide, Touchdown, on Monsanto's Roundup-ready soybeans. Zeneca already sold Touchdown outside of the United States and was preparing to sell in the United States after September 2000. In mid 1998, Monsanto sued Zeneca, saying it illegally acquired Roundup-ready soybean seed for testing Touchdown. The British company responded by suing Monsanto, charging that the company's requirement that farmers use its brand of glyphosate on Roundup-ready crops was anticompetitive. In March 1999, the companies dropped their law suits against each other. In exchange, Monsanto agreed to allow Zeneca to use its Touchdown on seeds using Monsanto's Roundup-ready herbicide-tolerant technology. In return, Zeneca agreed to pay Monsanto an unspecified licensing fee.[61]

While the lawsuits were still pending, Monsanto entered into a number of separate agreements to sell glyphosate to five other agricultural chemical companies, including Dow Chemicals and Novartis. Under the terms of these agreements, which extended for five years and could be renewed thereafter, Monsanto also agreed to allow U.S. farmers to use glyphosate herbicides from these companies on Roundup-ready cotton and soybeans in 2000, and corn in 2001. Commenting on the Dow deal, a Monsanto spokesman noted that "We were concerned that Dow would go and build glyphosate plants and engage in a price war. By having Monsanto provide supplies of glyphosate, Dow will have better costs of production."[62]

Early Results and Looking Ahead Since 1996, the use of transgenic seeds has increased exponentially, from 4 million acres planted in 1996 to 70 million acres in 1998. In 1997, sales of transgenic crops totaled $4 billion. The worldwide market is projected to double by 2002. In 1996, only 1 million acres of Monsanto's Roundup-ready soybeans were planted. In 1998, around half of the U.S. 75-million-acre soybean crop will be Roundup-ready. If growth continues, in 1999 Monsanto will have earned almost $300 million in royalties from sales of soybean seeds alone. *Bt* cotton is also expected to be used on more than half of the U.S. cotton acreage planted in 1999. Moreover, adoption is also occurring quickly overseas. China will use Mon-

FIGURE 2

Major Players in the
Agricultural Seed and
Chemical Industry:
Projected 1999
Revenues

Source: Monsanto Investment Conference, May 3, 1999.

santo's *Bt* cotton for about a quarter of its planting in 1999. Of the nearly 70 million acres planted with genetically modified crops worldwide in 1998, Monsanto varieties accounted for more than 70 percent. Monsanto claims that it could have sold a lot more if it had the seed (see Figure 2 for details).[63]

Human Pharmaceuticals

During the 1990s Monsanto's Searle unit launched a number of products, cumulating in the launch of Celebrex, the COX–2 inhibitor, in early 1999. The first of these, Ambien, a treatment for insomnia, was introduced in 1993 and by 1998 was generating more than $450 million in annual revenues. This was followed by Daypro, a once-a-day NSAID treatment for osteoarthritis and rheumatoid arthritis, which generated annual sales of $308 million in 1998, and Arthrotec, another NSAID drug that also has ulcer prevention properties, which generated revenues of $346 in 1998. Revenues from all three of these drugs, however, could well be dwarfed by sales of Celebrex.[64]

Aware that Merck's competing COX–2 inhibitor, Vioxx, would probably be on the market by mid 1999, Searle entered into a co-marketing agreement with Pfizer. The goal was to leverage the reach of Pfizer's large sales force, reckoned by many to be among the best in the industry. To jump-start market adoption, Searle and Pfizer sent 45,000 "patient starter kits" to physicians and pharmacies. In each free kit there were ten bottles, each containing a twenty-five day supply of Celebrex. Using a sophisticated data base, Searle gave its samples to doctors who most often prescribe arthritis-related painkillers (NSAIDs)—rheumatologists, orthopedic surgeons, and podiatrists. Searle also aimed the kits at physicians in big medical practices who prescribe large amounts of NSAIDs.[65]

As might be expected, the marketing pitch emphasized that Celebrex offers the same pain relief as traditional NSAIDs but causes fewer side effects, such as intestinal bleeding and ulcers. Pricing was perhaps the most difficult issue. Searle and Pfizer tested some 700 different pricing models before settling on a cost to consumers of about $2.42 per day. This was significantly more than generic NSAIDs, which can cost as little as 10 cents per day, but less than most analysts had initially expected. In part, the lower price was a concession to managed care organizations that were trying to get control of soaring prescription costs. Following a formal launch meeting of February 22, hundreds of sales representatives from both companies fanned out to doctors offices in what was one of the most intense marketing efforts ever. The aim was to acquaint the nation's 150,000 doctors with the virtues of Celebrex within six months. This was to be followed by a consumer advertising blitz. The cost of this effort was forecasted to exceed $100 million.[66]

The initial results from this launch effort were nothing short of spectacular. By April, Searle was reporting that it had already directly contacted 70 percent of the nation's doctors. According to independent research data, two months after the launch, about 100 percent of rheumotologists surveyed were aware of the drug and 98 percent had prescribed it. This compared with averages of 85 and 54 percent for new arthritis treatments.[67] It was soon apparent that Celebrex was experiencing the second fastest sales ramp-up of any drug product launch in U.S. history, outpaced only by sales of Pfizer's male impotence drug, Viagra. Two months after the launch, analysts were predicting first-year sales in excess of $550 million, and sales of $3 billion annually by 2002. To put this in context, in 1998 Monsanto's total sales were $8.65 billion, and that of its Searle unit $2.42 billion.

LOOKING AHEAD

In September 1997, Monsanto confirmed its commitment to life sciences when it spun off its commodity chemical businesses to stockholders as an independent unit with sales of close to $3 billion. What remained of Monsanto was focused on agricultural and human life sciences. In both areas, the company had ambitious long-term plans.

Agriculture

The success of the first wave of Monsanto's transgenic crops was based on the benefits farmers gained in the form of improved yield and economies in the use of inputs. Although these products offered no direct benefits to consumers, there was an indirect benefit from the increase in productivity; consumers needed to spend less of their disposable incomes on food. The second wave of transgenic crops, which Monsanto and others were set to introduce in the 1999–2004 time period, offered quality and nutrition traits—in other words, value-added outputs. Examples include oilseed rape with high lauric, stearate, oleic and GLA contents (all nutritionally beneficial), soy-

beans containing proteins that reduce cholesterol or have a medical value in combating osteoporosis or hormonal cancer, maize with enhanced oil and protein contents, and high-starch potatoes, which would take up less fat when fried. The last of these was a Monsanto product scheduled for market introduction in 2000. Monsanto had altered the genetic sequence of the potatoes to make them higher in starches and lower in water. When cut into french fries, the potato absorbs less fat in the deep fryer. The result is that the fries taste the same but have fewer calories and a better texture.[68]

A third wave of genetically modified crop products further down the pipeline could best be described as "plants as factories." Examples under development at Monsanto, Du Pont, and Novartis included using tobacco plants to produce albumin and growth hormones, corn to produce humanized monoclonal antibodies for treating diseases, and transgenic oilseed rape for producing modified fatty acids. Rape could also be modified to produce high levels of beta carotene—much greater than the amounts produced in crops such as carrots. This could be significant for meeting dietary deficiencies in some developing countries. There is also research under way to engineer plants that produce fibers, polymers, or intermediaries that otherwise could come from petrochemicals.

To accelerate the process of developing new transgenic crop varieties, in 1997 Monsanto entered into an alliance with Millennium, a biotechnology firm with expertise in screening genes to identify the causes of diseases—an area known as genomics. The terms of the deal called for Monsanto to pay Millennium $118 million over five years for *exclusive* access to Millennium's gene research in agriculture. In addition, Monsanto stated that it would start a gene research unit in Cambridge, Millennium's base, which would employ up to 150 scientists by the end of 1998. Millennium will hire most of the staff. According to a Monsanto spokesman, "By greatly increasing the speed and precision with which we can analyze new product leads, this agreement will help us rapidly bring future Monsanto life sciences products to market,"[69] The Millennium announcement came one day after Monsanto said it was extending an existing collaboration with another genomics firm, Incyte Pharmaceutical, also in agricultural genetics.

FIGURE 3

COX–2 Technology
Platform

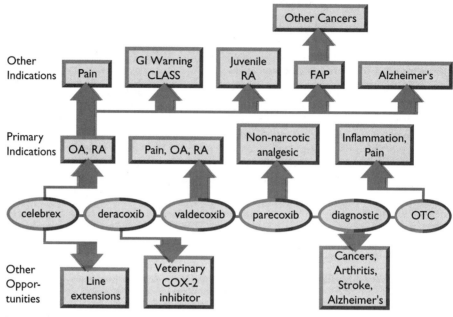

Source: Monsanto.

Pharmaceuticals

In pharmaceuticals, Monsanto has set itself the goal of continuing to grow its product portfolio and development pipeline in arthritis, oncology, and cardiovascular by adding one new chemical or biological entity to the pipeline every year (on average), and one new "technology platform" every three years. The concept of a technology platform refers to the notion of adding multiple indications for the same drug, or using an understanding of a basic biological process to develop a family of drugs.

The concept of technology platform can best be understood by considering how Monsanto hopes to exploit its technology platform in COX–2 inhibitors (see Figure 3). COX–2 enzyme expression is suspected of playing a role in Alzheimer's disease and some cancers, such as colon cancer (FAP). This raises the possibility that a COX–2 inhibitor, such as Celebrex, might be a useful treatment for these diseases. Searle is conducting phase III trials to explore the use of Celebrex in treating FAP, has data from a phase II trial using Celebrex to treat Alzheimer patients, and on the basis of this intends to move forward with a phase III Alzheimer trial later this year. Searle is also looking at producing different COX–2 in-

hibitors, such as deracoxib for the veterinary market, or valdecoxib, a second generation COX–2 inhibitor.

The Concerns of Analysts

While impressed by Monsanto's plans, analysts worried that the company lacked the resources required to grow its business, given its debt load. Of particular concern was the pharmaceutical area, where Monsanto was still a small player relative to industry leaders. There were fears that Searle, with its smaller research budget and sales force presence, would not be able to fully exploit and extend its strong product pipeline.

In mid 1998, Monsanto seemed to have found a solution to these issues when it announced a merger with American Home Products (AHP). AHP had a world-class pharmaceutical sales force and a strong financial position, but lacked Monsanto's deep product pipeline. However, the merger talks collapsed in October 1998, reportedly due to clashes between the top management of both companies over layoffs and attitudes to R&D spending and risk taking. In the aftermath of the collapse, Monsanto's management vowed to go it alone. [70]

TABLE I

Monsanto's Financial Position, 1996–1998

A: Statement of Consolidated Income (dollars in millions, except per share)

	Three Months Ended December 31		Twelve Months Ended December 31	
	1998	1997	1998	1997
Net sales	$ 2,148	$ 1,820	$ 8,648	$ 7,514
Costs, expenses, and other:				
Cost of goods sold	971	749	3,593	3,091
Selling, general, and administrative expenses	675	557	2,421	2,023
Technological expenses	391	326	1,358	1,044
Acquired in-process research and development	213	75	402	684
Amortization of intangible assets	281	59	487	173
Restructuring and other special charges—net	307		272	
Interest expense	98	59	312	170
Interest income	(11)	(9)	(50)	(45)
Other expense—net	69	7	96	8
Income (loss) from continuing operations before taxes	(846)	(3)	(243)	366
Income taxes	(243)	(8)	7	72
Income (loss) from continuing operations	(603)	5	(250)	294
Income from discontinued operations				176
Net income (loss)	$ (603)	$ 5	$ (250)	$ 470
Basic earnings / (loss) per share				
Continuing operations	$(1.00)	$ 0.01	$(0.41)	$ 0.50
Discontinued operations				0.30
Total	$(1.00)	$ 0.01	$(0.41)	$ 0.80
Diluted earnings / (loss) per share				
Continuing operations	$(1.00)	$ 0.01	$(0.41)	$ 0.48
Discontinued operations				0.29
Total	$(1.00)	$ 0.01	$(0.41)	$ 0.77
Weighted average common shares—basic (in millions)			603.5	590.2
Weighted average common shares—diluted (in millions)			603.5	610.5
Earnings before interest and Tax expense (EBIT)	$ (748)	$ 56	$ 69	$ 536

B: Segment Data (dollars in millions)

	EBITDA[1]			
	Three Months		Twelve Months	
	1998	1997	1998	1997
Segment				
Agricultural products	$ 35	$(11)	$1,092	$ 939
Nutrition and Consumer Products	88	109	405	440
Pharmaceuticals	222	197	451	422
Corporate and other	(25)	(26)	(183)	(94)
Total	$ 320	$ 269	$1,765	$1,707

[1]EBITDA (earnings before interest expense, taxes, depreciation and amortization excluding unusuals) is EBIT excluding depreciation, amortization, and the effects of unusual items.

C: Statement of Consolidated Financial Position (dollars in millions)

	December 31, 1998	December 31, 1997
Assets		
Current assets:		
Cash and cash equivalents	$ 89	$ 134
Trade receivables	2,404	1,823
Prepaid assets and other receivables	1,141	692
Deferred income tax benefit	567	243
Inventories	2,004	1,374
Total current assets	6,205	4,266
Net property, plant and equipment	3,254	2,400
Intangible assets	6,047	2,837
Investment and other assets	1,233	1,271
Total assets	$16,739	$10,774
Liabilities and Shareowners' Equity		
Current Liabilities		
Payables and accruals	$ 2,998	$ 1,813
Short-term debt	1,069	1,726
Total current liabilities	4,067	3,539
Long-term debt	6,259	1,979
Postretirement liabilities	871	735
Other liabilities	536	417
Shareowners' equity	5,006	4,104
Total liabilities and shareowners' equity	$16,739	$10,774
Working capital	$ 2,138	$ 727
Debt to capital ratio	59%	47%

Endnotes

1. J. Vorman, "China Seen Swiftly Adopting Transgenic Cotton," *Reuters*, April 26, 1999.
2. Monsanto, "In the Pipeline" (www.monsanto.com).
3. J. Rifkin, "Perils of Unnatural Science," *Financial Times*, June 20, 1998, p. 9.
4. C. Blackledge, "Benefits That Go Against the Grain," *Financial Times*, March 15, 1999, p. 4.
5. R. J. Mahoney, "The Player's Point of View," *Institutional Investor*, June 1989, p. 23.
6. D. Leonard Barton and G. Pisano, "Monsanto's March into Biotechnology," *Harvard Business School Case* 9–690–009.
7. K. Schneider, "Betting the Farm on Biotechnology," *New York Times* Business World Magazine, June 10, 1990, sec. 3, pt. 2, p. 26.
8. R. Steyer, "BST Is Monsanto's Splice of Life," *St. Louis Post Dispatch*, April 25, 1994, p. 12.
9. K. Drlica, *Understanding DNA and Gene Cloning* (New York: Wiley, 1997).
10. Company history (summarized at www.gene.com).
11. Schneider, "Betting the Farm."
12. Ibid.
13. "Offer of Top R&D Post Lured Him Off Campus," *Chemical Week,* January 23, 1980, p. 48.
14. "The Reworking of Monsanto," *Chemical Week,* January 12, 1983, p. 42.
15. Schneider, "Betting the Farm."
16. Steyer, "BST Is Monsanto's Splice of Life."
17. E. B. Fiske, "Monsanto Research Pact Aims to Cut Academic Controversy," *New York Times*, June 4, 1982, p. 21A; D. Sanger, "Corporate Links Worry Scholars," *New York Times*, October 17, 1982, sec. 3, p. 4.
18. Ibid.
19. Fiske, "Monsanto Research Pact."
20. B. J. Spalding, "Monsanto's Bid for the Lead in Biotechnology," *Chemical Week,* June 11, 1986, p. 41.
21. Ibid.
22. "The Reworking of Monsanto," *Chemical Week,* January 12, 1983, p. 42.

23. "Monsanto-Searle: A Biotech Coupling," *Chemical Engineering*, August 19, 1985, p. 26.
24. J. E. Ellis and E. K. Spragius, "Why Monsanto is Bucking the Odds," *Business Week,* August 5, 1985, p. 76.
25. "Monsanto-Searle: A Biotech coupling."
26. Ibid.
27. Spalding, "Monsanto's Bid for the Lead in Biotechnology."
28. Ibid.
29. Ibid.
30. K. Schneider, "Biotech's Stalled Revolution," *New York Times*, November 16, 1986, sec. 6, p. 43.
31. Ibid.
32. Ibid.
33. Schneider, "Betting the Farm."
34. C. S. Gasser and R. T. Fraley, "Genetically Engineering Plants for Crop Improvement," *Science*, June 16, 1989, p. 1293.
35. "Plant-Genetics Advance; Antibiotic-Resistant Petunias," *Popular Science*, 222, (April 1983), p. 19.
36. Gasser and Fraley, "Genetically Engineering Plants for Crop Improvement."
37. Schneider, "Betting the Farm."
38. Ibid.
39. B. J. Feder, "Out of the Lab, a Revolution on the Farm," *New York Times*, March 3, 1996, p. 3.
40. Steyer, "BST Is Monsanto's Splice of Life."
41. K. Schneider, "U.S. Approves Use of Drug to Raise Milk Production," *New York Times*, November 6, 1993, p. 1.
42. R. Steyer, "Discovery of Arthritis Drug Began in WU Lab," *St. Louis Post Dispatch*, April 6, 1998, p. A1.
43. Ibid.
44. These figures come from the FDA's own data base and were compiled by Analysis Group Economics, a drug industry consulting firm.
45. T. M. Burton, "A Pharmaceutical Plumb in Monsanto's Basket," *Wall Street Journal*, June 2, 1998, p. B1.
46. Figures come from Monsato's May 3, 1999, presentation to securities analysts (posted at www.monsanto.com).
47. M. Groves, "Canada Rejects Hormone That Boosts Cow's Milk Output," *Los Angeles Times*, January 15, 1999, pt. C, p. 1.
48. Ibid.
49. K. O'Sullivan, "EU Scientific Committee Casts Doubt on Safety of Injected Hormone Used to Boost Milk Yield," *Irish Times*, March 17, 1999, p. 2.
50. J. Swiatek, "Business of Seeds Changing in Big Ways," *Indianapolis Star*, January 12, 1997, p. E1.
51. R. Steyer, "Monsanto Buys Seed Corn Firm," *St. Louis Post-Dispatch*, January 7, 1977, p. C6.
52. P. Downs, "Badseed: Company Has Near Monopoly on the Seed Industry," *Progressive*, 63 (February 1999), 36.
53. T. M. Burton, "Monsanto's Cost Cutting Steps to Raise Cash for Seed Company Acquisitions," *Wall Street Journal*, November 12, 1998, p. A4.
54. S. Kilman and S. Warren, "Old Rivals Fight for New Turf Biotechnology Crops," *Wall Street Journal*, May 27, 1998, p. A4.
55. R. Steyer, "DuPont's Purchase of Pioneer Validates Big Bet Monsato Made on Seed Companies," *St. Louis Post Dispatch*, March 21, 1999, p. E1.
56. S. J. Willis, "Farmers Torn Over Use of Pest Fighter," *Arizona Business Gazette*, May 29, 1997, p. 16.
57. Monsanto, Bollgard Cotton Update (March 1997).
58. R. Steyer, "Super Soybean," *St. Louis Post Dispatch,* February 25, 1996, p. E1.
59. R. Steyer, "Monsanto Reports Success for New Roundup," *St. Louis Post Dispatch*, December 22, 1996, p. 1E.
60. Figures come from Monsato's May 3, 1999, presentation to securities analysts (posted at www.monsanto.com).
61. R. Steyer, "Monsanto, British Firm End War Over Herbicides," *St. Louis Post-Dispatch*, March 19, 1999, p. C9.
62. R. Steyer, "Monsanto Will License Roundup Rights to Dow," *St. Louis Post Dispatch*, January 20, 1999, p. C1.
63. R. F. Service, "Chemical Industry Rushes Toward Greener Pastures," *Science*, October 23, 1998, p. 608; J. Vorman, "China Seen Swiftly Adopting Transgenic Cotton," *Reuters*, April 26, 1999.
64. Data from Monsanto's May 3, 1999, presentation to securities analysts (posted at www.monsanto.com).
65. "Safe Painkiller Set to Launch Pharmaceuticals World War," *Financial Times,* February 5, 1999, p. 26.
66. A. Barrett and R. A. Melcher, "Why Searle Is Feeling No Pain," *Business Week*, February 15, 1999, p. 36.
67. Data from Monsanto's May 3, 1999, presentation to securities analysts (posted at www.monsanto.com).
68. R. Lenzner and B. Upbin, "Monsanto v. Malthus," *Forbes*, March 10, 1997, p. 58–60.
69. R. Rosenberg, "Millennium Inks Pact Worth as Much as $218M," *Boston Globe,* October 29, 1997, p. C2.
70. T. M. Burton and E. Tanouye, "Another Drug Industry Megamerger Goes Bust," *Wall Street Journal*, October 14, 1998, p. B1.

CASE 36

Tyco International

This case was prepared by Cynthia Montgomery, Robert Kennedy, Lisa Chadderdon, and Harold F. Hogan, Jr., of Harvard Business School.

On October 6, 1995, Tyco International, a diversified U.S. conglomerate, received some very unflattering news. A respected investor monitoring organization, the Council of Institutional Investors (CII), had included the firm in its list of the twenty worst-performing S&P 500 companies. CII generated its list annually, based on a mechanical formula that calculated total shareholder returns over a five-year period.[1] One commentator described the annual rankings as "the corporate equivalent of being put on the school detention list."[2]

The choice of Tyco as one of the twenty culprits was quickly challenged. Tyco's own management described the result as an artifact arising from an abnormally high share price during a narrow window at the start of CII's measurement period. Robert Monks, head of Lens, Inc., an activist money management firm and former member of Tyco's board of directors, also took exception to the report. In a letter of protest to the executive director of CII, Monks asserted that based on his own experience, he believed Tyco was a responsible company fully committed to enhancing shareholder value. He wrote:

> On balance we conclude that this is a first-rate company successfully adding value in the difficult mode of a conglomerate. Our criteria [for evaluating] companies ultimately is—what can we, as informed and effectively involved own-

ers, do to enhance value? Our answer in the case of Tyco is—virtually nothing. What are we missing? [See Appendix].

Was Monk's belief in Tyco justified? Or had the conglomerate form of organization in fact become outdated?

TYCO'S BUSINESSES

Tyco International was a diversified manufacturer based in Exeter, New Hampshire. In fiscal 1996, it had sales of $5 billion and net income of $310 million, up 12 percent and 45 percent, respectively, from the previous year. The company operated more than 300 individual profit centers in over sixty countries. Until recently, many people had been unaware of Tyco's existence, and many still confused it with a toy maker of the same name. In the last few years, however, Tyco had begun to make bids for more visible companies, such as American Standard and ADT, and had gained greater recognition in the press and on Wall Street. In 1997, *Business Week* described Tyco as one of the "stars you may never have heard of" and listed it among its top fifty companies.[3]

Traditionally, Tyco thrived in converter businesses, producing finished goods from raw materials. Each year the company purchased over 1 million tons of steel, 24 million pounds of cotton, and 1 billion pounds of polyethylene. Tyco generally ran its machines and factories twenty-four hours a day, seven days a week, and most of its businesses had at least a 50 percent share of their respective markets. The combination of volume purchasing, efficient production, and dominant market positions helped

Tyco become a low-cost producer and price leader in each of its core industries.

In 1997, the company had six primary operating divisions:[4]

- *Fire protection.* Manufactured, installed, and maintained detection systems, sprinklers, extinguishers, hydrants, hazardous equipment, and other related products. Major company: Grinnell.

- *Flow control.* Manufactured a variety of pipes, fittings, meters, valves, and other pipe-related products. Major companies: Grinnell; Allied Tube and Conduit; Mueller.

- *Disposable medical products.* Produced disposable medical supplies such as gauze; incontinence, urological, and anesthetic supplies; vascular therapy products; and medical electrodes. Major company: Kendall International.

- *Simplex Technologies, Inc.* Produced transoceanic fiber optic cable, underwater power cable, flexible pipe, and other undersea cable products.

- *Packaging materials.* Manufactured a wide variety of packaging materials for industrial and commercial use. Major companies: Armin Plastics; Ludlow Laminating and Coating; Carlisle Plastics.

- *Specialty products.* Described by one company executive as Tyco's "catch-all group, the pieces of the business that didn't really fit with anything else, a conglomerate within a conglomerate." Major companies: Earth Tech (environmental); Tyco Printed Circuit Board Group (printed boards); Twitchell (fabrics); Accurate Forming (metal parts).

Each of the six divisions was headed by its own president, who, in many ways, functioned as a CEO. The presidents were responsible for developing group-level strategy and building sets of related businesses within their respective domains.

There were very few transactions or resource flows among Tyco's divisions. Brad McGee, president of the specialty products division, commented:

> Across the six divisions, there's very little synergy. If you look at the percentage of things that are synergistic versus the size of the businesses, it's really just tiny little opportunities that we find here and there. And where those do occur,

it's generally just because we happen to belong to the same company and somebody out at a factory finds something that could make sense. For example, someone from one of my companies buys something from Kendall.... It's done only if they get a better price than in the market, and only because they happen to know they [Kendall] are there.[5]

The closely related fire protection and flow control divisions ("fire/flow"), which until 1993 had been one large segment, were the exception to this rule. The synergies between these divisions were multifold. Many of the flow control products manufactured by Grinnell, for instance, were used in the installation of the systems sold by the fire protection division. Nevertheless, both divisions were encouraged to negotiate the best terms available in the marketplace, and occasionally would buy from another company.

When Tyco's chairman, L. Dennis Kozlowski, was asked why Tyco ran its six divisions under one umbrella instead of spinning them off as independent companies, he responded:

> If at any time there was better value to be created for the shareholders by spinning off a business or breaking up the company, we would do that in a heartbeat. I own a million shares of the stock—I'm a big stockholder—so if a $70 share price would become a $100 share price, I wouldn't even hesitate—I'd do it right away.
>
> At least once a year we bring in someone from the outside who is highly incentivized to break up the company—for instance someone from J.P. Morgan, Merrill Lynch, or Goldman Sachs—and we tell them, "take a good look at us, break us up, and tell us what we're going to get per share for it. Then tell us if you think we should break up." It's the only way to get an objective look at it. And they have always said that we should stay as we are. Then I take what they say and give it to the Board.
>
> Looking at these factors, I come to the conclusion that the sum of the parts here is a lot less than the value of the whole. And it usually goes the other way for a diversified company. Someday breaking up the company may be the right thing to do. When I took over the company at the beginning of fiscal 1993, our market capital was 1.2 billion dollars. When we finish all these deals now, it will be about 20 billion

dollars—that's four years later. We have created an awful lot of value in the marketplace. I think if we can continue to do that, we will continue to be rewarded.[6]

THE MAKING OF A CONGLOMERATE

Tyco, Inc., was founded by Arthur J. Rosenberg in 1960 as a research and development laboratory. The company went public in 1964, and Rosenberg pursued a vision of rapid growth through acquisitions. By 1973, Tyco had completed twenty acquisitions, sales had increased to over $40 million, and the company had been transformed from an R&D provider into a manufacturing concern.

Inconsistent stock performance and widespread operational problems led to a change in management, and in April 1973, Joseph P. Gaziano was named president, chairman, and CEO. Gaziano established the goal of making Tyco a $1 billion company by 1985. It soon became clear that he intended to pursue his vision through a series of aggressive acquisitions. The business press observed that he made "a habit of hostile raids before that was the fashion."[7]

Gaziano's favored method of takeover was to begin buying a target company's stock on the open market. While he often failed to win the company, several of his aborted takeover attempts left Tyco with handsome profits. For example, a hostile bid for the electronics company Leeds and Northrup ended in failure, but still garnered Tyco $6.4 million in profit. In another instance, Gaziano bought 4.9 percent of the stock in Trane, a manufacturer of air conditioners. When confronted by Trane's chairman, Gaziano agreed to sell back the stock—for 21 percent above the market price. Three failed attempts in the 1970s alone added $15 million to Tyco's earnings.[8] Gaziano soon acquired a reputation as a corporate raider, which made him angry. "Nobody likes to be called nasty names," he says, "but it's like saying a linebacker hits too hard. What's too hard?"[9]

By 1982, Gaziano had transformed Tyco from a small, $41 million manufacturer to a $574 million conglomerate with substantial market share in a variety of industries. The story, however, was not universally positive. One commentator described the company as a "glamorous, shoot-from-the-hip buyer of small companies—a kind of mini-conglomerate

long after conglomerates had gone out of fashion."[10] The recessions of 1979 and 1982 also hit Tyco hard, with profits falling more than 20 percent between 1980 and 1982.

JOHN FORT, 1982–1992

Gaziano did not live to see the day that Tyco reached $1 billion in revenue. He died unexpectedly of cancer in 1982 and was succeeded by John F. Fort, an aeronautical engineer with degrees from Princeton and MIT. Fort had started working at Simplex in 1965 and was president when Tyco acquired the business in 1974. Soon afterward, Fort was named Tyco's COO.

The company Fort inherited in 1982 was "choking on high debt and chaotic management."[11] Fort discarded Gaziano's goal of becoming a $1 billion company and instead strove for improved operating performance. He implemented numerous cost-cutting measures, eliminating perks like corporate jets and apartments, and reducing the staff at corporate headquarters to thirty-five people. *Financial World* reported that "under Fort, all the glamour is gone. So are the jets, and so is much of the management. With the loss of the old management's glamour has come renewed respect from Wall Street."[12]

Fort also pruned nonproductive assets from Tyco's portfolio. He sold $68 million in equity accumulated during eight failed takeover attempts. In one transaction alone, he liquidated over 500,000 shares of Allied Corporation for $54.3 million and netted $11.3 million in profit.[13] At the same time, he jettisoned a number of unrelated businesses, and used some of the proceeds to reduce Tyco's heavy debt. Between 1982 and 1985, the company's long-term debt dropped from 119 to 8 percent of shareholders' equity.[14]

Fort reorganized the firm into three core business segments, each centered on a leading company: fire protection flow control (Grinnell); packaging materials (Armin and Ludlow); and electronic and electrical components (Simplex and the Printed Circuit Board Group).

Building a Disciplined Organization.

Fort focused on careful growth and disciplined, lean operations. Early on, he restructured the compensation system to create powerful incentives and

FIGURE I

Stock Price Analysis for Alternative Corporate Structure

Three investment banks conducted independent analyses to determine whether Tyco's shareholders would be better off if the company was split into several pieces. All three investment banks used similar methodologies. They valued each of Tyco's four business segments using market multiples for similar companies. The studies concluded that Tyco trades at a higher multiple than comparable firms in the printed circuit board and fire/flow industries, and at a multiple slightly below firms in the packaging industry. Thus, the analysts concluded that spinning off Tyco's business segments would not create value for shareholders.

[a]Market capitalization/(*relevant measure*) based on closing stock prices on April 2, 1993.

The comparable companies were the following:

Fire/flow: Amcast Industrial, BWIP Holding, Duriron Company, Gould Pumps, Graco Incorporated, IDEX Corporation, Keystone International, Mark Controls, Watts Industries, Central Sprinkler, and Figgie International.

Packaging: Ball Corporation, Bemis Company, Engraph, Inc., PCI Services, Inc., Sealed Air Corporation, and Sonoco Products Company.

Printed circuits: Altron Incorporated, Benchmark Electronics, Circuit Systems, Diceon, Hadco Corporation, Micronics Computers, and VLSI Technology.

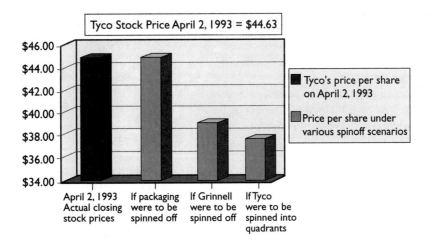

long-term thinking. Base salaries were set low, but performance bonuses could be very high. When an executive took over a division, a target was set for operating profit as a percentage of sales. Going forward, that person's bonus would be a percentage of operating profits above that target. As long as executives ran their divisions, their target rates never changed. Performance bonuses were paid in restricted shares, which vested slowly over time, thus keeping the executive team focused on continued improvement. Fort viewed this system as a way to mimic the incentives that leverage-buyout firms offered their managers:

> Our corporate structure is a very capitalistic system. There is very little central planning. We don't tend to set up a lot of rules. We develop incentives for our people, and it works. All of the earnings and incentives are geared to a higher stock price. Top management receives straight salary and stock options. Middle managers receive a percentage of profits from the profit centers they manage. You have to provide that—the greatest competition for good managers today is the entrepreneurial world. The way to hold onto them is to give them a business of their own within your business.[15]

Fort built a powerful controllers' organization as a complement to the decentralization effort. Managers had great freedom to improve performance, but they had to account for every dollar. Fort's focus on earnings was legendary. He once said, "The reason we were put on earth is to increase earnings per share."[16]

Based on his own experience as president of the fire/flow unit, Kozlowski explained the impact on executives: "… while they have the backing of an old-line, financially secure, capable company, they have all the entrepreneurship of a small entrepreneur who can go out and do what needs to be done without all the encumbrances by the corporation."[17]

Fort's Acquisition Policies

Fort's approach to acquisitions was radically different from his predecessor's. "Joe had a terrific instinct for acquisitions," Fort explained less than a year after becoming CEO. "But my background is in operations. I think we'll use a little more analysis now."[18] Fort believed that a good acquirer had to really understand a target. Someone had to walk around the factories, talk to the workers, and assess the operations. Only then could one decide "whether the managers know what they are doing, or don't. It's not something you can record on a piece of paper. It's very important to get a feel for the company, to judge what you can do with it."[19] Wall Street seemed to agree. Edward Cimilluca, who ran the Special Situations Group for Shearson Lehman Brothers commented, "Fort is a guy who knows how a factory works. He's not romanced by investment banking. His notion of making a company work is to get the best out of what Tyco owns. In doing that, he's completely changed the corporate culture of the place."[20]

During his tenure, Fort made several large acquisitions in the fire/flow division including Grinnell (1986), Hersey Water Meters (1986), Allied Pipe (1987), and Mueller (1988). The acquisitions were designed to make the firm a single source of manufacturing, contracting, and supply for its customers. In 1990, Tyco's fire/flow unit expanded overseas when it acquired Wormald, a manufacturer of fire protection equipment with operations in Europe, Australia, and New Zealand. This significantly expanded Tyco's worldwide presence in fire protection equipment, giving it more than 200 offices in thirty countries. By 1991, the fire/flow group had grown to nearly 80 percent of Tyco's sales.

Performance Under Fort

During Fort's eight years at the helm, Tyco's return on equity averaged 18 percent, and EPS increased an average of 25 percent per year. Tyco's stock price on the NYSE stood at $1.55 in January 1982 and was $29.56 in July 1990, a 41 percent compound growth rate. Total sales hit $1 billion in 1988, $2 billion in 1990, and $3 billion in 1991.

After this phenomenal growth, Tyco was again jolted by recession. The company's fire/flow business was hit particularly hard, as it depended on the highly cyclical construction industry. Between July and October 1990, Tyco's stock price declined 35 percent, to $19.19. EPS decreased from a high of $2.90 in fiscal 1990 to $1.58 in June 1993.

From the very beginning of his chairmanship, Fort had made it known that he planned to step down after ten years. He kept this promise and passed the leadership of the firm to L. Dennis Kozlowski on July 1, 1992.

TABLE 1

Tyco's Consolidated Statement of Income (in thousands, except per share data)

	Year Ended							
	June 30, 1997	June 30, 1996	June 30, 1995	June 30, 1994	June 30, 1993	June 30, 1992	June 30, 1991	May 31, 1990
Sales	$6,597,629	$5,089,828	$4,534,651	$3,262,832	$3,114,500	$3,066,485	$3,107,891	$2,102,740
Costs and Expenses:								
Cost of sales	4,751,987	3,692,885	3,313,301	2,534,322	2,428,406	2,390,218	2,406,077	1,603,054
Selling, general, and administrative	1,066,991	814,179	735,917	482,490	467,404	455,906	438,893	271,256
Merger and restructuring costs	—	—	37,170	—	39,325	25,612	—	—
Interest	90,762	58,867	63,385	45,017	50,453	63,261	73,856	41,256
	5,909,740	4,565,931	4,149,773	3,061,829	2,985,588	2,934,997	2,918,826	1,915,566
Income before income taxes and extraordinary items	687,889	523,897	384,878	201,003	128,912	131,488	189,065	187,174
Income taxes	268,887	213,750	168,285	76,441	56,532	36,222	71,580	68,055
Net income before extraordinary items	419,002	310,147	216,593	124,562	72,380	95,266	117,485	119,119
Extraordinary items	—	—	(2,600)	—	(71,040)b	—	—	—
Net income	$419,002	$310,147	$213,993	$124,562	$1,340	$95,266	$117,485	$119,119
Net Income Per share:a								
Before cumulative effect of account changes	$2.61	$2.03	$2.87	$2.70	$1.58	$2.06	$2.57	$2.90
Cumulative effect of accounting changes	—	—	(0.3)	—	(1.55)b	1.58	—	—
Net income	2.61	2.03	2.83	2.70	.03	2.06	2.57	2.90
Common equivalent shares	160,268	152,862	75,509	46,062	45,750	46,290	45,760	41,020
Cash dividends per common share	$.20	$.20	$.40	$.40	$.38	$.36	$.35	$.31

Note: All figures as reported each year. They are not restated for merger activity or stock splits. See Table 2 for restated figures.

aTwo transactions significantly affected the number of shares outstanding: In October, 1994 Tyco issued 30.4 million shares as part of its merger with Kendall. On October 18, 1995, the company announced a two-for-one stock split effected in the form of a stock dividend.

bEffective July 1, 1992, Tyco adopted the provision of Statement of Financial Accounting Standards ("SFAS") 109 "Accounting for Income Taxes" and SFAS 106 "Employers' Accounting for Post-Retirement Benefits Other than Pensions." These accounting changes resulted in a $71.04 million charge to earnings.

Source: Company documents.

DENNIS KOZLOWSKI, 1992–1997

L. Dennis Kozlowski joined Tyco in the mid 1970s. Within a few years, he had become president of the packaging business; he later headed the fire/flow division; and became Tyco's COO in 1989. In these roles he had worked closely with John Fort. Although he would make a number of changes as CEO, many of Fort's innovations and institutions would remain intact. As Senior Vice President Irving Gutin, a seventeen-year veteran at Tyco, explained, "We are very much the same, and we have changed dramatically at the same time."[21]

During Kozlowski's first year as CEO, the company's name was changed to Tyco International in order to better reflect its evolution into a worldwide provider of branded industrial products and services. The fire/flow division, which was four times as large as the other two divisions combined, was split into two independent segments, creating four divisions in all.

Shortly after he became CEO, Kozlowski initiated a strategic planning process. The end result was to set out two goals for the company: doubling EPS to $5 per share in five years (coined "five in five"), and reducing Tyco's operating cyclicality. Looking back at that period, CFO Mark Swartz commented:

> During the 1980s, we grew the fire/flow division, but electrical and packaging really became the stepsisters of the company. Tyco really was not a diversified company in 1991—it was almost entirely fire and flow. During the recession, we saw that it was in the electrical and packaging areas that we were able to continue 15% earnings growth year over year, while fire and flow were more cyclical. The goal since then has been twofold: to build those other two segments and make them strong, sequel partner businesses that can continue to grow during an economic downturn; and to increase the noncyclical parts of fire/flow [i.e., service].[22]

Finding Growth Because Tyco's core businesses were not expanding at a 15 percent rate, achieving that level of earnings growth would require cost cutting or acquisitions. Although Kozlowski was a fervent cost cutter, he believed that alone would not be sufficient to meet the firm's targets. Instead, he believed that sustained growth would require a number of acquisitions. In the fire/flow division,

Tyco had been pursuing a strategy of industry consolidation through acquisition. These acquisitions were designed to achieve economies of scale and to improve Tyco's relative competitive position. Kozlowski explained:

> If you look at our businesses, we're in industries for the most part that are consolidating—consolidating in manufacturing, distribution, and aftermarket. And so we have no one big competitor or one big customer in any one of our businesses. So that puts us in a very opportune position to continue this and consolidate more.[23]

In addition to pursuing this strategy in the firm's existing core businesses, Kozlowski was also eager to extend it to other industries ripe for consolidation.

Reducing Cyclicality The recession-induced earnings plunge was also a pressing concern for Kozlowski when he took office. He commented on the problem:

> After years of earnings growth in the eighties, Tyco hit a wall in 1991. We hit the wall because nonresidential construction was down in every English-speaking country in the world . . . and at that point in time we were highly dependent on nonresidential construction. Our investor group looked at us and said, "Oh my gosh—I didn't know we had a cyclical diversified company here, I thought we had a long-term sustainable diversified company." . . . So, having faced the cyclicality issue, I really thought we could add a lot of value in Tyco over the long term by addressing that issue. I wanted new growth [acquisitions] to be in long-term, sustainable businesses over the long term.[24]

One effort to address the cyclicality issue was to increase Tyco's service offerings in core businesses. Kozlowski explained:

> We want to service everything we sell in the aftermarket. Service is something that other competitors don't necessarily want to fool around with. There's a 24-hour-a-day, 365-days-a-year commitment, and you need to have infrastructure—the trucks, the systems, the communications—to do that. So we now pursue servicing on a worldwide basis, and will continue to pursue it. Service also happens to carry a margin in excess of 20%, probably 25%–30%.[25]

Service, which was only 15 percent of Tyco's fire protection business in 1993, grew to 45 percent of that business's revenues by 1997. Tyco also combated cyclicality through geographic expansion, so that it was unlikely that a recession in one part of the world would drive down performance across all of its businesses.

When interviewed in 1997, Kozlowski firmly believed that reduced cyclicality led to a premium for the company's stock. CFO Swartz agreed: "if you were to look right now at each of the single line businesses we're in, take the average multiple for each of those businesses and add it all up, you wouldn't come up with [our current] stock price."[26]

Corporate Headquarters

To achieve the firm's goals, Tyco's corporate executives, like its business managers, were expected to perform in ways that boosted shareholder value. This involved oversight and control of the businesses, allocating capital, and managing the firm's compensation system. Corporate headquarters also facilitated the mergers and acquisitions process, provided a minimum of overhead functions, and fulfilled the legal reporting requirements and investor relations needs of a large public company. One division president remarked, "Tyco takes care of a lot of things for us. They provide insurance, treasury functions and cash, investor relations and stock issues. Since I don't have to be concerned with those things, that allows me to really focus on growing my business."[27]

The headquarters of the $6 billion company was located in a small, two-story wooden building. Consistent with the company's philosophy and strategy, headquarters staff and overhead were kept to a minimum. The staff, including secretarial assistants, totaled 50—only 0.1 percent of Tyco's 40,000 employees. Although Tyco had experienced explosive growth for two decades, the corporate staff had increased only slightly. Tyco's had always been keen to eliminate bureaucracy, and headquarters reflected that antibureaucratic zeal. Meetings were kept to a minimum, and communication was direct and efficient—telephone calls or face-to-face discussions were far more common than memos. Formal support staff for senior executives was limited to a single shared secretarial assistant, although the CEO had a dedicated assistant.

Corporate executives were expected to be intimately familiar with the operating businesses. Jack Guarnieri, the corporate controller, explained: "We don't manage at arm's-length. We are making judgments all the time. When I first came [to Tyco] ... the one thing that struck me was how much the corporate people knew about the businesses. And I don't think we've lost a lot of that over the years."[28] Corporate executives came from a variety of backgrounds, including accounting, engineering, and law. Something they all had in common, however, was that they spent a considerable amount of time away from headquarters, traveling to Tyco divisions, working with managers, and assessing potential acquisitions.

There was no general charge on divisions to help cover the costs of corporate overhead, nor was corporate overhead in any way built into the divisions' budgets. Divisions were only billed by corporate for identifiable services, such as the provision of an outside environmental consultant or a lawyer to handle a specific problem. Beginning in 1995, all businesses were charged for the capital they employed and goodwill amortization on acquisitions. The cost of capital uniform across divisions was competitive with market rates.

Control and Compensation

Control of capital was highly centralized at Tyco. Cash was swept daily from the bank accounts of the divisions, and held in a central corporate account. Businesses were not paid interest on the monies held at corporate, and there were no guarantees that the divisions generating the cash would later be able to spend it. Capital expenditures between $100,000 and $150,000 required the approval of the corporate controller, between $150,000 and $500,000 that of the CFO, and beyond $500,000 the approval of the CEO and board of directors.

Under Kozlowski's leadership, decentralization and financial control continued to be at the core of Tyco's approach. The company used financial systems to push responsibility and accountability deep into the organization. Prior to joining Tyco, many of the companies' businesses had been unable to track profitability by product line. Senior Vice President Gutin emphasized the critical role of the company's financial controls: "Our systems are extremely important to us. I think they're our lifeline, our bloodline, because they enable us to know at each one of these 300-odd profit centers what's happening very quickly. Our systems are focused on the bottom line, on earnings. The numbers are very clear and specific."[29]

Given the importance of Tyco's financial systems, corporate management felt it was absolutely critical to have a first-rate controller staff, both at headquarters and within the operating units. One corporate officer noted:

> I would characterize the controller group as being stronger than in most other companies. Generally speaking, in the larger divisions, we try to put someone in the controller job who really is partnering up with the person running the operation. They're not considered bookkeepers. Ninety-nine percent of the ideas that we have for acquisitions surface from the business units and we expect a lot of input from the controllers on the local level before that information gets here. And you really can't do that if you are just keeping the books.[30]

Budgeting

Tyco's budgeting process was top-down, and budgets for the divisions were renegotiated from scratch each year. Since EPS had to increase 15 percent annually in order to reach the "five in five" goal, the budgets in aggregate had to yield that number. This did not translate into automatically setting a 15 percent earnings target for each division. Rather, budgets were set individually, reflecting Tyco's varying goals for each division. Some divisions had earnings targets of 25 percent, others of 12 percent. Additionally, since each business group was expected to strive to be the leader in its industry, each was expected to outperform its industry average in any given year. Swartz commented:

> We try to instill throughout the corporation that our goal is year in, year out to deliver to shareholders a minimum of 15% growth in earnings at the corporate level. We want all our people to really be reaching in the budgeting process. If we had a 15% across the board budgeting plan, I don't think we'd be getting all the potential from the ones who are growing faster. Plus, we have to consider the ones who are in a tough business environment. There might be a business in which being flat year to year would be a success.[31]

The process of setting budgets was rigorous and engaging. One division president, who headed a conservative, risk-averse company Tyco had recently acquired, described his first encounter with the process:

> Dennis [Kozlowski] was taking the group to an off-site strategic planning meeting in the middle of the budgeting process. He said, "You know, we're going to do the budget at this meeting and I expect everyone to meet the levels we've set." He told us he wanted a 15% increase, saying "I don't want to fight with you or any of the other guys. Just come down and show me how you get 15. If you think you can't get it, I want a one-on-one meeting with you—no finance guys."
>
> Well, I knew we were hitting a tough pocket here at my business. Although we were in the process of making an acquisition that was going to help tremendously, it was part of our culture historically that if you give a number when forecasting and setting budgets, you have to know there's a road map to get you there ... So we never put in new products, never put in acquisitions, when we calculated our budgets—those were support. I decided I needed to have a meeting with Dennis because I couldn't in good faith say that I was going to get 15% growth.
>
> So I called Dennis maybe a week later and set up an appointment. He called me back two days before the meeting. He wanted to find out why I was coming down, because I don't meet with him very often—primarily when they bring us in for meetings. I said, "Well, this is in response to your request that we meet with you if we can't bring 15% growth to the off-site we're having." He said, "Well, what do you mean, what's the problem?" And I said, "Well, I just have some trouble." He said, "Where are you now?" I said, "somewhere around 5 percent." And he said, "You don't want to come down here and meet with me and tell me that. It's just not a good thing for you to do.... It would be an ugly meeting." He went on to say, "This is when I have trouble with management. It's always around budget time. Management says one thing and I need something else, and then it's at the end of the day that we have to make fundamental changes."
>
> When I heard that, I just gulped, and said "maybe we ought to make sure we have this meeting because I don't think it would make

sense for me to go to the off-site meeting and find out there needs to be a fundamental change." Dennis finally agreed and we had the meeting. He listened to the issues and saw that there were some things that were really preventing us from getting to that number. He took these into consideration when setting our target, but I think the actual number was about 12 percent.

So, he's tough, but he did give in a little. But, you know, we do the same thing here in our business. We try to intimidate the folks into thinking that they have to do their best or incur the wrath of God. Dennis seems to be more effective at this than I am, though. [Laughter] I don't think that anyone here feels like I did after that phone call. But he simply said, "You've got to make sure these things happen. That's your job. And that's what you are doing—[building the business], acquisitions, cost reductions."

Dennis puts you out there. We're more at risk than we were before we were acquired by Tyco. If you can operate in a pressure cooker environment, though, you really get high rewards. But you're really out there. I know that if I don't deliver that number, I don't think there will be a lot of longevity.[32]

Once budgets were finalized, division presidents independently determined how to pass the budgets down to their direct reports. The budgets would continue to be passed down in this fashion to the line managers at each of Tyco's profit centers.

Remuneration   Complementing Tyco's control systems was an incentive system that provided high rewards for outstanding performance. Base salaries for operating managers were relatively low, but bonuses could be large. Unlike Fort, Kozlowski revised incentive plans annually. CFO Swartz commented on the change:

Dennis thought that the old compensation system (which rewarded managers on the cumulative performance of their businesses) may have boosted an entrepreneurial spirit, but it didn't take into account the money corporate had invested in a business and the return that was required, nor did it provide a powerful incentive for managers to maintain a high-level of performance. What we are supposed to do is grow the business for the shareholders every year—year in, year out. We are not supposed to be paying managers in down years and up years. That's

why we put into place a compensation plan that is focused on year over year results, with a built-in consideration of the costs of generating those results.[33]

Bonuses were based on operating performance, measured against three plateaus.[34] The first plateau was set at the level a manager had to reach to get any bonus, and usually was reached when there was minimal growth over the prior year's earnings. The second plateau was set at the level corporate believed the business should get, without anything going "incredibly right or wrong." Although significant variations existed, in the typical business this plateau was generally set at a 15 percent earnings increase. The third plateau was set at a point at which managers dramatically exceeded expectations. This could occur, for example, if they moved more quickly than expected on the integration of facilities, or put into place new capital expenditures to create additional earnings. Often this plateau coincided with an increase in earnings of 22 percent or greater.

Bonuses escalated rapidly as managers achieved higher performance plateaus. Bonuses for level one were approximately 10 to 20 percent of salary; for level two, 80 percent of salary; and for level three, bonuses increased from there. Management was quick to point out that managers who performed at level one for several years were unlikely to keep their jobs—that, they said, was "the ultimate discipline."

Plateau levels were announced after budgets for each of the operating divisions were determined. When asked about the degree of correspondence between incentive plateaus and budgets, managers differed in their views. Some at headquarters claimed that the linkage was relatively straightforward:

[Businesses] are going to generate what they generate, regardless of what the budget ends up saying—because the budget is a game of cat and mouse. Tyco may agree to a lower budget for a business if the company insists that it can't make a higher one—but the plateaus will be based on corporate's level of expectation at the higher budget level. We pretty much know the plateaus before the budgets are finalized, based on the investments we've put into them, as well as what the competition is doing.[35]

Others claimed that the relationship was less direct. One even praised this ambiguity: "I think the fact that bonus plateaus are a bit of a mystery is one of the strengths of the system. It's very flexible. It can change." Kozlowski himself subscribed to this view and emphasized that there was no direct correlation between incentive plateaus and budgets:

> If you talk to the operating people, they might tell you that their budget is important to their incentive plan. I maintain that it isn't. I never wanted budgets to be part of what a person was going to negotiate for their incentives. That would make the budget take on a whole different view. That makes them think, "How many cookies can I keep under the rug to guarantee that I'm going to max out in the process?" I know—when I was in their position—I would lowball my budget as much as possible, and argue violently for it. So for the operating people, we get their levels of performance over the prior year, and they don't know what the bonus plans are going to be until after their budgets are approved.[36]

Since its inauguration, management believed that the system had been working well. One corporate executive noted:

> To date, there haven't been any catastrophic events that have driven a change in a budget for a business. There have been skirmishes that have broken out, but when that happens, there are other things one can do to make up for that, through cost reductions elsewhere, or moving more quickly to put in new technology to lower costs. Managers are expected to take such steps.

Dennis wants everybody operating at the maximum all the time. So he pushes people to make an aggressive commitment—not an unrealistic one, but an aggressive one—and then he pushes them hard to come up with the results."[37]

Stock was an important element of compensation plans. For corporate executives, earned bonuses were paid 90 percent in stock; for division heads, the percentage was 60 to 70 percent; and for operating managers in individual profit centers, 10 percent. These bonuses often accumulated to large shareholdings. By 1996, seven Tyco executives had accumulated more than $1 million in stock.

The Acquisition Process

Acquisitions were a key activity at Tyco, and one in which the firm had a significant amount of expertise. For most acquisitions, the process started when a division recommended an acquisition to corporate. Division President Brad McGee explained:

> Generally, a lot of the acquisition process takes place in a decentralized fashion. So the guy that runs fire protection in Europe, who reports to the global president of fire protection, is always on the lookout for ways that he can enhance his business. He's always asking, "where are the gaps in my product line, and how can I fill those gaps?" When he finds an opportunity, he brings it back to the worldwide president, and they talk about where else that potential acquisition might fit into the organization. How would it benefit fire protection in Asia? How would it

TABLE 2

Selected Data from Consolidated Statements of Income, 1991–1996
(in millions, except per share amounts)

	1997	1996[a]	1995	1994[b]	1993[b]	1992	1991
Sales	6,598	$5,090	$4,535	$4,076	$3,919	$3,066	$3,108
Net income	419	310	214	189	21	95	117
Per share, net income	2.61	2.03	1.42	1.28	0.14	1.03	1.28

Note: Restated to reflect hypothetical combined operations prior to the Kendall acquisition—for FY 1993 and 1994—and stock splits.
[a]On October 18, 1995, the Company announced a two-for-one stock split effected in the form of a stock dividend. Results for all years presented have been restated to reflect the split.
[b]On October 19, 1994, a wholly owned subsidiary of Tyco merged with Kendall International, Inc. in a transaction accounted for as a pooling of interests. The financial results of Tyco and Kendall have been restated for fiscal years 1993 and 1994 to reflect this pooling.
Source: Company documents.

TABLE 3

Tyco's Consolidated Balance Sheet (in thousands, except per share data)

	Year Ended							
	June 30, 1997	June 30, 1996	June 30, 1995	June 30, 1994	June 30, 1993	June 30, 1992	June 30, 1991	May 31, 1990
Current Assets	2,446,524	1,695,524	1,451,901	1,048,404	1,133,105	1,107,262	1,097,940	732,424
Long-Term Assets								
Property and equipment, net	1,020,457	725,742	658,471	407,200	418,497	413,715	423,197	303,669
Goodwill and other intangible assets	2,106,900	1,232,617	1,004,463	864,416	832,561	910,070	859,082	362,257
Reorganization value in excess of identifiable assets	96,179	102,591	108,801	—	—	—	—	—
Deferred income taxes	58,183	69,823	101,678	65,610	60,281	—	—	—
Other assets	160,086	127,639	56,147	30,748	14,897	20,490	12,747	18,206
Total Assets	5,888,329	$3,953,936	$3,381,461	$2,416,378	$2,459,341	$2,451,537	$2,392,966	$1,416,556
Current Liabilities	1,735,265	1,291,810	1,084,715	810,683	868,541	832,984	854,713	512,651
Long-Term Liabilities								
Deferred income taxes	24,728	19,226	9,599	13,698	8,032	26,791	23,847	26,755
Long-term debt	919,308	511,622	506,417	412,913	562,059	534,951	609,255	269,776
Other liabilities	157,451	192,839	146,049	100,025	100,999	16,260		
	1,101,487	723,687	662,065	526,636	671,390	578,002	633,102	296,531
Shareholders' Equity								
Common stock at par value	84,203	76,488	38,183	23,176	23,161	23,503	23,527	21,018
Capital in excess of par value	1,412,041	627,985	620,633	371,785	366,278	377,634	370,628	119,334
Currency translation adjustment	(100,395)	(34,571)	(9,451)	371,785	366,278	377,634	370,628	119,334
Retained earnings	1,655,728	1,268,537	985,316	720,991	614,967	631,679	553,347	459,265
	3,051,577	1,938,439	1,634,681	1,079,059	919,710	1,040,551	905,151	607,374
Total Liabilities and Shareholders' Equity	5,888,329	$3,953,936	$3,381,461	$2,416,378	$2,459,341	$2,451,537	$2,392,966	$1,416,556

Source: Company documents.

benefit the U.S.? The operating managers don't just think about their individual regions.[38]

After potential acquisitions were identified by operating managers, Tyco's corporate headquarters employed a structured evaluation process. Corporate headquarters started by projecting adjusted EBIT and ROI for the acquisition. The ROI hurdle was generally set in the high teens. Two additional criteria were also important. Only friendly deals were considered and all acquisitions had to be *immediately* accretive to earnings. Acquisitions that hurt short-term EPS were never considered. Kozlowski emphasized that the process was very conservative:

> We do not use revenue enhancements as part of the return. We *want* revenue enhancements—we push them—but that's on *our* account for *our* shareholders, and we refuse to pay somebody else for our ability to increase revenues. Chances are we're going to share some cost reductions in the pricing of the business, but we *know* we're going to get the cost reductions. We will not miss on those because they're laid out—either you're going to consolidate this manufacturing facility, you're going to consolidate this distribution facility, or do away with dual HQ—you know those things are going to happen. But you're not always sure about revenue enhancements. So as a result, we don't use those. And we're absolutely not afraid at all to walk away from a marginal deal.[39]

When a potential candidate had passed the preliminary tests, operating people and corporate personnel began due diligence. In most cases the process was completed in a week to ten days, and sometimes even faster. If the acquisition passed this hurdle, operating managers immediately began to plan how the company would be folded into Tyco. Estimates were made of how many people would be laid off, which plants would be closed, and where the greatest synergies could be exploited. McGee noted:

> In acquisitions done to build existing divisions, we're either trying to use a common distribution channel, or maybe a common sales force, or we're looking for common manufacturing so that we can close down some manufacturing plants. In every acquisition, there's always something that we're going to force the acquired company to do that they did not do before so that we can reduce costs.[40]

While the operating divisions were developing these plans, corporate initiated the negotiation process. To ensure that the lowest price was paid, operating divisions were never involved in the actual negotiations. One senior executive explained,

> It's discipline. You don't let emotions get in the way. You don't let egos get in the way. You don't throw another million, 5 million, or 10 million bucks at a deal once you've set down what it's worth. If someone else tops your bid, you walk. We keep the discipline, and we therefore have a very good record of acquisitions with very strong rates of return.[41]

Tyco's key negotiator for all deals was Senior Vice President Gutin, whom many of his coworkers described as the best negotiator they had ever known. Kozlowski joked, "Irving was born to negotiate—he wakes up negotiating in the morning."[42]

Every acquisition required a corporate "champion" to see the deal through. Most often, the champion was the president of the division into which an acquisition would be folded. Sponsoring an acquisition carried with it a high level of commitment and accountability. The champion, in essence, pledged his or her bottom line that the promised cost reductions and performance levels relating to that acquisition would be met. When an acquisition was completed, the incentive plateaus for the sponsoring division president would be adjusted accordingly.

Growing by Leaps and Bounds

Since 1992, Tyco had completed more than seventy acquisitions. Most of these were "bolt-on acquisitions," undertaken to strengthen Tyco's leadership position in one of its existing core businesses. Examples include Keystone International, bolt-on to flow control, and AT&T's Submarine Systems, a bolt-on to Simplex.

Tyco also made several "platform" acquisitions that provided new opportunities for long-term growth and reduced Tyco's exposure to the business cycle. One of these was the acquisition of Kendall International, a $816 million health care products company. Kozlowski described the merger as one which "turned us overnight into a global force in the expanding market for disposable medical products."[43] The acquisition came at a time when the healthcare industry was on the

TABLE 4

Tyco's Acquisitions

Calendar Year	Selected Bolt-ons	Platforms
1990	National Pipe & Tube Allied Tube & Conduit Wormald and 2 others	
1991	Canvil Anvil Fluorotec	
1992	Neotecha U-Brand Machine shops and 3 others	
1993	Hindle Cockburns Charles H. Winn Stanley Flagg and 13 others	
1994	Preferred Pipe Medical Products Division of Labeltape Meditect and 10 others	Kendall International, Inc.
1995	Smith Valve Tectron Unistrut Automatic Sprinkler and 12 others	
1996	Star Sprinkler Nashua Corp. Betham Corp. Sentry Medical Products Thorn Security ARBO Group Stockham Valves & Fittings Rochester Corp. Triangle Wire & Cable Zettler GmbH and 24 others	Earth Technology Carlisle Plastics
1997 (through May)	Electro Star Babcock Sempell Valve American Fence Sherwood Medical AT&T Keystone Inbrand and 5 others	ADT

Source: Company documents.

verge of a major consolidation and restructuring. A smaller "platform" acquisition was Earth Technology Corp., purchased in January 1997. Earth Tech, a $108 million firm, was involved in both environmental consulting and the development of water and wastewater treatment facilities.

In 1997, Tyco consummated its largest acquisition ever when it bought ADT Ltd., a $1.7 billion home security systems provider.* ADT's business complemented Tyco's service operations in the fire protection sector and would allow Tyco to offer one source to customers for both security and fire monitoring.

After a spate of sizable acquisitions in 1997, some analysts warned that Tyco's pace was not sustainable. Board member Phil Hampton stated: "As you get larger, it takes more to keep producing the same kind of percentage returns. Either you do lots of small deals or you have to find larger ones that make sense. Those are harder to do because there are fewer of them and there is greater risk in each of them."[44]

---

*Tyco's acquisition of ADT was structured as a reverse merger. This means that, technically, ADT purchased Tyco and then changed its name to Tyco International. The purchase was structured in this manner for tax reasons. Tyco executives assumed all key executive positions in the new company.

WHAT'S SPECIAL ABOUT TYCO?

Under Kozlowski, revenues had grown by 66 percent, and earnings by 226 percent between 1992 and 1996. During this period, the company's market capitalization had increased from $1.60 billion to $6.23 billion. In January 1992, a Lehman Brothers analyst report concluded that "Tyco has the strongest fundamentals and best business mix of the diversified companies in our universe."

What *was* so special about Tyco? What accounted for its success? Here is what some people had to say in response to this question:

Corporate Controller Jack Guarnieri:

Everything here at corporate is done in controllable elements, and the people who run the individual businesses really feel like entrepreneurs. The decision levels are pushed down, everything's within the control of the people who run the business. The compensation system reflects [this fact], and people in the businesses make a considerable amount of money. That's what drives the whole place.[45]

The president of the specialty products division, Brad McGee:

FIGURE 2

Tyco International versus S&P 500 Total Monthly Returns, July 1992–June 1997

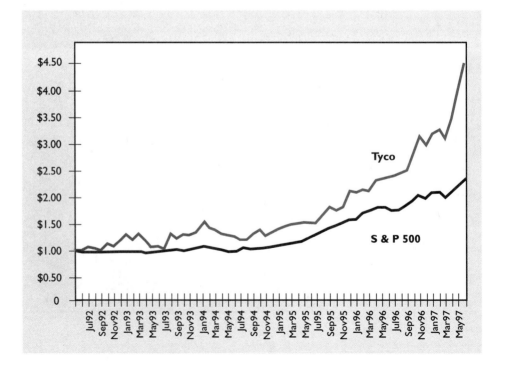

Everybody within the organization understands what Tyco is trying to do . . . we are focused on consistent EPS growth. We do whatever it takes to get there. Earnings per share drives the budgeting process, and since the businesses know that, it also drives their individual acquisition strategies, and their quest for growth. It also drives their desire to have the leanest cost structure, because the first place they can get earnings growth is through cost reduction. But, as Dennis has said before, nobody ever cuts their way to greatness. And so what people focus on most is "how are we going to get growth in this business?"[46]

CEO L. Dennis Kozlowski:

There are a few reasons why no one else is doing what we're doing. Most of the companies we buy are competitors. If you look at our businesses, we're in industries for the most part that are consolidating—consolidating in manufacturing, distribution, and aftermarket. And so we have no one big competitor or one big customer in any one of our businesses. So that puts us in a very opportune position to continue this and consolidate more.

Also, it's boring. It's not as glamorous as other things to tell someone you make fire hydrants and sprinkler heads. I've had a lot of very capable MBAs who have responded to the effect, "I've got a lot of education here, so I'm really not that interested in making fire hydrants or adhesive bandages—that's just not where I see my world." That's an advantage for somebody like us. Everybody wants to be the next Cisco Systems, so everybody is chasing that. In the meantime, we're quietly grinding it out in Rust Belt America. You know, if Bill Gates or other people like that got involved in our kind of businesses, we'd probably be in trouble. But fortunately there aren't a whole lot of people bothering us in our markets, and it's a real advantage.[47]

A VIABLE ORGANIZATION FORM?

Many in academic and business circles debate the viability and merit of conglomerates. In addressing this issue, John Thackeray wrote:

One could easily fill a football stadium with business academics and consultants who deride the strategy of diversification—unrelated diversification, that is to say, like a steel company running a pizza chain, or a real-estate firm owning a baseball team. And to back up their case, they can point to half a dozen studies in the past decade that document the wastefulness of most diversification, which in big companies is invariably done via acquisition.

On the other hand, the number of academics who believe in unrelated diversification could just about fill a phone booth. The conventional wisdom is emphatic: the massive diversification by U.S. business in the '60s, '70s, and early '80s was a red herring. What companies should have been doing instead was improving the global competitive positions of their original businesses.

Analysts and institutional investors have seen it happen a thousand times. A company unravels its diversification through disinvestment and, bingo, the stock price goes up. Which leads the moneymen to think that any management that clings to a passionate attachment to diversification must be wacko.

So, who's right and who's wrong? Perhaps, neither side. The answer seems to be relative: the oft-cited studies against diversification tend to look at the average outcomes—which are indeed lackluster—and don't focus on the few companies that have talent in this type of endeavor. Some years back, Stephen C. Coley of McKinsey & Company isolated a group of large companies that have got to be among the best managed in the country. All with sales of more than $500 million, they've earned a return on equity of more than 15% in every year from 1970 to 1988. There are only 30 of them. Of these, 13 were multibusiness companies. What's more, when all 30 are ranked for total shareholder return, in every five-year period since 1970 the multibusiness companies win hands down. Says Coley: "I suspect that the people who are good at diversifying do it all the time. They have mechanisms in place, they've been through the process a number of times. They know what kinds of business they can and can't manage."

It is the neophytes who push up the casualty rates. Which is why companies recently released from the straitjacket of regulation—notably those in the transportation, telecommunications, and power utilities industries—have squandered billions of their shareholders' money in recent years.

TABLE 5

Tyco's Sales and Operating Income by Segment, 1989–1996 as Reported Each Year (in $ thousands)

	Year Ended June 30				
	1996	*1995*	*1994*	*1993*	*1992*
Fire protection					
Sales	$1,991	$1,703	$1,526	$1,588	$1,616
Operating income	128	86	69	47	84
Flow control					
Sales	1,159	1,014	914	745	721
Operating income	114	90	70	38	33
Electrical					
Sales	481	430	437	413	392
Operating income	88	76	70	67	53
Disposable and safety products[a]					
Sales	1,459	1,387	—	—	—
Operating	292	261	—	—	—
Packing material[a]					
Sales	—	—	386	368	337
Operating income	—	—	54	45	41

[a]Following the Kendall acquisition in October 1994, the packaging business segment was combined with Kendall to create the disposable and safety products division.
Source: Company documents.

...There are many pathways to triumph through unrelated diversification. Successful diversification is like great art. It knows no rules. But its presence is unmistakable.[48]

APPENDIX: LETTER FROM ROBERT MONKS OF LENS, INC., TO THE COUNCIL OF INSTITUTIONAL INVESTORS (OCTOBER 6, 1995)

"The Council of Institutional Investors' ("CII") annual list of 'focus companies' is an important event. We spend much energy and time in trying to identify such companies. The 1995 CII list includes one company in particular which we evaluate very differently—**TYCO INTERNATIONAL**. I am writing to learn about differences in our methodologies—to find out what we don't know, so to speak.

"I know Tyco well. Indeed, I served as a direc-tor for ten years, from 1985 till 1994. Since that time I have only the information available to all shareholders. In our analysis there are at least three aspects of Tyco that bring it into our preliminary pool of potential 'focus companies':

"First, its five year total return is in the lowest decline of all companies we follow. As I look back five years to the third calendar quarter of 1990, I recollect the acquisition of Wormald—the largest transaction the company had ever entered into and one which made Tyco a worldwide business.... The stock price soared—briefly—up to a high of $60^{7/8}$ on July 25, 1990.... Thereafter, cyclical downturn of the nonresidential construction business resulted in a reduction of earnings and lowering stock price down to a low of $31^{3/4}$ (July 27) in the summer of 1992 which happened to be the time the current chief executive officer took his position. Our own calculations indicate an annual return (calculated on a "total return" basis) for holders of Tyco stock on September 19, 1995 ... of 35.4% for the previous year; 20.9% for three years; and 3.1% for five years....

"Second, Tyco is a multi-industry company—a traditional conglomerate. Our experience (Litton in the 1960s, ITT in the 1970s, Sears and others in recent times) suggests that this is a commercial mode in which it is extremely difficult to add value competitively over a long period of time. Some companies manage it—most notably GE under Jack Welch. Is Tyco a GE or an ITT? This is a question that the directors asked often and pointedly. We periodically engaged independent investment bankers—DLJ was the most recent—to analyze the 'spin off' values available to shareholders and compare them with the current market.... It is apparent that this company has achieved an enviable record of increasing earnings, cash flow, and earnings per share over a decade. It has made a great deal of money for its owners save only those who bought between June and September 1990.

"Third, the Board contains in addition to the CEO, the former CEO and the general counsel, resulting in three out of eight members being "insiders." ... The Tyco directors for many years have invested their entire compensation in common stock. The average value of the shareholdings of each of the seven 'nonmanagement' directors is in excess of $1 million.... For several years, United Shareholders of America ranked the largest American companies with a composite measure containing equal weighting for 'governance' and for 'performance.' On two occasions, Tyco was ranked in the top ten companies in the country and publicly given appropriate awards.... It is probably the only company incorporated in the Commonwealth of Massachusetts to have timely opted out of the statutory requirement for staggering election to boards of directors (disgracefully rushed through the legislature to "save" the Norton Company in 1988) ...

"On balance we conclude that this is a first rate company successfully adding value in the difficult mode of a conglomerate. Our criteria for 'focus companies' ultimately is—what can we, as informed and effectively involved owners, do to enhance value. Our answer in the case of Tyco is—virtually nothing. What are we missing?"

Source: Company documents.

Endnotes

1. CII used the following methodology to determine which companies were listed: First, a list of S&P 500 companies that underperformed their industry median in five-year and one-year total returns were identified. Those that outperformed the S&P 500 average for five-year total shareholder returns were dropped from the list. For the remaining companies, the difference between the industry's median five-year returns and each company's five-year returns was calculated to establish ranking. The lowest 20 firms were selected for the list.
2. Richard Thomson, "An Investor Calls," *Management Today,* December 1995, p. 62.
3. "The Business Week 50," *Business Week,* March 24, 1997, p. 79.
4. For external reporting purposes, Tyco divided its businesses into only four segments.
5. Interview with Brad McGee, April 28, 1997.
6. Interview with Dennis Kozlowski, June 23, 1997.
7. Laura Jereski, "Synergy, synergy, synergy," *Forbes,* November 14, 1988, p. 194.
8. Mitchell Lynch, "Tyco's Success Acquisition Still Leaves Questions About Gaziano's Grand Design," *Wall Street Journal,* August 27, 1981, p. 21.
9. Aimee Morner, "The Man Who Would Be Geneen," *Fortune,* March 12, 1979, p. 108.
10. Stephen Kindel, "The Guy Who Knows Factories," *Financial World,* June 30, 1987, p. 36.
11. "Tyco: Pursuing Profits as Relentlessly as It Once Pursued Growth," *Business Week,* March 5, 1984, p. 96.
12. Kindel, "The Guy Who Knows Factories," p. 36.
13. "Turning the Tables at Tyco," *Business Week,* August 29, 1983, p. 65.
14. Dougald MacDonald, "Grinnell Acquisition Pushes Tyco Revenue Past $1 Billion Mark," *New England Business,* February 3, 1986, p. 32.
15. "John Fort: CEO, Tyco Laboratories," *The Business of New Hampshire* (February 1991), 38.
16. John Thackray, "Diversification: What It Takes to Make It Work," *Across the Board* (November 1991), 17.
17. Mark McLaughlin, "Flat and Happy at the Top," *New England Business* (March 1990), 19.
18. "Tyco Official Adds Post of Chairman," *New York Times,* July 14, 1983, sec. D, p. 2.
19. Thackray, "Diversification," p. 17.
20. Kindel, "The Guy Who Knows Factories," p. 36.
21. Interview with Irving Gutin, April 25, 1997.
22. Interview with Mark Swartz, June 12, 1997.
23. Interview with Dennis Kozlowski, June 23, 1997.
24. Ibid.
25. Ibid.
26. Interview with Swartz.
27. Interview with Tyco executive.
28. Interview with Jack Guarnieri, May 9, 1997.
29. Interview with Gutin.
30. Interview with Tyco executive.
31. Interview with Swartz.
32. Interview with Tyco executive.
33. Interview with Swartz.
34. Two calculations were used to determine the level of compensation each division head would receive. The first was a

straightforward EBIT calculation. If certain target EBIT levels, called plateaus, were met, a percentage of base salary was awarded as a bonus. Second, a cash flow modifier was included. Corporate headquarters looked at inventory, receivables, contracts in process, payables, and accrued expenses on a quarterly basis to determine if cash flow trailed or exceeded its projected target. The EBIT-based bonus was then adjusted by a multiple of this percentage variation. If a business made an acquisition during the year, the target was reset to reflect the acquisition, but only at the acquisition's pre-Tyco level of performance.

35. Interview with Tyco executive.
36. Interview with Kozlowski.
37. Interview with Tyco executive.
38. Interview with Brad McGee, April 28, 1997.
39. Interview with Kozlowski.
40. Interview with McGee.
41. Interview with Tyco executive.
42. Interview with Kozlowski.
43. 1995 Tyco Annual Report, p. 4.
44. "Corporate Focus: Tyco International Isn't Playing, It's Out on the Prowl," *The Wall Street Journal,* Jan. 17, 1997, p. B4.
45. Interview with Jack Guarnieri.
46. Interview with McGee.
47. Interview with Kozlowski.
48. John Thackray, "Diversification: What It Takes to Make It Work," p. 17.

CASE 37

Philips Versus Matsushita: Preparing for a New Round

This case was prepared by Christopher A. Bartlett of Harvard Business School.

Throughout their long histories, N.V. Philips (Netherlands) and Matsushita Electric Industrial (Japan) had followed very different strategies and emerged with very different organizational capabilities. Philips built its success on a worldwide portfolio of responsive national organizations while Matsushita based its global competitiveness on its centralized, highly efficient operations in Japan.

During the 1980s, both companies experienced major challenges to their historic competitive positions and organizational approaches that forced major changes, and throughout the 1990s, both companies were struggling to reestablish their competitiveness. With the twenty-first century around the corner, observers were divided on the effectiveness of the massive strategic and organizational changes both companies had implemented, and how it would affect their long-running competitive battle.

PHILIPS: BACKGROUND

In 1892, Gerard Philips and his father opened a small light bulb factory in Eindhoven, Holland. When their venture almost failed, they recruited Gerard's brother, Anton, an excellent salesman and manager. By 1900, Philips was the third largest light bulb producer in Europe.

From its founding, Philips developed a tradition of caring for workers. In Eindhoven, it built com-

This case is intended to be used as a basis for class discussion rather than as an illustration of either effective or ineffective handling of the situation. This case was prepared by Christopher A. Bartlett, Harvard Business School. Used by permission.

pany houses, bolstered education, and paid its employees so well that other local employers complained. When Philips incorporated in 1912, it set aside 10 percent of profits for employees.

Technological Competence and Geographic Expansion

While larger electrical products companies were racing to diversify, Philips made only light bulbs. This one-product focus and Gerard's technological prowess enabled the company to create significant innovations. Company policy was to scrap old plants and use new machines or factories whenever advances were made in new production technology. Anton wrote down assets rapidly and set aside substantial reserves for replacing outdated equipment. Philips also became a leader in industrial research, creating physics and chemistry labs to address production problems as well as more abstract scientific ones. The labs developed a tungsten metal filament bulb that was a great commercial success and gave Philips the financial strength to compete against its giant rivals.

Holland's small size soon forced Philips to look beyond its Dutch borders for enough volume to mass produce, and in 1899, Anton hired the company's first export manager. Soon the company was selling into such diverse markets as Japan, Australia, Canada, Brazil, and Russia to establish new markets. In 1912, as the electric lamp industry started to show signs of overcapacity, Philips started building sales organizations in the United States, Canada, and France, and other cartel-free countries. All other functions remained highly centralized in Eindhoven. In many foreign countries, Philips created joint ventures with domestic companies to gain acceptance in local markets.

In 1919, Philips entered into the "Principal Agreement" with General Electric, giving each company the use of the other's patents. The agreement also divided the world into "three spheres of influence": General Electric would control North America; Philips would control Holland; but both companies agreed to compete freely in the rest of the world. (General Electric also took a 20 percent stake in Philips.) After this time, Philips began evolving from a highly centralized company whose sales were conducted through third parties to a decentralized sales organization with autonomous marketing companies in 14 European countries, China, Brazil, and Australia.

During this period, the company also broadened its product line significantly. In 1918, it began producing electronic vacuum tubes; eight years later its first radios appeared, capturing a 20 percent world market share within a decade; and during the 1930s, Philips began producing x-ray tubes. The Great Depression brought with it trade barriers and high tariffs, and Philips was forced to build local production facilities to protect its foreign sales of these products.

PHILIPS: ORGANIZATIONAL DEVELOPMENT

One of the earliest traditions at Philips was a shared but competitive leadership by the commercial and technical functions. Gerard, an engineer, and Anton, a businessman, began a subtle competition where Gerard would try to produce more than Anton could sell and vice versa. Nevertheless, the two agreed that strong research was vital to Philips' survival.

During the late 1930s, in anticipation of the impending war, Philips transferred its overseas assets to two trusts, British Philips and the North American Philips Corporation; it also moved most of its vital research laboratories to Redhill in Surrey, England, and its top management to the United States. Supported by the assets and resources transferred abroad, and isolated from their parent, the individual country organizations became more independent during the war.

Because waves of Allied and German bombing had pummeled most of Philips' industrial plant in the Netherlands, the management board decided to build the postwar organization on the strengths of the national organizations (NOs). Their greatly increased self-sufficiency during the war had allowed most to become adept at responding to country-specific market conditions—a capability that became a valuable asset in the postwar era. For example, when international wrangling precluded any agreement on television transmission standards, each nation decided at different times whether to adopt PAL, SECAM, or NTSC standards. Furthermore, consumer preferences and economic conditions varied: in some countries, rich, furniture-encased TV sets were the norm; in others sleek, contemporary models dominated the market. In the United Kingdom, the only way to penetrate the market was to establish a rental business; in richer countries, a major marketing challenge was overcoming elitist prejudice against television. In this environment, the independent NOs had a great advantage in being able to sense and respond to the differences.

Eventually, responsiveness extended beyond adaptive marketing. As NOs built their own technical capabilities, product development often became a function of local marketing conditions. For example, Philips of Canada created the company's first color TV; Philips of Australia created the first stereo TV; and Philips of the United Kingdom created the first TVs with teletext.

While NOs took major responsibility for financial, legal, and administrative matters, fourteen product divisions (PDs), located in Eindhoven, were formally responsible for development, production, and global distribution. (In reality, the NOs' control of assets and the PDs' distance from the operations often undercut this formal role.) The research function remained independent and, with continued strong funding, set up eight separate laboratories in Europe and the United States.

While the formal corporate-level structure was represented as a type of geographic/product matrix, it was clear that NOs had the real power. NOs reported directly to the management board, which Philips enlarged from four members to ten to ensure that top management remained in control of the vital NO operations. The board encouraged interaction with the highly autonomous NOs, and each NO regularly sent envoys to Eindhoven to represent its interests. Top management, most of whom had careers including multiple foreign tours of duty, made frequent overseas visits to the NOs. In 1954, the International Concern Council was established to formalize regular meetings among the principal managers from all the NOs and the board of management.

Within the NOs, the management structure mimicked the legendary joint technical and commercial leadership of the two Philips brothers. NOs were led by a technical manager and a commercial manager. In some locations, a finance manager filled out the top management triad that typically reached key decisions collectively. This cross-functional coordination capability was reflected throughout the NOs organization. On the front lines, product teams, comprising junior managers from the commercial and technical functions, set product policies and carried out administrative functions. Cross-functional coordination also occurred at the product group level through group management teams, whose technical and commercial members met monthly to review progress and resolve inter-functional differences. Finally, the senior management committee of each NO (with top commercial, technical, and financial managers) reviewed progress to ensure that product group directions fit with national strategies and priorities.

The overwhelming importance of foreign operations to Philips, the commensurate status of the NOs within the corporate hierarchy, and even the cosmopolitan appeal of many of the offshore subsidiaries' locations encouraged many Philips managers to take extended foreign tours of duty, working in a series of two- or three-year posts. This elite group of expatriate managers identified strongly with each other and with the NOs as a group, and had no difficulty representing their strong, country-oriented views to corporate management.

PHILIPS: ATTEMPTS AT REORGANIZATION

In the 1960s, the creation of the Common Market eroded trade barriers within Europe and diluted the rationale for maintaining independent, country-level subsidiaries. New transistor- and printed circuit-based technologies demanded larger production runs than most national plants could justify, and many of Philips' competitors were moving production of electronics to new facilities in low-wage areas in East Asia and Central and South America. Despite its many technological innovations, Philips' ability to bring products to market began to falter. In the 1960s, the company invented the audiocassette but let its Japanese competitors capture the mass market. A decade later, its R&D group developed the V2000 videocassette format—superior technically to Sony's Beta or Matsushita's VHS—but could not successfully market the product. Indeed, North America Philips rejected the V2000, choosing instead to outsource, brand, and sell a VHS product under license from Matsushita. Within three years, Philips was forced to abandon V2000 and produce a VHS product.

Over three decades, six chairmen experimented with reorganizing the company to deal with its growing problems. Yet in the late 1990s, Philips's financial performance remained poor and its global competitiveness was still in question. (See Tables 1 and 2.)

Van Reimsdijk and Rodenburg Reorganizations, 1970s

Concerned about what *Management Today* described as "continued profitless progress," newly appointed CEO Hendrick van Reimsdijk created an organization committee to prepare a policy paper on the division of responsibilities between the PDs and the NOs. Their report, dubbed the "Yellow Booklet," outlined the disadvantages of Philips' matrix organization in 1971:

> Without an agreement [defining the relationship between national organizations and product divisions], it is impossible to determine in any given situation which of the two parties is responsible.... As operations become increasingly complex, an organizational form of this type will only lower the speed of reaction of an enterprise.

On the basis of this report, van Reimsdijk proposed rebalancing the managerial relationships between PDs and NOs—"tilting the matrix" in his words—to allow Philips to increase the scale of production, decrease the number of products marketed, concentrate production, and increase the flow of goods among national organizations. He proposed closing the least efficient local plants and

TABLE 1

Philips Group Summary Financial Data, 1970–1997 (millions of guilders unless otherwise stated)

	1997	1996	1995	1990	1985	1980	1975	1970
Net sales	F76,453	F69,195	F64,462	F55,764	F60,045	F36,536	F27,115	F15,070
Income from operations (excluding restructuring)	5,065	2,537	4,090	2,260	3,075	1,577	1,201	1,280
Income from operations (including restructuring)	4,960	1,812	4,044	-2,389	N/A	N/A	N/A	N/A
As a percentage of net sales	6.5%	2.6%	6.3%	-4.3%	5.1%	4.3%	4.5%	8.5%
Income after taxes	3,278	685	2,889	F-4,447	F1,025	F532	F341	F446
Net income from normal business operations	3,291	723	2,684	-4,526	n/a	328	347	435
Stockholders' equity (common)	19,457	13,956	14,055	11,165	16,151	12,996	10,047	6,324
Return on stockholders' equity	16.6%	5.0%	20.2%	-30.2%	5.6%	2.7%	3.6%	7.3%
Distribution per common share, par value F 10 (in guilders)	F2.00	F1.60	F1.60	F0.0	F2.00	F1.80	F1.40	F1.70
Total assets	59,441	55,072	54,683	51,595	52,883	39,647	30,040	19,088
Inventories as a percentage of net sales	18.6%	17.9%	18.2%	20.7%	23.2%	32.8%	32.9%	35.2%
Outstanding trade receivables in month's sales	1.7	1.7	1.6	1.6	2.0	3.0	3.0	2.8
Current ratio	1.7	1.7		1.4	1.6	1.7	1.8	1.7
Employees at year-end (in thousands)	270	263	265	273	346	373	397	359
Wages, salaries and other related costs				F17,582	F21,491	F15,339	F11,212	F5,890
Exchange rate (period end; guilder/$)	2.02	1.74	1.60	1.69	2.75	2.15	2.69	3.62
Selected Data in Millions of Dollars								
Sales	$39,207	$40,944	$40,039	$33,018	$21,802	$16,993	$10,098	$4,163
Operating profit	2,543	1,072	2,512	1,247	988	734	464	NA
Pretax income	2,174	541	2,083	-2,380	658	364	256	NA
Net income	2,940	(349)	1,667	-2,510	334	153	95	120
Total assets	29,426	31,651	32,651	30,549	19,202	18,440	11,186	5,273
Shareholders' equity (common)	9,632	8,021	8,784	6,611	5,864	6,044	3,741	1,747

Source: Annual Reports; Standards & Poor's *Compustat*; Moody's Industrial and International Manuals.

TABLE 2

Philips Group, Sales by Product and Geographic Segment, 1985–1997 (million guilders)

	1997		1996		1995		1990		1985	
Net Sales by Product Segment										
Lighting	F10,024	13%	F8,860	13%	F8,353	13%	F7,026	13%	F7,976	12%
Consumer electronics	23,825	31	24,039	35	22,027	34	25,400	46	16,906	26
Domestic appliances	—		—		—		—		6,644	10
Professional products/systems	12,869	17	11,323	16	11,562	18	13,059	23	17,850	28
Components/semiconductors	15,003	20	11,925	17	10,714	17	8,161	15	11,620	18
Software/services	13,009	17	11,256	16	9,425	15				
Miscellaneous	1,723	2	1,783	3	2,381	4	2,118	4	3,272	5
Total	76,453	100%	69,195	100%	64,462	100%	F55,764	100%	F64,266	100%
Operating Income by Sector										
Lighting	1,151	23%	702	39%	983	24%	419	18%	F 910	30%
Consumer electronics	772	16	10	1	167	4	1,499	66	34	1
Domestic appliances	—		—						397	13
Professional products/systems	502	10	0	0	157	4	189	8	1,484	48
Components/semiconductors	2,262	46	1,496	83	2,233	55	-43	-2	44	13
Software/services	1,173	24	490	27	886	22				
Miscellaneous	188	4	199	11	423	10	218	10	200	7
Increase not attributable to a sector	(1,090)	(22)	(1,085)	(60)	(805)	(20)	-22	-1	6	0
Total	4,960	100%	1,812	1,006	4,044	100%	2,260	100%	F3,075	100%

Notes: Totals may not add up due to rounding.
Product sector sales after 1988 are external sales only; therefore no eliminations are made. Sector sales before 1988 include sales to other sectors; therefore eliminations are made.
Data are not comparable to consolidated financial summary due to restating.
Source: Annual Reports.

converting the best to International Production Centers (IPCs), each supplying many NOs. In so doing, van Reimsdijk hoped that PD managers would gain control over manufacturing operations. Due to the political and organizational difficulty of closing local plants, however, implementation was slow. By the end of the decade, several IPCs had been established, but the NOs seemed as powerful and independent as ever.

In the late 1970s, his successor as CEO, Dr. Rodenburg, continued this thrust. He reinforced matrix simplification by replacing the dual commercial and technical leadership with single management at both the corporate and national organizational levels. Yet the power struggles continued.

Wisse Dekker Reorganization, 1982

Unsatisfied with the company's slow response and concerned by its slumping financial performance, upon becoming CEO in 1982, Wisse Dekker outlined a new global strategy. Aware of the cost advantage of Philips's Japanese counterparts, he created more IPCs and closed inefficient operations—particularly on the Continent where 40 of the company's more than 200 European plants were shut. He focused on core operations by selling some businesses (for example, welding, energy cables, and furniture) while acquiring an interest in Grundig and Westinghouse's North American lamp activities. Dekker also supported technology-sharing agreements and entered alliances in off-shore manufacturing.

To deal with the slow-moving bureaucracy, he continued his predecessor's initiative to replace dual leadership with single general managers. He also continued to "tilt the matrix" by giving PDs formal product management responsibility, but leaving NOs responsible for local profits. And he energized the management board by reducing its size, bringing on directors with strong operating experience, and creating subcommittees to deal with difficult issues. Finally, Dekker redefined the product-planning process, incorporating input from the NOs, but giving global PDs the final decision on long-range direction. Still sales declined and profits stagnated.

Van der Klugt Reorganization, 1987

When Cor van der Klugt succeeded Dekker as chairman, Philips had lost its long-held consumer electronics leadership position to Matsushita, and

was one of only two non-Japanese companies in the world's top ten. Its net profit margins of 1 to 2 percent not only lagged behind General Electric's 9 percent, but even its highly aggressive Japanese competitors' slim 4 percent. Van der Klugt set a profit objective of 3 to 4 percent and made beating the Japanese companies a top priority.

As van der Klugt reviewed Philips's strategy, he designated various businesses as core (those that shared related technologies, had strategic importance, or were technical leaders) and non-core (stand-alone businesses that were not targets for world leadership and could eventually be sold if required). Of the four businesses defined as core, three were strategically linked: components, consumer electronics, and telecommunications and data systems. The fourth, lighting, was regarded as strategically vital because its cash flow funded development. The noncore businesses included domestic appliances and medical systems, which van der Klugt spun off into joint ventures with Whirlpool and GE, respectively.

In continuing efforts to strength the PDs relative to the NOs, van der Klugt restructured Philips around the four core global divisions rather than the former fourteen PDs. This allowed him to trim the management board, appointing the displaced board members to a new policy-making group management committee. Consisting primarily of PD heads and functional chiefs, this body replaced the old NO-dominated international concern council. Finally, he sharply reduced the 3,000-strong headquarters staff, reallocating many of them to the PDs.

To link PDs more directly to markets, van der Klugt dispatched many experienced product line managers to Philips' most competitive markets. For example, management of the digital audio tape and electric shaver product lines was relocated to Japan, while the medical technology and domestic appliances lines were moved to the United States.

Such moves, along with continued efforts at globalizing product development and production efforts, required that the parent company gain firmer control over NOs, especially the giant North American Philips Corp. (NAPC). Although Philips had obtained a majority equity interest after World War II, the U.S. company did not always respond to directives from the center. Referring to its much publicized choice of Matsushita's VHS video cassette format over its parent's V2000 format, NAPC's chairman said, "We made the best decisions for the parochial interests of our stockholders. They were not always parallel with those of Philips worldwide." To prevent replays of such experiences, in 1987 van der Klugt repurchased publicly owned NAPC shares for $700 million.

Reflecting the growing sentiment among some managers that R&D was not market-oriented enough, van der Klugt halved spending on basic research to about 10 percent of total R&D. To manage what he described as "R&D's tendency to ponder the fundamental laws of nature," he made R&D the direct responsibility of the businesses being supported by the research. This required that each research lab become focused on specific business areas (see Table 3).

Finally, van der Klugt continued the effort to build efficient, specialized, multimarket production facilities by closing 75 of the company's 420 remaining plants worldwide. He also eliminated 38,000 of its 344,000 employees—21,000 through divesting businesses—shaking up the myth of lifetime employment at the company. He anticipated that all this restructuring would lead to a financial recovery by 1990. Unanticipated lossed for that year—more than 4.5 billion Dutch guilders ($2.5 billion)—provoked a class-action lawsuit by angry American investors, who alleged that positive projections by the company had been misleading. In a surprise move, on May 14, 1990, van der Klugt and half the management board were replaced.

Timmer Reorganization, 1990

The new president, Jan Timmer, had spent most of his thirty-five-year Philips career turning around unprofitable businesses. In an early meeting with his top 100 managers he distributed a hypothetical—but fact-based—press release announcing that Philips was bankrupt. (There had already been rumors of a takeover or a government bailout.) "So what action can you take this weekend?" he challenged.

Under "Operation Centurion," headcount was reduced by 68,000, or 22 percent, over the next eighteen months, earning Timmer the nickname "The Butcher of Eindhoven." Because European laws required substantial compensation for layoffs—Eindhoven workers received fifteen months' pay, for example—the first round of 10,000 layoffs alone cost Philips $700 million. To spread the burden around the globe, and to speed the process, Timmer asked his PD managers to negotiate cuts with NO managers. According to one report, however, country managers were "digging in their heels to save local jobs." But the cuts came—many from overseas operations. In addition to the job cuts, Timmer vowed to "change the way we work." He established new performance rules and asked hundreds of top managers to sign contracts that committed them to specific financial goals. Those who broke those contracts were replaced—often with outsiders.

To focus resources further, Timmer sold off various businesses, including integrated circuits to Matsushita, minicomputers to Digital, defense electronics to Thomson, and the remaining 53 percent of appliances to Whirlpool. Yet profitability was still well below the modest 4 percent on sales he promised. In particular, consumer electronics lagged with slow growth in a price-competitive market. The core problem was identified by a 1994 McKinsey study that estimated that value added per hour in Japanese consumer electronic factories was still 68 percent above that of European plants.

TABLE 3

Philips Research Labs by Location and Specialty, 1987

Location	Size (Staff)	Specialty
Eindhoven, The Netherlands	2,000	Basic research, electronics, manufacturing technology
Redhill, Surrey, England	450	Microelectronics, television, defense
Hamburg, Germany	350	Communications, office equipment, medical imaging
Aachen, W. Germany	250	Fiber optics, X-ray systems
Paris, France	350	Microprocessors, chip materials and design
Brussels, Belgium	50	Artificial intelligence
Briarcliff Manor, New York	35	Optical systems, television, superconductivity, defense
Sunnyvale, California	150	Integrated circuits

Source: Philips, in *Business Week,* March 21, 1988, p. 156.

In this environment, most NO managers kept their heads down, using their distance from Eindhoven as their defense against the ongoing rationalization.

After three years of cost-cutting, in early 1994 Timmer presented a new growth strategy to the board. His plan was to expand software, services, and multimedia to become 40 percent of revenues by 2000. He was betting on Philips' legendary innovative capability to restart the growth engines. Earlier, he had recruited Frank Darrubba, Hewlett-Packard's director of research, and encouraged him to focus on developing fifteen core technologies. The list, which included interactive compact disk (CD-i), digital compact cassettes (DCC), high definition television (HDTV), and multimedia software, was soon dubbed "the president's projects." But his earlier divestment of some of Philips' truly high-tech businesses and a 37 percent cut in R&D personnel left the company with few who understood the technology of the new priority businesses.

By 1996, it was clear that Philips's HDTV technology would not become industry standard, that its DCC gamble had lost out to Sony's Minidisc, and that CD-i was a marketing failure. While costs were lower, so too was morale, particularly among middle management. Critics claimed that the company's drive for cost cutting and standardization had led it to ignore new worldwide market demands for more segmented products and higher consumer service. When Timmer stepped down in October 1996, the board decided to replace him with a radical choice for Philips—an outsider whose expertise was in marketing and Asia rather than technology and Europe.

Boonstra Reorganization, 1996

Cor Boonstra was a fifty-eight-year-old Dutchman whose years as CEO of Sara Lee, the U.S. consumer products firm, had earned him a reputation as a hard driver and a marketing genius. Joining Philips in 1994, he had headed the Asia Pacific region and the lighting division before being tapped as CEO. Unencumbered by tradition, he immediately announced sweeping changes. "There are no taboos, no sacred cows," he said. "The bleeders must be turned around, sold or closed. And we must change an organization that has been a closed system."

Within six months Boonstra had sold off eighteen businesses he described as "bleeders" and had reduced commitments to thirteen more perpetual loss makers, including a withdrawal from troubled German giant Grundig. To reach his target of increasing return on invested capital from 17 to 24 percent by 1999, he also initiated a major restructuring of Philips's worldwide operations, promising to transform a structure he described as "a plate of spaghetti" into "a neat row of asparagus." He said:

> How can we compete with the Koreans? They don't have 350 companies all over the world. Their factory in Ireland covers Europe and their manufacturing facility in Mexico serves North America. We need a more structured and simpler manufacturing and marketing organization to achieve a cost pattern in line with those who do not have our heritage. This is still one of the biggest issues facing Philips.

Within a year, he had begun to rationalize the global structure and redeploy its resources. Over and above the restructuring, 3,100 jobs were eliminated in North America and 3,000 employees were added in Asia Pacific during 1997, emphasizing Boonstra's determination to shift production to low-wage countries and his broader commitment to Asia. ("With Europe's slow growth, Asia is key to our rebuilding task," he said.) And he restructured the company around 100 business units, each responsible for its profits worldwide, effectively eliminating the old PD/NO matrix. Finally, to the shock of most employees, he announced that the 100-year-old Eindhoven headquarters would be relocated to Amsterdam.

By early 1998, he was ready to announce his strategy. Despite early speculation that he might abandon consumer electronics, he proclaimed it as the center of Philips's future. Betting on the "digital revolution," he planned to focus on established technologies such as cellular phones (through joint ventures with Marantz and Lucent), digital TV, digital videodisc, and web TV. More radically, he committed major resources to marketing, including a 40 percent increase in advertising to raise awareness and image of the Philips brand.

Record profits for 1997 boosted spirits in Philips, but, as the *Financial Times* pointed out, from such a low profit base, "the first few percentage points are comparatively easy to achieve."

MATSUSHITA: BACKGROUND

In 1918, Konosuke Matsushita (or "KM" as he was affectionately known), a twenty-three-year-old inspector with the Osaka Electric Light Company, invested ¥100 to start production of double-ended sockets in his modest home. The company grew rapidly, expanding into battery-powered lamps, electric irons, and radios. On May 5, 1932, Matsushita's fourteenth anniversary, KM announced to his 162 employees a 250-year corporate plan broken into 25-year sections, each to be carried out by successive generations. His plan was codified in a company creed and in the "Seven Spirits of Matsushita" (see Table 4), which, along with the company song, continued to be woven into morning assemblies worldwide and provided the basis of the "cultural and spiritual training" all new employees received during their first seven months with the company.

TABLE 4

Matsushita Creed and Philosophy (Excerpts)

> *Creed*
> Through our industrial activities, we strive to foster progress, to promote the general welfare of society, and to devote ourselves to furthering the development of world culture.
>
> *Seven Spirits of Matsushita*
> Service through Industry
> Fairness
> Harmony and Cooperation
> Struggle for Progress
> Courtesy and Humility
> Adjustment and Assimilation
> Gratitude
>
> *KM's Business Philosophy (Selected Quotations)*
> "The purpose of an enterprise is to contribute to society by supplying goods of high quality at low prices in ample quantity."
>
> "Profit comes in compensation for contribution to society. . . . [It] is a result rather than a goal."
>
> "The responsibility of the manufacturer cannot be relieved until its product is disposed of by the end user."
>
> "Unsuccessful business employs a wrong management. You should not find its causes in bad fortune, unfavorable surroundings or wrong timing."
>
> "Business appetite has no self-restraining mechanism. . . . When you notice you have gone too far, you must have the courage to come back."

Source: "Matsushita Electric Industrial (MEI) in 1987," *Harvard Business School Case* No. 388–144.

In the postwar boom, Matsushita introduced a flood of new products: TV sets in 1952; transistor radios in 1958; and color TVs, dishwashers, and electric ovens in 1960. Capitalizing on its broad line of 5,000 products (Sony produced 80), the company opened 25,000 domestic retail distribution outlets. With more than six times the outlets of rival Sony, the ubiquitous "National Shops" represented about 40 percent of all appliance stores in Japan in the late 1960s. These not only provided assured sales volume, but also gave the company direct access to market trends and consumer product reaction.

When postwar growth slowed, however, Matsushita had to look beyond its expanding product line and excellent distribution system for growth. After trying many tactics to boost sales—even sending assembly line workers out as door-to-door salesmen—the company eventually focused on export markets.

The Organization's Foundation: Divisional Structure

Plagued by ill health, KM wished to delegate more authority than was typical in Japanese companies. In 1933, Matsushita became the first Japanese company to adopt the divisional structure, giving each division clearly defined profit responsibilities while creating a "small business" environment to maintain growth and flexibility. This divisional structure generated competition among divisions, spurring them to drive growth by leveraging their technology assets into new products. After the innovating division had earned substantial profits on its new product, however, company policy was to spin it off as a new division to maintain the "hungry spirit."

Under the "one-product-one division" system, each product line was managed almost like an independent corporation. Corporate management provided each autonomous division with initial funds, deliberately underestimating working capital requirements to motivate it to work hard to generate retained earnings. Divisional profitability was determined after deductions for central services such as R&D and interest on internal borrowings. KM expected uniform performance across the company's thirty-six divisions, and division managers whose operating profits fell below 4 percent of sales for two successive years were replaced.

Matsushita ran its corporate treasury like a commercial bank, reviewing divisions' loan requests for which it charged slightly higher-than-market interest, and accepting deposits on their excess funds. Each division paid 60 percent of earnings to headquarters and financed all additional working capital and fixed asset requirements from the retained 40 percent. Transfer prices were based on the market and settled through the treasury on normal commercial terms.

While basic technology was developed in a central research laboratory (CRL), product development and engineering occurred in each of the product divisions. Matsushita intentionally underfunded the CRL, forcing it to compete for additional funding from the divisions. Annually, the CRL publicized its major research projects to the product divisions, which then provided funding in exchange for technology for marketable applications. While it was rarely the innovator, Matsushita was usually very fast to market—earning it the nickname "Manishita," or copycat.

MATSUSHITA: INTERNATIONALIZATION

Although the establishment of overseas markets was a major thrust of the second 25 years in the 250-year plan, in an overseas trip in 1951 KM had been unable to find any American company willing to collaborate with Matsushita. The best he could do was a technology exchange and licensing agreement with Philips. Nonetheless, the push to internationalize continued.

Expanding Through Color TV

In the 1950s and 1960s, trade liberalization and lower shipping rates made possible a healthy export business built on black and white TV sets. In 1953, the company opened its first overseas branch office—the Matsushita Electric Corporation of America (MECA). With neither a distribution network nor a strong brand, the company could not access traditional retailers, and had to resort to selling its products under their private brands through mass merchandisers and discounters.

During the 1960s, pressure from national governments in developing countries led Matsushita to open plants in several countries in Southeast Asia and Central and South America. As manufacturing costs in Japan rose, Matsushita shifted more basic production to these low-wage countries, but almost all high-value components and subassemblies were still made in its scale-intensive Japanese plants. By the 1970s, projectionist sentiments in the West forced the company to establish assembly operations in the Americas and Europe. In 1972, it opened a plant in Canada; in 1974, it bought Motorola's TV business and started manufacturing its Quasar brand in the United States; and in 1976, it built a plant in Cardiff, Wales, to supply the Common Market.

Building Global Leadership: Dominating through VCRs

The birth of the videocassette recorder (VCR) propelled Matsushita into first place in the consumer electronics industry during the 1980s. Recognizing the potential mass-market appeal of the VCR—developed by the Californian broadcasting company Ampex in 1956—engineers at Matsushita began developing VCR technology. After six years of development work, Matsushita launched its commercial broadcast video recorder in 1964 and introduced a consumer version two years later.

In 1975, Sony introduced the technically superior "Betamax" format, and the next year JVC launched a competing "VHS" format. Under pressure from MITI, the government's industrial planning ministry, Matsushita agreed to give up its own format and adopt the established VHS standard. During Matsushita's twenty years of VCR product development, various members of the VCR research team had moved from central labs to the product divisions' development labs and eventually to the plant. In 1976, as sales at home and abroad began to take off, Matsushita celebrated the unit's first profitable year.

The company quickly built production to meet its own needs as well as those of OEM customers like GE, RCA, and Zenith that decided to forgo self-manufacture of VCRs. Between 1977 and 1985, capacity was increased thirty-threefold, to 6.8 million units (In parallel, the company aggressively licensed the VHS format to other manufacturers, including Hitachi, Sharp, Mitsubishi, and eventually, Philips.) Increased volume enabled Matsushita to slash prices 50 percent within five years of product launch, while simultaneously improving quality. By the mid 1980s, VCRs accounted for 30 percent of sales—over 40 percent of overseas revenues—and provided 45 percent of profits.

MATSUSHITA: MANAGING INTERNATIONAL OPERATIONS

In the mid 1980s, the growing number of overseas companies reported to Japan in one of two ways: wholly owned, single-product global plants reported directly to Matsushita's product divisions, while overseas sales and marketing subsidiaries and overseas companies producing a broad product line for local markets, reported to Matsushita Electric Trading Company (METC), a separate legal entity. (See Figure 1 for METC's organization.)

Changing Systems and Controls

Throughout the 1970s, the central product divisions maintained strong operating control over their offshore production units. Overseas operations used plant and equipment designed by the parent company, followed manufacturing procedures dictated by the center, and used materials from Matsushita's domestic plants. Growing trends toward local sourcing, however, gradually weakened the divisions' direct control. By the 1980s, instead of controlling inputs, they began to monitor measures of output (for example, quality, productivity, inventory levels).

About the same time, product divisions began receiving the globally consolidated return on sales reports that had previously been consolidated in METC statements. By the mid 1980s, as worldwide planning was introduced for the first time, corporate management required all its product divisions to prepare global product strategies.

Headquarters-Subsidiary Relations

Although METC and the product divisions set detailed sales and profits targets for their overseas subsidiaries, local managers were told they had complete autonomy on how to achieve the targets. "Mike" Matsuoko, president of the company's largest European production subsidiary in Cardiff, Wales, however, emphasized that failure to meet

FIGURE 1

Organization of METC, 1985

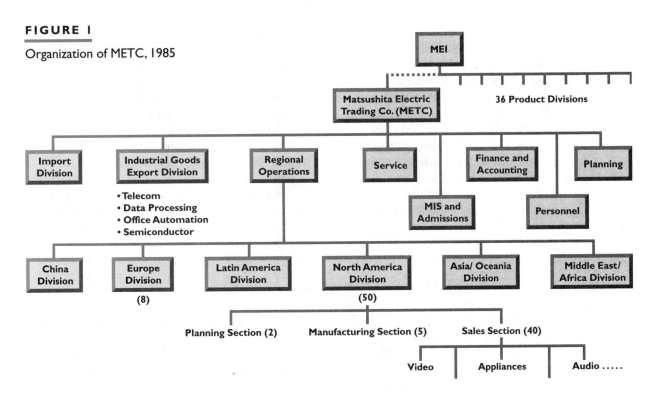

Note: ( ) = number of people.
Source: Harvard Business School Case No. 388–144.

targets forfeited freedom: "Losses show bad health and invite many doctors from Japan who provide advice and support."

In the mid 1980s, Matsushita had more than 700 expatriate managers and technicians on foreign assignment for four to eight years but defended that high number by describing their pivotal role. "This vital communication role," said one manager, "almost always requires a manager from the parent company. Even if a local manager speaks Japanese, he would not have the long experience that is needed to build relationships and understand our management processes."

Expatriate managers were located throughout foreign subsidiaries, but there were a few positions that were almost always reserved for them. The most visible were subsidiary general managers, whose main role was to translate Matsushita philosophy abroad. Expatriate accounting managers were expected to "mercilessly expose the truth" to corporate headquarters; and Japanese technical managers were sent to transfer product and process technologies and provide headquarters with local market information. These expatriates maintained relationships with senior colleagues at headquarters, who acted as career mentors, evaluated performance (with some input from local managers), and provided expatriates with information about parent company developments.

General managers of foreign subsidiaries visited headquarters at least two or three times each year—some as often as every month. Corporate managers reciprocated these visits, and on average, major operations hosted at least one headquarters manager each day of the year. Face-to-face meetings were considered vital: "Figures are important," said one manager, "but the meetings are necessary to develop judgment." Daily faxes and nightly phone calls between headquarters and expatriate colleagues were a vital management link.

Yamashita's Operation Localization

Although international sales kept rising, as early as 1982, growing host country pressures caused concern about the company's highly centralized operations. In that year, newly appointed company president, Toshihiko Yamashita, launched "Operation Localization" to boost offshore production from less than 10 percent of value-added to 25 percent, or half of overseas sales, by 1990.

To support the target, he set out a program of four localizations—personnel, technology, material, and capital.

Over the next few years, Matsushita increased the number of local nationals in key positions. In the United States, for example, U.S. nationals became the presidents of three of the six local companies, while in Taiwan, the majority of production divisions were replaced by Chinese managers. In each case, however, local national managers were still supported by senior Japanese advisers, who maintained a direct link with the parent company. To localize technology and materials, the company developed its national subsidiaries' expertise to source equipment locally, modify designs to meet local requirements, incorporate local components, and adapt corporate processes and technologies to accommodate these changes.

By the mid 1980s, offshore production subsidiaries were free to buy minor parts from local vendors as long as quality could be assured, but still had to buy key components from internal sources. They could also carry out routine production tasks independently, calling on corporate technical personnel when plans called for major expansion or change. And sales subsidiaries had more choice over the products they sold. Each year the company held a two-week internal merchandising show and product-planning meeting, where sales subsidiary managers negotiated over features, quantities, and even prices of the products they wanted to buy from the parent's product divisions. Corporate managers, however, could overrule the subsidiary if they thought introduction of a particular product was of strategic importance.

The overall localization thrust sparked opposition from managers in Japan. In a low-growth environment, increased foreign production would come at the expense of export sales. "What will that mean for employment in Japan?" said one senior manager. "Protecting the interests of employees is one of our greatest moral commitments. We cannot sacrifice that for any reason." Even some foreign subsidiary managers feared localization would reduce their access to central resources and expertise. If localized operations caused export income to contribute less, they reasoned, the central product division managers could give priority to domestic needs over foreign operations.

Nonetheless, between 1980 and 1988, Matsushita added twenty-one manufacturing companies and twelve sales companies abroad to bring those respective totals to sixty and forty-one. In 1990, Matsushita employed 50,000 workers overseas, twice the number of a decade earlier. Despite these efforts, in 1990 overseas production stood at only ¥600 billion—still less than half Matsushita's 25 percent target.

Yamashita's greatest wish was that Operation Localization would help Matsushita's overseas companies develop the innovative capability and entrepreneurial initiatives that he had long admired in the national organizations of rival Philips. (Past efforts to develop such capabilities abroad had failed. For example, when Matsushita acquired Motorola's TV business in the United States, its highly innovative technology group atrophied as American engineers resigned in response to what they felt to be excessive control from Japan's highly centralized R&D operations.) In an unusual act for a Japanese CEO, Yamashita publicly expressed his unhappiness with the lack of initiative at the TV plant Cardiff. Despite the transfer of substantial resources and the delegation of many responsibilities, he felt that the plant remained too dependent on the center.

Tanii's Integration and Expansion

Yamashita's successor, Akio Tanii, expanded on his predecessor's initiatives. In part because Matsushita's product divisions received only 3 percent royalties for foreign production against at least 10 percent return on sales for exports from Japan, he felt that product divisions were not giving their full attention to developing operations outside Japan. To correct the situation, he brought all foreign subsidiaries of Matsushita under the control of METC in 1986, thus consolidating the company's international operations in one administrative entity. To further integrate domestic and overseas operations, in April 1988, Tanii merged METC into the parent company. Then, to shift operational control nearer to local markets, he relocated major regional headquarters functions from Japan to North America, Europe, and Southeast Asia. Yet still he was frustrated that the overseas subsidiary companies acted as the implementing agents of the Osaka-based product divisions.

Through all these changes, however, Matsushita's worldwide growth continued generating huge reserves. With $17.5 billion in liquid financial assets at the end of 1989, the company was referred to as the "Matsushita Bank." Several top executives felt that if they could not develop innovative overseas companies, they should buy them. Flush with cash and international success, in early 1991 the company acquired MCA, the U.S. entertainment giant for $6.1 billion, with the objective of obtaining a media software source for its hardware. Within a year, however, Japan's economic bubble had burst, plunging the economy into recession. Almost overnight, Tanii had to shift the company's focus from expansion to cost containment.

Morishita's Restructuring

Despite Tanii's best efforts to cut costs, the problems ran too deep. The company's huge capacity, its full line of products, and its network of 27,000 retailers turned from assets to liabilities. With 1992 profits less than half their 1991 level, Tanii was forced to resign in February 1993.

His replacement, Yoichi Morishita—at fifty-six the most junior of the firm's executive vice presidents—immediately implemented a major restructuring designed "to eliminate laxness and extravagance." Central to his effort was a commitment to cut headquarters staff and decentralize responsibility to operating units, including overseas companies. Under the slogan "simple, small, speedy and strategic," over the next eighteen months he eliminated a layer of management and transferred 6,000 corporate staff to operating jobs. To the shock of many, he even began questioning the sanctity of lifetime employment. By contrast, he consolidated twenty research centers into nine, centralizing decisions to speed up new product introductions. Unwilling to respond to MCI's management pressure for more funding and greater independence, Matsushita sold off 80 percent of the company to Seagram at a $1.2 billion loss in early 1995.

Meanwhile, stimulated by a rising yen that raised the export prices, product divisions were aggressively moving value-added offshore, particularly to Southeast Asia. Attracted by booming markets, lower costs, and strong local partners, the company began investing in major production facilities, not just the knockdown assembly plants of the 1970s and 1980s. For example, production of all 1.5 million of Matsushita's export air conditioners was transferred to Malaysia. In that country alone,

TABLE 5

Matsushita, Summary Financial Data, 1970–1997[a]

	1997	1996	1995	1990	1985	1980	1975	1970
In billions of yen and percent:								
Sales	¥7,676	¥6,795	¥6,948	¥6,003	¥5,291	¥2,916	¥1,385	¥932
Income before tax	332	77	232	572	723	324	83	147
As % of sales	4.3%	1.1%	3.3%	9.5%	13.7%	11.1%	6.0%	15.8%
Net income	¥138	¥(58)[b]	¥90	¥236	¥216	¥125	¥32	¥70
As % of sales	1.8%	(0.8%)	1.3%	3.9%	4.1%	4.3%	2.3%	7.6%
Cash dividends (per share)	12.50	12.50	13.50	¥10.00	¥9.52	¥7.51	¥6.82	¥6.21
Total assets	8,696	8,011	8,202	7,851	5,076	2,479	1,274	735
Stockholders' equity	3,696	3,398	3,255	3,201	2,084	1,092	573	324
Capital investment	415	381	316	355	288	NA	NA	NA
Depreciation	345	292	296	238	227	65	28	23
R&D	435	399	378	346	248	102	51	NA
Employees (units)	270,651	265,538	265,397	198,299	175,828	107,057	82,869	78,924
Overseas employees	116,279	107,530	112,314	59,216	38,380	NA	NA	NA
As % of total employees	43%	40%	42%	30%	22%	NA	NA	NA
Exchange rate (fiscal period end; ¥/$)	124	106	89	159	213	213	303	360
In millions of dollars:								
Sales	$61,902	$64,102	$78,069	$37,753	$24,890	$13,690	$4,572	$2,588
Operating income before depreciation	3,015	2,495	2,924	4,343	3,682	1,606	317	NA
Operating income after depreciation	2,678	723	2,609	2,847	2,764	1,301	224	NA
Pretax income	1,112	(536)	1,017	3,667	3,396	1,520	273	408
Net income	70,128	75,583	92,159	1,482	1,214	584	105	195
Total assets	29,804	32,053	36,575	49,379	21,499	11,636	4,206	2,042
Total equity				20,131	10,153	5,129	1,890	900

[a] Data prior to 1987 are for the fiscal year ending November 20; data 1988 and after are for the fiscal year ending March 31.
[b] 1996 results include a write-off of ¥164 billion in losses stemming from the sale of MCA in June 1995.
Source: Annual reports; Standard & Poor's *Compustat;* Moody's Industrial and International Manuals.

TABLE 6

Matsushita, Sales by Product and Geographic Segment, 1985–1997 (billion yen)

	1997		1996		1995		FY 1990		FY 1985	
By Product Segment:										
Video equipment	¥1,342	17%	¥1,225	18%	¥1,272	18%	¥1,598	27%	¥1,947	37%
Audio equipment	576	8	518	8	555	8	561	9	570	11
Home appliances	1,026	13	914	13	916	13	802	13	763	14
Communication and industrial equipment	2,492	32	2,013	30	1,797	26	1,375	23	849	16
Electronic components	1,055	14	1,020	15	893	13	781	13	573	11
Batteries and kitchen-related equipment	472	6	405	6	374	4	312	5	217	4
Others	710	9	700	10	530	8	573	10	372	7
Total	7,676	100%	6,795	100%	6,948	100%	¥6,003	100%	¥5,291	100%
By Geographic Segment:										
Domestic	4,046	53%	3,727	55%	3,455	50%	¥3,382	56%	¥2,659	50%
Overseas	3,630	47	3,068	45	3,493	50	2,621	44	2,632	50

Notes: Total may not add due to rounding.
Source: Annual Reports

Matsushita had established sixteen companies producing a wide range of products and employing 20,000 people. Subsequently, the air conditioning and television companies expanded their commitment by establishing substantial Malaysian design and development centers. Similar levels of commitment were also being made to facilities in China, India and Vietnam.

By fiscal year 1997, profit margins had risen from 2.8 percent when Morishita took over to 4.3 percent. Besides restructuring the company, he had successfully repositioned its product portfolio, reducing low margin consumer electronics from 50 to 35 percent of sales and moving into digital technologies such as cellular phones, digital cameras, and digital video discs. Yet Morishita was discouraged that still less than half of its overseas sales were manufactured abroad. Equally troubling was the company's slow transition to local senior-level management in its overseas companies, and the even less successful attempts to integrate foreign managers at senior levels in the parent company.

CASE 38

ABB in China: 1998

This case was prepared by Suzanne Uhlen, Lund University (Sweden), under the supervision of Professor Michael Lubatkin of the University of Connecticut.

"I want to make ABB a company that encourages and demands innovation from all of its employees, and a company that creates the environment in which teamwork and innovation flourish," declares ABB's CEO Göran Lindahl. In seeking new growth, Lindahl is moving out of the long shadow of his predecessor, Percy Barnevik, considered one of the most successful international managers in Europe.

Technology giant ABB, the world leader in electrical engineering, is a $35 billion electrical engineering group, with companies all over the globe. It operates primarily in the fields of reliable and economical generation, transmission, and distribution of electrical energy.[1] Much has been written about the worldwide company. In 1996, ABB was ranked in the top forty of the first 500 companies listed by *Fortune* magazine. Recently, the company has announced its newest reorganization, which will make it more up-to-date globally according to Lindahl.[2] Lindahl took over from Barnevik as CEO in 1997.

ABB has different priorities in different markets. Western Europe and North America are the company's biggest markets. However, the high-potential markets are the Middle East, Africa, Latin America, and Asia. These markets are growing fast, and ABB expects to have half of its customers in these regions not long into the next century. The priority is on building local manufacturing, engineering, and other forms of added value. ABB wants to integrate these operations into the global networks to get full synergy effects and scale economies.

During 1998, the industrial production in OECD countries, in which ABB performs about 75 percent of its total business, has continued to grow, although at a slower pace than the strong growth rates of the previous year. Overall, industrial production in Europe is lower than a year ago, but still high compared with historical levels. Current economic activity in North America is slowing compared with the strong economy of recent years. In Latin America, high interest rates are delaying the financial closing of projects in an environment of reduced economic activity. The Indian economy is slowing, also due to reduced exports as a result of its strong currency compared with others in the region. Southeast Asia is gradually stabilizing at a low level, with reduced consumption and investments.

As a result of the ongoing economic uncertainty, overall global demand is forecast to remain soft in the near future. ABB expects to benefit with its well-established local presence around the world from higher demand in various industries and world markets. Appropriate cost cutting, continued selective tendering, and successful working capital reduction programs are expected to continue contributing positively to the ABB Group results. The company recognizes the world to be rapidly changing and increasingly unpredictable. Efforts have paid off and the group has taken advantage of opportunities in Asia and positioned itself for future growth in what is seen to be "the world's most dynamic market over a long term—China."[3]

The interest in China is growing steadily, and companies in Japan, the western European countries, the United States and elsewhere today view the Chinese market as having enormous potential.

This case was prepared by Suzanne Uhlen (Lund University, Sweden) under the supervision of Professor Michael Lubatkin (University of Connecticut). The case is intended to be used as a basis for classroom discussion rather than to illustrate either effective or ineffective handling of the situation. Used by permission.

C528

Given China's population of a billion and a growing economy, it has appeared to be worthwhile to make a major effort to gain a foothold in the market.[4] On the one hand, China represents a huge and largely untapped market. It is potentially bigger than that of the United States, the European Community, and Japan combined. On the other hand, China's new firms are proving to be very competitive, and China's culture is quite different from that of the West. However, in the Chinese market the growth remains at a relatively good level for enterprises such as Procter & Gamble, Motorola, Nestlé, and ABB. This market is regarded as a lifeboat to a lot of worldwide companies suffering from the financial crisis in the rest of Southeast Asia. Nevertheless, there is talk about China devaluing its currency, which might also drag China down into the crisis. However, the country has not shown any visible scratches from the surrounding crisis. China seems to be unshakable, and analysts are still valuing China as the country of the future.[5] Thus, the changes in China are creating both opportunities and threats for established worldwide companies. According to *Management Today,* China will be one of the top ten economies in the world by the year 2010.[6]

CHINESE INFLUENCE

A recruiters' guide to the country proclaims that "China will enter the next century as the rising power in Asia after two decades of astonishing economic growth that has transformed the country and that has given rise to new challenges."[7] Many cities in China have more than 5 million inhabitants. China has had a growing economy that cannot be compared with any other country's economy during almost three decades.[8] It is argued that China is not like any other developing country because of the rapid changes that are taking place in certain areas. In some areas, such as home electronics,[9] the development has surpassed the development in western countries, while in other areas China lags far behind.

The Chinese culture and society stretch back more than 5,000 years. There is a unique cultural heritage of philosophy, science and technology, societal structures, and traditional administrative bureaucracy.[10] With this in mind, it is no wonder, according to researchers, that conflicts often occur between Chinese and foreign cultures. Foreign managers are

accustomed to other values and norms, some of which may hardly be acceptable in China.[11]

In the current half-year reports from worldwide companies, a distinct trend is noticeable, according to Dagens Industri.[12] The more focus that the companies have put on basic industry, the more the Asian crisis tends to affect these companies. However, China is the country that can save these companies and others, but especially those companies operating in the business of infrastructure.[13] Now that the Cold War with China has ended, economic growth is stabilizing and the country is demanding a speedy reconstruction. The country has begun to enjoy unprecedented strategic latitude for the first time in 200 years and it no longer faces the threat of aggression from superior powers.[14] This has enabled it to focus on economic developments as the driving force of both its domestic and foreign policies. According to Professor Michael Yahuda, China's leaders also have come to base their legitimacy on providing the conditions of stability in which people can look forward to continued high levels of prosperity. The need for economic development is fueled by many other factors, such as providing employment for a vast population that increases by some 15 million a year. Additionally, there are significant regional inequalities that can only be addressed by further economic development.[15]

China is expected to evolve into a hybrid system of authoritarianism, democracy, socialism, and capitalism. Also recognized are the internal problems the country faces such as environmental disasters, political struggles, and tensions between the emerging entrepreneurial economy and the vast parts of China still under state control.[16] Today China receives the most direct investment and foreign aid of any developing country. Many companies are eager to establish their presence in China, which, it is argued, attracts more than its proportionate share of investments.[17] However, concluding remarks are, "... westerners cannot expect to know how China will develop and need to expect that the Chinese will always be different from them. Instead of trying to change China, they should look for positive steps that take their differences into account."[18]

According to China's Premier Zhu Rongji, China is indeed the largest market in the world. However, because of duplicate construction, there is a problem of oversupply in some areas. Nevertheless, the premier states that the market is far from being saturated.[19] Since China opened its doors to the outside world in the late 1970s, a large number of foreign investors have gained rich returns from their investments, yet some have ended in failure. The *China Daily* offers this guideline for ensuring business success in China:[20]

- Make long-term strategies for the Chinese market. Competition is intensifying and market exploitation needs time and patience. Foreign companies eager to get a quick return are usually disappointed at the results.

- Localize staff. They are familiar with the local business environment.

- Be aware of changes in policies and regulation. China is in the process of transforming from a planned economy to a market economy. Various policies and regulations are being revised and replaced, while new ones are being issued. Foreign investors must keep informed of the ongoing changes.

- Undertake practical market research. Because of social, economic, and cultural differences, practical and down-to-earth market research is a must before and during investment in China.

CHINESE CULTURAL INFLUENCE

There is a consensus among several authors that the Chinese have a traditional respect for age, hierarchy, and authority.[21] It originates from the Confucian concept of *li* (rite, proprietary), which plays an important role in maintaining a person's social position. *Li* can be seen today in the existing traditional bureaucracy and in vertical relationships concerning centralization of decision making, and in corruption to some extent, which is acceptable in such a cultural context.[22]

Second, the family is viewed as an essential social unit and there is a strong tendency to promote the collective or the group. Members within the family or group must maintain harmonious relationships and these social relations are seen as more important than the individual.[23] Thus, the family or clan norms are adopted as the formal code of conduct, and members are bound to these standards. Other research has found that in modern China, business and industrial enterprises were perceived as an extension of the family system.[24]

Third, the concept of *mianzi* ("face") is seen as an important characteristic. As Yanan Ju has noted, the general idea of *mianzi* is related to "a reputation achieved through getting on in life through success and ostentation."[25] *Mianzi* also serves to enhance harmony within the family or group, so that the positive is expressed publicly and any conflicts remain private.[26] Yung Lee Hong has found that the concept of *mianzi* still plays an important role in social relationships and organizational behavior.[27] However, Lu Yuan points out that there are two sides to this concept.[28] The first includes the individual's moral character, and the strong fear of losing this limits the person's behavior. The second aspect of *mianzi* involves assertions about a person, which is not seen quite as serious as the loss of face.[29]

The importance of personal relations (*guanxi*) is the fourth characteristic. According to Hong, persons with *guanxi* usually share a common birthplace, lineage, surname, or experience, such as attending the same school, working together, or belonging to the same organization.[30] A comparative study of decision making in China and Britain has revealed that Chinese managers use their personal *guanxi* more widely to exchange information, negotiate with planning authorities, and accelerate decision-making processes than managers from British firms.[31] As it is, the network transmits information, and because contacts and co-operation are built on trust, it is seen as very serious if that trust is broken. If a trust is broken the whole network will soon know about the incident and the person involved will have a hard time doing business again.[32]

ABB has been doing business in the Chinese market since 1919. At that time this was the first product delivery to China, and it was not until 1979 that ABB established its first permanent office. Nearly eleven years later hearing the words *Asia* and *electricity* made the heart pound with excitement in almost every chairman of an energy company. There were billions to be had from the booming demand for electricity in Asia.[33] But in recent years, the emerging Asian market has slowed down due to the financial crisis in the area. At the moment it seems as though China is the only country not affected by this financial crisis, and consequently, there are many companies that are now trying to be successful in China.

ABB is argued to be a company with a good position on the Chinese market due to good performance, delivery, autonomy, and also its good name. Today the company has nine representative offices and fifteen joint ventures; the number of employees has grown in four years from approximately 1,000 to 6,000 employees in China.

LOCAL ROOTS

The strategy of ABB is to use its global strength to support the needs of its local customers around the world. However, in China, ABB has a fairly high import duty on its products, which limits how much the company can sell. The idea of setting up local production in China was to increase market share, due to the fact that most Chinese customers do not have foreign currency[34] and are consequently forced to buy locally produced goods with the local currency. The reason for ABB to localize in China was not to achieve lower production costs, as some locally supplied components are more expensive in China than elsewhere. It was rather to be closer to the local market, and therefore facilitate a few local modifications to the products and provide shorter delivery times to the customer.

The phrase "think global, act local" is said to reflect ABB's fundamental idea of strong local companies working together across borders to gain economies of scale in many areas.[35] In spite of ABB claims to be able to respond swiftly and surely to market conditions,[36] some of the products in China are not truly adapted to the local market. Most of the products are designed for the IEC—international standard association based in Europe. The company manufactures products, which have to be tested according to different norms and standards. For example, North America ABB follows the ANSI-standard and in Canada the CSA-standard.

However, some of ABB's products would not pass a type test based on the Chinese standards. That is not because the quality is too low; on the contrary the quality of ABB products is sometimes too high. The quality of some of the products has evolved far beyond the requirements of Chinese standards—therefore these ABB products cannot meet the standards. The Chinese standards are based on what the local manufacturer can produce because the country does not have much other information. As one manager at ABB in China stated,

We are not going to redesign our products in order to meet the standards for the obvious rea-

sons, why should we take our quality out, why shall we take the advances out? It does become an issue from time to time, Chinese are very risk averse, if we have not done the type test in China. It is more to cover themselves in case something goes wrong.

Some other managers said that though ABB tries to adapt the products to the Chinese local standard there was a negative response because customers regard Western standards as superior and are asking for the superior product. The Chinese customers are seen as tough and sometimes demand more tests than ABB's products have gone through. Furthermore, insufficient feasibility studies for new joint ventures set up in China delay work when new information has to be collected about market conditions. This problem arises from the speed of changes in China and the difficulty for a company to catch up with what is going on.

However, when the so-called type tests of the product have been done, the company cannot change the design because of the high costs involved in this test. Some critics have suggested that ABB should adapt more to the Chinese situation, but then the tests would have to be redone. For some products, though as one manager said, the company must "adapt to the configurations the customers have a demand for, because they have an option—go to the competitor."

Still, in most cases, the local ABB companies in China are not allowed to change the products other than according to agreements with the licensee. The reason for that is that the technology partners[37] have the overall view of the quality and performance. The ABB corporation does not want to have different product performance for different countries. To be seen as the same product all over the world, the products must have the same descriptions. Consequently, the local ABB company can do only a few modifications to the standard product for the specific customer and cannot change the technology involved. The technology partners have a few alternatives that meet the demands of the Chinese customers and these products are also tested, but do not necessarily meet the Chinese standards.

The local ABB company tries to follow the ABB Group's policy, to be close to the customer and responsive to his or her needs.[38] In China, however, contracts are not commonly used, and this frequently obstructs satisfying the many customer demands.

> They keep on saying this is China and you should adapt to the Chinese way: Ok, if you want to buy a Chinese product that's fine, but this is our product—here are the terms and conditions. You can't just give in to that; otherwise you will kill your company, because they expect you to accept unlimited liability and lifetime warranty and the risks to which you would expose your company would eventually lead to its shutting down, so you just cannot do that.

The ABB view is that being close to the customer is the best guarantee that local requirements will be met.[39] However, the headquarters in Zurich has also set up some rules about the kind of contracts that the local subsidiaries shall sign worldwide. In China, contracts are something new and many Chinese customers do not want them. Consequently, some ABB companies in China do not use the standard ABB contract and are actually responsive to the customers' needs. When another ABB company comes to the same customer to set up a standard contract, the customer will point out that the previous ABB company did not seem to find the contract necessary.

PROFIT CENTERS

ABB's strategy is to take full advantage of its economies of scale while at the same time being represented by national companies in many home markets where some 5,000 entrepreneurial profit centers serve local customers. These companies are quite independent and have to stand on their own economically. In addition, the individual company's profit can easily be compared with revenue. In other words, the individual ABB company is measured on its own performance and needs, a profit when selling products or parts, even though it is within the ABB Group. It is recognized that the profit centers are efficient for decentralization and that the organization can act relatively fast. This also enables the company to be sensitive and responsive to potential problems. Each company has a fair amount of autonomy, which in turn makes the individual company flexible in the decision-making process. Even though ABB brochures state that the strategy of having profit centers enables

the easy transfer of know-how across borders,[40] it is argued that the direction is pretty much one way—from the technology partners, business areas, and country level to the subsidiary—rather than a two-way exchange.

Nevertheless, some conflicts of interest have occurred. For example, the local ABB company and all other licensees are more or less dependent on their licensors in Europe.[41] In the local ABB company's case, a factory in X-city that is one of its technology partners is measured, like everyone else, on its performance and on its profit. If it gives the local ABB company support, it will cost the former money, and likewise, if it sells the local ABB company components, it wants to make a profit. The consequence is that it is charging the local ABB company 25 to 100 percent over and above the cost of its parts.

> So in the end you end up calling them as little as possible and we end up buying parts from local suppliers that probably we should not buy from local suppliers. And we reduce our quality. They have great profit figures, we have some profit figures but there are some real serious problems along the way.

The technology partner argues, on the contrary, that the prices are high because it first has to buy from its supplier and then sell to the local ABB company, which makes the products more expensive. Besides, the technology partners pay for the type tests and all the product development.[42]

Such disagreements or conflicts have been occurring for a long time within ABB, but nobody has yet found a solution. It is said to be difficult for a company, like ABB, which is working with so many different products, markets, and in different cultures to have anything else than sole profit centers. If the profit centers did not aim for a profit when selling within the ABB Group, it is argued that the companies would no longer be independent companies. Being independent is seen as a strength, and therefore it would be against the laws of nature if the companies were not always aiming for a profit. Nonetheless, among these independent companies with profit centers there are some extreme examples:

> Our partner in Y-country was selling the finished product in China before. Now he sells the parts to the joint venture in China and wants to charge more for the parts than he did for the finished

product, and that is because it is in his interest and he will be evaluated on his performance. If he does not do that, his profits will be too low and he will be blamed for it. So he has got to do what he has got to do. That is what he is motivated to do and that is what he is going to do.

To some extent the technology partners are even selling indirectly to the Chinese market using nonofficial agents to avoid a high import tax and slip under the high market price that exists on the Chinese market. ABB China has sought to stop the use of these agents and is trying to force ABB companies to use only two official channels for ABB goods into the Chinese market. They are to rely on goods produced locally by the local ABB company and on direct imports from a technology partner.

STRUCTURE

ABB is a huge enterprise with dispersed business areas. They encompassed three segments—power generation, transmission and distribution, and industrial building systems—but these segments have recently been divided into six. Before the reorganization every country had its national ABB head office, with a country management that dealt with all the company business in that particular country. The other dimension of the matrix structure reflects the clustering of the activities of the enterprise into thirty-six business areas (or BAs). Each business area represents a distinct worldwide product market. Simplified, each BA is responsible for worldwide market allocation and the development of a worldwide technical strategy for that specific product line. Additional responsibilities for the BA are to coordinate who shall supply or deliver where, and also to work as a referee in potential disagreements between companies within the ABB Group.

In China, however, as in most developing countries, there is no BA in place and the decision power of the country management is consequently closer at hand. Hence, it is argued, decisions tend to be made at the country level rather than at the BA level. Disagreements between licensees in Western countries and subsidiaries in China have been, and are occurring, due to different business orientations. The local subsidiary in China has two or more licensors in Western countries, from which it buys components. Some of the licensees sold these

components themselves before the local subsidiary was taken up in China. Some licensees feel that the market in China was taken from them and that they therefore can compensate for potentially lost sales only by charging the Chinese subsidiary a higher cost. Consequently, if the disagreeing partner seeks the BA as a referee in this kind of case, the following happens, as one manager explains:

> The BA are looking at the global business—we can increase our global business if we set up a joint venture in China. But the technology partner can't increase their business if we set up a joint venture in China. If we set up a joint venture in China the technology partner wants to increase its business also, they are going to do some work, and of course want something for it. The BA is really powerless to push those along.

To date, the licensors have also been paying for all the technology development, which is, from their point of view, the reason for charging a higher price for the components they are selling. Because the enterprise is divided into 5,000 profit centers and because each of these profit centers wants a profit when selling a component or product, there have been some shortcomings in the coordination and cooperation between the licensors and the local Chinese subsidiary.

For example, the licensor in X-country makes the same breakers that the local ABB company does. When the licensor runs into a quality problem, it is ineffective at informing its licensee in China, which will probably also run into the same quality problem in the near future. The problem may be discussed at the local ABB company, but if it suggests changes to the licensor, the licensor will evaluate the situation on the basis of benefits to itself. Since it is going to invest its own resources, it is, of course, going to invest in areas beneficial to itself first or charge the local ABB company extra. Thus, "We have had some things that would really help us here in China. But I don't even bother, because I know the reaction."

More than eighty percent of what the Centers of Excellence produce is going to be exported,[43] which makes it especially important that the partners of the licensor can manage the contemporary challenges and opportunities that can emerge. However, the BA divides the world markets into different areas in which the specific ABB companies are to be a so-called first source.[44] Between some of the licensors and the local ABB company this has resulted in certain disputes. For example,

> We are responsible for the Peoples Republic of China's market and are supposed to be the sole source (or rather first source) because we have the expertise for this market. Our technology partner in X-country quotes into this market on a regular basis, does not inform us, and competes against us, and takes orders at a lower prices. This can destroy our position in the market place.

According to the licensor, it does not quote in the local ABB company's market because if the final customers have foreign currency, they will prefer imported products. The licensor states that it does not go into the Chinese market and offer its products, but does get inquiries from ABB in Hong Kong and delivers to that company. The Hong Kong Company in turn sells the products directly to the Chinese customer after having increased the original price up to the market price, which is often several times higher in China than in Europe, for example. It is a decision of the ABB China management that the Hong Kong coordinated sales force shall sell the local ABB company's products on the Chinese market among imported products and those of the local joint venture. It is argued that it helps to have sales coordination, that is the decision as to whether the products should be imported or not.

The technology is owned today by the Centers of Excellence in Europe, the licensors, which are also the ones paying for all the product development. ABB has chosen these licensees to be responsible for becoming the company's world source of this specific technology. These units are responsible for developing new products and ensuring quality by arranging technical seminars about the technology and by keeping special technology parts—so-called "noble parts"—only at their factory. The strategic decision to keep special parts and the drawings of these parts at only one chosen factory enables the company to secure itself against competitors copying its products. Consequently, these parts will not be localized or purchased in China. However, for one product group (THS) there has been an organizational change, including the establishing of a unit called CHTET, which shall now own all new technology that is developed and also pay for the product development. This change now involves all product groups.

MULTICULTURAL

The current fashion, exemplified by ABB, is for firms to be "multicultural multinationals," which means that the company must be very sensitive to national differences.[45] Barnevik, the former CEO, has argued that a culturally diverse set of managers can be a source of strength. According to Barnevik, managers should not try to eradicate these differences and establish a uniform managerial culture. Rather, they should seek to understand these cultural differences, to empathize with the views of people from different cultures, and to make compromises for such differences. Barnevik believes that the advantage of building a culturally diverse cadre of global managers is to improve the quality of managerial decision making.[46]

ABB in China is typified by a culturally diverse set of managers, with a mixture of managerial ideas derived from the different managers' national backgrounds, different values, and different methods of working. It then depends on which stage in personal development the manager has reached if he or she is going to be influenced by and absorb the new climate. As one manager said, "If you are close to being retired you might not change so much, there isn't much point. But you can't work in the same way as you do at home—it just wouldn't work."

According to another manager, ABB is a very international company with a great deal of influence from Scandinavian culture. However, it is a mixture of many cultures, and the mix depends on where the ABB company is located. In China, the ABB culture is influenced by Chinese culture, by the environmental circumstances, and by the laws. It is stricter in China than it is, for example, in Europe, because there are more rules. In spite of that, the managers do not feel that the result is a subculture of the ABB culture, but rather a mixture of managers from different cultures—"we are a multidomestic company."

The top level of the ABB management, however, is seen as far away from the daily life at the subsidiary level in China, such as at the local ABB company. According to one of the managers, "between that level and here, it's like the Pacific Ocean." Most of the managers say, though, that what the top level, including Barnevik and Lindahl,[47] says sounds very good and that is how it should be. Some disagree:

> Sounds like I'm working for a different ABB than these guys are. What they talk about is re-

ally good and that is how it should be. But then when I sit back and go into the daily work and say that's not at all how it is. Somewhere along the line something gets lost between the theory and ideas at that level which is quite good. But when you get down to the working level and have to make it work something really gets lost along the way.

EXPATRIATES

It is the BA with its worldwide networks that recommends, after suggestions from local offices, who is going to be sent as an expatriate to China or any other country. Thereafter, the BA and the country level cooperate, but it is the latter that finally decides which potential foreign expatriate is appropriate. The expatriate must be able to fit into the system in China, for the costs involved are very high. It is estimated that an expatriate costs the company about $250,000 a year, due to the high taxes the company is paying to have a foreign employee.

As a corporation, ABB's identity is supported not only by its possession of a coordinating executive committee but also by an elite cadre of 500 global managers, which the top management shifts through a series of foreign assignments. Their job is intended to knit the organization together, to transfer expertise around the world, and to expose the company's leadership to differing perspectives.[48] However, ABB in China is not yet a closely knit country unit, for several reasons. First, the expatriates come from the outside and most of their contacts are back in the home country. Most expatriates claim that the home office does not understand how difficult it can be to work abroad and that they need support. As one expatriate put it, "sometimes it just feels like I'm standing in the desert screaming." The home office, on the other hand, often views the expatriates as a burden because they need so much support. The home office, along with the BA, chooses the candidates for foreign placement, even though it is argued it has little knowledge, or no knowledge at all, of how it really is to work in a given country. But it would be almost impossible for all the local offices to have insight into the working conditions in other countries.

As to growing a strong country unit, the expatriates themselves say that they are stationed in China for a relatively short time and thus are less able to build up informal networks. Apparently, lit-

tle effort is made to establish an informal network because the few contact persons the managers have today will return home after a while and there is no formal way of contacting the replacing person. The formal LOTUS notes, a computer-based network that includes all managers worldwide, cannot compensate for this deficiency and help build the preferred strong country unit within China. Finally, the managers do not feel that they can offer the time, or the effort, to establish informal networks if these have to be rebuilt every two to three years due to the replacement of expatriates. A worldwide policy within the company limits the expatriates to operating as such for not more than five years at a time. Executives have questioned this policy, for, they say, "It is during the first year you learn what is going on and get into your new clothes. During the second year you get to know the people and the system, the third year you apply what you learned and the fourth year you start to make some changes—and this is very specific for developing countries."

Three years ago, the expatriates did no get any information or education about the country-specific situation before being sent out to ABB's subsidiaries in China. Today, when there are about 100 expatriates of twenty-five different nationalities in China, the approach has changed to some degree, but it is still mostly up to the prospective expatriate to collect material and prepare so that the acclimatization works out. Within the worldwide corporation, there is no policy of formal training for foreign assignments; rather, it is up to the expatriate's home office to prepare individuals. Some argue that "you could never prepare for the situation in China anyway, so any education wouldn't help." Others say that this attitude has resulted in a lot of problems with the expatriates, raising the company's costs even higher if the expatriate fails.

When it is time for the expatriates to return to the home office, they may feel unsure whether there are jobs for them back home. Thus, it is argued that it is very important for the expatriate to have as close a contact with the home office as possible and also to make use of the free trips home offered by the company.

THE CHINESE CHALLENGE

According to ABB, it wants to send out managers with preferably ten to fifteen years of experience. The task, however, is difficult, especially when the location may be in a rural area overseas and most managers with ten to fifteen years' experience have families, which are less likely to want to move to these areas. Sometimes, apparently, a manager gets sent to China rather than being fired—"they send the manager to where the pitfalls are greater and challenges bigger and potential risks are greater."

Research indicates that most expatriates have strong feelings about living in and adapting to the new environment in China. Newly arrived expatriates seem to enjoy the respect they get from the Chinese, and several managers said delightedly, "I love it here, and how could you not, you get a lot of respect just because you're a foreigner and life is just pleasant."

Some of the expatriates got to dislike the situation greatly after a longer stay, and a number of expatriates have asked to leave because their expectations about the situation in China have not been fulfilled.[49]

Some country-specific tasks have to do with teaching the Chinese employees to work in teams. The worldwide company ABB is especially focusing on creating an environment that fosters teamwork and promotes active participation among its employees.[50] This is, however, a big challenge for Western managers (the expatriates) because, it is argued, the Chinese employees have a hard time working in a group due to cultural and historical reasons. Some of the local ABB companies are said to have failed radically in their attempt to create teams, ad hoc groups, and the like because they have been in too much of a hurry. As was pointed out, "Here in China the management needs to encourage the teamwork a little bit, because it is a little against the culture and the nature of the people. This is not a question of lack of time for the managers, but I do not think we have the overall commitment to do it. Some of us feel strongly that we should, others that we can't." Because the expatriate management does not have the understanding or the commitment to teach local employees the company values, the quality at some companies has not been acceptable.

It is stated that ABB has a great advantage compared with other worldwide companies because of its top priority of building deep local roots by hiring and training local managers who know their local markets.[51] Replacing expatriates with local Chinese employees, where the local employees are set to be successors to the expatriates after a certain amount of years, shows the commitment to the philosophy of having a local profile. However, as the Chinese employees are coming from an extremely different system from that of the Western expatriates, it is argued that it takes them quite a long time to get exposed to Western management practices. To ease this problem, and to teach Western management style, ABB China, among other companies, has recently set up an agreement with a business school in Beijing to arrange training for Chinese employees with good management potential. This is in a way specific for ABB China because in developed countries the employees are responsible for their own development.[52] Just recently ABB had its own school in Beijing for Chinese employees to learn ABB culture and management. The school had to close, however, because of the profit center philosophy that required the school to charge the individual ABB companies for teaching their employees. As few companies wanted to pay for the education, the school had to close.

ABB is also regularly sending about 100 local Chinese employees to an ABB company in a Western country every year. Having had several employees quit after the invested training, ABB has now taken precautions against this risk with a service commitment. It requires that the employee (or the person's new employer) pay back the training investment if he or she quits or sign an agreement to continue working for ABB a certain number of years. The problem of local employees quitting after ABB's investment in their training is evidenced by the personnel turnover rate—approximately 22 percent within ABB China. Many local employees seek the experience of working for an international company such as ABB and then move on to another job, which might be better paid.

However, by having local employees, the local ABB company is responsive to local conditions and sensitive to important cultural objectives, such as the Chinese "guanxi."[53] It has been decided that the local employees should take care of the customer contact since the expatriates are usually only stationed for a few years at one location and are consequently not able to build up strong connections with customers.

REORGANIZATION

ABB is a decentralized organization, based on delegated responsibility and the right to make decisions in order to respond quickly to customers' requirements. In the core of this complex organization are two principles: decentralization of responsibility and individual accountability. These principles have been very relevant in China, which is a relatively young country for ABB to be operating in.[54] Decentralization is highly developed and the expatriate[55] managers have a wide responsibility that would normally demand more than one specialist in a Western company. However, in some instances the organization is criticized for being too centralized, such as that the country manager needs to accept if an employer is flying overseas.

The changes in China happen very fast, and according to ABB brochures, the greatest efficiency gains lie in improving the way people work together.[56] Within the ABB China region, communication has, however, its shortcomings when companies with overlapping products or similar products do not exchange their information to any large degree or coordinate their marketing strategies. On the technical side, communication is frequent: a manager during one day usually receives up to 100 E-mails from other ABB employees. But procedures for building up effective informal communication are lacking between most ABB companies operating in China. The distances are large, and so a meeting demands a greater effort than in almost any other country in the world.

According to the former CEO, Percy Barnevik, the aim of the matrix organization is to make the company more bottom heavy than top heavy— "clean out the headquarters in Zurich and send everybody out, have independent companies operating in an entrepreneurial manner," as one respondent mentioned. It is further maintained in the company brochures, that these entrepreneurial business units have the freedom and motivation to run their own business with a sense of personal responsibility.[57]

However, the result from the matrix organization in China is that the ABB subsidiaries have ABB China's objectives (the country level) and the business area's (BA) objectives to follow. ABB China is measuring how the different companies are performing within China. The BA, on the contrary, is measuring how the specific products are performing on a worldwide basis and what the profitability is for the products. Each BA has a financial controller, and each country level also has one. "Rarely are the two coordinated, or do they meet. So you end up with one set of objectives from each . . . Duplication! Which one shall you follow?"

According to the ABB Mission Book, the roles in the two dimensions of the ABB matrix must be complementary.[58] It demands that both the individual company and headquarters are flexible and strive for extensive communication. This is the way to avoid the matrix interchange becoming cumbersome and slow. It is seen as the only way to "reap the benefits of being global (economies of scale, technological strength, etc.) and of being multidomestic (a high degree of decentralization and local roots in the countries in which we operate)."

For many years, ABB was widely regarded as an exemplary European company, yet it is undergoing a second major restructuring within four years. CEO Lindahl's restructuring is aimed at making the organization faster and more cost efficient.[59] Due to the demands of a more global market, there are reasons for getting rid of the regional structure and to concentrate more on the specific countries. The reorganization has basically dismantled one half of the matrix: the country management. Henceforth, the BAs will manage their businesses on a worldwide basis, and it is said that there will no longer be the confusion between BA and country management setting different objectives. At the same time, segments are split up (many BAs form a segment) to make them more manageable (for example, the transmission and distribution segment has been split into two segments: transmission and distribution). Thus, the general managers of the individual joint ventures and other units will have only one manager above them in the organization who has a global view of the business. In China, it also means the dismantling of the Hong Kong organization as well as the Asia Pacific organization.

According to Lindahl, the reorganization is preparation for a much faster rate of change in the markets and for the company to be able to respond more effectively to the demands of globalization. It is seen as an aggressive strategy to create a platform for future growth.

FUTURE VISION

CEO Lindahl's view of the future is that it can no longer be extrapolated, but has to be forecasted by creativity, imagination, ingenuity, and innovation, leading to action based not on what was, but on what could be. The corporate culture needs to be replaced by globalizing leadership and corporate values. ABB is focusing on this by creating a unified organization across national, cultural, and business borders.

On the path toward the next century, ABB is going to focus on several essential elements: a strong local presence; a fast and flexible organization; the best technology and products available; and excellent local managers who know the business culture, are able to cross national and business borders easily, and can execute the company's strategy faster than the competition.[60] The company's view is that "We are living in a rapidly changing environment, and our competitors will not stand still. In the face of this great challenge and opportunity, enterprises that adapt quickly and meet customer needs will be the winner, and this is the ultimate goal of ABB."[61]

Endnotes

1. "100 Years of Experience Ensures Peak Technology Today," ABB STAL AB, Finspong.
2. *Dagens Industri,* August 13, 1998, p. 25.
3. Ibid.
4. Jean-Claude Usunier, *Marketing Across Cultures.*
5. *Dagens Industri,* July 2, 1998.
6. David Smith, *Management Today* (April 1996), 49.
7. Ahlquist, Magnus, as editor; *The Recruiters' Guide to China,* by preface of Professor Michael Yahuda.
8. *Bizniz,* September 30, 1997.
9. Examples include VCD-player, CD-ROM player, mobile telephones, beepers, and video cameras.
10. Jeffrey E. Garten, "Opening the Doors for Business in China," *Harvard Business Review* (May–June 1998), 160–172.
11. *Månadens Affärer,* No. 11, November 1996 (searched through AFFÄRSDATA via http://www.ad.se/bibsam/).
12. *Dagens Industri* August 19, 1998 (searched through AFFÄRSDATA via http://www.ad.se/bibsam/).
13. Ibid.
14. Ahlquist, Magnus, as editor; *The Recruiters' Guide to China,* by preface of Professor Michael Yahuda.
15. Ibid.
16. Garten, "Opening the Doors for Business in China," pp. 167–171.
17. See the report from *Economist,* October 1998 (www.economist.com).
18. Hong Yung Lee, "The Implications of Reform for Ideology, State and Society in China," *Journal of International Affairs,* 39, no. 2, pp. 77–90.
19. An interview with Premier Zhu Rongji in *China Daily,* March 20, 1998, p. 2.
20. *China Daily, Business Weekly,* Vol. 18, No. 5479, March 29–April 4, 1998, p. 2.
21. Hoon-Halbauer, Sing Keow; *Management of Sino-Foreign Joint Ventures.*
21. Yuan Lu, *Management Decision-Making in Chinese Enterprises.*
22. Ibid.
23. Jun Ma, *Intergoveral Relations and Economic Management in China.*
24. Oiva Laaksonen, *Management in China during and After Mao in Enterprises, Government, and Party.*
25. Yanan Ju, *Understanding China,* p. 45.
26. Quanyu Hwang, *Business Decision Making in China.*
27. Hong Yung Lee, "The Implications of Reform."
28. Yuan Lu, *Management Decision-Making in Chinese Enterprises.*
29. Ibid.
30. Hong Yung Lee, "The Implications of Reform."
31. Yuan Lu, *Management Decision-Making in Chinese Enterprises.*
32. *Månadens Affärer,* No. 11, November 1996.
33. *Economist,* Oct. 28, 1995 (searched http://www.economist.com).
34. Because China is still a quite closed country, Chinese people are not able to obtain foreign currency except in very limited amounts.
35. ABB, "The Art of Being Local," ABB Corporate Communications Ltd., printed in Switzerland.
36. ABB brochure, "You Can Rely on the Power of ABB," ABB Asea Brown Boveri Ltd., Department CC-C, Zurich.
37. Technology partner (in this case) = Center of Excellence (CE) = Licensors.
38. ABB's Mission, Values, and Policies.
39. HV Switchgear, ABB, ABB Business Area H. V. Switchgear, printed in Switzerland.
40. ABB, "You Can Rely on the Power of ABB."
41. Licensing is defined here as a form of external production where the owner of technology or proprietary right (licensor) agrees to transfer this to a joint venture in China, which is responsible for local production (licensee).
42. During the study, this has changed to some degree due to a unit called CHTET being introduced.
43. http://www.abb.se/swg/switchgear/index.htm (November 1997).
44. First source = you are the first source, but if you cannot meet the customer's requirements the second source steps in.
45. *Economist,* Jan. 6, 1996 (searched from http://www.economist.com)
46. ibid.
47. Göran Lindahl is the present CEO and chairman of the board.
48. *Economist,* Jan. 6, 1996.
49. There are two types of common but false expectations expatriates have when coming to China. Either they believe they are going to make a lot of money or they think they are going to experience the old Chinese culture—a culture that most of the time does not correspond to the culture of today's China.
50. ABB's Mission, Values, and Policies, Zurich, 1991.
51. ABB, "The Art of Being Local."
52. ABB's Mission, Value, and Policies.
53. Guanxi = connections, relations.
54. ABB set up its first office, a representative office, in 1979.
55. Expatriate is a person who has a working placement outside the home country.
56. ABB, "You Can Rely on the Power of ABB."
57. Ibid.
58. ABB's Mission, Values, and Policies.
59. *Dagens Industri,* August 13, 1998, p. 25.

60. "Meeting the Challenges of the Future," presentation given to the Executives' Club of Chicago, October 16, 1997.
61. ABB, "Leading the Way in Efficient and Reliable Supply of Electric Power," ABB Transmission and Distribution Ltd., Hong Kong.

APPENDIX

Motorola

Motorola was involved with their business in Russia and faced some problems with Glasnost and the decline of the country. At that time, the founder of the company, Galvin, realized that there was no future in Russia and declared that China was the country where the growth was to be. Consequently, Motorola established its first representative office in China in 1987, and has grown very fast ever since. Today, China generates more than 10 percent of Motorola's sales and the company has its major businesses in China.

Motorola has found that modernization in China happens very fast and all its competitors are present in the country, but it is still predicting China to be the potential leader in Asia for its kind of business. The customers also have high expectations of the products Motorola is offering because the products are considered very expensive. However, the problem the company is facing in China "is that Motorola is growing very fast and it is like chasing a speeding train and trying to catch up with it."

At present, Motorola has 12,000 employees and 200 expatriates in China, whereas the goal is that Chinese successors will take over the job of the expatriates. The expatriates are sent out on assignments for two to three years, with the possibility of renewal with a one-two rotation, but limited to a maximum of six years as an expatriate. The expatriates must meet high demands and cope with the difficulties of teaching teamwork to local employees. That aspect is very important within the company since all the strategy planning is done in teams. When the contract time for the expatriate has expired,

> You have done your job when the time comes and you have left the company and everything is working smoothly, but if everything is falling apart, you are a failure as an expatriate and have not taught a successor.

However, progress has been made in developing the company's local employees. Motorola has set up training abroad. The training, nevertheless, is preferably held within China, with rotation assignments and training at Motorola University. This company university was set up in 1994 when the company found that the Chinese universities did not turn out sufficiently well-trained students. Within the company there is, however, a requirement that every employee worldwide shall have at least forty hours of training, which is argued to possibly be exceeded in China. The view is that there must be a combination of good training and mentor development to get successful people. Motorola admits that it does make a mistake by not providing enough training for foreign expatriates before they come to China. It is also said that they have noticed that overseas Chinese often do not do well fitting into the system, even though they speak Chinese, or as quoted: "You get more understanding if you look like a foreigner and make some mistakes than if you don't. Overseas Chinese are measured through other standards than other foreigners."

Other problems the company is facing concerning expatriation, is that some expatriates just cannot handle the situation in China. If an expatriate fails, this has to be handled with care; otherwise the person looses face when coming back to the home office. The company also has pointed out that it needs expatriates with ten to fifteen years of experience in order to teach the local employees the company values and to transfer company knowledge. However, the people who are willing to change addresses and move to China are the younger employees with less than five years of experience.

The expatriates are often responsible for transferring technology knowledge and helping to get projects started, especially in the case of the newly set-up Center of Excellence in Tianjin, where $750 million was invested. This was Motorola's first manufacturing research laboratory outside the United States. In all the company has invested $1.1 billion in China and plans to invest another $1 to 1.5 million. Motorola has also set up two branches of worldwide training universities to educate customers, suppliers, and government officials, as well as its own employees. The money invested in China is said to be from the earnings within the whole enterprise, with the motivation that the Chinese market is going to be huge. Sincere commitment has been made and the present CEO, Gary Tucker, is said to have expressed the following:

"When Motorola has come to your country they never leave ... We manufacture in China, because this is where our market is. We get wealth by going to a lot of countries around the world and then doing well in that country."

The expansion strategy in China is through joint ventures. However, since it is important that the Chinese partners bring something of value, they have to be approved by the CEO. Other than that, it is argued that the company has become "so decentralized that it has become bad," and that the company desires to reorganize more along customer than product lines. A practical reorganization has taken place to move everybody operating in Beijing to the same newly built headquarters. However, entrepreneurial activities are also argued to be of importance, but difficult in practice due to financial motivation and autonomy.

In China the products are localized by having Chinese characters on the cellular phones and pagers. In 1987, Motorola started selling pagers and thought there would not be a big market because the telephone network was not well established, but then the company invented codebooks, which made possible two-way communication, and it also worked in Hong Kong, Singapore, and Taiwan. After five years of operation in China, the company has not yet been able grow deep roots in the market. Nevertheless, the investments in the country and efforts to make the company a Chinese one are argued to be the reason for the depth of the localization and make the company unshakable. To show its seriousness about putting in deep roots in China, Motorola has invested huge sums in sponsoring environmental protection, providing scholarships to students, building labs at universities, and donating money to primary schools in rural areas.[1]

The worldwide organization is seen as a "pyramid," with the corporate on top and business units underneath—"then put the apex at the bottom." The corporate office works as the glue that holds the organization together. In 1997, Motorola conducted a reorganization to better reflect the global nature of the business.[2] The coordination is also said to be safeguarded by this new formal structure. However, the informal information flow is argued to be better, but pointed out as probably overused. The information flow is mostly through E-mails. A manager gets approximately 70 to 100 a day, of which less than 30 percent are regarded as really useful.

All the controllers or general managers in the joint ventures get together quarterly to counsel, to solve problems, and give support to each other. Information is encouraged, but no system is developed to track what is going on in all the six districts in China where the company is operating. Competition between the different units is a common problem and is said to confuse customers. This problem cannot be solved because of the matrix organization.

What makes Motorola a worldwide company is argued to be that it has a set of key common beliefs or guiding principles from the role model and father figure of the company, Galvin: "uncompromising integrity and constant respect for people—that is what makes us Motorola." This is the principal code of conduct that Motorola practices, and which the management has to reread and sign every two years.

Motorola has made it clear that it has had to change the way it does things because it is operating in the Chinese market: it needs to show face, build relations, and have its people go to ceremonial meetings. Regarding relations, it is essential to make sure that the partner is reliable, that the business makes sense, and that it is legal, which is pointed out to be opposite from the West. However, it is then stated that the Motorola company always looks the same all over the world; it is the expatriates and their families that have made an effort to adapt to the surroundings.

China is a very difficult country for a huge company like Motorola to be operating in "because they would like to control the system and everything takes a long time because they will make sure that you are not cheating. You must be able to work with all the people that come from different departments and to let them trust you. Ordinary things like getting water, electricity, etc. is a huge problem. Doing business in the Chinese system is a challenge and therefore creates pressure because you get frustrated.

Procter & Gamble

In August 1998 China's largest international employer had been in China for ten successful years. Procter and Gamble, or P&G, has approximately 5,000 employees and 100 expatriates spread over eleven joint ventures and wholly owned enterprises in the country. This year it was ranked on *Fortune* magazine's "World's Most Admired Companies" list. Currently, the biggest market for the company is China, where new companies are being established. Before establishing companies in China, P&G did a feasibility study. However, as with most other feasibility studies done in China, the information was outdated even though it was only a year old, and people were criticized for not having sufficient knowledge about the country's specific situation.

The expatriates sent to China for the P&G account are said to have no other preparation than the company's deep culture, which will support them. Furthermore, a constant effort is being made within the company to put different cultural backgrounds together. Cultural values are also written down and are consistent all over the world. However, due to that, the different expatriates have a wide variety of cultural backgrounds and their management style is colored by their culture. It is pointed out that this mixture of management styles might confuse the local Chinese employees.

The main benefit gained for an expatriate is the one offered in the daily work. One exception are the expatriate salespeople, who get a whole year of orientation and language training. In line with the localization demands, the number of expatriates is decreasing. Because of the high costs involved of having expatriates, who are mostly three to four levels up in the organization, one of the key strategies is to develop local employees. Everybody who is an expatriate for P&G has a sponsor back home, a contact. It is deemed essential to keep in touch with the sponsor, and people are also encouraged to go back home once a year at the company's expense. There is no official limit in expatriate policy within the company on the length of stay for expatriates, but most of them are on a three-year contract. The expatriates are said to be a very close group—"we are all in this together and we have a common vision"—although as yet there is no expatriate network.

The optimal goal for P&G is to develop the organization so that it can be a Chinese-run company. Today, everything is made in the Chinese P&G factories for internal use and, just a couple of months ago, the company opened up a research center in Beijing, in cooperation with a prominent university.[3] A reason for opening a research center in Beijing is a bet on the future that the world's largest group of consumers will have a large say on how P&G will market and develop in the rest of the world. If the company has developed a good idea in China, the company will analyze how to reapply those ideas in the rest of the world. The same would be true of ideas developed at the headquarters in Cincinnati or in the previous Center of Excellence in Brussels.

Counterfeits are the greatest competition for the company, and an extensive problem. However, P&G does not sell all its products in China, and the quality of the products sold is not as high as it is in Western countries. The Chinese customers are said to be unable to pay for better value. Nevertheless, the company is trying to offer a consistency of quality the Chinese consumers are willing to pay for.

In the Chinese P&G organization, fewer layers are developed and the decision making takes a shorter time within the organization, because the company evolved very quickly and the market is said to be so dynamic and changing that P&G has not had the time to implement the layer. Consequently, the Chinese organization and structure are not the same as in other countries, but it is argued that the Chinese organization is, by all accounts, more efficient and that P&G will implement some of its features in other countries. At the current time a reorganization is taking place within the worldwide P&G, and the culture and reward system are being changed as well—all to make the company more flexible.[4]

As for the Chinese situation, "*guanxi*" is mentioned, which is said to be difficult for the expatriates to establish and consequently the company relies on the local staff. The local employees get an immense amount of education at P&G's own school. Also, expatriates at the company have the explicit responsibility to deal with company principles, values, and all the technical specifics for P&G. However, "they are so into running the business that sometimes the coaching of the locals is not possible."

One of the challenges Procter & Gamble faces in China is the difficulty in dealing with the government. The company has dealt with this by searching for a sophisticated government-relations manager who shall report not only to the head of operations in China but also to the chief executive of the company.[5]

Nestlé

In the beginning of the 1980s, China asked the world's largest food company, Nestlé, to come build "milk streets" in the country. China was unfamiliar with how to produce milk and turned to Nestlé, whose core business is actually milk powder. From that time the company has grown strongly in China and now has almost 4,000 employees, 200 of them foreign expatriates.

Today, Nestlé is regarded as having come from Swiss roots and turned into a transnational corporation.[6] The company has a history of being locally adaptive. During the First World War, Nestlé gave its local managers increasing independence from the beginning, to avoid disruptions in distribution.[7] This resulted in a great deal of Nestlé's operations being established at other locations than at their headquarters in Switzerland. Another cause was the company's belief that the consumers' taste was very local and that there were no synergy effects to be gained by standardizing the products. However, in 1993 the company started to rethink its belief in localization due to the increasing competition in the industry. Nestlé has acquired several local brands, influenced by its own country culture, which has caused it to standardize wherever possible.[8]

However, although the company is growing in China, it must be pointed out that it is not always selling products with as much margin as desired. The company is said to have as high a quality of products as they have in other countries, but the downside is that they must have lower margins in order to be competitive, which might not always be profitable. On the question "Why Nestlé has to be in China"? the following was expressed:

> "It is because China is a large country and if you have a company that is present in more than 100 countries, you see it as a must for all international companies to be present there. We supply all over the world and it is our obligation to bring food to the people—which is the company's priority."

Nestlé entered China with a long-term strategy to be in the country for a long period of time and from then the strategy was always set to focus on the long-run perspective. Nestlé's overall approach is "Think global and act local!" The company's strategy is guided by several fundamental principles, for instance, that "Nestlé's existing products will grow through innovation and renovation while maintaining a balance in geographic activities and product lines."[9]

With regard to the local Chinese employees, they get a few days of Nestlé education to learn about the Nestlé culture, but the expatriates have less training about going to another country. It is up to the home country to decide if it is necessary to train expatriates before sending them on an often three-year foreign assignment. However, leadership talent is highly valued within the company and consequently Nestlé has developed courses for this. The managers can independently develop their leadership talent, without any connection with the specific company style or culture. Community centers have been established to help expatriates with their contacts, supporting these expatriates psychologically and even offering language training.

In 1997, Nestle's "The Basic Nestlé Management and Leadership Principles" was published. It aims to make "the Nestlé spirit" generally known throughout the organization by means of discussions, seminars, and courses.[10] According to the CEO of Nestlé China, Theo Klauser, this publication is the key factor in Nestlé's corporate culture and started the company's international expansion 130 years ago.[11]

Within the organization of Nestlé China, the company has developed a specific structure due to the joint venture configuration. The information flow is seen as easy and smooth between these regions, thanks to the company concentrating its activities in only three regions in China. However, communication is said to be on a very high level, although it is argued that it is not even necessary to get all levels involved. As an example, only one unit in China takes care of all the marketing. At the same time each Nestlé company in China is responsible for its own turnover rate, which is said to create the flexible and decentralized company Nestlé is today. Quite unique for a worldwide company, Nestlé does not have any external E-mail network, and this is believed to concentrate the flow of information within the company.

A major challenge indicated for Nestlé in China is the effort in building long-term relationships to establish Nestlé as the leading food company. The difficulty is bringing the products to a more acceptable level in terms of profitability. Legal difficulties are also more important than in any other country. Other challenges are the issues concerning change, summed up as follows:

> Change happens every couple of months here, that is how the environment is, a lot of employees come from other more stable countries and sometimes find it difficult with all the changes. Change is how things are in China—it is nor-

mal. It is when something doesn't change, that is when you get worried! It is expected to change! Different from other countries where changes can be difficult to get.

Appendix Endnotes

1. Jeffrey E. Garten, "Opening the Doors for Business in China," *Harvard Business Review* (May–June 1998), 174-175.
2. Motorola Annual Report, 1997.
3. Qinghua University.
4. Procter & Gamble Annual Report, 1998.
5. Garten, "Opening the Doors for Business in China," *Harvard Business Review* (May–June 1986), 59-60.
6. http://www.Nestlé.com/html/home.html (September 1998).
7. J. A. Quelch and E. J. Hoff, "Customizing Global Marketing," *Harvard Business Review* (May–June 1986), 59-60.
8. Brorsson, Skarsten, Torstensson; *Marknadsföring på den inre markanden—Standardisering eller Anpassning,* Thesis at Lund University, 1993.
9. http://www.Nestlé.com/html/h2h.html (September 1998).
10. Nestlé Management Report, 1997.
11. Interview with CEO of Nestlé China, Theo Klauser, *Metro* (July 1998), 27.

CASE 39

Sandvik AB (A)

This case was prepared by Robin Teigland, Assistant Professor Julian Birkinshaw, and Professor Roderick E. White of the Richard Ivey School of Business, The University of Western Ontario, Canada.

In the fall of 1996, Clas Åke Hedström, CEO of the Sandvik Group, was reviewing the progress of the three initiatives he had undertaken since assuming leadership of the group in 1994. First, his push for corporatewide profitable growth, helped along by a strengthening global economy, had been successful. During 1995, revenues rose by 17 percent, while net profits went up by 54 percent. Further growth was expected. Second, Hedström had also changed the group's conservative financial policy. Dividends were increased to 50 percent of net profits over the business cycle. Third, Hedström was actively pushing for greater synergies among the six Sandvik business areas. But here progress was proving more difficult to measure.

All of these initiatives were intended to enhance shareholder value. Sandvik was viewed by most investors as a highly dependable, if unglamorous, asset. (See Figure 1 for shareprice performance.) As explained by one analyst,

> Sandvik is reliable . . . year after year, Sandvik's results are on the plus side of our expectations . . . it is seldom exciting, it never surprises by bolting in some unexpected direction, nor does management make the kind of bold plays that put butterflies in the stomach.

IVEY

Robin Teigland, Assistant Professor Julian Birkinshaw, and Professor Roderick E. White prepared this case solely to provide material for class discussion. The authors do not intend to illustrate either effective or ineffective handling of a managerial situation. The authors may have disguised certain names and other identifying information to protect confidentiality. Ivey Management Services prohibits any form of reproduction, storage, or transmittal without its written permission. This material is not covered under authorization from CanCopy or any reproduction rights organization. Copyright ©1998, Ivey Management Services.

At the same time, Sandvik received its share of pointed questions. For example, what did management intend to do with its cash hoard? An analyst stated:

> We expect more action from an essentially debt-free company with liquid assets exceeding SEK 5 billion . . . we wonder if Sandvik has ever heard of something called "leverage" to enhance return on shareholders' equity.

Hedström had taken action on this matter by increasing the dividend, lifting the overall growth ambition for the Sandvik Group and putting plans in place for a share repurchase.

Another line of inquiry was directed at Sandvik's portfolio of businesses. Some observers saw Sandvik as six stand-alone businesses, several with few, if any, operational links to the others. In many countries, the corporate strategy of unrelated diversification had become decidedly unpopular. A wave of corporate refocusing, sell-offs, and demergers resulted.[1] It was suggested that Sandvik could enhance shareholder value by selling one or more of its business areas. Indeed, takeover, or the threat of takeover, had forced some major corporations to restructure their business portfolios. Even though there was not as active a market for corporate control in Sweden, Sandvik did have reason to be concerned about changes in ownership and control. Sandvik's largest shareholder (25 percent) had recently announced its intention to sell its Sandvik holding. (See Table 1).

Sandvik's six businesses shared a common history, corporate culture, and corporate identity. While there was a historical relationship (see Figure 2), their activities had diverged over time. Since 1984, Sandvik's different business areas had operated with

FIGURE I

Monthly Share Price
Performance for
Sandvik, 1986–1996

a very high level of autonomy. Even so, Sandvik corporate management was averse to any suggestions that the group be broken up. "You would not put these six businesses together today, but that does not mean you should break them up either," explained Leif Sunnermalm, the executive vice president. It was believed there were many benefits for Sandvik businesses to be part of the group, and

there were many other areas where additional benefits could be gained. These potential benefits lay behind the current drive for greater cooperation among businesses. But Hedström recognized that if the benefits of being part of the group could not be realized, then the argument for breaking the group apart became more compelling. The whole had to be worth more than the sum of its parts.

TABLE I

Largest Shareholders of Sandvik AB as of December 1995

	Percentage of Voting Rights	Percentage of Shares
Skanska AB	26.1	20.3
Investment funds of the Swedish savings banks	10.4	10.1
National Swedish pension fund	7.8	6.2
Svenska Handelsbanken pension foundation	5.0	3.9
The Swedish staff pension foundation	3.9	3.6
SEB Investment funds	2.7	2.3
Folksam	2.4	1.9
National Swedish pension insurance fund	2.3	1.8
Labor market insurance AB	2.2	1.8
Skandia	1.9	1.8
Svenska Handelsbanken's investment funds	1.8	1.7
Nordbanken's investment funds	1.5	1.2

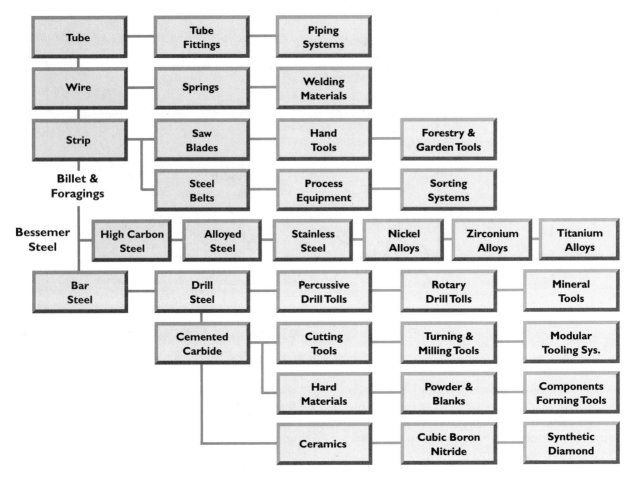

FIGURE 2

The Sandvik Evolution

Hedström and the executive group had begun to look for ways of achieving synergies among the businesses *without* centralizing decision making. At every opportunity, the executive group communicated its belief that Sandvik had to become a more integrated organization, to ensure that "the whole was greater than the sum of the parts." The corporate executives' enthusiasm for building an integrated Sandvik was tempered by a recurring worry: that employees throughout the company would see the changes as a step backward, as a reestablishment of central control over the six autonomous business areas. While this was not the intention, corporate management recognized the need to proceed very carefully, ensuring that the push for synergies did not jeopardize the effectiveness of Sandvik's existing organizational structure.

The process of change would not be easy because many managers at all levels did not see the need for greater integration. Hedström and his team began to consider the best ways of moving ahead.

SANDVIK HISTORY

The Early Years—1862 to 1941

Sandvik AB had its origins in a small steel company, Göransson Högbo Stål & Jernwerks, founded in 1862 in the town of Sandviken, 200 kilometers north of Stockholm, Sweden. The company was the first in the world to manufacture and sell steel using the Bessemer method. A reorganization of the company in 1868 led to the establishment of Sandvikens Jernverks AB, which was renamed Sandvik AB in 1972.

From its historical roots in steel and in a provincial Swedish town, Sandvik developed over the next century into a global materials technology engineering company, and one of Sweden's largest exporters. In 1995, Sandvik comprised more than 200 companies and employed more than 30,000 people in 130 countries. Its sales were SEK30 billion (approximately $4.5 billion), with 90 percent of sales outside of Sweden. (See Table 2)

Like many other Swedish industrial firms, Sandvik had developed an export orientation and an innovation-driven business philosophy. The company's operating philosophy evolved during the late nineteenth century. It could be summarized as

1. a conscious striving for the manufacture of high value-added products, which could bear the costs of transportation.
2. a firm commitment to R&D.
3. the identification of global needs for advanced niche products, which could be standardized to provide economies of scale but were uninteresting for bulk steel producers.
4. product development in close cooperation with customers.
5. the marketing of products through its own distribution channels, either wholly owned subsidiaries or exclusive agents.

Throughout its history, Sandvik had remained true to these principles.

TABLE 2

Sandvik Financial Results, 1990–1995*

	1995	1994	1993	1992	1991	1990
Invoiced sales, SEK M	29,700	25,285	21,770	17,217	17,558	18,256
Operating profit before depreciation and financial increase	6,265	4,550				
Profit after financial income and expenses, SEK M	5,620	3,811	1,764	1,486	1,776	2,842
as % of invoicing	19	15	8	9	10	16
Net profit for the year, SEK M	3,727	2,436	1,069	1,112	1,248	2,380
Earnings per share, SEK	13.40	8.75	3.85	4.05	4.55	8.70
Dividend per share (1996: as proposed), SEK	6.00	3.75	2.25	1.90	1.80	1.70
Pay-out ratio, %	45	40	58	47	40	20
Equity capital, SEK M	18,503	16,013	14,364	13,538	12,693	11,928
Equity ratio, %	64	59	60	59	57	54
Debt/equity ratio, times	0.1	0.2	0.2	0.2	0.3	0.4
Liquid assets, SEK M	6,893	6,591	5,171	4,864	4,814	5,251
Return on equity capital, %	21.6	16.0	7.7	8.5	10.1	21.8
Return on net assets, %	28.0	21.7	12.0	10.4	12.9	19.2
Investment in property, plant, and equipment, SEK M	2,050	1,229	886	886	1,021	1,161
Total investments, SEK M	2,092	1,575	964	1,311	1,761	1,715
Cash flow, SEK	164	1,215	1,425	1,645	882	1,486
Number of employees, 31 Dec.	29,946	29,450	26,869	28,617	26,237	25,781

*Key figures for 1994 and earlier have been adjusted to reflect the revised definitions that have been applied from 1995.

Around the turn of the century, Sandvik's emphasis on high-value added products led the company to expand from its base in Bessemer steel production into the emerging markets for specialty steel. For example, the company moved into markets that required hardness, cleanliness, dimensional stability, and blemish-free surfaces. End products made with Sandvik steel included corsets, gramophone needles, pens, umbrellas, and pocket watches. One important new product introduced in this era was Sandvik's cold-rolled strip steel, which became widely used for the manufacture of wood saws. This led to the development of a large saw product line. It eventually became the Saws and Tools Business area. Sandvik was one of the first companies to produce steel conveyer belts. Steel belts became a major product line and provided the base for the creation of a distinct business area, Process Systems.

International growth developed rapidly, and by 1914, 80 percent of Sandvik's sales occurred outside Sweden. The company experienced a downturn during the First World War and in the interwar period, but export levels remained high. By 1937, the company had established subsidiaries in thirteen countries in Europe and North America.

Diversification and Growth—1941 to 1981

In 1941, the management group made the critical decision to invest in an emerging technology called cemented carbide. Cemented carbide is a powdered metallurgical product, made primarily of tungsten, carbide, and cobalt, and it has a hardness approaching that of diamonds.[2] One of Sandvik's key competitors, Fagersta Bruks AB, had already begun experimenting with cemented carbide. It appeared to have great potential in the metalworking, mining, and forestry industries. Sandvik acquired the necessary cemented carbide technology. The new business, named Coromant, was placed under the direction of Wilhelm Haglund.

For the first few years, Coromant struggled to commercialize its cemented carbide technology. The Sandvik board even considered shutting down the business. But Haglund's foresight and determination were eventually rewarded, and cemented carbide rapidly became one of Sandvik's core technologies. By the 1980s, the Coromant business area was the largest and most profitable in the Sandvik Group. In addition, the Hard Materials and Rock

Tools business areas both evolved out of the group's cemented carbide technology.

While the cemented carbide product lines began to flourish, the steel operations experienced a downturn in demand during the 1950s. In order to reduce the effect of future downturns, Sandvik decided to focus on value-added steel products. One of these was seamless stainless steel tubes. After big investments during the 1960s, it became an important product for the Steel business area.

Throughout the 1950s and 1960s, Sandvik experienced a high level of growth, driven both by increased demand for cemented carbide products and by further internationalization. Under Haglund's leadership, the company increased the number of its foreign subsidiaries from thirteen in 1957 to thirty-five in 1967. In the 1970s and early 1980s, Sandvik continued to grow, but with an increasing reliance on acquisitions, which were typically relatively small companies in closely related areas of expertise. By 1980, Sandvik had 33,289 employees. However, in 1981 the world economy experienced the worst industrial recession since the 1930s. Sandvik was severely affected, and its profits fell from SEK746 million in 1979 to SEK310 million in 1982.

Crisis and Renewal—1982 to 1994

In order to return Sandvik to previous profit levels, the management group realized that significant changes needed to be made. In addition to reducing the work force to 24,000, management proposed some major organizational changes. For a long time Sandvik had been structured into divisions under a parent company. Managers reported to division management, as well as to functional management in the parent company. This dual reporting system had created a high level of bureaucracy, and delayed decision making.

In 1983 a decentralized organizational structure was established. Six independent business areas, two service companies, and three regional companies for peripheral markets were established. The organization structure still closely resembled the one created in 1984 (see Figure 3). The parent company was reduced to a management group with a staff of just fifty people. Sandvik announced to the public, "Our goal with the new structure is to delegate responsibility as well as to achieve an awareness of results and costs at all levels and a decreased bureaucracy with shorter decision routes."

FIGURE 3

The Sandvik Organization

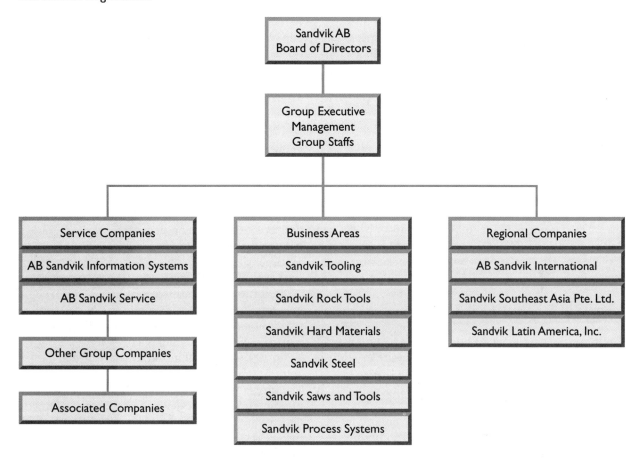

The structure of the Sandvik organization is shown in the diagram above. The underlying principle was established in 1983 and it consists of six separate business areas that are responsible for development, production, and sales of the group's products. Each business area has subsidiaries, or divisions, within joint Sandvik companies, in all major markets.

Outside the main markets, Sandvik's products are marketed by three regional companies that operate through local subsidiaries, sales offices, and agents.

Two companies provide general services; their principal customers are the Sandvik units in Sweden, but they also sell services to subsidiaries outside Sweden and to external customers.

Sandvik's organization also comprises a number of associated companies whose operations generally pertain to one of the business areas. The other group companies sector includes companies or groups of companies whose marketing strategies differ from those of the six business areas.

However, the financial problems were not over. In August 1983, Sandvik lost SEK219 million largely due to an unforeseen rise of the dollar against the Swedish krona. The company's major shareholder, Skanska AB, decided that it needed to take a stronger stand regarding the management of Sandvik. In 1984, Skanska increased its holding in Sandvik from 11 to 37 percent. Percy Barnevik, a former Sandvik employee and at that time CEO of ASEA, was appointed nonexecutive chairman, and Per-Olof Eriksson, formerly president of Seco Tools, was named CEO.

With the new organization and management team, Sandvik quickly returned to profitability.

Eriksson emphasized the need for clearly defined accountability. Each business was assessed on its return on net assets worldwide. Foreign-based businesses reported directly to their respective business heads, with only a token line of reporting into their country operation (in order to satisfy legal requirements). The corporate staff was kept very small.

Unlike his predecessors, Eriksson saw profitability as his primary objective, and growth as secondary. He became known as a cost-conscious leader, careful to avoid unnecessary expenditures and cautious in his growth plans. He was also visibly frugal in his own lifestyle and was frequently seen cycling to work from his home in Sandviken. Under Eriksson's leadership, Sandvik became a consistent performer, with ten unbroken years of profitable growth. In 1994, Eriksson retired and was replaced by Hedström, president of Sandvik Coromant since 1980.

SANDVIK'S BUSINESSES

There were six principal business areas and a number of service and regional companies. Sandvik Steel and Sandvik Tooling were by far the largest, with 33 percent and 32 percent of net sales, respectively. Rock Tools, Hard Materials, Saws and Tools, and Process Systems were the remaining business areas, each with between 9 and 15 percent of net sales. (See Tables 3 to 5.)

Sandvik Tooling

Sandvik Tooling had three parts: Sandvik Coromant; CTT Tools; and a small automation business.

Coromant   Coromant was consistently the highest return business in the Sandvik Group. It provided a product line of cemented carbide tools and tooling systems for metalworking products. These products had a very high value-to-weight ratio, and were typically transported by airfreight. The company supplied all major markets. In the United States, Coromant had two major competitors, Valenite and Kennametal. These competitors were expanding their activities through acquisitions in Europe, where Coromant was the market leader. Coromant was also the most solidly established non-Japanese competitor in Japan.

Coromant was recognized as the leading global player in its industry. In large part, this leadership position stemmed from a stream of product and process innovations. Products introduced during the last five years accounted for approximately 50 percent of total sales. Coromant was also the first company to introduce industry-scale diamond-coated carbide cutting inserts. Six per cent of annual turnover was invested in R&D.

Coromant was considered innovative in order processing, production, and logistics. Starting in 1984, a team developed a computer-aided purchase processing system (CAPP), which streamlined the entire order, design, and production process.[3] At the same time, Coromant introduced flow groups at its worldwide manufacturing facilities in order to promote flexibility. These changes enabled the company to reduce lead time from 50 days in 1984 to 2.3 days in 1995. A further aspect of Coromant's strategy was the development of its direct delivery system. In 1995, a change in the roles of the two European central warehouses (Gimo, Sweden, and Schiedam, the Netherlands) made possible a faster and more reliable supply of products to continental Europe and U.S. customers. Deliveries were made directly to the end users, generally within twenty-four hours.

In 1995 Coromant introduced its *CoroKey* program, to simplify the sales of Coromant's products. The program included a catalogue with a condensed product program, packaging with essential cutting data printed on the label, and coding and marking of the inserts to facilitate identification and ensure optimal use. Coromant also led the industry in information technology developments. In 1996, the company developed an extensive Intranet application, which provided immediately feedback on the relative cost and service levels of the different plants around the world. The CAPP system also speeded up the processing of tailored customer orders.[4]

In order to meet increasing demand, the business area made a substantial number of investments in 1994 and 1995. Management expanded the Gimo and U.S. facilities, acquired MKTS, a Russian cemented carbide company, and established a wholly owned production facility in China.

CTT Tools   CTT Tools was acquired in 1993 from the Swedish ball-bearing manufacturer SKF. CTT complemented Sandvik's cemented carbide product line with high-speed steel cutting tools and tooling systems. CTT Tools had approximately 10 percent of the global market. A comprehensive rationalization and restructuring program was performed at CTT between 1992 and 1994. Positive

TABLE 3

**Key Figures for Sandvik Business Areas
(in SEK millions)**

I. Tooling	1995	1994	1993	1992	1991
Invoiced sales	9576	8178	7184		
Profit before financial items	2436	1509	972		
Investment	747	397	240		
Number of employees	11010	10995	9919		
Ia. Coromant					
Invoiced sales	7184	6124	5287	4584	4884
Investment	616	364	200	218	332
Number of employees	7892	7911	6606	7186	7783
Ib. CTT Tools					
Invoiced sales	2334	2050	1897		
Investment	129	33	40		
Number of employees	3047	3084	3313		
II. Rock Tools					
Invoiced sales	2015	1955	1812	1510	1579
Profit before financial items	219	219	130	—	—
Investment	49	45	29	45	31
Number of employees	1877	1814	1840	1894	2063
III. Hard Materials					
Invoiced sales	1224	1029	893	808	655
Profit before financial items	185	135	51	—	—
Investment	102	60	46	73	43
Number of employees	1447	1446	1390	1574	1316
IV. Steel					
Invoiced sales	9807	7752	6450	5267	5570
Profit before financial items	1623	1014	461	159	279
Investment	452	293	289	253	277
Number of employees	7257	6903	5951	5917	6178
V. Saws and Tools					
Invoiced sales	2674	2583	2363	2049	1437
Profit before financial items	184	185	3	−82	−16
Investment	102	86	74	117	136
Number of employees	2998	3050	3060	3275	3676
VI. Process Systems					
Invoiced sales	1810	1603	1190	1190	1290
Profit before financial items	101	156	43	21	166
Investment	65	44	48	37	49
Number of employees	888	1037	789	755	755

TABLE 4

Overview of Sandvik's Business Areas

Hard Materials
R &D   Stockholm, Coventry (England), France
Manufacturing   United Kingdom and Denmark: two large highly specialized units for global market
                   10 local manufacturing units to supply customized production locally (five in Europe, five in
                   rest of world)
Sales   Direct market coverage in 50 countries (own units in 25, direct sales in 25)

Rock Tools
R&D   Stockholm
Manufacturing   In 13 countries with 30% of total production in Sweden
Sales   Direct market coverage in 50 countries

Coromant
R&D   Stockholm
Manufacturing   Main production in Gimo, Sweden
                   In 20 countries, including the United States (Fairlawn, N.J.), the United Kingdom (Feather-
                   stone), Russia, Poland (JV)
Sales   Direct market coverage in 60 countries

CTT Tools
R&D   Stockholm, Halmsted, Frankfurt, Zell, Sheffield (each brand has its own development)
Manufacturing   13 units, 10% within Sweden
Sales   Direct market coverage in 30 countries (12 units), and indirect via agents in most other
                   countries

Steel
R&D   Sandviken
Manufacturing   Main production in Sandviken
                   16 units, in Canada, Argentina, Czech Republic, Spain, United Kingdom, France, Brazil, India,
                   Finland
                   JV in Brazil, the United States (Scranton, Pa.), with Sumitomo, China
Sales   Direct market coverage in 55 countries

Saws and Tools
R&D   No central R&D; product development conducted at 8 product centres in Sweden (4),
                   Switzerland, Germany, the United States, and Portugal
Manufacturing   15 plants in 7 countries
Sales   Direct market coverage in 40 countries

Process Systems
R&D   Sandviken
Manufacturing   x units, including Korea

Sales   Direct market coverage in 25 countries

TABLE 5

The Competitive Environment of Sandvik's Business Areas

Tooling	**SEK 70 billion world market**
Cemented carbide	Sandvik about 20% market share
	Kennametal, Valenite (U.S.)
	Mitsubishi, Toshiba, Sumitomo (Asia)
	Number of local companies in Europe
High-speed steel	Sandvik about 10% market share
	Few large producers, but many small ones
Rock Tools	**SEK 8 billion world market**
Top hammer drilling	Sandvik, Uniroc (Sweden), Boart (S. Africa) with 67% of market
	10 companies with remaining 33%
Mineral tools	Kennametal, American Mine Tool
Down-the-hole drilling	Ingersoll-Rand (U.S.)
	Atlas Copco (Sweden)
	Large number of local suppliers
Hard Materials	**Sandvik Largest in Industry with 15% share**
	Four major competitors in Europe (Sandvik, Ceremetal, Plasee, Hertel), plus 50 small-medium firms
	Similar concentration in North America and Asia, but different competitors in each case
Process Systems	**Large Number of Companies, Limited Geographically or by Product Segment**
Steel	
Seamless tubes	Sumitomo (Japan), DMV (Europe)
Wire and bar	Ugine
	Number of smaller independent drawing mills
Strip	Hitachi Metals (Japan), Daido, Böhler Uddeholm
	Number of independent cold-rolling mills
Saws and Tools	**SEK 100 Billion World Market**
	Sandvik, Stanley and Falcon share 15% of market in Europe; remaining 85% is split among 500 competitors. U.S. market is more consolidated. Five competitors account for 50% of market. Remaining 50% is split among hundreds of smaller firms (including Sandvik)

effects of this program were achieved in 1995 since CTT was able to reduce costs as well as increase sales, partly due to its entrance into new markets provided by Coromant's global marketing organization.

Management worked to exploit synergies between the two companies in logistics, distribution, and product development. Dormer, one of the CTT Tools' companies, established a central warehouse with Coromant in the Netherlands. But some synergies were difficult to realize because of operational differences. As Coromant's president stated, "The devil hides in the details." One example was customer distribution. Seventy-five percent of Coromant's sales were direct, while only 30 percent of CTT's sales were direct and these were primarily to one customer.

Automation   Automation accounted for SEK58 million in sales in 1995. The business area was responsible for developing and marketing products such as computer systems for tool monitoring, tool administration, and production follow-up.

Sandvik Steel

Sandvik Steel was more of an engineering company than a conventional steel company. It developed, manufactured, and marketed only about 200,000 tonnes of specialty steel products annually. The steel business's main operations and R&D were located in Sandviken. In 1995, Sandvik Steel sold SEK 9.8 billion in stainless and high-alloy steel strips, wire, bars, and seamless tubes. The company was the world's largest producer of seamless tubing and rock-drilling steel. The products were used in a wide range of applications, from knives to surgery equipment and airplanes.

This business experienced an upsurge in demand in 1994. Invoiced sales increased by 20 percent in 1994 and 27 percent in 1995, resulting in a backlog of orders. In order to meet demand, capacity was expanded in Sweden and NAFTA. A tube mill was acquired and expanded in the Czech Republic and a jointly owned company (60 percent) was established in Quingdao, China. A joint venture was also developed in Brazil in 1994. Avesta Sandvik Tube, owned 25 percent by Sandvik Steel, grew substantially in this period due to access to Sandvik Steel's sales channels, particularly in Europe and Asia.

Although many of the business areas within Sandvik required steel in their product line, the Steel business area supplied only limited amounts to other Sandvik businesses. Steel provided 2,000 tonnes of steel to Saws & Tools, which was about 50 percent of the steel required in its saws, and SEK20–30 million value added to the Process Systems business area. As the world's largest producer of drill steel, the steel business provided a considerable amount of steel to Rock Tools, and to Rock Tools' competitors. The Steel business also shared the same trucking and shipping services with Rock Tools and Saws and Tools for its products from Sandviken to Europe.

Saws and Tools

The Saws and Tools area manufactured and marketed saws and hand tools for use in engineering, construction, metalworking, forestry, and horticulture. Eighty percent of product sales were to industrial and professional customers; the remaining sales were to individuals for personal use. With 1995 sales of SEK2.7 billion, the company was one of the largest in the hand tools industry, which was highly fragmented. The Saws and Tools business represented 9 percent of the group's total sales.

Competitive advantage in the saws and tools industry depended primarily on product adaptations and improvements rather than on basic research. In 1994, for example, Saws and Tools introduced the Ergo product line, which utilized a new design process to create ergonomically superior tools.[5] But some basic materials research was conducted in cooperation with the steel business and Coromant.

In order to improve profitability and delivery reliability, a series of productivity improvement programs and a new production organization were introduced between 1990 and 1994. The flow group organization was adapted from Coromant and was implemented at the production unit in Bollnäs, Sweden.

The hand tool industry experienced a rationalization during the 1994–1995 period, particularly with respect to the distribution system. The Saws and Tools area adapted Coromant's centralized warehousing concept and built a central European warehouse in the Netherlands, close to Coromant's Schiedam facility. Northern Europe was served by the Sandviken warehouse. North American distribution was being consolidated in a facility near Scranton, Pennsylvania.

Rock Tools

Representing 7 percent of the group's sales in 1995, the Rock Tools business area produced cemented carbide and steel-tipped rock-drilling tools for use in mining, civil engineering, and water-well drilling. Rock Tools was the only company in the rock-drilling industry that supplied a full line of rock-drilling tools.

The industry was mature, with Rock Tools and one or two other companies controlling the main markets. Continuous product improvement was essential to remain competitive. There was a trend toward increasing mechanization and more sophisticated, capital-intensive machinery. As a measure of progress, drilling speed increased from 10 meters per hour in the 1940s to 160 meters per hour in the 1990s. Rock Tools was able to lead the industry in technology development due to its membership in the Sandvik Group. The group had substantial research, development, and production of both cemented carbides and special steels, the materials that accounted for most of the components in rock-drilling tools. Rock Tools conducted its cemented carbide research in Stockholm in the same building as the Coromant and Hard Materials research teams, and also pooled its resources with the Steel business area in Sandviken.

In 1988, Rock Tools terminated its forty-one-year distribution agreement with Atlas Copco. Atlas Copco had purchased Fagersta, Rock Tools' main competitor. As a result, Rock Tools was left overnight without a sales and distribution organization. However, within three months Rock Tools was able to leverage the group's worldwide presence and build a new sales force of 200 people (many coming from Atlas Copco). Rock Tools was able to regain its market share and endure the subsequent price war, although with reduced margins. During this period, the Sandvik Group bought 25 percent of Tamrock, a Finnish producer of rock-drilling machinery and a competitor of Atlas Copco. This holding was increased to 49 percent in 1996.

In addition to product development and marketing support, Rock Tools also benefited from a series of best practices developed in the Coromant business area. When Lars-Anders Nordqvist was transferred from Coromant logistics and production to become the president of the Rock Tools business area, he brought with him the CAPP system as well as the logistics system. The introduction of a new work organization (self-managed flow groups) on the shop floor, together with new logistic systems for production loading and other improvements, led to a 60 percent rise in productivity from 1990 to 1996.

In order to achieve better market coverage, Rock Tools expanded its operations in Asia, Eastern Europe, and Latin America during 1995. A number of new development projects were also initiated with Tamrock.

Process Systems

Process Systems had 1995 sales of SEK 1.8 billion, 6 percent of the total for the group. The business originated in the early 1900s when the Steel business area began to make steel belts for chemical processing. In the early 1970s Process Systems was moved to Stuttgart, in order to be closer to the heart of the worldwide chemical processing industry. However, Process Systems developed applications for a wide variety of industries, including goods sorting and food processing in many countries, notably in the United States, Japan, and other parts of Asia. In 1996, the decision was made to relocate the head office for Process Systems back to Sweden.

In 1995, Process Systems delivered the world's largest package sorting system to UPS in Chicago (180,000 packages per hour). A new chemical processing production center was established in Korea for deliveries in Southeast Asia and China. In order to further broaden its product line, the business area acquired CML, an Italian company providing high-speed sorting systems of postal packages, magazines, and newspapers, in 1995. Other developments included the introduction of a new steam cooker as well as a dryer for the food processing industry.

The outlook for Process Systems was mixed. The competitive environment had become more difficult in the last few years. While the business continued to be profitable, management warned in the 1995 Annual Report that "weaker demand will be countered with continuing rationalization measures."

Hard Materials

The Hard Materials business area accounted for 4 percent of the Sandvik Group's total sales in 1995 and was the largest company in the hard materials industry. Hard Materials was formally created as a result of the 1984 reorganization, at which point it defined its product portfolio as "all cemented carbide applications not provided by Rock Tools and Coromant." Over time this definition became more focused, so that by 1996 Hard Materials competed in three areas: mechanical components, blanks for toolmakers, and rolls for the steel industry. This business needed finer grades of cemented carbide than either Rock Tools or Coromant. It was also involved in research into biocompatible ceramics. As a result, Hard Materials undertook much of its own research, in Stockholm, England, and France, though there were also frequent cooperative projects with Coromant and Rock Tools.

Hard Materials sold a small percentage of its products to other Sandvik businesses, for example, drill bits and carbide blanks to Sandvik Tooling, but most were to external customers (which were sometimes competitors of other Sandvik businesses). Hard Materials worked to coordinate purchases of tungsten and cobalt with Coromant and Rock Tools.

In the period 1991 to 1993, the hard materials industry experienced a recession and many companies became unprofitable. As a result, there were a number of bankruptcies and shutdowns. Sandvik made several acquisitions during this time (and in the years before 1987), including companies in the United Kingdom, France, and the United States. Subsequent to these acquisitions, Hard Materials underwent a restructuring of its manufacturing activities that resulted in a specialization of its European activities around five product centers. Currently, this business area was experiencing high demand as cemented carbide replaced steel in many industrial applications. In order to improve

its competitiveness, Hard Materials planned to further increase its R&D programs and accelerate the introduction of new materials and processes.

Corporate-Level Activities

Sandvik had a corporate staff consisting of approximately fifty people. The executive group comprised Hedström, the president and CEO; Leif Sunnermalm, executive vice president and CFO; and Lars Östholm,[6] executive vice president. In addition there were corporate managers responsible for Human Resources, Research and Development, Finance, and Corporate Relations (See Table 6).

Finance was one function that had always been performed centrally. A group of seven people in Sandviken, plus six in Switzerland and two in Singapore, were responsible for cash management, lend-

TABLE 6

The Sandvik Management Group

- *Clas Åke Hedström,* chief executive officer. Prior to being elected to CEO in 1994, Hedström was president of Sandvik Coromant, with a total of twenty-nine years of experience within the Sandvik Group.
- *Leif Sunnermalm,* executive vice president and chief financial officer. Sunnermalm joined the Sandvik Group in 1971 and moved from EVP in Coromant to EVP for the group in 1994.
- *Lars Östholm,* executive vice president, R&D. Östholm was employed by the Sandvik Group in 1958 and worked for it continuously except for the period 1971–1977, when he worked for ABB Steel. Prior to becoming EVP, he worked at Rock Tools.
- *Gunnar Björklund,* president, Sandvik Steel. Björklund joined Sandvik in 1959 and was elected to this position in 1982.
- *Göran Gezelius,* president, Sandvik Saws and Tools since 1988. Member of the Sandvik Group since 1982.
- *Lars-Anders Nordqvist,* president, Sandvik Rock Tools. Nordqvist started with Sandvik in 1967 and was elected president in 1991. Prior to this position, he was responsible for logistics and production at Sandvik Coromant.
- *Lars Pettersson,* president, Sandvik Coromant. Prior to joining Coromant, Pettersson worked in Steel. He was promoted to president in 1994.
- *Lars Wahlqvist,* president, Sandvik Hard Materials. Wahlqvist joined Rock Tools in 1969, left Sandvik to join Esab in 1975, and rejoined Sandvik in 1981. President of Hard Materials since 1984.
- *Roland Setterberg,* president, International Operations. Setterberg joined Hard Materials in 1986 after working with British Oxygen and Cabot Corporation. He became president of International Operations in 1997.
- *Rune Nyberg,* head, Human Resources. In 1983 Nyberg was hired by Sandvik into Coromant. After Nyberg had been two years outside Sandvik, Hedström recruited him to headquarters.
- *Peter Lundh,* head, Information Services. Member of Sandvik group since 1983.
- *Anders Illstam,* president, CTT Tools since its start in 1990. Previously president of SKF Tools.

ing and investments, and foreign exchange activities. The individual businesses were responsible for screening investment opportunities, presenting them to the board for approval.

Information systems (IS) had not been completely decentralized in 1984. Each business unit was made fully responsible for its IS needs. This meant businesses could establish their own resources, acquire external resources, or utilize the central IS function. The central IS function provided IT-services to the business units but also handled some of the common resources (the network, central operation, and so forth) in order not to lose scale and synergy effects. The decentralization of IS was not uniform. Most notably, Coromant built its own information systems group in 1988 by taking over its development resources from the central IS function. By 1996, Coromant had almost 65 people working in IS, compared with 170 in the central group. Other business areas still relied on the central resource and had smaller numbers of IS employees.

There was also a central component to the management of the group's technology. Sandvik's technology base had evolved over the years. In 1996, the company was positioned as "materials-driven," with technological strength in three areas:

1. Steel and alloyed steel
2. Cemented carbide and other hard material
3. Materials coatings

These technologies, in various combinations, formed the foundation for the six business areas.

While all R&D occurred in the business areas, there was a small technical advisory group responsible for the strategic direction of Sandvik's R&D. This group consisted of Lars Östholm, a staff researcher, and the heads of research from Tooling, Steel, Hard Materials, and Rock Tools. The advisory group met every three months to evaluate strategic R&D projects and to support projects that "fell between the lines" of the business areas or were pure research projects outside the company's mainline interests.

The executive group was also responsible for business development activities that fell beyond the boundaries of the existing six business areas. The possibility of a seventh Sandvik business, for example, had not been ruled out, but as Leif Sun-nermalm explained, "It would have to meet some very strict criteria, in terms of core technologies, customer base, expected return on investment, and growth opportunities."

Other Sandvik Operations

Sandvik had three regional companies. Sandvik International was responsible for exporting into Africa, the Middle East, and parts of the former USSR. Sandvik South East Asia and Sandvik Latin America, based in Singapore and Miami, respectively, were responsible for coordinating marketing activities in their particular regions. There were also two service companies: Sandvik Central Service, responsible for various support activities in the Sandviken area, and Sandvik Information Systems (see above).

Foreign Subsidiaries

Sandvik had extensive operations throughout the world, with approximately 200 foreign affiliates in 130 countries (see Table 7). In most of the smaller country markets, Sandvik had a single holding company, which represented all six business areas. Infrastructure and support functions were often shared, but the country manager had little or no influence over the day-to-day running of the various businesses. In the larger markets, such as the United States, the United Kingdom, and France, the business areas were more separate from one another. In these countries, there was little attempt made to share support functions or infrastructure. Following the 1984 reorganization, the country manager job was no longer a full-time responsibility. This role was usually assumed by the head of the largest business area in each country.

THE SANDVIK CULTURE

In many ways, Sandvik was the quintessential Swedish industrial company. The company was built on technological innovation around the turn of the century, and it rapidly gained a major overseas presence. Sandvik was also very "Swedish" in its style of doing business: conservative, understated and rather traditional, but with a strong work ethic and a strong corporate culture. As

TABLE 7

Geographic Distribution of Sales

	Invoiced Sales by Market Area (SEK million)		
	1995	1994	1993
Sweden	2370	1807	1494
European Union, excluding Sweden	13755	11506	9110
Rest of Europe	1419	981	1428
Total, Europe	17544	14294	12032
NAFTA	5626	5361	4572
South America	1422	1359	1210
Africa, Middle East	763	641	651
Asia, Australia	4345	3630	3305
Group Total	29700	25285	21770
	Invoiced Sales in the Ten Largest Country Markets (SEK million)		
	1995	1994	1993
United States	4863	4657	3872
Germany	4016	3453	3015
France	2533	2096	1857
Sweden	2370	1807	1494
Italy	2193	1658	1332
Great Britain	1893	1576	1263
Japan	1510	1307	1309
Brazil	831	752	682
Australia	817	748	623
Canada	620	587	543

stated by Percy Barnevik, "Sandvik cannot be described as a company given to excesses—put simply, the company does a darn fine job without a lot of fuss and without seeking any particular recognition for it." Sandvik was far and away the largest employer in the small town of Sandviken, two hours' drive north of Stockholm. Almost all senior managers were Swedes, and many had also grown up in Sandviken or the surrounding towns.

THE SEARCH FOR SYNERGIES

When Hedström was appointed CEO of the Sandvik Group in 1994, he brought with him an expansionist attitude. In addition to a goal of a 2 percent

return on net assets over a business cycle, he set a goal for annual sales growth at 6 percent for a ten-year period (compared with 4 percent in the past). In order to reach the aggressive growth goals, he encouraged managers to focus in particular on Asia, Central and East Europe, and the North American Free Trade area.

A key item on Hedström's agenda was to create greater synergies between the business areas and more value added by the corporate headquarters. To assist him, Hedström appointed Sunnermalm, a former colleague in the Coromant business area, as an executive vice president, and Rune Nyberg, an ex-Coromant manager, as corporate head of human resources. In the years following the 1984 reorganization, the six business areas had been encouraged to optimize their own profitability, with the result that the cooperative links between them had lessened over the years. Thus, while there were historical ties between the business areas, the current linkages were very mixed. Rock Tools, Hard Materials, and Tooling, for example, all drew from Sandvik's cemented carbide technology, but Saws and Tools and Process Systems were relatively independent of their sister business areas. Table 8 lists some of the synergies that were currently being exploited.

Hedström and his colleagues in the executive group were keen to see much greater synergies between the business areas. They felt there was considerable potential for cost savings if more activities were coordinated or combined, and also

TABLE 8

Existing and Potential Synergies in the Sandvik Group

Management and Administration	Profitability focus Use of management by objectives technique Parenting synergies Worldwide use of Sandvik IT network (common order, invoicing and financial) Group financing Shared back-office functions at smaller-scale subsidiaries Tax management
Human Resources	Common management planning system Internal career market Availability of corporate expatriate management Intercompany task forces (e.g., U.S.) Creating "center of excellence" Incentive system
Marketing and Sales	Sandvik brand Joint advertising and trade shows Joint customer education Customer file swapping Package sales to big customers and distributors
Logistics and Purchasing	Coromant and some CTT products sharing logistics Steel and Rock Tools sharing shipping Common purchasing of raw materials for the Group Coordinate purchase of travels, telecommunications, etc.
Production	Technology for Coromant, Rock Tools, and Hard Materials Manufacturing equipment for same Joint manufacture of carbide powder Flow-group concepts (developed by Coromant) CAPP system for Coromant, Rock Tools, and CTT
Research and Development	Materials research for Coromant, Rock Tools, Hard Materials, and partially for CTT Steel research for Rock Tools Steel grades with optimum machinability together with Coromant Boundless sharing of materials and application know-how

some opportunity for sales growth through, for example, cross-selling products between business areas. In order to get things moving, the Sandvik Group management put forward organizational initiatives in Human Resources and Information Technology. In the United States, a task force was formed to look for synergies among the sixteen U.S. operations. It was headed by Jim Baker, manager for Coromant's U.S. operations.

The U.S. Task Force

Of Sandvik's sixteen companies in the United States, many had been established through acquisition. Hedström convened a meeting of the sixteen company presidents in November 1995 to discuss the need to build synergies between these businesses. They identified purchasing, marketing, and human resources as areas where the greatest potential for synergies existed. Three task forces were set up, each headed by one of the company presidents and with representatives from each company. Jim Baker, the head of Coromant U.S., took overall responsibility.

A follow-up meeting between the U.S.-company presidents in December 1996 indicated that good progress had been made. As Baker observed, "we have 95 percent commitment to use the programs." The purchasing task force had looked at common purchasing agreements in all areas. They had in place agreements that were expected to save $13 million annually. The marketing task force agreed on standardized logos and a joint presence at trade shows. They also planned to launch a corporate advertising campaign in 1997 directed at senior managers in major user companies. The HR task force wanted to make movement of people between the Sandvik companies "seamless," and to this end it began the difficult task of harmonizing the different benefits packages in the sixteen companies. A further review was scheduled for June 1997, to look for further synergies in these areas and to consider other areas in which similar task forces could be established (for example, logistics, IT, distributor representation).

Human Resources

Rune Nyberg, the newly appointed corporate vice president of human resources (HR), observed that HR had "no co-ordination whatsoever." In an at-

tempt to develop greater cooperation among the business areas, Nyberg organized a conference in March 1996 for sixty senior HR managers from around the world. They discussed the key HR issues facing Sandvik as a group and identified six specific areas in which groupwide systems could be developed, such as compensation and benefits packages and benchmarking practices. International project groups were created to develop state-of-the-art systems in each area and establish "competence centers" that other parts of the Sandvik group could then draw on. While some systems, such as the new compensation and benefits system, would be mandatory, most would be at the discretion of the business areas. Nyberg's hope was that the involvement of these managers would encourage them to make use of the competence centers as they became established and to maintain relationships between one another. Nyberg also started a corporate HR newsletter to share the results of the project teams' research and to foster a dialogue between participants.

Another important issue was career management. Most managers had traditionally followed careers exclusively in a single business area. By 1996 only about 20 percent of managers had experience outside their current business areas. Hedström and Nyberg both felt that this proportion had to be increased in order to enhance the opportunities for cross-fertilization of ideas.

The Information Technology Council

Since 1984, some business areas had invested in their own proprietary information systems. As a result, the central IS group's ability to control groupwide systems was seriously compromised. In 1996, the Data Council, which had been established in 1985, was reorganized and given more precise tasks. At the same time a cooperation committee—the Information Technology Council—was formed. This council consisted of the president of Sandvik Information Systems and the heads of the IS groups in each business. Together they were responsible for defining policies and procedures, and analyzing major investments to ensure one set of standards, while not taking away each business area's responsibility for adapting these standards to its specific needs. The head of IT stated, "It has now dawned on many of the business units that there are significant opportunities for a common approach towards the setting of standards." The council met once a month and reported to the Sandvik Group Data Council.

INSTILLING THE NEED FOR CHANGE

Hedström hoped that the business area managers would see the changes he was putting forward as positive for the Sandvik Group and that they would also attempt to explore further synergies between the business areas. However, he realized that the business area presidents saw differing levels of potential and had different priorities. Gunnar Björkland, the former vice president of Sandvik Steel, believed that there might be distribution synergies for the various businesses due to a common customer base. However, he stated, "I can get more out of talking to Sumitomo with whom we do not directly compete than by talking to Coromant." Lars Wahlqvist, president of Hard Materials, observed that a "formal integration process is often rather less effective than an informal one." Göran Gezelius, president of Saws and Tools, went further when stating that "the search for synergies should not drive a major reorganization."

Hedström had several concerns about the search for greater synergies. First, it was not clear where the most valuable potential synergies lay. Hedström was aware of many of the obvious opportunities—hence the initiatives in HR, IT, and the U.S. task force—but many others would only be apparent to frontline managers in Sandvik's 200 international affiliates when they focused on identifying and exploiting the possibilities. Second, promised synergies often proved to be less significant than first anticipated, as the CTT-Coromant *relationship* had shown.[7] Finally, the exploitation of synergies was never costless. Lars Pettersson, president of Coromant, pointed out the possibility of conflicting needs between business areas, meaning that the optimum course of action for one business area could negatively impact another. The decision by Saws and Tools to build a new warehouse facility in the Netherlands, rather than build on Coromant's existing facility in Schiedam, was often cited as an example of business area needs taking precedence over group synergies. But Gezelius disagreed: "The fact is that we would have used the Schiedam facility, but the building was too small, there was no room to extend it, and Schiedam itself is extremely congested. In addition, Saws and Tools have very

different warehousing requirements from Coromant—we have pallet goods, they don't; we ship products in one to three days, they air-freight products within 24 hours. Once again, the devil hides in the details."

There were also concerns about the transfer of best practices between business areas. Historically, many innovative practices had come from Coromant. Thus, for the other business areas, adopting Coromant's practices meant "identifying a need and being humble enough to copy." Some business areas, such as Rock Tools, had been very good at this, but others had preferred to develop their own systems.

An underlying reason for most managers' concerns about the changes was the worry that increased synergies between the businesses would lead to a de facto recentralization of power and a corresponding loss of autonomy in the six business areas. The executive group was fully aware of this concern. As explained by Sunnermalm, "We are raising a warning flag as we proceed. Are we making roles unclear? Are we damaging the clear accountability that has served us so well? We need to move forward very carefully." The actions taken by the executive group had been focused on communication and voluntary cooperation. Hedström, Sunnermalm, and Östholm all traveled frequently to Sandvik's operations around the world, explaining the need for greater synergies between business areas and emphasizing that they were not trying to move back to the centralized approach of the early 1980s.

But they recognized that the "preaching stage" may not be sufficient to create and sustain the changes in behavior that were being sought. The goal was to get Sandvik employees acting with regard to their business *and* the group, rather than just their business. The U.S. task force and the HR and IT initiatives represented specific steps toward this goal. But Hedström felt that further changes were needed to expand and sustain the search for and exploitation of synergies within the Sandvik group. He pondered what further actions he should take.

Endnotes

1. The United States (e.g., 3M, AT&T) and the United Kingdom (e.g., ICI, Hanson) were two countries in which demergers and spinoffs were being increasingly employed to drive corporate restructuring and refocusing. However, there were

also signs of such things happening in Sweden, with Trelleborg's demerger of Boliden and Volvo's sale of its food and beverages businesses.

2. Tungsten and other carbides such as titanium were ground into powder and mixed with another metallic powder, usually cobalt. The powder was then pressed into the desired form and exposed to high temperatures. The result was a material which was both hard and durable for use in metal cutting.

3. Using this system, a salesperson entered an order in the company's computer, and it was then directly transmitted to the production floor, bypassing any administrative personnel.

4. Customers could input specifications for a desired product with the help of a Coromant representative. Within ten minutes, the customer would receive by fax a scale drawing of the product, as well as delivery and cost information.

5. Ergonomic tools were designed to reduce the risk of workplace injuries and promote greater productivity.

6. Gunnar Björkland, president of Sandvik Steel, was due to join the executive group in early 1997 when Lars Östholm retired.

7. Coromant and CTT had almost 100 percent overlap in customer groups, but on closer inspection Coromant had about 70 percent direct sales and 30 percent distributors, while CTT had the reverse.

CASE 40

PBS (A): The Joint Venture Decision

This case was prepared by Stanley D. Nollen, Karen L. Newman, and Jacqueline M. Abbey of Georgetown University.

Richard Kuba had brought a decision to his board of directors. A joint venture proposal between První Brněnská Strojírna (PBS), of which he was the general manager, and Asea Brown Boveri (ABB), the Swiss-Swedish engineering company, was on the table. Kuba had worked more than a year on these negotiations. A majority of his board members had been opposed to a joint venture with ABB and had initially rejected it. Now ABB had a new proposal to offer. Kuba and his board would reconsider the joint venture decision in a new board meeting. It was the board's decision to make, and it would not be easy.

As the general director (chief executive officer) of a sizable Czech company struggling to make the transition from central planning to a market economy, Kuba was in uncharted managerial waters. He believed that PBS had to take a decisive step to adapt to the challenge of international competition in the post-Soviet era. He felt responsible for the welfare of his employees and fellow managers, and he had a sense of national duty. PBS, a power plant equipment engineering and manufacturing company, had a continuous history from its founding in 1814 (the company name means "First Brno Machinery") through two world wars and the recently ended communist period. Now PBS once again had to adapt in order to survive.

This case is intended to be used as a basis for class discussion rather than as an illustration of either effective or ineffective handling of the situation. This case was prepared by Stanley D. Nollen, Karen L. Newman, and Jacqueline M. Abbey, Georgetown University. Used by permission.

PBS

The Company's Business

At the time of the Velvet Revolution, PBS's principal business was the manufacture of turbines and boilers, which accounted for a large majority of its revenue. (See the Appendix for a description of the change in government and general business conditions under central planning.) The company also built complete power and heating plants, serviced and reconstructed old plants, and manufactured miscellaneous industrial parts. The company listed its product lines as follows:

- *Turbines.* Steam turbines for industrial heating and power plants, small to mid-size gas turbines, turbochargers, and accessories.

- *Boilers.* Oil-fired, gas-fired, and coal-burning industrial boilers and accessories.

- *Power plants.* Complete power and heating plants made on a turnkey basis; service and reconstruction of existing plants.

- *Other products.* Burners, heaters, railcar shock absorbers, power plant measurement and regulation instruments, gas meters, castings, and forgings.

In 1992, PBS booked orders worth Kč 4,857 million (about $175 million (Table A-1) and earned revenue of Kč 3,472 million (about $125 million). Profit was Kč 365 million ($13 million). The level of employment was just under 8,000 and falling steadily (Table A-2).

The company's headquarters and most of its manufacturing facilities were in Brno, where it had made steam turbines for ninety years and gas tur-

TABLE A-I

PBS Sales Booked by Product Line, 1990–1992
(Kč million current)

Product	1990	1991	1992
Total sales	1,484	3,307	4,857
Turbines	527	1,080	782
Steam turbines	234	270	557
Gas turbines	63	54	27
Turbochargers	230	756	198
Boilers	549	724	1,823
Industrial boilers	415	563	1,099
Piping	134	161	724
Assemblies	85	288	299
Repairs	171	191	162
Central heating equipment	68	111	119
Aircraft equipment	101	14	18
Other (see text)	282	898	1,653

Notes: Freeing of prices in 1991 resulted in price inflation in Czechoslovakia of 58 percent in that year. Gas turbines includes expansion turbines.
Source: První Brněnská Strojíma (PBS), Annual Report, 1992.

TABLE A-2

Selected Financial and Operating Data for PBS, 1990–1992
(Kč million current except where indicated otherwise)

Variable	1990	1991	1992
Total revenue	2,052	3,412	3,472
Production revenue	1,842	3,207	3,255
Profit	224	369	365
Total assets	3,338	5,399	6,187
Fixed assets	2,246	2,688	2,972
Trade receivables	377	1,411	1,635
Trade payables	322	814	857
Bank loans	752	1,107	931
Exports as percent of booked sales—to COMECON	20	19	10
Exports as percent of booked sales—worldwide	24	28	53
Employees (number)	9,564	8,857	7,946
Labor productivity (Kč 000 revenue per employee)	215	385	437
Average monthly wages (Kč)	3,629	4,410	5,299

Notes: Data include the Velká Bítes plant. Figures for revenue in this table do not match sales figures in Table A-1 because the figures in Table 1 represent sales orders booked, not revenue received.
Source: První Brněnská Strojírna (PBS), Annual Report, 1992; and communication with PBS managers.

bines for thirty-five years. Four plants were located in smaller towns in Moravia, dating from post–World War II years. The plant in Trebič made boilers and accessories (burners, heaters), and the plant in Mikulov made blades for turbines. The plant in Velká Bíteš made turbochargers and had received most of the new capital investment that came to PBS from the central planning authorities during the 1980s. This plant's output was exported mostly to the Soviet Union until its breakup in 1991; this business then fell by 80 percent. The plant in Oslavany made a variety of products and parts, such as railcar shock absorbers, nuts, bolts, and screws that were not central to PBS's main turbine and boiler businesses.

By 1992, PBS had begun to concentrate on environmentally friendly power plant and heating plant systems. Much of its recent boiler business was to overhaul and reconstruct existing boilers to meet higher regulatory standards. In precommunist Czechoslovakia, PBS was a leader in the power generation equipment industry, with a reputation for good products and service. The early years of central planning were economically satisfactory as well. However, relative competitive decline set in at PBS after the "normalization" that followed Prague Spring in 1968. Investment in plant and equipment and in new technology was insufficient for more than twenty years. By 1992, PBS product quality was below Western standards, concern for the customer was low, and employee willingness to take initiative was lagging.

Yet PBS was better off than many other Czech companies that also suffered from little investment, aging capital equipment, and outdated products. Unlike most companies during central planning, PBS had its own engineering capabilities in-house, and as a result had developed its own coal-fired boiler and steam turbine technology. In addition, PBS had a long-standing but small turnkey business. It not only made boilers and turbines, but it also did all the work necessary to construct or reconstruct complete electric power generation plants and steam-heating plants. PBS was not just a manufacturing plant.

Distribution

Before 1989, PBS used two state trading companies for export sales: Škoda-export and Technoexport. Exports accounted for about one-quarter of PBS business, about three-quarters of which went to So-

viet bloc countries. Domestic sales of turbines and boilers were uncomplicated, partly because the product was tailor-made; also, there were few potential customers, orders were big, and there were no direct domestic competitors. PBS customers were the contractors that built the power plants or end users (usually companies or city governments) if PBS did the project on a turnkey basis.

Employee Wages and Production Costs

Wage rates at PBS as in all Czech companies were quite low—an average of Kč 5,400 per month in 1992 (about $190). The skill level of the work force was very good. However, productivity was also quite low because, PBS managers asserted, of the lack of investment in recent years. However, PBS did not have a production cost advantage compared with German companies. As Kuba said,

> We figured the German company's hourly rate for value added to engineer and produce turbine blades. We added up their wage rates and rental rates and depreciation rates, but we excluded the price of raw materials and parts they purchased from outside suppliers. Then we did the same calculation for ourselves. We found that our hourly rate was one-third of theirs. But then we looked at how long it took the Germans to make the turbine blades compared to how long it took us. It turned out that the German company used one-third the time that our company used. So our production costs were about the same as theirs.

Managers

The top managers at PBS were mostly technically educated (as expected in Czech industrial companies), and most had been employed at PBS for their entire careers. Kuba, the first post-revolution general manager, fit this pattern.

He had joined PBS in 1965 after graduating from Brno Technical University, where he studied power generation and turbine design. Early in his career, he spent some time in PBS's turnkey business. In 1968, Kuba began to attend economics courses from the Prague School of Economics, but when Prague Spring was crushed and tighter government control reasserted, he dropped his studies.

Kuba's ascent to the upper levels of PBS management was slow because he chose not to join the Communist Party. Despite his refusal to join the party, he was given the opportunity to travel abroad and work with foreign customers in Bulgaria, Romania, Sweden, and Syria. After completing graduate studies in power grid management in 1989, he was promoted to director of the engineering department in the power plant division. His promotion to general manager in 1990 at the age of forty-seven (he was selected by the head of Škoda Konzern) came as a surprise, even to Kuba himself.

Corporate Culture

The PBS corporate culture was influenced strongly by the requirements of central planning. PBS was the monopoly producer of boilers and turbines in its size range (small to medium sizes) in the Czech/Socialist Republic. There was no competition. Producing to meet a plan was the most important criterion of success. Cost control did not matter, and costs and prices were determined by central planners rather than market forces.

The work force was dominated by engineers. Boilers and turbines were over-engineered to stand up under extremely adverse conditions. Building a tough, sturdy, long-lasting product was far more important than building efficiently. PBS collaborated with the local technical university on research and development and took pride in its ability to design sophisticated equipment. More employees than necessary worked for PBS, a function of the government's full-employment policy. The enterprise was driven by production and engineering concerns. Employees were more excited about a well-engineered boiler than financial results.

The Investment and Finance

During the years of central planning, investment decisions from the Czechoslovak government were heavily influenced by the needs of major national or Soviet projects (for example, the development of nuclear energy or the construction of a natural gas pipeline). Profits earned by enterprises were remitted to the state and new investment capital came from the state, but there was no linkage between the two. In the case of PBS, most of the investment that came to it went into the outlying plants, especially the plant at Velká Bíteš which made turbochargers, mainly for the Soviet Union. However, these investments were of little value in 1992 because they were designed for the Soviet market that diminished so rapidly and dramatically.

Conversion of these plants to meet Western needs was difficult and costly because of differences in product specifications.

Interest rates were quite high in Czechoslovakia during this time, even in real terms, and loanable funds were very scarce. Short-term finance was also difficult to obtain, and a liquidity crisis ensued during 1992 and 1993. Since trade credit was scarcely available, many companies responded by simply not paying their bills. In PBS's case, trade receivables at their worst exceeded payables by a factor of two, and were Kč 1,635 million ($57 million) at the end of 1992, just below half of that year's sales revenue (Table A-2).

Privatization

The Czechoslovak government's objective for privatization was to transfer most of the country's large enterprises to widespread private ownership quite quickly. Because local citizens did not have the financial resources to "buy the economy" overnight, much of it was "given away." Under voucher privatization, each adult citizen was entitled to buy a book of vouchers containing 1,000 points for Kč 1,000 (which in early 1992 was an average week's wages). The voucher holder could bid for shares of individual companies or spend voucher points on mutual funds that in turn bought shares of companies. Other methods of privatization included auction (for smaller companies), tender offers (usually with conditions attached about future employment levels), management buyouts, direct sale to a predetermined buyer, transfer at no cost to a municipality, and restitution to the family from which property had been confiscated by the state.

PBS was converted to the legal form of a joint stock company to become PBS a.s. in 1991. All of the shares in the company were owned by the National Property Fund (NPF), which was the Czech government agency established to hold shares of enterprises until they could be sold to private buyers. The company, which had the usual functional structure of large enterprises in centrally planned economies (Figure A-1), reorganized into a divisional structure of product-centered businesses (Figure A-2). The Ministry of Industry put PBS a.s. into the first wave of voucher privatization in 1992. Thirty-six percent of PBS a.s. shares were purchased by individuals and investment funds; 60 percent remained with the NPF; and 4 percent were set aside for restitution, which was the standard practice. The

FIGURE A-1

PBS Organization Chart (partial) in 1989

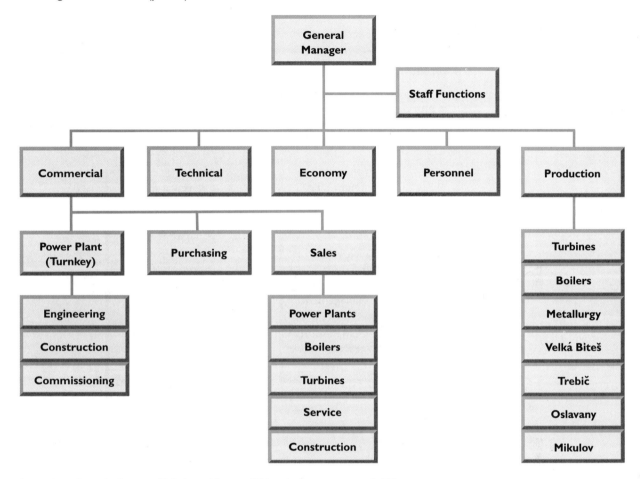

Source: První Brněnská Strojírna (PBS), Annual Report, 1991; and communication with PBS managers.

fact that the NPF held the majority of PBS shares meant that privatization was not complete and that further ownership changes would occur.

The Search for a New Business Strategy

To successfully make the transition from central planning and become competitive in world markets, PBS managers proposed two different types of strategies. PBS had been an industry leader before the central planning era. Some managers believed it could regain this position through increased efficiency and product innovation. These people, who included most of the deputy

general directors and department heads, placed their hopes for PBS in an ambitious new business strategy that called for maintaining independence and becoming more competitive by increasing quality standards, cutting production costs, producing products to meet international environmental standards, improving the fuel efficiency of products, and creating a climate for change within the company.

Financing this strategy, however, was a problem. There was very little capital available from Czech banks in the form of multiyear loans at reasonable interest rates, and PBS had not met with success in finding affordable financing from Western banks.

FIGURE A-2

PBS Organization
Chart in 1992

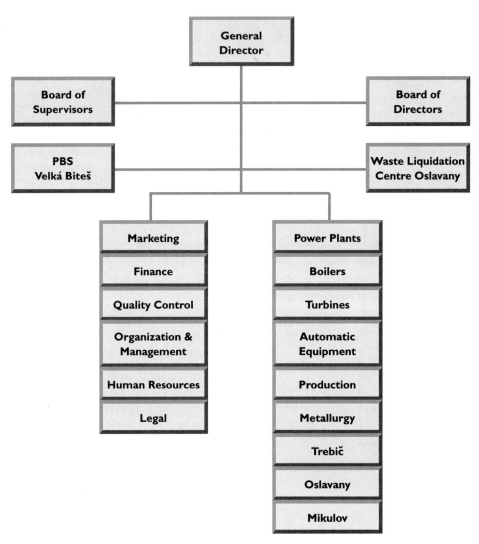

Source: První Brněnská Strojírna (PBS), Annual Report, 1992.

Other managers believed the choice was to decide which among several alternative relationships with other companies was best. They thought a go-it-alone approach could not succeed. The range of possibilities included some type of technology licensing or manufacturing link with a foreign company, some type of marketing agreement, a strategic alliance of some sort that would have technology transfer gains for PBS, the establishment of a joint venture with a foreign or domestic company, or purchase by a foreign or domestic company. When several Western companies—including General Electric, GEC-Alsthom, Deutsche Babcock, Siemens, and ABB—discussed business relationships with PBS beginning in 1991, PBS management listened, but only reluctantly.

THE JOINT VENTURE NEGOTIATIONS

Points of View and Kuba's Role

When foreign companies initially discussed partnership proposals with PBS, managers were ambivalent. They knew they needed capital to modernize, to gain access to Western technology, and to get assistance in developing export markets. But they also had a strong wish to remain independent and not lose their brand name. PBS was, according to the Czechoslovak Ministry of Privatization, the "family silver." Most managers were unwilling to consider breaking up the company or entering into a relationship that rendered PBS "just an equipment manufacturer." Many of the initial partnership proposals from Western companies would have led to one or both of these unattractive outcomes. Some PBS managers declared that the company had operated successfully for nearly two centuries and could survive without any Western equity partners. The trend toward environmentally clean power plants and heating plants by itself would bring substantial new business to PBS's repair and reconstruction unit. The PBS order book was full in 1991. Maybe no foreign partner was needed.

Kuba, however, thought differently. He knew that PBS did not have the latest technology. He discovered that Western companies could deliver a product in 25 percent less time than PBS could. While Kuba thought that PBS could upgrade its technology by itself, it would take more than five years because the investment capital was not available. With a foreign partner, it would go faster. In addition, turnover among young engineers at PBS was making internal technology development harder.

Kuba also believed PBS did not have the market economy experience to implement the company's strategy for improving its international competitiveness. In 1991 and 1992, he visited several PBS customers in foreign countries such as Pakistan and Iran.

They knew about Škoda Plzen and Škodaexport, but not about us. Škoda Plzen had ten businesses. If one of their businesses fails, they have nine others. We had one, and we had no name. ... There are four big international companies— General Electric, Siemens, ABB, and Mitsubishi— that control a big majority of the world market. There are tens of smaller companies like us, and some will not survive.

As Kuba saw it, these two facts—that PBS was not diversified and that world markets did not know his product—were as important as the need for technology updates.

The Czechoslovak economy, with economic reforms initiated in January 1990, was still getting worse. Industrial production had fallen about 40 percent since the Velvet Revolution, and GDP was off 26 percent (Table A-3). An upturn in business conditions was not predicted until 1994.

Kuba came to believe that it would be necessary to bring in a foreign investor, for both technological and market reasons.

I was not enthusiastic about bringing in a foreign investor, but I knew that we had to do it if we wanted to keep the company whole and not split it up. To keep the company together was more important than keeping it independent.

TABLE A-3

Economic Conditions in Czechoslovakia, 1989–1992

Variable	1989	1990	1991	1992
Gross domestic product, real % change[a]	0.7	−3.5	−15.0	− 7.1
Industrial production, real % change	0.9	−3.7	−23.1	−12.4
Consumer price inflation, %	1.4	10.0	57.8	11.5
Interest rate %[b]	5.5	6.2	15.4	13.9
Exchange rate, Kč/$, annual average	15.1	18.0	29.5	28.3
Unemployment rate, %	na	0.3	6.8	7.7

[a]Net material product.
[b]Lending rate to state enterprises.
Sources: Economist Intelligence Unit, *Country Report: Czech Republic and Slovakia,* 2nd quarter 1993. 2nd quarter 1990. London, 1993, 1990. International Monetary Fund, *International Financial Statistics,* March 1994. Washington, D.C., 1996, 1994.

Although the company could survive for several more years on the strength of its existing assets, order book, work force, and customer base, he thought that only a strong Western partner could ensure that PBS would flourish and remain the pride of Czechoslovakia.

As was common practice in the centrally planned Czechoslovakian economy, the general director of PBS decided most issues of company policy himself within the framework of the five-year plan. In 1992, Kuba was, in theory, accountable to a board of directors elected by the shareholders of PBS and to the state. In practice, however, these bodies had little experience with corporate governance. Committing the assets of PBS to a venture with a Western company that meant a foreign ownership stake was a controversial decision with major ramifications. Kuba expected to be criticized no matter which course the company chose. Therefore, he would not make this decision alone.

The International Finance Corporation

At the recommendation of the Ministry of Industry, which was keenly interested in the fate of PBS, Kuba met with advisers from the International Finance Corporation (IFC), the consulting arm of the World Bank. The first meeting occurred in March 1992. Kuba was impressed with the work the IFC advisers had done earlier in the Czech Republic, particularly in facilitating the conclusion of Škoda Plzen's joint venture negotiations. Kuba hired the IFC to structure a tender process and oversee negotiations for a joint venture.

The IFC advisers made two important recommendations to Kuba. First, PBS should secure government approval to enter into a joint venture with a Western partner in advance of negotiations. This would ensure that PBS, not the state, would be the ultimate decision maker. PBS acted on this recommendation immediately.

Second, the IFC advised that PBS should separate its turbine, boiler, and turnkey businesses from its other activities. Only by packaging the core businesses together, without adding in peripheral businesses and unrelated assets of dubious value, would PBS attract a Western partner. The advisers explained that they were trying to create an auctionlike situation, and in order to do that they had to package the most valuable parts of the company separately from the rest. Though most managers and board members were very skeptical, Kuba convinced them to allow the IFC advisers to restructure the company on paper in order to find the best potential partners.

Kuba remained noncommittal throughout the discussions, supporting the IFC advisers and facilitating negotiations but always in the name of "exploring options." He communicated that he was willing to take a risk to improve the company's prospects, but he did not challenge the sometimes passionate objections of his fellow managers to the need for a foreign investor in the company.

As the discussions continued, General Electric proposed to license technology to PBS, but General Electric would have imposed conditions that were unattractive and would not have invested any equity. The other potential partners fell into secondary positions. Siemens, GEC Alsthom, and Deutsche Babcock did not put forward sufficiently comprehensive proposals, or they did not offer enough technology transfer. The remaining contender was ABB.

ABB

ABB, formed by the merger in 1988 of Asea of Sweden and Brown Boveri of Switzerland, was one of the world's major engineering and industrial equipment companies. It had revenue of $29.6 billion in 1992 and net income of $505 million, which gave it a return on equity of 11.8 percent (from ABB web site http://www.abb.ch/abbgroup/investor). The company, with 213,000 employees, came out on top of both the 1994 and 1995 Financial Times–Price Waterhouse polls of European executives as the most respected company in the world (*Financial Times,* September 19, 1995).

The ABB corporate culture was more market- and efficiency-oriented than PBS's. Operating throughout the world in competitive markets, ABB's emphasis was on high quality at the right price. The customer dictated technical specifications as much as design engineers in ABB. ABB was accustomed to competing against other industry giants on big contracts. The firm was lean, renowned for having one of the smallest corporate staffs of any firm its size. Subsidiaries generally were given semiexclusive rights to a geographic area, but if the subsidiary failed to win bids or failed to make a profit, its geographic area might be changed or it might be sold.

ABB had five main businesses: industrial and building systems, power generation, power transmission and distribution, transportation, and financial services. The power generation business, into which PBS's business would fall, was the second largest of ABB's businesses, accounting for one-quarter of all ABB revenue. This business had experienced rapid growth; it had nearly tripled its revenue since 1988, despite declining prices. ABB's main competitors in its main businesses were Siemens of Germany, GEC Alsthom of Britain and France, Mitsubishi of Japan, and General Electric of the United States.

ABB was an example of a truly global corporation. The company had product-oriented business units with worldwide responsibilities ranging from design through manufacturing to marketing and customer service. ABB had a very small headquarters group in Zurich and dozens of wholly owned or majority-owned companies on six continents.

ABB was no stranger to negotiating foreign joint ventures. Its approach to negotiations—which emphasized relationship building, patient persistence, and resolving issues one at a time—had been honed through experience. In the power generation business, its corporate strategy was to locate the complete range of boiler production, turbine production, and power plant design activities into each of several ABB companies around the world rather than to separate boilers from turbines and put them in different companies. This approach allowed ABB to reduce the high costs of engineering labor and to compete in the high-value-added turnkey plant market.

Drawn by the country's skilled work force, low relative labor costs, proximity to western Europe, and successful conservative government, the company began investing in the Czech Republic in 1991. PBS would be the fourth and largest of seven Czech companies in the ABB network; other acquisitions had already been made in Poland, Hungary, and Romania.

In particular, ABB identified four main attractions of a joint venture with PBS:

1. ABB expected the market for power plants in the Czech Republic and in other central and east European countries to develop over time and become large, stimulated by the effort to clean up old plants; ABB wanted to be a "local" company inside this market.
2. ABB needed to develop a low-cost export platform—to export components to other ABB companies and to export complete products to other countries. Low-cost east European components could be combined with high-cost German or Swedish components to make an attractive total product package.
3. PBS had boilers and turbines in one company (one location), while ABB did not have boiler capacity in Europe. (It is easier to build a power plant if boiler and turbine production are located together because they frequently communicate with each other.)
4. PBS had considerable installed capacity to service; this would provide good short-run business even though the Czech Republic was not a major growth market in the power plant business at present.

ABB gave no thought to a licensing arrangement. According to an ABB negotiator,

> It is not the ABB way. We wanted equity. Anyway, in this case, we wanted just about the whole company, and that is not as easy to license as, say, the production of gas turbines like General Electric does. . . . We wanted to develop the power generation business in east and central Europe, and that required the hands-on management that only a controlling interest in a joint venture allowed.

The ABB team made it clear that it sought to buy into both the turbine and boiler businesses and to expand the turnkey operations. The other bidders were interested in smaller segments of the business. The ABB team's desire to incorporate both the turbine and boiler business made it more attractive to PBS management. ABB presented opportunities for technology transfers, training, market access, and investment capital that could build up PBS instead of simply absorbing it.

ABB sent representatives from its Power Ventures unit to negotiate the deal. Their task was to establish the joint venture and to manage its startup. The representatives had contact with PBS management and employees at different levels. Meetings with ABB's top corporate executives, including a lunch in Zurich with Percy Barnevik, the chief executive officer, were arranged for Kuba. ABB also engaged the head of its Prague office to emphasize to PBS management the advantages that ABB offered as a joint venture partner and ABB's vision for creating with PBS an efficient engineering firm capable of serving the turbine, boiler, and turnkey markets using advanced technologies and creative engineering solutions. ABB recognized PBS's capabilities in coal-fired power plants and intended to keep the joint venture a full-fledged company, not just a manufacturing plant. ABB also included environmental indemnifications in its offer. Substantial sums were invested in developing and presenting the pitch.

Among all potential western partners, only ABB was seemingly unfazed by PBS's lack of unified commitment to the concept of a joint venture. ABB sought to identify specific concerns of PBS management and responded with detailed presentations.

THE DECISION

After several months of negotiations, PBS managers had all the information needed to make a decision and several proposals before them to consider, the most attractive of which was from ABB. The meeting of the PBS board to decide on the proposals was held in late December 1992; it lasted twelve hours and became contentious. Everyone realized the gravity of the situation.

The board members returned to the issue of whether PBS should enter into a joint venture with a large western partner. Strong concerns were voiced; many of the managers had worked for PBS for decades and feared that PBS was inviting ruin by surrendering its independence. They feared the intrusion of western management. They saw the joint venture proposals as giving up, and they weren't ready to do that. Finally, after several hours, one member stood up and said "I'm going to say what I think everyone else is afraid to say—we don't like it. We don't want a deal." The board took a poll and decided that PBS should reject all joint venture proposals.

After the poll, the IFC advisers addressed the board for a further six hours, emphasizing that PBS's negotiating position was not likely to improve with time. Its market position would decline in the absence of needed investment and technology improvement. Further, if they simply broke off negotiations with the companies courting them now, they should expect that any future discussions on cooperation would meet with a much less favorable response. In short, PBS's negotiating leverage would steadily decrease over time and eventually, given its economic prospects, the company

would be forced to accept a much less desirable arrangement than was currently available. The time to form a joint venture was now or never; the company needed to decide now whether it would pursue its business objectives without a foreign partner or tell the existing bidders why their proposals were not satisfactory and invite revised bids. After further deliberation, the board resolved to solicit improved bids.

ABB responded quickly with a multifaceted approach, directing its attention not only to the board members but also to managers at lower levels and employees whose voices they knew could flow upward to persuade board members to change their minds in favor of a deal. Several ABB executives and engineers arrived in Brno the weekend following the marathon board meeting to address the issues that PBS had identified as most troublesome. They arranged to meet with employees at several different levels in order to hear and address the most common concerns. They believed it was important to provide a formal avenue for these employees to express their fears and reservations.

The ABB team presented a new proposal within a few days. A new board meeting was scheduled in which a decision would be made.

APPENDIX: BUSINESS UNDER CENTRAL PLANNING AND THE VELVET REVOLUTION

The Czechoslovak economy was nearly totally state-owned and mostly closed to trade and investment with the West from 1946 until the end of 1989. Most industries had only a few large enterprises, and in many instances they were monopoly producers of individual products. This meant that enterprises were typically very big (relative to the size of the market) and specialized in the production of just one product or a narrow product line. Enterprises in an industry were typically combined under a single "koncern." PBS was part of the Škoda Koncern group of companies, which consisted of Škoda Plzen (a heavy machinery maker with 30,000 employees), PBS (10,000 employees), CKD (a maker of railroad cars with 4,000 employees), SES (a Slovak company with 8,000 employees), and several smaller companies. Škoda Koncern was organized differently from most other Czech industrial groups insofar as it did not separate research and engineering into an enterprise apart from manufacturing units. Each company was a stand-alone enterprise.

The needs of the Soviet Union shaped the production program of many enterprises. Producers in centrally planned economies typically were only manufacturing plants (an enterprise was termed a "statni podnik" or state plant). They were producers, but they did not do other business functions, such as marketing and finance. Distribution and sales were handled by separate state-owned trading companies, research and development was either centralized or assigned to a separate enterprise, and capital investment decisions were made by the state. Banks disbursed funds and collected "profits" but did not make lending decisions. There were no capital markets.

The goal of the firm that all managers understood was to meet the production plan set by the central ministry. Successful managers were those who could skillfully negotiate a favorable plan and who knew how to produce the required quantity. Another goal imposed on firms by the state was to provide employment for everyone. There was little concern about costs, prices, money, or profits. Most managers were technically trained, and all top managers were necessarily members of the Communist Party; selection depended on political as well as business considerations.

Enterprises were centralized and hierarchical and typically had a functional organizational structure in which the production function was the biggest and most important. Other functions usually included a technical function, a commercial function (this was mainly order-filling and shipping), an economy function (mainly financial recordkeeping), a personnel function, and others depending on the company's type of business. Large enterprises during the socialist era typically provided a wide range of housing, recreation, education, and medical services to their employees.

The Velvet Revolution occurred in late November 1989 in Czechoslovakia, a few months after the fall of the Berlin Wall. The name, Velvet Revolution, comes from the fact that the existing Communist government resigned without bloodshed, after massive peaceful demonstrations in Prague, giving way to a democracy almost overnight. The first post-Communist government was led by Václav Havel, a playwright who had been imprisoned under the former regime for his political views. Havel, though inexperienced in government, was a strong symbol of the moral underpinnings of the Velvet Revolution and the future for Czechoslovakia. One of the first orders of business was rapid transformation of the economy (one of the ten largest in the world between World Wars I and II) from the most thoroughly state-owned of all Soviet bloc economies to a market economy based on private ownership of property. Many of the people who rose to power in companies had been active in the "Prague Spring" of 1968, a period of liberalization. The reforms were put down by an invasion of troops and tanks from Russia and other Soviet client states in August 1968. Many business leaders who sympathized with Prague Spring reforms were demoted.

PBS (B): The ABB PBS Joint Venture in Operation

The PBS board meeting to make the decision whether to accept the ABB proposal for a joint venture lasted eighteen hours. In the end, the PBS board voted in favor and the joint venture was agreed to. Several legal and contractual issues were quickly resolved, and the deal was signed in late December 1992.

STRUCTURE AND ORGANIZATION

ABB První Brněnská Strojírna Brno, Ltd. (ABB PBS) was a joint venture in which ABB had a 67 percent stake and PBS a.s. had a 33 percent stake. The PBS share was determined nominally by the value of the land, plant and equipment, employees, and goodwill. ABB contributed cash and specified technologies and assumed some of the debt of PBS. The new company started operations on April 15, 1993.

The ABB PBS company was a joint venture in its formal structure and governance. PBS a.s. had seats on the board, had part ownership, and was a supplier to the joint venture. The core operations of PBS a.s. were its Brno-based power generation business, its experience with turnkey operations, and its engineering and manufacturing capabilities with its customer base of installed equipment. The joint venture included the turnkey power plant business, boilers, and turbines (but not turbochargers). All of the PBS facilities in Brno and the outlying plant in Mikulov that made turbine blades went into the joint venture (refer to Table A-2). In sum, about 4,000 employees from PBS a.s. went to the joint venture; about 3,400 remained in PBS a.s. About 80 percent of the revenue of PBS a.s. became part of the joint venture.

Profit was to be divided in 2/3 to 1/3 shares according to ownership when it was earned and distributed; initial plans called for reinvestment of all profits and no dividends paid out to corporate parents.

ABB PBS was organized by product lines: power plants, turbines, boilers, and external services (the latter was added in 1995). Centralized functions such as marketing, finance, human resources, quality control, and information systems reported vertically to the general director and were matrixed horizontally with the business units or product divisions. The internal service division (maintenance) served the four product divisions. Each product division also had some of the same functions (Figure B-1).

ABB PBS was assigned geographic regions as its market territories by the ABB power generation segment and used the ABB selling network in these territories. Other ABB companies in the same lines of business had other territories, so head-to-head competition among ABB sister companies for the same customers was minimized.

The ABB regional selling network assisted ABB PBS in identifying business opportunities. ABB PBS was the prime contractor for the projects obtained. For turbines and boilers that were not part of a turnkey project, or in cases in which another ABB company was the primary contractor, ABB PBS participated as a subcontractor. ABB PBS had its own vice president for export sales and an export sales force for direct selling, as well as selling in cooperation with the ABB regional network.

In the domestic market, ABB PBS continued to use its own sales force and customer contacts. There were two domestic competitors, Škoda Turbiny (a company in the Škoda Koncern) and Vitkovice, whose principal business was steel.

FIGURE B-I

ABB PBS Organizational Chart in 1995

```
                              Managing
                              Director
   ┌──────────┬──────────┬──────────┼──────────┬──────────┬──────────┐
 Power      Turbines   Boilers   External   Internal   Controlling  ABB PBS
 Plants                          Service    Service                 (Slovakia)
```

Power Plants: Turnkey delivery of industrial steam and thermal power plants; flue glass cleaning ash handling systems; district heating applications; design, engineering, and feasibility studies.

Turbines: Steam turbines for power generation and mechanical drives; low-power gas turbines and co-generation units; gas flow meters; steam and gas turbine halls.

Boilers: Heat recovery steam generators; fluidized bed boilers; coal, gas, and oil fired boilers; preheaters; heat exchangers; heaters and condensers, boiler houses, and heat exchanger stations.

External Service: Repairs, overhauls, and modernization of power generation equipment and plants; retrofit and upgrading; spare parts; technical assistance, measurement, testing, and diagnostics.

Internal Service: Maintenance of company facilities

Controlling:
- Quality Assurance
- Finance & Accounting
- Human Resources
- Information Systems
- Sales Management
- Supply Management
- Marketing
- Law Services

Source: ABB PBS, Annual Report, 1995.

BUSINESS RESULTS

Financial Performance

Business for the joint venture in its first two full years was good in most aspects. Orders received in 1994, the first full year of the joint venture's operation, were the highest in the history of PBS. Orders received in 1995 increased 7 percent over 1994 in nominal terms. Revenues for 1995 were two and a half times those in 1994 (Table B-1). The company was profitable in 1995 and ahead of 1994 results with a rate of return on assets of 2.3 percent and a rate of return on sales of 4.5 percent (Table B-2).

The 1995 results showed substantial progress toward meeting the joint venture's strategic goals adopted in 1994 as part of a five-year plan. One of the goals was that exports should account for half of total orders by 1999. (Exports had accounted for more than a quarter of the PBS business before 1989, but most of this business disappeared when the Soviet Union collapsed.) In 1995, exports in-creased as a share of total orders to 28 percent, up from 16 percent the year before.

The external service business, organized and functioning as a separate business for the first time in 1995, did not meet expectations. It accounted for 5 percent of all orders and revenues in 1995, below the 10 percent goal set for it. The retrofitting business, which was expected to be a major part of the service business, was disappointing for ABB PBS, partly because many other small companies began to provide this service in 1994 (including some started by former PBS employees who took their knowledge of PBS-built power plants with them). However, ABB PBS managers hoped that as the company introduced new technologies, these former employees would gradually lose the ability to perform these services and that the retrofit and repair service business would return to ABB PBS.

ABB PBS dominated the Czech boiler business with 70 percent of the Czech market in 1995, but managers expected this share to go down in the fu-ture as new domestic and foreign competitors ap-

TABLE B-1

Orders and Revenues for ABB PBS Businesses in 1994 and 1995

Business	1994		1995	
	Kč million	% of total	Kč million	% of total
Power plants				
Revenue	490	23	3,062	52
Orders	3,230	49	3,687	47
Turbines				
Revenue	707	34	1,118	19
Orders	938	14	1,389	18
Boilers				
Revenue	900	43	1,353	23
Orders	2,439	37	2,452	31
Services				
Revenue	(not reported separately		314	5
Orders	in 1994)		381	5
Total	2,097	100	5,847	100
	6,607	100	7,909	100

Notes: Kč are in nominal terms. The sum of revenues and orders across businesses in this table exceeds the total revenue and orders figures re-ported in the income statement data in Table B-2; the percent distributions in this table are figured on the sum of revenues and orders in this table.
Source: ABB První Brněnská Strojírna s.r.o., 1995 Business Report and 1994 Business Report.

TABLE B-2

Selected Income Statement, Balance Sheet, and Other Operating Data for ABB PBS, 1994 and 1995
(Kč million current)

Variable	1994	1995
Revenue	1,999	5,015
Orders received	6,208	7,088
R & D expenditure	29	64
Investment	435	388
Total assets	5,115	9,524
Fixed assets	1,773	2,186
Trade receivables	451	509
Trade payables	197	817
Bank loans	690	710
Equity	1,130	1,110
Exports (percent of orders)	16%	28%
Employees (number)	3,600	3,235
Labor productivity (value added/salaries)*	Kč109/Kč	Kč 163/Kč

*Value added is revenue minus purchased inputs. The labor productivity figures are not meaningful as absolute numbers but rather are used for overtime comparisons.
Sources: ABB První Brněnská Strojírna s.r.o., 1995 Business Report and 1994 Business Report.

peared. Furthermore, the west European boiler market was actually declining because environmental laws caused a surge of retrofitting to occur in the mid 1980s, leaving less business in the 1990s. Accordingly, ABB PBS boiler orders were flat in 1995.

Top managers at ABB PBS regarded business results to date as respectable, but they were not satisfied with the company's performance. Cash flow was not as good as expected. Cost reduction had to go further. "The more we succeed, the more we see our shortcomings," said one official.

Restructuring

The first round of restructuring was largely completed in 1995, the last year of the three-year restructuring plan. Plant logistics, information systems, and other physical capital improvements were in place. The restructuring included the following:

■ Renovating and reconstructing workshops and engineering facilities

■ Achieving ISO 9001 for all four ABB PBS divisions (awarded in 1995)

■ Transfer of technology from ABB (this was an ongoing project)

■ Installation of an information system

■ Management training, especially in total quality assurance and the English language

■ Implementing a project management approach

A notable achievement of importance to top management in 1995 was a 50 percent increase in labor productivity, measured as value added per payroll crown. However, in the future, ABB PBS expected its wage rates to go up faster than west European wage rates (Czech wages were increasing about 15 percent per year), so it would be difficult to maintain the ABB PBS unit cost advantage over west European unit cost.

The Technology Role for ABB PBS

The joint venture was expected from the beginning to play an important role in technology development for part of ABB's power generation business worldwide. PBS a.s. had engineering capability in coal-fired steam boilers, and that capability was expected to be especially useful to ABB as more countries became concerned about air quality. (When asked if PBS really did have leading technology here, a boiler engineering manager remarked, "Of course we do. We burn so much dirty goal in this country, we have to have better technology.")

However, the envisioned technology leadership role for ABB PBS had not been realized by mid 1996. Kuba, the ABB PBS managing director, realized the slowness with which the technology role was being fulfilled, and he offered his interpretation of events:

> ABB did not promise to make the joint venture its steam boiler technology leader. The main point we wanted to achieve in the joint venture agreement was for ABB PBS to be recognized as a full-fledged company, not just a factory.... We were slowed down on our technology plans because we had a problem keeping our good, young engineers. The annual employee turnover rate for companies in the Czech Republic is 15 or 20 percent, and the unemployment rate is zero. Our engineers have many other good entrepreneurial opportunities. Now we've begun to stabilize our engineering workforce. The restructuring helped. We have better equipment and a cleaner and safer work environment.... We also had another problem, which is a good problem to have. The domestic power plant business turned out to be better than we expected, so just meeting the needs of our regular customers forced some postponement of new technology initiatives.

ABB PBS had benefited technologically from its relationship with ABB. One example was the development of a new steam turbine line. This project was a cooperative effort among ABB PBS and two other ABB companies, one in Sweden and one in Germany. Nevertheless, technology transfer was not the most important early benefit of the ABB relationship. Rather, one of the most important gains was the opportunity to benchmark the joint venture's performance against other established western ABB companies on variables such as productivity, inventory, and receivables.

MANAGEMENT ISSUES

The toughest problems that ABB PBS faced in the early years of the joint venture were management issues. There were two: How to relate to ABB sister companies in other countries and how to transform the human capital of the company.

Relationships with Other ABB Companies

Managing a joint venture company was always difficult, and joining a global corporation compounded the start-up challenges. The Czech managers at ABB PBS had to learn fast. One set of problems arose from the relationship of ABB PBS to its ABB sister companies. Kuba and his colleagues were accustomed to working together with other companies on big projects; before the Velvet Revolution, PBS worked with other companies in the Škoda group. But ABB was different. Cooperation coexisted with competition, and that was outside Kuba's experience. Sibling rivalry among companies was very much a fact of business life, he discovered. After relating an unhappy episode about his company's unfamiliarity with these business relationships, he commented:

> We underestimated the cultural differences between Czechs and other west European people. We have to learn how to say "no." We have to be better in claim management. We have to fight more in order to succeed in this environment.

This fact of corporate life was confirmed by Erik Fougner, the ABB country manager in the Czech Republic, who also noted that excess capacity in Europe caused the older ABB companies to be particularly anxious about the arrival of the Czech newcomer. Some were concerned that there would not be room for three ABB power generation industry companies in Europe in the future.

Human Capital Transformation

The physical and organizational restructuring of ABB PBS was nearly completed by 1996. The transformation of the thinking and behavior of employees had just begun. The ways that were adaptive, or at least tolerated, under central planning would not succeed in a competitive market economy. Changing employees' "mentality"—the term used by Czech managers—was human capital restructuring. It was proving very difficult to do, and it was going very slowly.

In several respects, ABB PBS was nicely positioned to accomplish human capital restructuring. The top management of the joint venture was stable; it was thoroughly Czech but with a keen awareness of the mentality issues; and the ABB parent company tried to offer assistance in a variety of ways. Czech management was supported by two or three expatriates taking nonexecutive positions in project management, supply management, and workshop planning.

The ABB PBS managers believed a background of knowledge of local history, culture, and business practices was essential. These Czech managers, as in most Czech companies, knew they had to change the attitudes and behaviors of their employees. Kuba said,

> It is easy to change the structure of the company, and it is easy to change the facilities, but it is not easy to change people's minds. . . . Employees don't yet understand the consequences of their actions. They don't take responsibility. There is low unemployment so they can leave and get a less stressful job instead of taking responsibility here.

ABB PBS had never laid off any employees for lack of work. Managers appreciated the good reputation this brought the company, but they also wondered if it dampened employees' motivation to work hard. Without the threat of layoff, would managers' human resource initiatives be followed?

Fougner, a Norwegian located in Prague since 1992, saw the same "mentality" problem:

> This is a bigger challenge than I thought it would be. The first level of change in Czech companies comes easily. To make nice new offices and new factory layouts is quite simple. But the transfer of real human resource learning is slow. . . . Responsibility and initiative are poor because it was not rewarded for two generations in these formerly centrally planned economies. Under central planning, you were given a task, you did it, and nothing bad would happen to you. The tasks themselves were compartmentalized—I did mine and you did yours. I did my duty so I'm okay. Even managers did not see the whole picture and could not take responsibility for it. The functional organization of companies [with the archetypal "functional chimneys"] made it worse.

What could be done? The company took three approaches. At the corporate level, ABB PBS tried to instill a sense of mission. The annual report for 1995 noted the efforts of top management to find agreement on corporate goals and values in order to strengthen employee identification with the company.

ABB, the parent company, tried to assist, but did not want to send too many expatriates to ABB PBS. Rather, local managers had to bring about the mentality changes themselves. ABB loaned some of the people from its internal consulting unit to the joint venture on a part-time basis. Their job was to train the (local) trainers and to sit beside the production and engineering managers and supervisors and work through attitude change material with them. Line managers were the ones who would implement the human capital restructuring, not personnel managers.

The compensation system was the third line of attack. Before the Velvet Revolution, factory-worker pay at PBS was based on a piece rate system that was surprisingly common in the Czech Republic. However, it was badly manipulated so that it did not motivate workers to raise output. Real or imagined equipment problems or shortages of parts—both of which occurred frequently—would excuse workers from meeting desired rates of output, or workers would stockpile output and then slack off. The system fostered the attitude among some workers that "you get a wage to show up, and anything extra you do gets you extra pay." This attitude reflected working conditions under communism, where wages were an entitlement rather than a payment for labor services rendered.

ABB PBS introduced a new incentive pay scheme, which was not without its problems. Employees were accustomed to stability and predictability in earnings. Another problem was that the time horizon for the incentive pay was too long—year-long profit-sharing schemes were too distant for production workers because they could not see the link between their performance and their reward that far ahead. The scheme was modified in 1996 to reintroduce some smaller discretionary bonuses, which were granted when the bonus-worthy work took place.

THE FUTURE

The ABB PBS joint venture was only three years old in the spring of 1996. By that time, the legal privatization of industry in the Czech Republic was essentially completed. The first five years of the transition from central planning to market economy for Czech companies was over. This meant

TABLE B-3

Economic Conditions in the Czech Republic, 1993–1995

Variable	1993	1994	1995
Gross domestic product, real % change	−0.9	2.6	4.6
Industrial production, real % change	−5.3	2.3	9.0
Consumer price inflation, %	20.8	10.0	8.9
Interest rate, %	14.1	13.1	12.8
Exchange rate, Kč/$, annual average	29.3	28.8	26.3
Unemployment rate, %	3.5	3.2	3.0

Sources: Economist Intelligence Unit, *Country Report: Czech Republic and Slovakia,* 1st quarter 1996; 2nd quarter 1994. International Monetary Fund, *International Financial Statistics,* March 1996, January 1994. Washington, D.C., 1996, 1994.

that some of the most extreme external stresses on companies, such as loss of markets and lack of finance, were behind them. The Czech economy appeared to be strong and growing (Table B-3).

By 1996, most of the major restructuring of ABB PBS was completed. Most of the easier internal changes had been made. Plant and equipment had been improved, and product quality was in good shape. Kuba and his colleagues had accomplished a lot, but they were not satisfied. Some of the hard changes were yet to be made, and the outlook for the company was mixed.

Doing business in competitive western markets was much more rugged than Kuba expected. Financial results were sufficient, given the difficult busi-

ness conditions the company faced, but they were not good enough for a mature market economy. Kuba knew there was overcapacity in the industry worldwide. There were tons of relatively small companies like his, and some of them would not survive. Belonging to the ABB network had advantages of course, but it also brought problems. Cooperation with ABB sister companies in marketing and technology was mirrored by competition and sibling rivalry with companies from cultures with which Kuba and his colleagues were unfamiliar. Internally, the transformation of ABB PBS's considerable human capital required renewed focus. Kuba could not rest easily yet.

CASE 41

The Boeing Company: The Merger with McDonnell Douglas

This case was prepared by Isaac Cohen of San Jose State University.

On December 10, 1996, Boeing CEO Philip Condit and McDonnell Douglas CEO Harry Stonecipher met in a hotel suite in Seattle to negotiate what *Fortune* magazine called "the sale of the century." Approved by both boards four days later, the merger of Boeing and McDonnell Douglas ended the longest-running rivalry in the aerospace industry. Boeing offered the McDonnell Douglas shareholders a stock swap that amounted to a premium of 21 percent over the price of McDonnell stock on the New York Stock Exchange—the equivalent of $14 billion in company stock. McDonnell Douglas's shareholders readily accepted the offer.[1]

To Stonecipher, the merger with Boeing represented an opportunity. With only one-third of its revenues and almost no earnings derived from its commercial products, McDonnell Douglas's commercial aircraft business was fast declining. The rapid consolidation of the defense business in the hands of a few large corporations (Lockheed Martin, Raytheon, Northrop Grumman, Boeing), coupled with the steady shrinkage of the defense budget, seriously threatened McDonnell Douglas's defense business. To survive, McDonnell Douglas had to merge with other defense firms. Stonecipher, therefore, was faced with a difficult decision: should McDonnell Douglas buy other defense businesses and pay a premium to the seller, or should it merge with the leading commercial aircraft maker and one of the largest defense companies, and be paid a premium by the buyer? Clearly, the high premium offered by Boeing tipped the balance in favor of a Boeing–McDonnell Douglas merger. Following the deal, Stonecipher became Boeing president.[2]

To Condit, the takeover of McDonnell Douglas also represented an opportunity. Because the commercial aircraft industry was subject to deep cyclical movement of booms and busts, and because the demand for defense products was relatively stable, Boeing could have benefited from the acquisition of a major military aircraft maker. Recalling two major slumps in Boeing's history, Condit explained: "We found ourselves moving in a direction ... of 80 percent commercial 20 percent defense and space, and at 20 percent, defense doesn't provide much pad for the next downturn on the commercial side."[3]

Condit acquired McDonnell Douglas just four months after he made a successful bid to purchase Rockwell's military and space division for $3.2 billion. He made both acquisitions during his first year at Boeing's helm, departing from Boeing's longstanding tradition of relying on in-house expansion rather than outright acquisition.[4] Condit continued serving as Boeing CEO following the takeover of McDonnell Douglas.

Although top management at Boeing and McDonnell Douglas had been discussing the possibilities of a merger for nearly three years, Condit's decision represented a strategic gamble. Would the Boeing Aircraft Company gain or lose from the merger with McDonnell Douglas? Would the merger enhance Boeing's worldwide competitive position relative to Airbus Industrie (a consortium formed by aerospace firms in four European countries), its only remaining rival? Or would it rather result in climbing costs and diminishing profits, because of the difficulties in integrating the two companies?

THE AEROSPACE INDUSTRY

Commercial Aircraft

The structure of the commercial aircraft industry resembled that of a pyramid, with a few airframe integrators at the top, dozens of primary subcontractors at the middle, and thousands of secondary subcontractors at the base. Subcontracting of aircraft production had grown in importance as aircraft components became more and more complex. In the 1930s, subcontracting made up less than 10 percent of the industry's operation; in the 1950s, 30 to 40 percent; and by the 1970s, subcontractors fabricated between 60 and 70 percent of the value of American airframes.[5] As aircraft production became increasingly more risky, subcontracting became associated with risk sharing. Over time, aircraft manufacturers extended subcontracting throughout the world, partly as a result of the demand made by foreign customers and their governments. As overseas carriers bought aircraft, their governments required airframe integrators to share design work and production with overseas firms.[6]

Entry into the business of manufacturing large commercial aircraft had always been very limited. One barrier to entry was the high and increasing cost of product development. The Boeing 747, for example, cost $1 billion to develop, the Boeing 767 cost $1.5 billion, the Airbus A320 cost $2.5 billion, and the total cost of developing the Boeing 777 in the early 1990s exceeded of $5.5 billion.[7]

Another entry barrier was the need to establish learning curves and achieve economies of scale. To break even on an entirely new aircraft, it took sales of 400 to 500 units and a minimum of fifty sales per year. Not only was it necessary for a company to wait up to ten years in order to reach the break-even point, but there was no guarantee that the company would ever break even, let alone make profits. As one group of industry analysts concluded, "economic failure is the norm in the civil aircraft business."[8]

The need to control costs gave rise to the "family concept" in aircraft design. Producing families of planes rather than single models, aircraft manufacturers built flexibility into the design of a given aircraft so that the fuselage could be stretched in the future to add more passenger seats in the cabin. Pioneered by Boeing, model stretching did play an important role in enhancing aircraft productivity.

These cost-cutting measures notwithstanding, commercial aircraft makers were unable to survive without government support. In the past, military contracts were extremely beneficial to commercial aircraft and engine makers, especially insofar as expensive new technologies like jet propulsion and swept wings were concerned. Since the mid 1960s, however, military and commercial developments had diverged, and consequently, government support to commercial projects declined. The Department of Defense continued to fund research with potential military implications, but by the late 1980s such funding amounted to less than 5 percent of Boeing's research and development. NASA also provided some direct funding, but again, only for technology development, not commercial product development.[9]

An additional factor that influenced the dynamics of the aircraft industry was airline deregulation. Deregulation of the domestic airlines in 1978 resulted in a substantial increase in air travel, intense air-fare competition among carriers, the entry of new low-cost, low-capacity airlines into the industry, and the growing utilization of the hub-and-spoke system by the major carriers. On the one hand, the explosion in air travel led to a steep growth in demand for new aircraft of all kinds. On the other, the proliferation of low-cost, short-haul airline companies (for example, Southwest Airlines, American West), combined with the extensive use of hubs by the large carriers, brought about an increased demand for short-range, single-aisle airplanes like the Boeing 737, the McDonnell Douglas MD80, and the Airbus A320. Additionally, the deregulatory environment shifted the focus of airline competition from performance to cost and from service to price. As Frank Shrontz, Boeing CEO between 1988 and 1996 observed, "In the old days airlines were infatuated with technology for its own sake. Today the rationale for purchasing a new plane is cost savings and profitability".[10]

In Europe, too, the airline industry experienced progressive deregulation during the 1980s and 1990s. By 1998, about one half of all worldwide air travel took place within a competitive, deregulated environment.[11] Such a trend—which was expected to continue—was likely to encourage foreign air carriers to become more cost conscious and more profit oriented in the future. Thus, in both the domestic and foreign markets, the economic deregulation of airline travel promoted increased competition among aircraft manufacturers.

Defense and Space

The defense and space industry differed from the commercial aircraft industry in three important respects. First, the U.S. government was the only primary customer for noncommercial aerospace products and services, and consequently, the total output of the industry was determined by political considerations. On the one side, the production of domestic military aircraft, missiles, and space products and services was subject to congressional debate over the budget; on the other, foreign military sales were restricted by the administration's foreign policy.[12]

Second, the defense and space industry operated under favorable contractual arrangements with the government. Unlike investments in commercial aircraft manufacturing, investments in defense and space were neither subject to excessive risks nor to volatile changes in market demand. The potential for unforeseen obstacles in developing defense and space products was so large that cost estimates prior to production were almost impossible to obtain. Accordingly, the government provided contractors with a special shelter—a contractual arrangement known as "cost plus," under which a defense contractor was guaranteed fixed profits regardless of the level of the final costs. Contractors competed for projects by submitting bids, but such bids were later supplemented by additional funds to cover overrun costs.[13] To control cost overrun, the U.S. government introduced "fixed-price contracts" in the late 1980s, but as a result of intense lobbying efforts on the part of the defense contractors, the fixed price contracts were replaced again by "cost reimbursement contracts" in the early 1990s.[14]

Third, the government's importance as a customer for aerospace products and services had diminished (Table 1). With the breakup of the Soviet Union in 1990, the Cold War was over and projected defense spending plummeted. Between 1987 and 1997, the Pentagon budget declined by 30 percent and its weapon procurement budget declined by 54 percent in 1997 dollars.[15] The shrinking defense budget led to large-scale mergers and acquisitions among defense contractors and to the growing consolidation of the industry. (Table 2). Following the merger of Boeing and McDonnell Douglas, four defense and space conglomerates ruled the aerospace industry: Lockheed Martin, Boeing-McDonnell Douglas, Raytheon, and Northrop Grumman. All four competed for leadership, and all were joined in a dense web of alliances and subcontracting arrangements that allowed each to prosper.[16]

HISTORY OF THE BOEING-DOUGLAS RIVALRY

In 1917, William Boeing founded the Boeing Airplane Company in Seattle, Washington. Three years later, Donald Douglas established what would become in 1926 the Douglas Aircraft Company. During the early 1920s, both companies were building

TABLE 1

U.S. Aerospace Industry Sales by Customer, 1982–1996, Selected Years

Year	Total Sales	% of Total Sales to U.S. Government	% of Total Sales to Other Customers
1982	56.4 billion	69.0%	31.0%
1984	69.6	74.9	25.1
1986	88.5	73.9	26.1
1988	95.5	72.6	27.4
1990	112.0	63.9	36.1
1992	115.5	55.7	44.3
1994	92.1	60.5	39.5
1996	93.9	54.6	45.4

Source: Aerospace Facts and Figures, 1997–98 (Washington: Aerospace Industries Association of America, 1997), p.13.

TABLE 2

The Ten Largest Defense Mergers and Acquisitions, 1992–1996

- March 1993   Lockheed acquired General Dynamics' aircraft and military businesses for $1.52 billion.
- April 1993   Martin Marietta acquired General Electric's aerospace assets for $3.05 billion.
- December 1993   Loral Corporation Acquired IBM's Federal Systems' Division for $1.57 billion.
- May 1994   Northrop Corporation acquired Grumman Corporation for $2.17 billion.
- December 1994   Martin Marietta merged with Lockheed in a transaction valued at more than $10 billion.
- April 1995   Raytheon Company acquired E. Systems for $2.3 billion.
- March 1996   Northrop Grumman acquired the defense electronics business of Westinghouse for $3.2 billion.
- April 1996   Lockheed acquired most of the assets of the Loral Corporation for more than $9 billion.
- August 1996*   Boeing acquired the defense business of Rockwell International Corporation for $3.2 billion.
- Dec. 1996**   Boeing acquired McDonnell Douglas for $14 billion.

*Sources: Wall Street Journal, December 16, 1996, *New York Times, December 16, 1997; **Business Week, December 30, 1996, p.38.*

a variety of flying machines—made of wood and fabric—for the military. The market for commercial aircraft evolved during the 1930s. As Boeing supplied United Airlines with its first sixty B-247s, Douglas went ahead with the development and production of a similar but superior aircraft: the DC1 (Douglas Commercial). The DC1 served as a prototype, but the larger DC2 outclassed the B-247, and the improved DC3 established Douglas as the world's largest manufacturer of commercial aircraft.[17]

Unable to compete with Douglas in the commercial aircraft business, Boeing redirected its efforts toward the military. Boeing's principal success during World War II was the development and production of the B-17 "Flying Fortress"—a giant four-engine bomber. Douglas, too, put its resources into the war effort, building attack bombers (A-20 Havoc) and Navy bombers (SBD Dauntless) and suspending its commercial production.[18]

The steep decline in military orders at the end of the war brought the aircraft industry to the verge of collapse. Douglas met the crisis by reestablishing itself as the world's largest manufacturer of commercial aircraft, producing the last great American piston transports: the DC6 and DC7. Boeing survived the downturn by producing an early gen-

eration of jet aircraft for the military: the B-47 and B-52 strategic bombers.[19] Having stayed out of civil aviation for more than ten years,[20] Boeing reentered the air transport market only after the jet had become operational for commercial use.

Boeing's first jet, the 707, followed closely the design of the military tanker KC-135, which Boeing had first produced under government contract. Douglas had no such advantage. By contrast to the Boeing 707, Douglas's first jet, the DC8, was a financial disaster: the company did not sell a sufficient number of units to recover its development cost.[21] Douglas's second jet, the smaller DC9, also failed to compete successfully with its rival, the Boeing 727. Altogether, twice as many 727s as DC9s were delivered (Table 3), Douglas's expenses were higher than Boeing's, and Douglas was selling the DC9 below cost. To avoid bankruptcy, Douglas merged in 1967 with the stronger McDonnell Aircraft Corporation, a defense contractor.[22]

The newly formed McDonnell Douglas Corporation became the largest manufacturer of military aircraft in the United States. McDonnell's premier aircraft in the 1960s and early 1970s was the F-4 Phantom, the Air Force's top fighter in Vietnam. To replace the Phantom, the McDonnell Douglas Corporation developed and produced the Air Force F-15 Eagle Attack fighter (1972), and the Navy

TABLE 3

Total Number of Best Selling Commercial Airplanes Delivered by Boeing and McDonnell Douglas, 1959–1997

Boeing		McDonnell Douglas	
B–707	1,010 (retired)	DC–8	556 (retired)
B–727	1,831 (retired)	DC–9	976 (retired)
B–737	2,975	MD80/90	1,221
B–747	1,136	DC–10	446 (retired)

Source: Boeing, Commercial Airplane Group, *Announced Orders and Deliveries as of 12/31/97.*

F/A–18 Hornet strike fighter (1978). Both fighters were still in production in the 1990s, both were used in the Gulf (1991) and Kosovo (1999) wars, and both were principal contributors to McDonnell Douglas's revenues on the eve of the merger with Boeing. On the eve of the merger, the McDonnell Douglas Corporation also produced the C-17 Globemaster—the Air Force's most advanced military transport, first introduced in 1995. Other defense products manufactured by McDonnell Douglas at the time of the merger included attack jump jets for the Marines (AV–8B Harrier), training aircraft for the Navy (T–45 Goshawk), attack helicopters (AH–64 Apache), and guided missiles (Harpoon, Cruise, and Tomahawk Cruise). In 1993 and 1994 respectively, foreign orders of F/A–18s (Switzerland) and F-15 (Israel) boosted the company's military business.[23]

In contrast to its defense sector, McDonnell Douglas's commercial business lagged far behind Boeing's. Between 1959 and 1996, Boeing produced 8,200 commercial jetliners and Douglas only 3,300. Defined by range of travel, Boeing families of airframes included the 737 for short-range, the 757 and 767 for medium-range, and the 747 and 777 for medium- to long-range travel. Boeing's most successful models were the 737 and 747 series. Going into service in 1967, the B–737 had become the top-selling commercial jetliner in history, with 3,300 units delivered by early 1999. Boeing offered the 737 in a variety of models of different ranges (2,000 to 3,200 miles) and different seat capacities (108 to 189 seats).[24]

The 747 family was introduced in 1970. Its development and tooling costs had almost bankrupted the company, but by 1978 sales reached the break-even point and thereafter the 747 became Boeing's most profitable aircraft.[25] Responding to Boeing's challenge, both the McDonnell Douglas and the Lockheed corporations launched a new wide-body aircraft, and both failed. The DC10, like the L1011, carried only two-thirds of the passenger load of the 747, cost two-thirds as much, and had one-half the travel range of the 747; besides, the market for such an airplane could not sustain two competing models. Lockheed exited the market in 1981 after selling only 244 units, and Douglas rolled out the last passenger version of the DC10 in 1980, unable to recover the airplane's high development costs.[26]

Still, McDonnell Douglas introduced two other commercial aircraft models. To compete with the B–737, Douglas upgraded and stretched the DC9 into the MD–80 (1980) and MD–90 (1995). Although an initial success, the MD–80/90 series did not generate sufficient orders to sustain sales (Table 4). By 1996, less than 150 units were on order (against more than 750 B–737 units on order),[27] sales were slowing down, costs were going up, and the MD program was losing money. After the merger with McDonnell Douglas, Boeing decided to discontinue manufacturing the two MD models, effective in 1999.[28]

Finally, McDonnell Douglas made one last effort to enter the market for large wide-body aircraft. In 1989, the company put into service the three-engine

TABLE 4

Shipments of Large (over 33,000 lbs.) U.S.-manufactured Civil Transport Aircraft During the Five years preceding the Boeing–McDonnell Douglas Merger, 1992–1996

Company and Model	1992	1993	1994	1995	1996
B 737	218	152	121	89	76
B 747	61	5	40	25	26
B 757	99	71	69	43	42
B 767	63	51	40	36	42
B 777	—	—	—	13	32
Boeing total	441	330	270	206	218
MD–11	42	36	17	18	15
MD–80	84	42	22	18	12
MD–90	—	—	—	14	24
McDonnell Douglas total	126	78	39	50	51
Total	567	408	309	256	269

Source: Aerospace Facts and Figures, 1997–98, p.34.

("tri-jet") MD–11, a derivative of the DC10.[29] Again, sales of the MD–11 languished, and Douglas soon faced competition from Boeing's newest jetliner, the 777. Entering into service in 1995, the 777 outsold the MD11 by a margin of 2 to 1 within a year (Table 4). Following the merger with McDonnell Douglas, Boeing management decided to limit future production of the MD11 to its freighter version.[30]

Product Development

Product development in the commercial aircraft industry had long been the preferred growth strategy undertaken by competing manufacturers. The occasional development of a new family of planes was essential for securing market share in the future, and accordingly, both Boeing and McDonnell Douglas undertook such a strategy in the 1990s. Yet only Boeing managed to deliver the new product.

Early in 1996, McDonnell Douglas announced a plan to develop a new twin-engine, wide-body aircraft. Named the MD-XX, the new jetliner (8,000-mile range, 300 to 400 seats) was intended to broaden the McDonnell Douglas product line and thereby reestablish the company's role as a major player in the commercial aircraft industry in the twenty-first century. During the spring and summer of 1996, engineers at Douglas facilities in Long Beach, California, worked on the design of the MD-XX, the company received orders for forty to fifty units from customers, and it made preparations to launch the new aircraft at the end of the year. Yet, on October 24, it decided to terminate the project. Stonecipher, McDonnell Douglas's CEO, urged the company board to forgo the development of the MD-XX because of its prohibitive cost: the project would have required an initial investment of $3 billion and an additional capital of $12 billion spent over a ten-year period. "Fundamentally, it wasn't an MD-XX decision," Stonecipher admitted, "it was a question of how far, how fast, and at what rate" Douglas could compete in the commercial aircraft business. "The market may be too tough for us to battle through" and "I have . . . other alternatives." Six weeks later, Stonecipher negotiated with Philip Condit the sale of McDonnell Douglas to Boeing.[31]

Condit led the 777 program to completion. Condit's role in developing the 777 paved his way to the top: Midway through the 777 development program, Boeing's board of directors elected him president and gave him a seat on the board. Four years later, in 1996, the board promoted Condit to CEO.

Launching the Boeing 777 in 1990, Boeing management sought to ensure the company's future.

"This is an offensive, not a defensive strategy," Condit noted, predicting that the 777 family would remain in production for fifty years. A wide-body aircraft with two gigantic jet engines ("the most powerful ever built"), the 777 went into service two years after Airbus had introduced its own new wide-body models: the two-engine A320 and the four-engine A340.[32]

Competition—and Cooperation—in Space

Boeing and McDonnell Douglas had long competed over NASA contracts, but such competition did not rule out partnership. On the contrary, the typical NASA project was extremely demanding and therefore required the joint efforts of several competing contractors. In the 1960s, Boeing built the lunar orbiters that circled the moon and the first stage of the rockets used in the Apollo space program; McDonnell created the Mercury and Gemini capsules; and Douglas developed the Delta expendable launch vehicle, the world's most reliable space launcher. Following the successful moon mission, both Boeing and McDonnell Douglas competed for NASA's contract to build Skylab, America's first space station, and McDonnell Douglas won. In the 1980s, the Rockwell Corporation led the development of the space shuttle program, with Boeing and McDonnell Douglas as key partners. Boeing produced the upper stage of the shuttle, and McDonnell Douglas provided the structural parts for the booster that lifted the shuttle into space.

In the 1990s, Boeing was in charge of leading the development of the International Space Station—the largest and most complex structure ever assembled in space—and McDonnell Douglas served as a subcontractor to Boeing, responsible for producing the station's structural backbone. As the two companies merged in 1997, the International Space Station contract was a major contributor to Boeing's revenues, just as the Delta II space launcher contract was a principal contributor to McDonnell Douglas's revenues. After its merger with Rockwell (1996) and McDonnell Douglas, the new Boeing became NASA's single largest contractor.[33]

The Challenge of Airbus Competition

The new Boeing had one formidable rival: Airbus Industrie. While Airbus's production rates in the 1980s were still low, its booking of new aircraft orders skyrocketed, and subsequently, the consortium was fast expanding its capacity. Airbus orders surpassed those of McDonnell Douglas in 1986, and its deliveries exceeded those of McDonnell Douglas in 1991. As Airbus gained, Boeing's new orders fell below the 50 percent mark for the first time in more than two decades. In 1990, the 777 launch year, Boeing booked 45 percent of the total industry orders, Airbus 34 percent, and McDonnell Douglas 21 percent. In 1996, the year in which Boeing announced its merger with McDonnell, Airbus booked nearly 50 percent of the worldwide industry orders, and delivered close to one-third of the worldwide output of commercial jetliners (Table 5). The merger created a duopoly, which was supposed, in theory, to reduce competition and give each of the two companies a price advantage in a seller's market. On the contrary, however, the merger intensified the battle between Boeing and

TABLE 5

Market Share of Actual (1992–1998) and Forecast (1999–2000) Shipments of Commercial aircraft, Boeing, McDonnell Douglas(MD), and Airbus.

	1992	1993	1994	1995	1996	1997	1998	1999	2000
Boeing	61%	61%	63%	54%	55%	67%	71%	68%	61%
MD	17	14	9	13	13				
Airbus	22	25	28	33	32	33	29	32	39

Sources: Aerospace Facts and Figures, 1997–98, p. 34; Wall Street Journal, December 3, 1998, and January 12, 1999; The Boeing Company 1997 Annual Report, p. 19; data supplied by Mark Luginbill, Airbus communication director, November 16, 1998.

Airbus, leading each company to slash aircraft prices by as much as 20 percent.[34]

In 1970, aerospace companies in France, Germany, Britain, and Spain had formed Airbus. Pooling their resources together to create a consortium, the participating companies served as both shareholders of and subcontractors to Airbus. The participating companies competed with each other over the development and production of particular aircraft components, and thus different shares of a given program were distributed among the partners. The partners, in addition, received generous subsidies from their governments to finance Airbus projects and ensure the consortium's long-term survival. Airbus received nearly $10 billion in government assistance for the development and manufacture of its first three models, and an additional $4–5 billion for initial work on its A330/340 models. These subsidies led to a trade war. The United States government, together with representatives of Boeing and McDonnell Douglas, claimed that Airbus' subsidies violated the General Agreement on Tariffs and Trade (GATT), and called for their removal. Again and again, the parties failed to reach a compromise. In 1992, at long last, Airbus and Boeing signed a bilateral agreement that limited government subsidies to 33 percent of Airbus's total development costs. In exchange, the agreement limited federal indirect R&D funds to 3 percent of the total revenues received by American aircraft manufacturers. In 1995, after twenty-five years of losses, Airbus finally generated profits.[35]

Although government assistance helped Airbus stay in the aircraft industry for the long haul, the consortium's success was impossible to understand without considering its strategy. In developing its long-term plans, Airbus sought to build on Boeing's rich experience, mimicking three elements of the old Boeing strategy: technological leadership, cost controls, and the development of families of planes.

Technological Leadership   "You cannot compete with a dominant . . . player if you don't offer something different," former Airbus President Roger Beteille said. He added that to persuade the major airlines to switch to a new supplier, Airbus had to differentiate itself from Boeing by incorporating the most advanced technology into its planes.

Among Airbus's technological firsts, the fly-by-wire system was perhaps the most famous. Introduced in 1988, the A–320 was the world's first fly-by-wire commercial aircraft, an aircraft controlled by a pilot transmitting commands to the rudder and flaps electrically, not mechanically.[36]

Cost Controls   As competition with Boeing intensified during the recession of the early 1990s, Airbus sought to reduce costs through deep cuts in jobs, the streamlining of the production process, and the speed-up of deliveries. Each of the consortium's partner companies participated in these cost-cutting efforts. In Britain, British Aerospace cut its wing-production time by 50 percent in two years while trimming its Airbus work force from 15,000 to 7,000 in five years. In Germany, Daimler-Benz (later Daimler-Chrysler), which built fuselages, reduced its production costs by 33 percent and production time by 50 percent, in six years (1992–1998). And in France, state-owned Aerospatiale, which produced cockpits, reduced its work force by 17 percent between 1993 and 1996.[37]

Families of Planes   Boeing was the first company to use the family concept in aircraft design. Airbus made the concept the foundation of its manufacturing and marketing strategy. A family of planes was made up of derivative jetliners built around a basic model. Since all derivatives of a given model shared maintenance, training, and operation procedures, as well as replacement parts and components, the use of such derivative airplanes to serve different markets enabled airline carriers to cut costs. Airbus used this family-based strategy in two ways. First, it produced and marketed derivative jetliners, and second, it introduced common design features ("commonalities") across the entire range of its models, not just the members of a single family, thus providing airline carriers with additional sources of savings.[38]

Airbus's strategy served the consortium well. By the mid 1990s, Airbus competed with Boeing in every travel market except the one served by the 747. The A320 family challenged the 737 in the short-range 120-plus seat market, the A300/A310 family competed with the 757 and 767 in the medium range 200+ seat market, and the

A330/A340 family went after the market for medium- to long-range travel, anticipating the coming of the 777.

THE RESULTS OF THE MERGER

The Boeing–McDonnell Douglas merger was completed on August 1, 1997, eight months after Condit and Stonecipher had originally announced it. Upon the completion of the merger, Boeing became the world's largest producer of military aircraft and the second largest supplier to the U.S. Department of Defense. The newly merged company quickly consolidated its holdings. It turned McDonnell's Saint Louis headquarters into Boeing's headquarters for military aircraft and missile program, put Boeing's space division (based in Seal Beach, California) in charge of all Boeing and McDonnell Douglas space-related programs, and developed detailed plans to phase out the McDonnell Douglas commercial aircraft business.[39]

Yet the merger failed to produce the expected results. In 1997, Boeing recorded a net loss of $178 million, the worst financial performance in fifty years. In 1998, a United Airlines executive called Boeing a "dysfunctional organization,"[40] a *Wall Street Journal* reporter described Boeing's revised projections for 1999–2000 (Table 6) as "shock[ing],"

and Boeing President Harry Stonecipher conceded that the crisis was likely to last from "two to five" years.[41] Over a two-year period following the announcement of the merger, Boeing shares lost one-third of their value.[42] What, then, was the source of Boeing's post-merger difficulties?

Defense and Space

Boeing's defense and space business units had performed well right from the early days of the merger. Defense and space revenues accounted for 39 percent of the total company sales in 1997, up from 25 percent in 1996, 23 percent in 1994, and 20 percent in 1992.[43] The Defense Department was Boeing's largest customer, spending nearly four times as much as NASA (Table 7). Boeing's Defense and Space Group was profitable in 1997, generating a 7.3 percent return on sales and thus offsetting, almost entirely, the large loss incurred by the company's Commercial Airplane Group. As shown in Table 6, Boeing's defense and space business units were profitable in 1998 and were expected to continue generating profits through the year 2000, with the group's margins steadily improving.

Boeing Defense and Space Group gained from recent changes in the defense budget. Following a decade-long decline in U.S. military spending, the

TABLE 6

Highlights of Boeing's Financial and Operation Data: Actual (1997–1998) and Projected (1999–2000)

	1997	*1998*	*1999*	*2000*
Operating revenues (bm)	$46	$56	$58	$50
R&D spending (bm)	$1.9	$1.9	$1.6–1.8	$1.5–1.7
Comm. aircraft shipped	374	559	620	490
Employment (thousands)	238	231	200–210	185–195
Profit margins:*				
Comm. aircraft	– 6.6%	0%	2%–3%	1%–3%
Defense and space**	7.3%	7.7%	7%–9%	8%–10%

*Operating earnings returns on sales.
**Including "Information."
Sources: For 1997 and 1998, The Boeing Company 1997 Annual Report, pp. 19, 24, 35, 72, and The Boeing Company 1998 Annual Report, pp. 35, 51, 76; for 1998–2000, Frederick M. Biddle and Andy Pasztor, "Boeing May Be Hurt Up to 5 Years," *Wall Street Journal,* December 3, 1998.

TABLE 7

Boeing's Defense and Space Group:*
Sales by Customer, 1997

Air Force	30%
Navy	18%
Army	6%
NASA	15%
Foreign	22%
Other	9%
Total	$18 billion

* Including information.
Source: The Boeing Company 1997 Annual Report, p. 24.

defense budget stabilized in 1997 at about $250 billion and was expected to increase moderately between 1998 and 2003. NASA's budget was expected to remain flat on an inflation-adjusted basis.[44] With no further spending cuts projected in either defense or space, and with a slight increase in the military procurement budget, the prospects of the industry were fast improving. Lockheed Martin, Raytheon, and to a lesser extent, the Northrop Grumman Corporation, were Boeing's principal competitors in this segment.

The largest defense contractor, Lockheed Martin, was a highly diversified company, producing a well-balanced mix of aircraft, electronics, and missiles. Lockheed held the most lucrative Defense Department contract in the 1990s: the development and production of the Raptor fighter jet (F–22), a successor to McDonnell Douglas's "still unchallengeable" F–15. The Pentagon ordered 340 F–22s at a "minimum" cost of $75 million each. In 1997, Lockheed delivered the first test model to the Air Force, but the Raptor was not expected to go into full production until 2004. Although Lockheed was the project's prime contractor, Boeing served as a subcontractor to Lockheed, producing about one-third of the Raptor, including the wings and the aft fuselage.[45]

Raytheon was Boeing's major competitor in aerospace electronics. Of the total cost of a given fighter aircraft, electronics made up one-third; the airframe and engine accounted for the remaining two-thirds. Raytheon had acquired Hughes electronics in 1997 and as a result became a powerful rival to Boeing, specializing in the development

and production of radar systems, night vision equipment, avionics gear, and missiles.[46]

Northrop Grumman was a much smaller company than either Lockheed or Raytheon. Building one of the last B–2 Stealth bombers in 1997, Northrop had become the industry's principal subcontractor and Boeing's single largest supplier. Northrop manufactured the aft fuselage for the Navy's Super Hornet fighter and the tail assembly and surface controls for the C–17 military transport, both produced by McDonnell Douglas, later owned by Boeing. In addition, Northrop served as a major supplier to Boeing Airplane Commercial Group, building half of the 747's fuselage and the doors for most of Boeing's passenger jetliners, including the 747.[47]

Boeing's position in the industry was unique. Boeing had no recent experience in building fighter jets and therefore its merger with McDonnell Douglas was critical, especially insofar as long-term government contracts were concerned. First, McDonnell held the second largest Defense Department contract in the industry: the production of the Super Hornet F/A18E/F aircraft fighter, the latest addition to the Navy fleet. The Navy ordered a total of 500 Super Hornets at a cost of $45 million each. Production of the F/A18E/F had begun in 1997 and was expected to continue until 2010.[48]

More important, the merger strengthened Boeing's competitive position in the contest over the richest military-aircraft contract ever: the development and production of the Joint Strike Fighter (JSF), a successor to Lockheed's F–16. In October 1996, the Defense Department selected Boeing and Lockheed, not McDonnell, to compete for the JSF project. The exclusion of McDonnell Douglas played a key role in Stonecipher's decision to sell the company to Boeing. A multipurpose low-end fighter, the JSF was expected to cost less than half as much as the high-end Raptor, yet the sheer size of the Pentagon's projected order was staggering: 2,850 JSFs in three different versions (Air Force, Navy, and Marine models) at the total estimated cost of more than $200 billion. The fly-off contest between Boeing and Lockheed was scheduled for 2001, and according to defense analysts, Boeing had the edge both because it was better equipped to master the complex manufacturing process required and because it was able to control costs better, having had the discipline of the commercial marketplace. In 1999, Lockheed reported a $150 million cost overrun for work on the design of an entrant to the JSF fly-off competition, a problem that was likely to hurt the company's prospects of winning the contract.[49]

The merger with McDonnell Douglas also provided Boeing with ample engineering and manufacturing resources. In the long run, the potential of transferring technological know-how back and forth between commercial and military business units gave Boeing an enormous advantage over its rivals, as even Boeing's competitors acknowledged. To mention one example, Boeing had developed expertise in composite materials while working on the B-2 bomber and then used this expertise to build the tail wing of the 777, which, in turn, was used to develop its advanced wing design for the proposed JSF jet.[50]

Commercial Aircraft

Boeing Commercial Aircraft Group lost $1.8 billion in 1997, the first year of the merger. In 1998, the group barely generated any profits, and during the next two years (1999–2000), its profits were expected to remain low, with the margins ranging from 1 to 3 percent (see Table 6).

One source of Boeing's post-merger troubles was its acquisition of the McDonnell Douglas MD model series. At the time of the merger, McDonnell's commercial jetliner business was losing money, and consequently, Boeing's management decided to phase it out, taking a special $1.4 billion pretax charge[51] which resulted in a larger than expected reported loss in 1997 (see Table 6).

Another source of difficulties was Condit's neglect of Boeing's commercial aircraft business. A newly promoted CEO, Condit focused almost exclusively on expanding Boeing's military business. He developed a long-term strategy of turning Boeing into the world's largest aerospace and defense company and implemented it at once, first buying Rockwell's military units, and then the McDonnell Douglas Corporation. Eager to complete the deal with McDonnell and preoccupied with lobbying the U.S. government for its approval, he overlooked mounting assembly-line problems that crippled Boeing Commercial Airplane Group. When it became apparent in the summer of 1997 that Boeing's assembly line was falling behind, Condit still underestimated the problem, acknowledging just a month-long delay in deliveries of commercial jets.[52]

But Boeing production problems were serious. A rapid ramp-up in aircraft production led to shortages of raw materials (aluminum, titanium, and other composites) and to delays in deliveries of parts and subassemblies. The hiring of thousands of inexperienced, "green," workers resulted in productivity inefficiencies.[53] So severe were the shortages and inefficiencies that the company was forced to shut down its 737 and 747 production line for one month in order "to bring work back into sequence."[54] Although largely unrelated to the Boeing–McDonnell Douglas merger, these problems did affect the post-merger results.

Other problems affected the post-merger results as well. Increased competition with Airbus drove Boeing's management to protect the company's market share at almost any cost. Caught in the competition, Boeing's management overlooked expenses, slashed prices, and gave up technological leadership. In the market for single-aisle, narrow-body aircraft, for example, Boeing competed with Airbus on price rather than technology, often selling the B-737 below cost. Because the A-320 was slightly more advanced than the B-737 (and its cabin a bit larger), a growing number of airline carriers favored the first over the second, citing passengers' preferences as the reason. United Airlines' 1996 decision to extend an Airbus A-320 order was a case in point.[55]

Still, Boeing's most pressing problem was cost escalation. In 1998, Boeing used 20 to 30 percent more labor hours to produce a jetliner than it had done in 1994.[56] As the company's four-year efforts to contain costs had stalled, Boeing lost $1 billion on the sale of its first 400 new-model 737s.[57] Although the company had launched a two-year program to modernize production, it continued to operate 400 separate computer systems that were not linked together.[58] While Airbus had already adopted a flexible, lean-production manufacturing system, Boeing was still utilizing a standardized, mass-production system that had barely changed since World War II. Hence the gap in labor productivity. In 1998, Boeing employed 211 workers for every commercial aircraft (560 jets made by 119,000 employees), and Airbus just 143 (230 jets produced by 33,000 workers).[59]

Finally, the merger of Boeing and McDonnell Douglas coincided with the Asian economic slump. The slump prompted the Asian airlines to cancel or defer aircraft orders. The slump affected both Airbus and Boeing, but not in the same way. On the one hand, Asian orders of wide-body jets were the most vulnerable and the first to be canceled; on the other, Airbus booked fewer such orders than did Boeing. Since Boeing, unlike Airbus, was highly dependent on the Asian market for the sale of its wide-body jets, the 747 and 777, Boeing's potential losses were greater than those of Airbus.[60]

CULTURE AND LEADERSHIP

The merger of Boeing and McDonnell Douglas posed a challenge to the new Boeing of integrating the two companies' corporate cultures and leadership styles. To be sure, both Boeing and McDonnell Douglas were aerospace firms dominated by an engineering culture. Their respective corporate images embodied the values and attitudes of engineers, that is, logic, precision, professionalism, and authority. Their professional work force was made up, first and foremost, of engineers, and their skilled work force of aircraft mechanics.

Still, there was a difference. According to industry analysts, McDonnell had long been known for its top-down management style, which had been formed through close alliance with the defense industry. Its organizational structure was rigid, its decision-making procedure centralized, and its chain of command quasi-military. Boeing, by contrast, had developed a more progressive management structure, based partly on team work and partly on employees' participation in decision making.[61] Boeing's management practices were shaped, above all, by the need to compete in the marketplace.

Condit's leadership style reflected Boeing's managerial tradition. An inspirational leader endowed with exceptional social skills, Condit led by example. Always preferring to work in groups, he regularly assigned tasks to teams rather than individuals. To promote camaraderie, loyalty, and a strong sense of bonding among Boeing's executives, he developed a ritual. Periodically, he would invite a new group of managers to his house to sit around the fire and tell anecdotes about their experience at Boeing. Each executive would than write on a piece of paper a positive and a negative story about Boeing, toss the paper with the negative story into the fire, and keep the paper with the positive story to carry it around and show others.[62]

Stonecipher's style was different, reflecting, to some extent at least, McDonnell's managerial philosophy. A strong executive with a track record of corporate turnaround, downsizing, and outsourcing, Stonecipher was a blunt talker and an aggressive leader, feared by his subordinates and highly respected on Wall Street. A nonplayer, he led by explicit command rather than persuasion. Asked once (in 1998) to compare his managerial style with that of Condit, he replied: "I'm more likely to shoot you and then ask your name; Phil is likely to ask your name and then shoot you."[63]

Condit had joined Boeing in 1965, after receiving a master's degree in aeronautical engineering from Princeton University. A gifted engineer, he rose quickly at Boeing, becoming vice president in 1983, president in 1992, and CEO in 1996.[64] Stonecipher had spent twenty-seven years at General Electric, rising through the ranks to become head of GE's jet engine division. He subsequently spent seven years at the Sunstrand Corporation (a military contractor making aerospace components), turning the company around, and three years at McDonnell Douglas, improving the firm's financial performance before selling it to Boeing.[65] At Boeing, Stonecipher served as president and as a director of the board.

The contrast between Condit's and Stonecipher's leadership styles raised an interesting question: Would the two executives cooperate successfully during the post-merger years or would they clash? Apparently, as Boeing's financial performance worsened, Stonecipher had gained power relative to Condit. Stonecipher was now one of Boeing's largest shareholders—Condit owned a relatively small amount of stock—and he enjoyed wide support among the company's investors. Nevertheless, he had two handicaps. First, he lacked the backing of Boeing's board of directors. Only four of Boeing's thirteen board members (including Stonecipher and John F. McDonnell, son of the company's founder) were McDonnell Douglas affiliates, and fully eight directors represented the old Boeing and were loyal to Condit. Second, he was sixty-three years old (in 1999) and Boeing's top executives were required to retire at sixty-five.[66]

TURNAROUND

As Boeing's crisis deepened, Condit, Stonecipher, and other top executives laid out a turnaround strategy. The strategy was based on a combination of four elements: the reorganization of Boeing's two major product groups, the replacement of the executive responsible for running the company's commercial airplane division, the introduction of radical cost-cutting measures, and the hiring of a new chief financial officer from outside the company.

On September 1, 1998, Condit ousted Ronald Woodward, head of Boeing's Commercial Airplane Group, who was next in line to become CEO, and replaced him with Alan Mulally. Mulally, who had served as Condit's chief engineer on the 777 project, had a reputation of a skillful team leader and headed Boeing's Defense and Space Group after the merger with McDonnell Douglas.

In consolidating the businesses of Boeing and McDonnell, Mulally quickly reorganized the Defense and Space Group. Taking a page from Alfred Sloan's reorganization of General Motors in the 1920s, he grouped all products and services into separate, autonomous divisions, drew carefully the divisional boundaries, and rendered each division responsible for its own financial performance. He then took charge of Boeing's Commercial Airplane Group and did the same. He reorganized it into three independent divisions: one responsible for single-aisle (narrow-body) planes, one for twin-aisle (wide-body) planes, and one for customer service. Again, each division was expected to generate its own profits, and each was responsible for its own loses. In the past, Boeing's executives rarely knew the exact cost of the planes they produced. Now they were fully accountable.[67]

Next, Boeing undertook several steps to cut costs, the most significant of which was downsizing. During the two-year period 1999–2000, Boeing planned to cut 30,000 to 50,000 jobs (see Table 6), most of them in the commercial aircraft division. Early in 1999, Boeing introduced a new computerized system designed to control the supply and stock of parts and components, and thereby reduce inventory costs. At the same time, Boeing renewed its efforts to build a flexible, integrated production-management system that would link its separate computer systems. In addition, the company was trying to reduce the number of special features it introduced into a variety of aircraft models sold to different airlines, and by so doing, cut its expenses further (without, of course, turning away customers).[68]

Lastly, in December 1998, in a move initiated by Stonecipher, Deborah Hopkins, former chief finan-

cial officer at General Motors, Europe, replaced Boeing's chief financial officer for thirty-two years, Boyd Givan. A forty-four year-old financial analyst, Hopkins was the youngest senior executive at Boeing, and the only woman occupying such a high position. She spelled out her plans at once. To help Boeing recover, she sought first to obtain more accurate cost data and deliver the data to line supervisors in a timely fashion; second, to determine the risks of undertaking large projects in a more methodical way; third, to discontinue unprofitable projects; and fourth, to increase Boeing's reliance on the outsourcing of aircraft components, systems, and equipment. "Teaching the business" to Boeing managers and workers, she had quickly proved she could deliver, helping the company improve its financial results.[69]

Hopkins's early success at Boeing raised the issue of succession. On the one side, Alan Mulally represented the traditional CEO candidate. A Boeing engineer groomed and promoted by Condit, he occupied the immediate position leading directly to the top. On the other, Deborah Hopkins embodied anything but the traditional. An outsider brought in by another outsider, she was a woman working in a company dominated by a tribal culture of white male engineers. An ambitious and outspoken executive, she said she was interested in running the company following Condit's retirement, a statement that created some tension within the leadership.[70] Whoever succeeded Condit, the rivalry between Mulally and Hopkins was likely to underlie Boeing's difficult journey to recovery and comeback.

FUTURE CONCERNS

Despite its initial promise, Boeing's turnaround strategy failed to adequately address two major concerns that could have affected its recovery. One concern pertained to the state of labor relations, and the other to the prospects of product development.

Labor Relations

Following the merger of Boeing and McDonnell Douglas, about half of all Boeing's employees were covered by collective bargaining agreements. Boeing's two largest unions were the International Association of Machinists (IAM), representing 30 percent of its employees, and the Seattle Professional Engineering Employees Association (SPEEA), representing 12 percent of the employees. In 1999, Boeing was expected to negotiate new union contracts with 54,000 machinists, 24,000 engineers, and 8,000 other workers, the vast majority of whom were employees of the old Boeing, working in four states (Washington, Oregon, California, and Kansas). In 2001, Boeing was scheduled to negotiate an additional IAM contract with 10,000 machinists, all of whom were former employees of McDonnell Douglas in the Saint Louis area.[71]

During the 1995–96 round of union negotiations, just before the merger, both Boeing and McDonnell Douglas experienced bitter and costly strikes. In 1995, the Boeing machinists struck for sixty-nine days, and a year later, the McDonnell machinists struck for ninety-nine days. The two strikes erupted over the issue of job security.

At Boeing, the machinists had voted down two proposed contracts before ratifying a third with an approval rating of 87 percent. Described by analysts as "overly generous," the Boeing IAM 1995 agreement provided the machinists with the best job security provisions in the industry (management was required to discuss outsourcing decisions with the union before implementing them) and with excellent health benefits. Financially

weak, Boeing was unwilling to undergo another lengthy strike with the engineers. Instead, it offered the SPEEA a labor agreement closely modeled on the IAM's.[72]

At McDonnell Douglas, the striking machinists ratified the contract with only 68 percent of the vote. Described by some analysts as "rich," the McDonnell Douglas–IAM agreement, like Boeing's contract a year earlier, contained several clauses restricting the company's ability to subcontract jobs. In addition, the agreement required McDonnell management to compensate displaced workers with adequate job training and/or limited severance pay.[73]

Following the strikes of the mid 1990s, negotiations in 1999 were particularly difficult because of Boeing's commitment to produce a record of 620 commercial jets throughout the year—a goal that enhanced the union's bargaining power relative to management's. Still, as the IAM contract expired in the summer of 1999, Condit and his team managed to avoid a Boeing strike, reaching an agreement with the machinists on a three-year contract. Ratified by the majority of the membership, the agreement provided the machinists with job security (no layoffs as a result of outsourcing), while granting the company the right to decide which jobs should be outsourced. Both the union president and a Wall Street analyst praised Condit for the successful ne-

TABLE 8

Highlights of Financial and Operating Data for Boeing Before the Merger with McDonnell Douglas (1994–96) and After the Merger (1997–98) (in $ millions except per share data)

	After merger		Before merger		
	1998	1997	1996	1995	1994
Sales and other Operating Revenues:					
Commercial jets	$35,545	$26,929	$16,904	$13,933	$16,851
Defense and space	19,872	18,125	5,777	5,582	5,073
Other revenues	730	745			
Total	56,154	45,800	22,681	19,515	21,924
Net earnings (loss)	$1,120	($178)	$1,095	$393	$856
Earnings per share (loss)	1.16	(0.18)	3.19	1.15	2.51
R & D expense	1,895	1,924	1,200	1,267	1,704
Number of employees	231,000	238,000	112,000	109,000	119,000

Source: Boeing Annual Report for 1996, p. 64; Boeing Annual Report for 1998, p. 78.

gotiations of the agreement; yet in the long run, the contentious issue of outsourcing had not been resolved.[74] Because Boeing was fast increasing its reliance on subcontracting and at the same time was reluctant to give union leaders a greater voice in outsourcing decisions, labor relations at the company were likely to remain strained as it entered the twenty-first century.

Product Development

Similarly, Boeing's decision not to develop a new aircraft had far-reaching implications on the long-term competitive advantage of the company. Historically, the aviation industry had rewarded risk taking. On the eve of the jet age, Boeing upstaged Douglas with the 707, gambling the entire company on the success of the jet technology. In the 1970s, Boeing revolutionized air travel with the introduction of the 747, taking another huge risk and leaving McDonnell Douglas further behind. At the dawn of the twenty-first century, Boeing suddenly turned conservative. Not only was the company reluctant to develop a new family of planes, but its R&D budget was shrinking: between 1998 and 2000, Boeing's research and development spending was projected to decline from $1.9 billion to as low as $1.5 billion (see Table 6).

Airbus, in the meantime, was developing an entirely new aircraft, the "super jumbo" A3XX. A giant double-decker designed to carry 550 to 650 passengers, or 230 more than the largest standard 747, the A3XX was projected to go into production in 2000 and into service in 2005, at the earliest. Airbus intended to use the A3XX to compete with the 747 "from above."[75]

During the twenty-year period 1999–2019, Airbus management forecasted a need for 1,400 "super jumbos" valued at $300 billion. Boeing disputed these figures, contending that about three-quarters of Airbus's projected demand for the "super jumbo" was, in fact, a demand for the 747. Given its projections, Boeing management concluded that there was no justification for spending more than $10 billion (Airbus's estimate of the project's cost) on replacing the jumbo. Instead, Boeing decided to introduce derivative airplanes built around the 747. Looking for ways to stretch and upgrade the thirty-year-old jumbo, Boeing engineers were examining a 550-seat 747 equipped with improved wing aerodynamics and a fly-by-wire technology.[76]

Boeing also decided to delay another project, its most ambitious one: the development and production of a supersonic jet. In November 1998, Boeing postponed until the year 2020 the date on which its projected supersonic jetliner would enter service. A 300-foot-long mockup built in 1970—now under restoration in a San Francisco museum—represented the most advanced progress Boeing had ever made toward completing the project.[77]

Endnotes

1. David Whitford, "Sale of the Century," *Fortune*, February 17, 1997, p. 100; Andy Reinhardt, "Three Huge Hours in Seattle," *Business Week*, December 30, 1996, p. 38; Jeff Cole, "Air Power: Boeing Plan to Acquire McDonnell Douglas Bolsters Consolidation," *Wall Street Journal*, December 16, 1996.
2. *Fortune*, February 17, 1997, pp. 96, 98, 100; Anthony Velocci, "Vertical Integration Looming Larger at McDonnell Douglas," *Aviation Week and Space Technology*, March 6, 1996, pp. 58–59.
3. Quoted in *Fortune*, February 17, 1997, p. 96.
4. Lawrence Fisher, "Boeing Chairman Offers 'Exuberance and Dynamism,'" *New York Times*, December 16, 1996.
5. David C. Mowery and Nathan Rosenberg, "The Commercial Aircraft Industry," in Richard R. Nelson, ed., *Government and Technological Progress: A Cross Industry Analysis* (New York: Pergamon Press, 1982), p. 116; Michael L. Dertrouzos, Richard K. Lester, and Robert M. Solow, *Made in America: Regaining the Productive Edge* (New York: Harper-Perennial, 1990), p. 204.
6. Mowery and Rosenberg, "The Commercial Aircraft Industry," p. 116; Dertouzos et al., *Made in America*, p. 204.
7. David C. Mowery and Nathan Rosenberg, *Technology and the Pursuit of Economic Growth* (New York: Cambridge University Press, 1989), p. 172. For the Boeing 777, see Eugene Rodgers, *Flying High: The Story of Boeing* (New York: Atlantic Monthly Press, 1996), p. 431; and for the A320, Eric Vayle, "Collision Course in Commercial Aircraft: Boeing—Airbus—McDonnell Douglas, 1991 (A)," *Harvard Business School Case* No. 9-391-106, October 1993, p. 3.
8. Dertouzos et al., *Made in America*, p. 203.
9. Ibid., pp. 206, 214.
10. Quoted in Janet Simpson, Lee Field, and David Garvin, "The Boeing 767: From Concept to Production," *Harvard Business School Case* No. 9-688-040, p. 6.
11. The Boeing Company 1998 Annual Report, p. 45.
12. For more on this argument, see Barry Bluestone, Peter Jordan and Mark Sullivan, *Aircraft Industry Dynamics: An Analysis of Competition, Capital, and Labor* (Boston: Auburn House, 1981), pp. 9–10.
13. Ibid., pp. 163–164.
14. Form 10-K of the Boeing Company for the Year Ended December 1, 1997, p. 3.
15. Lee Smith, "Air Power: Warplane Contracts Give a Lift to the New Aerospace Conglomerates," *Fortune*, July 7, 1997, p. 136.
16. *Fortune*, July 7, p. 135.
17. John B. Rae, *Climb to Greatness: The American Aircraft Industry, 1920–1960* (Cambridge Mass.: MIT Press, 1958), pp.

9-11, 63-72, 171; Boeing Commercial Airplane Group, *Backgrounder*, August 1997, p. 2.

18. Irving B. Holley, *Buying Aircraft: Material Procurement for the Army Air Force* (Washington: GPO, 1964), pp. 550, 576-77.

19. Rae, *Climb to Greatness*, p. 206.

20. Almarin Phillips, *Technology and Market Structure: A Study of the Aircraft Industry* (Lexington, Mass.: D.C. Heath, 1971), p. 110.

21. Rodgers, *Flying High*, p. 199.

22. Ibid., pp. 225-26.

23. Rae, *Climb to Greatness*, pp. 187-188; *Aerospace Facts and Figures, 1997-98*, pp. 47, 52-54; Boeing, *Backgrounder*, August 1997, pp. 5, 7-8; *Hoover's Handbook of American Business, 1997* (Austin: Hoover's Business Press, 1997), pp. 892-93.

24. Boeing, *Commercial Airplane Group, Announced Orders and Deliveries as of 12/31/97*, p. 1, in conjunction with The Boeing Company 1997 Annual Report, p. 19, and *Aerospace Facts and Figures 1997-98*, p. 35.

25. Rodgers, *Flying High*, pp. 287-88; Boeing, *Backgrounder*, August 1997, p. 6.

26. Rodgers, *Flying High*, pp. 284-85.

27. *Aerospace Facts and Figures 1997-98*, p. 33.

28. The Boeing Company Annual Report, p. 23.

29. Rodgers, *Flying High*, p. 413.

30. The Boeing Company 1997 Annual Report, p. 35.

31. Anthony L. Velocci, "MD-XX Termination May Seal Douglas' Fate," *Aviation Week and Space Technology*, November 4, 1996, pp. 24-25. See also *Fortune*, February 17, 1997, p. 98; and Bruce Smith, "Douglas Looks at Twin-Engine Design," *Aviation Week and Space Technology*, September 2, 1996, p. 78.

32. The quotations are from Jeremy Main, "Betting on the 21st Century Jet," *Fortune*, April 20, 1992, pp. 103-104, but see also Rodgers, *Flying High*, p. 420.

33. *Hoover's Handbook of American Business, 1997*, pp. 272-73, 892-93; Boeing, *Backgrounder*, August 1997, pp. 8-9; Rodgers, *Flying High*, p. 327; Form 10-K of the Boeing Company for the Year Ended December 31, 1997, p. 3.

34. *Rodgers, Flying High*, p. 422; Dertouzos et al., *Made in America*, p. 208; Vayle, "Collision Course in Commercial Aircraft," p. 18.

35. Dertouzos, et al., *Made in America*, pp. 210-214; Rodgers, *Flying High*, chap. 12; "Airbus 25 Years Old," *Le Figaro*, October 1997 (reprinted in English translation by Airbus Industrie), p. 6.

36. Equally important, Airbus made an aggressive use of composite materials to reduce aircraft's weight and simplify aircraft's construction (for example, it used composites to build a vertical fin, reducing the fin's parts-count from 2000 to 100). Similarly, in the area of aerodynamics, Airbus designed a wing that featured a distinct twist at the root to reduce drag, and a gust alleviation system to improve efficiency in cruise as well as reduce passenger discomfort in turbulence. "Airbus Industrie: 25 Flying Years," Airbus Industrie, 1997, pp. 13, 14, 17; Dertouzos et al., *Made in America*, pp. 212-213.

37. Together, these efforts enabled Airbus to slash its deliveries "lead time" (the period lasting from the time a customer gave specifications until delivery) from fifteen to nine months (single aisle) and from eighteen to twelve months

(wide body), and thereby reduce costly inventories by 30 percent. Charles Goldsmith, "Re-engineering: After Trailing Boeing for Years Airbus Aims at 50% of the Market," *Wall Street Journal*, March 16, 1998.

38. Dertouzos et al., *Made in America*, p. 212. A typical Airbus ad read: "Airbus' unique use of the latest fly-by-wire technology … enables airlines to operate … a whole set of aircraft types ranging from 120 to over 400 seats in capacity…. with a single pool of pilots" at a saving of "$1 million per aircraft per year." "Airbus: the Airbus Family," Airbus Industrie, 1997.

39. The Boeing Company 1997 Annual Report, p. 3; Jeff Cole, "Boeing Names New Managers, Alters Structure," *Wall Street Journal*, August 7, 1997.

40. Lawrence Zuckerman, "Boeing's Man in the Line of Fire," *New York Times*, November 8, 1998.

41. Frederick Biddle and Andy Paszor, "Boeing May be Hurt Up to 5 Years," *Wall Street Journal*, December 3, 1998.

42. "Fearful Boeing," *Economist*, February 27, 1999, p. 59.

43. The Boeing Company 1997 Annual Report, p. 72.

44. Jeanne Cummings, "President, in State of the Union Address, Offers Most Ambitious Agenda Since 1995," *Wall Street Journal*, January 20, 1999; The Boeing Company 1997 Annual Report, p. 27; *Fortune*, July 7, 1997, p. 134.

45. *Fortune*, July 7, 1997, pp. 133-136.

46. Ibid., p. 136.

47. Ibid.

48. The Boeing Company 1997 Annual Report, p. 25; *Fortune*, July 7, 1997, p. 136.

49. *Fortune*, February 17, 1999, p. 100, July 7, 1997, p. 136; Jeff Cole, "Lockheed Warplane has Racked Up Cost Overruns," *Wall Street Journal*, February 5, 1999.

50. Adam Bryant, "Boeing Offering $13 Billion to Buy McDonnell Douglas," *New York Times*, December 16, 1996.

51. The Boeing Company 1997 Annual Report, p. 36; Frederick Biddle, "Boeing Is still Waiting for the Merger Results to Take Off," *Wall Street Journal*, March 2, 1998.

52. Frederick Biddle and John Helyar, "Flying Low: Behind Boeing's Woes: Clunky Assembly Line, Price War with Airbus," *Wall Street Journal*, April 24, 1998.

53. Form 10-K of the Boeing company for the Year ended December 31, 1997, p. 4; Form 10-Q of the Boeing Company for the Quarterly Period ended June 30, 1998, pp. 14-15.

54. "Out-of-sequence work is an especially costly problem on an aircraft assembly line," says The Boeing Company 1997 Annual Report (p. 3), "as it causes efficiency to plummet to a small fraction of what it should be." See also p. 37.

55. "Bouncing Boeing," *Economist*, June 13, 1998, p. 72; *Wall Street Journal*, April 24, 1998.

56. According to Harry Stonecipher, cited in the *New York Times*, December 3, 1998.

57. "Aircraft Making: Boeing Woeing," *Economist*, August 8, 1998, p. 55, June 13, 1998, p. 72.

58. *Wall Street Journal*, April 24, 1998.

59. "Aerospace: Hubris at Airbus, Boeing Rebuilds," *Economist*, November 28, 1998, p. 65. My figures are slightly different from those of the *Economist* because I used the actual number of jets produced and the *Economist* used the projected number.

60. *Wall Street Journal*, December 3, 1998.

61. *Business Week*, December 30, 1996, p. 39.

62. Rodgers, *Flying High*, pp. 428–430.
63. Laurence Zuckerman, "Boeing's Leaders Losing Altitude," *New York Times*, December 13, 1998.
64. Rodgers, *Flying High*, pp. 427–28.
65. *New York Times*, December 13, 1998.
66. *New York Times*, December 13, 1998; Seanna Brower, "Comeback: Boeing Breathes Easier," *Business Week*, May 3, 1999.
67. *New York Times*, November 8, 1998; *Economist*, November 28, 1998, p. 65.
68. *Economist*, November 28, 1998, p. 65.
69. Jeff Cole, "New CEO's Assignment: Signal a Turnaround," *Wall Street Journal*, January 26, 1999.
70. Ibid.
71. The Boeing Company 1998 Annual Report, p. 39; Jeff Cole, "Boeing Co. May Give Unions Say on Subcontracts," *Wall Street Journal*, April 5, 1999.
72. Rodgers, *Flying High*, pp. 449–62; for the quotation see Anthony Velocci, "Healing Begins at McDonnell Douglas as

Strikers Return to Work," *Aviation Week and Space Technology*, September 16, 1996, p. 90.
73. Robert Rafalko and James Fisher, "Business as Warfare at McDonnell Douglas Corporation," Paper presented at the 1998 meeting of the North American Case Research Association, Durham, New Hampshire, pp. 1–7. For the quotation, see *Aviation Week and Space Technology*, September 16, 1996, p. 90.
74. *Wall Street Journal*, April 5, 1999; Ann Marie Squeo, "Boeing, Union leaders Reached Pact on Contract," *Wall Street Journal*, August 30, 1999.
75. Frederic Biddle, "Pulled Off Its Cloud, Boeing Suspends Quest for the Next Generation Jumbo Jet," *Wall Street Journal*, December 3, 1998; "Airbus May Be About to Challenge the Jumbo Jet's 30-Year-Old Monopoly," *Economist*, March 27, 1999, pp. 61–62.
76. *Economist*, March 27, 1999, pp. 61–62.
77. *Wall Street Journal*, December 3, 1998.